1999

University of St. Francis Library

3 0301 00203978 8

W9-AOX-608

SOCIAL WORK
PROCESSES

SOCIAL WORK PROCESSES

SIXTH EDITION

Beulah R. Compton
University of Southern Mississippi

Burt Galaway
University of Manitoba

LIBRARY
UNIVERSITY OF ST. FRANCIS
JOLIET, ILLINOIS

Brooks/Cole Publishing Company

I(T)P® An International Thomson Publishing Company

Pacific Grove • Albany • Belmont • Bonn • Boston • Cincinnati • Detroit • Johannesburg • London
Madrid • Melbourne • Mexico City • New York • Paris • Singapore • Tokyo • Toronto • Washington

Sponsoring Editor: *Lisa I. Gebo*
Marketing Team: *Steve Catalano, Aaron Eden, and Kyrrha Sevco*
Editorial Assistants: *Susan Wilson and Shelley Tweddell*
Production Coordinator: *Laurel Jackson*
Production Service: *Graphic World Publishing Services*
Manuscript Editor: *Bernard Gilbert*

Permissions Editor: *Catherine Murray Gingras*
Interior Design: *Pati Pye*
Cover Design: *Roy R. Neuhaus*
Cover Photo: *PhotoDisc*
Art Editor: *Graphic World Publishing Services*
Typesetting: *Graphic World, Inc.*
Printing and Binding: *R. R. Donnelley & Sons/Crawfordsville Division*

COPYRIGHT © 1999 by Brooks/Cole Publishing Company
A division of International Thomson Publishing Inc.
I(T)P The ITP logo is a registered trademark used herein under license.

For more information, contact:

BROOKS/COLE PUBLISHING COMPANY
511 Forest Lodge Road
Pacific Grove, CA 93950
USA

International Thomson Publishing Europe
Berkshire House 168–173
High Holborn
London WC1V 7AA
England

Thomas Nelson Australia
102 Dodds Street
South Melbourne, 3205
Victoria, Australia

Nelson Canada
1120 Birchmount Road
Scarborough, Ontario
Canada M1K 5G4

International Thomson Editores
Seneca 53
Col. Polanco
11560 México, D. F., México

International Thomson Publishing GmbH
Königswinterer Strasse 418
53227 Bonn
Germany

International Thomson Publishing Asia
60 Albert St.
#15-01 Albert Complex
Singapore 189969

International Thomson Publishing Japan
Hirakawacho Kyowa Building, 3F
2-2-1 Hirakawacho
Chiyoda-ku, Tokyo 102
Japan

All rights reserved. No part of this work may be reproduced, stored in a retrieval system, or transcribed, in any form or by any means—electronic, mechanical, photocopying, recording, or otherwise—without the prior written permission of the publisher, Brooks/Cole Publishing Company, Pacific Grove, California 93950.

Printed in the United States of America

10   9   8   7   6   5   4   3   2   1

Library of Congress Cataloging-in-Publication Data

Compton, Beulah Roberts.
    Social work processes   /   Beulah Roberts Compton, Burt Galaway.   —
6th ed.
        p.   cm.
    Includes bibliographical references and index.
    ISBN 0-534-35870-5
    1. Social service.   2. Social case work.   3. Social service—
United States.   4. Social case work—United States.   I.   Galaway,
Burt.   II.   Title.
HV37.C62   1998
362.3′2′0973—dc 21   98-21140
                                                                CIP

361.008
@ 734
6 ed

3-5-99 USF SOCIAL WORK DEPT. BT

*Dedicated to the many social work faculty
colleagues and students who have provided
comments and suggestions for strengthening
previous editions.*

Contents

Exhibits

Contributors

Eustolio Benavides
Consultant in private practice
St. Paul, Minnesota

Gale Burford
Professor
School of Social Work
Memorial University
St. John's, Newfoundland

Katharine V. Byers
Assistant Professor
School of Social Work
Indiana University
Bloomington, Indiana

John Victor Compher
Social Work Administrator
Philadelphia County Children and
Youth Agency
Philadelphia, Pennsylvania

Barry R. Cournoyer
Associate Dean and Professor
School of Social Work
Indiana University
Indianapolis, Indiana

Edith Fein
Research Director
Dunne, Kimmel, & Fein, LLC
Hartford, Connecticut

Cynthia Franklin
Associate Professor
School of Social Work
University of Texas, Austin

Jane F. Gilgun
Associate Professor
School of Social Work
University of Minnesota
Minneapolis, Minnesota

Jan L. Hagen
Professor
School of Social Welfare
State University of New York
Albany, New York

W. David Harrison
Professor
School of Social Work
University of Alabama
Tuskaloosa, Alabama

Howard Hess
Associate Dean and Professor
Graduate School of Social Service
Fordham University
New York, New York

Peg McCartt Hess
Associate Dean and Associate
Professor
School of Social Work
Columbia University
New York, New York

Miriam M. Johnson
Assistant Professor
College of Social Work
University of South Carolina
Columbia, South Carolina

Catheleen Jordan
Professor
School of Social Work
University of Texas, Arlington

Lyle Longclaws
Therapist and Consultant in Private
Practice
Winnipeg, Manitoba

Michelle MacKenzie
Social Worker
Halton Regional Police Service
Oakville, Ontario

Reima Ana Maglajlic
Ph.D. Student
School of Community Health and
Social Studies
Anglia Polytechnic University
Cambridge, England

Anthony N. Maluccio
Professor
Graduate School of Social Work
Boston College
Chestnut Hill, Massachusetts

Susan MacLeod
Social Worker
Community Health
St. John's, Newfoundland

John McKnight
Professor and Co-Director of the
Asset-Based Community
Development Institute
Institute for Policy Research
Northwestern University
Evanston, Illinois

Elijah Mickel
Associate Professor
Department of Social Work
Delaware State University
Dover, Delaware

Addie Morris
Assistant Director
Education and Outreach
Arkansas Division of Mental Services
Little Rock, Arkansas

Uma Narayan
Associate Professor
Philosophy Department
Vassar College
Poughkeepsie, New York

Kwane Owusu-Bempah
Lecturer in Psychology
School of Social Work
University of Leicester
Leicester, England

Edward J. Pawlak
Professor
School of Social Work
Western Michigan University
Kalamazoo, Michigan

Joan Pennell
Professor
School of Social Work
Memorial University
St. John's, Newfoundland
and Visiting Professor
Social Work Program
North Carolina State University
Raleigh, North Carolina

Craig Rennebohm
Director
Mental Health Chaplaincy
Seattle, Washington

Dennis Saleebey
Professor
School of Social Welfare
University of Kansas
Lawrence, Kansas

David Schatzky
Psychotherapist in private practice
Toronto
Ontario, Canada

Barbara Bryant Solomon
Vice Provost for Faculty and Minority
 Affairs
University of Southern California
Los Angeles, California

Harry Specht
Professor (deceased)
School of Social Welfare
University of California, Berkeley

Ilene Staff
Assistant Professor
Department of Pediatrics
University of Connecticut Health
 Center
Farmington, Connecticut

Susan Steiger Tebb
Associate Professor
School of Social Service
Saint Louis University
St. Louis, Missouri

Elizabeth M. Tracy
Associate Professor
Mandel School of Applied Social
 Service
Case Western Reserve University
Cleveland, Ohio

Joan Velasquez
Research Director (retired)
Ramsey County Community Human
 Services Department
St. Paul, Minnesota

Marilyn E. Vigil
Associate Professor
Department of Social Work
Metropolitan State University
St. Paul, Minnesota

Robert W. Weinbach
Professor
College of Social Work
University of South Carolina
Columbia, South Carolina

James K. Whittaker
Professor
School of Social Work
University of Washington
Seattle, Washington

Ralph Woehle
Associate Professor
Department of Social Work
University of North Dakota
Grand Forks, North Dakota

Felix Yaroshevsky
Psychiatrist in private practice
Toronto
Ontario, Canada

Preface

This is the sixth edition of a text that was first published in 1974. In our revisions, we have been helped immeasurably by suggestions from faculty and students who have used the text over the past 25 years.

As in earlier editions, the material is organized around three key concepts: ecosystems, social work as a problem-solving process, and worker-client partnership. We have integrated into this framework new material on social support, the development of helping communities, spirituality, the development of client competence, and the strengths perspective.

Faculty and students have had mixed reactions to the inclusion of readings in the text. Some have found these a helpful supplement to material presented in the chapters; others have found that the readings make the text too long and have preferred to use other supplemental readings. In response to this feedback, we have reduced the overall number of readings, increased the proportion of original readings, and tried to ensure that the chapters stand on their own. Faculty and students who use the readings will find that they supplement the material in the chapters but are not essential to the themes of the book. Thus, if you wish to use just the chapters, you will find that the book provides a coherent model for social work practice.

Further, some students have found it difficult to move from the chapters to the case material printed in the appendix without losing the flow of ideas. In this edition, we have used the longer cases in Appendix A primarily for the learning exercises included at the end of each chapter. You should be able to read each chapter without referring to Appendix A. Very short case excerpts are included as exhibits within each chapter to illustrate the ideas developed.

Social work practice has undergone many changes in the last 25 years. The major changes—a renewed interest in working with clients' strengths; the idea of social workers as facilitators and partners who help clients increase their competence; recognition of the importance of spirituality for some clients; and the ecosystem framework to guide both assessment and intervention—are very consistent with the practice model outlined in this text.

In 1998, social work celebrated its centennial. Our first 100 years have been marked by an ongoing debate between proponents of social reform and advocates of social services to individuals in need of help. Despite considerable efforts, the profession has not made very substantial progress towards merging these two perspectives. In this text, we have expanded the material on communities and argued that practitioners from an ecosystemic approach must incorporate both micro and macro approaches in assessment and intervention. The major challenge for the profession, as its second century begins, is to find a way of organizing social services and social work practice so that each individual social worker will direct change efforts to individuals and to larger social systems, as appropriate. This will require us to resist the pressures to define human problems in terms of individual pathologies. In the early 21st century, we must work toward a social work practice that focuses on the development of clients' strengths, client competencies, and communities in which people are supportive of one another.

We extend our thanks and appreciation to the many social work faculty and students who have offered helpful suggestions regarding this text. We hope that you will use the form at the back of the book to forward your comments and suggestions on this edition. Our special thanks go to Claudette Cormier, Faculty of Social Work,

University of Manitoba, who labored long and hard in the preparation of the manuscript. The original readings in the text have been prepared by outstanding social work scholars, to whom we extend our deep appreciation. We would also like to thank Susan Wilson, Laurie Jackson, and Lisa Gebo of Brooks/Cole Publishing for their support, persistence, and helpfulness in developing this edition. We appreciate the work of Catherine Gingras to secure permissions and of Anne E. Gassett, who served as production editor. Bernard Gilbert provided yeoman service as copyeditor and helped make this a shorter and better book. Finally, we have been enriched and guided by colleagues who have provided reviews for the fifth edition as well as the manuscript of this edition. Thanks

for suggestions and comments go to the following reviewers: Raymond Albert, Bryn Mawr College; Yvonne Asamoah, Hunter College; David Cousert, University of Southern Indiana; Katherine M. Dunlap, University of North Carolina at Charlotte; Alice Lieberman, University of Kansas; Robyn Lugar, Indiana State University; Sonja Matison, Eastern Washington University; and Phyllis Ross, Western Connecticut State University.

We have enjoyed working on this edition and hope that it will provide a foundation for your generalist practice in the 21st century.

—*Beulah R. Compton*
Burt Galaway

part I

CONTEXT FOR DECIDING WHAT TO DO

chapter 1

Key Themes for Social Work Practice

CHAPTER PREVIEW

We welcome you on a journey to skillful social work practice. We assume that you have been introduced to social welfare and to the social sciences in previous courses. We begin with a brief review of the definitions of social welfare, social work, and social science, so as to place the book in the context of your total social work education.

We then introduce three key themes (or concepts), which provide an organizing framework for our model of social work practice. These themes are:

- an ecosystem perspective, sometimes called the person-in-situation focus
- social work as a problem-solving process
- client-worker partnership

These themes will be further developed in Chapters 2 through 4 and will recur throughout the book.

We conclude with a discussion of the self-discipline and self-awareness that skilled practitioners need. If you are uncomfortable with either self-discipline or self-awareness, you may not be ready for the rigors of social work practice. We strongly recommend that you discuss any discomfort with your advisor.

We include a reading by Harry Specht, who suggests that the purpose of social work is to assist with developmental socialization, and another by Dennis Saleebey, who describes a strengths perspective for social work practice.

SOCIAL WELFARE, THE SOCIAL SCIENCES, AND SOCIAL WORK

Social Welfare

It is important to distinguish the concepts of social welfare, social work, and the social sciences. By social welfare, we mean an organized set of norms and institutions through which we carry out our collective responsibility to care for one another. Our responsibilities are often carried out through formal organizations, such as child welfare services, family services, criminal justice services, and mental health services. But social welfare can also be a set of norms (commonly held expectations of each other) that define our mutual responsibilities.

For example, in cultures where extended family and clan systems are still intact, shared norms may require members of such systems to provide care for dependent children or aging persons. In Reading 17–2, John P. McKnight suggests that formal social services may deter the work of informal helping systems.

Social welfare policy refers both to the goals of our collective responsibilities and to a set of services for carrying out those responsibilities. We often refer to public social welfare policy, meaning a set of laws and administrative rules that define the purposes of public social welfare and authorize organizations to work toward accomplishment of these purposes. Thus, we have laws providing income for dependent children and establishing a set of organizations to provide this income. Likewise, we have laws that provide for the protection of dependent populations such as children and infirm aged individuals, and that authorize agencies to provide protective services.

Social welfare policy addresses a number of fundamental questions: What are our collective responsibilities to each other? What structures and arrangements enable us to carry out these responsibilities? To what extent are the collective responsibilities to be carried out through formal organizations, and to what extent through informal help giving and self-help? What is the relationship between formal institutions and informal help giving? How and to what extent can public agencies, private nonprofit agencies, and for-profit agencies be involved in the formal social welfare delivery system? As we enter the 21st century, the development and articulation of views on these social welfare questions should be regarded as part of a liberal education. If you intend to practice within the social welfare system, you will be expected to provide informed leadership and direction to that system and to social policy. But this book is not about social welfare; that knowledge will come from other courses.

The Social Sciences

The social sciences, such as sociology, psychology, political science, economics, and anthropology, provide knowledge regarding the nature of society and the human condition. Knowledge generated by the social sciences is important to social welfare and guides social work professionals as we work with people to solve

problems that they are experiencing. Drawing knowledge from the social sciences, social workers attempt to understand the nature of human beings, the nature of societies, and the nature of interactions between social institutions and human beings. We also contribute our own knowledge regarding the nature of assessment (how to view and define problems) and the nature of the interventions used in social work. Thus, we borrow knowledge from the social sciences, translate that knowledge into forms useful to us in our practice, and use knowledge regarding assessment and intervention.

But is social work a social science? We think not. Social work is a profession that uses knowledge developed by the social sciences to further the goals of social welfare. Nevertheless, as we discuss in Chapters 2 and 17, social workers have a responsibility to generate knowledge and to use that knowledge in combination with knowledge borrowed from the social sciences. The practice of social work requires discipline and scientific rigor; we view the social worker as a practitioner/researcher.

Social Work

This is a book about social work and, specifically, about social work practice. Social work is the central—though not the only—profession within the formal social welfare system. The distinction between social work and social welfare resembles the distinction between teachers and the educational system or that between health professionals—doctors and nurses—and the health care system. One is the set of organizations and norms designed to accomplish policy goals; the other is the profession on which the organizations rely. This book introduces a model for social work practice that will guide your work as a professional within the social welfare system. We refer to it as the problem-solving model.

What do social workers do? Where and how do they intervene? For most of us, these are perplexing questions—questions made more perplexing by our lack of contact with social workers and the variety of social work practice. From our life experiences, we have little difficulty identifying the job of the doctor as healing the body—mediating between the physical organism and the environmental influences that threaten health. (The doctor's job becomes less clear and less understood, however, when we consider the treatment of mental illness.) Likewise, we know that the lawyer's job is to mediate between the individual and the legal institutions that ensure a reasonably orderly society. And few of us have any difficulty identifying the job of the teacher as transmitting the accumulated knowledge of the culture.

But what about social workers? What is their job? To William Schwartz (1961), the job of social work is to "mediate the process through which the individual and . . . society reach out for each other through a mutual need for self-fulfilment" (pp. 150–151). Schwartz assumes here that the interests of the individual and the interests of society are essentially the same. In a complex and changing society, however, the individual's desire to belong as a full and productive member may be blocked, as may society's ability to integrate and enrich its people. Social work intervention is directed toward these blockages and toward freeing the "individual's impetus toward health, growth, and belonging; and the organized efforts of society to integrate its parts into a productive and dynamic whole" (Schwartz, 1961, pp. 150–151).

What Schwartz calls blockages between the individual's impetus toward growth and the organized efforts of society will be experienced by the individual as problems. The problems may be varied—finding a job, caring for a child, maintaining communications in a marriage, getting along with others, dealing with threats of mugging in the street, boredom because of inactivity, lack of adequate housing, discrimination, and so on. We speak of social work as a problem-solving process; problem solving is the way social workers and clients put Schwartz's concept of mediation into action. Thus, problem solving mediates between the person and the resources of the environment; it addresses what's sometimes called the person-in-situation.

Key Themes

We present a model of social work practice built on three key themes or concepts—the ecosystem perspective, the problem-solving process, and client-worker partnership. All three concepts are well-established in social work practice and provide a framework for practice in all settings and with diverse populations. We will briefly introduce these concepts in the present chapter.

They are further developed in Chapters 2 through 4 and recur throughout the book.

Before we proceed, we must emphasize the distinction between practice, process, and intervention; these are often confused by social workers. Social work practice is the totality of what social workers do. It encompasses both a process (the problem-solving process) and planned change actions (methods of intervention). Although methods of intervention are often called social work practice, they are only one piece of practice. The focus of this book is on the problem-solving process, which you will need to understand and master before you turn to intervention techniques.

ECOSYSTEM PERSPECTIVE
Person-in-Situation

Alex Gitterman and Carel Germain have proposed a life model that "integrates the treatment and reform traditions, by conceptualizing and emphasizing the dysfunctional transactions between people and their social and physical environments" (Germain & Gitterman, 1980, pp. 10–13.) Social workers focus on problems that fall into three areas: (1) problems and needs associated with tasks involved in life transitions; (2) problems and needs associated with tasks in using and influencing elements of the environment; and (3) problems and needs associated with interpersonal obstacles that impede the work of a family or a group as it deals with transitional and/or environmental tasks (Germain & Gitterman, 1996, 1980). An ecosystem (or ecological) model focuses on the transactions of individuals and their environments, which are assumed to be in a constant state of reciprocity, each shaping the other. Social work interventions are directed toward the interface of the individual and the environment or at problems of living generated by the person-in-situation interaction. According to the ecosystem approach, individuals experience problems when there is a poor fit between their needs and wants and the resources made available by their environment—in particular, the community.

The ecosystem focus has been emerging as a framework for social work practice since the 1950s. Exhibit 1–1 is a 1969 statement of the function of social work. Like other definitions of social work from the 1950s, 1960s, and 1970s, it directs social work intervention toward the interaction between individuals and their

| EXHIBIT 1-1 | Social Work Practice as Matching Something in the Person and Situation |

Here is a classic statement of the focus of social work. What are the implications of this concept for social work practice? What are its implications for social work's claim to be a profession? Do you agree or disagree with Gordon's view? Why?

The central focus of social work traditionally seems to have been on the person-in-life-situation complex—a *simultaneous dual focus* on persons and environments. This focus has been concentrated at some times on the side of the organism as interpreted by psychological theory and at other times on the side of environment as interpreted by sociological and economic theory. The mainstream of social work, however, has become neither applied psychology nor applied sociology.

The simultaneous dual focus on organism and environment, however unbalanced at times in terms of trying to adjust one to the other, has remained essentially non-normative. So far social work has avoided identifying with or setting specific norms of human behavior or specifications of an ideal environment beyond the most general notion of human freedom and availability of resources for meeting basic needs. In oversimplified terms, emphasis has been on *individualizing* the person-situation complex in order to achieve the best match between each person and environment, in which either person-behavior or environmental situation may deviate widely from the typical or normative. We conclude, therefore, that the central target of technical social work practice is *matching* something in person and situation—that is, intervening by whatever methods and means necessary to help people be in situations where their capabilities are sufficiently matched with the demands of the situation to ``make a go of it.''

While social work has never very explicitly defined what is regarded as ``making a go of it,'' there has been, again with some imbalance, a simultaneous dual concern for outcome or consequences for both the individual and environment. Some of the consequences desired for individuals are verbalized as satisfaction, maintenance of a sense of dignity and feeling of worth, relief of stress, et cetera. Regarding the consequences of the environment, more is implied than stated in the term, ``living a socially productive life.'' We conclude, therefore, that the social work perspective in its practice is consequence—or outcome-oriented with the simultaneous dual focus on person and situation maintained in the outcome of the matching.

Source: W. E. Gordon. Basic contracts for an integrative and generative conception of social work. In G. Hearn (Ed.), *The general systems approach: Contributions toward a holistic conception of social work.* New York: Council on Social Work Education (1969), pp. 6–7.

environments (Baer & Federico, 1978; Boehm, 1958; Germain, 1973; Meyer, 1970; Peterson, 1979; Pincus & Minahan, 1973). Similarly, the National Association of Social Workers has developed (1981): the following working statement: "The purpose of social work is to promote or restore a mutually beneficial interaction between individuals and society in order to improve the quality of life for everyone" (p. 6). Among the items in this purpose statement is the following

Social workers focus on person-and-environment *in interaction*. To carry out their purpose they work with people to achieve the following objectives:

- Facilitate interaction between individuals and others in their environment.
- Help people enlarge their competence and increase their problem solving and coping abilities.
- Influence social and environmental policy.

These definitions are all consistent with Schwartz's mediating approach and foreshadow the ecosystem approaches formulated by Gitterman and Germain.

Social work intervenes or mediates between people and their social environments.

According to Harriett Bartlett (1970), social work focuses on social functioning, which she defines as the "relation between the coping activity of people and the demand from the environment" (p. 116). For Bartlett, social functioning does not refer to the functioning of individuals or groups, but instead to what goes on between people and the environment through the exchange between them. Thus, people and environment are encompassed in a single concept, which requires that they be constantly reviewed together.

The consensus, then, is that social work intervention is directed to the interaction between humans and their environments. But do social workers change the individual or change the environment? This is an old issue in social work (Fook, 1993; Franklin, 1990; Lee, 1929). Social workers do both. The debate about whether the profession should focus primarily on individual change or on environmental change (Wood & Middleman, 1991) results from failure to understand the ecosystem perspective. The parties to this debate miss the central focus on the interaction between the individual and the environment.

In a historical review, Barbara Levy Simon finds that a dual focus on people and environments is a necessary element of the empowerment tradition in American social work (1994).[1] Research suggests that most practicing social workers are able to integrate clinical and social orientations in their work (Taber & Valtano, 1970; Reeser, 1991). Moreover, a focus on the person-situation interaction is consistent with concepts of politically progressive (Barber, 1995) and radical casework: "a radical casework approach would mean not merely obtaining for clients social services to which they are entitled or helping them adjust to the environment, but also trying to deal with the relevant people and institutions in the clients' environment that are contributing to their difficulties" (Rein, 1970, p. 19).

Recently, social work has developed a system for classifying problems from the person-in-situation perspective (Karls & Wandrei, 1992). The person-in-environment (PIE) system was developed so as to provide the profession with a problem classification system consistent with social work's dual focus on person and environment; in part, it is a response to dissatisfaction with the diagnostic and statistical manual (DSM) of the American Psychiatric Association (1994). DSM was designed to reflect psychiatric problems and carries a heavy disease or pathology orientation. PIE provides a system for classifying problems in both the role performance of an adult and the available environmental supports.

Social Science Knowledge for Practice

If social workers mediate the person-situation interaction to assist clients in the resolution of problems, three main types of knowledge will be relevant: (1) knowledge about the person—individual behavior and patterns of adaptation and all that affects them; (2) knowledge about the situation—the community, its institutions, and the various resource structures; and (3) transactional concepts to help us understand "trans-

actions between people and environments that, on one hand, promote or inhibit growth, development, and the release of human potential and, on the other hand, promote or inhibit the capacity of environment to support the diversity of human potential" (Germain, 1981, p. 325). Our profession borrows most knowledge about the person and the situation from supporting social sciences. In Chapter 2, we discuss some of the types of knowledge and theories useful for social work practice and offer guidelines for selecting knowledge.

Prevention or Intervention?

Throughout the history of the profession, there has been a divisive debate between those who advocate individual change and those who prioritize social change. The ecosystem model demands that social workers develop interventive skills in both areas. The social worker in The House on Sixth Street (Appendix A–7) organized the tenants to work toward better housing; this intervention was aimed at social change. In different circumstances, however, the same social worker might have focused on assisting a family to secure more adequate housing or assisting a family to develop the skills and ability to improve existing housing—that is, on individual change.

There has been equally fierce disagreement within social work between advocates of rehabilitation and proponents of prevention. Critics have argued that social workers spend too much time with the casualties of our society, instead of attacking root problems in efforts at prevention. To a large extent, this is a restatement of the debate about social change versus work with individuals. Prevention is seen as requiring social change, while rehabilitation is perceived as helping individuals to cope with immediate situations. In reality, all social work is both preventive and rehabilitative. Helping a mentally ill person is rehabilitative but also prevents future distress. Efforts to provide deprived children with adequate nutrition, clothing, and, where necessary, substitute living arrangements are both rehabilitative and preventive.

PROBLEM SOLVING
Beyond Casework, Groupwork, and Community Organization

Traditionally, social workers have been segregated into three major categories: caseworkers, group workers,

---

[1] The other necessary elements are collaborative partnerships with clients, emphasis on strengths and capacities, recognition of clients' rights and responsibilities, and a focus on historically disempowered groups.

EXHIBIT 1-2	Generalist Social Work Practice Compared to Method-Focused Agency Practice	
GENERALIST SOCIAL WORK FOCUS		**AGENCY METHOD FOCUS**
Not predefined	←PROBLEM→	Predefined by setting
No client system until contract	←CLIENT→	Presumed to be agency client
Not predetermined	←CLIENT→	Predetermined (whether family, group, couple, individual, etc.)
Target = client system and/or others	←CLIENT→	Client = sole target
Includes environment as potential target of social worker action	←ASSESSMENT→	Environment viewed primarily in terms of client responses and behavior
Not predefined; multimethod	←METHODS→	Predefined
Includes client and social environments as targets; multilevel interventions	←INTERVENTION→	Primary focus on client as target
Social worker: generally multiple primary roles (such as counseling and/or linking to resources and/or case management)	←STAFF ROLES→	Technical: generally one primary role (such as counseling or information services)

Source: Rosemarie Carbino, Clinical Professor, School of Social Work, University of Wisconsin, Madison.

or community organizers. These categories, by encouraging a focus on one side or the other of the person-situation interaction, tend to obscure the range of problem definitions and change strategies that might be considered. Schwartz (1961) notes that it is inappropriate to define the method on the basis of the number of persons with whom the worker interacts and suggests that we regard casework, groupwork, and community organizing as terms characterizing the relational system within which the method is implemented. For Schwartz, method is "a systematic process of ordering one's activity in the performance of a function. Method is function in action" (p. 148). In other words, method is the systematic way in which social workers mediate between the individual and the social environment.

When a study of 226 children seen at a child guidance clinic found a high frequency of family and social problems, the authors concluded that "these findings provide support for a traditional social work concept—the person-in-environment perspective . . . a focus on only the individual yields an incomplete picture. Social workers need to provide a sufficiently comprehensive assessment to detect problems in the broader social context" (Proctor, Vosler, & Sirles, 1993, p. 261). Likewise, Susan Stern and Carolyn A. Smith (1995) studied 864 adolescents and their families and found that both parenting and delinquency were affected by the social

environment. Thus, interventions must be directed to the context in which the family lives as well as to internal family processes (Coady, 1993).

Martin Rein (1970) notes that the association of social change with community organization and of individual change with social casework may be an oversimplification, inasmuch as work with individuals can be directed toward change in social standards and work with groups or communities can be directed toward helping people adapt to their current situations. We agree, but this distinction is often missed in social work. The expectation remains that the community organizer works at community change, the caseworker works to produce individual change, and the group worker to do either, depending on the nature of the group. This expectation diverts the focus of social work from the person-situation interaction to either the person or the situation, depending on the particular method in which the practitioner has been steeped.

The ecosystem perspective has led to the idea of a generalist social work practitioner, who assesses problems in the person-situation interaction and considers a range of possible solutions (Kemp, Whittaker, & Tracy, 1997). In Exhibit 1–2, Rosemarie Carbino summarizes the differences between a generalist focus and the older focus on methods. The problem-solving model developed in this text provides a model for social work generalists to use in work with individuals, families, and other groups—including groups representative of communities—to resolve problems they are experiencing in their interactions with their environments.

A Process for Practice

Abraham Kaplan (1964) has referred to a law of the instrument. "Give a small boy a hammer, and he will find that everything that he encounters needs to be pounded. It comes as no particular surprise to discover that scientists formulate problems in ways which require for their solution just those techniques in which they themselves are especially skilled" (p. 23). The same difficulty is found in social work, especially when practice is understood in terms of models of intervention. Social workers need the ability to define problems independently of intervention models and, on that basis, to select the most appropriate model for intervention.

It is important to be very clear about the difference between social work process and social work intervention. Intervention, which is a conscious, planned effort to produce change, is only one component of social work process. Before intervening, we must understand the nature of the problem we are attempting to resolve, as well as the objectives and purposes of intervention. Social work process is a broader concept than intervention; it encompasses all of the elements of practice. Any effective intervention depends on a clear understanding of social work process and the development of skills for managing this process. This is a book about social work process, and intervention will be considered as one component of that process; it is not a book on models of intervention.

Two sets of skills are necessary for social work: skills in knowing what change strategies to use; and skills in the actual use of change strategies (Bisno, 1969; Kidneigh, 1969). Kidneigh believes that social workers must possess both the capability of deciding-what-to-do and the capability of doing-the-decided. In other words, social work practice involves making decisions about what needs to be done and decisions about how to carry out intervention.

Social workers engage in problem-solving behavior in order to resolve problems arising in the interaction between persons and their situations. An overview of the problem-solving model is presented in Chapter 3; the various components of the Model are considered in more detail in Chapters 8–18. Problem solving is a rational, goal-directed process that includes actions to define the problem; to collect information on which to base decisions; to engage the client in goal setting and decision making; to produce change; and to evaluate progress.

Problem Solving and Strengths

Describing a change process by means of a problem-solving model is quite different from employing a problem-focused model. Social workers do start with a problem—some sense of distress or discomfort in the relationship between an individual and his or her broader community or environment. Developing a solution to that problem will call upon strengths brought by the client, you, and the environment. Thus, the problem-solving model is strengths-focused. Identification of strengths is a very important part of the assessment process; planning for use of these strengths is part of developing a service plan.

Intervention Models for Practice

Intervention refers to deliberate planned actions undertaken by the worker and the client to resolve a problem. Thus, intervention occurs after defining a problem and identifying the desired resolution (or objectives). An intervention model is an organized set of procedures that, on the basis of research (including our practice experience), are thought to be useful for the resolution of the specific problem confronting the client and worker. As we have already noted, intervention is a part, but not the totality, of social work practice; the purpose of this book is to present a model for social work practice and not to present models of intervention (that comes later, after the practice model has been understood and mastered).

Beware of two errors often made by social workers. One is to assume that practice is only intervention. A second, equally serious, error is to inflexibly adopt an intervention model—especially a model developed in a discipline external to social work—and to apply it indiscriminately, without regard for the definition of the problem or for client objectives. Haphazardly applying transactional analysis, reality therapy, Adlerian psychology, behavioral modification, or any other system of thought is not the same as doing social work.

Social Work and Case Management

The term *case management* has different meanings. To some, it means assisting clients to access resources—that is, to manage the resources of their communities (Rose, 1992). To others, it means managing the client; it often carries the connotation of rationing or controlling access to community resources, usually formally organized resources. The first definition—assisting clients to assess and utilize the resources of their communities—is central to social work practice. In Chapter 13, we talk about case management and the role of the professional as a social broker, who links clients with community resources. An example is provided in Reading 13-1, where Miriam M. Johnson and W. David Harrison illustrate the practice of community care, which plays a central role in social work practice in the United Kingdom.

Social work practice is case management that helps people link to the resources of their community (Dinerman, 1992)—not only to formal service providers but also to neighbors, extended family members, clubs and organizations, churches and other religious groups, recreational and mutual aid groups, and so forth.

Social Work and Therapy

Harry Specht (1990) traces the relationship of social work to psychiatry, humanistic psychology, and what he calls the popular psychotherapies. Specht believes that an overemphasis on psychotherapy has led social work to focus on individual cases, rather than its original vision of improving social conditions for all. He argues that, as social workers,

> our mission must be to build a meaning, a purpose, and a sense of obligation for the community, not one by one. It is only by creating a community that we establish a basis for commitment, obligation, and social support. We must build communities that are excited about their child care systems, that find it exhilarating to care for the mentally ill and the frail aged. Psychotherapy will not enable us to do that. (Specht, 1990, pp. 354–355)

We agree with Specht that the mission of social work must be in building community, but we disagree with his view that building community cannot occur on a one-by-one, individual-by-individual basis. We hope that many of you will become community development workers and will find the concepts that we are developing in this text useful in that work. Work with individual clients, however, can also contribute to building communities, provided it is focused on assisting persons to become community participants, to access informal networks, and to make contributions to the overall welfare of their communities. This is our vision of social work and is, historically, the mainstream of social work. It is not therapy.

Our primary mission is to build communities and to assist persons to participate in communities. Is there any role at all for therapy in social work? Yes, but it is a relatively minor role. Social work therapists are like heart surgeons. Clearly, highly skilled doctors are needed to perform bypass and other heart surgery; but this is a relatively minor role within the medical profession, and only a few heart surgeons are needed. It would be disastrous for public health if heart surgery became the model for all of medicine. Likewise, we regard therapy as a specialty within social work; it requires considerable advanced training, and only a few social workers will need this training. It would be a disaster for community and social development if therapy were to become the model of training for all social workers.

Settings for Practice

Where can social workers do the kind of social work we're talking about—building community, linking persons to resources, assisting persons in mobilizing informal support networks, and helping persons contribute to the well-being of their communities? The best opportunities are still to be found in the areas of greatest need—child welfare work, probation services, and work with community centers that serve either geographic communities or communities of interest (aged persons, individuals with chronic mental illness in nonresidential settings, homeless people, and so forth). Much of this work is done by public agencies; there are unusually good opportunities to practice social work in public child and family service agencies. However, innovative private agencies also provide excellent opportunities for social work focused around developing social networks, social-ization, and normalization.

Generalists and Specialists

We have argued that social work skills can be classi-fied in two broad areas: skills necessary for assessment or for deciding what to do; and skills necessary for inter-vention or doing the decided. Does this imply that all social workers must be able to do all things for all people? The problem-solving model provides a sound basis for thinking of general social work practice and for the development of specialists in highly technical and com-plex models of intervention.

In this approach, a social worker in general practice is a person who is skillful in deciding what to do. These practitioners will not be limited in their vision by any preferred relational system (individual, family, small group, and so on) or commitment to a particular change strategy. Thus, they will be able to focus attention on the person-situation interaction. In deciding what to do, the practitioner is free to examine variables in the person, in the situation, and in the interaction of the two. Skills in engaging the applicant in data collection and assessment are essential to defining the problem and arriving at a practical and workable decision about what needs to be done.

The profession must provide clients with a wide range of interventive strategies for doing the decided. Some of these models may require skilled specialists. In some situations, the generalist practitioner will possess skills in the necessary interventive strategies and may imple-ment the intervention plan. In other situations, the generalist will call in a specialist for assistance. Some service plans may call for specialists from outside the profession, while other plans will involve specialists from within the profession. In some instances, the specialist may carry most of the responsibility for imple-menting the service plans; in others, most of the imple-mentation will be the responsibility of the generalist, who will work as a team member with the specialist in meeting the objectives of the service plan. We will discuss teamwork in Chapter 16.

Sometimes it is suggested that social workers might specialize by setting or field of practice—child welfare, mental health, corrections, family services, schools, hos-pitals, and so forth. Recent research from a sample of over 2500 master's degree social workers working in five different fields of practice, however, found that the frequency with which workers in different fields of practice performed 131 specific tasks was essentially the same (Raymond, Teare, & Atherton, 1996). The authors concluded that curricula organized on the basis of an advanced generalist model will be more congruent with the actual work done by social workers than will those based on a field-of-practice model. Mastering the skills necessary for implementing a generalist practice model, such as the problem-solving model, will equip you for practice in a variety of settings.

Knowledge Development, Research, and Practice

We require knowledge of the problem-solving pro-cess. This involves problem definition and assessment, as well as knowledge of intervention models. You will be expected to understand the knowledge base of your profession and to keep informed about new develop-ments. You will be performing regular literature searches in libraries and on the world wide web (Giffords, 1998) in order to learn from what others have done and to make that knowledge available to your clients. Exhibit 1–3 provides an introduction to the relevant tools.

Social workers have a responsibility to expand their knowledge of the problem-solving process and of social work assessment and intervention. We also borrow and integrate practice concepts from other professions; developing, testing, and transmitting knowledge about social work practice—both the process and the models of intervention—is a central responsibility for social work-ers. You are responsible for research to evaluate your own practice and to contribute to the profession's knowledge base. The Code of Ethics of the National Association of Social Workers (NASW) (1996) makes development of knowledge an ethical duty: "Social workers should con-tribute to the knowledge base of social work and share with colleagues their knowledge related to practice, research, and ethics" (p. 24).

Knowledge can be used in two very different ways. For some, the possession of knowledge provides a means to exercise power over persons who do not have that knowledge; this is the power of the expert. But knowl-edge can also be made available to persons and organi-zations for their own decision making. This occurs when

---

EXHIBIT 1-3   Tools for Searching the Social Work Literature

These tools will assist you to conduct searches of the social work literature.

American Psychological Association. (1994). *Publication manual* (4th ed.). Washington, DC: Author.

This is the manual of style used by most social work journals and is widely used by publishers of other social and behavioral science materials.

Social work abstracts. Washington, DC: National Association of Social Workers.

Published four times a year; the winter (December) issue contains a cumulative index for the year. A CD-ROM version that can be searched electronically is available in many libraries.

Barker, R. L. (1995). *The social work dictionary* (3rd.ed.). Washington, DC: National Association of Social Workers.

The first social work dictionary, containing definitions of over 3000 terms commonly used in social work.

Edwards, R. (Ed.). (1995). *Encyclopedia of Social Work* (19th ed.). Washington, DC: National Association of Social Workers.

Two volumes of articles on topics related to social work and social welfare.

Ginsberg, L. (1995). *Social work almanac.* Washington, DC: National Association of Social Workers.

A collection of descriptive statistics of interest to social workers organized by field of practice.

World wide web resources for social workers: http://pages.nyu.edu/~holden/gh-w3-f.htm

---

we, as experts, offer information to clients for their use. In the worker-client partnership, which is central to social work practice, we avoid using our expertise to consolidate our power. Instead, we make knowledge available to clients, to assist them in their own decision making and planning.

Generally speaking, professional knowledge is generated by research. However, it is wrong to draw a sharp distinction between research and practice. Social work practice is research, and social work practitioners are researchers. Social work practice involves: the systemic definition of a problem; collection of data to assist in defining the problem and working toward a solution; a clear statement of objectives; development of an intervention plan; and systematic implementation of that intervention plan. Research consists of precisely the same processes, although different language is used to describe them. Defining a research problem, for example, is essentially the same as defining a problem for work. What in research are called dependent variables are, in social work practice, the objectives to be accomplished with the intervention plan. The intervention itself is analogous to the independent variables; we expect the interventions to lead to the accomplishment of objectives. The research plan is a description of how the research project will be implemented and is essentially the same as the service plan, a description of how the intervention will be carried out. There is a wide range of approaches to research, just as there is a wide range of

approaches to intervention. Disciplined and systematic practice is research and, as a social worker, you are a practitioner/researcher.

WORKER AND CLIENT AS PARTNERS
Social Work as a Partnership Arrangement

The client and social worker function as partners throughout the problem-solving process; the client is fully involved and participates in all of the decisions. Some students come into the profession because they want to reform or change people. If this is your interest, you are likely to find social work a frustrating experience. Our function as social workers is not to reform or to change people; rather, we engage people in a problem-solving process by which they resolve their own problems. As Dennis Saleebey notes in Reading 1-2, people can heal themselves.

The concept of partnership is becoming well developed in the field of community economic development (CED). This area for social work practice has been evolving from our community organization and community development roots; merging practices of community development, social development, and economic development, its practitioners assist whole communities—often underdeveloped and marginalized communities—to control their own resources and destinies. Community economic development often involves the need for partners that are external to the communities. In Exhibit 1–4, Teresa MacNeil describes some of the pitfalls when the external partner is a government agency. Alexander Lockhart (1982) discusses the dialectical nature of partnership between an insider and outsider working toward a community economic development plan for a Canadian Aboriginal community. Each partner brings resources and information for the work to be done; while the contributions by each partner are different, they are of equal importance to accomplishing the tasks. Lockhart (1982) stresses that, "if a current fashionable term 'social impact assessment' is to mean anything beyond a cheap strategy to usurp the ability of a community to determine what kinds of development are most consistent with its own sense of being, then such assessment must ensure that community insiders learn as much about themselves from the process as do any outsiders who may be involved" (p. 167).

We will return to this concept of assessment as joint learning and joint decision making in Chapters 10 and 11. At this point, we want simply to alert you that all aspects of social work processes involve worker and client partnership; none is the exclusive jurisdiction of the worker. This concept of joint decision making may be at variance with your own image of professional practice;

perhaps you think of the professional as an expert who knows what needs to be done. If so, we invite you to seriously consider the possibilities of partnership and to discuss this notion with your colleagues.

Values for Practice

Values guide and direct practice, as we will discuss in Chapters 4 and 6. One aspect of the value orientation should be clarified at the outset. Social workers have long held a commitment to increasing the opportunities available to clients and to assisting clients in making use of available resources. Harold Lewis (1972) asserts that "institutionalized restrictions which limit opportunities, as well as the personal shortcomings of the client which may curtail options, are legitimate targets for change" (p. 411). By working to increase the client's opportunities for meaningful choice, you attempt to increase client self-determination.

READINESS FOR PRACTICE

The model of social work practice that we are developing is based on three central concepts: an ecological

---

EXHIBIT 1-4   Governments as Community Economic Development (CED) Partners

Populations are generally aware of factors affecting their fragile economy but the citizens usually do not engage actively in altering the conditions which cause the economies of their communities to be forever insecure and reliant upon extraordinary measures. They view such work as belonging to government. Thus, announcements of plans from above are the perennial expectation of a population which has learned to be helpless. Governments as partners in CED must take into account the current state of learned helplessness and follow processes to enable the population to see and take hold of ways to transform their community through its economy.

Development of communities, and especially less-advantaged communities, must follow a strategy which places responsibility for formulating and realizing change firmly in the hands of the people of the community who, in turn, learn to grasp and deal with that responsibility. Ideally, this approach involves all levels of the nation's

governmental and corporate forces. First and foremost, it requires citizens to understand the facts of their economic circumstances and the causes of their underdevelopment. It then requires them to identify, choose, and act on their development options. To place responsibility more squarely in the hands of citizens does not mean that governments must abandon their responsibility for economic development. Rather, government is situated as a stage-setter, as an enabler, and as the sponsor of a process which will transform a community according to the choice and determination of its population. Government is the force to handle those functions and activities which are otherwise impossible for citizens to handle themselves. The role of specialists is shifted from being decision makers who specify development policy to being the major source of support for citizens who would determine the direction of development in their local economy. This is a formidable role shift.

Source: T. MacNeil. Governments as partners in community economic development. In B. Galaway & J. Hudson (Eds.), *Community economic development: Perspectives in Canadian research and policy.* Toronto: Thompson Educational Publishing (1994), p. 179.

perspective, a problem-solving process, and worker-client partnership. Before developing these themes, however, we need to address two matters that will have a bearing on your readiness to practice social work: self-discipline and self-awareness.

Social Work as Disciplined Practice

Social work is a skilled profession. Learning any skill-based activity—whether figure skating, dancing, swimming, basketball, or chess—requires hard work and disciplined practice. It's sometimes said that social work is simply doing what comes naturally. Remember, though, that it takes a skillful person to make difficult work look natural. The graceful movements of a figure skater are only possible after many hours of practice.

Spontaneity grows out of discipline because discipline moves you beyond the limitations of your own past into new areas of responding. Much of what you will be learning in social work practice may seem unnatural; you may need to challenge your customary patterns of behavior and to consider alternative responses. In the process, you may develop skills that look natural and spontaneous but are new for you. We invite you to a journey of disciplined examination of past ways of behaving; it will be hard work.

Self-Awareness

Social work practice requires us to know ourselves and become so comfortable with ourselves that we do not need to impose our own views on others. It will help you in your studies if you already feel a level of comfort with yourself. You'll find that your social work education will validate some of your past experiences, beliefs, and views but challenge others as you are exposed to new ideas and experiences.

As you begin this course, spend a little time in honest self-examination. Are you committed to the discipline necessary to learn new skills? Are you sufficiently secure that you don't need much validation of who you are? Are you sufficiently secure that you are able to have some of your views and ideas challenged? If you have any concerns, discuss them with your advisor, who will help you to sort out whether you are ready for the grueling, emotionally challenging practice of social work.

CHAPTER SUMMARY

By now, you have been introduced to the central concepts found in this book—the themes that will be recurring in subsequent chapters. Here are the important ideas:

• The focus of social work intervention is on the person-situation interaction. A focus solely on the individual or on the situation is inappropriate. The long debate in the social work profession about individual services versus social reform detracts from this focus.

• The function of social work is to facilitate a problem-solving process—specifically, to assist clients in resolving problems in person-situation interactions.

• Social work involves a partnership with clients to engage in problem solving.

• Social workers are case managers, in the sense that their primary mission is to help link individuals to the resources of their environments, including informal social networks and support systems.

• An overemphasis on therapy in the education of social workers and in practice will detract from the profession's mission of community building.

• A distinction must be made between social work practice and models of intervention. Social work practice encompasses all components of the problem-solving process, including deciding what to do and doing the decided. Models of intervention relate only to doing the decided—that is, to carrying out a plan designed to produce change.

• Preparation for social work requires hard work, self-discipline, and self-awareness.

A LOOK FORWARD

Harry Specht presents his concept of social work as developmental socialization in Reading 1-1 and argues that an overemphasis on popular psychotherapies has detracted from the primary vision and mission of social work. In Reading 1-2, Dennis Saleebey discusses strengths-based perspective for social work.

In the next three chapters, we will further develop the concepts introduced in this chapter. In Chapter 2, we introduce general systems theory, place ecosystems within this framework, and discuss its value in social work practice.

In Chapter 3, we consider the problem-solving process in more detail. (We will return to the various phases of this process in Chapters 8–18.) As we will see, the strengths-based perspective is consistent with the problem-solving model, which, in turn, is consistent with the general systems perspective.

In Chapter 4, we consider values in the context of social work practice and examine how social workers can increase client self-determination and enhance client dignity.

READING 1-1 *Social Work's Mission*

Harry Specht

Is there a difference between social work and psychotherapy? Does social work have a mission of its own that distinguishes our profession from the psychotherapies? Generally, as I have noted elsewhere, the major function of social work is concerned with developmental socialization, while psychotherapy is concerned with resocialization and restoration (Specht, 1988). The concern of developmental socialization is with helping people perform in their appropriate social roles by providing information and knowledge, social support, social skills, and social opportunities. It is also concerned with helping people deal with interference and abuse from other individuals and groups, physical and mental disabilities, and overburdening responsibilities they have for others (Specht, 1988). The concern of resocialization is with helping people deal with feelings, perceptions, and emotions that prevent them from performing their social roles adequately because of impairment or insufficient development of emotional and cognitive functions intimately related to the self (Specht, 1988).

Professional social workers will recognize the close relationship between—and the overlapping of—these two social functions. However, to say that social work is similar to and overlaps with the work of other professions (e.g., law, medicine, education, and psychotherapy) is not to say that all these professions are identical. We must, if we desire to give direction to our profession, take on the difficult task of drawing boundaries between ourselves and other professions. The drawing of boundaries can be difficult and painful because it may lead us to establish priorities and require us to exclude some functions and practices that, no matter how socially desirable, are diversionary and subversive to our mission.

The central point of this article is that the psychotherapies have diverted social work from its original vision, a vision of the perfectibility of society, the building of the "city beautiful," the "new society," and the "new frontier." There is a yet-unfulfilled mission for social work that might be resuscitated. It is a mission to deal with the enormous social problems under which our society staggers: the social isolation of our aged, the anomie experienced by our youths, the neglect and abuse of children, homelessness, drug addiction, and AIDS. Psychotherapy is not useful in dealing with these great problems.

Let us not be confused over the fact that there is some overlapping knowledge about human growth and development that social workers and psychotherapists share, or the fact that we both make focused use of interpersonal relationships, or that there are some small similarities we share in respect to practice. All human services professions share similar knowledge, but the uses they make of that knowledge are determined by their respective missions.

Our mission must be to build a meaning, a purpose, and a sense of obligation for the community, not one by one. It is only by creating a community that we establish a basis for commitment, obligation, and social support. We must build communities that are excited about their child care systems, that find it exhilarating to care for the mentally ill and the frail aged. Psychotherapy will not enable us to do that, and the farther down the psychotherapeutic path we go, the less effective we will be in achieving our true mission. There are models for doing this: the Civilian Conservation Corps of the 1930s, the War on Poverty of the 1960s, Alcoholics Anonymous, the civil rights movement, the Peace Corps, and the National Service Corps now being discussed in Congress are all models by which we can build communities that change people, communities that give a purpose and meaning to people's lives and, most important, communities that enable us to care about and love one another. To take that as our professional mission requires us to make a great change in our way of thinking and practicing.

This is a task that is tantamount to the cleaning of the Augean stables. We have, all of us, been socialized to think and act in psychotherapeutic terms and to prize one-on-one interventions. We educate our students to follow suit, and it is therefore not surprising that they, too, prize the psychotherapeutic role. Social services, whether public, voluntary, or for profit, are organized to make individualized psychotherapeutic forms of helping the most significant we have to offer. Whether we are dealing with child abuse and neglect, addictions, loneliness, anxiety, economic dependency, or other physical and mental disabilities, it is psychotherapeutically oriented work with individuals that is considered to be the key.

Use of groups, community associations, and voluntary associations are usually considered to be secondary means for change. At best, they provide significant "social support" and "helping networks"; somewhat less important, they are good informational resources, recreational experiences, and they provide respite for caregivers and backups and reenforcement for individual treatment. Rarely are they perceived by professionals to be the primary and most desirable means for change. There are occasional episodes—usually at times of national crises—when we rediscover the group and the community. This occurred during the two world wars, the Depression, and the civil rights revolution. When there are cuts in allocations for social programs, agencies retreat unhappily to offering group treatment in place of psychotherapy. But when the crises subside, we quickly return to individualized therapy as our major means for dealing with social problems. For the most part, all

nonpsychotherapeutic interventions are perceived by professionals to be inferior.

We have these perceptions of social treatments because, as Americans, our belief in the individual's capacity for change is strong, and our faith in the power of the group and community is weak, evidence to the contrary notwithstanding. It would, indeed, require a very great change in the profession, in professional education, in the organization of our service systems, and most of all, in our systems of belief for social work to provide the community with a social program to deal with social problems.

It may be too late. We have been socialized for 70 years to believe that psychiatry, psychoanalysis, and humanistic psychology are appropriate means for dealing with social problems. We are about to be engulfed by popular psychotherapy. We must differentiate between these two practices and stop deluding ourselves that they are not different. The difference between them is vast. We should not be secular priests in the church of individual repair; we should be the conscience of the community. We should not ask, "Does it feel good?" We should help communities create good. We must have a vision of social work that enables us to direct our energies to the creation of healthy communities. That is how we make healthy people.

From *Social Service Review,* Sept. 1990, pp. 345–357. © 1990 by The University of Chicago. All rights reserved.

READING 1-2 *The Strengths Perspective: Principles and Practices**
Dennis Saleebey

Over the past decade or so, strengths-based approaches to case management and direct practice have been developed in a number of fields of practice—mental health (Kisthardt, 1997; Rapp, 1998; Sullivan, 1997), juvenile justice (Clark, 1997), gerontological social work (Fast & Chapin, 1997; Parsons and Cox, 1994), families (Kaplan & Girard, 1994), substance

*An original reading prepared for this edition.

abuse (Miller & Berg, 1995; Rapp, 1997), communities (Kretzmann & McKnight, 1993), schools (Benard, 1997a), and public welfare (Bricker-Jenkins, 1997). In addition, there are parallel developments in other areas of research, program, and practice; developmental resilience and youth development (Henderson, 1997; Werner & Smith, 1992); health and wellness (Gazzaniga, 1992; Mills, 1995; Weil, 1995); social constructionism (Franklin, 1995; Freedman & Combs, 1996); and solution-focused therapy (De Jong & Miller, 1995).

Significantly, some of the impetus for the development of a strengths/resilience-based practice comes from our society's unabashed fascination with pathology, problems, moral and interpersonal aberrations, violence, and victimization. Add to that the unstinting effort to medicalize and pathologize almost every human behavior pattern, habit, and trait, and you have a heady mix of diagnoses, labels, and identities at the ready—all advertising our abnormalities, disorders, weaknesses, fallibilities, and victimization. An influential cartel of professions, institutions, businesses, and individuals—from medicine to the pharmaceutical industry, from the insurance business to the media—stands to assure us that we all have a storehouse of vulnerabilities and failings born of toxic and traumatic experiences (usually in childhood) that put us at risk for an astonishing array of pathologies: from caffeine addiction to post-traumatic stress syndrome to dissociative identity disorder (Kaminer, 1993; Peele, 1989; Peele & Brodsky, 1991; Rieff, 1991). Victimhood has become big business, as many adults—prodded by a variety of therapies, gurus, and ministers—search out their wounded inner children and memories of the poisonous ecology of their family background. This phenomenon blurs the distinction between people who have been seriously traumatized and victimized and those who experience the expectable trials and tribulations of real life (Dineen, 1996).

To practice from a strengths perspective does not require us to blithely ignore or mute the real pains and troubles that afflict children, groups, families, and classes of people. Child sexual abuse is real; violence is real; cancer is real; schizophrenia is real; racism is real. But from the vantage point of a strengths perspective, it is as wrong to deny the possible as it is to deny the problem. The strengths perspective decries the fact that the recovery movement, now so far beyond its original boundaries and intent, has

> pumped out a host of illnesses and addictions that were by earlier standards, mere habits, some good, some bad. Everywhere in public we find people talking freely, if not excitedly, even proudly about their compulsions—whether it be gambling, sex, exercise, or the horrible desire to please other people. We are awash in a sea of codependency, wounded inner children, and intimacy crises. (Wolin & Wolin, 1993, p. 7)

The strengths perspective calls us back to a more balanced view of the human condition: a view in which we respect the power of human beings to overcome and surmount adversity.

PRINCIPLES OF THE STRENGTHS PERSPECTIVE

Like any theory, the strengths orientation is a construction of symbols, language, rhetoric, and diction. In this case, the language is ordinary. As Goldstein (1997) points out:

> Strength and resilience are social constructions with some vintage built into, over time, the ordinary, plebeian, or folk vocabulary. Terms—or really value judgments—such as virtue, willpower, integrity, fortitude are common, culturally defined ways of referring to the character and worth displayed in the face of the travails of living. (p. 28)

I would add words such as empowerment, membership, competence, potential, responsibility, growth, assets, and vision. These stand in stark contrast to the esoteric and sometimes remote vocabulary of the medical, mental health, and human service professions. Words have power: They can elevate and ennoble; or they can subvert and destroy. They can encourage and motivate; or they can dishearten and enervate.

In a sense, we are asking those who have been hurt and discouraged—those who have been clients, often unwilling, of the human service industry—to engage in both insurrection and resurrection. Many people who are thought to have disorders are the objects of a totalizing discourse (Gergen, 1991). This discourse, based on a wildly expanding deficit language and taxonomy, eventually suffuses into the identities of individuals, so that they become their designation—a schizophrenic, a borderline, a victim, an alcoholic, and so on. Insurrection involves getting the stories of oppressed and suffering people out to those who need to hear them—schools, agencies (maybe your agency), hospitals, legislators, other professionals, even family members. Unfortunately, the media and various therapeutic enterprises are now busily creating cultural stories from which many of us draw our sense of who we are—the adult child of an alcoholic, the codependent, the hapless victim. Resurrection refers to an individual's or family's or even a community's rediscovery of their capacities and resiliencies once they begin to shed the mantle of totalizing discourse and to get their own stories and narratives heard. We need to heed the words of

Edward Roberts (1992), the late president and founder of the World Institute on Disability and an individual with severe disabilities since childhood: "Never underestimate the power within any individual. Their limbs may be withered and useless but their spirit and souls are intact." Once people begin to remember and weave their own stories, their own realities, and get the word out, they often experience a resurrection of will and hope.

Major Principles of the Strengths Perspective

We know that strengths-based approaches differ from pathology-based approaches in their language. They also differ in the basic principles that guide and direct practice.

EVERY INDIVIDUAL, EVERY FAMILY, EVERY COMMUNITY HAS STRENGTHS, ASSETS, AND RESOURCES. While sometimes hard to invoke, this principle asks you to discern the resources and competencies that people have and to respect those strengths and the potential they have for reversing misfortune, countering illness, easing pain, and reaching goals. To detect strengths, you must be genuinely interested in, and respectful of, clients' stories, narratives, and accounts—the interpretive slants they take on their own experience; these are the most important theories that guide practice. You need to assume a respectful and open mindset.

TRAUMA AND ABUSE, ILLNESS AND STRUGGLE MAY BE DEVASTATING BUT THEY ALSO MAY BE OPPORTUNITIES FOR GROWTH AND SOURCES OF CHALLENGE AND OPPORTUNITY. Clearly, there are traumas that can overwhelm the coping capacities of any child or adult. Sometimes extraordinary measures are required to help such individuals get back on track. But the literature on the resilience of children and adults shows that most individuals—even children—when confronted with persistent or episodic crisis, disorganization, stress, trauma, or abuse somehow are able to surmount the adversity. They do not fall into a welter of psychopathology and the replication of their own family's chaos and disorganization. Children are active and developing individuals who, through these trials, learn skills and develop attributes that stand them in good stead in adulthood (Masten, 1994; Werner & Smith, 1992; Wolin & Wolin, 1993). In almost every study, the majority—sometimes a significant majority—of children who have experienced a very painful childhood develop into competent adults who have avoided many pitfalls and created a relatively satisfying and productive life for themselves (Benard, 1997b; Swadener & Lubeck, 1995). Not that these children and adults don't suffer or bear the scars of past hurts and cruelties; they certainly do. But along the way, thanks to resources within themselves and factors in their environments, they acquire knowledge, traits, and capacities that are preservative and life-affirming.

ASSUME THAT YOU DO NOT KNOW—NOR CAN YOU KNOW—THE UPPER LIMITS OF ANY INDIVIDUAL'S CAPACITY TO GROW AND CHANGE. A diagnosis or assessment seems to set limits on what professionals think is possible for an individual or family. Being diagnosed as schizophrenic closes doors, abridges possibilities and opportunities, subverts hopes and dreams. But we cannot know, except in the crudest of ways, what the limits are. We cannot know that; we cannot even know that about ourselves. And, if we cannot know it, then why assume it? Why not assume at the outset that there are many unknown possibilities (Deegan, 1996)? Why not assume that all of us have innate wisdom and health even though it may lie uncultivated? In his health/realization/community empowerment projects, Roger Mills (1995) noticed that

> if we treated people as healthy and showed confidence in their healthy side, they gained hope and managed things better . . . When we treat people as if they are one and the same as their problems . . . they tend to become more and more diseased . . . We concluded that we could help people much more by teaching them their own intrinsic health, rather than encouraging them to explore their dysfunctions.

The limitations we assume are often a product of the diagnosis and the process of being diagnosed.

TAKE INDIVIDUAL, FAMILY, AND COMMUNITY VISIONS AND HOPES SERIOUSLY. The basic equation of the strengths perspective is disarmingly simple. You account for and summon up the strengths, resources, and capacities of individuals and families and put them in the service of meeting needs, minimizing risks, and realizing hopes and dreams. To do this, of course, you have to know the assets of individuals and families and their environments and to take their dreams seriously. As George Vaillant (1993) notes:

> Our capacities for creativity, for mature self-deception, and for religious wonder are all facilitated in *dreaming*—both day and night dreams—as we review the past and rehearse the future. (p. 338)

Dreams fuel hopes; hopes fuel intention; intention fuels action. It does not even matter if the dream is never fully achieved in the drama of daily life. What does matter is that it is taken seriously, it is made palpable through belief and elaboration, and steps are taken to move, however haltingly, in that direction. It is, in other words, a project.

EVERY ENVIRONMENT IS FULL OF RESOURCES. No matter how harsh an environment, no matter how it may test the mettle of its inhabitants, it is also a potentially lush topography of assets and resources (Kretzmann & McKnight, 1993; McKnight, 1995; Shaffer & Anundsen, 1993; Sullivan, 1997) containing informal consolidations of individuals, families, and groups, associational networks of peers, systems of intergenerational mentoring, and individuals willing to give time and succor. In the strengths model of case management (Rapp, 1998), natural resources are preferred and sought before seeking resources in the service system. In the words of McKnight (1995), the community vision of society

> understands the community as the basic context for enabling people to contribute their gifts. It sees community associations as contexts in which to create and locate jobs, provide opportunities for recreation and multiple friendships, and become the political defender of the right of labelled people to be free from exile. (p. 169)

Subsidiary Principles of the Strengths Perspective

There are other principles of the strengths perspective, many of which flow from those just discussed.

DON'T TAKE NO FOR AN ANSWER. People who are in trouble or in crisis don't tend to think in terms of their strengths. It takes some diligence and artful demonstrations on your part to move them in the direction of seeing some of their virtues.

HELP CORRECT THE EFFECTS OF BEING LABELED. Many people who have been a part of the welfare, social service, mental health, or health systems have been taught deficit- and problem-based self-definitions very well. For some, these designations have become a central part of their identity. You must be active in pointing out (in terms of their daily life, in their real time, in their actual place) how, in fact, they are much more than a label, a reputation, or a case.

TAKE ADVANTAGE OF THE CONSIDERABLE RESOURCES OF CULTURE AND ETHNICITY. Every culture is rich in resources— people, rituals, symbols, healing practices, support sys-

tems, spiritual bounty—that may be used in helping people right and redirect the course of their life. Curanderismo, the medicine wheel, sweatlodge, and other rituals and healing practices will serve to provide support, tranquility, instruction, and healing. Cultural narratives of origins, of migration and settlement, of triumph over adversity and oppression may solidify identity, provide comfort, stimulate pride, and suggest future paths.

NORMALIZE AND EXTERNALIZE. To normalize requires that we work with individuals and families to turn problems into wants and possibilities. People often get stuck in a rut of conflict, disorganization, and confusion when they are trying to solve a problem, to figure out what the problem is, or to meet needs. Helping people to look toward what they want, how they would like to be, or how they might otherwise meet needs often helps to break the logjam of difficulties and stresses. Externalizing means of getting people's stories out to those individuals, associations, agencies, and institutions that need to hear them.

The problem-based approach and the strengths approach are compared in Exhibit 1–5; the contrast is drawn a little dramatically to make the point.

ASSESSMENT

The strengths perspective requires that we broaden the scope of our work and our assessment. It reminds us that individuals and families have not always had problems, and that they do not have these difficulties every waking moment; they also have successes. The emphasis is on knowing them in a more holistic way: acknowledging their hopes and dreams, their needs, their resources and the resources around them, their accomplishments, their capacities, and their gifts. The strengths perspective invites a more affirming interaction with individuals and families; as a professional, you engage them conversationally as collaborators and peers, recognizing that they and you are both experts and have a mutual interest in improving their quality of life.

Part of the work during assessment is toward normalization—understanding problems as expressions, in part, of attempts to meet needs and realize possibilities. Many problems have evolved as distorted, anguished ways to meet common human needs—for love, respect, control, tranquility, choice, stability, security, and so on. Assessment is based on an exploration of

EXHIBIT 1-5	Comparison of Strengths- and Problem-Based Approaches

Problem/dysfunction	**Strengths**
Safety and security of children and vulnerable family or group members is first concern	Safety and security of children and vulnerable family or group members is first concern
Individuals/groups are seen as vulnerable and at risk and charaterized in terms of pathologies/disorders/trauma	Individuals/groups are seen as having innate resilience, strengths, and assets in spite of problems
Individuals/groups are defined as cases and/or problems to be dealt with	Individuals/groups are defined as unique: the sum total of their talents, resources, capacities, and assets, as well as their problems
Problem- and pathology-focused vocabulary of victimization and recovery	Possibility- and development-focused vocabulary of resilience and mastery
Individual/familial/group accounts sought in service of naming the problem, deficit, abuse, pathology	Individual/familial/group accounts sought in the service of discovering who this individual or family is
Knowing the individual/family/group from the outside in	Knowing the individual/family/group from the inside out
Skeptical of individual/family accounts, which are seen as excuses, rationalizations	Disposed to believe individual/family accounts, which are seen as stories/narratives
Centerpiece of work is the treatment/work plan: goals set by professionals and protocols	Centerpiece of work is the goals and aspirations, the needs and strengths of the individual, family, or group
Professional is the ultimate expert on and arbiter of the individual's/family's/group's life	Individual/family/group are the experts on their lives—past, present, and future
Professional designs and carries out the plan of helping or treatment	Work is a collaborative effort driven by the aspirations of the individual/family/group
Possibilities for choice, control, and development are seriously limited by age and the effects of abuse, addiction, pathology	Possibilities for choice, control, and development are always open
Resources for work are primarily the knowledge and skills of the professional/service delivery system	Resources for work are primarily the strengths, capacities, and assets of the individual or family/group members and the community
Help is centered on solving the problems, controlling the symptoms, eliminating the addiction, etc.	Help is centered on getting on with life, affirming and developing values and commitments, making and finding membership in the community

the needs that are crying to be met, the hopes and dreams of individuals and family members, and the strengths and resources that they have at their disposal or can develop.

The strengths approach to assessment does not come naturally for many of us. It has to be learned, and many conceptual, professional, institutional, and interpersonal barriers need to be overcome. If the strengths and assets of colleagues are not acknowledged and employed, it will be hard for you to affirm and summon up the capacities of your clients. Mills (1995) argues strongly that the first order of business is to create the organizational and interpersonal conditions for the health of staff. In our assessments, we should always strive to be possibility-focused, goal-focused, solution-focused, and strengths-focused. The rankest amateur can find pathology in some individuals and families; it takes skill, determination, and a different standpoint to find strengths.

What Are Strengths, and How Do You Find Out about Them?

Almost anything might turn out to be a strength, depending on the context, the contingencies, and the demands in people's daily lives. Following are some of the experiences, traits, and environmental and interpersonal transactions that have been found to be strengths at one time or another.

WHAT PEOPLE LEARN AS THEY STRUGGLE. People discover inner resources as they confront demands and challenges—whether abuse, illness, death, oppression, or chronic stress. Or they may develop personal traits and qualities that help them master the trauma. As Wolin and Wolin (1993) point out, children in chaotic, disorganized, or violent families often learn interpersonal skills and develop intrapsychic habits of mind that help them survive—a sense of humor, insight into others' motives and behavior, a strong moral imagination, and creativity, for example. Some people not only learn from the successes but from their trials as well, even those they may inflict upon themselves. For example, most people quit or moderate drinking on their own because they do not like what they see in the mirror, and because they have come to cherish other values and principles of living (Peele & Brodsky, 1991).

WHAT INDIVIDUALS/FAMILIES KNOW. People learn intellectually or educationally about their world as well as discerning and distilling things through their own life experience. Perhaps an individual who, as a child, cared for an ailing parent has developed the frame of mind and interpersonal skills to tend to the needs of vulnerable or sick individuals. Another individual may be able to use an artistic medium to entertain and educate others. We cannot know what it might be unless we take the time to find out.

PERSONAL QUALITIES AND VIRTUES. Forged in the fires of trauma and hardship, these qualities might include loyalty, perseverance, independence, insight, steadfastness, self-discipline, and a sense of humor and fun; the list could be extended indefinitely. To balance the considerable invalidating weight of DSM, we need a Diagnosis of Strengths Manual, in which we account for, develop criteria of, and describe in detail the substantial virtues that people may possess.

TALENTS THAT PEOPLE HAVE. These talents may surprise not only the professional but also the talented individual, in whom they may have lain dormant for years. Playing a musical instrument, carpentry, telling stories, cooking, landscaping, painting, home repair—it could be anything. Like all strengths, these may provide tools and resources to assist individuals, families, groups, and communities in reaching their goals. In addition, they may be assets that can be shared and given to others, thereby fostering solidarity, strengthening mentorship, or cementing friendship.

CULTURAL AND FAMILY RITUALS, BELIEFS, STORIES, AND LORE. Often profound sources of strength, guidance, stability, comfort, or transformation, these resources tend to be overlooked, minimized, or distorted by official or professional orientations and definitions.

SURVIVOR'S PRIDE. People who have confronted and surmounted challenges to their integrity, health, and even existence often have, deep inside, survivor's pride. As Wolin and Wolin (1993; 1992, p. 6) note, "survivor's pride drives the engine of change, shame jams the gears!"

DREAMS AND HOPES. Individual and family dreams and hopes are as much a motivating dynamism as pride. Strengths-based practitioners aim to give palpable shape to aspirations and then help people employ their strengths and resources in a project designed to take steps toward their dreams.

THE COMMUNITY. Any community, even the most impoverished, has people, institutions, associations, organizations, and natural resources that may contribute to the well-being of individuals and families. Asked to help out another child or adult, many individuals in a public housing community, for example, will be able and willing to provide succor, respite, guidance, or material resources.

SPIRITUALITY/FAITH. For many individuals and families, the wellspring of strength and resilience is the belief in some transcendent power and in the possibility of transformation, surcease of pain, or the summoning of strength to face life's challenges.

Discovering and Uncovering Strengths

LOOK AROUND YOU. When you are with a client, do you see evidence of interests, talents, competencies? A young social work student who was visiting Mrs. G. a 35-year resident of public housing who had successfully raised 11 children, noticed the family pictures and cross-stitching with Biblical quotations on the walls. Prompted by this observation, she and Mrs. G. developed a plan in which Mrs. G. would lead a Bible study course for young mothers. It was the student's hope that Mrs. G. would also teach the young women about parenting. Mrs. G. adamantly declared that she would stick strictly to Bible instruction. But in the course of the study, Mrs. G. did pass along a lot of information about parenting. Interestingly enough, in all her years as a resident, Mrs. G. had never been asked to share her wisdom.

Here's another example. Michael, with moderate mental retardation, lived in a group home. Now an adult, he was assigned a new case manager. The social worker noticed at their first meeting that the walls of Michael's room were decorated with elegantly wrought maps of the local area, the state, and the nation. Michael told the worker that he had hand drawn them from memory; there was no record of this in Michael's extensive file. Impressed with Michael's uncanny ability, the social worker, with Michael's collaboration, brought the maps to public attention through a feature story in the Sunday supplement. As a result, Michael's maps were displayed at a local art museum. However, Michael's pride in his accomplishments was perhaps the most important outcome—an outcome that was immanent when the worker looked around.

LISTEN TO CLIENT STORIES. Stories—especially stories of survival—are often the richest source of clues about interests, hopes, strengths, and resources. When Jonelle told the story of her struggle with alcoholism, she mentioned that drawing was an important, though tenuous, source of respite for her. However, no one knew she had this talent. The social worker wondered if Jonelle would be willing to use her talent in planning a mural that children were going to paint in the community recreation room. She agreed. This project brought Jonelle great satisfaction and a little notoriety. Her struggle with alcohol continued, but she clearly had more reserves to draw upon and more determination to become sober.

LET PEOPLE KNOW YOU ARE INTERESTED IN THEIR CAPACITIES, HOPES, AND DREAMS. We have to let people know that we want to hear about their talents, their accomplishments, their virtues, and the resources within and around them. We should never dismiss their dreams as impracticable. Jim, diagnosed with chronic undifferentiated schizophrenia, wanted to work; to him, this was the sign of being a fully endowed citizen. His previous case managers, because of Jim's demeanor and appearance and his occasional hallucinations, thought that this was not practicable. A new case manager took Jim's dream seriously. They worked together to get Jim ready for the job market, rehearsing, giving shape to his dream of real work. Soon after, Jim interviewed for a job and was hired; he has now worked for two years. Jim, in fact, had much to offer any employer, but it was buried underneath official designations and opinions of who he was and what his limitations were.

Exhibit 1–6 provides several kinds of questions you might ask to discover strengths. These obviously do not exhaust likely questions; and they are not meant to be a protocol or format. Rather, they are designed to stimulate possible lines of thinking during engagement and conversation. Exhibit 1–7 is an example of a form that can be used to record strengths.

ELEMENTS OF STRENGTHS-BASED PRACTICE

Acknowledging the Pain

For many individuals and families, there is real use and purpose in addressing, acknowledging, reexperiencing, and putting into perspective the pains and trauma of life, especially those that now seem insistent. Catharsis, grieving, expression of rage and anxiety, and the metabolization of these feelings are important in developing an understanding of where individuals have been, what their current struggles are, and what emotional and

---

EXHIBIT 1-6	Questions to Discover Strengths

Survival questions. How have you managed to survive (or thrive) thus far, given all the challenges you have had to contend with? How have you been able to rise to the challenges put before you? What have you learned about yourself and your world during your struggles? Which of these difficulties have given you special strength, insight, or skill?

Support questions. What people have given you special understanding, support, and guidance? Where are they now? What did they respond to in you? What associations, organizations, or groups have been especially helpful to you up to now?

Exception questions.[1] When things are going well in life what is different? In the past, when you felt that your life was better, more interesting, or more stable, what about your world, your relationships, and your thinking was special or different? In those times in your life when your problems did not seem to be troubling you, what was different?

Possibility questions. What do you want out of life now? What are your hopes, visions, and aspirations? How far along are you toward achieving these? Which of your special talents and abilities will help you realize your dreams? How will you know when things are going well in your life—what will you be doing, who will you be with, how will you be feeling, thinking, and acting? How can I help you achieve your goals? What do you think is the first step we can take in reaching your goals?

Esteem questions. When people say good things about you, what are they likely to say? What is it about your life, yourself, and your accomplishments that gives you real pride? What gives you genuine pleasure in life? When did you begin to believe that you might achieve some of the things you wanted in life?

---

[1] Thanks to the practitioners of solution-focused therapy for this terminology. (De Jong & Miller, 1995).

EXHIBIT 1-7 **Strengths Assessment Form**

Life Domains:
 Survival/daily living: Shelter, safety, security, food, health
 Economic well-being: Income, employment, education, training
 Personal and social well-being: Personal/spiritual growth, values, mutual support, hopes and visions, physical and
  mental health, citizenship, connection

Life domain to be worked on: _____

Aspirations, interests, and needs (what do we want?) _____

_____

_____

Individual and family strengths and exceptions:

_____

_____

_____

Community and social resources available for meeting needs, achieving aspirations, and fostering a healing mind
and environment:

_____

_____

_____

Immediate goal: _____

Steps to be taken toward goal	Persons and resources involved	Target date
1.		
2.		

---

cognitive baggage they carry with them. This is also an important step in letting go of the past and conceiving a different, and better, present and future. For some, it may even be beneficial to explore the roots of trauma in family, community, and culture. It is also important to assess current risks—for example, in a family in which there has been abuse. But the purpose is always to look for the seeds of resilience and rebound, the lessons taken away from the adversity; the cultural, ethnic, and familial sources of adaptability; and resources to be used in lessening risk factors. This is the resiliency attitude (Henderson, 1997) in action!

Stimulating the Discourse and Eliciting Narratives of Resilience and Strength

Individuals often exhibit great resistance to acknowledging their competence, reserves, and resourcefulness. In addition, many traits and capacities that are signs of strength are hidden by years of self-doubt, the blame of others, and a diagnostic label. The revelation of indi-

---

EXHIBIT 1-8 **Language of the Seven Resiliencies**

The Wolins have created a model of resiliency that includes not only the damage done to individuals but seven resiliencies that individuals may develop over time—from childhood to adolescence to adulthood. These personal qualities, traits, and capacities, forged in the fire of trauma, include:

Insight: What begins in childhood as a sense that there is something wrong ends in adulthood as a deep understanding of oneself and other people.

Independence: What begins in childhood as a moving away from painful family scenes ends in adulthood as a rational and reasoned separation from (or redefined relationship with) their family.

Relationship: What begins in childhood as a search for connection to available, positive adults ends in adulthood as the ability to consciously form gratifying attachments to others.

Initiative: What begins in childhood as a way of exploring the world away from parents ends in adulthood as the ability to become focused on goals and aims and to accomplish them with energy and purpose.

Creativity and humor: What begins in childhood as playing, supposing, and pretending that one is something valued or powerful ends in adulthood as the ability to compose and make things out of nothing or to mix the terrible with the ironic and absurd and to laugh at what one has created.

Morality: What begins in childhood as questions about why one is hurt and judgments regarding the rights and wrongs of one's life ends in adulthood as dedicated service to others or to an ideal.

Source: S. J. Wolin & S. Wolin, *The resilient self: How survivors of troubled families rise above adversity.* New York: Villard (1993).

---

vidual strengths may be hindered by lack of words, by disbelief, or by lack of trust. The social worker may have to begin to provide the language—to look for and give name to those resiliencies that people have demonstrated in the past and in the present. Some names for resiliencies are listed in Exhibit 1–8. To develop such a language in the context of clients' lives, the social worker elicits stories and narratives of their daily struggles and triumphs—what they have done, how they survived, what they want, and what they want to avoid. People need to acknowledge their strengths, play them out, see them in the past and the present, feel them, and have them affirmed by the worker and others. In this way, they write a better text for themselves. The social worker can assist by reframing—not in the manner of so many family therapies, but by adding brush strokes that depict the clients' capacity and ingenuity.

Stimulating a strengths discourse involves at least two acts on your part: providing a vocabulary of strengths (in the language of the client); and mirroring—providing a positive reflection of the client's abilities and accomplishments and helping the client to find other positive mirrors in the environment (Wolin & Wolin, 1994).

Acting in Context: Education, Action, Advocacy, and Linkage

Education is the process by which individuals learn about their capacities and resiliencies, as well as their hopes, goals, and visions. Having found such competencies, the individual is encouraged to take the risk of action. Through continuous, collaborative action with the worker, individuals begin to employ their strengths as they move toward well-formed, achievable goals. The goals should be positive and verifiable and should reflect changes in behavior, knowledge, status, and/or feelings. This process is not easy for many clients. But as they decide and act, as they identify multiple strategies for achieving outcomes, they are encouraged to put their assets, resources, strengths, and resiliencies to work. Inevitably, they will also discover the limits of their resilience and the effect of still-active sore spots and scars. But, in the end, their decision making and activity, along with the mobilization of internal and external resources, will lead to changes in thinking, feeling, and relationship that are more congruent with their goals and their strengths.

It is important that the individual or family begin to use available community resources to move toward their goals. For you, this means advocacy: You must discover what natural or formal resources are available and accessible, and to what extent they are adequate and acceptable to the client (Kisthardt, 1993). The environment is full of resources: people, institutions, associations, and families who are willing and able to provide instruction, succor, relief, services, time, and mirroring. When people begin to plan ways of achieving their goals and to exercise their strengths, the effect is synergistic. They can do more personally, and they find themselves closer to connection to a community. Here's an example. The director of a respite program identified a creative strategy for providing respite to parents of children with special needs. In collaboration, a worker from the agency and the family developed a plan for the scheduling of respite, including the parents' particular needs. The worker and the parents identified potential respite givers among friends, relatives, or neighbors. The worker then assisted the family in making requests for respite. When someone agreed, all the parties worked together to formulate a contract for care. The worker also helped the respite providers identify what they expected to receive in return for their services. In some cases, parents swapped respite services. In others, the agency gave $10 to the parents, who, in turn, paid the provider (Rupe, 1997).

Normalizing and Capitalizing on Strengths

Over a period of time—often a short period of time—you and the individual or family will begin to consolidate the strengths that have emerged, reinforce the new vocabulary of strengths and resilience, and bolster the capacity to discover resources. Furthermore, you and the family periodically make an accounting of and celebrate the goals and successes that have been realized. The purpose is to cement the strengths and to assure the synergy of their continuing development and articulation. One important avenue to normalization for many who have been helped through a strengths-based approach is to teach others what they have learned in the process, a kind of mentorship. This also facilitates disengagement between worker and client, with the assurance that the personal strengths and the communal resources are in place.

CONCLUSION

The strengths perspective requires that you and your clients develop a different way of looking at what you do together. Practitioners who apply the strengths perspective report that, once clients are engaged in building up strengths and employing assets in daily living, they develop a desire to do more, to become more absorbed in daily life, and to be drawn by future possibilities.

By way of summary, Kaplan and Girard (1994) suggest that we can empower families (and individuals) in six ways:

- by believing in their ability to change and helping them to believe in that ability
- by providing families with a perspective that is hopeful and full of possibilities
- by educating families and helping them increase their own skills
- by recognizing and building upon their assets and strengths and the resources around them
- by helping families realize that they do have options and alternatives
- by designing strategies that support and strengthen cultural and ethnic backgrounds (p. 41)

LEARNING EXERCISES

1. Prepare one- or two-sentence definitions for each of the following terms, or briefly explain each term's meaning to a friend.
   developmental socialization
   ecosystem
   generalist model of practice
   partnership
   person-in-situation
   problem solving
   resiliency
   self-awareness
   social science
   social welfare
   social work intervention
   social work process
   spontaneity
   strengths perspective
   totalizing discourse

2. Review the case of the House on Sixth Street (Appendix A-3). How does this illustrate a shift in perspective from working with individuals to working with communities? How does it illustrate the idea of a social work generalist who brings in specialists when necessary to accomplish objectives?

3. In what ways did the social worker in the case of the House on Sixth Street (Appendix A-3) involve clients in decision making?

4. What implications does the idea of partnership with

clients have for your responsibilities as a professional? Try to summarize these implications in one paragraph, or briefly explain them to a friend.

5. Explain how Specht's concept of developmental socialization (Reading 1-1) relates to the ecosystem perspective or the person-in-situation focus discussed in this chapter. In your view, what is the usefulness of Specht's concept for social work assessment and intervention?

6. Does the strengths perspective presented by Saleebey in Reading 1-2 fit with the problem-solving model? Does problem solving imply an emphasis on problems or deficits and an inadequate acknowledgement of strengths?

EXHIBIT 1-9   Mrs. Warren's Profession

George Bernard Shaw wrote *Mrs. Warren's Profession* in 1894. The play, published in 1898, was so controversial that it was banned in London and was not produced until 1905 in New York. (The American producer was arrested for producing the play but was acquitted.) Mrs. Warren was an entrepreneur and successful businesswoman who had amassed considerable wealth. She had put her daughter, Vivie, through the University of Cambridge, where Vivie was one of the first female students and excelled in mathematics. Mrs. Warren worked as a prostitute and owned a chain of brothels across Europe. The play centers around the mother-daughter relationship as Vivie becomes aware of the nature of her mother's business; Mrs. Warren has hopes that Vivie will take over management of the business. This dialogue occurs in Act 2:

Mrs. Warren: You! you've no heart. *(She suddenly breaks out vehemently in her natural tongue—the dialect of a woman of the people—with all her affectations of maternal authority and conventional manners gone, and an overwhelming inspiration of true conviction and scorn in her)* Oh, I won't bear it: I won't put up with the injustice of it. What right have you to set yourself up above me like this? You boast of what you are to me—to me, who gave you the chance of being what you are. What chance had I? Shame on you for a bad daughter and a stuck-up prude!

Vivie: *(sitting down with a shrug, no longer confident; for her replies, which have sounded sensible and strong to her so far, now begin to ring rather woodenly and even priggishly against the new tone of her mother)* Don't think for a moment I set myself above you in any way. You attacked me with the conventional authority of a mother. I defended myself with the conventional superiority of a respectable woman. Frankly, I am not going to stand any of your nonsense; and when you drop it I shall not expect you to stand any of mine. I shall always respect your right to your own opinions and your own way of life.

Mrs. Warren: My own opinion and my own way of life! Listen to her talking! Do you think I was brought up like you? able to pick and choose my own way of life? Do

you think I did what I did because I liked it, or thought it right, or wouldn't rather have gone to college and been a lady if I'd had the chance?

Vivie: Everybody has some choice, mother. The poorest girl alive may not be able to choose between being Queen of England or Principal of Newnham; but she can choose between ragpicking and flowerselling, according to her taste. People are always blaming their circumstances for what they are. I don't believe in circumstances. The people who get on in this world are the people who get up and look for the circumstances they want, and, if they can't find them, make them.

Mrs. Warren: Oh, it's easy to talk, very easy isn't it? Here! Would you like to know what my circumstances were?

Vivie: Yes: you had better tell me. Won't you sit down?

Mrs. Warren: Oh, I'll sit down: don't you be afraid. *(She plants her chair farther forward with brazen energy, and sits down. Vivie is impressed in spite of herself)* D'you know what your gran'mother was?

Vivie: No.

Mrs. Warren: No, you don't. I do. She called herself a widow and had a fried-fish shop down by the Mint, and kept herself and four daughters out of it. Two of us were sisters; that was me and Liz; and we were both good-looking and well-made. I suppose our father was a well-fed man: mother pretended he was a gentleman; but I don't know. The other two were only half sisters: undersized, ugly, starved-looking, hard-working, honest, poor creatures: Liz and I would have half-murdered them if mother hadn't half-murdered us to keep our hands off them. They were the respectable ones. Well, what did they get by their respectability? I'll tell you. One of them worked in a whitelead factory twelve hours a day for nine shillings a week until she died of lead poisoning. She only expected to get her hands a little paralyzed; but she died. The other was always held up to us as a model because she married a Government laborer in the Deptford victualling yard, and kept his room and the three children neat and tidy on eighteen shillings a week—until he took to drink. That was worth being respectable for, wasn't it?

UNIV. OF FRANCE
JOLIET LIBRO

EXHIBIT 1-9 **(continued)**

Vivie: *(now thoughtfully attentive)* Did you and your sister think so?

Mrs. Warren: Liz didn't, I can tell you: she had more spirit. We both went to a church school—that was part of the ladylike airs we gave ourselves to be superior to the children that knew nothing and went nowhere—and we stayed there until Liz went out one night and never came back. I know the schoolmistress thought I'd soon follow her example; for the clergyman was always warning me that Lizzie'd end up jumping off Waterloo Bridge. Poor fool: that was all he knew about it! I was more afraid of the whitelead factory than I was of the river; and so would you have been in my place. That clergyman got me a situation as scullery maid in a temperance restaurant where they sent out for anything you liked. Then I was waitress; then I went to the bar at Waterloo station: fourteen hours a day serving drinks and washing glasses for four shillings a week and my board. That was considered a great promotion for me. Well, one cold, wretched night, when I was so tired I could hardly keep myself awake, who should come up for a half of Scotch but Lizzie, in a long fur cloak, elegant and comfortable, with a lot of sovereigns in her purse.

Vivie: *(grimly)* My aunt Lizzie!

Mrs. Warren: Yes; and a very good aunt to have, too. She's living down at Winchester now, close to the cathedral, one of the most respectable ladies there. Chaperons girls at the county ball, if you please. No river for Liz, thank you! You remind me of Liz a little: she was a first-rate business woman—saved money from the beginning—never let herself look too like what she was—never lost her head or threw away a chance.

When she saw I'd grown up good-looking she said to me across the bar, "What are you doing there, you little fool? Wearing out your health and your appearance for other people's profit!" Liz was saving money then to take a house for herself in Brussels; and she thought we two could save faster than one. So she lent me some money and gave me a start; and I saved steadily and first paid her back, and then went into business with her as her partner. Why shouldn't I have done it? The house in Brussels was real high class; a much better place for a woman to be in than the factory where Anne Jane got poisoned. None of our girls were ever treated as I was treated in the scullery of that temperance place, or at the Waterloo bar, or at home. Would you have had me stay in them and become a worn out old drudge before I was forty?

Vivie: *(intensely interested by this time)* No; but why did you choose that business? Saving money and good management will succeed in any business.

Mrs. Warren: Yes, saving money. But where can a woman get the money to save in any other business? Could you save out of four shillings a week and keep yourself dressed as well? Not you. Of course, if you're a plain woman and can't earn anything more; or if you have a turn for music, or the stage, or newspaper-writing; that's different. But neither Liz nor I had any turn for such things: all we had was our appearance and our turn for pleasing men. Do you think we were such fools as to let other people trade in our good looks by employing us as shopgirls, or barmaids, or waitresses, when we could trade them in ourselves and get all the profits instead of starvation wages? Not likely.

Source: Bernard Shaw, *The Complete Plays of Bernard Shaw*. London: Paul Hamlyn (1965), pp. 75–76. (First published in 1898.)

---

7. Exhibit 1–9, an excerpt from one of George Bernard Shaw's plays, presents a conversation between Mrs. Warren and her adult daughter, Vivie. How does this illustrate the person-in-situation concept? Do you agree more with Vivie or with Mrs. Warren? What are the reasons for your views? Now, try to state reasons in support of the opposing view. How does this excerpt help us understand people at the beginning of the 21st century—over 100 years after it was written? What does it suggest about our responses to clients?

REFERENCES

American Psychiatric Association. (1994). *Diagnostic and statistical manual of mental disorders* (4th ed.). Washington, DC: Author.

Baer, B. L., & Federico, R. C. (1978). *Educating the baccalaureate social worker.* Cambridge, MA: Ballinger.

Barber, J. G. (1995). Political progressive casework. *Families in Society,* 76(1), 30–37.

Bartlett, H. M. (1970). *The common base of social work practice.* New York: National Association of Social Workers.

Benard, B. (1997a). Fostering resiliency in children and youth: Promoting protective factors in the school. In D. Saleebey (Ed.), *The strengths perspective in social work practice* (2nd. ed., pp. 167–182). New York: Longman.

UNIV. OF ST. FRANCIS
JOLIET, ILLINOIS

Benard, B. (1997b, Winter). Resiliency research: A foundation for youth development. *Resiliency in Action, 2,* 13–18.

Bisno, H. (1969). A theoretical framework for teaching social work methods and skills with particular reference to undergraduate social welfare education. *Journal of Education for Social Work, 5*(2), 5–17.

Boehm, W. W. (1958). The nature of social work. *Social Work, 3*(2), 10–19.

Bricker-Jenkins, M. (1997). Hidden treasures: Unlocking strengths in the public social services. In D. Saleebey (Ed.), *The strengths perspective in social work practice* (2nd ed., pp. 133–150). New York: Longman.

Clark, M. (1997). Strengths-based practice: The new paradigm. *Corrections Today, 59*(2), 110–111, 165.

Coady, M. F. (1993). An argument for generalist social work practice with families versus family systems therapy. *Canadian Social Work Review, 10*(1), 27–42.

De Jong, P., & Miller, S. D. (1995). How to interview for client strengths. *Social Work, 40*(6), 729–736.

Deegan, P. (1996). Recovery as a journey of the heart. *Psychiatric Rehabilitation Journal, 19,* 91–97.

Dineen, T. (1996). *Manufacturing victims: What the psychology industry is doing to people.* Montreal: Robert Davies.

Dinerman, M. (1992). Managing the maze: Case management and service delivery. *Administrators in Social Work, 16*(1), 1–9.

Fast, B., & Chapin, R. (1997). The strengths model with older adults: Critical practice components. In D. Saleebey (Ed.), *The strengths perspective in social work practice* (2nd. ed., pp. 115–132). New York: Longman.

Fook, J. (1993). *Radical casework: A theory of practice.* St. Leonards, Australia: Allen & Unwin.

Franklin, C. (1995). Expanding the vision of the social constructionist debates: Creating relevance for practitioners. *Families in Society, 76*(7), 395–407.

Franklin, D. L. (1990). The cycles of social work practice: Social action vs. individual interest. *Journal of Progressive Human Services, 1*(2), 59–80.

Freedman, J., & Combs, G. (1996). *Narrative therapy: The social construction of preferred realities.* New York: W. W. Norton.

Gazzaniga, M. S. (1992). *Nature's mind: The biological roots of thinking, emotions, sexuality, language, and intelligence.* New York: Basic Books.

Gergen, K. J. (1991). *The saturated self: Dilemmas of identity in contemporary society.* New York: Basic Books/Harper Collins.

Germain, C. B. (1973). An ecological perspective in casework practice. *Social Casework, 54*(6), 326–331.

Germain, C. B. (1981). The ecological approach to people: Environmental transactions. *Social Casework, 62*(6), 323–331.

Germain, C. B., & Gitterman, A. (1980). *The life model of social work practice.* New York: Columbia University Press.

Germain, C. B., & Gitterman, A. (1996). *The life model of social work practice: Advances in theory and practice.* New York: Columbia University Press.

Giffords, E. D. (1998). Social work on the Internet: An Introduction. *Social Work, 43*(3), 243–251.

Goldstein, H. (1997). Victors or victims? In D. Saleebey (Ed.), *The strengths perspective in social work practice* (2nd. ed., pp. 21–36). New York: Longman.

Henderson, N. (1997). Resiliency and asset development: A continuum for youth success. *Resiliency in Action, 2,* 23–27.

Kaminer, W. (1993). *I'm dysfunctional, you're dysfunctional.* New York: Vintage Books.

Kaplan, A. (1964). *The conduct of inquiry: Methodology for behavior science.* San Francisco: Chandler.

Kaplan, L., & Girard, J. (1994). *Strengthening high-risk families: A handbook for practitioners.* New York: Lexington Books.

Karls, J. M., & Wandrei, K. E. (1992). PIE: A new language for social work. *Social Work, 37*(10), 80–85.

Kemp, S. P., Whittaker, J. K., & Tracy, E. M. (1997). *Person-environment practice: The social ecology of interpersonal helping.* New York: Aldine de Gruyter.

Kidneigh, H. C. (1969). A note on organizing knowledge. In *Modes of professional organization: Vol. II. Tulane Studies in Social Welfare* (pp. 153–160). New Orleans: School of Social Work, Tulane University.

Kisthardt, W. E. (1993). A strengths model of case management: The principles and functions of a helping partnership with persons with persistent mental illness. In M. Harris & H. Bergman (Eds.), *Case management for mentally ill persons: Theory and practice.* Langhorne, PA: Harwood Academic Publishers.

Kisthardt, W. E. (1997). The strengths model of case management: Principles and helping functions. In D. Saleebey (Ed.), *The strengths perspective in social work practice* (2nd ed., pp. 97–114). New York: Longman.

Kretzmann, J. P., & McKnight, J. L. (1993). *Building communities from the inside out.* Evanston, IL: Northwestern University, Center for Urban Affairs and Policy Research.

Lee, P. R. (1929). Social work: Cause or function. In National Conference on Social Welfare (Ed.), *Proceedings of the National Conference on Social Work* (pp. 3–20). New York: Columbia University Press.

Lewis, H. (1972). Morality and the politics of practice. *Social Casework, 53*(6), 404–417.

Lockhart, A. (1982). The insider-outsider dialectic in native socioeconomic development: A case study in process understanding. *The Canadian Journal of Native Studies, 2*(1), 159–168.

Masten, A. S. (1994). Resilience in individual development: Successful adaptation despite risk and adversity. In M. C. Wang & E. W. Gordon (Eds.), *Education resilience in inner-city America: Challenges and prospects* (pp. 3–25). Hillsdale, NJ: Lawrence Erlbaum.

McKnight, J. L. (1995). *The careless society: Community and its counterfeits.* New York: Basic Books.

Meyer, C. H. (1970). *Social work practice: A response to the urban crisis.* New York: Free Press.

Miller, S. D., & Berg, I. K. (1995). *The miracle method: A radically new approach to problem drinking.* New York: W. W. Norton.

Mills, R. (1995). *Realizing mental health.* New York: Sulzberger & Graham.

National Association of Social Workers. (1981). Conceptual frameworks II [Special Issue]. *Social Work, 26*(1), 6–75.

National Association of Social Workers, (1996). *Code of ethics.* Washington, DC: Author.

Parsons, R. J., & Cox, E. O. (1994). *Empowerment-oriented social work practice with the elderly.* Pacific Grove, CA: Brooks/Cole.

Peele, S. (1989). *The diseasing of America.* Lexington, MA: Lexington Books.

Peele, S., & Brodsky, A. (1991). *The truth about addiction and recovery.* New York: Simon & Schuster.

Peterson, K. J. (1979). Assessment in the life model: A historical perspective. *Social Casework, 60*(10), 586–596.

Pincus, A., & Minahan, A. (1973). *Social work practice: Model and method.* Itasca, IL: Peacock.

Proctor, E., Vosler, N., & Sirles, E. (1993). The social-environmental context of child clients: An empirical exploration. *Social Work, 38*(3), 256–261.

Rapp, C. A. (1998). *The strengths model: Case management with people suffering from severe and persistent mental illness.* New York: Oxford University Press.

Rapp, R. (1997). The strengths perspective and persons with substance abuse problems. In D. Saleebey (Ed.), *The strengths perspective in social work practice* (2nd ed., pp. 77–96). New York: Longman.

Raymond, G. T., Teare, R. J., & Atherton, C. R. (1996). Is "field of practice" a relevant organizing principle for the MSW curriculum? *Journal of Social Work Education, 32*(1), 19–30.

Reeser, L. C. (1991). Professionalization, striving, and social work activism. *Journal of Social Science Research, 14*(3/4), 1–22.

Rein, M. (1970). Social work in search of a radical profession. *Social Work, 15*(2), 13–33.

Rieff, D. (1991, October). Victims All. *Harper's Magazine,* pp. 49–56.

Roberts, E. (October, 1992). Keynote address. Annual conference of social workers and psychologists working with closed head and spinal cord injuries. Las Vegas, Nevada.

Rose, S. (Ed.). (1992). *Case management and social work practice.* White Plains, NY: Longman.

Rupe, M. (1997). *Strengths model for family preservation and family reunification.* Training manual. Lawrence, KS: School of Social Welfare, University of Kansas.

Schwartz, W. (1961). Social worker in the group. In National Conference on Social Welfare (Ed.), *Social welfare forum* (pp. 146–171). New York: Columbia University Press.

Shaffer, C. R., & Anundsen, K. (1993). *Creating community anywhere: Finding support and connection in a fragmented world.* New York: Jeremy P. Tarcher/Putnam.

Simon, B. L. (1994). *The empowerment traditions in American social work: A history.* New York: Columbia University Press.

Specht, H. (1988). *New directions for social work practice.* Englewood Cliffs, NY: Prentice-Hall.

Specht, H. (1990). Social work and the popular psychotherapies. *Social Service Review, 64*(3), 345–356.

Stern, S. B., & Smith, C. A. (1995). Family processes and delinquency in an ecological context. *Social Service Review, 69*(4), 703–731.

Sullivan, W. P. (1997). On strengths, niches, and recovery from serious mental illness. In D. Saleebey (Ed.), *The strengths perspective in social work practice* (2nd ed., pp. 183–197). New York: Longman.

Swadener, B. B., & Lubeck, S. (Eds.). (1995). *Children and families "at promise": Deconstructing the discourse of risk.* Albany, NY: State University of New York Press.

Taber, M. A., & Vattano, A. J. (1970). Clinical and social orientations in social work: An empirical study. *Social Service Review, 44*(1), 34–43.

Vaillant, G. E. (1993). *The wisdom of the ego.* Cambridge, MA: Harvard University Press.

Weil, A. (1995). *Spontaneous healing.* New York: Alfred A. Knopf.

Werner, E., & Smith, R. S. (1992). *Overcoming the odds: High risk children from birth to adulthood.* Ithaca, NY: Cornell University Press.

Wolin, S. J., & Wolin, S. (1992). The challenge model: How children can rise above adversity. *Family Dynamics of Addiction Quarterly, 2*(2), 1–9.

Wolin, S. J., & Wolin, S. (1993). *The resilient self: How survivors of troubled families rise above adversity.* New York: Villard.

Wolin, S. J., & Wolin, S. (1994, October). *The challenge model of helping.* Workshop sponsored by Kansas City Employee Assistance Programs. Kansas City, MO.

Wood, G. G., & Middleman, R. R. (1991). Advocacy and social action: Key elements in the structural approach to direct practice in social work. *Social Work with Groups, 14*(3/4), 53–76.

chapter 2

The Ecosystem Perspective and the Use of Knowledge

CHAPTER PREVIEW

Your supporting social science courses will have provided you with some of the knowledge base on human behavior and the social environment that you need to be an effective social work practitioner. Social work educators often refer to these as the HBSE (human behavior and social environment) foundation courses required for social work practice. This language reflects the ecosystem or person-in-situation focus that we introduced in Chapter 1.

In this chapter, we will summarize aspects of the ecosystem focus central to our model of practice. Here are the main ideas:

1. In the general systems framework, systems are regarded as goal-directed, or purposeful, and have boundaries; systems may be nested within one another.

2. The concept of ecosystems, or the person-in-situation, is adapted from general systems theory and provides a focus for social work practice.

3. This framework requires the practitioner to possess knowledge regarding the environment, the person, and their interaction; much of this knowledge is borrowed from the supporting social sciences, especially role theory and egopsychology. The profession, however, is responsible for organizing and focusing this knowledge to guide practice.

4. Social work also develops and organizes knowledge for practice from its own professional experience; this is primarily knowledge about assessment and intervention.

5. Knowledge is never complete. Thus, we must

always be concerned about how to act in the absence of knowledge and about how knowledge is used in the service of clients.

The three readings at the end of this chapter elaborate on these ideas. In Reading 2-1, Felix Yaroshevsky and David Schatzky argue for the importance of a family (that is, system) assessment before medication is prescribed to regulate the behavior of troubled children. In Reading 2-2, Lyle Longclaws points to the importance of considering culture, including spirituality, in work with Native people. Finally, in Reading 2-3, Jane Gilgun describes how a system orientation can guide social work assessment. She uses genograms and ecomapping to understand individual and family placement in larger systems.

SYSTEMS THEORY

Theories used as a base for social work practice must inform us about the nature of person-environment interrelatedness and person-situation transactions. Systems theory meets this requirement. It offers a conceptual framework that shifts attention from the cause-and-effect relationship to the person and situation as an interrelated whole. We do not ask whether the environment causes the person to behave in a certain way or whether the person affects the environment in a certain way. Rather, the person is observed as a part of his or her total life situation; person and situation are a whole in which each element is both cause and effect in a complex set of relationships. These dynamic interactions, transactions, and organizational patterns are critical to the functioning of both the individual and the situation but are observable only when we study the whole system.

The whole is always more than the sum of its parts. You cannot understand a problem in social functioning by adding together, as separate entities, an assessment of the individual and an assessment of the environment. Rather, you must strive for understanding of the complex interactions between client and all levels of social systems, as well as the meaning that the client assigns to these interactions. Theory used by social workers must allow for problems to be identified in the transactions, lack of fit, opportunities, and limitations among individuals and the various levels of environment that make up our social systems. This is different than thinking of problems as individual or family pathology. The terms *dysfunctional individual* or *dysfunctional family* are to be avoided, because they do not reflect the interactional nature of individuals, families, and their environments.

A system is usually defined as a whole, a unit, composed of people and their interactions, including their relationships. Each person in the system is related to the others in a more or less stable way, within a particular time and space. However, the system is constantly changing, as it moves toward its goals. Kaplan (1986) has suggested that it is possible to compare a system to a tuning fork: "When you strike one end, the other end reverberates" (p. 16). Individuals within a social system are always interacting; the absence of overt interaction is itself an interaction. Systems theory serves social work well, in that its conceptual framework supports the purpose of the profession by shifting attention from either the person or the environment to problems in the interaction.

The systems perspective does not provide directives or prescriptions for action. However, it serves as a base from which to develop a model and a much-expanded repertoire of interventive actions. Systems theory holds that an intervention at any point in the system will affect the entire system; if you want one end of the tuning fork to reverberate, you may either strike that end directly or you may strike the fork at any place along its length. Thus, as a social worker, you will need to consider alternative actions that lead to the change sought. Plan-

ning careful and creative use of alternatives with your client will be an important part of your work.

Open and Closed Systems

Closed systems do not interact with any other systems; they neither accept input nor provide output. Closed systems tend toward less differentiation of their parts (all parts become alike) and lose organization and effective function; they are characterized by entropy. To grow and develop, systems must be open to input from other systems. A striking example is the problems that social workers find in children of families who have rigid, closed boundaries and do not permit input from other systems in the community. Another example is the problem of effectively and humanely governing prisons and other total institutions, such as nursing homes and residential treatment centers, given that they are relatively closed systems with only guarded input across their boundaries. In Chapter 6, we will ask you to consider whether confidentiality in social work practice can be used to create a closed worker-client system. And, if so, what are the implications of this?

A boundary is a closed circle around selected variables, or parts, such that there is less interchange of energy or communication across the circle than there is within the circle. Open systems have semipermeable boundaries; how open or closed the boundaries are will be different for different systems. All of us are familiar with communities that are very conscious of their identity and are unwilling to tolerate strangers or new behavior. In time, such communities, with relatively closed boundaries, may suffer some of the effects of entropy. Growing systems have well-defined semipermeable boundaries and have ways of maintaining those boundaries.

Suppose you are visiting a family because a child is in trouble with the school or community. If a parent greets you at the door with the statement that he needs none of your interference and can take care of his own children, you have two pieces of important data: You know that this parent is probably the person in the family charged with boundary maintenance, and you know that the boundaries around this family appear at first contact to be closed. You may expect that the system itself will be in trouble because of lack of input of new information and energy. You will also have questions about how you can be admitted inside the boundaries. Are the boundaries closed to you only because of the organization you represent or the purpose of your visit? Or is this the family's usual way of functioning? Is this a desperate attempt to protect the integrity of the system, or is it a cultural pattern of the family in relating to outsiders? Whatever the cause of the closed boundaries, you know that the health of the system depends on its becoming more flexible and open.

You will also encounter families in which boundaries seem too open and unguarded. You may be allowed to intrude at will; invited in, you find yourself sitting in the midst of chaos, with no sense that this is any more than a collection of individuals. The lack of boundary maintenance is your first clue that such families are in trouble.

In their work together, social workers and clients establish conceptual boundaries to define the phenomena that demand their attention; these are the boundaries of the system of concern. Typically, the definition of the problem and the definition of the system of concern are inextricably related. For example, when an individual brings a problem, do you define the problem as lying within the boundaries of the individual as a complete social system? Or do you define the problem in such a way that the family system becomes the focus of concern and the individual is seen only as a component of the system? (Yaroshevsky and Schatzky address this matter in Reading 2-1, in the context of medicating children with problem behavior.) Or do you believe that the problem falls within the sphere of another institution? In establishing the boundaries of the system of concern, you need to determine what transactions are central to the solution of the problem (Klenk & Ryan, 1974).

Nested Systems

The individual may be regarded as a system nested within a person-situation system. But the person is also composed of a set of subsystems, such as the physical-biological system, the cognitive system, the emotional system, and the action and reaction system. Beyond the level of the person-situation interaction are still larger systems. Thus, the person is embedded within a hierarchical arrangement of systems; each system is part of a larger whole and is also a suprasystem to other systems.

Smaller systems incorporate and assimilate the larger system into themselves. The familiar social work principle that we need to consider the individual and the environment could be restated as the injunction that we should consider the environment as found in the individual. The importance of culture is not only that it is a larger system surrounding the individual but also that it is part of the individual. Simon (1952) speaks of the layering of systems and points out that the individual, primary groups, organizations, and so on can best be considered as nests of Chinese blocks, in which any activity taking place in one system at one of these layers will be operating simultaneously in at least one other system at another level.

Each level in a system faces both ways, toward the smaller systems of which it is composed and toward the larger system of which it is a part. Any action that you take with any piece of the system may affect the whole system and may then spread like ripples outward into the larger system and inward to smaller divisions of the system. Thus, your action with an individual is going to affect the family or intimate group of which he or she is a part and will spread from there out into the larger social groups and organizations of which that group is a part. In the same way, actions taken with the individual will affect all systems of that individual—physical, psychological, cognitive, and so on. You may recall the familiar debate about the relationship between attitudes and behavior: Does a person's attitude need to change before behavior changes? Systems theory suggests that this is not a helpful discussion, because changing behavior is likely to result in attitude change, and vice versa.

Activity within a particular system relies on the performance of all systems at lower levels. Further, activity of a system at any given level is a part of, and may be controlled by, systems at higher levels. New properties emerge at each successively higher level (Magnusson & Allen, 1983b). This principle may be seen in the family system. The family as a larger system relies on individual members to play their parts if it is to function successfully. Family members who cannot fill their function in the family will require that the family make some adjustment and, depending on the extent of the failure, may severely impair the family's ability to function. If a parent loses a job, each family member will suffer individually, and the family system will be highly stressed. The parent will seek to find a new job within the larger social system. If the family is to continue to function at previous levels, the larger system must provide the parent with the resource (work) that is sought. The community will take action against jobless parents who steal to feed their children, and may also take legal action if the children are allowed to go hungry. In society, parents are expected to find appropriate ways to feed their children—for example, through work, welfare, and informal systems of support.

Power is the ability of larger systems to limit the behavior of smaller systems and to offer opportunities for their growth. This is a key concept in analyzing the relationships between the various levels of systems (Ullman, 1969). As social workers, we need to consider the relationship between power, powerlessness, and the processes of human growth and development. We must be aware of the ways in which power within larger social systems deprives smaller systems of adequate and effective solutions to problems of growth and development and thus decreases the individual's ability to select appropriate solutions to problems of social functioning. An individual may have the personal qualities and resources required to cope effectively with life, but may be deprived of access to appropriate resources by the larger social system.

Goal-Directed Behavior in Systems

Change and stability. Human systems are constantly in the process of change and movement. Such movements are the system's attempt to take purposive goal-directed action. Human systems strive for the enhancement and elaboration of internal order and for the ordering and selection of outside stimuli to maintain purposive movement toward a goal.

As it changes, a system maintains a dynamic equilibrium—a *steady state*. Movement toward a goal and the need for order and stability are both essential to systems. However, in some theories of human growth and behavior, the human need for stability and pattern is regarded as the central concern of the practitioner. They assert that, once a pattern is established, it cannot be changed by the system without help; the system maintains this homeostatic pattern, just as a thermostatically controlled heating system maintains a steady tempera-

ture. What this position ignores is that a system is always changing. A social system includes both forces for change and forces promoting stability. Change forces are generally used by the system to achieve goals, provided that they are not blocked by environmental factors. Thus, instead of attempting to oppose a force within the client, you may be concerned with finding ways to ally your strength with client strengths in order to overcome the obstacles to growth. If the direction of the client's movement appears to be destructive, you must first examine—and perhaps renegotiate—system goals, so that the push of the system toward change can be allied with your strengths.

Equifinality and multifinality. Equifinality is the capacity to achieve identical results from different initial conditions. There are many ways to accomplish the same objective. If a system is open, the final state or objective will not depend on the initial conditions. Such a system will have an objective of its own, and the results will depend on the interactions of the elements of the system and the transactions of the system with other systems in relation to that purpose. The concept of multifinality suggests an opposite principle: Similar conditions may lead to dissimilar results. Thus, similar initial conditions in any client may or may not be relevant to the establishment of the objective.

Patterns of recurring interactions. All systems develop patterns of recurring interactions. These patterns result in routine interactive behaviors between various subsystems. Patterns can be either rigid or flexible. Next time you are a member of a class, observe the seats that members take at the first and subsequent sessions. People tend to take the same seats each time, although there is no overt rule about where people should sit. This is an example of the patterned behavior that occurs in a system. Systems function better and meet the needs of both the system and the subsystems when they have a flexible pattern of action, are able to use many patterns, and adapt to a variety of situations. You can test the rigidity of the seating pattern in a class by taking a seat usually occupied by someone else and observing the behavior of that person. There may be an overt objection to your change of seats. Is the objection brief, or are some members very upset that have changed the pattern? If you try to explain that you were testing the rules of the system, is there general acknowledgement of what happened, or do some members give you good reasons why the pattern is important? Such patterns usually operate below the conscious level of the people in the system, particularly in family systems, and people are surprised when the pattern is identified and called to their attention.

Attempts to change a system are based on the identification of such patterns. Suppose that, in a family interview, the mother answers every time the worker asks the adolescent a question. This pattern in the family denies autonomy to the adolescent, especially in an interaction with someone outside the boundaries of the family system. It may be a rule of family behavior that the mother will answer for all members in the family when any outsider intrudes. Thus, each pattern of interaction in a system is based on rules about behavior within that system. The violation of these rules has consequences, because the system has power to limit individual expression. Rules are "implicit and unwritten; indirectly expressed and inferred; recurring over time; self-perpetuating" and are a parsimonious way of dealing with the complexity of interaction (Kaplan, 1986, p. 18). There are two types of system rules: (1) rules about behavior; and (2) rules about how to make rules. You will meet families in which there is an ongoing quarrel over how often the adolescent may date during the week, for example. In reality, these quarrels may not be over the actual rules but may represent the adolescent's demand to have some participation in rule making—that is, a desire to change the rules about how rules are made.

Rules operate when we move from one system to another. Because these rules are unconscious, they are generally accepted as reality—as the way things work. Thus, when two people marry, they may bring conflicting rules into their new family system. Since each assumes that his or her rule is the way things should be, there can be many conflicts over which rule is right. Neither rule represents a correct view of reality but is simply a residue from an earlier system. This perspective is also important when we are working with people from another culture. Neither our way of doing things nor their way of doing things represents the truth. We will fail in our helping role unless we understand the way larger systems' rules become a part of our reality and a part of ourselves.

Tension. Tension is characteristic of all systems that are open to transactions across their boundaries. It may manifest itself in either destructive or constructive ways. Identification of tensions and analysis of how and to what purpose they operate within and between systems is important for social work. Buckley (1967) argues that we should not regard inertia as a fixed quality of complex, adaptive systems, with tension as a disturbing factor; rather "some level of tension must be seen as characteristic of and vital to such systems although it may manifest itself as now destructive, now constructive" (p. 53).

Feedback and purposive systems. Feedback underlies purposive, goal-seeking mechanisms. Feedback is "a communications network which produces action in response to an input of information and includes the results of its own action in the new information by which it modifies its subsequent behavior" (Deutsch, 1968, p. 390). Human systems are feedback-controlled, goal-directed systems, "since it is the deviations from the goal state itself that direct the behavior of the system" (Buckley, 1967, p. 53). The goal-directed feedback loop underlying self-directing human and social systems involves accepting information from the outside, imputing meaning to the information, establishing priorities among information processed with respect to a goal, and activating appropriate behavior to bring the system in line with its goal (Buckley, 1967). Thus, feedback is central to the interaction between a system and its environment. In a complex adaptive system, there are multistage mediating processes between the reception of feedback and its use (Buckley, 1967).

Feedback may be negative or positive. Negative feedback carries information that the system is behaving in such a way as to make it difficult to achieve its goal; such feedback should result in behavioral correction in line with goals. Positive feedback indicates that the system is behaving correctly in relation to its goal and calls for more behavior of the same quality. Negative feedback corrects deviation, since it results in behavioral change back to the goal; positive feedback moves toward ever greater deviation from the previous state, since it calls for more of the same.

It is critical to understand that the system is goal-directed and will evaluate the usefulness of your input against its goals. To be optimally helpful, you need to know the goals of the system. If the goals of the client are ignored, for example, your helping effort will wander along with no direction, or you may inappropriately set goals yourself, rather than negotiating with the client. You will not be effective unless you understand how the client wants the problem solved and how that desired solution relates to the client's life goals.

Systems and Social Work Practice

Most of the examples of systems theory used so far have involved client systems. However, you will do some of your most important, time-consuming, and demanding work with people other than those traditionally viewed as clients. Your primary focus may involve work with other systems if you are to help clients solve problems in social living. If you are in child welfare services, you will work with court services, medical services, neighbors, police, attorneys, the school system, foster parents, and other child care services. In addition, you will work as part of an organized agency. Workers usually think of clients as the people they are there to help, but you may want to consider seriously who really benefits from your change efforts. Who is the client in the case of child abuse—the child, the parents, or the community that asked you to get involved? Who gives you the right to interfere in other people's lives? Who sanctions what you do? In your daily transactions, you will find that in order to achieve some overall goal, you are working with many different people about different things and for different reasons. We discuss this matter further in Chapters 3 and 4. The key point here is that, as a social worker, you will be interacting in many overlapping systems.

Pincus and Minahan (1973) suggest that you will be interacting with four types of social systems: the change agent system, the client system, the target system, and the action system. To these we add the professional system. Decisions about the purpose and the relationships that should be a part of each encounter will determine the specific definition of each system.

Change agent system. Social workers are change agents employed for the purpose of planning and working with other systems. The agency or organization of which you are a part can be thought of as the change agent system. Obviously, the change agent system will heavily influence your behavior, through policies that represent sanctions, constraints, and resources. These will be discussed in greater detail in Chapter 5, where we consider the source of authority for your professional actions.

Client system. People may be considered a part of the client system when they have asked for your services or have entered into an implicit contract with you. (For further discussion on defining clients, see Chapter 3.) Some people voluntarily seek your help, but you will often approach a person because of a responsibility to the community—for example, if you work in corrections, child welfare, protection for aged and persons with disabilities, and so on. It is not clear what the client system is in these cases; perhaps the community is the client. Also, neighborhood center staff (a change agent system) may identify a neighborhood need and ask you to form a group to deal with it. In this instance, the community or the change agent system itself may be considered the client. The people identified as the targets of your efforts are potential clients, until some sort of agreement is reached by which they sanction intervention in their lives and transactions. Without an agreement, they may be the target system. This important point will be discussed further in Chapter 3.

Target system. The people who change agents "need to change or influence in order to accomplish their goals" are the target systems (Pincus & Minahan, 1973, p. 58). The target system and the client system overlap if the client needs to change. However, much of social work practice involves working with the client system toward some desired change in some other system (a target system). Unless intervention is clearly with a person's agreement, a system cannot be considered a client system. If you approach a person at the request of someone else, or a person comes to you because he or she is ordered to do so, the person to whom your change efforts are directed is the target system; the person or agency who brought you together with the target system is the client system. Individuals who see you under the orders of another person become clients when they accept that you can help them and express a wish for help.

Action system. The action system consists of those with whom the social worker interacts in a cooperative way to accomplish the purposes of the change effort. You will be engaged in numerous action systems, such as neighborhood groups, family groups, mutual aid groups, and professional teams.

Professional system. This system is made up of professional associations of social workers, the educational system by which workers are prepared, and the values and sanctions of professional practice. The values and the culture of the professional system strongly influence both the required and the permitted actions for you as change agent. You will use the professional system in working to change your agency or in acting as an advocate of social change.

ECOSYSTEMS
Person-in-Situation

Social work has adapted a multilevel systems perspective to focus on persons interacting with their situation, or the person-in-situation. Bronfenbrenner (1979) has referred to ecological systems in his analysis of human development. This language was adopted by Carel B. Germain and Alex Gitterman (1980; 1996; Gitterman, 1996), who formulated an ecological model for social work practice. Their approach, known as the *life model*, has been widely adopted and expanded by several other scholars (Brower & Nurius, 1993; Kemp, Whittaker, & Tracy, 1997; Mattaini, 1990; Meyer, 1988; Rothery, 1993). Although criticized as unnecessary and less useful than domain-specific theories (Wakefield, 1996a, b), the ecosystem perspective is widely used in social work. It guides practice in many settings and with many different clients, including communities (Figueira- McDonough, 1995), schools (Clancy, 1995), families (Maddock, 1993, Rothery, 1993), groups of clients with sickle cell disease (Kramer & Nash, 1995), persons with dementia (Minahan, 1993), foster care (Osterman & Benbenishty, 1992), suicidal adolescents (Henry, Stephenson, Hanson, & Hargett, 1993), children with behavior problems (Fraser, 1996, Bernier & Siegel, 1994, 1997), and children adjusting to divorce (Lenqua, Wolchik, & Brauer, 1995). We will speak interchangeably of ecosystems, ecological systems, an ecological perspective, and the person-in-situation; in all cases, we are considering the relationship between person and environment.

In discussing the person-in-situation, we will be looking at environmental demands, internal demands, environmental supports, and individuals' coping or adaptive abilities. A problem exists when there is not a good fit between the individual's coping ability and the demands of the environment or between what an individual wants and desires and the supports of the environment. Germain and Gitterman (1996, 1980) suggest that these problems in living may occur at times of life transitions, because of maladaptive interpersonal processes relating to the individual's coping ability and because of either excessive demands or inadequate supports from the environment. The ecosystem focus of social work is reflected in a problem classification developed on the basis of the person-in-environment (PIE) system (Karls & Wandrei, 1994a, b). In this classification, social functioning is defined as "a person's overall performance in his or her social roles" (Karls & Wandrei, 1994b, p. 7), and four groups of roles are identified—family roles, other interpersonal roles, occupational roles, and specialized situation roles. (The specific roles within each group are displayed as Exhibit 10–5 in Chapter 10.) Roles are also identified in six environmental systems—economic and basic needs system, education and training system, judicial and legal system, health safety and social services system, voluntary association system, and affectional support system (Karls & Wandrei, 1994b).

Change efforts might be directed toward eliminating environmental sources of stress, alleviating or reducing the stress by reducing environmental demands, increasing the supports available from the environment, or strengthening the individual's coping ability. We will be considering these options in Chapters 12–16, when we discuss approaches to intervention in social work. For now, it is enough to understand that social work interventions are related to problems resulting from lack of fit between individuals and their environments. Thus, change efforts can be directed toward the environment, toward the individual, or toward the interaction between the two. Exhibit 2–1 provides a summary of practice principles derived from an ecological perspective.

As social workers, we need to be aware of how the structures and cultures of society are reflected in the self, the life structure of each individual, and how individuals' coping strategies affect all the rest of us. Yet we must also recognize that a person's life is unique—a reflection of self and choices. All human beings have their own particular world that presents them with opportunities, meanings, feelings, identities, and myths, which each individual selectively uses and internalizes (Levinson, 1978).

What Is the Environment?

Exhibits 2–2 and 2–3 show the complexity of the interaction between person and environment. As com-

EXHIBIT 2-1	Key Ecosystem Concepts

The ecosystem perspective in social work embodies a balanced emphasis on person and environment and is characterized by the following concepts:

1. The environment is a complex environment-behavior-person whole, consisting of a continuous, interlocking process of relationships, not arbitrary dualisms.
2. The mutual interdependence among person, behavior, and environment is emphasized.
3. Systems concepts are used to analyze the complex interrelationships within the ecological whole.
4. Behavior is recognized to be site-specific.

5. Assessment and evaluation should be through the naturalistic, direct observation of the intact, undisturbed, natural organism-environment system.
6. The relationship of the parts within the ecosystem is orderly, structured, lawful, and deterministic.
7. Behavior results from mediated transactions between the person and the multivariate environment.
8. The central task of behavioral science is to develop taxonomies of environments, behaviors, and behavior-environment linkages and to determine their distribution in the natural world.

Source: P. Allen-Meares, & B. A. Lane, Grounding social work practice in theory: Ecosystems, *Social Casework: The Journal of Contemporary Social Work, 68*(9), 518, (1987).

plex as Exhibit 2–2 appears, it deals only with the social environment, which consists of several levels—the individual, the group, the family, the community and class, and the culture. In addition to the social environment, we must also consider the physical environment, consisting of the natural physical environment, such as climate, and the constructed environment, such as the shelters we build.

Third, we need to be aware of the temporal environment, consisting of time and space. Because human life is finite and is lived within certain defined spaces, time and space are critical environmental qualities. They can be further divided into two subclasses: general and personal. Most human beings construct shelters to protect them from the environment but, in so doing, they also construct a personal and/or family space that gives them some privacy from the group. The construction of shelter and the marking of private space may differ from culture to culture. In North America, we demand a shelter that is readily accessible to our place of employment or education, that has certain electrical appliances, heat, and perhaps air conditioning, and that is attractive, according to our personal definition. The private space we create then interacts with our feelings about ourselves.

Fourth, we need to consider the transpersonal or spiritual environment (Cowley, 1993; Canada, 1991), which encompasses all culturally supported ways and opportunities to seek meaning in life. This realm includes beliefs about existence and the possibility of relationship with a higher being, but is not confined to formal or informal religious practices (Frankl, 1987;

Guttman, 1996). In Reading 2-3, Lyle Longclaws notes that spirituality must be considered in work with Native clients; spirituality infuses the culture and provides for a sense of wholeness (Yellow Bird, 1995). A lack of fit between an individual's need for meaning and transpersonal experience and the opportunities available in society may lead to signs of spiritual crisis or malaise (Cowley & Derezotes, 1994; Sermabeikian, 1994). These signs may be misinterpreted as indicators of mental illness unless the practitioner is sensitive to the transpersonal environment. The transpersonal and spiritual environments have received only limited attention in social work (Derezotes, 1995; Sheridan, Bullis, Adcock, Berlin, & Miller, 1992), although a recent survey of 284 social work educators from 25 U. S. schools of social work found that 82% favored inclusion of work on spirituality within the curriculum (Sheridan, Wilmer, & Atcheson, 1994).

For social work practice, the environment may be defined as a combination of people and their interactions and transactions in a particular geographic, socially defined, and constructed space. The transactions occur over a particular period of time in the individual and family's life and in the life of the social and cultural system (Germain, 1979; Pincus & Minahan, 1973; Siporin, 1975).

Integration of Person and Environment

We cannot regard environment as something outside ourselves—as another billiard ball with which we collide

EXHIBIT 2-2 | **What Individuals Are**

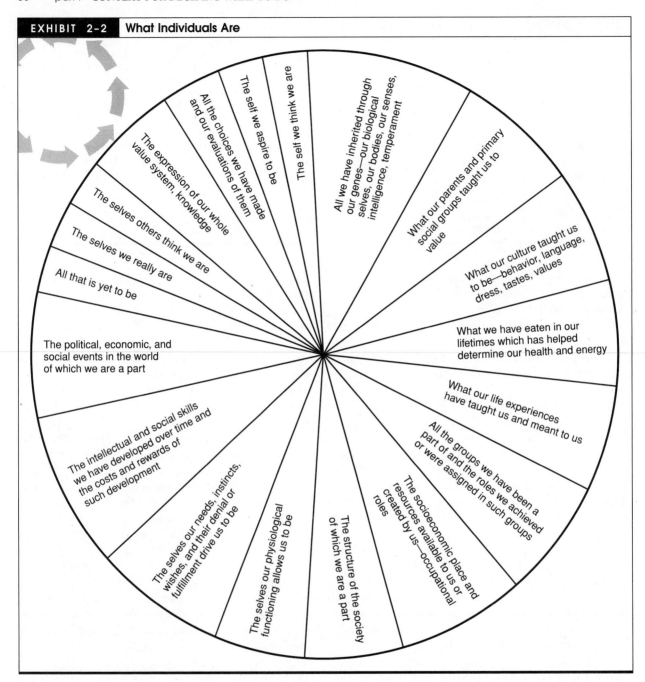

The self we think we are

The self we aspire to be

All the choices we have made and our evaluations of them

The expression of our whole value system, knowledge

The selves others think we are

The selves we really are

All that is yet to be

The political, economic, and social events in the world of which we are a part

The intellectual and social skills we have developed over time and the costs and rewards of such development

The selves our needs, instincts, wishes, and their denial or fulfillment drive us to be

The selves our physiological functioning allows us to be

The structure of the society of which we are a part

The socioeconomic place and resources available to us or created by us—occupational roles

All the groups we have been a part of and the roles we achieved or were assigned in such groups

What our life experiences have taught us and meant to us

What we have eaten in our lifetimes which has helped determine our health and energy

What our culture taught us to be—behavior, language, dress, tastes, values

What our parents and primary social groups taught us to value

All we have inherited through our genes—our biological selves, our bodies, our senses, intelligence, temperament

once in a while. Environment is of us, and we are of it. From the moment of our birth, our environment becomes an intimate part of us and presents us with the material from which we construct our lives, through the choices we make and the social transactions in which we engage. As an example, consider John and Richard, two 18-year-olds who have just graduated in the upper 10% of their respective classes. They look very much alike and are both attractive and in good health. John's family was an established professional family with a more than

EXHIBIT 2–3	Interacting Factors That Influence Individual Development

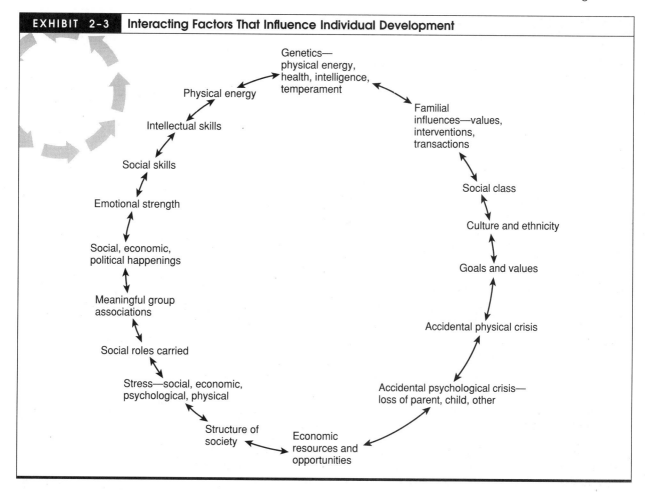

adequate financial base. From birth, John had little exposure to other than a professional life, and he was expected to complete high school and go on to a university. Thus, John attended his father's alma mater and became a professional man. His choice of this life pattern was highly approved in his environment; to make another choice would have been extremely difficult.

Richard, by contrast, was the oldest of five siblings. His father was a farmer, but the family sold the farm and exhausted its assets to pay for his father's care during a long terminal illness. His mother and the children then lived in a small rural community, where his mother ran a small grocery store. Money was extremely tight; the family had no social security support because Richard's father was not covered. Richard was very bright and much interested in farming. He would have liked to attend a university and major in agribusiness. However,

the university was 100 miles away, and Richard could see no way to pay for his education. In addition, his mother needed both his financial and emotional support. A job was open in the local creamery, and Richard took it. After 10 years he became manager of the creamery. It was a good, steady, and adequately paying job. It meant that Richard had daily contact with the farm life he loved, but it was far short of the contribution he could have made and of the life of which he had dreamed. Both these men constructed their lives from the choices the environment offered them, as they saw them. Starting their adult life with very similar internal resources, they became very different through the opportunities the environment offered and the choices they made.

Thus, our individual lives are shaped by the choices we make in response to the environmental opportunities presented us. By our choices and activities, we in turn shape the environment. Richard was concerned about how certain farm practices were destroying the topsoil and depriving birds and small animals of their habitat. He organized a group of concerned farmers, who arranged for a representative of the local university to come and help them understand better land use. The farmers learned to cooperate with the needs of their environment and grew more prosperous for it. Through our interactions and our transactions, we shape both our future and the future of our environment. Much of social work practice is devoted to helping clients analyze the impact of the environment on their problems and making a planned effort to change undesirable conditions.

The concept of adaptation is useful in considering the transactions between any level of human system and the larger system within which it is embedded. Adaptation is often seen as a process in which the smaller system capitulates to the power of the larger environment—that is, as a form of submission. However, submission is only one method of adaptation. Adaptation includes all of the transactional processes by which people shape their environment—physical and social—and in turn are shaped by it.

The Environment as a Series of Mediating Layers

Attempting to define the environment of any social system is complex. Think of the environment as a set of nested boxes, stacked in order of size. The environment of any box in the set is not only the next larger box but all of the boxes that are larger. Yet each larger box will have its own characteristics that are different from—but shaped by—the still larger boxes that constitute its environment. The impact of the largest box on the smallest box will be mediated by all of the intervening boxes. Thus, for an individual, the impact of the community is mediated through the next larger box, usually the family.

We find it helpful to distinguish four levels of environment: the individual's situation at a particular point in time, the micro level, the meso level, and the macro level. Each level is embedded in the higher levels, and the functioning of each level is determined in large part by its interaction with the higher level (Bronfenbrenner, 1979; Magnusson & Allen, 1983a, b). The situation is the part of the environment accessible to the individual's perception at any given moment. As Magnusson and Allen

(1983a) note, "It is in actual situations that we encounter and form our conceptions about the world and develop specific kinds of behavior for dealing with it." Situations present "the information that we process, and they offer the feedback necessary for building valid conceptions of the outer world. Knowledge about the actual situations that an individual has encountered, along with the accompanying physical, social, and cultural microenvironments, will help us understand behavior at different stages of development" (p. 11).

The micro level of environment is "that part of the total physical and social environment that an individual is in contact with and can interact with directly in daily life during a certain period of time" (Magnusson & Allen, 1983a, p. 11). This level of environment includes the individual's experiences in his or her family, experiences at school, at work, during leisure time, and so forth. To a large extent, the microenvironment is specific to the individual, in that no other person experiences the same environment in the same way. The microenvironment is very important in the development of an individual, because it determines the types of situations an individual will encounter.

The meso level of the environment is "that part of the total environment that in some way or another influences and determines the character and functioning of the microenvironment" (Magnusson & Allen, 1983a, p. 11). It includes relationships between major groups, organizations, and institutions that the individual encounters in daily life, such as school, work, church, recreation, and community resources.

The macro level of environment is common to most members of the groups living in it and involves the physical, social, cultural, economic, and political structure of the larger society, including technology, language, housing, laws, customs, and regulations. We have five systems of different sizes, from individual to macrosystem. Each system is part of a larger whole and itself is a suprasystem to other systems (remember our nested boxes). The whole is reflected or contained in each of its parts, and all parts are complementary aspects of the whole. Thus, language, an element of the larger macrosystem, is also a critical part of each individual. Since the macro level of environment is a part of each individual system, it is easy for social workers to overlook the meaning of the macroenvironment to the smaller individual system.

There are some factors in the environment that operate at all levels. Perhaps the most important of these is the extent to which the environment sets limits on the behavior of individuals and offers opportunities for their development. The actual environment does have an impact on behavior and development, but it is through the individual's perception and interpretation of the environment and the meaning assigned to these perceptions and interpretations that the environment has the most influence. Thus, you must be concerned about three environments:

- the actual environment
- the environment as perceived by the client
- the environment as perceived by you

It is very tempting to conclude that your perception of the actual environment is more accurate than the client's, but it is dangerous to act on this belief. Such an assumption will probably result in an inability to understand the meaning that the client assigned to his or her perception. (Besides, your perception may be more distorted than the client's.)

The Ecosystems Perspective and the Knowledge for Social Work Practice

The distinguishing mark of a profession is the ability of its practitioner, through an active thinking process, to convert knowledge into professional services tailored to the unique requirements of the client. Students and social workers often think first of action, rather than of knowledge as a basis for action. However, as we saw in Chapter 1, you will fail as a professional if you develop a high level of interventive skill, no matter how demanding and complex, and then apply it indiscriminately to all situations, regardless of the problem, the objective, or the capacity of the system. A profession demands that interventive skills be used selectively, on the basis of a body of knowledge and theory, a process for deciding, and the purpose and values of the profession. Social work confronts us with tasks that are complex, constantly changing, and nonroutine. These tasks do not yield to the rote application of specific techniques.

In the professions, in contrast to the basic sciences, knowledge is sought for use rather than for its own sake. The presumed purpose of social work "defines the boundaries of relevant knowledge as well as stimulating the search for new knowledge. Part of what makes a given profession distinctive is the nature of action or practice evolving from placing knowledge within a particular frame of reference" (Kamerman, Dolgoff, Getzel, & Nelson, 1973, p. 97). The frame of reference is dictated by the purposes and values of the profession.

Thus, knowledge and purpose have an interactive relationship. As purposes change, new knowledge is sought to deal with the new purposes; similarly, as knowledge expands within a given purpose, it is sometimes found that the purpose itself is changed by the new knowledge (often more slowly than we might wish). For example, when the polio vaccine was developed, its wide use resulted in significant reduction in the numbers of children crippled by polio. As a result, a large world-famous center devoted to the rehabilitation of polio patients found the demand for its services so reduced that it had to reconsider its mission. To make use of its highly trained specialists, it began to offer rehabilitative services to persons with spinal cord injuries or brain damage. New knowledge changed the purpose.

Selecting and organizing knowledge for social work is difficult because we cannot define with any precision the necessary areas of expertise. According to Schwartz (1961), "Every profession has a particular function to perform in society: it has received a certain job assignment for which it is held accountable" (p. 150). What is the job assignment of social work? As we saw in Chapter 1, the purpose of the profession, according to the National Association of Social Workers (NASW), is to assist persons who experience some disequilibrium between their own resources, abilities, and knowledge and the situations in which they find themselves. A secondary purpose is to engage in activities aimed at preventing such disequilibrium. Thus, the principal focus for knowledge building should be the development of theories to account for such disequilibrium in various situations and of models to guide assessment and intervention in these situations.

On that basis, we can classify the knowledge we need as follows:

1. Knowledge that contributes to understanding the complex interactions in which the client is involved and of the meaning the client assigns these interactions.

2. Knowledge that contributes to understanding the individual and the impact of environmental factors on the psychological, social, and physical development and functioning of the person.
3. Knowledge that contributes to understanding the interrelatedness of person and situation (environment) as a continuously emerging and ever-changing process over time.
4. Knowledge that contributes to understanding assessment and its relationship to planning and intervention.
5. Knowledge that contributes to understanding what is involved in effective social work intervention.

Social work both borrows knowledge from the social and behavioral sciences and develops knowledge to guide practice. One of our major problems with borrowing knowledge is that we have borrowed rather indiscriminately. We have huge lumps of knowledge from various disciplines, but we do not have any way to integrate them into a coherent base.

When we borrow knowledge, we need to ask what that knowledge contributes, in terms of our purpose. Does it contribute to our ability to further the purposes of the profession? Much of the borrowed knowledge in social work is derived from the perspective that personality is the overriding influence in social functioning or the perspective that environment is the overriding influence. In building social work knowledge, by contrast, our interest is in how these factors, in interaction over time, influence social functioning. We need theory and knowledge that deal with the developmental and adaptational interrelatedness of personality and environment. Social workers have recognized this problem but, in their search for appropriate theory, they have tended to accept the view that the environment and the individual are interrelated but separate entities. This focus has resulted in a mental model in which the person and the environment affect each other in much the same way as billiard balls do—by striking one another. In this transaction, only the course of each ball is changed; the essential nature of each remains unaffected.

BORROWED KNOWLEDGE

In social work, as in all other professions, we often borrow knowledge that provides us with helpful explanations for our purposes. All professions rely on borrowed knowledge generated and tested in the basic disciplines. In social work, adopting an ecological perspective, we borrow knowledge from our supporting social sciences to help us understand transactions between people and their environments, the nature of people, their responses to their environments, and how environments are or are not responsive to individuals. What follows is a summary of some of the borrowed knowledge used by social work. (You may have already considered this material in your supporting social science courses and your social work human behavior and social environment courses.) We will look at knowledge borrowed from role theory and from ego psychology.

Role Theory

Role theory helps to enrich and expand our understanding and use of systems theory. It can help us to understand interactions within a system; it also serves as a transactional, or bridging, concept between individuals and the larger social systems in which they are embedded. Roles are the expected behaviors of a person occupying a particular social status or position in a social system. Some informal roles are only of importance to persons within a system, such as the role of family joker or the scapegoat. But formal roles within a smaller system (such as the family) carry important implications for both the individual (the subsystem in this case) and the family, because the larger social system (society) has established rules, patterns, and expectations for this particular role within the smaller system. Roles may be either achieved or ascribed. *Ascribed roles* are occupied because of a demographic characteristic. Examples are man, daughter, adolescent, and African American. Individuals have no choice about this role but, of course, they interact with expected behaviors associated with the role to mold performance. *Achieved roles* are acquired on the basis of choice and accomplishments; examples include social worker, wife, parent, Methodist, and student.

As we noted earlier, larger systems depend on smaller systems and have the power to give or withhold opportunities for growth. For example, a person who occupies the role of parent within a family may be punished by the larger system for violating society's standards for the performance of that role, even though the smaller system, the family, has no complaint about how the role is being enacted. Thus, larger systems offer opportunities and impose limitations on smaller systems through the power to define acceptable role performance. Accordingly, role, in combination with power, is a bridging concept that provides a linkage between larger and smaller systems. Both the larger system and the smaller system have socially constructed notions of what the behavior should be and what it means to fulfill the role. The larger system—society or a culture—maintains role performance standards and expectations and may have a tremendous investment in the fulfillment of certain roles in prescribed ways (Biddle & Thomas, 1966).

Social norms provide guides for the attitudes, feelings, and behavior that are permitted, expected, or prohibited for the individual filling that role. These norms, or expectations of role performance, are communicated by persons within the system or from another system. Norms will differ from culture to culture. For example, all cultures have prescribed behavior for a woman filling the role of mother within the family system. However, these prescribed behaviors may differ significantly according to the cultural environment of the particular family system. They also differ over time in any specific culture. This has importance for the social worker in problem definition, data collection, assessment, and intervention.

Social roles are elements of all social systems and are generally ascribed or achieved on the basis of our positions within various social systems. Beyond overt behavior, these expectations encompass what we are and feel like as we interact with the other, whose nature, behavior, and feelings are also prescribed (Perlman, 1961). In open systems, role prescriptions are more general and allow for changes in behavior; moreover, changes in the way system elements fill their role (acting, feeling, and being) may result in significant system changes. Thus, change in a system may be brought about by some change in how an element within the system is, feels, or behaves or by a change in the system's role behavior that affects the transactions with larger social systems.

Role complementarity. Role positions, or statuses are usually paired. For every parent, there is a child; for every wife, there is a husband. If the position of husband is no longer filled in the family system, the role of wife changes to the role of widow, divorced person, or separated or abandoned woman. If a system is to enjoy some stability and integration, there must be some reciprocity

of expectations between role partners. If an industrial organization is to be free to pursue its goals, there must be some agreement between persons occupying management and policy-making roles and those occupying labor roles. If a husband and wife are to create a family system with some stability, they must reach some agreement about how their roles will be performed.

The patterns of expected role behavior grow from the need of social systems to have a steady state—to have the stability that comes from being able to predict, within some acceptable limits, the behavior of elements within the system. These patterns of expectation grow from two types of interaction. First, the opportunities, deprivations, and needs among parts internal to the system will establish role expectations related to system maintenance and growth. For example, children need protection and nurture if they are to grow and make their contribution to life. The system must determine what position, or positions, within the system will be given that job and what behavior from that element will ensure effective care of the child. The second source of the expectations is found in the system's transactions with other systems and environments. For example, all individuals need food, clothing, and shelter; the patterns that develop to meet these needs will depend on the geographic and climatic environment within which people find themselves. When individuals group themselves into larger systems, differentiation of functions essential to the well-being of the system will develop. In this process, roles will be assigned to system parts, and expected role patterns will develop. When the environment changes, problems may arise within the system as the various elements of the system continue previously patterned behavior. Thus, conflict between parents and children—or old and young people—may be largely conflict between expected role patterns and a changing environment that appears to make some of these patterns dysfunctional.

Role expectations allow for individual interpretations and behaviors. However, under the expectations of ascribed or achieved roles, certain aspects of the self will be developed, while other aspects will be neglected or even consciously repressed. An example of such repression may be seen in sex role stereotyping and the way it has limited opportunities for women. In this context, we need to examine our expectations regarding the role of client. Do we expect dependency and helplessness, or do we expect clients to actively engage their environments—and us? How do we communicate these expectations?

In general, if role expectations are rigid and circumscribed, individuals in a particular role may feel considerable stress. Currently, many women are actively trying to change their ascribed roles in society, which they perceive as unduly constrictive. These efforts evoke discomfort and resistance in some members of society who have been conditioned to gender-role differentiation.

Role set and role conflict. An individual's *role set* is the array of roles that he or she fills at any particular time (Merton, 1968). For example, we may simultaneously be a mother, a daughter, a wife, a social worker, a supervisor, a church member, and so on. If a role set includes two different roles in two different systems, and the expected behaviors of the roles are defined so that the roles cannot be simultaneously filled, the individual suffers from role conflict, which can be very painful. To rebut charges of discrimination against women, employers sometimes assert that women are not as interested in advancement as men and will not fulfill expected behaviors for management roles, such as night work or travel. For the women involved, this type of demand may conflict with the roles of wife and mother in their family system. Role expectations may conflict in at least three ways:

- The social system of which the person is a part may provide no acceptable alternative for a different solution.
- The person's own internalized notions about acceptable behavior within the role may limit alternatives.
- The other occupant of the role pair may hold role expectations that clash with the person's wishes and generate conflicted interaction between these two primary elements of the system involved.

Role incongruity. Role incongruity exists when one's own perception of one's role differs from the expectations of significant others in the system or the environment. Because of expectations about women in the role of mother, women may be denied the resources of child care that would allow them also to occupy with some comfort the role of employee in occupational systems. Role incongruity arises in social work when the practitioner's expectations for the behavior of the client differ from the client's expectations, or when the client's notion of the social worker's role differs from the social worker's notion. The client may expect to be told what to do, but the interview takes a different course. In correctional systems, the social worker may have a self-image as a helper, while the client perceives a role of surveillance and control.

Role incongruity is likely in attempts to interpret the role performances of an individual from another culture; the two cultures may hold very different—or conflicting—views about the attitudes and behavior appropriate to the role. This can lead to serious and often unrecognized problems in social work. For example, a Native American social work student was working with a Native American woman who desperately needed medical care but was too frightened to go to the clinic. In an attempt to act as a broker for her troubled client, the student went to talk to the doctor at the clinic. Her interview with the doctor made her very angry; she felt that the doctor had been rude, suspicious, and rejecting. She told her field instructor that the doctor began immediately to question her about the client and continued to ask many very direct questions; this behavior was incongruent with her norms about the way strangers should treat each other. If the worker misinterpreted the doctor's behavior, imagine how the doctor would have appeared to the client.

Role ambiguity. Role ambiguity exists when a person is unclear about the expected behaviors of a particular role. For example, a young father may be unclear about his expected child care responsibilities; or an applicant for social services may be unclear about worker expectations regarding what information is to be shared. Role ambiguity may occur because expectations have not been clearly communicated or have been clearly communicated but have not been understood. Role ambiguity is likely to occur at times of transition—for example, starting a new job, retiring, living with a new partner, or joining an organization. Any new role, such as university student or parent, calls for clarification of the associated role expectations.

When you work with applicants and clients, you will need to clarify their role expectations. We recommend that you spend some time learning what the applicant or client expects of you and believes that you expect. Determining the client's expectations and clarifying any ambiguities; negotiating any differences early in your contact will help reduce later confusion and conflict. In addition, much of your work will involve preparing applicants and clients for experiences that are new to them, whether court appearances, admission to a residential facility, placement in a nursing home, or placement in a foster home. Many applicants and clients are likely to be unclear as to the expected behaviors of the new role. Discussing what the expected behaviors are and preparing the person for the transition will reduce anxiety and ease the transition. For example, young people being sent to correctional or residential treatment facilities are often very unclear and anxious about what is going to happen to them and what behaviors are expected. It is advisable to spend time orienting such clients and their families by discussing admissions processes and their expected behaviors.

Role set and social support. Social support is a central concept in social work practice. You may think of social support as the resources provided by other persons in your role set that enable you to cope with the demands of your environment and your life transitions. We can think of four types of social support (Cameron & Rothery, 1985; Rothery, 1993):

1. Concrete or instrumental supports—that is, the goods and services used to cope with life's demands, such as money, child care, or homemaker services.

2. Information and knowledge, including information about life's demands and experiences and information about available resources in the community.

3. Emotional supports, including opportunities to discuss feelings and to consider life experiences in a safe environment.

4. Affiliational supports that provide a sense of importance and belonging.

Social support is provided either formally or informally (Cameron, 1990; Erickson, 1984; Whittaker & Garbarino, 1983). Formal social supports are those provided by agencies and persons paid to deliver the service. Informal social supports are those you and your client receive from neighbors, friends, families, work colleagues, and so forth. Much of social work practice consists of assessing the extent and nature of applicants' social support network and working with clients to change their interaction with their social support systems. In Reading 2-3, Jane Gilgun introduces the techniques of ecomapping, which are designed to assess the nature of social supports and relationships within families and their relationship to the broader environment.

Elizabeth M. Tracy and James K. Whittaker provide another tool for assessing social support in Reading 14-1.

Interventions may be designed to do the following:

• Increase the size of the social support network by increasing the number of persons in the client's role set.

• Strengthen the social support network by increasing or intensifying the type of social support provided.

• Change the social support network by discontinuing interactions with some persons in the role set and adding new ones. This might be appropriate, for example, when clients are receiving negative unhelpful messages rather than support that is helpful and positive.

• Change the nature of the interaction with a member of the role set in order to increase positive, helpful interactions and decrease negative ones.

• Help clients to understand the reciprocal nature of social support and to follow through on that understanding by providing support to other persons in their role set.

As a social worker, you will need to understand the different types of social support, how to assess the nature of the social support network in relation to any client, and how to intervene in the client's social support networks. We will return to formal social support systems in Chapter 13 and to informal social support networks in Chapter 14.

Ego Psychology

Because ego psychology is based on psychoanalytic concepts regarding the human personality, we will begin with a brief consideration of psychoanalytic theory, whose principles were first outlined by Sigmund Freud. We will not try to present any coherent summary of psychoanalytic theory; you may want to consult other sources for a more comprehensive account.

Psychoanalytic constructs. Psychoanalytic theory conceives of the human being as a dynamic energy system consisting of basic drives and instincts. Interaction with the environment serves to organize and develop the personality, through a series of developmental stages. From birth, we are pushed by largely unconscious and irrational drives toward the satisfaction of desires that are also largely unconscious and irrational. Thanks to the structure of the mind and the operation of an unconscious defense system, we tend to be unaware of these irrational forces. Nevertheless, they have a tremendous effect on our behavior and on the way we relate to others. The behavior that others observe and our own knowledge of our behavior and our purposes provide a very incomplete picture of who we are as individuals and what drives us. Most of the motivating forces of personality are beneath the surface and are available to our conscious and rational understanding and direction only through a careful exploration of these buried regions. Thus, our personality is primarily an elaboration of the unconscious irrational drives with which each of us is born and a response to the vicissitudes of early childhood.

According to psychoanalytic theory, the personality is a semiclosed energy system that operates to conserve energy by resisting stimulus and change. Individuals are driven by unconscious forces and struggle to maintain a homeostatic balance. Consequently, real change in behavior after childhood can only come through an experience that reaches the deepest levels of personality. The environment and events in the world around us have an impact on us and on our behavior only through the meanings we assign such events as a result of our unconscious needs and defenses.

Freud held that the personality was structured into three divisions. "The id comprises the psychic representatives of the drives, the ego consists of those functions which have to do with the individual's relation to his environment, and the superego comprises the moral precepts of our minds as well as our ideal aspirations" (Brenner, 1955, p. 45). The ego is expected to act as the executive officer of the personality, dealing with impulses from the id and with moral signals of the superego, as well as with the realities of the environment.

Psychoanalytic theory does not serve social workers well, because of the assumptions on which it rests. It assumes that people primarily seek freedom from discomfort and will choose comfort and peace rather than growth. The theory is deterministic, in that the human personality is seen as a semiclosed rather than an open system. A semiclosed system is analogous to mechanical devices such as the thermostat; according to Freud, people strive to conserve energy and to return to their previous state, homeostasis. The need of the system is for stability, rather than for some balance between stability and change. Correspondingly, there is always great resistance to change. The primary motivating factor is freedom from internal conflict, and people can be pushed into change only by unendurable discomfort. The notion of goals and the importance of hope in motivation are not a part of this theory.

Ego psychologists have reexamined the concepts of psychoanalytic theory in the light of observations of human behavior. They assign the central place in human functioning to the rational processes of the ego, rather than the irrational and instinctual forces of the id. They hold that the individual comes into this world with both rational and irrational instincts. The personality develops and becomes differentiated in relation to environmental interactions, concerns, goals, and unconscious needs; it is not simply an elaboration of inner instinctual drives. Rather than being fixed early in life, personality is constantly developing.

Ego psychology constructs. Eric Erikson held that, although early experience was significant, the personality system remains open, all through life, to meaningful interaction with both the inner and outer life experiences. The notion that new tasks and new biopsychosocial demands continually present human beings with opportunities for growth and change was a fundamental departure from psychoanalytic beliefs. The manner in which these opportunities are used will reflect the individual's success and failure in dealing with earlier life tasks (Hartman, 1970).

Ego psychologists began to challenge the psychoanalytic view of the conservation of energy and the notion of a semiclosed system. They argued for an open personality system, because of evidence that human beings are born with an ego need to seek both difference and stimulus from the environment. Thus, personality development is the result of active interaction with the environment. Discarding the emphasis on homeostasis, the ego psychologists argued that, while the personality needs a certain stability, people also seek new experiences, in pursuit of growth and development.

They retained the psychoanalytic notion of the ego as the executive officer of the personality—the part that takes action. "The main categories of ego functions are its clusters of cognitive, affective, motoric, executive, and integrative operations" (Perlman, 1975, p. 214). Cognitive functions are the thought processes, consisting of facts, notions, concepts, memories, and beliefs and the way that this material is acquired, stored, retrieved, organized, and reorganized. The affective functions of the ego have to do with feeling processes: anger, guilt, hate, love, caring, and excitement. The executive function of the ego involves decision making and action. Decision making rests on the ability to perceive the natural and external environment accurately, to think logically and analyze, and to integrate thinking, feeling, and a sense of mastery and also on the possession of action skills with which to carry out decisions that have been made.

All these ego functions are interrelated, and each affects the others. Feeling affects thought; thought affects feeling. Action can bring significant change in both thinking and feeling. Thus, we may begin work with thinking, feeling, or action. Where we will begin depends on how we assess the client, the problem, the objective, the situation, and what the client wants.

Competence and mastery. Robert White (1959, 1963) further developed the notion that individuals are motivated from childhood to interact actively with the environment, not merely as a result of drives such as hunger, thirst, and sex, but because of a need to explore the world and to import new experiences and stimuli into the system. Competency is developed as individuals master a new experience in line with their standards and with the approval of the real world; people are innately motivated to try new and more complex tasks. White called this motivational force a push toward mastery. Trader (1977) identifies this as part of the base for effective work with oppressed groups.

Experiences of competency result in a sense of mastery—a belief that one can change the environment by obtaining knowledge of how to change it and using skills that one has developed. These concepts support the notion that, given a relatively benign environment, individuals actively seek control of their lives and welcome new experiences.

Motivation. A feeling of mastery—or control over one's internal reactions and relevant external events—is a significant force in motivating human behavior (Liberman, 1978). Laboratory investigations about the importance of control are summarized by Lefcourt (1966): "When individuals are involved in situations where personal competence can affect . . . outcomes, they tend to perform more actively and adequately than when . . . situations appear less controllable" (p. 188).

Thus, "insofar as individuals believe that their actions and inactions affect their well-being, the achievement of a sense of mastery becomes a major goal throughout their lives" (Liberman, 1978, p. 36). If an individual is to acquire a sense of mastery, there must be a framework that links his or her performance to self-esteem. This link is governed by the person's background and current situation, task relevance, task difficulty, attribution of performance, and the attitudes of significant others.

Client motivation, capacity, and opportunity are central to problem resolution. Motivation is what a person wants and how much he wants it. The two driving forces of motivation are: (1) hope that one can achieve the chosen goals; and (2) discomfort because one has not yet achieved them (French, 1952). Workers need to address hope in the first interview if clients are to engage in effective problem solving (Ripple, Alexander, & Polemis, 1964). People will not move toward change unless they see that change will aid them in achieving their (not your) goals and they have significant commitment to achieving those goals. The commitment to the goal will be determined by the balance between hope that they can achieve the goal and discomfort with not having achieved it. These principles were tested by a research and demonstration project that sought to discover whether clients labeled untreatable could actually be reached and helped. This project found that the concepts of hope and discomfort were key to helping people, although ideas about discomfort needed to be refined (Compton, 1979). If it is to serve as an impetus to problem solving, discomfort must be at a manageable level and must be focused on the problem to be solved. Clients whose experience has resulted in failure in all aspects of living develop an all-pervasive sense of discomfort, which results in a deterioration of goal-directed efforts, with the onset of helplessness and apathy.

Hope increases the amount of pressure that can be withstood before the disintegration of goal-directed efforts begins. Individuals who are hopeful that they can effectively move toward what they want are willing to forego other satisfactions and withstand pressures from other needs and wants in order to realize their primary goal. This is why it is important to establish a tentative goal in the first interview. Doing so supports and expands the client's hope of achieving a desired outcome and thus generates motivation. A sense of hope develops from (French, 1952; Perlman, 1957; Towle, 1948, 1950; Ripple and Alexander, 1956; Ripple, Alexander, & Polemis, 1964; White, 1959, 1963):

- a sense of trust that there is some relationship between one's needs and the intentions of the world around one
- a sense that one has meaning for others, that one's actions are important
- a sense of who one is
- a sense of competence built on evaluation of past efforts (past successes as one evaluates them)
- perception of the opportunities in the environment around one
- one's experience with frustration in the past
- a generalized sense of mastery
- a relationship between one's perception of one's competence and one's perception of the skills needed to reach the goal

Ripple, Alexander, and Polemis (1964) attempted to assess the importance of motivation, capacity, and opportunity on the client's effective use of social work services. The client's level of hope and the opportunities available were the critical factors in use of services. The personality functioning of the client and the type of problem did not appear to be of critical importance. Ripple recommended that, in the beginning stages of client-worker interaction, the worker make a careful assessment of the hope-discomfort balance and be concerned with the impact of his or her activities on this critical balance.

Frustration is important to motivation. It is possible to avoid frustration by avoiding a commitment to an objective. Severe and repeated frustration will move an individual in this direction. Frustration is the realization that the objective to which one is committed is unattainable and is increased to the extent that previous commitments to the purpose have been thwarted. If goal-directed striving is frustrated, perhaps it is possible to find substitute objectives, so that the pressure can be rechannelled. If substitute objectives are not found, the pressure and desire may be discharged in destructive forms such as rage. Hope is destroyed and overt rage is produced when the individual has been pursuing an objective with confidence and the objective becomes unattainable. The experience of frustration over time is destructive of the individual's sense of competence and mastery and ends with the disintegration of goal-directed striving. Loss of hope culminates in apathy and learned helplessness.

Learned helplessness. The concept of learned helplessness fits with White's concepts of competence and aids in understanding unmotivated and apathetic clients. It is troubling to hear social workers say that they cannot help people who are unmotivated and apathetic. Apathy and lack of motivation are responses to lack of environmental opportunities in individuals' struggles to be competent. The environment limits individuals' efforts to cope with life. If they are to develop competence and autonomy in social functioning, they must be able to make valid predictions about the response of the environment to their action. They must have some confidence that what seems to be a problem is reasonably responsive to their efforts. If events are uncontrollable, helplessness sets in. In this psychological state, people believe that nothing they do makes any difference in their lives. According to Seligman (1975), "Learned helplessness produces a cognitive set in which people believe that success and failure is independent of their own skilled actions" (p. 38). If people are to develop competence, initiative, and autonomy, the response of the environment to their efforts and their actions must be comprehensible, ordered, and consistent. We should not be surprised when people whose coping strategies have produced inconsistent responses or failure appear helpless.

Greer, Davison, and Gatchel (1970) studied the relationship between stress and perceived control; individuals who believed they had control over the aversive stimuli in the experiment found these conditions much less stressful than did those who believed they had no control over them. The subjects who experienced less stress did so because their belief in the ability to control the aversive stimuli allowed them to label the condition as one in which they were not helpless.

Before we label clients as apathetic and lacking motivation, we must examine what has been happening in their lives. What kind of control do they have over life events? How does the situation respond, if at all, to their efforts? Does the environment constantly respond to their efforts in a negative or inconsistent way? Individuals who cannot see that their actions make a difference are less motivated to try. "Learned helplessness may develop when individuals believe they have no control over events—even when those events could actually be affected by their behavior" (Hooker, 1976, p. 194).

Resiliency. The study of resiliency is a logical extension of research identifying personal and environmental risk factors for emotional and behavioral dysfunction. (Fraser, 1997). One such risk factor is adversity in early life, which has long been associated with social and psychological difficulties in later life. John Bowlby (1951) made the connections between deprivation of love and care in the early years and antisocial behavior in adolescence and adulthood. However, an experience that places one person at high risk for damaging repercussions may roll off the back of the next person, because of differences in how they perceive the experience, their genetic predisposition, and the psychosocial environment in which they grow and live (Anthony, 1987).

Epidemiological studies have identified a series of risk factors for children's mental health outcomes (Rutter, Maughan, Mortimore, Ousten, & Smith, 1979; Rutter, 1979). These include parental marital discord, father's low-skilled and nonskilled employment, familial overcrowding, paternal criminal behavior, maternal mental illness, and the child's admission to out-of-home care. Moreover, the likelihood that youngsters will be exposed to stressful life events, their intellectual functioning, general competency, ability to engage with others and with activities, and tendencies toward disruptiveness are all related to the socioeconomic status of the child's family and to familial stability, cohesiveness, and organization (Garmezy, 1987).

Recent research has focused on successful adaptation in spite of childhood adversity. It is unusual for more than half of children exposed to significant risk factors to develop serious disability or persistent problems (Werner & Smith, 1992). Norman Garmezy (1971) has identified what he calls a group of invulnerable children

whose prognosis could be viewed as unfavourable on the basis of familial or ecological factors but who upset our prediction tables and in childhood bear the visible indices that are hallmarks of competence: good peer relations, academic achievement, commitment to education and to purposive life goals, early and successful work histories. (p. 114)

Instead of invulnerability, we now speak of resiliency. The resilient youngster suffers both the short- and long-term effects of adverse experiences and relationships, but can incorporate these experiences into a coping core, which may be strengthened by adversity. One respected longitudinal study showed that resilience in children is highly correlated with flexibility, which allows them to break free from failures, avoid self-defeating repetitions, and try many different problem-solving techniques in their efforts to cope (Murphy & Moriarity, 1976). Garmezy (1983) found that resilient children shared three categories of protective factors in almost all their experiences:

1. The children themselves were easy to relate to, felt good about themselves, believed they were in control of their lives, and were self-reliant.
2. In most families, there was a warm relationship with at least one adult, the family felt close, and order and organization were in evidence.
3. In the neighborhood or elsewhere in the community, there was a support system to help the child move toward self-defined goals, and there were role models with whom the youngster could identify.

Both Rutter (1987) and Garmezy (1987) questioned whether there might be processes or mechanisms in the lives of children and young people to make them more resilient. Rutter (1987, p. 329) suggested four categories of resiliency-building experiences:

• experiences that alter exposure or involvement in the risk
• experiences that reduce the likelihood of chain reactions from the risk encounter
• experiences that promote self-esteem through service and supportive personal relationships or successful task accomplishment
• experiences that open up opportunities

There is little literature with respect to building resilience in child welfare practice. Festinger (1983) found that a large sample of young adult graduates of foster care in New York City fared no better or worse than a control group of young adults from a similar class background, except with respect to education and employment, where the foster care graduates were at a disadvantage. (Outcomes for youngsters substantially raised in foster family were significantly better than those for individuals raised in group home care.) In a British study, 75% of adult foster home graduates manifested largely satisfactory outcomes from their experiences in care (Triseliotis, 1980). A study of 585 graduates from a program providing high-quality, planned, long-term foster care for children and youth with troubled behavioral patterns and multiple placement histories found that graduates from the program often achieved levels of comfort and well-being in young adulthood that could not have been predicted from the adversity of their early experiences (Fanschel, Finch, & Grundy, 1990).

The development of resilience appears to depend on how youngsters integrate potentially damaging events into their worldview. They seem to benefit from repeated opportunities to develop an integrated view of their histories. In one study of female incest survivors, those women who could make sense of the incestuous victimization were more likely to exhibit effective adult coping, including less psychological distress, better social adjustment, and higher levels of self-esteem (Silver, Boon, & Stones, 1983). Research findings suggest that individuals from family backgrounds characterized by child maltreatment (Herrenkohl, Herrenkohl, & Egolf, 1994) and parental mental illness (Beardslee, 1989) have a better chance of adult well-being if they can reach some understanding of their childhood history and their lack of responsibility for shortcomings of parental and family functioning.

Stress and coping. Much social work involves engagement with the client when a stress situation appears threatening, and the client's coping devices have been exhausted or the client is depressed and apathetic because resolution of the troubles appears impossible. The concepts of stress and coping provide links between the person and the environment.

Stress is the tension that arises in a system—individual, family, or group—from the perception that an event involves uncertainty and risk. For many, stress may precipitate appropriate problem solving activities, leading to effective choice of alternatives, appropriate choice-directed action, and a satisfying solution. Often, the feeling of stress has some element of pleasure; we gear ourselves up to meet a challenge. Some people, however, interpret most events as beyond their capacity to influence and are therefore stressful, and accordingly may not attempt to problem-solve.

Social workers must understand coping patterns—the generalized coping resources of the client and how these resources are used. They must also determine the client's ability or inability to mobilize these mechanisms. The most basic category of coping resources consists of beliefs and attitudes toward life. If the driving forces of motivation are hope and discomfort, then someone who does not believe that effort will produce results will not be motivated to marshal coping resources. Likewise, individuals who do not see that they have any effect on what happens will be apathetic. According to Antonovsky (1980), people who believe that life is orderly and purposive, that processes can be understood, and that outcomes are generally for the best, suffer less debilitating illness than others, no matter how severe the level of stress. Perhaps the most powerful coping mechanism is a belief in life.

Other coping mechanisms include the individual's knowledge, successful experiences with life tasks, and cognitive capacities and ability to reason; the ability to control and use emotional and affective responses to stress; and skills to carry out planned action, which usually come from past successful experiences (Antonovsky, 1980). Notable among the environmental resources that assist with coping are money and power. Money provides the means to purchase services or things we may need; power serves to assure us that we are worthwhile and capable of controlling our own destiny. Another environmental resource is the individual's network of supporting social systems. In a time of stress or crisis, a network of family, friends, neighbors, and colleagues can provide emotional support, information, and other resources. Much of your practice as a social worker will involve assisting clients to identify, access, strengthen, and develop informal systems of social support.

Transpersonal psychology and spirituality. Social work needs to give more systematic attention to the emerging research from transpersonal psychology, which examines the forms that spirituality takes and the ways in which spirituality may assist people to cope with environmental stresses. Carl Jung, one of Freud's students, came to believe that spirituality is a primary human drive and rejected Freud's theory of the pleasure principle. Jung did not deny biological drives but argued that "the wheel of history must not be turned back, and man's advance towards a spiritual life, which began with the primitive rites of initiation, must not be denied" (Jung, 1933, p. 123). Until recently, however, Jung's views have had relatively limited impact on social work.

Transpersonal practitioners focus on the human search for meaning in life and the ways in which a failure to find meaning leads to difficulties in coping (Frankl, 1997; Guttman, 1996). In that context, spirituality has been incorporated into the treatment of alcoholic substance abusers (Berenson, 1987; Krystal & Zweben, 1989). The 12-step program, which originated in Alcoholics Anonymous and is now widely used to help people with addictions cope with environmental stresses, explicitly acknowledges the existence of a higher being. Transpersonal approaches that incorporate spirituality may help clients deal with a sense of alienation, hopelessness, and grief (Breen, 1985; Cowley & Derezotes, 1994; Klein, 1986). Exhibit 2–4 presents a definition of spirituality that transcends any particular religious ideology.

As a social worker, you will need to understand and foster clients' searches for meaning in their lives and to appreciate the consequences of clients' sense that life has no meaning. Echoing Jung, Patricia Sermabeikian (1994) suggests that

> spirituality is a human need; it is too important to be misunderstood; avoided; or viewed as regressive, neurotic, or pathological in nature. Social workers must . . . acknowledge that spirituality in a person's life can be a constructive way of facing life's difficulties. (p. 181)

Diversity, difference, and stability. Social workers need to comprehend how cultures develop, how, over time, opportunities and deprivation shape the culture of a people, and how a given culture becomes a part of the human systems that transact with it. We also need to appreciate the importance of difference in the development of human societies, to understand that human organizations develop through the expression of individual differences, and to respect diversity. Standards of health and normality must include a broad range of coping behaviors and values, so as to accommodate individual diversity and cultural or ethnic differences

(Greene, 1994). Exhibit 2–5 offers a simple example of human difference. What do you see as you look at it? Do you see a vase? Or do you see two faces? Both perceptions are correct, but could you imagine an argument between two people over which view is normal?

This notion of equal but different is difficult to understand, because of the human tendency to assume that, if two objects are different, one must be innately better than the other, or one must be right and the other wrong. It appears that no society exists without some oppression of the different by those in possession of power and resources. The resources may be money, cattle, physical strength, knowledge, or education. Those who have the power to impose their will on groups that are different tend to assign the highest value to the qualities that they possess. Other groups are viewed as having less desirable qualities.

Our difficulty in acknowledging individual differences derives, in part, from the nature of human learning. We learn by categorizing people, objects, and experiences and assuming a certain commonality within each category. We use these categories to communicate with others. For example, when we speak of a tree, our companions know that we mean a growing thing of a certain type. However, an expert in forestry would want to know much more detail. With each additional piece of knowledge, a particular tree is specified more precisely. Social workers, as specialists in human interaction, cannot be satisfied with putting people in broad categories based on innate characteristics such as sexual organs, skin color, or even presenting problem. Neither can we assume that all people who are of a common ethnic origin or who subscribe to certain common ways of life are alike. We must know enough about each individual to see that person as unique. Systems theory and ego psychology point to the importance of diversity in the

---

EXHIBIT 2-4   The Spiritual Dimension of the Person

The spiritual element of the person is the aspect of an individual's psyche, consciousness and unconsciousness, that is also called the human soul. It is in terms of the spiritual dimension that a person strives for transcendental values, meaning, experience and development; for knowledge of an ultimate reality; for belonging and relatedness with the moral universe and community; and for union with the immanent, supernatural powers that guide people and the universe for good and evil. The spiritual aspect of the person is not subsumed or dealt with in psychoanalytic ego theory or in cognitive theory, though it has a place in Jungian and existentialist therapies.

Source: M. Siporin. Current social work perspeactives on clinical practice, *Clinical Social Work Journal, 13,* 210–211 (1985).

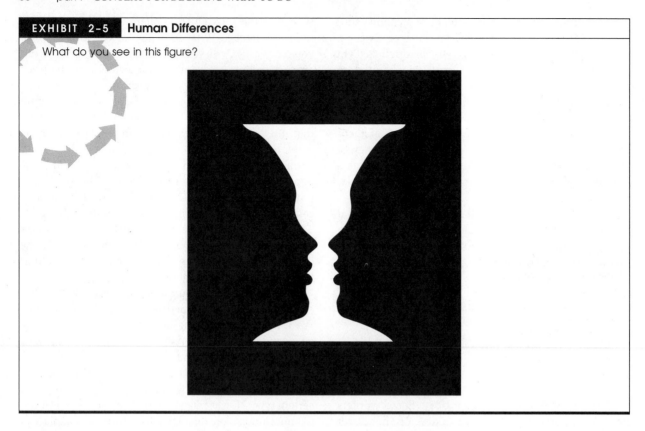

EXHIBIT 2-5 | **Human Differences**

What do you see in this figure?

development of human systems. Without difference, human systems would not develop.

On the other hand, the notions of patterned expectations (from role theory), steady state (from systems theory), and homeostasis (from psychoanalytic theory) all suggest resistance to change, to diversity, and to difference. Human systems need stability. Knowing that the behavior of others will be broadly predictable in some dimensions of human life allows systems to shape and control their own actions.

Because of this need, role expectations tend to become internalized as value systems. Thus, in human systems, role behaviors will often be categorized as right or wrong, regardless of any benefits they may have for the development of the system. As an example, consider family systems. Society cannot exist without some system for the creation, protection, and socialization of children—the family system. However, family systems in different cultures will have different notions about what behaviors are necessary to safeguard children and who performs this

role. In North America, middle-class white families usually assign this role to the mother, but it could be assigned just as effectively to an aunt, grandmother, uncle, father, or even a person outside the family. Members of human systems that assign this behavior to the mother tend to view the assignment of these tasks to any other person as wrong or abnormal and needing change. In contemporary society, the grandmother, uncle, or other extended family members may be regarded as part of another system. Social workers must distinguish carefully between their own internalized expectations of role performance and their knowledge of the needs of human systems and what transactions are truly damaging.

Definitions of pathology and health reflect the expectations of dominant groups in society about role behaviors and the meanings attached to these behaviors. Social workers, however, need definitions for pathology and health that are based on knowledge of the minimum required needs of individuals and of the maximum allowable transactional behavior.

Using Borrowed Knowledge

Harriet Trader (1977) asks that we examine borrowed knowledge from the perspective of social work's function in society. Her questions, summarized in Exhibit 2–6, reflect concern with the congruency between the purposes and values of social work and the theory base used to guide practice. Knowledge developed to serve a profession whose function is different from that of social work may not serve us well without considerable adaptation. For example, social work has found much that is useful in knowledge of human growth and development originating in psychology, psychiatry, and medicine. However, in borrowing this knowledge, we have not always considered the difference in the functions of the professions. In particular, social work—especially social work involving individual clients—has often accepted the goals of psychiatry and borrowed approaches focused on the cure of illness rather than on solving problems of social functioning. Thus, clients' problems have become the clients' pathology.

KNOWLEDGE DEVELOPED BY SOCIAL WORK

In addition to using borrowed knowledge, social workers develop their own theories and their own models of practice through a commitment to an orderly discovery process. Berkowitz (1969) speaks of the wisdom that social workers acquire in and through practice. This knowledge, regarding both practice methods and human behavior, is passed on to new social workers. Since the founding of the profession, we have been concerned with understanding clients' problems from the clients' perspective and learning more about how to help them.

The Tension Between Research and Practice

Theory grows through the collection of observations and the development and testing of assumptions about the meaning of these observations. Although the literature of social work is rich with important observations of

---

EXHIBIT 2-6	**Criteria for Borrowing Theory and Knowledge from Other Disciplines**

1. *Pathology-health balance.* Do the concepts focus on illness or deficit rather than on well-being and strengths? Are the definitions of pathology and health based solely on the expectations of the dominant group in society? Do standards for health include a range of potentials that allows for group differences? Are class differences implied or stated in the models for either normality or abnormality?

2. *Practitioner-client control balance.* Does the theory suggest that the worker carries more responsibility than the client in the process of changing the client's situation? Are clients perceived, even subtly, as being inferior to practitioners? Are practitioners seen as being obliged to use their knowledge and skills to increase clients' coping abilities? Does the theory view human beings as primarily dependent, interdependent, or independent? Can the theory allow for shared control? From what source does the practice derive its legitimacy?

3. *Personal-societal impact balance.* Does the theory embody a personal-deficit model rather than a societal model in assigning causation for problems? Does the theory take into account historical as well as current societal conditions? Can the theory account for

political-economic influences on behavior? Does the theory assign importance to variations in socialization experiences among oppressed groups? Does the theory allow for linking of the personal to the social and environmental aspects of behavior?

4. *Internal-external change balance.* Does the theory emphasize internal, psychic change in preference to changes that occur in society? Does the theory assume that the nature of society is primarily punitive rather than supportive? Are the definitions for change based primarily on the dominant societal patterns, or do they allow for a variety of patterns? To what extent is the view of change synonymous with adjustment?

5. *Rigidity-flexibility balance.* Does the theory allow for the adjustment of concepts to the needs of particular groups? Do abstract principles lend themselves to creative and differential application in practice? Can the theory accommodate new information about oppressed groups? Does the theory relate to a view of the class structure of society? Does the theory demand an uncritical adherence to its postulates? Are there built-in criteria for continual assessment of the utility of the theory?

Copyright 1977, National Association of Social Workers, Inc. from *Social Work, 22*(1), pp. 10–13. Reprinted with permission.

the interactions between client and practitioner, these observations have tended to remain at the level of idiosyncratic accounts of professional experiences. Perhaps one reason for this is that social workers have tended to regard only a narrow range of knowledge as acceptable in the profession.

As social work was emerging, the professions were beginning to adopt a new notion, fostered by industrialism, technology, and the scientific movement—the notion that the only significant knowledge about the world was based on empirical observations and that "all disagreements about the world could be resolved, in principle, by reference to observable facts. Propositions which were neither analytically nor empirically testable were held to have no meaning at all. They were dismissed as emotive utterance, poetry, or mere nonsense" (Schon, 1983, pp. 32–33). Empirical science was not just a form of knowledge; it was the only source of positive knowledge in the world. "According to the positive epistemology of practice, craft and artistry had no lasting place in rigorous practical knowledge" (Schon, 1983, p. 34).

Social work research also embraced this approach, sometimes known as logical positivism. Many researchers focused not on the questions that social workers need to answer but rather on the best techniques for examining and testing a phenomenon; they became methodologists. As a result, researchers failed to examine phenomena that were central to the everyday experience of practitioners, who consequently found research publications of little help in responding to people in trouble. A split developed between research and practice: Practitioners accused researchers of not producing knowledge that would be useful for practice (Bergmark & Oscarsson, 1992); researchers, in turn, accused practitioners of not being interested in hard knowledge and of lacking discipline and intellectual rigor. Practitioners are involved in the messy problems of human life and speak of experience, trial and error, intuition, and even of muddling through. Researchers, however, tend to be devoted to technical rigor and solid competence. Given their strong belief that real knowledge depends on a particular research methodology, researchers sometimes adopt an elitist and patronizing attitude toward practitioners: They contend that researchers know, whereas practitioners only feel. Practitioners, on the other hand, may be disdainful of research, reluctant to consider its usefulness for practice, and uninclined to think clearly

about what they are doing. Some practitioners would do well to describe more carefully the person-in-situation and their interventions. Further, some do not take seriously their ethical obligation to contribute to the knowledge base of the profession.

Despite the lingering view that social work is not a hard science, we now have the opportunity—and the obligation—to generate knowledge for practice on the basis of a wide range of methods. In particular, many social workers are drawn to the phenomenological approach which focuses on the lived experience of each individual and suggests that we may best understand another person by experiencing the world as the other person does. This approach is consistent with social workers' training in understanding the client's feelings. "The practitioner is in the ideal position to be a researcher. A new paradigm would relieve the need to apologize for the unscientific anecdotal nature of the data, for it is in that direction that the most appropriate understanding of human processes can be found" (Haworth, 1984, p. 355).

Social work, like most other professions, draws on an extensive body of practice wisdom. Over time, practitioners discover what works and what does not. These precepts represent a collective wisdom that has accumulated now for more than 100 years. Practice wisdom is transmitted informally from supervisor to practitioner and is organized and transmitted in educational institutions and publications. It is accepted solely on the basis of practitioners' experience; very little of it has been verified through rigorous research. Waldo Klein and Martin Bloom (1995) suggest that practice wisdom emerges as practitioners employ unarticulated knowledge and develop on-the-spot hypotheses to guide their practice and make progress with a case. Identifying and articulating these practice hypotheses will contribute to both theory development and testing of the knowledge used by the profession (Gilgun, 1994; Harold, Palmiter, Lynch, & Freedman-Doan, 1995; Klein & Bloom, 1995; Millstein, 1994).

Scientific inquiry and practice can be integrated on the basis of the problem-solving process which is used by both practitioners and researchers (Allen-Meares & Lane, 1990): The best of scientific inquiry is an attempt to solve a problem, and the best of practice is an attempt to join a client in problem solving. In this respect, the process of research and practice are similar. In each, a problem must be defined, a hypothesis must be stated with greater or lesser confidence (assessment, in practice terms), data must be collected, a methodology must be stated (plan of intervention, in practice terms), and an outcome must be evaluated. Mullen (1985) suggests that, because of the tension between research and practice, both researchers and practitioners are losing their focus on purpose and becoming narrowly preoccupied with method "out of context with purpose":

> A refocus on purpose directs attention to the type of knowledge needed to facilitate the profession's mission. The knowledge that is required is the type that would facilitate problem solving and be close to the context of practice. There are various approaches to problem solving, ranging from the traditional to the modern and cutting across both familiar and novel situations. The profession needs practice and research approaches that are responsive to these problem-solving alternatives. (p. 18)

The integration of research and practice can be seen in the movement toward empirical practice (Fischer, 1993; Reid, 1994; Thyer, 1996). Social workers have a responsibility to systematically develop the knowledge base for the profession, to increase the quantity of research being done, and to contribute to research that meets the profession's need for knowledge to address complex social problems (Lindsey & Kirk, 1992).

Theory and Practice

There is a debate within the profession about whether theory is necessary for practice (Simon, 1994; Thyer, 1994). We agree with Briar and Miller (1971) that

> the choice for the practitioner is not whether to have a theory but what theoretical assumptions to hold. All persons acquire assumptions or views on the basis of which they construe and interpret events and behavior, including their own. These assumptions frequently are not explicit but are more what has been called "implicit theories of personality." Thus, the appeal for practitioners to be atheoretical amounts simply to an argument that theory ought to be implicit and hidden, not explicit and self-conscious. (p. 53)

Briar and Miller (1971) indicate that social workers' assumptions about the possibilities of human change will probably affect the degree of optimism with which they approach their clients. Further, the premises about what can be changed will largely determine what workers attempts to change. Knowledge-based theory (hypotheses regarding the nature of the phenomenon and the strategies that will help) and values (what social workers see as desired ends) interact with the problems clients bring and the solutions sought. As a practitioner, your work with any client will be determined by the purposes and values of the profession; by your understanding of the situation, developed on the basis of social work knowledge and theory; and by your appraisal of the client's state and attitudes, an appraisal based on your interpretation of what the client says will

- be explicit about goals—what is to be changed, who sets the goals, and how this is done.
- be optimistic to searching for more effective and powerful ways to bring it about.
- specify what is required of the client.
- specify, in behavioral terms, what the practitioner must do to bring about the desired changes.
- indicate what the practitioner needs to do in order to make sure that the changes are carried over into the client's real life.
- tell the practitioner how to assess the outcome of intervention.

It is the social worker's responsibility to analyze and understand the situation before taking action. All professional practice requires rapid, continuous, and expert selection of generalizations from the profession's body of knowledge; at the same time, the practitioner must remain open to feedback from the client and willing, on that basis, to abandon the first hypothesis and select another. Social workers put their professional knowledge to its first important use through their ability to know where the client is, so that the client and worker may be actively involved in assessing the situation with which they are dealing.

Social workers are continually trying to identify the knowledge base on which the profession rests. But this is difficult, for a number of reasons.

1. The primary knowledge of the profession is drawn cumulatively from the immense range of human problems revealed by individuals in particular situations.
2. Knowledge needed for many problem-solving activities in the profession must be drawn from allied

disciplines, which poses problems of appropriate selection, translation, and use.

3. The relevant knowledge is changing constantly and advancing rapidly.
4. Because the profession is engaged in a wealth of activities, it's not always clear where the boundaries of relevant knowledge lie.

There has been a shift in the profession from concern with the internal state of individuals and their adaptive functioning to a broader view of individuals as participants in an interactional field of psychological and social forces. This shift calls for a different organization of our knowledge base and an expanded range of approaches and techniques.

Knowledge and Values

Values and knowledge are often confused because all value dimensions of human life influence the knowledge base of practice in one way or another. Values are what we hold as desirable; they express what ought to be. When we describe what is, we are using knowledge. Values imply a preference for certain "means, ends and conditions of life, often accompanied by strong feeling" (Pumphrey, 1959, p. 23). Knowledge, on the other hand, is information about the world and its qualities, about people and their interrelationships.

Values relate to the question of whether a proposition is right or wrong, while knowledge relates to the question of whether it is true or false. This distinction is very important to social work. For instance, we may be destructive to our child clients and their families if the value of freedom to choose is not tempered with the knowledge that children, as they develop, also need firm, consistent limits. If we have test-based evidence that a particular proposition is true and also believe that it is right, there will be no desire to change it. Some of our greatest conflicts in social work arise where knowledge and values do not agree. For example, significant research findings indicate that many people believe parents have the right to punish their children in any manner they please. To challenge this value, social workers call on knowledge—specifically, research evidence about child care that shows the negative effect of certain punishments. Another important conflict centers on treatment of the poor. There is significant evidence that living in abject poverty, with inadequate nourish-

ment, can be severely damaging to children, both physically and psychologically. However, a widely held value system says that people should stand on their own two feet and not take help from anyone, no matter what. Social workers must remember that, in a democratic society, all individuals have the right—within limits—to their own value system. These values can only be challenged by empirical evidence that shows them to be damaging to human beings. We cannot demand that people change their values to conform to ours; however, people can be asked to consider test-based knowledge when it is available.

William Gordon (1962, 1965) has discussed two kinds of knowledge: (1) knowledge that has been confirmed by empirical testing and/or observation; and (2) assumptive knowledge—knowledge that is accepted and acted on as though it were true but has not yet been confirmed, although the intent is to confirm it eventually. Assumptive knowledge may be true or false. It must be subjected, in due course, to testing based on accepted guidelines for research. if there is resistance to efforts to test a notion, that notion may be a value, rather than an item of assumptive knowledge. Much knowledge in social work is assumptive knowledge; its acceptance is conditional on the professional's willingness and commitment to test it.

Acting on Incomplete Knowledge

Because the amount of knowledge needed is so vast and some of it is so uncertain, social workers must accept that, like all other practitioners in the human services, they intervene in people's lives on the basis of incomplete knowledge. This raises some hard questions: How can we help people to feel some confidence in us as helpers when we are often uncertain about what we know? How can we doubt our effectiveness and still be effective?

The stress of acting on incomplete knowledge confronts all professionals in the human services but it bears heavily on social workers, because of our commitment to individuals and their worth. Some social workers handle their discomfort by trying to forget what they do not know. They become dogmatic, certain of their own knowledge; this renders them unable to grow, because a person who already knows cannot learn. Some social workers handle the discomfort by emphasizing what they do not know and how helpless they are. They search

EXHIBIT 2-7	A Social Work Pledge in the Face of Incomplete Knowledge

This is my solemn vow to my client:

- I will try everything I know to help the client with whom I am involved.
- I may not know what way is best in all instances, but I will think carefully about my procedures.
- I will be willing to assume the responsibility for my actions.
- I will not be blinded by preconception, nor will I impulsively follow a fleeting impulse or an easy answer.

- I will draw thoughtfully and responsibly upon every bit of knowledge that is available, and I will constantly and actively search for more.
- I will be an insistent questioner rather than a passive taker; I will remain identified with the profession while I vigorously question it.
- I will be open to new knowledge; I will not be so committed to a course of action that I cannot change when new knowledge is developed.

for other authorities, while their client suffers from the lack of a secure helper. Some practitioners blame the profession for their discomfort. They then find themselves representing a profession in which they have no confidence and with which they have no identification; this is a truly uncomfortable position. These workers never come to grips with their need to know. If they had read the literature of other professions, they would understand that all professions are woefully lacking in knowledge of human beings and their interaction.

Our role as a helping person in complex and ever-changing situations demands that we act on uncertain knowledge. The best way of living with this is to commit ourselves to becoming active learners and to the scientific method. Exhibit 2–7 offers a pledge that may help you live with the reality of incomplete knowledge.

CHAPTER SUMMARY

We have organized this chapter as a funnel: We began with the broad topic of systems theory and moved to a discussion of the knowledge generated in social work and its incompleteness. We emphasized that systems are goal-directed, may be open or closed, and have boundaries. We then considered ecosystems and the notion of person-in-situation, which is central to social work practice. According to the ecosystem approach, individuals are in constant interaction with their environment, and social work practice aims at changing the transactions between people and their environments. Further, the ecosystem approach suggests the types of knowledge that are necessary for social work practice.

Some of this knowledge is borrowed—largely from role theory and egopsychology. The profession also has a responsibility to generate knowledge for its own use, primarily in the areas of assessment and intervention. Much of this knowledge is embodied in the practice wisdom of the profession, which is handed down from one generation of social workers to the next. As a profession, we have a responsibility to further test and systematize this knowledge.

Systems theory and the ecosystem approach provide a useful organizing framework for social work for these reasons:

- The concepts relating to the development, function, and structure of systems are equally applicable to all the clients served by social workers, including individuals, groups, and communities.
- Systems theory clarifies the range of elements that bear on social problems, including the social units involved, their interrelationships, and the implications of change in one element for all the others.
- Systems theory shifts attention from the characteristics possessed by individuals or their environments, by focusing on interfaces and the communication process. Social work sees individuals and their environments as part of a complete whole.
- Systems theory sees people as active systems capable of self-initiated behavior and thus able to contribute to, and alter, their environment or even to create new environments. Adaptation of the environment is as much a property of human systems as is the tendency to respond to the environment. These concepts negate the

tendency to see disturbances as pathology and move the worker into the present life of the client.

• Once they accept the concept of systems as purposive, along with the concepts of equifinality and multifinality, social workers must modify their attitude to causation and the possibilities for change. These concepts support self-determination, client's participation in the change process, and the necessity of knowing and considering client goals in assessment and planning of intervention.

• Systems theory encourages social workers to focus on the purpose of the system and, in consequence, to support client self-determination and to relate professional feedback to client purpose.

• A living, open system requires constant transactions with other systems and the environment for progressive development; social workers must provide and maintain interchange opportunities for all clients.

• To avoid closed systems, social workers must be aware of populations and systems that are heading toward isolation, the strains in society that result in isolation, and already-isolated populations within society.

• Change and tension are inherent in open systems; social workers must explore why suggested changes are resisted and why such changes become unbearable for a system. This entails meeting clients where they are and fostering self-determination. In this perspective, tension or conflict is not pathology.

• The concept of system boundaries gives us a way of evaluating the systems with which we work. Healthy systems will respond to external influences with caution and a degree of testing; systems that are too open or too closed are a cause for concern. We respect clients' rights and recognize the need for careful consideration of the ways we cross the clients' boundaries.

• Recognition that change in one part of a system can effect the whole means that we must be aware of the impact of intervention on clients' the broader transactions.

• In the systems perspective, the agency is regarded as a social system, and the agency, the worker, and the client are all in the same transactional field. Social workers constitute a social system and are also components of the social agency system.

• The person-situation system exists within a hierarchical arrangement of systems that extends from the individual to the macro level of society and culture.

The notion of ecological systems also creates two related problems in social work assessment: (1) the social worker may be overwhelmed by the mass of data and the multitude of possible connections between an individual and various components of the environment; and (2) the worker may never move beyond the assessment phase, as one connection leads to another connection and then another, in a potentially infinite chain. We will return to these problems in Chapter 10. For the moment, you can begin to reflect on how you might usefully limit or focus assessment. In Reading 2-3, Jane Gilgun offers a useful example of an ecosystem assessment that remains focused despite the wide range of data considered.

The ecosystem approach suggests that we need knowledge about the transactions or interactions of persons and their environment. Social work both borrows and generates such knowledge. Borrowed knowledge from role theory and from ego psychology is helpful for understanding our focus on the person-in-situation.

Role theory provides social workers with the following useful insights:

• Many expected behaviors are prescribed (by us and by other elements of our social system) relative to our position within that system.

• Every role involves both our own expectations and abilities and those of one or more other people.

• The notion of role expectation implies norms that set the outside limits of congruent, nonconflicted interactions and transactions between positions within the system and across systems.

• There are emotionally charged value judgments about how people carry out their roles on the part both of the person occupying the role and of others.

• Social functioning may be seen as the sum of the roles performed by a human system.

• The concepts of role, role functioning, role expectations, and role transactions may be used to increase the knowledge base for assessment of the problem situation. Role failure and/or role conflict will tend to follow:

a. When resources necessary for a person's ability to perform a role are lost or absent.

b. When people are thrust into new roles without knowing the role expectations.

c. When there is a conflict in role expectation on the part of interacting systems.

d. When there is conflict of role expectations within the cluster of roles carried by a person.
e. When there is ambiguity on the part of other systems about role expectations.
f. When the individual as a system, or as a member of a social system, does not have physical, intellectual, or social capacities adequate to the role.
g. When high feeling or crisis disrupts previously effective role patterns.

• Individuals receive instrumental, information, emotional, and affiliational social support through interaction with other persons in their role set. These interactions and the flow of social support provide a focus for social work assessment and intervention.

Ego psychology makes the following useful contributions:

• If the ego has its own needs and drives and is autonomous, and if the human personality develops over the life cycle, efforts directed to present life experiences are of particular importance.
• If the personality is an open system, day-by-day input from transactions with the environment are of great importance; the client needs to be actively involved with the environment.
• The idea that the individual strives for competence and mastery offers an optimistic view of the possibilities of human growth and change, while stressing the importance of input from other social systems and the environment.
• In ego psychology, individuals are seen as actively and consciously participating in their own destiny, rather than simply reacting to stimuli or to needs beyond their control. This leads to the concept of partnership between the social worker and the client.
• The idea that human beings seek active experiences and control of their own destiny provides guidance in assessment, demands that clients be active participants in planning and change, and supports the social work values of self-determination and respect for the individual.
• The notion that motivation is what the client wants and how much he or she wants it, together with the concept of goal-in-systems theory, reminds us of the importance of client goals and client self-determination.
• Hope is a stimulus for active problem solving and

gives us a view of the meaning of apathy that challenges other views of what produces dependency.
• The human search for meaning in life suggests the importance of considering clients' transpersonal and spiritual experiences.
• Research in ego psychology indicates that a continuous relationship from a caring adult plays a key role in the development of resiliency in children and youth. This raises an important question for both social work practice and the organization of social services: Should we work at strengthening and preserving relationships, rather than disrupting them?

In borrowing knowledge, we need to ensure that it fits with the person-in-situation focus of the profession and, thus, can make a helpful contribution to our practice.

Social workers also generate knowledge—specifically, in relation to assessment and intervention. Historically, there has been controversy in the profession regarding the nature of knowledge; researchers' empirical approach contrasts strongly with practitioners' more intuitive knowledge. Researchers' traditional emphasis on logical positivism has now been broadened to include knowledge gained from phenomonological approaches. The conflict between researchers and practitioners will be eased if we expect researchers to provide knowledge that is useful for practice, and we expect practitioners to more systematically describe their practice and organize the practice wisdom of the profession. In Chapter 6, we will discuss our ethical obligation as practitioners to apply, and contribute to, the knowledge base of the profession.

A LOOK FORWARD

The three readings in this chapter will deepen your understanding of the ecosystem focus in social work practice. A brief article by Yaroshevsky and Schatzky emphasizes the importance of a family assessment before prescribing medication to control the behavior of young people; the authors suggest that, in some situations, the behavior is the result of interactions in the ecosystem, rather than a symptom of illness within the youth. Lyle Longclaws argues for the importance of considering culture, including spirituality, in work with Native people. And, finally, Jane Gilgun discusses an ecosystemic approach to assessment, with a case illustration that suggests practical, concrete steps for assessment.

In the next chapter, we will discuss the problem-solving process. In Chapter 4, we will examine client-worker partnership and, in Chapter 5, we will argue that the preferred source of authority for your action comes from an agreement with your client. These ideas have important implications for the ways in which you use knowledge. Knowledge can be used to help people seek new alternatives and opportunities or to regulate and control them. Social workers have a responsibility to make their knowledge available as tools and resources, so as to assist clients in expanding their range of opportunities and choices, in redefining problems so that change is possible, and in selecting appropriate courses of action for achieving their objectives. It is improper for social workers to withhold knowledge or to use it in an effort to control people.

READING 2-1 *Ritalin, Ritalin, Who's Got the Ritalin?**

Felix Yaroshevsky and David Schatzky

This year, thousands of young children in Canada will get hooked on a powerful prescription drug called Ritalin. This addiction will be initiated by well-intentioned parents, teachers and physicians who want to eliminate the children's restless, angry, frustrated, self-destructive behavior—instantly.

This chain of delegated responsibility for hooking a child on pills often starts with teachers, already under stress because of too few resources and classes that are too large. They may pressure parents to take hard-to-handle kids to the doctor, and create parental anxiety by convincing them that without medication these children will not learn. The doctor feels obliged to alleviate this anxiety and prescribes Ritalin.

The International Narcotics Control Board reports that, in 1995, 250 million doses of Ritalin (methylphenidate) were prescribed in the United States, and goes on to warn "all governments to exercise the utmost vigilance in order to prevent . . . medically unjustified treatment with methylphenidate." The U. S. Drug Enforcement Administration says that "abuse of methylphenidate can lead to tolerance and severe psychological dependence." Even the manufacturer of Ritalin, in its letter to Canadian physicians dated November 23, 1994, advised them to prescribe the drug "when remedial measures such as psychological counselling and educational tutoring alone are insufficient."

Nevertheless, when they hear the words "restless" and "lack of attention," doctors all too frequently give Ritalin without first asking more about what's going on in the life of the child.

In summer, change is in the air. Children change schools and teachers. Some spend part of the summer at the cottage, attend camps, or visit their grandparents. They are forced into different routines and relationships and must adjust to each new situation. They are exposed to attitudes expressed by one member of the family who is critical of others; children are very vulnerable to these messages containing the truth about how family members feel about each other, even when stated subtly and sometimes without a word being spoken.

Consider the typical story of a 7-year-old we'll call Kevin. He's a very active child who drives his parents crazy at bedtime by devising new ways to extend his hours of play. His parents strongly disagree about how to discipline him and are completely inconsistent when putting him to bed.

Last summer, Kevin spent a month at his grandparents' cottage. His parents visited on weekends. During the week, the grandparents had no problems with Kevin at bedtime; but on the weekends, when his father tried to put him to bed, the grandparents felt their son-in-law was too strict and looked at each other in a way that conveyed their profound disapproval. Then they raised the subject with Kevin's mother and father when they thought Kevin was out of earshot. Kevin's mother supported her parents; his father felt isolated and unsupported and grew so angry that he returned alone to the city.

The usually well-hidden marital difficulties between Kevin's parents flared up and, by the time Kevin came

---

* Reprinted from Toronto Globe and Mail, September 3, 1996; Reprinted by permission of the authors.

home, his parents were on the verge of divorce. Kevin felt it was all his fault.

Now he could go to bed as late as he wanted, because his parents were so busy fighting. He didn't get enough sleep. He became restless, fidgety, bored, and defiant. When he went back to school, he continued to withdraw and rebel. The teacher complained about his behavior, and his mother took him to a doctor. The doctor, who had no way of knowing the real context of Kevin's life without a proper family assessment, prescribed Ritalin.

Now Kevin is heavily drugged and behaving better, but no one is helping him with his confusion and anger over the stresses and instability of his family life. A family assessment would have helped his mother and father sort out their differences in a way that would give Kevin the support and appropriate consistent attention that every child needs in order to function normally.

In families already preoccupied with a separation and lengthy litigation, the pressure on children is even greater.

When a doctor takes the time to perform an assessment, and the family is ready to understand and appreciate what the child is going through, remedial help can be made available and medication can be avoided. The assessment takes into account the family history, power structure, communication system, and group politics. The child may be a power broker between subtly feuding parents. Imagine a teeter-totter with a parent at each end and the child in the middle; where the child goes, so goes the weight, and the power shifts. With family therapy, balance can be restored and the child's behavior changes, generally without Ritalin.

People who advocate medication as the first way to make children behave, without exploring their life situation and real needs, might as well treat unhappiness with cocaine.

READING 2-2 *Social Work and the Medicine Wheel Framework**

Lyle Longclaws

The ecological or person-in-situation approach is used by social workers to better understand the person and environment. This approach cannot be appreciated in isolation of cultural factors. This paper describes cultural factors associated with the Anishinabe (Ojibway/Saulteaux Indians) medicine wheel and compares principles central to the ecological and medicine wheel models.

THE ECOLOGICAL MODEL AND SOCIAL WORK

Social work has always been interested in the person and the environment, despite an emphasis on one or the other throughout the development of the profession. Several decades ago, social workers may have been viewed more as psychologists than as sociologists, with only a secondary and indirect interest in peoples' relationships with their environments. However, since the late 1960s, a definite reciprocal interest in environment has emerged. Brower (1988) recognizes that the ecological model, often defined as the social environmental approach, developed from the profession's dual commitment to the person and environment; it grew directly from the profession's roots. Germain and Gitterman (1980) adopt the ecological perspective and view social work as being at the interface between people and the environment. They see a reciprocal relationship between the person and environment, in which each shapes the other, and advocate treatment of the person within the context of the environment. Bryant (1980) applies an ecological formula to treatment of inner-city families, while Compher (1982) limits his analysis to the educational environment. Both suggest that it is possible for social workers to effectively intervene in order to ensure appropriate relationships and productivity within such settings.

The ecological framework assists us in organizing information about people and environments in order to understand the interconnectedness. In this approach, human beings are regarded as engaging in constant adaptive and evolutionary interchange with all elements of their environments. Human needs and problems are

---

*An original paper revised for this edition.

generated by the transactions between people and their environments. Additionally, like all living systems, people need to maintain a notion of fit in order to match human needs to environmental resources.

Stress results from lack of fit and the cognitive appraisal of imbalance between perceived demand and perceived capability. Produced by either external or internal demands, stress occurs in a cyclical form: One stressful event leads to another. In this way of thinking, stress is part of any transaction; social workers may intervene in the cycle to help mobilize the client's ability to deal with the perceived demand. Social workers may also reframe the situation or provide supportive interventions.

The client's ability to cope depends on personality attributes and also situational elements such as the incentive system and societal preparation and support for coping. The social work profession forms part of the social environment and acts a mediator with the external environment. Social workers offer emotional support by providing problem-solving skills and may be responsible for advocating at the case level while working with the person. Further, social workers may advocate on behalf of a class, such as single mothers, and in areas of policy.

Individuals move through a series of life transitions, all of which require environmental supports and coping skills and may result in stress if there is not a good fit between internal and external demands and resources (Germain & Gitterman, 1980). Common life transitions include stages of human development, changes in occupation, and relocation from rural to urban areas. In general, the environment may either assist or hinder life transitions. It is helpful to think of different layers in the environment. The first two layers include the natural world and the built world and their effects on people's behavior. The third layer, which consists of three sublayers, is the social world and deals with people in terms of organizations. Examples of the first sublayer include neighbors and self-help groups. The second sublayer includes service organizations, such as school systems. The last sublayer consists of culture, which is broadly shared across families and organizations and includes values and political systems. Most of the attention of social work has been on the third layer. Meanwhile, the built and social worlds are in continual interaction among these layers and the individual.

The profession of social work is interested in the person, the environment, and transactions between the two. In contrast to labeling that fosters a deficit view of the person, transactional concepts can help focus assessment and intervention on the relations between person and environment. Transactional ideas view adaptation as a process of shaping physical and social environments; people in turn are also shaped by the environment. The goal of intervention in transactions is to release adaptive capacities and to improve the environment. Social workers are interested in transactions that either promote or inhibit growth and development.

Thus, social workers assess the nature of transactions and intervene in them. Such interventions are often oriented toward stress reduction and enhancement of coping. Network intervention tries to increase mutual aid among those within the social network and supports the development of self-esteem, personal autonomy, sovereignty, and other experiences that will increase individuals' well-being. An adaptation evaluation takes account of emotional and situational stress in order to help people discover their inner resources and enhance their self-esteem and confidence.

The ecological approach is appealing to social workers of Anishinabe ancestry because it suggests the possibility of culturally appropriate treatment for the Anishinabe Indian people within their environments. Redhorse and his colleagues (Redhorse, Lewis, Fest, & Decker, 1978) challenge the profession to apply ecological standards to Indian families, who may be vanishing as rapidly as the buffalo. However, caution is necessary; the Anishinabe social worker cannot afford to be drawn to yet another mirage, in hopes of quenching a very real thirst in the midst of a vast desert.

THE ANISHINABE MEDICINE WHEEL TEACHINGS

Medicine wheel teachings are passed down orally by Anishinabe elders from Waywayseecappo First Nation (located in West Central Manitoba, near the town of Rossburn). Waywayseecappo elders teach that four laws or ceremonies were given to the Anishinabe in order for them to obtain balance and harmony. These are the midewewin, aniba-gwayshimoong, anishanabe-nee-mide-wing, and ape-tong. (Exhibit 2–8 provides a glossary of selected Anishinabe concepts.) Of the four, the midewewin is most frequently practiced by Anishanabe. The other three have been modified; the council dance, for example, is now held for peaceful purposes, and not

---

EXHIBIT 2-8   **Glossary of Anishinabe Concepts**

Aniba-qwayshimoong: one of the four lodges or laws of the Anishinabe.

Anishinabe: literally, the original people (in the Ojibway/Saulteaux language).

Anishinabe-nee-mide-wing: one of the four lodges or laws of the Anishinabe.

Ape-tong: one of the four lodges or laws of the Anishinabe.

Bad medicine: the destructive use of medicine and knowledge to harm an individual.

Council dance: ceremony traditionally performed in time of war but now modified to promote peace and goodwill.

Eshkabes: individuals who assist a teacher elder during ceremonies. These individuals may also be apprentices who are learning the teachings.

Giveaway: traditional ceremony in which personal possessions are distributed to those in attendance.

Indian Country: common term for land traditionally held by First Nations.

Kitche Manitou or Manitou: literally, the great mystery.

Medicine wheel: an organizing and clarifying framework, dynamic in nature, for thinking about existence in the universe.

Midewewin: one of four lodge or laws of the Anishinabe; currently, the most frequently practiced of these laws.

Mother earth: the earth as giver and sustainer of life.

Naming ceremony: a ceremony in which an individual is given his or her spiritual or Indian name.

Oda aki: literally, heart of the earth or center.

Ojibway: common English term for the Anishinabe.

Powwow: a social gathering usually with dancing and feasts.

Saulteaux: common French term for the Anishinabe—specifically, those who historically lived at present-day Sault Ste. Marie and later migrated to present-day Manitoba and Saskatchewan.

Shake tent: sacred ceremony practiced for specific purposes and only on rare occasions.

Sundance: ceremony held for four days every June, commencing on the longest day of the year; the general purpose is to strengthen the commitment of participants in the ways of the medicine wheel teachings.

Sweatlodge: purification and healing ceremony.

Sweetgrass: one of four sacred cleansing medicines used by the Anishinabe.

Turtle Island: North America.

---

for war as in traditional tribal times. Elders continue to practice age-old ceremonies in which the four laws are handed down. In order to fully appreciate and participate in the four major ceremonies, or laws, Anishinabe must travel the medicine wheel journey. Exhibit 2–9 presents a diagram of the medicine wheel, which serves as a framework for learning the significance of ceremonies and rituals.

The medicine wheel approach views the universe and a person's position in it as critical to understanding the meaning of a good life. It acknowledges the interconnection of all beings and forces existing on physical and spiritual worlds. The medicine wheel framework has teachings essential for the physical world, while recognizing the direct link to oda aki (centeredness). Centeredness, the ultimate goal to be achieved within the medicine wheel circle, is the achievement of balance—peace and harmony with oneself and all other living things. Individuals travel within their own medicine wheel but are guided by the teachings given to all Anishinabe. Each life affects all others in the circle of life, in both the present and the future. All living things are born with a spirit, but only human beings must find

harmony within the circle, because all other living things, such as the plants, animals, and elements, are already in balance with the universe. A philosophy of interdependence is paramount to achieving harmony and balance in the medicine wheel. The medicine wheel demonstrates the absence of a hierarchy. It has no top or bottom; all living things have their place and responsibility in the natural order of life within the wheel. People and nature are viewed as interdependent and connected. Whatever happens to one happens to all. Thus, utmost respect and reciprocity is practiced within the medicine wheel circle.

Given this worldview, the purpose of the medicine wheel is to provide a framework for ensuring the balance and harmony of Anishinabe within the circle of life. Those who disregard the medicine wheel teachings experience imbalance and disharmony with all around them. To ensure balance and harmony, the medicine wheel proposes a way of living that emphasizes responsibilities, values, and ethics. Ceremonies assist individuals in centering themselves and give them strength to participate in a lifelong learning process. People are born good. Throughout life, the teachings of the medicine

EXHIBIT 2-9   The Anishinabe Medicine Wheel

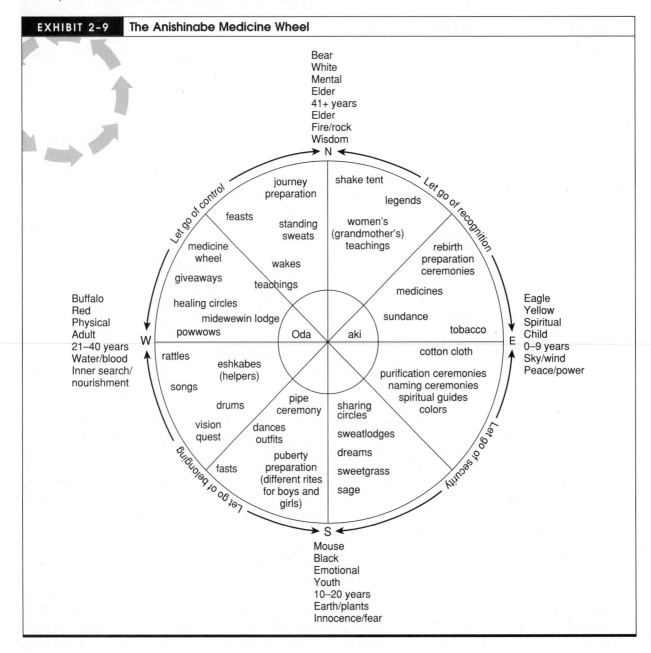

Bear
White
Mental
Elder
41+ years
Elder
Fire/rock
Wisdom

N

Let go of control

Let go of recognition

journey preparation

shake tent

legends

feasts

standing sweats

women's (grandmother's) teachings

medicine wheel

wakes

rebirth preparation ceremonies

giveaways

teachings

medicines

healing circles

sundance

midewewin lodge

Oda   aki

powwows

tobacco

rattles

eshkabes (helpers)

cotton cloth

songs

purification ceremonies
naming ceremonies
spiritual guides
colors

drums

pipe ceremony

sharing circles

vision quest

dances outfits

sweatlodges

fasts

puberty preparation (different rites for boys and girls)

dreams

sweetgrass

sage

Let go of belonging

Let go of security

Buffalo
Red
Physical
Adult
21–40 years
Water/blood
Inner search/ nourishment

W

E

Eagle
Yellow
Spiritual
Child
0–9 years
Sky/wind
Peace/power

S

Mouse
Black
Emotional
Youth
10–20 years
Earth/plants
Innocence/fear

wheel provide guidance and protection from evil forces that can lead people astray—off the good or red road. These evil forces are found all across Turtle Island, mother earth, and Indian country. Evil forces of the spiritual world are manifested in the physical world through the use of bad medicine. Evil forces are also found in physical substances such as alcohol and drugs.

The values of materialism, greed, jealousy, and dishonesty are also seen as evil forces, as they prevent the individual from reaching personal centeredness. People who are involved with these evil forces are lost, not only to themselves but to the nation. Therefore, feeling a direct connection to the spirit world, Anishinabe are careful not to offend any of their relations, living or dead, through their actions or thoughts, lest they be the recipient of that spirit's wrath. This worldview reinforces the ethics and values of the Anishinabe. Most aspects of life are defined and given significance within the context of the spiritual world.

Central life principles of the Anishinabe include respect, kindness, caring, sharing, honor, and the attainment of wisdom, strength, and truth. These values are operationalized within extended family groups and clans, which take on specific roles and responsibilities; the bear clan, for example, is responsible for protection within the nation or tribe, while the responsibility of extended family groups is to ensure the survival of the family.

Particular ethical principles are defined for use within the extended family groupings, within the tribe, and in dealings with other nations. All Anishinabe are either part of an extended family or members of a clan. They participate in the circle of life, with different responsibilities in different phases. The circle is a powerful symbol of the interconnection and interdependence of all the phases.

A child enters the circle at birth. The parents make a gift of tobacco and cotton cloth to an elder who will conduct a naming ceremony, so that Manitou will recognize the child's spirit. Later in life, if the child states his or her Indian name before praying, Manitou will hear the prayers. The naming ceremony reinforces group identification, as family members accept their responsibilities to raise the child in a prescribed way. The ceremony includes the burial of the child's umbilical cord, signifying that the child is forever a member of the nation. The child is not the property of the parents; the name reinforces a deep connection to all of mother earth and enables the child to grow in spirit. The name also provides guidance; with deepening understanding of the name, the child begins to distinguish his or her individual gifts. Frequently, the child receives personal colors, related to the name; the meaning of the colors is elaborated in traveling through the circle. When worn by the child, colors are believed to give strength.

After receiving traditional gifts, the elder prepares for the ceremony. When the time is right to share the naming celebration, a pipe ceremony is conducted at sunrise with family members. Prayers of gratitude are expressed. Through the dreams of the elder, the spirits give the name to the child. The name signifies the belief that a spirit guide will protect and direct the child over the life journey. As part of the ceremony, the extended family holds a feast to celebrate its commitment to the child.

As clan members travel through the circle of life, they grow in ways of knowledge, spirit, and wisdom. The four directions of the medicine wheel possess teachings to assist in the search for knowledge and wisdom. Anishinabe believe that the east is associated with illumination, peace, and spiritual influence. These gifts are represented by the eagle, who flies closest to Manitou and is believed to have great vision or farsightedness. Because the sun rises in the east, this is the direction of the child and of the color yellow, signifying the sun's rays. In recent interpretations, the east is associated with Asian peoples. The eastern direction is also represented by the elements such as wind and is the domain of the sky.

Moving in the direction of the sun as it crosses the sky, the next direction is south. The south is represented by the mouse; the gifts received there include innocence and fear. This direction corresponds to the emotional realm; within the circle of life, it is associated with the ages of 10–20 years. The south represents the worlds of plants; mother earth is represented by the color black, signifying a time of letting go of security and belonging, which can be a dark or unknown time. Ceremonies such as sweatlodges, pipe ceremonies, vision quests, and male and female puberty rites are introduced to assist youth. These ceremonies are enriched with sharing circles, songs, chants, and dancing. The young Anishinabe person may be given the right to hold sharing circles in which sweetgrass, sage, and other medicines are used, depending on his ability to respect these gifts. The south begins making contact with the center of the circle, known as oda aki. The individual is conscious of experiences of harmony and balance. As the frequency of these experiences increases, the individual begins to develop the ability to visit the spiritual world, and the likelihood of having a meaningful journey increases.

The next direction in the medicine wheel is the west, represented by the buffalo. Buffalo are leaders of the hoof clan and represent the gifts of nourishment and introspection. This direction is associated with people aged 21–40 and is the physical domain of the circle. The corresponding color is red, representing the setting sun and the blood or water of the physical world. Like buffalo, people in this phase of life protect and provide nourishment for their young and also protect the weak and old. In this phase, there is opportunity for searching inwardly, which provides the strength for letting go of control; this is necessary in order to remain in balance and harmony with all living things. During this phase, the vision received in youth is given meaning and is strengthened by participating as an eshkabe (helper) to an elder or medicine person. Gifts of songs, drums, and rattles reinforce the teachings and provide greater insight. With greater understanding of the medicine wheel teachings at this phase, the individual has greater influence in healing circles and a place of credibility in the midewewin lodge. Giveaways are a necessary part of benefiting from such spiritual nourishment. This phase is associated with a different style of songs and dances at social gatherings such as powwows.

The fourth direction is the north, represented by the bear. The gifts of this direction are knowledge, guidance, and wisdom. This phase is the mental sphere in the circle of life; having lived more than 40 years, Anishinabe are teachers of young and old alike. This direction is represented by the color white, to denote the blanket of wisdom in the winter of an Anishinabe's life cycle. The elements of fire and rock are powerful symbols of completing the foundation within the medicine wheel. The rocks, as the oldest substance on mother earth, are referred to as grandfathers and used in the sacred sweatlodge ceremony. They are heated in a fire and then placed with great reverence in the center of the sweatlodge. Water is sprinkled on the rocks with medicines, so that the spirits of grandfather rocks are released and heal the participants in the sweatlodge ceremony. In this phase in life, having practiced the ways of the people as outlined in the medicine wheel teachings, the elder will now be prepared to assume leadership in ceremonies. Elder Anishinabe conduct the sweatlodge, pipe ceremonies, standing sweats, sundance, shake tents, council dance, naming ceremonies, burial rites, and feasts, and pass on teachings through stories. They are healers, with knowledge of the medicines available from the plant world. Anishinabe are very respectful of elders and their wisdom and look forward to taking this role in the clan. Elders have let go of control and recognition, so that they live life for their Manitou and all creation. In addition, elders are seen as returning to the beginning of the circle, which is the spiritual world; they are becoming a child once again, particularly toward the end of their life in the physical world.

The last three directions within the Anishinabe medicine wheel are the vertical, which represents Kitche Manitou; the horizontal, which represents mother earth; and the inward, which represents the heart or center. There are many ways of traveling on the medicine wheel circle. For example, contrary people will do everything backward; others may travel vertically or horizontally within the circle; still others will start at a certain direction and work their way around the circle. The process is not linear but cyclical. Anishinabe may be born in one direction, learn those teachings, but never progress throughout their lifetime; these people are referred to as warriors. A chief or clan mother will travel through two phases and receive the teachings and gifts. An elder will travel and obtain the gifts and teachings of three phases, while the medicine person will have completed or traveled through all four phases and will be knowledgeable of the teachings and gifts. Medicine people supervise others in their journey through the medicine wheel.

ECOLOGICAL PRACTICE AND ANISHINABE HEALING PRINCIPLES

The ecological and medicine wheel frameworks have been presented as independent models. However, they overlap. For example, the respect of person and environment embraced within the ecological approach has parallels in Anishinabe belief. Another similarity is that both approaches recognize the value of intervention by an expert within the culture; when people require assistance, they involve another party. As part of the process, all experts identify problems in relationship to the environment as they understand it. In social work, experts exercise authority that they have obtained through academic preparation and certification that emphasizes intellectual ways of helping clients. These experts often operate within a spiritual anomie and consider spiritual values taboo; help is secular in nature. Professional principles hold that experts must be objective in order to be effective. Emotional and personal involvement with clients is discouraged, in the belief that this will cloud the expert's judgment.

The Anishinabe tradition offers useful insights to ecological practitioners. One is the importance of expertise based on life experience, wisdom, and recognition within one's culture. Further, for the Anishinabe, spirituality is an essential element of centeredness, although spiritual needs are often ignored by social workers. The individual is seen as part of an extended family and clan network, with reciprocal responsibilities to other members of the extended family and clan.

The Anishinabe healing principles recognize the inherent rights and dignity of the individual but assert the interconnectedness of all, so that the healing of the individual is necessary not only for the person, but for family and clan. Holistic values, with ceremonial supports, contribute balance to the spiritual dimensions of life. Anishinabe experts base their qualifications on life experience and giftedness. The key is to respect the family and clan in order to establish a relationship, so that reciprocity can occur. Reciprocity is necessary for the person to become centered, so that balance and harmony can be restored both to the person and to those affected, such as family and clan; in this way relationships within the environment are strengthened.

Because elders have gained the wisdom to understand the family's reality, they can use the dynamics of that reality to guide people to healthier lives. Therefore, elders serve as mentors in guiding unhealthy families beyond their trapped reality. This guidance, provided within the medicine wheel framework, suggests that behavior is determined by environment. To change behavior means that the environment must be changed. Yet, the principle of a centered self (including harmony with spiritual needs) will effectively balance the realities of the physical world or environment.

Becoming centered is an empowering process. Less emphasis is placed on expertise; self is the principal resource. The utilization of extended family is encouraged to support this self-empowering process and contributes to the overall healing of the person within the environment. The process includes isolating parts of the person that do not permit self to provide leadership. Ceremonial activities support the person in reaching an agreement with all parts of the self. These healing practices are driven by spiritual principles. Holistic principles are rooted in ancient wisdom, are humanistic in nature, and do not permit the isolation of person or problem from environment.

The interconnectedness of all cannot be overemphasized, but assistance is personalized in order to provide meaning and mutual healing. The person is not viewed as a client but referred to as family. This is in direct contrast to labeling people as clients or patients, where the emphasis is on the problem. A person-oriented focus exists throughout an indefinite treatment time span. Unlike short-term intervention, where independence is viewed as progress, the Anishinabe healing principles emphasize the restoration of balance and harmony, which can only occur if there is interdependence.

CONCLUSION

This comparison of the ecological approach to social work and Anishinabe healing principles suggests that there are similarities—in particular, the idea of interconnectedness and a focus on both person and environment. But there are different emphases. Elders identify problems in terms of the spiritual relationship to environment. Healing occurs primarily from the inside out (in the spiritual realm) and not from the outside in (in the environment). Can social workers, with their secular traditions, accommodate spiritual aspects within their practice?

The involvement of extended family is central to Anishinabe healing. The extended family is also a part of the ecological system of all people. How can extended-family involvement be made a more central part of social work practice?

The encouragement of professional resources that provide arms-length treatment will discourage voluntary requests for assistance from most Anishinabe people. The authoritarian attitude that the expert knows what is best for the client will not result in client independence. Can a personal relationship evolve if the person seeking assistance is viewed simply as a client in the worker's overflowing caseload? Is it reasonable to expect a professional to ignore an academic training that encouraged objectivity and authority in order to practice Anishinabe beliefs when helping people in need?

The Anishinabe medicine wheel is not a model of social work, but the teachings can provide social workers with useful tools. Social workers need to recognize the important roles played by elders, ceremonies, spirituality, and family in the ecological systems of clients from Native cultures. Supporting the client's participation in traditional culture, and not getting in the way of these practices, may be the most useful way of restoring balance and harmony between the person and environment.

An Ecosystemic Approach to Assessment*

Jane F. Gilgun

A defining characteristic of social work practice is its focus on the person-environment interaction. Such a focus requires an assessment and an intervention plan that encompasses the person, the environment, and the interactions between them. An ecosystemic approach to assessment involves understanding the "interrelated, complex reality in people's lives" (Meyer, 1983, p. 30). The starting point for an ecosystemic assessment is the client's perception of the environment. Its major emphasis is on observation of the client's interaction with members of the interpersonal environment, usually the family.

The environment can be sliced into several categories. The client's most immediate environment is interpersonal, composed of individuals with whom the client interacts. This slice of the environment frequently is called the micro level (Bronfenbrenner, 1979; Garbarino, 1982). The family, friendship networks, and relationships in schools, the workplace, and governmental agencies are examples of settings where interpersonal connections are made. The interpersonal environment also can be historical, such as the family of origin or the death or birth of persons who affect present interactions. Interpersonal patterns from the past often influence present interactions.

Another dimension of the interpersonal environment is the stage of the individual and family life cycle. Interactions change depending on developmental stage. For example, parents are doomed to frustration when they attempt to force a 2-year-old to share toys happily; sharing is not characteristic of a child at this age. The family with three young children under 5 will have far different issues and interactions with each other than they will when the children are between the ages of 10 and 15, although there also will be continuities.

A person's environment is also physical—for example, the presence or absence of businesses or other facilities that can offer employment. Access to schools, job training programs, grocery stores, playgrounds, and recreation can have an enormous impact on the person's

quality of life and opportunity. The relationship that exists between two micro-level settings is called the meso level by Bronfenbrenner (1979) and Garbarino (1982). The school-home, church-home, and work-home relationships are examples. An isolated family has few meso-level relationships, while a socially integrated family is characterized by numerous, rich, and supportive meso-level relationships.

Often, environments with which individuals do not come into direct contact may have a profound impact on their interpersonal interactions. The workplace environment can affect family life; actions of the federal government can affect taxation and thus the individual and the family; changes in policy made by the county welfare office can deeply affect many individuals who have no direct contact with the office itself. This is the exo level of the environment (Bronfenbrenner, 1979; Garbarino, 1982).

Even more nebulous than the effects of the exo level of the person's environment is the macro level. Here, aspects of the environment are shaped by customs, norms, and practices that can be—and often are—fair to most people but can also be racist, sexist, and ageist. These aspects of the environment can be thought of as part of a stratification system where opportunity, power, privilege, and prestige are allocated along the dimensions of age, sex, social class, race, and sexual orientation, to name just a few. The consequences of stratification systems are experienced through social, economic, and political policy and practice, which often are exo-level influences, as well as by the daily micro-level interactions. These interpersonal interactions give individuals feedback on their social standing and either open or close opportunity for education, income, and social and political power.

Individuals usually are not aware of how profoundly macro-level forces affect the course of their lives. Thus, a 27-year-old divorced mother of three children under age 10 may believe that her personal inadequacies are causing the family's financial troubles. She may become depressed and isolated. When she does seek opportunities for education and job advancement, there may be

*An original article prepared for this text.

nothing available for her, resulting in more depression, feelings of inadequacy, and isolation. In fact, more than her individual choice has led to her poverty and discouragement. Through public policy, as well as more individualized micro-level actions, many women live in poverty because of lack of encouragement and opportunity—and sometimes outright negation of their potential to develop a well-paying and meaningful career. The status that most persons have achieved results largely from socialization practices, opportunity structures, and beliefs, all macro-level forces, over which individuals have little control and of which they usually are unaware.

This reading provides an example of how to conduct an ecosystemic assessment. Guidelines for doing this assessment will be developed out of case material. Thus, the approach is presented as it would be experienced by the practitioner: from the assignment of the case, to gathering and organizing assessment data, to thinking about the data, and, finally, to developing an initial intervention plan. You, in effect, will be looking over the shoulder of an experienced practitioner who does an ecosystemic assessment; the reader will be privy to the practitioner's self-talk.

AN INITIAL ASSESSMENT

You are a social work practitioner in a family service agency. Your supervisor gives you a face sheet and a file folder that is empty except for a few lines recording a phone intake. Your supervisor says, "I'd like you to take this case." The face sheet tells you the initial contact was made by Mary Smith, 23, married to John Smith, 23, for five years. They have a 2½-year-old son, Billy, and a 1½-year-old daughter, Kelly. Mary is at home with the children, although prior to the birth of Kelly, she worked as a computer operator. John is a diesel mechanic, earning $32,000 a year. He also has a tow truck business that provides a net income of $25,000 a year. Both are white and high school graduates. They went to the same high school. Their last names are Anglo-Saxon, and their religion is Catholic. Mary's parents are alive, and she has two older sisters and one younger sister. John's mother died when he was 14, and he left his father's home at 16 to live with an aunt and uncle. He has one younger brother. John's father has not remarried.

The intake note states that Mary has requested help in dealing with John's physical violence. She left the family home three times in the last six months. Twice she left without the children, and she feels guilty about that; one time, she left home with slippers on, and it was December and cold outside. She told the intake worker that John would not come in for consultation.

Knowledge of Content Area

Trained in ecosystemic thinking, you also have some knowledge of violence against women in families. Your first thought is whether Mary has a protection plan, which is a preplanned set of actions she will take in the event of an abusive episode. When you phone to make an appointment, you will check on the protection plan. You also intend to make an early appointment because, in domestic abuse situations, a person's life may be in danger. If the case had involved an area with which you weren't familiar, you would have discussed the case in depth with your supervisor before making the appointment, and you would also have gone to the agency library to educate yourself about the subject area. Accurate knowledge of the content area of a case is essential for effective practice.

You are, in fact, knowledgeable about violence against women in families, and through experience you have gained confidence in your ability to deal effectively with such cases. Knowledge in a content area goes hand in hand with doing the assessment. You would not have known about the centrality of a protection plan had you not had knowledge of domestic abuse as a content area.

You phone Mary, and she answers with a soft "Hello." You hear children crying in the background. You identify yourself and tell her you've called to schedule a time when she can come into the office for an appointment. Mary says, "I'm so glad it's you. I've been walking on eggs around here. John's tow business has been slow, and he's been so touchy. The kids are driving me crazy. I can't get Billy to play with Kelly, and they fight all day long. Just a few minutes ago, Billy hit Kelly with a toy truck. I'm afraid he's going to be just like his father." The softness is gone from her voice; she sounds hoarse and distraught.

You negotiate a mutually agreeable time to meet with Mary. You check to see if she is willing to ask John to come in, too, and she says that she doesn't want him there this time. "I need to see someone all by myself," she said. For most forms of work with married persons, the agency has a strict policy that the couples are seen together, but an exception can be made for domestic abuse situations. If, after a few sessions, it appears that the husband and wife both want to remain together, the policy is to involve the other spouse in treatment. The rationale for involving both spouses is that each spouse is a significant part of the other's interpersonal environment. Each spouse mutually influences the behavior of the other, although a host of mediating variables may influence the couple's interaction. When a spouse in a domestic abuse situation is seen alone, the purposes are: (1) to develop a protection plan; (2) to establish that responsibility for stopping the abuse lies with the batterer; and (3) to clarify whether the spouse wants to remain with the batterer. Thus, there are very good reasons to see a married person alone in such cases. The agency has a similar policy when the presenting problem is alcohol or drug abuse, compulsive gambling, and compulsive sexual acting-out.

You ask Mary if she would like to take a few minutes to talk about ways of protecting herself from battering. She says she would. You give her an example of a typical protection plan: having the names and phone numbers of shelters and of friends and family who will provide refuge if she finds herself in physical danger; keeping a spare car key and some money where she can get to them in an emergency; and not hesitating to call the police if she finds herself in danger. She listens intently and tells you she hadn't thought of calling the police, and she doesn't know the names and phone numbers of any shelters. You encourage her to call the police, and you provide her with information on the shelters. You tell her that she can phone the shelter at any time to get advice and support. You also tell her that the shelters have ongoing groups for women in battering relationships. She expresses a great deal of gratitude for the information and for your interest in her well-being. She cries just a little. When she has left the home during episodes of violence in the past, she has gone to stay at her parents. "They let me stay, but they don't understand. It gets tense there after a while, and I go home," she says.

Initial Assessment of Environmental Supports

Because you think in terms of systems, you are able within a few minutes to assess Mary's environmental supports. She does have her parents' home as a safe environment during the violent periods, but she had no knowledge of shelters and the police as resources. When you discover this, you provide her with the necessary information. Thus, when doing ecosystemic assess-

ments, the interventions can follow immediately, as they did in this case. Mary did not know about some key resources, and the practitioner immediately provided her with the information.

Before you ask about the children's safety during the battering episodes, Mary tells you that John does not hit the children. A few times, he has thrown objects at Mary and just missed the tops of the children's heads, but that is the extent of his physical violence toward them. Mary said that, when she has left the home only to return within an hour or two, John has fed the children, bathed them, and read them bedtime stories. "He loves the kids," she said, "and he says he loves me. I don't know if he really loves me, but he works on being a good father."

You are concerned that the children are witnesses to their father's violence. There is ample evidence that simply witnessing violence can affect children negatively. Children tend to identify with victims and have affects similar to persons who are the direct target of violence. In addition, children who witness violence are at risk of perpetrating violence themselves, while they are still children and later, in adolescence and adulthood.

As you hang up the phone, you realize that this case has serious issues, but there is reason to hope for a good outcome. Mary is bright and articulate. Despite being in a battering situation, she has her wits about her. Although she is speaking for John, he appears to have some strengths: He states his love for Mary and the children, and apparently he enjoys parenting his children. You are not clear about the strengths of the marital relationship. That Mary is not saying she wants to leave John suggests that the marriage may provide a degree of satisfaction.

The face sheet, the intake data, and your initial phone call have provided you with the beginnings of an ecosystemic assessment. This type of assessment involves the generation of a great deal of data. The genogram and the ecomap are two ways of organizing data.

The Genogram

A genogram is a diagram of the family's generational configuration (Guerin & Pendagast, 1976; Hartman, 1979). It helps organize both historical and contemporary data on the major figures in the client's interpersonal environment. Thus, it helps the social worker understand how family patterns are affecting the current situation. Births, deaths, mental illness, alcoholism,

EXHIBIT 2–10   **An Initial Genogram of the Smith Family**

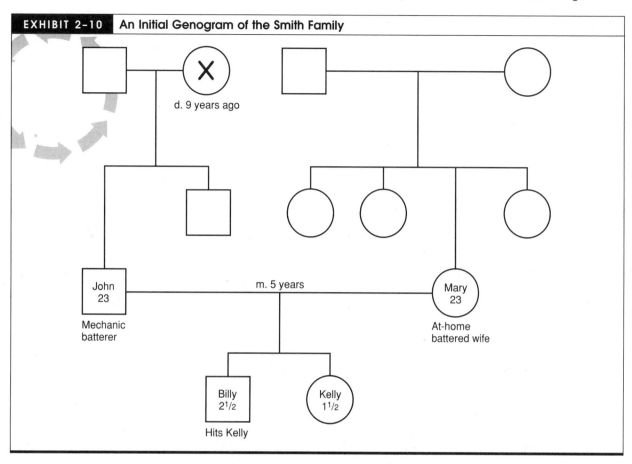

divorce, separation, adoption, incest, and family occupation are some of the types of family data present on genograms, which provide a concise means for organizing complex and significant information helpful to intervention planning. The following symbols signify family events and relationships.

> ○ = Female   □ = Male
> ▽ = Pregnancy   – – – = Marital separation
> ✕ = Death   . . . . = Divorce

Names and ages customarily are placed on the genogram. Exhibit 2–10 is a genogram of the Smith family, based on the information the practitioner has gathered so far. As work with the family proceeds, information will be added to the genogram. The genogram provides a representation of the family generational structure. The initial information suggests John might have issues related to his mother's death, and his reasons for leaving his father's home at age 16 might be important. Neither set of

grandparents were divorced, and John's father did not remarry. This, along with the couple's Catholicism, suggests the possibility that divorce is discouraged by family tradition. On the basis of the genogram information, the worker hypothesizes that John and Mary may be committed to staying together and that John may need to do some family-of-origin work—that is, to work out his thoughts and feelings regarding his mother's death and possible cut-off from his father. Mary is likely to have family-of-origin issues related to her parents, but there are no data yet to support or disconfirm this.

The Ecomap

An ecomap is a diagram of the family within its social context, and it includes the genogram (Hartman, 1978; Seabury, 1985). The purpose of the ecomap is to organize and clarify data on the supports and stresses in the family's environment. The major meso-level and exo-level social systems that affect the family are placed

EXHIBIT 2-11	An Initial Ecomap of the Smith Family

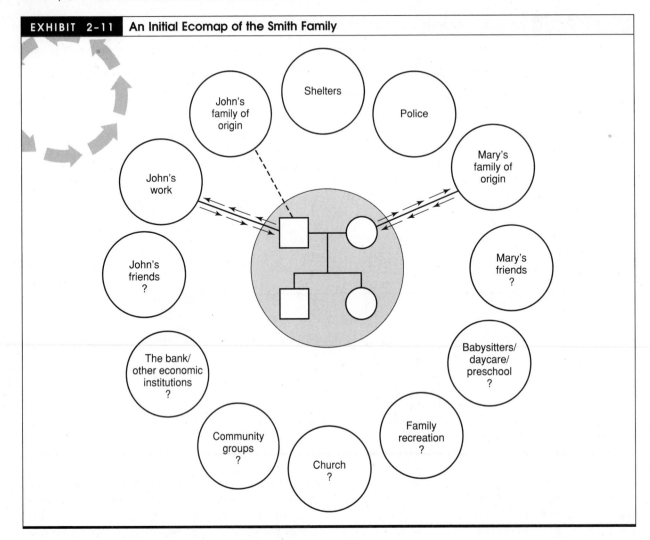

within circles; and the family genogram is placed within the center circle. The symbols for the ecomap are

strong relationship $\underset{\rightarrow}{\leftarrow}$
stressful relationship ++++++
tenuous relationship − − − − −

No line at all means no relationship. Exhibit 2–11 is an initial ecomap of the Smith family.

Many of the possible community groups, support groups, and friendship networks are not known at this time. During your first interview with Mary, you intend to explore some of the other environmental supports she might have. The only two types of outside relationships

that are known to you are John's with his work and Mary's with her parents. Chances are good that there are a few more relationships outside the family. Typically in families who come in for treatment, however, a major task is helping them to hook into the already-existing support networks within their communities. As the practitioner, you expect to explore ways that Mary and her family can make more connections outside of the nuclear family.

The Stratification Assessment

The face sheet information also provides a set of facts that will help you do a stratification assessment. A stratification assessment involves looking at the family's and the individual family members' place in the social structure. Race, age, social class, and gender-role issues all are involved in a stratification assessment. These attributes greatly influence a person's access to opportunities, power, and prestige. Mary and John are both white European Americans and, thus, are not likely to have suffered from racism. Because they are Catholic, and the area in which they live is predominantly Catholic, religious prejudice might also not be an issue for them. They are a working-class couple, and they have a good income. Thus, they are not suffering from economic deprivation, but they are not likely to be leaders and policy makers in their communities or on a wider level; their social power, therefore, is likely to be limited.

Gender-role issues in this family may be significant. John has two jobs, while Mary appears to have almost sole responsibility for the children. This suggests an imbalance in parenting and breadwinner roles, which may be a source of stress in the family. Possible support for this hypothesis comes from Mary's report that the kids are driving her crazy and the sound of children screaming at each other during your phone conversation with Mary. John may be overworking, and you wonder what motivates him to work two jobs when his income from one job appears adequate. You wonder if Mary would like to go back to work. You know that, in families where battering occurs, the battering spouse often has traditional gender-role expectations. You plan to explore whether this is contributing to the battering.

You also wonder if child care is available in the neighborhood or if there is a play group. This would provide Mary with some respite from child care and offer her the possibility of adult company. John is likely to have control over the family assets, which would contribute to his power in the family. Mary, on the other hand, is not earning money and is home with children a great deal of the time. She may feel quite powerless within the family.

Developmental Assessment

It is important to analyze the stages of individual and family development in assessing families. John and Mary are the same age, and they married at age 18, right after high school graduation. Thus, they are in a high-risk group for divorce, and they are likely to have had to struggle with late-adolescent issues at the same time they were adapting to marriage and then to parenthood.

Because they were married for about two years before Mary became pregnant with Billy, they had some opportunity to establish themselves as a couple before becoming parents. Identity issues, which are salient in adolescence, might still be a source of contention. These might be related, in part, to gender-role practices, as already noted. They have two very young children, which might be stressful to both parents: John might be worried about financial support, and Mary might be overburdened with parenting.

The children are not at an age where they would play quietly with each other. If they are cooped up in a house all day with each other, and with Mary, the stress level of the mother-children interaction might be quite high. John's battering of Mary not only increases her stress level but may be undermining the children's sense of security, which would make them even more difficult to manage. John's working two jobs would contribute further stress: He would provide Mary with minimal companionship, and he would not be available to share child care responsibilities. In sum, they are likely to be in a tough spot developmentally, as individuals and as members of a family.

THE FIRST INTERVIEW

Planning for the First Interview

After completing the genogram, the ecomap, and the stratification and developmental assessments, and after thinking about the data you've gathered so far, you make a plan for your initial interview with Mary. Your first priority is to assess whether she has developed an adequate protection plan. Then you plan to gather more data on her perception of the presenting problem—the battering and its effects on her and the children. You intend to allow Mary to tell her story in her own words, but you also intend to guide her gently, so that you can continue to assess the extent to which she has a supportive or potentially supportive environment.

As you do the initial assessment, you are hoping that the process itself will help Mary to see her own situation more clearly. If this happens, she may, on her own, discover some action plans that could protect her from further violence. You intend to keep yourself open to many possibilities. You are taking no stand on whether she should stay with John. You simply don't have enough information on which to make a judgment. You also don't know how strongly Mary feels about working on her relationship with John. Out of respect for the client and because you truly want to start where Mary is, you plan not to make premature judgments about what you think she should do. If she or the children are in danger of serious physical or psychological injury, you will recommend physical separation from John until she and the children are safe.

As you listen to Mary and draw her out, you will be on the alert for data on environmental supports and stresses. How much time does John spend working? How might this affect the couple and family interactions? What kinds of friendship networks do John and Mary have? What kinds of recreation does the family enjoy? Is the interpersonal environment outside the nuclear family supportive or is it a source of additional stress? As Mary tells you about the presenting problem and family interaction, you are confident that much of these data will be part of her narrative. If there are some blanks, such as information on friendship networks or recreation, you intend to ask about these.

You also will be interested in understanding how stratification and gender-role issues play out in the family. Who makes decisions for the family? Is there conflict over family roles? Does Mary wish she were back at work? Does she want John to work less and spend more time with her and the children? You expect to gather a lot of information about these issues as Mary tells you her story.

As Mary describes the presenting problem, you plan to observe her account of her interactions with John, examining such issues as hearing the other out versus interrupting; asking for clarification and drawing the other out versus assuming knowledge of what the other is thinking and feeling; the ability to express a range of thoughts and feelings versus being able to express a limited range; self-centeredness versus other-centeredness; taking responsibility for one's self versus blaming; patterns of pushing the other around versus cooperation; and the extent of problem-solving behavior versus premature closure of discussion, unilateral actions, and high-handedness. These interactions are part of the interpersonal environment and form a significant part of an ecosystemic assessment.

You also realize that much of what you will learn from Mary's description will be self-report data. If Mary decides that she would like to work on the marital relationship and John comes in for marital therapy, then you will have an opportunity to observe their interactions at first hand. However, Mary will be reporting her perceptions of the interactions, and it is on the basis of her perceptions that she thinks, feels, and acts.

The Presenting Problem

Your intercom buzzes. "Mary Smith is here," the receptionist announces. You walk to the waiting room. Sitting on the edge of the red vinyl chair and biting her lower lip is a fair-skinned, freckled young woman with full, dark hair. "Mrs. Smith?" you say. You introduce yourself and exchange the usual pleasantries as you walk to your office. "No," she says, "I had no trouble finding the office. The kids' pediatrician is right across the street." You note that she takes the children to a pediatrician, and the environment of the agency is familiar to her.

Mary quickly unburdens herself. She loves her husband, but he flares up and hits her. He gets mad at the drop of a hat. You ask her to describe a recent incident when he became angry and hit her. She said, "John always has two of his buddies over. They sit around and drink beer, eat chips, and watch football on TV. I'm the maid. John orders me around. I fetch the beer and fill up the chip bowls." You wonder if John wants to show his friends that he has a wife who is willing to wait on him. Is having such a wife some kind of proof that he is a competent male? Why does Mary wait on the men? Does she think that is her role? These kinds of thoughts relate to the stratification section of the assessment. You are trying to understand the gender-role structure of the couple. Often, traditional gender roles work very well for couples, but when the partners each have different ideas of appropriate gender-role behavior, or if partners are being exploited, the scene is set for conflict.

Mary reports that all three of the men make fun of her: They say she's got a fat can, tell her she ought to smile more, and ask why she doesn't keep the kids quiet. Last Saturday, she got angry and told them to leave her alone. She refused to wait on them. "I slammed the door of the bedroom shut, and Kelly started to cry and banged on the door. Then Billy cried. John yelled at the kids to be quiet. I took the kids to the playground." Mary says that when she got home, John was alone. "He started yelling at me for humiliating him in front of his friends. I yelled back, demanding that he apologize for treating me like a maid and for letting his friends make fun of me. He yelled that they were only kidding. I started swearing, and then he did. He hit me on the side of the head, and I swore some more. He started punching. I ran out of the house. I remember hearing the kids cry. I walked around for about an hour. When I came home, John was calmly feeding the kids. We didn't talk about the fight. In bed that night, he wanted to make love. I didn't feel like it. He got mad again, but we didn't fight. After a while, we went to sleep." The next day was Sunday. They hardly spoke, and John was out all day and night towing cars with his two buddies. Mary was alone with the children.

Assessing the Content of the Presenting Problem

When doing an ecosystemic assessment, asking for a description of a recent incidence related to the presenting problem is an efficient way of obtaining data on which to base your continuing assessment.

The material for the ecomap, the stratification assessment, and the interactional assessment is plentiful. John has two close friends with whom he spends a lot of time. Certainly these men provide John with companionship, but they also might be a wedge between John and Mary if, indeed, they are always at the house. Mary feels rejected by them. Whether or not their teasing is intended to be good-natured, she feels put down by their remarks. These men also seem to think that it is appropriate for Mary to serve them beer and chips and to keep the children quiet. If Mary wanted to protest these assigned roles, John would be able to cite the rightness of the roles because he and his two friends all think they are appropriate. Thus, on the ecomap, Mary's relationship to these two men would be characterized as stressful, while John's relationship to them would be strong. That Mary did not call on anyone else when she left the home suggests that she has a tenuous support system. No new lines showing social support for Mary can be drawn. The presence of a playground is a positive aspect of the environment, and it should be indicated on the ecomap.

The material for the stratification assessment is quite rich. Mary and John are not in agreement about roles when John has friends over. Mary does not want to wait on them, while John expects her to. John also expects her to go along with teasing, which Mary doesn't like and wants stopped. The disagreement over appropriate roles was the reason Mary went to her room and then left the home to take the children on an outing. That she took the children instead of leaving them in John's care suggests

that she considers child care her responsibility. John did not object when she took the children. Thus, he is likely to agree that the children are largely her responsibility. Drinking beer, eating chips, and watching football on television also are activities strongly associated with the male gender role. It is possible that John is a traditional male, behaving in ways the culture suggests males ought to behave. John's two jobs suggest that he values work highly. Some men believe that their value lies in their wallets: If they earn more money, they feel more valued and more confident that they are competent men. You wonder what Mary's and John's beliefs are about this.

The interactional assessment leads to the hypotheses that John and Mary apparently have few problem-solving skills; that they are not able to draw each other out and hear each other's point of view; that they have a restricted range of expressiveness of thoughts and feelings; and that much of their behavior is unilateral and each becomes frustrated. After a cooling-down period, they are not able to discuss or resolve conflict. They deal with frustration by swearing, yelling, and leaving the field. John has one additional and dangerous behavior: He beats his wife.

Assessing Strengths

As you are listening to Mary and making your assessment, you decide that you need a clearer picture of what the couple's strengths might be. You ask Mary to describe a recent incident in which things went smoothly between her and John. She says, "Three weeks ago on a Saturday morning, before John went off on his towing business, I suggested we go on a picnic next to a lake where we could swim. I know he likes picnics and swimming. His mother used to take him and his brother swimming a lot. I like picnics, and so do the kids. John wanted to go. He agreed to be home by noon. He got home by 12:30, and we were off by 12:45. We had a great day. John cooked. I set the table and cleaned up. He played with the kids in the water. I did, too. The kids fell asleep on the way home. We both unloaded the car and put the kids to bed. We made love that night." This story shows that the couple does share some recreation. Again, the tasks performed generally fall along gender-typed lines, but there was a great deal of cooperative effort also. The couple apparently can take great pleasure in shared activities. The story also provides further data on the amount of time John spends at work and Mary spends with the children. Further data gathering will clarify the reasons for the amount of time the couple spends apart. You hypothesize that staying away is a means of avoiding conflict, a way for John to earn extra money, and an opportunity for John to be with his friends.

Without much pause, Mary's story about the happy family outing spills into her telling you how much John had wanted a family when they were going out. His father used to beat his mother. One time, John drew a knife on his father to stop the beating. His father didn't beat John, but he used to make fun of him and had little time for him. John sees his father once a year at Christmas. She says her own father was not a batterer, but he was an alcoholic and was verbally abusive.

Developmental and Historical Assessment

Mary's narrative provides a great deal of developmental and historical information. As a young family, they are able to participate in appropriate family activities. A picnic outing at a lake is something both the children and

the adults enjoy, and they were able to interact with each other in mutually pleasurable ways. Some of the information, however, was Mary's interpretation of John's history, and you would prefer hearing John's story from John. Since, however, you have the data, it does help you to formulate additional hypotheses about the wife battering and the future of the marital relationship. John may well have had a close relationship with his mother. Her death may have been a serious and difficult loss. That his father used to beat his mother suggests that John had very poor modeling for problem solving and for conflict management and resolution. He may well be bringing what he knows into his marriage. John, like all of us, would carry his earlier environment with him. If he had a close relationship with his mother, that might provide a basis for building a nonviolent relationship with Mary. Mary's report of her father's verbal abuse and drinking behavior suggests that she, too, came from a family with poor interpersonal skills of problem solving and conflict

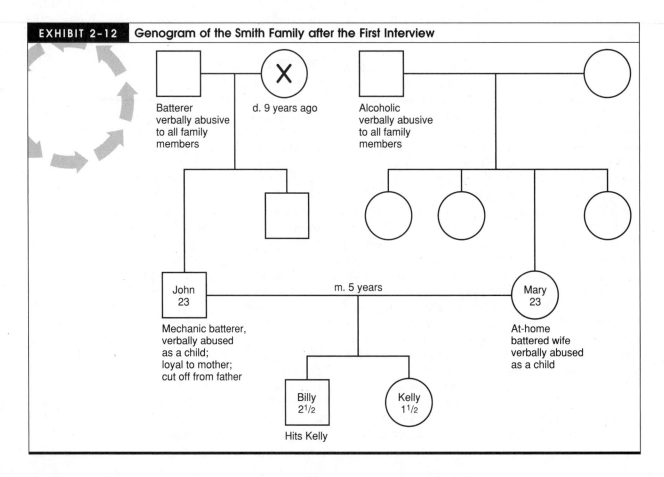

EXHIBIT 2-12 **Genogram of the Smith Family after the First Interview**

management and resolution. Finally, John's history of witnessing his father's beating of his mother adds to your thinking that John's children—especially Billy—are at risk for becoming physically violent themselves. You've learned that Mary's father is an alcoholic and is verbally abusive, that John's father also was verbally abusive and beat his wife but not the children, and that John defended his mother against his father. You will place that information on the genogram when the interview is over.

These developmental and historical data provide you with a context in which to understand Mary and John.

That there is a dovetailing of the family histories of each spouse does not surprise you. Commonalities in background, particularly emotional constellations, are the rule rather than the exception in couples work. The dovetailing makes the job of intervention much simpler. Each spouse has a part to play in clearing up communication difficulties. John, of course, has the additional task of coming to terms with his physical violence and learning and using alternatives to violence. The interview has given you rich data, and you add information to the genogram and the ecomap (Exhibits 2–12 and 2–13).

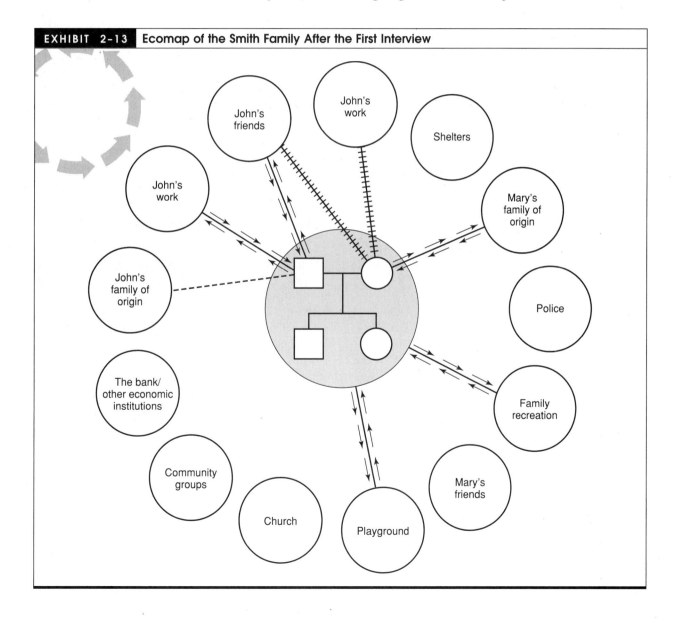

| EXHIBIT 2-13 | Ecomap of the Smith Family After the First Interview |

PLANNING INTERVENTIONS

Your initial assessment with Mary has provided you with multiple intervention points. If she were a computer, you could easily reprogram her: You could hook her up to day care, play groups, a battered women's group, a job, a host of supportive friends, and the entire gamut of interpersonal skills. If John were a computer, you could program him to stop the violence immediately and come in for marital therapy. You could hook him up to a group for battering men and some friends who would help him to foster his relationship with Mary. He could instantly acquire a gamut of interpersonal skills and motivation to work less and spend more time with Mary and the children. Neither, of course, is a computer, nor are they programmable. These lists of changes you would like to make, however, are based on your ecosystemic assessment; they are, in fact, the recommendations you intend to make to the couple over the course of your work with them. Exhibit 2–14 shows how you would like the family ecomap to look. The ecomap, then, helps you visualize treatment goals.

Your assessment, of course, is not complete. As you continue your work with Mary, and possibly John, you will gather further data, which will suggest further possible points of intervention. The data you have thus far, however, touches on all the levels of ecosystemic assessment. From this point on, your assessment will continue, but the balance of your work will tip toward ecosystemic interventions and evaluation of the effectiveness of the interventions.

You start the intervention planning at the place where the client is. Mary is the client you have in your office, and it is with her that you plan the interventions. What she wants and experiences as most pressing will be the focus of the intervention planning. The most pressing issues for her are likely to be: (1) stopping the battering; (2) improving communication; and (3) redistribution of breadwinner and parenting roles. As you continue to work with her, she is likely to be ready to look at and change other aspects of her interpersonal environment. John may also come in for service. This is likely to facilitate more change in the couple's ecosystem.

The work you do with the family will proceed in microsteps, building on the foundation the clients provide. Your ecosystemic assessment will prove a blueprint for how you would like the family to be. The assessment will help you keep your focus as you work on small pieces of the couple's ecosystem. The couple, however, is ultimately in charge of the directions taken. Client self-determination is a fundamental right, superseded only by the right to protection of life. It is also a therapeutic necessity. Your assessment and intervention planning may be first-rate, but careful, respectful, and empathic work with clients to help them define their goals is the means by which you will achieve some of the goals suggested by the ecosystemic assessment.

In doing ecosystemic interventions, practitioners have many choices. You will be working on more than one level. Often major issues are on the micro level—that is, the interpersonal, interactional level—but the micro-level issues often are supported by, affected by, and affect meso-level, exo-level, and macro-level issues. In short, interactional, stratification, developmental, historical, exo-level, and meso-level issues are in dynamic and reciprocal interaction. Concurrent interventions at two or more systems levels appear to be more effective than interventions on one level alone. Advocacy, lobbying for legislative change, working toward policy changes in your own agency, and setting up special community service programs may develop from your micro-level work with individual client systems.

SUMMARY AND DISCUSSION

In doing an ecosystemic assessment, practitioners are gathering data on mutually interacting environmental systems. The genogram helps to organize some of the historical and developmental data that influence present interactions. The ecomap helps organize meso-level and exo-level environmental contingencies that are part of the client's ecosystem. The interactional assessment provides information on the micro level. The stratification assessment helps organize data on gender roles, distribution of power (in decision making, for example), and the family's and the individual's place in the social structure, as determined by age, gender, race, ethnicity, social class, sexual orientation, and occupation, to name a few. The influence of the macro level is seen in all four types of assessments.

The starting point for the ecosystemic assessment is the clients' perceptions of their multiple environments. Observation is often an important source of assessment data, but an ecosystemic assessment can be done with an individual client. An ecosystemic assessment provides many possible points of intervention. Where to

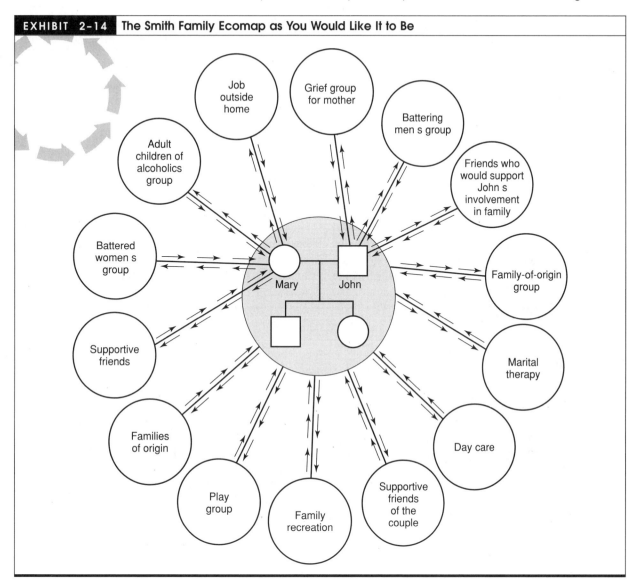

EXHIBIT 2-14   The Smith Family Ecomap as You Would Like It to Be

start the intervention is determined by where the client is—that is, what the client wants and experiences as most pressing.

In involuntary situations, where a client is court-ordered into treatment, an ecosystemic assessment is especially desirable, because the client might experience many aspects of the environment as painful. If the practitioner begins where the client is and contracts to facilitate changes that the client requests, the client may be more likely to work to change behavior that is harmful and illegal. For example, abusive parents are often court-ordered into treatment. By definition, they are not choosing to work with a practitioner, and they may be quite reluctant to set treatment goals. An ecosystemic assessment might help client and practitioner discover environmental contingencies that support the abusive behavior. Some of these contingencies might be experienced by the client as noxious. Feelings of isolation are common among abusive parents and often are both a source of pain and a contributing factor to the abuse.

An ecomap would quickly reveal social isolation. If the client would like to decrease social isolation, then this goal would be responsive to the client's request. Increased social integration might also decrease the likelihood of the parent abusing again. Many other mutually agreed-upon ecosystemic goals would need to be developed and pursued in order to deal with the complex problem of child abuse. The ecosystemic assessment is a solid foundation on which to plan intervention into such complex situations.

Ecosystemic assessments and interventions respond to the heart of the definition of social work direct practice. As social workers, we are enjoined to treat the person-environment interface, and we are enjoined to start where the client is. The ecosystemic approach helps us do this. In involuntary situations, this approach has a great deal of promise in bringing about change in the client's interactions with the myriad aspects of an envi-ronment that the client undoubtedly experiences as painful. Finally, the ecosystems approach can also help us accept that there are some situations that we, together with our clients, may not be able to change. Sometimes, the effects of racism, sexism, ageism, and classism on an individual client or family have been so devastating that we are practically helpless. Widespread change in the social structure is the intervention that would facilitate solution of the client's presenting problem. Social workers have a part to play in changing the social structure through research, client advocacy, lobbying legislators, and writing model laws and policy, and by becoming planners, policymakers, or managers in human service agencies. The ecosystems approach, then, opens up many possibilities for intervention on the micro, meso, and macro levels both for direct practitioners and for social work planners, managers, policy makers, researchers, and educators.

LEARNING EXERCISES

1. Here are some important concepts discussed in this chapter. Try to briefly define each term and identify how the concept applies to social work practice.

adaptation
change agent system
closed system
ecomap
ecosystems
ego
equifinality
feedback
genogram
learned helplessness
macro level
meso level
micro level
nesting of systems
open system
power
resilience
role
role ambiguity
role conflict
role incongruity
role set
system
target system
transpersonal

2. Consider the social worker and client as a system and think about your present understanding of social work practice. What might contribute to the client-worker system becoming a closed system? What are the dangers if this system is closed? How can this be prevented?

3. Review the case of the house on Sixth Street (Appendix A-3). How does this illustrate the layering of systems? Who or what is the client? What (or who) is the target system? What other means might the change agent and client have used to accomplish their objectives?

4. Review the Stover family case (Appendix A-2). When did Mrs. Stover become the client? What did the worker do that assisted Mrs. Stover to decide to accept service?

5. In Reading 2-3, Jane Gilgun discusses an ecosystemic approach to assessment. Do you see any difference between the approach she describes and the three key concepts we identified in Chapter 1? (*Hint:*

You may wish to quickly review the material in Chapter 4.) How might you modify the way you carry out an ecosystemic assessment in order to reduce any possible discrepancy between her approach and the model of practice we are discussing?

6. Finding fault or blaming a system is unlikely to produce change. On the basis of the ideas developed by Felix Yaroshevsky and David Shatzky in Reading 2-1, how could you encourage the family to consider interventions other than the use of medication, without appearing to blame the parents?

7. Exhibit 2–15 is a brief case excerpt from the first contact with an Appalachian family resettled in a southern urban center. How are environmental factors impacting the Birky family? Try to do an ecomap of this family following the suggestions made by

---

EXHIBIT 2-15 | **The Birky Family**

John Birky is a 4-year-old white boy enrolled in a full day care program. The day care center is located in a predominantly African American public housing project in a southern city of 90,000. This center provides services to low-income families where both parents work or the only parent works or is disabled. John was referred to the staff social worker a few weeks after his enrollment because he demonstrated possible neglect. He usually arrived at the center at 8:00 A.M. unfed and inadequately dressed, and his frequent illnesses (cold, strep throat) were very often untreated. His language development was limited and he was poorly toilet trained. Staff were required to change his clothes frequently and expressed resentment of and dislike for the child. The center teaching staff had made routine attempts to contact the mother—sent notes home, phoned—but thus far with no success.

On the social worker's first phone call, she reached the mother, who was obviously upset; only the day before, her 2-year-old son had drowned in the uncovered drainage ditch behind the apartment. This incident had been on the late news broadcast the night before, but none of the staff had realized it was John's brother. The ditch ran the length of the housing project, which was located in an underserviced, low-income part of the city and had been the scene of a previous drowning. Although the city had promised to cover the ditch, there were no indications of any efforts to do so.

The social worker made an immediate visit and found the mother in tears but pathetically eager to talk to someone. She said her mother and most of her large extended family were coming for the funeral the next day; they lived about 75 miles away in a rural Appalachian section of the state. From what the mother said, the social worker gathered that Mr. and Mrs. Birky had grown up together and married very early. Their first child had been stillborn. Tears rolled down her cheeks when she told this. "It looks like God don't want us to raise no children," she said. She had resented the day care staff changing John's clothes; he never soiled himself at home. She also said, "They told John to eat

breakfast before he came. John eats when we eat—don't none of us eat much. But we have enough and we never, none of us, been on welfare." The remains of a lunch of hominy and red beans could be seen on a card table in the almost bare living room.

Wiping her eyes, Mrs. Birky explained that the 2-year-old, Robert, was too young for the day care center, which takes only ages 3–5. A neighbor had been keeping Robert and several children who were under 3 or otherwise ineligible, but Robert was at home with his father the day he drowned, because Mr. Birky had been laid off from his service station job. The phone had rung and Mr. Birky had run into the next room to answer it, hoping it was about his job. Somehow Robert got out the back door and was gone. Mr. Birky hadn't missed him at first. Here Mrs. Birky broke off. Then she said, "Children are bound to get into things. I don't know—it's the Lord's will, I guess. My whole family has had a lot of sadness." She said her husband had gone to see about the funeral. She hoped they could borrow some money to pay for it when the families arrived.

Mrs. Birky said she felt strange in the city. Most of her neighbors were "colored—I mean black." She explained, as if for the benefit of the African American social worker, that there were no blacks where she grew up and their ways were strange to her, "but there's good and bad in all people." But she didn't like living around people who were on welfare, "colored or white." Her family would "do without" first.

Although the day care center's records show Mrs. Birky's age as 20, she looked 35 or more, was thin, and needed dental work. She picked up a book from the battered coffee table and said she had enrolled in a GED course; that's where she was "the day it happened." Her husband, aged 21, could barely read and write, and she wanted to "learn more so I can help him." She had never done "public work" and had no plans to get a job, though some of her sisters did waitress work or factory work "back home." Mr. Birky had worked in a factory which closed; that was why they had moved to the city.

Jane Gilgun in Reading 2-3. What messages have the parents internalized from their rural environment that may be interfering with their ability to improve the fit between their current needs and environmental resources? If you were this worker, on which problem would you like to begin work with—Mr. and Mrs.

Birky? Why? If you suggest coping with the grief, indicate at least three approaches to intervention that you might use. And if you selected dealing with the grief as the initial area to begin work, what would be your second area of focus after the family had made some progress with the first? Why?

REFERENCES

Allen-Meares, P., & Lane, B. A. (1990). Social work practice: Integrating qualitative and quantitative data collection techniques. *Social Work, 35*(5), 452–458.

Anthony, E. J. (1987). Risk, vulnerability and resilience. In E. J. Anthony & B. J. Cohler (Eds.), *The invulnerable child* (pp. 3–49). New York: The Guilford Press.

Antonovsky, A. (1980). *Health, stress, and coping.* San Francisco: Jossey-Bass.

Beardslee, W. R. (1989). The role of self-understanding in resilient individuals: The development of a perspective. *American Journal of Orthopsychiatry, 59*(2), 266–278.

Berenson, D. (1987). Alcoholics Anonymous: From surrender to transformation. *Family Therapy Networker, 11,* 24–31.

Bergmark, A., & Oscarsson, L. (1992). The limits of phenomenology and objectivity: On the encounter between scientism and practice. *British Journal of Social Work, 22*(2), 121–132.

Berkowitz, S. J. (1969). Curriculum models for social work education. In *Modes of professional education* (Tulane Studies in Social Welfare) (pp. 228–234). New Orleans: New Orleans School of Social Work, Tulane University.

Bernier, J. C., & Siegel, D. H. (1994). Attention deficit hyperactivity disorder: A family and ecological systems perspective. *Families in Society, 75*(3), 142–151.

Biddle, B. J., & Thomas, E. J. (1966). *Role theory: Concepts and research.* New York: Wiley.

Bowlby, J. (1951). *Mental care and mental health.* Geneva: World Health Organization.

Breen, J. (1985). Children of alcoholics: A subterranean grieving process. *Psychotherapy Patient, 2,* 85–94.

Brenner, C. (1955). *An elementary textbook in psychoanalysis.* New York: Doubleday.

Briar, S., & Miller, H. (1971). *Problems and issues in social casework.* New York: Columbia University Press.

Bronfenbrenner, V. (1979). *The ecology of human development.* Cambridge, MA: Harvard University Press.

Brower, A. M. (1988). Can the ecological model guide social work practice? *Social Service Review, 62*(3), 411–429.

Brower, A., & Nurius, P. (1993). *Social cognition and individual change: Current theory and counseling guidelines.* Newbury Park, CA: Sage.

Bryant, C. (1980). Introducing students to the treatment of inner-city families. *Social Casework, 61*(10), 629–636.

Buckley, W. (1967). *Sociology and modern systems theory.* Englewood Cliffs, NJ: Prentice-Hall.

Cameron, G. (1990). The potential of informal support strategies in child welfare. In M. Rothery & G. Cameron (Eds.), *Child maltreatment: Expanding our concept of helping* (pp. 145–168). Hillsdale, NJ: Lawrence Erlbaum.

Cameron, G., & Rothery, M. (1985). *An exploratory study of the nature and effectiveness of family support measures in child welfare.* Toronto: Ontario Ministry of Community and Social Services.

Canda, E. R. (1991). East/west philosophical synthesis in transpersonal theory. *Journal of Sociology and Social Welfare, 18*(4), 137–152.

Clancy, J. (1995). Ecological school social work: The reality and the vision. *Social Work in Education, 17*(1), 40–47.

Compher, J. V. (1982). Parent-school-child systems: Triadic assessment and intervention. *Social Casework, 63*(7), 415–423.

Compton, B. (1979). *Family-centered project revisited.* Minneapolis: School of Social Work, University of Minnesota.

Cowley, A. D. (1993). Transpersonal social work: A theory for the 1990s. *Social Work, 38*(5), 527–534.

Cowley, A. S., & Derezotes, D. (1994). Transpersonal psychology and social work education. *Journal of Social Work Education, 30*(1), 31–41.

Derezotes, D. S. (1995). Spirituality and religiosity: Neglected factors in social work practice. *Arete, 20*(1), 1–15.

Deutsch, K. (1968). Toward a cybernetic model of man and society. In W. Buckley (Ed.), *Modern system and research for the behavioral scientist* (pp. 387–400) Hawthorne, NY: Aldine.

Fanshel, D., Finch, S., & Grundy, J. (1990). *Foster children in a life course perspective.* New York: Columbia University Press.

Festinger, T. (1983). *No one ever asked us: A postscript to foster care.* New York: Columbia University Press.

Erickson, G. D. (1984). A framework and themes for social network intervention. *Family Process, 23*(2), 187–204.

Figueira-McDonough, J. (1995). Community organizing and the underclass: Exploring new practice directives. *Social Service Review, 69*(1), 57–85.

Fischer, J. (1993). Empirically based practice: The end of ideology? *Journal of Social Service Research, 18*(1/2), 19–64.

Frankl, V. G. (1997). *Man's search for ultimate meaning.* New York: Insight Books.

Fraser, M. W. (1996). Aggressive behavior in childhood and early adolescence: An ecological developmental perspective on youth violence. *Social Work, 41*(4), 347–361.

Fraser, M. (Ed.). (1997). *Risk and resilience in childhood: An ecological perspective.* Washington, DC: NHSW Press.

French, T. M. (1952). *The integrating behavior: Basic postulates.* Chicago: University of Chicago Press.

Garbarino, F. (1982). *Children and families in the social environment.* New York: Aldine.

Garmezy, N. (1971). Vulnerability research and the issue of primary prevention. *American Journal of Orthopsychiatry, 41*(1), 101–115.

Garmezy, N. (1987). Stress, competence, and development: Continuities in the study of schizophrenic adults, children vulnerable to psychopathology, and the search for stress-resistant children. *American Journal of Orthopsychiatry, 57*(2), 159–174.

Germain, C. B. (1979). Ecology in social work. In C. B. Germain (Ed.), *Social work practice: People and environments* (pp. 1–22). New York: Columbia University Press.

Germain, C. B., & Gitterman, A. (1980). *The life model of social work practice.* New York: Columbia University Press.

Germain, C. B., & Gitterman, A. (1996). *The life model of social work practice: Advances in theory and practice.* New York: Columbia University Press.

Gilgun, J. F. (1994). A case for case studies in social work research. *Social Work, 39*(4), 371–380.

Gitterman, A. (1996). Life model theory and social work treatment. In F. J. Turner (Ed.), *Social work treatment: Interlocking theoretical approaches* (4th ed., pp. 389–408). New York: The Free Press.

Gordon, W. E. (1962). A critique of the working definition. *Social Work, 7*(4), 3–13.

Gordon, W. E. (1965). Knowledge and value: Their distinction and relationship in clarifying social work practice. *Social work, 10*(4), 32–39.

Greene, R. R. (1994). *Human behavior theory: A diversity framework.* Hawthorne, NY: Aldine de Gruyter.

Greer, J. H. , Davidson, G. C., & Gatchel, R. I. (1970). Re-education of stress in humans through non-veridical perceived control of aversive stimulation. *Journal of Personality and Social Psychology, 16*(4), 731–738.

Guerin, P. J., & Pendagast, C. G. (1976). Evaluation of family system and genogram. In P. J. Guerin (Ed.), *Family Therapy Theory and Practice* (pp. 450–464). New York: Gardner.

Guttman, D. (1996). *Logotherapy for the helping professional: Meaningful social work.* New York: Springer.

Harold, R. D., Palmiter, M. L., Lynch, S. A., & Freedman-Doan, C. R. (1995). Life histories: A practice-based research technique. *Journal of Sociology and Social Welfare, 22*(2), 23–43.

Hartman, A. (1970). To think about the unthinkable. *Social Casework, 51*(8), 467–474.

Hartman, L. A. (1979). The extended family as a resource for change: An ecological approach to family-centered practice. In C. B. Germain (Ed.), *Social work practice: People and environments,* (pp. 239–265). New York: Columbia University Press.

Haworth, G. O. (1984). Social work research practice and paradigms. *Social Service Review, 58*(3), 355.

Henry, C. S., Stephenson, A. L., Hanson, M. F., & Hargett, W. (1993). Adolescent suicide families: An ecological approach. *Adolescence, 28*(110), 292–308.

Herrenkohl, E. C., Herrenkohl, R. C., & Egolf, B. (1994). Resilient early school-age children from maltreatment homes: Outcomes in late adolescence. *American Journal of Orthopsychiatry, 64*(2), 301–309.

Hooker, C. E. (1976). Learned helplessness. *Social Work, 21*(3), 194–198.

Jung, C. G. (1933). *Modern man in search of a soul.* New York: Harcourt, Brace & World.

Kamerman, S. B., Dolgoff, R., Getzel, G., & Nelson, J. (1973). Knowledge for practice: Social science in social work. In A. J. Kahn (Ed.), *Shaping the new social work* (pp. 97–148). New York: Columbia University Press.

Kaplan, L. (1986). *Working with multiproblem families.* Lexington, MA: Lexington Books.

Karls, J. M., & Wandrel, K. E. (Eds.), (1994a). *Person-in-environment system: The PIE classification system for social functioning problems.* Washington, D.C.: NASW Press.

Karls, J. M., & Wandrel, K. E. (1994b). *PIE manual: Person-in-environment system.* Washington, D.C.: NASW Press.

Kemp, S. P., Whittaker, J. K., & Tracy, E. M. (1997). *Person-environment practice: The social ecology of interpersonal helping.* New York: Aldine de Gruyter.

Klein, B. (1986). A piece of the world: Some thoughts about Ruth. *Women and Therapy, 5,* 33–40.

Klein, W., & Bloom, M. (1995). Practice wisdom. *Social Work, 40*(6), 799–807.

Klenk, R. W., & Ryan, R. M. (1974). *The practice of social work* (2nd ed.). Belmont, CA: Wadsworth.

Kramer, K. D., & Nash, K. B. (1995). The unique social ecology of groups: Findings from groups of African Americans affected by sickle cell disease. *Social Work with Groups, 18*(1), 55–65.

Krystal, S., & Zweben, J. (1989). The use of visualization as a means of integrating the spiritual dimension into treatment: Part 2. Working with emotions. *Journal of Substance Abuse Treatment, 6*(4), 223–229.

Lefcourt, H. M. (1966). Belief in personal control: Research and implications. *Journal of Individual Psychology, 22*(2), 185–195.

Lenqua, L. J., Wolchik, S. A., & Brauer, S. L. (1995). Understanding children's divorce adjustment from an ecological perspective. *Journal of Divorce and Remarriage, 22*(3/4), 25–63.

Levinson, D. J. (1978). *The seasons of a man's life.* New York: Alfred A. Knopf.

Liberman, B. (1978). The role of mastery in psychotherapy: Maintenance of improvement and prescriptive change. In J. Frank, R. Hoehn-Saric, S. Imber, B. Liberman, & A. Stone (Eds.), *Effective ingredients in successful psychotherapy* (pp. 35–72). New York: Bruner/Mazel.

Lindsey, D., & Kirk, S. A. (1992). The continuing crisis in social work research: Conundrum or solvable problem? *Journal of Social Work Education, 28*(3), 370–382.

Maddock, J. W. (1993). Ecology, ethics, and responsibility in family therapy. *Family Relations, 42*(2), 116–123.

Magnusson, D., & Allen, V. L. (1983a). An interactional perspective for human development. In D. Magnusson & V. L. Allen (Eds.), *Human development: An interactional perspective* (pp. 3–34). New York: Academic Press.

Magnusson, D., & Allen, V. L. (1983b). *Human development: An interactional perspective.* New York: Academic Press.

Mattaini, M. A. (1990). Contextual behavior analysis in the assessment process. *Families in Society, 71*(4), 236–245.

Merton, R. (1968). *Social theory and social structure* (4th edition). New York: Free Press.

Meyer, C. H. (1983). The search for coherence. In C. H. Meyer

(Ed.), Clinical social work in the eco-systems perspective (pp. 5–34). New York: Columbia University Press.

Meyer, C. (1988). The eco-systems perspective. In R. Dorfman (ed.), *Paradigms of clinical social work* (pp. 275–294). New York: Brunner/Mazel.

Millstein, K. H. (1994). Building knowledge from the study of cases: A reflective model for practitioner self-evaluation. *Journal of Teaching in Social Work, 8*(1/2), 255–279.

Minahan, D. J. (1993). Assessment of dementia patients and their families: An ecological family centered approach. *Health and Social Work, 18*(2), 123–131.

Mullen, E. J. (1985). Methodological dilemmas in social work research. *Social Work Research and Abstracts, 21*(4), 12–20.

Murphy, L. B., & Moriarity, A. (1976). *Vulnerability, coping and growth: From infancy to adolescence.* New Haven: Yale University Press.

Osterman, D., & Benbenishty, R. (1992). Keeping in touch: Ecological factors related to foster care visitation. *Child and Adolescent Social Work Journal, 9*(6), 541–554.

Perlman, H. H. (1957). *Social casework: A problem-solving process.* Chicago: University of Chicago Press.

Perlman, H. H. (1961). The role concept and social casework: Some explorations. *Social Service Review, 35*(4), 370–381.

Perlman, H. H. (1975). In quest of coping. *Social Casework, 56*(4), 213–225.

Pincus, A., & Minahan, A. (1973). *Social work practice: Model and method.* Itasca, IL: Peacock.

Pumphrey, M. (1959). *The teaching of values and ethics in social work education.* New York: Council on Social Work Education.

Redhorse, J. G., Lewis, R., Fest, M., & Decker, J. (1978). Family behavior of urban American Indians. *Social Casework, 59*(2), 67–72.

Reid, W. J. (1994). The empirical practice movement. *Social Service Review, 68*(2), 165–184.

Ripple, L., & Alexander, E. (1956). Motivation, capacity, and opportunity as related to casework services: Nature of client's problem. *Social Service Review, 30*(1), 38–54.

Ripple, L., Alexander, E., & Polemis, B. (1964). *Motivation, capacity and opportunity: Studies in casework theory and practice.* Chicago: School of Social Service Administration, University of Chicago.

Rothery, M. (1993). The ecological perspective and work with vulnerable families. In M. Rodway & B. Trute (Eds.), *Ecological family practice: One family, many resources* (pp. 21–50). Queenston, Ontario: Edwin Mellen.

Rutter, M. (1979). Protective factors in children's response to stress and disadvantage. In M. W. Kent & J. Rolf (Eds.), *Primary prevention of psychopathology, social competence in children* (Vol. III, pp. 49–79). Hanover, NH: University Press of New England.

Rutter, M., Maughan, B., Mortimore, P., Ouston, J., & Smith, A. (1979). *Fifteen thousand hours: Secondary schools and their effects on children.* Cambridge, MA: Harvard University Press.

Rutter, M. (1987). Psychosocial resilience and protective mechanisms. *American Journal of Orthopsychiatry, 57*(3), 316–331.

Schon, D. A. (1983). *The reflective practitioner: How professionals think in action.* New York: Basic Books, Inc.

Schwartz, W. (1961). Social worker in the group. In National Conference on Social Welfare (Ed.), *Social welfare forum* (pp. 146–171). New York: Columbia University Press.

Seligman, M. E. P. (1975). *Helplessness: On depression, development and death.* San Francisco: W. H. Freeman.

Sermabeikian, P. (1994). Our clients, ourselves: The spiritual perspective and social work practice. *Social Work, 39*(2), 178–183.

Sheridan, M. J., Bullis, R. K., Adcock, C. R., Berlin, S. D., & Miller, P. C. (1992). Practitioners' personal and professional attitudes toward religion and spirituality: Issues for education and practice. *Journal of Social Work Education, 28*(2), 190–203.

Sheridan, M., Wilmer, C., & Atcheson, L. (1994). Inclusion of content on religion and spirituality in the social work curriculum: A study of faculty views. *Journal of Social Work Education, 30*(3), 363–376.

Silver, R. L., Boon, C., & Stones, M. H. (1983). Searching for meaning in misfortune: Making sense of incest. *Journal of Social Issues, 39*(2), 81–102.

Seabury, B. A. (1985). The beginning phase: Engagement, initial assessment, and contracting. In F. Laird & A. Hartman (Eds.), *A handbook of child welfare* (pp. 335–359). New York: Free Press.

Simon, B. L. (1994). Are theories for practice necessary? Yes! *Journal of Social Work Education, 30*(2), 144–148.

Simon, H. (1952). Comments on the theory of organization. *American Political Science Review, 46*(4), 1130–1139.

Siporin, M. (1975). *Introduction to social work practice.* New York: Macmillan.

Thyer, B. A. (1994). Are theories for practice necessary? No! *Journal of Social Work Education, 30*(2), 148–152.

Thyer, B. A. (1996). Forty years of progress toward empirical clinical practice? *Social Work Research, 20*(2), 77–81.

Towle, C. (1965). *Common human needs.* New York: National Association of Social Workers (Original work published in 1945).

Trader, H. (1977). Survival strategies for oppressed minorities. *Social Work, 22*(1), 10–13.

Triseliotis, J. (1980). Growing up in foster care and after. In J. Triseliotis (Ed.), *New developments in foster care and adoption* (pp. 131–162). London: Routledge & Kegan Paul.

Uliman, M. (1969). A unifying concept linking therapeutic and community process. In F. Duhl & N. Rizzo (Eds.), *General systems theory and psychiatry.* Boston: Little, Brown.

Wakefield, J. C. (1996a). Does social work need the ecosystems perspective? Part 1. Is the perspective clinically useful? *Social Service Review, 70*(2), 1–32.

Wakefield, J. C. (1996b). Does social work need the ecosystems perspective? Part 2. Does the perspective save social work from incoherence? *Social Service Review, 70*(2), 183–213.

Werner, E. E., & Smith, R. S. (1992). *Overcoming the odds: High risk children from birth to adulthood.* Ithaca, NY: Cornell University Press.

White, R. W. (1959). Motivation reconsidered: The concept of competence. *Psychological Review, 66*(5), 297–334.

White, R. W. (1963). *Ego and reality in psychoanalytic theory.* New York: International Universities Press.

Whittaker, J., & Garbarino, J. (1983). *Social support networks: Informal helping in the human services.* New York: Aldine.

Yellow Bird, M. J. (1995). Spirituality in First Nations story telling: A Spanish-Hidatsa approach to narrative. *Reflections, 1*(4), 65–72.

chapter 3

Problem Solving: A Process for Social Work Practice

CHAPTER PREVIEW

In this chapter, we provide an introduction to the problem-solving process that underlies social work practice. We will discuss four key ideas:

- Problem solving is an orderly life process directed toward accomplishing goals.
- The application of problem solving, including the use of client strengths, may help the social worker accomplish the goals of the intervention.
- The problem-solving process may be resolved into a series of important phases.
- In social work, practitioners interact with a wide range of individuals, under a wide range of circumstances. To refer to all of these individuals as clients is imprecise and unhelpful.

We also develop a restricted and more appropriate definition of the term *client*. In addition, we will address some of the criticisms of the problem-solving process: that it is too linear, that its fundamental rationality results in an undervaluing of emotions, and that it does not recognize the importance of strengths. All of these criticisms are based on an inadequate understanding of the problem-solving process.

In Reading 3-1, Ralph Woehle discusses some of the limitations of the problem-solving process and suggests modifications to accommodate these limitations.

In Chapters 8–18, we will discuss the phases of the problem-solving process in more detail.

PROBLEM SOLVING AS A LIFE PROCESS

Dewey and Problem Solving

John Dewey (1933) described the thought processes of human beings when confronted with problems. According to Dewey, our problem-solving behavior is based on reflective thought that begins with a feeling of perplexity, doubt, or confusion; we want to eliminate the difficulty. To do this effectively, we must follow a rational procedure. Otherwise, we may act uncritically or impulsively, leap to inappropriate conclusions, mistake the nature of the problem, or search for the answer to the wrong problem. Any of these behaviors may compromise our capacity to cope with the situation and will make it likely that the problem will remain unsolved.

Dewey reduced effective problem solving to a set of procedural steps in a well-defined and orderly sequence. He referred to these steps as the five phases of reflective thinking:

1. Recognizing the difficulty
2. Defining or specifying the difficulty
3. Raising suggestions for possible solutions and rationally exploring the suggestions, including data collection
4. Selecting an optimal solution from among many proposals
5. Carrying out the solution

Problem solving involves a preferred model for orderly thought and action that, once laid out in progressive steps, points toward the attainment of a solution. Conscientious implementation of the model increases the likelihood that our objectives will be achieved.

Dewey's list failed to include evaluation of the effectiveness of the attempted solution. Evaluation introduces feedback loops into the process and permits modifications in the procedures even as we are employing them. The problem-solving process for social work practice may be divided into four primary phases:

1. Engagement
2. Assessment
3. Intervention or action
4. Evaluation

Each of these phases can be further subdivided. Specific activities must be accomplished during each phase; we will discuss these activities in Chapters 8–18.

Problem solving has been applied in many different fields of human activity. In the early 1940s, George Polya (1957) developed a model intended, specifically, to help mathematics instructors teach mathematical problem solving but more broadly, to provide guidance for all problem solvers. His model includes four phases:

1. Understanding the problem, which includes understanding the problem situation, the goal of the problem solver, and the conditions for solving the problem
2. Devising a plan by which the goal could be attained
3. Carrying out the plan
4. Evaluating the plan, its implementation, and the results

The scientific method may be considered a model of problem solving. Bennis, Benne, and Chin (1969) proposed problem-solving strategies for effecting change in human systems. Exhibit 3–1 displays the steps of a problem-solving process used to assist large organizations.

Problem Solving as Growth and Change

Misunderstandings often surround the idea of problem solving in social work practice. One misconception is that competent people do not have problems. This is unrealistic. Problems in living do not represent mistakes or weaknesses; rather, they are a part of growth and change. We all need to accept ourselves and our life struggles.

| **EXHIBIT 3–1** | **The Simplex System To Improve Organizational Problem Solving** |

Min Basadur proposes an eight-step problem-solving process:

Step 1: Problem finding. A skilled problem finder learns to uncover problems rather than waiting to be overwhelmed. For example, a single customer complaining may be enough to reveal a potential problem in the distribution process.

Step 2: Fact finding. Once a problem has been identified, all the relevant information needs to be gathered to understand the size and importance of the problem. Useful questions to answer are: ``How often . . . ?''; ``How much . . . ?''; and ``How long . . . ?'' Beware of taking facts for granted; some may turn out to be assumptions.

Step 3: Problem definition. This requires stating the problem in a way that can be resolved. ``How might we . . . ?'' is often a good way of defining a problem.

Step 4: Idea finding. This requires the generation of a number of alternative approaches to achieve a desired goal. Brainstorming is a useful way of avoiding the premature exclusion of certain options.

Step 5: Evaluation and selection of solutions. Sifting the possible solutions down to the best approach usually requires listing the criteria against which various options will be evaluated. Eventually the best overall approach is adopted.

Step 6: Action planning. Finding a solution is not enough; it has to be implemented. Develop a specific action plan, including who will do what and when. The plan must be realistic and take account of organizational constraints.

Step 7: Gaining acceptance. Action planning usually identifies people who have to provide approval—or even active support—for the plan to succeed. Many proposals for change fall apart because of inadequate attention to how to win over the necessary people.

Step 8: Taking action. Finally, the time comes to take action. Set a deadline, share your plans with others, and break big tasks into smaller pieces.

Source: M. Basadur, *The power of innovation*. Langham, MD: Pitman (1995).

Some social workers define the purpose of social work as meeting needs; they seem to believe that to speak of a client's need is less assaultive on the client's sense of self or competence than to speak of a problem in living. We disagree. The notion of fulfilling the client's need is grandiose and poorly defined; it can mean whatever the worker wants it to mean. Too often, the professional will determine what the client needs, in a travesty of the medical model of practice.

We prefer to think of clients' wants. A need is usually something that the client lacks, whereas a want is usually something that the client desires. When we listen for client wants, we are hearing the client's desires and goals, rather than busying ourselves in trying to assess need or lack. Exhibit 3–2 illustrates the difficulties that occur when social workers act solely on their view of client needs.

Life itself is a problem-solving process. Reid (1978, p. 26) says it well: "A want . . . experienced without satisfaction becomes a problem." Human wants are endless; when one is satisfied, another immediately takes its place. Thus, we all are constantly involved in problem solving. Those who are good problem solvers do it so automatically that they often do not understand the process, concentrating only on the result. For example, when we awake in the morning, we are immediately confronted with a problem: Do we get up? If so, when? We quickly and sometimes quite unconsciously collect data about this problem. What do we anticipate accomplishing today? How important is it to us? What will be the reaction of meaningful people to our decision? Will those around us impose certain sanctions on us because we have not done this? As we perceive and integrate the data, we come to a decision and take action. We will have difficulties if we incorrectly perceive the implications of the problem we want to solve. For example, we may try to get up when physically we cannot or should not. Or we may decide to remain in bed when getting up and taking certain actions are important to our well-being. Those who are successful in life are not without problems, but they solve problems well.

The steps we use to solve problems in living are the same as those that social workers use to help clients. First, we must perceive a want and define the problem that must be solved in order to satisfy this want. Wants often arise out of our goals for ourselves, and a satisfactory solution must relate to these goals. Given the goals, we start to gather data related to the situation. As we consider solutions, we need to consider again the data we have acquired. Given the data, we must plan for possible action to reach our goal. Action is then taken to carry out the decision and to evaluate the results of the action, so that we can learn from the process. In this evaluation, we assess whether the action taken has moved us toward the goals we selected.

If our evaluation is negative, we often go back and try to assess what step in the problem-solving process was not done well. We say, "If only we had known. . . ." When we say this, we are usually saying that we perceived or defined the problem incorrectly or that we did not have the knowledge and information necessary to an appropriate decision. Sometimes it may mean that our method of action was not effective. Some of us suffer a great deal at this point in the problem-solving process, because we hold ourselves totally responsible for a negative outcome. Actually, the only 20/20 vision in life is hindsight; we approach all problems in living with incomplete

---

EXHIBIT 3-2	Determining Client Needs: A Case Example

Mr. K's wife had to be hospitalized, leaving him with no care for three preschool children. Mr. K was referred to an agency to plan for child care, a need defined by the court. The assigned worker in the child care agency accepted the referral information that Mr. K's need was child care. However, Mr. K was struggling primarily with worry about his wife's illness. He wanted desperately to understand the cause and the course of the illness and to know when she could come home. The worker's attempt to meet client need as she saw it was not related to the help Mr. K wanted; she ignored questions about the meaning of his wife's illness. As a result, Mr. K's level of functioning became more and more pathological, in her eyes. Also, Mr. K continued to struggle with his problem a year later, while the worker was still struggling with Mr. K's need for child care. Thus, neither the worker nor the client had achieved their goals, because there was not a common understanding of Mr. K's problems or goals.

knowledge, and we can never be sure of the solution. Our only security is the process.

PROBLEM SOLVING IN SOCIAL WORK

Helen Harris Perlman (1957) is the originator of the problem-solving framework for social work. The principal difference between our knowledge base and that used by Perlman is that ours is based on systems theory. Correspondingly, we extend the problem-solving process to groups, organizations, and communities, and we broaden our model to include more emphasis on transactions with, and change in, other social systems. Perlman presented problem solving as a casework process; we see the problem-solving process as the base for generalist practice.

Perlman emphasizes the practitioner's responsibility for thinking about the facts, diagnosis, and planning. We agree that the worker carries responsibility to do this hard headwork and to see that the process moves forward. However, the worker must also test out his or her thinking with the client, so that responsibility is shared at every phase of problem solving, including assessment and intervention. Perlman sees problem solving as both a process and a method of helping; we see it as a process that will include the selection of appropriate interventive methods but is not itself a method of intervention. We expect the worker to engage in a broader array of helper roles than does Perlman. She emphasizes the enabler role of the worker. Furthermore, Perlman does not distinguish as sharply as we do between the various stages of the process; she says that treatment begins with the first glance between worker and client. However, she does emphasize, as we do, that the work cannot proceed until the applicant accepts the role of client.

Phases of the Problem-Solving Process

Each phase of problem solving requires specific social work skills and must be accomplished before the next phase can be completed. You will be successively involved with the following tasks:

1. Engagement with clients, including exploration of the presenting problem and preliminary setting of objectives
2. Data collection, assessment of the situation, setting objectives, and planning of action

3. Intervention, or the carrying out action
4. Evaluation

Our model of the process is the only one that has a goal or objective at two phases. We add preliminary objective setting immediately following, or concurrent with, problem identification. This objective is a statement of what the client wants; it may be changed later. Early setting of objectives based on what the client wants will increase client motivation, especially if the want is strongly held. Early clarification of objectives also moves the relationship toward a partnership and results in active client engagement. Objectives are reconsidered and finalized as a part of assessment and before service planning.

The problem-solving process is a series of interactions between client and social worker; it involves the integration of feeling, thinking, and doing and is guided by a purpose and directed toward achieving an agreed-upon objective. The process is expected to bring about a solution to the problem. To be effective, it must involve interaction supported and guided by appropriate knowledge. The process is conducted within the values and sanctions of the profession, and a collaborative relationship must develop between worker and client.

Relationship and understanding do not develop just because two people find themselves in a common enclosed space. (We discuss the development and use of the relationship in detail in Chapter 6.) Relationship is embodied in emotions and attitudes that sustain the problem-solving process as practitioner and client work together in partnership toward some objective. Thus, the problem-solving process rests on the ability of each partner to relate and communicate with the other. The client has information about:

- what brings him in contact with the social worker
- the emotions, fears, and conflicts generated by the problem
- what she or he expects of this contact and the social worker

The social worker has at hand:

- a body of knowledge about a variety of problems
- access to resources that may be available to bring to bear on the problem
- methods and skills of helping
- an orderly way of proceeding that will move client and worker toward a problem solution

Our notion of a problem-solving process rests on the principle that troubles in living stem from difficulties in effectively coping with specific situations in daily life. Difficulties in coping may stem from a combination of:

- motivation: an imbalance of hope and discomfort relative to the achievement of objectives
- capacity: the needed knowledge, social skills, rational skills, relationship with external reality, and interplay of current and past biopsychosocial factors in development
- opportunity: access to support systems, needed resources, and helping relationships

Effective movement toward a desired goal depends on the motivation and ability of the person (or system) to engage in a problem-solving process and to use (or develop) opportunities in the environment.

Engagement. Engagement involves initial contact with the applicant. It includes activities directed toward understanding the nature of the presenting problem and identifying the preliminary goals, usually in terms of what the applicant wants. Successful engagement will result in an agreement with the applicant—who may then be considered a client—to proceed to assessment, for the purposes of specifying the problems and developing a service plan; this agreement is a preliminary contract. We will discuss the engagement phase in Chapters 8 and 9.

It is important to begin with the problem as seen by the applicant, in whatever way he or she may present it. You will run into difficulty if you are so focused on your definition of the problem or your concern with applicant capacity that you cannot hear the person. Some workers are often unaware of how their understanding of the problem differs from the applicant's. Social work requires active engagement of applicants, and that engagement must be around concerns consistent with applicants' expectations and problem definitions.

People who have little ability to weigh and measure alternative courses of action, and who have no reason to trust the help that you offer, will neither express their problems in your terms nor express their objectives in terms of learning a more productive way of living. Often, they express problems in terms of basic survival needs. You can join with the applicant in setting objectives at this level—to secure necessary repairs on the refrigerator or to find a way to get a new stove. These are worthy objectives; they help to make the applicant's life more satisfying, and they are the applicant's objectives. Such problems and objectives are the stuff of the beginning engagement. By helping to solve this problem, you can begin to build trust and a sense of success, which can then be used to move on to other problems and other objectives, if there are others. Exhibit 3–3 offers a tongue-in-cheek story about starting with the

---

EXHIBIT 3-3	**Starting Where the Client Is**

Suppose that we were out in the woods and we came upon a man who had accidentally got his foot caught in a bear trap. There he is, howling and carrying on frightfully, weeping and straining in a most profane fashion. Then two psychologists come by and one of them wants to give the man the Rorschach test and an intelligence test and take a case history. The other psychologist, however, has undergone a different kind of training; and he says, "No let's start intensive psychoanalysis right now." So, they talk it over. They have their differences, of course, but they agree eventually that what this man in the bear trap needs is obviously psychotherapy. If he would just be trained to be a more mature individual; if he could have the release therapy he needs; if he would undergo the needed catharsis, achieve the necessary insight, and work through the essential abreaction, he would develop more maturity, he would understand the difficulty he is having, and he would then be able to solve his problem himself. Obviously, the psychologists agree, that is the only sound way to deal with the poor fellow. Suddenly, however, a farmer comes by and lets the man out of the bear trap. To the utter amazement of the psychologists, the man's behavior changes greatly and quickly. Besides, he seems to take a great liking to the farmer, and goes off with him, evidently to have a cup of coffee.

Source: W. Johnson, Being understanding and understood: Or how to find a wandered horse. *ETC: A Review of General Semantics,* 8(1), 176–177 (1951).

presenting problem—or the problem the applicant brings. You will have difficulty with the problem-solving model unless you are able to start where the applicant is—which is usually not with cause but with relief of symptom.

Discussion of applicant objectives is a part of engagement. Defining the problem and setting tentative objectives are a part of framing the problem and deciding what will be our focus in helping the client. The applicant's engagement with the problem-solving process will be increased by selecting an objective that the applicant believes is a reasonable answer to his want. This problem and goal formulation may change over the period of exploration and data collection, but you and the client must have some agreement on a tentative objective in order to begin working together. Don't be surprised if the applicant does not seem motivated in the absence of a tentative agreement. For an example of what may happen in the absence of agreement on goals, see Exhibit 5–1, which depicts a conflict between the authority a worker received from her agency and the authority she received (or needed) from her client. Clarifying tentative objectives when the applicant and worker first come together is critical both to partnership building and to the applicant's motivation to work on the problem. The problem, the objective, and the situation will set the parameters for data collection. Without this, data collection may be unfocused and may stray fruitlessly into unrelated areas of the applicant's life.

Assessment. Assessment is the use of information to make decisions about the problem and what can be done about it. It involves refinement and specification of the problem, consideration of alternative approaches to solving the problem, selection of a preferred solution or objective, and development of a detailed action plan to accomplish the goal. Assessment results in a service plan.

To facilitate assessment, in general, data must be collected on:

- internal emotional response or feelings
- beliefs and the way the applicant views that situation
- the feelings and wishes of others who are important to the applicant
- possible environmental responses, sanctions, and opportunities
- the applicant's abilities, strengths, and skills to carry out the action proposed

You will consider alternatives, guide the selection of an alternative, and develop a plan to achieve the objective sought. With increase in the number of alternative responses or solutions that you and the client consider, the appropriateness of the final action will also increase. It may also be devastating for clients to be tangled in so many alternatives that they cannot act. Thus, you will face alternatives that are the most feasible.

We discuss assessment in detail in Chapters 10 and 11. Some people regard data collection and assessment as two distinct phases in the problem-solving process. However, the needs of assessment determine the data that you will collect. Thus, we see the activities of data collection and interpretation of data as intertwined.

Intervention. The service or action plan devised in the assessment process is carried out by you and your client. You will make a very wide range of intervention activities available to your clients; we introduce several of these in Chapters 12–16. As we saw when considering the ecosystem approach in Chapter 2, intervention can be directed toward the environment or toward the client-environment interaction, and so it will be important to have access to a wide range of intervention approaches.

Evaluation. Evaluation is the final phase of the problem-solving process. It includes activities to determine whether you and the client are carrying out the action or intervention plan as agreed and whether the desired objectives are being accomplished. On the basis of the evaluation, the action plan may be modified, if necessary. In addition, you may use evaluation with your client to reformulate the problem or to change objectives. Evaluation may also lead to decisions to terminate service, because the objectives have been accomplished, because they are unlikely to be accomplished, or because the client may be better served by another worker or another agency. Finally, evaluation can assist you and the client to determine whether the intervention is producing unexpected results. We discuss evaluation in Chapter 17.

Strengths and Problem Solving

Proponents of the strengths perspective in social work practice have criticized the problem-solving model on the grounds that the focus on problems obscures client strengths (Weick, 1992). This criticism, however, misses the central point that problem solving is directed toward objectives desired by the client. In the engagement phase, we move very quickly to identify client objectives and to set a preliminary goal; problem solving is goal-oriented. While problems in the person-situation interaction are the basis for the initial engagement between client and worker, the ensuing formulation and implementation of solutions calls upon client strengths, strengths in the environment, and worker strengths. Assessment involves a systematic identification of strengths as they relate to the desired objectives; intervention will include a plan to draw on these strengths. The identification and use of strengths has always been a part of the problem-solving process. As problem-solving practitioners, we welcome the emerging literature on the strengths perspective (Chapin, 1995; Rapp, 1998; Saleebey, 1992, 1997).

Emotion, Knowledge, and Relationship

The solution of problems in living always involves emotions, the knowledge that we have available to us, our perceptions of the world, and an orderly way of thinking. These elements interact in a complex way. It is painful to perceive that we have a problem that we cannot solve alone, a problem that represents a serious threat to our goals, or a problem that seriously threatens the needs and wants of those around us. The pain we feel usually obscures parts of the problem; it interferes with data collection and our consideration of alternative solutions and blocks effective action toward a solution. When clients feel such paralyzing emotional pain, the social worker must help to dissipate the feeling. If the client has the appropriate knowledge, skills, and resources, problem-solving activities that concentrate on the dissipation of feeling and self-acceptance may enable the client to solve the problem. However, dissipation of feeling is not enough for most clients, who will need additional knowledge about the problem, about what data is relevant, or about appropriate solutions; most importantly, they may need resources to enable them to take the necessary action.

All effective helping processes draw upon the worker's and the client's feelings. These feelings become a necessary and vital part of problem solving and create the climate in which helping takes place. Problem solving takes place in a context of feelings. It is, however, a rational process.

The problem-solving model requires a lot of rational headwork. Accordingly, you may suppose that it is appropriate only for clients who have the ability to weigh and measure alternative courses of action. Nothing could be further from the truth. You bear the primary burden of rational headwork; but you must also ensure that the client participates in decisions about the course of action to be followed. We have used this approach successfully with families judged by other professional helpers—schools, mental health clinics, and social agencies—to be unreachable and beyond help. Fraser (1996) identifies the importance of cognitive problem solving in family preservation services and work with aggressive youth. It is particularly helpful to clients who do not possess problem-solving skills adequate to their living situation.

Problem Solving as a Spiral Process

We have portrayed problem-solving as an orderly, sequential process; any one phase depends on the successful completion of the preceding phase. In practice, however, you may be operating in more than one phase at once. The phases follow each other in some rough order, but one phase does not wait upon the completion of another before it begins. Problem solving in social work proceeds as a spiral process, in which action does not always wait upon the completion of assessment, and assessment often begins before data collection is complete. In fact, you may become aware that you have not collected enough facts, or the proper facts, only after you have started trying to sum up all you know. When you and your client begin to take action toward some solution for the problem, you may discover that you have selected an unworkable course or are proceeding on the wrong problem and must start all over again. However, you begin again with the distinct advantage of having knowledge, observations, and a working relationship.

Perlman (1957) states that treatment begins with the first glance between client and worker. We would say that the beginning of the relationship comes with that first glance. This incipient relationship will help shape problem identification, assessment, and solution. As problem solving progresses through its various phases, the relationship will change.

You will find that problem solving is a squirming, wriggling, living process that embraces the social reality between you, the client, and all the systems of which you and the client are a part. In practice, it is difficult to identify and track each phase of the process, or to discern the logic of the process. It is your business to know what phase is the primary focus at any time and to check constantly to see that you deal with all phases. An impulsive leap to some action, with no pause for thought or consultation with your client, will not be successful. Problem solving may be characterized as the process by which worker and client decide:

- what problem or question on which to work
- the desired objectives of the work
- what accounts for the persistence of the problem even though the client wants something changed
- what procedures should be undertaken to change the situation
- what specific actions are to be undertaken to implement the procedures
- how the actions have worked out

For the social worker, successful problem solving calls for skill and the ability to keep both a clear head and an understanding heart. However, the problem-solving framework does not provide specific guides to specific procedures; it does not promise that a particular type of thinking and exploring will yield the answer. Rather, it promises that this type of thinking and exploring, conducted consciously and knowingly, in about this order, will increase the probability of finding an effective answer that is consistent with the client's goals. What the answer is will depend on what the question is, what the client wants, and what knowledge, understanding, resources, and capacity for joint action you and the client can bring to the process.

CLIENTS, APPLICANTS, PROSPECTS, AND RESPONDENTS

We need to alert you to a rather serious problem of terminology in the social work profession. Historically, the term *client* has been used to describe a very broad category of people with whom the social worker inter-

acts. For Helen Harris Perlman, as we have seen, an individual who came to an agency for help was an applicant; only after reaching an agreement with the worker on goals did the applicant become a client. We agree with this distinction. However, we believe it can be taken further.

The conditions under which you initiate services will be markedly different for different individuals. We can identify at least three major categories:

1. A person or group initiates a request for service—for instance, a couple who contact a family service agency for assistance in resolving marital difficulties; parents who approach an agency for help in managing a rebellious adolescent; or a young adult seeking assistance with symptoms of depression.

2. You reach out to offer services to persons or groups who have not requested the services. Often, this will involve marketing your services. Examples include outreach workers who establish contact with youth gangs or young people who may be attracted to gangs, who contact homeless persons to connect them with services, or who reach out to prostitutes both to encourage safe sex practices and to offer services. Family resource centers may reach out through advertising and personal contact to encourage parents to participate in the centers' programs.

3. Individuals are told, under pressure of outside authority, that they must see a social worker. This mandatory referral may be associated with crime, drug abuse, child neglect, or some types of mental illness. For instance, in Exhibit 3–4, hospital officials believe that commitment proceedings are necessary to protect Joe, who is being held against his will under a 72-hour hold. The social worker has been asked to discover if the parents would be willing to commit Joe. In this case, who is the client? Is it Joe? Is it the physician? Is it the hospital? Or is it society at large, acting through the social worker to protect Joe?

The interactions and role relationships between you and persons called clients will differ in different phases of the work—for example, when you are exploring whether a problem exists and when you are implementing an intervention. Perlman (1957) identified this difference when she referred to applicants and clients. Others have noted the need to make distinctions among those with whom the practitioners work (Gambrill, 1983, Germain & Gitterman, 1980, Reid, 1978).

EXHIBIT 3-4   **Joe, A Potential Suicide**

Joe, an 18-year-old single white male, was admitted to the hospital on a 72-hour medical hold. Two nights prior to this hospitalization, Joe had attempted to end his life by slashing his wrists. Tonight, Joe made an additional attempt to take his life. In addition, he self-inflicted wounds (2–3 inches long) on his right arm, cuts (3–4 inches long) on the left side of his abdomen, and long scratches on his sternal chest area. He explains that he has recently broken up with his girlfriend (Karen) and that he attended a party this evening at which the girlfriend was present with a new boyfriend. According to Joe, Karen is pregnant with his child. Seeing her proved very difficult for him. Thus, he left the party, broke into Karen's home, and obtained a paring knife from the kitchen to inflict his injuries. I was asked by the attending physician to learn if Joe's parents would be willing to petition to have him committed for inpatient treatment. It is the physician's belief that Joe is not stable enough psychologically to refrain from harming himself if released. Since he is refusing the recommended help, and the physician believes that he is dangerous to himself, commitment is the only alternative to pursue within the 72-hour hold.

Nevertheless, any person, family, group, or organization with whom the social worker interacts for purposes of defining a problem or producing change still tends to be referred to as a client. Such use of the term shows little regard for the differing sources of authority for the interaction, the differing circumstances under which the interactions occur, the differing levels of client desire for the interactions, and the difference between interactions for purposes of problem definition and interactions for purposes of intervention. We believe the profession must develop a more precise nomenclature as a step toward clarifying our thinking and acting.

In this book, we define the client as any individual, group, family, or organization with whom the social worker has an explicit agreement regarding the nature of the problem to be resolved and an intervention plan. Thus, there is no client until we have a clear agreement regarding the problem and the steps to resolve it. Obviously, we also interact with individuals, groups, families, and organizations in order to develop this clear agreement. In these earlier phases, we use the following terms:

• An *applicant* is a person, group, or organization who voluntarily seeks out our services.
• A *prospect* is a person, group, or organization to whom we are reaching out.
• A *respondent* is a person, group, or organization who is required to interact with us.

Many applicants will enter into agreements with you and become clients, but others may not. Also, prospects and respondents may find a basis for work with a social worker and become clients. Ron Rooney (1988, 1992) has developed a framework in which he suggests ways that the social worker might go about converting respondents (involuntary clients, in Rooney's terminology) to clients.

Having made these distinctions, we need a concise way of referring collectively to applicants, prospects, and respondents. We are going to adopt the convention of using the term *applicant* to mean any potential client, unless the context clearly suggests that prospect or respondent would be a more appropriate term. Similarly, for the sake of brevity, we will use the term *person* to mean an individual, family, group, organization, or community.

CHAPTER SUMMARY

The problem-solving model does not in any way deny people's irrational and instinctive characteristics. Studies in mental hospitals have found that even the most regressed psychotic patients are at least as responsive to changes in external reality as to their internal fantasies. Altering their external reality alters their ways of coping and "given a chance to participate in making decisions that affected their lives, inmates generally did so in a responsible manner and with constructive results for all concerned—professionals as well as themselves" (Lerner, 1972, p. 161).

This model further accepts the view that social work processes are not a set of techniques by which experts who understand what is wrong seek to improve, enlighten, plan for, or manipulate clients. Rather, social work processes are an attempt "by one human being with specialized knowledge, training, and a way of working to establish a genuinely meaningful, democratic, and collaborative relationship with another person or persons in order to put one's special knowledge and skills at the second person's (or group's) disposal for such use as can be made of it" (Lerner, 1972, p. 11). Decisions about what individuals and groups of individuals should be, have, want, and do are cognitive decisions in which "every person is a legitimate expert for oneself and no person is a legitimate expert for others" (Lerner, 1972, p. 161). The model rests on the assumption that every human being has a desire to be active in his or her own life—to exercise meaningful self-control for his or her own purposes.

Living systems are purposive. Practitioners are more effective when they start with the applicant's purposes and the obstacles to their achievement. The push toward change comes from the discomfort of unfulfilled wants, but the pull toward change comes from hope that these wants can be fulfilled. This does not imply ignorance about unconscious and irrational factors. It simply means that the practitioner starts with the rational, with consciously expressed problems and goals. Such objectives may appear totally irrational and impossible, but the model demands that they be respected and seen as a valuable statement of applicant wants.

We like the problem-solving framework for a number of reasons:

1. No assumptions about the cause, nature, location, or meaning of the problem are built into the model itself. Thus, the framework allows the problem to be defined as associated with the client, with the other systems with which the client has transactions, with lack of social resources that should be supplied by the environment, or with transactions among these factors. The existence of a problem does not imply impaired functioning or personality malfunctioning.

2. The framework is based on a belief in the growth potential of all human systems. Attention is turned away from personal deficits and toward social transactions and human struggles toward growth.

3. The model is not based on any particular theoretical orientation and allows you and your client to agree on any method of intervention appropriate to the problem, the problem location, the objectives, the client, and your competence and resources.

4. The framework gives a prominent place to client objectives. This is congruent with social work values such as the importance of the individual, of individual differences, and of self-determination, and recognizes the importance of the client's purposes.

5. The way that the problem is defined and goals are established determines which data are relevant and where the emphasis and direction of inquiry will lie. This facilitates data collection that is relevant, salient, and individualized, and minimizes intervention in the client's life.

6. The framework supports the client's right to personal definition of the problem. If you have a different view, you must negotiate a joint statement of the problem to be worked. You and the client must agree on what you are going to undertake together.

7. The process is applicable to a wide variety of situations and settings in which social work is practiced and to client systems of different sizes and types. The problem-solving framework demands that the tasks and activities of the social worker be stated at a very specific level and related to client objectives. This is a distinct advantage over frameworks that allow for a more abstract service plan.

Specific social work skills and activities are required for each phase of the problem-solving process. The skills and activities for the four phases—engagement, assessment, action or intervention, and evaluation—are summarized in Exhibit 3–5.

A LOOK FORWARD

In Reading 3-1, Ralph Woehle reviews some of the problem-solving literature and offers suggestions to reduce the linearity of the process. Assessment is continuous, and decisions made by social workers and clients are always nested in higher-order decisions by the agency and the professional identification of the worker. (Does this seem similar to the layering of systems we noted in Chapter 2? We noted there that higher-order systems both limit and provide opportunities for lower-order systems.) Woehle suggests that we limit the process of generating alternatives to those that are feasible in solving problems with available strengths; that we clearly prioritize alternatives; and that we commit resources to the alternatives of higher priority. Woehle consistently draws from the literature of the task-centered models. In that literature, tasks are defined as actions to be carried out by the client (Epstein, 1988; Reid & Epstein, 1977; Reid, 1978, 1992). Because of our emphasis on partnership, we prefer to define tasks as specific actions that either the

EXHIBIT 3-5	Phases of the Problem-Solving Process

I. Engagement phase
  A. Activities
    1. Securing applicant participation
    2. Defining the presenting problem
    3. Establishing a preliminary objective (what applicant wants)
    4. Negotiating a preliminary agreement regarding data collection and continuing to work together
  B. Skills needed
    1. Ability to use self in the interests of the applicant on the basis of self-awareness and understanding of resources
    2. Listening—not only listening with ears to words and with eyes to body language but a total kind of perceptiveness (listening with the third ear) that involves attending carefully, both physically and psychologically, to the applicant
    3. Communication of empathy, genuineness, trustworthiness, respect, and support
    4. Encouragement of applicant participation through techniques such as paraphrasing, clarifying, perception checking, focusing, questioning, reflecting, informing, confronting, interpreting, assuring, and reassuring

II. Assessment phase
  A. Activities
    1. Exploration, investigation, data collection
    2. Organizing data and thinking about information to develop statement of:
       a. the problem for work
       b. objectives
    3. Formulation of an action plan
  B. Skills needed
    1. Skill in the use of a range of data collection methods—not only client interviewing but also the use of records, test data, other written materials, interviews or conferences with other than the client, observations, and documentary evidence
    2. Ability to focus on the collection of necessary data
    3. Ability to use knowledge—of growth and development, human diversity and culture, human functioning and malfunctioning, and the interactions and transactions of human systems—in order to analyze and interpret the data collected
    4. Ability to identify applicant/client strengths

5. Ability to prioritize and organize data in such a way as to suggest useful action
6. Ability to partialize, in order to select an area of work
7. Ability to generate a range of alternative plans and to determine the feasibility of each alternative
8. Ability to involve applicant/client in all decision making
9. Ability to specify problems for work
10. Ability to develop specific action plans

III. Action or intervention phase
  A. Activities
    1. Carrying out action plan
    2. Supporting client in these change activities
    3. Following through on actions you have agreed to take
  B. Skills needed
    1. Skills in use of a range of social work interventions and roles necessary to carrying out the action plan
    2. Communication skills as needed to implement the plan
    3. Ability to keep focus on the objectives and the corresponding action plan
    4. Ability to support and involve client in carrying out the action plan

IV. Evaluation phase
  A. Activities
    1. Reviewing implementation of action plan; was the plan carried out as agreed?
    2. Determining the extent to which objectives were attained
    3. Ending services through termination or transfer
  B. Skills needed
    1. Ability to involve client in determining whether the plan is being carried out
    2. Ability to measure attainment of objective
    3. Ability to confront client who does not follow through
    4. Ability to accept responsibility for own failure to follow through
    5. Ability to reconsider problem statement, goals, and service plan
    6. Ability to develop new plans
    7. Ability to end services, through either termination or transfer

worker or client have agreed to carry out in the intervention phase.

In Chapter 4, we will further develop the theme of worker-client partnership. As we have already noted, partnership, along with the ecosystems focus and problem solving, is one of the central concepts in this model of practice. Some of the difficulties in orchestrating partnership emerge in Chapter 5, where we discuss the three sources of authority for you as a social worker: your client, your profession, and your agency.

Variations on the Problem-Solving Theme*

Ralph Woehle

Perlman (1957) wrote that any attempt to describe casework should be regarded as an exercise in problem solving, because the subject matter is complex and in motion. It was necessary, she said, to carve out some essential qualities of the whole and to view them as parts on a continuum. In this paper, weaving variations on Perlman's theme, we will examine problem solving as part of a continuum in a systems context. The problem-solving model will be combined with the strengths perspective of Saleebey (1996) and incorporated within the general model of mixed scanning provided by Etzioni (1986).

PROBLEM SOLVING

Originally, Perlman (1957) saw three components in the problem-solving process: (1) study or fact finding; (2) organizing the facts into a goal-oriented explanation; and (3) implementing the conclusions in some action on the problem. She recognized that these three steps did not differ radically from the three steps of the previous diagnostic schools; the major difference was that problem solving was conceived as a cooperative process with the client. Therefore, problem solving had to abandon the Freudian preoccupation with the unconscious, and adopt an emphasis on conscious rationality.

Many other writers have outlined problem-solving processes. Sheafor, Horejsi, and Horejsi (1997), drawing from Epstein (1988) and the problem-solving approach of Pincus and Minahan (1973), as well as other authors, describe a change process having five stages: (1) intake and engagement; (2) data collection and assessment; (3) planning and contracting; (4) intervention and monitoring; and (5) evaluation and termination.

Epstein (1988), along with Reid (1978), has integrated client tasks and time limits into the problem-solving framework. The task-centered model focuses on the achievement of tasks and problem reduction (Epstein, 1988), by restating the particular problem, undertaking continuous assessment, generating alter-

natives, negotiating support from other agencies, and implementing agreed-upon task strategies. Implementation of the strategy includes further development of the tasks; support of task performance; and verification and monitoring of tasks, effects, and problem reduction. Finally, termination may lead to extension of the work if the client wants and is committed to further services, to monitoring (if required by some authority), or simply to ending the services. The task-centered work is to be completed within a limited time period, which is clearly stated at the beginning of the process.

More recently, Saleebey (1996) has cautioned that the language of problem solving tends to become the language of pathology, in which professionals name clients according to their problems. Such naming can entrap clients in the pathologizing system, a contention supported by this writer's research (Woehle, 1994). Saleebey (1996) would have us honor the ability of the self, with environmental help, to heal.

By the mid-1980s, Macht and Quam (1986) claimed that problem solving and planned change had become accepted as the key commonality of social work. This has placed rational thought at the core of social work. However, few social work writers have made this rational base explicit. Exceptions include policy analysts, who have drawn on a rich literature in political science and sociology (DiNitto, 1995).

As DiNitto (1995) has indicated, social science has fallen far short of the requirements for purely rational change. All of the alternative actions and outcomes cannot be specified in advance; neither are actions easily related to effects. As Fox (1987) has further pointed out, facilitative, or incremental, goals may be easier to see than goals describing outcomes. Such short-term goals are also easier to relate to specific actions than are outcomes. The functional or normative goals Fox (1987) identified may be more consistent with systems theory. However, such goals are not specific solutions to problems. Finally, decision-making parties often disagree. As Barker (1987) has indicated, incremental social change is an effort to take into account a variety of political and pluralistic influences. In brief, incrementalist theories

---

*An original reading revised for this edition.

have questioned whether it is possible to consciously bring about solutions to problems.

Lindblom's (1977, 1980) work spanned the range of thought on rationality and incrementalism. He referred to the first as the root approach and to the latter as the branch approach. Originally, he preferred the branch approach, which he called muddling through. In his magnum opus, however, Lindblom (1977) came to praise the possibilities of both approaches and their traditions. On a practical level, Etzioni (1986) integrated the two approaches in his mixing-scanning model.

SYSTEMS THEORY IN SOCIAL WORK

Social work theory has considered the limitations of rational thought via systems theory. Systems theory takes account of the environment and usually adds a feedback loop to the problem-solving model. Feedback loops provide the client and social worker with information about reactions to the problem-solving activities, including reactions from the environment (Fordor, 1976). However, some social work writers using the systems approach have not altered the problem-solving model significantly. Pincus and Minahan (1973) did not move beyond traditional problem solving. Others adopt a more complex cybernetic model (Fordor, 1976), in which the traditional problem-solving model is expanded to include feedback loops. Such views are consistent with systems theory but avoid major issues raised by systems theory. They leave rational and scientific reductionist assumptions in place, even if they are multicausal (Auerswald, 1987). The causes have remained additive in such models, whereas in ecological systems the whole is greater than the sum of its parts.

The ecological issues raised by systems theory are its greatest contribution. In fact, Auerswald (1987) says this is a new epistemology. Unlike the old epistemology, which saw things as true or false on the basis of the scientific method, this epistemology sees truth as heuristic. Science and rationality are also heuristic devices in this new epistemology and are therefore acceptable ways of understanding. However, Auerswald no longer represents science and rationality as an underlying truth. Thus, systems theory is important because it takes us from a static view of rationality as a reflection of the underlying truth to rationality as an abstraction of the far more complex and socially structured reality, which cannot be fully expressed by the abstraction.

Systems theory is also important because it points to the environmental factors in the functioning of systems. In this respect, it has had great impact on social work. Pincus and Minahan (1973) moved social work boldly into the social environment with their practice model. Similarly, Etzioni (1986) pointed to the importance of structural factors in decision making in his mixed-scanning model. But he later indicated that considerations of the mixed-scanning approach had largely ignored such factors. By combining the contributions of systems theory, the strengths perspective, problem solving, and mixed scanning, it is possible to generate variations of the problem-solving model that are compatible with practice as social workers have always found it.

SYSTEMS, SCANNING, STRENGTHS, AND PROBLEM SOLVING

Lantz (1986) added to the problem-solving model in family therapy by adding reflexive feedback loops. He saw 10 stages. The first six were conventional problem solving. Then Lantz added a problem-escalation stage, which followed task preparation; this stage limited the ability to resolve the original problem. In one possible feedback loop, escalation leads back to assessment; in another, task preparation is followed by resistance, reflection, and insight. The therapist must respect the resistance, Lantz (1986) said, and explore the family's catastrophic expectations about the dangers of change. Insight might then reveal the nature of the family's resistance, and the therapist and family would be able to move back to the task preparation stage. Thus, Lantz added feedback loops within the client system.

Auerswald (1987) drew on systems theory to describe an approach to family therapy that was very similar to problem solving, especially to the task-centered approach. However, he added problem-solving sequences that went outside the client system. While he recognized that work might have been directed at the client's larger environment, and he claimed to draw on a revolutionary development, he did not go as far as he might have. His model still appeared to consist primarily of reductionist, sequential problem solving.

Etzioni's (1986) mixed-scanning approach, while originally intended for policy-making processes, might also be used in personal decisions about careers, marriage, health, and financial security. Mixed scanning is a hierarchical mode of decision making. Fundamental decisions are seen as of a high order; within them are nested lower-order, more incremental decisions. Scanning, according to Etzioni (1986), consists of the gathering, evaluation, and use of information in order to come to conclusions. In social work terms, scanning is assessment. But the hierarchical nature of the decision making offers something more: It recognizes that most decisions are made in the larger context, a context partly consisting of larger policy decisions and organizational structures. The limitations imposed by the context make the rational consideration of all alternatives less productive, because many alternatives are not possible in that context. Scanning is therefore less demanding than the full rational search for solutions, but it is more strategic than pure incrementalism. Rational approaches demand an evaluation of all possible solutions, and incrementalism deals with just the trouble spots; scanning strikes some middle ground.

Etzioni (1986) listed four major steps that made the mixed-scanning approach operational. First, all relevant known alternatives should be listed on strategic occasions. (In social work terms, alternatives are explored). Second, the implementation should be fragmented (or in social work, partialized) into several sequential steps. Third, steps should be reviewed as they are implemented. (This resembles continued assessment). And, fourth, a rule for the allocation of time and assets (strengths) among the various levels of scanning should be formulated. (Policies should be reviewed.)

Scanning or assessment of the alternatives might lead to elimination of those that will not be pursued. Etzioni (1986) suggested three criteria for elimination: (1) utilitarian—the lack of means or strengths to pursue the alternatives; (2) normative—the violation of basic values of the decision makers; and (3) political—the violation of values or interests of the actors whose support seems necessary for making a decision and implementing it. For alternatives not so rejected, examination in greater detail is in order. Basically, this involves repetition of the scanning process in ever greater detail, until only one or some other small number of alternatives remain.

Before implementing a remaining alternative, it should be broken down into parts in three ways (Etzioni, 1986). First, for administrative clarity, it is broken down into sequential parts. Second, for political purposes, commitment to implement is made in serial steps.

Resources or strengths are committed a piece at a time, while maintaining a strategic reserve. Furthermore, arranging commitments so that the most costly ones can be made later will make the process more reversible and less costly. Finally, scanning or assessment should continue on scheduled occasions and as the need arises. At important turning points, assessment at higher system levels would be desirable.

As each subset of increments is completed, scanning or assessment at the level of that subset should be undertaken (Etzioni, 1986). Even if things seem to be working, assessment should continue, though less intensively. Trouble requires more intensive assessment. Alternative strategies may appear more desirable in light of experience with the present alternative. If the goal has been achieved or become undesirable or too costly, the effort may be discontinued. Use of resources or strengths is required for assessment itself (Etzioni, 1986). Assessment takes time and energy, some of which should be reserved for occasions when its use is triggered by set intervals or by emergencies.

Assessment proceeds on the assumption of limited foresight. Each step is a hypothesis that needs evaluation; or, in more practical terms, each step is a trial that may be more or less successful. Likewise, each set of steps, which constitutes a larger step, is a trial. When a course of action is failing, assessment is a way of learning about the reasons for failure and considering alternative courses of action.

This literature review suggests several generalizations and task processes that modify problem solving. Let's consider each of these in turn.

GENERALIZATIONS

On the basis of the literature, some conclusions may be drawn regarding the continual use of assessment; the recognition of higher-order decisions in which task decisions are nested; the generation, elimination, and prioritization of alternative tasks; and the commitment of system strengths. Each of these topics will now be discussed in greater detail.

Assessment

Assessment is present in every part of the social work process. Everything that happens provides information to the worker and client. Participants in the process do not adhere strictly to a particular task process, even when they have agreed to do so; assessment continues naturally as practitioners and clients look at their situations and adjust their work. However, the assessment process must be orderly if the work is to maintain some direction. Clients and workers can strategically guide the assessment process by emphasizing it at certain times and deemphasizing it at others. There are at least three occasions when assessment should be the primary work of the process. The first is the assessment associated with problem, strength, and task identification in each task process; this is assessment as described traditionally in problem-solving and task-centered approaches to social work.

The second strategic use of assessment occurs on specified occasions. Often these occasions are specified by institutional or individual policies—for example, by governmental policy for review of cases or by a supervisor's practice of directing a periodic case review. Alternatively, the need for further assessment may emerge from the process itself. For instance, if a task process develops a problem that requires the ongoing task process to be modified, the worker and client may need to shift the work to assessment of the emerging problem and the strengths needed to address it.

Finally, assessment occurs at the end of each task process. This is usually referred to as evaluation but, given that one task flows from another, evaluation will often be the assessment for the next task.

Assessment should review strengths as well as problems. In fact, a problem is not a problem unless some available system has the means to resolve it. Thus, by definition, problems can only be assessed in relation to the strengths of systems that can address those problems.

Nested Decisions

A second important modification of the traditional problem-solving process is the recognition that decisions in the work process are nested in higher-order decisions. Generally, this means that social work occurs within the context of decisions made in larger social structures. Such structures might include the agency and the larger public bureaucracy in which the agency is typically located; professional associations; client interest groups; and communities with their particular cultural values. For example, Rothman, Smith, Nakashima, Peterson, and Mustin (1996) report that practice is sometimes directed by client protection policies and procedures,

which may give rise to ethical quandaries. Thus, both agency and professional/licensing organizations nest the practice decisions, and their directives may conflict.

In some circumstances, higher-order decisions may themselves emerge as social work issues. If so, the work will move out of the client system to some external system. For example, changing agency policy may be a proper work task if a particular policy limits desirable tasks at the client level.

As we have already noted, all client-worker efforts are nested within a professional association and licensing agency and also within governmental agencies and policymaking bodies, all of which have procedures to guide social work decisions and practice (Rothman, Smith, Nakashima, Peterson, & Mustin, 1996). This nesting implies the political nature of work decisions; decisions will often be political compromises between competing prescriptions rather than rational conclusions. If rationality is to limit pure muddling, however, it must also guide decision making. The compromise between these two approaches is to make relatively limited commitments to tasks that we are quite certain we will be able to complete.

Finally, since the problems and strengths may be located in a variety of systems and at various system levels, assessment may at times be directed at systems other than the one where work is presently located. It is therefore necessary to assess such issues not just when they emerge in relation to an individual case, but in some systematic fashion. Such assessments must take account of strengths as well as problems.

Generating Feasible Alternatives

Although Epstein (1988) also recommended the generation of alternatives, this account will focus on Etzioni's (1986) approach. First, Etzioni suggested the generation of known alternatives on strategic occasions, following assessment. Basically this is a matter of working with the client to identify as many options as strengths and knowledge allow. Thus, even in the initial assessment, social workers recognize that their job is limited by present knowledge and strengths.

Second, Etzioni (1986) recommended the elimination of alternatives by tests of feasibility—by looking at resources or strengths and at the values of participating parties. In social work, the relevant values are those of clients, workers, and sanctioning bodies such as agencies and professional associations. This is closely related to Epstein's (1988) suggestion that tasks be prioritized in terms of clients', workers' and referral-source priorities, since a low-priority task will probably be eliminated. Note that, as the assessment of strengths and problems continues, priorities may change, or new tasks of high priority, consistent with available strengths, may emerge.

Use of Strengths

Commitment to tasks may change if the availability of system strengths to complete tasks changes. Available strengths of social service agencies are subject to fluctuation, because society's commitment is politically unstable and demands for services fluctuate. Economic conditions and fluctuations, as well as a variety of individual, family, and macrosystem conditions, may otherwise affect available strengths. Consequently, long-term tasks always face uncertainties with regard to systems strengths. Furthermore, the ability to judge strengths in advance is limited. Thus, it is generally not rational to commit to a long-term task at any cost.

Etzioni (1986) suggests a fragmented commitment of resources to task completion. Basically, this means limiting the early commitment of strengths to small amounts, pending the accomplishment of small tasks. He also suggests leaving the biggest commitments to last, where possible. The short-term tasks of Reid (1978) and Epstein (1988) obviously help to meet this requirement. Just as it should not be assumed that strengths will be adequate, it should not be assumed that they are nonexistent. Workers should be prepared to work with clients to seek support for task completion from the larger social environment, inside or outside of the agency's network, as Epstein (1988) suggests. This is the essence of Cowger's (1994) assessment for strengths.

TASK PROCESS

Given the generalizations identified here, various modifications of the task process can be suggested. Modifications suggested here are: extended sequential task processes, three task processes with feedback loops, the terminated task process, and simultaneous-task processes.

Sequential Task Processes

As Epstein (1988) recognizes, the work with the client does not necessarily end when a specific set of tasks is completed. If the worker, client, and other involved parties agree, additional tasks may be undertaken. If this work begins after the completion of a task cycle, then the next set of tasks is a repetition of the original process, with different goals, tasks, and so on. In brief, this variation is merely the sequential continuation of repetitions of the problem-solving process.

Processes with Feedback

As already noted, variations of the task-centered approach with internal feedback loops have been identified by Lantz (1986). Lantz indicated that two types of feedback loops involving work with the family may emerge. One such loop may occur when tasks are being identified. If family members resist at this stage, exploration of that resistance can lead to reflection, insight, and return to the prescribed tasks. Alternatively, if problem escalation occurs as tasks are being undertaken, it may be necessary to return to the assessment stage to redefine tasks. Lantz sees these loops as reflexive, and both involve work within the family system.

Auerswald (1987) did not describe the diagram suggested by his approach. He might, in fact, have disagreed with an attempt to reduce it to a diagram. While his model was described earlier as sequential, it can also be represented as feedback loops that spiral into the social environment or into subsystems. Auerswald recognized that the family's problem may not exist in the family system. Thus, problem solving undertaken in the family might not work. Returning to assessment may indicate that the problem may lie in an individual or in the larger environment—the school, for example. If such problems are identified, the worker then takes up the problem-solving process in the appropriate system.

Whether the problem lies within or outside of the system, the strength to resolve the problem must be located in a system that can be brought to bear on the problem. It follows that strength assessment must also move between systems and may be successful in a system other than that in which the problem is located.

The Terminated Process

Because feasibility is continually being evaluated, the process may be discontinued at any stage. Indeed, the process may end almost as soon as it begins. The inability to bring strengths to bear on a problem may end the process. For example, if an agency refers a client with goals for certain services but the services are not authorized by some overriding authority, then the start-up suggested by Epstein (1988) may lead to discontinuation of services. In fact, tasks may be discontinued at any time that the ongoing assessment reveals a lessening of the priority of the problem or unavailability of requisite strengths.

Simultaneous Task Processes

Simultaneous task processes are appropriate when an initial task process can proceed only if another is undertaken. For example, if a family has a child with behavior problems, the parents may undertake consistent discipline as a task. But the child also has to develop behavior control. A task for the child may include working on positive behavior. Thus, simultaneous work on discipline and the behavior of the child may be undertaken.

CONCLUSION

The new ecosystem paradigm has suggested that rational problem solving is an analogy for the social work process. However, it does not represent the underlying truth of the process. Thus, it would also be possible to propose another model for the work process and to reject scientific rationality. Rather than rejecting traditional

social work, however, this paper suggests that there is much to be said for the traditional approaches to social work.

Nevertheless, once we begin to challenge the assumption of rationality underlying the idea that social work is a linear process, we are free to consider nonlinear approaches. Information about such processes suggests several modifications of traditional problem solving: (1) the liberal use of assessment, both on a continuous basis and on special occasions; (2) the nesting of decisions in higher-order decisions, which directs work to other levels on occasion and situates decisions within political processes; (3) limitation of the number of alternatives generated, on the basis of the feasibility of problem solving with the available strengths; and (4) the need to commit strengths appropriately among prioritized alternatives. Task processes may be modified from the traditional problem-solving model by (1) making them sequential; (2) adding feedback loops at various system levels; (3) terminating them at any point; and (4) running them simultaneously.

This paper represents a small step. Two larger steps seem obvious at this point. First, any or all of the above task processes may be used in a given case; case diagrams may be permutations and combinations of those here described. Second, the release from scientific rationality as an underlying truth frees us to consider a wide variety of nonrational approaches.

LEARNING EXERCISES

1. Write a brief description for each of these key terms, or orally define the term for a colleague.
   applicant
   capacity
   client
   engagement
   motivation
   opportunity
   problem solving
   prospect
   respondent
   want

2. Reread Exhibit 3–2. How might you have handled this situation differently?

3. In the case of Debbie Smith (Appendix A–1), the worker, representing a child welfare agency, initiated contact by calling on Debbie Smith at her home because of possible concerns about child neglect. There is no indication at all that Debbie Smith requested the services. Who is the client here? What are the reasons for your views?

REFERENCES

Auerswald, E. H. (1987). Epistemological confusion in family therapy and research. *Family Process, 26*(3), 317–330.

Barker, R. (1987). *The social work dictionary.* Silver Spring, MD: NASW.

Bennis, W., Benne, K., & Chin, R. (Eds.). (1969). *The planning of change.* New York: Holt, Rinehart & Winston.

Chapin, R. K. (1995). Social policy development: The strengths perspective. *Social Work, 40*(4), 506–514.

Cowger, C. D. (1994). Assessing client strengths: Clinical assessment for client empowerment. *Social Work, 39*(3), 262–268.

Dewey, J. (1933). *How we think* (rev. ed.). New York: Heath.

DiNitto, D. (1995). *Social welfare: Politics and public policy.* Boston: Allyn and Bacon.

Epstein, L. (1988). *Helping people: The task-centered approach.* Columbus, OH: Merrill.

Etzioni, A. (1986). Mixed scanning revisited. *Public Administration Review, 46,* 8–14.

Fordor, A. (1976). Social work and systems theory. *British Journal of Social Work, 6*(1), 8–14.

Fox, R. (1987). Short term goal oriented family therapy. *Social Casework, 68*(8), 494–499.

Fraser, M. W. (1996). Cognitive problem solving and aggressive behavior among children. *Families in Society, 77*(1), 19–32.

Gambrill, E. (1983). *Casework: A competency-based approach.* Englewood Cliffs, NJ: Prentice Hall.

Germain, C. B., & Gitterman, A. (1980). *The life model of social work practice.* New York: Columbia University Press.

Lantz, J. E. (1986). Integration of reflective and task oriented techniques in family treatment. *Child Welfare, 65*(5), 261–270.

Lerner, B. (1972). *Therapy in the ghetto.* Baltimore: John's Hopkins Press.

Lindblom, C. E. (1977). *Politics and markets.* New York: Basic Books.

Lindblom, C. E. (1980). *The policy making process.* Englewood Cliffs, NJ: Prentice Hall.

Macht, M., & Quam, J. (1986). *Social work: An introduction.* Columbus, OH: Merrill.

Perlman, H. H. (1957). *Social casework.* Chicago: University of Chicago Press.

Pincus, A., & Minahan, A. (1973). *Social work practice: Model and method.* Itasca, IL: Peacock.

Polya, G. (1957). *How to solve it.* Princeton, NJ: Princeton University Press.

Rapp, C. A. (1998). *The strengths model: Case management with people suffering from severe and persistent mental illness.* New York: Oxford.

Reid, W. J. (1978). *The task-centered system.* New York: Columbia University Press.

Reid, W. J. (1992). *Task strategies: An empirical approach to clinical social work.* New York: Columbia University Press.

Reid, W., & Epstein, L. (1977). *Task-centered practice.* New York: Columbia University Press.

Rooney, R. (1988). Socialization strategies for involuntary clients. *Social Casework: Journal of Contemporary Social Work, 69*(3), 131–140.

Rooney, R. (1992). *Strategies for work with involuntary clients.* New York: Columbia University Press.

Rothman, J., Smith, W., Nakashima, J., Paterson, M. J., & Mustin, J. (1996). Client self determination and professional intervention: Striking a balance. *Social Work, 41*(4), 396–405.

Saleebey, D. (Ed.). (1992). The strengths perspective in social work practice. New York: Longman.

Saleebey, D. (1996). The strengths perspective in social work practice: Extensions and cautions. *Social Work, 41*(3), 296–305.

Saleebey, D. (Ed.). (1997). *The strengths perspective in social work practice* (2nd ed.). New York: Longman.

Sheafor, B. W., Horejsi, C. R., & Horejsi, G. (1997). *Techniques and guidelines for social work practice.* Boston: Allyn & Bacon.

Weick, A. (1992). Building a strengths perspective for social work. In D. Saleebey (Ed.), *The strengths perspective in social work practice* (pp. 18–26). New York: Longman.

Woehle, R. (1994). Case management and labelling in a rural family agency. In B. Locke & M. Egan (Eds.), *Fulfilling our mission: Rural social work in the 1990's.* Morgantown: West Virginia University.

chapter 4

Client-Worker Partnership

CHAPTER PREVIEW

In this chapter, we discuss client-worker partnership—the third key theme underlying our model of practice. We will be presenting three sets of ideas:

- the nature of client-worker partnership in decision making about the problem-solving work
- partnership as enhancing respect for the dignity and uniqueness of the individual
- partnership and client self-determination

In Reading 4-1, Susan Tebb notes that the typical medical problem-oriented model for recording is in violation of client self-determination. She offers a partnership approach to recording (the CREW model), in which clients are involved in writing their own records.

We introduced the notion of worker-client partnership in Chapter 1 and returned to it in our discussion of the problem-solving process in Chapter 3. In this chapter, we will develop the concept further and link it to the social work values of promoting human dignity and self-determination.

NATURE OF WORKER-CLIENT PARTNERSHIP

Barbara Levy Simon (1994), in her history of the empowerment tradition in American social work, notes that a collaborative relationship with clients has been one of the key elements of empowerment. Collaboration means working together, and working together creates a partnership in which worker and client both participate to achieve the goal of the problem-solving effort. Through participation, people develop their strengths, take ownership of their lives, and contribute to a democratic process.

Various authors have described the relationship between worker and client as a partnership (Bricker-Jenkins, 1991; Coady, 1993; Maluccio, Washitz, & Libassi, 1992; Reid & Epstein, 1977; Reid, 1978, 1992). Bricker-Jenkins (1991) describes the worker-client partnership as open, egalitarian, and mutual. Clients are viewed as capable of making their own decisions and are to be a part of any decision making. Worker and client enter into a collaborative relationship based on trust, respect (Coady, 1993), and mutual involvement (Tebb, 1991). Applicants and clients are involved and participate in all decisions, including assessment and the development of intervention plans (Valentine, 1993). The ideas of mutuality and equality, which are necessary to partnership, are also central to feminist approaches to social work practice (Bricker-Jenkins, 1991; Collins, 1986; Nes & Iadicola, 1989; Rosewater & Walker, 1985; Russell, 1989). Mutuality is a critical foundation for working with Native people (Kelley, McKay, & Nelson, 1985) and is necessary for reducing the power distance between you and your clients. We see partnership as involving the negotiation of decisions; worker and client make equally important but different contributions to problem solving.

Negotiating Decisions

Partnership means that you and your client, as partners, jointly negotiate key decisions in the problem-solving process. In particular, you agree on a definition of the problem to be solved, the objectives to be achieved, and the action plan to accomplish those objectives. Partnership means negotiation, not unilateral decision making. You do not stipulate the nature of the applicant's problem or the objectives to be achieved; nor do you passively acquiesce in the applicant's perception of the problem or statement of objectives. At the same time, we encourage you to accept and work within the applicant's perception of the problem and wants whenever this seems reasonable and consistent with your professional responsibilities. On occasion, however, you will ask the applicant to consider different ways to frame the problem statement or to consider alternative problems or alternative objectives.

Exhibit 4–1 presents excerpts from a National Association of Social Workers (U.S.) policy on end-of-life decisions by persons with a terminal illness. Note that the policy acknowledges the right of competent individuals to make their own choices, but only after being informed of all the available options. This provides an opportunity to identify and negotiate other choices with a person who is considering ending his or her own life.

In negotiation, both parties place their points of view on the table and try to find a common area of agreement.

In Chapter 11, we will talk about negotiation of the problem statement, desired objectives and solutions, and the action plan. You need to be aware that many applicants will perceive you as a person of power, because of the position you occupy in the agency or because of the expertise you bring to the partnership. Accordingly, you must take care to express your views in a way that will enhance applicant participation and self-determination. It is advisable first to secure the views of your applicant and then to frame your own views to support applicant views, or else to clearly label your views as alternatives for consideration.

There are two dangers to avoid in negotiating with applicants: (1) dominating the process by expressing your views too early or too authoritatively or by failing to create a climate in which the applicant can express his or her point of view; and (2) accepting the applicant's views without presenting your views, which results in a denial of client self-determination.

EXHIBIT 4–1   **Client Self-Determination and End-of-Life Decisions**

NASW's position concerning end-of-life decisions is based on the principle of client self-determination. Choice should be intrinsic to all aspects of life and death.

The social work profession strives to enhance the quality of life; to encourage the exploration of life options; and to advocate for access to options, including providing all information to make appropriate choices.

Social workers have an important role in helping individuals identify the end-of-life options available to them. This role must be performed with full knowledge of and compliance with the law and in accordance with the NASW Code of Ethics (National Association of Social Workers, 1993). Social workers should be well informed about living wills, durable power of attorney for health care, and legislation related to advance health care directives.

A key value for social workers is client self-determination. Competent individuals should have the opportunity to make their own choices but only after being informed of all options and consequences. Choices should be made without coercion. Therefore, the appropriate role for social workers is to help patients express their thoughts and feelings, to facilitate exploration of alternatives, to provide information to make an informed choice, and to deal with grief and loss issues.

Social workers should not promote any particular means to end one's life but should be open to full discussion of the issues and care options. As a client is considering his or her choices, the social worker should explore and help ameliorate any factors such as pain, depression, need for medical treatment, and so forth. Further, the social worker should thoroughly review all available options including, but not limited to, pain management, counseling, hospice care, nursing home placement, and advance health care directives.

Social workers should act as liaisons with other health care professionals and help the patient and family communicate concerns and attitudes to the health care team to bring about the most responsible assistance possible.

Because end-of-life decisions have familial and social consequences, social workers should encourage the involvement of significant others, family, and friends in these decisions. Social workers should provide ongoing support and be liaisons to families and support persons (for example, caregivers, significant others) with care to maintain the patient's confidentiality. When death occurs, social workers have an obligation to provide emotional and tangible assistance to the significant others, family, and friends in the bereavement process.

Copyright 1997, National Association of Social Workers, Inc. from *Social Work Speaks: NASW Policy Statement*, 4th edition, p. 66. Reprinted with permission.

Equally Important but Different Contributions

You and the applicant do not bring the same things to the problem-solving work, but your differing contributions are equally important to accomplishing the objectives.

The applicant will bring:

- knowledge regarding his situation
- knowledge as to how the problem emerged
- expectations regarding how you can help
- a network of social relationships
- views as to what she would like to have done
- strengths for use in reaching objectives

You will bring:

- expert knowledge to help assess the situation and select service plans most likely to accomplish applicant objectives
- skills in the problem-solving process
- professional views for consideration by the applicant
- skills to help the applicant formulate problems in ways that are solvable
- skills in assisting an applicant to mobilize internal and external strengths in the service of specific objectives
- skills in creating an environment in which the applicant can participate
- the resources of your agency
- connections with other community resources

It is not your job to cure clients. Rather you assist them in recognizing and using strengths that they bring, as well as the resources of their environments. You do this by helping them to set goals and work toward those goals. As a result of partnership, clients become active participants in the problem-solving process. The contributions of both you and the client are necessary to the problem-solving work; neither is sufficient without the other.

Partnership and Your Professional Identity

The concept of partnership with applicants or clients may require you to rethink your own emerging professional identity. Some social workers believe that they know what is best for people and try to impose their knowledge on clients; they use their expertise to control their clients. William Gordon (1969) argued that social work is nonnormative, in the sense that we hold only

very general concepts of the ideal environment or the ideal person (see Exhibit 1–1 in Chapter 1). The notion of nonnormative practice supports the diversity that enriches us all; it is inconsistent with the idea of the social worker as expert about what is best for people.

A number of elements are conducive to an effective and beneficial client-worker partnership:

1. Concern for the other and purposeful expression of feelings between you and the client (Biestek, 1994). You care for clients by showing concern and encouraging them to create change for themselves.
2. Acceptance—a nonjudgmental attitude, recognition of the client's dignity, equality (Biestek, 1994), and uniqueness, sensitivity to the client's feelings, and understanding of the client's wants.
3. A sense of commitment and obligation to the plan (Biestek, 1994). This is essential if the goals of the partnership are to be achieved.
4. Empathy. The empathetic worker will more easily identify strengths and options, by attempting to see the problem from the client's point of view.
5. Authority—your right to make decisions regarding issues pertinent to the client-worker partnership (McIvor, 1991). Those decisions, however, still require the consent of the client who is responsive to your authority (Palmer, 1983).

Your professional identity is based on these five elements—that is, on your ability to manage a problem-solving process in which clients are full participants. This concept of partnership is what distinguishes social work from the other professions.

Social Work Values

Efforts to make definitive statements about social work values stir heated controversy. Is there a value base that all social work practitioners must accept? Does social work possess a set of values that is in some way unique in our culture? Are there interventive methodologies that social workers should not use because they are inconsistent with professional values? Henry Miller (1968) noted some of the value dilemmas encountered by social work practitioners and suggested that we should withdraw from settings in which treatment is imposed or coerced. Elizabeth Salomon (1967) suggested the possibility of inherent conflict between the humanistic stance of social work and scientific methodology. Scott Briar and Henry Miller (1971) advanced the intriguing suggestion that client-self-determination might be conceptualized as a treatment technique rather than a value, on the basis that clients in one-to-one relational systems make faster progress when they are extended maximum opportunities for self-determination. In other words, self-determination might be viewed simply as a means of facilitating client progress rather than as a fundamental social work value.

Webster's Ninth New-Collegiate Dictionary (1991) defines value as "something . . . intrinsically valuable or desirable." William Gordon (1965) noted that values denote things that are preferred, and Charles Levy (1973), developing this idea, indicated that values might be classified as preferred conceptions of people, preferred outcomes for people, and preferred instrumentalities for dealing with people. In other words, values can be thought of as the profession's beliefs about people and appropriate ways of dealing with them. Paul Halmos (1966), an English sociologist, concluded from an extensive literature review that the helping professions operate on the basis of tenets of faith concerning the nature of people. This faith, Halmos argued, is accepted without proof and provides guidance and direction for the professions. Thus, values are the profession's unproved—

and probably unprovable—beliefs about human nature; these beliefs provide direction to the practitioner's day-to-day work.

But are a profession's values the source of its uniqueness? We think not. The social work profession exists within a larger cultural context; it identifies and operationalizes value premises already existing in society. Schwartz (1961) has identified social norms as one of the three factors limiting professional social work practice. Because our complex culture is characterized by a wide range of values, some of which are in conflict, the social work profession selects the values it will support in practice. Thus, the profession may operationalize values in a distinctive way, but the values themselves are shared with other parts of the culture.

One way of thinking of values is to picture an inverted triangle (Exhibit 4–2). The broad top of the triangle represents values in a remote, general, or abstract sense, while the narrow bottom corresponds to proximate, specific, and concrete values. If values are to guide practice, the challenge is to take abstract concepts—such as client self-determination or the innate dignity of the individual—and apply them in specific situations. We can move from the general to the specific by asking "How?" questions. "Why?" questions, seeking an expla-

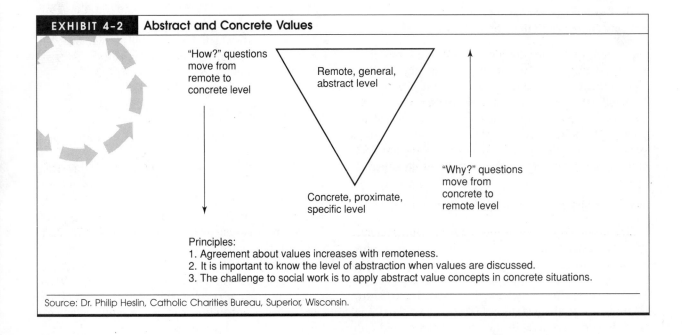

EXHIBIT 4–2   Abstract and Concrete Values

"How?" questions move from remote to concrete level

Remote, general, abstract level

Concrete, proximate, specific level

"Why?" questions move from concrete to remote level

Principles:
1. Agreement about values increases with remoteness.
2. It is important to know the level of abstraction when values are discussed.
3. The challenge to social work is to apply abstract value concepts in concrete situations.

Source: Dr. Philip Heslin, Catholic Charities Bureau, Superior, Wisconsin.

nation of actions, move us from the specific to the remote. In general, agreement increases with abstractness. Social workers readily agree, for example, to the abstract principle of client self-determination, but there may be considerable controversy over how to make this principle concrete when working with a 15-year-old who is determined to steal cars.

As you move from abstract value statements to specific practices, you will be both establishing client rights (Allen, 1993; Biehal & Sainsbury, 1991) and limiting the uses to which the profession's methodology can be placed. Group processes, for example, may be used to stir up fear and hysteria, which threaten diversity, self-determination, and community life. This use of group strategies is inappropriate because it is inconsistent with social work values. As we know, change strategies and methodology can be used for a variety of ends. Social work practitioners must ensure that their interventions support the values of the profession.

In summary, values can be construed as unproven beliefs that guide and direct the work of a professional. These beliefs are not unique to the profession but are shared with others in the culture. However, they may be operationalized in a distinctive way. What are the value premises with which the social work profession identifies, and how are these premises operationalized? We will consider two that are essential to worker-client partnerships:

- belief in the uniqueness and inherent dignity of the individual
- belief in client self-determination

PARTNERSHIP AS RESPECT FOR INDIVIDUAL DIGNITY AND UNIQUENESS

Social work has always held that each person is a unique individual with an inherent dignity that is to be respected. People are sufficient in themselves and are not to be treated as objects or as means to other ends. Diversity is welcomed. Paul Tillich (1962), a theologian who considered the philosophy of social work, referred to our human uniqueness as our existential nature. William Gordon's concept of social work function (see Exhibit 1–1 in Chapter 1) derives from the same notion. Gordon (1969) has suggested that the social work profession does not attempt to move either the environment

or the person toward some ideal model but rather strives to establish linkages between individuals and their environments, without attempting to limit the diversity of either.

How can the premise that every individual is unique—and has the right to be treated with respect and dignity—be applied in concrete social work situations? Social workers can operationalize this value in practice:

- by treating people as individuals and avoiding classifications
- by encouraging participation in problem solving
- by discovering and making use of client strengths
- by holding people—including ourselves—accountable
- by carefully considering what our communications convey about dignity

Dignity through Individualization

It can be difficult to strike a balance between classification and the responsibility to respond to persons as individuals. Classification—generalizing beyond individuals and organizing phenomena on the basis of common characteristics—is necessary in order to make sense out of a mass of raw data and to build knowledge. However, the pitfall of classifying people is that we may begin to respond to them as representatives of a particular category rather than as individuals. The consequences of this have been documented in a body of sociological literature on labeling and deviance (Becker, 1963; Lemert, 1967; Platt, 1977; Rubington & Weinberg, 1968; Schur, 1973; Simmons, 1969; Tannenbaum, 1951). Labeling, or classification, distorts individual differences. Further, once labeled deviant, individuals may find that they encounter responses determined by the label rather than by any of their particular characteristics. This sets up a self-fulfilling prophecy, in which individuals become what the label says they are (Merton, 1968). Reviewing cohort and other studies, Shireman and Reamer (1986) raise the possibility that the juvenile justice system may unwittingly promote crime by its labeling practices. Hans Toch (1970) states the problem succinctly:

> Playing the classification game in the abstract, as is done in universities, is a joyful, exhilarating experience, harmless and inconsequential. Classifying people in life

is a grim business which channels destinies and determines fate. A person becomes a category, is processed as a category, plays the assigned role, lives up to the implications. Labelled irrational, the person acts crazy; catalogued dangerous, the person becomes dangerous or stays behind bars. (p. 15)

One system of classification that you are likely to encounter in your practice is the American Psychiatric Association's Diagnostic and Statistical Manual of Mental Disorders (DSM) (1994). While some social workers (Jahn, 1986; Kline, Sydnor-Greenberg, Davis, Pincus, & Frances, 1993; Williams, 1981) find DSM useful for social work, we think its use raises fundamental ethical questions, as well as important malpractice considerations (Kirk & Kutchins, 1994; Kutchins & Kirk, 1987). Kirk and Kutchins (1992) have concluded that the third edition of DSM was created largely as a political document to lend credibility to psychiatrists' claim that they are scientific. Comments by psychiatrist Karl Menninger about the first version of DSM are presented in Exhibit 4–3.

There are two fundamental issues here: (1) It is inappropriate to relate to people on the basis of a diagnostic label; and (2) it is problematic for social work to use a typology or classification scheme developed for another profession. DSM may be useful for psychiatry, but social workers are not psychiatrists and have no business using psychiatric terms and labels. We may need to understand DSM in order to communicate with our psychiatric colleagues, but we do not need it as a guide to our own practice.

But isn't classification necessary? Or should we agree with Salomon (1967) that the scientific imperative to order and classify is inconsistent with the humanism of social work? Toch (1970) suggests that "the point of concern rests in any labels that lead to sorting or

disposition" (p. 15). Toch takes the position that labeling is necessary for thinking or theory building but is not particularly helpful in making dispositional decisions about people. Concern arises when decisions about what is going to happen to individuals are determined by a category in which they have been placed. And yet it is precisely at this point that classification appears most useful. Generally, classifications come into play when professionals are attempting to assess or diagnose a situation as a guide for selecting appropriate interventions. This danger is reduced if worker and applicant collaborate to develop an understanding of the problem and a service plan based on that understanding.

The PIE system for classifying adults' problems in social functioning (Karls & Wandrei, 1994a, b) provides a useful tool for social work and avoids the pitfalls of assigning a label and prescribing treatment on the basis of that label. PIE provides a mechanism for ordering information on the role performance—including coping abilities—of adult applicants, as well as environmental resources and supports. When problems are identified, either in the role performance of the individual or in the resource structure of the environment, worker and applicant can design an intervention plan to address those problems and are free to draw from a variety of theoretical perspectives in doing so. PIE helps us to classify problems within an ecosystem framework but does not prescribe that a particular intervention should be from a particular problem classification.

Dignity through Strength

Partnership with clients will reduce our occupational hazard of focusing on client weakness and problems. In Chapters 1 and 3, we noted that the problem-solving process focuses on mobilizing client strengths. Utilizing

---

EXHIBIT 4–3	**Karl Menninger on the DSM**

A committee of our worldly national body has just published a manual containing a full description of all the bewitchments to which all human flesh is err, with the proper names for each one, the minute suborder and subspecies listed and a code number for the computer. The colleagues who prepared this witch's hammer manual are worthy fellows—earnest, honest, hard-working, simplistic; they were taught to believe that these horrible things exist, these things with Greek names and Arabic numerals. And if patients show the stigmata, should they not be given the label and the number? To me this is not only the revival of medieval nonsense and superstition; it is a piece of social immorality.

Source: K. Menninger, *The crime of punishment.* New York: Viking Press (1968), pp. 117–118.

strengths can help improve the quality of life; to individuals with chronic mental illness, this is more important than is symptom reduction (Coursey, Farrell, & Zahniser, 1991). In studying social worker and client perceptions of treatment outcome and client functioning, Anthony Maluccio (1979) found that

> clients presented themselves as pro-active, autonomous human beings who are able to enhance their functioning and competence through the use of counseling service along with the resources operant in themselves and their social networks. Workers, on the other hand, tended to view clients as reactive organisms with continuing problems, weakness, and limited potentialities. (p. 399)

Social work assessment and intervention is best based on strengths brought by applicants and clients to their situations (Rapp, 1998; Saleebey, 1992, 1995; Weick, Rapp, Sullivan, & Kisthard, 1989). We should certainly be aware of weakness and pathology, but our focus will be on how to mobilize and use strengths brought by the applicant, the worker, and the environment to resolve problems in the person-situation interaction. Think about how different your own reactions are when your strengths are discussed, rather than your weaknesses. Most of us are more willing and able to address weaknesses when reminded of the strengths we can bring into play.

Maluccio (1979) concludes that "there is a need to shift the focus in social work education and practice from problems or pathology to strengths, resources, and potentialities in human beings and their environments. If this shift occurs, practitioners would be more likely to view clients as capable of organizing their own lives"

(p. 401). We agree. A focus on strengths is consistent with respect for individual dignity.

Dignity through Participation

Participation in decision making, planning, and action is essential to human dignity. Acknowledging this, the United Nations has included the right to participate in decisions as Article 12 of the Convention on the Rights of the Child (Exhibit 4–4). Weick and Pope (1988) suggest that social work practice needs to regard the client's own knowledge as primary, in order to counteract the traditional emphasis on professional expertise. Recognizing and developing client's wisdom contributes to self-determination, to the establishment of a caring partnership, and to effective service (Biehal, 1993; Itzhaky & York, 1991, 1994). These are keys to good social work practice.

In most dealings with professionals in our culture, the decision-making authority of the client is largely overshadowed by the expertise of the professional; essentially, the client is only able to decide whether to accept the professional's advice. Not so with the social work profession. The expertise of the social worker lies less in the substantive area of knowing what is best for the client and more in the process area of assisting clients to develop alternatives for themselves, make decisions among the alternatives, and implement the decisions. Matthew Dumont (1968) has pointed out the dangers of what he calls a rescue fantasy:

> a "rescue fantasy" in the therapist—a feeling that the therapist is the divinely sent agent to pull tormented souls from the pit of suffering and adversity and put

---

EXHIBIT 4-4   **Children's Right to be Heard**

The Convention on the Rights of the Child was adopted by the United Nations General Assembly on November 20, 1989 and has been ratified by most industrialized nations except for the United States. Three key themes in the convention are the importance of living in families; the right to identity, including cultural identity; and participation. Article 12 extends to children the right to express views about matters affecting them:

1. States Parties* shall assure to the child who is capable of forming his or her own views the right to express those views freely in all matters affecting the child, the view of the child being given due weight in accordance with the age and maturity of the child.

2. For this purpose, the child shall in particular be provided the opportunity to be heard in any judicial and administrative proceedings affecting the child, either directly, or through a representative or an appropriate body, in a manner consistent with the procedural rules of national law.

---

*Nations that have become party to the Convention by ratifying it.

them back on the road to happiness and glory. A major reason this fantasy is so destructive is that it carries the conviction that the patient will be saved only through and by the therapist. When such a conviction is communicated to patients, verbally or otherwise, they have no choice other than to rebel and leave or become even more helpless, dependent, and sick. (p. 6)

Exhibit 4–5 presents a stunning example of nonparticipatory decision making. How might J. J. have been given an opportunity to participate?

You may find it frustrating that you cannot be the fountainhead of all wisdom for the client. A certain humility is necessary to recognize that the client is the chief problem solver. This is not to deny that you play a major part in helping the client through the process and may, at times, serve rather forcefully as the client's agent. Indeed, Oxley (1966) suggests

> that the worker should learn to expect a little bit more than the client expects of himself. Social workers are very well versed in beginning where the client is but perhaps too often tend to stay where the client is. If they instead assume the responsibility for leadership and imparting realistic hope, they may more effectively strengthen a client's ego and help him to reach to achieve his full potential and assume social responsibility. (pp. 432–437)

Schwartz (1961) refers to this as lending a vision. Expecting and encouraging participation will strengthen applicants' and clients' sense of dignity.

Dignity through Accountability

Accountability is an aspect of dignity that is often overlooked. People's dignity is enhanced when they are regarded as responsible for their thoughts, their decisions, and their behaviors. To assume otherwise is to deny their strengths.

However, you need to understand what accountability does not mean. Accountability is not a matter of imposing consequences. In some fields, such as juvenile and criminal justice, the concept of accountability is used to justify harsh punishments. In other disciplines, professional staff may systematically control consequences in an effort to mold behavior. The concept of accountability as the manipulation or imposition of consequences is not appropriate for social work.

On the other hand, you should not attempt to protect applicants or clients from the consequences of their actions. From systems theory, we know that any behavior will result in a reaction from the environment. It is certainly appropriate for the social worker to provide an analysis of the likely consequences of a particular course of action as part of the decision-making process. What is not appropriate is for the worker to attempt to protect the client from these consequences (unless there is a clear legal mandate to do so, a topic to which we'll return in our discussion of self-determination) or to deliberately manipulate the consequences in an attempt to secure some specific behavior.

EXHIBIT 4–5	Nonparticipatory Decision Making

J. J. is a white, 14-year-old ninth grader at a suburban junior high school. His teachers and principal have identified him as an aggressive youth who is failing in the classroom, lacks motivation, and displays poor attendance and social skills. Until this year, J. J. did not have a history of problems and had been able to achieve satisfactory grades. All attempts to promote acquiescence within the school setting, by detention, suspension, tutoring and other means, have failed. The staff has been in frequent contact with the mother, who is verbally supportive but has been unable to impact J. J.'s current behavior. She has refused referral to outside assistance, because a previous experience resulted in loss of her job. At a case conference involving the principal, teacher, attendance clerk, and social worker, the consensus was that, if his behavior continued to decline, J. J. was in danger of failing ninth grade and being summoned before the juvenile court on a truancy petition. The staff was hesitant to adopt drastic action because they believed J. J. could be retracked toward appropriate behavior. He is of above-average intelligence, has athletic prowess, and is personable. Negative sanctions or stigmatization through the court might increase his level of frustration and prove harmful in the long run. Thus, he was temporarily assigned to a small group of delinquent, acting-out students in an attempt to discover whether he would be willing to discuss and work-through various problems in a group of students in similar situations.

Source: MSW student, School of Social Work, University of Minnesota.

How, then, can accountability enhance dignity? The partnership between the applicant or client and the social worker implies that each party has legitimate expectations of the other. When one person's behavior is not consistent with those expectations, that person can be properly held accountable for the behavior. For example, if clients do not follow through on a commitment, the social worker should explore what has happened and establish the firm expectation that they will follow through on commitments in the future.

As an example, let's imagine that the J. J. case in Exhibit 4–5 had been handled differently. The principal and teacher called the attendance, performance, and behavioral problems to the attention of the school social worker, who made contact with J. J. In these circumstances, as we discussed in Chapter 3, J. J. would be a prospect. He would become a client if he accepted services and developed a plan with the worker. Let's assume further, for the sake of illustration, that the worker and J. J. explored the problem areas and that J. J. did agree to participate in the group as a means of working on his problems. But then J. J. did not show up for the group meeting. Under this scenario, dignity through accountability would require the worker to contact J. J., to note that he has not followed through on what he has agreed to do, to discuss what might underlie J. J.'s nonattendance, to discover what J. J. plans to do about it, and to reinforce and maintain the expectation that J. J. will follow through on what he has agreed to do because he has the strength to do so. This concept of accountability does not require imposing consequences on J. J. for failure to attend. Exploring J. J.'s nonattendance means discussing with J. J. what happened; it does not mean asking him why he did not attend. We are not interested in justifications or rationalizations. We are, however, interested in learning what prevented J. J. from doing what he said he was going to do, and what he plans to do about that in the future.

Maintaining accountability will entail developing skills at confrontation (discussed in Chapter 17). Confrontation does not imply a harsh attack. Rather, you gently, but firmly, indicate to people that they have not lived up to their agreements, discuss any relevant circumstances, and reinforce your expectation that they will meet their commitments in the future. Confrontation grows out of your desire to assist people to become

responsible, not out of your anger that they have been irresponsible. Do you experience anger when a client fails to follow through? If so, you need to address this anger, with the assistance of your supervisor, in order to further develop your professional competence. Anger leads to a desire for harsh consequences and rejection; helping people to be responsible calls for a factual discussion of the behavior and a reinforcement of expectations.

Remember that, in a partnership, accountability goes both ways. The client has a right to expect you to be accountable. However, most clients will find it difficult to confront you when you act irresponsibly—when you fail to make telephone calls, to secure information you have promised, to be available when you have agreed to be available, or to follow through on other commitments. Accordingly, it is up to you to acknowledge your own irresponsibility, to apologize for your failures, and to be forthright with your client about what you plan to do. No person—client or worker—is infallible; thus, we will all, at times, fail to do what we have promised. When this happens, we can model a nondefensive way of handling our own fallibility by accepting accountability, apologizing, and moving ahead to correct the problems in our own performance.

Communicating Dignity

The dimensions of dignity—individualization, strength, participation, and accountability—are present in our communications with applicants and clients. Individuals' communications with others—the messages they receive about themselves—largely shape their self-image (Rose, 1962). And, if people feel good about themselves, see themselves as persons of worth, and have a sense of their own strength and capability, they will tend to be happier and more able to deal constructively and appropriately with their environment. Thus, as social workers, we have an obligation to constantly review what we are communicating. Does our language invite participation and enhance dignity? Exhibit 4–6 provides examples of such language. Does our behavior communicate that our applicants and clients are unique individuals to be highly prized? For example, what message is communicated if the worker safeguards an hour and provides a client with a specific appointment time? What message does it send if the worker has neither the

---

EXHIBIT 4-6 Language that Invites Participation

The language we use may encourage or discourage participation by families and persons we serve. Here are several examples, taken from the newsletter of the Family Support Network (Charleston, South Carolina):

OUT WITH THE OLD

Resistant families
Dysfunctional families
Case management
"We offer this"

Staffing a case

Disturbed child
Professionals as providers
"We need a placement for this child; where to next?"

"That's your job"
SED, CCRS, etc.

IN WITH THE NEW

Families with unmet needs
Families that are overwhelmed and underserved
Service coordination
"What do you need?"; a willingness to make it up as we go

Families and professionals creating intervention plans together

Child with emotional disturbance (person-first language)
Families as preferred providers
"Let's develop a community plan with this child and family"

Matching each other's offers
Say the words!

Adapted from: *Network News* Learn to Talk. (Winter, 1995).

---

courtesy nor the good sense to return a telephone call promptly?

And the worker's attitude to privacy—both in how the interview is conducted and in how the material gained from interviews is handled—communicates a powerful message about the esteem in which the interviewees are held. Emily Jean McFadden (1992) concludes that respecting the dignity of the child requires us to refrain from therapeutic interventions that invade privacy unless we have the child's permission. When attempting to operationalize the value of individual dignity, you may find it useful to repeatedly inquire, "What does this action on my part communicate to the client about my perception of her?"

PARTNERSHIP AND SELF-DETERMINATION

Self-determination implies permitting individuals to make decisions for themselves. Most of the time, applicants and clients will make decisions that are responsible—that is, consistent with the welfare of the community. Social workers generally try to balance client self-determination with responsibility to the total community (Ewalt & Mokuau, 1995). In a historical review, Freedberg (1989) suggests that social workers confront a

contradiction in their roles as client advocates and as agents of a society in which clients are disenfranchised. Nevertheless, barring some clear-cut indication of danger to others, the social worker in day-to-day contacts with clients will generally attempt to maximize opportunities for client self-determination. Thinking of clients as your customers—the consumers of social services—may enhance client choice and self-determination (Moore & Kelly, 1996; Tower, 1994).

Self-Determination as Alternatives

Self-determination implies making choices. There can be no self-determination without alternatives. Self-determination may be reduced by time limitations that preclude an adequate search for alternatives, by mental incapacity of the client (Abramson, 1988), and by a divergence of interests between the client and agency. Much of your activity with applicants and clients will involve searching for alternatives, in order to expand the opportunities for self-determination. You will help the person to develop new alternatives and resources within the environment or to develop new ways of responding to environmental demands. Expanding the range of alternatives available to clients may be difficult, in part because of entrenched institutional practices that limit client choice.

Self-determination is constrained—if not eliminated—when people believe there is nothing they can do to influence events. In that case, the task of the worker is to help the applicant or client to overcome this learned helplessness and to begin to exercise choice. Self-determination may also be increased by efforts to increase opportunities in the environment—both by removing blockages within the environment and by helping individuals to remove blockages within themselves that limit their abilities to utilize environmental opportunities. Internal blockages may include cognitive structures that prohibit the applicant or client from considering other alternatives—including alternative ways to think and behave—and patterned emotional responses to the social environment. People whose range of responses to their environment is limited by their own stereotyped and patterned cognitions, feelings, and behavior are as impoverished in terms of self-determination as are clients whose environment provides scant opportunities.

Self-Determination and Client Values

Both human dignity and self-determination imply respect for a great diversity of applicant and client value systems. However, that principle can be difficult to implement. For example, if we believe in the self-determination of all people, what do we do when a client coerces another person or seriously interferes with the rights of a vulnerable individual? What do we do with values—sometimes cultural beliefs—that call for the subordination of women to men, for genital mutilation of girls, for severe corporal punishment of children, for the denial of services to men, for ethnic cleansing, or for distrust of persons who are different? Does the principle of client self-determination require the social worker to support such value orientations among cultural groups in which they are dominant? It is our position that we cannot support client behavior that results in damage to another individual or group even if that behavior is based on client or cultural values.

Charles Levy (1972) identifies a number of areas in which social workers favoring planned change have value conflicts with applicants. There may be times when your conception of how to operationalize human dignity

and client self-determination is inconsistent with value orientations held by applicants. Such differences, when they arise, become a matter for discussion and negotiation between you and the applicant. The differences must be clarified and a workable resolution achieved before intervention efforts begin.

Applicant values may also serve as a limit to self-determination. For instance, a sense of collective responsibility to a community may provide such a limit (Ewalt & Mokuau, 1995). Dale Hardman (1975) suggests that values themselves become an appropriate target for change when they conflict with the welfare of others or with clients' ability to achieve the agreed-upon goals. When Hardman was working with a parolee whose values regarding sexual activity were likely to lead to illegal behavior and to damage the dignity and feelings of another, his unexamined belief in the right to self-determination at first left him uneasy but essentially uninvolved. However, when he realized that the person being damaged could be his daughter, the rights of the other suddenly became critical. Hardman had to confront not just the difference between his own value system and the respondent's but his responsibility, as a professional, to be concerned with the rights of all people. Another example is spouse abuse, which seems to be related to the value orientation that the proper role of a wife is subservience to the husband. Communities who still believe that to spare the rod spoils the child also pose a challenge to social workers.

Social work does not mean forcing people to change. The principle of self-determination suggests that, where appropriate, worker and client should pursue three avenues of inquiry:

- consideration of how values may restrict progress toward the objectives desired by the applicant
- consideration of possible alternatives and their consequences for achieving the objectives
- consideration of the rights and needs of others

Does the principle of self-determination imply that the worker puts the total responsibility of decision making on the applicant, without offering alternatives or discussing the results of particular choices? Not at all. Just as the extreme of making decisions for applicants is to be avoided, so is the extreme of never sharing a viewpoint. Withholding the benefit of your judgment may leave applicants and clients unaware of alternatives that would be relevant to their own decision making. Over 50 years ago, Charlotte Towle (1945/1965) noted, "The social worker's devotion to the idea that every individual has a right to be self-determining does not rule out valid concern with directing people's attention to the most desirable alternative" (p. 26). You have an obligation to share your own thinking—and perhaps your own experiences—with clients and applicants. However, you must take care to present your input as information to be considered, rather than as an edict to be followed. Schwartz (1961) offers some helpful suggestions. In contributing data—facts, ideas, and value concepts—you should inform the applicant that what you are offering is only part of the total available social experience. You must also clearly relate the data to the purpose of your work with the applicant. Opinions should be clearly labeled as such and not represented as facts. Successful practitioners are able to share knowledge and thinking without imposing a judgment, thereby allowing others to freely accept or reject their views.

Such worker input must be distinguished from self-disclosure. Feminist counselors (Bricker-Jenkins, 1991; Collins, 1986; Rosewater & Walker, 1985; Russell, 1989) and others believe that disclosing their personal life experiences is an important tool for strengthening relationship and communication and facilitating client progress toward counseling goals. We will be considering self-disclosure in Chapter 12. In the present context, we suggest relatively focused worker input directed toward assisting applicants and clients to perceive alternatives relating to the problem to be addressed, possible objectives, and intervention plans. Whenever possible, worker input will be supportive of clients' perceptions and wants.

Worker Self-Determination

Some workers confuse applicant and client self-determination with worker self-determination. Social workers agree to limit their own self-determination in the interest of others when they take on professional responsibility. Social work codes of ethics, including those of the National Association of Social Workers (U.S.) and the Canadian Association of Social Workers, clearly limit worker self-determination. According to those codes, you must practice within the knowledge and skill base of the profession, and you must give priority to serving your clients. You are called to limit your own self-determination in the other's behalf—for example, if your communication style or dress style arouses the antagonism of applicants and clients. In Exhibit 4–7, Alice is working as a community organizer. Does she have an obligation to set aside her own goals of changing the system and work with people who want to be successful within the system as it exists?

LEGAL AUTHORITY AND SELF-DETERMINATION

Fields of practice in which you possess legal authority to coerce respondents may challenge your commitment to self-determination. Authority is typically mandated, on different grounds, for two types of respondents:

1. To protect individuals perceived as being vulnerable because of their dependent status; such respondents include dependent children, persons with developmental disabilities, and infirm older people.

EXHIBIT 4-7	Worker Values and Frustration

In this excerpt, Alice is a social worker functioning as a community organizer. I remarked that it certainly must be satisfying to organize and be part of such an event. I was surprised when Alice shook her head slowly and said in a much more sombre tone of voice, "No, 99% of the time there is very little glamour to organizing." I asked her to explain further, and she went on to say that it is hard, hard work and that one of the most discouraging things for her to realize is that oftentimes the people you are organizing aren't necessarily looking for a change in the system, but rather to become a part of that system. Usually that means playing the same games that those in power play. She talked further about the frustration she deals with constantly. I, too, began to feel that organizing was not the glamorous, romantic job I had pictured it to be.

Source: BSW student.

2. To force rehabilitation for those who have violated the norms of society; such respondents include juvenile and adult offenders, persons with chemical dependency problems, and individuals with a mental illness.

Use of Authority to Protect

It is important to distinguish between the protective and helping functions of the social worker (Kelly, 1994; Murdach, 1996; Reid & Epstein, 1977). The practitioner must also make sure that the respondent understands this distinction. If, as we have argued (Chapter 2), available knowledge should direct our interventions and our knowledge base confirms that dependent children, persons with developmental disability, and frail older individuals may be victimized and may harm themselves, then responsible action requires some limitations on self-determination in the interest of providing protection. However, we still have a responsibility to develop as many practical alternatives as possible for decision making, within the limits necessary to protect the respondent.

For example, children who must be removed from their homes because of neglect or abuse can be involved in decision making regarding the alternative living arrangements. As already noted, the United Nations Convention on the Rights of Children provides children with the right to express views on matters affecting them (Exhibit 4–4). Involving children in decision making may reveal resources—such as relatives and neighbors—previously unknown to the social worker. Exhibit 4–8

provides an illustration; Arthur was placed with the Jelnicks, a family he suggested.

Likewise, our knowledge may indicate that an older person who is physically ill, may no longer be able to live alone at home, despite a wish to do so. Although the need for protection limits self-determination, you may well be able to engage the respondent in selection of the alternative living arrangement. Nicholson and Matross (1989) suggest ways in which social workers can enhance self-determination in persons—such as those with senile dementia and persons with advanced AIDS—who live beyond their ability to make autonomous decisions. One possibility is to use durable powers of attorney, living wills, and prerecorded oral communications, by means of which individuals can give instructions regarding their care after their decision-making ability has been impaired by disease.

When coercion is used to protect a respondent, you must be clear about the knowledge that justifies use of authority and about the source and extent of the authority. You must also communicate these matters clearly to the respondent. Use of authority can lead to abuse of power (Szasz, 1994) by social workers, especially if they are not sensitive to the possible consequences of their actions (Diorio, 1992). Because of that risk, respondents are entitled to request an appeal and review of your decisions. The involvement of courts or guardians (Downes, 1992) independent of you is an appropriate check against abuses. As individuals and as a profession, we have an obligation to continually reassess whether coercive authority is really necessary to protect the

---

| **EXHIBIT 4-8** | **Finding a Foster Home for Arthur** |

As a new probation officer, I had just been assigned to Arthur, a 16½-year-old inmate of the State Training School with a record of truancy and running away from home. He was ready for release to foster care, but no placement had been found. When I met Arthur, I asked him if he had any ideas—any relatives or other persons whom we might talk with about a possible placement. He seemed a bit hesitant, but said there was this neighbor he had lived with and worked for briefly during previous summers. I explored this as much as I could; Arthur believed he got along well with the neighbor but didn't have an opinion as to whether the couple would be interested in letting him live with them. After some further discussion, he agreed that the matter could at least be

looked into. Arthur agreed to write a letter that day indicating that I would be in touch with them to discuss his parole planning.

I waited about a week and then called the Jelnecks; Mrs. Jelneck indicated that they had received a letter from Arthur and agreed to let me come out and talk with her and her husband about parole planning.

We talked at length about their past contact with Arthur which, by and large, they perceived as positive; I indicated that we did not believe it would be appropriate for Arthur to return home and that he agreed with this; I wondered if they would be in a position to consider letting Arthur live with them. They agreed to consider the possibility.

respondent or is being used unnecessarily to impose a particular standard.

Use of Authority to Force Participation in Service Programs

The use of authority to force rehabilitation efforts on respondents creates a serious dilemma for the profession. There are at least two distinct ways in which this dilemma might be resolved: (1) by attempts to integrate the authority and service roles and, within the limitations imposed by the setting, to expand opportunities for self-determination; and (2) by the withdrawal of social work from coercive efforts to rehabilitate.

Usually, social workers attempt to integrate their authority and service functions (Behroozi, 1992; Hardman, 1960; Hatcher, 1978; Ivanoff, Blythe, & Tripodi, 1994; Klockars, 1972; Overton, 1965; Rooney, 1992). The presence of legal authority leaves some areas available for the exercise of self-determination. A probation officer enforces the legal requirement that the probationer must report; this is not a matter for self-determination. But the sensitive probation officer can allow for considerable self-determination in the frequency of reporting, the length of the interviews, the time of reporting, and the content to be discussed during the interviews. Respondents in correctional settings can be extended self-determination in how they use workers.

In an analysis of juvenile justice policy, and the concept of just deserts, Shireman and Reamer (1986) conclude that opportunities exist for social workers to work with respondents within rehabilitative programs. Ron Rooney (1988, 1992) has developed a conceptual framework for social work practice that calls for an effort to convert the respondent to a client, through the negotiation of a mutually acceptable service plan. Rooney suggests that, through creative social work practice, many persons who start seeing a worker as respondents may find an area in which they can voluntarily agree to work and thus may become clients. At the very least, respondents have the option of determining whether they are going to do anything more than the legal minimum, as well as the option of ignoring the requirements of the authority and accepting the consequences.

Some respondents will be unwilling to negotiate a service plan and will continue to see you only because they are under external coercion to do so. In this situation, as mentioned in Chapter 3, we might appropriately regard the state, through its formal institutions (courts, hospitals, prisons, and so forth), as our client. Bradley Googins and Bruce Davidson (1993) suggest that the organization may be the client for social workers practicing in employee assistance programs—a setting in which coercion is more subtle than in corrections. The social worker's authority to intervene in these settings derives from a contract with the organization or with the state; the goals of service are to reduce behavior that, collectively, we find undesirable. Thus, the person who meets with the social worker is the target of change. Some practitioners feel uncomfortable with the notion of the state as client, because it explicitly acknowledges the social control function of the profession. In our view, however, a straightforward identification of the relationships between the worker, the state, and the respondent will make it easier to forthrightly address the conditions under which you, as a representative of the state, can forcibly intervene in the life of the respondent. What are the limits of your power? What are the rights and obligations of the respondent?

As already noted, social work could uphold its value of self-determination by withdrawing from coercive services (Miller, 1968). This would imply the development of structures such that populations who are presently being subjected to forced rehabilitation could be provided with social services on a voluntary basis. In Exhibit 4–9, Gerald O'Connor offers an insightful discussion of self-determination in prisons.

Peter Rayner (1986) contrasts two scenarios for probation work. In one scenario, derived from the model of coerced treatment, probation becomes more and more repressive; social work has relatively little involvement, except to provide an ideological justification for repression. In the second scenario, the probation officer works in partnership with offenders; probation terms are mutually negotiated. Much of the change effort is directed toward developing social support networks and mobilizing community resources to meet needs and wants identified by the offender.

Respondents' willingness to work in partnership with social workers—and thus to become clients, in the strict sense—may hinge largely on the type of services offered and the manner in which they are made available. Many offenders are likely to enter into agreements with a social worker in order to resolve problems

---

EXHIBIT 4-9 **Self-Determination in Prison**

The principle of self-determination, the freedom to choose one's own destiny is based on an assumption of individual dignity . . . The recognition of people's right to free choice guarantees that they may choose to run their life as they see fit. This choice may run counter to society's welfare and even their own, yet essentially it is their choice and their prerogative. Society may censure, but it cannot take from them the right; nor should society strip them of personal dignity by a censure. The criminal then has a right to say ''crime is my choice and I am willing to pay the price. If you send me to prison, I am paying my debt to society and refuse to submit to your attempts to reform me.'' The principle of self-determination makes it incumbent upon society to honor such a plea. There are large numbers of inmates in correctional institutions who recognize a need for rehabilitation and are willing to become involved in programs for that end. An inmate's voluntary recognition of a need for assistance does not, in turn, give officials a free reign in outlining the inmate's rehabilitation program. It is reasonable that the offender have input into the definition of the offender's own problem and have this included in the official assessment. The inmate should have the opportunity to say what type of program would be of assistance and who should provide the services. Further, it seems appropriate that the inmates have a right, in part, to determine the conditions under which the services are delivered.

Source: G. O'Connor, Toward a new policy in adult corrections. *Social Service Review, 46*(4), 582 (1972).

---

that they are experiencing in their personal lives. This is also true for children (Silverman, 1977) and individuals with chronic mental illness (Coursey, Farrell, & Zahniser, 1991).

This issue will be debated for some time. Our inclination is to begin challenging the appropriateness of social work activity in coerced rehabilitative settings and to develop structures, policies, and programs that would permit a more voluntary association between respondents and social workers. Such efforts are consistent with the principle of client self-determination. This does not, of course, exempt persons who are found guilty of violating laws from being negatively sanctioned or punished by society. At the same time, we have a professional obligation to evaluate the penalties employed. Are they fair and humane? Do we rely too much on high-cost penalties such as jail and prison, which sap resources that might otherwise be available for social welfare and educational services? Is the effect of the penalties restorative and healing or alienating and divisive (Galaway, 1981; Galaway & Hudson, 1996; Van Ness & Strong, 1997; Zehr, 1990)? And, most importantly, are we using the criminal law where more informal sanctions might be at least as effective?

CHAPTER SUMMARY

In this chapter, we have developed the notion of worker-client partnership, which will recur frequently as we elaborate our model of social work practice. Partnership embodies two major social work values—respecting the uniqueness of each individual and encouraging client self-determination. The key ideas about partnership are:

1. The social worker and the client negotiate all important decisions about the problem to be solved, the objectives to be sought, and the service plan implemented to reach those objectives.

2. The social worker and the client bring different but equally important resources to the problem-solving work.

3. For the purposes of partnership, social workers must define their professional identity in terms of facilitating a problem-solving process and securing client participation. Social workers are not experts who know what is best for their clients.

4. Professional values are preferences; they cannot be proven true. The values of social work are adapted from the overall culture. Two fundamental values of social work practice are the innate dignity of the individual and the importance of self-determination.

In order to respect the dignity of the individual, we must:

1. Respond to people as individuals and avoid classification by means of diagnostic labels.
2. Focus on strengths in the problem-solving process.
3. Provide for maximum client participation.
4. Maintain joint accountability with the client.
5. Take care to communicate respect in all of our behaviors.

Five points have been made about self-determination:

1. Self-determination commits us and our clients to a quest for alternatives. Without alternatives, there is no opportunity to make decisions and no opportunity to engage in self-determination.

2. We are responsible for increasing applicants' and clients' opportunities for decision making. We are not experts who know what is substantively best for people and consequently we should avoid making decisions for applicants. Our skills are in guiding a process of joint decision making.

3. We have an obligation to offer our own viewpoints and suggestions to applicants and clients. We must be careful to offer our ideas as input to be considered, and not as an edict or the right answer.

4. Efforts to modify client values are consistent with the concept of self-determination if the values interfere with efforts to attain client objectives or with the welfare of others and if the client concurs with efforts to produce a change of values.

5. Client self-determination must be distinguished from worker self-determination. When we assume professional responsibility, we sharply limit our own self-determination. We accept the responsibility of behaving in ways that best meet the interests of applicants and clients and serve to increase their opportunities.

The concept of client self-determination is difficult to apply in work with respondents—individuals who interact with social workers unwillingly, under the authority of coercive agencies; respondents may be receiving protective services because of their perceived vulnerability and dependency or may be sub-mitting to rehabilitation services to address their socially proscribed behavior. To honor the principle of client self-determination in work with respondents, social workers must:

1. Recognize the potential for abuse of their power.
2. Clearly explain the limits on respondent choice and the opportunities that remain.
3. Identify and use as many opportunities for respondent choice as the situation allows.
4. Whenever possible, work within the framework of what the respondent wants.
5. Recognize the importance of an appeal or review process for respondents who are unhappy with workers' decisions.

A LOOK FORWARD

In the next chapter, we will examine three sources of authority for your practice—your client, your profession, and your agency—and consider possible conflicts among them. In Chapter 6, we will look at the ethics of social work practice, as well as some of the legal conflicts and dilemmas that you may encounter. In Chapter 7, we consider the concept of relationship; that discussion complements the material on partnership in the present chapter.

In Reading 4-1, Susan Steiger Tebb presents a client-focused approach to recording that puts the value of self-determination into practice. In this approach, the client becomes your partner in developing the written record of your work together.

READING 4-1 *The Record of Change: Client-Focused Recording**

Susan Steiger Tebb

Social work recording has changed over time in response to concerns about cost-effectiveness and worker accountability and to changes in practice, in the role of the social worker, in agency services, and in technology—from the advent of the typewriter to the use of the computer and Internet (Kagle, 1995). The effort to develop a record that reflects accountability and changing services and technologies has sacrificed a basic value of social work—client self-determination (Tebb, 1991a).

Recording often lacks relevance to social work practice, because popular recording methods do not recognize documentation as a tool that can reflect the thinking and responsibility of both the social worker

---

*An original reading prepared for this edition.

and client (Monnickendam, Yaniv, & Geve, 1994; Tebb, 1991a). A record is a data vessel of client history. The file, however, can provide very little on plans for client change; it does not usually present a clear picture of the relationship between the social worker and client, nor does it assist practitioners in their reflection, planning, and thinking. Records are often written after the important work between client and worker is done (Gelman, 1992).

"It is not the recording, as a wise case worker once said, which is difficult; it is the thinking which precedes it. If we can think clearly about a client's needs, his circumstances, and the treatment proposed, the record will shape itself easily and simply" (Hamilton, 1946, p. 207). Recording is used traditionally as an administrative aid (an agency-based file). A client-focused record, however, furthers client change and improves practice. The thesis of this article is that client involvement in record writing can strengthen the role of self-determination in social work practice.

GROUNDWORK FOR RECORD CHANGE

Background

Weed's (1969) problem-oriented record was introduced in the late 1960s and offered the medical field a way of reforming unwieldy and ineffective medical records. This model provided a very organized and simple framework for recording. The problem-oriented record (POR) consists of four segments: (1) a data base that gives both demographic and medical patient information; (2) a problem list gleaned from the data base; (3) strategies to solve each problem; and (4) ongoing plans for each problem. The acronym SOAP (subjective data, objective data, assessment of the subjective and objective data, and plan) is the outline for this recording model. This model was soon adapted to social work recording (Beinecke, 1984; Hartman & Wickey, 1978; Johnson, 1978; Kagle, 1984, 1991; Kane, 1974; Wilczynski, 1981). The social worker uses subjective information to decide which problem(s) to address; the problem-oriented medical record is often criticized for its subjectivity (Tebb, 1991a).

Another criticism of the problem-oriented record is that it does not address the interrelationship of client problems. Because problems are disconnected from clients, practitioners are able to view clients as objects,

instead of knowledgeable resources and partners in the change process. The client's problems or weaknesses are observed, rather than the client's strengths, and these problems are regarded as outside the client's control (Tebb, 1991a). The social worker selects the problem, gathers the objective and subjective information, makes an assessment, and develops a plan. The client is not expected to play an active part in this process. If what clients say about themselves is described as subjective and what social workers say is objective, the implication is that client information is only in the client's mind, whereas the practitioner's information is factual and verifiable. This method of recording places the social worker outside the client's situation; the social worker's role is then to observe and manipulate the client's situation.

Using the POR method, the professional accepts total responsibility for determining a plan for change and resolution of the problem. This method of recording violates the value of client self-determination. The emphasis of the POR is on biomedical rather than psychosocial factors and does not show the ongoing process or the complexity of services provided through the client-worker relationship. Although described as objective, the social worker's findings are actually observations. Addressing this concern, Donnelly and Brauner (1990) suggest that client data be described as the story and practitioner data as observations, but they maintain that, no matter what words are substituted, the mantra of subjective, objective, assessment, and plan will continue to be used, and a more radical solution needs to be developed. They note that social workers are only observers and can only understand clients through interaction and collaboration.

Client Involvement

The U.S. Privacy Act of 1974 provided clients with access to their files. In our litigious society, one of the best protections from possible liability is to collaborate with the client in writing the file (Gelman, 1992; Kagle, 1995). Several social workers (Badding, 1989; Doel & Lawson, 1986; Gelman, 1992; Houghkirk, 1977; Kagle, 1991, 1993, 1995; McDevitt, 1994; Monnickendam, Yaniv, & Geve, 1994; Schrier, 1980; Wilczynski, 1981) have involved the client in the recording process as part of the social work intervention and report that the experience is positive for all. Further, a record written together is less likely to be denied as evidence when subpoenaed by a court. Client involvement adds to the quality of the record.

Badding (1989) reports on a study to determine whether client involvement in the recording process had potential for improving practice and the client's ability to change. Practitioners used their judgments and included the client's input in the file, along with their own assessment; the record was then shared with the client. The findings indicated that this procedure increased client autonomy and encouraged the client to take responsibility for his or her actions and changes. This process helped the client express feelings more openly and enhanced communication between the social worker and client. It enabled both to correct any inaccuracies in their perceptions of the work. According to Goldstein (1988), using a recording process that highlights capability and potential "encourages clients to discover the richness of choice and the cornucopia of opportunity" (pp. 16–17). In collaboration with the client, the worker can use recording to construct an understanding of the situation and begin to look at ways to change it. Clients who share in recording tend to remember their plans better than those who do not (Badding, 1989).

Gelman's (1992) work with adolescents reinforced Badding's (1989) findings. Client changes were observed as a result of active client involvement in the recording process. While access to their file was important, actual involvement in the creation and writing of the file provided adolescents with a sense of investment in their change process (Gelman, 1992). Client participation also resulted in records that were better written and organized, shorter, more factual, and easier to read and use.

Child welfare agencies now require practitioners to involve families in developing service plans (McDevitt, 1994); what better way than to record together? In this approach, files are open for review by clients, and planning is conducted with client participation. Client access to records can lead to improvement in the quality of recording, and recording together tends to empower clients. The Family Service Association of America found that client reading of the file should be seen as part of the counseling process (Kagle, 1991). At the very least, clients should be given access to information requested by others, with the opportunity to amend or correct it and comment. Informed consent implies that the client should know what records say before authorizing their

release to others. Writing the record together is a natural way to reassure clients regarding the content of their file, and also eliminates the need to amend or correct. In addition, access to files can promote client-worker communication and trust.

Client Satisfaction

Higher levels of client satisfaction with the social work relationship and with outcomes were reported when the client was actively involved in the creation of the record (Gelman, 1992). Wilczynski (1981) found that the client's active involvement in the change process is as therapeutic as the achievement of a successful outcome. Recording enables the social worker to communicate the process of change and growth. By recording together, the worker and client can look critically at the meanings of this process.

CLIENT-FOCUSED RECORDING MODEL

The client-focused recording method has evolved out of dissatisfaction with SOAP, the problem-oriented medical record, which is incompatible with social work values (Goldstein, 1988; Weick, 1983, 1987). At the core of social work process is change, which is the norm in any intervention. Questions about change were used in generating a client-focused recording model that recognizes clients as knowledgeable participants in the social work process (Tebb, 1991a). The questions were (Weick, 1987):

1. How might such change occur?
2. What factors seem to contribute to change?
3. What forces constitute resistance to change?
4. How can change be fostered?

By answering these questions, the client and the social worker address the initial change process.

A replacement for the problem-oriented medical record should retain the strengths of the POR model: organization, simplicity, and ability to be remembered. One client-focused alternative to SOAP is known as CREW. The acronym is apt: A crew (the word is derived from the French verb *creistre*, to grow, according to *Webster's Ninth New Collegiate Dictionary* 1991) is a group of people banded together to work toward a goal. In using this acronym as a guide in recording, the following questions are asked (Tebb, 1991a):

Contributors: What factors contribute to the need for change?

Restraints: What factors constitute restraints or barriers to change?

Enablers: What factors seem to be enabling or contributing to change?

Ways: How can change be fostered?

Client-focused recording examines worker and client perceptions of the immediate situation; this method is not solely oriented toward the problems. Collaboration between worker and client provides the client with the opportunity to make choices, take responsibility, and practice self-determination (Badding, 1989). If the client is involved in the recording process, meanings can be examined, and ongoing review of the actual process and the overall plans for change is possible, with informed determination of the next steps. In client-focused recording, responsibility for change no longer rests exclusively with the professional, but is shared by the social worker and the client; the client is acknowledged as a knowledge source. Asking the CREW questions facilitates the active involvement of the client in the recording process.

Exhibit 4–10 summarizes the differences between the CREW and SOAP approaches.

Exhibit 4–11 is an example of a CREW record. It concerns Jane, who has recently reunited with her husband. Her husband has a history of alcoholism but has regained sobriety; Jane's intention is to make the marriage work. By addressing the CREW together, Jane and I were able to identify, evaluate, and assess Jane's concerns and establish ways to use the available resources to help her move on with her current marriage. As we wrote the record together, Jane had the opportunity to recall childhood memories of abuse and was convinced of the importance of continuing work on her parenting skills. The process of collaborative writing reassured Jane that I had heard her point of view.

The answers to the four CREW questions can be incorporated into any agency recording format. McDevitt (1994) suggests a flexible format consisting of three parts:

1. A structured set of summary sheets with demographic information on health, family, schooling, and goals.

EXHIBIT 4-10	Comparison of Client-Focused and Problem-Oriented Recording	
	CREW (client-focused record)	SOAP (problem-oriented medical record)
View of problem, need for change	1. Client defines the need for change and shares it with the professional. 2. Client sees self as an active player in the problem and need for change.	1. Professional defines the problem through careful observation. 2. Problem externally caused and separate from client.
Client-professional relationship	1. Professional relies on client's personal knowledge. 2. Professional supports client with expert knowledge as a consultant and enabler for change. 3. Professional's knowledge and relationship strengthen client's ability for change.	1. Client reliant on professional's expert knowledge. 2. Client is passive; professional is the leader and expert. 3. Specialized expert knowledge separates professional from client.
Nature/process of change	1. Client with the support of the professional is the change agent. 2. Client, in partnership with the professional, defines personal meaning of problem and change. 3. Client designs plans for change with professional input. 4. Change is a naturally occurring process directed by client with support of professional.	1. Professional is the change agent. 2. Professional is given power to create client's meaning of problem and change. 3. Change is initiated by the professional and client follows professional's plans.

Adapted from: S. Tebb, Client-focused recording: Linking theory and practice. *Families in Society, 72*(7), 429 (1991).

EXHIBIT 4-11 **A Crew Recording Written with Jane**

CONTRIBUTORS

Remarried followed by two years of struggling. Her present husband, an alcoholic, maintained sobriety for the first year of marriage. He relapsed and Jane left him for six months. Able to renew his sobriety during the six month separation, the couple are now back together and Jane has sought out help, wanting the marriage to have a chance.

RESTRAINTS

Jane is 28 years old, third youngest of seven children from a self-described very violent and turbulent childhood. Her father, an alcoholic, was victim along with the children to a wife and mother who physically, mentally and sexually abused the family. Father often retreated to the basement to avoid his wife's abuse. Jane felt safe with her two older brothers and looked to her older sisters as ``mom.'' She was not particularly attached to her younger two siblings; they were ``just there.''

There were many rules in her home. One rule was you could not be sick. She remembers at four years of age getting sick to her stomach, vomiting, and being beaten by her mother for throwing up. She also had to clean up after herself.

Her parents divorced when she was 11 years old and the children resided with their mother. After the divorce her mother began to speak of suicide. Social Service was involved and there were social workers coming into the home often, sometimes placing the children for short periods of time in foster care.

One day when Jane was in junior high she came home to blood all over the house. Her mother had slit her wrists. At this point the children were either placed with her father and his new wife or with an aunt. Jane stayed with her father for nine months and then was returned to her mother's. It was at this time that the sexual abuse began. The mother would fondle her and bathe with her. If Jane locked the bathroom and

refused to allow her mother in, the mother would beat her when she came out. Jane was also sexually abused by boarders whom her mother took in to help pay the rent. Her siblings were aware of what was happening but for their own self preservation they withdrew. She tried to tell people what was happening to her but they did not believe her. She began to overeat and became involved with drugs and alcohol at 15 years of age. Following high school at 19 she became pregnant and married the father of her child. He had a history of prison. She divorced him when she was 24 and the child custody battle over the terms is still waging.

ENABLERS

There were two significant people in Jane's life who showed her kindness, a teacher and a neighbor. Through all the turmoil at home she was able to finish high school. She quit drinking and abusing drugs at the time of the divorce and has been able to stay sober for over five years, through the current marriage's six month separation and her husband's misuse of alcohol. She is not an abusive mother and continues to fight for the custody of her child. She believes her health, sobriety and ability to parent are due in part to help she received from support groups and an occasional social worker.

WAYS

Jane acknowledges that couple counseling would probably be best but she knows she cannot make her husband participate. She is the one wanting the help and she is the one who will participate in counseling. She asked the social worker to invite her husband and also to offer to meet individually with him. Jane will continue to attend a sobriety support group and also to participate in a parenting support group. She finds both groups a source of emotional and social help to her. She credits the parenting group with helping her to learn to parent.

---

2. Ongoing service plans and assessments with shared client-worker recording.
3. Comprehensive closing and/or transfer summary.

The CREW record in Exhibit 4–12 was prepared with Mabel, who is the full-time caretaker for her husband, a person with Alzheimer's disease. The ability to establish control and time for herself added sparkle

to Mabel's eyes. She began attending the hospital's caregiver support group and actively encouraged other caregivers to use respite services and reconnect with friends. Reading the file validated for Mabel that she needed to begin to consider herself and her needs and not to internalize them. Our sharing in the writing also provided me with examples of what George was like before he became ill. By working with the

EXHIBIT 4-12	A Crew Recording Written with Mabel

Mabel participated in the recording process by reading the record at the beginning of each of our sessions.

CONTRIBUTORS

Using an assessment tool together Mabel shared with me things that she only dreamed about doing since she had become a full-time caregiver to her husband, George. I learned that she missed a quilting group; she was a founding member and they had been meeting over twenty years. She also had not attended church nor exercised on a regular basis for over three years.

RESTRAINTS

Concerned about Mabel's appearance the nurse in George's outpatient clinic asked that I see Mabel. George's diagnosis of Alzheimer's disease had confined her to her home and she had no means of socializing or having regular contact with others. Mabel was tired, listless and her doctor was concerned about her health and whether she would be able to continue providing round the clock care to George who needed constant watching because he was now wandering.

ENABLERS

Mabel willingly sat with me and completed the assessment tool. It offered Mabel an opportunity to share her loneliness and her doctor's concerns. It offered me a better understanding of the restraints Mabel was experiencing in her caregiving role.

WAYS

Keeping in mind Mabel's dreams we set about to make some changes in her caregiving situation. Mabel was supported to approach her minister and ask him to announce in church her need for volunteers to sit with her husband while she attended church. She would bring George to church with her if he was feeling well and a church volunteer would sit with him in an empty classroom while she attended early church. If it was not a good day the volunteer would come to her home. At my suggestion Mabel hired a neighbor high school boy to come over to her home each afternoon and sit with George while she went out walking. After much persuasion on my part and feeling renewed due to regular exercise and social contract, Mabel agreed to try the local Red Cross respite service. The respite worker came to her home once a week to be with George while Mabel attended her quilting group.

four CREW questions, we were able to make plans that could bring Mabel some enjoyment and hope again.

CONCLUSION

Client-focused recording (CREW) provides a method for social worker and client to critically address and examine the meanings that are made and those that need to be made. This recording process reflects the continuous growth of meaning constructed by the client and worker in their collaborative relationship. If social workers understand the process of continuous change, they will be able to facilitate the change procedure in the best interests of their clients.

It would behoove our profession to begin, once again, to learn about, discuss, and examine social work recording. Besides serving the needs of the agency, recording can also serve the needs of clients. Collaborative recording, as an integral part of the social work process, emphasizes the importance of values and self-determination. In doing so, client-focused recording becomes an important bridge connecting social work values with social work practice. Records that reflect the mutuality of the client-worker relationship provide meaningful knowledge, and agency personnel can use the recording process to extend every possible choice to the client. As a result, social work values are expressed in action.

LEARNING EXERCISES

1. If you are a student in the United States, contact one of your U.S. Senators to learn her views about ratifying the United Nations Convention on the Rights of the Child. We suggest either writing to your Senator or telephoning a staff person in the Senator's local office. You will need to wait patiently for a response. Once you get a response, decide whether you agree with the Senator's position. What are the reasons for your conclusion?

2. If you are a Canadian student, the Convention has the force of law in your province because it has been ratified by Parliament. Contact one of your local child welfare workers or supervisors to learn how he applies Article 12 (reprinted as Exhibit 4–4). Does the worker or supervisor know about this Article and his or her obligations under it?

3. Contact both the National Association of Social Workers (U.S.) and the Canadian Association of Social Workers using the information in Exhibit 5–2 and obtain their codes of ethics. In what ways do these codes create an ethical duty on your part to work in partnership with your clients?

4. Consider this excerpt from a letter of reference written on behalf of an applicant for admission to a school of social work:

> His main weakness is his tendency to prefer to believe the positive in clients, and he may therefore minimize pathology. With increased formal training in the social work program, I would anticipate significant improvement in this area.

Do you agree with the referee that a preference to believe the positive about applicants and clients is a weakness to be corrected by social work education? What are the reasons for your views?

5. Take a few minutes to study Reading 7-1 (Chapter 7), in which Addie Morris describes her experiences as a client of a large public welfare agency. Imagine that you are a worker in that agency. How might you have responded so as to show more respect for the dignity of Addie Morris and her children? Think about your responsibility as a social worker for what agency procedures and policies communicate to clients. How do agency procedures and their use express values?

REFERENCES

Abramson, J. S. (1988). Participation of elderly patients in discharge planning: Is self-determination a reality? *Social Work, 33*(5), 443–448.

Allen, J. A. (1993). The constructivist paradigm: Values and ethics. *Journal of Teaching in Social Work, 8*(1/2), 31–54.

American Psychiatric Association (1994). Diagnostic and statistical manual of mental disorders. Washington, DC: American Psychiatric Press.

Badding, N. C. (1989). Client involvement in case recording. *Social Casework, 70*(9), 539–548.

Becker, H. (1963). *The outsiders: Studies in the sociology of deviance.* New York: Free Press.

Behroozi, C. S. (1992). A model for social work with involuntary applicants in groups. *Social Work with Groups, 15*(2/3), 223–238.

Beinecke, R. H. (1984). Pork soap, strap, and sap. *Social Casework: The Journal of Contemporary Social Work, 65*(9), 554–558.

Biehal, N. (1993). Changing practice: Participation, rights and community care. *British Journal of Social Work, 23*(5), 443–458.

Biehal, N., & Sainsbury, E. (1991). From values to rights in social work: Some issues in practice development and research. *British Journal of Social Work, 21*(3), 245–257.

Biestek, F. P. (1994). Revisiting our heritage: An analysis of the casework relationship. *Families in Society: The Journal of Contemporary Human Services, 75*(10), 630–634.

Briar, S., & Miller, H. (1971). *Problems and issues in social casework.* New York: Columbia University Press.

Bricker-Jenkins, M. (1991). The propositions and assumptions of feminist social work practice. In M. Bricker-Jenkins, N. R. Hooyman, & N. Gottlieb (Eds.), *Feminist social work practice in clinical settings* (pp. 271–303). Thousand Oaks, CA: Sage Publications.

Coady, N. F. (1993). The worker-client relationship revisited. *Families in Society, 74*(5), 291–297.

Collins, B. (1986). Defining feminist social work. *Social Work, 31*(3), 214–219.

Coursey, R. D., Farrell, E. W., & Zahniser, J. H. (1991). Consumers' attitudes toward psychotherapy, hospitalization, and after care. *Health and Social Work, 16*(3), 155–161.

Diorio, W. D. (1992). Parental perceptions of authority of child welfare caseworkers. *Families in Society, 73*(4), 222–235.

Doel, M., & Lawson, B. (1986). Open records: The client's right to partnership. *British Journal of Social Work, 16*(4), 407–430.

Donnelly, W. J., & Brauner, D. J. (1990). Why SOAP is bad for the medical record. Unpublished manuscript, Medical Service, Department of Veteran Affairs, Edward Hines, Jr. Hospital, Hines, IL; Department of Medicine, Loyola University of Chicago Stritch School of Medicine, Maywood, IL; Department of Medicine, University of Illinois at Chicago.

Downes, B. R. (1992). Guardianship for people with severe mental retardation: Consent for urgently needed treatment. *Health in Social Work, 17*(1), 13–15.

Dumont, M. (1968). *The absurd healer.* New York: Viking Press.

Ewalt, P. L., & Mokuau, N. (1995). Self-determination from a pacific perspective. *Social Work, 40*(2), 168–175.

Freedberg, S. (1989). Self-determination: Historical perspectives and effects on current practice. *Social Work, 34*(1), 33–38.

Galaway, B. (1981). Social services and criminal justice. In N. Gilbert & H. Specht (Eds.), *Handbook of the social services* (pp. 250–280). Englewood Cliffs, NJ: Prentice-Hall.

Galaway, B., & Hudson, J. (1996). *Restorative justice: International perspectives.* Monsey, NY: Criminal Justice Press.

Gelman, S. R. (1992). Risk management through client assess to case records. *Social Work, 37*(1), 73–79.

Goldstein, H. (1988, May). *Strength of pathology: Ethical and rhetorical contrasts in approaches to social work practice.* Paper presented at the School of Social Welfare, University of Kansas.

Gordon, W. E. (1965). Knowledge and value: Their distinction and relationship in clarifying social work practice. *Social Work, 10*(4), 32–39.

Gordon, W. E. (1969). Basic concepts for an integrative and generative conception of social work. In G. Hearn (Ed.), *The general systems approach: Contributions toward an holistic conception of social work* (pp. 5–11). New York: Council on Social Work Education.

Hamilton, G. (1946). *Principles of social case recording.* New York: Columbia University Press.

Hardman, D. (1960). The constructive use of authority. *Crime and Delinquency, 6*(3), 245–254.

Hardman, D. (1975). Not with my daughter you don't. *Social Work, 21,* 278–285.

Hartman, B. L., & Wickey, J. M. (1978). The person-oriented record in treatment. *Social Work, 23*(4), 296–299.

Hatcher, H. A. (1978). *Correctional casework and counseling.* Englewood Cliffs, NJ: Prentice-Hall.

Houghkirk, E. (1977). Everything you've always wanted your clients to know but have been afraid to tell them. *Journal of Marriage and Family Counselling, 3*(2), 27–33.

Itzhaky, H., & York, A. S. (1991). Client participation and the effectiveness of community social work intervention. *Research in Social Work Practice, 1*(4), 387–398.

Itzhaky, H., & York, A. S. (1994). Different types of client participation and the effects in community social work intervention. *Journal of Social Service Research, 19*(1/2), 85–98.

Ivanoff, A., Blythe, B., & Tripodi, T. (1994). *Involuntary clients in social work practice: A research based approach.* Hawthorne, NY: Aldine de Gruyter.

Jahn, K. (1986). The usefulness of DSM-III and systematic interviews in treatment planning. *Women and Therapy, 5*(1), 91–99.

Johnson, H. C. (1978). Integration the problem-oriented record with a systems approach to case assessment. *Journal of Education for Social Work, 14*(3), 71–77.

Kagle, J. D. (1984). *Social work records.* Homewood, IL: The Dorsey Press.

Kagle, J. D. (1991). *Social work records* (2nd ed.). Belmont, CA: Wadsworth.

Kagle, J. D. (1993). Record keeping: Directions for the 1990s. *Social Work, 38*(2), 190–196.

Kagle, J. D. (1995). Recording. In *Encyclopedia of social work* (19th ed.)., pp. 2027–2033). Washington, DC: National Association of Social Workers.

Kane, R. A. (1974). Look to the record. *Social Work, 19*(4), 412–419.

Karls, J. M., & Wandrei, K. E. (Eds.). (1994a). *Person-in-environment system: The PIE classification system for social functioning problems.* Washington, DC: NASW Press.

Karls, J. M., & Wandrei, K. E. (1994b). *PIE manual: Person-in-environment system.* Washington, DC: NASW Press.

Kelly, T. B. (1994). Paternalism and the marginally competent: An ethical dilemma, no easy answers. *Journal of Gerontological Social Work, 23*(1/2), 67–84.

Kelley, M. L., McKay, S., & Nelson, C. H. (1985). Indian agency development: An ecological practice approach. *Social Casework: The Journal of Contemporary Social Work, 66*(10), 594–602.

Kirk, S., & Kutchins, H. (1992). *Selling of DSM-III: The rhetoric of science in psychiatry.* Hawthorne, NY: Aldine de Gruyter.

Kirk, S., & Kutchins, H. (1994). The myth of the reliability of DSM. *The Journal of Mind and Behavior, 15*(1/2), 71–86.

Kline, M., Sydnor-Greenberg, N., Davis, W. W., Pincus, H. A., & Frances, A. J. (1993). Using field trials to evaluate proposed changes in DSM diagnostic criteria. *Hospital and Community Psychiatry, 44*(7), 621–623.

Klockars, C. B. (1972). A theory of probation supervision. *The Journal of Criminal Law, Criminology and Police Science, 63*(4), 550–557.

Kutchins, H., & Kirk, S. (1987). DSM-III and social work malpractice. *Social Work, 32*(3), 205–211.

Lemert, E. (1967). The juvenile court quest and realities. In President's Commission on Law Enforcement and Administration of Justice, *Task force report: Juvenile delinquency and youth crime* (pp 91–106) Washington, DC: U.S. Government Printing Office.

Levy, C. S. (1972). Values and planned change. *Social Casework, 53*(8), 488–493.

Levy, C. S. (1973). The value base of social work. *Journal of Education for Social Work, 9*(1), 34–42.

Maluccio, A. (1979). *Learning from clients: Interpersonal helping as viewed by clients and social workers.* New York: Free Press.

Maluccio, A. N., Washitz, S., & Libassi, M. F. (1992). Ecologically oriented, competence-centered social work practice. In C. W. Lecroy (Ed.), *Case studies in social work practice* (pp. 5–13). Belmont, CA: Wadsworth.

McDevitt, S. (1994). Case records in public child welfare: Uses and a flexible format. *Child Welfare, 73*(1), 41–55.

McFadden, E. J. (1992). The inner world of children and youth in care. *Community Alternatives: International Journal of Family Care, 4*(1), 1–17.

McIvor, G. (1991). Social work intervention in community service. *British Journal of Social Work, 21*(6), 591–609.

Merton, R. K. (1968). *Social theory and social structure* (4th ed.). New York: Free Press.

Miller, H. (1968). Value dilemmas in social casework. *Social Work, 13*(1), 27–33.

Monnickendam, M., Yaniv, H., & Geve, N. (1994). Practitioners and the case record: Patterns of use. *Administration in Social Work, 18*(4), 73–86.

Moore, S. T., & Kelly, M. J. (1996). Quality now: Moving human service organizations toward a consumer orientation to service quality. *Social Work, 41*(1), 33–40.

Murdach, A. D. (1996). Beneficence re-examined: Protective intervention in mental health. *Social Work, 41*(1), 26–32.

National Association of Social Workers (1996). *Code of Ethics.* Washington, DC: NASW Press.

Nes, J., & Iadicola (1989). Toward a definition of feminist social work: A comparison of liberal, radical, and socialist models. *Social Work, 25*(1), 12–20.

Nicholson, B., & Matross, G. (1989). Facing reduced decision-making capacity in health care: Methods for maintaining client self-determination. *Social Work, 25*(3), 234–238.

Overton, A. (1965). Establishing the relationship. *Crime and Delinquency, 11*(3), 229–238.

Oxley, G. B. (1966). The caseworker's expectations in client motivation. *Social Casework, 47*(7), 432–437.

Palmer, S. (1983). Authority: An essential part of practice. *Social Work, 28*(2), 120–124.

Platt, A. (1977). *The child savers: The invention of delinquency* (2nd ed.). Chicago: University of Chicago Press.

Rapp, C. A. (1998). *The strengths model: Case management with people suffering from severe and persistent mental illness.* New York: Oxford University Press.

Raynor, P. (1986). *Social work, justice and control.* Oxford, England: Basic Blackwell.

Reid, W. J. (1978). *The task-centered system.* New York: Columbia University Press.

Reid, W. J. (1992). *Task strategies.* New York: Columbia University Press.

Reid, W. J., & Epstein, L. (1977). *Task-centered practice.* New York: Columbia University Press.

Rooney, R. (1988). Socialization strategies for involuntary clients. *Social Casework: Journal of Contemporary Social Work, 69*(3), 131–140.

Rooney, R. (1992). Strategies for work with involuntary clients. New York: Columbia University Press.

Rosewater, L., & Walker, L. (1985). *Handbook of feminist therapy: Women's issues in psychotherapy.* New York: Springer.

Rubington, E., & Weinberg, M. S. (1968). *Deviance: The interactionist perspective.* New York: Macmillan.

Russell, M. (1989). Feminist social work skills. *Canadian Social Work Review, 6*(1), 69–79.

Saleebey, D. (Ed.). (1992). *The strengths perspective in social work practice.* New York: Longman.

Saleebey, D. (1995). The strengths perspective in social work practice: Extensions and cautions. *Social Work, 41*(3), 296–305.

Salomon, E. L. (1967). Humanistic values and social casework. *Social Casework, 48*(1), 26–33.

Schrier, C. J. (1980). Guidelines for recordkeeping under privacy and open-access laws. *Social Work, 25*(6), 452–457.

Schur, E. (1973). *Radical non-intervention: Rethinking the delinquency problem.* Englewood Cliffs, NJ: Prentice-Hall.

Schwartz, W. (1961). Social worker in the group. In National Conference on Social Welfare (Ed.), *Social Work Forum* (pp. 146–171). New York: Columbia University Press.

Shireman, C. H., & Reamer, F. (1986). *Rehabilitating juvenile justice.* New York: Columbia University Press.

Silverman, M. (1977). Children's rights and social work. *Social Service Review, 51*(1), 171–178.

Simmons, J. L. (1969). *Deviants.* Berkeley, CA: Glendessary Press.

Simon, B. L. (1994). *The empowerment tradition in American social work.* New York: Columbia University Press.

Szasz, T. (1994). *Cruel compassion: Psychiatric control of society's unwanted.* New York: Wiley.

Tannenbaum, F. (1951). *Crime and community* (2nd ed.). New York: Columbia University Press.

Tebb, S. (1991a). Client-focused recording: Linking theory and practice. *Families in Society, 72*(7), 427–432.

Tillich, P. (1962). The philosophy of social work. *Social Service Review, 36*(1), 12–16.

Toch, H. (1970). The care and feeding of typologies and labels. *Federal Probation, 34*(3), 15–19.

Tower, K. D. (1994). Consumer centered social work practice: Restoring client self-determination. *Social Work, 39*(2), 191–196.

Towle, C. (1965). *Common human needs.* New York: National Association of Social Workers. (Original work published in 1945.)

Valentine, D. P. (1993). Children with special needs: Sources of support and stress for the family. *Journal of Social Work and Human Sexuality, 8*(2), 107–121.

Van Ness, D., & Strong, K. (1997). *Restoring justice.* Columbus, OH: Anderson.

Webster's Ninth New Collegiate Dictionary. (1991). Springfield, MA: Merriam.

Weed, L. L. (1969). *Medical records, medical education, and patient care.* Cleveland: The Press of Case Western Reserve University.

Weick, A. (1983). Issues in overturning a medical model of social work practice. *Social Work, 28*(6), 467–471.

Weick, A. (1987). Reconceptualizing the philosophical perspective of social work. *Social Service Review, 61*(2), 218–230.

Weick, A., & Pope, L. (1988). Knowing what's best: A new look at self-determination. *Social Casework: The Journal of Contemporary Social Work, 69*(1), 10–16.

Weick, A., Rapp, C., Sullivan, P., & Kisthardt, W. (1989). A strengths perspective for social work practice. *Social Work, 34*(4), 350–354.

Wilczynski, B. L. (1981). New life for recording: Involving the client. *Social Work, 26*(4), 313–317.

Williams, J. B. W. (1981). DSM-III: A comprehensive approach to diagnosis. *Social Work, 26*(2), 101–107.

Zehr, H. (1990). *Changing lenses.* Scottsdale, PA: Herald Press.

chapter 5

Authority for Social Work Practice

CHAPTER PREVIEW

In the previous chapters, we introduced the conceptual framework for the model of practice being developed in this book: a focus on ecosystems; social work practice as problem solving; and worker-client partnership. In this chapter, we discuss the sources of authority to develop and implement service plans with clients; in Chapter 6, we examine the role of ethics in guiding your social work practice; and, in Chapter 7, we discuss the professional relationship in social work. At that point, we will be ready to look at the phases of the problem-solving process in more detail.

In this chapter, we examine three sources of authority for your work as a social worker:

- the authority you receive from your client
- the authority you receive from the social work profession
- the authority you receive from your agency

We will then consider how to resolve conflicts when the expectations of these sources of authority are not in agreement. Resolving such conflicts may mean attempting to change your agency. In Reading 5-1, Edward J. Pawlak considers some techniques for producing change in your employing agency. He refers to this process as tinkering with the organization.

AUTHORITY FROM THE CLIENT

You will not be surprised to read that the client is one of the three sources of authority for your practice. In Chapter 3, we suggested that there is no client until you and the applicant reach an explicit agreement as to the problem to be solved, the objectives to be achieved, and the service plan to accomplish these objectives; through this agreement, the applicant has authorized you to carry out actions.

Change is most likely to occur if there is agreement among all parties about the change effort. Even when approaching respondents or prospects, you must try, during the engagement process, to find a common area for work, so that you may receive direct authority from the person being served. In Chapter 3, we mentioned the importance of focusing on applicant wants, rather than applicant needs. That perspective will assist you in receiving explicit authority from clients for the services you provide.

Focusing on Wants

The social work literature is replete with references to the client's needs. But how do we know what the client needs? All too often, a need is the professional's idea of what is good for the client. In Exhibit 5–1, William Reid suggests that it is better to consider the client's wants. A want is a "cognitive affective event consisting of an idea that something is desirable and a feeling of tension associated with not having it" (Reid, 1978, p. 25). Further, "when a want is experienced without means of satisfaction at hand or in sight, one has the sensation of having a problem" (Reid, 1978, p. 25). We agree with Reid that a person's wants provide a more useful focus for social work than do client needs.

A focus on what the client wants should help deter social workers from doing to people what they do not want done, in the name of meeting their needs. Even if well motivated, efforts to meet people's needs may violate individual liberties (Gaylin, Glasser, Marcus, & Rothman, 1978; Szasz, 1994). Partly in response to such incursions, a number of rights movements—children's

---

EXHIBIT 5-1	Wants as a Focus for Social Work

A focus on wants rather than needs may give us a different perspective on the unmotivated client. Usually, he is unmotivated to be what social workers or others believe he ought to be. He lacks "motivation" to be a better spouse or parent, or to be more law abiding. To our dismay we see vast numbers of people who do not have motives for self-betterment, as we define it. While many clients lack motivation in these terms, few lack wants. If the client's wants are our concern, then the essential questions become: What does the person want? Can we help him get it? Should we do so? Should we try to create wants he does not have? If so, by what means? These questions are not easily answered, but they may help clarify our position and thinking about the many people who are less than enthusiastic about our efforts to help them.

Source: W. Reid, *The task centered system.* New York: Columbia University Press (1978), pp. 25–26.

---

rights, students' rights, patients' rights, inmates' rights, gay rights, and so forth—have emerged. Clearly, large bureaucracies cannot be trusted to act consistently in the best interest of individuals. By focusing on the wants that individuals experience, rather than the needs attributed to them by some external agency, social workers are able to respect individual liberty and dignity and are more likely to secure clients' authority for intervention.

Agency or Society as Client

In your practice, you will work with many people who, at first, will not agree to a service plan; they will not grant you authority to intervene on their behalf. In Chapter 3, we categorized these individuals as respondents or prospects. In the engagement phase, you may negotiate an agreement with some of these individuals, who will become your clients. Others, however, may never reach an agreement with you.

You may find it troublesome to work with respondents and prospects, because the relationship is not voluntary. The worker establishes contact to carry out a legal mandate or to sell a service. To deal with this discomfort, two approaches are possible. One is to seek some common ground where you and the person can agree on the problem, objectives, and a service plan; if successful, these efforts would convert the respondent or prospect to a client. Scholars specializing in work with respondents suggest this course of action (Ivanoff, Blythe, & Tripodi, 1994; Rooney, 1988, 1991).

The second course of action is to rely upon the authority you receive from your agency, which has responsibility for carrying out a mandated service. Under these circumstances, it is inappropriate to refer to the persons with whom you are working as clients. Using the terminology in Chapter 2, these persons are the target systems. The client is society or, more specifically, your agency, which has a particular mandate to carry out change efforts on behalf of society. When working on behalf of your agency as client, you must still function within the knowledge and ethical limits of the profession: For example, you cannot carry out actions that are harmful to individuals; you are bound to enhance self-determination by trying to create opportunities for choice; you will use the least restrictive services possible; you will use the minimal interventions necessary to carry out the organization's mandate; and you will respect the rights of people being targeted for change. Agencies that provide mandated services often have broad legal power to intervene in people's lives. This raises the possibility of abuse of power (Coursey, Farrell, & Zahniser, 1991). When you recognize society and your agency as a client, your professional ethics will limit the ways in which you exercise your power.

AUTHORITY FROM THE PROFESSION

As we noted in Chapter 1, Schwartz (1961) emphasizes that every profession has an assigned function in society, for which the profession is accountable. Social work is no exception. Communities and clients need assurance that your services are within the recognized and approved parameters of society's assignment to the profession.

A profession develops with the recognition of a complex social problem whose solution demands specialized knowledge and skill. Because professionals' knowledge is so specialized, individuals using their services may not have the expertise to judge the adequacy of those services. Professionals usually demand the autonomy to make judgments, and take actions, independent of lay control; they consider themselves accountable only to their peers. Society grants the professional this power, on the understanding that it will be used in the interest of the community and not solely of the profession. Recognizing that condition, the profession establishes an ethical obligation of community service, to safeguard against the self-aggrandizement of its members and to ensure that its social function is fulfilled. For its part, the community sanctions the professional's right to practice through some combination of

- completion of a prescribed course of education
- proof of a level of competency through an examination
- regulation of the practitioner through licensing, registration, or certification

Professional Associations

All professions have professional associations. Professional organizations serve four purposes:

- to improve the performance of individual practitioners
- to police the membership in the interests of competent individual performance
- to protect the members' exclusive right to practice their profession
- to promote public policies consistent with the profession's mandate

The primary professional association in the United States is the National Association of Social Workers (NASW), a national association with chapters in each state. Individuals join NASW directly and are assigned membership in the appropriate state chapter. In Canada, social workers join provincial professional associations and thereby become members of the Canadian Association of Social Workers (CASW). Social workers at all levels have a duty to support improvement of practice and public policy through membership in a professional association; we encourage you to consider a student membership. (The addresses and contact numbers for the national organizations are found in Exhibit 5–2; Appendix B lists the addresses and contact numbers for the state and provincial associations.)

Organizations have also been established to promote improvements in professional education and to accredit educational programs that meet minimum standards: the Council on Social Work Education (CSWE) in the United States and the Canadian Association of Schools of Social Work (CASSW) in Canada. Most of the members of both CSWE and CASSW are departments, schools, or faculties of social work, along with faculty members who teach in social work education programs. Membership, however, is open to others. Each organization publishes lists of accredited social work education programs. (The addresses for CSWE and CASSW are also included in Exhibit 5–2.)

Licensure of Social Work

Licensing is a legal procedure that restricts who may practice social work (Hickman, 1994). Every state in the

---

EXHIBIT 5-2 Social Work Professional Associations

National Association of Social Workers (U.S.)
750 First Street NE, Suite 700
Washington, DC 20002-4241
Phone: 800-638-8799
FAX: 202-628-6800
E-mail: info @ naswdc.org
www: http://www.naswdc.org

Canadian Association of Social Workers
383 Parkdale Avenue, #402
Ottawa, Ontario K1Y 4R4
Phone: 613-729-6668
FAX: 613-729-8608
E-mail: casw @ casw-acts.ca
www: http://www.intranet.ca/ncsaw-acts/

Council on Social Work Education
1600 Duke Street
Alexandria, VA 22314
Phone: 703-683-8080
FAX: 703-683-8099
E-mail: info @ cswe.org
www: http://www.cswe.org

Canadian Association of Schools of Social Work
323 Chapel Street, Second Floor
Ottawa, Ontario K1N 7Z2
Phone: 613-236-3424
FAX: 613-237-5969
E-mail: by256 @ freenet.carleton.ca

United States has passed licensing legislation, but Canadian provinces have been slow to do so. To become licensed, an individual must complete an educational program accredited by the Council on Social Work Education. The states have different levels of licenses, depending on the qualifications and experience of the candidate. Most states require social workers to participate in ongoing educational experiences in order to keep their license current.

Licensing requirements vary from state to state. Some states require a wide range of practitioners to be licensed; others are less restrictive. In Colorado, for example, social workers and mental health practitioners must be licensed in order to practice psychotherapy; thus, if you don't profess to practice psychotherapy, you don't need a license in that state. Minnesota, by contrast, provides for four levels of licensure. Licensing is far from comprehensive, because some states exempt groups of workers on the basis of their employing agency—for instance, those employed in public welfare agencies or those employed in medical settings, which usually impose their own accreditation review and standards for staff qualifications. NASW has been lobbying, with some success, for comprehensive licensing legislation in all the states.

If you live in the United States, you will find it instructive to contact your social work licensing board (at the address provided in Appendix B) for information on who must be licensed in your state, as well as the licensing requirements. Does your board offer multilevel licensure based on various educational and experience requirements? Are all persons who wish to call themselves social workers required to have a license, or are certain groups exempted from this requirement? You may also contact your professional association to learn if the association is promoting any amendments or changes in your state's licensing law. Licensing is more limited in Canada than in the United States; if you are a Canadian student, you may find it interesting to learn the position of your provincial association on licensing.

Professional Autonomy

Social work, like other professions, maintains that the knowledge and skill of the professional are so different from general knowledge and skill that no one outside the profession can judge the professional. Every profession claims that it alone has the knowledge to regulate practice; this is one element of professional autonomy. One problem of professional autonomy, however, is that it may reinforce rigidity and conservatism within the profession. For example, especially in clinical practice, social work licensing may encourage the traditional viewpoint that problems are due to individual pathology.

However, the community is increasingly demanding that the people served by professions should have the right to judge professionals by the outcome of their service. In addition, there is concern that self-regulation could allow professionals to protect each other at the expense of the community and to suppress information on incompetent practitioners. You and your classmates may find it instructive to contact your state licensing board and find out how many licenses are in effect, how many disciplinary actions have been taken in the last year, the reasons for these actions, and whether disciplinary actions against social workers are made public.

Another element of autonomy is that professionals seek to be self-directing in their work—that is, to control the content and terms of the work. However, it is important to distinguish between the autonomy of the profession and the autonomy of the individual practitioner. In reality, the more that a profession is able to exercise autonomy, the more its members are controlled by a hierarchy of institutionalized expertise (Friedson, 1970, pp. 71–92). Note, however, that social welfare organizations are usually bureaucratic, not professional, organizations; many professionals operating in organizations have authority based on their positions, rather than their expertise.

Professional Culture

As practitioners interact in the course of their work and self-development, they tend to learn particular ways of thinking and acting and a particular language—in other words, a professional culture. Once they have internalized the values and culture of the profession, social workers feel constrained to work in ways consistent with established professional practice. This internalization of professional values and culture—a process known as socialization—is an important aspect of professional education, because it provides protection to the client. In the helping process, you rely on yourself and your judgment; no one intervenes to safeguard the client. Therefore, the only assurance the community has that you can be trusted with professional tasks is the belief that your actions and judgements stem from professional values and knowledge—that you have been immersed in the professional culture.

The tasks social workers are expected to perform are often unclear and may be contradictory. For example, social workers are often expected to control every expenditure of the welfare client but at the same time to promote independent behavior on the part of welfare recipients. Both expectations cannot be satisfied; one or the other must be chosen. Your professional culture will assist you in making this decision.

AUTHORITY FROM THE AGENCY

Social work began, grew, and developed to its present stage as a professional practice within an agency structure. While the private practice of social work is growing, practice within an agency is a reality of professional life for most social workers today. Thus, we need to understand agency sanctions as an important element of social work practice. Community agencies are organized to offer resources for the solution of clients' problems and specify policies under which those resources are available. The necessity of conforming to those policies may restrict client access to resources. Thus, our relationship with clients also involves the agency, its purposes, and its policies. Effective practice demands skill in utilizing agency resources, an understanding of the relevant network of agencies, and a working relationship with those agencies.

An Interstitial Profession

As we saw in Chapter 1, social workers are concerned with the interactions between the individual and society. In that sense, social work is an interstitial profession, serving both the client in need and society at large. This is a complicated situation. The agency (public or voluntary, traditional or nontraditional) by which a social worker is employed receives its sanction from, and is accountable to, the community or to some community group, whose members usually are not clients. The parameters of the service any professional can offer are determined by the parameters of the agency's mandate.

Social workers use two types of tools in their work. The first is internalized professional knowledge and skill.

Skill and knowledge cannot be used up and may be increased and sharpened by practice; professionals sell their knowledge to support themselves. Some professionals, such as lawyers and doctors, sell their services directly to their clients or patients. In the case of social work, however, most services to clients are paid for by the community and may be—at least in theory—available to all members of the community, even those who cannot themselves afford to pay for the services. Social workers may also dispense money, either directly to the client or for concrete resources. But money is usually scarce. Money to support social work is not your property; it belongs to the community. The community that allocates scarce resources to the support of social work services wants to assure itself that these resources are used responsibly.

Clients who go to a lawyer, or patients who go to a doctor may look elsewhere for help if they think the service they receive is not adequate. Thus, they express their evaluation of a professional's competence by depriving the professional of income. If these professionals want to support themselves and their dependents, they must practice in a way that satisfies the users of their services. However, since most clients do not pay the full cost for social work services, their withdrawal in disappointment and disgust from the inadequate social work practitioner seldom directly penalizes that practitioner. Social workers (and their agencies) are well protected from their client's evaluations. They are open to the evaluation of their supporting community, but the supporting community neither pays nor evaluates workers directly; rather, it gives money to an organization, usually called an agency, that hires the professional practitioners. The agency, in interaction with its supporting community through representative groups, both sets the parameters of practice within which workers must operate and evaluates their performance within those parameters.

To give your clients maximum service, you must understand the organization for which you work and know how its structure and function were determined. If you are going to be actively involved in change, you need to know the possible points of intervention. Three major factors affect the organization of agencies: source of support, source of sanction, and areas of concern. Agencies obviously cannot operate without a source of funds. An agency's funds come from public tax funds, from private voluntary contributions, and from fees for services. Any agency's policy and structure, procedures, and flexibility will be determined by the source and adequacy of its funding. As a general rule, funds are not adequate to demands that workers wish to meet, and so difficult choices among real needs must be made.

The public tax-supported agency will usually operate within legislation and will be dependent on a legislative body for its broad policy and for the appropriation of public funds for its support. In some cases, the board or commission of a public service may be appointed by an elected executive officer (such as a governor). Administrators of public agencies determine procedures and more detailed policy issues within the legislation that established and maintains the agency. Some social work departments (such as the social service department of a school system, a hospital, or court) operate as part of a larger host agency. In this situation, the financial support and policy-making processes will be determined by those of the host agency, which is controlled by professional interests other than social work (Dane & Simon, 1991).

Private agencies usually operate under the general policy directives of a board of directors. Such a board has three primary functions: It establishes the right of the agency to carry on its program and sanctions the agency's activities; it is responsible for the agency's overall policy; and it is responsible for fund raising. Boards are often composed of an elite group of members, with little understanding of the daily realities of those for whom the programs were developed. Board members of private agencies are volunteers; members who are constantly on the losing side of an issue often drop out, unless they have a deep commitment. The board hires the executive of the agency, whose two goals are often to keep the board happy and to run the agency his or her way. The executive usually controls staff access to the board and the flow of information to the board about the agency's work. Attempts by social workers to represent clients and their interests in policy and program matters are often frustrated.

Agencies have both a function and a program. Its function is defined by the community; its program consists of the ways in which that function is carried out. Even if an agency's function remains constant, its program ought to be responsive to changing needs. Thus, an agency whose function is the care and treatment of children may initially have cared largely for orphaned or dependent children but now may be concerned primarily with disturbed children or with day care.

Agency Function

Social workers have always had to adapt to practice within agency function. The functional school of social casework, current from the early 1930s to the late 1950s, perceived that the role of the social caseworker was to carry out the function of the agency, which had a social mandate to provide a specific service (Smalley, 1967; Taft, 1935). Advocates of the diagnostic school (Hamilton, 1951), by contrast, also practiced in agencies but minimized the notion of agency function; in their view, the role of the agency was simply to provide the resources—such as offices and secretarial support—that practitioners required in order to diagnose and treat a wide variety of psychosocial ills. The debate between the diagnostic and functional schools of social work is an interesting part of social work history; in modern practice, these distinctions have largely been lost, with the adoption of a generalist problem-solving practice model.

But the notion of agency function is still very much a part of contemporary social work practice. You may be working in agencies with a specific function—child protection, child welfare, offender supervision, residential treatment of disturbed youth, care for the aging, independent living for persons with disabilities, and so forth. Further, in some large agencies, you may be a part of a special unit that further narrows the agency function. A public child welfare agency, for example, may include such specialized units as foster home recruitment and supervision, foster care placement, child protection for preschool children, child protection for adolescents, and independent living services. When we discussed the nesting and layering of systems in Chapter 2, we saw that higher-order systems provide both opportunities and limitations to lower-order systems. Your agency, as a system, will provide resources and opportunities for you and your client to work together toward accomplishing objectives; on the other hand, the concept of agency function may limit what you and your client can do. Exhibit 5–3 illustrates a conflict between an agency's view of its function and an applicant's request for service. Constrained by the agency's narrow definition of function, the workers were unable to start with what this applicant wanted and to develop a preliminary goal. As a

EXHIBIT 5-3   Conflict Between Agency Policy and Applicant's Wants

Mrs. Iverson called requesting services for Jody, her 15-year-old daughter, whom she described as being out of control. According to the mother, the daughter was attending school on a sporadic basis, lying, and stealing. The mother is a single parent currently separated from her second husband, who is not the child's father. The stepfather was reported by the mother to be chemically dependent and the children did not get along with him. There is one other child in the family, a son, who is currently not living in the family home. The mother works full-time as an aide at a nursing home. She wanted some type of temporary placement for her daughter. The intake worker explained that the purpose of our program is to keep the child in the home. The mother expressed a willingness to give the program a try.

After receiving the referral from intake, I contacted the mother and set up a meeting in the family home. I learned that the mother had recently kicked her daughter out of the home and the girl was staying with an adult friend.

The daughter was not present, apparently because of the mother's refusal to allow Jody back in the home. Mrs. Iverson told me that she does not trust her daughter because she steals and lies. Jody does not follow house rules, which include doing chores and being home by curfew. Money is also a factor contributing to the stress between mother and daughter. Jody is responsible for some bills that the mother cannot afford to pay; this was the reason Mrs. Iverson decided to kick Jody out of the home.

Mrs. Iverson's recent marital separation resulted in the loss of a second income; financial ends are not being met even though she took on a second job. I asked about her marital situation. She stated that they had been separated for about two months and she intended to file for divorce.

I inquired about mother's support network at this point in her life. She stated that she had a sister with whom she is very close. This sister was recently diagnosed with cancer, and Mrs. Iverson feels very concerned. She also talked about a close woman friend who has children. Both she and her daughter have talked with this woman in the past and it was helpful, although she feels that the situation has gotten so bad now that even this friend cannot help.

I asked her about possible community resources. She stated that she and her estranged husband briefly saw a Christian marital counselor, but stopped because it did not help with their problems. She and her daughter also saw a counselor once about a month ago. Mrs. Iverson said she does not believe in counseling.

Mrs. Iverson reported that she does not spend very much time with her daughter because she works in the evenings. When they do talk, they argue a lot. I asked

what, if anything, had been done to alleviate some of the problems between them. Mother told me about a written contract that was drawn up at the suggestion of her woman friend. The contract dealt with house rules such as curfew, chores, and not yelling at her mother. The mother stated that her daughter was good about following the contract for a few days but then she started breaking it on a regular basis. As a consequence, the mother grounded the child, but she was never home to follow through on it.

I told the mother that it was my hope to be of some assistance to both her and her daughter and I asked her how she thought I could help. The mother stated that she didn't know how I could help and that she basically saw the situation as pretty hopeless.

At this point I felt as if I needed to begin applying some pressure on Mrs. Iverson to start formulating some concrete steps toward getting her daughter back in the home. As I did this I was very conscious of two things: The mother did not want the child back in the home and the goal of the program is to keep children in the family home and avoid placement.

I told the mother that since she was the child's legal guardian she was responsible for caring for the child, and that part of that care was to allow the child to come back home. I again asked the mother what she saw as my role in this situation and how I might possibly be able to help. The mother did not provide any concrete response. I told her once again that I did not view the situation as hopeless, but that some hard work needed to be done before any real changes would be made.

I asked the mother what would have to happen in order for Jody to be able to return home. She stated three things: (1) get a part-time job, (2) follow house rules regarding chores and curfew, and (3) go to school on a regular basis. I felt very positive about the fact that she had identified these very concrete stipulations.

The mother appeared to be fairly resistant to exploring possibilities for goal setting and also seemed apathetic to the idea of having a social worker involved, stating that she did not know what good it would do. I felt frustrated by the negative attitude of mother, but also tried to be empathetic.

After spending about an hour talking, the mother was providing both nonverbal and verbal feedback indicating that she did not see any real solutions nor did she particularly see where I could be of assistance. Before the meeting had completely ended, I suggested a meeting with the mother, daughter, and myself. The mother agreed to this if I was willing to set it up. We ended with the understanding that I would contact the daughter and get back to the mother about a specific meeting date and time.

Source: Anonymous MSW student.

result, the applicant became angry and the agency was unable to provide service to this family.

In such situations, you may focus on persuading your agency to consider the broadest possible interpretation of its function. Recall the Birky case in Exhibit 2–15. The social worker in this case was from a preschool center and was initiating contact because of concerns about the 4-year-old's behavior in school, as well as possible child neglect. At the first interview, the worker was informed that the youngest child in the Birky family had just drowned in an uncovered ditch near the housing development. After the death of another child, the city had promised to cover the ditch but had not done so. Suppose that Mr. and Mrs. Birky and the worker agree to direct attention to the ditch, which presents a hazard to children. The goal is clear—to get the ditch covered and thus produce a safe environment for children. The worker and the family will be able to consider a number of alternatives for accomplishing this goal—for example, securing an attorney to bring suit against the city; contacting the city council member who represents that area; applying pressure to get the city to do what it has previously agreed to do; and organizing a group of neighbors in the housing development to bring greater pressure on the city. However, the worker is employed by a day care center. Is there any inconsistency between actions to get the ditch covered and the function of the agency? If so, how might the worker go about handling the inconsistencies?

Social workers must beware of defining the applicant's problem in terms of the agency's function. Often it becomes almost second nature to assume that the problems fall within the agency's purpose. A worker within a child-placement agency may tend to assume that placement is a good solution for any child's problem. Such a narrow focus can do great harm to applicants and clients, by limiting the consideration of alternatives for solution of the applicant's problem. Clearly, it is not possible to offer all services within a single agency. However, if the applicant's problem is not one your agency is capable of addressing, or the desired solution is not one you can offer, then you must be willing to make a referral.

The Agency as a Bureaucracy

Most formal organizations are structured as bureaucracies. Sociologist Max Weber (1947) summarized the defining characteristics of bureaucracies—most notably, they are hierarchical and promotion is dependent on the judgment of superiors—and cited the examples of the Roman Catholic Church, the modern army, large-scale capitalistic enterprises, and various charitable organizations. Bureaucracy is usually seen as the most efficient way to organize any large group of people. However, it has certain dysfunctional characteristics:

> timidity, delay, officiousness, red tape, exaggeration of routine, and limited adaptability. (Wilensky & Lebeaux, 1958)

Bureaucracies try to achieve efficiency by standardizing tasks. They do this by breaking tasks into smaller and smaller parts, in order to standardize them. Barbara Lerner (1972) notes that "standardized procedures are rational only if one is striving to produce a standard product [but] each human being is a unique entity and wants to remain so" (p. 170). The bureaucratic agency is organized around "abstract, standard parts: specific programs organized around specific problems that are dealt with by specific procedures" (p. 171). Clients are "then defined in terms of the particular problems around which programs are organized" and are "processed to and through those programs and subjected to the various procedures and techniques which constitute them" (p. 173) rather than seen in terms of their own goals and expectations.

Conflict between professionals and bureaucracies occurs in any organization staffed by personnel who spend years developing expertise. As Weissman (1973) points out:

> Professionals share a desire for and expect a large degree of autonomy from organizational control; they . . . tend to look to other professionals to gain some measure of self-esteem, are not likely to be devoted to any one organization, and accept a value system that puts great emphasis on the client's interest.
>
> Bureaucrats are different from professionals. They perform specialized and routine activities under the supervision of a hierarchy of officials. Their loyalty and career are tied up with their organization. Therefore, conflict results when professionals are required to perform like bureaucrats. (p. viii)

In social work, professionals and bureaucrats are not two different sets of people; more typically, a professional person occupies a bureaucratic role.

Bureaucratic forms of organization are useful in social

services, because no other feasible organizational model has properties as well suited to carrying out the very complex functions required of social services (Pruger, 1978). Each agency has a bureaucratic structure by which it delegates its tasks and stabilizes its operations. The executive director is the primary administrative officer and has direct responsibility for the day-to-day functioning of the agency. Executive directors are usually responsible for getting the money to run the agency; this responsibility may occupy most of their time and thought. They report to the board of directors or a public body. They are usually involved in working with other agencies toward community social work goals and in the public relations functions of the agency.

Below the executive, you may find a bewildering array of division directors, unit supervisors, consultants, and line supervisors. A small agency may have only three levels of hierarchy: the executive, the supervisors, and the workers. Line workers are most conscious of their relationship to their direct supervisor, whose two functions may seem contradictory: (1) helping workers to improve their skills in the interests of getting the present job done at the best level possible; and (2) applying performance standards to workers and evaluating their performance relative to those standards. Like workers, supervisors differ; some may be more interested in job security and tenure than in the client's needs for service or your need for support and learning opportunities. As a beginning worker, you will benefit from the supervisor's assistance in increasing your self-awareness, improving your way of working, and enlarging your fund of knowledge about people, resources, and helping processes.

You may need considerable support from supervisors in dealing with day-to-day job frustrations. Harry Wasserman (1970) found that, in a large public agency, what workers were able to offer clients was more likely to be determined by structural constraints than by the workers' knowledge and skills; of the 12 workers studied, eight had left the agency after two years. Wasserman (1970) concluded that "the two principal feelings expressed by the 12 new professional workers during the two-year period were frustration and fatigue" and that "they were exhausted by having day after day to face critical human situations with insufficient material, intellectual and emotional resources and support" (p. 99). Supervisors cannot wave a magic wand and undo the effects of structural constraints on your capacity to help. But a

supervisor can, through support and the offer of intellectual and emotional resources, make a difference in what you are able to do and how you grow on the job.

You will find it necessary to work within a bureaucratic structure; it will not help you or your applicants and clients to regard the bureaucracy as your enemy. Rather, it must be understood as a reality—a complex system within which both you and clients are subsystems. You will need to learn to work within, to use, and to change bureaucracy, rather than to simply make yourself feel good by seeing bureaucracy as bad (Pruger, 1978).

MANAGING CONFLICTS AMONG THE SOURCES OF AUTHORITY

In Chapter 2, we introduced role theory and the notion of a role set. As a social worker, you are part of a role set in which you receive expectations about your practice from your applicant or client, your profession, and your agency. Sometimes, these expectations will be in conflict, and you will need to find a way to resolve or manage the conflict (Drolen & Harrison, 1991; Globerman & Bego, 1995). Commonly, this conflict is between the expectations of the agency, derived from its function or its bureaucratic structure, and the expectations of the profession. Less frequent is conflict between the applicant or client's expectations of what you will do and the profession's expectations of what you should do. Conflict between the client's expectations and the agency's expectations is also conceivable, but it tends to be contained within the conflict between agency and profession, as long as the client's expectations are reasonable, ethical, and legal.

Conflict between Agency and Professional Expectations

On many occasions, the judgment that you and your client form about how best to move toward the client's objective will conflict with what is possible, given the resources and parameters of your agency. You may find yourself discouraged and angered by the unavoidable compromises that you must make between your client's wants and the demands of the agency in particular and of society in general. If you better understand the bureaucracy within which you practice, some of this frustration can be avoided, and you will be more effective in bringing about change in agency functioning.

Accountability and evaluation. Weissman (1973) points out that professionals who are working to change the bureaucratic structure need to recognize the difference between nonprofit and profit-making organizations: "Money serves as an alarm system in private enterprise" (p. vii). For nonprofit organizations, there is only an indirect connection between the product produced and revenue. Thus, the alarm system that should bring change is severely flawed. Both professionals and agency executives may prefer to be judged by effort expended, rather than by the success or failure of the effort. However, social agencies cannot solve their problems without an effective accountability system. With no risk of being penalized, the administration has little need to seriously consider the views and ideas of lower-level staff or clients. It may be that the profession's increasing reliance on third-party payments and managed care will increase pressure for accountability. We need to ensure, however, that accountability is defined in terms of outcomes acceptable to clients as well as efficient service delivery.

Who should evaluate the effectiveness of social work? Is it to be the worker, the supervisor, the executive, the board, the general public, or the client? To achieve objectives is the appropriate outcome of service, and service objectives for clients are determined by client and worker, not by the agency. Yet the agency has a vital stake in both what the objectives are and how they are reached. Agencies may define four or five broad classes of goals appropriate to their function, but these broad goal classifications must be operationalized and made concrete with individual clients. Thus, the agency policy becomes an important part of objective setting. It will take skill for you to negotiate agency policy and client desires so that the objective set is both realistic and desired, effective alternative means to achieve the objective are considered, and an action plan is selected.

Standardized means. Specialization and standardization of tasks and the rational allocation or assignment of these tasks in accordance with an overall plan is central to bureaucracy (Weber, 1947). Collective tasks may be broken down into component tasks that are means to a collective end. Two assumptions underlie this concept:(1) that there is a clear, consistent, complete, and generally agreed-upon definition of the ulti-

mate end toward which the organization is working; and (2) that the end is achievable through standardized means (Lerner, 1972).

A social agency usually states the ends it intends to pursue in such general terms (for example, the support of healthy family life) that the extent to which they have been achieved cannot be measured. Alternatively, the ends may be expressed in programmatic terms—such as crisis intervention, an aftercare program, a family therapy program, a drug program—with the consequence that the clients' problems are defined in relation to programs rather than to clients' objectives. Further, we do not have standardized means to apply, even if the client could fit within a standardized objective.

In working with individual human beings, we are simply not able to say, "If this, then that." There are too many variables in each ecosystem. A profession works by applying principles and methods to resolve problems determined by unique client input and professional judgment, rather than by employing standardized procedures toward some predetermined objective established by a hierarchical authority. The individual objective of any client must both fit within the agency's generalized goal and be specific to the client. Your goals with clients will be specific statements about what must be achieved for this particular client in this particular situation. Most generalized agency goals easily lend themselves to the development of particular client objectives if you understand the purpose and function of goals in the helping process; the important point is that the overall agency goals must be individualized for each client.

Orientation toward authority. The professional regards authority as residing in professional competence; the bureaucrat sees authority as residing in the position held. Correspondingly, professionals orient themselves toward serving the best interests of the client, whereas the bureaucrat seeks to serve the best interests of the organization. Professionals usually identify with their professional colleagues, both on an individual basis and in their professional association; bureaucrats identify with the bureaucracy. Morgan (1962) notes that, in exercising power, "the professional norm is to influence clients and peers by modes which are oriented toward the pole of free exchange while the bureaucratic norm is oriented toward the pole of coercion supported by invoking of sanctions" (p. 115).

Working within the Bureaucracy

When you accept a position on an agency staff, accept a salary from the agency, and use agency resources to help clients, you cannot disregard agency policies and procedures. You are bound by those policies. If they are unacceptable, you must either work to change them while remaining bound by them or else leave the agency and work for change from the outside. Robert Pruger (1973) suggests that, if you stay, you need to become a good bureaucrat, by developing the qualities and tactics summarized in Exhibit 5–4.

The policies and practices of an agency are communicated to clients through your words and actions. How you handle yourself, as a concerned professional, is important to clients when they have to deal with less than adequate resources. The agency is not a monolithic organization; bureaucracies are also systems and, as such, are amenable to change. You need to learn ways of changing agency policy and to recognize opportunities for their use. You are responsible for how you interpret policy and for being creative in making resources available. In addition, all policy, all procedures, and all rules

have some slippage, some room for maneuver. You must be alert for ways of using that slippage to help clients or to expand your autonomy in decision making.

Questioning agency culture. If you are to maximize clients' access to services, you will need an accurate understanding of the policies and procedures of your agency; you must thoroughly understand the parameters of agency policy and the authority available for interpretation. A policy is a broad statement. It has to be interpreted by some individual before it can be applied to a particular case. Too often, practitioners will either ask the worker at the next desk what the agency does in a particular circumstance or give the supervisor a quick call. We suggest, as an alternative, that you follow these steps:

1. In partnership with the client, decide what is needed.
2. Find out exactly what the written statement of the policy says.
3. Think about what that policy actually means and about all of the possible ways to interpret and apply it.
4. Test the various policy interpretations against the plan made with the client.

EXHIBIT 5-4 **The Good Bureaucrat**

Qualities of the good bureaucrat:

1. Staying power. Things happen slowly in complex organizations, but whatever changes workers have in mind cannot be implemented if they do not stay in and with the organization.

2. Vitality of action and independence of thought. Organizational life tends to suppress these qualities. Workers must resist such pressure.

3. The ability to provide room for insights and tactics that help individuals preserve and enlarge the discretionary aspect of their activity and, by extension, their sense of personal responsibility.

Tactics used by the good bureaucrat:

1. Understand legitimate authority and organizational enforcement. Most organizations' regulatory policies and codes allow individuals considerable autonomy if they recognize it. Within the limits of legitimate authority, individuals may expand their discretionary limits.

2. Conserve energy. Change agents should not thrash around and feel discouraged because they do not receive, in a large organization, the kind of support they receive from their friends. Also, master the paper flow of the organization. You should describe what can be changed and work on it, rather than bemoaning what cannot be dealt with.

3. Acquire a competence needed by the organization.

4. Don't yield unnecessarily to the requirements of administrative convenience. Keep in mind the difference between that which serves the organizational mission and that which serves the organization. Rules, standards, and directives as to the way things should be done are means that serve ends. In organizations, means tend to become ends, so that a worker may be more concerned about turning in the mileage report than about the results of the visit to a client. Ends and means should be clearly distinguished.

5. Remember that the good bureaucrat is not necessarily the most beloved one.

Adapted from: R. Pruger, The good bureaucrat. *Social Work, 18*(4), 27–32 (1973).

5. Select the interpretation that will best enable you to help the client with problem solving.
6. Write down that interpretation of the policy and its application to the client situation.
7. Submit this statement to your supervisor, for approval or simply as information. Whether approved or denied, the statement becomes part of the record of service to the client.

Asking colleagues or supervisors about policy is not the proper way to perform your role as an independent professional. Following this course increases the likelihood of receiving a directive that limits what you can do because, where a policy is in doubt or is unclear, the easiest thing for an administrator to do is to say no. Old patterns become stabilized and become harder and harder to change when workers rely on the traditional messages about policy that circulate on the office grapevine. Far too often, workers accept routine word-of-mouth statements about agency resources; they may gripe, but they do not question the interpretation. You can help keep the agency active as an ever-changing bureaucracy by really knowing policy and by using creative interpretations of policy.

A few years ago, one of us conducted a study to find out whether clients were receiving the aid they needed. Workers reported discouragement with the limitations of agency policies and felt that these policies prevented them from really helping their clients. However, the study revealed that the average client of that agency was receiving less than half of the services and resources to which the client was entitled under agency policies. What was limiting client access to services was not the policies themselves, but rather the narrow and traditional way in which workers and supervisors were interpreting them.

Service to the client is not limited to what you do when you sit with the client. Some of the most important work, requiring the most self-discipline and commitment, involves taking on the roles of broker and advocate with the agency's bureaucracy. Social workers often prefer to deal with people rather than with paper, but dealing with paper is an essential part of your professional responsibilities. You may fail the client in hurtful ways if you lack skills in advancing written proposals. Operating contrary to traditional grapevine interpretations of policy may involve you in uncomfortable differences with agency colleagues and your supervisor; it is not easy for an individual worker to move contrary to established patterns and relationships. However, if your interpretations conform to written policy, they can usually prevail in the client's interests, which is what social work is all about.

Changing policy. If policy does not permit adequate service to clients, you will need to seek empowerment strategies to produce change in your organization (Shera & Page, 1995). The first rule of policy change is that griping does not do it; neither does making eloquent statements of feeling. To change a policy, you must first define the problem concisely and document this definition in some detail, by organizing and verifying data. In Reading 5-1, Edward J. Pawlak suggests some tactics for tinkering with organizational structures, rules, and policies to bring about bureaucratic change.

You must be clear about what needs to be changed, about the likely obstacles to change, and about the cost of both the problem and its solution. People unfamiliar with the bureaucratic setting may take a drastic step to change the situation and be shocked by the repercussions. Let's consider, for example, the worker who feels that clients are being poorly served by a policy and resigns in anger and frustration. A newspaper reporter hears of the problem and interviews the worker. Seeing an opportunity to use the power of public opinion, and certain of the virtue of the cause, the worker describes the agency's problems to the reporter. However, when the story is published, many people in the community interpret it as an example of how poorly social workers administer public funds. Community pressure develops to cut the funds of the agency, to set up more stringent rules and regulations governing the social workers, and to replace the social work director with a business manager who will see that rules are followed.

Before acting, it is important to determine what forces inside and outside the organization are keeping the problem alive. What the worker in this example did not know was that the executive and the board were as deeply concerned as the staff with certain policies but had concluded that any attempt to change things would result in costly backlash. This is not to say that the threat of backlash should dissuade you from action. But you need to know the approximate strength of the backlash and to decide in advance how it should be met. For instance, the freedom fighters in the 1960s civil rights movement foresaw the likely response to their activities and drilled themselves in advance so that they would not be taken unawares by sudden hostile reactions.

You should also anticipate the difficulties of the solution. Almost any solution to a social problem brings other problems in its implementation. Be sure that the solution is not worse than the problem and figure out some ways of dealing with anticipated difficulties. Find out whether those with the power to make a decision are simply unaware of the problem, are strongly invested in present policy, or are opposed to any change because a clash of interests and values is involved.

Finally, determine who in the organization has responsibility for decision making in the relevant area and who or what can influence the decision. Timing can be crucial. Like individuals, agencies are most often open to change when they are in crisis—for example, when budgets are increasing or decreasing, when there are great decreases or increases in the number of clients served, when their performance reports are being questioned, or when new methods of dealing with the problem are being widely acclaimed.

Confrontation or collaboration? You will need to understand the process by which change takes place. For instance, the initiation of change often requires a different approach than does the implementation of change. Workers who fight a bruising battle for the initiation of change will lose the war if they are unwilling or unable to be active in the implementation of change. Changes in the way things are done are what makes a difference in how the client is served.

Consider whether change can be achieved more effectively in your situation by an advocacy strategy, a collaborative strategy, or both. Advocacy strategies employ an array of tools—for example, calling on citizen groups, unions, and professional organizations to engage with you in litigation, picketing, bargaining, and building pressure; contriving crises; bringing sanctions to bear through external authorities; and perhaps encouraging noncompliance with policy by workers and clients. Techniques appropriate to a collaborative strategy include:

- providing facts about the nature of the problem
- presenting alternative ways of doing things
- trying to develop an experimental project that involves different ways of doing things and getting permission to implement it

- seeking to establish a committee to study the situation and making recommendations for changes
- attempting to improve the working climate of the agency so that individuals feel trusted and safe and thus can look beyond securing their own position to the task to be done
- attempting to bring professional values and ethics to bear through use of a logical argument
- pointing out what is really happening under the present policy

Clients and Policy Change

Clients can be a powerful force in changing policy that does not serve them well; they can be our allies in policy change. We do not want clients to endanger themselves by social action or to relieve us of our responsibility for advocacy, but one way clients may act to help themselves is to push for policy changes in areas that affect their lives. They may choose to organize themselves collectively or to write individual letters or position statements about troublesome policies; enough letters to a governor or legislator can have an important impact. Too often, we see clients as helpless victims of circumstance and view ourselves as the knights in shining armor who defend them. In respecting client strengths, we should recognize that they can act for themselves in addressing life's difficulties.

At some agencies, clients who are dissatisfied with the services they receive can contact client advocates, ombudsmen, or client/consumer representatives. An advocate will serve as the client's representative to try to resolve the problem. An ombudsman takes on a neutral role, investigates the complaint, and makes recommendations; usually, ombudsmen have no authority to order changes. Consumer representatives also investigate complaints, and are more likely than an ombudsman to have the authority to make adjustments if they find that a client or customer has not been well served. You have a duty to routinely inform applicants and clients of the availability of these services.

Potentially, clients and applicants can also impact agency policy and the way services are delivered by appealing decisions that they believe are wrong and inconsistent with their wants. Most agencies have policies and procedures for client appeals of adverse decisions and hearings or reviews of their concerns. Some agencies, however, are reluctant to make this information fully known to applicants and clients. Clients may also request an appeal or review of decisions that you have made. While few workers like to have their decisions challenged, the right to appeal is a necessary protection against the abuse of power. You have the responsibility to inform clients of their appeal rights and to assist them in exercising those rights.

In some situations, clients and applicants may have recourse to litigation. As child protection work shifts from a helping process to a more adversarial basis, for example, increasing numbers of parents are challenging the decisions of child protection agencies in court. The high cost and long delays of court proceedings, in turn, make mediation seem an attractive means of resolving such disputes (Barsky, 1997a, 1995). Mediation is well established as a mechanism for resolving disputes between commercial firms and customers and between landlords and tenants, but its use in disputes between clients and social agencies is very recent. Using this mechanism, clients may be able to extend to you the authority you need to provide services that are in conflict with agency policy.

Alternative Structures for Practice

Prompted by the difficulties of practicing within a bureaucratic structure, some social workers are endeavoring to develop other structures for their practice. One of these is private practice. In the early 1970s, only about 3% of NASW members were in private practice; by the early 1990s, however, over 30% of NASW members were engaged in full- or part-time private practice (Karger & Stoesz, 1994). Interestingly, a recent survey of MSW students and faculty in graduate social work programs found that a majority of the MSW students expected to do private practice at some point in their career, but the faculty generally did not perceive themselves as preparing students for private practice (Brown & Barker, 1995).

The popularity of private practice among graduate students raises two concerns: First, most private practitioners are from the clinical wing of the profession. As we noted in Chapter 1, social workers doing therapy should have a relatively limited role within the profession. Second, most private practice has depended on user pay. This, together with the therapeutic orientation, has

meant that services are accessed primarily by persons from middle- and upper-class economic groups, which conflicts with social work's historic mission to serve the poor.

Some emerging developments may allay these concerns. First, roles for private practitioners are expanding. For example, there is an increasing demand for mediators to resolve a wide variety of conflicts. Like therapy, however, mediation is a specialist role. What about the generalist practice we are developing in this text? One possibility is the preparation of reports for defense counsel use at disposition or sentencing hearings for juvenile or adult offenders. As probation services become overwhelmed and relinquish this work, in favor of an oppressive law-enforcement orientation, private practitioners may be able to assist offenders in changing their behavior and taking advantage of legitimate opportunities in society. Private practitioners may also find work as case managers in service areas such as child welfare, juvenile and adult justice, and services for older individuals and persons with developmental disabilities.

Second, changes in funding patterns may improve the access of low- and moderate-income persons to private practitioners. As government agencies, insurance companies, and other third-party payers purchase services from a variety of organizations and practitioners, rather than attempting to deliver them directly, opportunities for private practice may increase. Without the huge administrative costs of bureaucratic structures, private practitioners can provide their services at low cost. The use of vouchers and other mechanisms to provide clients and applicants with the means to purchase services directly may also create opportunities for private practitioners (Bertsch, 1992).

Small collectives present another alternative to large bureaucratic organizations. In terms of standardization of functions and specialization of staff, collectives are at the opposite end of the continuum to bureaucracies. In collectives, all staff members participate in decision making. However, collective decision-making structures are very inefficient, because of the time required to discuss matters fully and to reach a consensus.

Can bureaucratic structures be made more responsive? One proposal is to use work teams, in which groups of workers take on joint responsibility for a set of activities (Katzenbach & Smith, 1993; Manz & Sims,

1995). This approach attempts to introduce collective decision-making processes into bureaucratic structures. However, team meetings, if not carefully planned and conducted, can absorb a large amount of time that would otherwise be available for client services.

Many corporations have downsized by eliminating entire levels of middle management. This type of downsizing flattens the corporate hierarchy and reduces the hierarchical rigidity, but requires a highly competent and self-directed worker at the line level. Organizational flattening is likely to be contemplated by governmental and nonprofit agencies (Peters, 1992; Treacy & Wiersema, 1995).

CHAPTER SUMMARY

In this chapter, we have introduced the sources of authority for social work practice, the possibility of conflict among these various sources of authority, and some approaches to resolving such conflict. Here are the major ideas we have discussed:

• As a social worker, your most important source of authority is your clients, who reach an agreement with you to work jointly in defining problems and moving toward mutually agreed-upon objectives. You are most likely to secure authority from clients if you keep your focus on client wants. However, two other sources of authority must also be considered.

• Your second source of authority is your profession. You are expected to practice within the knowledge and value frameworks of social work and to be a competent practitioner.

• Your third source of authority is your agency, which has been allocated resources from taxpayers, donors, or shareholders for use in carrying out its socially mandated function.

• The conflict that you are most likely to experience is between the expectations of your agency and your professional duties to your client. A bureaucratic agency's need to standardize functions may be inconsistent with the autonomy required for professional practice. Limiting definitions of agency functions may leave many client wants outside perceived agency interests. Your intervention plan may conflict with the agency's need to conserve resources or its impulse to self-protection.

• In the event of conflict between your agency and your professional values, you have a responsibility to consider the possibility of changing agency practices. We make the following recommendations:

1. Be aware of how the way in which you are delivering services is affecting clients.

2. Be aware of the written policies of your agency. Do not accept informal interpretations of agency practices that may be circulating within your agency culture if these interpretations appear to limit services or to be demeaning of clients.

3. Document and prepare specific statements of problems and proposals for change within the agency. Try to do this collaboratively with colleagues; a group of voices carries more impact than a single voice.

4. In framing your request for change, emphasize how your proposal will strengthen the agency's function, improve services, increase public support, and so forth. You will want to provide powerful decision makers within your organization with a reason to support the request.

5. Try to avoid publicly embarrassing the agency. Use public embarrassment only as a last resort; such techniques are likely to result in strong countermeasures. You will need a strong support system—both inside and outside the organization—in order to withstand those attacks.

6. Inform clients of their rights to appeal decisions and of the availability of client advocates, ombudsmen, or client representatives within the agency. We encourage you to work toward developing a process for the resolution of client-agency conflicts, if this process is not presently available within your agency.

• You may also experience conflicts between client expectations and your professional values. Some clients may expect you to do things that you think are professionally unsound; others may expect you to refrain from doing things you believe are required of you as a professional practitioner. In these situations, we recommend acting on your professional obligation; discuss clearly with the client the actions you will be taking and the reasons for taking these actions. Generally, we discourage you from doing things without the client's knowledge, even if your actions are inconsistent with the client's wants.

A LOOK FORWARD

In Reading 5-1, Edward J. Pawlak argues that you have a responsibility to work for change within your agency. He offers a number of incremental approaches to producing changes and also identifies some more radical approaches. Which of the approaches are you comfortable with? Which might you have difficulty using?

In the next chapter, we look at ethical practice, in the context of client wants and your responsibilities to your agency.

In Chapter 7, we move to the concept of relationship. Relationship—the pattern of communication you establish with applicants and clients—is the medium through much of your activity as a social worker will occur and is essential to the development and implementation of service plans. This chapter will further elaborate the notion of the client as the source of authority. In Chapter 8, we begin a more detailed discussion of the various phases of the problem-solving process.

READING 5-1 *Organizational Tinkering**

Edward J. Pawlak

Social services are usually provided through governmental and nonprofit organizations. The structures, policies, operating procedures, and regulations of these organizations have profound effects on social work practices and on the services and benefits provided to clients (Moore, 1992). In the interest of meeting clients' needs and increasing service effectiveness, practitioners must sometimes seek adjustments in these matters. For example, standardized nursing home rules regarding the use of physical restraints may have to be modified for particular patients. Some domestic assault shelters do not accommodate male children over 12 years of age, but exceptions to the rule may be desirable because chronological age is not equivalent to developmental age. Managed care policies often need to be challenged because they inappropriately limit access to diagnostic tests and specialists, the type and number of counseling sessions for particular mental health or substance abuse problems, and length of patient stay in hospitals.

Yet many direct service practitioners are not interested in intraorganizational change in the interest of their clients or of good practice. Haynes and Mickelson (1997) express similar concerns about social workers' lack of interest in—or even antagonism to—social action and identify factors within the profession that serve as barriers to such action. Many workers are overwhelmed,

cynical, disillusioned, or burned out by their dealings with organizations (Arches, 1991; Briar, 1968; Cohen & Austin, 1994; Dane & Simon, 1991; Gottlieb, 1974; Hanlan, 1971; Piliavin, 1968; Podell & Miller, 1974; Samanttai, 1992; Soderfeldt, Soderfeldt, Soderfeldt, & Warg, 1995; Specht, 1968; Weatherley, 1983).

Your position in social welfare organizations will usually preclude your pursuing ambitious organizational change from within. However, you can work at change in modest, makeshift, and experimental ways; your effectiveness as a practitioner may depend on engaging in such organizational tinkering. This reading will help you improve your talent in dealing with organizations by examining "both the mundane and the extraordinary as levers" (Weissman, Epstein, & Savage, 1983, p. 203) to tinker with organizational structure, modes of operation, rules, conventions, policy, and programs. I take a partisan stand on behalf of practitioners, but it does not follow that managers are necessarily the villains. The tactics identified here are directed toward those administrators who cause direct service staff to harbor severe misgivings about the organization.

You must bear in mind the pitfalls and dilemmas of organizational tinkering. It takes place in a political climate and in a structure of authority, power, norms, and sanctions (Epstein, 1968; Green, 1966; Gummer & Edwards, 1985; Jansson, 1994; Nader, Petkas, & Blackwell, 1972; Weisband & Franck, 1975). Before embarking on a change effort, it is advisable to assess the prospects for success, by identifying and analyzing

*Reprinted with permission. Copyright 1976, *Social Work*, National Association of Social Workers, Inc.

the factors that might facilitate or impede change (for assistance in organizational or policy assessment, see Brager & Holloway, 1992; Flynn, 1992; Netting, Kettner, & McMurtry, 1993; Neugeboren, 1966; Patti, 1974).

OPPORTUNITIES FOR TINKERING

Bureaucratic Succession

Bureaucratic succession usually refers to a change in leadership at the highest levels of an organization; here, it is defined more broadly, to include changes in leadership at all levels in the hierarchy. Bureaucratic succession is an opportunity to influence intraorganizational change. (Austin & Gilmore, 1993).

Organizations usually go into a period of inaction prior to an administrator's departure. This is a lame-duck phase of organizational life, when any major change is avoided until the new administrator takes office. To take advantage of this period, you can:

- speed up the completion of a pet project
- slow down the initiation or completion of a controversial project that lacks consensus
- organize fellow workers to propose changes that had been unacceptable to the outgoing administration
- suggest criteria for the selection of a successor
- seek membership on the search committee
- prepare a position paper for the new administrator
- propose a revision in the governance structure to enhance participatory decision making
- propose the formulation of a workgroup to facilitate transition

The resignation of a clinician who had served as director of staff development in a large family and children's services agency provided the staff with an opportunity to influence the transformation of the position into that of administrative assistant. The agency had recently undergone many changes—diversified sources of funding including purchase of service contracts, new programs, and rapid growth in staff size and diversity—without an accompanying increase in administrative staff. At the suggestion of the clinical staff, responsibility for staff development was decentralized to supervisors and staff within programs. The clinician's resignation became the occasion for examining whether the position should be modified to serve such administrative staff functions as program development and grants management.

The first one hundred days offer opportunities for change. New administrators tend to be conservative about implementing changes until they are more familiar with the organization; but they are still interested in developing and in making their own mark. This three-month period provides opportunities to orient and shape the perceptions of new administrators who, until they acquire their own intelligence about the organization, are both vulnerable and receptive to influence.

Bureaucratic succession provides an opportunity for an organization to take pause; to examine its mission, structure, policies, practices, accomplishments, and problems; and to decide what it wants to become. You can participate in these processes and take advantage of the structure of influence during this vulnerable phase.

Rules

Organizational rules invite tinkering. They act as mechanisms of social control and standardization, provide guidelines for decision making, limit discretion, and structure relationships between persons and units within the organizational structure and between separate organizations (Perrow, 1972). There are two types of rules—formal and informal. Formal rules are derived from law or are determined administratively or collectively. Informal rules, which may be as binding as formal ones, are practices so routine as to have become organizational conventions or traditions. Rules vary in specificity, in their inherent demand for compliance, in the manner in which compliance is monitored, and in their sanctions for lack of compliance.

You can tinker with rules either by adopting generous interpretations or by using discretion with an ambiguous or general rule. Rules do not necessarily eliminate discretion, but they may eliminate alternatives that might otherwise be considered (Thompson, 1967). Gottlieb (1974) describes rules as "not necessarily static. They appear to be a controlling force working impersonally and equally, but they vary both in adherence and enforceability and are used variously by staff in their adaptation to the 'welfare bind'" (p. 8).

Hanlan (1967) suggests that "in public welfare there exists an informal system that operates without invoking the formal administrative machinery of rules" (p. 93). The director of a community action program encouraged new workers to err on the side of generosity in determining eligibility for programs. A vocational rehabilitation counselor reported that he made it possible for many clients to receive dental services by liberally interpreting a rule that provided dental care only for those clients whose appearance and dental problems would otherwise have prevented them from being considered for employment involving public contact. It is possible to tinker with the manner in which rules are interpreted and enforced.

Another way of tinkering with rules is to avoid what Gottlieb (1974) calls rule interpretations by agents of the system alone. For instance, a client who was denied unemployment compensation benefits consulted his social worker, who called an attorney in Legal Aid. The attorney had a different interpretation of the qualifying criteria. The social worker informed the employment counselor of the lawyer's opinion, and shortly thereafter the client was approved for benefits. In another instance, a group of relatives of nursing home patients studied nursing home regulations, and used their understanding to influence changes in food services practices, including who could assist patients with feeding (p. 8).

A supervisor for public assistance eligibility once reported that a thorough knowledge of all the rules enables the welfare worker to invoke one rule over another in order to help clients get what they need. Gottlieb (1974) points out that rules allow for exceptions:

> For example, an 86-year-old woman with mild dementia had broken her pelvis. While in the hospital she was agitated and needed wrist restraints because she pulled out her IV and catheter, and tried to climb over the bed rails in spite of her pain. During the admission's process into the nursing home, the mother's son became alarmed upon learning that the ward supervisor wanted to rely on pain medication and bed railings to control the mother's movement. The son's report about his mother's behavior in the hospital did not persuade the supervisor to alter her plan. The supervisor reported that the nursing home was under pressure from state regulators to reduce reliance on restraints. The son told the ward nurse that he wanted to appeal her decision to the director of nursing. Upon reviewing the circumstances and regulations, the director ruled out the use of wrist restraints, but approved the use of a tray to secure the patient in her wheelchair and a possy to secure her in bed (a possy is a restraint that wraps around the patient's chest with straps tied to the bed that allow some movement). (p. 32)

A study of regulatory agencies (Nader et al., 1972) suggests that rules are both opportunities for action and potential obstacles. Major effort is frequently required to persuade the agency to follow its rules. In a related context, Haynes and Mickelson (1997) believe that practitioners have a responsibility to monitor the bureaucracy so as to ensure that rule implementation is consistent with legislative intent.

Another way of dealing with rules is to avoid asking for an interpretation. One agency administrator has suggested that personnel should not routinely ask for rulings and urges them to use their own discretion: "If you invoke authority, you put me in a position where I must exercise it. If I make a decision around here, it becomes a rule." Staff should examine the function of rules, discern the latitude they are allowed in interpreting them, and exercise discretion.

The Position Paper

Too often, practitioners rely on the anecdotal or case approach to influence change in an organization. Such an approach is easily countered by the rejoinder that exceptional cases do not require a change in policy but should be handled as exceptions. The white paper and position paper are much ignored means of tinkering with organizations.

A white paper is a report on a specific subject that emanates from a recent investigation. A position paper is a statement that sets forth a policy or a perspective. The first is usually more carefully reasoned and documented; the second may be argued instead of reasoned. Such statements strive for logic and are characterized by their use of both quantitative and qualitative data. Workers can take advantage of agency information and reporting systems, or they can collect and write up vignettes of their experiences with clients that provide scrupulous documentation, informed indignation, and the formulation of a compelling case (Pawlak, Jeter, & Fink, 1983). Both position papers and white papers demand a specific response. For instance, a student social worker wrote a position paper identifying the number of teenage pregnancies, the number of associated medical problems, and the high rate of venereal disease among adolescents. She argued for the redirection of the original planned parenthood proposal from the main office to satellite clinics in public housing developments and schools. The paper was well received and spurred the executive to obtain funding from the housing authority.

INCREMENTAL TINKERING

Lindblom (1970) has characterized decision making in organizations as disjointed incrementalism. Simon (1957) indicates that organizations "satisfice"—that is, they make decisions that are good enough. Uncertainties in the environment, the inability to scan all alternatives, and the unknown utility of a solution or decision all preclude optimal decision making. The complexity would be overwhelming if organizations were to try to comprehend all the information and contingencies necessary before making a rational decision. Thus, organizations are reluctant to make changes on a large scale, because this could lead to large-scale and unpredictable consequences. Resistance to change may often be attributed to organizational structure and processes, rather than to a malevolent or unsympathetic administrator. At the same time, the values and roles of administrators cannot be ignored.

Demonstration Projects

You may consider approaching innovation incrementally and on a small scale by first gaining authorization for a demonstration project. A demonstration project may be bounded by the duration of time or the proportion of the budget or staff time that is devoted to it. The problem with such projects is that the people for whom the demonstration is being carried out are not always specified; if identified, they are not always kept abreast of developments. Often there is a failure to articulate the ramifications and consequences of a successful or unsuccessful demonstration. You must develop a strategy of demonstration—a means of diffusing innovation throughout the organization or into other organizations and of obtaining commitments from the administration when the demonstration is complete. Here is an example. A social worker met with a group of suspended or expelled junior high school students after class to discuss their problems. Realizing that she needed to have a chance to intervene directly in their school behavior, she persuaded the agency supervisor, the principal, and the classroom teacher to develop a pilot project—the opportunity class—to be used as a last resort before expulsion. When the project was organized, the social worker remained in the classroom for several periods at least two days each week. She handled the acting-out behavior problems, while the teacher continued classroom instruction. Eventually, the teacher acquired skill in handling students who were acting out, and the social worker no longer attended. Ultimately, some students returned to a regular classroom, while others were expelled.

The partialization strategy (Rothman & Lubben, 1988) and sheltered experiments (Cohen & Austin, 1994) are other approaches to incremental organizational change. Partialization relies on the selection of a segment of the target population that has the potential for successful implementation of the innovation; this is vital if the innovation is to be implemented throughout the organization. In sheltered experiments, the change initiatives are contained in one workgroup or part of the organization, which is viewed as a laboratory where new ideas can be developed and tested before application to other units. In this approach, the agency views itself as a learning organization (Senge, 1994).

Restructuring Committees

Agency board committees are typically composed of elected members and the executive director of the agency. In addition, in some agencies, one or two staff members may also serve on the committee or occasionally attend meetings to make reports. One strategy for tinkering with the committee is to promote the idea that nonboard and nonstaff members with certain expertise be included on it. For example, a psychiatrist and a local expert on group treatment with children might be recruited to join a case services committee, in order to provide legitimation to innovations that board members were resisting.

Romancing Influentials

"Romancing, as the metaphor implies, requires solicitous sustained attention; it is a process rather than an event" (Pawlak et al., 1983, p. 5). Take advantage of opportunities to develop relationships with organizational influentials. They are more likely to listen to change proposals if made by someone who is well known, respected, and trusted. Such opportunities include going out to lunch, sharing coffee breaks, traveling to meetings and conferences, attending agency retreats and social events, working jointly on a community project, and volunteering to work on a project of interest to the influential.

Austin (1988) has proposed that middle managers should help the boss to do good, by what he calls managing up. Many of his recommendations can be adapted to the relation between front-line staff and supervisors or middle managers. He suggests that it is worthwhile to understand the cross pressures and role strains experienced by managers. Also, like all of us, they make mistakes, have blind spots, and sometimes feel isolated because of their position in the organization. Managing up could include:

- alerting supervisors to an emerging problem they might miss because they are no longer on the front lines
- covering for your boss with higher-ups when he or she makes an honest mistake
- filling in for your boss, if appropriate, when something unexpected comes up
- warning your boss that troubles are ahead
- giving helpful tips
- gently and respectfully helping your boss to recognize a blind spot
- volunteering to help out when your boss has to meet a deadline or is excessively busy

"The 'bottom line' for the managing up process can be captured in a simple question, 'How many times over the past year did you recognize and compliment your superior on a job well done?'" (Austin, 1988, p. 45). Change proposals initiated by front-line staff are more likely to be considered and well received by the boss if you have been supportive and have put some effort in developing a working relationship, thereby setting the stage for reciprocity.

Flynn (1995) asserts that effective advocacy depends in no small part on developing credibility as a person. You have a responsibility to keep on top of what's going on and to seize opportunities for change in a timely fashion. This means that you must purposefully work to create a reputation as a person who is prepared and who has to be reckoned with, rather than someone who is reactionary and who confronts long after a decision has been made or an action taken. This requires frequent and routine exchanges with officials. Credibility is not established by blindsiding officials, nor by setting them up for the shooting gallery.

Persistence

Organizational change "is inextricably bound up with the everyday routines of organizational life and requires a long-term perspective . . . Beliefs and expectations can be affected by frequent, consistent, and positive reinforcement" (Weissman et al., 1983, p. 203; see also Gil, 1987). Organizational change is not a sprint, but a long-distance race; it requires endurance and stamina. You should not give up on change proposals that are rejected during the first go-around. Perhaps adjustments and compromises have to be made; perhaps the proponents of change are too far out in front of other staff and officials; perhaps there is insufficient ownership of the proposal. Sometimes it just takes time for a problem or solution to sink in; officials or colleagues are likely to be more receptive to change upon repeated clobbering from clients or external agents. Staff turnover, changing conditions, new funding opportunities, a different political climate, or a crisis might provide the opportunity to give the change proposal another try. When that happens, seize the opportunity.

Bypassing

Bypassing means that, instead of taking proposals for change or grievances to your immediate superiors, you seek a hearing or decision from a higher level in the hierarchy. This form of bypassing is acceptable and even encouraged in an enlightened organization; government workers, in fact, are entitled to such bypassing as part of due process (Flynn, 1995). Bypassing is risky, however, in that it can discredit views of your judgment if the matter is trivial or if it appears that it could have been resolved at a lower level in the hierarchy (National Institute of Business Management, 1987). Bypassing also places the administration in a vulnerable situation; the tactic, if justified, reflects poorly on the judgment of the superior and the administrators who hired him or her. This may lead to questions of nonretention or spur a desired resignation. For example, when a clinician's complaints concerning the physical plant and security of a youth home went unheeded by the director, he demanded to meet with the executive committee of the board. The director admitted that his own sense of urgency differed from that of his staff, but arranged for the meeting. The executive committee approved some of the recommendations for change and authorized that they be implemented as soon as possible.

Cultivating your boss's boss over a long period is an indirect form of bypassing (National Institute of Business Management, 1987). If your boss shoots down your ideas, you may want to seek as much contact as possible with the person over your boss. This is risky if your boss is respected. However, if you have convictions about your proposal and believe that it should be championed, you may have to do some maneuvering so that higher officials have an opportunity to read your proposal. Alternatively, you may have to take advantage of an opportunity, such as a staff retreat, to communicate your ideas.

Technical Experts

Agencies often write grant applications for funds to support their programs. A critical phase of the application process occurs at a public review of the grant application, when the funding agency invites comment or a letter of support from the agency or from interested parties. If you are dissatisfied with a particular program, and it is an important matter, you can provide the agency that issues the grant with dissenting information, testify at the review of the grant application, or respond from the standpoint of an expert witness. The grant-review process may be an opportunity to voice concern about an agency's program and to influence the advisory group to give conditional approval or disapproval. You may attempt to influence the review process indirectly, by encouraging an expert third party to raise questions about the grant application, or directly. For instance, a social worker was asked to present a technical review of a volunteer program for young offenders in a regional planning advisory group. The program was modeled after an existing program in another part of the state. The documents supporting the application contained a manual that described the role of the volunteer. It suggested that a volunteer should report any violations of parole to the corrections authority but should not reveal this action to the offender. In seeming contradiction, it emphasized that the volunteer should be a friend of the offender. The social worker informed the advisory group of the reporting provision and of his strenuous objection to it. The director of the program had failed to read the manual thoroughly and was unaware of the statement. The advisory group approved the program on the condition that the volunteer not serve as an informer and demanded that the staff codify the conditions under which it may be morally imperative for the volunteer to reveal the offender's behavior.

You may be asked to endorse a program or a grant application perfunctorily, without having read the proposal. In other instances, programs and grants are endorsed in spite of strong reservations. Such exchanges of professional courtesy are questionable, notwithstanding the pressures toward reciprocity that exist among agencies. You should take advantage of requests for endorsement or participation in the grant-review process, particularly if you believe that certain aspects of a proposal or program are questionable. The desire for professional endorsement also underlies agency efforts to recruit social workers for board membership or as paid consultants. Refusal of such offers is a way of making a statement about a program.

Jansson (1990) asserts that technical expertise can be used in advocacy and in managing external controls over programs and agencies: "Technical staff should participate in—and provoke—arguments about technical data and their interpretation by offering alternative interpretations, different criteria and options, and alternative methodology" (p. 24). He urges technical staff to view projects as exercises in argumentation and to perceive the political aspects of their work, rather than viewing their work exclusively in technical terms. His suggestions can be adapted by front-line practitioners interested in changing organizations from within.

RADICAL TACTICS

Whistleblowing

Whistleblowing refers to the disclosure of information, publicly or anonymously, that you believe is evidence of wrongdoing, waste, or mischief: violations of law, rules, or regulations; mismanagement of agency funds or resources; abuse of authority; a threat to the staff's or clients' health, safety, or well-being; and so on. Imagine this scenario. Still concerned about the physical plant and security of a youth home, the clinician already mentioned notified the state monitor about the condition of the home. At the next site visit, the monitor raised questions about the residents' access to balconies and the roof and about the staff-client ratio on weekends.

Whistleblowing should be used only in grave matters, after all other remedies within the organization have been exhausted. You are obliged to have a thorough, accurate, and verifiable account of the objectionable situation. Although whistleblowing has legislative protection, it is not a fully institutionalized value that is universally accepted. Some whistleblowers have become targets of reprisals, including threats and intimidation from co-workers, false accusations of misconduct or mental illness, harassment, lowered performance evaluations, denials of promotion, and loss of employment.

When you consider whistleblowing, investigate the matter carefully before taking action. Initially, this can be accomplished easily by exploring sites on the world wide web that discuss whistleblowing laws, outlets such as hotlines and nonprofit organizations, strategies and tactics, procedures, and precautions (Exhibit 5–5). A search using the word *whistleblowing* will yield a number of useful sites. You should also seek legal counsel; whistleblowing can result in liability damages. You need to consider carefully the professional, moral, and legal standards that support such action (Nader et al., 1972; Reamer, 1992; Siegel, 1992). Consider this example. Several staff members of a program that served sexually assaulted children suspected that a law enforcement officer was not completing investigations of abuse that were assigned to him. They initially checked the allegation with the officer, who claimed that interviews had been conducted. Rather than go it alone, three workers decided to make a joint statement at an interagency team meeting that included law enforcement representatives; they reported that several parents had not been interviewed by the police investigator. The law enforcement agency representatives were upset with what they perceived to be unfounded charges. However, upon further inquiry, it was discovered that the officer had closed some cases without completing an investigation, and records were misplaced. Although the workers' claims were eventually vindicated, their relationships with some law enforcement representatives were never the same. As one worker put it, "No good deed shall go unpunished." However, the staff members did not regret their actions,

and they found support from other members of the program.

Resignation in Protest

Resignation in protest, or public defection, is another tactic that should be used only when you experience unbearable misgivings and find it both morally and professionally imperative to reveal them publicly. The major problem is that the organization has the financial and operational resources to counter the protest, but you are likely to have none. Also, with few exceptions, resignation in protest has a history of aversive consequences for the protester (Weisband & Franck, 1975). A resignation in protest may also discredit the agency. Therefore, you must be prepared to have your observations and conclusions verified, and your judgment subjected to public review and scrutiny. In addition, you must realize that future employers will wonder whether such a history of protest will continue. As an example, suppose that our clinician's concerns about the youth home went unheeded by the board, and he resigned in protest. Moreover, he informed the board and the director that he would discourage any professional worker from accepting employment at the agency. He was effective in discouraging local professionals from accepting employment at the agency unless firm commitments were made to modify policies and practices that were detrimental to clients.

The theory of escalation urges you to begin by using conventional and formal means to express grievances and influence change. Only after these have been exhausted, and traditional means have encountered failure and resistance, should you engage in a series of escalations to such radical forms of protest as boycotting, palace revolts, picketing, leaking information, whistleblowing, and the like. You should not begin by engaging in the most radical and abrasive strategy. Change must be approached incrementally, in order to document the intransigence of the organization. If this is not done, the

EXHIBIT 5-5	Whistleblowing on the World Wide Web
For an extensive international bibliography visit: http://helex.ucsd.edu/-bssinion/dissent1/documents/demaria/bib.html	Other useful sites include: http://www.reporter.org/hillman/courage/downside.html http://www.reporter.org/hillman/courage/levels.html

agency may point to your failure to follow administrative due process. Your lack of etiquette and failure to go through channels may become the bone of contention, and you may become the object of protest (Nader et al., 1972; Needleman & Needleman, 1974; Weisband & Franck, 1975).

CONCLUSION

Working to secure intraorganizational change is a professional right and responsibility and should be a condition of employment. You should have the opportunity to bring insights into the plans and programs of the organization for which you work; such participation requires that you acquire skill in dealing with organizations. Your participation in organizational activity should promote responsive service delivery systems and satisfactory work climates.

Attempting to secure intraorganization change, however, may expose you to risk of retaliation from your agency. You will need a strong support group both to reduce risk and to help you cope with the stress often associated with organizational tinkering. Your professional association is a potential source of support; you may be able to lodge a complaint if your agency is in violation of the personnel standards of your association. This, however, is a radical technique and requires caution. Your agency will probably have formal grievance procedures that you may use when you experience adverse action from your agency. If you are represented by a collective bargaining agent, your union will be a source of support and will have a formal grievance procedure available for you.

LEARNING EXERCISES

1. Review the following terms to be sure you have a clear understanding of the concept. Write a brief definition (two or three sentences), or try to explain the concept orally to a friend or classmate.

    agency culture
    bureaucracy
    bureaucratic succession
    client
    flattening of organizations
    informal rules
    interstitial profession
    organizational tinkering
    professional autonomy
    professional culture
    standardization of tasks
    whistleblowing
    work teams

2. If you are an American student, contact your state board responsible for licensing social workers. How many different types of licenses are available in your state? What are the qualifications for a social work license? Will you be eligible to apply for a license when you complete your degree work?

3. Contact the state or local office of NASW to determine if the professional association believes changes are needed in the licensing law. If so, what changes are advocated and why are these thought necessary?

4. If you are a Canadian student, contact your provincial professional association to determine if the association is involved in any efforts to secure licensure for social work in your province. If efforts are underway, what is being proposed by the professional association? If licensure is not being sought by the professional association, why has the association chosen not to do so?

5. Exhibit 5–6 is a possible service plan for the Birky family, introduced in Exhibit 2–15. Recall that the social worker for this family was employed by a preschool. As the worker, you have some concern as to whether this intervention plan is within the function of your agency. Write a memo to your supervisor to defend this service plan and explain why you think it should be followed.

6. In the memo to the supervisor that you prepared for the previous example, did you seek permission from the supervisor for the service plan, or did you focus your memo on informing the supervisor about the plan and the reasons why you believed it was appropriate? What was the reason for seeking permission or for informing? What do you regard as the advantages and disadvantages of each approach?

EXHIBIT 5-6	A Service Plan for the Birky Family

Suppose that the following service plan has been developed with Mr. and Mrs. Birky (see Exhibit 2–15) to get the ditch covered and to secure damages from the city for the loss of their son. The principle of equifinality discussed in Chapter 2 indicates that there are many ways to move from a problem to accomplish an objective; you may think of other alternative plans to accomplish the goal of getting the ditch covered.

Problem: An uncovered ditch creates a safety risk for children in the housing project in which Mr. and Mrs. Birky live. Two children, including their 1-year-old son, have drowned in the ditch.

Objectives: 1. To get the city to fulfill its commitment to cover the ditch.
2. To secure damages from the city for failure to follow through on a previous commitment to cover the ditch.

Service Plan:

Tasks	To be done by	Completion date
1. Contact legal aid and the family's minister to identify attorneys who specialize in this type of case	Mr. & Mrs. Birky	October 15
2. Make inquiries of legal experts to identify attorneys who have successfully sued the city for damages and accept cases on a contingency fee basis	Social worker	October 15
3. Meet to review the list of possible attorneys and develop a short list of three attorneys	Social worker and Mr. & Mrs. Birky	October 20
4. Arrange visits with the attorneys to discuss the case and fee arrangements	Mr. & Mrs. Birky	October 25
5. Meet with the three attorneys	Mr. & Mrs. Birky and social worker	November 10
6. Meet to discuss whether to retain an attorney to file suit against the city	Mr. & Mrs. Birky and social worker	November 15
7. If decision is to retain an attorney, secure and review retainer agreement	Mr. & Mrs. Birky and social worker	November 20
8. Sign retainer agreements	Mr. & Mrs. Birky	November 24
9. If, after consultation with their attorney, the decision is against suing the city, meet to consider other possible alternatives	Mr. & Mrs. Birky and social worker	November 25

7. Identify at least three ways in which professional autonomy may conflict with the bureaucratic organization of most agencies.

8. Assume that you are the social worker with Mrs. Iverson in Exhibit 5–3. How might you have handled the agency's limited definition of services differently in this case? What steps might you take within the agency to try to change agency policy? Are any of the techniques for organizational tinkering suggested by Edward Pawlak in Reading 5-1 potentially useful? Why or why not?

9. Consider how the various agency representatives who came in contact with Mrs. Morgan in

Reading 7-1 could have been more helpful. How could they have communicated a different climate in the agency, without any change in agency policy or procedures?

10. Do you think Mrs. Morgan in Reading 7-1 might be able to organize and lead an organization of former welfare clients in an effort to humanize the welfare agency? How might you, as a social worker, assist her in doing so? What are the risks of assisting Mrs. Morgan to develop an organization of welfare clients if you are employed by one of the public agencies she encountered? What would you do to reduce these risks?

REFERENCES

Arches, J. (1991). Social structure, burnout, and job satisfaction. *Social Work, 36*(3), 202–207.

Austin, M. J. (1988). Managing up: Relationship building between middle management and top management. *Administration in Social Work, 12*(4), 29–46.

Austin, M. J., & Gilmore, T. N. (1993). Executive exit: Multiple perspectives on managing the leadership transition. *Administration in Social Work, 17*(1), 47–60.

Barsky, A. E. (1995). Mediation in child protection. In H. Irving & M. Benjamin (Eds.), *Family mediation: Contemporary issues* (pp. 377–406). Thousand Oaks, CA: Sage.

Barsky, A. E. (1997a). Mediation and empowerment in child protection cases. *Mediation Quarterly, 14*(2), 111–134.

Barsky, A. E. (1997b). Child protection mediation. In E. Kruk (Ed.), *Mediation and conflict resolution in social work and human services* (pp. 117–139). Chicago: Nelson-Hall.

Bertsch, E. F. (1992). The voucher system that enables persons with severe mental illness to purchase community support services. *Hospital and Community Psychiatry, 43*(11), 1109–1113.

Brager, G., & Holloway, S. (1992). Assessing prospects for organizational change: The uses of force field analysis. *Administration in Social Work, 16*(3/4), 15–28.

Briar, S. (1968). The casework predicament. *Social Work, 13*(1), 9–10.

Brown, P., & Barker, R. (1995). Confronting the "threat" of private practice: Challenges for social work educators. *Journal of Social Work Education, 31*(1), 106–115.

Cohen, B., & Austin, M. J. (1994). Organizational learning and change in a public child welfare agency. *Administration in Social Work, 18*(1), 1–19.

Coursey, R. D., Farrell, F. W., & Zahniser, J. H. (1991). Consumers' attitudes toward psychotherapy, hospitalization, and aftercare. *Health and Social Work, 16*(3), 155–161.

Dane, B. A., & Simon, B. L. (1991). Resident guests: Social workers in host settings. *Social Work, 36*(3), 208–213.

Drolen, C. S., & Harrison, D. W. (1990). State hospital social work staff: Role conflict and ambiguity. *Administration and Policy in Mental Health, 18*(2), 127–129.

Epstein, I. (1968). Social workers and social action. *Social Work, 13*(2), 101–108.

Flynn, J. P. (1992). *Social agency policy: Analysis and presentation for community practice* (2nd ed.). Chicago, IL: Nelson-Hall.

Flynn, J. P. (1995). Social justice in social agencies. In *The encyclopedia of social work* (19th ed., pp. 2173–2179). New York: NASW Press.

Friedson, E. (1970). Dominant professions, bureaucracy, and client services. In W. R. Rosengren & M. Leften (Eds.), *Organization and clients* (pp. 71–93). Columbus, Ohio: Charles E. Merrill.

Gaylin, W., Glasser, I., Marcus, S., & Rothman, D. J. (1978). *Doing Good: The limits of benevolence.* New York: Pantheon Books.

Gil, D. (1987). Individual experience and critical consciousness: Sources of change in everyday life. *Journal of Sociology and Social Welfare, 14*(1), 5–20.

Globerman, J., & Bego, M. (1995). Social work and the new integrative hospital. *Social Work in Health Care, 21*(3), 1–21.

Gottlieb, N. (1974). *The welfare bind.* New York: Columbia University Press.

Green, A. D. (1966). The professional social worker in the bureaucracy. *Social Services Review, 40*(2), 71–83.

Gummer, B., & Edwards, R. L. (1985). A social worker's guide to organizational politics. *Administration in Social Work, 9*(1), 13–21.

Hamilton, G. (1951). *Theory and practice of social casework* (2nd ed.). New York: Columbia University Press.

Hanlan, A. (1967). Counteracting problems of bureaucracy in public welfare. *Social Work, 12*(7), 93.

Hanlan, A. (1971). Casework beyond bureaucracy. *Social Casework, 52*(4), 195–198.

Haynes, K. S., & Mickelson, J. S. (1997). *Affecting change: Social workers in the political arena.* New York: Longman.

Hickman, S. (1994). Social work licensing—what's it all about? *The New Social Worker, 1*(1), 4–7.

Ivanoff, A., Blythe, B., & Tripodi, T. (1994). *Involuntary clients in social work practice: A research based approach.* Hawthorne, NY: Aldine de Gruyter.

Jansson, B. (1990). Blending social change and technology in macropractice: Developing structural dialogue in technical deliberations. *Administration in Social Work, 14*(2), 13–28.

Jansson, B. (1994). *Social welfare policy: From theory to practice* (2nd ed.). Belmont, CA: Brooks/Cole.

Karger, H., & Stoesz, D. (1994). *American social welfare policy.* New York: Longman.

Ketzenbach, J. R., & Smith, D. K. (1993). *The wisdom of teams: Creating a high performance organization.* Cambridge, MA: Harvard Business School Press.

Lerner, B. (1972). *Therapy in the ghetto.* Baltimore: Johns Hopkins Press.

Lindblom, C. E. (1970). The science of muddling through. In F. Cox, J. Erlich, J. Rothman, & J. Tropman (Eds.), *Strategies of community organization* (pp. 291–300). Itasca, IL: F. E. Peacock.

Manz, C., & Sims, H. P., Jr. (1995). *Business without bosses: How self-managing teams are building high performance companies.* New York: Wiley.

Moore, S. (1992). Case management and the integration of services: How service delivery systems shape case management. *Social Work, 37*(5), 418–423.

Morgan, R. (1962). Role performance in a bureaucracy. In National Conference on Social Welfare (Ed.), *Social work practice* (pp. 111–126). New York: Columbia University Press.

Nader, R., Petkas, P. J., & Blackwell, K. (1972). *Whistle-blowing.* New York: Grossman.

National Institute of Business Management. (1987). *How to win at organizational politics—without being unethical or sacrificing your self-respect.* Personal report for the executive. New York: National Institute of Business Management.

Needleman, M. L., & Needleman, C. E. (1974). *Guerrillas in the bureaucracy.* New York: Wiley.

Netting, E. F., Kettner, P. M., & McMurtry, S. L. (1993). *Social work macropractice.* New York: Longman.

Neugeboren, B. (1996). *Environmental practice in the human services.* New York: Haworth Press.

Patti, R. (1974). Limitations and prospectives of internal advocacy. *Social Casework, 55*(9), 537–545.

Pawlak, E. J., Jeter, S. C., & Fink, R. L. (1983). The politics of cutback management. *Administration in Social Work, 7*(2), 1–10.

Perrow, C. (1972). *Complex organizations: A critical essay.* Glenview, IL: Scott Foresman.

Peters, T. (1992). *Liberation management.* New York: Knopf.

Piliavin, I. (1968). Restructuring the provision of social services. *Social Work, 13*(1), 34–36.

Podell, L., & Miller, R. (1974). *Professionalism in public social services* (Study Series, Vol. 1, No. 2). New York: Human Resources Administration.

Pruger, R. (1973). The good bureaucrat. *Social Work, 18*(4), 27–32.

Pruger, R. (1978). Bureaucratic functioning as a social work skill. In B. L. Baer & R. C. Federico (Eds.), *Educating the baccalaureate social worker* (pp. 149–168). Cambridge, MA: Ballinger.

Reamer, F. G. (1992). Should social workers blow the whistle on incompetent colleagues? Yes. In E. Gambrill & R. Pruger (Eds.), *Controversial issues in social work* (pp. 66–72). Boston: Allyn & Bacon.

Reid, W. (1978). *The Task centered system.* New York: Columbia University Press.

Rooney, R. (1988). Socialization strategies for involuntary clients. *Social Casework: Journal of Contemporary Social Work, 69*(3), 131–140.

Rooney, R. (1991). *Strategies for work with involuntary clients.* New York: Columbia University Press.

Rothman, J., & Lubben, J. E. (1988). The partialization strategy: An empirical reformulation of demonstration project planning. *Administration in Social Work, 12*(3), 45–60.

Samantrai, K. (1992). Factors in the decision to leave: Retaining social workers with MSWs in public child welfare. *Social Work, 37*(5), 454–458.

Schwartz, W. (1961). Social worker in the group. In National Conference on Social Welfare (Eds.), *Social welfare forum* (pp. 146–171). New York: Columbia University Press.

Senge, P. (1994). *The fifth discipline: The art and practice of the learning organization.* New York: Doubleday Currency.

Shera, W., & Page, J. (1995). Creating more effective human service organizations through empowerment strategies. *Administration in Social Work, 19*(4), 1–15.

Siegel, D. (1992). Should social workers blow the whistle on incompetent colleagues? No. In E. Gambrill & R. Pruger (Eds.), *Controversial issues in social work* (pp. 74–77). Boston: Allyn & Bacon.

Simon, H. A. (1957). *Administrative behavior* (2nd ed.). New York: MacMillan.

Smalley, R. (1967). *Theory for social work practice.* New York: Columbia University Press.

Soderfeldt, M., Soderfeldt, B., & Warg, L. (1995). Burnout in social work. *Social Work, 40*(5), 648–655.

Specht, H. (1968). Casework practice and social policy formulation. *Social Work, 13*(1), 42–43.

Szasz, T. (1994). *Cruel compassion: Psychiatric control of society's unwanted.* New York: Wiley.

Taft, J. (1935). *The dynamics of theory in a controlled relationship.* New York: Macmillan.

Thompson, J. D. (1967). *Organizations in action.* New York: McGraw-Hill.

Treacy, M., & Wiersema, F. (1995). *The discipline of market leaders.* Reading, MA: Addison-Wesley.

Wasserman, H. (1970). Early careers of professional workers in a public child welfare agency. *Social Work, 15*(3), 98–101.

Weatherley, R. A. (1983). Participatory management in public welfare: What are the prospects? *Administration in Social Work, 7*(1), 39–50.

Weber, M. (1947). *The theory of social and economic organization.* New York: Free Press.

Weisband, E., & Franck, T. M. (1975). *Resignation in protest.* New York: Grossman.

Weissman, H. (1973). *Overcoming mismanagement in the human service professions.* San Francisco: Jossey-Bass.

Weissman, H., Epstein, I., & Savage, A. (1983). *Agency based social work: Neglected aspects of clinical practice.* Philadelphia: Temple University Press.

Wilensky, H. L., & Lebeaux, C. N. (1958). Industrial society and social welfare. New York: Russell Sage Foundation.

York, R. O., & Henley, H. C. (1986). Perceptions of bureaucracy. *Administration in Social Work, 10*(1), 3–13.

chapter 6

Ethical Practice

CHAPTER PREVIEW

In this chapter, we will focus on the professional duties of a social worker—professional ethics. Codes of ethics are usually in written form and established by professional associations.

In this chapter, we will:

- define ethics
- identify your primary ethical duty to your client
- identify your ethical duty to contribute to competent practice by being a competent practitioner; by using, generating, and sharing knowledge; and by taking reasonable actions to ensure that all social workers function in a professional manner
  - identify your responsibility—to both your client and society—to engage in advocacy for social justice and identify some possible conflicts between advocacy on behalf of individual clients and advocacy for larger classes of clients
  - consider the matter of dual relations and the ethical concerns about maintaining both a professional relationship and another relationship with the same person
  - consider confidentiality and suggest that the profession rethink this issue

In Reading 6-1, Kwane Owusu-Bempah argues that confidentiality is not applicable to social work with African families.

Because you have multiple ethical duties—to clients, society, agency, colleagues, and profession—conflict among these duties is likely. You will need to give careful thought to ethical decision making and to resolving these conflicts; besides seeking the advice of your colleagues and supervisor, you should encourage your agency to hire a professional ethicist as a consultant.

We recommend that you obtain the codes of ethics, from the National Association of Social Workers (U.S.) and the Canadian Association of Social Workers, using the contact information in Exhibit 5–2. You will need to be familiar with the relevant national code. Take some time to compare the two codes; you will notice that there are many more similarities than differences in the two.

VALUES AND ETHICS

We have defined values as unprovable assumptions or tenets of faith that guide social work practice. Levy (1973) categorizes values as preferred conceptions of people, preferred outcomes for people, and preferred instrumentalities for dealing with people. In our discussion of innate human dignity and self-determination, we focused on ways of putting these values into effect in day-to-day social work practice. Accordingly, it might seem that these values fall into the category of preferred instrumentalities for dealing with people. These values, however, also incorporate preferred conceptions of people, as they imply that people are capable of making decisions and participating, are to be respected for individual differences and diversity, and can choose among alternatives. We have said little about the preferred outcomes for people, except to indicate that they must be consistent with the value premises; to a large extent, the outcomes of service provisions are subject to the values themselves and thus are negotiated individually with applicants.

The concept of professional ethics is linked to the notion of values. Professional ethics, which are usually codified, relate to the duties of professionals in their relationships with other persons—including clients, other professionals, and the general public—and represent a set of obligations that we accept on assuming the role and status of a professional. You will find a number of codes of ethics in social work; the various state licensing boards, social work professional associations, and other professional associations to which social workers belong have all formulated codes that are binding on members. Barker (1988) has concluded that these codes are so similar as to be indistinguishable and should be given equal consideration. You accept the obligation to practice in accordance with a code of ethics when you join a professional association or become licensed or registered by a licensing authority.

Although the ethical codes of the National Association of Social Workers (U.S.) and the Canadian Association of Social Workers differ in structure and organization, there is considerable similarity in their

substance. The structures of the codes are summarized in Exhibit 6–1. The NASW code "does not specify which values, principles, and standards are most important and ought to outweigh others in instances when they conflict" (NASW, 1996, p. 3), whereas the Canadian code does establish seven ethical duties and obligations, as well as three ethical responsibilities. The ethical duties and obligations are of higher priority than the ethical responsibilities; violation of the duties and obligations can subject the worker to disciplinary action.

DUTY TO CLIENTS

Most codes provide that your primary ethical duty is to work in the best interests of your clients. This must supersede your own personal interest and, perhaps, your

---

EXHIBIT 6–1 Organization of the NASW and CASW Codes of Ethics

NASW CODE

1. Preamble
2. Purpose of code
   - Identifies core values
   - Summarizes ethical principles
   - Designed to help identify relevant considerations when professional obligations conflict or ethical uncertainties arise
   - Provides ethical standards
   - Socializes practitioners to mission, values, ethical principles, and ethical standards of the profession
   - Articulates standards to assess whether social workers have engaged in unethical conduct
3. Ethical principles derived from values of the profession
   - To help people in need and address social problems
   - To challenge social injustice
   - To respect the inherent dignity and worth of the person
   - To recognize central importance of human relationship
   - To behave in a trustworthy manner
   - To practice within area of competence; to develop and enhance professional expertise
4. Ethical standards
   - Responsibilities to clients
   - Responsibilities to colleagues
   - Responsibilities in practice settings
   - Responsibilities as professionals
   - Responsibilities to the social work profession
   - Responsibilities to the broader society

CASW CODE

1. Definitions
   - Best interest of client
   - Client
   - Conduct unbecoming
   - Malpractice and negligence
   - Practice of social work
   - Social worker
   - Standard of practice
2. Preamble
   - Philosophy
   - Professional practice conflicts
   - Nature of this code
3. Ethical duties and obligations
   - Primary professional obligation to client
   - Integrity and objectivity
   - Competence in the provision of social work
   - Limit on professional relationship
   - Confidential information
   - Outside interests
   - Limit on private practice
4. Ethical responsibilities
   - Responsibility to the workplace
   - Responsibility to the profession
   - Responsibility for social change

personal values. This ethical duty may also, at times, be in conflict with your responsibilities to your agency, especially in situations where the agency defines function narrowly or limits action plans on the basis of cost. Recall the case of Mrs. Iverson (Exhibit 5–3 in Chapter 5); there was clearly a conflict between Mrs. Iverson's request for service and the agency policy.

Carrying out your ethical responsibilities to serve the best interest of the client requires that you be clear about who the client is. This is often difficult. For example, in a child protection situation, is the client the young person, the family, or the agency and taxpayers who are providing the resources for the service? In a marital dispute, is the client the couple, the wife, or the husband? There are no easy answers to these questions. You must be clear in each situation, however, as to where your primary responsibility lies and then discuss this matter with the people involved. Another difficulty occurs when working with respondents. Is your primary ethical duty to the respondent or to the person or organization who is requiring the respondent to see you?

In some settings—such as child protection or corrections—social workers have legal power to impose requirements on the people being served. This creates an opportunity for the abuse of power or its oppressive use. We do not like to think that social workers may abuse their power. It happens, however, and consequently we need to have open and clear discussions about how social workers exercise power and how it may be abused. Consider, for example, the experiences of Native peoples in North America, whose children, historically, have been needlessly consigned to boarding schools by social workers.

To guard against abuses of power, we recommend two principles:

1. Always use the least intrusive intervention possible, especially when you are relying upon legal power to impose a requirement. Exhibit 6–2 reports a situation in which young children were erroneously removed from their home late at night because of a social worker's lack of understanding and knowledge. This worker's

---

EXHIBIT 6-2   An Instance of Abuse of Power

Nackawic, N. B.—A family is angry and shaken after three terrified toddlers were spirited away in the night by a social worker who mistook birthmarks for bruises.

Joshua Martin, 3, Jason, 2, and 10-month-old Lolita were returned home with an apology after social workers confirmed the blue marks on the children's backsides were birthmarks, said their father, Denis Martin.

But that was after 12 hours of anguish that has left the children upset and unable to sleep.

Last Thursday, Martin and his Philippines-born wife, Gloria, hired a 17-year-old baby-sitter to care for the children while the couple went grocery shopping in Fredericton, about 40 kilometers to the south.

"When we got back, the baby-sitter was gone and so were the children," said the 36-year-old father.

"And there was a note from a social worker."

Martin said he tried to persuade authorities of their mistake and even spoke to the social worker who took the children. But he was told nothing could be done until morning.

"We told them most children in the Philippines get that birthmark," said Martin.

"But they didn't buy that. They wouldn't even discuss it."

The Canadian Medical Association's Home Medical Encyclopedia says the birthmarks—called Mongolian blue spots—are commonly found on Asian and black children.

The encyclopedia describes them as blue-black pigmented spots found singly or in groups on the lower back and buttocks at birth and notes they "may be mistaken for a bruise."

Russ King, health and community services minister, defended the actions of his staff.

"We did review the situation and the (Family Services) act was complied with fully," King said Wednesday. "The department also has protocol procedures and these were complied with."

Asked if it's normal procedure to remove children when the parents aren't home and leave a note, he said: "The act was followed."

Replied Denis Martin: "Their procedure may have been followed, but the procedure they had was lousy as far as coming into my house and taking my children when we weren't home. They should wait until the parents come home."

From "Terrified Toddlers Taken From Home" in the *Winnipeg Free Press*, October 1, 1992, p. A16. Reprinted with permission.

decision to take the children into care constitutes an abuse of power. It would have been more ethically appropriate to remain in the home with the youngsters—or to arrange for someone else to provide this coverage—until the parents returned and the alleged abuse could have been clarified. In that way, the youngsters would have been spared the traumatic removal from familiar surroundings.

2. Avoid taking precipitous action without first consulting the people involved—whether applicants, respondents, or clients—and carefully considering their views. Exhibit 6–3 contains several recent instances of abuse of power by social workers and social agencies, taken from the files of a single child placement agency. Some of these abuses would likely have been avoided if the social workers had taken the time to secure the wishes and views of the respondents before making a decision.

To sum up, professional legal power may be exercised in ways that are ethically unsound because they do not further the best interest of the client. We suggest three guidelines to assist you in avoiding this ethical problem:

1. Be aware that power can be abused, and consider this possibility in your decision making.
2. Choose the least intrusive services possible when using power to force people into services.
3. Carefully secure and consider the views of respondents before you use power to force people into service.

| EXHIBIT 6–3 | **Abuses of Power in Child Placement** |

Here are recent instances of abuse of power by social workers, taken from the records of a private agency that provides out-of-home services to children and youth served by public social service agencies.

1. Jane, 16 years old, was doing very well in her foster home and her school. She was also active in her community; among other things, she volunteered at a homeless shelter. At a shopping center one day, she had an unexpected encounter with her mother, who pressured her to come home. Jane felt ambivalent about this, and discussed her confusion with the public child welfare case worker. The worker became angry, in the belief that Jane did not appreciate the good home she was in, and took steps to move her to a more restricted setting: The worker telephoned the foster parent on the day after the meeting and told her to pack Jane's clothes. The worker planned to pick up Jane and her clothes when Jane returned home from school and to move her to a shelter, where she would remain until there was an opening in a group home. Jane had no warning of this pending change.

2. Jose, 7 years old, and Carlos, 9 years old, were placed in a Spanish-speaking home in the city where their mother lived. The mother maintained contact with Carlos and Jose, as well as with the foster mother; her behavior was sometimes inconsistent and disturbing to the youngsters, but the foster mother was able, with the assistance of the private agency social worker, to help the mother become more dependable and clear in her communications to Carlos and Jose. One of the public agency workers who had previously served the boys disliked the mother intensely and saw her as undermining placements; the worker had also had conflicts with the private agency social worker who supervised the foster home around the mother's involvement with the two boys. Further, this worker had two older siblings of Carlos and Jose placed with a non–Spanish-speaking home about 200 miles away. This public agency worker successfully pressured her colleague, who had Carlos and Jose on her caseload, to move the boys from the culturally appropriate placement close to their mother and place them with their older siblings in the English-speaking family 200 miles away.

3. Eric, a 16-year-old who identified as gay, had completed a residential treatment program for sexual perpetrators. Extensive planning had been completed—including a number of preplacement visits—to place Eric with a foster family who were comfortable with his sexual identity. Arrangements had been completed for him to receive counseling from a therapist in the community; school coordination had been completed, so he was ready to start school. When he had been in the placement about a month and was preparing for the opening of school, the administrator of a public agency that had legal and financial responsibility for Eric became angry that the private agency would not negotiate a lower rate for Eric, overrode the placement decision of his own social worker, and ordered that Eric be immediately removed from the foster home.

Source: Files of a private social agency that wishes to remain anonymous.

DUTY OF COMPETENT PRACTICE

Both the NASW and CASW codes require that you practice within the limits of your knowledge and skill and the parameters of the profession. You have an ethical duty to be a competent practitioner. This includes the use of supervision and ongoing training to improve your competence, keeping up to date with the professional literature, clear discussion with clients of any limitations in your skills, and referral to others when necessary to carry out a service plan.

The responsibility to be familiar with current professional literature is clear in the NASW code (and implied in the CASW code). Many social workers fail to meet the responsibility of using such knowledge in their decision making. In a study of 73 social workers meeting with 151 clients of family service agencies, Aaron Rosen (1994) examined the knowledge used to make decisions about problems and to select both outcomes and interventions. Value-based normative assertions were the most frequently used knowledge for all decisions; some use was made of theoretical knowledge and policy rationales, but there was almost no use of research-based knowledge. Research knowledge was used much less often for decisions about interventions than for the other decisions.

Generating and Sharing Knowledge

The NASW code states very explicitly that you have an ethical duty to share the knowledge arising from your practice by making presentations at professional conferences and writing for professional journals; this duty may also be inferred from the CASW (1994) provision that "a social worker shall promote excellence in the social work profession" (p. 23). Writing is an essential social skill for communication, advocacy, and sharpening one's own thinking skills (Walker, Carrell, & Roemer, 1996). Williams and Hopps (1988) encourage greater partici-

pation in research and publishing by those involved in the day-to-day practice of social work, as a means of expanding social work knowledge; they offer several suggestions to assist you in getting your work published. Exhibit 6–4 lists some helpful tools for professional writing.

We hope that you will take seriously your ethical obligation to present materials at professional conferences and submit materials for publication. Writing for publication is different from other types of professional writing: Generally, it will be more formal and in the third person, will involve a review of the literature presented in summary form, will include the presentation of case material or other data, and will involve your own analysis or interpretation of the material. In professional writing, the goal is to share your material and your interpretation, rather than to regurgitate what others have said.

If you are to develop presentations and articles for publication, you will need skill at preparing abstracts. Conference program committees make their selections on the basis of abstracts of the proposed presentations. Preparing a paper for a conference is generally the first step toward getting your work ready for publication. Unfortunately, writing courses often overlook this skill; many students progress through a university without ever writing an abstract. Exhibit 6–5 presents material on abstract writing. We suggest that, as an exercise, you prepare abstracts for all of the course papers you are now writing.

Reacting to Incompetent Practice

You have a duty to take action when you become aware of incompetent or unethical practice by other social workers. The NASW code, which is more explicit than the CASW code, suggests that you first approach the colleague to discuss his or her incapacitation, incom-

EXHIBIT 6-4	Tools For Professional Writing

American Psychological Association (1994). *Publication manual* (4th ed.). Washington, DC: Author. (Order by phone at 1-800-374-2721.)

Beebe, L. (1993). Professional writing for the human services. Washington, DC: National Association of Social Workers. (Order by phone at 1-800-638-8799.)

Mendelsohn, H. N. (1992). An author's guide to social work journals (3rd ed.). Washington, DC: National Association of Social Workers. (Order by phone at 1-800-638-8799.)

EXHIBIT 6-5 | **Preparing Abstracts**

The abstract is intended to provide sufficient information that readers can make decisions about whether the publication will be of use in their work or a conference committee can decide whether to invite the writer to prepare a paper. Abstracts are to be both short and specific. Try to avoid general terms that do not convey clear meaning, use as few words as possible, and avoid repetition.

Here is an example of a poorly written abstract:

There are a number of dimensions that are common to professions. The author examines the concept of a profession through exploration of literature sources and interviews with persons who consider themselves to be professionals. A group of five particular dimensions is noted. The article discusses these five dimensions and arrives at

an operational definition of a profession. The author then explores the operability of this definition by applying it to the practice of social work.

Here is another abstract of the same paper:

A definition of profession is developed by examining five dimensions of the concept—body of knowledge, particular skills and techniques, delivery of service to clients, common culture, and public sanction. Elements of all five dimensions are found in social work, although body of knowledge and skills and techniques may be less apparent than the other dimensions.

How does this second abstract differ from the first? In what way is it more helpful in supporting a judgment regarding the entire paper?

---

petence, or unethical behavior and to develop a plan for remediation. If this is not successful, your responsibility is to file a complaint with the professional association—the NASW or the CASW. If you are practicing in a jurisdiction in which licensing is required, you may also have a duty to file a complaint with the licensing board. We recommend that you be quite sure of the facts before you make an allegation. However, we have a duty to our profession, to the clients we collectively serve, and to society to take reasonable actions when we become aware of ethical or incompetent practice by colleagues.

Actions alleging social worker malpractice—in the form of lawsuits, complaints filed with licensing boards or complaints filed with professional associations—have been relatively rare, but they are always a possibility. As a prudent practitioner, you will need to conduct your practice so as to reduce the risk of a successful malprac-

tice suit or complaint (Bullis, 1990; Houston-Vega & Neuhring, 1996; Reamer, 1994a, 1995b). Exhibit 6–6 provides some tips as to how you might do this. If you are subject to a malpractice suit or complaint, your case records will be your best defense; therefore, it is important that these be complete, clear, concise, and written in objective and professional language (Gelman, 1992). The records should support the decisions made. Case recording is an essential part of the service you provide to clients and, as we'll see in Chapter 17, goes well beyond case management. Richard Imbert, president of the American Professional Agency, which handles most social workers' malpractice insurance, recommends that you take the following steps should you be subject to a malpractice suit ("Malpractice," 1997):

1. Call your insurance company.
2. Admit nothing.

EXHIBIT 6-6 | **Tips for Avoiding Successful Malpractice Actions**

Carole Mae Olson, social worker and member of the Board of Directors, National Association of Social Workers, offers the following rules for risk management:

1. Don't even think about writing an incorrect diagnosis.
2. Take threats of suicide seriously.
3. Know your areas of skill and competence and refer clients to other practitioners if you are not qualified to provide the service they need.

4. Follow up on referrals; do not abandon the client.
5. Reveal complete information about your practice to the client, including qualifications, business practices, and confidentiality limits.
6. Monitor the fees due; don't let bills mount up.
7. Avoid dual relationships.
8. Obtain the necessary signed releases.
9. Establish a simple written contract with a client.
10. Use consultation often.

Source: Malpractice: How to sidestep the pitfalls, *NASW News*, p. 5 (1997, February).

3. Cease all contact with the client involved.
4. Do not change or destroy records.
5. Don't discuss the case with anyone other than your lawyer.

DUTY TO ADVOCATE FOR SOCIAL JUSTICE

Both the NASW and the CASW codes establish an ethical duty to provide case and class advocacy. Social work advocacy is goal-oriented activity carried out on behalf of clients and aimed at influencing systems that threaten, or impinge upon, clients' survival, freedom, equal opportunity, and/or dignity. Case advocacy is partisan intervention by a social worker with the goal of improving services and resources for a particular client. In class advocacy, the goal is to improve services for a particular class of people. Advocacy has a long tradition in social work (Ad Hoc Committee on Advocacy, 1969; Gilbert & Specht, 1976; Rothman, 1985; Wood & Middleman, 1991).

Social Justice and Private Practice

There has been extensive discussion of social workers' commitment to promoting social justice (Benn, 1991; Brown, 1990; Ezell, 1991, 1993; Hardina, 1995; Poppendieck, 1992; Specht, 1990; Specht & Courtney, 1994; Stoesz, 1986; Wakefield, 1988a,b). Does the increased attractiveness of private practice and employment in profit-making firms threaten social work's traditional mission of working for social justice? Schriver (1990) reached the conclusion that a clinical gentry is emerging, with little or no commitment to the NASW code. Complex trends, including the incursion of large profit-making firms into health and social welfare service delivery (Karger & Stoesz, 1994; Specht & Courtney, 1994; Stoesz, 1994; Wakefield, 1988a,b), have led social workers into such diverse practice arenas as employee assistance firms, health maintenance organizations, home health corporations, and health management companies (Karger & Stoesz, 1994). Independent private practice is only the tip of the privatization iceberg.

This is not a new debate. Early in the 20th century, reformers from the settlements were accusing the charity organization societies of trying to take the social out of social work (Axinn & Levin, 1982; Leiby, 1978; Lubove, 1977; Trattner, 1989). Porter Lee (1929) asserted that both cause (social reform) and function (direct practice) were legitimate tasks for social work.

Traditionally, the mission of social work has been both to promote social justice and to deliver direct services. Contemporary trends threatening this dual mission need to be addressed deliberately (McCullagh, 1987; Schriver, 1990; Strom & Gingerich, 1993). Also, more humanistic organizational structures must be developed, in the interests of both clients and workers (Fabricant & Burghardt, 1992; Hoff, 1995).

In practical terms, what do social workers do to express their concern for social justice? Borenzweig (1981) found that the majority of social workers in both private and public practice reported no involvement in political activities; those in private practice were just as likely to be involved in political advocacy as were those in public practice. Wolk (1981) found that social workers were more politically active than was the general population; the social workers most likely to be politically active were white, older, of higher educational and economic achievement levels, and involved in macropractice. Ezell (1991) found that administrators are more active in advocacy than are caseworkers. Studying the significance of social workers' role orientations, Reeser (1991, 1992) found that neither social workers with agency (bureaucratic) orientation nor those with a professional orientation were supportive of social activism, although those with a client orientation did tend to be active, especially if they also had a professional orientation. Wagner (1989) concluded that idealistic social workers with a strong commitment to social justice often feel that these concerns are not dominant in the social work community. In a study of social workers' donations of money or time to community service, Hoff, Huff, and Ord (1996) concluded that "social workers in the public and non-profit sectors may be in as much danger of losing their commitment to social justice and reform as those in private practice" (p. 59). However, 68% of social workers in private practice and for-profit agencies reported doing pro bono work as compared to 12% in the nonprofit and public agencies.

Conflicts between Class
and Case Advocacy

Social workers are ethically mandated to carry out both class and case advocacy. However, class advocacy raises complex issues (Torczyner, 1991). At this macro-level of advocacy, you are charged with attempting to speak for potentially thousands of other individuals, without the possibility of an agreement with each individual involved. In other words, you risk infringing upon the self-determination of those for whom you claim to speak. Who is the client? Who decides the purpose and objectives of your actions? Who decides what actions will be taken?

If resources are limited, advocacy poses another ethical dilemma. In those circumstances, your actions in advocating for a specific client or class will also affect the dignity, freedom, and well-being of others. Suppose that you have clients who are low-income Southeast Asians.

Is it ethically justifiable for you to advocate for the installation of a food shelf that would stock foods conforming to your clients' nutritional needs and eating customs? This activity would potentially restrict the access of other needy individuals to limited funds and resources. Thus, while advocating for this service meets your duty to give primary attention to your clients, it might be inconsistent with your duty to uphold the right to equal opportunity for all human beings. George Hoshino offers another illustration of the dilemma in Exhibit 6–7. Public budgets for income maintenance are limited; thus, if some clients receive more than they are entitled to, the amounts available for other equally needy persons will be reduced. What is the worker's duty in this situation?

Requests for advocacy may bring out a conflict of values between you and your client. For example, a group of refugees asked their social worker to advocate

---

EXHIBIT 6–7   The Means Test: A Dilemma in Social Work Practice

In a session on the means test, I gave the example of a professional social worker in a family service agency counseling a public assistance recipient and learning in the confidential relationship that the client was earning a weekly income from baby-sitting. How should the worker handle the situation? One student said he had been an eligibility worker, and used to tell his clients, in effect, ``Don't tell me anything I shouldn't know.'' Another student fell back on the confidentiality rule: What went on between the worker and the client in the interview room was strictly confidential; otherwise, how could the client relate to the worker? It was pointed out that there is a difference between confidentiality in the professional sense and privileged communication in the legal meaning, which applies to the attorney-client, doctor-patient, priest-confessor, husband-wife, and certain other relationships. But even those are not absolutes; for example, doctors must report suspected child abuse.

Assuming that they know what the general public assistance policies are, including the responsibility of the recipient to report any changes in income that affect eligibility, how should social workers behave? The fact is that, in a means test program, any increase in income and assets will reduce the amount of the grant or disqualify the recipient entirely. One student even mentioned that he had lived with a woman who was a recipient. Did his presence and any support he provided the woman and her children

constitute income or resources? Would they affect the grant?

As the discussion proceeded, it was clear that the students tended to resort to various subterfuges to get around the effects of the means test: It is the recipient's responsibility to report; it is not a concern of the worker. If the worker becomes aware of income or assets in the course of his or her professional relationship with the client, he or she has a responsibility to inform the client of the requirement to report additional income. What if the client refuses to notify the public assistance agency and so advises the worker? Our county, for example, has a general policy that all staff who learn of unreported income must report that information to the public assistance unit, whether or not the client does. Some students stated that, if they informed the client that they were reporting the income to the public assistance agency, the client would terminate service immediately. Thus, the dilemma: How can the worker maintain the relationship with the client and, at the same time, ensure that the laws are obeyed? What happens when the worker, while encouraging the client to find work and get off assistance, is told by the client that this would mean loss of Medicaid protection for herself and her children, since most jobs that public assistance recipients can get are not covered by health insurance? Some recipients would regard the advice that they should get a job as simply insane, since they also would have the added cost of day care, which few could afford.

Source: Dr. George Hoshino, Professor Emeritus, School of Social Work, University of Minnesota, Minneapolis.

for the repeal of legislation prohibiting the marriage of children under the age of 16. According to the refugees, this law infringes upon their right to maintain their cultural practices since, in their culture, it is traditional for young women to marry early, sometimes at the age of 12 or 13. The social worker was faced with a conflict of values. She believed that her clients had the right to preserve their cultural heritage, but she could not support the marriage of children at such an early age. Not only would this conflict with her culturally determined viewpoint on the proper age of marriage, but she believed it might present health risks to the young girls. Because of a strong cultural preference for large families, they would probably become pregnant shortly after marriage.

Advocacy might also engender a conflict between you and your agency. For instance, a social worker employed in a shelter for undocumented·Central American refugees was prohibited by the agency from participating in advocacy to reduce violence and harassment directed at the shelter residents by neighbors. The agency was interested in maintaining a low profile in the community. There may also be a conflict between ethical duty and law. Having decided to advocate for these Central American clients, the social worker might be charged with a felony for conspiring with undocumented aliens. To avoid breaking the law, the worker must refrain from any affiliation with the clients that would support their presence in this country. Should the worker abide by the law or give primacy to the clients' needs?

It may also be difficult to determine when an individual case of injustice should be expanded into a cause for social change. Suppose that a school social worker is requested to advocate for the safe passage of Native American students to and from school, because they are frequently assaulted and harassed by other students. Conversations with other school social workers reveal that similar attacks are taking place in other communities. Should the worker continue to devote attention to individual cases of victimization or direct energies, instead, toward larger-scale change—keeping in mind that the worker already has a heavy work load?

One of the keys to working through ethical issues is to ask all of the questions relevant to a given situation. If you do so, you are less likely to charge ahead thoughtlessly. While there are few absolutes in solving ethical problems, some methods of working toward choices are more ethically sound than others. A good place to start is with a firm awareness of social work values. Because social work places a high value on client self-determination, client input is to be elicited as much as possible, by:

- attending to client relationships, with the goal of understanding the full meaning of their wants
- utilizing all of the clients' available skills and resources
- respecting clients' ideas in planning advocacy efforts
- teaching skills necessary for clients to represent themselves without an advocate
- working to make inaccessible systems accessible to clients

In class advocacy, additional measures must be taken to promote client self-determination, including:

- working with client representatives
- keeping the larger population informed of all actions taken on their behalf
- monitoring group sentiment regarding these actions and their consequences

For example, before moving to class advocacy, the worker for the Native American students who were harassed while traveling to and from school should take the time to speak to the students. The worker should involve as many students, parents, and colleagues as are available in identifying the extent of the problem and potential solutions. The role of the social worker as an advocate must always be regarded as temporary. It is important to empower clients to speak effectively for themselves. The school social worker might form a task force of Native American youth to address the problem of victimization and help them develop the skills to speak for themselves. This approach both enhances client self-determination and facilitates the development of advocacy skills among the youth.

Deliberate Misdiagnosis

It appears that some clinical social workers resort to deliberate misdiagnosis in order to meet a client's perceived need for services within the context of funding limitations. Kirk and Kutchins (1988) surveyed a random sample of clinical social workers whose names were drawn from the NASW Register of Clinical Social Workers. Of those surveyed, 70% thought DSM was not a real help in diagnosing marital and family problems; 64% said that the primary reason for using DSM was because of third-party reimbursement; 80% indicated that third-party requirements often influence their diagnosis; 72% reported that deliberate overdiagnosis occurs either frequently or occasionally to help clients qualify for reimbursement from insurance; and 86% indicated that a diagnosis was deliberately used with an individual when the primary problem was in the family system. Deliberate overdiagnosis is, in effect, a way of defrauding a third-party payer—either an insurance company or the government (through a health funding program)—in order to provide payment for the services the social worker believes are necessary for clients.

The ethical dilemma concerning diagnosis is analogous to the means test dilemma presented in Exhibit 6–7. For the most part, social work clients are low-income people. Caught within the welfare system, they are regulated as to the types and amount of mental health counseling allowed by the third-party payor—the insurance company or Medicaid. Many clinical social workers find themselves considering whether to assign diagnoses that will grant clients the time and help they would not otherwise receive. This may mean assigning diagnoses other than the true diagnosis or assigning a very general disorder—such as generalized anxiety—in order to ensure payment.

This ethical dilemma raises a number of questions. For example, is the system really so inflexible that social workers must cheat in order to get services for their clients? Who should be able to determine the types of mental health care that clients need—social workers, the client, or insurance companies? Social workers may take huge ethical chances for the good of their clients if they believe that their clients' well-being comes first. The issues are more complex in the case of private social work therapists. In that case, not just services for the client but the therapist's fees are at stake. How can anyone know if the overdiagnosis is intended primarily to generate income or to provide service? Which is the more powerful motive? And is misdiagnosis ethical if the end result is the provision of service that, on the basis of an accurate diagnosis, may not have been necessary?

Duty to Provide Voluntary Public Service

You have a duty, under the NASW and CASW codes, to provide voluntary public service that benefits society as a whole. This might be thought of as paying your civic rent; we all benefit from community life and, therefore, incur a responsibility to contribute something back to the community (Bergel, 1994). You should give careful thought to how you will fulfill this ethical obligation. One possibility is to engage in class advocacy, especially if your agency job description does not recognize the importance of such advocacy and sets limits on what you can do. A professional association or other interest groups will welcome your consistent, thoughtful efforts toward the social justice aims of the organizations.

DUAL RELATIONS

Both the CASW and NASW codes provide clear boundaries for the professional relationship. You are not to invade the privacy of clients, by requesting information other than that necessary to meet the goals of your work together. Sexual relationships with clients or former clients are forbidden, although the CASW code hedges this by stating that client status ends two years after discharge. The NASW code indicates that social workers should not accept, as a client, any person with whom they have previously had a sexual or social relationship.

Dual relationships, including social relationships, are discouraged. A dual relationship exists when you know a client also as a neighbor, employee or employer, colleague, and so forth. Kagle and Giebelhausen (1994) view dual relationships as boundary violations and harmful to clients; even posttermination friendships between worker and former client are harmful, in their view. They recommend disciplinary action against workers who engage in dual relationships.

In small rural communities, however, the worker cannot avoid involvement in dual relationships (Brownlee & Taylor, 1995; Delaney, Brownlee, Sellick, & Tranter, 1997). The social worker is likely to see a person as a client and as a joint participant in community activities, informally on the street, and so forth. Then the issue is how to manage a dual relationship. We suggest a frank discussion with the client about the likelihood that you will encounter each other in different contexts and the negotiation of an agreement about how that could most comfortably be handled.

Ethical difficulties with dual relationships are most likely in therapeutic settings. Social workers involved in community organizing, community development, rebuilding viable neighborhoods, and developing and mobilizing informal systems of social support are unlikely to see any ethical problems at all in dual or multiple relationships. Indeed, such relations may be essential for their work.

Richard Bodde and Martha M. Giddings (1997) suggest that the avoidance of nonsexual dual relationships may be impossible in today's practice environment and argue that, in the interests of sound ethical decision making, we need to have a more open and balanced discussion of dual relationships within the profession. They offer three suggestions:

1. Nonsexual dual relationships should be viewed from a neutral perspective, in order to facilitate professional discussion of the topic.
2. Social workers need to admit the complexities of nonsexual dual relationships and to differentiate between appropriate and inappropriate dual relations.
3. The key professional issues are exploitation, coercion, and manipulation, which can occur in either dual or single relationships; the focus needs to be on how to prevent these negative behaviors.

RETHINKING CONFIDENTIALITY

Both the NASW and CASW codes identify the social workers' duty to hold material shared by client in confidence. Many social workers treat confidentiality as a fundamental value of the profession, on the same level as client self-determination and respecting human dignity. We disagree, for two reasons. First, the duty of confidentiality with a client has been eroded (Dickson, 1997); both the CASW and the NASW codes establish a duty to report matters such as child abuse or abuse of vulnerable people, a duty to warn persons whose safety may be threatened by a client, and a duty to protect clients from self-inflicted harm. Second, the duty of confidentiality to individuals may result in unintended negative consequences.

Duty to Warn

The duty to warn and the duty to report have created a large number of situations in which confidentiality must be breached. All states and provinces require reporting of child abuse and neglect, and many have statutory requirements to report the abuse of vulnerable adults. These reporting requirements may create ethical dilemmas for family counselors (Butz, 1985; Watkins, 1989). A series of court decisions and statutes impose a duty on social workers to warn potential victims if a client reveals intention to harm someone, even if the information is transmitted in the context of a confidential relationship (Schwartz, 1989).

The duty to warn was established as a legal requirement by the Tarasoff case (Fulero, 1998; Kagle & Kopels, 1994; Kopels & Kagle, 1993). In this case, Prosenjim Toddar confided to his therapist that he intended to kill a woman when she returned from vacation. The therapist took the matter seriously and contacted both his supervisor and the police, who briefly detained the man but had no grounds for holding him. Toddar subsequently killed the woman, Tatiana Tarasoff. Tatiana's family successfully sued the therapist, on the grounds that he failed in his duty to warn her of the danger from Toddar. The Tarasoff case has provided the legal basis for the position that social workers have an ethical duty to warn third parties when a client expresses serious threat that may place the third party in eminent danger. Professional judgment, consultation with supervisors and colleagues, and the resources of an ethics consultant will guide you in determining when threats are serious, when the danger is eminent, and how the warning should be conveyed. You also have a duty to let your client know that a warning must be provided to the third party and to involve the client in deciding how to do so.

AIDS poses a significant ethical challenge for the social worker (Reamer, 1991): If you are working with a client who is HIV-positive, do you have a duty to warn the client's partners (Abramson, 1990; Gelman & Reamer, 1992; Gray & Harding, 1988; Lamb, Clark, Drumheller, Frizzell, & Surrey, 1989; Reamer, 1988, 1991; Ryan, 1988; Schlossberger & Hecker, 1996; Taylor, Brownlee, & Mauro-Hopkins, 1996)? How do you weigh your duty of confidentiality to your client against your duty to warn partners of the client's HIV-positive status? Exhibit 6–8 offers three scenarios that illustrate this dilemma. We propose the following guidelines:

1. You have a duty to ensure that persons who are engaging in sexual activity with an HIV-positive client are informed of the client's HIV-positive status.

EXHIBIT 6-8   The Duty to Warn Partners of HIV-Positive Clients

These scenarios highlight the matter of balancing your duty of confidentiality to clients and your duty to warn partners of HIV+ clients.

1. Joe is a social worker in an HIV anonymous testing clinic. Susan, a 24-year-old married woman, tested HIV+. Joe encouraged Susan to inform her husband Frank of her positive status, and to abstain from unsafe sex practices until she had discussed her health with him. Two weeks later, Susan returned to see Joe. She was very distraught and confused. Susan told Joe that she had been having unprotected intercourse with her husband so that he would not suspect anything was wrong. She still had not found the courage to tell Frank about her status for fear of losing him. Joe is unclear how to proceed in his role. He could take more time with Susan toward disclosing her HIV+ status to her husband, but he is also concerned about warning Frank so that he can protect himself.

2. Mary is a student social worker placed at a community college. She has been working with an HIV+ student for seven months. Mary has been helping Steve to cope with the pressures of school, health and relationships. Steve is afraid to inform new partners of his HIV+ status for fear of being rejected. Recently, Mary has discovered that Steve's new partner of three weeks is a male friend of hers. To her knowledge, the friend is not aware of Steve's HIV+ status. Mary wonders if Steve would inform his partner of his positive status if the couple were to engage in sex. Mary feels obligated to work with Steve toward disclosure, but is inclined to inform her friend about Steve's status. She is also considering removing herself from a position of conflict of interest.

3. Barb is an addiction counselor in a drug/alcohol treatment center. She has been working with Michelle for three months. Michelle is an HIV+ recovering injection-drug user. Barb has recently learned that Michelle is using again. Barb has also received reports of Michelle prostituting herself to raise drug money. Further, she has been sharing her needles with other users. Barb realizes that relapses happen and wants to work with Michelle toward recovery. Barb also feels a responsibility to report Michelle's behavior to the proper authorities. However, Barb wonders if it should be up to Michelle's sexual and needle-sharing partners to protect themselves responsibly.

From "Confidentiality *versus* the duty to protect: An ethical dilemma with HIV/AIDS clients" by S. Taylor, K. Brownlee, and K. Mauro-Hopkins in *The Social Worker/Le travailleur social, 64*(4), pp. 9–10. Copyright © 1996 Canadian Association of Social Workers.

---

2. You should discuss this responsibility openly with your client and jointly develop a plan for informing the partner.

3. If the client fails to follow through on the plan, you will need to take action to inform the partner, but you should first discuss your plan for doing so with the client.

Confidentiality is particularly problematic for social workers practicing in police settings (Curtis & Lutkus, 1985) and in schools (Berman-Rossi & Rossi, 1990; Garrett, 1994). A New Jersey survey found social workers more likely than psychiatrists or psychologists to report that they would breach confidentiality; the groups were presented with a series of vignettes relating to duty to warn and duty to protect others (Lindenthal, Jordan, Lentz, & Thomas, 1988). With so many limitations on confidentiality, social workers might seriously reconsider whether to offer it at all. We believe you do have an obligation, however, to clearly discuss with the client what information you will be sharing, with whom you will be sharing it, and the reasons for such disclosures.

Negative Consequences of Confidentiality

There are additional reasons to reconsider the importance of confidentiality. First, the concept may deprive applicants and clients of responsibility for their own oral statements. In Exhibit 6–9, Warren, having shared certain information with Mr. Corrado, has a responsibility to share this information with the court. To deny him this responsibility would imply that Warren is incapable of facing his obligations and would be a threat to his dignity. But what do you do if an applicant says, "I would like to tell you something but I want you to keep it secret"? You might reply that you can only determine how to use the information after it is shared, that the applicant should be aware of this in deciding whether to share the information, and that you will discuss with the applicant how and in what way the information will be used.

EXHIBIT 6-9	Does Warren Have Confidentiality?

Warren Duffy, a 15-year-old six footer, was charged with armed robbery. In a juvenile court hearing Warren denied this charge. He claimed complete innocence and suggested that this might be a case of mistaken identity. He was remanded to Youth House while the charge was investigated. Orlando Corrado was assigned to be his social worker. While	Mr. Corrado was evaluating his background, Warren admitted that he committed the crime with which he was charged. Corrado suggested that it might be best if Warren himself informed the judge of this. Warren refused to do so and added that what he had told the social worker was said in strictest confidence.

Source: F. Loewenberg & R. Dolgoff, *Ethical issues for social work practice* (3rd ed.). Itasca, IL: F. E. Peacock (1988), p. 57.

A second problem with confidentiality is that it may reduce the options available to you and your client. Worker and client constitute a system, and strict confidentiality would result in a closed worker-client system. We discussed some of the dangers of closed systems in Chapter 2. Confidentiality may deprive the system of the opportunities for growth and change generated by outside influences. In particular, confidentiality may be inconsistent with the utilization of larger support systems and social networks. In Reading 6-1, Kwane Owusu-Bempah suggests that confidentiality may be harmful to African clients, because its individualistic focus will undermine traditional African support systems based in the family and community.

We are not arguing for an abandonment of the concept of confidentiality, but only a serious appraisal of its limitations. The best practice will be to jointly decide who is going to share what, in what way, and then to proceed on the basis of a jointly developed service plan. Confidentiality is a resource that a social worker may offer, but it should not be used as a justification for failure to act, a justification for shielding clients from responsibility for their own oral behavior, or a justification for failure to assist clients in building support systems and mutual support groups. Perhaps confidentiality should be considered as one of the negotiated conditions of service, rather than a value.

ETHICAL DILEMMAS

Resolving Ethical Conflicts

Social workers have simultaneous ethical obligations to several people. Conflict among these obligations poses an ethical dilemma (Proctor, Morrow-Howell, & Lott, 1993), in which you cannot meet your obligations to one party in your role set without violating your ethical commitment to another. To resolve an ethical dilemma, it is necessary to establish a hierarchy of values or principles; the more important provisions take precedence and provide guidelines for resolving the dilemma (Loewenberg & Dolgoff, 1988; Reamer, 1993b, 1994b). Exhibit 6–10

EXHIBIT 6-10	A Hierarchy of Principles to Guide the Resolution of Ethical Dilemmas

1. Rules against basic harms to the necessary preconditions of action (such as life, health, food, shelter, mental equilibrium) take precedence over rules against harms such as lying or revealing confidential information or threats to additive goods such as recreation, education, and wealth.
2. An individual's right to basic well-being (the necessary preconditions of action) takes precedence over another individual's right to freedom.
3. An individual's right to freedom takes precedence over his or her own right to basic well-being.

4. The obligation to obey laws, rules, and regulations to which one has voluntarily and freely consented ordinarily overrides one's right to engage voluntarily and freely in a manner which conflicts with these laws, rules, and regulation.
5. Individuals' rights to well-being may override laws, rules, regulations, and arrangements of voluntary associations in cases of conflict.
6. The obligation to prevent basic harms such as starvation and to promote public goods such as housing, education, and public assistance overrides the right to retain one's property.

Source: F. G. Reamer, *Ethical dilemmas in social services* (2nd ed.). New York: Columbia University Press (1993), pp. 60–65.

EXHIBIT 6-11   **Tasks for Ethical Decision Making**

1. Identifying ethical principles in a situation.
2. Establishing priorities among the principles.
3. Assessing the potential risks and consequences of a course of action.
4. Identifying compelling conditions that could supersede normal application of ethical principles.
5. Enumerating provisions and precautions necessary to cope with a course of action.
6. Evaluating decisions in the context of ethical and professional responsibility.

Source: C. S. Levy, *Social work ethics on the line.* New York: Haworth Press (1992), Chapter 3.

---

provides the hierarchy of principles suggested by Reamer (1993b).

Charles Levy (1992) uses the concept of ethical decision making. He believes that social work practice is inherently conflictual and identifies six tasks to complete as you struggle with your conflicting duties (Exhibit 6–11). Loewenberg and Dolgoff (1988) suggest that the concept of ethical dilemmas or ethical problems may not be quite correct; they prefer to think of ethical aspects of practice.

Sorting out your multiple ethical duties to individual clients, families, colleagues, your agency, and society is a complex task. You will need to give careful thought to ethical decision making; we hope that you will have regular conversations about this matter with your professional colleagues and your supervisor. You will also benefit from the services of a professional ethicist for consultation on ethical questions (Reamer, 1995a). Unfortunately, very few agencies will provide such a consultant. This is an important deficiency in the support services available to social workers; we suggest that you and your colleagues discuss this matter and raise it appropriately within your agency.

Recognizing Bad Practice

In some circumstances, what is initially described as an ethical dilemma may prove, on closer examination, to be simply an example of bad practice. Consider Exhibit 6–9: Is this really an example of an ethical dilemma? We do not see an ethical dilemma; rather, we see the very strong likelihood of serious practice errors. It appears that Mr. Corrado did not inform Warren of whom he represented. Further, the purpose of their meeting was unclear, and what use would be made of the information shared had not been clearly communicated. Our view is that Mr. Corrado failed to recognize that he was dealing with a respondent (not a client) and may have had a distorted view of confidentiality.

Exhibit 6–12 provides another purported example of an ethical dilemma regarding confidentiality. We fail to see how this could be seen as an ethical dilemma, except by a very distorted application of the idea of confidentiality. In our view, good practice dictates that this worker join with Debbie, either as a prospect or a respondent, in planning how she will discuss this matter with her parents. This girl and her parents need to be moving quickly to assess the situation, including the

---

EXHIBIT 6-12   **Who Tells Debbie's Parents?**

Debbie Roberts, a 12-year-old sixth grader, is 10 weeks pregnant. She has been a good student. Her teacher reported that she never has had any trouble with her. Until now she has not been known to the school social worker. She was sent to the worker only because she refused to talk to the school nurse about her condition. In her conversation with Debbie, the social worker learned that Debbie did not want to have an abortion, but wanted the social worker to help her make arrangements so that she could carry to full term. She stressed that she did not want her parents to know that she was pregnant.

Source: F. Loewenberg & R. Dolgoff, *Ethical issues for social work practice* (3rd ed.). Itasca, IL: F. E. Peacock (1988), p. 30.

health risk of a 12-year-old carrying a pregnancy to full term.

At least three factors contribute to the tendency to portray bad practice as an ethical dilemma. First, there may be confusion about who the client is. In Exhibits 6–9 and 6–12, Warren is a respondent and Debbie is a prospect; in both cases the social worker has been asked to intervene by another party. Good practice requires us to share this fact with Debbie and Warren (there is no indication in the examples that this occurred) and then to be guided by our practice knowledge.

Would this situation have been any different if Debbie had voluntarily approached the social worker and requested services? We think not, for a second reason. The social worker's knowledge—about the handling of stress, the thought processes of a 12-year-old, the risks of pregnancy to a 12-year-old, and the expected and normal tensions between an early adolescent and her family—should have been brought to bear on this situation. Partnership depends on input from the worker—specifically, the worker's practice knowledge. It is bad practice for the social worker to comply with an applicant's initial request, without drawing on practice knowledge. But what happens, even after this interaction, if the 12-year-old adamantly maintains that she does not want her parents told? We think, at that point, that good practice dictates that the parents be told anyway and that the social worker assist in making protective service arrangements, if necessary. The worker will, of course, discuss with Debbie the actions being taken.

A third factor contributing to the identification of bad practice as an ethical dilemma is an over-emphasis on confidentiality. Many authors treat confidentiality as a value for social work practice; as already noted, we believe there are some fundamental problems with this concept. Confidentiality is very important in some limited areas of social work practice, such as psychotherapy, where people are revealing past feelings, rather than current actions; even in a psychotherapeutic relationship, however, the worker has a duty to warn if a client reveals a plan to hurt others.

CHAPTER SUMMARY

In this chapter, we have introduced the idea of professional ethics as a set of duties that you take on because of your decision to become a social worker. These duties are stated in written codes of ethics; you should obtain those of the National Association of Social Workers (U.S.) and the Canadian Association of Social Workers (using the contact information in Exhibit 5–2) and compare them.

Your primary ethical duty is to your clients. You have a duty to be a competent practitioner; this includes being knowledgeable about new developments in the profession. You also have a duty to contribute to the knowledge base of the profession and to take reasonable steps to assure that other social workers are competent practitioners.

You have a duty both to your clients and to society to engage in advocacy for social justice. But advocacy may create conflicts between your duty to an individual client and your duties to society as a whole.

The duty to avoid dual relationships has been included in the code of ethics, although this will be very difficult for many workers, especially those practicing in small communities or in closely knit cultures and neighborhoods. Concern about dual relationships stems from an overemphasis in the profession on the therapeutic function; it is likely to be less of a problem for social workers practicing in nontherapeutic settings.

The duty to hold what a client tells you in confidence is emphasized in the codes and is often considered a primary value of the profession. Confidentiality, however, has been eroded by other duties, including the duty to warn and the duty to report behaviors such as child abuse. In some situations, confidentiality may be harmful because it undermines the work of traditional cultures and informal social support networks in providing resources and support for problem solving. Thus, you will need to rethink the place of confidentiality in practice.

The fact that you have multiple duties—to clients, to colleagues, to your agency, to the profession, and to society at large—creates difficulties in ethical decision making. You may not be able to simultaneously meet all of these obligations. Thus, you will need to carefully consider the ethical aspects of practice and develop guidelines to assist you in ethical decision making. You should regularly discuss the ethical aspects of practice with colleagues and your supervisor. Agencies should also provide a professional ethicist as a consultant to assist you in working through and resolving ethical questions.

A LOOK FORWARD

In Reading 6-1, Kwane Owusu-Bempah considers confidentiality in an African context and warns that its individualistic focus may undermine traditional support systems.

In this book, we present an approach to social work practice that is both humanistic and scientific. Classification is minimized; clients are involved in a partnership with workers; and individuality is maximized. In Chapter 7, we consider the concept of a professional relationship and, in Chapter 8, we move onto engagement, the first phase of the problem-solving process.

READING 6-1 *Confidentiality and Social Work Practice in African Cultures**

Kwane Owusu-Bempah

Many writers have argued against the rigid application of Western social work principles and values in African settings, on the grounds that they are foreign to African cultures (for example, Silavwe, 1995). Often principles such as confidentiality are inimical to African cultural values (Owusu-Bempah & Howitt, 1995). This discussion argues that the Western notion of confidentiality, so central to Western social work practice, is not applicable to social work with African families in Africa, and may be harmful to them. Its relevance for work with African families in Western societies is equally questionable.

The principle of confidentiality is based on the concept of individuality, which is alien to African traditional societies and other non-Western cultures (Huang, 1994; Owusu-Bempah & Howitt, 1995; Silavwe, 1995). Confidentiality in social work assumes an individual-community dichotomy; it perceives the individual and his or her family, group, or community as separate entities. The notion is based on the assumption that the individual (and his or her actions) and the community of which he or she is a member are more or less independent of each other. African cultures hold a contrary belief. In these cultures, the individual is embedded in the community—so much so that one derives psychological and spiritual sustenance, a sense of selfhood or being,

only through the corporate being of one's family, group, or community.

The Western concept of confidentiality is problematic in an African setting because African societies are characterized by *gemeinschaft* relationships. In such societies, personal problems become group problems and are collectively resolved by the community. In African traditional societies, whatever happens to the individual is felt also by the community, and vice versa. For this reason, as Silavwe (1995) points out, social work or welfare services are typically provided by the extended families, with the support and assistance of the wider community.

Personal problem-solving mechanisms are built into kinship and community relationships. No personal problem escapes the attention and concern of one's extended family or group. Even a matrimonial problem, such as adultery, is treated as a matter that affects the whole community and is to be resolved—or at least discussed—at the community level. Similarly, the group empathizes with, counsels, and supports a rape victim. It would be a mistake, if not bad practice, to disregard this deep sense of communalism when working with African families; one might well be imposing an alien conception of confidentiality (or individuality) on clients who require a sense of kinship or group solidarity. For confidentiality to be appropriate to social work with African families, it must be defined more broadly as information held within the family, the group, or the

---

*An original reading prepared for this volume.

community—that is, information or knowledge that is not shared with out-groups. Confidentiality is of significance to African societies only in so far as it safeguards the group or community rather than its individual members.

Confidentiality in social work demands that information disclosed in the worker-client relationship be kept secret, concealed, private, or personal. However, African societies are more exposed; people's lives are open to scrutiny. Thus, the Western concept of confidentiality does not have the same meaning or importance to them (Clifford, 1996). African societies are characterized by a deep sense of communalism or social consciousness; there is a community of fate. In these societies, people are in communion with one another; they share both the benefits and misfortunes of life; they do not have personal problems, but rather community problems. Hence, an interview with a client, for instance, is very likely to turn into an open forum involving the family, friends, and sympathizers, whose main objective is how best they can mobilize their efforts to help or support the client. As opposed to Western societies, which are characterized by individualism, people in African traditional societies are more concerned about what they can give to one another—the family, group, or community—than what they can take; they strive collectively to meet the survival needs of the community at large, as opposed to individual needs. Africans in traditional societies are social and empathic beings, who thrive on group thinking, group feeling, and group action. To be relevant, social work with African families must accept this and adapt its methods accordingly.

In a traditional African setting, the handling of information about a person who is HIV-positive, for instance, is a simple matter and involves no dilemma. To put the client's selfish need for confidentiality before the health needs of his or her family or the general welfare of the community would be regarded as immoral. The problem would automatically be treated at least as a family problem, and resources would be mobilized to protect the family. The well-being of the client's spouse and children (and the community as the whole) would be given priority over the client's individual need for confidentiality or privacy. In brief, adherence to confidentiality is not a sound practice in situations where decisions

have an impact on everyone within the client's family, group, or community. Such are the situations that prevail in African societies.

Implicit in the principle of confidentiality is the belief in individualism. Its rigid application across cultures may be regarded as Eurocentric. The individualism (or selfishness) of the West would be moral turpitude in many African cultures, where the well-being of the community is dependent upon the cooperative action of its members. What strengthens the life of the community is held to be good and right, and what weakens it is held to be unacceptable, a threat. The community, therefore, has a right to know those factors that weaken it or threaten its survival—including personal problems—so that it may rectify them. Everitt, Hardiker, Littlewood, and Mullender (1992) concur with this view in suggesting that, in participatory projects, confidential knowledge be shared among all concerned parties.

Silavwe (1995) recommends that social work adopt a community approach in order to be meaningful and effective in traditional African settings. This approach is also likely to be relevant and helpful in work with African families in Western societies. In the latter case, however, community must be defined as a group of people with whom the family or the client has close relationships, who are interested in the client's well-being, and with whom the client has *gemeinschaft* relationships, rather than a group of individuals living in close physical proximity with the client or the family.

The level of westernization may determine the amount of confidentiality that would be appropriate in social work with African families in Western societies. Nonetheless, no matter how westernized, African families will not have divested every vestige of their own cultures or forgotten their traditional ways of life; they will always carry with them the cultural baggage that identifies them as Africans. Africans in the West cannot be farther than one or two generations away from their counterparts in Africa. Some will continue to practice African customs traditionally, while others modify them. Indeed, many Africans in Africa are more westernized than a number of those in Western societies. Relevant social work practice with African families in Western societies, therefore, requires consideration of their African backgrounds.

LEARNING EXERCISES

1. Prepare brief definitions (one or two sentences) for each of these terms, or briefly explain the term to a friend.
   advocacy
   class advocacy
   code of ethics
   dual relationship
   duty to warn
   ethics
   value

2. In the section on advocacy as an ethical duty, we identified a conflict of values between a social worker and a group of refugees who wanted assistance in changing legislation so as to permit girls younger than 18 to marry. Do these clients have a right to advocacy? How does the social worker reconcile her own beliefs about early marriage and pregnancy with her loyalty and responsibility to her clients? If the social worker refuses to advocate for her clients, should she also refuse any assistance that might aid their legal action, which she believes is potentially harmful to many young women? It's likely that, even if the legislation is not changed, the practice of early marriage will continue. Does that information influence your views?

3. What would you do in the situation in Exhibit 6–13, which could easily happen to a social worker practicing in a small community? What parts of the NASW or the CASW codes would guide your decision making?

4. In Exhibit 6–7, George Hoshino describes an ethical dilemma posed by the means test. How would you resolve this dilemma? Explain your reasoning. What provisions of either the CASW or NASW codes guide your decision making?

5. Review the instances of abuse of power in Exhibit 6–3. Put yourself in the position of a social worker at the private agency serving the young people who have been subjected to these abuses by workers at the public agency. What action would be appropriate for you to take? Is your decision influenced by the fact that your salary and other expenses of the private agency depend on the fees paid by the public agency for your services?

6. In Reading 6-1, K. Owusu-Bempah discusses the appropriateness of confidentiality in work with African clients. Might these concerns extend to other groups and communities? If so, provide examples. Are there urban neighborhoods where the same concerns might be relevant?

7. Think about how you might fulfill your duty to warn when working with the HIV-positive clients described in Exhibit 6–8. Then team up with a classmate and role-play how you might discuss the duty to warn with your client; if possible, get a third or fourth person to observe your role-play and to provide some constructive feedback.

EXHIBIT 6-13 Dual Relationships and Confidentiality

You are a child protection social worker. Recently you apprehended two young children against their father's wishes. On more than one occasion he threatened harm to you and your family, to the police and the Family Court judge. After the court session, the police officer involved said that "the man was under stress, probably didn't mean what he said, and nothing could be done unless a criminal act occurred."

Later that week you obtain quotes to have your kitchen floor repaired, sign a contract with a local firm, and pay a deposit. The work crew arrives and quite unexpectedly the young man whose children you recently apprehended is in the crew to work in your house. You have to go to a very important meeting that morning and are just leaving as the workers arrive. Your baby-sitter will be at home with your two young children. Given the constraints of professional ethics and confidentiality, how would you handle this situation?

Source: K. Brownlee & S. Taylor, CASW Code of Ethics and non-sexual relationships: The need for clarification. *The Social Worker/Le Travailleur Social*, 63(3), 136 (1995).

REFERENCES

Abramson, M. (1990). Keeping secrets: Social workers and AIDS. *Social Work, 35*(2), 169–173.

Ad Hoc Committee on Advocacy. (1969). The social worker as advocate: Champion of social victims. *Social Work, 14,* 16–20.

Axinn, J., & Levin, H. (1982). *Social welfare: A history of the American response to need.* New York: Longman.

Barker, R. (1988). Just whose code of ethics should the independent practitioner follow? *Journal of Independent Social Work, 2*(4), 1–5.

Benn, C. (1991). Social justice, social policy and social work. *Australian Social Work, 26*(3), 239–244.

Bergel, V. R. (1994). The many (unexpected) advantages of volunteering. *The New Social Worker, 1*(1), 22–23.

Berman-Rossi, T., & Rossi, P. (1990). Confidentiality and informed consent in school social work. *Social Work in Education, 12*(3), 195–207.

Bodde, R., & Giddings, M. (1997). The propriety of affiliation with clients beyond the professional role: Non-sexual dual relationships. *Arête, 22*(1), 58–70.

Borenzwei, H. (1981). Agency vs. private practice: Similarities and differences. *Social Work, 26*(3), 239–244.

Brown, P. (1990). Social workers in private practice: What are they doing? *Journal of Clinical Social Work, 18*(4), 407–421.

Brownlee, K., & Taylor, S. (1995). CASW code of ethics and non-sexual dual relationships: The need for clarification. *The Social Worker/ Le Travailleur Social, 63*(3), 133–136.

Bullis, R. K. (1990). Cold comfort from the Supreme Court: Limited liability protection for social workers. *Social Work, 35*(4), 364–366.

Burstow, B. (1992). *Radical feminist therapy: Working within the context of violence.* London: Sage.

Butz, R. (1985). Reporting child abuse and confidentiality in counseling. *Social Casework, 66*(2), 83–90.

Canadian Association of Social Workers. (1994). *Social work code of ethics.* Ottawa, ON: Author.

Clifford, W. (1996). *A primer of social work casework in Africa.* Oxford: Oxford University Press.

Curtis, P., & Lutkus, A. (1985). Client confidentiality in police social work settings. *Social Work, 30*(4), 355–360.

Delaney, R., Brownlee, K., Sellick, M., & Tranter, D. (1997). Ethical problems facing northern social workers. *The Social Worker/ Le Travailleur Social, 65*(3), 55–65.

Dickson, D. T. (1997). *Confidentiality and privacy in social work.* New York: Free Press.

Everitt, A., Hardiker, P., Littlewood, J., & Mullender, A. (1992). *Applied research for better practice.* London: Macmillan.

Ezell, M. (1991). Administrators as advocates. *Administration in Social Work, 15*(4), 1–17.

Ezell, M. (1993). The political activity of social workers: A post Reagan update. *Journal of Sociology and Social Welfare, 20*(4), 81–97.

Fabricant, M., & Burghardt, S. (1992). *The welfare state crisis and the transformation of social service work.* New York: M. E. Sharpe.

Fulero, S. M. (1988). Tarasoff: 10 years later. *Professional Psychology: Research and Practice, 19,* 184–190.

Garrett, K. J. (1994). Caught in a bind: Ethical decision making in schools. *Social Work in Education, 16*(2), 97–105.

Gelman, S. R. (1992). Risk management through client access to case records. *Social Work, 37*(1), 73–79.

Gelman, S. R., & Reamer, F. G. (1992). Is Tarasoff relevant to AIDS-related cases? In E. Gambrill & R. Pruger (Eds.), *Controversial issues in social work* (pp. 342–355). Boston: Allyn & Bacon.

Gilbert, N., & Specht, H. (1976). Advocacy and professional ethics. *Social Work, 21,* 288–293.

Gray, L. A., & Harding, A. K. (1988). Confidentiality limits with clients who have the AIDS virus. *Journal of Counselling and Development, 66,* 219–223.

Hardina, D. (1995). Do Canadian social workers practice advocacy? *Journal of Community Practice, 2*(3), 97–121.

Hoff, M. D. (1995). The welfare state and social justice: An interdisciplinary study. In G. Magill & M. D. Hoff (Eds.), *Values and public life* (pp. 169–198). Landham, MD: University Press of America.

Hoff, M. D., Huff, D. D., & Ord, L. M. (1996). The social worker's ethical obligation to society: An assessment of charity and justice contributions of social workers. *Arête, 21*(1), 47–60.

Houston-Vega, M. K., & Neuhring, E. (1996). *Prudent practice: A guide for managing malpractice risk.* Washington, DC: NASW Press.

Huang, L. N. (1994). An integrative approach to clinical assessment and intervention with Asian-American adolescents. *Journal of Clinical Child Psychology, 23,* 21–31.

Kagle, J. D., & Giebelhausen, P. N. (1984). Dual relationships and professional boundaries. *Social Work, 38*(2), 213–218.

Kagle, J. D., & Kopels, S. (1994). Confidentiality after Tarasoff. *Health and Social Work, 19*(3), 217–222.

Karger, H., & Stoesz, D. (1994). *American social welfare policy.* New York: Longman.

Kirk, S. A., & Kutchins, H. (1988). Deliberate misdiagnosis in mental health practice. *Social Service Review, 62*(2), 225–237.

Kopels, S., & Kagle, J. D. (1993). Do social workers have a duty to warn? *Social Service Review, 67*(1), 101–126.

Lamb, D. H., Clark, C., Drumheller, P., Frizzell, K., & Surrey, L. (1989). Applying Tarasoff to AIDS-related psychotherapy issues. *Professional Psychology: Research and Practice, 20*(1), 37–43.

Lee, P. R. (1929). Social work: Cause or function? In National Conference on Social Welfare, *Proceedings of the National Conference of Social Work* (pp. 3–20). New York: Columbia University Press.

Leiby, J. (1978). *A history of social welfare and social work in the United States.* New York: Columbia University Press.

Levy, C. S. (1973). The value base of social work. *Journal of Education for Social Work, 9*(1), 34–42.

Levy, C. S. (1992). *Social work ethics on the line.* New York: Haworth Press.

Lindenthal, J., Jordan, T., Lentz, J., & Thomas, C. (1988). Social workers' management of confidentiality. *Social Work, 33*(2), 157–159.

Loewenberg, F., & Dolgoff, R. (1988). *Ethical issues for social work practice* (3rd ed.). Itasca, IL: F. E. Peacock.

Lubove, R. (1977). *The professional altruist: The emergence of social work as a career 1880–1930.* New York: Atheneum, 1977 (originally published Cambridge: Harvard University Press, 1965).

Malpractice: How to sidestep the pitfalls. (1997, February). *NASW News*, p. 5.

McCullagh, J. G. (1987). Social workers as advocates: A case example: *Social Work in Education, 9*(4), 253–263.

National Association of Social Workers (1996). *Code of ethics.* Washington, D.C.: Author.

Owusu-Bempah, J., & Howitt, D. (1995). How Eurocentric psychology damages Africa. *The Psychologist, 18*(10) 462–465.

Poppendick, J. (1992). Values, commitment and ethics of social work in the United States. *Journal of Progressive Human Services, 32*(2), 31–44.

Proctor, E. K., Morrow-Howell, N., & Lott, C. L. (1993). Classification and correlates of ethical dilemmas in hospital social work. *Social Work, 38*(2), 166–177.

Reamer, F. G. (1988). AIDS and ethics: The agenda for social workers. *Social Work, 33*(5), 460–464.

Reamer, F. (1991). AIDS, social work, and the duty to protect. *Social Work, 36*(1), 56–59.

Reamer, F. (1993b). *Ethical dilemmas in social service* (2nd ed.). New York: Columbia University Press.

Reamer, F. G. (1994a). *Social work malpractice and liability: Strategies for prevention.* New York: Columbia University Press.

Reamer, F. G. (1994b). *Social work values and ethics.* New York: Columbia University Press.

Reamer, F. G. (1995a). Ethics consultation in social work. *Social Thought, 18*(1), 3–16.

Reamer, F. G. (1995b). Malpractice claims against social workers: First facts. *Social Work, 40*(5), 596–601.

Reeser, L. C. (1991). Professionalization, striving, and social work activism. *Journal of Social Service Research, 14*(3/4), 1–22.

Reeser, L. C. (1992). Professional role orientation and social activism. *Journal of Sociology and Social Welfare, 19*(2), 79–94.

Rosen, A. (1994). Knowledge use in direct practice. *Social Service Review, 68*(4), 561–571.

Rothman, G. (1985). *Philanthropists, therapists, and activists: A century of ideological conflict in social work.* Cambridge, MA: Schenleman.

Ryan, C. C. (1988). The social and clinical challenges of AIDS. *Smith College Studies in Social Work, 59*(1), 3–20.

Schlossberger, E., & Hecker, L. (1996). HIV and family therapists' duty to warn: A legal and ethical analysis. *Journal of Marital and Family Therapy, 22*(1), 27–40.

Schriver, J. M. (1990, March). *The gentrification of social work: Philosophical implications and value issues.* Paper prepared for presentation at the 1990 annual program meeting of the Council on Social Work Education, Reno, NV.

Schwartz, G. (1989). Confidentiality revisited. *Social Work, 34*(3), 223–226.

Silavwe, G. W. (1995). The need for a new social work perspective in an African setting: The case of social casework in Zambia. *British Journal of Social Work, 25,* 71–84.

Specht, H. (1990). Social work and the popular psychotherapies. *Social Service Review, 64*(3), 345–357.

Specht, H., & Courtney, M. (1994). *Unfaithful angels: How social work has abandoned its mission.* New York: Free Press.

Stoesz, D. (1986). Corporate welfare: The third stage of welfare in the United States. *Social Work, 31*(4), 245–249.

Stoesz, D. (1994). Is privatization a positive trend in social welfare? Yes. In H. J. Karger & J. Midgley (Eds.), *Controversial issues in social policy* (pp. 108–110). Boston: Allyn & Bacon.

Strom & Gingerich (1993). Strom, K. J., & Gingerich, W. J. (1993). Educating students for new market realities. *Journal of Social Work Education, 29*(1), 78–87.

Taylor, S., Brownlee, K., & Mauro-Hopkins, K. (1996). Confidentiality versus the duty to protect: An ethical dilemma with HIV/AIDS clients. *The Social Worker/Le Travailleur Social, 64*(4), 9–17.

Torczyner, J. (1991). Discretion, judgement, and informed consent: Ethical and practice issues in social action. *Social Work, 36*(2), 122–128.

Trattner, W. I. (1989). *From poor law to welfare state: A history of social welfare in America* (4th ed.). New York: Free Press.

Wagner, D. (1989). Fate of idealism in social work: Alternative experiences of professional careers. *Social Work, 34*(5), 389–395.

Wakefield, J. (1988a). Psychotherapy, distributive justice and social work, part 1. *Social Service Review, 62*(2), 187–210.

Wakefield, J. (1988b). Psychotherapy, distributive justice and social work, part 2. *Social Service Review, 62*(3), 353–382.

Walker, M. A., Carroll, M. M., & Roemer, M. (1996). Teaching writing in social work education: Critical training for agents of social change. *Journal of Teaching in Social Work, 13*(1/2), 43–56.

Watkins, S. (1989). Confidentiality and privileged communications: Legal dilemma for family therapists. *Social Work, 34*(2), 133–136.

Williams, L., & Hopps, J. (1988). On the nature of professional communication: Publication for practitioners. *Social Work, 33*(5), 453–459.

Williams, L., & Hopps, J. (1987). Publication as a practice goal: Enhancing opportunities for social workers. *Social Work, 32*(5), 373–376.

Wolk, J. (1981). Are social workers politically active? *Social Work, 26*(4), 283–288.

Wood, G. G., & Middleman, R. R. (1991). Advocacy and social action: Key elements in the structural approach to direct practice in social work. *Social Work with Groups, 14*(3/4), 53–76.

chapter 7

Relationship in Social Work Practice

CHAPTER PREVIEW

This chapter will focus on the social work relationship—the helping relationship that develops between worker and client. When discussing systems theory in Chapter 2, we saw that human systems, individuals, and groups—in fact, all open systems—need input from the world around them if they are to survive and grow. The concept of relationship is central to all social work practice.

This chapter will introduce you to:

- definitions of relationship in social work
- the development of relationships through clarity of purpose and collaboration
- the elements of relationships, including: concern for the other, commitment and obligation, acceptance, expectation, empathy, authority and power, and genuineness and congruence
- qualities of the helping person, including: maturity and courage, creativity, self-awareness, and sensitivity and acceptance of difference

Reading 7-1 is a first-hand account by Addie Morris of her experiences with social workers. Her experiences, which we hope are not typical, illustrate how both agency policy and worker behavior may create conditions in which a helping relationship cannot flourish.

DEVELOPMENT OF RELATIONSHIP

Toward a Definition

The relationship between worker and client was emphasized in earliest conceptions of social work

activity. True, it was the worker who decided which goals would be redemptive for the client and beneficial for society; nevertheless, there was a fledgling acknowledgement of the principle of self-help and a clear conviction of the importance of personal influence (Pumphrey & Pumphrey, 1961; Reynolds, 1963; Richmond, 1899, 1917).

A clearly defined concept of the social work relationship has yet to be articulated, despite the early recognition of relationship as a basic concept in social work theory and the years of experience in the practical development and use of relationship. The importance of human relationships in the promotion of growth and change is universally acknowledged, but there is little agreement about how relationships exert their effect. Many authors merely describe qualities of the relationship that they consider important or record very specific instances of their use of relationship.

Felix Biestek (1957) sees the relationship between caseworker and client as "the channel of the entire casework process; through it flow the skills in intervention, study, diagnosis and treatment" (p. 4). The casework relationship is defined as "the dynamic interactions of attitudes and emotions between the caseworker and the client, with the purpose of helping clients achieve better adjustments between themselves and their environments" (Biestek, 1957, p. 12).

To Helen Harris Perlman (1957), the identifying mark of a professional relationship "is in its conscious purposiveness growing out of the knowledge of what must go into achieving its goal" (p. 64), and "all growth-producing relationships, of which the casework relationship is one, contain elements of acceptance and expectation, support and stimulation" (p. 68). She also identifies authority as an element of the professional relationship and clearly differentiates between the relationship and other aspects of the helping process. Perlman (1971) sees the caseworker as helping people to deal with their problems through (1) the provision of resources, (2) the problem-solving work, and (3) the therapeutic relationship, which she defines as the "climate and the bond" between workers and clients that "acts to sustain and free clients to work on their problems" (p. 58).

In a groupwork context, Grace Coyle (1948), defined relationship as "a discernible process by which people are connected to each other, and around which the group takes its shape and form" (p. 91). Helen Northen (1988) says that relationship consists "primarily of emotional responses which ebb and flow from person to person as human behavior evokes different affective reactions" (pp. 53–58). Describing relationship as one of the major means available to the social group worker, Gisela Konopka (1963) identifies its elements as purpose, warmth, and understanding. According to Konopka (1963), the relationship between the social worker and the small helping group differs from the relationship between the social worker and an individual in the following ways:

1. Members support each other and are not alone with authority.
2. There is greater informality.
3. Members are surrounded by others in the same boat, and there is a feeling of identification that would be impossible in casework.
4. Members are not bound to accept other members.
5. The worker is shared.
6. There is a lack of confidentiality within the group.

Alan Keith-Lucas (1972) defines the helping relationship as "the medium which is offered to people in trouble and through which they are given the opportunity to make choices, both about taking help and the use they will make of it" (p. 47). The characteristics of the helping relationship, he says, are: (1) mutuality, (2) reality, (3) feeling, (4) knowledge, (5) concern for the other person, (6) purpose, (7) the fact that it takes place in the here and now, (8) its ability to offer something new, and (9) its nonjudgmental nature.

According to Pincus and Minahan (1973), a relationship can be thought of as an affective bond between workers and other systems with which they may be involved and may involve an "atmosphere of collaboration, bargaining or conflict" (p. 73). They identify the common elements of all social work relationships as (1) purpose; (2) commitment to the needs to the client system; and (3) objectivity and self-awareness on the part of the worker.

Some recent literature refers to relationship as a therapeutic alliance (Bachelor, 1995; Barnard & Kuehl, 1995; Gady, 1993; Horowitz, 1991; Kokotovic & Tracey, 1990; Marziali & Alexander, 1991). Reviewing therapeutic alliance research, Coady (1993) suggests that social work's historical emphasis on the helping relationship has been diluted in recent years and calls for a renewal of this emphasis. Horowitz (1991) believes that relationship, even though difficult to measure, is at the heart of long-term psychiatric rehabilitation. Marziali and Alexander (1991), reviewing the psychotherapy research, found that a productive relationship includes agreement between client and worker on the objectives of therapy, the tasks to accomplish those objectives, and an interpersonal bond between client and worker.

Descriptions of the professional relationship have largely focused on the one-to-one or one-to-group relationship. However, as Pincus and Minahan (1973) point out, social workers engage in many other types of relationships. In working on behalf of their clients, workers may be involved with landlords, teachers, employers, and even boards of directors and executives of other agencies.

When social workers engage in administration, policy, planning, and organization activities, the system in which they are involved may be regarded as their client in some circumstances, but the social workers' responsibilities within this relationship are different from those in the helping relationship: They carry no responsibility to help the other system with personal problems or to provide personal growth experiences for any individual member of the group or the group as a whole. Rather, they are involved in helping the client to change the professional policies and programs of another (target) system. All social work relationships, however, have purposes and reflect values of the profession. Moreover, all social work relationships involve elements of power and authority; especially in situations that involve policy-making or organizational change, however, that power and authority may reside in persons other than the social worker.

All professional relationships in social work involve self-discipline and self-knowledge, together with the capacity for free, genuine, and congruent use of self. Further, you can deal with other persons and systems better if you have some sensitivity to their situation and goals and some empathy for them. However, the content of the empathic understandings will vary greatly, because social work relationships are emergent and are affected by time and place. How the professional relationship is used will also be different in different circumstances; Exhibit 7–1 summarizes the relevant variables. Nevertheless, all practitioners share a commitment to client welfare as a base for their professional activities.

In focus group research with public child welfare clients and public child welfare workers in Missouri, Brett Drake (1994) found considerable agreement between clients and workers regarding the worker competencies required for child welfare: "The most frequently mentioned competencies, both by social workers and clients, involved the worker's ability to

foster an appropriate relationship with the client" (p. 595). The competencies identified by workers and clients are summarized in Exhibit 7–2.

Purpose

Purpose is a part of all relationships. What makes the social work relationship special is that its purpose and goal are conscious and fall within the overall purpose and value system of the profession.

As we saw in Chapters 1 and 2, the purpose of social work practice is to change something in the interaction between individuals and their environment so as to improve their capacity to cope with their life tasks and, in so doing, to make their aspirations and values more attainable. The purpose and values of the profession focus the purpose of the social work relationship so that influence is not used capriciously. In other words, they shape the *normative purpose* of the social work relationship, which is to change or develop a human or social system so as to improve individuals' ability to cope with their life tasks and to attain their aspirations and values.

Each social work relationship will also be influenced by what's called its *operational purpose*. The operational

---

EXHIBIT 7–1   Variables Affecting How the Social Work Relationship Is Used

1. The purpose of the relationship.
2. The position of the practitioner in the change agent system.
3. The role of the worker and the role of the other in interaction (remember the discussion of the differing perceptions of role in Chapter 3).
4. The role and position of the other in the larger social systems of which both worker and other are a part (the community, church, social groups).
5. The goal toward which the social worker is directing change activities.
6. The goal toward which the other systems are directing their activities. Note that, in the relationship between client system and change agent system, it is assumed that the goal is to develop a relationship that allows for working together. However, relationships between the change agent and individuals in the target system or the action system may

involve relationships of cooperation, negotiation, or conflict.
7. The form of communication. In the direct helping relationship between an individual client and the practitioner as the change agent, communication is usually verbal. However, in the relationship between practitioners and their own change agent system, or between the change agent and action or target systems, many other forms of communication—such as letters and reports—may be used. It is important that the practitioner be skilled in the use of all methods of communication.
8. The skill of the worker in decision making and the use of appropriate intervention methods.
9. The type of system with which the worker interacts. Practitioners may work toward change in a client system that consists of an individual, group, organization, or community; or may work with individuals or groups representing nonclient systems.

Adapted from: Y. L. Fraley, A role model for practice. *Social Service Review, 43*(2), 145–154 (1969).

EXHIBIT 7-2   Relationship Competencies For Child Welfare Practice

COMPETENCIES IDENTIFIED BY CHILD WELFARE CLIENTS	COMPETENCIES IDENTIFIED BY CHILD WELFARE WORKERS
Workers must show clients basic human respect.	Workers must be able to express an appropriate attitude.
Workers must not be pushy or rude.	Workers must avoid presenting a judgmental or blaming demeanor.
Workers must ask permission of clients to look in rooms or examine contents of cupboards.	Workers must not impose their own values on clients.
Workers must be willing to spend time with clients.	Workers must be able to see the situation from the client's point of view.
Workers must be consistently honest with clients.	Workers must project an attitude that is assertive but not aggressive.
Workers must be aware of the dehumanizing context of child welfare work.	
Workers must be able to effectively communicate with clients.	Workers must be able to effectively communicate with clients.
Workers must speak at the client's level.	Workers must use clear, unambiguous language.
Workers must use direct language.	Workers must relate to clients at the client's level.
Workers must be able to really listen to what the client says.	Workers must use body language and eye contact appropriately.
Workers should be able to use small talk as an aid to establishing effective communication.	Workers must avoid the use of threatening terms.
	Workers must use good listening skills.
Workers must be able to develop a comfortable relationship with clients.	Workers must not prejudge situations.
Workers should have the ability to develop relationships that are warm, not simply nonhostile.	Workers must understand situations as they see them and should be open to input from clients.
Workers must use an empathic presentation.	Workers must not base their assessments on prior occurrences as documented in the case files.
Workers must not prejudge families on the basis of reports from other workers or the nature of the initial report.	Workers must clearly acknowledge the client's right to participate in the process.
	The client's role must be explicitly delineated.
	The worker must allow the client to define the situation as he or she sees it.
Workers must have the ability to remain calm and to defuse client anger, especially in initial meetings.	Workers must have an awareness of the impact of child protective services (CPS) intervention.
	Workers must understand the intrusive nature of CPS intervention.
	Workers must have skill in dealing with and diffusing anxiety.

Copyright 1994, National Association of Social Workers, Inc. from *Social Work, 39*(5), pp. 597, 599. Reprinted with permission.

---

purpose of the helping relationship is to increase the coping capacity of the client or to secure needed resources from the environment. By contrast, a social worker who is lobbying state government for an increase in special education funding has a very different operational purpose. The different purpose of this interaction will be critical to the way the relationship develops and is utilized. Even though they share a normative purpose, different types of social work relationships are governed by different operational purposes. The operational purpose determines the outer parameters of a relationship within the overall limits set by the normative purpose.

Finally, each social work relationship has a unique *individual purpose*, which will vary over time; the immediate purpose of this particular interaction will differ from the long-range purpose of a series of interactions. Thus, Mrs. Jones may have become involved in a helping relationship because she wants to have an enduring and happy marriage (a long-term purpose) but, when she comes in today, she may want help regarding the way she responded this morning to her husband's criticism of her housekeeping (an immediate objective that is a step to the long-term purpose). The outreach worker at a community center may be involved with a street gang in discussions about using the center for its meetings. The worker's immediate purpose is to provide the group with a better meeting place, but the long-term purpose may be to help the group develop less destructive activities.

The normative and operational purposes of any social work relationship may be implicit, but you must be able to formulate clearly the immediate purposes of professional contacts with others and to describe such purposes to them. The success of your work will depend upon it. Mayer and Timms (1970) found that clients' lack of understanding of the purposes and values of the professional may obstruct the development of a helping relationship. The unique purpose in the helping relationship should come out of mutual consideration of what the client wants; but it is your obligation to see that purpose is established.

It is important to clarify the operational purpose of the relationship when your primary role is not that of helping—for instance, when a court, community, or other institution expects you to control, or modify the behavior of an individual that is harmful to others and is causing distress to the community. In these circumstances, you must state clearly and honestly the purpose that brought you to the family's door. The statement of purpose may lead you into a discussion of the authority and power you carry in the situation. You must explain carefully and clearly to the family why you are there, your responsibilities to agency or institution or community, and the limits of your authority.

Purpose affects two other related issues: your role as helper and confidentiality. When you enter a situation uninvited, you must not pretend that your only motivation is to help the family. The family realizes that this is patently untrue and that you have other responsibilities; if you are perceived as dishonest, you are giving the family permission to be dishonest in turn. Within the limitation of purpose, you may be able to maintain an honest identification as someone who wants to help; nevertheless, you must communicate that you are entering the situation for other than helping purposes. You should also be aware that help can mean very different things to you and to respondents. Families who have had difficult experiences with self-styled helping professionals may regard the word as a danger signal. Or suppose we are helping an offender in the criminal justice system. Are we helping the offender achieve what he or she wants? The offender may simply want to be left alone. Alternatively, are we helping by changing the offender's behavior, so that—from our perspective—he or she can have a better life?

Your purpose in entering the situation also affects your approach to confidentiality. At the very beginning of your relationship, you must inform respondents what information may be shared outside your relationship, how it will be shared, with whom it will be shared, and whether the respondent will be informed when it is shared. Most people respond favorably to this approach. Such honesty and directness respects their right to share information as they see fit, removes their nagging sense of uncertainty about what happens to information, and results in a more appropriately open response. You should avoid attempts to push respondents to trust you; rather, you should invite them to decide your trustworthiness for themselves, on the basis of their experiences with you.

However, when you explain your purpose to respondents, you must be prepared for a reaction of anger, distrust, and rejection and you must be able to discipline personal feelings and responses. Your ability to understand and appropriately use all the elements of the situation is important if a working relationship is to develop.

Working Together

Relationship does not emerge spontaneously out of some mysterious interpersonal chemistry. It develops out of purposive interaction—out of the business with which worker and applicant concern themselves. On entering the social work situation, the applicant is not looking for a helping relationship but for the redress of specific difficulties. The relationship develops out of communication about these difficulties. You need to be aware that the professional relationship is not necessarily pleasant or friendly. Sometimes the problem is worked out in reaction and anger. Keith-Lucas (1972) writes that "the attempt to keep the relationship on a pleasant level is the greatest source of ineffectual helping" (p. 18); if you seek relationship as a goal, it will generally elude you. But a helping relationship will grow wherever you demonstrate to others that you respect them, that you care what happens to them, and that you are willing both to listen and to act helpfully.

Because the relationship develops out of purposive work, it grows and changes; when the purpose has been achieved, it comes to an end. The relationship that develops between you and the applicant will depend on the purpose, combined with:

- the setting in which you and the applicant come together
- the time limits of the process
- the individuals or groups involved and the interests that they represent
- the capacities, motivations, expectations, and purposes of those involved
- the problem that brings you and the applicant together and the goals each has for its resolution
- the qualities you bring, including knowledge and skills
- the actual behaviors of the parties to the relationship in transactions over time

In the helping process, the relationship may be used in two ways. First, you may use the relationship to sustain clients as they work on the problem. Second, consideration of the relationship itself may become the task; you and the client may focus on the way the client uses this relationship as a prototype of his or her problems in other meaningful interactions. In problem-focused groups, members' interpersonal transactions with the worker and with one another may be the problem under consideration. In task groups, the relationship between worker and group and the relationships among the members are used to sustain them as they work on some other problem that they share.

Both you and the applicant bring irrational elements (bits and pieces from past relationships and experiences that do not fit the present), nonrational elements (emotion, feeling, affect), and rational elements (intellectual and cognitive qualities) to the relationship. These elements come from (Goldstein, 1973):

- past experiences that have influenced the ability of the individuals to relate to others

- the here-and-now physical and emotional state of those involved
- the here-and-now thoughts or mental images of each individual about self, the process, and the problem
- each person's anxiety about the present situation and about the persons in it
- each person's expectations of how to behave and what should come out of the interaction
- each person's perception of the others involved
- the values and ideals shared by the participants in the process
- the influence of other social and environmental factors

You present yourself as a professional and expect to share in the private thoughts and feelings of vulnerable people. Accordingly, you carry special responsibilities for what you bring to the helping process.

ELEMENTS OF RELATIONSHIP

Social workers have used different words to characterize the helping relationship, but the worker qualities regarded as necessary for that relationship have remained consistent. These qualities can be classified into seven groups: (1) concern for the other, (2) commitment and obligation, (3) acceptance, (4) expectation, (5) empathy, (6) authority and power, and (7) genuineness and congruence.

Concern for the Other

Concern for the other means that you sincerely care about what happens to the person and are able to communicate this feeling. Such concern is an unconditional affirmation of applicants' life and needs; you want them to be all they can be and to do all they want to do, for their own sake. You may find it difficult to express unconditional affirmation for applicants. When you enter a situation at the request of a court, a community, or an agency, the family or the individual whom you confront may be angry and hostile and may behave or dress in ways that you find offensive. In those circumstances, it is essential to be aware of your negative feelings and judgments, so that you do not unconsciously communicate anger and rejection.

Don't confuse concern for others with liking. You don't have to like everyone. If you believed that you did, you would be inclined to deny or repress your feelings, rather than to change them. Concern is a sense of so caring for the other that personal feelings of liking or disliking are no longer relevant (Keith-Lucas, 1972).

If we are to help others, we must become deeply involved with them. However, there is a risk that, as our emotional relationship with an individual deepens, we will become overinvolved, out of a desire to see their problems solved. We are overinvolved when we take on someone else's problem as our own and focus on what we want rather than what the client wants.

Concern for another in the helping relationship means that we offer our skills, our knowledge, ourselves, and our caring for clients to use (or not use, if they choose) in their movement toward desired objectives. It means that, within the limits of purpose, time, and place, we respond as they need us to, rather than as our need to help demands; we need to care enough for clients that we leave them free to fail. For most of us, it is easier to do, rather than to stand and wait, but active waiting may be the most appropriate expression of concern. To be truly concerned means that we are willing to be the "agent of a process rather than the creator of it" (Keith-Lucas, 1972, p. 104).

Concern for the other means respecting applicants' and clients' privacy rights. We seek only as much understanding and knowledge of others as is necessary for the helping process. It is always disturbing to hear a social worker use the extent of the material that the client shares as the measure of a helping relationship. Sharing private information with a helping person is never easy; it may give rise to feelings of shame or violation. To seek knowledge of others for the sake of knowing is to make them the object rather than the subject of our efforts.

We communicate concern and respect by being on time for interviews and conferences. Making appointments for home visits says that you respect others' privacy and want them to have the opportunity to present themselves as they wish. We communicate respect by ensuring that the interviewing or conference room is as attractive as possible, by dressing in a culturally appropriate manner, and by concerned listening. Concerned listening is not passive; it is an active search for the meaning in the applicant's communication. You may disagree with what is being said, but must value the sharing that it represents. You also need to hear accurately. You must find ways to convey recognition of the value of the applicant's communication and your desire to understand it—for example, by responding with relevant questions or comments; an expressed desire to understand often conveys concern better than does a statement of already achieved understanding.

Concern for the other means that you view applicants as uniquely valuable human beings, transcend your own needs and view of the problem, and lend yourself to serving the applicant's interests and purposes.

Commitment and Obligation

You cannot enter into relationships with others without assuming the accompanying responsibilities. Both you and the applicant accept commitments and obligations so that the purposes of the relationship may be achieved. The terms of these commitments and obligations are explicitly shared. Commitment to the conditions and purposes of the relationship allows applicants to feel safe and reduces the testing behavior and trial-and-error searching that often mark the beginning of a relationship; they can turn their attention and energy to the task at hand, rather than to self-protection.

Any person asking for help from another is aware of the need to accept commitments and obligations; anxiety regarding what those commitments and obligations may involve often keeps the person from seeking help. The general obligations expected of clients are an open and honest presentation of the problem, their situation, and their ways of coping and also an accommodation to the conditions of the helping relationship—for example, agreement to come to a certain place at a certain time for an interview and to work as they can on the selected problem. Clients' commitments can be renegotiated.

As a social worker, you also assume commitments and obligations. In particular, you have a responsibility to meet the conditions of the relationship in the fullest way:

- by being present at prearranged times and places and also in certain emergency situations
- by keeping the focus of the work on the applicant's problem
- by offering a relationship that is conducive to sharing, growth, and change

Applicants will question your desire to help if these commitments are violated without adequate reason and adequate explanation; they may conclude that you do not consider them important.

Commitment cannot be qualified by our idiosyncratic personal needs; it is a freely determined wish to further the purpose of the helping relationship, without the expectation of returns that support our sense of worth, add to our self-esteem, or preserve our status. Commitment is communicated through resolute consistency, constancy, responsible follow-through, and the preservation of the other's dignity and individuality. You must assume responsibility and accountability for what you say and do.

You can hardly expect that a family will have any sense of obligation or commitment to you when you enter a situation at the request of a third party. However, it is critical that you be aware of your commitment to the family and that you totally fulfill any obligations that you assume. Many of these families have had extremely negative experiences with professionals, and they are prepared to examine every promise in great detail. Any variation in a plan may reinforce their impulse to distrust. Moreover, they may decide to test you. It is not comfortable to be mistrusted. However, we must recognize that many respondents are simply acting on the basis of their previous experience with our peers. We must earn trust, not expect it.

Acceptance

Often, acceptance is thought to mean the communication of a nonjudgmental attitude and the ability to differentiate between the person and the person's actions. We prefer a more active definition: to accept means to regard as true, to believe in, to receive what the other offers. If we accept others, we receive what they offer of themselves, with respect for their capacity and worth, with belief in their capacity to grow and mature, and with an understanding that their behaviors are attempts at survival and coping.

Acceptance involves knowing, individualization, and trust or expectation. *Knowing* relates to your efforts to take in and understand other people's reality, experience, values, needs, and purposes and to acquire some idea of where other people come from—some idea of their life and frame of reference. *Individualization* means the capacity to see the person as a unique human being, with distinctive feelings, thoughts, and experiences. The individual must be differentiated from all others, including ourselves. Assumptions about others must not be based on generalized notions about a group, a class, or a race, although it is important to understand the manner in which race, class, and gender influence client-worker transactions. *Trust* or *expectation* means that you have faith in the capacity of individuals for self-determination and self-direction; you maintain a positive attitude and do not depersonalize families or individuals (Drake, 1994). You consider it the right and responsibility of each individual to exercise maximum self-determination in the person's own life with due regard for the welfare of others.

Acceptance does not mean that we always agree with the other person; it does not mean that we forego our own values and support the applicant's values; it does not mean that applicants' and clients' behavior is excused because of the challenging circumstances in which they must live. It means, rather, that we emphasize the importance of behaving in socially appropriate ways and of observing established laws and regulations as we also seek to understand the intense anger that drives applicants to act impulsively against limits and regulations. It is not hard to empathize with their need to strike out. We need to understand that people act as they must in the complexity of their particular human situation; they are what their nature and their environment—coupled with their vision—permit them to be.

Self-determination, nonjudgmental respect, sensitivity, individualization, expectation of growth, and understanding are all part of the notion of acceptance. One of the most effective ways to communicate acceptance is to try to understand applicants' positions and feelings. By commenting appropriately on what they say or by asking relevant questions, we confirm that we have heard and are motivated to understand them.

Expectation

Expectations of the future affect present well-being and behavior, which, in turn, affect future well-being and behavior. Expectation is a potent force; it must be reckoned with in all our transactions with other humans. As a social worker, you will need to consider:

• your expectation about the applicant's ability or willingness to change

- your expectation of your own effectiveness in the change process
- the applicant's expectation of your behavior
- the applicant's expectation of the effect of the helping process

If you expect that the applicant is capable of growth and change, learning, and problem solving, your effectiveness as a helper will be much increased. Ripple, Alexander, and Polemis (1964) found that clients tend to continue with social workers who are strongly encouraging and optimistic about outcome, whereas bland or neutral attitudes are associated with discontinuance. The social workers who are most effective in the helping process are those who expect that their clients will change, given appropriate help and support. You must be convinced of the human impulse toward growth if you are to be an effective change agent.

Applicants' expectation of what we will do to help will also have a major influence on outcomes. Consider this example:

> My husband's gambling was driving me around the bend and I thought maybe the Welfare could help me do something about it. But all the lady wanted to do was talk—what was he like when he gambled, did we quarrel and silly things like that. She was trying to help and it made me feel good knowing someone cared. But you can't solve a problem by talking about it. Something's got to be done. (Mayer & Timms, 1969, p. 1)

This woman received some help through her contacts with the social worker, but failed to return after several sessions, because she could not see that anything was being accomplished. Applicants will not be helped unless their expectations are in accord with what actually happens in their transactions with you. As the applicant's and worker's notions about their work together become more congruent, that work will be more effective (Marziali & Alexander, 1991). An applicant whose expectations of your behavior are not met will withdraw from the relationship.

When you intervene at the request of third parties, expectation will have a critical effect on problem solving. The family or individuals may expect nothing but trouble from contact with you, and the problem will be made worse if you harbor a belief that the family is hopeless. When both parties have negative expectations, they can only reinforce each other, and you will have a total impasse. You can attempt to change the family's expectations in two ways.

The first is through careful exploration of the family's expectations and attempts to discuss inaccurate perceptions. It is not usually helpful to inform respondents that you are different from other social workers they may have encountered. You must begin by examining your ideas and feelings about the family, by realizing that the family has valid reasons for its position, and by setting aside your own judgments and conclusions in order to focus on understanding the family. It is important to avoid becoming defensive. The family is not angry at you. Family members are reacting to an invasion of their home, on the basis of their previous experience of such invasions. Ask them what they think about your presence and respond to their comments with understanding.

The second way involves challenging respondents' inaccurate expectations of you by asking them to compare the expectations with your actual behavior. Exhibit 7–3 presents an example. Developing a clearly stated set of expectations between you and the respondent is essential if the respondent is to accept your services and become a client.

EXHIBIT 7-3   Challenging a Respondent's Inaccurate Perception of the Worker

In an interview, a social worker was encouraging a young Native American prisoner to enroll in some of the prison's vocational training groups. The man refused. The following conversation ensued.

Client: There's no need to try and do anything with you people. You are all alike.
Worker: What do you mean, we are all alike?
Client: You all lie to us. You never do anything that you promise to do. We can't trust you.
Worker: When have I lied to you? When have I failed to follow through on a promise?
Client: You haven't, but everybody else around here does.
Worker: But I am not everybody. I am me. If I haven't lied to you or failed you, then I think you should try trusting me until I do. When I do fail, I want you to tell me about it so I can change. But until that time . . .

Thus, it is important to explore what the applicant expects. Is this expectation congruent with what can be done in the given situation? If not, you will need to discuss what can be done, what you are prepared to do, and what ought to be done. These discussions are important to both the helping process and the helping relationship. If you are to be helpful, this discussion must prompt changes in the applicant's behavior or your behavior, so that they are congruent.

The applicant's belief that a relationship with you will have a good outcome is also important; trust and faith are necessary if change is to occur. In trusting you, applicants must perceive you as competent and helpful, both at the present and over time. For example, in a study of clients seen for approximately six weeks in a mental health clinic, the clients' hope scores before treatment showed a positive correlation with improvement after their cases were closed (Gottschalk, 1973). There are other examples of this in medicine; for instance, patients' scores on an acceptance scale before open heart surgery were found to be considerably better predictors of postoperative recovery than the actual severity of their disease (Frank, 1978).

Empathy

Empathy is the capacity to enter into the feelings and experiences of another—to know what the other feels and experiences—without losing oneself in the process (Rogers, 1966). The social worker uses the understanding that empathy provides in order to help the other person. According to Keith-Lucas (1972), empathy involves understanding the feelings the other has about the situation, knowing inside oneself how uncomfortable and desperate these feelings may be for the client, but never claiming these feelings for oneself as the helping person. In Exhibit 7–4, he differentiates between pity, sympathy, and empathy.

Empathy requires the capacity to feel an emotion deeply and yet to remain separate enough from it to be able to use the resulting knowledge. To many beginning workers, these may seem to be antithetical qualities. But remember that clients are not looking for someone to share their feelings, no matter how relieving that may be; rather, they need help in coping with a situation that feeling alone cannot resolve. Clients value a worker who can build strong personal bonds with them (Drake, 1994; Marziali & Alexander, 1991) but they also need a worker who, by standing apart, can bring some difference in feeling and thinking—a worker who is able, with a clear head, to secure resources that were unavailable to clients, were unknown to clients, or were not thought of by them.

Authority and Power

Authority may be defined as power delegated to you by the client and the agency; you are seen as having the power to influence or persuade, as a result of your possession of knowledge and experience and your position. Thus, in the helping relationship, your authority has an institutional aspect, deriving from your position and function within the agency's and a psychological aspect—the power granted by applicants and clients

---

EXHIBIT 7-4 Pity, Sympathy, and Empathy

Consider three reactions to someone who has told us that he strongly dislikes his wife. The sympathetic man would say, "Oh, I know exactly how you feel. I can't bear mine, either." The two of them would comfort each other but nothing would come of it. The pitying man would commiserate but add that he himself was most happily married. Why didn't the other come to dinner sometime and see what married life could be like? This, in most cases, would only increase the frustration of the unhappy husband and help him to put his problem further outside himself, onto his wife or his lack of good fortune. The empathetic person might say something like, "That must be terribly difficult for you. What do you think might possibly help?" And only the empathetic person, of the three, would have said anything that would lead to some change in the situation.

Source: A. Keith-Lucas. *Giving and taking help.* Chapel Hill: University of North Carolina Press, pp. 80–81 (1972).

because they accept you as a source of information and advice, as an expert in your field. A person in need of help seeks someone who has the authority to be of help. If you assume this authority, the relationship may provide a sense of safety and security to a client whose powers of self-dependence are ebbing.

Power and authority in the helping relationship are neither good nor bad; they will always be present in some form or other. If you pretend that you carry no authority, applicants will be troubled by suspicions and doubts about why you are unwilling to admit what they know so well. Incongruence between what the applicants feel and what you say makes an authentic relationship impossible.

As a social worker, you will need to be able to deal with authority both when you exercise it and when others exercise it over you. This is especially true if you work as a community organizer, a researcher, or a consultant. If what authority means for you and those with whom you work is unexamined or denied, you will lack the knowledge that you need to guide your clients.

Goldstein (1973) points out that when one requires from another what "cannot be obtained elsewhere—whether one is seeking the adoption of a child, financial assistance, help with a personal problem, or professional services to assist in a social action enterprise—the relationship cannot be equalized" (p. 83). Because the worker's needs have no relevance to the task, "the seeker cannot reciprocate or supply the provider with any reward that can restore the balance" (p. 84). The fact that the seeker has limited alternatives to meet personal needs is further heightened by the fact that workers are seen as having competence and knowledge (pp. 84–86). When you refer clients elsewhere, when you say, "We will meet once a week on a Monday if that is convenient for you," or when you decide to include another family member in service, you are setting the conditions of the relationship. You are exercising your authority.

Questions of power and authority are particularly relevant when we are required to enter a situation by court order or agency decision. Prior experiences of the misuse of professional authority may underlie the family's negative expectations, lack of trust, and fear of commitment. When we intervene in people's lives at the request of others, we must be prepared to explain very clearly—many times, if necessary—what authority and power we carry, what the limits of our authority and power are, and how we will use it. This is often difficult because of our own feelings about authority.

Genuineness and Congruence

Research shows that effective helping relationships require the social worker to communicate empathy, acceptance, concern for the other, and congruence (Truax & Crakhuff, 1967; Truax & Mitchell, 1971). Congruence means that what we say and what we do must always match (be congruent); we must be consistent, honest, open, and real. To be congruent and genuine, we must seek three things:

- honest knowledge of ourselves
- clear knowledge of agency procedures and policies and of the professional role
- internalization of our concern for the other, acceptance of clients, commitment to their welfare, and acknowledgement of our authority

Those who are real, genuine, and congruent in a helping relationship know themselves, are unafraid of what they see in themselves, and are comfortable with who they are. They can enter a helping relationship without anything to prove or protect; thus, they are unafraid of others' emotions. To be congruent, we must have faced and examined our own feelings about many life experiences that applicants and clients share with us, so that we know which feelings are ours and which are theirs. What are our feelings about the lies applicants tell us?

Another aspect of congruency relates to how you present yourself to the applicant and how the applicant sees you, as a representative of a particular agency or service. Usually the applicant does not pay the full—or any—costs of service, and so you are paid by someone else. What does the structure of the agency, its position in the community, and the source of its funds mean to the applicant? Workers who have not honestly examined these questions may appear distant from the reality of the applicant's life. If you have examined your roles and tasks in relation to agency, applicants, and target systems, you can assume the roles and tasks fully and honestly, with an openness about all their aspects and about their impact on applicants.

Our popular culture tends to portray true caring as impulsive and instinctive, from the heart, uninhibited, and natural. There is a common misconception that to think about a feeling distorts it and makes it less an expression of who people are. In reality, congruent people need a warm and nurturing heart; an objective, open, aware, and disciplined mind; and an open channel of communication between them.

Professionalism and objectivity should not be interpreted to mean coldness, cautiousness, and an impersonal, restricted reaction to the expressed feeling of others. Practitioners who relate in these ways are acting out of a need to be self-protective or a fear of self and hence of others. Both an impersonal mode of relating and the undisciplined expression of transient impulses are self-serving and are equally destructive of the capacity to communicate congruence and genuineness in the helping relationship.

To illustrate this point, consider a world-class figure skater. Spectators feel the spontaneity and creative force of her performance. But the performance required years of slow and painful learning—self-discipline, persistence, gradual growth, and change in the use of self. This skater's creative free movements are unnatural to the untrained beginner. Yet the skater does not think of each movement or gesture. She has so internalized the demands of the task that she can give herself to it entirely; she can respond freely and spontaneously to what is in herself in the here and now. The skater knows herself and her capacity, and there is a joy in what she does. Similarly, social workers enter their professional relationships with a clear knowledge of what can and cannot be done, a sense of competence, and a belief in what they are doing. Effectively helping others demands no less preparation, work, discipline, and self-knowledge than does virtuoso figure skating.

THE HELPING PERSON

Social work practitioners bring about change through their use of self—of who they are and what they have made a part of themselves, including their thoughts, their feelings, their belief systems, and their knowledge. Many people do not have the capacity to help others, in the same way that many people do not have the capacity to design computers or to perform surgery. None of these jobs is simply a matter of knowledge; they all call for certain kinds of people with certain kinds of talents. According to Keith-Lucas (1972), people will not be good helpers if they:

- are interested in knowing about people rather than in serving them
- are impelled by strong personal needs to control, to feel superior, or to be liked
- have solved problems similar to those of the people in need of help but have forgotten what it cost them to do so
- are primarily interested in retributive justice and moralizing

On the other hand, qualities that a helping person needs are maturity and courage, creativity, self-awareness, and sensitivity and acceptance of difference.

Maturity and Courage

The most effective helping people are deeply involved in the process of becoming; they find change and growth exciting rather than threatening. They do not exclude themselves from the human condition but view all people, including themselves, as engaged in problem solving. Not only are they unafraid of life, but they enjoy being alive, with all the struggles that this may involve. Because their anxiety and tension are at an optimum level, they are free to take on new experiences. They are mature human beings.

With maturity, we want to increase the ability of others to control their own lives. Effective social work relationships cannot be created and sustained without this desire, which takes the form of a commitment to ourselves.

Maturity provides the courage to take the risks that social work relationships inevitably demand: the risks of failing to help; of becoming involved in difficult, emotionally charged situations that people do not know how to handle; of having your comfortable world and ways of operating upset; of being blamed and abused; of being constantly involved in the unpredictable; and perhaps of being physically threatened. This courage is not based on ignorance or insensitivity; rather, we are fully aware, yet do what must be done.

It takes courage to think honestly about ourselves and others and to confront clients with the reality of their problems, which will seem threatening and hurtful. Courage calls on us to be skeptical and inquiring in our thinking yet trusting of others.

Creativity

Creativity, which includes originality, expressiveness, and imagination, is critical to social work, because the most effective practice involves the search for alternative ways to define a problem and to solve it. Applicants come to us because they are stuck in the ways they define the problem and in the solutions they see. We are of no help if we propose only pedestrian definitions and solutions; we must create something new. Creativity involves openness to all life experiences, the ability to hold knowledge in suspension, curiosity that is never satisfied, and disregard for conformity.

Helping people must be nonconformist.[1] Conformity involves accepting prevailing opinion as fact, and this hinders the search for new solutions. Social workers need to regard most solutions to life problems as tentative and provisional. Intellectual openness and receptivity imply the freedom to shake loose from accepted theoretical positions or systems of thought. Creative individuals are committed to finding a solution to a problem; they are not committed to any particular solution. In spite of the heavy investment they have made in educating themselves, they are able to hold their knowledge tentatively. This may seem paradoxical; certainly, it is a challenge, because we tend to hold tenaciously to things in which we have invested ourselves.

---

[1] However, it is important to distinguish nonconformity from counterconformity, an unthinking rejection of authority or accepted ways of doing, which may be motivated by personal insecurity and hostility.

Another paradoxical quality of creative people is that they may be deeply committed to a problem but at the same time detached from it. Creative people like complexity. They can maintain an openness and joy in the contradictory or obscure; they have a tolerance for conflict; they do not seek premature closure.

Self-Awareness

Along with feelings, cognitive and irrational elements may be identified in the professional relationship. The cognitive element includes the knowledge and values that applicant and worker bring to the relationship, as well as the reflections and thought processes that the relationship engenders. At the cognitive level, the worker relates what is said and done to his or her knowledge and makes sense out of the interchange of feelings.

Irrational elements are not called forth by the present situation but derive from earlier relational experiences; they may be feelings, attitudes, or patterns of behavior. These elements are irrational in that they are usually unconscious and inappropriate to the present situation. Consider the case of Bob, an emotionally disturbed boy. Observation of his family revealed that the mother treated Bob differently from the other children. Informed of this, she burst into tears and said that she couldn't deny him anything, because he was just like her. Like him, she had been the smaller of a set of twins, and so she was sure that, like her, he always felt picked on. She had no evidence to support her opinion; it was irrational.

The irrational also emerges in our attempts to create a congruent, honest working relationship across racial, cultural, or social class barriers. If we study the history and culture of another race and we plan rationally how to proceed in the helping relationship, we may still find that, when we meet a member of that race, the feelings and thoughts that rise within us are not what we would wish. Though we condemn ourselves for these forbidden feelings and deny them to ourselves and others, they persist because they are irrational responses that we learn as a part of our culture. All of us live and grow up in a racist society; we all absorb, to a greater or a lesser extent, the irrational attitudes of that society. These attitudes become a part of us. The fact that they are irrational makes them all the more difficult to understand and eradicate.

If we recognize that irrational elements are present in the helping relationship, we will be more able to understand and accept the expressions of clients. Moreover, the recognition that irrational elements are part of us all implies a constant need for self-awareness, if we are to prevent such elements from intruding inappropriately into the helping relationship.

Working with groups will make special demands on your self-awareness. Each individual in the group may call up a different response from you. You need to be aware of favoritism, rejection, avoidance, and demands for special attention. In addition, you must monitor power and status problems, sibling rivalries, competitions, and aggressions. Self-awareness and self-discipline are necessary to maintain focus and purpose, while weaving the many strands of individual needs and rivalries into a meaningful process. It takes particular skill to remain focused on the needs of others in the face of the group's questioning of your judgment and authority. In groupwork, you will need to develop self-discipline based on an understanding of your own status needs, your needs to preserve face before a group, and your innate responses to open conflict.

In individual work, by contrast, you can depend less on immediate client feedback. Thus, there is a greater need to be aware of any feelings and responses that are aroused in the transactions with the client. You must be particularly aware of your own dependency needs and how they affect your reactions to others' dependency needs and feelings about authority; you must be conscious of any feelings of omnipotence and the need for client approval; and you must be aware of any need to take too much, or too little, responsibility with your clients. What are your expectations and how do these affect client relationships? Are there points at which the client's needs and problems touch off feelings in you that may hinder the helping process? Self-discipline is required to control such feelings.

Problems in the helping relationship may be caused by lack of self-awareness about attitudes toward racial, ethnic, and gender difference. Davenport and Reims

(1978) found that stereotyped reaction to women clients was not correlated with the worker's theoretical position but was associated with the individual's biased belief systems. You must be aware of your belief systems and their impact on your practice and find ways of working without bias.

Self-awareness implies flexibility, a sense of humor, readiness to learn, acceptance of one's limitations, and openness, all of which are important qualities for a helping person. Most of all, self-observation demands courage: We need to be unafraid of what we will find. All of us, to some extent, distort feelings that we do not want to acknowledge; by so doing, however, we impair our ability to help others. The need for self-protection gets in the way of sincerity, openness, genuineness, and honesty.

Sensitivity and Acceptance of Difference

Even when we are committed to sharing ourselves with others, such endeavors are awkward and imperfect. For troubled people, these efforts are complicated by all of their feelings about their problems, their self-perception as people with problems, and the threat of the unknown in the helping process. Accordingly, sensitivity is essential to social workers; we must be able to observe even small movements and changes in others, to put ourselves into the feeling and thinking of others, and to avoid stereotypes. This is closely related to our capacity to be open to the new and to our readiness for change.

We must also be sensitive to the impact of difference in gender, sexual preference, race, age, class, and culture on the professional relationship. Cultural norms related to differences are powerful forces that are part of our unconscious; they seem right to us. Such attitudes are so deeply embedded in society that it is impossible for any of us to have escaped their impact. We should quit denying that we have such attitudes and accept them as a part of us, work at identifying them, be aware of how we express them, and then try to change them.

Gender roles are particularly relevant to social work, because most clients are women. For example, how do we feel when a middle-aged woman comes to us over and over again with tales of spouse abuse and brutality but refuses to leave the situation? Do we recognize social, economic, and moral constraints that may hold her in place, in spite of a strong desire to change her situation?

Shirley Cooper (1978) points out that white people "influenced by a culture rampant with racism and unfamiliar with the intricacies and nuances of the lives of ethnic people may, even with the best of intentions, fail to recognize when social and cultural factors predominate" in their professional attitudes. By contrast, "ethnic therapists are vulnerable to the opposite form of clinical error. Because they are so centrally involved, they may exaggerate the importance or impact of ethnic factors" (p. 78).

Cooper (1978) also discusses the unavoidable guilt experienced by white practitioners who are aware of their privileged position in a segregated society and cautions that this guilt may lead them to "unrealistic rescue fantasies and activities—a form of paternalism" (p. 78). When white guilt remains unconscious, it can lead to overcompensation, denial, reaction formation, an intense drive to identify with the oppressed, and a need to offer them special privileges and relaxed standards of behavior that are no more acceptable to their communities than to the general population.

Gitterman and Schaeffer (1972) suggest that institutional racism results in social distance between worker and client. As they point out, however, the helping process is a mutual endeavor between active participants, and so the participants must listen to each other. Goodman (1974) says:

> The profession of social work cannot afford to sustain practices that would diminish the humanity of any group. It must deny that only blacks can treat blacks, or only whites can treat blacks, or only people of the same culture can understand each other well enough to provide help. Social work must . . . propagate a multiracial set of identities that will continue and extend the search for a common basis in humanity. (p. xiii)

CHAPTER SUMMARY

Relationship is an important theme in the social work literature. Our review of some definitions established that the professional relationship involves an exchange of feelings, thoughts, and perceptions between worker and client. Relationship is the medium through which most social work change is carried out. We made the following key points:

• The professional relationship can be thought of as a climate between worker and client that is characterized by open communication of thoughts, perceptions, and feelings.

• The worker bears the primary responsibility for developing conditions under which a relationship will develop.

• Relationship is purposeful. Its goal is to accomplish objectives that are sought by the applicant and acceptable to the worker and agency. The nature of the relationship will depend on the objectives sought.

• The relationship develops from the worker's joint problem-solving work with applicants and clients. The problem-solving work should begin immediately; the relationship will evolve as work progresses. It is counterproductive to delay problem solving until a relationship exists because, without joint activity, there will be no basis for the relationship to evolve.

• There are seven essential elements of a professional relationship: (1) concern for the other, (2) commitment and obligation, (3) acceptance, (4) expectation, (5) empathy, (6) authority and power, and (7) genuineness and congruence.

• Qualities conducive to a professional relationship include maturity and courage, creativity, self-awareness, and sensitivity and acceptance of difference.

A LOOK FORWARD

In Reading 7-1, Addie Morris vividly describes her experiences in attempting to seek assistance from a public welfare agency. Imagine you are a social worker in this agency. What are your responsibilities, as a social worker, to try to improve the climate that clients experience at your agency?

This chapter concludes our consideration of the framework you will be using for social work practice. We now begin a more detailed examination of the four major phases of problem solving: engagement, assessment, intervention, and evaluation. We group engagement and assessment together, as the process of deciding what to do. Then intervention and evaluation may be grouped together as the processes involved in implementation—that is, doing the decided.

READING 7-1 # Four Pennies to My Name: What It's Like on Welfare*

Addie Morris

I had to get up at 3:30 A.M. and start getting the kids dressed. Sally was five and the oldest, so I started with her. Then I dressed Sam; he was three. I did the baby last. All I had to do was change her diaper and wash her face because I had dressed her before putting her to bed.

It was cool that morning and I didn't have a coat for Sam. He never had a chance to go any place in the winter anyway, so there had been no reason to buy him one. I decided to use Sally's coat that Aunt Jean had given her two years ago. He wouldn't know the difference, and I could care less about what people would say.

I wrapped the baby snugly and the four of us started off for the bus stop. At 4:45 a bus finally came and the four of us boarded. I put forty-five cents in the box and we took a seat in the rear. But I hadn't settled down before the driver called, "Lady, you owe me another fare." I had only forty-five cents left and if I gave that to him, I wouldn't have any money to return home. I approached the front of the bus with the baby in my arms. By this time, I had tears in my eyes. Couldn't this black man understand what was happening to me? Didn't he realize that if I had the money I would have gladly put it in the box?

I stood holding on to the rail beside the driver, unable to say anything. Every time I tried to speak the words choked in my throat. Finally, I got the words out tearfully, "Mister, I am on my way to the social service office. I don't have but forty-five cents to my name. I will need that to return home on."

A lady that was sitting a couple of seats behind the driver said, "Aw, let the woman go. Can't you see what she's going through?"

The driver looked straight ahead and mumbled, "Go on and sit down, lady." That is exactly what I did. I returned to my seat too ashamed to look at anyone.

I sat in my seat silently with tears streaming down my cheeks. Sally put her arms around my neck and asked,

"What's wrong, Mama? Do you need my shoulder?" I reached over Sam and gave Sally a big hug.

"No, darling, I don't need your shoulder," I replied.

I heard someone in back of me whisper, "Wasn't that sweet?"

It was a thirty-minute drive to the social service department. My kids and I went out the side door of the bus. I couldn't bear to face all of the people by walking out the front door. I felt relieved that only one other lady got off at the bus stop. She walked so fast ahead of us I thought she must be going to some place important. I had to take my time walking because I was carrying the baby and Sam couldn't walk too fast.

When we arrived at the social service office, it was 5:05. The door of the office was still locked, and people were standing around waiting for it to open. After standing for a few minutes, I decided it would be better if I sat on the steps for awhile. It was then that I noticed the lady who got off the bus with us. She quickly turned her head when she saw me looking at her. The door finally opened at 5:30. Everyone rushed in and took a number or crowded half in line around the desk. I didn't know what to do so I took a number, too. Then I went to the front desk. I waited in line for at least ten minutes before my turn came to talk to the receptionist.

I came straight to the point, saying, "I'd like to see someone about getting food, clothes, and shelter for me and my children." The receptionist told me I would have to wait and talk to an intake worker but they didn't just hand out money like that. Then she took my name and said someone would call me later. I felt a little sick to my stomach that she thought I was looking for a handout.

Around 9:00 the kids became restless. I kept getting up to give them a drink of water, but the water wasn't relieving their hunger. There was a snack bar next to the information desk and some people were buying things to eat. Naturally this made the kids want food even more. But the only money I had I needed for carfare to get home. Finally, Sam stood up and said, "Mom, can I have one piece of candy?" I was embarrassed and I couldn't think normal. I slapped Sam hard. He began to cry loudly—

*Reprinted with permission of the American Public Welfare Association from *Public Welfare* (Spring 1979), pp. 13–22. Copyright 1979 by the American Public Welfare Association.

maybe because he was hurt but also because he was hungry. I told him he better stop crying right away. And of course, not wanting another slap, he did.

By 11:00 the waiting room was crowded. Some people had to stand. However, when noon came everyone that worked there went out to lunch. By this time, my insides felt like they were melting together. I knew how Sally and Sam must feel. But I wasn't thinking much about them because I was too busy feeling sorry for myself.

All of the employees came back to work at 1:00 o'clock. I approached the receptionist again to find out why I hadn't been called. She told me flatly, "Everyone has to wait their turn; they will call you when they get to your name." I tried to explain that my two older children hadn't had breakfast or lunch and I couldn't afford to purchase them anything from the snack bar. She looked up from her scratch pad and said, "What do you expect me to do? I hear this kind of thing all day long." I quickly took my seat hoping too many people hadn't heard our conversation.

Finally, at 1:15 a lady came out and called, "Mrs. Morgan." My name never sounded so beautiful. I hurried to the front desk. A woman instructed me to follow her to a small room I assumed was her office. She began by saying, "I am Mrs. Jenkins and you are Mrs. Morgan."

"Yes," I replied.

She said, "What can I do for you?"

I began, "My husband left me because he was constantly being laid off. He said we could make it better without him."

"Do you know where your husband is?"

"No, ma'am," I replied.

Giving me an application blank, she said, "Fill this out and bring it in tomorrow by 5:30."

It seemed Mrs. Jenkins had finished, but I continued to sit there. After a few seconds, she said, "You may go now."

"But . . . but Mrs. Jenkins, I don't have any food for my two older children. I do have some milk for my baby. Plus I don't have bus fare to return tomorrow." She went into another room and returned with two bus tickets. I said, "I brought two walking children with me that are sitting in the waiting room." She went out again and returned with two more tickets. Then she told me that she would be unable to provide me with a food order; my application would have to be approved first.

As I left the room I thought to myself, "Anyone who thinks being on welfare is fun has to be mentally unstable." The wait alone is enough to make you go out of your mind. Then after the long wait, what did I get? Four bus tickets. Well, at least the bus driver wouldn't be able to embarrass me.

I walked slowly to where Sally and Sam sat. I was thinking hard. I could tell they were glad to see me—it showed in their eyes. But they were afraid to show me because I had been acting so strange and they thought I might lash out at them again.

Someone was sitting in the chair that I was in earlier, so I asked Sam to stand so I could sit down and compose myself. I decided that since I didn't have to use forty-five cents for bus fare, I could buy a snack. I gave the baby to Sally and went to the snack bar. I bought one pack of potato chips and two candy bars. Now, all I had was four pennies to my name.

When I returned with the candy and potato chips, I could see the joy in Sally and Sam's eyes. I gave them each a candy bar and the three of us shared the potato chips. Afterwards, we filled up with water at the fountain.

As we left the building, I was thinking we might go to Aunt Jean's instead of going home. After all, she didn't live too far away. Maybe she would ask us to spend the night and then it would be easier to return to the social service office the next morning. Besides, we didn't have any food at home and she might offer us a little something to eat.

We took a bus going west toward Aunt Jean's house. I was pleased to have two tickets to put in the box when we boarded the bus. It wasn't long before we had arrived at our stop. We got off and started walking to Aunt Jean's home. Sally and Sam realized where we were going and started skipping instead of walking. I was sure they realized that they would get a meal there. Aunt Jean always gave us food.

Aunt Jean was happy to see us. She was even happier that John had finally decided to leave. I didn't bother to explain how desperate I was. It would have only encouraged her to remind me how bad John was. Right then, I could do without hearing that. I tried to make it appear that I was paying her one of those long awaited visits. She was really pleased and indicated that she knew that John was the reason I could never visit before.

Aunt Jean was full of southern hospitality and offered us food immediately. It wasn't long before Sally, Sam, and

I were sitting down to a hot meal. It wasn't the greatest, but it was food: salmon, biscuits, syrup, and grape-fruitade to drink. I washed the dishes for Aunt Jean.

Then we sat down to talk and watch television. It wasn't long before Aunt Jean started to encourage me to spend the night. Of course, this was what I had been waiting for, but I didn't want to let on. "I am going to fool you this time," I said. "We are going to spend the night." She was happy with this. The children were pleased, too. And I was glad at the way Sally and Sam had been conducting themselves.

The next morning we were able to get up a little later because we were closer to social services. I didn't have to start dressing the children until 4:30. Either Aunt Jean didn't hear our noise or she didn't want to be bothered. I was hoping she would get up and offer us breakfast. At the last minute, she got up and fixed us coffee with a lot of cream. We enjoyed this because we love coffee with lots of cream.

As I boarded the bus, I thanked the Lord again that I was able to put two tickets in the box. I was also thankful that my insides were not clinging together from hunger.

We arrived just as the door of the social services office was opening. People rushed in to take a number. Others formed lines at the receptionist's desk. I rushed to take a number, too. Then I remembered that I had taken one the day before and hadn't returned it. The next number was fifteen. My number from the day before was six. Naturally, I kept the number six. Then I wondered if that was a wise decision. The worker I get with the number fifteen might help me more than the one I would get with the number six.

We waited in the waiting room the same as we did the previous day. People walked back and forth to buy snacks. I know that Sam and Sally were hungry, but neither of them asked for anything. They were probably afraid. In my heart I wanted to be able to buy goodies for my children just like everyone else. I knew this was why I lashed out at them for every little thing. I realized that I wasn't making things any better by doing this, so I promised myself that I would do better.

I was daydreaming about being able to afford things for my children when I heard my name over the paging system, "Mrs. Morgan, front desk." I rushed up to the front desk and identified myself.

A lady said, "This way, please."

She offered me a chair and identified herself as Mrs. Jones. I handed her my application and she began to look it over. She didn't say a word with her mouth, but she said a lot with her facial expressions. I would have felt better if she had spoken. I began perspiring until my hands felt slippery. My knees began to tremble so that it appeared I was shaking my baby. I wondered whether Mrs. Jones was enjoying my extreme anxiety. She certainly wasn't trying to alleviate it by breaking the silence.

I suppose it took Mrs. Jones ten minutes to read my application. To me it seemed like ten years. She finally looked up at me and said, "Mrs. Morgan, do you know where your husband is now?" I told her that I didn't have any idea of where he could be. Then she proceeded to tear apart each of my answers on the application. She asked, "Do all three of your children have the same father?" I suppose I was partly to blame on this one. I didn't indicate their last names on the form because I assumed anyone would know their last name was Morgan. Mrs. Jones wanted to know about the length of time I had lived at our address. She threw one question after another at me: "Why don't you have . . . ?" "What have you been doing up to now for . . . ?" "How come you haven't . . . ?" Either Mrs. Jones was asking the questions in a downgrading manner, or I had a complex and was taking all of her questions the wrong way. But I was meek as a lamb answering all of her questions.

My father always said, "Take it easy when you have your head in a lion's mouth." This was certainly true now, and I needed this woman for my survival.

As she continued to question me, I became choked up. When I began to answer her question on what I had been doing for food, I broke down. Here I was a grown woman crying. Mrs. Jones did or said nothing to comfort me. She just sat there. When I managed to control myself, she said, "Maybe I should tell you a little about what we can do for you. We are not intended to be an agency for people to live off. We are designed to help you out with aid until you are able to manage alone. We only take care of things that are essentials or necessities . . . " She rambled on and on but still wasn't saying anything that I wanted to hear. I wanted to know what they were going to give me.

Finally she told me she would work out a budget for me and tell me how much it was when she got back. She left and was gone for thirty minutes. I was relieved because I knew that at least I would be getting some help.

I wasn't even angry when I saw her joking and laughing with her friends instead of working on my budget.

She came back with the budget that the department allowed for me. It included the following:

Rent	$100
Lights	15
Gas	20
Food, clothes	120
Total	$255

I was currently paying $130 for rent, but she said the department only allowed $100. She further explained that my checks would arrive on the first and sixteenth of each month. Each check would be for $127.50. She told me about the food stamp program that I was eligible for. The way I understood it I could pay $10 and get enough stamps to buy $15 worth of food.

I was very thankful. In fact, I was so happy I walked right out of her office without asking for bus tickets to get home or a food order to keep us until the following week. I turned around and went back into the office, stumbling over the chair I had been sitting in. "I don't have any food for my two older children," I told her. "I also don't have any money or bus tickets to get home."

"I see your kind every day," she said. "Want everything you can get. Have a seat outside and they will call your name to pick up the tickets and food order."

I was so thrilled. I went back outside, sat down next to my kids, and hummed "Thank You, Jesus." Suddenly, things had begun to look up for me. I could really pray to God now. Before, I was too depressed to pray as I should.

They didn't call my name until 3:00. When I went up to the front desk, Mrs. Jones gave me a $20 food order and $2 worth of bus tickets. I was so hungry and weak, I just thanked her, got the children, and left.

On the way to the bus stop I decided what I was going to do. I would take a bus to the supermarket that was six blocks from my house. We got off the bus and walked proudly to the supermarket. We were going to be able to buy some groceries.

I was careful to add up every item I put into the basket. I knew I couldn't go over $20. I bought potatoes, eggs, milk, bread, sugar, corn flakes, beans, spinach, beef neck bones, chicken livers, and other items that were reasonable and would stretch a long way. After I had finished, I only had a little over $18 worth of groceries. I told Sally and Sam they could go and pick one thing they wanted.

I've never seen two happier kids. Sam got a box of six Baby Ruth candy bars; Sally picked a box of vanilla wafer cookies. I was so full of pleasure with their joy that tears rose in my eyes.

When the cashier finished, I had two bags full of groceries. I realized I couldn't carry the groceries and my baby, too. There were drivers by the door calling, "Transportation. Transportation." I sure needed transportation, but I couldn't afford it.

I pushed my groceries outside and decided to give one of the bags to Sally to carry. I carried the other bag and the baby. But I hadn't gone very far when my load became unbearable. I absolutely couldn't go any farther. I managed to get my bag to the ground before it burst.

For about five minutes, I was out of breath. Sally and Sam seemed to sense what was happening to me because they stood there silently with me. I was trying to stuff some of the groceries into Sally's bag when a car pulled to the curb and stopped.

It was one of the men who was at the supermarket calling, "Transportation." He said, "Lady, do you need a ride?" I told him yes but I didn't have any money. "Get in," he said. Sally, Sam, and I crowded in as he held the seat forward. I told him where we lived. To make conversation, I talked about the weather. I offered him some of my groceries for pay but he refused.

The dinner I prepared that evening was a tasty one. I fried the chicken livers with onions and we had rice, spinach, and corn bread. We felt like saying grace before eating for a change. During our meal, I explained my success of the day. "Now we will be able to eat a meal three times a day. And I won't be so worried and upset."

Sam asked, "Is three times a day a lot of times?" I laughed and assured him that it was enough times that he wouldn't be hungry.

We had never been able to afford story books or television in our home. So I decided I must think of something to entertain the kids. As the three of us sat on the floor, I told them stories. I started with "The Three Little Pigs," continued with "Snow White," and ended up with "The Four Little Rabbits." When I finished, Sally said, "Mom, I didn't know you could tell stories."

The following week was beautiful: three meals each day, peace of mind, and most of all giving love and receiving my children's love.

Saturday was the sixteenth of the month and my check was due. My groceries were getting thin. However, I knew I could make it a few more days. I waited for the postman. He finally came around 1 P.M. He left something in my mailbox. I was so excited. I rushed downstairs and found a sample of Ultra Sheen.

I refused to let my disappointment get the best of me and told myself the check was delayed because of the weekend and would definitely be there on Monday. Meanwhile, things would be all right. I must admit that the weekend wasn't a pleasant one. In fact, it was the longest weekend I've known. I wasn't harsh with kids, though. I just wasn't motivated to talk, clean house, or do anything but the necessities.

Finally, Monday came. The postman always came earlier during the week. But today he didn't stop. My heart was beating so hard, I thought it was going to come through my skin. Without thinking, I ran outside after the postman with only my robe and slippers on. He stopped and went through his bag of mail again but didn't find anything for me.

I ran back inside and fumbled through my purse until I found Mrs. Jones' telephone number. I hurried out to the corner telephone booth with my last dime. I dialed the number but every time the line was busy. At twelve noon, I finally got through but no one answered. Then I realized everyone was out to lunch. But I was determined not to hang up until someone answered.

Around 1:00 someone finally answered the phone. I asked to speak to Mrs. Jones. When she came to the phone she asked, "Was that you letting the phone ring for a whole hour?" She hadn't identified herself.

"Yes," I said, "I'd been calling all morning, and the line was busy. I was determined to reach you." I identified myself and told her about my check not coming in the mail. She said that sometimes it takes two to three weeks for checks to get started. She told me to be down at the office at 8 A.M., and she would have a check for me.

Our food was more than thin at this point. We had been eating generously because we thought we'd be getting more food in two weeks. Anyway, I felt at ease because I would be getting a check the next day.

Tuesday morning I was up bright and early. But it suddenly dawned on me that I didn't have any money to take the bus. I decided I would have to walk. I awakened Sally and told her about feeding the baby and where she could find bread to toast for Sam and herself. I told her to give the baby one bottle in the morning and the other

when she wakes from her nap. She agreed to do this faithfully and off I went.

It was a long walk. Although I wasn't wearing a watch, I could tell it was already much later than 8:00. I was so tired I thought my legs would fall from under me. But I couldn't stop. I had to get my check so I could buy food for my children.

Finally, I arrived. I was so exhausted that I had to lean on the receptionist's desk to ask to see Mrs. Jones. She told me to have a seat and Mrs. Jones would call me. There were no vacant seats in the waiting room so I went over to a large ash tray in the corner and sat on it. I was absolutely too tired to stand any longer. As I sat there catching my breath, I looked at the clock on the wall and it said 10:10. Gee whiz, it had taken me more than four hours to walk from home.

Mrs. Jones came out and called different people but not me. Some of the people she called I thought had come in after I had. But I didn't have any proof. And even if I had proof, there was nothing I could do about it.

Just before noon Mrs. Jones came out and called me. As soon as I approached the desk, she handed me a check and two bus tickets. I reached out and tried to shake her hand but she refused. I said, "Thank you so very, very much!" I left humming an old spiritual, "Yes, God Is Real."

What a thrill it was to have a check of my own for $127.50. I had never had a check this large in my whole life. All I could do was sing and pray a thankful prayer all the way to the bus stop.

I got off the bus near the supermarket. Going inside, I asked them to cash my check. Of course, they asked, "Do you have any identification?" All I had was my marriage certificate that I had forgotten to take out of my purse after I'd taken it to the social service office two weeks before. I gave my marriage license to the clerk and told her that was the only identification I had. She smiled and initialed my check and told me that the cashier would cash it after I had made a purchase. Then she asked me whether I would like an identification card so I could cash all of my checks there. Of course, I was pleased and thanked the clerk. She gave me a wallet-size card.

I was so happy walking around the store picking up my groceries. I began to feel as though I was a princess.

After I finished getting my groceries, I still had $90 left. I felt great. The same men were across from the checkout counter saying, "Transportation. Transportation." I walked across and asked the one that had given the children and me a ride two weeks before.

After he had helped me take my groceries in, I asked him would $1 be enough. He said, "Whatever you want to give." So I gave him a dollar and he thanked me.

Then I noticed something different about my house. My children had attempted to clean the house while I was gone. They jumped up and down with joy when they realized that I was bringing food home. I jumped right along with them for the good job they had done. Then Sam and Sally happily assisted me in putting the groceries away.

After I cooked dinner, we sat down to eat. Everyone was quiet. I thought I would break the silence by asking whether anyone had anything they would like to talk about. Sam spoke up, "Mama, aren't you glad Daddy is gone?"

I quickly replied, "No! Why?"

He began to stammer a bit and continued, "We can eat good food all the time since he's away. I hope he stay gone."

"Oh, don't talk like that," I said. I was sorry I had broken the silence. And I had spoken in such a defensive manner. I knew I wasn't letting my children open up and tell me what was on their minds. Yet, I couldn't seem to help myself.

The rest of the week went fine. I told the children stories and even played games with them—games like guessing who has the penny, or who is knocking at my door. All our games had to be things that didn't require a game set. I decided to do exercises and play running games, too. The house had very little furniture—only the necessities: stove, refrigerator, one bed, a mattress on the floor for Sally and Sam to sleep on, and a cradle. So, there was plenty of space available for running.

On Friday, Mr. Perry came over for the rent. I didn't want to give him all of the money that I had. And, even if I did give him all of the money I had, I would still have a balance due to him. The rent was $130 and I had a little more than $88. I decided to give Mr. Perry $65 of the rent and promised to mail him the balance in two weeks. He wasn't pleased because he'd had trouble with my husband in the past. But he agreed. And I felt more secure with the $23 I kept in case of an emergency.

I kept pretty much to myself the following two weeks and enjoyed my children and having decent food to eat. Before I expected it, my check arrived. It was the first of the month, but somehow I expected it to be late. I now had $150. Happy, I mean I was happy. I only owed a $15 gas bill and a $10 light bill.

I left my children alone, instructing them to keep the door closed and not open it for anyone. First I walked to the grocery store. This way I could get my check cashed. I decided not to get groceries until I was on my way home. After getting my check cashed, I took a bus to the post office and bought three stamped envelopes and three money orders to pay my light, gas, and rent balance.

Then I returned to the supermarket. I spent $30 for groceries. I also paid the driver $1 to take my groceries home. So I had $29 left—not a lot of money, but some in case of an emergency.

The money I received from social services could pay the rent, utilities, and buy some food. However, the food would have to be mostly second rate such as neck bones, chicken livers, or bacon ends. But I couldn't complain because I could at least live.

The time came for Sally to start school and I began to wonder what we would do for clothes. I started looking for a night job, but I couldn't find work doing anything. I would even have taken a job sweeping the street. I knew there had to be more to life than this. I was barely surviving.

The day before school, I made starch out of flour and ironed Sally's best dress which wasn't much. It was old plus it was up to her butt because she had gotten it two years before. I bought her a pair of gym shoes and socks at the supermarket.

The first day of school I dressed Sally along with Sam, the baby, and myself. Of course, today was Sally's day and the rest of us didn't matter that much. But as we waited in line to register, I noticed the way the other children were dressed.

After being in school for several weeks, Sally began to act strangely. One afternoon she came home and asked, "Mama, why do all of the children laugh at me?" I didn't want to tell her it was because I couldn't afford to buy her nice clothes like the others had. She seemed to sense that I didn't want to talk about it, so she never mentioned it again. But she began to withdraw and talk less and less. That winter she had a mental breakdown and was hospitalized for two weeks. When the doctor told me he thought this had happened because of the way she had been treated by her peers at school, I became even more determined to get a job so I could buy us some clothes.

I soon found the Lord was looking out for me. The day Sally was discharged from the hospital, her doctor told me about a job at a nursing home working nights as a nurse's aide. He said the man that was the administrator was a friend of his. He told him about me and the administrator had agreed to give me a try. I felt all I needed was a chance like this. I was so elated I had tears in my eyes when I thanked the doctor. He told me to take good care of my children.

I was due to start to work on Sunday night. I knew I couldn't afford to hire anyone to look after the children when I was at work. So I took time and explained to Sally what I was going to do. I told her in order to get money to buy a few toys and clothes like other people, I had to work. I would need her help with Sam and the baby. I assured her they would be asleep most of the time anyway.

I bought a white uniform with my light bill money and used the rest of my emergency savings to catch the bus to and from work.

It was three weeks before my first paycheck, but it was well worth the wait. I cleared $120 and had some money to buy clothes. I went to K-Mart and bought Sam a suit, Sally a dress, shoes and socks, and the baby a new dress, socks, and shoes because she had never had any shoes before.

That Sunday when I got home from work, I dressed everyone; and we all went to church. I was sleepy that night at work, but I was pleased we went. The kids enjoyed it and my heart felt all good inside.

From that time forward Sally kept the kids for me while I worked at night. We had better food and clothes—and I even started saving a little. We went to church every Sunday and sometimes during the week. Sally and Sam began to love Sunday school and looked forward to going.

Sometimes I felt a little guilty for accepting money from social services and working, too. But I rationalized to myself that I couldn't survive on either one alone. So I took the better of two evils and risked going to jail if I got caught.

One night at work an inservice instructor gave a class on "Treating the Patient As a Human Being Through Reality Orientation." I dearly enjoyed the class. Afterwards, I went to the instructor and asked her about continuing my education. She was happy about my interest, especially since I wanted to be a nurse. (I had

been thinking about this for some time.) She agreed to bring me literature and an application to a junior college. Of course, I was happy about her promise, but I never expected her to fulfill it. So often people had made promises and never kept them.

The next evening when I arrived at work, I was surprised to find a catalog about a nearby community college and an application. During my lunch break that night I read as much as I could of the catalog and filled out the application.

I wrote a letter to my high school for my transcript. I felt like I was really doing something worthwhile. But in the back of my mind I kept reminding myself that I might not be accepted. Maybe my southern education hadn't been adequate. But I was optimistic. I talked about going back to school with my co-workers and they made fun of me. Even the licensed practical nurse in charge made sarcastic remarks. But this made me keep my head up and try harder.

In less than a month I received a letter from the school to come down for an interview. I became apprehensive, but I decided to go. Surely it couldn't be any worse than my first few visits to social services. Besides, all they can tell me is "yes" or "no."

The interview wasn't as difficult as I expected. The director of nursing was black—although she talked and tried to act like she was white. She was blunt and direct. She informed me that with my academic background I would need one year of liberal arts before entering the nursing program.

I registered early in the summer for the fall semester. I planned to take four courses: English 1, Chemistry 1, Humanities 200, and Speech 200. My classes began at 8:00 A.M. and were over at 11:00. Two were on Monday and Wednesday, and the other two were on Tuesday and Thursday. This meant I would be home by 12:30 every day so Sally could go to school in the afternoon.

Soon summer was over and it was time for Sally and me to start to school. I sat down and explained my plans to Sally. I told her she would be caring for Sam and the baby (now a year and a half old) in the morning while I attended classes. She already knew how to prepare cereal for them. That would be all they would need until I returned home at 11:30. Then I would prepare lunch and dress Sally for school. (Sally was better now and able to return to school.)

This plan worked out well. During that first year, I made two A's in chemistry, four B's in my other courses, and two C's in English. I managed to pay my own way through school in addition to buying our clothing. (I enjoyed dressing Sally each morning after I arrived home from work. I continued to thank the Lord for decent clothes to dress her in.)

In April, I received a letter from the Nursing Evaluation Committee to come for an interview for the nursing program. I was put through the third degree at that interview. I managed to answer their questions and remain calm on the outside. But sometimes two of them would ask a question at the same time. I would answer one. Then, when the opportunity presented itself, I answered the other. At the end of the interview, the director of the program told me that I was accepted to the nursing program and was to begin classes in September. I couldn't have been happier.

The next week I made an appointment to see Mrs. Jones at social services. I told her of my acceptance in the nursing program. She questioned me about my getting into the program without prior preparation. I told her about attending classes for the past eight months. Then she asked me, "What do you want me to do?" I told her the first thing I would need was money for a babysitter. To this she replied, "You didn't seem to have any trouble getting a babysitter for the past eight months." At this point my hands became sweaty. Couldn't this lady see the sacrifices I had made? I composed myself and told her of the arrangement I had made with Sally.

But Mrs. Jones continued the questioning. She asked how I got the money to attend college. Silently I said, "Lord, forgive me for this lie," before I told her that my boyfriend had paid for my schooling. I added that we had broken up now and I wouldn't be receiving any more help from him. At last, she told me that social services could allow me $30 a week for child care but nothing for tuition. She told me to try the financial aid office at the school.

I did exactly as Mrs. Jones said and went to the financial aid office at the college. I was able to get a loan and a grant to cover my entire tuition. But I decided to continue to work. I planned to save the loan money in case I had to stop working. However, if I didn't use the loan money I could pay the loan back upon completion of the program.

So I continued to work at the nursing home. The jokes and remarks about my going to school became less frequent as I progressed in the nursing program. At the request of the nursing director, I even took charge when the supervisor was unable to come in.

At times, working along with going to school and taking care of my children would get the best of me. Sometimes I would catch myself nodding in class, and once I fell asleep. Everyone was leaving the classroom when I awakened. I was so embarrassed. I immediately went up and explained to my instructor that I was working nights.

Finally I graduated. It was a small graduation, but an extremely happy occasion for me and my children. As I walked across the stage for my associate degree in nursing, my baby Nell stood up in her seat in the rear of the auditorium and said, "That's my mama!" The audience turned to her and cheered and clapped.

I am now off AFDC and I am very thankful to God that he helped me through those years. I am very proud to be a nurse, and it feels great to be able to go to the supermarket and pay for my groceries with cash rather than food stamps. I always felt people were watching me when I paid with food stamps. It doesn't mean that I have that much more money now, but I do have more dignity which seems to make the money go further. Bank tellers and checkout clerks seemed to sneer at me when I cashed my welfare check. With a check I've earned, these people respect me and I feel that I am not a burden to society. I feel good about having earned that money.

I can see now that children act in the same way their parent acts. When I was on welfare and barely able to make ends meet from one month to the next, my kids were sad and struck out at each other. Now that I am more content, they are nice to each other. Another factor that has changed their attitude is that they can do things other children do and have things other children have. Now I am able to buy Sam a truck for his birthday. I can afford to take the kids to the zoo or on a picnic in the park. Sally has pajamas so she can spend the night with a friend. Our life is very different from before.

It's a great feeling to be off welfare.

LEARNING EXERCISES

1. Write brief definitions (one or two sentences) of the following concepts, or briefly explain the concept to a friend:

   acceptance
   authority
   commitment
   concern
   concerned listening
   congruence
   creativity
   empathy
   expectation
   maturity
   normative purpose of relationship
   operational purpose of relationship
   self-awareness
   sensitivity
   understanding
   white guilt

2. Examine the case of Debbie Smith in Appendix A-1. Ms. Smith is a respondent; the social worker is entering this case in the interests of child protection. This worker shows considerable skill, however, in establishing conditions under which the relationship with Ms. Smith is likely to develop. What specific things did this worker do to foster a positive working relationship with Ms. Smith?

3. How do you react to the idea that the way professionals dress communicates concern and respect for others? What do you see as the implications of this?

4. Think of an experience you have had in establishing a relationship with a friend. Write a one-paragraph discussion of the process, focusing on what you did. What can you learn from this about how to establish a relationship with an applicant or client? What makes a relationship with a friend different from a relationship with a client?

5. In *Jordi*, Theodore Rubin (1969) describes work with an autistic child. After reading the book, identify the qualities that Sally, the worker, brought to her work with Jordi. What specific things did Sally do to help Jordi?

REFERENCES

Bachelor, A. (1995). Client's perception of the therapeutic alliance: A qualitative analysis. *Journal of Counselling Psychology, 42*(3), 323–337.

Barnard, C. P., & Kuehl, B. P. (1995). Ongoing evaluation: In session procedures for enhancing the working alliance and therapy effectiveness. *American Journal of Family Therapy, 23*(2), 161–172.

Biestek, F. (1957). *The casework relationship.* Chicago: Loyola University Press.

Coady, N. F. (1993). The worker-client relationship revisited. *Families in Society: The Journal of Contemporary Human Services, 74*(5), 291–300.

Cooper, S. (1978). A look at the effect of racism on clinical work. *Social Casework, 54*(2), 78.

Coyle, G. L. (1948). *Group work with American youth.* New York: Harper & Row.

Davenport, J., & Reims, N. (1978). Theoretical orientation and attitudes toward women. *Social Work, 23*(4), 306–311.

Drake, B. (1994). Relationship competencies in child welfare services. *Social Work, 39*(5), 595–602.

Frank, J. D. (1978). Expectation and therapeutic outcome: The placebo effect and the role induction interview. In J. D. Frank, R. Hoehn-Saric, S. Imber, B. Liberman, & A. Stone (Eds.), *Effective ingredients of successful psychotherapy* (pp. 1–34) New York: Bruner/Mazel.

Gitterman, A., & Schaeffer, A. (1972). The white professional and the black client. *Social Casework, 53*(5), 280–291.

Goldstein, H. (1973). *Social work practice: A unitary approach.* Columbia, SC: University of South Carolina.

Goodman, J. A., (Ed.) (1973). Preface. In James A. Goodman (Ed.), *Dynamics of racism,* in Social Work Practice (pp. ix-xii). Washington, DC: National Association of Social Workers.

Gottschalk, L. (1973). A study of prediction and outcome in a mental health crisis clinic. *American Journal of Psychiatry, 130,* 1107–1111.

Horowitz, R. (1991). Reflections on the casework relationship: Beyond empiricism. *Health and Social Work, 16*(3), 170–175.

Johnson, W. (1951). Being understanding and understood: Or how to find a wandered horse. *ETC, 8*(1), 161–179.

Keith-Lucas, A. (1972). *Giving and taking help.* Chapel Hill: University of North Carolina Press.

Kokotovic, A. M., & Tracey, T. J. (1990). Working alliance in the early phase of counselling. *Journal of Counselling Psychology, 37*(1), 16–21.

Konopka, G. (1963). *Social group work: A helping process.* Englewood Cliffs, NJ: Prentice-Hall.

Marziali, E., & Alexander, L. (1991). The power of the therapeutic relationship. *American Journal of Orthopsychiatry, 61*(3), 383–391.

Mayer, J. E., & Timms, N. (1969). Clash in perspective between worker and client. *Social Casework, 50*(1), 32–40.

Mayer, J. E., & Timms, N. (1970). *The client speaks: Working class impressions of casework*. New York: Atherton Press.

Northen, H. (1988). *Social work with groups*. New York: Columbia University Press.

Perlman, H. H. (1957). *Social casework: A problem solving process*. Chicago: University of Chicago Press.

Perlman, H. H. (1971). *Perspectives on social casework*. Philadelphia: Temple University Press.

Pincus, A., & Minahan, A. (1973). *Social work practice: Model and method*. Itasca, IL: Peacock.

Pumphrey, R., & Pumphrey, M. (1961). *The heritage of American social work*. New York: Columbia University Press.

Reynolds, B. C. (1963). *Uncharted journey*. New York: Citadel Press.

Ripple, L., Alexander, E., & Polemis, B. (1964). *Motivation, capacity and opportunity. Studies in casework theory and practice*. Chicago: School of Social Service Administration, University of Chicago.

Richmond, M. E. (1899). *Friendly visiting among the poor: A handbook for charity workers*. New York: Macmillan.

Richmond, M. E. (1917). *Social diagnosis*. New York: Russell Sage Foundation.

Rogers, C. (1966). Client-centered therapy. In C. H. Patterson (Ed.), *Theories of counselling and psychotherapy* (pp. 403–439) New York: Harper & Row.

Rubin, T. (1969). *Jordi*. New York: Macmillan.

Truax, C. B., & Carkhuff, R. (1967). *Toward effective counselling and psychotherapy: Training and practice*. Hawthorne, NY: Aldine Publishing.

Truax, C., & Mitchell, K. (1971). Research on certain interpersonal skills in relation to process and outcome. In A. Bergin & S. Garfield (Eds.), *Handbook for psychotherapy and behavior. Change: An empirical analysis* (pp. 299–344). New York: Wiley.

part II

TOOLS FOR DECIDING WHAT TO DO

chapter 8

Engaging Potential Clients

CHAPTER PREVIEW

In this chapter, we discuss engagement, the first phase of the problem-solving process. Engagement begins as we establish communication with an applicant, respondent, or prospect and ends when we have a preliminary agreement to work together; the preliminary agreement will also include tentative objectives. Engagement is a process, not a set period of time. It may take only a few minutes for some applicants, but a full interview for others; especially for respondents and prospects, it may spread over several weeks or months and involve multiple contacts. The engagement process will differ depending on whether you are engaging an applicant, a respondent, or a prospect. Engagement is a process of communication. Accordingly, we start with a discussion of communication and barriers to communication. In Chapter 10, on data collection

and assessment, we will discuss interviewing, a structured form of communication used in most social work practice.

In this chapter, we will:

- outline the communication process
- suggest how you might prepare for engagement, including the use of past case records
- introduce you to procedures appropriate to engaging applicants, respondents, and prospects
- discuss the preliminary agreement that results from engagement, including how to identify the initial objectives wanted by the potential client

In Reading 8-1, Craig Rennebohm discusses how to engage individuals who are homeless and mentally ill; in this case, engagement may extend over several contacts. Finally, in Reading 8-2, Barry R. Cournoyer and

Katharine V. Byers discuss the communication skills necessary for engaging groups.

COMMUNICATION

Basic Principles

Engagement is based on communication, an interactional process that gives, receives, and checks out meaning (Exhibit 8–1). Some communication theory concepts provide a useful framework for understanding problems that may arise in engagement: *Encoding* involves putting the message to be sent into symbolic form, in preparation for transmission; *transmitting* is the process of sending the encoded message; *receiving* and *decoding* are the processes of receiving and interpreting the stimuli that were sent; and *noise* consists of extraneous influences that may have distorted reception of the message transmitted. Finally, *checkout* or *feedback* provides a way of overcoming problems created by noise, by inadequate encoding or decoding, or by faulty transmission or reception.

The checkout phase of the communication process is essential; it was discussed as an interviewing technique by Robert Brown (1973). Suppose that A sends a message to B, which B receives. How does B know that the message received is the message A intended to send? Perhaps B's receptors were faulty; perhaps A's transmitter was faulty; or perhaps there was noise or interference between A and B that distorted the message. B checks out the message by telling A what has been received.

From time to time, you will use feedback to be sure that you are accurately interpreting the applicant's words and feelings. For example, you might restate what you have heard in similar but fewer words, submit a tentative summary of the applicant's discussion, or connect things that the applicant has left unconnected. At times, you will offer a tentative interpretation: "Is it possible that what you are telling me means . . . ?" Often you will be tempted to use reassurance: "I understand . . . "; "That is hard . . . "; "Most people would be upset . . . " It is natural to want to support the applicant by an expression of understanding. Be very careful, however, because such phrases may cut off the applicant's further exploration of the difficulty.

In discussing potential communication problems in social work, John Cormican (1978) speaks of difficulties arising from the existence of different dialects. By this, he means, for example, that the symbols encoded and transmitted by one party may be received by the other party, but may not be decodable; or the message may be decoded incorrectly—that is, may be misinterpreted. Lewis and Ho (1975) give an example of a problem in nonverbal communication with Native American clients.

> In an effort to communicate more fully, the social worker is likely to seat himself facing the client, look him straight in the eye, and insist that the client do likewise. A native American considers such behavior to be rude and intimidating; contrary to the white man, he shows respect by not staring directly at others. (p. 380)

Cormican (1978) asserts that labels such as borderline state, depressive, and personality disorder create barriers

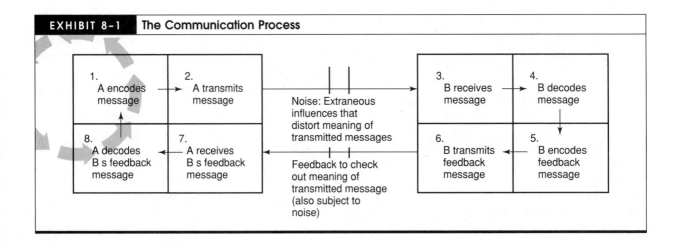

| EXHIBIT 8–1 | The Communication Process |

to communication. These labels will distort the decoding process if you interpret the message sent by an applicant in relation to your understanding of the labels rather than in relation to what the applicant intended. You should use feedback to check out whether you got the message the sender intended. In Reading 8-2, Cournoyer and Byers identify empathetic communication skills in a groupwork setting. Empathetic communications derive from your understanding of an applicant's or client's frame of reference and reflect content, feeling, thinking, and meaning. Such reflective skills can be used with client systems of any size to check out the messages received. As illustrated in Exhibit 8–2, however, checkout or feedback is subject to the same potential communication problems as the original message-sending process.

We can never completely understand what another is saying, thinking, and feeling, and we should not delude ourselves into thinking otherwise. However, we have a responsibility to improve clarity and understanding in our communications. We must strive both to understand the applicant and to make our own communications as clear as possible. Bloom (1980) offers good advice: "Communications to clients ought to be simple, clear, accurate, and direct. Social workers should choose words that are precise and cannot be misunderstood, words that are not evasive and vague" (p. 337).

Communications occur simultaneously on many levels—verbal and nonverbal, overt and covert. We sometimes speak of the denotative and metacommunication levels of messages. The denotative level refers to the literal content of the symbols used (usually words),

whereas metacommunications are messages about the message; voice inflection, gestures, manner of speaking, and other factors all provide clues to the intended meaning. The ability to communicate several messages simultaneously provides an opportunity for the famous double bind—the simultaneous transmission of contradictory messages, so that the receiver thinks, "I'm damned if I do, and damned if I don't" (Bateson, Jackson, Haley, & Weakland, 1963; Esten & Willmott, 1993).

Barriers to Communication

Barriers to communication may occur at any phase in the communication process—encoding, transmitting, receiving, decoding, and checkout. Many of these barriers are obvious: inability to conceptualize and use symbols (encoding problems); speech impediments (transmitting problems); hearing or receptor impediments (receiving problems); failure to understand the concepts received (decoding problems); and environmental influences (noise that interferes with the messages between transmitter and receiver). These barriers, while very relevant to engagement, are also reasonably obvious. In this section, we will consider a series of subtler but equally serious barriers to communication. In addition to applicant resistance, we look at five worker barriers to engagement: anticipation of the other; assumption of meaning; failure to make the purpose explicit; premature change activities; and inattentiveness.

Anticipating the other. We do not listen carefully if we believe we know what the other person is going to say—that is, if we anticipate the message. We will distort

---

EXHIBIT 8-2 **Feedback as a Communication Problem**

The client in treatment struggles to express a feeling or thought that troubles her. She finally manages to say something that perhaps approximates what is on her mind. The social worker's response is, "I really appreciate where you are coming from." What does the social worker's response mean? What does it reveal and what does it conceal? What contribution, positive and negative, does this remark make toward furthering the treatment of the client and fostering a therapeutic relationship? This phrase is a duplicitous expression of confusion, concealment, and lack of understanding and empathy. If one were to ask the therapist what he intended to convey to the client by using the phrase, he would presumably say something like, "I mean that I understand what the client is feeling." But his every word proves otherwise. First, nobody can truly understand what another person is feeling. One can come close, and such approximations of empathy are surely what social workers strive toward in their work, but understanding inevitably remains an approximation.

Source: A. Bloom, Social work and the English language. *Social Casework*, 60(6), 333 (1980).

the message by selectively hearing and decoding. We may think we know what an applicant is going to say if the individual has already been assigned a diagnostic label (Cormican, 1978) or conforms to one of our stereotypes.

Stereotyping can be very subtle. After noting similarities between several applicants, you may begin to develop a stereotype of that particular kind of person. The stereotype then interferes with your perception of new applicants and may serve to block any communications that are inconsistent with the stereotype. Anticipation of the other occurs when you permit an existing stereotype to distort the current communication. We may develop stereotypes from our own practice experience or from summaries or background information provided by our agency. Suppose that you have been asked to provide service to the family whose agency record contains the summary in Exhibit 8–3. This summary creates powerful images that will affect your interpretation of communications from the Shasta family. Remember, though, that this summary is only a description of certain discrete behaviors of Mr. and Mrs. Shasta; without additional data, you will not know enough about the situation to make inferences about the meaning of the behavior for the Shastas. You will be well advised to listen carefully to what they have to say.

Assumption of meaning. In this case, you receive an ambiguous message, fail to check out its meaning with the applicant, and proceed on the basis of a meaning that you have read into the message. The words themselves may be ambiguous, the way in which they are uttered may convey unclear feelings or thoughts, or the applicant's behavior may be communicating messages inconsistent with the words. Checking the meaning with the applicant may prevent you from making erroneous assumptions that interfere with communication and engagement. As an example, consider this brief excerpt from an interview with a respondent—a 16-year-old boy just released from an institution on parole.

> I asked how things had gone this past week. He looked at me with a grin and said, "Fine." He added that he had not done anything. During this time he kept leafing through the magazine and pointed out someone's picture to me. At this point I told him that we were here to talk and that he should put the magazine away. It is very obvious that this boy knows very little or at least practices few of the common courtesies of everyday living.

Because the boy grinned and was leafing through a magazine, the worker assumed that he was trying to avoid conversation. However, the worker acted on this assumption without first checking it out. Taking a few minutes to ask the boy what it was about the magazine that interested him or to make a more direct checkout—"I get the message that you are not too interested in talking with me now"—might have clarified the situation and moved the worker toward a more helpful engagement with the youth.

Failure to make the purpose explicit. If you fail to make the purpose of an interview explicit, you and the

---

EXHIBIT 8–3 **Stereotypes in a Case Summary**

The family has been known to the agency for the past 15 years on the basis of 13 applications, mainly because of nonsupport of husband or his jailing. Family consists of Mr. Shasta (age 32), Mrs. Shasta (age 27), and six children. Mr. Shasta has been in and out of court since a young boy due to delinquent and antisocial behavior. He received a dishonorable discharge from army. In last few years his drinking has increased to near alcoholism. Mrs. Shasta came from a family also long known to the agency. She married Mr. Shasta at age 17 to escape an alcoholic father. Recurring pregnancies, health trouble, and abuse by her husband have left her in poor shape to cope with him, let alone child rearing and managing the home. The case is looked on by staff as one of the most unpleasant in the agency because of several incidents of fraud, continued misuse of funds, and Mr. Shasta's refusal to seek and keep work. Mr. Shasta is avoided by workers as much as possible due to his violent temper and drinking. Returning him to employment is seen as hopeless; he has quit or been fired from at least 20 jobs. Mr. Shasta's behavior after drinking seems to affect his disposition toward looking for work and toward his wife and children. Adequacy of child care is a concern, with reports that the mother neglects her children. Neighbors have reported that the father beats the children when drunk while Mrs. Shasta tries to protect them. Health problems of mother and children are an ongoing issue but the family is indifferent to need for medical care.

applicant may have different—perhaps contradictory—ideas of what the purpose is and will interpret each other's communications in the light of your different ideas. As these subtle distortions continue, the two of you will be heading in entirely different directions.

Exhibit 8–4 provides another example. Mr. Allen says clearly that he has come to pay his taxes, but the social worker is concerned about his health. It takes several questions before the worker understands the importance of responding to the applicant's concerns.

Premature change activities. Social workers are committed to change. Difficulties occur, however, when we attempt change efforts without clearly understanding what the applicant wants and whether that change is feasible. Change efforts should be based on valid and reliable data and on a considered decision by the applicant and the worker to engage in such efforts. The purpose of engagement is to understand the presenting problem and what the applicant wants done about it. To urge change at this early stage may create a barrier to communication and thereby limit the availability of important information relevant to decision making. A secondary problem is that change

efforts in these early contacts frequently take the form of directive approaches—such as persuasion and advising—that are seldom effective until trust has been developed.

Inattentiveness. If your mind wanders during an interview—if you start thinking about other cases, say, or planning future activities—you create a barrier to continued communication with the applicant. Applicants can reasonably expect you to give undivided attention to their present communications; your responsibility is to honor that expectation. But even the most experienced workers will have moments when thoughts wander and attentiveness wanes. M. Ellen Walsh (1981) recommends owning up to these lapses with a simple comment,

for example, "Excuse me, Frank. What you were saying made me think of something else that's going on, and I haven't been paying close attention for a minute, here. Can you go over that again? I was with you up to the point where you said Jan had no business interfering with the kids." Despite most therapists' fears of revealing such incidents, clients are probably aware of these lapses anyhow, and the admission wins respect for its honesty. (p. 461)

EXHIBIT 8-4   Failure to Respond to Client's Concerns

When Mr. Allen came into the office, the worker was completely surprised at the growth on his head. Actually, Mr. Allen gave the appearance of having two heads, one on top of the other. I asked about it and Mr. Allen said that it had just started, but that wasn't what he had come to see the worker about. He came because he wanted to pay his taxes. He said he had saved some money out of his grant, and with the extra $5 this month, he had "settled" with the tax offices. He declared Mrs. Allen still wouldn't pay taxes, but he was going to. The worker told him we would budget the entire tax bill in his grant, and that he would receive a $4 raise or a total of $37. The worker again asked about his head. He had been told that when he was a baby he had fallen off the bed, and has had a small knot since. He said he wanted to keep his taxes current, and would never again be talked out of paying them. The worker assured him his taxes would be included in the future in his grant alone because I knew of Mrs. Allen's attitude. The worker wanted to know when this knot had started growing. Mr. Allen said it suddenly started getting bigger about two months ago. Before getting a breath

he started talking about taxes again. He must have had a hard time saving enough money to pay up. He said they "settled" for $18, and he had a "clean slate." He told of how he had done without his newspaper, hadn't been running his fans much nor watering his flowers as he should. I remarked I wished he had come to us sooner, but now that the taxes were paid, and the future ones budgeted, suppose we talk about his head. What had he done for it? He replied he had not done anything, and again changed the subject to taxes. I told him I noticed each time I mentioned his head, he changed the subject to taxes. It made me wonder if he didn't want to talk about his head, or if there was some connection with his head and taxes. He looked surprised, and then slowly, as if explaining to a child, said, "Long ago the doctors told me if this ever started growing in a hurry I would have to have it cut off. I am 77 years old and may or may not get out of that operating room. If I die, my wife can live on her old age pension if she has a home, if not, she can't. So, I have to get those taxes paid before I go to a hospital or even see a doctor."

Applicant resistance. The barriers that applicants create may be thought of as forms of resistance against entering into a problem-solving process. Resistance is a specialized kind of defense used by the applicant to ward off the worker and avoid any discomfort involved in problem solving. Three sources of resistance can be distinguished. First, resistance may stem from the usual discomfort and anxiety involved in dealing with a strange person and a new situation. Second, resistance may stem from cultural and subcultural norms regarding involvement with service agencies and asking for help. Studies have found that, whereas some cultural groups feel relatively comfortable about seeking help from professionals, others prefer to rely on their informal support system (Cleary & Demone, 1988; Daniel, 1985; Griffith & Villavicencio, 1985; Logan, Freeman, & McDay, 1990; Marlow, 1990; McGoldrick, 1988). Because of cultural norms, some persons may find it particularly difficult to admit the existence of a problem and to seek a solution. Agencies may exacerbate cultural differences by establishing procedures that intensify applicant discomfort; an emphasis on scheduled appointments and office visits, for example, may aggravate the resistance of clients from lower socioeconomic groups and hamper their ability to use more traditional social service agencies. As Renate Frankenstein (1982) notes, what is recorded as resistance may instead be an indication that certain agency practices and worker expectations inhibit communication with troubled families. Third, some applicants may be securing a degree of gratification from their problems. This is a serious source of resistance; it interferes with the applicant's ability to communicate, reduces self-determination, and makes problem solving more difficult.

Overcoming barriers to communication. If obstacles to communication arise, dealing with them will be a necessary preliminary goal, before any other problem-solving work can begin. Exhibit 8–5 describes some turn-offs to avoid in your communications with applicants during engagement, as well as other phases of problem solving.

Here are some final thoughts about communication:

1. The questions asked determine the answers given, and it is your responsibility to determine the questions.

2. How you behave in the presence of the applicant communicates how you regard your relationship with that person. The same is true of how the applicant behaves.

3. Silence is as much a part of human communication as what is said and how it is said. Therefore, you must be aware of what issues the applicant is not addressing, and you must recognize that the applicant will interpret your silence in his or her own way.

4. Individuals become dependent and shirk responsibility for their actions when someone else takes responsibility for their thinking, feeling, and planning. On the other hand, not doing appropriate things for applicants may further break down their coping skills and deepen their apathy.

5. You can communicate by action as well as talk. For some clients, nonverbal communication may be more effective for engagement (Middleman & Wood, 1991).

EXHIBIT 8-5	Communication Turn-Offs

Suzette Haden Elgin identifies these turn-offs during intimate conversations. You should avoid them in your communications with applicants.

- Unsolicited advice: "Let me tell you what I'd do . . . "
- Prophesies: "You're going to hate yourself tomorrow."
- Hijackings: "You think you had a bad day? Let me tell you what happened to me!"
- Reassuring squelches: "A year from now you'll look back on this and laugh."
- Contradictions: "You're not tired; you couldn't be."

- Cutesipation: "Of course I think your little stories are worth reading; they're charming."
- Interrogations: "Why did you do that? Why didn't you talk to me first? What was going on in your head?"
- Evaluations: "You lost your job because you weren't willing to turn in your work on time."
- Diagnoses: "You're only saying that because you're tired; you don't really mean it."
- Sermons: "The money you spend on suits would clothe an orphanage."

Source: S. H. Elgin, *Genderspeak.* New York: Wiley (1993).

The messages that you want to send to applicants (summarized in Exhibit 8–6) will probably be communicated more through your behavior and your nonverbal metacommunications than through anything you say.

GETTING STARTED

You and a potential client will usually come together in one of three different ways:

1. The individual, family, or group may reach out for help with a problem they have identified as being beyond their means of solution.

2. You may reach out to offer services to persons who are not initially seeking help—for example, gang members, prostitutes, runaways on the streets, or homeless persons.

3. Someone else may identify an individual, a family, or a group as having a serious problem that threatens the welfare of themselves or others and request that you intervene. You may go out to the family or individual, or they may report to the agency under duress by the referral source.

Preparing for Engagement

Your initial contact may involve your interaction with an individual, a family, or some other group. To prepare, you will collect and review any pertinent data you have about the applicant and the purposes of the coming encounter. In addition, you may want to discuss with others in your agency the kinds of help that the agency can offer. Beginnings are important and establish the pattern of ongoing relationships. You wish to demonstrate respect and concern for potential clients. Thus, you will want to do everything possible to reduce unnecessary obstacles to communication. An understanding about the time and place is essential, as are arrangements to ensure that the meeting will be comfortable, private, and as free from interruptions as possible. You will give thought to contact with collaterals—that is, persons, other than the applicant, whose interest and/or participation may impinge on the change endeavor. For example, you may want to contact the family of a referred adolescent. However, we suggest that, whenever possible, contacts with collaterals be delayed until after the first meeting with the respondent so that you have an opportunity to discuss the purpose of the collateral contact together.

Sometimes, though, there may be compelling reasons for a collateral contact before you see the appliacant. In these circumstances, we suggest the following guidelines:

1. Applicants are the primary source of information, although not necessarily the only source.

EXHIBIT 8-6   Elements of the Worker's Presentation of Self

1. Compassion: I deeply care about you.
2. Mutuality: We are here on a common human level; let's agree on a plan, and then let's walk the path together.
3. Humility: Please help me to understand.
4. Respect: I consider you as having worth. I treat your ideas and feelings with consideration. I do not intrude upon your person.
5. Openness: I offer myself to you as you see me; real, genuine, and authentic.
6. Empathy: I am trying to feel what you are feeling.
7. Involvement: I am trying to share and help in your efforts.
8. Support: I will lend my conviction and back up your progress.
9. Expectation: I have confidence that you can achieve your goals.
10. Limitation: I must remind you of your agreed-upon obligations.
11. Confrontation: I must ask you to look at yourself.
12. Planning: I will always bring proposals, but I would rather have yours.
13. Enabling: I am here to help you become more able, more powerful.
14. Spontaneity and control: I will be as open as possible, yet I must recognize that, in your behalf, I need to exercise some self-control.
15. Role and person: I am both a human being like you and represent an agency, with a special function to perform.
16. Science and art: I hope to bring you professional skill, which must be based on organized knowledge, but I am dealing with people, and my humanity must lend art to grace the science.

2. You should not acquire data that you would be unwilling to share with the applicant. In addition, you should be willing to disclose the process by which the data was secured and to explain why you resorted to that means.

3. Any data that you have about a particular aspect of the problem—for example, from agency files—should be shared with the applicant before you ask how he or she feels and thinks about that topic. In this way, you scrupulously avoid trapping the applicant and provide an opportunity for the applicant, before taking a position, to reconcile what you know with what she thinks and feels.

4. If you must seek information in advance of initial contact with the applicant, you should limit that data to the situation that brings you and the applicant together—nothing more. By amassing large amounts of data unrelated to the problem at hand, you will limit your ability to hear and understand what the applicant is saying in the here and now.

5. Usually, you can wait until after the first meeting with the applicant before you obtain information from other sources. At that meeting, you and the applicant can establish the need for such information and the purposes it serves. Most data collection will take place after you and the applicant have agreed to work together and have a preliminary definition of the problem on which you will work and the objectives that will be sought— that is, after the applicant has become a client.

Initial contacts may be scheduled in a number of ways. The applicant may have telephoned the agency for an appointment, or the appointment may have been scheduled by letter. Remember that the process of scheduling the initial contact may be the first communication the potential client has with your agency; you want the communication to be clear and to create a positive, friendly impression. We recommend the letters be specific as to date, time, and place but that they also be informal and written in the first and second person. If you have not spoken directly with the applicant, because the initial meeting has been scheduled by letter, or by some other staff person, we suggest that you telephone at least a day in advance of the meeting to confirm the appointment, briefly respond to any questions that have come up about the appointment, and indicate that you are looking forward to meeting with the applicant. This short person-to-person communication will help lay the groundwork for engagement.

For some respondents, such as families in which there is an allegation of child abuse, you may be required to make an unannounced home visit as your initial contact. We believe this is ill-advised and will unnecessarily escalate the respondents' anger. We encourage you to work within your agency to develop policies that permit you to telephone in advance—if only a few hours—to let the respondent know that you will be visiting. Unannounced visits, if required, can become a part of the plan that is negotiated with the respondent during the first visit; the ground rules will then be clear and known. If the respondent has no telephone, or if you are required to make an unannounced visit as the first contact, we suggest that you start the visit by briefly introducing yourself, stating the name of the agency you represent, establishing whether the person who answered the door is the parent or caretaker of the child in question, and indicating that you need their assistance in determining if a child in the household has been neglected or abused. At that point, we recommend asking permission to come into the house. What do you do if permission is denied? We will discuss your options shortly.

In the process of engagement, you will cross the boundaries of the applicant. What you do and say will affect the course of your relationship and your ability to be of help. This requires that you always be sensitive to the meaning of boundaries for the applicant and show respect for the boundaries.

Engaging Applicants

Applicants are seeking help from you and your agency. Thus, we suggest that you start with a relatively brief exploration of the presenting problem; start where the applicant is (Pilsecker, 1994). You may find it useful to begin with a relatively open-ended question—for example, "Could you tell me what brings you to the agency?" You may also wish to explore how long the presenting problem has existed and how frequently it occurs, as well as past efforts to resolve it. We suggest that, after these initial explorations, you quickly shift attention to what the applicant wants to have done. The applicant is more likely to agree to work with you if the focus is on desired solutions, rather than on the problem.

You will also need to have a preliminary discussion of what the applicant expects from you and what you expect from the applicant. In the engagement process, all of these discussions—about presenting problems, desired solutions, and expectations—are preliminary, but they provide the starting point for data collection, assessment, and the development of a service plan.

In dealing with applicants, you will need to understand what it means to help someone. Keith-Lucas (1972) defines help as something offered by one person or group to another in such a way that the helped person or group can use it to achieve some solution of the issue at hand. Thus help has two important elements: (1) what is given; and (2) how it is given and used. To be helpful, what is given must be of value to the recipients, and it must be given in such a way as to leave the recipients free to use it in their own way, without loss of self-esteem or loss of control. Applicants become clients when they decide that it is possible to accept the help offered.

In our culture, accepting help from professionals often implies a considerable loss of self-esteem. The difficulty is increased if the problem is attributed to some defect of the applicant; we erect barriers to problem solving when we assume that problems in living are signs of personality malfunction or devalued personal qualities.

Asking for help may be painful and difficult for people who have been taken advantage of or who have made previous unsuccessful attempts to live in a better way. On the other hand, some parents will support a groupwork agency financially so that their children can have rich developmental experiences. Although the enrollment of their children in these programs is an acknowledgement that they need help, the parents see it as a positive step. Likewise, the neighborhood group that seeks a social worker's help in advocating change in another system—a school or a housing project—may see this as a positive step toward controlling their own situation. However, because the social problems of poverty and unemployment are often regarded as the consequences of individual pathology, a family wrestling with these problems may feel inadequate and afraid to ask for help. If you're ever driven through miles of confusing streets before stopping to ask for directions, you may wonder why you had to waste so much time, gas, and energy before you could admit you were lost. Were you attempting to preserve a sense of adequacy?

You can be helpful to applicants only when you understand what they would like to change. Thus, in the engagement phase, you and the applicant must clarify the problem on which you will work; you determine the applicant's expectations and wants regarding your work together. Both you and the applicant must understand the realities and boundaries of your abilities and the agency's resources. The applicant needs some realistic understanding of what the work will require.

Engaging Prospects

Engaging prospects is different from engaging applicants. The roles seem to be reversed. You will be reaching out to contact a prospect with an offer for service. Prospects may not want service, and probably have little awareness of your potential helpfulness. In the past, they may have found service provision demeaning; perhaps service was offered on terms that were not acceptable to them. Examples of prospects include runaway youth, homeless populations, individuals with chronic mental illness (who are often also homeless), prostitutes, and those with alcohol and drug problems. Many of these people have given up hope. It will require considerable communication skill, patience, and persistence to engage a prospect.

Engaging prospects means that you must be accessible (Snell, 1991). There are at least three dimensions of accessibility. You must be available to prospects at times that are convenient for them, in places where they are, and in a manner that the prospect finds acceptable. In Reading 8-1, Craig Rennebohm describes walking the streets of Seattle each day to make contact with people who are homeless and chronically mentally ill. Outreach workers working with youth gangs must be on the streets, accessible, and in places where young people congregate. Making contact with roadside prostitutes means getting out on the road to meet and talk with these young women. These approaches will also require consistency and patience. It is unlikely that meaningful contact will occur with one walk through a neighborhood, one evening out where young people congregate, or one visit to the roadside rest stops where prostitutes solicit business. You will need to patiently establish a continuing presence and invite trust.

Successfully engaging prospects is likely to require the offer of concrete services and resources. The initial service for work with prostitutes might be to offer condoms, in order to reduce the risk of sexually transmitted disease. This may serve as a stepping stone to conversations with the young women regarding their objectives, whether the sex trade is contributing to those objectives, and what other options are available to them. Marcia Cohen (1989) found that engagement with individuals who are homeless and mentally ill requires a clear offer of service addressed to client wants and is provided on a voluntary basis. Actively engaging such prospects requires a commitment to empowerment types of practice, in which prospects maintain control over the helping process.

You will think of yourself as a salesperson as you engage prospects. Any good salesperson will be persistent, consistent, and patient in making contacts. You will also need to be skillful at determining what the prospect wants and to offer a service that empowers the prospect and provides something that they want. Reaching out to prospects is an aspect of social work practice that has often been overlooked. It is very important, however, if we are to successfully offer services to groups of people who have been marginalized.

Engaging Respondents

You engage respondents because someone else recognized a problem and either asked you to intervene or required the respondent to seek service from you. Many, if not most, of the people you see will be respondents. When you accept a referral, it is your responsibility to determine why the respondent is being referred and what the referral source's perception of the situation is—that is, to determine what the referral source sees as the problem, how the source identifies it as a problem, what the facts are that bear on the problem, how the source sees the possibility for change, and what objectives the referral source seeks.

Exercise caution, however, in giving the referral source any assurance that you will work toward those objectives. You will also want to consider the objectives desired by the respondent. If the objectives desired by the referral source are inappropriate or impossible, you should discuss this before you agree to intervene. For example, a goal that we could not accept would be the demand by a referral source that we remove six children

from a neighbor who appears to be neglecting them and place them in a foster home. You will also explore the respondent's view of the reason for referral. You court disaster when you accept someone else's view without making your own professional assessment and without understanding the meaning of the referral to the respondent.

The respondent may or may not be willing to provide an opinion regarding the problem. Usually, however, advance information about the problem has been supplied by the referral source. The respondent may not have given permission for information to be shared with you and may not know what information was shared. Consequently, it is important for you to share the advance information and, if possible, the source of that information with the respondent. Sometimes you cannot reveal the source of information—for example, in cases involving child neglect and abuse in which the informant asks not to be identified; in the interest of protecting the children, such requests are granted. But suppose that you are a court intake worker and have on your desk the police report of a car theft. The young man accused of stealing the vehicle is sitting in your office. Begin the interview by showing him the police report and asking him to comment on it. Does he agree with it? Are there statements that should be corrected? If his story differs markedly from that of the police officer, you may suggest that this will need to be cleared up during the court hearing, when both parties are under oath.

It is not your function to catch people in lies or distortions. Rather, you try to establish honest and open communication. When respondents have been directed to report to you—for example, if you are seeing young people or adults who are under a court order such as probation—you will find it useful to begin with a discussion of their perception and recall about the process that brought them to you. What do they recall about the court hearing? What did the judge—or whoever made the referral—say about the reason for referral? Respondents are often not clear about what prompted the referral. Exploring this will give you an opportunity to help respondents clarify their perception. You may consider alternative perceptions and understandings, if you believe there is some distortion in respondents' recall. Having begun the discussion in this relatively neutral area, you may then be able to move into a consideration of respondents' perceptions of the problem and wants. In examining family preservation services to families of abused children, Ronald Rooney (1993) found "that the interaction with the social worker who explains services and helps to create a contract may be the critical factor as a family moves from varied levels of scepticism to a generally favorable view about the services" (p. 14). The nature of the initial experience with a social worker had a greater impact on the family's decision to accept or reject services than does their initial status as applicant or respondent. Recommendations regarding engagement with the family in cases of alleged child abuse are offered in Exhibit 8–7.

EXHIBIT 8-7   **Engaging Respondents in Situations of Alleged Child Abuse**

Begin the interview by introducing yourself. Be direct and clear in explaining who you are and why you are there (Baily & Baily, 1983). An example is: ``My name is Debbie. I am a social worker from Child and Family Services. I have come because it has been reported that Nicolas is in potential danger. Are you Nicholas's mom?''

At this point, you should try to gain entry into the house. You could say, ``It must be awkward for you with me standing in the doorway like this. Would you like to discuss this inside?'' The parent may let you in; or refuse to talk anymore and shut the door; or continue to talk, but not let you in the door. In the latter case, you should continue to try to gain trust by explaining that you are there to learn what happened and you need the parents' help. You should make it clear that this is something you can work on together. As you develop more of a relationship with the parent, you should again request access to the house. If the parent refuses to talk at all or consistently refuses to grant entry, you must go back to the agency and get the necessary court order or other authority to take protective action.

Once inside the house, you should refrain from accusing the parents of abuse, but instead state your concern for the child and explain that it is your job to protect children (Bross, Krugman, Lenherr, Rosenburg, & Schmitt, 1988). You should ask the parent for help in understanding this mutual problem. Remember that you have walked uninvited into this situation, and the client will probably be angry. You could say, ``I understand some bruises were noticed at school today. I need your help in understanding how he may have gotten these bruises. Have you noticed them?'' It is important for the parent to be able to talk to you. You may ask for an explanation of the situation from the parent's point of view. For example, ``How do you think Nicolas got those bruises?''

Kadushin and Martin (1988) believe that the primary focus should be on what the agency and the parents can do together to help the child. They recommend that you make the following assumptions during the initial contact:

1. The parents are not deliberately willful in their behavior. Neglect, abuse, and exploitation are responses to the social and/or personal difficulties that the parents face.

2. Change is possible.
3. The parents are unhappy about the situation but will be defensive.
4. The first efforts should be directed at helping the parents make the changes that would permit the children to remain in their own home without danger.

You should now ask to see the child. The parent is not given the right to refuse an exploration (Kadushin & Martin, 1988); however, you should try to develop a good relationship with the parent(s), and try to keep all actions and information voluntary. If at this time, or at any other time during the interview, the parent objects or expresses resentment, you should acknowledge his or her feelings and reinforce his or her role as a parent (Oppenhein, 1992). An example of this is: ``I understand how difficult it must be to see your son hurt. Maybe it would be easier for Nicolas if you hold his arm while I examine it.'' Examine the child carefully, in the presence of the parent, who preferably is involved in the process (Oppenhein, 1992). You need to reassure the child as this is going on and to get a sense of the child's general well-being. As the examination proceeds, you should also be assessing the parent-child relationship (Oppenhein, 1992).

If the child is seen alone, you must reassure the child that you have the permission of the parent to talk to the child and that what the child says to you will not be shared with the parents unless the child agrees (Kadushin & Martin, 1988).

Examine the child for any physical injuries, including missing teeth, bruises or other skin discoloration, scabs covering healing cuts, rope burns, pin marks, scratches, and any difficulties the child might display in walking or manual dexterity (Kadushin & Martin, 1988). If there is any evidence of injury, make an appointment with a pediatrician. You must be upfront with the parent and get the parent involved. Oppenhein (1992) gives an example of this: ``We have a problem here. To me it looks like someone has deliberately hurt him. He will have to see a doctor. I can help arrange that. We need to be clear about how and when these injuries happened. Could someone in the household have hurt him?'' This statement is straightforward, but does not blame the parent.

Source: Debbie Scora, BSW student, Faculty of Social Work, University of Manitoba, Winnipeg, Manitoba.

Your communications with respondents are designed to encourage them to participate with you as a partner. As much as possible, you want to share power with respondents and form a partnership in problem solving. Asking permission is a good strategy. Drake (1994) notes that, when workers ask permission, child welfare clients feel respected and empowered. In child welfare work, you can ask for permission to enter the house or to see a child. More generally, you can ask for permission to explore any area of concern. For example, instead of saying to a youth, "I'd like to talk about the offense," say, "Is it all right if we talk about the offense?" Instead of saying, "How are things going at home?" you might ask, "Would it be all right with you if we talk a little about how things are going at home?" In these simple ways, you can assist respondents to share in the decision making and encourage their continuing participation. Asking for permission, however, creates the possibility that the respondent will say no. When you stand on the front step and ask, "May I come in and visit?" the family may say no. If you ask, "May we talk about the offense?" the answer may be: "No, I'd rather not." Our experience has been that this does not happen often. When it does, you have three options.

Your first option is to honor the respondent's request but leave the option of returning to the subject later. For example, you might say, "All right, we don't need to talk about that now, but I'll be wanting to return to that matter with you." Your second option is to explore what lies behind the respondent's refusal. You might say, "Can you tell me what's in back of your not wanting to invite me in?" or "Can you tell me the reasons you don't want to talk about the offense?" You shift the focus from the negative decision to what lies behind it. We don't recommend, however, that you ask why. To do so usually produces defensive or angry responses, which are unhelpful. We are not much interested in the respondent's justification or explanation for a decision; we want to understand the reasons for it.

Your third option is to turn to persuasion and to explain the reasons for your request. Try to convince the respondent that it is important for you to come in and visit, or to discuss the offense. If you outline your reasons in a rational manner, you may be able to avoid resorting to your authority. However, we generally recommend against this third option. Our preference is for option two, exploring what lies behind the respondent's deci-

sion. If the respondent appears uncomfortable with that, we suggest moving to option one.

When you engage respondents, you will be expected to provide reports to referral sources. In particular, you will let the referral source know whether contact was made with the respondent and whether you and the respondent have agreed to work together. Exercise caution in reporting to the referral source; do not share information about the respondent unless this sharing was first discussed with the respondent and was either approved by the respondent or is required by law or court order. Consider with the referral source how to proceed if you think that you cannot help, that there is no problem, or that the respondent is unwilling to become a client. The referral source may become the client. For example, parents who come to the agency to report a child's problem quite often become the clients, and the child may or may not be seen. Or suppose that a neighborhood group is upset over the behavior of a family that has recently moved to the neighborhood. A visit by the social worker reveals that the new family is functioning well but differently from the neighbors. Perhaps the neighborhood group becomes the client, and the problem to be examined is difficulty in accepting difference. Or your initial contact may reveal that the respondent really does want help with some difficulties, but the help to be given does not fall within the function of your agency. In that case, you may suggest that the referral source seek help elsewhere. You must engage in a problem-solving process with the source and bring the contact to an orderly termination. This usually takes only one telephone call.

When you intervene in people's lives at a third party's request, you are likely to stir up anxiety and perhaps anger. It will be difficult for the family or the individual to engage with you until they understand why you have come, what you know about them, and what you are trying to do to them. If they are to answer your questions, you must first share yourself and your purpose with them; there must be no hidden agenda. Often, you will be contacting people whose previous experiences with social agencies or other institutions have left them feeling rejected, judged inadequate, or betrayed. The initial response to you may be shaped by the respondents' negative image of social workers and what they do to people.

There are three important principles here. First, you have walked uninvited into the situation. Thus, respondents have the right to their anger; they have the right to challenge you. In fact, those responses may demonstrate appropriate system boundaries. On the other hand, the respondent who threatens you with physical violence and the respondent who welcomes you and hands you the problem have poor boundary structures. You should not placate the respondent, nor try to allay the anger by talking about your intent to help. Instead, deal openly, realistically, and compassionately with the problem as you understand it. You want to be able to say, "This is my understanding of what brought me here. I know my coming into your life may bring trouble. But if we can agree on the reality of the problem and what you want done about it, I think we can work through to some better way of operating."

The second principle concerns your own feelings about your role. We have been brought up to be polite and not to confront people with negative observations about themselves. So we have very little experience of being direct in this way, unless we are angry at someone. As professionals, we need to learn to share negative facts with compassion and caring. While our words may transmit difficult information, our voice must convey concern. You may need to practice before you are able to share negatives simply as facts, in a supportive manner.

The third principle is that you must share negative facts and evaluations as if they are a problem to be solved. Tell the respondent that this is your information; don't say that it is the truth, and don't accept the respondent's word that it is false. The fact that you have this information creates a problem for both you and the respondent. What do you do with the information? Also, don't tell the respondent how he or she ought to behave. Rather, say, for example, "Most of the things I read say that kids get along better if their parents don't use physical punishment as the only method of discipline. Have you heard this? Have you ever tried other ways of correcting your kids? What did you do and how did it work?" This approach avoids setting you up as the authority and allows the respondent to reject your suggestions without rejecting you. It also involves the respondent, by presenting a problem.

Transfer Cases

We have been discussing engaging applicants, respondents, and prospects as if these were individuals or groups new to your agency. As a new worker, however, you are likely to have cases transferred to you from current or previous workers with your agency. These individuals and groups will be known to the agency and most will probably be clients, in the sense that they and their previous worker will have arrived at an agreement regarding the problem, objectives, and service plan. Others, however, may still be respondents and prospects.

Ideally, the transfer process will involve at least one joint meeting with you, the previous worker, and the individual or group being served. This meeting will provide an opportunity for discussion of the progress made by the individual or group and the previous worker; the previous worker can introduce you and facilitate your own engagement with the person or individual. Unfortunately, this ideal is often not met. The transfer process may consist of the delivery of a case file, perhaps with a transfer summary, and instructions to provide service to the individual, family, or group. You will then need to consider how to engage this person or group, whether applicant, respondent, or prospect. What use do you want to make of the existing written material? How you will go about your first contact?

We suggest that you read the case file and begin the interview by offering the applicant a brief summary of what you learned from the file. Then ask for comments and for any corrections the applicant wants to make. This is preferable to asking applicants to talk about their problems. On one memorable occasion, that inquiry prompted a long sigh and the response: "You are the fifth worker I have had, and you all ask me to start over. Don't you people ever write anything down?" Another client commented, at termination, "The most important thing is that you cared, and I knew that you did because the first time I saw you, you told me you had read our record and you still came out to help. We had been in such a mess for so long that I was surprised to know that anyone who knew about us would think we were worth coming to see."

This discussion of the applicant file can be brief. You will quickly move to understanding the desired solution and the applicant's view about the progress being made. You and the applicant can then focus on what needs to be done and how you might be a part of this.

THE TASKS OF ENGAGEMENT
Inviting Participation

Partnership is one of the underlying principles of social work practice. Applicant and worker participate together in decision making and other processes. As we saw in Chapter 4, participation implies respect for the dignity of each applicant. One of your tasks in engagement is to create a climate that invites and encourages participation from applicants.

If you talk too much, you will deprive applicants of the opportunity to participate and inhibit their future participation. As we have seen, you must share certain basic information. With respondents, for example, you need to identify yourself and your agency, the referral source, and your understanding of the reason for contact. With a transfer client, you should briefly summarize the file material and ask for confirmation or correction. Practice sharing this information very concisely—preferably in no more than one or two sentences—and then follow up with an open-ended question that encourages participation; open-ended questions are framed so that they cannot be answered with a yes or no (Chapter 10). Exhibit 8–8 provides an example of failure to encourage participation. In this example, a worker responsible for aftercare and discharge planning attempts to engage a youth in a juvenile correction institution.

The following suggestions may be helpful in encouraging applicants' participation:

1. Keep your introduction brief and then ask an open-ended question designed to secure the applicant's perceptions.
2. As quickly as possible, focus on solutions; most people are more interested in talking about what they want done about a problem than about the problem itself.
3. Avoid advice or direction at this early stage of the process.

4. Try not to be uncomfortable with silences; it is all right to let the applicant proceed at his or her own pace.
5. Be aware that many of us talk too much, especially when we're uncomfortable; if this is your pattern, consciously try to limit your own talking.
6. Always remember that your task is to create a comfortable climate in which the applicant feels able to participate.

Applicant participation may be blocked by overuse of reassurance, especially in early phases of work. Reassurance is seldom appropriate during engagement, though that may be hard to accept if you feel the applicant's pain and have the impulse to remove it. Try to remember that the purpose for which the applicant came to you is not the removal of the pain but the solution of the underlying problem. Pain is a signal that there is trouble. Understanding the pain will help you to understand the problem as the applicant perceives it and move toward solutions.

Understanding the Presenting Problem

Starting with the applicant's perspective. You will use your skills of interviewing and communication to understand the applicant's perception of the problem. What brings the applicant to ask for help? One of your primary tools is the ability to empathize. You must put all other considerations aside and fully hear what the applicant is saying—the words used, the feeling carried by the words, and the unspoken messages conveyed by body language. While you will be aware of the need to focus the interview and to collect relevant data, you must also remember that proceeding too quickly to data collection

---

EXHIBIT 8–8	How Not to Start an Interview

This excerpt is from an interview by a social worker responsible for discharge planning and community supervision of youth released from a juvenile correction institution. This is the first interview between David and this worker and takes place at the institution. What do you see to be the difficulty here? How might this social worker have started the interview differently?

I introduced myself to David and he shyly acknowledged the introduction. I asked him to sit down and I sat across from him where I proceeded to interpret my role and my interest in working with him and his family. I told

him that I knew what the reason was for his being at the Hillside School and that I was here to begin planning with him for his return home. I also indicated to David that I would be talking to him and his parents to help them with any problems that they may have. I also related to David that I had seen his mother, and that I had planned to see both his mother and father as soon as possible. At the beginning he had come into the office looking very apprehensive and seemed to maintain an air of cockiness about him. I also had the impression that David viewed me with suspicion.

is counterproductive: If the applicant is able to share, it is better to listen than to question. Make brief comments or ask simple questions related to what the applicant has just said, as encouragement to continue; let the applicant tell the story in his own way, while you seek to understand.

Don't become preoccupied with formulating your own judgment or collecting information for your purposes; the critical issue is to understand the applicant's view of what brings you together (Pilsecker, 1994). If you don't understand, don't despair or feel inadequate. Honestly admit your difficulty in understanding, and ask if the applicant can say more. In working with an applicant very different from you, it is unrealistic to expect immediate mutual understanding. Reach into yourself and try to recall an occasion when you felt something similar to what the applicant expresses. You may not have lost a spouse or a child, but surely you have suffered some loss that left you in despair. The depth of feeling may be different, but the similarities help you to understand. The commonalities of human emotions and experience allow us to relate to one another. However, the other side of the coin is the danger of assuming that you understand the applicant because you have had a similar experience—or, worse, that, because you successfully dealt with a similar problem, what worked for you should work for the applicant. No two people experience the same event in the same way. If you are to be of help, you must start where the applicant is, which means understanding the applicant's view of what brings you together.

The process will go astray if you become so focused on your definition of the problem that you do not hear what applicants are saying. Without applicant input, the objectives that you adopt cannot reflect what the applicant wants. Given the lack of a common objective, things will not go well and, in looking for an explanation, you might mistakenly attribute your lack of progress to the client's supposed psychopathology.

Exhibit 8–9 provides an example. Mr. Keene was referred to a private family agency following the hospitalization of his wife for mental illness; the court believed that Mr. Keene would need help in caring for the three children, ages 4, 2, and 1. At the end of Exhibit 8–9, after 14 months of working with Mr. Keene, the worker is again asking him how he wants to solve the child care problem. However, it seems that, for Mr. Keene, the primary problem is the absence of his wife. The second is

his lack of comprehension of mental illness, and the third is the guilt he carries about what has happened. It can be expected that there will continue to be problems with child care as long as the worker does not recognize Mr. Keene's feelings and begin with Mr. Keene's problem. This case is a good example of how, if we want to be of help, we must start where the applicant hurts. If we cannot start there—as in emergency situations involving child abuse—we can at least discuss with the respondent what the situation is about and realize how our views differ. We can, through our behavior, convey that we hear the respondent and that his or her view of the problem is understood.

Partializing. You begin with the problem that the applicant identifies. But these may be more than one. Because you cannot do everything at once, you must engage with the applicant in deciding which problem to address first. Partialization is the process of selecting, from the universe of applicant problems, the specific problem that is to become the focus of worker-client attention (often called the problem to be worked or the problem for work). This process improves the likelihood of finding common ground. You and the applicant don't have to agree on all the problems, just on the first.

Ideally, you will go with the applicant's selection of a starting point. However, if the applicant's choice is dangerous to self, or others, or if it promises more trouble and failure, you have the responsibility of pointing out the risks. You cannot be a party to planning that is destructive. On the other hand, you must be very sure of your ground before rejecting the applicant's chosen starting place.

Finding common ground. There can be no engagement between the applicant and you without a common understanding of what problem needs to be addressed. You and the applicant must spell out your respective definitions of the problem and agree on an order in which to proceed.

If the applicant does not have any suggestions about where to start, you may introduce suggestions about a starting place. Sometimes you and the applicant may find that where to begin will turn into the immediate problem to be worked. The inability of the various interests to perceive the situation in the same way may well be a central problem. Consider Mr. Keene in Exhibit 8–9. In that case, the worker had a problem identified by a referral system: Mr. Keene's children needed care. While

EXHIBIT 8-9 **Incongruence Between Worker and Client Goals**

Mr. Keene had need of and sought a great deal of help in financial management. He looked to the worker as to a parent to decide on specific expenditures. His major problems in financial management were an uncontrollable impulse to overspend on useless gifts to his wife and an inability to deny the children toys, sweets, and recreation jaunts. He would agree with the worker when she carefully figured out with him what would be reasonable and appropriate spending on these items, but he would persistently overspend. He talked persistently about his wife, about the fact that he had not known she was ill, about not knowing the cause of her illness, about his concern as to when she would come home. The worker did not respond directly to these concerns but concentrated on the children's needs. In 12 months, however, he was able to afford a housekeeper.

His relationship to the children was characterized by anxious fretting over them, indulging them, and demanding the utmost in care for them from the housekeeper. Momentary sternness with them would be quickly replaced by petting and indulgence. Any illness or behavior deviations caused extreme worry. Certain comments indicated that he connected the children's symptoms with their mother's behavior. He persisted in taking the children to visit their mother even though the worker advised against it and he himself would agree that the visits meant little to his wife and were exhausting and disturbing to the children. The worker's efforts to help him largely involved giving recognition to his desire to be a good parent and using his concern for the children's welfare to argue for consideration of their health and emotional comfort. Mr. Keene always presented problems to the worker with an earnest request for advice, and the worker gave sound child guidance advice freely. However, Mr. Keene was able to use the advice only fragmentarily.

The worker observed repeatedly in the record that Mr. Keene was very devoted to his wife. He visited regularly and excessively, taking gifts and writing letters. He talked repeatedly of her eventual return. He would react to any slight improvement in her condition with great optimism and with urgent demands for her discharge. Recently he brought her home against medical advice. She became disturbed, and after she disrupted a smoothly running home, he was forced to return her to the hospital. It was recorded that he often referred to his wife's competence prior to her illness, adding, ``And I didn't know she was ill.'' This statement was not explored.

Mr. Keene's relationship to the housekeepers had been problematic. The first housekeeper probably was incompetent, but this was not clear because of Mr. Keene's nagging and his constant comparisons of her activities with those of his wife. He fired this woman because she was unkind to the children.

The second housekeeper, a competent person who got along fairly well with the children, quit because she could not endure his demands or his competitive undermining of her efforts with them. Mr. Keene was remorseful about this, recognizing too late that she was a good housekeeper and mother substitute.

The third housekeeper was a competent, motherly woman who got along smoothly with Mr. Keene through joking with him, mothering him, and bossing him. She mended his clothes and packed his lunches. She allowed the children to play without restraint, and they became more quiet and contented. Mr. Keene assumed more responsibility with chores and reported enthusiastically to the worker that now his problems were solved and he would not be needing help much longer. Impulsively, without consulting the worker or the housekeeper, he brought his wife home from the hospital with grudging medical consent but on the basis of his reports of favorable conditions for her care at home. Later he justified his actions through saying that he had been unhappy that his wife was not at home to enjoy everything with them. The housekeeper could not put up with the wife's very disturbed behavior and threatened to leave. Mr. Keene turned to the worker, who helped him face the fact that his wife was not ready to live outside of a hospital. In returning her, Mr. Keene had to call plainclothes police and win her cooperation through deception.

Now, following this episode, Mr. Keene is anxious and undecided as to future plans. He thinks he probably can mend matters with the housekeeper, but she is still angry and fearful and on the verge of leaving. How will he ever bring his wife home if no one will give her a trial? Will she ever get well? This is a good housekeeper, and perhaps he should urge her to stay. Certain comments show some anger with her for not putting up with his wife, even though Mrs. Keene was irrational and clearly unable to assume responsibility or to permit anyone else to do so in her home. Foster home care was discussed, but he thought he could not face not seeing his children every day. The pros and cons of the two plans—foster care and a continuation of the present plan—were reviewed. Mr. Keene left the interview undecided but leaning toward another trial of the housekeeper service.

that represents a possible problem to be worked out. Mr. Keene's definition of the problem must also be recognized, along with his views as to where to begin the work.

Sometimes a common ground for work can be established quickly; sometimes a series of interviews is necessary; and sometimes no common ground can be found. However, without a common place to begin, you and the applicant cannot proceed; both parties may need to acknowledge this fact and, for the present at least, terminate the process. In an authority-related setting, where you have a legal mandate to provide supervision and the respondent has a legal mandate to report his or her activities, there are two possibilities. You may return to the court, acknowledge the impasse, and ask that the court decide the next steps. This may be wise if, for example, you have been mandated to work with a mother who has been abusing her child and you are concerned about the child's physical well-being. Alternatively, you may agree to meet only the responsibilities mandated by the court. In either of these situations, however, the possibility of future negotiations should be left open.

Before we move on, let's make one more important point about problem definition: You must be careful not to confuse the problem and the cause. Consider the case of a 13-year-old boy, James C., who (1) has just stolen a car, (2) comes from a home in which the father has just died in an automobile accident, and (3) has a mother who says that she may overprotect her son. Most students will write that the problem is the mother's overprotection and the lack of a father. The central problem at the moment, however, is that the boy has just been apprehended by the police while driving a stolen car.

If you focus on the mother's overprotection, you have shifted the problem from the son's behavior to the mother's. Moreover, you may be terribly wrong. Asked to tell what happened, the boy may say, for example, that he was a candidate for gang membership and the initiation rites required that he steal a car. If so, assessment requires that the two possible explanations (those offered by the mother and the son) be considered together. Perhaps, in the course of the exploration and assessment, you and the family will redefine the problem to be worked as the mother's overprotection.

Another underlying cause of James' behavior may be his father's death, through its impact on the mother's feelings and actions. Should the mother's feelings be the problem to be worked? What would happen to the mother's sense of adequacy and her ability to treat her son differently if the problem to be worked was defined as her reaction to her husband's death, and that reaction was assessed as a normal response to overwhelming stress and crisis? And what about her son's reaction to his father's death? You need to think about these questions and raise them with the mother and son. Data will be collected on all the life stresses that may have led to the problem behavior. In Chapters 10 and 11, we will discuss how to integrate these data into some meaningful assessment of the situation and plan the work together. For now, be aware of the danger of confusing the presenting problem with the cause.

Understanding What the Applicant Wants

What does the applicant hope will happen as a result of working with you? Knowing the answer, you will be able to understand what the applicant wants to see changed.

Often, applicants want help in implementing some already-decided solution, rather than in examining alternatives to action. This makes sense. When confronted with a problem, our inclination is to search for some desired end. Goal seeking is what gives the problem-solving process its thrust and purpose, and the consideration of applicant objectives is an important part of each phase of the process.

In the beginning contact, however, it is important that you separate the problem from the objective, so that each may be considered separately. When a mother comes to your child welfare agency saying that she needs to place her child, that may be her answer to any one of a whole range of problems. You must identify the problem to which placing the child is the applicant's answer. You and the applicant may be able to find a better solution for her. Do not dismiss applicant objectives lightly; simply seek to separate objective and problem for more effective work.

Exhibit 8–10 illustrates a skillful engagement with a respondent—a 16-year-old at an institution for delinquent youth, whose objective was to secure his release. The worker's acceptance of this objective provided a

EXHIBIT 8-10   Engaging a Respondent

John, age 16, was sentenced to a term of open custody for five months for charges of Break & Enter, and Failure to Comply with his Undertaking.

The initial session began with discussion about what problem areas John would like to focus on during our meetings. I explained that we would try to define one to three target problems that he felt were of the most importance to him.

John immediately indicated that his primary goal was to obtain a review of his sentence in order to get out of custody early. John felt that the problem was: ``Being in custody for five months poses a barrier for John to show others that he can manage his life well without getting into further trouble.''

We held a brief discussion on some of the requirements that would be expected by a judge in granting a review and felt that in most cases, they were both desirable and within John's means to achieve.

I continued to initiate discussion around John's interest in showing others of what he was capable. John described that people viewed him as having a negative attitude—that he often wants things his way and doesn't care to compromise, that he is impatient and won't follow rules or requests that don't suit him, that he is too sarcastic in his tone with others and that he is jeopardizing his schooling. John stated that he wanted to show them that he could follow rules and get along and could complete his schooling. His goal was to show others (parents, teacher, authority) an improved attitude. I pointed out how closely linked this issue was with his interest in a review in order to strengthen motivation and rationale for this goal.

John indicated that not obtaining his schooling was a serious problem for him. His goal was to attend school full time and continue work on his grade eleven and twelve credits.

Source: L. Kallies, *Task-centered social work with young offenders*. MSW practicum report, Faculty of Social Work, University of Manitoba, Winnipeg (1997).

basis for the two of them to develop an appropriate service plan.

Understanding the applicant's frame of reference. Perhaps the most severe handicap in problem solving is our tendency to define applicant's problems within our own frame of reference. When applicants insist that we look at the problem from their point of view, we may interpret that as resistance to seeing things accurately and, thus, as proof of our fixed ideas. To illustrate, connect the dots in Exhibit 8–11 as directed.

After you have tried to solve the problem, turn to Appendix C for the solution. Are you surprised? Most people fail to solve this problem, because they assume that the dots compose a square and that the solution

EXHIBIT 8-11   Our Limited Frame of Reference

Connect these dots by means of four straight lines, without lifting your pencil from the paper. (See Appendix C for the solution.)

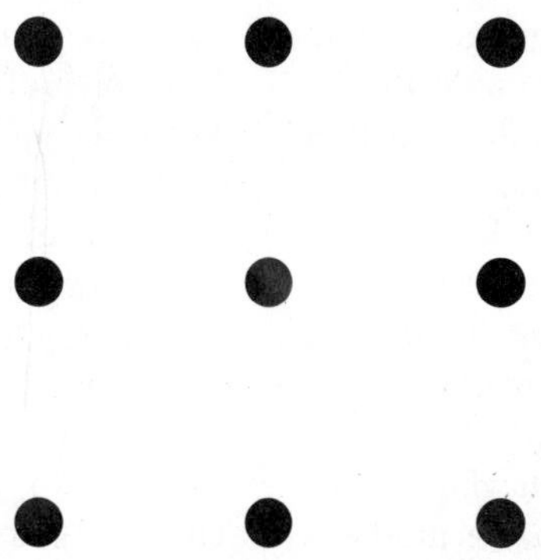

must fall within the boundaries of the square. Thus, the failure to solve the problem does not lie with the difficulty of the problem, but with self-imposed assumptions; unconscious assumptions can get in the way of problem solving. You must be aware of your assumptions and make initial contact within the applicant's frame of reference.

Levels of goals and objectives. There are different levels of goals. You may be concerned with an optimal or ultimate goal—the final desired outcome to which the effort is directed. Or you may be concerned with interim objectives that are significant steps on the journey toward the optimal goal; often, these intermediate objectives provide a way of testing whether the ultimate goal is sound.

In Exhibit 8–12, we see how analysis of the different levels of objectives allows us to find common ground. Each of the significant participants in Ms. Bates' case have a personal view of the problem and a corresponding objective or solution. Professional people involved with Ms. Bates want her to accept both the inevitability of her physical deterioration and a realistic plan for care— although they differ on the plan. She, desperately needing to deny the prognosis, is determined to get well and return to teaching; all she wants is recognition of this objective and help in achieving it. How can these disparate objectives be reconciled?

If we examine the different levels of solutions, we find that the participants' interim objectives are not different.

All the professional people want Ms. Bates to participate in rehabilitative efforts that will keep her functioning as well as possible for as long as possible. These same efforts are necessary if she is to achieve her ultimate goal of returning to teaching.

The worker may inform Ms. Bates (1) that the medical staff and she see the problem differently; (2) that they are in strong disagreement over the ultimate goals; (3) that the worker questions whether Ms. Bates can return to full-time teaching; but (4) that the place to start is with her ability to work on objectives that are necessary to either ultimate goal. If she wants to return to the classroom, she must struggle to walk again, to read braille, and to physically care for herself. Eventually, there will come a time when the worker and Ms. Bates put the results of their efforts together and make an ultimate plan: Either she will return to the community as an independently functioning person, or she will accept some alternate goal for at least partially sheltered care. Ms. Bates soon discovered, through trying to cope with self-care, that she would be unable to return to the classroom and decided that part-time work in a nursing home was a realistic objective. The worker did not have to force a change in goal; with experience, Ms. Bates made her own decision.

Beginning with objectives as steps towards longer-term goals enhances hope as a motivating factor. If you tell applicants that their goals are unrealistic, they will not be inclined to engage with you; you have

---

EXHIBIT 8-12 **Conflicting Objectives**

Ms. Bates, a 29-year-old school teacher, was admitted to a rehabilitation service following a massive stroke. She has been diabetic since she was 5 years old, and despite constant medical attention and rigid personal self-discipline in diet and medication, the disease was becoming progressively worse. During the past five years she has been losing her sight, and now she is considered legally blind. The stroke, which was also related to the diabetic condition, resulted in paralysis of her right side. Ms. Bates has always been a very goal-directed person and, in spite of an ever more disabling illness, has an advanced degree in the education of children with disabilities. She sees her problem as one of getting well quickly so she can return to her classroom, and she has a somewhat unrealistic notion of what is involved in such an accomplishment, denying the hard and difficult work of learning to walk with a cane and of learning to

read by braille. She is angry with the nurses and often refuses to cooperate with them because she feels that they are trying to keep her dependent. Her prognosis (which has been shared over and over again with her) is that she is in the last stages of an irreversible terminal condition and that she can never return to teaching. From their view the problem is that Ms. Bates is unwilling to accept the prognosis and behave properly. The staff feels that the problem is that the patient won't accept the massive damage that she has and will not participate with them in the small, painful, and difficult tasks necessary to achieving minimal self-care. A social worker sees the problem as getting Ms. Bates to apply for welfare because her own funds are almost exhausted and to engage Ms. Bates in planning for a move to a nursing home, as the rehabilitation facility cannot keep her much longer.

destroyed hope. If you can begin with lower-level objectives, applicants will usually abandon unrealistic goals on the basis of the experience they gain. In the engagement phase, you and the applicant work toward a common understanding of lower-level objectives, which serve to engage you both in unearthing the information required to establish a service plan. The problem-solving model demands that the client's purposes and expectations be explored and understood; lack of attention to client perceptions in the engagement phase—and the inappropriate selection of a starting place that results—has been identified as major source of failures in the helping process (Mayer & Timms, 1969).

Clarifying Expectations and the Preliminary Agreement

Engagement culminates in a preliminary agreement between you and the applicant about the presenting problem and the desired objectives. In addition, you must clarify the realities and boundaries of what can be offered and help the applicant understand the nature of further work together. As you convey to the applicant any limits on the service offered, you should also express confidence in your ability to help within those limits. If the service that can be offered is too limited, you must help the applicant find another resource. You must not promise more than you can deliver and raise false hopes; equally, you do not want to engender hopelessness. The applicant will only become involved in action with you if you offer hope that something can be done about the applicant's pain, despair, or anger.

Applicants are often confused about how the helping process will work. What do social workers do? There is no visible technology to offer clues. Your behavior in engagement provides an example of social work in action; that is one reason this phase is so important.

At the end of engagement, you will have identified the presenting problems and determined the applicant's initial objectives and desired solution. You and the applicant will then decide whether you wish to continue together. If so, the next stage is to collect the data on which assessment and planning will be based (Chapter 10).

CHAPTER SUMMARY

Engagement is accomplished through communications to involve applicants, prospects, and respondents in an understanding of presenting problems and their desired solutions. The process involves giving, receiving, and checking out meanings. Communications with potential clients may be impaired by these barriers:

- anticipation of what the other is going to say
- assumptions of meaning about communications from the other
- inexplicit purposes for the interview
- premature efforts to produce change
- inattentiveness
- applicant resistance

The tasks of engagement include:

- creating a climate in which the other person can participate
- understanding the presenting problem and situation as perceived by the applicant
- understanding what the applicant wants done and what solutions he or she perceives
- developing an initial agreement to continue working together

The process of engagement will be different with applicants, prospects, and respondents. Applicants actively seek service, and you can usually begin with a straightforward discussion of their perception of the problem and move quickly to their desired solutions. With respondents, you will need to be clear about your own purpose, role, and responsibilities but also engage them in a discussion of their perception of their situation and your presence in it. You may spend considerable time negotiating an understanding of the presenting problem, as well as respondents' view of the desired solutions. With prospects, you will be working, like a salesperson, to establish communication and to learn what the prospect wants that might be made available through your agency.

Engagement lays the groundwork for all future work and establishes the partnership essential for effective social work practice. You will work to understand applicants' perceptions of their situation, their presenting problem, and their desired solutions. Engagement ends when you have a preliminary agreement to collect data for use in formulating and evaluating alternative ways of achieving the desired objectives.

A LOOK FORWARD

In Chapter 9, we discuss communication across cultures. Interracial and intercultural communication places even greater responsibility on you to ensure that messages are being clearly received and transmitted.

In Chapter 10, we move to a discussion of data collection and assessment, and in Chapter 11 we discuss the service agreement that provides the basis for intervention. Engagement, data collection, assessment, and development of a service agreement are not discrete linear processes; they are interwoven, as we loop back from one to another. Consequently, you will find many common themes in these chapters.

In Reading 8-1, Craig Rennebohm describes outreach and engagement with individuals who are chronically mentally ill and homeless. He outlines a continuum of care, moving from approach through companionship and partnership toward a goal of growing mutuality. The values essential to outreach and engagement are respect, recognition of our essential human equality, and clear commitment to a healthy future.

In Reading 8-2, Barry R. Cournoyer and Katharine V. Byers identify communication skills for work with groups. They distinguish between two general forms of communication—empathic and expressive. Empathic communications draw from the client's frame of reference and are attempts to communicate your understanding of the client's expressions. Expressive communications draw from the worker's frame of reference and are efforts to share knowledge, experience, ideas, feelings, and so forth. We think the ideas in Reading 8-2 are equally useful for communication with individuals.

READING 8-1 *Approach and Companionship in the Engagement Process**

Craig Rennebohm

The primary concern of the Mental Health Chaplaincy is for individuals on the streets of downtown Seattle who are homeless and mentally ill. The chaplain and volunteers seek out those who are most vulnerable, isolated, and lacking in care. Walking a daily route, the chaplain observes, gently approaches, builds trust, and assists with appropriate resources. The aim of the Chaplaincy is to share with each individual the journey from the street to stability and to do all we can to foster the healing process.

Basic to our work is the notion of story. Each of us has a story—the narrative of our unique history and journey. Our story is neither right nor wrong. It may be deeply confused or disturbed, but it still our story. That is where

the work begins. There may be profound difficulties or struggles affecting this individual's life; a person may be fearful or wary, hopeless or hostile; yet the story is there, waiting to be told, if we will be patient and listen.

I cannot stress enough the importance of beginning with deep respect for each person we meet. We regard each individual not as a client or patient or case, but as a brother or sister in the human family. Much of what we do in the Chaplaincy is guided by simple courtesy and kindness. Part of that is to understand that peoples about the world have their own ways and traditions; we don't just barge in.

Many individuals are hardly able to speak of their situation. One man stood in the doorway of a department store. He may have been waiting for a bus, or just waiting. Later in the day, he was still there, and again the next morning. His clothes looked a little slept in. I said hello; he nodded. A day or two later, he was again at his post. I stopped and asked him how things were going. He said ok. For a week or so, we exchanged greetings, perhaps a

---

*An original reading prepared for this edition. I acknowledge my colleagues in the Seattle Mental Health Chaplaincy and in the community who share this work of outreach and engagement. These thoughts have taken shape through continuing conversations and consultations with many good, wise, and caring souls.

couple of sentences. One morning, I asked if he wanted to join me for coffee. He agreed. As we sat together he responded to a few questions. He was sleeping out. That was hard, I commented. The conversation quickly died; a spare narrative at best, almost nothing. A few days later, still with no job, the man went with me to a shelter, where he was able to get a regular mat each night, and I began seeing him there each morning. I found he had a pattern. At 7:00 A.M., when the shelter emptied, he looked for a newspaper on the ground or in the trash. He took it back to the shelter again at 9:00, when it opened for the day, and looked in the want ads. He circled one or two, and then sat.

This he explained in five or six sentences and with great effort at concentration. I told him that I had noticed how, after we talked a little, he would stop. I asked if he could tell me what happened; we were sitting on the floor, our backs to the wall. "It's embarrassing," he said. "I start something, then I just stop. I can't go on." A long pause. "Like right now. My thoughts are just floating away. Everything is just floating away." Silence.

I told him that I thought there was something we could do to help. "I'd like to talk to a friend here about this. See what she thinks. Just get some ideas." I looked at the man to see how this might seem to him. Slowly, he nodded. I consulted with one of the shelter counselors. Our sense was that this individual might be struggling with some form of thought disorder, a subtle type of schizophrenia. With the man's permission, I introduced him to the counselor. After a couple of visits in which he tried laboriously and valiantly to respond, we made a plan together to see the shelter psychiatrist. The four of us met. The man again shared his pain and embarrassment at being "so slow," and was unable to answer most of the questions or follow the mental status exam exercises. At the doctor's suggestion, he did begin with a small dose of medication. The physician explained that the medicine was intended to help the brain function better, to help the man keep his thoughts together, to take a few more steps each day.

The process was slow. The man continued to meet with the team. Gradually, he was able to stretch out his thinking and conversation over longer and longer periods of time. He began to talk a little of his family and past. We were able to pinpoint when the illness had begun to burden his life, several years earlier, and to

trace how things had deteriorated for him into homelessness. We went together to apply for benefits, and shared a walk to a nearby clubhouse program specializing in helping folks prepare for and find work. Today, this man is employed; he has his own apartment; he is in touch with his family. It appears that the medicine may be a lifetime necessity. The man tells his story with clarity and feeling. It includes the episode of illness and his ongoing vulnerability; it includes the experience of his isolation and also the account of his reconnection with others.

The process of reconnection involves four phases of relationship: approach, companionship, partnership, and mutuality. Each phase ends with a change in the relational field. The approach phase ends with the establishment of a one-to-one relationship. The companionship phase concludes as others begin to be part of the circle of healing and partnerships develop with other caregivers. As stability is reached in the community, healing and supportive partnerships may continue to be important, but our life is increasingly characterized by a growing number of mutual relationships with friends, peers, co-workers, family, and neighbors.

In the approach phase of outreach and engagement, the Chaplain or volunteer first observes and then, on the basis of the observation, chooses a mode of introduction. These are quite natural behaviors. In observing, we simply evaluate how comfortable a person is with others, how formal or informal we might want to be, how close we may come, how much conversation a person may be able to tolerate, and what their actions may tell us of their condition and sensitivities.

Careful observation reveals moments appropriate for small introductory steps. The work is incredibly slow; at first a second or two, then four or five seconds of contact. After a month, our encounters may last less than a minute.

Often, when students or interns or guests are walking with me to learn a little about outreach and engagement, I suggest we stop for a while at the corner or in the park and just watch. We see who comes by, what occupies a person, how much space they claim or need. After a while, I ask my colleague simply to go and say hello to someone, nothing more. If the person responds and wants to talk, fine. Sometimes, my colleagues have difficulty with this. They want a reason; they want to have a role, a professional frame. You have what you need, I say. You are a neighbor; you share this world; it is enough.

One day, a man sat slumped on a park bench, the rain pouring off him. His hands were grimy from days without washing. On his feet were broken shoes with no laces; all he wore was a light jacket on the cold November day. I went toward him a few steps. He took no notice. Quietly, I asked if it would be all right if I shared the bench. He said nothing. Tentatively I sat down with him in the rain. Perhaps after ten minutes, I spoke again. "My name is Craig. I'm a Chaplain." A pause, then I asked, "Can I help?" Again no response. From his demeanor, I guessed that the man might be experiencing a serious depression. I did not expect that it would be easy for him to speak. Minutes more went by. "It can be hard, very hard," I said. Once more, nothing. We sat together for almost half an hour. Slowly he lifted his head a little. "Nothing can be done," he said.

A bare thread, the merest, thinnest line between us. It took an hour or more to weave a few more such threads of conversation into enough of a connection that he was willing to go with me to a nearby drop-in center. There, over a cup of coffee, he was able to share a little of his story. He was homeless; he didn't know the shelters; he hardly ate any more; he didn't think anyone could help. I invited him to go with me to the shelter. His hopelessness was overwhelming, almost totally paralyzing. He just shook his head. We waited. I was prepared to let things rest and try again the next day. What we did or did not do, how far we got that day was not nearly so important as how we treated each moment together.

As it happened, we did go to the shelter. He was registered for the night, and I alerted the staff that he was new, and struggling. He had not wanted to talk with anyone else. We visited again together over several days. He had been in the army and afterward managed a law office. While in that job, he became "very tired," listless. He started drinking and lost his position. He went into an alcohol treatment program and had been sober ever since. But again, the great tiredness came. He stopped going to his aftercare appointments and simply stayed in bed. His benefits were stopped, and he was evicted. He had been to treatment, but it hadn't helped; he didn't know what to do. I suggested that one of the staff at the shelter had some knowledge of this sort of thing, and we could possibly talk with him. I let the idea sit for a while. The next week, with the man's agreement, a colleague

from the mental health team joined us, just to get acquainted.

The three of us met several times informally, in the shelter or on the street. It was awhile before the man was ready to go to the counselor's office. The visits continued, and slowly the possibility of depression was raised as something to look at. A diagnosis can be hard to hear. Stigma, myth, fear of being crazy make it difficult to accept that this is something affecting our lives. A visit with a doctor was arranged, a time to ask questions and talk over what might be involved in care. Medications were explained and started. He applied for benefits again. A small apartment was arranged. Still, the man was doubtful. It was a month to six weeks before the medication took effect. Today, the man is an assistant manager of the building; he helps welcome and settle in others. He is a quiet and modest man, but very much part of our community, the man at the door.

All of our introductions rest on a basic truth: we are neighbors. Wherever I am, on the street, in the shelter or drop in center, on the bus, out for a walk, I try to practice the simple hospitality of greeting, a nod, a smile, a hello. I may introduce myself a number of times and begin a conversation again and again with a particular individual. When a person tells me his or her name and entrusts me with a little of its meaning and history, I feel that the approach has achieved some success.

In meeting another, few of us reveal all of ourselves at once. Who we are emerges a little at a time, as we begin to feel safe. Whether on the street or in the office, after I have met someone and talked a little, I thank the person, and ask if it would be ok to say hello or to meet again. I don't assume that privilege.

Partly, I think the response depends on how I have acted. Has there been some sharing back and forth? As in any conversation, the other person is interested in me. What do I do? Where I am from? What do I think and feel and believe? Always, I find that we have some common ground in our stories; we are never complete strangers to one another. I do take care with self-disclosure, just as the other is careful about how much to say to me. I try to be open, honest, thoughtful—not a blank screen, but a real person.

As we deepen our introductions, as we begin to share more of ourselves, we are entering into companionship. A companion is one who walks alongside, listens, helps with the road ahead, works with us to overcome obstacles and barriers, carries some of the load. A good companion helps us learn the way, interprets if necessary, reflects with us about our efforts and needs. A companion has sympathy, empathy, compassion for us. A companion knows what it is like and is able to feel with us as we move through our experiences.

First, a good companion needs to listen well. I have found it important to listen intently, to give the other my undivided attention, even through pauses and silences. People need time to find a word, to name a feeling, to remember, especially if their brain is disturbed or their life situation is fraught with struggle. Though colleagues have suggested I carry a pager or cell phone, I don't. I don't want to be interrupted when listening to another. When I am with someone in need, I want to listen as deeply and as long as is necessary, with as much attention and care as I can muster.

Second, I listen not so much for details as for feelings and for the themes of the conversation. How can I acknowledge the wealth of sensations, the emptiness or turmoil that another is going through? There are a range of common human themes: the need for shelter, food, survival, the yearning for safety and security, issues of relationship, struggles with decision, right and wrong, the desire for understanding and acceptance, questions of meaning and purpose, a desire for useful and produc-tive work, health. What are the life themes that are important to this person?

Third, when I am listening, I keep in mind that no one thing ever defines or determines another person. Only over time and in the context of community can I begin to fully know and understand who an individual may be.

Fourth, I take great care with responses. I often ask for clarification. "Help me understand." "I'm not sure what that means. Could you say more?" "How so?" "What are you experiencing?" "Is this something that has happened with you before?"

Fifth, as I listen to another, I listen also to myself. What feelings are being stirred in me? What thoughts and memories are emerging? Not that I will share all this, but it helps me to begin to empathize. Listening to myself is a reminder that, in sharing this journey with another, I am opening myself to a new experience. In engaging, I will be affected.

Sixth, as I listen to another, I listen especially for the possibilities—the future that is available in this journey. What strengths, what resources, what capacities does

this person carry and have available? I listen for the hope, the dreams, the meanings that are important to this person. What draws the person on? What gives the person a sense of purpose and power?

Seventh, as I listen, I ask how I can best promote the journey toward health and wholeness. I always test my intuitions and ideas with the other person and with the helping team. "What do you think?" "Is this agreeable?" "How do you feel about doing this?" "Does this seem helpful?" These ways of listening honor the other. More than anything I can give, these are the ways that make for companionship.

In approaching another person, we start with an understanding that, no matter how delicate or tenuous, a relationship is there. The question is what we will make of our encounter. Our task as we observe and introduce ourselves is to strengthen the fragile ties, to come to some gentle agreement that we can walk and perhaps work together.

It may be that this will not happen. Even then, my hope is that we will have approached in such a way that keeps open possibilities for someone else down the line to join the journey.

As companionship develops, our aim is also clear. The relationship we build seeks always to strengthen and encourage the other, to increase that person's capacity for choice, decision, life chance. Being a companion is an art; it requires a capacity to listen, a willingness to serve, and skill in helping find a way toward a worthy destination. As companions, we develop a common language. We discern the territory around us, scout out the best paths forward, and make connections with others who may be important for the journey.

As a circle of care and community forms, the process of engagement comes to fruition. Sustained in a period of companionship, a person is increasingly able to partner with other caregivers and enter into friendships, explore a vocation, exercise citizenship and civil rights, and take an active part in family home and neighborhood. In our view, companionship does not abruptly end. It is ground-work out of which a range of other helping relationships can grow.

Companionship honors our human needs and sows the seeds of mutuality. On the journey together, we talk about tomorrow, about our hopes, about the kind of life this person is working toward. Our aim is not to keep another dependent upon us or our services. In companionship, we recognize that we all require to be part of a circle of support and also that we are created for interdependence, for a life of sharing, for a life in community. None of us can make the journey alone.

As the journey continues, the experience of companionship takes its place in our relational memory; we can refer back to this fundamental experience of being accompanied and cared for.

A woman I once knew summed it up clearly. Involuntarily committed to a mental hospital, she was discharged after three months with a referral to a new mental health program, which declined to serve her. Homeless and without care, she rapidly deteriorated and ended up in jail. Her defense attorney arranged for me to visit before her trial; I agreed to assist when she was released on parole the next morning at 10:00 A.M. At midnight, the jail cut her loose, and she was long gone when I arrived. I began looking in the places where she mentioned she had found refuge in the past. Early that afternoon, we connected and began the journey together—to a nurse for medication, to a shelter, to the clothes bank, to a mental health center to start the process of enrollment once again. Sometime later, a note came to the Chaplaincy office. "Thank you for coming to find me," it read. "Thank you especially for not leaving me."

We are privileged to approach another and to share his or her journey in its most troubling moments. Of course, our efforts will not always be successful. Our approach may be declined, our companionship brief. Even then, I trust we have made an important attempt. Perhaps with the next person, the connection will hold.

READING 8-2 *Basic Communications Skills For Work With Groups**

Barry R. Cournoyer and Katharine V. Byers

A well-developed competence in communications skills is important for all forms of social work practice. However, when you work directly with client systems of more than one person, proficiency in communications skills becomes indispensable. Communication with a dyad, a family, or a small group for the purpose of problem solving is a much more complex interactional process than communication with an individual client alone. In the group setting, you must attend closely not only to the communications between you and each group member but also to the communications between each member and every other member and to communications between you and the group as a whole.

As Schwartz (cited in Shulman, 1992) and others so significantly suggest, the group worker has two clients: the individual and the group. Shulman (1992) extends this idea to all social work practice, terming it the *two-client construct*. Social workers, because of our dual emphasis on person and environment, always consider elements beyond the individual person. In group work,

the two-client construct is especially applicable. As a group leader, you continuously shift focus and redirect communications from the individual to the group and from the group to the individual. These connecting processes occur over and over again throughout the life of the group. In such complex contexts, accurate reception and understanding of messages require close observation and careful listening. Similarly, accurate transmission of messages to the several potential recipients requires well-developed skills in direct and clear communication.

Two general forms of communication have relevance for social work with dyads, families, and small groups: communication based on empathic skills; and communication based on expressive skills. The major distinction between them, which is of remarkable significance for both the sender and receiver of messages, is that empathic communications from the worker to a client—whether individual or group—derive from the client's frame of reference, whereas expressive communications derive from the worker's frame of reference and only indirectly—if at all—from the client's. In empathic

---

*An original article revised for this text.

communications, you attempt to reflect or mirror the client's expressions. You paraphrase, as accurately as possible, the client's own message. Expressive skills enable you to share knowledge, ideas, experience, feelings, and expectations for the purpose of helping clients go beyond where they are likely to progress on their own.

EMPATHIC COMMUNICATION SKILLS

From its inception, social work has recognized the importance of empathy. The frequent references to starting where the client is and the concept of client self-determination reflect an emphasis on understanding, appreciating, and respecting clients' feelings, thoughts, and experiences: "Empathy is an understanding *with* the client, rather than a diagnostic or evaluative understanding *of* the client" (Hammond, Hepworth, & Smith, 1977, p. 3). Cournoyer (1996) states that it "is not an expression of 'feeling for' or 'feeling toward,' as in pity or romantic love. Rather it is a conscious and intentional joining with others in their subjective experience" (p. 7). In most contexts, empathic understanding is probably the single most important quality that you must regularly demonstrate in your work with clients.

Empathic communication skills are responsive or reflective in nature. The content of empathic reflections originates in the subjective experience of the client; such reflections may be responsive to the nonverbal as well as the verbal expressions of the client. When you communicate empathically, you help clients feel understood, respected, and accepted. Empathic reflections encourage clients to continue their exploration of thoughts, feelings, and experiences that are meaningful to them. Their use also supports the development of the rapport with the social worker, which helps clients feel valued and facilitates the "use of existing strengths to develop a more positive self-image" (Brown, 1991, p. 59).

Consistent with the groupwork notion of two clients, the individual and the group, empathic communications may reflect the expressions of an individual member, one or more subgroups, or the group as a whole. For example, when you observe a group member smiling and laughing and you say, "Bill, you seem pleased today," you are utilizing an empathic skill. Of course, even when your empathic communications are directed toward one individual, they often affect other members in the group and the group as a whole. Your responses promote the development of an empathic culture. As the group

members follow your empathic lead, the group becomes a context to communicate understanding, acknowledge strengths, and celebrate positive outcomes.

You can also empathically communicate understanding of the expressions of subgroups or the whole group. For example, suppose you observe that, when one group member, Joan, begins to talk, most other members cross their arms or legs, change facial expressions, or tilt their heads and eyes downward. In response, you may utilize an empathic communication by saying, "The group seems to be impatient with Joan just now."

As a social worker, you may communicate empathy through the use of several distinct skills. All of the empathic skills, however, require that you (1) nonverbally attend, observe, listen, and remember; and (2) accurately reflect what the client has communicated. In doing so, you acknowledge the individual and cultural meanings of the client's nonverbal and verbal expressions.

Attending (Kadushin, 1995) involves communicating nonverbally that you are open and available to others. Keep your hands, arms, shoulders, and legs in appropriate but relaxed positions. In group settings, you should periodically make eye contact with each and every member. For many social workers, this occurs naturally as a part of listening. However, be sure to also establish occasional eye contact when a group member is not talking. By attending in this way, you demonstrate recognition that members contribute to the group through their interest and involvement as well as through their words and actions. Keep in mind, however, that patterns of eye contact are usually culturally determined. "In many cultures, regular eye contact is experienced as positive, but in several others it is not" (Cournoyer, 1996, p. 83). As Ivey (1988) notes, "Some cultural groups (for instance, certain Native American, Eskimo, or aboriginal Australian groups) generally avoid eye contact, especially when talking about serious subjects" (p. 27). Sensitivity to these differences will help you avoid misinterpretations of eye contact and other culturally relevant nonverbal behaviors. Your knowledge in these areas may also aid you in facilitating communication among group members with different ethnic and cultural backgrounds. Head nods and facial expressions that are congruent with the other's communications represent further aspects of nonverbal attending. In meetings with families and groups, be aware that, if you attend more intently to one person, others may experience you as taking sides or having favorites. In addition to listening closely and remembering the verbal expressions of the clients, attending also involves observing carefully the nonverbal communications of group members. Observing, listening, and remembering are essential if you are to engage in accurate reflections of what group members have expressed. You may convey your understanding of clients' expressions through specific empathic communication skills: reflection of content; reflection of feelings; reflection of thinking or meaning; combined reflection; and summarization.

Reflection of Content

Reflection of content involves communicating your understanding of the clients' expressions about problems, circumstances, or other aspects of their lives (Carkhuff & Anthony, 1979). Frequently, you begin by inviting group members to talk about their problems and situations. After someone makes a few statements, you may reflect your understanding of the content, by accurately paraphrasing the message. For example, a group member might share a problem by saying, "I didn't see it coming. She just packed her bags and left without a word. Two weeks ago I received a notice that she is filing for divorce." You might empathically reflect of the content of the message by saying, "She left suddenly without telling you and now she wants to end the marriage."

You may also reflect content expressed by subgroups or the group as a whole. Such a response might begin, "So the group is saying . . . ," followed by a statement that demonstrates your understanding of a group-identified concern or situation. For example, several members of a group might express their difficulties in meeting at the time and on the days scheduled. You might reflect the content by saying, "Meeting at this time represents a real problem for many of you."

Reflection of Feeling

Reflection of feeling (Carkhuff & Anthony, 1979) involves communicating understanding of the client's verbal and nonverbal expressions of feelings about the problem or situation, other group members, or the worker. A typical reflection of feeling might begin, "You feel . . . " or "You're feeling . . . ," followed by a restatement of the feeling or feelings expressed. Be sure to use an equivalent feeling word, rather than repeating the words used by the other person. You are a human being, not a tape recorder; exact repetitions can seem mechanical and phony.

When you wish to reflect expression of a subgroup or the group as a whole, you might begin by saying, "Johnny and Sue feel . . . " or "The group seems to feel . . . " For example, following another group member's comments concerning marital conflict, Jack says, "I'm very ashamed about the way I berated my wife in our arguments. I don't know how I can make it up to her." You could reflect the feelings by saying, "You're feeling guilty and despondent about how you treated your wife."

Should you observe downcast eyes, slouched body positions, and yawns on the part of a large number of the group members, you might reflect their probable feelings by stating, "The group seems to be tired and perhaps a little bored just now." Sometimes, feelings expressed by an individual or the group relate specifically to you, the group worker. For example, a member might express frustration and resentment when questioning the effectiveness of your style of group leadership. When you accurately reflect such feelings, you accomplish a great deal indeed. First, you demonstrate that you are personally and professionally competent enough to respond to all kinds of messages, including those about yourself. Second, you immediately increase the safety within the group. If you can communicate understanding of feelings, even those that relate personally to you, others may feel safe to express their feelings as well. Third, by reflecting these feelings as you would others, you encourage a greater level of cohesion and intimacy.

For example, suppose that a social worker asked a member of a teenage group to leave a meeting because the youth had been drinking beer; the smell of alcohol was obvious. After the boy left, the remaining members became silent. They furtively looked at one another and at the worker. In such a context, the worker might reflect the group's feelings by suggesting, "The group seems to be feeling kind of stunned right now. Are you surprised that I would ask Johnny to leave because he had been drinking?" By demonstrating to Johnny that professional service sometimes extends to the maintenance of agreed-upon rules, the worker may help to enhance his individual functioning. By reflecting the other members' feelings about Johnny's departure, the worker contributes significantly to the group's growth and development.

Reflection of Thinking or Meaning

Reflection of thinking or meaning (Carkhuff & Anthony, 1979) involves communicating your understanding of the thoughts or the meaning that an experience has for a client. A group member might share a beginning description of the problem or situation and perhaps express some associated feelings. You may encourage the individual to explore the thoughts about these experiences by saying, "You think . . . " and then reflecting the message the client has implicitly or explicitly sent. When reflecting messages from the group you may begin with, "Do you mean . . . ?" Alternatively, you could lead into the reflection by saying, "The group seems to think . . . ."

For example, suppose a group member describes concerns in this manner: "I am really mad at my folks. They want me to get all A's in school, to help out at home, and to work part-time too." The meaning can be reflected by suggesting, "You think that your parents expect too much of you; you believe that their demands are unreasonable."

In one meeting, following several group sessions in which one person had taken up a large and disproportionate share of the group's time, several other members began to express their disapproval. A social worker might reflect the meaning of their message by asking: "Are you thinking it might be time to explore the issue of time-sharing? By time-sharing, I mean the process by which we as a group assure that each member has a fair opportunity to speak. Is that what you're thinking about just now?"

Combined Reflection

Combined reflection involves responding to a client's direct or indirect expression of a mixture of content, feelings, thought, and meaning. Such expressions may reflect the client's view that two or more experiences seem to relate to one another but are not necessarily linked in a causal way. At other times, the client may see one experience as the result of, or caused by, another. When the relationship is associational rather than causal, you may connect the two or more empathic reflections with the words *and, but,* or *yet.* When the relationship is seen by the client as causal, the connecting word changes to *because.* Consider the following examples of combined reflections:

- "You have just lost your job *and* you feel devastated, as if the world just caved in."
- "You feel devastated *because* you lost your job."
- "You feel devastated *because* right now you think you will never get another decent job."
- "You just lost your job *and* you think you'll never get another one."

Combined reflections may also be used to respond empathically to expressions from the group as a whole. Here are three examples:

- "The group feels annoyed with me just now because I carried out my obligation to report to the judge those of you who failed the drug-screening tests."
- "Jean, you're angry with Judy because she told you to grow up."
- "You feel proud that Susan has progressed so far but, since it means that she will be leaving the group, you also feel sad."

Summarization

In summarization (Kadushin, 1995), the worker reflects a number of expressions communicated by one or more of the group members over a period of time. It may involve a single empathic skill, such as reflection of content or feeling; often, however, it takes the form of a combined reflection. A summarization might begin with a statement such as, "You've shared a number of important things here today. Let me try to summarize what the group members have said." You would then go on to outline the major elements of the session. For example, you might summarize a group meeting in the following way:

> We've explored a number of personal experiences and concerns today. Let's see if I have understood the major ones accurately, and maybe I can pull some of them together. Joseph and William are going through divorces and are experiencing feelings of guilt, anger, and loss. Maria's husband has recently died, and this has left her feeling uncertain about the future; she wonders whether she'll be able to make it on her own. Wanda has lost her job and thinks she may never find another one. It seems that, in one way or another, all of you in this group are trying to cope with some major changes in your lives, and it's really a struggle to see any bright spots, any hope.

Summarization can contribute to the identification of concerns, issues, and themes that the group members may choose to explore. Especially when used to highlight commonalities among clients' experiences, summarization can aid in the development of cohesiveness—an important ingredient in successful groups (Schopler & Galinsky, 1995). This process of finding common ground is especially important in heterogenous groups, where members differ from one another in age, race, socioeconomic class, or sexual orientation. For example, suppose that, during one session of a grief therapy group for parents whose children have died, the members discuss the ways in which death is handled in their respective cultures. In summarizing that discussion, the worker could make special note of the common feelings of loss experienced by all the parents in the group. By mentioning the commonalities while respecting the differences, the worker contributes to a sense of group membership and belonging.

Although groups composed of diverse members can be quite challenging to social workers, they can also be extremely energizing (Chau, 1990). Heterogenous groups can be especially successful when "group members get to know each other, appreciate and value the vitality of diversity, learn how to use their diversity for creative problem solving and enhanced productivity, and internalize a common superordinate identity that binds them all together" (Johnson & Johnson, 1994, p. 449).

EXPRESSIVE COMMUNICATION SKILLS

In expressive communication, the worker communicates from his or her own frame of reference, rather than the client's. You will introduce new material or extend client-initiated material. When you share knowledge, feelings, perceptions, expectations, judgments, or hypotheses, you are using expressive skills. Your selection and use of expressive skills should be guided by professional values, knowledge, and experience. In groups, a worker most often utilizes group theory, communication theory, role theory, and the values and ethics of the social work profession. Group workers today also rely upon strengths (Weick, Rapp, Sullivan, & Kisthardt, 1988) and ethnic-sensitive (Devore & Schlesinger, 1996) and ethnic competence (Green, 1982) perspectives to guide their use of expressive skills, especially in work with at-risk, vulnerable, and diverse population groups.

Because the expressive skills are generated by the worker rather than the client, they must be used with sensitivity, care, and respect.

Expressive communication skills also help group members understand your role, the purpose of the group experience, and your expectations of the participants. The expressive skills help clients to become aware of additional resources and to consider new ways of thinking, feeling, and behaving. They may also be used to promote and enhance the interaction among group members. Among the expressive communication skills commonly used in work with groups are: clarification of purpose, roles, and expectations; questioning; partializing; focusing; sharing information; self-disclosure; reframing; and confrontation.

Clarification of Purpose, Roles, and Expectations

Perhaps the most fundamentally important of all the expressive skills used by social workers is the clarification of purpose, roles, and expectations (Shulman, 1992). This is usually among the very first communication skills used by social workers as they meet with a new individual client or a group. Through such clarification, a preliminary direction for work is established. In addition, this process constitutes an important aspect of informed consent.

As they begin a group experience for the first time, many members commonly experience a good deal of ambivalence and anxiety. They may ask themselves, "What will this be like? What will the social worker think of me? Who are these other people? Will they understand my concerns? Will they like me? Will they reject me?" Because of their cultural backgrounds and previous experiences, certain people (for instance, some Asian Americans) may be uncomfortable with the prospect of sharing private feelings and family issues within a group context.

You can help to alleviate many of these concerns by clearly stating your view of the general purpose for the group, by clarifying your role in regard to the group's work, and by outlining the expectations you have for the group members. You may also outline some of the norms to be observed within the group. Meeting with each group member individually prior to the first group session provides a context for initial explanation of purpose and roles. Later, during the first group meeting, further exploration and clarification can follow from the foundation established during the individual meetings.

You should, of course, vary the way in which you clarify purpose and roles according to the nature of each group experience. For example, suppose you were beginning a group for women who had been battered by their spouses. You might initiate the exploration and clarification of roles, purpose, and expectations in the following way:

> Now that we are seated, I'd like to introduce myself and share my views about how we might use these times together. My name is Sue Walker and I'm a social worker here at the counseling center. As we have discussed individually, the general purpose for this group is to provide an opportunity to share your problems, concerns, and hopes with others who are also experiencing violence and aggression in their homes. I don't see myself as an expert who listens to your problems and then tells you what you should do. Rather, I see my role as helping you help each other. Together, you have an enormous amount of wisdom that, I hope, you will share with one another. I'll get things started each time we meet and try to make sure that everybody gets a chance to be heard. I'll also identify some topics and share information about family violence that may be helpful to you. What I'd like each of you to do in the group is to share your own concerns, experiences, and ideas with one another; to listen to others express themselves; and to join in as together we work to resolve the problems that are presented. How does this approach sound to you?

Of course, your use of the clarification skills will also vary according to the particular purpose for each group, the role that the social worker assumes in regard to the group, and the characteristics of group members. Typically, clarification of purpose, role, and expectations needs to be more elaborate with groups than with individuals. Groups are inherently more complex and, during the beginning stages, there tend to be relatively high levels of anxiety and ambivalence among the members. With clients who are more or less forced to participate, the clarification process should be quite extensive and detailed. Also, because differences among group members (in gender, ethnicity, age, and so on) may initially inhibit free and full expression, you can contribute to the development of a climate of trust and safety by clarifying group guidelines for interaction. By verbalizing norms (Middleman & Wood, 1990) early in the process, you can encourage respect for differences within the group.

Questioning

The communication skill of questioning (Kadushin, 1995) or probing (Cournoyer, 1996) typically occurs when the worker asks questions or makes comments that function as questions. Questioning is a powerful, multipurpose tool that social workers may use in helping clients learn and grow. Too many questions, however, especially when asked one after another, may lead clients to feel interrogated rather than interviewed. Fortunately, after a group has been together for a while, members tend to ask questions of one another. Also, if you regularly use empathic reflecting skills, you will probably find that fewer questions are needed.

Questions may be open-ended or closed-ended. Open-ended questions encourage clients to express themselves freely and openly: "How did that occur?" "What were your thoughts?" "How do you feel?" "What did that mean to you?" "How do you explain that?" Closed-ended questions, on the other hand, tend to yield short responses, sometimes even yes or no , but they can provide a great deal of information in a short period: "How many children do you have?" "Are you married?" "When did you move there?" "Have you ever been in a group before?"

When asking questions, be aware that some may contain an implied suggestion or judgment. For example, you might say to a group member, "John, have you told your mother yet?" You may intend this as a simple request for information. However, John may conclude that you think he would not follow through on his commitment to discuss the topic with his mother; or he might believe that you would be disappointed in him if he had not yet talked with his mother; or he might interpret this as a suggestion that, if he has not yet done so, he *should* tell his mother as soon as possible.

Questioning skills are often especially appropriate in conjunction with certain other expressive skills, such as clarifying purpose and roles or sharing information. In such contexts, you may use questions to check out clients' reactions to what you have said. For example, you could ask, "How does that sound?" or "Does that make sense?" or perhaps "I'm wondering what you think about this?"

In problem-solving groups, questions are not only used to encourage members to share personal experiences but also as a means of facilitating group interaction. For example, one group member, Diane, might have talked about the fear and embarrassment she felt when her son had a seizure in the grocery store. You might then seek input from another group member whose daughter has epilepsy: "Bill, I wonder if you'd share with Diane some of the experiences you've had with your daughter." Other examples of a social worker using the questioning skill include, "Mary, I'd be interested in your reaction to that" or "Jack, would you like feedback from the group as to how we see you?"

As the group proceeds and develops a sense of cohesion, you can become more active in promoting interaction. For example, you could say, "Sam, would you move over next to Tammy and speak directly to her about this?" You can also facilitate interaction by seeking expression from the group as a whole. For example, you might say, "I'd like to hear how the group feels about what Steve just said." As the group continues to develop and becomes more cohesive, the members themselves often facilitate group interaction by asking questions of one another and directly expressing their thoughts and feelings.

Partializing

Partializing (Cournoyer, 1996) is a skill that helps clients to break down problems, concerns, and other complex phenomena into more manageable parts to greater facility in problem solving. When problems are viewed individually or in small pieces, they tend to seem less overwhelming and can be more readily addressed in a logical or prioritized order. For example, following a lengthy list of concerns by a group member, the worker might say, "You have a lot going on right now. I wonder if it might be easier for you and the other group members if you identified one concern that we could focus upon first. Could you select one that we could explore today?"

Focusing

Focusing (Bertcher, 1979) is an expressive communication skill through which social workers highlight or call attention to something that is, or could be, of importance to the group's work. In their discussions, group members may sometimes wander away from their agreed-upon purpose and goals; you may need to redirect

them back toward the work to be done. Also, there could be interpersonal dynamics or processes that should be highlighted for the group. For example, a social worker leading a group for persons experiencing depression might focus by saying, "I noticed that, when Sheila said she sometimes thinks of doing away with herself, the rest of us suddenly got quiet and then went on to some other topic. I'd like to back up a little and really respond to what Sheila tried to say." If a group member has expressed a desire to improve interpersonal relationships, a worker using the focusing skill might say, "Rita, you've said that you have experienced the men in your life as irresponsible and undependable. Since I'm a man and there are other men in the group, I wonder if you'd share what reactions you have had to us?"

In heterogenous groups, prejudices and biases may need your specific attention and intervention. If unaddressed, such attitudes may interfere with group functioning and inhibit group cohesiveness. For example, suppose you are leading a group composed of two noticeable subgroups: a younger set of people in their early 20s; and an older set of individuals in their late 40s. You observe that the younger members consistently fail to respond to pertinent comments made by the older members. In using the focusing skill to address this issue, you might say, "I noticed that when Esther and Nellie made suggestions based upon their life experience, Julie and Heather, who are quite a bit younger, did not respond. What do you think? Might the age differences in this group affect the way we interact with one another?"

Sharing Information

Sharing information (Kadushin, 1995; Shulman, 1992) or educating (Cournoyer, 1996) is a vital skill in social work practice. Sometimes, clients do not readily identify available resources within their own natural environment. When appropriate, social workers will share information about community programs and services, which can be very tangible resources for some clients. There are less tangible resources, as well. By helping group members identify unrecognized assets and underutilized strengths, a worker may contribute to a sense of individual and group empowerment (Delgado & Humm-Delgado, 1982). In the real world, social workers frequently function as educators or trainers. When conducting training sessions or leading educationally oriented groups, social workers regularly share large amounts of information in their teaching function.

Social workers leading problem-solving groups may sometimes encourage group members to discover certain information on their own. Indeed, seeking out information can be empowering to individual members and to the group as a whole. For example, members of a support group for parents of disabled children may seek information about ways to involve their boys and girls in community recreation programs from which they have previously been excluded. When successful, such independent knowledge seeking can be enormously satisfying for all group members. On occasion, however, group members individually or collectively may not be able to access relevant, accurate, or complete data. As a group leader, you may appropriately offer information that is relevant to the purpose and current work of the group. Indeed, in many cases, you would have a professional responsibility to do so. In sharing information, however, you should clearly distinguish between fact and opinion, and you should convey the data in such a way that clients are free to accept or reject it. When sharing opinions, you should qualify your expressions by saying, "In my view . . . " or "It's my opinion that . . . " Here are two examples of a social worker sharing information:

- "I know something about the topic you're discussing. The fees for that particular program are based on a family's ability to pay. The more income a family has, the more services cost. The lowest fee is $5 and the highest fee is $80 per visit. Most of the members of this group would pay between $15 and $25 each week."
- "In my opinion, as their children grow older, parents would usually be wise to gradually loosen the rules and modify their methods of discipline. I think that most adolescents of 13 should be treated in a manner quite different from most young adults of 17. What do you think?"

Self-Disclosure

When, as a social worker, you appropriately disclose your own feelings and experiences (Hammond, Hepworth, & Smith, 1977), the group members are likely to perceive you as a sincere and genuine human being. You may also contribute to group cohesion and mutual understanding when you share some of your personal feelings and experiences. Through your own self-disclosure, you also help to model open communication for the group members. However, you should be careful not to share so many feelings and experiences that group meetings become contexts for you to focus on yourself. Group members may find it difficult to deal with their own concerns when the social worker takes up most of the time with self-disclosure. It is helpful to ask yourself, "Will my self-disclosure support the group's work in relation to its purpose and goals?" If your answer is yes, you may appropriately disclose relevant personal feelings and experiences. However, even in that case, you should express yourself in such a way that you maintain ultimate responsibility for your own feelings and actions. Other persons—and especially clients—should not be identified as the cause of your feelings and behavior. For example, suppose a social worker says to a group member, "You make me feel very sad today." This sentence suggests that the client is causing the social worker's feelings; in effect, the worker holds the client responsible for the worker's own emotional reaction. Such a communication is neither personally nor professionally appropriate. It would be better to say, "When I listen to your feelings of loss and sadness, I feel like crying right along with you." In this form of self-disclosure, the social worker maintains personal responsibility for his or her own feelings and actions.

Here are some examples of a social worker using the skill of self-disclosure:

- "Jim, your feelings about your Vietnam experience really hit home with me. I, too, was in Nam and, when I came back, I felt more like a foreigner than an American."
- "I'm feeling uneasy about what just happened here. Judy was talking about her disappointment in us as a support group and we just seemed to skip over her feelings. I'd like to go back to that point now and tell you, Judy, what I felt when you expressed your feelings of disappointment. Honestly, I felt defensive when you complained about the group. I felt that if the group isn't meeting your needs then it must be my fault. I began to feel guilty and wondered what I could do to fix it for you."
- "Jack, when you raise your voice and point your finger at me, I begin to think that you're angry at me. At that point, I start to feel angry, too."

• "Yes, I do feel annoyed when you arrive late for our group meetings. Sure, I'd like it better if you were here on time. However, I'd be much more disappointed if you didn't come at all."

Reframing

Reframing (Brown, 1991; Toseland & Rivas, 1995; Cournoyer, 1996) can help group members view a problem or situation in a new or different way. Often this involves identifying positive aspects of a negative situation. For example, a parent who experiences her teenager's rebellious attitude as a complete negative may benefit from the idea that her daughter's capacity for independent thinking will help her manage the complexities of life as she enters young adulthood. Reconceptualizing negatives as positives may help group members feel hopeful about the potential for change and may contribute to the problem-solving process. Such reframing processes can lead to individual and group empowerment, as members realize that many problems and situations can be viewed from several perspectives. They may experience a genuine sense of personal competence and freedom when they recognize that alternate explanations exist and that they can select the perspective that best fits their own particular circumstances. For example, when a group member complains about the inquisitiveness and interference of her mother-in-law, the group worker might say, "It sounds like your husband's mother cares very deeply about her son and continues to be concerned about his welfare. How would you like her to show her interest and concern in him?"

Confrontation

The use of confrontation (Cournoyer, 1996) involves directly pointing out to a client a discrepancy or an inconsistency between statements and actions. In effect, the social worker asks an individual or group to examine an apparent contradiction or inconsistency in thoughts, feelings, and behavior. This skill should be used with considerable caution, since some clients will experience strong emotional reactions when confronted. Typically, when confrontation is used in groups, it is communicated with warmth, understanding, and concern for the members. It is good practice to utilize empathic communi-

cations before and after confrontations. Also, be sure to deliver confrontations in such a way that you assume responsibility for the content of the messages and acknowledge that others may see things differently. Here are a few examples of confrontations used by social workers in their work with groups:

• "Jason, you say that you want to get good grades but you also tell us that you don't do much studying. Help us understand how your desire to get good grades fits with your reluctance to put in time with the books."
• "George, you've identified a number of goals that you want to work on in the group. Some of them seem terribly ambitious—more than what most of us could achieve and more than anything you've been able to accomplish in the past. What do you think? Are you setting up goals that are impossible to reach?"
• "Each one of you is in this group because you accepted the judge's offer to participate in counseling sessions rather than go to jail. All of you have come to the meetings, but several of you arrive late and do not participate in the group discussions. Could it be that some of you are just going through the motions?"

SUMMARY

Successful work with groups requires that you maintain a dual focus at all times. As a group worker, you have two clients: each individual member and the group as a whole. You must continuously attend to them both, through the use of two major categories of social work skills. Through empathic skills, you communicate understanding of the experiences of the group members. By accurately reflecting their verbal and nonverbal messages, you help to build cohesion and facilitate group development. When you regularly convey empathic understanding, you contribute to the growth of an active, interactive group culture, where thoughts, feelings, and experiences are freely shared. Through expressive communication skills, you contribute your own thoughts, feelings, and information from your social work frame of reference. The expressive skills enable you to assist the group members as they proceed into uncharted territory, exploring and experimenting with new information, new experiences, and new perspectives.

LEARNING EXERCISES

1. Here are some concepts introduced in this chapter. Write a one- or two-sentence definition of each, or briefly explain the concept to a friend:

   accessibility
   anticipating the other
   assumption of meaning
   collaterals
   decoding
   double bind
   empathic communications
   encoding
   expressive communication
   feedback
   metacommunications
   partialization
   preliminary goal
   presenting problem
   reframing
   resistance

2. In the case of the House on Sixth Street (Appendix A-3), Mrs. Smith came to a neighborhood service center to complain that there had been no gas, electricity, heat, or hot water in her apartment house for more than four weeks. She asked the agency for help. Mrs. Smith was 23 years old, African American, and the mother of four children, three of whom had been born out of wedlock. At the time, she was unmarried and received public assistance. She came to the center in desperation because she was unable to run her household without utilities. How did Mrs. Smith and the worker view the presenting problem? How did the differences get resolved? How did the presenting problem and the problem to be worked differ?

3. Reread the case of Mrs. Iverson and her daughter (Exhibit 5–3 in Chapter 5). Note how the interview floundered as the worker moved from topic to topic in an attempt to find a focus for the work, while Mrs. Iverson's level of anger increased. Suggest how Mrs. Iverson might have been successfully engaged.

4. Exhibit 8–13 describes an incident that occurred when 200 young people arrived at a summer camp. Identify some reasons why the engagement process went so poorly. If you were a management level staff member at this summer camp, how would you have handled the engagement differently? It isn't enough to argue that these young people should have been better prepared, and their expectations clarified, before they arrived at the camp, although that may be important feedback for future planning. You must figure out some way to engage these young people as you find them, not as you would like to find them.

5. Here are several typical situations in which social workers engage potential clients:

   5.1. Sixteen-year-old Leslie spends a great deal of time hanging around a local shopping center and youth drop-in center. Leslie has been experiencing serious conflict with parents and is suspected of engaging in prostitution. You are a social worker from

---

EXHIBIT 8-13   A Failure of Engagement

In this case, a problem arose when 200 young people arrived at a summer camp in a Caribbean country. The young people were from four different districts of the country.

The campers arrived in the afternoon and were registered and assigned sleeping quarters. At 7:00 P.M., the orientation program began. Camp staff and volunteers were introduced, and the aims and objective of the camp were outlined. The objective was to establish a half-acre vegetable garden on the campsite.

At this announcement, the campers from district C became restive. Staff believed tiredness was the cause of the behavior, but soon district B campers started to react in the same fashion. The campers said that they were not informed at district level of the activities at the camp and were not prepared for such hard work; they requested to be sent home immediately. This request could not be granted, as the transport that brought the groups had left for the return journey, and it was now 10:30 P.M.

The campers began behaving outrageously, and the director summoned the police, who found the groups involved in vandalism and destruction of property and arrested 25 participants. The police had to spend the rest of the night at the camp in order to maintain law and order.

the drop-in center and have had several brief, informal contacts with Leslie. At the center you try to engage Leslie in discussion regarding what's going on and whether Leslie wants to make changes.

5.2. Eric, age 16, has just pleaded guilty in juvenile court to a charge of home burglary and has been placed under probation supervision. You are his probation officer; he is reporting to you for the first time. This is your first contact.

5.3. Cynthia, a 19-year-old single woman, has scheduled an appointment with a neighborhood counseling service to discuss persistent feelings of sadness, which she has been experiencing over the past several weeks. You are seeing her for the intake session.

5.4. You are a child protection worker and are calling on a home where a 5-year-old child is alleged to be without adequate clothing and remains in a home without adequate heat; the complaint was received in January. You are visiting the home on the same day that the complaint was taken.

5.5. You are a school social worker visiting with the mother of 10-year-old Carlos, who has been in five fights with peers in the last two weeks. The teachers believe that Carlos is the aggressor in these situations. You have telephoned to schedule a home visit and have arrived at the home to discuss this matter.

Team up with colleagues and role-play getting these interviews started. Each role need only last 2–3 minutes. Invite an observer to give you feedback on these questions:

- Did you briefly identify yourself?
- Did you briefly state your understanding of the reason for getting together?
- Was this introduction accomplished with one or two sentences at most?
- Did you follow this with an open-ended question to encourage applicant participation?

6. Attend a task, therapeutic, or informal group and observe the extent to which the group leader uses the empathic and expressive skills discussed in Reading 8-2. In addition, how well does the leader demonstrate sensitivity to the diversity of culture represented in the group by modifying his or her style of involving members in the group process? What would you have done differently, had you been the leader?

7. Videotape yourself leading a group discussion. Review the tape, noting the frequency and appropriateness with which you used empathic and expressive skills. How did your leadership affect the group process? What skills might you have used to make the group discussion more effective? You may also ask group participants or external observers to review the tape and provide additional feedback on your use of basic communication skills. Watch the tape with the sound off to focus on your use of nonverbal communication cues.

REFERENCES

Baily, T., & Baily, W. (1983). *Child welfare practice*. San Francisco: Jossey-Bass.

Bateson, G., Jackson, D., Haley, J., & Weekland, J. (1963). A note on the double bind. *Family Processes, 2*(1), 154–161.

Bertcher, H. J. (1979). *Group participation: Techniques for leaders and members*. Newbury Park, CA: Sage.

Bloom, A. (1980). Social work and the English language. *Social Casework, 60*(6), 332–338.

Bross, D., Krugman, R., Lenherr, M., Rosenburg, D., & Schmitt, B. (1988). *The new child protection team handbook*. New York & London: Garland.

Brown, L. N. (1991). *Groups for growth and change*. New York: Longman.

Brown, R. A. (1973). Feedback in family interviewing. *Social Work, 18*(5), 52–59.

Carkhuff, R. R., & Anthony, W. A. (1979). *The skills of helping*. Amherst, MA: Human Resource Development.

Chau, K. L. (1990). Social work with groups in multicultural contexts. *Groupwork, 3*(1), 8–21.

Cleary, P. D., & Demone, H., Jr. (1988). Health and social service needs in a Northeastern metropolitan area: Ethnic group differences. *Journal of Sociology and Social Welfare, 15*(4), 63–76.

Cohen, M. B. (1989). Social work practice with homeless mentally ill people: Engaging the client. *Social Work, 34*(6), 505–509.

Cormican, J. D. (1978). Linguistic issues in interviewing. *Social Casework, 59*(3), 145–152.

Cournoyer, B. R. (1996). *The social work skills workbook* (2nd ed.). Pacific Grove, CA: Brooks/Cole.

Daniel, J. H. (1985). Cultural and ethnic issues: The Black family. In E. H. Newberger & R. Bourne (Eds.), *Unhappy families: Clinical and research perspectives on family violence* (pp. 145–153). Littleton, MA: PSG.

Delgado, M., & Humm-Delgado, D. (1982). Natural support systems: Source of strength in Hispanic communities. *Social Work, 27*(1), 83–89.

Devore, W., & Schlesinger, E. G. (1996). *Ethnic-sensitive social work practice* (4th ed.). Boston: Allyn & Bacon.

Drake, B. (1994). Relationship competencies in child welfare services. *Social Work, 38*(5), 595–602.

Esten, G., & Willmott, L. (1993). Double bind messages: The effects of attitude toward disability on therapy. *Women and Therapy, 14*(3/4), 29–41.

Frankenstein, R. (1982). Agency and client resistance. *Social Casework, 52*(1), 24–28.

Green, J. W. (1982). *Cultural awareness in the human services.* Englewood Cliffs, NJ: Prentice-Hall.

Griffith, J. E., & Villavicencio, S. (1985). Relationship among acculturation, sociodemographic characteristics, and social support in Mexican American adults. *Hispanic Journal of Behavioral Sciences, 7,* 75–92.

Hammond, D., Hepworth, D., & Smith, V. (1977). *Improving therapeutic communication.* San Francisco: Jossey-Bass.

Ivey, A. E. (1988). *Intentional interviewing and counselling: Facilitating client development* (2nd ed.). Pacific Grove, CA: Brooks/Cole.

Johnson, D. W., & Johnson, F. P. (1994). *Joining together: Group theory and group skills.* Boston: Allyn & Bacon.

Kadushin, A. (1995). Interviewing. In R. L. Edwards & J. G. Hopps (Eds.), *Encyclopedia of social work* (19th ed., pp. 1527–1537). Washington, DC: NASW Press.

Kadushin, A., & Martin, J. (1988). *Child welfare services* (4th ed.). Pacific Grove, CA: Brooks/Cole.

Keith-Lucas, A. (1972). *Giving and taking help.* Chapel Hill: University of North Carolina Press.

Lewis, R. G., & Ho, M. K. (1975). Social work with native Americans. *Social Work, 20*(5), 379–382.

Logan, S. M. L., Freeman, E. M., & McDay, R. G. (Eds.). (1990). *Social work practice with Black families.* New York: Longmans.

Marlow, C. (1990). Management of family and employment responsibilities by Mexican American and Anglo American women. *Social Work, 35*(3), 259–265.

Mayer, J. E., & Timms, N. (1970). *The client speaks: Working class impressions of casework.* New York: Atherton Press.

McGoldrick, M. (1988). Ethnicity and the family life cycle. In B. Carter & M. McGoldrick (Eds.), *The changing family life cycle: A framework for family therapy* (2nd ed.). New York: Gardner.

Middleman, R. R., & Wood, G. G. (1990). *Skills for direct practice in social work.* New York: Columbia University Press.

Middleman, R. R., & Wood, G. G. (1991). Communicating by doing. *Families in Society, 72*(3), 153–156.

Oppenhein, L. (1992). The first interview in child protection: Social work method and process. *Children & Society, 6*(2), 132–150.

Pilsecker, C. (1994). Starting where the client is. *Families in Society, 72*(3), 153–156.

Rooney, R. H. (1993). When the client is unwilling. *CURA Reporter, 23*(2), 11–14. (Published by University of Minnesota, Center for Urban and Regional Affairs.)

Schopler, J. H., & Galinsky, M. J. (1995). Group practice overview. In R. L. Edwards & J. G. Hopps (Eds.), *Encyclopedia of social work* (19th ed., pp. 1129–1143). Washington, DC: NASW Press.

Shulman, L. (1992). *The skills of helping individuals and groups* (3rd. ed.). Itasca, IL: F. E. Peacock.

Snell, C. L. (1991). Help seeking behavior among young street males. *Smith College Studies in Social Work, 28*(3), 293–305.

Toseland, R. W., & Rivas, R. F. (1995). *Introduction to group work practice* (2nd ed.). Boston: Allyn & Bacon.

Walsh, M. E. (1981). Rural social work practice: Clinical quality. *Social Casework: The Journal of Contemporary Social Work, 62*(8), 458–464.

Weick, A., Rapp, C., Sullivan, W. P., & Kisthardt, W. (1988). A strengths perspective for social work practice. *Social Work, 34*(4), 350–354.

chapter 9

Communicating Across Cultures

CHAPTER PREVIEW

Engaging a person from a different culture requires considerable sensitivity, openness to difference, willingness to acquire knowledge of other cultures, and understanding of self (Dungee-Anderson & Beckett, 1995). These matters surface in the engagement process but will be a part of all your cross-cultural communications. Your educational program will probably include one or more courses on human diversity; numerous books examine the relationship of cultural diversity to social work and the organization of social services (Asamoah, 1997; Devore & Schlesinger, 1996; Ewalt, Freeman, Kirk, & Poole, 1996; Harper & Lantz, 1996; Herberg, 1995; Lynch & Hanson, 1992).

In this chapter, we will consider issues that arise as we engage and work with persons from other cultures:

- how to recognize different styles of communication
- how to develop cross-cultural competence through study, use of cultural guides, and asking applicants
- how to avoid pitfalls such as failure to recognize that variation exists within a cultural group, that some cultural practices may be a source of stress for some clients, that culture is only a part of identity, and that not all clients want a worker of the same culture or gender

In Reading 8-1, Ellen Velasquez, Marilyn E. Vigil, and Eustolio Benavides provide a framework for cross-cultural communication illustrated by work with Latino clients. In Reading 8-2, Uma Narayan discusses working across insider and outsider differences with particular attention to gender differences.

DIFFERENT COMMUNICATION STYLES

Differences in Help-Seeking Behavior

There are cultural differences in help seeking and the type of help sought. For instance, African Americans (Boyd-Franklin, 1989; Daniel, 1985; McGoldrick, 1988), Caribbean Canadians of African ancestry (Brice-Baker, 1996; Gibson & Lewis, 1985; Ho, 1983), and Latinos (Griffith & Villavicencio, 1985; Vasquez-Nuttall, Romero-Garcia, & DeLeon, 1987) often prefer to seek help from family, friends, and churches. These attitudes will be reflected in communication patterns during engagement. African Americans and Caribbean Canadians, for example, may become inarticulate or belligerent (Brice-Baker, 1996; Christiansen, Thornley-Brown, & Robinson, 1982; Daniel, 1985), may see questions as prying (Chapman, 1995), and may take more time than whites to become comfortable with the worker and to develop trust (Boyd-Franklin, 1989; Gibbs, 1980). Latinos' cultural norms concerning privacy discourage discussion of family matters with children and strangers (Dana, 1983). Persons from some Asian cultures are likely to deal with problems by internalizing them to avoid a loss of face (LeResche, 1992; Tamura & Lau, 1992). In addition, many Asian immigrants are distrustful of officials (Duryea & Gundison, 1993) and thus will avoid contact with agencies. Jewish Americans, by contrast, may be quick to seek help, including psychotherapy, because they are less likely to regard it as a sign of weakness (McGoldrick, Garcia-Preto, & Lee, 1989; Sanua, 1985; Srole, Langer, Michael, Opler, & Rennie, 1962).

Understanding differences in help-seeking behavior will help you interpret initial reactions from applicants. In particular, applicants from cultures that discourage help seeking from outside agencies may feel reluctant to see you. Help-seeking behavior also holds implications for the types of services most acceptable. Persons comfortable discussing problems with family members, friends, and other informal helpers may be open to your support for doing so. They may then be able to use you as a forum, to sort out the types of action they want to take on the basis of the advice they have received. Be careful about recommending services such as psychiatric or psychological counselling that may have negative connotations. Exhibit 9–1 provides a cautionary example and also illustrates the problem of the assumption of meaning (discussed in Chapter 8); this worker might have proceeded differently if she had checked out what the group meant by support.

Taylor, Neighbors, and Broman (1989) analyzed 1979–1980 U.S. survey data regarding the use of social service agencies by African Americans. In a sample of 2079, 64% (1322) indicated having a serious personal problem at some time in their lives. Of these, 90% sought help from at least one member of their informal network, while 49% (631) sought professional assistance; only 91 used social services. Extended kin networks are important sources of service for African Americans (Billingsley, 1992; Dilworth-Anderson, 1992; Luckey, 1994), as well as Puerto Ricans (Delgado, 1995). Providing services to African Americans and other cultural groups will probably require maintaining positive relationships with gatekeepers (members of stature and trust in these communities), who will help to link persons who need services with agencies (Gibbs, 1993).

Distinctive Communication Styles

Cultural styles of communication are often distinctive. Failure to understand these distinctive practices will result in miscommunication and misunderstanding. In many Native American cultures, direct eye contact is considered insulting and is avoided; to European Americans, however, avoiding eye contact seems evasive and dishonest. Likewise, many American and Canadian native cultures value noninterference, and direct questioning may be perceived as a violation of this value. Indirect approaches—including use of analogy, stories, and hypotheticals—will be more acceptable (Tafoya, 1989). Use of metaphors and folk sayings (dichos) will help your communications with Latino clients (Zuniga, 1992).

Many Asian cultures expect a period of polite conversation at the beginning of a visit; rushing to the reason for the visit, without exchanging pleasantries, is considered rude. In some cultures, failure to accept coffee or tea would be discourteous. Some cultures place importance on silence as a form of respect; others tend to be very expressive. White social workers sometimes misunderstand the expressiveness of African Americans. At a meeting to consider the importance of the church in the life of African Americans, a white social worker who worked in a nursing home noted with concern that African American seniors were spending so much time in religious activities—singing hymns, prayer, and Bible study—that they did not have time to meet with her, so that she could assist them with grieving. Did this worker misunderstand the importance of this expressive behavior for the African Americans? If she were less preoccupied with her own particular style of helping, the worker would be more able to assist these seniors in a manner consistent with their own traditions and culture.

To sum up, you need to be aware that cultures differ in their patterns of communication, in the meaning of words, in the way things are said, and in the meaning of

---

EXHIBIT 9-1 **Misdirected Advocacy**

A worker was requested to advocate on behalf of Southeast Asian clients for increased support services during their resettlement. The worker immediately directed her attention toward increasing psychological support services, through the enlistment of numerous psychologists and psychiatrists, on the assumption that psychological support was a desired component of support services. The result of this action was that the clients immediately severed their relationship with the worker and declined all further offers of assistance from her agency. The clients felt that they had been misrepresented by the worker in her efforts to seek support services and had been deeply insulted. In their culture, a referral to a psychologist meant that a person was crazy or deranged. To these Southeast Asians, support services were associated with financial, material, or educational assistance.

SOURCE: Kathleen Behrens, MSW student, School of Social Work, University of Minnesota, Minneapolis.

gestures. Sensitivity to these differences is necessary as you work at engaging people from cultural backgrounds other than your own. As you learn more about the cultures of the particular clients you serve, you will become more effective at engagement and helping. No one can be expected to be conversant with all cultures. You are, however, expected to become knowledgeable about the culture of those you are attempting to serve.

CULTURAL COMPETENCE

Cultural competence consists of our attitudes, knowledge, and behaviors regarding cultures other than our own. The elements of cultural competence are (Cross, 1988):

- acceptance and respect for difference
- high esteem for culture
- continuous self-assessment
- attention paid to the dynamics of difference
- seeking to expand knowledge of cultures and their strengths

Recognizing culture as a resource and a source of strength for people is a necessary condition for cultural competence. Culture is an important—though not the only—contributor to our sense of identity. People can draw from the resources of their culture—for example, the expressive singing, prayer, and Bible study of the African American seniors in our earlier example—to help cope with stress and life transitions.

Your understanding and appreciation of clients' cultures will increase as you move toward competent practice. You will become more aware of the strengths of their cultures and will find yourself supporting alliances that help people to draw on these strengths. To increase your understanding of cultural differences, you will rely on library and field study, cultural guides, and your clients.

Research and Study

In Chapter 6, we noted your ethical duty to keep current through regular reading of the practice literature. You also have an ethical duty to become knowledgeable about the cultures of your clients. *Social Work Abstracts* and your local library will yield a rich literature on the relevant cultures. A large body of material is also available on the world wide web. Spend a little time on the web to locate information about a cultural group of your choice; Exhibit 9–2 will help you get started.

EXHIBIT 9-2	Human Diversity on the Internet

Here is a list of Internet sites related to topics of human diversity. Use these to begin your exploration.

Native Americans: http://www.nucleus.com/4worlds/future.html
Resiliency in Action: http://resiliency.com
Biracial/multicultural experience: http://www.agate.net/~wordshop/biracial.html
National Organization of Women: http://www.now.org
Simon Wiesenthal Center: http://www.wiesenthal.com/index.html
ACLU: http://www.aclu.org/index.html
Human Rights Campaign: http://www.gayspace.com/hrc.html
National Multicultural Institute: http://www.nmci.org/nmci/index.html
Anti-Defamation League: http://www.adl.org
Foundation for Women's Health:
    http://www.gnomes.org:80/forward/

Just Cause: http://www.webcom/~justcaus
Net Hate (the dark side of the net): http://www.vir/Shalom/hatred.html
Definition of terms: http://www.tmn.com/Artswire/www/CALIFORNIA/06eq.html
WWW Library of Migration and Ethnic Relations: http://www.ruu.nl/ercomer/wwwvlwwwvlmer.html
Universal Black Pages: http://www.gatech.edu/bgsa/blackpages.html
African-American Forum: http://mailer.fsu.edu/~afroamhm/index.html
Latino culture: http://galaxy.tradewave.com/galaxy/community/culture/Latino.html
WWW Latino/Hispanic Research and Dissemination Networks: http://www.care.panam.eduresearch/web-search/wwwlatino.html
Disability info: http://www.prostar.com/%7Ethe.arc/dis-link.html
MED WEB: http://www.medweb.net

SOURCE: L. Chadiha, J. Miller-Cribbs, & D. Wilson-Klar. Human diversity (course syllabus). In W. Devore & B. J. Fletcher (Eds.), *Human diversity content in social work education*. Alexandria, VA: Council on Social Work Education (1997), pp. 103–130.

Another way of learning about cultures is to participate in cultural events and celebrations—African American church services, powwows, Cinco de Mayo parades, Catholic feast day events, Chinese New Year, Kwanzaa (Karenga, 1995), and so forth. Large cultural groups are likely to be served by their own newspapers; a subscription to these newspapers will provide regular information about upcoming cultural events for you to explore. Your local library can also put you in touch with cultural organizations in your community.

Cultural Guides

A cultural guide is a person familiar with a culture, to whom you can turn for advice and assistance, especially when messages from your applicants or clients seem confusing or your work with clients of other cultures is stalling. A cultural guide may be a worker within your agency, another professional colleague, or a friend or acquaintance. Normally, people enjoy talking about their cultures; you can expect helpful responses to sincere inquiries. Don't forget that you may also serve as a guide to others regarding your own culture.

The Client as a Resource

The applicant or client is the best expert about his or her situation, including the cultural aspects of relationship. Like cultural guides, clients will often enjoy sharing their culture with you if your inquiry is perceived as sincere interest. A gentle inquiry of your client may be helpful when you sense that communications are strained. Remember that directness is considered rude in some cultures; many clients will be uncomfortable saying anything that might be construed as criticism of you. Indirect questions may be more appropriate: "How is this usually handled in your culture?" "How is disagreement usually dealt with in your culture?" "How do people express unhappiness in your culture?"

SOME PITFALLS

Pitfalls to avoid in your cross-cultural work include the assumption that cultures are homogeneous, overbroad concepts of cultural relativism, the idea that human personality can be reduced to cultural identity, and the assumption that applicants always want a worker of the same culture.

Misconceptions About Cultural Homogeneity

You need to be aware of two types of variation: variation within a culture and variation in the extent to which an individual client identifies with his culture. Differences within any culture may be almost as strong as cross-cultural differences. Among Latinos, those who trace their ancestry to Mexico, Cuba, Puerto Rico, and other South and Central American countries have significantly different cultures (Santiago, 1993). There are over 300 Native American tribes in the United States and over 50 in Canada, with "tremendous variation among tribes regarding gender roles, language, religion, acculturation, and relationship with non-Indians" (Tafoya, 1989, p. 73). The culture of African Americans is different from that of Caribbean American populations, and different again from the various African cultures practiced by recent immigrants. And, of course, there are many very diverse Asian cultures, all with long histories (Berg & Miller, 1992). You need to be aware of differences within cultures and the extent to which your client considers these differences important.

Further, individual clients will differ in the extent to which they identify with a particular cultural tradition. Many Latinos, for example, remain active in cultural organizations, speak Spanish at home, and actively identify with their cultural tradition; others do not. Some Native Americans practice their traditional religions, participate in cultural ceremonies, and have kept their language alive; others have adopted Christianity and limit their cultural activities largely to powwows. Longclaws (1996) identifies the following categories of cultural identification among Native Americans: traditionalists, transforming or new traditionalist, assimilated, universalist, and anomic.

It is important to respect applicants' and clients' wishes regarding their cultural identification. In your practice, you will be sensitive to the extent to which a particular client identifies with his or her cultural background, whether the client wishes to have a closer identification, and whether the client wishes to take on a different identification.

Misconceptions about Cultural Relativism

Cultural relativism, at its extreme, means that all values are relative to a particular culture; there are no cross-cultural absolutes. This idea surfaces in news accounts of the ongoing international debate about human rights. If all values are relative, there can be no universal standard of human rights. Obviously, social workers need to accept some level of cultural relativism. For example, research evidence (Beavers, 1986; Moon & Williams, 1993), indicates that different cultures differ in their views of what constitutes abuse; acknowledging this, attempts have been made to introduce the notion of cultural relativism into the assessment of child abuse (Exhibit 9–3). But how far should social workers take cultural relativism? Remember our example of a social worker asked to assist efforts by Hmong refugees to lower the legal age for marriage to 12, in line with their cultural practices (Chapter 6). How should the worker respond?

We believe that, in your efforts to communicate across cultures, the wisest course of action is to work at becoming informed about, and sensitive to, cultural differences, without romanticizing any other culture. All cultures offer considerable strengths to people; all cultures also have the potential to oppress some members. Your communications with clients will help you discover what features of their culture they find empowering and want to strengthen. It is also appropriate to consider what features they find troubling and would like to change.

Misconceptions about Identity

While culture is an important part of human identity, it is not the only determinant of identity and behavior. As we saw in Chapter 2, each of us has our own role set. We simultaneously occupy many roles, all of which contribute to our sense of identity and to our behavior. We may be a member of the dominant culture or one of the many other cultures; we may be straight or gay; we

may be a spouse or a parent; we may occupy an occupational role; we may live in a rural community or an urban neighborhood; and so forth. We are more than our culture. Who we are depends on the relative weight we give to the various roles we occupy. For some, cultural identity is the most important and permeates all other roles; for others, their primary identification may come, for example, from an occupational role or a family role. Many lesbians and gay men are active in groups based around sexual orientation, which may be more important to them than their identification as European American, Latino, African American, and so on. Communication with clients will be enhanced if you do not emphasize culture to the exclusion of other roles and if you are open to learning from clients what they perceive as the most important contributors to who they are and who they want to be.

Two additional factors complicate cultural considerations. First, we are born into some cultures and adopt others. Perhaps you were born into a particular Latino or Native American culture, but then you may choose to adopt other cultures—gay culture, rural culture, a professional culture, and so forth. You must sort out this complex interplay with each client, and make decisions about which cultural identities are most important. How can the client draw from each?

Second, an increasing number of persons are of mixed culture. What is the culture of a child whose father is African American and whose mother is Irish American? This question underlies the controversial proposal to add a mixed-race category to the U.S. census. This cultural complexity may seem problematic, but it creates an opportunity for individuals to select strengths from various cultures and to be more active in determining who they are and what

---

EXHIBIT 9-3	Cultural Relativism and Assessment

PIE attempts to avoid defining social roles in a culture-specific context. It is imperative that the social worker using the system take into account the specific cultural and societal role definitions influencing the client. For example, in the African American community, physical punishment of children may be viewed as a more socially acceptable method of disciplining a child than in some other communities. To determine whether or not an African American parent has a parent role problem, the social worker must take into account whether the parent's discipline of the child would be considered excessive within the norms of the client's reference group and, of course, whether the discipline meets the legal conditions of physical child abuse.

SOURCE: K. E. Wandrei, & J. M. Karls. Structure of the PIE system. In J. M. Karls & E. K. Wandrei (Eds.), *Person-in-environment system: The PIE classification system for social functioning problems.* New York: NASW Press (1994), pp. 24–25.

they want to be (Gibbs & Moskowitz-Sweet, 1991; Weaver, 1996).

Misconceptions about Client Preferences

Evidence as to whether clients prefer a worker of the same culture is mixed. Some studies have suggested that a helper of a different race is perceived as less helpful (Davidson, 1992; Morrow-Howell, Lott, & Ozawa, 1990; Terrell & Terrell, 1984). A study of 53 Veterans Administration counselors found that both white and nonwhite counselors perceived themselves as about equally effective in their work with white clients, but that white counselors perceived themselves to be less effective than nonwhite counselors in work with nonwhite clients (Davis & Gelsomino, 1994). Taylor, Neighbors, & Broman (1989) found that 62% of the African Americans who received social services received them from a white worker; of these, 26% would have preferred an African American social worker, 15% did not want an African American social worker, and it made no difference to 59%. Arguments that it may be easier to communicate with a worker of the same culture or gender must be weighed against the risk of creating segregated services in which African Americans serve African Americans, Latinos serve Latinos, women serve women, and so forth.

As much as possible, applicants' preferences should guide this decision. If you sense that an applicant is uncomfortable working with you, initiate a discussion of whether the client would prefer to be seen by a worker of the same gender or the same race. Your willingness to discuss the matter openly will satisfy many applicants. Should the applicant or client prefer to be seen by a worker of the same gender or race, we recommend that you try to meet the preference, if that is possible within your agency. If the agency cannot meet the client's preference, discuss with the client; that can be defined as a problem. You and the client need to struggle with this problem and to find a reasonably satisfactory solution within the resource limits of your agency.

We have been discussing cross-cultural communication primarily from the perspective of a worker from the dominant culture working with persons from other cultures. However, increasing numbers of African Americans, Native Americans, Latinos, Asian Americans, and others have been entering social work and will be working with white clients. The fact that these practi-

tioners were raised in a society dominated by white culture may help them to work with white clients. Nevertheless, they will be involved in cross-cultural communication and will need to be sensitive both to their white clients' reactions and to their own latent feelings toward whites. Davis and Gelsomino (1994) found that all workers, no matter what their cultural background, tended to perceive the source of white clients' problems as internal and the source of other clients' problems as external; they interpreted this finding as a possible bias against white clients, on the part of all practitioners.

CHAPTER SUMMARY

In a sense, all communication is cross-cultural, because all individuals are different. As a worker, you are reaching out to engage with others, establish communication, and work toward the solution of problems that they are experiencing in their ecosystems. But communication is made more difficult to the extent that we do not share a common pool of symbols, styles, and gestures. Thus, the further apart you and the applicant are, in terms of life experiences and culture, the more you will need to work at understanding the applicant's experiences and perspectives. This will necessitate acceptance of difference, holding in abeyance some of your own preconceptions, and actively but sensitively seeking to understand. Exhibit 9–4 offers some suggestions for communicating with persons with disabilities. You may find these suggestions useful in all of your communications.

We have made these points:

1. Cultural differences may affect both help-seeking behavior and communication styles.

2. Cultural competence occurs when you respect differences, have high esteem for culture, conduct a continuous assessment, pay attention to the dynamics of difference, and seek to expand your knowledge of cultures and their resources.

3. You can enhance your cultural competence by reading, participating in cultural events, seeking consultation from cultural guides, and talking with clients about their cultural experiences and expectations.

4. You need to recognize that cultures are not homogenous, individuals vary in their sense of identification

| EXHIBIT 9-4 | Interacting with a Person with a Disability |

The American Association of Retired Persons' Disability Initiative suggests that, when interacting with someone who has a disability, you proceed as follows:

- Relax, act naturally; be yourself. If you aren't sure how to behave, *ask* the person what you should do.
- Don't assume the person needs or wants your assistance, but don't be afraid to ask politely—not patronizingly—if she does.
- In meeting or parting, shake whatever the person offers: hand, prosthesis, hook, or elbow.
- If the person is visually impaired, immediately identify yourself and anyone with you.
- Remember that most people with visual impairments are not hard of hearing; use a normal tone of voice when addressing them.

- If the person is deaf or hard of hearing, look directly at her when you talk rather than at any interpreter or other assistant who may be present. Don't shout; that distorts your voice and makes it even harder to understand.
- Remember that people who are deaf depend heavily on facial expressions, hand gestures, and body language for communication.
- If the person is visually impaired or hard of hearing, don't avoid words like see or hear; she doesn't. Stumbling for other words to use will make an otherwise natural conversation awkward.
- Above all, remember that people with disabilities are people first; their disabilities are only one part of who they are.

SOURCE: L. Burgess. Myths are the greatest barriers. *Modern Maturity, 37*(1), 6–7 (1994).

with a particular culture, and there may be limits to cultural relativity.

5. Culture is not the only determinant of identity and behavior.

6. Applicants do not always want a worker of the same culture.

A LOOK FORWARD

In Reading 9-1, Joan Velasquez, Marilyn Vigil, and Eustolio Benavides offer some suggestions for commu-

nication with Latino families. In Reading 9-2, Uma Narayan offers some suggestions for working across gender differences. In Chapter 10, we move from the process of engaging an applicant to assessment; in Chapter 11, to developing a service agreement; and, in Chapter 12, to the process of intervention. Note that engagement, assessment, and developing a service agreement are continuous processes and are not separated by clear boundaries, even though, of necessity, we must deal with them as sequential processes in this text.

| READING 9-1 | *A Framework for Establishing Social Work Relationships Across Racial/Ethnic Lines**

Joan Velasquez, Marilyn E. Vigil, and Eustolio Benavides

It is well documented that disproportionately large numbers of social work clients, particularly in public agencies, are racial or ethnic group members. When we examine the use of social work services by

these clients, we find a substantially higher rate of discontinuance than among white clients (Miranda, 1976). It is our assumption that many of these clients drop out of service because they do not perceive what they are offered as helpful and that the partnership which ideally evolves from engaging a client in a positive, purposeful relationship does not develop.

*An original article prepared by the authors.

Our purpose here is to explore the development of the social work relationship across racial ethnic lines within a framework of biculturalism. Although this framework has evolved primarily from social work with Latinos, we believe it applies to work with any ethnic or racial group.

If we define culture as a relatively unified set of shared values, ideas, beliefs, and standards of action held by an identified people, numerous cultural groups can be identified within this country. The dominant culture integrated the values and norms of European immigrant groups, as each was encouraged to drop its language and become assimilated by the majority. Groups with recognizable physical characteristics—notably, skin color—have also been pushed to accept the dominant culture as their own, yet have been responded to as separate and inferior groups and thus not allowed to participate fully in it. As a result of this exclusion and a desire on the part of some to retain their original culture, distinct groups continue to exist. We view the retention of one's culture of origin as desirable and see multiculturalism as a perspective that encourages acceptance of difference and the capacity to work with it.

Let us diagram a bicultural continuum to reflect this perspective.

Relationship

Dominant Anglo/ white culture	Other group culture
Values, norms, role expectations	Values, norms, role expectations

Each group's cultural system is based on a set of values manifested in norms and role expectations that are distinct from those of the dominant cultural system. Though a wide range of individual differences exists within each group and parts of one group's system may be similar to that of others, recognizable boundaries exist and must be bridged if relationships are to be developed across them.

At either end of the continuum are located those who function within the boundaries of that cultural system. They identify and interact primarily with other members of the same group, govern their behavior according to its values and norms, and often speak a common language.

Movement across the continuum in either direction indicates exposure to another cultural system and generally occurs as one interacts with members of the other group. At least one participant in a relationship which crosses racial or ethnic lines must move toward the other in order to develop common ground for communication. If movement does not occur, interaction remains on a superficial level. As noted earlier, such movement in society has generally been from right to left on this continuum. Members of the dominant group have traditionally expected others to move toward them—to understand their cultural system and adapt to it. We maintain that the preferred alternative is for the social worker to develop the capacity to move across the continuum to wherever the client is located on it.

Let us consider the implications of this perspective for social work practice. Movement across the continuum essentially requires that one understand the values and norms of another cultural system and of one's own system, be aware of where differences lie, and accept both as legitimate. The Anglo/white worker, then, must acquire a substantial knowledge base, including the values, expected role behaviors, historical experiences, and language of the group to which the client belongs. It is essential that the worker accept both self and other before this knowledge can be integrated and applied effectively. Workers, as they offer service to the client, then draw from this understanding and acceptance to assess where the particular individuals involved are located on the continuum.

Social workers who are members of a nondominant racial or ethnic group have, when working with other members of the same group, the advantage of understanding from life experience what is expected and appropriate within the group. They also have the advantage of being identified by physical characteristics as people with common experiences, more likely to be trusted than Anglo/white workers, who must overcome this immediate barrier if service is to be used. In addition to understanding their own system, however, workers from nondominant cultures must develop the capacity to interact effectively within the Anglo/white system as well, since its members predominantly control needed services and resources. When working with members of other groups, such workers move across two continua, developing their capacity to interact within both the dominant culture and the clients' culture.

Anglo worker/Native American client

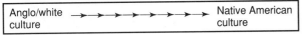

Latino worker and client/Anglo service system

Asian American worker/Anglo client

African American worker/Latino client/
Anglo service system

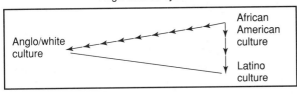

Worker movement across the bicultural continuum is diagrammed in the accompanying examples. The arrows indicate that workers move from wherever they are located both to where the client is and toward competence in interacting with the Anglo/white system.

In order to establish helpful, purposeful relationships across racial/ethnic lines, workers of all groups must be able to move along each continuum to interact within the cultural context that has meaning for the client.

The purpose of the social work relationship is to help clients to become the kind of people they want to become, or to do something they have chosen to do, by overcoming barriers and dealing more effectively with the stresses of life. The magnitude of this task for the client will not be understood by a worker who lacks empathy—the capacity to enter into the feelings and experiences of another without losing oneself in the process.

Unless workers have some knowledge of the values, norms, and expectations of the culture of the client and of this particular client, they will not be able to understand either the client's goals or the barriers impeding progress toward these goals. It is easier for each of us to work with clients who share the same cultural values,

norms, expectations, and worldview, since it is easier to be appropriately empathic with such clients. A more conscious effort is required to work effectively with clients of another culture, who have a different frame of reference, particularly in regard to perceptions of the importance of activity, the dynamics of relationships, and human nature.

Empathy, which requires openness to the reality of another person's feelings, experiences, and perceptions, facilitates the conscious efforts of workers in establishing relationships with clients of a different culture. Work with clients of a different culture requires, in addition, an openness on the part of workers to values, norms, and worldviews that their own culture may not share. This requires workers to understand and respect their own culture and the role it has played in their development and to feel free to respect the culture of the other. It demands from workers a belief that no culture is inherently superior to another, but that each is merely different.

We have chosen three dimensions of Latino culture—the culture with which we are most familiar—in order to illustrate factors relevant to the development of the social work relationship across racial or ethnic lines. The three dimensions considered—language, locus of control, and worldview—are not the only, or perhaps even the most important, dimensions of Latino culture. However, they provide examples of how the bicultural framework can be applied in client-worker situations and illustrate points of possible incongruities between the perceptions of the worker and those of a Latino client.

Although these incongruities may not exist if either the Latino client or the worker has ease of movement on a bicultural continuum, nevertheless the onus of movement on the bicultural continuum is on the worker if he is to meet the client wherever the client is and if there is going to be any possibility of establishing a working relationship.

Verbal and nonverbal communications express a person's feelings, ideas, and worldview developed in a particular cultural context. The meanings assigned to verbal and nonverbal communication can result in incongruities between worker and client.

A nonverbal gesture, such as lowering of the eyes or not looking at someone directly, is interpreted by some persons as a sign of respect and deference to authorities and elders, but by others as a sign of lack of veracity.

Nonverbal communication is much more open to mis-interpretation than is verbal communication. However, verbal communication can also be misinterpreted when one language does not allow for full expression of the nuances and concepts behind another language. This is especially true in regard to Spanish and English.

In Spanish, there are two means of addressing another person, depending on their status in terms of both age and social role. Tu is the personal pronoun used to address peers or persons who are younger, whereas Usted is used to address elders and persons in positions of authority. To address an authority or an elder by using tu, the familiar form, is not seen as a misuse of language but rather as a lack of respect to that individual. This is not a cause for embarrassment, for there is no such term in Spanish. Rather, it is a cause for shame, since disre-spect is never seen as a matter to be taken lightly.

The use of *you,* the familiar pronoun in English, is appropriate at all times, since English usage does not distinguish its salutation according to either function or age. The general trend in the usage of English in this country is to do away with distinctions and to become acquainted with one another on a first-name basis. To do the opposite, in English, is sometimes viewed as an attempt to create an artificial distance between the two parties.

In dealing with persons who are of Spanish heritage, the emphasis is not on creating an artificial distance but rather on acknowledging what is already so—namely, that some people have more power by virtue of position and some have more experience by virtue of age. To address another who is older or in authority on a first-name basis is not viewed as an attempt to get closer to the other but rather as an attempt to challenge authority or to discount experience. A person who did this would be viewed as ill-bred or, at a minimum, ill-mannered and disrespectful.

Respect, then, becomes the key for dealing with authority. Respect, however, is not the same as *respeto.* In English, one can respect another while *strongly* oppos-ing the opinions that that person holds; the word *respect* does not contain the element of acceptance of another's view as one's own. *Respeto,* on the other hand, means that one must not challenge the opinions of others. It means that, if one chooses not to adopt the opinions of another, one must at least pay deference to the other person's views by not saying anything. Thus,

for Latinos, the locus of control tends to be much more external than internal, whether the locus is God, fate, nature, authority, or age, and this condition is con-stantly reinforced by means of language.

Because the respect for authority is essential to the highly structured and hierarchical worldview of Latinos, relationships do not occur as often between equals as they do in the dominant culture. Relationships are perceived as occurring between one who is in author-ity and one who is not. A social worker is seen as a person with authority. The purpose of the social work relationship—the conscious and deliberate use of self for the benefit of the client—remains the same. How-ever, the way that the purpose is viewed by Latino clients may be different from the way it is viewed by Anglo clients.

A Latino client entering a social work relationship views the relationship as unequal. The worker is assigned a sense of authority and *respeto.* The client may disagree with the worker but remain silent rather than appear disrespectful. A worker unaware of this culturally deter-mined approach may view the silence as resistance. Errors in assessment resulting from culture-based mis-interpretations lead to antagonistic relationships and the selection of inappropriate methods of intervention. Con-sider the discordant perceptions that may result from differences on the dimensions of locus of control and worldview. Latinos tend to see many aspects of their lives in which the control is external. Anglos consider more aspects of their lives to be under internal control. Efforts to foster independence and self-reliance, if taken at face value, can be viewed by Latinos as a lack of concern for others and as representing a pompous and unrealistic attitude. This logically follows from a Latino worldview in which there is a balance of pain and pleasure and the natural order is controlled by God. In the white/Anglo worldview, the individual is the powerful force; individu-als are in charge of themselves and can change what they want to change about themselves or their world. Latinos view themselves as much more interdependent and not solely in charge of themselves. What they, as individuals, can do is more dependent on others and the external environment.

If not recognized and addressed, such contrasting views impede work toward common goals. For example, the worker may decide to deal with an adolescent client on a one-to-one basis. However, the Latino mother may view this as inappropriate, since she sees herself as in control of her child. Failure to recognize and acknowledge the mother's position is likely to result in discontinuance from service. The reason might never be shared with the worker, because of the authority element in the relationship.

In empathizing with a Latino client, a worker may want to move too quickly from recognizing the difficulty the client is experiencing to identifying what could be done to help. For the client, it may be more helpful to dwell on the difficulty longer—even to the point where the worker might interpret this as resistance or as evidence that the client does not have the capacity to use the service. From the Latino client's point of view, dwelling on the difficulty could be viewed as helpful, since the client knows that pain is balanced by pleasure. The worker could acknowledge that cultural element and use it with the client, to prepare for the more pleasant phase of life; this would result in a more useful service for the client.

We have presented a framework for viewing cross-cultural social work relationships as developing across a bicultural continuum. The dimensions of language, locus of control, and worldview illustrate points of possible incongruities between the perceptions of an Anglo worker and a Latino client, which, in turn, create difficulties in establishing effective social work relationships. Empathy is required if workers of one culture are to move on a bicultural continuum toward clients of a different culture. We believe that recognizing the necessity of, and developing the capacity for, such movement will increase the likelihood of engaging clients of a different culture in positive, purposeful, and effective relationships.

READING 9-2 *Working Together Across Differences**
Uma Narayan

TAKING EMOTIONS SERIOUSLY

Communication and working relationships are often hard to initiate or sustain between people who differ in class, race, ethnicity, gender, or sexual orientation, despite the presence of common interests and shared goals. I think it would be helpful for individuals with different backgrounds and groups with heterogenous components to reflect on the difficulties of communication between people who share, and people who do not share, the experience of oppression. The emotions—and hence the sense of self—of members of the oppressed group are unintentionally violated by nonmembers who participate in the dialogue.

I have tried to analyze a number of ways in which this can happen. I hope that the cases considered, though by no means exhaustive, will provide a starting point for people to talk together about, and work through, problems in dialogue. Working across differences is a morally and socially important enterprise in every context—in political groups, in relationships between social workers (and other professionals) and their clients, and in friendships. Such differences in background and identity can be enriching resources, epistemologically, socially, and personally. Learning to understand and respect these differences can make more complex our understanding of ourselves and our societies, can broaden the range of our politics, and enrich the variety of connections we have as persons. But such efforts are not without costs; I shall focus on these costs.

For the sake of convenience, I shall use the term *insider* to refer to a member of an oppressed group and the term *outsider* to refer to nonmembers. These terms have a disadvantage in that they lack an explicit sense of hierarchy but have the advantage of reversing conventional ideas of what is central and what is marginal. People are insiders or outsiders only with respect to specific forms of oppressive social structures—racism, sexism, compulsory heterosexuality, and so forth. An individual who is an insider with respect to one form of oppression (say, by being a woman) may be an outsider with respect to another form of oppression (say, by being white).

*Revision of paper originally published in *Hypathia*. Revised by author for this book.

These problems in communication may have different implications in the context of political and professional relationships than when they occur between friends. Friends may more easily be able to articulate such problems, and insiders may be more willing to make allowances for outsiders who are friends. Moreover, outsiders may be more concerned about having caused offense to insiders who are friends and, hence, more willing to understand the nature of the problems that arise. However, working across differences is an unavoidable project in all of these contexts. We need to understand the costs of communicating across differences and try to minimize those costs.

My focus on emotions in problems of communication follows the injunction of several strands of feminist theory that the emotions must be taken seriously and not regarded as mere epiphenomenal baggage. Thus, although I shall be addressing problems that have to do with communicating across all sorts of difference, and not gender differences alone, my project is still primarily inspired by the feminist commitment to take emotions seriously.

Much feminist writing about the importance of emotions has focused on the positive contributions that emotions make to knowledge and communication. This is both understandable and appropriate, since feminist theory is a response to perspectives where the emotions have been regarded as antithetical to reason and as impediments to knowledge.

A strength of feminist thinking is its commitment to contextualizing its statements. Skeptical of claims that emotions are always a hindrance to knowledge, it would prefer to examine the specific roles of emotions in particular contexts. In keeping with this commitment, feminist theory would fail to live up to its own standards if it adopted another absolutist perspective on the emotions—that emotions always had a positive contribution to make in the domain of knowledge and communication.

Differences of class, race, gender, sexual orientation, and so on often correlate with significantly different opportunities, values, and social experiences for insiders and outsiders. Factors like race, class, and gender have historically been part of deep and divisive social structures, which have engendered conflict, tension, hostility, and mistrust between insiders and outsiders. Communication between insiders and outsiders is in

constant danger of breaking down unless people learn to trust one another across divisive social differences and to sustain working relationships in contexts of distrust and disagreement. Even when people are working together for common social, political, professional, or personal goals, communication cannot be sustained unless the problems that arise between insiders and outsiders are addressed.

So, working together across our differences seems to be unavoidable. We are condemned to either ignoring differences at the cost of conflict and mistrust or working tenuously across them to form always risky bonds of understanding.

EPISTEMIC PRIVILEGE AND THE POLITICS OF DIFFERENCE

My starting premise is that goodwill is not enough. A simple resolution by individuals or groups to try and understand the experiences of more disadvantaged persons or groups, whose oppression they do not share, and to try and empathize with their interests is not going to resolve the thousands of problems that crop up in communication. Too often, even the most resolute possessors of goodwill will find themselves baffled and angered by failures of communication.

Such resolute goodwill toward members of more disadvantaged groups may be an important foundation for trust-building experiences. But this will not be sufficient to cause strong, historically constituted networks of distrust to simply evaporate into thin air.

Annette Baier (1986) says that trust "is accepted vulnerability to another's possible but not expected ill will (or lack of good will) toward one" (p. 235). Members of disadvantaged groups may be willing to set aside their mistrust of members of advantaged groups with whom they work, to the extent of accepting the existence of goodwill on the part of these advantaged outsiders. But they *cannot* fail to be aware that the outsiders' goodwill is not enough to overcome assumptions and attitudes born out of centuries of power and privilege.

Insiders realize that being hurt by the insensitivity of outsiders they endeavor to work with is often more difficult emotionally than being hurt by the deliberate malice of outsiders they expect no better of. Here, insiders render themselves more vulnerable by acknowledging the outsiders' goodwill.

In considering the difficulties in communicating across differences, I start by examining the claim that members of oppressed groups have epistemic privilege (Harding & Hintikka, 1983; Hartsock, 1983). Epistemic privilege means that members of an oppressed group have a more immediate, subtle, and critical knowledge of their oppression than do nonmembers. The claim of epistemic privilege need not imply that the insiders have a clearer or better knowledge of the *causes* of their oppression. Since oppression often includes the denial of access to education and hence to the means of theory production (detailed knowledge of the history of their oppression, conceptual tools with which to analyze its mechanisms, and so on), the oppressed may not have a detailed analysis of how their oppression originated and has been maintained and of all the systemic purposes it serves. Explanatory theories and conceptual tools—such as class structure and patriarchy—that help us understand the specificities of oppression are often developed by people who, as nonmembers of the oppressed group, have greater access to the means of theoretical production.

However, the oppressed have epistemic privilege when it comes to immediate knowledge of everyday life under oppression—all the ways in which the oppression affects their social and psychic lives. The emotions play an important role in this knowledge.

Second, the claim to epistemic privilege for the oppressed does not mean that nonmembers of the oppressed group can never come to understand the experiences of the oppressed. Such a claim would have very undesirable political consequences; it could excuse those who are not members of an oppressed group from any concern with that oppression. After all, if outsiders can never understand most significant aspects of a form of oppression, how could they meaningfully take an interest in it or help fight against it? Taken this way, the claim to epistemic privilege would make communication between insiders and even sympathetic outsiders close to useless. Besides, this interpretation is not supported by experience. Many of us know a few men who understand a good deal about feminist concerns, for instance, or white people who understand a good deal about issues of race.

But I think that the claim to epistemic privilege does imply that nonmembers of the oppressed group will have to make a great effort to apprehend the details of lived oppression. Having insiders as friends and colleagues, sharing in aspects of their lifestyle, fighting alongside them on issues that concern them, and sustaining a continuous dialogue with them can all help outsiders develop a more sophisticated understanding of what oppression involves. But outsiders who simply have an abstract sort of goodwill toward insiders are unlikely to have a clear awareness of the forms in which an oppression is experienced.

Outsiders should not deceive themselves that they can learn nothing about oppression unless educated about it by insiders. True, if insiders have epistemic privilege about their oppression, outsiders cannot educate themselves about insiders' situation except by listening to, or reading about, their experience of their situation. But concerned outsiders must recognize a responsibility to actively seek out and acquire such knowledge.

Third, the claim that the oppressed have epistemic privilege does not mean that the knowledge they have of their oppression is in any way incorrigible. Members of an oppressed group, like human subjects in general, can always be mistaken about the nature of their experience. Insiders may differ in the way they perceive or interpret certain incidents; not all of them can be right. At times, it may even be that all of them are wrong.

However, epistemic privilege does have some implications for outsiders who want to argue that the understanding of an insider is wrong. Such outsiders must proceed with methodological humility and methodological caution. By methodological humility, I mean that the outsiders must always be aware that, as outsiders, they may be missing something, and that what appears to be a mistake on the part of an insider may make more sense if they had a fuller understanding of the context. By methodological caution, I mean that outsiders should be careful to present their attempted criticism in such a way that it does not—nor even seem to—denigrate or dismiss the validity of the insider's point of view.

Fourth, the claim to epistemic privilege for the oppressed should not be identified with the claim that the oppressed should speak for themselves and represent their own interests. Even if insiders had no epistemic privilege whatsoever, there are several other good and important reasons why they should speak for themselves. Historically, those in power have always spoken as if their point of view is universal and represents the values, interests, and experiences of every-one. Many critiques of political, moral and social theory have been directed at showing how these allegedly universal points of view represent the viewpoints of the powerful and the privileged (Young, 1986).

Besides, the right to speak for oneself is closely tied to the oppressed group's sense of autonomy, identity, and self-respect. For that reason alone, the oppressed should speak for themselves.

EPISTEMIC PRIVILEGE AND THE EMOTIONS

In my view, an important aspect of epistemic privilege is that the oppressed have knowledge conferred by their emotional responses to oppression. Whereas concerned outsiders' knowledge of oppression is always more or less abstract and theoretical, the knowledge of insiders is enriched by their lived experience. Insiders' emotional responses to oppression enrich their knowledge of that oppression in at least three ways.

1. UNDERSTANDING THE EMOTIONAL COSTS OF OPPRES-SION. Sympathetic outsiders can react emotionally to incidents of racism, sexism, and so forth, even though they are not the targets of such oppression. But outsiders often fail to realize that insiders' emotional responses to the oppression may be much more complex than their own. Consequently, their understanding of the emotional costs of the oppression will be more sketchy than that of insiders. Sympathetic outsiders, when encountering a racist or sexist incident often feel anger at the perpetrator and sympathy with the victim. The insider victim, however, may feel a jumbled array of emotions: anger at the perpetrator, a deep sense of humiliation, a sense of being soiled by the incident, momentary hatred for the whole group of which the perpetrator is a part, rage at the history that sustains such attitudes, anger and shame at one's powerlessness to retaliate, a sense of solidarity with those who face the same problems, and maybe even pity for the stupidity of the perpetrator. Outsiders may fail to wholly grasp the effects of the oppression on its victims, and the full emotional costs.

2. APPRECIATING THE SUBTLER MANIFESTATIONS OF OPPRES-SION. Outsiders who have not experienced an oppression firsthand are likely to understand only the *general* and *commonplace* ways in which it is manifested. For instance, if a professor uses openly sexist examples or is openly hostile to female students, sympathetic male students may notice his attitudes. But if those attitudes are expressed more covertly—through dismissing wom-en's queries, not taking their contributions seriously, undervaluing their work, or lack of cordiality—outsiders may fail to see what is happening.

Insiders will often pick up cues ranging from facial expressions to body language that outsiders may fail to spot and will often also be alerted by their own feelings of unease about the person or situation. As a consequence, insiders are far more likely than outsiders to know the extent to which a form of oppression permeates a society and the very subtle forms in which it can operate.

3. MAKING CONNECTIONS OR SEEING OPPRESSION IN NEW CONTEXTS. Outsiders usually know about the more wide-spread and commonplace contexts in which an oppres-sion is manifested but may fail to recognize the same sort of phenomena in new or unusual contexts. Or, they may fail to make the connection between what they know in theory and what is taking place in a given situation. For instance, men who have been sensitized to the silencing of women in public forums may fail to see the same phenomenon in informal gatherings or between friends. Insiders are more likely to make these connections and to carry over what they have learned to new contexts, because exposure to the oppression makes them more vigilant.

EMOTIONAL COSTS OF WORKING ACROSS DIFFERENCE

Although oppression may confer epistemic privilege, it certainly constitutes a burden. Insiders are burdened by all the forms an oppression takes, from everyday and trivial manifestations to violent and life-threatening ones. Insiders pay a heavy social and psychological price that no outsider pays. Collaboration between insiders and outsiders is often fraught with difficulty, for, in any communication, the two groups are not equally vulner-able, as Maria Lugones and Elizabeth Spelman (1983) explain:

> We have had to be in your world and learn its ways. We have to participate in it, make a living in it, live in it, be mistreated in it, be ignored in it, and rarely, be appreci-ated in it. But there is nothing that necessitates that you understand our world; understand, that is, not as an observer understands things, but as a participant, as someone who has a stake in them understands them. So your being ill at ease in our world lacks the features of our being ill at ease in yours precisely because you can leave and you can always tell yourselves that you will soon be

out of there and because the wholeness of yourselves is never touched by us, we have no tendency to remake you in our image. (p. 576)

The insider pays the price of oppression. Even sympathetic outsiders, prone to blind spots and clumsiness, can hurt the insider more often than they imagine. Insiders cannot simply walk away from the problems and issues that permeate their lives, as the outsider always can, nor can they ever inadvertently hurt outsiders in quite the same way that outsiders can hurt them. Thus, since the brunt of possible hurt is most often on the insider, the burden of taking care not to cause offense can fairly be laid on the outsider. Outsiders often assume, wrongly, that goodwill on their part is a guarantee against causing offense to insiders; when insiders are offended and express their anger, the outsiders often react with honest bafflement and anger, since they cannot understand how someone as sympathetic to an oppressed group could conceivably be seen as having offensive views or attitudes.

I shall try to analyze a number of ways in which outsiders may cause affront and grief to insiders; the list is in no way exhaustive. These failures have in common the inability of outsiders to fully understand and respect the emotional responses of insiders. In some cases, the responses of outsiders violates insiders' sense of self-identity, self-worth, or self-respect. In others, the outsiders' responses violate insiders' sense of group identity, respect, and solidarity.

1. **DENIAL OF THE VALIDITY OF AN INSIDER'S RESPONSE.** Given the way differences work, it is hardly surprising that insiders and outsiders may often have very different understandings of what is involved in a situation. For instance, men and women often have very different understandings concerning where responsibility lies in cases of sexual harassment. Men often think women are responsible for attracting unwanted attention, because of the way they dress or conduct themselves. Women often see this as an attempt to absolve men of their real responsibility. When men blame women for the sexual harassment from which they suffer, they wholly deny the validity of the insiders' understanding of such harassment as something inflicted on them. Insiders will most often respond emotionally to such attempts to negate their understanding—with anger, tears, and so on. To insiders, the issue is not purely theoretical, and their anger and pain at what they have to endure is exacerbated

by the seeming inability of even well-intentioned outsiders to see their point of view.

The situation is complicated in that most outsiders and insiders have been socialized differently and understand and display emotions in very different ways. For instance, public (or even private) displays of emotion by women, which are experienced as natural and authentic by the women, often seem excessive and artificial to men.

Outsiders often react to insiders' emotional responses over a disagreement in two ways: by dismissing the emotional response as just one of those silly and irrational responses to which insiders are prone; by accusing the insider of using the emotional response as a manipulative measure. Insiders may be told that, since they could not muster arguments that were cogent enough to convince the outsider, they are now resorting to emotional tactics to win the argument.

When outsiders take both tacks, insiders are in a strange double-bind over their emotions. If the response is authentic and natural, it is also pathetic and a symptom of weakness, irrationality, and lack of self-control. If the response is not a symptom of weakness and irrationality, it is a calculated, manipulative, and inauthentic strategic move. To insiders, who already feel that displaying their emotions has made them vulnerable, such dismissals or accusations of manipulation add insult to injury. Outsiders must realize that denial of the validity of the insiders' responses will almost certainly cause a serious breach in the dialogue, since they deeply violate insiders' self-respect.

2. **ACCUSATIONS OF PARANOIA.** Outsiders often consider the reactions of insiders to be paranoid. They think that the insiders are imagining the existence of racist or sexist attitudes, say, in cases where outsiders fail to see such attitudes. (This is another way in which outsiders deny the validity of the insider's response.) Accusations of paranoia are usually incorrect, since even sympathetic outsiders may fail to pick up on subtle forms of prejudice and discrimination. They also undermine insiders' confidence that their judgments are accurate. Insiders are often aware that subtle instances of racism and sexism are open to interpretation and consequently are anxious and uncertain about their own perceptions.

But insiders are mostly correct in their suspicions. Sometimes less subtle manifestations follow, or else the insider meets other insiders who have the same feelings of unease about the same outsider. For instance, women students and students of color seem to largely agree in their individual judgments as to which of their professors are sexist or racist, often in the subtlest of ways.

Outsiders should refrain as far as possible from such accusations of paranoia, since they are likely to be wrong, and since such accusations undermine insiders' trust in their own perceptions. This may reduce their capacity for vigilance, something that those who are on the receiving end of oppression can ill afford.

3. INSENSITIVE REACTIONS TO AN INSIDER'S RESPONSE. Outsiders can be offensively insensitive to insiders' reactions without necessarily dismissing them as irrational, manipulative, or paranoid. Here's an example. A group of people were discussing whether it was important that women (rather than men) taught courses in feminist theory and that African American professors (rather than white ones) taught courses in African American literature, philosophy, and history. An African American talked about his experience with a white teacher who taught Richard Wright with little sensitivity to the context of African American culture and who constantly dismissed what his African American students had to say. A white participant responded by saying that it was better to include such works on syllabi, regardless of who taught them, than to exclude them because there were no teachers from appropriate backgrounds to teach them. This was an insensitive reaction because the insider's account of his unhappy experience was brushed aside. The same basic point could have been made by saying, for instance, "I can understand what you are talking about. Such experiences must be awful. But don't you think that it may be a good thing to push for African American writings to be included on syllabi, regardless of who is there to teach them?"

In this case, the outsider was white, a woman, and a feminist, and her response may be seen as an insensitive failure to analogize. If a woman had talked about how awful it was to do Virginia Woolf with a sexist male teacher, and a man had commented similarly, any feminist would have perceived it as a sexist response.

If working together across difference is to be possible, we must all learn to analogize from situations of oppression in which we have been insiders to those in which we are outsiders. It seems that understanding of one form of oppression does not necessarily sensitize one to other forms. But, if we make the effort to analogize, it may give us some clues as to how to avoid insensitive responses when we are outsiders.

4. FAILURE TO AVOID STEREOTYPIC GENERALIZATIONS. Sometimes, even the best-intentioned outsiders utter cliches and stereotypic generalizations about insiders. For instance, outsiders may see culturally mediated attitudes to birth control, family size, or work as the result of simple ignorance or backwardness on the part of insiders. Outsiders should carefully scrutinize their explanations of insiders' behavior for such insulting cliches.

5. FAILURE TO SEE WHY STATEMENTS ARE IMPLICITLY INSULTING. Outsiders are often taken aback by insiders' sharp reactions to certain statements. For instance, women in a group may react sharply to a man's statements that are insulting to *particular* women, who may not be present or even members of the group. The women present may suspect, with some justification, that the man's statements reflect his attitudes to women in general. To avoid that sort of reaction, outsiders must be very careful to specify what their criticism of a particular insider is and try to show why it is not an expression of a general negative attitude to insiders in general.

Outsiders often fail to understand why, for instance, a Latino may react negatively to implicitly derogatory remarks about, say, Chinese or African cultures. Outsiders fail to see that insiders may quite legitimately suspect that these remarks reflect negative attitudes toward all other cultures. It may be very difficult, but outsiders will have to focus on the more general implications of their statements for insiders, in order to avoid unintentional insult.

6. INAPPROPRIATE JUDGMENTS. Outsiders often think that their relationship with insiders entitles them to make judgments about what insiders ought to do or feel. These judgments, almost inevitably, turn out to be insulting to the insider. For instance, women philosophers and philosophers of color who are interested in areas like mathematical logic are offended by implications that they should be devoting themselves to political philosophy and/or feminist theory. Outsiders who imply this fail to see why it may be a matter of pride for members of oppressed groups to excel in a difficult field like mathematical logic. Similarly, many Western feminists imply that some non-Western feminists are too critical about their own cultures. They fail to see that women who have fought against some of the most oppressive aspects of those cultures cannot afford outsiders' more rose-tinted view. Good advice to outsiders is that they should learn from the perceptions of insiders, rather than telling insiders what they ought to do or feel.

There are, no doubt, several other ways in which communicating across difference can create problems. For instance, outsiders who desire to be praised for their interest in an issue that does not directly affect them may fail to understand insiders' resentment of that desire. Or outsiders may fail to understand why, at moments of crisis, even insiders whom they are close to may prefer to discuss their problems with other insiders.

These problems of communicating across difference will be easier to handle if both insiders and outsiders take seriously the idea of the epistemic privilege of the oppressed. Outsiders must try to understand that good-will on their part is not sufficient to guarantee that their perceptions and comments are inoffensive to insiders. They must realize that insiders may have a more subtle and complex understanding of the ways in which oppression operates and that insiders are especially vulnerable to insensitivities from outsiders whom they have begun to trust. Outsiders have good reason to proceed with methodological humility and methodological caution and to focus more careful attention on the implications of what they say.

While the exercise of methodological humility and methodological caution may cramp the spontaneity of outsiders' reactions and the ease with which they communicate, this seems a small price to pay in order to avoid offense to insiders and serious breaches in communication.

Is there anything insiders can do to help in working across differences? Perhaps the idea of epistemic privilege can make a difference to insiders as well. If they realize that outsiders have difficulty in understanding the subtlety of oppression, insiders may be able to deal with outsiders' insensitive perceptions or comments with greater charity. This is not to say that such insensitivities must be simply overlooked or forgiven, but the manner of confrontation may be different. For instance, instead of reacting with anger, which inevitably makes the outsider defensive, the insider could try instead to point out why the outsider's remarks were experienced as hurtful or offensive.

Even with the best intentions, it is very hard for insiders not to react to insensitivity with anger, for each insensitivity evokes memories of countless others. Besides, anger is a necessary emotion for those who must constantly exercise vigilance in the face of systematic social prejudice and discrimination. Insensitivities from trusted outsiders make insiders especially bitter and pessimistic about hopes for change, and anger is often an inevitable corollary.

Besides, revealing anger makes one less vulnerable than revealing hurt. In revealing anger, one seems to react from a position of strength, while revealing hurt may invite outsiders' pity or guilt, neither of which the insider can find very palatable. Moreover, insiders often resent the burden of constantly explaining themselves to outsiders and feel bitter that, while they must unavoidably live and function in the outsider's world, the outsider has no such imperative to understand their world and their experience. However, perhaps insiders must try, whenever possible, to raise issues of insensitivity with some rein on their anger. And outsiders, for their part, must try to understand the insiders' anger.

Certainly, continuing examination of communication across differences will reveal other kinds of problems. What is important is that these problems are seriously analyzed and addressed, to permit more sensitive perceptions on the part of outsiders and easier interaction between insiders and outsiders.

LEARNING EXERCISES

1. Write one- or two-sentence definitions for each of the following terms, or briefly explain its meaning to a friend:

   bicultural continuum
   cultural competence
   cultural guide
   cultural relativism
   epistemic privilege

2. The U.S. government's efforts to promote human rights have prompted resistance by some Asian governments, which argue that concepts of individual freedom and human rights are derived from Western thought and do not fit well with Asian values that emphasize the needs of society, the group, and the family. A news story on this issue is presented in

Exhibit 9–5. The excerpts in Exhibit 9–5 are from the Denver *Post* but this matter was also reported in the New York *Times* (July 29, 1997, p. A8) and the Toronto *Globe and Mail* (July 29, 1997, p. A10). What are your views? Are American efforts to impose the concept of human rights on Asian countries a form of cultural colonialism? If so, are there conditions under which this would be justified? Can you identify incidents in your work in which the client's community regards social work concepts— such as confidentiality, individual dignity, and self-determination—as less important than other values such as family and group solidarity and the survival

of the culture or as simply wrong? If so, does emphasizing these social work values constitute a form of oppression?

3. The novel *Snow Falling on Cedars* by David Guterson (1995), which revolves around the murder trial of a Japanese American, illuminates the Japanese American experience in the United States during World War II. Cite examples from the novel of how cultural differences resulted in misunderstandings. What steps might have been taken to improve understanding between the Japanese Americans and the European Americans? Identify at least two reasons why the reporter (Ishmael) failed to

EXHIBIT 9–5   Asian Values and Human Rights

KUALA LUMPUR, Malaysia—"Asian values" clashed head-on with the Western concept of human rights and individual freedoms Tuesday in an unusual public exchange between U. S. and Asian diplomats at a meeting normally devoted to celebrating their good relations.

At the heart of the dispute were questions simple and complex, including: What are human rights? Are there any universal values, such as belief in individual freedoms? Are some values more attuned to Western culture than to the East? Are Western countries that try to impart those values "interfering" in Asian nations' internal affairs?

The issue that prompted public debate was a suggestion by Malaysia's Prime Minister Mahathir Mahamad that it is time for the United Nations to "review" its 50-year-old Universal Declaration of Human Rights.

The rights document, Mahathir said earlier this week, was forced on the world by the superpowers at the end of World War II, and may now be outdated and unsuited for the needs of developing countries.

"Everybody knows that human rights does not consist of individual political and civil rights," said Indonesian Foreign Minister Ali Alatas during the debate. "People are now much more aware that economic rights, cultural rights, social rights are just as important."

Undersecretary of State Stuart Eizenstat called it "remarkable" that countries want to alter the human rights charter, and he took issue with the thesis that Western respect for individual freedoms runs contrary to the goal of stability and economic development.

"The respect for the individual is not contrary to social stability, it is not contrary to economic prosperity," Eizenstat said, in a spirited defense of the human rights charter. "It is essential."

The rights declaration, adopted December 10, 1948, has no legal force but has become recognized as a codification of civil, political, economic and other rights for all. Dec. 10 is celebrated as Human Rights Day around the world.

The backdrop to the debate is a lingering complaint in Asia that the West—particularly the United States—is heavy-handed and culturally insensitive in condemning the human rights situations in developing countries, and a widespread contention that paternalistic, authoritarian forms of government are more compatible with "Asian values" that stress the needs of society over the rights of individuals.

Underlying the "Asian values" debate is a new international assertiveness on the part of Asian countries that have been bolstered by years of economic success. Many of these Asian leaders, hailing from authoritarian countries, are holding up their nations as providing a competing formula for prosperity that challenges Western liberal democracies.

Eizenstat, supported by the European Union delegates, said the 20th century has seen some of the worst horrors—including genocides by the Nazis and the Khmer Rouge, and two world wars—and that it would be a mistake now for Asians to start tinkering with basic concepts of human rights agreed upon a half-century ago. "Universal values don't know a time period," he said.

From "Asian Values and Western Human Rights" by K. Richburg in *The Washington Post*, July 30, 1997. Reprinted with permission.

immediately report new evidence to the court. The book ends with this sentence: "The heart of any other, because it had a will, would remain forever mysterious." What meaning does that hold for you?

4. Select a cultural group and do a search of *Social Work Abstracts* for the last 10 years to identify materials that will help you understand that culture. Then do a search for additional material on the world wide web.

REFERENCES

Asamoah, Y. W. (1997). *Innovations in delivering culturally sensitive social work services.* Binghampton, NY: Haworth Press.

Baier, A. (1986). Trust and antitrust. *Ethics, 96*(2), 231–260.

Beavers, C. (1986). A cross-cultural look at child abuse. *Public Welfare, 44,* 18–22.

Berg, I. K., & Miller, S. O. (1992). Working with Asian American clients: One person at a time. *Families in Society, 73*(6), 356–363.

Billingsley, A. (1992). *Climbing Jacob's ladder.* New York: Simon and Shuster.

Boyd-Franklin, N. (1989). *Black families in therapy: A multisystem approach.* New York: Guilford.

Brice-Baker, J. (1996). Jamaican families. In M. McGoldrick, J. K. Pearce, & J. Giordano (Eds.), *Ethnicity and family therapy* (2nd ed., pp. 85–96). New York, Guilford.

Chapman, A. B. (1995). *Entitled to good loving: Black men and women and the battle for power and love.* New York: Henry Holt.

Christiansen, J. M., Thornley-Brown, A., & Robinson, J. A. (1982). *West Indians in Toronto: Implications for helping professionals.* Toronto: Family Service Association of Metropolitan Toronto.

Cross, T. (1988). Cultural competence continuum. *Focal Point, 3*(1).

Dana, R. H. (1993). *Multicultural Assessment Perspectives for Professional Psychology.* Boston: Allyn & Bacon.

Daniel, J. H. (1985). Cultural and ethnic issues: The Black family. In E. H. Newberger & R. Bourne (Eds.), *Unhappy families: Clinical and research perspectives on family violence* (pp. 143–153). Littleton, MA: PSG.

Davidson, J. R. (1992). White clinician-black client: Relationship problems and recommendations for change from a social influence theory perspective. *Journal of Multicultural Social Work, 1*(4), 63–76.

Davis, L. E., & Gelsomino, J. (1994). An assessment of practitioner cross-racial treatment experiences. *Social Work, 39*(1), 122.

Delgado, M. (1995). Puerto Rican elders and natural support systems: Implications for human services. *Journal of Gerontological Social Work, 24*(1/2), 115–130.

Devore, W., & Schlesinger, E. G. (1996). *Ethnic-sensitive social work practice* (4th ed.). Needham Heights, MA: Allyn & Bacon.

Dilworth-Anderson, P. (1992). Extended kin networks in black families. *Generations, 17*(3), 29–32.

Dungee-Anderson, D., & Beckett, J. O. (1995). A process model for multicultural social work practice. *Families in Society, 76*(8), 459–468.

Duryea, M. L., & Gundison, J. B. (1993). *Conflict and culture: Research in five communities in Vancouver, British Columbia.* Victoria, BC: University of Victoria Institute for Dispute Resolution.

Ewall, P., Freeman, E. M., Kirk, S. A., & Poole, D. L. (Eds.). (1996). *Multicultural issues in social work.* Washington, DC: NASW Press.

Gibbs, J. T. (1980). The interpersonal orientation in mental health consultation: Toward a model of ethnic variations in counselling. *Journal of Community Psychology, 8,* 195–207.

Gibbs, J. T. (1993). *After the L.A. riots: Social work's role in healing cities.* San Francisco: Many Cultures.

Gibbs, J. T., & Moskowitz-Sweet, G. (1991). Clinical and cultural issues in the treatment of biracial and bicultural adolescents. *Families in Society, 72*(10), 579–592.

Gibson, A., & Lewis, C. (1985). *A Light in the Dark Tunnel: Ten Years of Westindian Concern and Caribbean House.* London: Centre for Caribbean Studies.

Griffith, J. E., & Villavicencio, S. (1985). Relationship among acculturation, sociodemographic characteristics, and social support in Mexican American adults. *Hispanic Journal of Behavioral Sciences, 7,* 75–92.

Guterson, D. (1995). *Snow falling on cedars.* New York: Vintage Press.

Harding, S., & Hintikka, M. (Eds.). (1983). *Discovering reality: Feminist perspectives on epistemology, methodology, and philosophy of science.* Boston: Dordrecht & Reidel.

Harper, K. V., & Lantz, J. (1996). *Cross-cultural practice: Social work with diverse populations.* Chicago: Lyceum.

Hartsock, N. (1983). The feminist standpoint: A specifically feminist historical materialism. In S. Harding & M. Hintikka (Eds.), *Discovering reality: Feminist perspectives on epistemology, methodology, and philosophy of sciences* (pp. 283–310). Boston: Dordrecht & Reidel.

Herberg, C. D. (1995). *Frameworking for cultural and social diversity: Teaching and learning for practitioners.* Toronto Canadian Scholars' Press.

Ho, C. G. T. (1993). The internationalization of kinship and the feminization of Caribbean migration: The case of Afro-Trinidadian immigrants in Los Angeles. *Human Organization, 52*(1), 32–40.

Karenga, R. (1995). Making the past meaningful: Kwanzaa and the concept of Sankofa. *Reflections, 1*(4), 36–46.

LeResche, D. (1992). Comparison of the American mediation process with a Korean-American harmony restoration process. *Mediation Quarterly, 9*(4), 323–339.

Longclaws, L. (1996). New perspectives in healing. In J. Oaks & R. Rieve (Eds.), *Issues in the North* (Vol. 1; Occasional Publication Series No. 4). Winnipeg, MB: Department of Native Studies, University of Manitoba.

Luckey, I. (1994). African American elders: The support network of generational kin. *Families in Society, 75*(2), 82–89.

Lugones, M. C., & Spelman, E. V. (1983). Have we got a theory for you! Feminist theory, cultural imperialism and the demand for "the women's voice." *Women's Studies International Forum,* 6(6), 573–581.

Lynch, E. W., & Hanson, M. J. (1992). *Developing cross-cultural competence: A guide for working with young children and their families.* Baltimore, MD: Paul H. Brookes.

McGoldrick, M. (1988). Ethnicity and the family life cycle. In B. Carter & M. McGoldrick (Eds.), *The changing family life cycle: A framework for family therapy* (2nd ed.) (pp. 69–90). New York: Gardner.

McGoldrick, M., Garcia-Preto, N., Hines, P. M., & Lee, E. (1989). Ethnicity and women. In M. McGoldrick, C. M. Anderson, & F. Walsh (Eds.), *Women in families: A framework for family therapy* (pp. 169–199). NY: Norton.

Miranda, M. R. (1976). *Psychotherapy with the Spanish-speaking: Issues in research and service.* Los Angeles: Spanish-Speaking Mental Health Center.

Moon, A., & Williams, O. (1993). Perceptions of elder abuse and help-seeking patterns among African-American, Caucasian-American, and Korean-American elderly women. *The Gerontologist,* 33(3), 386–394.

Morrow-Howell, N., Lott, L., & Ozawa, M. (1990). The impact of race on volunteer helping relationships among the elderly. *Social Work,* 35(5), 395–404.

Santiago, J. M. (1993). Hispanic, Latino, or Raza? Coming to terms with diversity. *Hospital and Community Psychiatry,* 47(7), 613.

Sanua, V. D. (1985). The family and sociocultural factors of psychopathology. In L. L'Abate (Ed.), *The handbook of family psychology and therapy* (Vol. 2), pp. 847–875. Homewood, IL: Dorsey.

Srole, L., Langer, T. S., Michael, S. T., Opler, M. K., & Rennie, T. A. C. (1962). *Mental health in the metropolis: The midtown Manhattan study.* New York: McGraw-Hill.

Tafoya, T. (1989). Circles and cedar: Native Americans and family therapy. *Journal of Psychotherapy and the Family, 6,* 71–98.

Tamura, T., & Lau, A. (1992). Connectedness versus separateness: Applicability of family therapy to Japanese families. *Family Process,* 31(4), 319–340.

Taylor, R. J., Neighbors, H. W., & Broman, C. L. (1989). Evaluation by Black Americans of the social service encounter during a serious personal problem. *Social Work, 34(3),* 205–211.

Terrell, F., & Terrell, S. (1984). Race of counselor, client sex, cultural mistrust level, and premature termination from counseling among black clients. *Journal of Counseling Psychology,* 31(3), 371–375.

Vazquez-Nuttall, E., Romero-Garcia, I., & DeLeon, R. (1987). Sex roles and perceptions of femininity and masculinity of Hispanic women: A review of the literature. *Psychology of Women Quarterly, 11*(4), 409–425.

Weaver, H. N. (1996). Social work with American Indian youth using the orthogonal model of cultural identification. *Families in Society,* 77(2), 98–107.

Young, I. M. (1986). Impartiality and the civic public: Some implications of feminist critiques of moral and political theory. *Praxis International, 5*(4), 381–401.

Zuniga, M. E. (1992). Using metaphors in therapy: *Dichos* and Latino chants. *Social Work,* 37(11), 55–60.

chapter 10

Data Collection and Assessment

CHAPTER PREVIEW

In Chapter 8, we introduced the process of engaging applicants, prospects, and respondents. In Chapter 9 we introduced considerations involving cross-cultural communication; you will be sensitive about the extent to which your communication style is encouraging cross-cultural communication in all phases of the social work process. In this chapter, we consider the processes of data collection and assessment. We will introduce the following ideas:

1. Assessment is the use of information for decision making about the problem and what is to be done about it.
2. Data are collected and processed to provide the information necessary for decision making.
3. The applicant is the primary source of data, but data may be collected from other sources.
4. Data are collected regarding the strengths brought by the applicant and the worker and those found within the situation of the applicant, as well as data necesary to formulate a statement of the problem to be worked.
5. Assessment focuses on the feasibility of accomplishing the solutions desired by the applicant.
6. Data are collected regarding alternate ways of accomplishing desired solutions, to assist in determining the most feasible alternative.
7. Decision making is a joint process involving both worker and applicant; it is not solely a professional responsibility.
8. The worker makes a knowledge base available to the applicant for use in considering how feasible the desired solutions are and in selecting the alternative most likely to lead to the desired solutions.

In Reading 10-1, Gale Burford, Joan Pennell, and Susan MacLeod describe the application of family group conferences, an assessment process that shifts power and authority for decision making to families; the role of the professional is to provide information needed by families for decision making and to facilitate the process.

In Reading 10-2, Cynthia Franklin and Catheleen Jordan discuss four assessment models—psychosocial, cognitive behavioral, life models, and family systems—and develop a fifth, which they call technical eclecticism, to integrate methods from the other four models. In contrast to the approach taken in this text, they describe assessment as the responsibility of the professional, with minimal involvement of the applicant.

ASSESSMENT

Definition

Assessment—the collection and processing of data to provide information for use in making decisions about the nature of the problem and what is to be done about it (Ivry, 1992)—is a cognitive, thinking process; it involves thinking about data that have been collected. The outcome of assessment is a service plan, which provides a definition of the problem for work, objectives or solutions to be achieved, and an action plan to accomplish the objectives.

There are four key questions in assessment:

1. What data are needed for assessment?
2. Who has the data?
3. How are the data to be collected?
4. Who processes the data and develops a service plan?

We first need to make a distinction between data and information, to emphasize the purpose of assessment as the development of a service plan, to note the difference between assessment and diagnosis, and to identify assessment as a continuous, ongoing process.

Data and Information

Data are the bits and pieces of perceptions, thoughts, and feelings collected about applicants and their situations. You may think of data as facts, or things that are accepted as facts. However, data are of no use until they have been organized. Think back to the case of Mr. Keene in Exhibit 8–9. Several bits and pieces of data were collected over 14 months: Mrs. Keene was hospitalized; Mr. Keene had depended on her to handle the household finances and the children; Mr. Keene was not accepting the seriousness of his wife's condition; Mr. Keene had difficulty having homemakers in the household; and so forth. These data had not been organized so as to guide intervention.

Information is processed data. Assessment is the process of organizing and processing data and making decisions on the basis of the information obtained from the processed data. The relationship between data and information is illustrated in Exhibit 10–1.

The Purpose of Assessment

The purpose of assessment is to reach an understanding of applicant wants and solutions, the presenting problem, and the person-in-situation so that worker and

applicant can construct a plan to alleviate the problem. Note that assessment is not conducted in order to understand the applicant; its purpose is to develop the understanding necessary for appropriate planning. It culminates in an action plan designed to accomplish agreed-upon objectives.

The process of assessment is an attempt to

- comprehend the key elements in the problem situation
- understand the meaning of the problem to the applicant
- identify strengths in the applicant and his or her environment
- clarify the feasibility of applicant objectives
- direct professional knowledge in an active thinking process aimed at identifying what needs to be altered in the situation
- plan how these desired changes may be accomplished

Through the assessment process, the applicant achieves an understanding of the problem, a belief in its manageability, and a sense of what a solution can mean.

The purpose of assessment is to develop a service plan, which, as we'll see in Chapter 11, consists of:

- a statement of the problem to be worked
- a statement of specific objectives to be accomplished
- an action plan to accomplish the objectives

Assessment and Diagnosis

Sometimes assessment is seen as putting the client in a category or attaching a label. That is not the purpose of

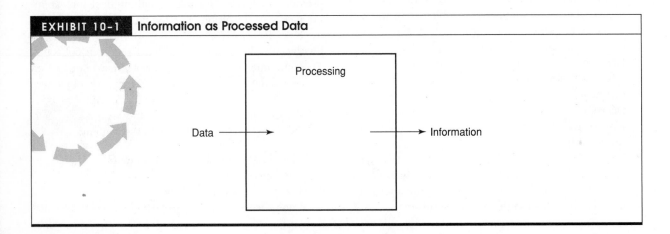

| EXHIBIT 10-1 | Information as Processed Data |

Data → Processing → Information

the process! Rather than focusing on the client alone, assessment is focused on the client, the problem, desired solutions, and the situation, in a systematic interaction. Systems theory teaches us that problems are the result of complicated interactions among all system variables. To seek a single ultimate cause or reason invites frustration and failure. Our aim is to order information about the client-situation-problem for the purposes of decision making concerning goals and actions.

Some social workers still speak of *diagnosis* (Turner, 1994). We dislike this term for several reasons. First, this term implies that there is something wrong with the applicant and, further, that the decision about what is wrong is made by the professional person through an examination; it does not connote dynamic interaction and joint responsibility. Moreover, diagnosis is often seen as a process by which a professional assigns a label (Mattaini & Kirk, 1991; Weick, 1986). When doctors diagnose, they assign labels signifying what is wrong, and they usually tell their patients what would be the most satisfactory form of treatment. As we saw in Chapter 4, this is inconsistent with the social work goal of individualizing the person-in-situation. Finally, there is evidence that the diagnosis may be more related to agency and agency function than to the client (Safer, 1995; Kutchins & Kirk, 1986; Desgranges, Desgranges, & Karsky, 1995).

The debate about diagnosis within social work cen-

ters around use of the *Diagnostic and Statistical Manual* (DSM-IV) of the American Psychiatric Association (1994). Some social workers, especially those working in mental health settings, strongly support the use of DSM-IV and believe it is appropriate for social workers to be involved in diagnosing mental disorders (Jarman-Rohde, McFall, Kolar, & Strom, 1997; Williams-Finch & Spitzer, 1995). Others argue just as strongly that DSM-IV is inappropriate for social work (Kirk & Kutchins, 1992, 1995, 1997). The arguments for and against the use of DSM-IV are summarized in Exhibit 10–2.

The idea of the social worker as an expert in describing and diagnosing mental disorders is inconsistent with the notions of partnership, participation, and building on strengths developed in this book. Thus, we agree that DSM-IV is inappropriate in social work, although you will certainly encounter social workers who make use of DSM-IV diagnostic categories. The person-in-environment (PIE) system (Karls & Wandrei, 1994a, b), developed specifically for social work, overcomes many of the objections to DSM-IV and is a more appropriate tool for classifying the problems that social workers encounter with applicants.

Assessment as a Continuous Process

In Chapter 3, we described problem solving as a spiral, rather than a linear step-by-step process. You will be

EXHIBIT 10-2	Arguments for and Against the Use of DSM-IV
ARGUMENTS FOR	**ARGUMENTS AGAINST**
1. Provides a common language for mental health professionals 2. Meets administrative requirements of clinical, governmental, and reimbursement agencies 3. Criteria and descriptions improve diagnostic relationship 4. Is the most advanced classification of mental disorders available	The approach taken in DSM contradicts many basic tenets of social work. Important social work perspectives—systems theory emphasizing the crucial role of families, small groups, and communities; a growth and development model of human behavior; the individualization of the client; a sensitivity and commitment to multicultural diversity; the emphasis on client abilities and strenghts; concerns about distributive justice; and the focus on the client empowerment model for interventions—are all neglected if not negated by the individual pathology–oriented DSM.

Source: B. W. Williams-Finch & R. L. Spitzer. Should DSM be the basis for teaching social work practice in mental health? Yes! *Journal of Social Work Education, 31*(2), 148–153 (1995).
Source: H. Kutchins & S. A. Kirk. Should DSM be the basis for teaching social work practice in mental health? No! *Journal of Social Work Education, 31*(2), 159–165 (1995).

engaging potential clients in assessment and intervention on several different levels—and perhaps on several different problems—at the same time. You and your client are constantly collecting new data and processing it to secure new information for decision making. This may result in a reassessment or a reconsideration of the problem for work, the desired objectives, or the action plan. Newly emerging problems and wants may need to be addressed, or you may examine matters whose consideration you had intended to postpone.

Assessment of a situation, problem, or person and the impact of the environment is a continuous process from the time you enter a situation until termination. You will be engaging in assessment on an ongoing basis with your client.

Types of Assessment

Depending on how your agency defines its function and the limits it places on your work, three types of assessment are possible:

- service specific
- applicant specific-global
- applicant request specific

A service specific assessment is conducted to determine if an applicant is eligible for the service provided by your agency; this is sometimes referred to as eligibility determination (Kropf, Lindsey, & Carse-McLocklin, 1993; Leutz, Abrahams, & Capitman, 1993). You may not be able to provide services to applicants who do not meet the eligibility criteria of your agency; however, you have a responsibility to refer them to other services that will meet their wants.

Applicant specific-global assessment begins with a presenting problem presented by the applicant, which expands to a more general review of the applicant's person-situation interaction. The focus is on the applicant and the presenting problem, rather than on the service provided by the agency. You will, however, ask the applicant to move through an extensive data collection phase to review the person-in-situation interaction before arriving at a service plan.

Applicant request specific assessment begins with the presenting problem, moves quickly to what the applicant wants done about the problem, and then addresses the feasibility of accomplishing applicant objectives. For this type of assessment, only data necessary to understand the presenting problem, to determine the feasibility of applicant objectives, and to consider the most effective ways of accomplishing these objectives are collected. You work within this limited framework, rather than attempting a more comprehensive review of the person-in-situation.

In reality, you must always take into consideration the agency function and whether or not the applicant is eligible for services. In some agencies, however, the function is defined broadly enough that you and your applicant have leeway to develop a range of service plans. At some point in your career, you are likely to provide service from an agency that defines function narrowly and has a fairly definite set of eligibility criteria. Applicant specific-global assessment is used in settings where it is necessary to reach a comprehensive understanding of the applicant's social functioning before developing a service plan and making a commitment to providing service. However, this type of assessment may dampen applicant enthusiasm and hope, and reduce motivation. Progress is more likely if you can quickly move in a direction the applicants desire.

Our preference is for applicant request specific assessment, which focuses on what the applicant wants. The organization of this chapter is based on applicant request specific assessment, but the material is applicable to the other two types.

TYPES OF DATA

The ecosystemic focus for social work practice suggests that we will need to collect:

- data regarding the applicant's wants and objectives
- data regarding the presenting problem as perceived by the applicant
- data regarding the applicant's level of hope and discomfort
- data regarding the opportunities available to the applicant

Data collection for assessment is a continuation of the process of engagement (Chapter 8). There is no sharp separation between the two; engagement flows into assessment and data collection. Thus, you and the applicant are continuing efforts to understand the presenting problem and to frame it so that it is amenable to change. You will be considering applicant wants and objectives and collecting data to determine how feasible they are and to identify alternative methods of achieving them. Thus, you will be looking at the strengths brought by the applicant, strengths brought by you, and the opportunities and strengths available in the environment.

Client Wants and Desired Solutions

In the engagement phase, we encouraged you to identify and discuss the applicant's initial wants. What does the applicant want done? What are your objectives? The engagement process ends with a preliminary agreement in which these wants and objectives are formalized. Typically, the preliminary agreement will provide a basis for the collection of data necessary for decisions about accomplishing the objectives. You will need to collect and organize data to permit decisions in four areas:

1. How feasible is it to accomplish the objectives?
2. Are the objectives to be short-term or long-term?
3. What strengths in the applicant, you, and the situation might contribute to the objectives?
4. In what alternative ways might the objectives be accomplished?

Feasibility of desired solutions. You and the applicant will need to evaluate the feasibility of the applicant's desired solutions. Can they be achieved? A key part of feasibility is whether the objectives involve changes that are reasonably within the control of you and the applicant. A woman who is being abused by her spouse, for example, may want to have the spouse stop hitting her and may propose this as an objective. This is not a very feasible objective, however, because neither you nor the woman can reasonably accept responsibility for controlling the man's behavior. Thus, you will assist the applicant in identifying alternative objectives that may be feasible—for example, moving to a safe place or activating community agencies, such as the police, to secure a restraining order.

You will need data about possible barriers to accomplishing the objectives. Barriers may relate to the objectives themselves or to specific action plans; they may be within the applicant, within the applicant's situation, or within limitations imposed by your agency or professional commitments. For example, an applicant's strong feelings of worthlessness may serve as a barrier to an objective of strengthening communication with a neighbor or friend. High crime rates may serve as a barrier to older persons' objective of engaging in neighborhood activities outside the home. In that case, you would need to collect data so as to establish whether the barrier is in fact the high crime rates (a barrier in the situation) or an exaggerated fear of crime (a barrier within the applicant). To illustrate the barriers that you bring, recall the Birky case (Exhibits 2–15 and 5–6), in which the social worker was employed by a day care center. It's quite possible that this agency's view of function would limit the worker's involvement in political action designed to cover the ditch in which the Birkys' son had drowned. You will need data to identify possible agency barriers and to make decisions about the chances of overcoming the barriers. As a result of assessment, you may define overcoming the barriers as your initial service plan.

Ethical concerns may also prevent your consenting to certain action plans. Suppose you are working with an agency that serves African Muslim refugees and immigrants. Some of these families, new to your community, may ask you to help them arrange for the circumcision of their prepubescent daughter. Should you agree to this objective, which reflects their traditional culture? You are also likely to encounter requests in which the action plan—the means used to achieve the objectives—poses ethical difficulties. Recall Exhibit 6–7, in which a woman on public assistance was declining to report outside sources of income. You probably have no ethical problem with the objective of increasing the income available to a family on public assistance, but does this means of doing so create any ethical concerns for you? Would you propose a similar action plan for other families on public assistance?

Collecting data about the feasibility of an objective or action plan creates two possible sources of disagreement between you and the applicant: disagreement about which objective is the most important; and disagreement about the feasibility of pursuing a particular objective or action plan. How can such disagreements be resolved? In accordance with our notion of partnership, we suggest that differences of view between you and the applicant be discussed and negotiated.

EXHIBIT 10-3 Whimspire Mission and Goals

The mission of Whimspire is to assist young people to achieve social integration and prepare them to live in a democratic society by serving as an alternative to institutional care and providing opportunities to live in family settings.

The mission will be accomplished to the extent that we can assist young people in our care to move toward outcome goals necessary for interdependent adult living in a democratic society. As an adult, the person will

1. Work and be self-supporting.
2. Actively participate in the community, including voluntary associations, recreational interest groups, religious organizations, or other community organizations, and contributing to the benefit of the overall community.
3. Respect the rights of others, appreciate difference, and avoid victimizing others through illegal behavior.

4. Live in a family or other intimate relationship where one gives and takes emotional support.
5. Manage personal and household matters including budget, cleaning, shopping, cooking, and laundry.
6. Accept responsibility for one's own behavior including taking steps to make amends for mistakes and omissions.

These are long term outcome goals. Whimspire services will contribute to assisting young people to accomplish these goals. Youths who emancipate from Whimspire programs into interdependent adult living will be relatively skillful in all of these areas. Youth who are discharged to some permanency plan other than emancipation should be further along towards accomplishing these outcomes than when they came into the Whimspire program but they cannot be expected to have sufficient skills to fully accomplish the goals.

SOURCE: Whimspire, Inc. *Whimspire Practice Guide: A Social Integration Model.* Grand Junction, Colorado: Author (1997), pp. 1–2.

What if where the applicant wants to begin is not, in your view, the most important objective? We suggest that, if at all possible, you begin with what the applicant wants to do. But indicate to the applicant which objective you believe is important and mention that you will want to return to that objective as progress is made toward the applicant's initial objective. That puts the matter on the agenda.

In the event that you and the applicant disagree about the feasibility of a particular action plan or objective, we recommend thorough discussion and negotiation of the differences before proceeding. If agreement proves impossible, you and the applicant will need to consider a different objective or, perhaps, a different action plan that you both agree is feasible.

Long-term and short-term objectives. Do you and the applicant develop objectives that can be accomplished relatively quickly, or do you set longer-term goals? It is helpful to think of objectives in terms of their level of specificity. Much of the focus of your work will be on accomplishing very concrete and specific objectives; specific objectives may be accomplished in the short term. Considerable evidence indicates that people approach agencies for concrete, specific services (Drake,

1996; Goldberg & Stanley, 1985). Further, setting specific short-term objectives will provide clients with a sense of satisfaction and thus enhance motivation to pursue additional—perhaps more difficult—objectives.

We differentiate here between objectives and goals. Goals are the end states that you and your applicant desire in the long term; they are often stated in general terms. Examples might be to have a happy marriage or a good job, to be more assertive, or to make an important contribution to the community. Objectives, by contrast, are short-term, immediate, specific, and concrete; they describe the immediate solutions you and your client desire for the problem. Objectives represent a step toward a goal and are specific enough that you and your client will know if they have been accomplished. Given this distinction, most of your service plans will involve objectives.

Having short-term objectives does not preclude you and your applicant from also having long-term goals. Long-term goals may provide a framework in which to develop short-term objectives. In practice, your agency mission and function may provide a basis for long-term goals. For example, the long-term goals of the foster family care agency in Exhibit 10–3 provide a direction for the agency's services and supply a framework within which the social workers and clients can develop individualized objectives.

Alternative action plans. You and the applicant will also need data to support decisions about the action plan most likely to achieve the objective. As we saw in Chapter 2, the principle of equifinality suggests that there are many ways of reaching the same objective. Consider Exhibit 10–4. If your goal is to take home the tallest tree, which tree do you select? To make sure that you have selected the proper tree, please take a measuring stick and determine the height of all of the trees. Are you surprised? Failure to consider alternatives will often result in an inadequate action plan. Our vision is limited by past experience, preferred courses of action, and our own bias. Carefully considering alternative action plans is one step toward overcoming these limitations and, as we established in Chapter 4, choice among alternatives is what constitutes self-determination. Further, the experience of choice enhances motivation (Deci & Ryan, 1980; Deci, Spiegel, Ryan, Koestner, & Kauffman, 1982).

In the Birky case (Exhibit 2–15), social work students typically identify an initial objective of resolving or coping with the grief from the tragic death of their young son. Many students, however, have difficulty identifying alternative action plans by which this objective might be achieved. There are at least five: (1) counseling by the worker; (2) referral to a grief counselor in the community; (3) support and help in resolving the grief from members of their extended family; (4) support and assistance from neighbors, clergy, or members of religious organizations in their new community; and (5) connecting the family to a mutual aid group of parents who have lost young children to tragic accidents. Part of the assessment process will be to determine the feasibility of each of these options and to select the one Mr. and Mrs. Birky would like to follow.

Do you need to systematically consider all alternatives? Are there any situations in which you may simply accept the preferred alternative and pursue that, without considering others? Including all logical alternative courses of action could become very tedious; this would

---

EXHIBIT 10-4 **Selecting a Tree**

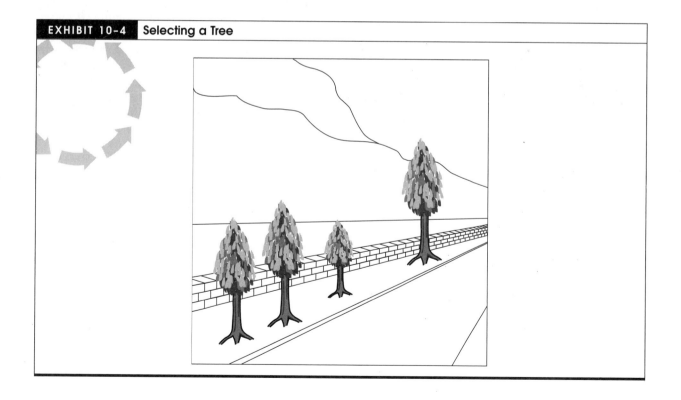

discourage applicants who, after all, come to us for a resolution of their problem and may not have much patience for exploring alternatives. You can reasonably rule out any alternatives that make no sense to you and the applicant. For example, you are not likely to agree to help an unemployed youth hold up a convenience store, even though that might accomplish the objective of obtaining enough money to buy food. In working with a young prostitute, however, do you seriously consider the viability of this trade as a source of support? Or would you insist on looking only at other alternatives? The reason for looking at alternatives is to avoid being entrapped by blinders that limit choice. We suggest that you consider only sufficient alternatives to be comfortable that there is choice for the applicant.

In some circumstances, you will not consider alternatives. If the applicant proposes a course of action that seems reasonable to you, this can simply be adopted; you can always introduce alternatives later, if the proposed course of action proves unsatisfactory. As we have noted, problem solving is a spiral process. You and your client will reconsider action plans, objectives, and even problem statements if progress toward the objectives falters.

Exploring the Presenting Problem

Focusing on the solution. Do you find it strange that we have discussed collecting data about desired solutions or objectives before talking about collecting data about the presenting problem? We have done so for three reasons:

1. Our focus is on objectives, wants, and solutions; this is a problem-solving not a problem-focused model for practice.
2. Starting with a focus on the feasibility of the applicant's desired solutions enhances motivation and hope. This follows from the engagement process, where we stress the importance of understanding client wants.
3. Problems and desired solutions are not separable. Discussion of the feasibility of the desired solutions will necessarily take you and the applicant back to a discussion of the presenting problem. You will be involved in a continuous process of testing out various ideas regarding the nature of the problem, the desired solution and whether it will address the problem, and alternative

ways of reaching the solution. You will be formulating hypotheses, testing these against the available data and information, rejecting some, and refining others, in a spiral process (Meyer, 1993).

Applicants come to agencies because they perceive a presenting problem; respondents are sent because someone else believes there is a presenting problem; and we reach out to prospects because we and our agency believe there is a presenting problem. Thus, we collect data regarding their perception of the presenting problem:

- What does the applicant want to have changed?
- Why did the problem first occur? How often is it experienced?
- What attempts have been made to resolve the problem? What have been the results of these attempts?

How should you divide your attention between exploring the presenting problem and collecting data regarding what the applicant wants and the feasibility of these objectives? Proponents of a solution-focused approach suggest that the worker should move very quickly to specifying the solution desired by the applicant and trying to accomplish that solution (Cowger, 1994; de Jong & Miller, 1995; de Shazer, 1988; Selekman, 1993, 1997). A problem-versus-solution debate, however, is largely a chicken-or-egg argument: Solutions are developed in response to a problem. Thus, attention to defining the problem allows you and the applicant to determine whether the proposed solution will in fact address the problem. We find the following guidelines helpful:

1. Try to understand the presenting problem and to formulate the problem for work in a way that points toward a solution desired by the applicant.
2. Begin collecting data regarding desired solutions as quickly as possible.
3. Be sure the desired solutions are linked back to the problem; will accomplishing the solution solve the problem presented by the applicant?
4. Be sure you and the applicant agree on the problem that you are trying to solve.

The person-in-environment (PIE) classification system. We have cautioned against any efforts to attach diagnostic or classification labels to clients. However, problem classification schemes that are consistent with the ecosystem focus have now been developed. These may be useful in conceptualizing the types of problems you are likely to encounter. Perlman (1968) described three categories of human problems: (1) deficiencies or deficits in tangible material means, deficiencies in personal capacity that restrict or thwart role performance, and deficiencies of knowledge and preparation; (2) personality disturbances or mental disorders; and (3) discrepancies in roles, including discrepancies between several valued roles, between expectations of self and others, or between personality needs and role requirements and discrepancies that result from ambiguous and contradictory definitions of roles.

William Reid and Laura Epstein (1977; Reid, 1978) have developed a classification scheme of eight problems they believe are amenable to the task-centered model of practice, which is a problem-solving model: (1) problems of interpersonal conflict, (2) dissatisfaction in social relationships, (3) dissatisfaction with formal organizations, (4) difficulties in role performance, (5) decision problems, (6) reactive emotional distress, (7) inadequate resources, and (8) psychological and behavioral problems. Building on Reid and Epstein's classifications, Northern (1982) added loss of relationships and cultural conflicts. Carol Germain and Alex Gitterman (1996) have developed a classification system consistent with their life or ecological model for social work practice. They identified three categories of problems: (1) life transitions involving developmental changes, status role changes, and crisis events; (2) unresponsiveness of social and physical environments; and (3) communication and relationship difficulties in families and other primary groups. Their work has made substantial contributions to the ecosystem approach in social work. A strength of these various approaches is that they classify the types of problems social workers address without linking problem classification to a particular service plan.

Recently, the National Association of Social Workers (U.S.) has developed and published the person-in-environment (PIE) system (Karls & Wandrei, 1994a, b), which is comprehensive, draws heavily from role theory, and is consistent with the ecosystem perspective. The PIE system describes, classifies, and codes the social functioning problems of adult social work clients. PIE creates uniform statements of social role; environmental, mental, and physical health problems; and client

strengths. The PIE system balances problems and strengths; it describes problems of both the person and the environment and qualifies them according to duration, severity, and the client's ability to solve or cope with them. PIE is not a diagnostic system, because it does not offer a cause-and-effect relationship for the problems identified. What it does is to provide social work with a language to describe its unique area of service.

PIE was developed out of concern about the inadequacies of other problem classification systems, especially DSM-IV. DSM-IV fails to meet the needs of social work, because the locus of the problem is placed in the individual and emphasis is on treatment of a specific disease or disorder. Social work needs a system that gives primacy to social functioning and recognizes the importance of interpersonal and environmental problems (Karls & Wandrei, 1994a).

The PIE system consists of four factors, in terms of which the applicant is described:

- Factor I: social functioning problems
- Factor II: environmental problems
- Factor III: mental health problems
- Factor IV: physical health problems

The focus of social work will be primarily on Factors I and II, although a description of the adult's functioning in all four is necessary to provide a complete picture. Social functioning is described in terms of the person's performance of social roles and includes the role in which the problem is identified, the type of problem in role performance, the severity of the problem, the duration of the problem, and the ability of the applicant to cope with the problem. Exhibit 10–5 lists the categories and subcategories of roles in which problems of social functioning may occur. The PIE manual (Karls & Wandrei, 1994b) provides descriptions and examples of nine different types of role performance problems. The applicant is rated on the severity and duration of the problem and ability to cope with the problem; for each index, you check one of six possibilities, each with a numeric value.

The descriptions of environmental problems focus on factors in both the physical and social environment that affect the applicant's social functioning and well-being. Six dimensions of the environment are considered (Exhibit 10–6). The PIE manual identifies specific potential problems in each of the environmental dimensions and

EXHIBIT 10-5	Social Roles Used for the PIE System

SOCIAL ROLE	CODES
Family Roles	1000.XXX
Parent Role	1100.XXX
Spouse Role	1200.XXX
Child Role	1300.XXX
Sibling Role	1400.XXX
Other Family Role	1500.XXX
Significant Other Role	1600.XXX
Other Interpersonal Roles	2000.XXX
Lover Role	2100.XXX
Friend Role	2200.XXX
Neighbor Role	2300.XXX
Member Role	2400.XXX
Other Interpersonal Role	2500.XXX
Occupational Roles	3000.XXX
Worker Role—Paid Economy	3100.XXX
Worker Role—Home	3200.XXX
Worker Role—Volunteer	3300.XXX
Student Role	3400.XXX
Other Occupational Role	3500.XXX
Special Life Situation Roles	4000.XXX
Consumer Role	4100.XXX
Inpatient/Client Role	4200.XXX
Outpatient/Client Role	4300.XXX
Probationer/Parolee Role	4400.XXX
Prisoner Role	4500.XXX
Immigrant Role—Legal	4600.XXX
Immigrant Role—Undocumented	4700.XXX
Immigrant Role—Refugee	4800.XXX
Other Special Life Situation Roles	4900.XXX

SOURCE: J. M. Karls & K. E. Wandrei, *PIE manual: Person-in-environment system.* Washington, DC: NASW Press, (1994), pp. 7–8.

provides for ratings of both their severity and duration, using the same indices as for role performance problems.

We find the PIE system attractive, for these reasons:

1. It presents a problem classification scheme consistent with the person-in-situation or ecosystem focus of social work.
2. It incorporates applicant strengths, coping abilities, and the environmental sources of problems and avoids labeling or stigmatizing.
3. It provides social work with its own classification scheme and should remove our need to use inadequate and inappropriate classification schemes that have been developed by other professions.
4. It will be an aid for conceptualizing, describing, and interpreting the types of problems that social workers encounter.

5. The system does not require a link between problem definition and intervention; you and the applicant are free to select the most appropriate interventions on the basis of the unique situation of the applicant and your knowledge base.

The weakness of the PIE system, as presented and described in the manual, is that assessment and problem classification are the responsibility of the worker. Thus, it retains the notion of assessment by an expert, rather than a participatory partnership between worker and applicant. According to Karls and Wandrei (1994a), the social worker should record what he or she perceives as a problem, even if the client would not necessarily agree. However, this responsibility is not inherent in the PIE system. We see no reason why problem classification cannot be jointly negotiated by worker and appli-

EXHIBIT 10-6	Environmental Systems Used for the PIE System

ENVIRONMENTAL SYSTEMS	CODES
1. Economic/Basic Needs System	5000.XX
Food/Nutrition	5100.XX
Shelter	5200.XX
Employment	5300.XX
Economic Resources	5400.XX
Transportation	5500.XX
Discrimination in Economic/Basic Needs System	5600.XX
2. Education and Training System	6000.XX
Education and Training	6100.XX
Discrimination in Education/Training System	6200.XX
3. Judicial and Legal System	7000.XX
Justice and Legal	7100.XX
Discrimination in Judicial/Legal System	7200.XX
4. Health, Safety, and Social Services System	8000.XX
Health/Mental Health	8100.XX
Safety	8200.XX
Social Services	8300.XX
Discrimination in Health, Safety, and Social Services System	8400.XX
5. Voluntary Association System	9000.XX
Religion	9100.XX
Community Groups	9200.XX
Discrimination in Voluntary Association System	9300.XX
6. Affectional Support System	10000.XX
Affectional Support	10100.XX
Discrimination in Affectional Support System	10200.XX

SOURCE: J. M. Karls & K. E. Wandrei, *PIE manual: Person-in-environment system.* Washington, DC: NASW Press (1994), pp. 24–25.

cant. If you find the PIE system attractive, we suggest that you use it as part of a helping partnership.

We also have some concern about the global nature of assessment in the PIE system. Many applicants and respondents expect prompt action to relieve the problems they are experiencing. Accordingly, we prefer assessment as a step-by-step, ongoing process. This does not preclude your using the PIE system, however. Once you and the applicant have identified a problem in one or two areas of the PIE classification, you can begin to identify solutions and action plans for these problems. Depending on your joint decision making, you may or may not return to other areas.

Linking problem classification to objectives and action plans. In Chapter 4, we suggested that classification is necessary as an aid to thinking but that it is unwise to base decisions about what to do on the classification, rather than on the specifics of the person-in situation. Does accepting a problem classification scheme, rather than completely individualizing

the problem statement, compromise the choice of an action plan?

The existence of a link between problem statement, objectives, and action plan is not, in itself, a warning sign. How a problem is stated implies the objectives, and the objectives sought are likely to at least limit the range of action plans that can be realistically considered. Formulating a problem for work with the client, however, is not the same as deciding what problem classification the client's ecosystem fits. The following guidelines will help you to struggle with this thorny problem:

1. Work from a specifically defined problem for work developed by you and the applicant in an ecosystem approach, rather than attempting to fit the applicant's problem into a preexisting problem classification.

2. If the stated problem for work fits a problem classification scheme, and if research evidence suggests that some action plans may be more successful for

resolving the problem than others, you must share this information with the applicant. Note that research evidence is a resource that you bring to the relationship for joint use by you and the applicant; it is not a source of authority that allows you to control the process.

3. Remember that research evidence is based on aggregated data and, consequently, only provides a probability that the action plan will result in the accomplishment of the goals; there will always be exceptions at the individual case level (Rubin & Babbie, 1997).

4. Within systems theory, the principle of equifinality suggests that there are many ways to reach a particular objective. You and the applicant have a responsibility to think hard about the objective you desire and the action most likely to achieve that objective, given the applicant's situation. Do not rely on any scheme that suggests that a particular problem classification automatically leads to a particular type of action plan.

Exploring the causes of problems. How important is it to understand the causes of a particular problem? At one time, this was thought to be essential; social workers spent considerable time trying to understand the causes of problems, through examination of the individual's developmental history and analysis of the environmental resources and opportunities. The notion that we need to understand the causes of the problem in order to seek solutions in the present and the future has been challenged, however (de Shazer, 1982, 1988; Kaplan & Girard, 1994; O'Hanlon & Weiner-Davis, 1989; Reid & Epstein, 1978).

Often the causes of current problems lie in the past but are intractable. We are interested in solving problems and accomplishing goals that will improve quality of living in the present; collecting data about past causes that cannot be changed will not contribute to present problem solving. Collecting data about present causes that can be subjected to change efforts may be helpful, but we must not become bogged down in trying to understand complex interconnections. While this may be a stimulating intellectual exercise, most clients want problems solved. We should move quickly to an understanding of their wants and how to accomplish these.

Another difficulty is that extensive exploration of causes, by dwelling on the negative, tends to diminish applicant hope and, as we know, hope is essential to motivation and the attainment of objectives. Hope is enhanced by exploring what the applicant wants, what can be done, and how we can do it.

Thus, exploring the causes of the problem is unlikely to be helpful early in work with the applicant; at that stage, the first priority is to understand applicant wants and develop an action plan. Later, if you encounter problems that appear intractable, and there is no progress toward objectives despite the implementation of an action plan, you and the applicant might agree to spend some time exploring what is contributing to the difficulty.

Discovering Strengths

Peter de Jong and Scott D. Miller (1995) find that developing well-formed objectives involves uncovering applicant strengths, because what objectives are achievable will depend on what strengths are available. In assessment, it is preferable to clarify competencies and resources, rather than to look for causes (Miley, O'Melia, & Dubois, 1995). We recommend a systematic discussion of the strengths and resources that the applicant brings to the work with you; this may take some patience and probing, because many people are unaccustomed to thinking in terms of their strengths (de Jong, 1998). You will also need to identify strengths and resources in the applicant's environment. What are the resources of the informal social support network? Can family, friends, neighbors, or others assist the applicant in reaching his or her goals? Finally, you are also an important resource to the applicant; identify strengths that you bring to the work, including the agency resources available to you.

Searching for exceptions, an approach developed in solution-focused brief therapy (Miller, 1992; Molnar & de Shazer, 1987; de Shazer & Berg, 1988), is useful for identifying strengths. Ask the applicant to describe exceptions to the problem. When does the problem not exist? What is different about those times? As exceptions emerge, you will be able to identify how the applicant or the situation contributes to the exceptions. In Reading 11-1 (Chapter 11), Michelle MacKenzie illustrates the use of this approach with a family disturbed by the aggressive behavior of the 7-year-old son. Once the family was able to discover times in which the behavior was not a problem, they were able to use their strengths to create similar circumstances. The search for exceptions underlines the importance of carefully considering times when things are going well, describing these times, and working at expanding and replicating these positive experiences.

Discovering strengths requires different questions than does discovering problems:

> Instead of asking, "what's wrong with this family?" the question becomes, "what are the strengths in this family that will help them grow and change?" Instead of asking, "why is this person mentally ill or delinquent or abusive?" the question can be, "what do they need to develop into more creative and loving adults?" (Weick, Rapp, Sullivan, & Kisthardt, 1989, p. 354)

Some guidelines for strengths assessment are provided in Exhibit 10–7, along with a case example.

DATA COLLECTION
Locating the Data

Where will you and the applicant collect the data needed to make an assessment? The applicant is the primary source of the data for decision making; the applicant is the expert on her situation, has struggled with the problem, and is the person most likely to know what she wants. It is important to give preeminence to the applicant's understanding of the facts and to believe them (Cowger, 1994).

You and the applicant may also find it necessary to collect data from other sources: from collaterals such as family members, friends, employers, and schools; and from other community professionals, agencies, and organizations. Remember that a primary goal of data collection is to identify strengths and resources within the community and within the applicant. In the case of the Birky family (Exhibit 2–15), it might be helpful to collect data about the availability of churches that the family would feel comfortable attending. The move to the city has disrupted their prior support systems; connections to religious organizations might help provide the support they need to cope with the loss of their child.

The files and records of your own agency will also provide data. However, we suggest caution in using file material. What you have is historic data; we are much more interested in present functioning and future goals. Moreover, file material may not bear on the present problem, may confuse the matter if it was gathered for a purpose unconnected with the present, and will reflect the biases, selective perceptions, and evaluations of the people who collected it. People change and grow; the agency record may no longer reflect the applicant and his situation.

Records usually represent the views of professionals who have worked with the applicant in the past and are artifacts of their time. They may not reflect the strengths

---

EXHIBIT 10-7	**Strengths Assessment**

Harry, a 45-year-old man, grew up in rural Kansas. He had been referred to the community support program upon discharge from the state hospital. Harry had been hospitalized 20 years ago, and carried a diagnosis of chronic schizophrenia. He had been placed in a board-and-care home that was located in a large urban area.

The community support staff became worried about Harry. It was reported that he was noncommunicative, had poor hygiene skills, and was hallucinating regularly. These problems were compounded by a report from the boarding home that Harry was packing his bags each night as if to leave. The staff predicted imminent rehospitalization.

Harry was referred to a social worker trained in the strengths perspective. Through the process of a strengths assessment, Harry's knowledge of and

interest in farm work came to the fore. The social worker took seriously this expression of interest and began working with Harry to find a place where he could use his skills.

They located a ranch on the edge of town where the owner was happy to accept Harry as a volunteer. Harry and the owner became friends and Harry soon established himself as a dependable and reliable worker. After a few months Harry recovered his truck, which was being held by his conservator, and began to drive to the farm daily. To the delight of the community support staff, Harry began to communicate and there was a marked improvement in his personal hygiene. At the time of termination with the case the owner of the ranch and Harry were discussing the possibility of paid employment.

Weick, C. Rapp, W. P. Sullivan, & W. Kisthardt. A strengths perspective for social work practice. *Social Work, 34*(4), 353–354 (1989).

orientation and optimism about growth that is central to social work in the early 21st century. All too often, records are a catalog of problems and deficits and may be of limited use in your current practice. If you do secure data from agency records, however, the applicant should be fully informed of this and should be a party to the data collection; you should discuss the resulting data openly and completely with the applicant. The applicant may disagree with much of the data and should have the opportunity to do so.

An important principle is that the applicant must be aware of the resources you are seeking and why they are being sought. If at all possible, the applicant's permission should be secured before any sources of data are accessed. Whether or not permission is secured, the applicant must know about the sources used, the data sought, and why the data is believed to be appropriate to the task at hand. You must share all the information on which decisions may be based if you are committed to the applicant's participation in decision making.

Interviewing in Social Work

There are five general sources of data: (1) the applicant's accounts; (2) the accounts of others; (3) questions and tests, either verbal or written; (4) observations; and (5) records of other professional or institutional systems. The most widely used tool for data collection is the interview, or group meeting, with the applicant, in which questioning and observation are used to gain data. You must decide the purpose of face-to-face meetings, what data are to be obtained, and how you want to structure the meeting. At one extreme is the nondirective interview or meeting, in which you follow the feeling and thinking of the interviewee or allow the group to reveal itself as it will. At the other extreme is the completely structured interview or meeting, in which you have a scheduled set of questions. You are also giving some structure to the interview and determining what data may be collected when you decide where and when it will be held, when you establish ground rules and norms for content and participation, and even when you arrange chairs for the persons involved. Careful thought should be given to the place of the first meeting. Is it to be on the applicant's turf or yours?

The nondirective interview, which allows applicants to tell their own story in their own way and at their own pace, is an important source of data that usually cannot be gained by direct questions. Listening carefully and observing body language will provide an understanding of the stress produced by the problem and something of the resources the applicant has tried to use or has found helpful. You begin to understand the applicant's cognitive pattern—the kind of reasoning he uses. You can collect knowledge about the applicant's coping strategies and strengths. In addition, you can gain considerable knowledge about relationships with others and with you. The applicant's understanding of social relationships and their utility can be estimated from his or her account of the problem, the way it came about, and what has been done to change it.

You will also use the interview to collect data from sources other than the applicant. In using these other systems, you should consider carefully the kinds of data they can provide and the need you have for those data. Be aware that some data sources may expect you to share data in return. You should discuss any data sharing with the applicant in advance. If you are unwilling to share data, you must make this known to the source when the interview is requested.

Excellent books have been written on the social work interview (Benjamin, 1987; de Jong & Berg, 1998; Epstein, 1985; Evans, Hearn, Uhlemann, & Ivey, 1998; Garrett, 1995; Gordon, 1992; Herson & Hassett, 1998; Kadushin, 1990; Schubert, 1991), and social work educational programs usually devote considerable time to interviewing skills. The distinguishing features of the social work interview are as follows:

1. It has a context or setting—often an agency that offers clearly defined services to applicants bringing specified problems, but sometimes the applicant's home, the offices of other agencies, or an informal community setting. The context provides a limit to the communications and a basis for the elimination of extraneous material.

2. It is purposeful and directed. Social work interviews are conducted to accomplish specific purposes; they are not casual exchanges of information or informal conversations. Once again, the purpose of an interview provides a basis for limiting communications and eliminating extraneous material.

3. It is limited and contractual. The social worker and applicant come together in a specific context for a

defined purpose; their communications are limited to those purposes.

4. It involves specialized role relationships. Worker and applicant interact with each other on the basis of their specialized roles. This, again, is a limiting factor, because their interactions will usually be confined to the expected behaviors of their specialized roles.

Interviewing as data collection. In Chapter 8, we discussed communication as an interactional process that involves giving, receiving, and checking out meaning. Interviewing is a specialized form of communication that, as we've just seen, is contextual, purposeful, and limited and involves specialized role relationships. You interview to secure data for use in decision making about the nature of the problem, desired solutions, and the service plan.

You must be concerned about the reliability and validity of your data collection procedures (Marlow, 1998; Rubin & Babbie, 1997). *Reliability* is the extent to which the interview produces consistent information. If different messages are received from an applicant at different times, you will need to be reasonably certain that the differences reflect actual changes in the person and are not a consequence of your interviewing style; otherwise, a reliability problem exists. *Validity* is the extent to which the information obtained reflects the actual perceptions, thoughts, feelings, and behaviors of the applicant. If the person is not sharing actual perceptions, thoughts, feelings, and behaviors, a validity problem exists, and you will need to adjust the interviewing

techniques. Concerns about validity and reliability have surfaced, for example, in interviewing children about sexual abuse. Separated from familiar settings and support systems and subjected to repeated interviewing and leading questions, the child may provide reports intended to please the interviewer, rather than accurate accounts of what took place. Likewise, critics of work on repressed memory syndrome have argued that repressed memories may be planted by therapists, whose clients endeavor, probably unconsciously, to provide what they want. (Loftus & Ketchamik, 1994; Barka, 1998; Wassel-Grimm, 1995). As interviewers, we are responsible for creating a climate in which the applicant is able to share valid and reliable information.

Creating a productive climate. By creating a climate in which the applicant can comfortably share thoughts, feelings, and perceptions, you increase the likelihood of securing valid and reliable data. This will call upon your skill in avoiding the barriers to communication noted in Exhibit 10–8 and in dealing with the obstacles to communication presented by applicant resistance.

Creating a productive climate for participation is integral to developing a helping relationship. In fact, one way to operationalize the concept of relationship is as a climate that is characterized by open and oral communications. You will need to ask questions in a manner that motivates and encourages applicant participation; your own participation may be minimal.

Providing a focus. With the applicant's participation, you will need to establish a purpose early and focus

---

EXHIBIT 10–8   Barriers to Productive Communication

1. Moralizing and sermonizing by using ``shoulds'' and ``oughts''
2. Advising and giving suggestions or solutions prematurely
3. Trying to convince client about right point of view through lecturing, instructing, arguing
4. Judging, criticizing, placing blame
5. Analyzing, diagnosing, making glib or dramatic interpretation; labeling client's behavior
6. Reassuring, sympathizing, consoling, excusing
7. Using sarcasm or employing humor that is distractive or makes light of clients' problems
8. Threatening, warning, or counterattacking
9. Stacking questions
10. Asking leading questions
11. Interrupting inappropriately or excessively
12. Dominating interaction
13. Fostering safe social interaction
14. Responding passively
15. Parroting or overusing certain phrases or cliches
16. Dwelling on the remote past
17. Going on ``fishing'' expeditions

SOURCE: D. H. Hepworth, J. A. Larson, & R. H. Rooney. *Direct social work practice* (5th ed). Pacific Grove, CA: Brooks/Cole (1997).

the interview in relation to the purpose. When pursuing what the applicant has said, you should pick up on areas related to the interview's central focus. Tangents are to be avoided; questions that lead into extraneous areas are not helpful. Material brought out in an interview may suggest a purpose and focus for subsequent interviews. You may choose not to respond to this material initially, but to bring it up later.

Aaron Rosen and Dina Lieberman (1972) report on an experimental study of the content relevance of workers' responses—that is, "the extent to which the content of an interactive response is perceived by a participant to be relevant and in agreement with the participant's own definition and expectations of the content to be dealt with in the treatment relationship" (p. 398). With compliant clients, workers with more training did significantly better at maintaining content relevance. Workers with less training had more content-relevant responses with aggressive clients, but many of their responses were harsh and retaliatory and ineffective in promoting communications. These findings point to the need for clear worker and client understanding of the purpose of the interview (Rosen & Lieberman, 1972).

Levels of response. In an interview, it is your responsibility to separate and identify the applicant's levels of response. Responses are typically on one of four levels:

1. Perceptual—interactions and communications around what the applicant perceives. What was seen and heard?
2. Cognitive—interactions and communications around what the applicant thinks. What meaning is attached to what was seen and heard?
3. Affective—interactions and communications around the feelings generated by the applicant's perceptions or cognitions. How does the applicant feel about what was thought or what was seen and heard?
4. Behavioral—interactions and communications around either past or anticipated behavior. How did the applicant behave in response to what was seen and heard? How might the applicant behave in the future.

You will interact with applicants at all these levels. For data collection, however, a thorough exploration of the perceptual and cognitive levels is necessary before moving to the feeling and behavioral levels.

Here's an example. Imagine that you are interviewing Chan, a 16-year-old boy who has frequent arguments with his father. Following a recent argument, Chan stormed out of the house and drove off in a neighbor's car. In discussing the situation, Chan will probably begin with the comment that he and his dad do not get along, that his dad does not understand him, or that his dad is unfair. These are all cognitive statements; they reflect his interpretation of perceived events. A frequent interviewing error is to accept the meaning that the applicant has reported and to move immediately into the areas of feelings and behavior. However, it is important to carefully explore Chan's perceptions: What took place? What did Chan see and hear? What did his father say? What did Chan say? What happened then? After exploring the incident in detail, you and Chan are both prepared to consider alternative interpretations of the events. After moving back to the perceptual level ("What did you see and hear?") and reconsidering the cognitive level ("What meanings do you attach to what you saw and heard?"), you may move the interview to the affective level ("What did you feel when this was occurring? Do I still detect a note of anger in your voice? As you look back on it now, what kinds of reactions are you having?"). And from the feeling level, the next logical step is to behavior ("What did you do when this happened? As you look back, what might have been other ways of handling yourself? In view of such experiences, if you and your father have future arguments, what are ways in which you think you might behave?"). You will expend considerable effort to collect an account of the incidents that occurred and to develop an interpretation of those incidents before moving into a consideration of Chan's feelings and behavior. Failure to explore the perceptual and cognitive levels in detail may lead to incomplete data for use in decisions about problem-solving plans.

Interviewing techniques. We regard interviewing as a disciplined art. But does discipline interfere with spontaneity? If you learn interviewing techniques, will you become mechanical and nonhuman? We think not. Learning appropriate techniques will increase your spontaneity for two reasons: (1) In the process of learning about interviewing, you become aware of—and able to deal with—barriers to communication in your usual responses to people; and (2) interviewing techniques expand the repertoire of responses available to you and consequently permit increased spontaneity because you are not locked into an earlier, limited set of responses. As Alfred Kadushin (1972) comments, "Technical skill is not antithetical to spontaneity. In fact, it permits a higher form of spontaneity; the skilled interviewer can deliberately violate the techniques as the occasion demands. Technical skill frees the interviewer in responding as a human being to the interviewee." (p. 2). As we have already noted, the graceful figure skater could not become spontaneous and free without many hours of disciplined practice; so it is with interviewing. Spontaneity and freedom do not come naturally but with discipline, with practice, and with learning.

We will consider five interviewing techniques for data collection, which are designed to encourage applicant participation: (1) open-ended questions, (2) probing, (3) avoiding biasing questions, (4) feedback, and (5) avoiding asking why.

Open-ended questions. An open-ended question— for instance, "Can you tell me a little about yourself?" or "What would you like us to do?"—cannot be answered yes or no; rather, it requires an essay-type answer. It is good to begin with open-ended questions, because they allow applicants to choose the starting point. If an applicant fumbles, you can come back with a more focused question. An interview can be thought of as a funnel; it begins with broad, open-ended questions and becomes more focused as you and the applicant narrow in on specific areas of concern. In the following example, a student is interviewing a social worker about her work:

> Following a brief statement by me concerning the purpose of the interview and an agreement by both of us concerning a time limit, I asked my first real question. "Do you view your work as social work?" In response, Joan asked, "What is your definition of social work?" I replied that rather than define social work at this point I would prefer to learn more about the work that she is doing, and perhaps at some time in another interview we could approach the topic of social work as it relates to her work. At this point in the interview I felt briefly that our roles in the interview situation had been reversed.

Starting this interview with an open-ended question might have both invited participation and brought focus to the purpose.

Probing. In probing, you invite applicants to say more about a particular topic. An open-ended question such as "Can you tell me more about that?" is probing. It relates to something the applicant has said and asks for more information. By gentle probing, you give direction to the interview. Exhibit 10–9 provides some examples of probing responses.

EXHIBIT 10-9 Probing Responses

Suppose that a client says, "I don't get along with my parents." Here are some possible responses that meet the two important requirements of interviewing: (1) encouraging the client to participate and (2) helping you to direct the interview.

- How do you feel about this?
- You don't get along with your parents.
- What do you mean when you say . . . ?
- Give me an example of how you . . .
- Tell me more about this.
- Oh?
- For instance?
- When did you first notice that . . .
- What are some of the things you and your parents disagree about?
- What is your dad like? What is your mom like?

- You seem to be very upset about this.
- Perhaps you could share some of your ideas about what has caused these problems.
- If your parents were here, what would they say about this problem?

And here are three rules of thumb:

1. Avoid asking a question that calls for a yes or no answer.
2. It probably never helps to ask the question why. If clients knew why they were having trouble, they wouldn't be seeing you.
3. Silence is a possible probing response. Because it tends to provoke anxiety, especially in adolescents, it generally loses its effect if too prolonged.

Richard J. Bealka, psychiatrist, Mental Health Institute, Independence, Iowa.

Avoid biasing questions. The data collection interview requires that you maintain neutrality. As Cournoyer and Byers noted in Reading 8-2, you must

> be aware that some questions may contain an implied suggestion or judgment. For example, you might say to a group member, "John, have you told your mother yet?" You may intend this as a simple request for information. However, John . . . might interpret this as a suggestion that, if he has not yet done so, he should tell his mother as soon as possible.

Tone of voice and nonverbal communications can betray bias as easily as your choice of words.

There is no inconsistency between the requirement of neutrality and your responsibility to provide input. The purpose of the data collection interview, however, is to secure reliable and valid information about the applicant's perceptions and interpretations; your input at this stage would have a biasing effect and should be avoided. Once you have learned the applicant's position and thinking, you may consider offering your own experience to the applicant, when various intervention strategies are under consideration.

Feedback. Feedback is an important technique for clarifying communication. In checkout, you use feedback that reflects back to the applicant what you are perceiving, in order to determine whether the communication is correct: "This is what I hear you saying"; "I seem to be hearing this"; "I see you're doing this"; "Am I understanding what you are saying is this?" This type of active listening may sometimes seem awkward, because it is seldom used in everyday conversation. However, it can avoid misunderstandings and also encourages the applicant to pursue conversation in a particular area. Rosen and Lieberman (1972) examined the use of feedback among social workers, on the basis of stimulus-response congruence—"the extent to which a response by one participant in the relationship provides feedback to the other participant that the message sent was actually received (p. 398)." They found that trained workers maintained a higher rate of congruent responses than untrained workers. This suggests that the use of feedback is a skill acquired by training.

Avoiding asking why. Asking why tends to produce defensive reactions. You will not usually be interested in asking applicants to explain their behavior. Rather, you

will ask them to describe their situation and to explore alternative ways of interpreting and reacting to that situation. In eliciting material for problem solving, it is more productive to ask, for example, "What was happening then? What seemed to be going on? Can you tell me what you were doing? What seemed to be the nature of the situation?"

Other Data Collection Tools

Observation. We all use observation of others in daily interaction; as a social worker, you will need to make deliberate use of the technique. As with oral questions, observation can be structured or unstructured, and you can be a totally uninvolved observer, a participant observer, or a leader-and-initiator observer. For example, you may give a group of children a game to play and then observe and record their actions without being in any way involved in the game; or you may be a committee member, both involved and observing; or you may serve as a committee chairperson while trying to observe the interactions of the members.

In the last example, it's reasonable to ask how effectively a chairperson can observe the interactions of other committee members. Another concern about observation involves the bias and selectivity of the observer. No one can possibly observe all the interactions of a group, or even all the facial expressions and changes in posture of a single interviewee. Observation requires sensitivity to others and the capacity to see small changes; it requires that you know yourself and your biases; and it requires you to reflect on what you want to learn through this process and how to do so. Since you cannot collect all the data on any one transaction, you must recognize that you collect only certain information and are therefore selective. You must know what framework guides your selectivity.

Questionnaires. You have been introduced to the development of questionnaires in your research courses (Marlow, 1998; Oppenheim, 1992; Rubin & Babbie, 1997) and will use these skills in your practice. Agencies often require new applicants to fill out intake forms. An anonymous written questionnaire may be helpful if a group is trying to decide a focus for future meetings and members seem reluctant to share their views openly with other members; it allows members to express an opinion without fear of penalty. Written exercises are sometimes used in family work to allow members to express themselves without the risk of directly attacking other members. A written questionnaire may also be useful for data collection in community organizing. Obviously, you will not use a written questionnaire with people who do not express themselves well in writing or see it as a dehumanizing device.

Data Collection by Applicants

We usually think of the social worker as doing the data collection, but the applicant may also be involved. For example, an applicant may be able to secure reports from other agencies, to collect data from friends and neighbors, and to research neighborhood resources—the availability of mutual aid groups, religious organizations, and so forth (Delgado, 1996). An interesting example concerns community service. In such programs, offenders have the opportunity to provide unpaid service to community organizations rather than to pay fines or serve jail time. In most probation agencies, the community service program is administered by a staff person who contacts public and nonpublic organizations and then places offenders in the available slots. An alternative approach is to help offenders develop a plan to go out and collect data about opportunities for community service at local organizations in their community and, in effect, to develop their own placement site. The respondent is involved as a participant in data collection and in deciding where to provide community service.

In community organizing, you will involve residents in data collection from other community members regarding matters that need to be changed and the desired goals. For example, returning to the Birky family (Exhibit 2–15), suppose that you and the family have decided to organize tenants in the housing development to reduce hazards to children, including the open ditch. Mr. and Mrs. Birky may assist in data collection by talking with neighbors to identify hazards to children and by helping to organize a neighborhood forum on the subject. We suggest that, in the assessment process, you and the applicant discuss your data needs and develop a plan that addresses how the data will be collected, by whom, and when.

You may also ask other persons to collect data for you. In some situations, a person close to the applicant and knowledgeable about the situation may interview the applicant for you. Also, you may have other professionals administer oral or written tests to collect data; psychologists, for instance, often use projective techniques, which allow applicants to impose their own frame of reference on some stimulus, such as a picture. Finally, to obtain a second source of information, you may ask another professional—or perhaps your supervisor—to interview the applicant.

PROCESSING DATA AND DECISION MAKING

Data are collected as a basis for decision making about the problem to be worked, the objectives, and the action plan. What is the role of the applicant in decision making?

Role of the Applicant

Views about the role of the applicant in decision making span a continuum from no involvement at all, at one pole, to the applicant as primary decision maker, at the other. At one of these poles, Cynthia Franklin and Catheleen Jordan in Reading 10-2 assume that the social worker will collect the data and take responsibility for decision making; no reference is made to involving the applicant. This may be due in part to their focus on workers in managed care behavioral health. Lack of applicant participation is not inherent in any of the assessment models that they describe.

At the other pole, Gale Burford, Joan Pennell, and Susan MacLeod in Reading 10-1 describe a Canadian experience with family group conferences. Family group conferences originated in New Zealand as a way of responding to youthful offenders and to children in need of care and protection (Hudson, Maxwell, Morris, & Galaway, 1995). In this approach, social workers and other professionals perform two functions. They facilitate a process of family decision making; and they provide the family with data for consideration in their decision making. The family also has data available from its own members and, in the case of youthful offenders, from the victims. The family then meets privately to develop a plan as to how to deal with the youthful misbehavior (often this involves making redress to the victim) or to provide for the safety, protection, and nurturance of their children. The plan that results from the family's assessment is presented to the professionals for their approval.

Family group conferences and other participatory approaches to assessment empower families and will enhance motivation to carry out the plan. Applicant participation in decision making also ensures that the applicant's frame of reference is adopted and facilitates the recognition of applicant strengths (Cowger, 1994; de Jong & Miller, 1995; Saleebey, 1997). As in all other phases of problem solving, you should negotiate assessment with your client (Dean, 1993). Exhibit 10–10 provides 11 guidelines for strengths assessment that incorporate client participation.

Use of Knowledge

Assessment is an active thinking and testing process that results in the integration of understanding and knowledge in such a way that the problem may be analyzed in terms of appropriate applicant actions and professional services. The test of a sound assessment is the contribution it makes to problem resolution and to guiding the actions that you and the applicant take. You will generate the assessment by posing a series of questions to yourself and to the applicant. The questions emerge from the material the applicant shares, from your professional knowledge of human beings, from the genesis and course of the problem, and from the effect of

common responses to the problem situation. You will be drawing on knowledge about key variables in situations similar to the applicant's—for example, knowledge regarding the meaning of loss if the applicant speaks of losing a spouse or knowledge regarding the stress of transition if the applicant has just retired.

In assessment, you need to determine the applicability of generalized knowledge to the particular situation of your applicant. You will ask questions in order to understand how your applicant's situation differs from the situation that would be constructed from generalized knowledge. For example, if the applicant has lost her husband, your generalized knowledge identifies the life tasks necessary after such a crisis and the feelings that usually accompany such an experience. You want to know whether the tasks and the feelings are problematic for the applicant and how she is coping with them. Thus, you might say, "It must be difficult to pick up the pieces and do all the things that have to be done around a house." Or a question may seem more appropriate: "Since your husband's death, has it been hard to do what you need to do around the house?" Or you may ask, "When two people live together, they tend to share a lot of household tasks. Has it been difficult for you to do all these things by yourself?" We suggest asking about tasks because it is usually easier for the applicant to talk about facts than about feelings. She may talk about feelings as she answers these questions. If not, you may make a more direct comment about feelings.

The problem-solving model asks you to consider the duration, previous occurrences, and precipitating

---

EXHIBIT 10-10 Guidelines for Strengths Assessment

These guidelines provide an alternative to existing normative and deficit models of diagnosis and treatment.

1. Give preeminence to the client's understanding of the facts.
2. Believe the client.
3. Discover what the client wants.
4. Move the assessment toward personal and environmental strengths.
5. Make assessment of strengths multidimensional.
6. Use the assessment to discover uniqueness.
7. Use language the client can understand.
8. Reach a mutual agreement on the assessment.
9. Avoid blame and blaming.
10. Avoid cause-and-effect thinking.
11. Assess; do not diagnose.

Source: C. D. Cowger, Assessing client strengths: Clinical assessment for client empowerment. *Social Work, 39*(3), 265–267 (1994).

factors of the problem. It is generally more difficult to solve a problem that has persisted for a long time. Applicants have usually formed some pattern of adjustment to a long-standing problem and may find it hard to consider a new approach. The factors influencing a recent problem are easier to understand; the applicant will not be so debilitated in trying to deal with it. If the applicant sighs and says the problem seems to have gone on forever, you may wonder how much energy is available to deal with it; the applicant may have a sense that it is unmanageable. In assessment, you must determine whether these assumptions abstracted from general knowledge are true for this particular person.

You must also understand why the applicant decided to ask for help. The answer to this question will tell you a lot. Something must be different now, or why would the applicant have come in today? Has the situation reached a point at which the applicant feels unable to go on without some sort of relief? Or did something happen that gave the applicant new hope or new urgency to attempt a solution?

You also need to know about previous occurrences of the problem and the applicant's prior attempts to change it. This information will permit some estimate of the applicant's capacity to plan, to look forward and predict outcome, and to invest energy and will provide some evidence of social skills and knowledge of social situations. You want to know whether the applicant possesses or is able to use the skills to deal effectively with problems. You also want to know how the applicant's situation has contributed to the inability to solve the problem. How much sustained action has the applicant been able to invest?

At the same time, you will use all your empathic skills to understand the meaning carried by the applicant's words and all your observational skills to read body language. Is the feeling that the applicant is expressing appropriate to the seriousness of the problem? If the problem is overwhelming, but the applicant appears untroubled and smiles a great deal, what theory might explain what is happening?

You will also be trying to apply your professional knowledge in order to understand the applicant's skills and environment. What does the applicant's account of the attempts at solution tell you about the available situational and environmental supports and resources and about the obstacles in the environment?

To illustrate the use of professional knowledge, let's return to Mr. Keene's situation in Exhibit 8–9. Assume that, at the point of the last recording, the worker left the agency and you were assigned to Mr. Keene. You are going to see him tomorrow. You have two tasks: to make a brief assessment of the situation on the basis of the information gathered by the last worker; and to plan for the interview, which will include testing your tentative assessment and considering the possibility of a different service plan.

In making the assessment, you will want to note the previous worker's definition of the problem and assessment of the situation. It appears that the worker focused on Mr. Keene's level of functioning relative to some notion of how an ideal father might relate to his children. There was no attempt to assess the systemic transactions of Mr. Keene's situation and Mr. Keene's development of parenting skills. Accepting that the children must have adequate care, do you agree with the previous worker that this is solely Mr. Keene's responsibility? The previous worker appeared to see Mr. Keene as a rather impetuous, dependent man, who was inconsistent in his relationship with the children and impulsive in his relationship with his wife. There was no evaluation of the meaning of the situation to Mr. Keene, the knowledge he had of the problem, or his social skills in dealing with all of the systems with which he suddenly had to interact. Do you think that the worker's focus on child care may have contributed to Mr. Keene's continuing problem? In attempting to develop a tentative assessment of the situation, you will want to go back to precipitating factors of the problem. What knowledge do you have of the situation and of the general meaning of such a situation to an individual? Let's take a look.

The problem began as a crisis for Mr. Keene. Suddenly his wife was out of contact with reality and had to be hospitalized. What do you know about the impact of crisis on people and their ability to cope? Would Mr. Keene have functioned better if the worker had given some attention to what the crisis meant to him? Moreover, a wife is more than just a child care person or a homemaker. What do you know about the relationship between Mr. Keene and his wife? And what do you know about the meaning of sudden loss of a spouse? Would the loss of his wife have been more difficult for Mr. Keene because of the relationship between them? How does he cope with this? Would he be able to be a better father if he had some help in coping with the loss of his wife? What is the meaning of Mr. Keene's dependency? Could it be a consequence, in part, of the crisis and the loss of his wife? Does your understanding of loss and crisis suggest possible interventions to help assess Mr. Keene's ability to cope and to offer him support?

Would all of the inconsistencies of Mr. Keene's behavior have been prevented if, at the beginning, the worker had assessed the situation differently? Suppose the worker had offered Mr. Keene support and help in dealing with the loss of Mrs. Keene. Did the first worker see the children or the home? What would it have meant to Mr. Keene if the worker had visited? What would it have meant to the homemaker?

Mr. Keene seemed unaware of the signs of Mrs. Keene's growing illness until the illness reached a crisis. Is it common for family members to be oblivious to changes in close family members? What does Mr. Keene understand about his wife's illness? Mr. Keene talks repeatedly about his lack of knowledge of her illness. How much knowledge does the average layperson have of the onset, course, and prognosis of mental illness? Did the hospital offer Mr. Keene any information about the cause of his wife's illness or the course of treatment? Can we expect applicants to deal effectively with a problem when they do not have the facts of the situation?

How much contact has the hospital staff had with Mr. Keene? What are their observations of his behavior and his relationship with Mrs. Keene? Would Mr. Keene like you to contact the hospital staff? Would he like you to visit his wife? Would he want to go with you? What would visiting the hospital contribute to your planning with Mr. Keene?

Your knowledge base should inform you that, in many instances of death and illness, family members feel remorseful, angry, or deserted. Is it possible that Mr. Keene's inconsistent relationship with the children and his wife comes from remorse and anger? Furthermore, our theories tell us that high levels of feeling restrict the ability to hear, understand, and use factual knowledge; when feeling is high, you may need to act to

reduce it before the applicant will hear what you say or be able to participate in planning. Does that information provide some guidance about whether to begin with information or with exploration of feeling? Would exploration of feeling help Mr. Keene develop a more consistent pattern of behavior?

In this case, the worker failed to consider Mr. Keene's situation or microenvironment and concentrated solely on his responsibility to care for the children. Yet an understanding of the total system is critical to the assessment of Mr. Keene's functioning. Further questions may be important. What is Mr. Keene's notion of the roles of husband and father? Does the macrosystem from which he comes set forth these roles in ways that conflict with the worker's and housekeepers' notions? Does Mr. Keene have an extended family support system? Can he turn to his neighbors? As you think about the plan for the first interview with Mr. Keene, what do you identify as the most helpful way to approach him? Your plan might look something like that in Exhibit 10–11.

Assessment Instruments

The various assessment instruments available (Boughner, Hayes, Bubenzer, & West, 1994; Reichertz & Frankel, 1993; Van Hook, Berkman, & Dunkle, 1996) can be grouped in three categories, on the basis of their intended purpose: (1) instruments to facilitate data collection; (2) instruments to aid in organizing and processing data; (3) instruments to contribute to decision making.

Instruments designed to facilitate data collection, including questionnaires and application forms, are used to speed up data collection; they may be computerized to ease data collection and tabulation for agency communication and statistical reports. While useful, these instruments should not be allowed to interfere with communication between you and the applicant. They need to be regularly reviewed. Are they balanced? Do they provide data that are actually needed? For example, an application form that asks for a description of the presenting problem should also ask what the applicant wants done about the problem; an application form that has a checklist for problem behaviors should also include a checklist for applicant strengths.

EXHIBIT 10-11   **An Interview Plan Reflecting a Systems Perspective**

Your plan for the first interview with Mr. Keene (Exhibit 8–11) might look something like this:

A. Problems that will need to be explored
  1. Reactions to change in workers
  2. Problems of grief and loss
  3. Problem of transition to single parent
  4. Care of children
B. Climate of the interview
  1. An attempt to convey caring for Mr. Keene and his feelings
  2. Acceptance and support
  3. Empathic and responsive; convey recognition of the value of his statements
C. Pace of interview
  1. Relaxed, try to match Mr. Keene's tempo
D. Data collection
  1. Be alert to clues; attempt to expand, amplify, and clarify client's meaning
  2. Ask Mr. Keene to amplify and expand meaning
  3. Within this climate, interview to explore support networks and hospital contacts,

knowledge of mental illness, and child care
E. Plan of interview
  1. Establish a beginning contact with Mr. Keene
  2. Learn more of Mr. Keene's struggles, worries, stresses
  3. Offer help to Mr. Keene in understanding his wife's illness
  4. Offer appropriate support to Mr. Keene
  5. Recognize Mr. Keene's struggles
F. Goal of interview
  1. A beginning understanding of the problems to be worked
  2. A beginning engagement with Mr. Keene that allows for working on the problem

In reading this plan, can you see how the questions related to assessment have been used to guide the interview? Notice how assessment of the loss, remorse, and pain of Mr. Keene over the illness of his wife affects the plan for the climate of the interview and its pace.

Instruments for organizing and processing data include outlines for organizing information; the format for the service plan presented in Chapter 11 and the sample case plan presented in Reading 11-2 (Exhibit 11–17) are examples. Other examples are genograms and ecomaps (Reading 2-3) and the social network map (Reading 14-1). These are tools for organizing data so as to obtain the information needed for decision making.

Instruments to contribute to decision making are usually designed to measure some underlying concept—self-esteem, social support, anger, family functioning, and so forth—that may be subject to change efforts. These instruments are usually scales or indices; the scale provides a score indicating the extent to which that concept is present or absent. Such assessment instruments have become very popular, because they lend a scientific aura to social work practice and they can often be administered quickly and cheaply.

These instruments need to be used with considerable caution. First, they are based on aggregated data. This means that there is a probability—usually known for a defined population—that the items on the questionnaire measure the underlying concept, but there will always be false positives—people for whom

this is not true. Findings from aggregated data cannot predict outcomes in individual cases; they can only be used to estimate the probabilities of an outcome (Rubin & Babbie, 1997). When using one of these scales, you need to know its validity. Scales are standardized for one or more populations; they may not be valid and reliable for other populations, although they are often used for populations for which they have not been standardized. You may feel more comfortable using the scale if it has been standardized on several different populations, at several different points in time, and has produced relatively consistent reliability and validity scores.

You have a professional responsibility to be thoroughly familiar with any assessment instruments employed; you must have detailed knowledge as to how the scale was developed, populations for which it has been standardized, and its known reliability and validity. We strongly recommend that you discuss any results of the tests and instruments with the applicant and treat this as information to be considered for decision making. You and the applicant should decide together whether the results from the assessment instrument are useful to decision making.

Assessment as Negotiation

The purpose of assessment is to develop a service plan acceptable to you and the applicant. This is most likely to occur if you negotiate the definition of the problem, the desired goals, and the appropriate action plan with applicants. Some social workers feel that they possess the power of professional expertise and are uncomfortable with the notion of negotiation. In our view, it is essential to a helping partnership. Negotiation has been recognized as a way of working with respondents (Murdach, 1980), working out differences of opinion regarding the problem, arriving at agreement on goals (de Jong & Miller, 1995), and reaching agreement regarding the action plan. Negotiation requires a communication process and respect for each other's views.

ASSESSMENT AS A CONTINUOUS PROCESS

Assessment involves collecting data, processing and organizing data, and making decisions by negotiation between you and the applicant. These processes will continue throughout your work with the client. Service plans will require revision; you and the client may decide to pursue different objectives; and previously unknown data will surface and require that decisions be modified. Thus, assessment is a continuous process.

Partialization

Partialization is the process of selecting which of the problems brought by the applicant will be addressed first. You cannot do everything at once; thus, it is necessary to make decisions about where to begin. For example, the Birky family (Exhibit 2–17) has a very large number of problems stemming from their ecosystem. Working with more than one or two would overwhelm the family and the worker.

But how do you partialize? As with most decisions, this is a matter to be negotiated between you and the applicant. One possibility is to start by asking what issues are troubling the applicant and what solutions are sought. You may start with either problems or solutions; the two will be linked as you formulate a specific service plan. The applicant can make a list, to which you will suggest additions on the basis of your own observations and experience. If the applicant disagrees with your perception of a problem area, you have two options: (1) to withdraw your proposed problem but to indicate that you would like to return to it at a later time; and (2) to explore the differences of view between you and the applicant. Be open to the possibility that your perception is incorrect. In the early contacts with applicants, the first option is preferable, unless the matter is very urgent and may involve the safety of others. You can always raise the topic again when the client is more comfortable with you.

Once you have generated a list, ask where the applicant would like to start. It is highly advisable to begin with the problem that is of most interest to the applicant, if at all possible. The work is more likely to be successful within the framework that the applicant chooses.

Sequencing of Service Plans

How many problems can you and the applicant attempt to resolve at one time? We suggest that you focus initially on a single problem area, along with the associated objectives and action plans. As you make progress in that area, you and the applicant may then take on additional problems, solutions, and action plans. These may be items from your original list, matters that you have held for reconsideration, or new problems that have developed from your work together. You can discuss, negotiate, and phase in new service plans as soon as you and the applicant feel comfortable in doing so. Once some successes have been achieved, applicant motivation will improve. Avoid overwhelming people. If you are unsure whether the applicant is ready to move into another area, ask; the applicant is your best source of information.

CHAPTER SUMMARY

Assessment is the use of information to make decisions about the nature of the problem, what is to be done about the problem, and how this is to be accomplished. It includes the collection and organization of data to provide the information needed for decision making. In the ecosystem approach, assessment enlists applicant participation and does not involve labeling; accordingly, we caution against using classification schemes such as DSM-IV. The person-in-environment (PIE) system may be useful, especially if it can be administered in partnership with the applicant. This system is based on the ecosystem perspective, does not link problem classification with preferred treatment, and does not have the stigmatizing effects of DSM-IV.

Data collection responsibilities may be shared with the applicant; in most situations, the applicant will be the primary source of data. Data collection usually involves interviewing. You are responsible for creating a climate in which the applicant can share; providing a focus for the data collection; distinguishing between the levels of response (perceptions, cognitions, behaviors, and feelings); and using interview techniques that encourage applicant participation. We recommend that your data collection efforts be guided by the following principles:

1. The applicant is the primary source of data.
2. The applicant must be informed of your data collection activity.
3. Data are collected for use.
4. You are willing to share data with the applicant.
5. You acknowledge what is known.

Data are collected regarding the applicant's desired solutions, the feasibility of these solutions, applicant and worker strengths, strengths in the applicant's environment, and the presenting problem.

You and the applicant will interpret the data collected in order to make decisions about the nature of the problem for work, the desired objectives, and the service plan most likely to accomplish the objectives. Decision making is participatory; to a large extent, assessment is a process of negotiation directed toward arriving at a service plan about which you and the applicant agree.

Finally, assessment is a continuous process. As you and the client work together, new data will be collected, new information will come to light, and new decisions will be made. You will be working with clients to solve problems and accomplish goals in sequential patterns and will be facing new problems and objectives as your work progresses. This requires the ability to partialize, especially at the beginning, when you must not take on more than you and the applicant can handle.

A LOOK FORWARD

At the beginning of this chapter, we indicated that a service plan results from assessment. In Chapter 11, we will pull together the major themes from the chapters on engagement, data collection, and assessment by considering the three components of the service plan:

• the statement of the problem for work
• specific objectives to be accomplished
• the action plan to accomplish these objectives

The action plan will include the specific activities that must be carried out to accomplish the objectives. We will discuss action plans in terms of tasks for the client and the interventive roles that the worker implements.

In Reading 10-1, Gale Burford, Joan Pennell, and Susan MacLeod describe family group conferences and provide a case illustration. Family group conferences, which originated in New Zealand (Hudson, Maxwell, Morris, & Galaway, 1996), reverse the traditional roles of social worker and applicant in data collection and assessment. The social worker and other professionals provide data to the family; the family processes the data and develops a plan. The family is empowered to do assessment, although the plan that results from their assessment is subject to approval by the professionals.

In Reading 10-2, Cynthia Franklin and Catheleen Jordan describe four assessment models that have been used in social work—the psychosocial, cognitive-behavioral, life, and family systems models. They examine the theoretical principles supporting these models and indicate how a social worker in a managed care behavioral health setting would use each one. Franklin and Jordan develop their own assessment model—technical eclecticism—by borrowing approaches from the other assessment models, even though the theoretical bases may be inconsistent. In contrast to the approach developed in this book, Franklin and Jordan perceive assessment as a process that is carried out by the professional and often involves labeling the applicant. They believe that categorization of the applicant's problem provides an indication of the treatment plan.

READING 10-1 *Family Group Decision Making**

Gale Burford, Joan Pennell, and Susan MacLeod

INTRODUCTION

Social workers have a historic commitment to enabling people to take charge of their individual and collective lives—what we today refer to as empowerment. At the same time, social workers are keenly aware of the dangers of leaving families to their own devices, especially in situations of violence against children and women (Pennell, 1995; Schechter, 1982; Sinclair, 1985). While social workers must be watchful that empowerment does not become a rationale for government cutbacks and off-loading of responsibilities onto families and communities, they still need to move ahead with strategies for advancing people's self-determination in safe and effective ways. This chapter provides an example of one means—family group decision making—by which social workers can fulfill their mandate, through encouraging partnerships in which family, community, and government representatives work together to resolve family violence.

In the Canadian province of Newfoundland and Labrador, the Family Group Decision Making Project tested the New Zealand approach of family group conferencing in situations of family violence—that is, abuse against child and adult family members. In this reading, the model is overviewed, and then a case example is used to highlight relevant practice elements, particularly for ensuring the safety of the participants.

BACKGROUND TO THE PROJECT

New Zealand's Children, Young Persons and Their Families Act (1989) outlines how the extended family is to be brought together and resourced as a decision-

*An original reading prepared for this book. It is based on a demonstration project that received funding from the Canadian federal departments of Health, Human Resources Development, Justice, Solicitor General, and Heritage, as well as the Newfoundland & Labrador Department of Social Services. In Nain, the project was cosponsored by the Labrador Inuit Health Commission. Support for the project also came from the Newfoundland & Labrador Department of Justice, Public Service Commission, Women's Policy Office; Correctional Services of Canada; Royal Newfoundland Constabulary; Royal Canadian Mounted Police; and the Provincial Association Against Family Violence.

making body in cases of child protection and youth justice. The model of family group conferencing has been described in detail, and some research has been carried out, especially on youth justice conferences (Atkin, 1991; Connolly, 1994; Maxwell & Morris, 1993, 1996; Paterson & Harvey, 1991; Walker, 1996).

To adapt an imported model to the Newfoundland and Labrador context, the university researchers teamed up with representatives from a broad cross section of groups, including women's groups, cultural organizations, police, child welfare, and correctional services. They formed into a provincial committee and local advisory committees in each site where the model was to be tested. This effort in itself took nearly two years and involved first working out a clear statement of philosophy and then policies for the project.

In discussion with local leaders, three sites in the province were selected for demonstration: Nain, an Inuit community in northern Labrador; the Port au Port Peninsula, a rural Newfoundland area with people of British Isles, French, and Micmac heritage; and St. John's, the province's capital and largest urban center, with residents of largely British and Irish descent.

During the course of the project, 37 conferences were held (32 families; four had reconvened conferences), with a total of 472 participants, of which the large majority were family, relatives, or other close supports (384) rather than professionals (88). In order to enhance the validity and reliability of the findings, research and evaluation information on the family group conferencing was collected through diverse methods and from a range of perspectives (Ristock & Pennell, 1996). Descriptions of the model and the results of an implementation study are available (Burford & Pennell, 1995a, b, 1996; Burford, Pennell, & MacLeod, 1995; Burford, Pennell, MacLeod, Campbell, & Lyall, 1996; Pennell & Burford, 1994, 1995, 1996). Reports will be available on the findings from a follow-up study and economic analysis of the project.

PHILOSOPHY AND MODEL

Family group decision making was predicated on the assumption that, in order for anyone in a family to be safe, everyone has to be safe. Focusing only on the abuse of a child when older teens or adults are also being abused does not solve the problem and may even put further at risk those other people who are being abused. In particular, a rationale was developed for avoiding the kind of blaming of mothers that can go on in child protection when the only leverage the authorities have is to intervene on behalf of the child, rather than strengthening families by empowering women (Callahan, 1993). The model challenges mandated authorities to work together with the extended family to bring a halt to the abuse, as an alternative to the marginalization of the family, that can occur in fragmented service systems (Stark & Flitcraft, 1988; Swift, 1991) and in judicial proceedings (Braithwaite, 1989).

Inherent in this philosophy is the notion that families can only come together safely and make appropriate decisions if emotional support and protection is provided throughout the process and if needed resources are made available to assist them in carrying out their decisions. In our adaptation of the model, safety was provided in a variety of ways. The university hired site coordinators who were known for their community work, especially in efforts to end violence. Training in the approach was provided not only to the coordinators but to a broad range of community and government participants, so that they could work together effectively.

In addition to a local advisory committee already mentioned, each site had either a community panel to advise the coordinator on working with the families or a professional consultant in the case of Nain, where the advisory committee recommended that the Labrador Inuit Health Commission both cosponsor and provide the consultancy. Each coordinator worked from the general guidelines provided by the project to flesh out specific procedures for safety at the local level (MacLeod & Campbell, 1996).

THE FAMILY GROUP CONFERENCE (FGC)

The coordinator then began to accept referrals from any protective services agency, or combination of agencies, who could pay for the costs of bringing the extended family together and could resource the family's decisions if they agreed with the plans the family developed. At first, some practitioners were reluctant to refer families, because they were concerned about safety issues, worried that the families could not come up with quality decisions or would not follow through on plans,

and wondered if the government would actually resource the plans and if involvement in the project would create extra work for them. The coordinators' tasks at this stage involved working to overcome systemic resistance to the use of an empowerment approach; some of the people who spoke the language of empowerment balked in the moment of letting go, as is often the case during times of restructuring and transition when powerful groups are seeking to reinvent themselves (Burford, 1994).

The coordinator contacted family members, assisted them in identifying who their family members were, prepared all persons for the meeting, facilitated the meeting, and ensured that the plan was specific before submitting it to the referring authorities. The meetings themselves consisted of an opening phase, during which the coordinator worked to set a climate of respect, safety, and clarity of purpose; an information-giving phase, in which the coordinator promoted a sense of authenticity and understanding by having the investigating authorities and other professionals express their concerns and provide information about the identified problems; a phase of family private deliberations, at which time the professionals left the room to foster ownership by family members over the plan that they developed; and a phase of firming up the plan, in which the coordinator returned to the room with the family and worked to anchor their ideas and clarify roles in writing.

REFERRAL AND PREPARATION

Wendy's story illustrates the model. Wendy, age 15, was referred to the Family Group Decision Making Project by a child protection worker, with the endorsement of the police, after she showed up at school with a black eye. She alleged that her father had hit her because she had taken some of his drugs to sell at school. Wendy's friend convinced her to talk to the guidance counselor outside of school. The guidance counselor subsequently contacted the child welfare department, as is mandatory, and an investigation was started. The investigation involved the police, because of the implication of drugs and the alleged assault. It was brought out during the investigation that the father had a lengthy criminal record and a history of violence; he admitted that he was currently an alcoholic. It also came out during the investigation that Wendy's younger sister, Natalie, and her father had had many physical altercations previously, including an occasion on which he assaulted her.

Wendy's older sister, Melanie, maintained that "none of this involves me." No charges were laid against Wendy for her alleged drug dealing, and no charges were laid against the father for assaulting Wendy, as he agreed to move out of the house. Everyone in the family admitted that the incidents as described by Wendy were true. This was the family's first involvement with the police and with child welfare in the province since their return a few months earlier.

Preparation is very important to the success of the meeting. Laying the groundwork for the conferences was the most time-consuming of all the coordinator's activities and usually took place over a period of three to four weeks. Tasks included:

1. Compiling the invitation list—ensuring that all sides of the family (including those of the biological fathers) were invited to the conference.

2. Identifying support persons—requiring that all young survivors be accompanied at the conference by an adult who would stay by them to provide support; and encouraging the same for all adult survivors, as well as for abusers and others who might feel at risk during the conferences.

3. Securing personal statements—having the participants (especially young people, mothers, and abusers) prepare in advance a written statement of their views, to be presented at the conference.

4. Training professionals—preparing the child protection workers, police, and other professionals on how to present their reports at the conference.

The coordinator's notes reveal her anxiety during the preparation phase of Wendy's case: "This is the one I was most concerned with in terms of safety of family members during the FGC process. The dad . . . has . . . history of violence, alcohol and drug abuse, and criminal behavior yet at present there are no social controls (parole or probation) monitoring his behavior." But she felt that she had paid careful attention throughout the planning to the safety of the family members:

> This family was a perfect example of how the safety measures this project utilizes are effective in keeping people safe . . . The offender as well as the mom and kids in the family chose a support person. He identified this as a way he could feel more in control of his emotions and a way that would ensure he would not blow up or leave during the FGC.

THE CONFERENCE

The hours leading up to the conference were typically an anxious time. The coordinators' skill in turning a last-minute obstacle into an opportunity was tested time and time again. In Wendy's case, the family decided three days prior to the conference to change its location. As the coordinator observed, "While this was a nightmare for me it was obviously the right thing for the family and added to their ownership of the process and the FGC." The arrival of the family members, their seeing one another's faces, and joining together in the circle demonstrated their willingness to overcome what were often considerable odds. For the children and young people, seeing their relatives come into the room "for them" proved therapeutic.

Opening the Conference

The task of the coordinator was to set a climate of respect for the family, including any rituals that might be important to them, while at the same time making the purpose of the meeting very clear. The coordinator would have had the opportunity to find out from the family members what would be a good way to open the meeting, in what order to introduce people in attendance, and who should be called upon to give an opening comment or prayer, if this was the family's preference. The coordinator would typically name the abused person or persons at this stage and repeat, for example, "We are here for Wendy, to make sure she is safe," thereby reinforcing the purpose of the conference.

The mother's eldest brother opened Wendy's conference with words of welcome. This was fitting, as all family members demonstrated a great deal of respect for this man; years before, he had taken on the role of parent with his younger siblings when both their parents died. He was now clearly viewed as the head of the family. In addition, he had organized the use of the meeting space at his community hall and was therefore also in the role of the host for the conference.

Information Giving

First, the authorities were asked to present the facts from the investigation or assessment, then other professionals or community leaders were invited to provide information on the general area of concern, and finally personal statements by family members were read to the group. When the authorities gave their reports, the conferences tended to be quite emotional, not only because the family—along with their relatives and other close supports—heard the facts, but because they witnessed each other's reactions. The coordinator's successful efforts in rehearsing the authorities for the presentations paid high dividends at this stage.

Reflecting back on Wendy's conference, where both the child protection worker and a police officer were present, the coordinator wrote:

> The impact of having the officer speak was significant in that it emphasized the seriousness of the situation for the family and criminalized for them what had become part of their daily life. Both the officer and the Child Protection Worker were respectful, clear and detailed in their presentations.

Later, when discussing the conference, the coordinator noted that the police officer

> made it clear what charges could have resulted . . . I think the family saw the police in a more positive role than in the past. The kids in the family have grown up with a "Don't tell the cops" ethic . . . They saw [the child welfare social worker] in a very positive light. She was clear and specific, didn't gloss over anything. She had good rapport with them. She hadn't antagonized any of them. No one [in the family] disputed the facts that the police officer and social worker presented.

Invited guests gave information to the family on a specific topic, such as the impact of sexual abuse, handling attention deficit disorder, or, in Nain, traditional practices of family support. Normally, the coordinators and investigative authorities were discouraged from acting in the role of information giver in order to keep their roles distinct. In Wendy's family, the guest speaker on alcohol and violence was unexpectedly unable to attend, as the coordinator noted in her journal, "The child protection worker and I shared this role of information provider and in this instance it worked fine because the family had a great deal of respect for this worker and saw her as a helper."

One of the most poignant moments in the conference was when the family members' prepared statements were shared:

> Most family members had their support person read their statement (except Mom). The children's statements had a major impact on the family. Dad used his statement as a way of taking responsibility for his behavior and

expressing his sorrow to his family. The uncle (mom's brother) who was his support person, cried when reading the Dad's statement as did most family members, however they did not let him off the hook at all and the statement was sincere rather than an attempt to glean sympathy and minimize the behaviors . . . The two uncles who attended the meeting were people the dad had respect for and he wanted their approval. It was imperative that they be present at the FGC as this ensured the Dad's attendance and his good behavior. It was they who made him feel shame about what he had done, not the officials present.

It was important at the end of this stage for the coordinator to again check with the family to find out if they still agreed that there was a problem. if they did not, we were always prepared to call the conference to a halt, thank everyone for coming, and refer the case back to the referring worker.

THE FAMILY'S PRIVATE TIME

Once the information stage was complete, including an opportunity to ask questions, and reassurances had been given that people could be brought back if the family had further questions, the moment came when the coordinator facilitated the transition to the family's private deliberation time. Of course, the coordinator was instructed not to leave if violence was imminent but that didn't happen at any of the 37 conferences. The professionals—especially the therapist—felt nervous at the idea of leaving the family on their own, with just themselves and their chosen support people; doubts were expressed that these dysfunctional families could talk purposefully without a professional in the room. Initially, even our own coordinators, and some family members, were skeptical, but any time a professional person was allowed to stay in the room the professional took over overtly or subtly, for lack of the patience to wait the family out, let them express their pain, and coalesce.

Perhaps the professionals had a blueprint in mind for how a family ought to reach a decision. In practice, our research confirms, it is not always by everyone having an equal say. In Wendy's conference, the observer's notes report that Natalie was

> very vocal . . . Wendy was the opposite. She hardly spoke at all, but quietly sanctioned any decisions by interpreting and writing all family decisions, thereby giving them her seal of approval. Melanie, unfortunately, said virtually nothing throughout the conference.

The families each had their own way of expressing themselves and of approaching their purpose. Like other groups who come together to work out solutions to problems, their strategies were not always orderly or elegant, but they got the job done. Only one of the 32 families failed to come up with a plan.

FIRMING UP THE PLAN

When the family groups felt that they had addressed all the issues in the plan, the coordinator and the referring worker were invited back into the room to review what the family was recommending. The emphasis was on making sure that roles and tasks were clear. At Wendy's conference, the plan was well in hand by the time the coordinator returned to the room:

> Wendy ensured she had control of the plan and the decisions agreed upon at the FGC by being the note taker during private deliberation time. She did a fabulous job and had all decisions recorded in great detail. When I asked her at the end of the FGC if she was satisfied with the plan, she grinned and said, "I wrote it, didn't I?"

Key points from the plan included:

- counseling for the two younger daughters
- counseling for the parents to deal with their addictions, their relationship, and their parenting, and the father's violent behaviors
- regular family outings (without involving intoxicants)
- curfews for the daughters
- separate housing for the father until he had completed his treatment
- a safety plan (for example, calling the police and relatives) in case the father arrived at the home inebriated or became violent
- a review meeting of the family and child protection to determine if and when it would be safe for the father to return home
- consistent monitoring by the child protection worker

The costs for the counseling and transportation were to be paid by Child Protection.

But what about the oldest daughter Melanie, who never spoke up? Does this plan represent her interests? It appears so. At the end of the conference, all the family members and the professionals said that they were quite satisfied with all aspects of the conference; the same was true two weeks later, when the researcher interviewed family members about the conference. The researcher wrote, "The three [daughters] seem to be very happy with their lives now that there is peace in the house and some routine in their lives." During the follow-up interview a year later with the aunt, the researcher reported:

> Overall, [the aunt] felt that the FGC left the family better off. It essentially eliminated the abuse evident in the family and made [the mother] a "better person." [The mother] quit drinking, smoking and did all of the extra counseling that was suggested in the plan. According to [the aunt], up until their departure to [another province], [the mother] was doing quite well. The girls also held up their end of the deal by keeping their curfews [and attending counseling]. [The father] on the other hand, did not put as much effort into it, in [aunt's] opinion. She's pretty sure that he did not attend any of the counseling sessions that he said he would.

The aunt's progress report corresponds with the national police records and provincial child welfare records, which indicated that there had been no further reports, allegations, or investigations of abuse with this family during the 12 months following the conference.

Reflecting on her experience with the family and the conference, the social worker from children's protection services said: "As a worker, we are so used to going out and confronting people on the issues . . . it's so much more effective with everyone there." Before transferring the family to another worker, she visited the family home two months after the conference and again at six months. The father was even present for the second visit but was not living in the home. The mother and daughters said on both occasions that the plan was working and, in particular, the father was not drinking.

STRENGTHS AND LIMITATIONS OF THE MODEL FOR SOCIAL WORK

The strengths of the model for social work are numerous:

1. The abuse is brought out in the open where it can be discussed.
2. The abuser is shamed in a way that does not endanger, but rather serves to safeguard, survivors.
3. The family group is empowered to make important decisions.
4. Nonadversarial relationships between the family and the professionals are fostered.
5. Family and community resources are mobilized on behalf of survivors.

On the other hand, the model calls for a substantial commitment to community development and requires coordinators with considerable communication skills. The model will seem counterintuitive to administrators in many service delivery systems, which are operated in a top-down, expert-driven manner, and some professionals are not used to a more collaborative environment that empowers families nor to the pressure for accountability. It is best used in systems that are committed to developing thorough and ongoing case review and planning models. Moreover, the use of the model illuminates problems of interdisciplinary collaboration, especially around cooperative resource allocation. The idea that different departments will flexibly allocate their resources in the service of an individual family's plan challenges the status quo. Typically, a block of services is purchased in the hope that the professionals' assess-

ments and recommendations will mesh up with those purchases.

The model also challenges the ways in which many professionals like to work, because it operates around the family's needs; hence, the conferences typically took place outside of normal working hours and lasted on average around six hours. We did not experience resistance from professionals to meetings in the evenings or on weekends, but this was a demonstration project. Would the same cooperation exist on an ongoing basis?

The entire process lends itself to the empowerment philosophy of the social work profession. After a number of conferences had been held, and general anxiety about the use of the model had dissipated, the assistant director of child welfare commented, "Once you understand it, family group decision making seems . . . well, really, it's just good social work practice."

READING 10-2 *The Clinical Utility of Models and Methods of Assessment in Managed Care**

Cynthia Franklin and Catheleen Jordan

Social work practice is changing with the advent of managed care and managed behavioral health care. Managed care is a way of financing health, mental health, and social services in which the focus is on cost containment and increasing the quality of clinical services delivered (Strom-Gottfried, 1997). Managed care systems are changing the way that social workers and other professionals conduct their practices in both public and private agencies. Indeed, the managed care context is blurring the boundaries so that the distinction between public and private practice no longer applies (Franklin & Johnson, 1996).

The current trend in managed behavioral health care is to finance brief and effective service delivery models (Corcoran & Vandiver, 1996; Franklin & Johnson, 1996; Strom-Gottfried, 1997; Winegar, 1993). These systems mandate the development of best practices, accurate assessment, and diagnosis to see that clients are referred to the most effective, cost-efficient interventions, with an emphasis on the measurement of case

outcomes. To compete in market-driven social services and mental health care delivery systems, practitioners will need a variety of skills in empirically based assessment and an ability to monitor systematically the effectiveness of their practices (Blackwell & Schmidt, 1992; Corcoran & Gingerich, 1994; Giles, 1991; Lazarus, 1995; Sabin, 1991).

Therefore, greater sophistication in assessment and measurement techniques is necessary for competent practitioners. In social work practice, assessment denotes different but related processes: (1) the determination of what interventions and resources are needed to help a client solve problems; (2) an evaluation that leads to a clinical diagnosis—for instance, assignment of an accurate diagnostic label from DSM-IV; (3) a set of interventions that reveal relevant information about the client but also introduce information that produces change; and (4) an ongoing evaluation of a client's progress toward treatment goals.

Over the past 20 years, social work has moved toward the use of standardized measures as part of clinical assessment; a broad literature advocates that

*An original reading prepared for this edition.

single-case designs be used to monitor the progress of outcome goals (Blythe & Trippodi, 1989; Fischer & Corcoran, 1994; Hudson, 1989; Jordan & Franklin, 1995; Levitt & Reid, 1981). Many academic social workers saw the need to produce clinical researchers and wanted students to practice in ways that would contribute to the empirical knowledge base concerning practice effectiveness. The impulse to train practitioners as researchers arose, in part, out of social work's failure to produce outcome studies that contribute to its own knowledge base (Franklin, 1994).

This approach did not prove very successful. The responsibility for producing clinical research should be the role of the academic social workers whose job description entails research; it should not be a primary role of practitioners, who have little time to produce clinical research—and are likely to have even less time in the managed care environment. Practitioners are required to familiarize themselves with research incorporating the best-known empirically based practices for different problems. Further, they must demonstrate that what they are doing with their clients is cost-effective. Diverse skills in assessment and outcome measurement are needed in order to practice in an effective and accountable manner.

In this reading, we build on previous work (Franklin & Jordan, 1992; Jordan & Franklin, 1995) to provide a knowledge of various assessment models that may be useful in managed care. We review four practice models—the psychosocial, cognitive-behavioral, life, and family systems models—and identify the assessment strategies of each. We further discuss the utility of these models in managed care environments. An integrative framework for combining the best practices from the models is presented, along with an integrative skills checklist to guide decisions concerning what is needed in a brief assessment.

PSYCHOSOCIAL ASSESSMENT MODEL

In the psychosocial and related ego approaches, associated with Florence Hollis, Gordon Hamilton, and others (Blanck & Blanck, 1974; Goldstein, 1986, 1988; Hollis & Wood, 1981; Maluccio, 1981; Parad & Miller, 1963; Perlman, 1957, 1986; Woods & Robinson, 1996), the goal is to determine a diagnosis of the client. Factors such as past history and developmental processes are taken into account in making this diagnosis and in

implementation of the change efforts. Ego psychology provides the psychosocial assessment framework, and an appreciation for the interplay of biopsychosocial processes is built into the model. Goldstein (1986) explains that, compared to the classical psychoanalytical ideas dominant in early social work practice, ego psychology presented a more optimistic and sociocultural view of human behavior:

> Ego psychology concepts were used to refocus the study and assessment process on (1) the client's person-environment transactions in the here and now, and particularly the degree to which he is coping effectively with major life roles and tasks; (2) the client's adaptive, autonomous, and conflict free areas of ego functioning, as well as her ego deficits and maladaptive defenses and patterns; (3) the key developmental issues affecting the client's current reactions; and (4) the degree to which the external environment is creating obstacles to successful coping.

Psychosocial theory has integrated ego psychology with other ideas, including role theory, systems theory, and factors such as ethnicity, values, and power (Turner, 1988). Over the years, psychosocial assessment and treatment have incorporated new ideas from the social sciences. The current model emphasizes more of a systems perspective; the focus of the social worker is on modifying the aspects of persons and environments that are easiest to change. Psychosocial theory has incorporated many ideas from systems theory—for instance, that a change in one part of a system may influence other parts of a system, and that small changes may create a big difference in client functioning. Practitioners focus on clients' strengths and coping abilities and work to help people make the best adaptations possible. The model has taken on a more collaborative approach, with a focus on problem solving, although it retains the major assumptions of ego psychology concerning personality functioning.

Psychosocial Assessment in Current Practice Environments

One of the strengths of the psychosocial model in today's practice environments is that it is consistent with the medical model, which involves study, diagnosis, and treatment. Its biopsychosocial perspective meshes with that of medically based behavioral health care settings. The focus of the psychosocial model on support, strengths, coping, problem solving, and a quick return to adaptive functioning also meets the current demands of managed care. The model's basis in ego psychology, however, may prove to be a challenge. In managed care settings, there is little time for detailed history taking and study of the developmental processes associated with problem patterns; and there is no time for the long-term fostering and use of the therapeutic relationship in the psychosocial approach (Budman & Armstrong, 1992; Sabin, 1991).

Current practice environments offer short-term treatment sessions; evidence suggests that clients rarely see practitioners for more than six to eight sessions, regardless of therapeutic orientation (Koss & Shiang, 1994). Some practitioners have advocated a course of intermittent work, similar to a primary care model; in this approach, practitioners would offer fewer sessions spaced over a long period of time (Cummings & Sayama, 1995). Another model being used is intensive outpatient treatment, where clients are seen two to three times a week for a short period. Even single-session therapies are being used (Talmon, 1990). In general, psychoanalytic ego psychologies and associated treatment models that rely on long-term therapy have fallen out of favor. Some social work authors have linked the advent of managed care to the demise of psychodynamic theories (Alperin & Phillips, 1997). There have also been efforts to develop shorter-term psychodynamic models that can be used in brief therapy (Davanloo, 1980; Levenson & Butler, 1994; Sifneos, 1992; Worchel, 1990). The psychosocial model has aligned itself with brief psychodynamic perspectives.

Over the years, the psychosocial model has adapted by taking on variations of other models—for example, aspects of the functional case work model, which deemphasizes history and focuses on solving problems in the here and now through the use of agency resources. Some of these adaptations include abbreviating history taking in the diagnostic interview and working more collaboratively with the client to solve problems (Woods & Robinson, 1996). To offer a viable assessment model for today's practice environment, the psychosocial model will need to continue to move toward a shorter-term perspective that relies less on history and ongoing therapeutic relationship and more on rapid assessment and helping clients to quickly resolve their presenting problems.

The psychosocial model's usefulness for managed care settings is also limited by the paucity of empirical outcome research demonstrating that this model is successful at resolving a client's presenting problems. Most research on the psychosocial model has been based on qualitative case studies (Woods & Robinson, 1996), which do not provide the efficacy and effectiveness data required if the method is to become an acceptable treatment alternative. Qualitative methods are useful in practice but may have limited utility for managed care (Franklin & Jordan, 1995).

Methods Used in Psychosocial Assessment

Turner (1988) suggested that psychosocial diagnosis is an ongoing process involved with the identification and labeling of problems and with the recognition of client strengths. Detailed psychosocial interviewing has become a key component of assessment in the model. Specific assessment techniques include: (1) classical psychiatric interviewing for the purposes of making a diagnosis; (2) the use of standardized and projective testing to aid accurate diagnosis; (3) psychosocial and developmental study to identify problem patterns; and (4) observations and interpretations of the client-social worker relationship for the purpose of helping clients understand their problem patterns and providing a corrective emotional experience. Social workers in managed care environments will particularly appreciate two aspects of the psychosocial model: the use of standardized interviews to obtain an accurate mental health diagnosis; and the monitoring of symptoms to make sure that they change during the treatment plan.

To practice in managed care, social workers need to be skillful in various types of diagnostic assessments and the use of the DSM-IV (Jarman-Rohde, McFall, Kolar, & Strom, 1997). Increasing the validity of these assessment activities is consistent with the historic focus of the psychosocial model on detailed study leading to a diagnosis. Many diagnostic tools are currently available to help practitioners make an accurate diagnosis on the basis of established criteria; several involve semistructured interviews using standardized formats. Interviewing for diagnostic purposes is an important part of the psychosocial model.

To use the best practices in clinical assessment, practitioners must learn to identify and evaluate various standardized assessment tools on the basis of their psychometric properties and clinical utility. Exhibit 10–12 provides a useful evaluation form for assessment instruments.

Standardized interviews guide the practitioner in making a quick and accurate diagnosis and allow the practitioner to closely scrutinize diagnostic decisions. In other words, practitioners are no longer relying only on their own clinical judgments in an informal interview process but have a valid measure to aid their judgments. This will decrease the likelihood of inaccurate diagnosis, which leads to time wasted on treatments that do not match the problems, and increase the likelihood that clients will receive treatments in a timely manner.

Managed care companies are very concerned that clients receive the correct level of care necessary to solve problems. In particular, most managed behavioral health care companies require a DSM-IV diagnosis as a basis of payment for mental health treatment. The practitioner has to communicate to the payor (the managed care company) that the client actually has the diagnosis and needs a certain level of treatment. Companies usually prefer that problems be solved at the outpatient level, instead of automatically opting for more expensive residential treatments. Managed care companies have review panels and experts who evaluate the practitioner's treatment plan and determine if his or her clinical judgments concerning diagnosis and treatment are warranted. Being able to establish diagnosis through the use of standardized interviewing adds credibility, so that it is easier to justify a regimen of treatment. It may also provide methods to monitor changes in symptoms during the course of treatment, in which the payor is also interested. Sauter and Franklin (1998), for example, review five instruments for assessing posttraumatic stress disorder in children.

COGNITIVE BEHAVIORAL ASSESSMENT MODELS

Cognitive behavioral therapy focuses on clients' present functioning and attributes clients' problem behavior to learning processes, the formation of maladaptive cognitive schemas, information processing, and proactive cognitive structures or meaning systems. It has moved to the forefront in psychotherapy within professional psychology and is also one of the most popular forms of brief psychotherapy (Turner, 1992). In social work, it has been integrated into competency-based, problem-solving, and task-centered models, as well as the empirical practice model (Berlin, 1996; Brower & Nurius, 1993; Franklin & Jordan, 1998; Franklin & Nurius, 1996; Gambrill, 1983; Gambrill, Thomas, & Carter, 1971; Granvold, 1996; Mattaini, 1990; Rose, 1977, 1988; Shorkey & Sutton-Simon, 1983; Stuart, 1980; Thyer, 1983, 1985, 1987, 1988). Brower and Nurius (1993) have integrated the knowledge from cognitive science into a new practice model, the cognitive-ecological model. The cognitive behavioral model is more a school of thought than a unitary set of practices or theory; it has been influenced by theoretical positions ranging from psychoanalytic to behavioral therapies.

The underlying theoretical base of the cognitive behavioral model is taken from experimental psychology—particularly, learning theories and work in cognition and memory, information processing, and social cognition. Recently, cognitive theory has also borrowed from developmental theories such as attach-

EXHIBIT 10-12	Evaluation Form for Standardized Assessment Measures
Name of measure: Author: Date of publication: Purchase availability: Availability of manual: Cost: Time for administration: Ease of use: Clarity of directions:	Scoring procedures: Level of training needed: Purpose of the measure: Theoretical orientation: Standardization and appropriateness of norms: Evidence for validity: Evidence for reliability: Evidence for clinical utility:

SOURCE: C. Jordan & C. Franklin. *Clinical assessment for social workers: Quantitative and qualitative methods.* Chicago: Lyceum Books/ Nelson Hall (1995), p. 89.

ment theories, and integrated newer systems theories, such as complexity systems theory (Guidano, 1991; Mahoney, 1991, 1995). Meichenbaum (1993) describes how cognitive behavior therapy has changed over time by identifying three metaphors that have guided the model.

1. Conditioning as a metaphor: Cognitions are viewed as covert behaviors subject to the same laws of learning as overt behavior.

2. Information processing as a metaphor: The mind is a computer. The language of information processing and social learning theory (for example, decoding, encoding, retrieval, attributional bias, cognitive structure, schemata, belief systems, cognitive distortion, and cognitive errors) is employed.

3. Constructive narrative as a metaphor: Humans construct their personal realities and create their own representational models of the world. Personal meanings, multiple realities, and consequences of cognitive constructions are emphasized. The therapist helps clients to alter their narratives and life stories and to reframe stressful life experiences and emotions as normal. The focus is on strengths, resources, coping abilities, and narrative reconstruction.

Cognitive behavioral models are beginning to emphasize that behavioral and cognitive sequences are complex, interactional, circular, and self-perpetuating (Arrington, Sullaway, & Christensen, 1988; Mattaini, 1990). Constructivism is a central theoretical construct for contemporary cognitive therapies (Ellis, 1989; Mahoney, 1991; Meichenbaum & Fitzpatrick, 1993). According to Mahoney (1991), constructivism

1) emphasizes the active and proactive nature of all perception, learning and knowing, 2) acknowledges the structural and functional primacy of abstract (tacit) over concrete (explicit) processes in all sentient and sapient experience; 3) views learning, knowing and memory as phenomena that reflect the on-going attempts of body and mind to organize (and endlessly reorganize) their own patterns of action and experience—patterns that are, of course, related to changing and highly mediated engagements with their momentary worlds. (p. 95)

Many of the principles of the newer cognitive therapies are supported by research relating to memory (Brower & Nurius, 1993), social cognition (Fiske & Taylor, 1984), ecological psychology (Greenberg & Pascual-Leone, 1995), narrative psychology (van den Broek & Thurlow 1991), new social cognitive, applied developmental, and learning theories (Aldridge, 1993; Bandura, 1989; Prawat, 1993), complexity systems theory (Mahoney, 1995; Warren, Franklin, & Streeter, 1996), and evolutionary epistemology, which is the study of how humans construct knowledge (Mahoney, 1991). Brower and Nurius (1993), for example, review empirical research from cognitive, personality and social psychology, as well as ecological psychology, and describe the importance of the constructivist perspectives (Franklin, 1996).

Cognitive Behavioral Assessment in Current Practice Environments

Cognitive behavioral assessment has considerable promise for work in managed care settings. In fact, given the compatibility of cognitive behavior therapy with brief practice settings, some social workers have advocated that student training focus on cognitive behavioral methods (Jarman-Rohde et. al, 1997). Cognitive behavioral therapies have rejected Freudian psychology, with its emphasis on long-term treatment and pathology. Instead, these therapies developed an understanding of human behavior based on learning and cognitive theories, the importance of environmental modification, self-efficacy, and adaptive change. The principle of parsimony was incorporated in the models, and practitioners were taught to be pragmatic, efficient, and effective in their approach to human problems. For these reasons, cognitive therapy has always been a brief form of therapy (Wilson, 1981).

In cognitive therapy, practitioners are active, and sessions are structured and goal-directed. The relationship between the client and worker is collaborative; there is an emphasis on gathering evidence and exploring personal hypotheses, with the notion of testing out faulty ideas and personal coping strategies. Efforts are made to develop a clear conceptualization of the case on the basis of theory, and cognitive behavioral techniques are chosen according to the client's goals. In general, the practitioner's tasks are psychoeducation, increasing client cognitive and behavioral skills for better functioning, and helping the client plan for relapse prevention. This active and systematic approach is very consistent with brief treatment models and managed care.

Four attributes of the cognitive behavioral model make it especially useful for managed care:

1. It is a short-term model that focuses on the rapid assessment and treatment of mental disorders. Cognitive behaviorists primarily emphasize the resolution of the presenting problem; they work with history only as it relates to the client's current functioning. The main focus is to identify faulty learning and cognitive mechanisms that maintain the presenting problem and then to guide, educate, and facilitate the client in getting past the current difficulties.

2. Cognitive behavior therapies are the best researched of all psychotherapies. The methods that they use rest on a strong empirical base. Researchers in academic psychology and psychiatry have supported the efficacy studies on cognitive behavioral therapies and produced impressive outcome studies on their effectiveness.

3. Cognitive behavior therapists have provided detailed treatment manuals that guide practitioners in helping clients resolve problems such as depression, substance abuse, personality disorders, and posttraumatic stress disorders (Barkley, 1997; Beck, Rush, Shaw, & Emery, 1987; Beck & Freeman, 1990; Beck, Wright, Newman, & Liese, 1993; Linehan, 1993; Meichenbaum, 1994). Such manuals make practice more systematic and outline procedures that are known to work. By following the manuals, practitioners can be sure that they are using the best practices, which is an important consideration in managed behavioral health care.

4. Cognitive behavior therapies advocate that practitioners systematically monitor the effectiveness of their practices; many of the early behavior therapists advocated the use of single-case designs (Barlow & Hersen, 1984). This emphasis is very consistent with managed care principles.

Methods Used in Cognitive Behavioral Assessment

The goal of cognitive behavioral assessment is to specify the behavior (thoughts, feelings, or overt behavior) that is to be changed, along with its antecedents and consequences and underlying cognitive mechanisms. From a nine-step procedure (Gambrill et al., 1971), behavioral assessment today has evolved into a multidimensional contextual model (Barth, 1986; Gambrill, 1983; Mattaini, 1990; Whittaker & Tracy,

1989). Gambrill (1983) identified sources of influence over clients' behavior, including the actions of others, thoughts, emotions, physiological factors, setting, events, physical characteristics of the environment, ethnic and cultural factors, material and community resources, past history, societal factors, and developmental factors. Specific assessment techniques used in the cognitive behavioral model include behavioral analysis theory, interviewing, identifying underlying cognitive schemas, logs, self-anchored scales, and standardized measures (Bellack & Hersen, 1988; Hudson, 1982; Kanfer & Schefft, 1988; Sharkey & Sutton-Simon, 1983).

In assessment systems, cognitive behaviorists focus on theoretically and experimentally based approaches for identifying and tracking specific behaviors and cognitions that need to be changed. Popular earlier models, such as the ABC model, focused on tracking antecedents, behaviors, and consequences of a particular problem. Collecting data on the frequency and duration of cognitions and behaviors is important for observing the difficulties that clients are experiencing and monitoring their changes. Self-observation, self-monitoring, and self-recording are hallmarks of assessment approaches; in newer constructivist models, these activities are also central to change efforts (Brower & Nurius, 1993).

With a focus on developing standardized measures to assess maladaptive cognition and behavior (Clark, 1988), cognitive behavior therapists have been forerunners in advocating valid and reliable methods for client assessment. Computerized assessment systems (Hudson, 1990; Jordan & Franklin, 1995; Nurius & Hudson, 1988); systematically track behaviors using standardized measures. For instance, the Hudson (1982, 1989) Clinical Assessment System (CAS) provides approximately 20 scales to measure intrapersonal and interpersonal client problems, such as generalized contentment and marital satisfaction. The system is designed so that clients (or the practitioner) may enter and graph the data on computer for single-system analysis. Standardized rapid assessment instruments (RAIs) are becoming popular in social work practice (Fischer & Corcoran, 1994; Jordan & Franklin, 1995). Behavioral practitioners also endorse computer-based expert systems, which aim to help practitioners make clinical decisions—for example, in child welfare and in mental health (Mullen & Schuermann, 1990; Stein, 1990; Wakefield, 1990).

EXHIBIT 10-13	Essential Questions for a Brief Therapy Assessment Interview

1. Why is the client entering therapy now?
2. Are there any signs of psychosis, delusions, or thought disorders that would indicate that the client needed immediate medical or psychiatric treatment?
3. Are there signs of organicity indicating the need for neurological or other medical treatment?
4. Is there evidence of depression or of suicidal or homicidal ideations?
5. What are the presenting complaints?
6. What important factors are antecedent to the client's problem and to seeking help?
7. Who or what is maintaining the problem?
8. What does the client wish to derive from therapy?
9. What are the client's preferences for therapy style? How can you match that style?
10. Are there clear indications for a specific modality for treatment based on the BASIC ID?
11. Can a therapeutic alliance be maintained or should the client be referred?
12. What are the client's positive attributes and strengths?

It is impossible to describe a full spectrum of cognitive behavioral approaches to assessment, because of the increasing numbers (currently more than 20, according to Franklin, 1995) of specific models and their unique features. One comprehensive assessment framework developed from the cognitive behavioral approach is multimodal assessment, which helps practitioners evaluate client problems in great depth and detail across different modalities, including behavior, affect, sensory, imagery, cognitions, interpersonal relationships, and physiological factors of client functioning, as well as their interactive effects (Lazarus, 1989). Lazarus (1991) developed a Multimodal Life History Inventory to help practitioners gain information about the different modalities. The comprehensive components that go into a behavioral assessment are summarized by the acronym BASIC ID: Behavior, Affect, Sensation, Imagery, Cognition, Interpersonal, and Drugs; the latter represents the broader biological realm.

In the multimodal model, practitioners formulate a brief but comprehensive assessment by developing a modality profile, which organizes information according to the BASIC ID assessment. Using the BASIC ID, practitioners can make differential decisions about effective treatments. It is also possible to scale the modality preferences, so as to determine whether a client shows a more favorable response to treatment in particular areas (Lazarus, 1981). For example, some clients may experience their difficulties more through their behavior, while others have more difficulties with affects. Even a client with a presenting problem such as anxiety (an affect) may respond to treatments that focus

on another modality. For example, one of the authors had a client who experienced anxiety attacks mainly as physiological sensations (rapid heart, tight muscles). The modality profile suggested a treatment focused on the sensation modality. As it turned out, the client difficulties were effectively helped by teaching him progressive muscle relaxation exercises. Using the BASIC ID, it is possible for a practitioner to plan interventions systematically on the basis of the client's assessment profile.

Exhibit 10–13 lists the 12 essential questions that a practitioner should ask in a brief therapy interview, according to the multimodal model.

LIFE MODEL ASSESSMENT

The life model for social work practice was developed by Germain and Gitterman (Gitterman, 1988). The underlying theory is ecological, concerned with interactions between people and their environments (Johnson, 1981). Important concepts include stress, coping, and adaptation, as well as competence, autonomy, social networks, and organizations. The goal of the life model assessment is for client and worker to collaborate together in order to understand the problem, and then to set objectives and plan the intervention (Johnson, 1981). Gitterman (1996) explains assessment as concerned with "the interplay of dynamic forces within the life space, including the influence of the agency as a presence in the client's ecological context" (p. 391). The primary tool of assessment is the problems-in-living formulation, which distinguishes between three areas of the life space: life transitions, environmental pressures, and maladaptive interpersonal processes (Gitterman, 1996).

Gitterman (1988) identified five major aims of the life model: (1) to develop a perspective that gives equal attention to people and to the environment; (2) to develop a model of practice that bridges the traditional specializations of casework, administration and planning, and family therapy; (3) to mirror life processes closely, so that social workers fit in with clients, instead of requiring clients to fit in with their theoretical orientation; (4) to build on people's strengths, rather than on their pathologies and to avoid labeling, which is seen as blaming clients for their problems; and (5) to build bridges between treatment and social reform.

Life Model Assessment in Current Practice Environments

While considerable information can be conveyed through the ecological assessment, this information does not provide a direct set of interventions to address the various difficulties in functioning. This limits the life model's utility as a set of practice activities for managed care. The assessment phase of the life model relies on a detailed social study, which is inconsistent with the time and resource constraints of brief therapy environments. In the managed care setting, assessment information must permit immediate selection of a solution to a problem. The life model has yet to provide this degree of specificity. Mattaini's (1990, 1992a) efforts to combine the ecological assessment model with specific targeted interventions from behavioral practice may be a step in the right direction.

Wakefield (1996a, b, c) has pointed out several weaknesses of ecological systems theory that limit its clinical utility in managed care. First, this approach is not an intervention model but rather relies on other social science theories—such as cognitive therapy and ego psychology—for its interventions. Wakefield suggests that, because the life model does not add anything new to existing models, it is unnecessary. We might add that ecological models such as the life model impose a cumbersome overlay of metatheory on other theoretical approaches, with no benefit for managed care. Second, Wakefield suggests that to integrate different areas of social work practice, as the ecological systems theory hopes to do, is not possible, because each field has to develop its own unique perspectives and interventions

on the basis of extant theories. We might add that direct practice in managed behavioral health care requires very specialized skills in clinical assessment and intervention. While some knowledge of community systems, management, and policies (for example, information technology, advocacy, and health care reforms) is needed, generalist training and skills will not serve clinical practitioners very well. Finally, Wakefield argues that ecological systems theory is nonempirical and does not offer a research base for its effectiveness. The nonempirical status of the life model also limits its clinical utility for managed care.

According to Warren, Franklin, and Streeter (1996), some of the difficulties of the ecological systems theory mentioned by Wakefield can be transcended through the use of newer systems theories, which concentrate on how ordered systems—such as human social systems—develop and change. These theories, based on chaos and complexity systems theory, come from empirical research in other fields, such as mathematics and biology, and provide mathematical and empirical tools to study systems. Such tools have been lacking in the life model and other ecological approaches. In addition, with their focus on change, these approaches may be useful for modeling change processes in brief therapies and may provide decision tools for facilitating naturally occurring change processes in current practice environments.

Methods Used in Life Model Assessment

Assessment techniques include the interview, ecomaps or social network mapping, and standardized social support assessment instruments (Cheers, 1987; Hartman & Laird, 1983; Streeter & Franklin, 1992). Social support can be linked empirically to improvements in social and mental health functioning and is an important area for assessment (Streeter & Franklin, 1992). Tracy and Whittaker (1990) have improved upon the information that can be obtained through ecomapping by combining it with card sort techniques and an interview grid approach to perform clinical assessment of social network characteristics. In its current form, however, this assessment instrument is too cumbersome for use in brief therapy. Mattaini (1992b) has provided computer software for developing ecomaps and a variety of graphic-based assessments within the ecosystems approach. In their brevity and clarity, the computerized versions of these assessments are promising for integration into managed care settings, especially when computerization of graphic methods is combined with a specific set of treatment recommendations.

Reviewing the literature on social support, Streeter and Franklin (1992) identify eight measures that may be used in clinical practice. The use of standardized measures for social support may greatly improve social work assessments.

FAMILY SYSTEMS ASSESSMENT MODELS

The family therapy field has developed multiple methodologies for assessing families as a system. These new methods focus on whole-systems functioning and assess the interactional, interpersonal, and systemic functioning of family groups. Assessment of whole-systems family functioning is based on systems theory and assumes that the interactions of a family group take on measurable and/or observable behavior patterns and characteristics that extend beyond the individual behaviors of each of its family members (Franklin & Jordan, 1998).

Family systems assessment focuses on the systemic or relational network characteristics of family functioning and the associated presenting problems. Systemic functioning specifically refers to the circular, patterned ways in which family groups are believed to behave. Behavior patterns in family systems are nonlinear, recursive, repetitive, and reflexive (Becvar & Becvar, 1988; de Shazer, 1982; Hoffman, 1981; O'Hanlon & Wilk, 1987; Selvini, Boscolo, Cecchin, & Prata, 1980; Tomm, 1987). Some family clinicians believe that systemic family patterns have meaning or serve a function for the family system—by helping the family to stay intact or to avoid marital conflict, for example (Haley, 1990; Madanes, 1984; Palazoli, Cirillo, Selvini, & Sorrentino, 1989). Other clinicians focus more on the behavioral aspects of the systemic functioning or the self-reinforcing nature of the pattern and make few interpretations about its meaning or function (Cade & O'Hanlon, 1993; Fisch, Weakland, & Segal, 1982; Watzlawick, Weakland, & Fisch, 1974).

To effectively assess family systems, clinicians need methods that can focus on the interactive sequences and relational network patterns of the entire family. Assessment is both a way to discover how a family system is functioning and a method for intervening in the patterns of a family system. Correspondingly, assessment

and change interventions are not distinct but, rather, are interactive and circular; assessment methods may function both as information-gathering strategies and as interventive methods (Tomm, 1987). Viewing assessment as intervention blurs the boundaries between which methods are for assessment and which are for change (Franklin & Jordan, 1998; O'Hanlon & Wiener-Davis, 1989).

Family Assessment in Current Practice Environments

Family assessment methods focus on introducing rapid change and are especially suited for brief therapy settings. The brevity of this approach adds to its utility for managed behavioral care. However, all the interventions are based on systems theory, which holds that the presenting problem will be resolved if we alter the functioning of the whole system. Although some family approaches, such as the Mental Research Institute (MRI) and solution-focused therapy—have the resolution of the presenting problem as a goal, not all approaches are so goal-directed. Managed care companies may accept the idea that family relationships are an important target of intervention when the client's difficulties are primarily interpersonal (for instance, marital conflict or battering); greater reluctance is likely, however, in the case of individual mental health issues (for instance, depression or psychosis).

Fortunately, a body of empirical literature points to the importance of relationship issues in mental health problems such as depression (Jacobson & Christensen, 1997; O'Leary & Beach, 1990), although some of the theoretical notions concerning the possibility of eliminating client problems by changing family patterns remain open to question. Nevertheless, there is support for the effectiveness of family therapy with a variety of mental health disorders (Pinsof & Wynne, 1995). The process-driven nature of the family assessments and interventions may make it difficult to tell where the assessment ends and the intervention begins. In family therapy, assessment is treated as just another intervention or change effort. This is positive in that there are no delays in treatment, but negative in that it is difficult to specify what assessment means. For example, how does assessment help us determine which interventions to choose or monitor the progress in treatment? The development of standardized family assessment measures may clarify this question.

Methods Used in Family Assessment

Assessment methods designed for family systems may also be used to facilitate change within those systems. Change happens as the system is assessed; assessment and change are part of the same process, as patterns are successively identified and modified. Family assessment relies on questioning techniques that are used to simultaneously gather information and introduce information into a family system. Franklin and Jordan (1998) review such techniques, including circular questions; conversational/therapeutic questions; hypothesizing, circularity, and neutrality; tracking problems, solutions, and/or exceptions to problems; and pretherapy change assessment.

Family assessment models and standardized measures derived from research on the classification and assessment of family systems functioning include the Olson circumplex family model (Olson, 1986; Olson et al., 1985; Olson, Sprenkle, & Russel, 1979), Beavers' levels of family functioning and competence model (Beavers, 1981; Beavers & Hampson, 1990; Beavers & Voeller, 1983); and the McMaster family model (Epstein, Baldwin, & Bishop, 1982, 1983).

INTEGRATIVE SKILLS ASSESSMENT

To master a range of effective skills in assessment, it is important to learn assessment techniques from the various practice models. We call this approach an integrative skills assessment approach (Franklin & Jordan, 1992). The following assumptions underlie the integrative skills assessment approach:

1. Practice is empirically based.
2. Assessment is brief but comprehensive enough to be effective.
3. A larger-lens or systems approach is useful in grasping the complexities of problems.
4. Measurement is essential.
5. Ethical practitioners evaluate their clinical work.
6. Well-qualified practitioners are knowledgeable about numerous assessment methods and can apply multiple methods in developing assessments.

Such an approach to assessment is compatible with the demands of managed care and will prepare practitioners to be effective in their work. The integrative skills approach to assessment assumes that practice

methods from different theoretical models may be used together, without consideration for inconsistencies in the underlying assumptions among the models. This approach is based on the theory of technical eclecticism (Hepworth & Larsen, 1989).

Technical eclecticism assumes that the complexities of practice require effective practitioners to be eclectic but acknowledges that the inconsistencies inherent in the underlying assumptions and principles of the different models preclude integration at the theoretical level (Lazarus, 1981). Instead, without necessarily embracing any underlying theory, technical eclecticism allows practitioners to borrow techniques (outcome-producing methods) from various treatment models, to seek empirical validation for the choices made, and to exercise some flexibility in trying out techniques on an exploratory basis (Rosen, 1988).

Integration of skills, therefore, relies on the empirical connections between methods and client outcomes. Technical eclecticism is a prescriptive, problem-solving, and outcome-driven approach. Any treatment techniques may be used together if empirical evidence suggests they can solve client problems. A technique with no empirical support—in particular, a technique from the practice wisdom—may be used on an exploratory basis, as long as the practitioner seeks to monitor its effectiveness. This type of tinkering with practice methods is similar to the approach recommended by Blythe and Briar (1985) in developing empirically based models of practice.

Within technical eclecticism, the practitioner selects a battery of assessment techniques from different treatment models in order to produce a valid and reliable assessment of client attributes. Techniques and empirical outcomes are organically connected. Assessment and treatment techniques are chosen because of their effective outcomes, and positive outcomes happen on account of effective techniques. There is a continuous interaction between knowledge derived from clinical techniques and knowledge derived from empirical outcomes. This approach is consistent with the managed care context and will serve practitioners well.

The integrative skills checklist in Exhibit 10–14 formulates a brief assessment model on the basis of the four assessment models considered here and allows practitioners to make decisions about which techniques to use in any assessment. The focus of the checklist is

EXHIBIT 10-14	Checklist for Brief Integrative Skills Assessment Protocol

Instructions: (1) Check off the sections below as they apply to the client and/or the client's problems. (2) Next, go to the Integrative Skills Assessment Protocol and complete only the sections checked.

I. Identifying information
_____ 1.-12.

II. Nature of presenting problem
_____ 13.a.   List all problems
_____ 14.a.-k.   Specification of particular, discrete problem behavior(s)
_____ 15.a.   Prioritize problem(s)

III. Client
_____ 16.a.-i.   Intrapersonal issue
_____ 17.a.-d.   Interpersonal—family
_____ 18.a.-b.   Interpersonal—work or school
_____ 19.a.   Interpersonal—peers

IV. Context and Social Support Networks
_____ 20.a.-b.   Agency consideration
_____ 21.a.-c.   Client's environmental context

V. Assessment Measures
_____ 22.   Family functioning
_____ 23.   Marital (or significant other) functioning
_____ 24.   Individual functioning
_____ 25.   Social supports

VI. Strengths and Resources
_____ 26.   Client strengths
_____ 27.   Environmental strengths

VII. Assessment Summary and Treatment Recommendation
_____ 28.a.   Baseline
_____ 29.a.   Practitioner impressions
_____ 30.   DSM
_____ 31.a.   Problem(s) targeted for intervention
_____ 32.a.-b.   Recommended treatment alternatives

VIII. Methods Used in Assessment
_____ 33.   Standardized interview
_____ 34.   Ethnographic interview
_____ 35.   Nonstandardized interview
_____ 36.   Background information sheets and questionnaires
_____ 37.   Standardized assessment measures
_____ 38.   Behavioral observations
_____ 39.   Projective measures
_____ 40.   Self-anchored or self-rating scales
_____ 41.   Client logs or diaries
_____ 42.   Graphs or maps
_____ 43.   Experiential and task assignments
_____ 44.   Information from collateral sources
_____ 45.   Previous treatment or other social service records
_____ 46.   Other (PLEASE SPECIFY: _____)

SOURCE: C. Jordan & D. Franklin. *Clinical assessment for social workers: Quantitative and qualitative methods.* Chicago: Lyceum Books/ Nelson Hall (1995).

assessing the client in the environmental context. Not every question or technique may be relevant for every client, but the checklist gives a sense of areas that could be important in obtaining an accurate picture of the client and outlines several methods by which this information may be collected. In brief assessment, the practitioner must be able to determine which areas to focus on and must develop a method for including some data and excluding others. The following guidelines are suggested:

1. Always begin by reviewing information on the presenting problems (for instance, the client's depression and anxiety).

2. Focus the assessment initially on the resolution of the presenting problems, by forming concrete and specific goals for change. How does the client experience the presenting problem? How is it a problem for him or her? What is needed to make immediate progress on the depression and anxiety?

3. Next, focus on the resolution of associated or secondary problems that may prevent the resolution of the presenting problem or that need attention once the presenting problem is resolved (such as marital conflicts).

4. Think about the other sections (developmental history, family situation, and so on) and decide what information is affecting the presenting problems and how it needs to be considered in the treatment process

(for instance, the client's report of childhood abuse). Just skim these sections to see if anything might be relevant for maintenance and relapse prevention (for example, a cognitive schema of lack of self-worth that perpetuates the depressive pattern).

5. Look at all the assessment information and treatment goals you have obtained and construct a set of recommendations for the client that can begin to be implemented in the first session.

SUMMARY

Managed care demands that social workers develop sophisticated skills in clinical assessment; they need to know the most effective empirically based techniques. Redressing the lack of information on assessment methods for managed care, we have evaluated four assessment models—the psychosocial, cognitive behavioral, life, and family systems models—in terms of their clinical utility for managed behavioral health care settings. We have examined the potential for integrating diverse methods across practice models within the framework of technical eclecticism and presented an integrative skills checklist that aids practitioners in making decisions about which areas to cover and which techniques to use in a brief assessment.

LEARNING EXERCISES

1. Provide one- or two-sentence definitions of the following terms, or explain them briefly to a colleague:
   cognitive behavioral
   cognitive level of response
   data
   family group conferences
   information
   open-ended question
   partialization
   perceptual level of response
   psychosocial
   strengths assessment
   technical eclecticism

2. Franklin and Jordan discuss four different assessment models that are in use in social work:

   • psychosocial model
   • cognitive behavioral model
   • life model
   • family systems model

   For each model write one paragraph identifying the major contrast between that model and the approach to social work assessment and practice in this book.

3. Review the plan for the interview with Mr. Keene presented in Exhibit 10–11. How have questions related to assessment been used to guide the interview? How does assessment of the loss, remorse, and pain of Mr. Keene over the illness of his wife affect the plan regarding the climate and pace of the interview?

4. In Appendix A, the case of the house on Sixth Street (A-3) involves working with applicants who are seeking help, while the cases of Debbie Smith (A-1) and the Stover family (A-2) involve working with respondents referred by an agency or institution. Compare the process of problem identification and description in these cases. How did the process differ? What evidence do you see of negotiation? What do you find useful and what do you question in the problem identification process for each case?

5. On page 272, we used an example of an applicant whose husband had recently died and suggested that, in the course of your interactions, you might want to ask, "When two people live together, they tend to share a lot of household tasks. Has it been difficult for you to do all these things by yourself?" Here are four different ways this applicant might respond. What does each example tell you? What knowledge do you use to interpret each response?

   • "Oh, I haven't really done anything since he left me. The house is in a terrible mess and I don't have anything in the kitchen except some casseroles the neighbors brought over before the funeral. I feel awful when I look around my house, but we always did things together and I just can't get up the courage to tackle it by myself. I just sit and feel lost and cry."

- "Well, you know, Tom never was very good about helping me with the house or other things. He went off to work and I did the rest. So I have kept busy doing things I usually do. Somehow I seem to miss him less if I keep busy. It's at night, when we used to watch TV together and discuss the programs, that I really feel alone."
- "Oh, my daughter lives down the street, and she comes and keeps things going for me. I guess that I just sit. Somehow I don't want to do anything."
- "Oh, my kids live close, and my daughter comes about three times a week and helps me. She brings groceries that she knows I need. When she can, she stays for supper and we talk about Dad. It is so good to talk to someone about all the things we did together and meant to each other. Somehow it's like he is there with us. My son comes maybe a couple of times a week and the three of us have supper and talk. It makes me feel so much better to remember all we had together and to know that the kids still remember and always will."

6. Compare the coping resources of Ms. Smith (Appendix A-1), and Mrs. Stover (Appendix A-2). What resources does each use to deal with his or her situation? Draw an ecomap of each client situation.
7. Interview two social workers, one from a mental health setting and one from another setting, about DSM-IV. Do they use DSM-IV in their practice? In what way? What do they see as the strengths of DSM-IV? What are its limitations for social work?

REFERENCES

Aldridge, J. (1993). Constructivism, contextualism, and applied developmental psychology. Perceptual and Motor Skills, 76(3), 1242.

Alperin, R. M., & Phillips, D. G. (1997). The impact of managed care on the practice of psychotherapy: Innovation, implementation, and controversy. New York: Brunner/Mazel.

American Psychiatric Association. (1994). The diagnostic and statistical manual of mental disorders (4th ed.). Washington, DC: Author.

Arrington, A., Sullaway, M., & Christensen, A. (1988). Behavioral family assessment. In I. R. H. Falloon (Ed.), Handbook of behavioral family therapy. New York: Guilford.

Atkin, B. (1991). New Zealand: Let the family decide: The new approach to family problems. Journal of Family Law, 29(2), 387–397.

Baker, R. A. (Ed.). (1998). Child sexual abuse and false memory syndrome. Amhurst, NY: Prometheus Books.

Bandura, A. C. (1989). Human agency in social cognitive theory. American Psychologist, 44, 1175–1184.

Barkley, R. A. (1997). Defiant children: A clinician's manual for parent training. New York: Guilford.

Barlow, D., & Hersen, M. (1984). Single case experimental designs: Strategies for studying behavior change. New York: Pergamon.

Barth, R. (1986). Social and cognitive treatment of children and adolescents. San Francisco: Jossey-Bass.

Beavers, W. R. (1981). A systems model of family for family therapists. Journal of Marital and Family Therapy, 7, 229–307.

Beavers, W. R., & Hampson, R. B. (1990). Successful families: Assessment and intervention. New York: W. W. Norton.

Beavers, W. R., & Voeller, M. N. (1983). Family models: Comparing the Olson circumplex model with the Beavers systems model. Family Process, 22(1), 85–98.

Beck, A., & Freeman, A. (1990). Cognitive therapy of personality disorders. New York: Guilford.

Beck, A., Rush, J., Shaw, B. F., & Emery, G. (1987). Cognitive therapy of depression. New York: Guilford.

Beck, A., Wright, F. D., Newman, C. F., & Liese, B. S. (1993). Cognitive therapy of substance abuse. New York: Guilford.

Becvar, D. S., & Becvar, R. J. (1988). Family therapy: A systemic integration. Needleham, MA: Allyn & Bacon.

Bellack, A. S., & Herson, M. (1988). Behavioral assessment: A practical handbook (3rd ed.). Elmsford, NY: Pergamon.

Benjamin, A. (1987). The helping interview: With case illustrations. Boston: Houghton Mifflin.

Berlin, S. B. (1996). Constructivism and the environment: A cognitive-integrative perspective for social work practice. Families in Society, 77(6), 326–335.

Blackwell, B., & Schmidt, G. L. (1992). The educational implications of managed mental health care. Hospital and Community Psychiatry, 43, 962–964.

Blanck, G., & Blanck, R. (1974). Ego psychology in theory and practice. New York: Columbia University Press.

Blythe, B. J., & Briar, S. (1985). Developing empirically based models of practice. Social Work, 30, 483–488.

Blythe, B. J., & Trippodi, T. (1989). Measurement in direct practice. Newbury Park, CA: Sage.

Boughner, S. R., Hayes, S. F., Bubenzer, D. L., & West, J. D. (1994). Use of standardized assessment instruments by marital and family therapists: A survey. Journal of Marital and Family Therapy, 20(1), 69–75.

Braithwaite, J. (1989). Crime, shame and reintegration. New York: Cambridge University Press.

Brower, A. M., & Nurius, P. S. (1993). *Social cognition and individual change: Current theory and counselling guidelines.* Newbury Park, CA: Sage.

Budman, S. H., & Armstrong, E. (1992). Training for managed care setting: How to make it happen. *Psychotherapy, 29,* 416–421.

Burford, G. (1994). Editorial: Getting serious about humanism in administration: The real unsolved mystery. *Journal of Child and Youth Care, 9*(3), v–viii.

Burford, G., & Pennell, J. (1995a). Family group decision making: An innovation in child and family welfare. In J. Hudson & B. Galaway (Eds.), *Child welfare in Canada: Research and policy implications* (pp. 140–153). Toronto, ON: Thompson Educational.

Burford, G., & Pennell, J. (1995b). *Family group decision making project: Implementation report summary.* St. John's, Newfoundland, Canada: Family Group Decision Making Project, School of Social Work, Memorial University of Newfoundland.

Burford, G., & Pennell, J. (1996). Family group decision making: Generating indigenous structures for resolving family violence. *Protecting Children, 12*(3), 17–21.

Burford, G., Pennell, J., & MacLeod, S. (1995). *Family group decision making: Manual for coordinators and communities.* St. John's, Newfoundland, Canada: Family Group Decision Making Project, School of Social Work, Memorial University of Newfoundland.

Burford, G., Pennell, J., MacLeod, S., Campbell, S., & Lyall, G. (1996). Reunification as an extended family matter. *Community Alternatives, 8*(2), 33–55.

Cade, B., & O'Hanlon, W. H. (1993). *A brief guide to brief therapy.* New York: Norton.

Callahan, M. (1993). Feminist approaches: Women recreate child welfare. In B. Wharf (Ed.), *Rethinking child welfare in Canada* (pp. 172–209). Toronto: McClelland & Stewart.

Cheers, B. (1987). The social support network map as an educational tool. *Australian Social Work, 40*(3), 18–24.

Clark, D. A. (1988). The validity of measures of cognition: A review of the literature. *Cognitive Therapy and Research, 12,* 1–20.

Connolly, M. (1994). An act of empowerment: The Children, Young Persons, and Their Families Act (1989). *British Journal of Social Work, 24*(1), 87–100.

Corcoran, K., & Gingerich, W. J. (1994). Practice evaluation in the context of managed care: Case recording methods of quality assurance reviews. *Research on Social Work Practice, 4*(3), 326–337.

Corcoran, K., & Vandiver, V. (1996). *Maneuvering the maze of managed care.* New York: Free Press.

Cowger, C. D. (1994). Assessing client strengths: Clinical assessment for client empowerment. *Social Work, 39*(3), 262–266.

Cummings, N. A., & Sayama, M. (1995). *Focused psychotherapy: A casebook of brief, intermittent psychotherapy throughout the life cycle.* New York: Brunner/Mazel.

Davanloo, H. (Ed.). (1980). *Short-term dynamic psychotherapy.* New York: Jason Aronson.

de Jong, P., & Berg, I. K. (1998). *Interviewing for solutions.* Pacific Grove, CA: Brooks/Cole.

de Jong, P., & Miller, S. D. (1995). How to interview for client strengths. *Social Work, 40*(6), 729–736.

de Shazer, S. (1982). *Patterns of brief family therapy: An ecosystemic approach.* New York: Guilford.

de Shazer, S. (1988). *Clues: Investigating solutions in brief therapy.* New York: W. W. Norton.

de Shazer, S., & Berg, I. (1988). Constructing solutions. *Family Therapy Networker, 12*(5), 42–433, 43.

Dean, R. G. (1993). Constructivism: An approach to clinical practice. *Smith College Studies in Social Work, 63*(2), 127–146.

Deci, E. L., & Ryan, R. M. (1980). The empirical exploration of intrinsic motivational processes. In L. Berkowitz (Ed.), *Advances in experimental social psychology* (Vol. 13, pp. 40–80). New York: Academic.

Deci, E. L., Spiegel, N. H., Ryan, R. M., Koestner, R., & Kauffman, M. (1982). Effects of performance standards on teaching styles: Behaviour of controlling teachers. *Journal of Educational Psychology, 74*(6), 852–859.

Delgado, M. (1996). Community asset assessments by Latino youths. *Social Work in Education, 18*(3), 169–176.

Desgranges, K., Desgranges, L., & Karsky, K. (1995). Attention deficit disorder: Problems with preconceived diagnosis. *Child and Adolescent Social Work Journal, 12*(1), 3–17.

Drake, B. (1996). Relationship competencies in child welfare services. *Social Work, 39*(5), 595–602.

Ellis, A. (1989). Is rational emotive therapy (RET) "rationalist" or "constructivist"? In A. E. Ellis & W. Dryden (Eds.), *The essential Albert Ellis* (pp. 114–141). New York: Springer.

Epstein, L. (1985). *Talking and listening: A guide to the helping interview.* St. Louis: Times Mirror/Mosby.

Epstein, N. B., Baldwin, L. M., & Bishop, D. S. (1982). *McMaster family assessment device (FAD) version 3, manual.* Providence, RI: The Brown University/Butler Hospital Family Research Program.

Epstein, N. B., Baldwin, L. M., & Bishop, D. S. (1983). The McMaster family assessment device. *Journal of Marital and Family Therapy, 9*(2), 171–180.

Evans, D. R., Hearn, M. T., Uhlemann, M. R., & Ivey, A. E. (1998). *Essential interviewing: A programmed approach to effective communication* (5th ed.). Pacific Grove, CA: Brooks/Cole.

Fisch, R., Weakland, J. H., & Segal, L. (1982). *Tactics of change: Doing therapy briefly.* San Francisco: Jossey-Bass.

Fischer, J., & Corcoran, K. (1994). *Measures for clinical practice* (2nd ed.). New York: Free Press.

Fiske, S. T. & Taylor, S. T. (1991). *Social Cognition* (2nd ed.). New York: McGraw-Hill.

Franklin, C. (1994). Must social workers continually yield current practice methods to the evolving empirically supported knowledge base. Yes. In W. W. Hudson & P. S. Nurius (Eds.), *Controversial issues in social work research* (pp. 271–282). Boston: Allyn & Bacon.

Franklin, C. (1995). Expanding the vision of the social constructionist debates: Creating relevance for practitioners. *Families in Society, 76*(7), 395–407.

Franklin, C., & Johnson, C. (1996). Family social work practice: Onward to therapy and policy. *Journal of Family Social Work, 1*(3), 33–47.

Franklin, C., & Jordan, C. (1992). Teaching students to perform assessment. *The Journal of Social Work Education, 28*(2), 222–241.

Franklin, C., & Jordan, C. (1995). Qualitative assessment: A methodological review. *Families in Society, 76*(5), 281–295.

Franklin, C., & Jordan, C. (1998). *Family practice: Brief systems methods for social work.* Pacific Grove, CA: Brooks/Cole.

Franklin, C. & Nurius, P. (1996). Constructivist therapy: New directions in social work practice. *Families in Society, 77*(6), 323–325.

Franklin, C., & Streeter, C. L. (1993). Validity of the 3-D circumplex model for family assessment. *Research on Social Work Practice, 3*(3), 258–275.

Gambrill, E. (1983). *Casework: A competency based approach.* Englewood Cliffs, NJ: Prentice-Hall.

Gambrill, E., Thomas, E., & Carter, R. (1971). Procedure for sociobehavioral practice in open settings. *Social Work, 16,* 51–62.

Garrett, A. (1995). *Interviewing: Its principles and methods* (5th ed.). Milwaukee, WI: Families International.

Germain, C., & Gitterman, A. (1996). *A life model of social work practice: Advances in theory and practice.* New York: Columbia University Press.

Gitterman, A. (1996). The life model theory and social work treatment. In F. Turner (Ed.), *Social work treatment; Interlocking theoretical approaches* (4th ed., pp. 389–408.) New York: Free Press.

Giles, T. R. (1991). Managed mental health care and effective psychotherapy: A step in the right direction? *Journal of Behavior Therapy and Experimental Psychiatry, 22,* 83–86.

Gitterman, A. (1988, March). *Alternative practice explanatory frameworks: A debate.* Presentation at the Annual Program Meeting, Council on Social Work Education, Atlanta, GA.

Goldberg, E. M., & Stanley, S. J. (1985). Task-centered casework in a probation setting. In E. M. Goldberg, J. Gibbons, & I. Sinclair (Eds.), *Problems, tasks and outcomes* (pp. 89–159). London: George Allen & Unwin.

Goldstein, E. G. (1986). Ego psychology. In F. J. Turner (Ed.), *Social work treatment* (3rd ed., pp. 375–405). New York: Free Press.

Goldstein, E. G. (1988, March). *Alternative practice explanatory frameworks: A debate.* Presentation at the Annual Program Meeting, Council on Social Work Education, Atlanta, GA.

Gordon, R. C. (1992). *Basic interviewing skills.* Itasca, IL: F. E. Peacock.

Granvold, D. K. (1996). Constructivist psychotherapy. *Families in Society, 77*(6), 345–357.

Greenberg, L., & Pascual-Leone, J. (1995). A dialectical constructivist approach to experimental change. In R. A. Neimeyer & M. J. Mahoney (Eds.), Constructivism in psychotherapy (pp. 169–191). Washington, D. C.: American Psychological Association.

Guidano, V. F. (1991). *The self in process.* New York: Guilford.

Haley, J. (1990). *Problem solving therapy.* San Francisco: Jossey-Bass.

Hartman, A., & Laird, J. (1983). *Family centered social work practice.* New York: Free Press.

Hersen, M., & Hassett, V. B. (Eds.). (1998). *Basic interviewing: A practical guide for counsellors and clinicians.* Mahwah, NJ: Lawrence Erlbaum.

Hoffman, L. (1981). *Foundations of family therapy.* New York: Basic Books.

Hollis, F., & Wood, M. E. (1981). *Social casework: A psychosocial therapy* (3rd ed.). New York: Random House.

Hudson, J., Maxwell, G., Morris, A., & Galaway, B. (Eds.). (1995). *Family group conferences: Perspectives on policy and practice.* Monsey, NY: Criminal Justice Press.

Hudson, W. W. (1982). *The clinical measurement package.* Homewood, IL: Dorsey Press.

Hudson, W. W. (1989). *Computer assisted social services manual.* Tempe, AZ: Walmyr.

Hudson, W. W. (1990). Computer-based clinical practice: Present status and future possibilities. In L. Videka-Sherman & W. J. Reid (Eds.), *Advances in clinical social work research* (pp. 105–117). Silver Spring, MD: National Association of Social Workers Press.

Ivry, J. (1992). Teaching geriatric assessment. In M. J. Mellors & R. Solomon (Eds.), *Geriatric social work education* (pp. 3–22). New York: Haworth.

Jacobson, N. S. & Christiansen, A. (1996). *Integrative couple therapy: Promoting acceptance and change.* New York: Norton.

Jarman-Rohde, L., McFall, J., Kolar, P., & Strom, G. (1997). The changing context of social work practice: Implications and recommendations for social work education. *Journal of Social Work Education, 33*(1), 29–46.

Johnson, L. (1981). *Social work practice: A generalist approach.* Boston: Allyn & Bacon.

Jordan, C., & Franklin, C. (1995). *Clinical assessment for social workers: Quantitative and qualitative methods.* Chicago: Lyceum Books/Nelson Hall.

Kadushin, A. (1972). *The social work interview.* New York: Columbia University Press.

Kadushin, A. (1990). *The social work interview: A guide for human service professionals* (3rd ed.). New York: Columbia University Press.

Kanfer, F. H., & Schefft, B. K. (1988). *Guiding the process of therapeutic change.* Champaign, IL: Research Press.

Kaplan, L., & Girard, J. L. (1994). *Strengthening high-risk families: A handbook for practitioners.* New York: Lexington.

Karls, J. M., & Wandrei, K. E. (Eds.). (1994a). *Person-in-environment system: The PIE classification system for social functioning problems.* Washington, DC: NASW Press.

Karls, J. M., & Wandrei, K. E. (Eds.) (1994b). *PIE manual: Person-in-environment system.* Washington, DC: NASW Press.

Kirk, S. A., & Kutchins, H. (1992). The selling of DSM: The rhetoric of science in psychiatry. Hawthorne, NY: Aldine de Gruyter.

Koss, M. P., & Shiang, J. (1994). Research on brief psychotherapy. In A. E. Bergin & S. L. Garfield (Eds.), *Handbook of psychotherapy and behavior change* (4th ed., pp. 664–700). New York: Wiley.

Kropf, N. P., Lindsey, F. W., & Carse-McLocklin, S. (1993). The eligibility worker role in public welfare: Worker and client perceptions. *Aretê, 18*(1), 34–42.

Kutchins, H., & Kirk, S. (1986). The reliability of DSM-III: A critical review. *Social Work Research and Abstracts, 22*(4), 3–12.

Kutchins, H., & Kirk, S. A. (1995). Should DSM be the basis for teaching social work practice in mental health? No! *Journal of Social Work Education, 31*(2), 159–165.

Kutchins, H., & Kirk, S. A. (1997). *Making us crazy: DSM, The psychiatric Bible and the creation of mental disorders.* New York: Free Press.

Lazarus, A. (1981). *Multi-modal therapy.* New York: McGraw-Hill.

Lazarus, A. (1989). Multimodal therapy. In R. Corsini & D. Wedding (Eds.), *Current psychotherapies* (4th ed., pp. 503–544). Itasca, IL: F. E. Peacock.

Lazarus, A. (1991). *The multi-modal life history inventory.* Champaign, IL: Research Press.

Lazarus, A. (1995). Preparing for practice in an era of managed competition. *Psychiatric Services, 46,* 184–185.

Leutz, W., Abrahams, R., & Capitman, J. (1993). The administration of eligibility for community long term care. *The Gerontologist, 33*(1), 92–104.

Levenson, H., & Butler, S. F. (1994). Brief dynamic individual psychotherapy. In R. Hales, & S. Yudofsky (Eds.), *Textbook of psychiatry* (2nd ed., pp. 947–967). Washington, DC: American Psychiatric Press.

Levitt, J. L., & Reid, W. J. (1981). Rapid assessment instruments for practice. *Social Work Research and Abstracts, 17*(1), 13–19.

Linehan, M. (1993). *Skills training manual for treating borderline personality disorders.* New York: Guilford.

Loftus, E., & Ketcham, K. (1994). *The myth of repressed memories and allegations of sexual abuse.* New York: St. Martin's Press.

MacLeod, S., & Campbell, S. (1996). Family group decision making: A strategy to help families and communities keep women and children safe. In M. Russell, J. Hightower, & G. Gutman (Eds.), *Stopping the violence: Changing families, changing futures* (pp. 170–174). Vancouver, BC: Benwell Atkins.

Madanes, C. (1984). *Behind the one-way mirror: Advances in the practice of strategic therapy.* San Francisco: Jossey Bass.

Mahoney, M. J. (1991). *Human change processes.* New York: Basic Books.

Mahoney, M. J. (1995). Continuing evolution of cognitive sciences and psychotherapy. In R. A. Neimeyer & M. J. Mahoney (Eds.), *Constructivism in psychotherapy* (pp. 39–68). Washington, DC: American Psychological Association.

Maluccio, A. N. (Ed.). (1981). *Promoting competence in clients: A new/old approach to social work practice.* New York: Free Press.

Marlow, C. (1998). *Research methods for generalist social work* (2nd ed.). Pacific Grove, CA: Brooks/Cole.

Mattaini, M. A. (1990). Contextual behavioral analysis in the assessment process. *Families in Society, 7*(4), 236–245.

Mattaini, M. A. (1992a). *More than a thousand words: Graphics in clinical practice.* Washington, DC: NASW Press.

Mattaini, M. A. (1992b). *Visual Ecoscan for clinical practice (Software on Macintosh and MS DOS).* Washington, DC: NASW Press.

Mattaini, M. A., & Kirk, S. A. (1991). Assessing assessment in social work. *Social Work, 36*(3), 260–266.

Maxwell, G., & Morris, A. (1993). *Family, victims and culture: Youth justice in New Zealand.* Wellington, New Zealand: Social Policy Agency and Institute of Criminology, Victoria University of Wellington.

Maxwell, G., & Morris, A. (1996). Research on family group conferences with young offenders in New Zealand. In J. Hudson, A. Morris, G. Maxwell, & B. Galaway (Eds.), *Family group conferences: Perspectives on policy and practice* (pp. 88–110). New York: Criminal Justice Press.

Meichenbaum, D. (1993). Changing conceptions of cognitive behavior modification: Retrospect and prospect. *Journal of Consulting and Clinical Psychology, 61*, 202–204.

Meichenbaum, D. (1994). *A clinical handbook/practical therapist manual for assessing and treating adults with post-traumatic stress disorder (PTSD).* Waterloo, ON: University of Waterloo, Institute Press.

Meichenbaum, D., & Fitzpatrick, D. (1993). A constructionist, narrative perspective on stress and coping: Stress inoculation applications. In L. Goldberger & S. Breznitz (Eds.), *Handbook of stress: Theoretical and clinical aspects* (2nd ed., pp. 706–723). New York: Free Press.

Meyer, C. H. (1993). *Assessment in social work practice.* New York: Columbia University Press.

Miley, K. K., O'Melia, M., & Dubois, B. L. (1995). *Generalist social work practice: An empowering approach.* Toronto: Allyn & Bacon.

Miller, S. D. (1992). The symptoms of solution. *Journal of Strategic and Systemic Therapies, 11*, 1–11.

Molnar, A., & de Shazer, S. (1987). Solution-focused therapy: Towards the identification of therapeutic tasks. *Journal of Marital and Family Therapy, 76*(7), 421–433.

Mullen, E. J., & Schuermann, J. R. (1990). Expert systems and the development of knowledge in social welfare. In L. Videka-Sherman & W. J. Reid (Eds.), *Advances in clinical social work research* (pp. 119–142). Silver Spring, MD: NASW Press.

Murdach, A. D. (1980). Bargaining and persuasion with non-voluntary clients. *Social Work, 25*(6), 458–461.

Northern, H. (1982). *Clinical social work.* New York: Columbia University Press.

Nurius, P. S., & Hudson, W. W. (1988). Computers and social diagnosis: The client's perspective. *Computers in Human Services, 5*(1/2), 21–36.

O'Hanlon, W. H., & Weiner-Davis, M. (1989). *In search of solutions: A new definition of psychotherapy.* New York: W. W. Norton.

O'Hanlon, W. H., & Wilk, J. (1987). *Shifting contexts: A generation of effective psychotherapies.* New York: Guilford.

O'Leary, K. D., & Beach, S. R. H. (1990). Marital therapy: A viable treatment for depression and marital discord. *American Journal of Psychiatry, 147*(2), 183–186.

Olson, D. H. (1986). Circumplex model VII: Validation studies and FACES III. *Family Process, 25*(3), 337–351.

Olson, D. H. (1991). Commentary: Three-dimensional (3-D) circumplex model and revised scoring of FACES III. *Family Process, 30*, 74–79.

Olson, D. H., McCubbin, H. I., Barnes, H., Larsen, A., Muxen, M., & Wilson, M. (1985). *Family inventories: Inventories in a national survey of families across the family life cycle* (rev. ed.). St. Paul, MN: Family Social Science, McNeal Hall, University of Minnesota.

Olson, D. H., Sprenkle, D. H., & Russel, C. S. (1979). Circumplex model of marital and family systems: Cohesion and adaptability dimensions, family types and clinical applications. *Family Process, 18*, 3–28.

Oppenheim, A. N. (1992). *Questionnaire design, interviewing, and attitude measurement.* New York: Pinter.

Palazoli, M. S., Cirillo, S., Selvini, M., & Sorrentino, A. M. (1989). *Family games: General model of psychotic processes in the family.* New York: Norton.

Parad, H. J., & Miller, R. (Eds.). (1963). *Ego oriented casework.* New York: Family Service Association of America.

Paterson, K., & Harvey, M. (1991). *An evaluation of the organisation and operation of care and protection family group conferences.* Wellington, New Zealand: Department of Social Welfare.

Pennell, J. (1995). Encountering or countering women abuse. In P. Taylor & C. Daly (Eds.), *Gender dilemmas in social work: Issues affecting women in the profession* (pp. 89–105). Toronto: Canadian Scholars' Press.

Pennell, J., & Burford, G. (1994). Widening the circle: Family group decision making. *Journal of Child and Youth Care, 9*(1), 1–11.

Pennell, J., & Burford, G. (1995). *Family group decision making: New roles for "old" partners in resolving family violence: Implementation report* (Vols. 1–2). St. John's, Newfoundland, Canada: Family Group Decision Making Project, School of Social Work, Memorial University of Newfoundland.

Pennell, J., & Burford, G. (1996). Attending to context: Family group decision making in Canada. In J. Hudson, A. Morris, G. Maxwell, & B. Galaway (Eds.), *Family group conferences: Perspectives on policy and practice* (pp. 206–220). New York: Criminal Justice Press.

Perlman, H. H. (1957). *Social casework: A problem solving process.* Chicago: University of Chicago Press.

Perlman, H. (1986). The problem solving model. In F. Turner (Ed.), *Social work treatment* (3rd ed.). New York: Free Press.

Pinsof, W. M., & Wynne, L. C. (1995). The efficacy of marital and family therapy: An empirical overview, conclusions and recommendations. *Journal of Marital and Family Therapy, 21*(4), 585–613.

Prawat, R. S. (1993). The value of ideas: Problems versus possibilities in learning, *Educational Research, 22*(6), 5–16.

Procidano, M., & Heller, K. (1983). Measures of perceived social support from friends and from family: Three validational studies. *American Journal of Community Psychology, 11*, 1–24.

Reichertz, D., & Frankel, H. (1993). Integrating family assessment into social work practice. *Research on Social Work Practice, 3*(3), 243–257.

Reid, W. J., & Epstein, L. (1972). *Task centered casework.* New York: Columbia University Press.

Reid, W. J., & Epstein, L. (1977). *Task centered practice.* New York: Columbia University Press.

Reid, W. J. (1978). *The task-centered system.* New York: Columbia University Press.

Ristock, J., & Pennell, J. (1996). *Community research as empowerment: Feminist links, postmodern interruptions.* Toronto, ON: Oxford University Press.

Rose, S. (1977). *Group therapy: A behavioral approach.* Englewood Cliffs, NJ: Prentice-Hall.

Rose, S. (1988, March). *Alternative practice explanatory frameworks: A debate.* Presentation at the Annual Program Meeting, Council on Social Work Education, Atlanta, Georgia.

Rosen, A., & Lieberman, D. (1972). The experimental evaluation of interview performance of social workers. *Social Science Review, 46*(3), 395–412.

Rosen, H. (1988). Evolving a personal philosophy of practice towards eclectism. In R. Dorfman (Ed.), *Paradigms of clinical social work* (pp. 388–412). New York: Brunner/Mazel.

Rubin, A., & Babbie, E. (1997). *Research methods for social work* (3rd ed.). Pacific Grove, CA: Brooks/Cole.

Sabin, J. E. (1991). Clinical skills for the 1990's: Six lessons from HMO practice. *Hospital and Community Psychiatry, 42*, 605–608.

Safer, D. J. (1995). An outpatient/inpatient comparison of child psychiatric diagnosis. *American Journal of Orthopsychiatry, 31*(3), 298–303.

Saleebey, D. (Ed.). (1997). *The strengths perspective in social work practice.* New York: Longman.

Sauter, J., & Franklin, C. (1998). Assessing post-traumatic stress disorder in children: Diagnostic and measurement strategies. *Research on Social Work Practice, 8*(3), 251–270.

Schechter, S. (1982). *Women and male violence: The visions and struggles of the battered women's movement.* Boston: South End Press.

Schoech, D. (1989). The University of Texas at Arlington. Private conversation.

Schubert, M. (Ed.). (1991). *Interviewing in social work practice* (rev. ed.). Alexandria, VA: Council on Social Work Education.

Selekman, M. (1993). *Pathways to change: Brief therapy solutions with difficult adolescents.* New York: Guilford.

Selekman, M. (1997). *Solution focussed therapy with children.* New York: Guilford.

Selvini, M. P., Boscolo, L., Cecchin, G., & Prata, G. (1980). Hypothesizing-circularity-neutrality: Three guidelines for the conduct of the session. *Family Process, 19*(1), 3–12.

Shorkey, C. T., & Sutton-Simon, K. (1983). Reliability and validity of the Rational Behavior Inventory with a clinical population. *Journal of Clinical Psychology, 39*(1), 34–38.

Sifneos, P. E. (1992). *Short-term anxiety provoking psychotherapy: A treatment manual.* New York: Plenum Press.

Sinclair, D. (1985). *Understanding wife assault: A training manual for counsellors and advocates.* Toronto, ON: Publications Ontario, Publications Services Section.

Stark, E., & Flitcraft, A. (1988). Women and children at risk: A feminist perspective on child abuse. *International Journal of Health Services, 18*(1), 97–118.

Stein, T. J. (1990). Commentary: Issues in the development of expert systems to enhance decision making in child welfare. In L. Videka-Sherman & W. J. Reid (Eds.), *Advances in clinical social work research* (pp. 503–546). Silver Spring, MD: NASW Press.

Streeter, C. L., & Franklin, C. (1992). Defining and measuring social support: Guidelines for social work practitioners. *Research on Social Work Practice, 2*(1), 81–98.

Strom-Gottfried, K. (1997). The implications of managed care for social work education. *Journal of Social Work Education, 33*, 7–18.

Stuart, R. (1980). *Helping couples change: A social learning theory approach to marital therapy.* New York: Guilford.

Swift, K. (1991). Contradictions in child welfare: Neglect and responsibility. In C. T. Baines, P. M. Evans, & S. M. Neysmith (Eds.), *Women's caring: Feminist perspectives on social welfare* (pp. 234–271). Toronto, ON: McClelland & Stewart.

Talmon, M. (1990). *Single session therapy.* San Francisco: Jossey-Bass.

Thyer, B. A. (1983). Behavior modification in social work practice. In M. Hersen, P. Miller, & R. Eisler (Eds.), *Progress in behavior modification* (Vol. 15, pp. 173–226). New York: Academic.

Thyer, B. A. (1985). Textbooks in behavioral social work: A bibliography. *The Behavior Therapist, 8*, 161–162.

Thyer, B. A. (1987). Contingency analysis: Toward a unified theory for social work practice. *Social Work, 32*, 150–157.

Thyer, B. (1988). Radical behaviorism and clinical social work. In R. Dorfman (Ed.), *Paradigms of clinical social work* (pp. 123–148). New York: Brunner/Mazel.

Tomm, K. (1987). Interventive interviewing. *Family Process, 26*(2), 167–183.

Tracy, E. M., & Whittaker, J. K. (1990). The social network map: Assessing social support in clinical practice. *Families in Society, 71*(8), 461–470.

Turner, F. (1988). Psychosocial therapy. In R. Dorfman (Ed.), *Paradigms of clinical social work.* (pp. 106–122). New York: Brunner/Mazel.

Turner, F. J. (1994). Reconsidering diagnosis. *Families in Society, 75*(3), 168–171.

Turner, R. (1992). Launching cognitive behavioral therapy for adolescent depression and drug abuse. In S. H. Budman, M. F. Hoyt, & S. Friedman (Eds.), *The first session in brief therapy* (pp. 135–155). New York: Guilford.

Van den Brook, P., & Thurlow, R. (1991). The role and structure of personal narratives. *Journal of Cognitive Psychology, 5,* 247–259.

Van Hook, M. P., Berkman, B., & Dunkle, R. (1996). Assessment tools for general health care settings: PRIME-DM, OARS, and SF-36. *Health and Social Work, 21*(3), 230–234.

Wakefield, J. C. (1990). Commentary: Expert systems, Socrates, and the philosophy. In L. Videka-Sherman, & W. J. Reid (Eds.), *Advances in clinical social work research* (pp. 485–502). Silver Spring, MD: NASW Press.

Wakefield, J. C. (1996a). Does social work need the ecosystems perspective? Part 1. Is the perspective clinically useful? *Social Service Review, 70*(1), 1–32.

Wakefield, J. C. (1996b). Does social work need the ecosystems perspective? Part 2. Does the perspective save social work from incoherence? *Social Service Review, 70*(2), 183–213.

Wakefield, J. C. (1996c). Does social work need the ecological perspective: Reply to Alex Gitterman. *Social Service Review, 70*(3), 476–481.

Walker, H. (1996). *Whanau hui,* family decision making, and the family group conference. *Protecting Children, 12*(3), 8–10.

Warren, K., Franklin, C., & Streeter, C. L. (1996). *New directions in systems theory: Chaos and complexity.* Austin, TX: University of Texas at Austin, School of Social Work.

Wasel-Grimm, C. (1995). *Diagnoses for disaster: The devastating truth about false memory syndrome and its impact on accusers and families.* Woodstock NY: Overlook Press.

Watzlawick, P., Weakland, J. H., & Fisch, R. (1974). *Change: Principles of problem formulation and problem resolution.* New York: Norton.

Weick, A. (1986). The philosophical context of a health model of social work. *Social Casework, 67*(9), 551–559.

Weick, A., Rapp, C., Sullivan, W. P., & Kisthardt, W. (1989). A strengths perspective for social work practice. *Social Work, 34*(4), 350–354.

Whittaker, J., & Tracy, E. (1989). *Social treatment: An introduction to interpersonal helping in social work practice* (2nd ed.). New York: Aldine de Gruyter.

Williams-Finch, B. W., & Spitzer, R. L. (1995). Should DSM be the basis for teaching social work practice in mental health? Yes! *Journal of Social Work Education, 31*(2), 148–153.

Wilson, G. T. (1981). Behavior therapy as a short-term therapeutic approach. In S. H. Budman (Ed.), *Forms of brief therapy* (pp. 131–166). New York: Guilford.

Winegar, N. (1993). Managed mental health care: Implications for administrators and managers of community-based agencies. *Families in Society, 74,* 171–177.

Woods, M. E., & Robinson, H. (1997). Psychosocial theory and social work treatment. In F. J. Turner (Ed.), *Social work treatment* (4th ed., pp. 555–580). New York: Free Press.

Worchel, J. (1990). Short-term dynamic psychotherapy. In R. A. Wells & V. J. Giannetti (Eds.), *Handbook of brief psychotherapies* (pp. 193–216). New York: Plenum.

chapter 11

The Service Agreement

CHAPTER PREVIEW

Engagement, data collection, and assessment culminate in the formulation of an explicit service agreement; and at that point the applicant becomes a client. In practice, as we have noted, all the phases of the problem-solving process will be occurring simultaneously. An explicit service agreement will guide subsequent intervention activities but, as new assessments or reassessment arise, you and the client will modify the service agreement accordingly.

In this chapter, we will explore the three aspects of the service agreement: the problem for work, the agreed-upon objectives, and the corresponding action plans. We also discuss your participation in the action plan in terms of five interventive roles: enabler, teacher, social broker, mediator, and advocate.

In Reading 11-1, Michelle MacKenzie reviews a solution-focused brief therapy model of practice and illustrates its application to a family that includes a hyperactive 7-year-old. This reading illustrates how, within the framework of a partnership, a focus on solutions, objectives, and strengths can quickly produce change by alleviating stress.

In Reading 11-2, Edith Fein and Ilene Staff offer guidelines for setting objectives and creating action plans with birth parents of children in out-of-home care. Despite its specific application here, we believe that this approach is useful for a broad range of client settings.

ASPECTS OF THE SERVICE AGREEMENT

Definition

Terminology. In previous editions of this book (for example, Compton & Galaway, 1989), we used the term *service contract*. However, despite its wide currency (Bassin, 1993; Goulding, 1990; Maluccio & Marlow, 1974; Preston-Shoot, 1989; Reid, 1966; Rowe, 1996; Saxon, 1979; Shulman, 1992; Thomlison & Thomlison, 1996; Turner & Jaco, 1996; Wickham, 1993), the concept of contracting has provoked some controversy (Croxton, 1988; Davis, 1985; Hoshino, 1989; Miller, 1990; Rojek & Collins, 1987, 1988). The critics argue that the concept of contracting is misleading in social work practice. Because of the more powerful position of the worker, applicants are unable to negotiate what they need and cannot hold the worker accountable; moreover, this concept does not accurately reflect the complexity of work with some clients. On the other hand, some writers suggest that contracting encourages more ethical practice by making objectives explicit and by recognizing that applicants have options (Bloom & Fischer, 1982; Ivanoff, Robinson, & Blythe, 1987; Tutty, 1990). Wood (1978) has linked the lack of an explicit contract with negative results from service.

We believe concerns about contracts are legitimate, but they are addressed by the partnership concept that we have emphasized. Power sharing between worker and applicant is very different from the notion of behavioral contracting, sometimes practiced in corrections agencies and schools, in which youth are told what they must do and informed of the consequences for failure to comply, without any negotiation at all. Although contracting does partialize work with clients, partialization has long been a part of social work and helps to motivate clients, by breaking the work into a series of manageable pieces and permitting small successes.

Acknowledging criticisms from colleagues, however, we will refer here to the *service agreement;* this term expresses the mutuality of the process and avoids the legalistic implications of the term *contract*. The *action plan* is the part of the service agreement that describes the specific actions to be undertaken in order to reach the objectives. Related terms in the literature include intervention plan, therapy plan, and treatment plan.

Mutuality. We have emphasized the partnership, or mutuality, of worker and applicant in all phases of the problem-solving process—engagement, data collection, and assessment. In the service agreement, however, the partnership concept is fully developed and made explicit. The service agreement is

> the explicit agreement between the worker and the client concerning the target problems, the goals, and the strategies of social work intervention, and the roles and tasks of the participants. Its major features are mutual agreement, differential participation in the intervention process, reciprocal accountability, and explicitness. In practice these features are closely interrelated. (Maluccio & Marlow, 1974, p. 30)

However, the concept of partnership does not mean that you and the client contribute the same knowledge, understanding, feeling, and activity. Your contributions are different but of equal importance.

As we have noted, an initial or exploratory agreement is developed in the engagement phase, to facilitate data collection. The differences between an exploratory agreement and a working agreement are explained in Exhibit 11–1.

Negotiation. The service agreement calls for input, decision making, planning, and commitment from both applicant and workers. It is your responsibility to respect the applicant's individuality and to maximize opportunities for applicant self-determination in the process of arriving at a service agreement. You will provide the applicant with opportunities for meaningful decisions about self and situation, through discussions, negotiations, choosing among available alternatives, or developing new alternatives. Negotiating a service agreement entails answering these questions:

1. Is the problem for work still the one that was initially identified?
2. Why has the problem persisted despite earlier attempts to solve it?
3. What is the desired solution? Specifically, what objectives should guide the action plan?
4. How will this solution be achieved?

EXHIBIT 11-1 **Ingredients of a Social Work Service Agreement**

A working agreement is essentially an understanding between at least two people and should cover:

1. The objectives or goals (the what) toward which each party shall work. These objectives should be specific, discrete, and, whenever feasible, observable.
2. The specific responsibilities of each party to the agreement in terms of rights and obligations.
3. The technique or means (the how) to be used in achieving the objectives.
4. The administrative procedures to be involved—when to meet, where to meet, and so on.

These four ingredients cover the essential terms of an agreement and should be explicit and detailed, so that each party knows clearly what is expected.

It is possible to specify at least two types of agreements: *exploratory and working.*

1. The exploratory agreement represents a commitment, by both parties, to explore and negotiate the terms of a working agreement. No other commitment is made at this stage.
2. A working agreement may or may not grow out of an exploratory agreement; this will depend on the negotiation that takes place.

Therefore, it is possible to specify the following sequence:

1. Acceptance of an *exploratory* agreement.
2. The development of a *working* agreement.
3. Review and evaluation of the accomplishments of the working agreement.
4. Renegotiation resulting in a new working agreement or termination. This is essentially a repetition of stage 1.

Source: Joe Hudson, Professor, Faculty of Social Welfare, University of Calgary, Calgary, Canada.

Remember that the applicant may be an individual, a family, a group, or an organization and that you may be interacting with applicants in a variety of settings.

In negotiating a service agreement you and your client will be confronting differences—of perception, thinking, and worldview—that must be resolved (Murdach, 1982; Seabury, 1979). You should not try to avoid conflict. To do so is counterproductive and results in corrupt contracts, which do not reflect an honest agreement on objectives (Seabury, 1979). Your goal should be to tease out differences and then negotiate them. Even if the conflict cannot be resolved, and no agreement is reached, at least no time or energy will have been wasted on a corrupt contract. An agreement between you and an applicant not to pursue service because of recognized differences or conflict is, in fact, an agreement.

If you are to be helpful, you must find a common ground with the applicant regarding problem definition, objectives, and an action plan. This will involve bargaining and negotiating and will generally call for perseverance. Workers who announce to a supervisor after a single contact with an applicant that they are closing the case, because agreement could not be reached, do not understand the nature of negotiation.

The Problem for Work

Developing a service agreement involves joint assessment and decision making. In the engagement phase, you and the applicant have arrived at an initial definition of the problem, set initial objectives, collected some data, and done some exploration of the identified problem and objectives. On that basis, you and the applicant must now define the problem for work, what can be done about it, and how you are going to do it. This will involve ordering and organizing the available information, intuitions, and knowledge into some pattern that explains the problem and suggests a number of possible solutions. This process includes two components: "analysis of a situation to identify the major factors operating within it" and "identification of those factors which appear most critical, definition of their interrelationships, and selection of those to be dealt with" (Bartlett, 1970, p. 144). Both you and the applicant will need to do hard and independent thinking in

assembling and ordering the information and in making judgments about its meaning; for you, this is a professional obligation.

The problem for work—the problem defined by you and the applicant on the basis of the completed assessment—may be the same as the presenting problem, may be a further specification or restatement of the presenting problem, or may be entirely different. Depending on the circumstances, the problem for work may be defined as residing with the applicant, as outside the applicant, or as the result of the applicant-situation interaction. The target of change may or may not be the applicant.

Ideally, the definition of the problem will suggest an effective solution and will be reflected in a problem statement (Reid, 1992). Here's a useful checklist for problem statements:

1. Does the statement describe something in the applicant's current situation as a source of discomfort that the applicant wants changed? Is the statement specific and explicit? A broad general statement—for example, "Tom does poorly at school"—is not useful. A much more specific statement is: "Tom is failing mathematics" or "Tom has been absent 25 of the last 60 days of school."

2. Is the applicant in the problem statement? If not, it is someone else's problem. For example, a service plan for the applicant cannot be supported by a problem statement such as: "The mathematics teacher has too high a grading standard" or "The staff at the school do not like Tom." A useful statement would be: "Tom is experiencing disfavor from his teachers" or "Tom's mathematics skills do not meet passing standards for his class." Either of these latter statements would allow for action plans directed toward changing Tom's behavior, changing the mathematics standards, or changing the way teachers relate to Tom.

3. Do you and the applicant have the capacity, power, and resources to solve or reduce the problem? It is not useful to formulate problems that have no possibility of solution.

4. Does the statement describe a problem for work, rather than a solution? The problem statement should suggest possible solutions but should not itself be a statement of the desired solution. Avoid statements of

objectives such as: "Tom needs to pass his mathematics course" or "Tom needs to improve school attendance."

Objectives and Solutions

What are the desired objectives of the joint work? What is the appropriate solution for the problem? To answer these questions, you will adopt the same process as in defining the problem for work. Your first responsibility is to use interviewing skills to discover applicant views of desired solutions. You may then share your view of the desired objective with the applicant. If the two views are not congruent, this difference must be negotiated, just as incongruent perceptions of the problem were negotiated. Unless you and the applicant can arrive at mutually agreeable solutions, there is no sense in proceeding, because you will be working in different directions.

Some professionals believe that the problem-solving model is only of value to applicants capable of highly rational functioning. But every human being wants something (if only to get rid of the worker), and these wants can be translated into wishes and hence into objectives. For many applicants, securing essential survival needs is the only objective worth setting. In that case, you and the applicant can agree that securing these essentials is the first and most important objective.[1] Some practitioners have strong views on what objectives are worthy of social work. In our view, however, what is most important is that applicants should be actively involved in thinking about objectives and that the objectives should relate to their wishes. If you feel that small concrete objectives are unimportant and that supplying concrete needs to apathetic, withdrawn, depressed, or angry people need not involve mutual problem definition and objective setting, you need to reexamine your assumptions about what meaningful professional interaction is.

Research into the outcomes of social work practice indicates that failure is often linked to a divergence of purpose between worker and applicant (Goldberg & Stanley, 1985; Lerner, 1972; Mayer & Timms, 1969;

Polansky, Bergman, & de Saix, 1973). Individuals who expect an agency to provide a certain kind of help, toward a certain kind of solution, will be confused if you offer something they do not understand and were not aware they wanted. In such situations, applicants will often leave the agency in frustration and disappointment.

In Chapter 8, we indicated that engagement includes identifying the solutions that applicants want for the problems they are encountering. Through assessment, you consider these solutions—and, if appropriate, other possible solutions—and examine their feasibility. The service plan records your joint decisions regarding the desired objectives or solutions. The solutions with which you are working—whether the initial wants, the initial wants reframed or revised, or an entirely different set—are negotiated and jointly agreed upon by you and the applicant (Berg & Miller, 1992; Cowger, 1994; Berg & de Jong, 1996).

In a qualitative study of workers' initial contact with applicants, Thomas Kenemore (1987) found that workers often needed to negotiate the services provided but were uncomfortable with this, for lack of explicit practice theory regarding the negotiation of applicant preferences.

In setting objectives, as in defining the problem for work, you will be looking for common ground with the applicant. Your task, as the worker, is to find a common objective to which you and the applicant can direct your change efforts. Once you have identified an objective that is important for the applicant and consistent with your professional obligations, begin at that point, even if there are other objectives that you deem more important or even more urgent. Opportunities to define other objectives will occur as you work together.

Consider the case of Mrs. Troy in Exhibit 11–2. The Troy family is experiencing what Germain and Gitterman (1980) call "problems and needs associated with tasks involved in life transitions" (p. 32). From the worker's viewpoint, important objectives would be to help Mrs. Troy develop skills in managing her children or handling stress. After exploration and negotiation, however, the worker agreed to Mrs. Troy's objective of getting John out of the house. Working toward this objective provided an opportunity for the worker to provide immediate assistance for Mrs. Troy. The objective also meets

---

[1] This may well entail pursuing changes in the environment, which runs counter to a tendency in social work to define problems and objectives in terms of personal qualities of the applicant (Rosen, 1993).

EXHIBIT 11-2   Getting John Out of the House

Mrs. Troy was referred to this agency for help in coping with her children. She was referred by a welfare department social worker who is providing brief individual counseling for Margaret, the 16-year-old daughter, regarding plans for her 2-month-old baby. The family consists of Mrs. Troy, age 42; John, age 19; Joe, age 17; Margaret, age 16; Robert, age 2 months (Margaret's baby); Marcel, age 14; and Raymond, age 12.

The social worker who made the referral thought Mrs. Troy needed help in handling the kids, especially the oldest boy, John. Before I saw Mrs. Troy, a second referral was made by the nurse who is working with Mrs. Troy, who is diabetic. The nurse stated that Mrs. Troy would become so upset with the kids, John in particular, that she would forget to take her medication. She thought that Mrs. Troy was at her wit's end and was threatening to leave the kids and disappear.

Mrs. Troy was not as desperate when I interviewed her two days later. She did, however, make it clear that she wanted some help to get John out of the house.

She also wanted the other kids to do what they were told. Mrs. Troy saw John as the main problem. He deliberately aggravated the other kids, ordered them around, would sit around the house all day and have his friends over, refused to obey her, and called her profane names. Mrs. Troy's boyfriend moved out a few months ago because of the frequent arguments he had with John. She also felt that John's bad example was causing her to lose control of the other kids.

Mrs. Troy's primary request was for help in getting John to move out of the house, but she didn't seem to feel there was much hope of doing it. She had tried putting his clothes out, locking him out, and changing the locks. Each time, John persisted in his efforts to get back in by shouting and pounding on the doors and windows. Mrs. Troy, feeling powerless and seeing no alternative, would let him in. On one occasion when John became belligerent after coming home drunk, she called the police. They simply drove him a few blocks away and released him.

---

two important tests: specificity and attainability. Let's consider these two qualities.

First, objectives should be sufficiently specific and concrete to be measurable. Indeed, explicitness is a criterion for all parts of the service plan—problem statement, objectives, and action plan (Lundy, 1993). The establishment of measurable objectives is necessary to integrate social work practice with research and evaluation (Greene, 1989). It permits applicant and worker to determine whether the objectives have been accomplished and provides the basis for accountability within the profession. Broadly stated objectives—such as helping a person feel better, increasing opportunities for socializing experiences, or improving parent-child relationships—are meaningless and do not provide the relief wanted by applicants (Epstein, 1980; Berg & Miller, 1992; Reid, 1992).

Second, there should be a reasonable chance of attaining the objectives. The attainability of an objective will depend on the applicant's degree of interest and abilities and also on the available resources; these factors are sometimes referred to, respectively, as motivation, capacity, and opportunity (Ripple & Alexander, 1956). Increasing motivation, capacity, or opportunity in a particular area might itself be selected as an objective, in some circumstances.

Feminist and other scholars have noted the benefits of selecting small objectives, which are relatively easy to meet, rather than large objectives, which may be difficult to achieve and discouraging for the applicant (Russell, 1989; Berg & Miller, 1992). Short-term objectives that can be accomplished within a few weeks—or even a few days—are likely to be more concrete and attainable than longer-term objectives, which are usually stated in general terms. Thus, we suggest that you focus on short-term, immediate objectives. Once you have successful experiences, you and your clients can always develop new service agreements, with new objectives. Exhibit 11–3 lists criteria for well-formed objectives.

The Action Plan

The action plan lays out the detailed steps that you and the applicant will take to move from the problem for work to solutions. The process by which you and the applicant determine the action plan resembles that adopted in defining the problem and in arriving at objectives. You will first discover what the applicant would like to do to reach the solution and what the applicant expects you to do. You must also establish your own expectations of what you will do to accomplish the objectives and what the applicant will do. Any differ-

---

EXHIBIT 11-3 | **Well-Formed Objectives**

1. The objectives belong to the client and are expressed in the client's language.
2. The objectives are small. Small objectives are easier to achieve than larger ones.
3. The objectives are concrete, specific, and behavioral.
4. The objectives seek presence rather than absence.
5. The objectives have beginnings rather than endings.
6. The objectives are realistic within the context of the client's life.
7. The objectives are perceived by the client as involving hard work.

Source: J. K. Berg & S. D. Miller. *Working with the problem drinker: A solution focused approach.* New York: W. W. Norton (1992), pp. 32–44.

---

ences in these expectations must be negotiated and resolved.

The principle of equifinality suggests that there are many routes to any desired end state. A common error in social work is to offer an action plan without considering alternatives with your applicant. Consider Exhibit 11–4, which is an excerpt from the Stover case (Appendix A-2). There is agreement that the problem is Mrs. Stover's lack of knowledge about cooking and that the objective is for her to be able to prepare more attractive meals. The worker precipitously develops the action plan of providing Mrs. Stover with a recipe file. A better process would have been to involve Mrs. Stover in the discussion. What steps might enable her to improve her cooking skills? Perhaps she knows of friends, relatives, or neighbors from whom she could request recipes; perhaps she could make use of the public library; perhaps a county extension agency or some other organization could provide the services of a home economist. One possible action plan is summarized in Exhibit 11–5.

Offering an action plan too quickly denies applicants the opportunity to plan and work toward solutions to their own problems and thereby denies them the opportunity to display their strengths.

The development of a service plan should include a systematic review of applicant strengths. Develop a list of strengths and discuss with the applicant how these might be used to accomplish each objective. Strengths, of course, include the applicant's personal resources, as well as the resources of family, friends, and neighbors and cultural resources. Examples of strengths for Mrs. Stover might include: "talks at least once a week with her mother," "occasionally has coffee with the neighbor," and "has visited the local public library."

Time limits. Note that the agreement in Exhibit 11–5 contains time limits for completing the tasks. We suggest that you set a date for the accomplishment of each activity in the service plan. On that basis, you and the applicant can evaluate whether the plan was implemented as scheduled. Deadlines tend to motivate people. Reid and Epstein (1972) call this the goal gradient effect; When deadlines are approaching, people's efforts increase. Think of your own experience in completing course assignments. Would the work get done without deadlines?

Working with groups. Though most of our illustrations have involved individual clients, you will also be developing service plans in work with families

---

EXHIBIT 11-4 | **A Recipe File for Mrs. Stover?**

Mrs. Stover brought up a further problem in connection with running the household. She is now getting more interested in housework and cooking. She is realizing how little she knows about cooking. She attempted to cook a goose for the family, but due to improper cleaning of the goose beforehand, spoiled it. She claims the food that she knows how to prepare is plain and unattractive and she feels she is lacking in knowledge of skill in cooking. The children do some complaining about the food; George recently pointed out that other children he knows get more variety than he does. I agreed to bring a recipe file for Mrs. Stover containing a large variety of recipes and some instructions on food preparation and menus.

EXHIBIT 11-5   **A Sample Service Agreement with Mrs. Stover**

Date: February 3

Problem: Mrs. Stover is unable to prepare an attractive variety of meals for her family.

Objective: By February 10, Mrs. Stover will be able to prepare and serve her family a dish she has not previously prepared.

Action plan:

1. On February 4, Mrs. Stover will invite her neighbor to coffee and make inquiries about recipes for preparation of low-cost main dishes.
2. By February 5, Mrs. Stover will call at the public library and check cookbooks for two or three new recipes.

3. Worker will contact the county extension agency to determine if: (a) the service of a home economist consultant is available; and (b) the agency has recipes available for low-cost main dishes.
4. February 7. Worker will telephone Mrs. Stover to review progress on securing recipes. We expect that Mrs. Stover will be able to select a recipe to try over the weekend.
5. February 8 or 9. Mrs. Stover will prepare a new dish for her family.
6. February 10. Mrs. Stover and worker will meet at 10 A.M. to evaluate the plan and to decide about next steps.

(Anderson & Stewart, 1984; Fox, 1987; McClendon & Kadis, 1990; Schulman, 1992) and other groups (Preston-Shoot, 1989; Wickham, 1993). The group dynamics will introduce some additional complexities. Family and group members may have different views about problems, solutions, and action plans. Working as a mediator, you will assist the group or family to resolve these differences, so that a service agreement can be negotiated. Some group or family members may have hidden agendas that interfere with the development of a service agreement. Exhibit 11–6 offers some ideas for helping a group to reach a decision.

Focusing on results. Donald Campbell (1975) distinguishes between two types of agency administrators. Trapped administrators are so concerned with a particular program or set of activities that they cannot adapt or change. Experimental administrators, on the other hand, are committed to accomplishing the objectives and goals of the agency; they are prepared to change, to adapt, and to replace programs and activities as necessary in order to accomplish the objectives and goals of their agency.

There are also trapped practitioners—social workers who focus on particular activities or services rather than

---

EXHIBIT 11-6   **Helping a Group Reach a Decision**

1. State the problem clearly.
   Examples: ``The purpose of this meeting is . . .''
   ``Our job for today is . . .''
2. If the problem or a given statement is not clear, ask for clarification.
   Examples: ``I'm not sure I understand the purpose of this meeting. Would you mind restating it?''
   ``I'm sorry, I missed that point. Will you say it again?''
3. Stay on focus and help others to do so.
   Examples: ``I don't quite see how that relates to our problem.''
   ``It seems to me we're digressing.''
4. Summarize.
   Examples: ``Here are the points we have made so far . . .''
   ``Thus far we have agreed . . .''

5. Test the workability of proposals.
   Examples: ``Do you think the members would support that proposal?''
   ``Where would we get the money to do that?''
6. Test willingness to carry out the proposal.
   Examples: ``Would you be willing to . . .''
   ``Who can take this responsibility?''
7. Test readiness for decision.
   Examples: ``Are we agreed, then, that . . .''
   ``Well, are we ready to make that decision?''
8. Call for the decision.
   Examples: ``I move that . . .''
   ``Will someone put this into a motion?''

on accomplishing objectives. They tend to see every problem and objective in terms of a particular approach to interaction, such as advocacy, family counseling, or twelve step programs for addictions treatment. We must be able to think about alternative courses of action if we want our clients to do so. Further, if we can generate a greater number of possible solutions to a problem, we are likely to generate higher-quality solutions (D'Zurilla, 1986; Heidrich & Denny, 1994; Nezu & D'Zurilla, 1981). To avoid becoming a trapped practitioner, follow these guidelines:

1. Be open to the action plan the applicant prefers.
2. Carefully consider alternative action plans to accomplish any objective.
3. Carefully consider what research evidence supports your favorite or preferred interventions or the activities that you like to see in action plans.
4. Be open to action plans that call for an intervention beyond your range of interest or skill. In these situations, the initial action plan will include steps to find those skills within the community.

Limitations on worker activity. When negotiating an action plan, you must be aware of four important limitations on your activity: time, skill, ethics, and agency function.

Time. You cannot responsibly commit yourself to activities that extend beyond the time you have available; conversely, a client can reasonably expect you to do what you say you will do. Consider this incident. A social worker placed a 14-year-old boy in a foster home. Knowing that the youth might have some initial adjustment problems, the worker indicated that they would meet weekly to talk about them. Burdened by a heavy caseload, however, the worker was unable to visit the boy until four weeks after placement, and the boy, disillusioned and angry, rejected the worker's efforts to become involved. The youth ran away and eventually became institutionalized. Had this worker made a realistic agreement—to see the boy once a month instead of once a week—client and worker might have been able to maintain communication and to engage in more effective problem solving. Don't confuse intensity of service with quality of service. Poor-quality service is provided when you make commitments that you cannot meet; conversely, frequent contacts between worker and client do not necessarily imply high-quality service. You must plan your time so that you do not make unrealistic commitments.

Skill. You should not enter into service agreements calling for activity that exceeds your skills. When a client requires a specialized skill that you do not possess—such as marriage counseling or bargaining with a large bureaucracy—the negotiated action plan will include the participation of an appropriate expert or specialist. In the proposed service plan for Mrs. Stover (Exhibit 11–5), for example, the worker secured information about the service of a home economist; we don't expect social workers to be experts in cooking or nutrition.

Ethics. You will avoid involvement in intervention plans that commit you to unethical behavior. For example, the applicant's economic crisis might be alleviated by a burglary, but it would obviously not be appropriate for you to participate in such an action. You will also be unlikely to agree to a plan that involves the exploitation of others or racial, ethnic, or gender discrimination.

Agency. As we noted in Chapter 5, social services tend to be organized around specific functions (Wilensky & Lebeaux, 1958) that sets limits on worker-client agreements (Murdach, 1982). You have the options of interpreting agency function broadly, requesting exceptions to agency limitations, and working within your agency to secure a broader definition of its functions (Chapter 5) but, as long as agencies have community-sanctioned functions, you must take account of these limitations when making commitments to clients.

Written Agreements

The service agreement, including the action plan, may be in oral or written form. Written agreements have some clear advantages. As Barker (1987) notes, written agreements, although underused in social work, are effective tools for explicating objectives and mutual expectations. They help identify ambiguities and improve the specificity of the plan, thereby reducing the likelihood of misunderstanding and aiding evaluation (Wilcoxon, 1991). Written agreements are more effective in reaching objectives than are oral agreements (Klein, Fein, & Genevo, 1984; Tolson, 1988). Putting agreements in written form will also provide a useful learning experience, especially in your early attempts to develop agreements. A possible written agreement for the Stover case appears in Exhibit 11–5.

Another important consideration is that workers, like clients, are more likely to follow through on commitments that have been made explicit in a written agreement. In our view, clients must be able to hold social workers accountable (Chapter 17). The profession needs effective channels by which clients may file complaints against workers who have not competently followed through on their commitments. Possibilities include agency appeals, consumer services that incorporate worker/client mediation, and professional malpractice complaints filed against workers. A worker's failure to follow through on an agreed-upon intervention plan constitutes professional malpractice.

INTERVENTIVE ROLES

Definition

The action plan requires you to assist your client in identifying and implementing a solution to the problem for work. To do so, you will take on a variety of interventive roles.

We define intervention in a relatively restricted sense, as activities undertaken subsequent to the development of a service agreement so as to achieve objectives specified in the service agreement. Some social workers use the term in a more global way, to refer to all social work activities, including data collection and assessment. However, we believe that defining intervention as distinct from data collection and assessment will keep these three aspects of social work in a more balanced perspective and place proper emphasis on the need to reach an agreement with the applicant before any change activities can begin. In line with this definition, the worker's interventive roles constitute the behavior expected of the worker by both client (individual, family, group, or community) and worker to accomplish the objectives specified in the service agreement.

We will consider five interventive roles—social broker, enabler, teacher, mediator, and advocate. Some authors conceptualize social worker roles differently; for example, Charles Grosser (1965) has discussed the roles of broker, enabler, advocate, and activist in community development work. The literature also includes

references to additional roles such as therapist (Briar, 1967b), encourager (Biddle & Biddle, 1965), ombudsman (Payne, 1972), bargainer (Brager & Jorcin, 1969), lobbyist (Mahaffey, 1972), and validator (Tobias, 1990).

The interventive roles of broker, enabler, teacher, mediator, and advocate provide a framework for thinking about interventive activity with systems of any size, from individual to community. This framework is independent of specific change modalities, which tend to wax and wane over time; several authors have assembled lists of interventive modalities (Roberts & Nee, 1970; Rothman & Tropman, 1987; Tropp, 1968; Whittaker, 1974). In Chapter 12, we discuss some useful change methods that have withstood the test of time.

Social Broker

To understand the role of social broker, let's consider an analogy. Stockbrokers assist clients to define their resources, assess risk tolerance, and develop investment objectives. They then use their contacts and knowledge of the market to select stocks consistent with clients' objectives. How about real estate brokers? Realtors help to analyze clients' resources and needs and defining objectives about the desired type of home, and then draw on their knowledge of the available housing resources to meet the clients' objectives. Similarly, a social work broker links the client with other community resources, in order to accomplish the objectives specified in the service agreement. Serving as a social broker requires a broad knowledge of community resources, as well as knowledge of agency operating procedures, so that effective connections can be made.

You are acting as a social broker when you arrange for a client to receive marital counseling, for job placement, or for improved housing; when you bring outside experts to provide valuable information to groups; or when you assist a community group by identifying sources of program funding or additional outside expertise.

Referral is a basic activity of the social broker. In many cases, the most important service you can provide is to help a client find and use a needed resource—not only formal social agencies and community programs but also clubs, organizations, and associations in which they might wish to participate.

Enabler

In the enabler role, you assist clients to find the coping strengths and resources within themselves in order to produce the changes required by the objectives of the service agreement. Change occurs because of client efforts; your responsibility is to facilitate—or enable—the client's accomplishment of a defined change. A common misconception is that the enabler only facilitates change within the client or in the client's pattern of relating. However, the enabler can also help the client find ways of altering the environment. In Reading 12-1, Barbara Solomon discusses an empowerment approach for work with families and identifies four empowerment strategies—enabling, linking, catalyzing, and priming.

You are an enabler when you assist a group of neighborhood residents to think through the need for a new day care center, identify factors that must be considered in establishing the center, and plan the steps that might be taken to provide day care; when you help a group to identify sources of internal conflict and other factors obstructing movement toward defined objectives and then to discover ways of dealing with these difficulties; and when you assist a mother to identify problems in her relationship with her child and to identify and select alternative courses of action to improve that relationship.

Enablers may encourage verbalization, facilitate the ventilation of feelings, examine the pattern of relationships, offer encouragement and reassurance, or engage in logical discussion and rational decision making. What Tobias (1990) calls the validator role may also be an aspect of enabling: "The function of the validator is to confirm, legitimize, substantiate, or verify the feelings, ideas, values, or beliefs of the client as well-grounded, correct, or genuine within the client's system" (p. 357). Tobias sees this role as particularly important for work with mentally ill clients, "who from the onset of their illness have experienced confusing and painful feelings

and ideas, distorted perceptions, and impaired judgment . . . compounded by years of institutional delegitimization, disqualification, and negation" (p. 35). The enabler role primarily involves contacts with the client, rather than with external systems.

Some social workers are disinclined to think of themselves as enablers because of the negative connotation of this word in the context of addiction. It might be useful to distinguish between positive and negative enabling. Negative enabling—for instance, justifying excessive use of alcohol because of stress, delinquency or crime because of unemployment, or spouse battering because of whining is inappropriate in social work. People are responsible for the decisions they make; our responsibility is to help clients sort through these decisions and their possible implications. On the other hand, positive enabling involves assisting individuals and groups to rally their strengths and respond to the problems they are experiencing. Stress, for example, might be handled through exercise, meditation, or joining a stress management group, rather than drinking.

Teacher

In the teacher role, you may provide clients with new information necessary for coping with problem situations, assist clients in practicing new behaviors or skills, or model alternative behavior patterns. You are performing a teacher role when you supply low-income parents with shopping and nutritional information or provide parents with information regarding child development for coping with difficult problems of children; when you demonstrate different ways for an adolescent to respond to the authority of teachers, by means of role-playing; when you teach a neighborhood group how to request more frequent refuse services from the city council; and when you carefully check out the meaning of words and phrases and model clear communication. Exhibit 11–7 illustrates the use of role-playing.

EXHIBIT 11–7	A Drop-in Neighbor

Mary Maki is a resident of a high-rise apartment building. Other residents are constantly dropping in on her, and she feels her privacy is being violated. On several occasions, Mary has become angry with these visitors. She wants to find a balance between protecting her privacy and maintaining friendships. The worker and Mary agree that alternative responses to anger are needed. Thus, Mary and the worker role-play situations in which Mary can learn to deal with a drop-in neighbor without harming a friendship.

Like the enabler, the teacher strengthens clients' abilities to cope and to change the problems in their situation. Whereas the enabler helps clients to mobilize existing resources, however, the teacher introduces additional resources into client systems.

Teaching is an important aspect of social work practice. In some cases, the information that you provide may be all that is needed in order to accomplish the objectives. However, don't confuse giving information with giving advice. Giving information implies supplying data, input, or knowledge that clients are free to use or not, as they see fit. Giving advice implies that you know what is best for the client; you will rarely give advice. Schwartz (1961) offers three important warnings about providing information:

1. You must recognize that the information you offer is only a small part of the available social experience.
2. The information should be related to the problem being addressed.
3. Opinions should be clearly labeled as such and not represented as facts.

Mediator

Mediation involves efforts to resolve disputes between the client system and other persons or organizations. If a young person has been expelled from school and the service agreement has the goal of getting the student back into school, you may need to serve as a mediator between the young person and the school authorities. If a neighborhood group wishes to secure a playground but has insufficient political power to do so, because of rivalries with another neighborhood organization, you may need to mediate between the two organizations. Exhibit 11–8 provides an illustration of mediation.

In the mediator role, you will assist clients and the other party to find a common ground on which to reach a resolution of the conflict. There is growing literature on mediation and conflict resolution (Dillon & Emery, 1996; Folger, Poole, & Stutman, 1993; Kruk, 1997; Leviton & Greenstone, 1997; Moore, 1986; Parsons, 1991; Savoury, Beals, & Parks, 1995; Severson & Bankston, 1995; Tolson, McDonald, & Moriarty, 1992; Umbreit, 1995). You will work at facilitating communication between the parties by encouraging them to talk to each other; information sharing and persuasion may also be helpful.

In serving as a mediator, you will:

- try to bring about a convergence of the perceived interests of both parties to the conflict
- help each party recognize the legitimacy of the other's interests
- assist the parties in identifying common interests in a successful outcome
- avoid a situation in which issues of winning and losing are paramount
- attempt to localize the conflict to specific issues, times, and places
- break the conflict down to separate issues
- help parties identify that they have more at stake in continuing a relationship than the issue of the specific conflict

When working with groups or families, the mediator role will also prove useful in resolving disputes *within* the client system. Such mediation can also be regarded as enabling, since resolving intrasystem disputes permits the client to mobilize resources and move toward the objectives of the service agreement. A debate about when mediation is mediation and when is it enabling is not particularly useful, although this does illustrate the overlap between the various interventive roles.

EXHIBIT 11-8	Mediating a Conflict in a Board and Lodging Home

Ida Wick, who lives in a board and lodging home, collects mementos and keeps old newspapers. The board and lodging operator has asked Ida to have some of the items moved, because of fire regulations. When Ida and the operator become irritated with one another, the social worker acts as a mediator. The worker first discusses the problem with Ida and then makes a request for a joint meeting with the operator. In the meeting, the worker negotiates a settlement by which the fire safety standards can be met. Ida is provided with a storage cabinet, in which to keep her more important mementos and with a scrapbook for newspaper clippings.

Like therapy, mediation is a specialist function in social work. Workers may specialize exclusively in mediation; some may specialize even more narrowly—in mediating parent-adolescent conflicts, for instance, or mediating child custody conflicts in divorce cases. From time to time, you will use mediation and conflict resolution skills in your practice and, as a broker, you will refer some clients to a specialist mediator.

Advocate

As an advocate, you present and argue the client's cause when this is necessary to accomplish the objectives of the agreement. Charles Grosser (1965) notes that in social work, as in the legal profession, the advocate is not neutral but a partisan representative for the client. Reviewing social work concepts of advocacy, Michael Sosin and Sharon Caulum (1983) concluded that a more precise definition was required and, to address that need, defined advocacy as

> an attempt, having a greater than zero probability of success, by an individual or group to influence another individual or group to make a decision that would not have been made otherwise and that concerns the welfare or interests of a third party who is in a less powerful status than the decision makers. (p. 12)

As advocate you will argue, debate, bargain, negotiate, and manipulate the environment on behalf of the client. Advocacy differs from mediation. In mediation the effort is to secure resolution to a dispute through give and take on both sides; in advocacy, the effort is to win for the client. Advocacy efforts are frequently directed toward securing benefits to which the client is entitled (Exhibit 11–9). Most social workers use advocacy (Ezell, 1994), although perhaps less frequently than other roles (Herbert & Levin, 1996).

Unlike the broker, enabler, teacher, and mediator roles, advocacy can be used without the direct involvement of the client. This creates the risk of proceeding without having a clear agreement with the client to do so (Torczyner, 1991). Lawyers do not become the representatives for clients until clients have retained them and authorized them to extend this service; likewise, you should be sure you have an explicit agreement with the client before engaging in advocacy.

Roles and Specialization

Because we have discussed the interventive roles separately, you may have concluded that these roles could serve as a basis for specialization in social work. Certainly, some of the roles, such as mediator, may be developed as a specialty practice. However, a generalist worker needs to be able to serve as broker, enabler, teacher, mediator, and advocate; to specialize will limit your ability to help clients. If you have skills in all roles, you and the client can select the most appropriate interventive role for each situation; this provides a range of possible means of achieving objectives.

Exhibit 11–10 presents a conversation between a social worker in a Head Start program and Mrs. B, who wants to enroll her child in the program. Note the development of a preliminary service contract. There is agreement that Mrs. B is having difficulty with Jimmy, and the objective is for her to learn new ways of handling him. The intervention proposed by the worker is to talk with Mrs. B about parenting skills; this involves the enabler and, possibly, the teacher role. However, the roles of broker, mediator, and advocate might also have been used. For example, further exploration about what happened at the child guidance center, about her perceptions of what the doctor said, about

---

EXHIBIT 11-9	**Advocacy with Social Security**
Hullie Mutton's benefits from the Social Security office have been summarily decreased, on the grounds that an overpayment was made to her. The Social Security office admits the error was theirs. The social worker discusses the decrease with the client and offers to contact the office in Mrs. Mutton's behalf. The worker stresses to the representative,	Miss Jones, that the error was not the client's and that the reduction in SSI is taxing to Mrs. Mutton. Further, the worker requests information on the appeal process and indicates that the client wishes to begin the proceedings. Miss Jones agrees to take a further look at Mrs. Mutton's situation and says that she will ask her supervisor for an exception.

EXHIBIT 11-10   How to Discipline Jimmy?

Mrs. B told me about taking Jimmy to the child guidance center and what the doctor had told her. Apparently the doctor had tested Jimmy and then talked to Mrs. B. She had complained of his bad behavior and that she didn't know how to discipline him. Apparently the doctor told her that the problem might be hers and not Jimmy's. He said that she was lonely and insecure and maybe needed some guidance in handling her children. She discussed this freely and admitted that this might be true. I asked her whether she would like to have me come over to talk to her about ways to handle Jimmy. She said definitely yes, that she couldn't do a thing with him.

her thinking and feelings concerning the experience, and about her willingness to return to the center might have led to an action plan in which the worker served as a broker and linked Mrs. B and the center. If there was a problem with the manner in which the center related to Mrs. B, the worker might have used a mediator role to solve these disputes or an advocate role to serve as Mrs. B's representative at the center. The objective remains the same—to help alter Mrs. B's way of relating to her son—but the action plan to accomplish this objective may involve counseling with Mrs. B, serving as the broker linking Mrs. B and the center, mediating differences between Mrs. B and the center, or acting as Mrs. B's advocate and representing her interests to the center. Your ability to use all the interventive roles and your willingness to explore the client situation thoroughly provide a wide range of options for action.

Note that an intervention plan may combine elements of various roles. As an illustration, let's consider the referral process, a major part of the social broker role. Referral involves three distinct steps: preparation of the client; preparation of the referral organization; and follow-up. In preparing the client, you discuss what the referral will involve and what the referral agency expects. Adopting enabler and teacher roles, you allow the client to make effective use of the referral agency.

In preparing the referral agency, you share information about the client, with the client's full knowledge and usually with the client's consent. In some situations, an agency may be reluctant to accept a referral; you may then need to use mediation or advocacy. After the client makes initial contact with the referral organization, you will follow up with both the client and the organization. Ideally, follow-up should be a part of the initial planning. As a result of follow-up, you may learn about resistances in the client or in the referral organization,

which may again call for enabling, teaching, mediation, and/or advocacy skills.

This model of social brokering, supplemented by the other interventive roles, is central to the use of formal social support and social care (Chapter 13). In order to provide a useful service, you must be skilled at involving the client in developing a service agreement and skilled at helping the client to find and use the resources necessary to meet the objectives of the agreement. Such an approach requires the ability to humanize the ways in which services are delivered and to assist agencies in meeting their responsibilities to clients.

CHAPTER SUMMARY

The service agreement is negotiated between worker and applicant. It defines the problem for work, specifies the objectives, and provides an action plan designed to move from the problem to the objectives. The service agreement is a commitment on the part of both worker and applicant to implement the plan; changes can, of course, be jointly negotiated. Here are three important principles:

1. Joint negotiation of the service agreement involves input from both worker and applicant. Don't be afraid to provide appropriate input; your professional judgment, experience, and background are all sources of knowledge and information that should be available to the applicant in decision making. The key is to arrive at a service agreement that represents the best collective judgment of both you and the applicant.

2. In the ecosystem approach, you and the applicant must be alert to the widest possible range of objectives and interventive approaches: The target of change may be the applicant, the environment, or their interaction.

No worker can be expected to master all change strategies, but you need to be aware of the repertoire of change strategies available to the profession and to be able to help the client select the most appropriate strategy. If you cannot provide the service, you should be able to locate it elsewhere in the community.

3. The development of a service agreement is a cognitive process involving thinking, reasoning, and decision making. Feelings are important, but planning should be done on a rational basis. The planning may, of course, involve plans to deal with feelings. Interventive efforts should be based on a deliberate rational service agreement negotiated with the client.

Intervention has been defined as the social worker's activity directed toward achieving the objectives of a service agreement. The five interventive roles discussed—social broker, enabler, teacher, mediator, and advocate—may often be used to reach the same objectives; this provides you and the client with alternative approaches to intervention. In addition, the roles may be used in conjunction with one another. The generalist social work will tend to focus on social brokerage, in which enabling and teaching are used to improve clients' access to community resources, and mediation and advocacy are used to influence the delivery of resources to clients.

As we saw in Chapter 10, you will move sequentially with a client from problem to problem, rather than trying to address all at once. Thus, you will also be continuously negotiating and phasing in appropriate service agreements and action plans. Service agreements must be flexible enough to be renegotiated as client needs and

wants change (Schulman, 1992; Tolson, Reid, & Garvin, 1994). New or revised agreements will build on what you have learned in your work together; social work is a developmental process (Rothery, 1980).

A LOOK FORWARD

In the remaining chapters, we consider various tools for implementing the service agreement: interventions that assist clients to mobilize power (Chapter 12), the use of formal (Chapter 13) and informal (Chapter 14) social support, the development of helping communities (Chapter 15), teamwork (Chapter 16), evaluation (Chapter 17), ways to end services (Chapter 18), and ways to avoid burnout (Chapter 19).

In Reading 11-1, Michelle MacKenzie describes the solution-focused brief therapy model, which focuses on assisting applicants to define the solutions they desire and moving quickly to accomplish these solutions. Prolonged discussion and clear definition of problems is not considered necessary. This approach has much to contribute to problem-solving models of practice. Problem solving is not problem-focused; it means identifying applicant wants, solutions, and objectives, and developing action plans to reach those solutions or objectives.

In Reading 11-2, Edith Fein and Ilene Staff describe a process for setting goals—in the terminology used in this book, objectives—with birth parents of children in care. The service planning involves identifying and stating goals, building on strengths and resources, and creating action plans. You will find their suggestions useful for work with most clients.

READING 11-1 *A Brief Solution-Focused Practice Model**
Michelle MacKenzie

Families often provide social workers with vague or conflicting descriptions of what they want to change. The worker typically attempts to help families articulate clear and specific goals and to develop a service plan against which the effectiveness of the treatment can be judged (de Shazer, 1975, 1982; Fisch, Weakland, &

*An original reading prepared for this book.

Seagal, 1982; Haley, 1963; Jacobson, 1985; Weakland, Fisch, Watzlawick, & Bodin; 1974). Solution-focused brief therapy (de Shazer, 1984, 1985) is designed to assist in developing a clear idea of the goals of service and in creating a positive context for change. De Shazer (1985) maintains that families often cannot recognize the solutions to their own problems that they already have at their disposal. Solution-focused therapy is designed to shift the focus from past to present and future and from problems to strengths and to promote expectations of change. The service focus emphasizes family resources and creates a context in which "change is not only possible but inevitable" (de Shazer, 1985, p. 137).

The solution-focused brief therapy model is optimistic and proactive (de Shazer et al., 1986) and offers both the family and social worker an efficient and practical means for solving problems. Because the focus is on solutions and what is working, the model promotes cooperation and hope.

The model focuses on solution construction with clients. What clients find helpful often has no direct relationship to the problems presented (de Shazer, 1985). Rather than trying to understand the problem, the worker asks clients questions and identifies tasks that help them focus on their own perception of needs and goals and their own existing and potential resources for solutions (Lipchik & de Shazer, 1986; Molnar & de Shazer, 1987). Discovering exceptions—times when the problem wasn't a problem (or was less severe—is more helpful than asking about the times it was a problem (Molnar & de Shazer, 1987).

The approach is based on Milton Erickson's ideas about people's resources (Durrant, 1992; de Shazer, 1982). Erickson was not particularly interested in helping people consciously understand their predicaments; he thought that insight and interpretation were largely useless. Three primary principles of Erickson's work have been assimilated into the solution-focused brief therapy model (de Shazer, 1982):

1. Meet the patient where he is at, and gain rapport.
2. Modify the patient's productions and gain control.
3. Use the control that has been established to structure the situation so that change, when it does occur, will occur in a desirable manner and a manner compatible with the patient's inner wishes and drives.

Brief therapy is time-limited; Weakland prefers to call his work efficient therapy (Weakland et al., 1974), as does Steve de Shazer (1988a): "Therapy should be as efficient and effective as possible, and brief therapy is built around ways of knowing when therapy is finished" (p. 29). Brevity is a metaphor for clarity about what needs to be changed, an attitude of being task-oriented (Budman & Gurman, 1988). Brief therapy has also been termed problem-solving therapy (Molnar & de Shazer, 1987; Miller, 1992). The premise is that problems are maintained by repetitive interactional patterns. Once the pattern has been identified, a solution can be developed to interrupt it and reduce or extinguish the problem (Haley, 1987).

Solution-focused practitioners do not accept that the problem and its underlying causes must be known in order to find a solution. Rather, they relate the continuation of the problem to the context in which it occurs and the expectation that it will continue (de Shazer, 1988a). Consequently, the focus is on the situation, rather than on the person. Solutions can be developed by amplifying nonproblematic patterns, without attempting to determine what caused the problem (de Shazer & Berg, 1988). The solution-focused brief therapist shifts from changing problems to constructing and initiating solutions (Lipchik & de Shazer, 1986).

Solutions, like problems, vary a great deal from individual to individual, but they are similar enough to allow researchers to formulate a description that fits for most (Miller, 1992). Solutions may be described "as the behavior and/or perceptual changes that the therapist and client construct to alter the identified difficulty, the ineffective way of overcoming the difficulty, and/or the construction of an acceptable, alternative perspective that enables the client to experience the complaint situation differently" (de Shazer et al., 1986, p. 210).

Problems or complaints requiring service are typically defined as involving a limited set of behaviors, perceptions, thoughts, expectations, and feelings (de Shazer, 1988a). The role of the therapist is to assist clients in discovering the solutions outside the complaint. "The solution focus emphasizes exceptions to the rules of the problem rather than the rules of the problem itself" (Molnar & de Shazer, 1987, p. 350). The therapist engages clients in developing solutions by asking when the complaint does not occur. By "generating discussion about such exceptions to the complaint, the clinician and client system create the opportunity for solutions to completely emerge" (Miller, 1992, p. 3). Any exception to the complaint is a potential solution, since it lies outside the constraint of the problem and the accompanying worldview. Often, clients can describe exceptions to the problem, but do not regard them as significant. "For the clients, these are not differences that make a difference; making these differences make a difference is the heart of the therapist's job" (de Shazer & Berg, 1988, p. 42).

To do so, the therapist needs to explore the constraints of the complaint (de Shazer et al., 1986). The solution needs to fit within those constraints (de Shazer, 1985, 1988a). The quality of fit will depend on the relationship between the social worker and the client(s) (in particular, the feelings of closeness and responsiveness within that relationship), the pathway the interview takes, and the goals (de Shazer, 1988b; Lipchik & de Shazer, 1986).

The solution-focused brief therapy model promotes collaboration between social worker and client system (de Shazer, 1984). Resistance is reframed as the client's way of informing the worker that the present intervention does not fit (de Shazer, 1988a). To promote and encourage collaboration,

> First we connect the present to the future (ignoring the past), than we compliment clients on what they are already doing that is useful and/or good for them, and then—once they know we are on their side—we can make a suggestion for something new that they might do which is, or at least might be, good for them. (de Shazer, 1988a, p. 15)

People come to therapy because they want to change their situation but their attempts to change have not worked (de Shazer, 1985; de Shazer et al., 1986). A small change in one person's behavior can produce far-reaching differences; specifically, a change in one part of the system leads to changes in the system as a whole. Accordingly, smaller changes are promoted because "the bigger the goal or the desired change, the harder it will be to establish a cooperative relationship and the more likely the therapist and client will fail" (de Shazer et al., 1986).

A primary task of intervention is to help clients change their method of constructing experience. If clients construct—and talk about—their experiences in a different way, they may begin to have different experiences, which, in turn, will prompt different depictions or reports in subsequent sessions (de Shazer, 1988a).

In the initial interview, the therapist works to build rapport and create a workable, task-centered, and cooperative therapeutic alliance with the client (Lipchik & de Shazer, 1986). The establishment of rapport leads to fit between the client and the social worker. Understanding and accepting the client's worldview is essential for the development of useful solutions and, correspondingly, the quality of the therapeutic alliance established in the first session predicts the outcome of contracted, short-term therapy (Marziali, 1984; Marizial & Alexander, 1991; Moras & Strupp, 1982). Furthermore, rapport promotes hopefulness about the therapeutic process, which is also significantly associated with a favorable outcome.

It is optimal to contract the goals of therapy early in the therapeutic process—preferably during the first interview—as success in therapy depends upon establishing criteria for change (Thomlison, 1984). Lipchik (1986) states that goals must be set "by the end of the first session so that there is a focus for the therapy and some way to evaluate progress" (p. 94). Also, "the family, in forming goals and in establishing the conditions to be changed, leads the therapy" (p. 495) and "the setting of goals fosters a truly collaborative effort that offers a paradigm for continuing problem-solving activity outside the therapeutic situation" (Fox, 1987, p. 495). The focus on goals is associated with positive change, as it is based on the principle of starting where the client is (Reid, 1990).

The solution-focused model differentiates clients as visitors, complainants, and customers (de Shazer, 1988a; Kral, 1990). The client is the person most irritated with the situation and, therefore, the person most willing to do something about it (Kral, 1990). Visitors are there because they have to be, the problem at hand is not a major concern for the visitor; some visitors do not even recognize that there may be a problem. Complainants are willing to discuss the problem but lack the desire to take any action. Finally, a customer relationship exists when clients explicitly identify the problem and their goals and are willing to do something (Kral, 1990). An essential task for the therapist is to identify these differing roles within families and to assist and encourage visitors and complainants to become customers.

The initial interview includes the search for exceptions to the problem. The search for exceptions is central to a solution-focused interview; exceptions are the beginnings of solution construction. If exceptions cannot be articulated, the therapist should continue exploration of the identified problem or complaint until exceptions emerge (Lipchik & de Shazer, 1986). The worker complements the search for exceptions by maintaining the attitude that change will occur. This positive, proactive attitude promotes the amplification of nonproblematic patterns of behavior within the system (de Shazer, 1984).

The solution-focused brief therapy model utilizes the miracle question. "Suppose one night there is a miracle and while you are sleeping the problem is solved: What will you notice different the next morning that will tell you there has been a miracle? What else?" (Berg & Gallagher, 1991, p. 96). When clients pretend that their complaint has miraculously been resolved, they see solutions more clearly. Further, the steps toward the solution become clearer; "clients queried in such a manner have been observed to become more concrete and behaviorally specific as well as become more self-confident, smile and even burst out laughing" (Miller, 1992, p. 5).

As an illustration of solution-focused work, consider the Davis family. Bobby and his family were referred to the Community Intervention Program (CIP) by the school guidance counselor on account of his low self-esteem, his emotional difficulties following the death of his grandmother, and his parents' concerns about his defiance and acting-out behaviors. Ten months earlier, at the recommendation of the guidance counselor, the family had attended one family therapy session but then declined further service. This second referral was prompted by the parents' increasing concerns about Bobby's behavior. The disposition summary written by the previous worker advised that the family was resistant to counseling and unwilling to engage. The family consists of Ben (37) and Mary (34), who have been married for 10 years, and their children Eve (9) and Bobby (7). This family is interracial; Ben is Jamaican Canadian and Mary is Anglo-Canadian. Mary works full time for Bell Canada, and Ben has been unemployed for almost a year on account of a back injury. He conducts some sporadic car repair work from his garage.

All sessions occurred within the family's home. In the first visit, the worker briefly explored perceptions of the problem; used the miracle question to search for exceptions, as a way of moving toward solutions; assessed the perceived seriousness of the problem and the motivation for change by means of scaling questions; and identified tasks to assist Ben and Mary in moving toward the solution they wanted.

Both Ben and Mary cited Bobby as a major source of anger and frustration because of his verbal defiance

and increasing aggression. They had similar—but less intense—concerns about Eve. Eve advised that her parents yelled a lot, which she found upsetting. Bobby remained very quiet and appeared withdrawn and uncomfortable, despite attempts at demystifying any possible misconceptions regarding therapy and/or therapists. Ben and Mary had told Bobby that they were in therapy because of him and his behaviors. The worker let Bobby know that lots of families have difficulties and/or problems and that he was not the problem; rather, it was the family as a whole that was experiencing some difficulties. However, Bobby remained relatively quiet throughout therapy and only engaged in discussions unrelated to any stated family issues.

During the first session, individual perceptions regarding the initial problem/complaint were explored. Ben and Mary concurred that Bobby had been a difficult child since the age of about 4 and that both children's behaviors had significantly deteriorated over the last two years, since the maternal grandmother's death. Both children were frequently defiant and did not follow simple parental instructions or directives. Ben clearly identified Bobby as their biggest problem, as he was increasingly aggressive and easily became frustrated and aggravated. In addition, Ben was concerned that Bobby seemed uninterested in school and his grades were not as good as his sister's. However, school personnel reported that, while Bobby did exhibit some difficulties with his reading, he was improving. Bobby remained relatively quiet throughout this session and became aloof when discussing personal issues that were problematic to his parents. He would not state his perceptions of why the family was seeking service and did not display any reaction to his parents' stated concerns. Eve advised that she and Bobby had a bad attitude and were at times bad, which made her parents very mad and upset.

Both children were quiet and presented as being shy and uncomfortable. They remained close to their mother and frequently hugged and kissed her or hid behind her as a means of declining to answer a question. In addition, before choosing to answer a question, they would look toward their father for approval and/or permission to continue. Mary spoke openly about her feelings and emotions, in a quiet voice, while Ben presented as a very logical and pragmatic person who spoke about facts and realities. Mary thought that Bobby's problem behaviors could possibly be attributed to the loss of his grandmother. On the other hand, Ben thought that these behaviors were based on Bobby's inability and/or unwillingness to follow simple rules and also his laziness. Whereas Mary said that Bobby and Eve required love, support, and guidance, Ben was punitive and said that reprimanding the children was the only way to rectify the situation. Ben frequently interrupted Mary and the children when they were speaking and often finished their statements or comments, with little consideration for their thoughts or what they were going to say. This obviously irritated Mary, who would comment, "Ben, you're not listening now, just like you never listen" or else would remove herself from the table, wave her arm, and laugh, as though saying, "Here he goes again."

Each family member was asked the miracle question: "If a miracle happened tonight while each of you was sleeping, what would you notice the next morning that was different and that would let you know that a miracle had occurred?" This was a little confusing for both Bobby and Eve, but they appeared interested and intrigued. Therefore, the question was restated. "If you had a magic wand and could wave it to make a wish so that something about your family would be different, what would your wish be?" Mary said that she would like to get along better. Asked what it would take to get along better, she said that she would like the family's communication to improve, so that they felt better about each other, and she would like her husband to listen to her and understand her feelings more. Ben agreed with Mary and also said that he would like his wife to yell less at the children and his children to listen more and do as they were told. Eve said that she too would like less conflict within the home. In addition, she would like her parents not to yell as often and wished that everyone would be happier. Bobby remained quiet and said that he did not know. In exploring the exceptions, Mary, Ben, and Eve said that there is less upset when the family does things together.

There appeared to be a lot of conflict between Mary and Ben and a sense of hopelessness, which was expressed both verbally and nonverbally, via their eye contact (or lack of it) and sighs indicating discomfort and/or difference of opinion. Given the children's increasing irritability, the worker asked if they could be excused for the rest of the session; Ben and Mary agreed.

The worker then shared some observations regarding the level of marital conflict. In response to this feedback, Ben and Mary engaged in a heated discussion regarding their unmet emotional needs. Mary reacted strongly to Ben interrupting her and to his oppositional demeanor; Ben appeared confused and upset by the exchange. Both appeared embarrassed by the worker's presence. The worker focused their attention on exceptions—times they had been able to share their differences of opinions, feelings, and thoughts without such heated conflict.

The next step in the interview was to ask scaling questions, which are used to measure clients' progress before and during therapy, to determine clients' investment in change, and to assess perceptions of solutions. An example of a scaling question is: "On a scale of 1 to 10, where 10 is when these problems are solved and 1 is the worst they have ever been, where are you today?" The score itself is not as important as the change that was accomplished to get to that point or the change expected to get to the next level. Thus, follow-up questions might be: "How did you manage to get to a 3? What would be different if you were at 4?"

The worker used: three scaling questions with Ben and Mary. The first was: "On a scale of 1–10, where 10 is the highest, where would you rate your sense of family satisfaction?" Ben answered, a little hesitantly, with a 6; Mary chose 4. To search for exceptions, the worker asked both Mary and Ben what it would take to move one number up the scale. Both advised that they would like to argue less; to understand each other better; to enjoy each other more, without feeling as though they were always stepping on eggshells; and to spend more positive time with the children, instead of yelling and disciplining them.

The second and third scaling questions, also based on a 10-point scale, concerned their personal motivation regarding therapy and their optimism that therapy would be worthwhile and beneficial. Mary rated her personal motivation at 9 and her sense of optimism at 7. Ben assigned a 5 in both cases. Mary appeared to be the customer of service, as she presented as the person most irritated with the situation and therefore, probably the person most willing to do something about it. Ben could be termed a complainant of service as he was willing to discuss the problem, but he was not as motivated to do anything about it.

Mary, Ben, and the worker contracted the following goal of therapy: to process and attempt to improve marital communication in order to decrease marital conflict, thereby decreasing family conflict.

In the remainder of the session, the worker delivered compliments and acknowledged Ben and Mary's strengths. Two tasks were discussed and assigned. The first was the formula first task: "Between now and next session, I want you to observe, so that you can tell me what happens in your family life and/or relationship that you want to continue." Formula first tasks are used to shift the focus from past to present and future and from problems to strengths and to promote expectations of change (Molnar & de Shazer, 1987). They are often provided at the end of a session.

Secondly, Mary and Ben were asked to do something different every time they felt the urge to argue and as soon as they sensed the stirrings of conflict or tension. Mary and Ben were both very receptive to these tasks. In addition, they decided to try and prioritize family outings and togetherness time, which were enjoyable for the whole family and appeared to reduce their conflict. Mary and Ben both said that they felt comfortable working on the contracted goal and agreed that Eve and Bobby did not need to be involved in subsequent sessions. All subsequent sessions were spent with Mary and Ben.

The worker visited this family's home for four additional sessions over the next three months. By the third session, Mary and Ben agreed that they had a better appreciation of each other and were able to come up with some interesting and unique ways of implementing the do-something-different task. Both agreed that they enjoyed spending time together without the children, as it decreased their feelings of animosity and conflictual exchanges and increased their ability to understand one another. Furthermore, Mary said that, since she and her husband had been spending more time together, she felt more supported and better equipped to deal with her children's behaviors and to meet their needs without yelling.

The conflict between Mary and Ben decreased as they directed increased energy and time to their marital relationship. They continued to have disputes and differences of opinions, but both felt better understood and were able on occasion to agree to disagree, without any unspoken or repressed feelings of anger or remorse. As their communication became more direct and open, Mary and Ben acknowledged that communication had

also improved with their children. There was less yelling and conflict. Both Mary and Ben noted that they were enjoying their children more and did not feel as antagonistic toward them for insignificant negative behaviors and occasional disrespect and/or defiance.

From one session to the next, there was an observable increase in positive communication and affect between Ben and the children. Ben was not as ill-tempered when talking to the children or asking them to do something, and he was more affectionate with them; he gave hugs and allowed Bobby to sit on his lap. The worker shared this observation with the parents, because it was such a sharp contrast to the first session.

At the fifth and termination session, both parents said that they had achieved their goal of improved marital communication and decreased marital conflict. They understood how the high level of marital conflict had affected not only their relationship but also their ability to deal with their children's needs. Their improved communication had a positive impact on their relationship with the children; it had served to decrease their children's negativity and increase their family's sense of cohesion.

During the initial session, the parents were able to identify the exceptions to their complaint/problem as times when they did things together. By the termination session, they had implemented activities to make these exceptions occur more frequently; they had become more the rules of family functioning, rather than the sporadic exceptions. Throughout the course of service, the family allocated more time and energy in discussing and planning family activities, which created increased family communication and positive time spent together.

Preliminary data indicated that clients reported clearer treatment goals following this intervention (de Shazer, 1985). Moreover, clients were judged to be optimistic about the possibility of change and more cooperative in therapy and often reported improvement in the presenting problem. According to de Shazer (1985), therapists also appeared more optimistic about the possibility of change.

Between 1978 and 1983, therapists from the Brief Family Therapy Center in Milwaukee saw 1600 cases for an average of six sessions per case (de Shazer et al., 1986). Follow-up phone calls by a person who had no connection with the case were made to a representative sample of 25%. Of this sample, 72% either met their goals for therapy or felt that significant improvement had been made, so that further therapy was not necessary (de Shazer et al., 1986). An earlier study (Weakland et al., 1974) reported similar success rates, with an average of seven sessions per client.

In 1988, David Kiser conducted a follow-up study (Sykes Wylie, 1990) by tracking the progress of 164 clients for 6, 12, and 18 months after therapy. Of 69 clients receiving 4–10 sessions, 93% (64) reported they had met, or made progress on, their treatment goal. At the 18-month follow-up, 51% reported that the presenting problem was still resolved, while about 34% said that it was not as bad as when they had initiated therapy. In other words, 85% of the clients reported full or partial success; further, 94% of the group had received 10 or fewer sessions. These findings suggest continued improvement, rather than deterioration after solution-focused brief therapy (de Shazer et al., 1986).

READING 11-2 *Goal Setting with Biological Families**

Edith Fein and Ilene Staff

"Goal-setting is one of the critical tasks of the social work problem-solving process" (Anderson, 1989). Goal-setting encourages procedures that give a clear picture of problems, support treatment planning and assessment of progress, and facilitate review and evaluation of outcomes.

This chapter presents policy and practice in setting goals with biological families whose children have been removed because of abuse or neglect. Using the experience of a demonstration program in operation since 1989 as illustration, the authors examine guidelines for the goal-setting process; set forth tools for helping workers in assessment, decision-making, and treatment-planning; discuss policy and practice aspects; and consider the application of results and conclusions from this example to family reunification practice in general.

THE FAMILY REUNIFICATION PROJECT

Casey Family Services is a voluntary long-term foster care and permanency planning agency founded in 1976 in Connecticut, currently serving over 200 children in six New England states. This chapter draws from the agency's experience with its Family Reunification Project, which assists families whose children are in foster care primarily because of abuse or neglect and who need a broad range of intensive or special services

if the family is ever to be reunited. The program offers families case management and clinical intervention services in their own homes. Unlike most time-limited, crisis-oriented family preservation programs, family reunification services may be provided for periods as long as two years. Professionals assigned to the families have low caseloads and are able to give sustained attention to the families.

Each family is assigned to a reunification team consisting of a social worker and a family support worker. The team provides such services as training in parenting skills; mental health counseling; respite care; group support; and assistance with housing, job training, transportation, and legal problems. Services begin before the child returns home, when the reunification team and the biological family create a service agreement setting forth treatment goals and plans, and continue after reunification for as long as needed, up to a two-year total.

Referrals to the program come from state agency workers who determine that reunification should be the permanent plan for an abused or neglected youngster, but who are not optimistic that it can be achieved unless intensive services are provided. The biological family must be willing and able to participate in formulating a service agreement and to work with the reunification team. In addition, the foster parents or residential care facility staff must be willing to work with the team, and the child must have been removed from the home within the previous 18 months. To protect children and

---

*Reprinted by special permission of the Child Welfare League of America from Fein, E. and Staff, I. *Together Again: Family Reunification in Foster Care,* 1993, pp. 67–97.

ensure the safety of workers, cases are not accepted if a sibling has died because of abuse or neglect or if life-threatening abuse has taken place in the past; if the child's safety would be jeopardized by reunification; if sexual abuse has taken place and the perpetrator lives in the home or is an active member of the family; if violence has taken place (or a potential for violence exists) toward people outside the family; or if caregivers are substance abusers with no willingness to participate in treatment.

GOAL-SETTING IN CHILD WELFARE

Since the 1970s, goal-setting has found expression in several areas of practice, including the development of task-oriented casework (Reid & Epstein, 1972), time-limited therapy (Mann, 1973), and goal-attainment scaling (Garwick & Lampman, 1972). The child welfare field has benefited from this emphasis on goals. Permanency planning—the mainstream movement in delivering child welfare services—stresses explicit formulation of problems, treatment planning, identification of permanent placement options, case management, review of plans, and timely decision-making based on the implementation of service agreements (Maluccio, Fern, & Olmstead, 1986). Permanency planning thus epitomizes goal-setting.

Functions

Service planning for family reunification using a goal and plan orientation, as Maluccio et al. (1986) suggest, fulfills the following functions:

- Encourages systematic thinking about many areas of family needs
- Structures service delivery activity so workers, supervisors, and clients are fully aware of what is occurring
- Aids in case planning and management, allowing for timely decision-making and corrective action when necessary
- Helps clients participate in what is happening to their families in achieving reunification
- Ensures program accountability
- Documents case progress for possible court testimony

In the child welfare field, intensive family preservation programs have given further impetus to the goal-setting orientation. Intensive family preservation programs typically are in-home, time-limited, crisis-oriented services, and are designed to prevent foster care placement of children at risk of removal from their homes (Whittaker, Kinney, Tracey, & Booth, 1990). Various family preservation training courses and handbooks underscore the usefulness of focus and goal-setting in delivering these services (Lloyd & Bryce, 1985; Tracy, Haapala, Kinney, & Pecora, 1991; Whittaker et al., 1990).

Some family preservation program advocates believe the family preservation model might make family reunification efforts more timely and more successful than they are at present (Maluccio, Kreiger, & Pine, 1991; Nelson, 1990). Many family reunification programs are superficially similar to family preservation services, having developed from the same roots. However, there are important differences. Most important, in intensive family preservation programs a family's motivation to develop and achieve goals and to work with service providers is tied to the fear that children will be removed from the home—a strong authoritative mandate. Families of children already in foster care, however, have different concerns.

First, family reunification readily occurs two-thirds to three-fourths of the time in the course of normal service delivery by state agencies (Fein, Maluccio, Hamilton, & Ward, 1983; Tatura 1989); parental motivation is not necessarily an issue. Second, those children not reunified with their families are typically victims of one or more unfortunate circumstances: the state agency may not be able to deliver the kind or depth of services the family needs; the children present almost insurmountable problems in adjusting to family life; or the families are too troubled to make use of the services available. Third, even children who are quickly reunited with their families face difficulties (Turner, 1984). When children stay out of the home for long periods, families achieve a new equilibrium without them, and parents may feel ambivalent about having the children return. As a result, reunification programs, which by their nature work with many families in situations such as those described above, are forced to deliver services without the motivation and authoritative mandate that family preservation programs command.

For all these reasons, goal-planning is an essential feature of family reunification practice and was made an integral part of the Casey program model. Family members and social workers alike can use the focus and structure that goal-planning provides, particularly when reunification aims at a level of reconnection short of living in the same household. In those cases, the goal-planning process enables the family and the social worker to identify the appropriate level of reconnection and achieve some success in attaining the selected level despite the family's inability to live together.

THE SERVICE PLANNING PROCESS

The process of service planning requires that workers and clients together (1) identify appropriate goals, (2) build on existing strengths and resources, and (3) create action plans to help the clients' progress toward the goals. Of the three, identifying and explicitly stating the goals is probably the most difficult, but all are crucial for a successful case plan.

Identifying and Stating Goals

To create a goal statement, the worker must consider what problems the family is facing (see Exhibit 11–11), what must change about the family's functioning to allow reunification to take place, and what the family will be like if the goals are achieved. Goals are statements of positive family functioning, as illustrated in Exhibit 11–12.

Building on Strengths and Resources

While goals are positive statements about changes the family can achieve, strengths and resources are abilities, ways of functioning, personal characteristics, environ-

mental conditioning, social connections, or any positive aspects of the family's life that are present or that can be found or mobilized in behalf of the family (see Exhibit 11–12).

Creating Action Plans

Particular actions must be taken by the reunification team and the family, separately and together, to achieve progress toward the family's goals. The plans should be specific, indicate a date by when they will be accomplished, and identify who will be working on each plan. For example, consider goal #1 in Exhibit 11–12. Ms. Parker and Mr. Vega will not abuse drugs or alcohol. Plans for them might include the following actions:

• Ms. Parker will no longer associate with the drug dealers she knew in the past, beginning immediately. *Responsibility:* Ms. Parker.
• Weekly until May 1, Ms. Parker and the social worker will discuss Ms. Parker's drug cravings, how she feels about herself, and how she is managing her new life. *Responsibility:* Social worker and Ms. Parker.
• Mr. Vega will continue attending AA meetings. *Responsibility:* Mr. Vega.

GUIDELINES FOR SETTING GOALS AND CREATING CASE PLANS

The following guidelines should be applied in developing an effective service plan.

EXHIBIT 11-11 Problem Areas

In creating goals and plans, each of the following problem areas should be considered for families whose children are in care because of abuse or neglect:

1. Parents' feelings toward selves.
2. Parents' relationship, including sexual relations
3. Parents' recognition of problems
4. Parents' capacity for child care
5. Parents' approval of children
6. Discipline of children
7. Supervision of children
8. Incidence of sexual abuse
9. Child's behavior
10. Relationship between parents and child

11. Child's relationship to family
12. Child's feelings toward self
13. Child's disabling condition
14. Child's developmental lags
15. Child's relationship to peers
16. Child's relationship to foster family
17. Child's educational needs
18. Health care
19. Home management (nutrition, clothing, sanitation, hygiene, physical safety)
20. Money management
21. Housing and transportation needs
22. Employment needs
23. Social networks

EXHIBIT 11-12	Goals and Strengths

GOALS

Ms. Parker and Mr. Vega will not abuse drugs or alcohol.

Ms. Parker and Mr. Vega will have enough money to pay for the basic needs of life, including housing, clothing, food, and utilities, and will manage their money carefully.

Ms. Parker and Mr. Vega will set limits and teach Jacob right from wrong.

Ms. Parker and Mr. Vega will have a good understanding of Jacob's needs.

Ms. Parker and Mr. Vega will develop a good relationship, free from abuse.

STRENGTHS AND RESOURCES

Mr. Vega has enrolled in a drug rehabilitation program.

Ms. Parker has already completed Phase 1 of day treatment and has been regularly attending AA meetings.

Ms. Parker currently has a stable job.

Mr. Vega is actively looking for a job.

Ms. Parker and Mr. Vega want very much to learn better ways to be good parents.

Ms. Parker and Mr. Vega intend to visit Jacob regularly and will provide their own transportation.

Mr. Vega and Ms. Parker are involved in counseling to improve their communication with each other.

Goals

A. A goal should state how the family situation will be different, not what the reunification team or family will do to make it happen.

> Confusing goals and plans is the problem most frequently encountered in writing goal statements. The goal is the end-state that is sought; details of the work that needs to be done will be written in the plans. They are related as strategy and tactics are related.

Not a goal: Mother will visit with her two sons.

Goal: Mother will give her children the affection and attention they need.

B. Each goal should be explicit and germane to the family's functioning and ability to cope. The language should be direct and informal.

> To participate productively in their plans, client families have to understand the concepts and language of their goal statements. Technical jargon is not helpful. The goals should define what the clients' life situation must be to have their children live with them.

Unclear goal: Mother will have a responsive support network.

Clear goal: Mother will be close to other people she can talk to and get help from them when she needs it.

C. Goals should be formulated to balance explicit and assessable expectations with the family's social and emotional needs.

The goals must specify the changes necessary for the family to attain reunification. Goals that define a better state but are irrelevant to the original reason for placement should not be identified.

Irrelevant goal: Mother should volunteer her time to help others.

Relevant goal: Mother will locate and use community resources.

D. Family members should be able to make progress on some goals in a fairly short time period so that a feeling of success can emerge from their interactions with the worker.

> Long-term goals should include more easily attainable short-term goals, to encourage the confidence that family members must have to work toward their larger achievements.

Long-term goal: Mother will earn sufficient money from employment to support her children on her own.

Short-term goal: Mother will obtain services to have enough to pay for such basic needs as housing, clothing, food, and utilities.

E. Goals should be stated in such a way that progress toward their achievement can be assessed.

> Progress toward a goal is an important concept. Some of the goals will never be fully reached—improvement is always possible in such areas as understanding a child's needs or providing needed affection. Goal achievement, moreover, is not always easily measured. Sufficient progress toward

the goal, however, can be evaluated through the social worker's observation of parent-child interactions.

Limited goal: Mother will interact with her children. Assessable goal: Mother will give her children more of the affection and attention they need.

Strengths and Resources

F. Family strengths and resources should be articulated so workers and family members begin to think positively about the family's potential.

Strengths may be dispositional attributes such as motivation, biological predispositions such as intellectual capacity, or positive events. They should always be the focus when formulating goals. Strengths should be germane to the particular case and explicitly stated.

Strength: Mother has had her own apartment in the past. Mother has begun to look at classified ads for affordable housing.

Goal #1: Mother will provide a home with space, furnishings, appliances, utilities, and so forth, adequate for essential household functions and for meeting the personal needs of family members.

Strength: Mother already receives food stamps and has dealt with state and local welfare offices.

Goal #2: Mother will have enough money to pay for basic needs, such as housing, clothing, food, and utilities, and will manage her money carefully.

Action Plans

G. Each action plan should be explicit, doable in a specified time period, and assessable.

The plans proposed to achieve each goal, that is, the work to be done, should be reasonable and specific enough so that the worker's and the family's actions can be monitored and measured.

Goal: Mother will give her children more of the affection and attention they need.

Plans: (A) Mother will visit children once a week at the agency office; (B) Social worker will bring children to mother's home once a week starting June 1st; (C) Mother will attend parent support group.

SUPPORTIVE RECORDKEEPING

Effective goal-planning requires a systematic recordkeeping procedure that is consonant with a program's philosophy and practice. The procedures suggested here are based on earlier work in goal-planning (Jones & Biesecker, 1980; Miller, Fein, Howe, Claudio, & Bishop, 1984; Maluccio et al., 1986), and incorporate concepts and techniques developed in permanency planning work in child welfare. The recordkeeping system is a logical extension of the service-planning process and guidelines discussed above, and was developed by the staff of the project on which this chapter is based.

The recordkeeping system uses a variety of forms to establish goals with the family, outline the plan of action, define responsibilities, document case activity, and monitor and evaluate case progress. The forms are described briefly below, and in the following section their use is illustrated with a case example.

The Case Plan Form

The case plan form (Exhibit 11–13) is the central document upon which most of the others depend. It defines what the case is about and what planning will lead to progress toward specified goals. The case plan requires that workers consider a multitude of potential problems, define applicable goals with the client, delineate resources and strengths that may be brought to bear, create plans that will help the client progress toward the goals, and identify responsibility for completion of the plans.

The Monthly Goal and Plan Rating Form

The monthly goal and plan rating form (Exhibit 11–14) allows for monthly review of goal and plan progress. It tracks changes in the amount of effort expended, monitors continuance or completion of the plan, and evaluates the past month's efforts. The form is completed by the reunification team and reviewed with the family. The monthly evaluation enables both team and family to be supported in the successes they have had and to be aware of the work that remains.

Other Forms

Additional forms include a referral sheet (see Exhibit 11–15), containing information provided by the state agency; a face sheet, with full demographic information; an assessment, using the Family Risk Scales (Magura, Moses, & Jones, 1987), at several key points in case progress; a status change form, documenting milestones in case progress; narrative recordings, comprising an

EXHIBIT 11-13	Sample Case Plan		

Family Name:	Smith	Case #:	01
Workers:	J. Jones		

Use as many pages as needed to identify all goals and plans to be worked on. Add new goals and plans as they emerge. In the right-hand columns, please indicate the date each goal and plan was identified and who will be working on each.

GOAL #: _____1_____	Date	Who
Mother will give her children the affection and attention they need.	2/10/90	

Strengths and Resources		
Mother loves to play with the boys when they visit.	2/10/90	1
Mother likes to read magazine articles about child care.	2/10/90	1

Plan A.		
Mother will visit children once a week at the agency office.	2/10/90	1

Plan B.		
Worker will discuss discipline and other child-rearing problems	2/10/90	2
at each home visit.		

Plan C.		
Social worker will bring children to mother's home	3/10/90	3
at each home visit.		

Plan D.		
Mother will attend parent support group.	3/10/90	1

Codes: 1-Family, 2-Family Support Worker, 3-Social Worker, 4-Other (specify)

(continued)

EXHIBIT 11-13	Sample Case Plan (continued)

Family Name:	Smith	Case #:	01
Workers:	J. Jones		

Use as many pages as needed to identify all goals and plans to be worked on. Add new goals and plans as they emerge. In the right-hand columns, please indicate the date each goal and plan was identified and who will be working on each.

GOAL #:	2	Date	Who
Mother will have enough money to pay for the basic needs of life,		2/10/90	
including housing, clothing, food, and utilities, and will manage her			
money carefully.			

Strengths and Resources

Mother already receives food stamps and has dealt with state and local
welfare offices.

Plan A.	Date	Who
Worker will help mother draw up a budget.	2/10/90	2

Plan B.	Date	Who
Worker will go with mother to open a bank account.	2/10/90	1, 2

Plan C.	Date	Who
Mother will not buy anything on layaway or credit.	2/10/90	1

Plan D.	Date	Who
Worker will help mother with shopping to take advantage of	2/10/90	1, 2
coupons, sales and bargains.		

Codes: 1-Family, 2-Family Support Worker, 3-Social Worker, 4-Other (specify)

| EXHIBIT 11-13 | Sample Case Plan (continued) |

| Family Name: | Smith | Case #: | 01 |
| Workers: | J. Jones | | |

Use as many pages as needed to identify all goals and plans to be worked on. Add new goals and plans as they emerge. In the right-hand columns, please indicate the date each goal and plan was identified and who will be working on each.

GOAL #: 3	Date	Who
Mother will not abuse drugs or alcohol.	2/10/90	

Strengths and Resources

Mother has been free of drugs for extended periods in the past.

Mother is determined to stay clean in the future.

Plan A.

| Mother will no longer associate with the drug dealers she knew in the past. | 2/10/90 | 1 |

Plan B.

| Mother will attend AA meetings each Wednesday evening. | 2/10/90 | 1 |

Plan C.

| Mother and social worker will discuss mother's cravings, how she feels about herself, and how she is managing her new life. | 2/10/90 | 1, 3 |

Plan D.

| Worker will attend parent support group at the agency. | 3/10/90 | 1 |

Codes: 1-Family, 2-Family Support Worker, 3-Social Worker, 4-Other (specify)

EXHIBIT 11-14	Sample Monthly Goal and Plan Rating Form

Family Name:	Smith		Case #:	01
Workers:	J. Jones, O. Doe		Rating Date	2/28/90

INSTRUCTIONS: At month's end, list all goals and plans by describing them briefly in the space provided. Rate goals and plans on focus and status; indicate this month's progress for goals, and an evaluation for plans, in the third column. The codes and scales are listed on the bottom of the form.

GOAL #: _____ 1	Focus	Status	Goal Progress
Mother will give her children the attention and	1	C	2
affection they need.			

Plan	Focus	Status	Eval.
A. Mother will visit.	1	C	3
B. Worker will discuss discipline, etc.	1	C	2
C.			
D.			
E.			
F.			
G.			
H.			
I.			
J.			
K.			
L.			

Codes:

Focus:
Over the past month, how much time has been spent by the family or the team on this plan? Toward achieving this goal?
1. A major amount of time.
2. A minor amount of time.
3. Goal or plan not worked on this month.

Status:
At this time this goal or plan is:
C. Continued
D. Discontinued

Plan Evaluation:
Over the past month, how well was this plan working?
1. Not at all.
2. Working a little.
3. Working very well.

Goal Progress:
How much progress, if any, has there been this month in approaching this goal?

0	1	2	3	4	5
Regress from goal	None	A little progress	Moderate progress	A lot of progress	Goal achieved

EXHIBIT 11-15	Sample Referral Form

Case # _____ Referral Date _____ Taken by _____ Team Assigned _____

State Worker _____ Phone # _____

Child Information

Name _____ DOB _____

Current Placement: Type _____ Name _____ Removal Date _____

Address _____

_____ Phone # _____

Sex _____ Race _____ Grade _____ School _____

Previous Placements: ☐ No   ☐ Yes   How many? _____

To be reunified with

Name _____ Relationship to child _____

Address _____

_____ Phone # _____

Biological Parents   Mother   Father

     Name   _____   _____

     Address   _____   _____

               _____   _____

     Phone #   _____   _____

Comments (mention siblings to be reunified)

_____

_____

_____

_____

_____

_____

_____

_____

_____

_____

_____

_____

_____

_____

_____

intake summary, periodic case updates, and case notes; an expense form; and the service agreement described above. The following case example illustrates the use of some of these forms for service planning and goal setting and for case documentation.

> Five-year-old Josh has been in family foster care for the past three months. Months before, he was admitted to a hospital clinic along with his two-year-old brother, Philip. Both had bruises, head lice, and scabbed sores around the hairline severe enough for the clinic to refer them to state care. Josh was not yet toilet trained, Philip seemed to be developmentally delayed, and both boys were poorly socialized.
>
> This was not the first time the two boys had been removed from their family. Earlier in the year they had been placed in family foster care and later returned home. But now their mother was not keeping medical appointments and was known to be associating with drug dealers. In light of this information, social workers from the public child welfare agency were pessimistic about the outcome of a second effort to reunite the family, but they referred the family to a private agency for intensive reunification services.

Josh and Philip's case plan contained seven goals, three of which are illustrated in Exhibit 11–13. The mother was involved in the creation of the goals and for each goal, family strengths were defined and plans made. The case plan identifies the date each goal and plan was established, as well as who is responsible for the plan. Note that for goals 1 and 3, additional plans were made a month after the original plans.

The Monthly Goal and Plan Rating Form (Exhibit 11–14) illustrates the first month's rating of progress on goal 1. (A rating form is normally completed for each goal.) The social worker and family support worker team complete the form together. This form is shared with the mother or can be completed with her participation. The rating form charts progress, shows where more work needs to be done, and keeps the goals and plans in everyone's consciousness.

PROGRAM AND PRACTICE ISSUES

As discussed above, the goal-setting process is a familiar, if not completely comfortable, procedure for social workers. When it is used systematically, benefits for clients and staff members are well documented (Klier, Fein, & Gener, 1984; Miller et al., 1984). Agency reunification programs, however, have not generally directed themselves to the particular fit between their reunifica-

tion objectives and a goal-setting orientation. For goal-setting (or goal-oriented service planning) to be an integral feature of family reunification programs, a number of factors must be considered.

WORKERS' SKILLS AND ATTITUDES

Social workers are often uncomfortable at first with formulating goals and plans. "We were struck by the meager reporting we found in most of the case records about the social worker's definition of clinical tasks and description of ongoing therapeutic work. A well-articulated service plan was often not present in the records" (Fanshel, Finch, & Grundy, 1989, p. 477). Indeed, many programs are not clear about their continuum of goals (Videka-Sherman, 1989). Even training courses designed to teach the procedure can add to the confusion—some define goals as the most general of the plans, others equate goals with mission statements, and still others confuse the workers' efforts with the clients' needs (Anderson, 1989).

Despite training and the availability of written guidelines, staff members may vary widely in their ability to articulate goals. Some workers may write goals that are action-oriented, rather than ones that describe new situations for the client. Consensus may not exist on the degree of specificity that differentiates a goal from a plan. Moreover, in some cases goals may correctly describe an improved family situation but their relationship to reunification may not be clear. A client's goal, for example, might be to become self-supporting, but having a job might not result in managing money well enough to achieve reunification.

To assist workers in the goal-setting process—in effect, to come to agreement on the proper scope for goals in relation to plans—the authors examined all the early goals and plans in the family reunification project being presented in this chapter. These goals and plans fell into fairly clear categories, addressing financial stability, child care, substance abuse treatment, and educational and vocational attainment. These categories were congruent with factors in the Family Risk Scales (Magura et al., 1987), already used in the project to assess families at intake, reunification, and case closing.

From this examination, a list of representative goals was created, amalgamating the workers' experience and the Family Risk Scale factors (see Exhibit 11–16). Workers and family members can select a pertinent goal from the list or use one as a guide or model. This

---

EXHIBIT 11-16   Representative Goals

The (parents) (family):

1. Will have and keep a clean, safe home, without physical dangers.
2. Will provide a home with space, furnishings, appliances, utilities, and so forth, adequate for essential household functions and meeting the personal needs of family members.
3. Will have enough money to pay for the basic needs of life, including housing, clothing, food, and utilities, and will manage their money carefully.
4. Will keep themselves and their children healthy by eating healthy, balanced meals and by getting medical and dental care when needed.
5. Will be close to other people they can talk to and get some help from when they need it.
6. Will get and use community services.

7. Will have a good relationship, free of abuse, with other adults in the home.
8. Will each feel that he or she is a good person and deserves to be treated well.
9. Will not abuse drugs or alcohol.
10. Will give their children the affection and attention that they need.
11. Will make sure that their children are safe from harm at all times, and that they are not left alone or left with someone who is not able to take care of them.
12. Will set limits and teach their children right from wrong without hurting them physically or with words.
13. Will have a good understanding of their children's needs.
14. Will make sure their children attend school regularly.

---

procedure, used in other goal-oriented programs (McCroskey & Nelson, 1989), can smooth out variations in specificity of goals and plans, and help to create goals that are germane to the reunification effort.

Role of Supervisor

The supervisor's importance in formulating, documenting, and monitoring goals and service delivery plans cannot be overestimated. Although an evaluation component within a program can help with monitoring and assuring consistency, it does not replace the supervisor. Service quality and oversight are managed by monitoring responsibility. For example, the case plan sets forth a clear overview of expected action for each case, indicates who is responsible for the action, and often provides a timeline. The supervisor can use the case plan to determine whether appropriate planning is taking place.

Supervisors also can use the Monthly Goal and Plan Rating form (Exhibit 11–14) as a summary of progress and a basis for case conferences with workers and families. The goal concentration minimizes the sometimes rambling nature of presentations based on narrative recordings.

Number of Goals

As discussed elsewhere by Fein and Staff (1991), various issues arise in goal-oriented reunification services that are not readily dealt with by extra effort or training. In particular, how many goals should be set at

the beginning of service? Some workers believe that it is most respectful of families if family members know from the beginning of service all they will need to do to have their families reunited. These workers advocate starting with as complete a list of goals as is necessary to effect reunification, with the understanding that other goals can be added if the situation changes during the course of the case. They reason that beginning with only a few goals and then adding others as early successes occur makes families feel they will never achieve the ultimate reunification.

Other workers fear that a complete list of goals will dishearten a family, that a few goals will lead to early successes, and that the original goals can easily be amended because the family will have had that understanding from the beginning. Some writers suggest that developing a complete list of goals is important; clients then rank goals and the most pressing receive attention first (Pomerantz, Pomerantz, & Colca, 1990).

No evidence documents that one method is superior to the others. Examination of various questions about goal-setting as a client motivator is sorely needed, particularly for neglectful families (Videka-Sherman, 1989).

CONCLUSION

The project described in this chapter is part of a small, financially healthy, voluntary agency that can afford the small caseloads, specialized programs, and individualization of clients good case management and effective casework for reunification require. How well would the method apply to large, publicly funded reunification services in public agencies? If a public agency has the resources, it can implement a goal-oriented intensive service. Alternatively, it can contract for such services from voluntary agencies. The principles of goal orientation and careful and systematic documentation, however, can be used to support any agency's reunification efforts.

EXHIBIT 11-17 Objectives and Intervention Plans with a Spouse Abuse Client

Jackie called the Geneva Women's Center early one morning and left a message on the answering machine saying she needed help and would like to meet with someone after work. Later that afternoon she came to the Center. I met with Jackie, who said that she had to come in because she couldn't take it anymore. Jackie detailed numerous incidents of physical, verbal, and emotional abuse by her husband Joe in the last two years. The last incident occurred over the weekend. Joe had come home drunk, found her sleeping, and flipped their double bed over with her in it. He then began screaming and shouting at her, calling her names, and saying that she was no good, lazy, and that he "ought to take care of her." The episode ended when Joe literally threw her out of the bedroom and slammed the door. Jackie eventually slept on the couch but decided she had to leave. She believed that Joe would come after her if he knew she was trying to leave, which is why she waited until he would be working to take any action. Jackie had heard about the Center from a woman at work and wanted help finding a place to stay until she could decide what to do.

I explained to Jackie about the shelter in Bluegrass (60 miles away) and the safehome network here in Geneva. Jackie felt she wanted to stay in Geneva so she could keep working. She was pretty sure Joe would not bother her at work. I told her that a safehome could be arranged. After determining Jackie's particular needs (smoker, not allergic to animals, no children, no personal items) I excused myself and alerted other staff, who began to make the arrangements. It was necessary to begin work on this immediately because of the lateness of the hour.

When I returned to the room, Jackie was crying. She said she didn't really want to leave, that she loved Joe, but she couldn't handle getting beat up all the time. She just didn't know what to do. I asked Jackie if she had thought about different things to do. Her list of possibilities included help for Joe, reconciliation and salvaging their marriage, and divorce. She hadn't made a decision as to which she should pursue. Jackie said she thought Joe would be mad if she didn't come home, but that she didn't feel she could return there until things changed.

We discussed the resources she had available to her through the Center: emotional support, assistance with filing an Order for Protection (OFP), legal advocacy, and assistance with financial and housing needs. I also mentioned the counseling program for abusive men offered by the Mental Health Center. We talked at length about an OFP and the functions it provides: removing an abuser from the home, ordering counseling or treatment, ordering financial support, preventing the abuser from further assaults or threats of assault, and so on. I explained that one of the primary functions of the order was to provide safety for the victim and to give up to one year for decision making.

After further review of the process of obtaining an OFP, Jackie thought she would like to file, but wanted to think about it for a while. I said that would be fine. Our discussion was interrupted by a staff-person who related that safehome arrangements had been made. I asked Jackie if she was ready to go; she was, and I drove her to the safehome. After getting Jackie settled, I gave her written information about the things we talked about and assured her that the woman she was staying with could answer any questions she might have. We then made arrangements to meet at the Center the next day, when she got off work, to see if she'd made any decisions.

Jackie and I met the next day. She reported that she hadn't slept very well the night before, but that the woman she was staying with was very nice. Jackie also said she called Joe, who was wondering where she was and asked her repeatedly to come home. He said that he loved her, that he was sorry, and that they could work things out. Jackie said she wanted to believe him but couldn't, and that she told him she needed some time to think about things. Jackie went on to tell me that she thought the OFP was a good idea and that she wanted to file. She thinks that Joe might get help if the court orders him to, and maybe things would work out. She wanted to include occupancy in the order until Joe shows that he's really willing to change.

Jackie and I filled out an OFP form before she returned to the safehome. We agreed that the following day she would get off work early and file with my assistance. I would call the court administrator's office and let them know we were coming and pick Jackie up after work. In the event the order could not be served to Joe that same day, Jackie would arrange to stay at the safehome one more night.

Source: Ellen Holmgren, MSW student, University of Minnesota School of Social Work.

LEARNING EXERCISES

1. Provide one- or two-sentence definitions of the following terms, explain each one briefly to a colleague:

   action plan
   advocacy
   intervention
   interventive role
   mediation
   miracle question
   mutuality
   negative enabling
   positive enabling
   problem for work
   search for exceptions
   service agreement
   social broker
   solution-focused brief therapy

2. Review the Stover case (Appendix A-2). What can you learn from the process used to develop a mutually acceptable objective with Mrs. Stover? How does this case illustrate high-quality but low-intensity service?

3. In Exhibit 11–2, Mrs. Troy and the worker reached agreement on the objective of getting John out of the house but no action plan was developed. Put yourself in the place of a worker and think about possible action plans. What possible strengths might you explore with Mrs. Troy? What are alternative ways to accomplish the objective? Draft a possible service agreement using the format in Exhibit 11–5. To keep this from becoming a one-sided effort, ask a classmate to play the role of Mrs. Troy. Pay particular attention to your ability to identify and focus Mrs. Troy's strengths in relation to the objective and your ability to explore with her alternative courses of action that might be used to reach the objective. You should secure her views first, using the material on interviewing in Chapter 10. Then you may share your experience related to the problem at hand.

4. Do you see any service agreements in the case example in Exhibit 11–17? Try to identify two oral agreements, the objectives for each, and the action plans. We recommend that you take a few minutes and put these into written form.

5. Review Appendix A-3. How does the action plan in this case illustrate the use of outside experts? Note that the action plan is implicit and not written. Using the format contained in Exhibit 11–5, prepare a service plan that includes the problem for work, the objectives, and the action plan.

REFERENCES

Anderson, C. M., & Stewart, S. (1983). *Mastering resistance: A practical guide to family therapy.* New York: Guilford Press.

Anderson, S. C. (1989, October). *Goal setting in social work practice.* Paper presented at the annual meeting of the National Association of Social Workers, San Francisco.

Barker, R. L. (1987). Spelling out the rules and goals: The written worker-client contract. *Journal of Independent Social Work, 1*(2), 67–77.

Bartlett, H. M. (1970). *The common base of social work practice.* New York: National Association of Social Workers.

Bassin, A. (1993). The reality therapy paradigm. *Journal of Reality Therapy, 12*(2), 3–13.

Berg, I. K, & de Jong, P. (1996). Solution to building conversations: Co-constructing a sense of competence with clients. *Families in society, 77*(6), 376–391.

Berg, I., & Gallagher, D. (1991). Solution focused brief treatment with adolescent substance abusers. In T. C. Todd & M. Selekman (Eds.) *Family treatment of adolescent substance abusers* (pp. 93–111). Boston: Allyn & Bacon.

Berg, I. K., & Miller, S. D. (1992). *Working with the problem drinker: A solution focused approach.* New York: W. W. Norton.

Biddle, W. W., & Biddle, L. J. (1965). *The community development process: The rediscovery of local initiative.* New York: Holt, Rinehart & Winston.

Bloom, M., & Fischer, J. (1982). *Evaluating practice: Guidelines for the accountable professional.* Englewood Cliffs, NJ: Prentice-Hall.

Brager, G. A., & Jorcin, V. (1969). Bargaining: A method in community change. *Social Work, 14*(4), 73–83.

Briar, S. (1967a). The social worker's responsibility for the civil rights of clients. *New Perspectives, 1*(1), 89–92.

Briar, S. (1967b). The current crisis in social casework. In National Conference on Social Welfare (Ed.), *Social work practice* (pp. 19–33). New York: Columbia University Press.

Budman, S. H., & Gurman, A. S. (1988). *Theory and practice of brief therapy.* New York: Guilford Press.

Chandler, S. (1985). Mediation: Conjoint problem solving. *Social Work, 30*(4), 346–349.

Compton, B., & Galaway, B. (1989). *Social work processes* (4th ed.). Pacific Grove, CA: Brooks/Cole.

Cowger, C. D. (1994). Assessing client strengths: Clinical assessment for client empowerment. *Social Work, 39*(3), 262–268.

Davis, L. V. (1985). Female and male voices in social work. *Social Work, 30,* 106–113.

de Shazer, S. (1975). Brief therapy: Two's company. *Family Process, 14,* 78–93.

de Shazer, S. (1982). *Patterns of brief family therapy.* New York: Guilford Press.

de Shazer, S. (1984). The death of resistance. *Family Process, 23,* 11–17.

de Shazer, S. (1985). *Keys to solution in brief therapy.* New York: W. W. Norton.

de Shazer, S. (1988a). *Clues: Investigating solutions in brief therapy.* New York: W. W. Norton.

de Shazer, S. (1988b). An indirect approach to brief therapy. *Family Therapy Collection, 19,* 48–55.

de Shazer, S., & Berg, I. (1988). Constructing solutions. *Family Therapy Networker, 12*(5), 42–43.

de Shazer, S., Berg, I., Lipchik, E., Nunnally, E., Molnar, A., Gingerich, W., & Weiner-Davis, M. (1986). Brief therapy: Focused solution development. *Family Process, 25*(2), 207–222.

Dillon, P. A., & Emery, R. E. (1996). Divorce mediation and resolution in child custody disputes: Longterm effects. *American Journal of Orthopsychiatry, 66*(1), 131–140.

Durrant, M. (1992). *Solution focused brief therapy: Work shop package.* Bradford, ON: Knowledge Unlimited.

D'Zurilla, T. J. (1986). *Problem solving therapy: A social competence approach to clinical intervention.* New York: Springer.

Epstein, L. (1980). *Helping people: The task-centered approach.* St. Louis: C. V. Mosby.

Ezell, M. (1994). Advocacy practice of social workers. *Families in Society, 75*(1), 36–46.

Fanshel, D., Finch, S. J., & Grundy, J. F. (1989). Foster children in life-course perspective: The Casey family program experience. *Child Welfare, 68*(5), 467–478.

Fein, E., Maluccio, A. H., Hamilton, V. J., & Ward, D. (1983). After foster care: Outcomes of permanency planning. *Child Welfare, 62*(6), 485–558.

Fein, E., & Staff, I. (1991). Implementing reunification services. *Families in Society, 72*(6), 335–343.

Fisch, R., Weakland, J. H., & Segal, L. (1982). *The tactics of change: Doing therapy briefly.* San Francisco: Jossey-Bass.

Folger, J., Poole, M., & Stautman, R. (1993). *Working through conflict: Strategies for relationships, groups, and organizations.* New York: Harper Collins.

Fox, R. (1987). Short-term, goal-oriented family therapy. *Social Casework: The Journal of Contemporary Social Work, 68*(8), 494–499.

Garwick, G., & Lampman, S. (1972). Typical problems bringing patients to a community mental health center. *Community Mental Health Journal, 8*(4), 271–280.

Germain, C. B., & Gitterman, A. (1980). The life model of social work practice. New York: Columbia University Press.

Goldberg, E. M., & Stanley, S. J. (1985). Task-centered case work in a probation setting. In E. M. Goldberg, J. Gibbons, & I. Sinclair (Eds.), Problems, tasks, and outcomes (pp. 89–159). London: George Allen & Unwin.

Goulding, M. M. (1990). Getting the important work done fast: Contract plus redecision. In J. Zeig & S. Gilligan (Eds.), *Brief therapy: Myths, methods, and metaphors* (pp. 303–317). New York: Brunner/Mazel.

Greene, G. J. (1989). Using the written contract for evaluating and enhancing practice effectiveness. *Journal of Independent Social Work, 4*(2), 135–155.

Grosser, C. (1965). Community development programs serving the urban poor. *Social Work, 10*(3), 15–21.

Haley, J. (1963). *Strategies of psychotherapy.* New York: Grune & Stratton.

Haley, J. (1987). *Problem solving therapy* (2nd ed.). San Francisco: Jossey-Bass.

Heidrich, S. M., & Denny, N. W. (1994). Does social problem solving differ from other types of problem solving during the adult years? *Experimental Aging Research, 20*(2), 105–126.

Herbert, M., & Levin, R. (1996). The advocacy role in hospital social work. *Social Work in Health Care, 22*(3), 71–83.

Hoshino, G. (1994). Contracting in social work: Another fad? In B. Compton & B. Galaway (Eds.), *Social work processes* (5th ed.) (pp. 406–407). Pacific Grove, CA: Brooks/Cole.

Ivanoff, A., Robinson, E., & Blythe, B. (1987). Empirical clinical practice from a feminist perspective. *Social Work, 32*(5), 417–423.

Jacobson, N. S. (1985). Family therapy outcome research: Potential pitfalls and prospects. *Journal of Marital and Family Therapy, 11*(2), 149–158.

Jones, M., & Biesecker, J. (1980). *Goal planning in children and youth* (DHHS publication No. OHDS 81-30295). Washington, DC: U.S. Government Printing Office.

Kenemore, T. (1987). Negotiating with clients: A study of clinical practice experience. *Social Service Review, 61*(1), 132–144.

Klien, J., Fein, E., & Genevo, C. (1984). Are written or verbal contracts more effective in family therapy? *Social Work, 29*(3), 298–299.

Kral, R. (1990). *Strategies that work: Techniques for solutions in the school.* Milwaukee, WI: Brief Family Therapy Centre.

Kruk, E. (1997). *Mediation and conflict resolution in social work and human services.* Chicago: Nelson-Hall.

Lerner, B. (1972). *Therapy in the ghetto.* Baltimore: Johns Hopkins Press.

Leviton, S. C., & Greenstone, J. C. (1997). *Elements of mediation.* Pacific Grove, CA: Brooks/Cole.

Lipchik, E., & de Shazer, S. (1986). The purposeful interview. *Journal of Strategic and Systemic Therapies, 5*(1/2), 88–90.

Lloyd, J. C., & Bryce, M. E. (1985). *Placement prevention and family reunification: A handbook for the family-centered service practitioner.* Iowa City, IA: National Resource Center on Family Based Services, The University of Iowa.

Lundy, M. (1993). Explicitness: The unspoken mandate of feminist social work. *Affilia, 8*(2), 184–199.

Magura, S., Moses, B. S., & Jones, M. A. (1987). *Assessing risk and measuring change in families.* Washington, DC: Child Welfare League of America.

Mahaffey, M. (1972). Lobbying and social work. *Social Work, 17*(1), 3–11.

Maluccio, A. N., Fein, E., & Olmstead, K. (1986). *Permanency planning for children: Concepts and methods.* London & New York: Taristock Publications.

Maluccio, A. N., Kreiger, R., & Pine, B. A. (1991). Preserving families through reunification. In E. M. Tracey, D. A. Haapala, J. Kinney, & P. J. Pecora (Eds.), *Intensive family preservation services: An instructional source book* (pp. 215–235). Cleveland, OH: Mandel School of Applied Social Sciences, Case Western Reserve University.

Maluccio, A., & Marlow, W. (1974). The case for the contract. *Social work, 19*(1), 28–36.

Mann, J. (1973). *Time-limited psychotherapy.* Cambridge, MA: Harvard University Press.

Marziali, E. (1984). Three viewpoints of the therapeutic alliance. *Journal of Nervous and Mental Disease, 7,* 417–423.

Mariziali, E., & Alexander, L. (1991). The power of the therapeutic alliance. *American Journal of Orthopsychiatry, 61*(3), 383–391.

Mayer, J. E., & Timms, N. (1969). Clash in perspective between worker and client. *Social Casework, 50*(1), 32–40.

McClendon, R., & Kadis, L. (1990). A model of integrating individual and family therapy: The contract is the key. In J. Zeig & S. Gilligan (Eds.), *Brief therapy: Myths, methods, and metaphors* (pp. 135–150). New York: Brunner/Mazel.

McCroskey, J., & Nelson, J. (1989). Practice-based research in the family support program: The family connection project example. *Child Welfare, 63*(6), 573–587.

McIntyre, E. L. G. (1986). Social networks: Potential for practice. *Social Work, 31*(6), 42–46.

McKnight, J. (1992). Redefining community. *Social Policy, 23,* 56–62.

Miller, K., Fein, E., Howe, G., Claudio, C. & Bishop, G. (1984). Time-limited, goal focused parent aide services. *Social Casework, 68*(8), 472–477.

Miller, P. (1990). Covenant model for professional relationships: An alternative to the contract model. *Social Work, 35*(2), 121–125.

Miller, S. D. (1992). The symptoms of solution. *Journal of Strategic and Systemic Therapies, 11,* 1–11.

Molnar, A., & de Shazer, S. (1987). Solution-focused therapy: Towards the identification of therapeutic tasks. *Journal of Marital and Family Therapy, 13*(4), 349–358.

Moore, C. W. (1986). *The mediation process.* San Francisco: Jossey-Bass.

Moras, K., & Strupp, H. (1982). Pretherapy interpersonal relations, patients, alliance and outcome in brief therapy. *Archives of General Psychiatry, 39,* 405–409.

Murdach, A. D. (1982). A political perspective in problem solving. *Social Work, 27*(5), 417–421.

Nelson, D. (1990). Recognizing and realizing the potential of family preservation. In J. K. Whittaker, J. Kinney, E. M. Tracy, & C. Booth (Eds.), *Reaching high-risk families: Intensive family preservation in human services* (pp. 13–30). Hawthorne, NY: Aldine de Gruyter.

Nezu, A., & D'Zurilla, T. J. (1981). Effects of problem definition and formulation on the generation of alternatives in the social problem solving process. *Cognitive Therapy and Research, 5,* 265–271.

Parsons, R. J. (1991). The mediator role in social work practice. *Social Work, 36*(6), 483–487.

Payne, J. E. (1972). Ombudsman roles for social workers. *Social Work, 17*(1), 94–100.

Polansky, N. A., Bergman, R. D., & de Saix, C. (1973). *Child neglect: Understanding and reading the parent.* New York: Child Welfare League.

Pomerantz, P., Pomerantz, D. J., & Colca, I. A. (1990). A case study: Service delivery and parents with disabilities. *Child Welfare, 69*(1), 67–73.

Preston-Shoot, M. (1989). Using contracts in groupwork. *Groupwork, 2*(1), 36–47.

Reid, W. (1985). *Family problem solving.* New York: Columbia University Press.

Reid, W. (1990). An integrative model for short-term treatment. In R. A. Wells & V. J. Giannetti (Eds.), *Handbook of brief psychotherapies* (pp. 55–77). New York: Plenum.

Reid, W. (1992). *Task strategies: An empirical approach to clinical social work.* New York: Columbia University Press.

Reid, W. (1996). Task-centered social work. In F. J. Turner (Ed.), *Social work treatment: Interlocking theoretical approaches* (4th ed., pp. 69–93). New York: Free Press.

Reid, W., & Epstein, L. (1972). *Task-centered practice.* New York: Columbia University Press.

Ripple, L., & Alexander, E. (1956). Motivation, capacity, and opportunity as related to casework service: Nature of the client's problem. *Social Service Review, 30*(1), 38–54.

Roberts, R. W., & Nee, R. H. (Eds.). (1970). *Theories of social casework.* Chicago: University of Chicago Press.

Rojek, C., & Collins, S. A. (1987). Contract or con trick? *British Journal of Social Work, 17*(2), 199–211.

Rojek, C., & Collins, S. (1988). Contract or con trick revisited: Comments on the reply by Gordon and Preston-Shoot. *British Journal of Social Work, 18*(6), 611–622.

Rosen, A. (1993). Correction of workers' personal versus environmental bias in formulation of client problems. *Social Work Research and Abstracts, 29*(4), 12–17.

Rothery, M. (1980). Contracts and contracting. *Clinical Social Work Journal, 8*(3), 179–187.

Rothman, J., & Tropman, J. (1987). Models of community organization and macro practice perspectives: Their mixing and phasing. In F. Cox, J. Erlich, J. Rothman, & J. Tropman (Eds.), *Strategies of community organization* (4th ed., pp. 3–26). Itasca, IL: F. E. Peacock.

Rowe, W. (1996). Client-centered theory: A person-centered approach. In F. J. Turner (Ed.), *Social work treatment: Interlocking theoretical approaches* (4th ed., pp. 69–93). New York: Free Press.

Russell, M. (1989). Feminist social work skills. *Canadian Social Work Review, 6*(1), 69–81.

Savoury, G. R., Beals, H. L., & Parks, J. M. (1995). Mediation in child protection: Facilitating the resolution of disputes. *Child Welfare, 74*(3), 843–862.

Saxon, W. (1979). Behavioral contracting: Theory and design. *Child Welfare, 58*(8), 523–529.

Schwartz, W. (1961). Social worker in the group. In National Conference on Social Welfare (Ed.), *Social welfare forum.* New York: Columbia University Press.

Seabury, B. (1979). Negotiating sound contracts with clients. *Public Welfare, 37*(2), 33–38.

Severson, M. M., & Bankston, T. V. (1995). Social work and the pursuit of justice through mediation. *Social Work, 40*(5), 683–690.

Shulman, L. (1992). *The skills of helping individuals, families and groups* (3rd ed.). Itasca, IL: F. E. Peacock.

Sosin, M., & Caulum, S. (1983). Advocacy: A conceptualization for social work practice. *Social Work, 28*(1), 12–17.

Sykes Wylie, M. (1990). Brief therapy on the couch. *Family Therapy Networker, 14*(3), 26–72.

Tatura, T. (1989). Characteristics of children in foster care. *Division of Child, Youth, and Family Services Newsletter* (American Psychological Association), *12*(3), 16–17.

Thomlison, B., & Thomlison, R. J. (1996). Behavior theory and social work treatment. In F. J. Turner (Ed.), *Social work treatment: Interlocking theoretical approaches* (4th ed., pp. 39–68). New York: Free Press.

Thomlison, R. (1984). Something works: Evidence from practice effectiveness studies. *Social Work, 29*(1), 52–55.

Tobias, M. (1990). Validator: A key role in empowering the chronically mentally ill. *Social Work, 35*(4), 357–359.

Tolson, E. (1988). *The metamodel and clinical social work.* New York: Columbia University Press.

Tolson, E. R., McDonald, S., & Moriarty, A. R. (1992). Peer mediation among high school students: A test of effectiveness. *Social Work in Education, 14*(2), 86–93.

Tolson, E., Reid, W., & Garvin, C. (1994). *Generalist practice: A task-centered approach.* New York: Columbia University Press.

Torczyner, J. (1991). Discretion, judgement, and informed consent: Ethical and practical issues in social action. *Social Work, 36*(2), 122–128.

Tracy, E. M., Haapala, D. A., Kinney, J., & Pecora, P. J. (Eds.). (1991). *Intensive family preservation services: An instructional source book.* Cleveland, OH: Mandel School of Applied Social Services, Case Western Reserve University.

Tropp, E. (1968). The group: In life and in social work. *Social Casework, 49*(5), 267–274.

Turner, J. (1984). Reuniting children in foster care with their biological families. *Social Work, 29*(6), 501–505.

Turner, J., & Jaco, R. (1996). Problem-solving theory and social work treatment. In F. J. Turner (Ed.), *Social work treatment: Interlocking theoretical approaches* (4th ed., pp. 503–522). New York: Free Press.

Tutty, L. (1990). The response of community mental health professionals to client's rights: A review and suggestions. *Canadian Journal of Community Mental Health, 9*(1), 1–24.

Umbreit, M. (1995). *Mediating interpersonal conflicts: A pathway to peace.* West Concord, MN: CPI Publishing.

Videka-Sherman, L. (1989). *Intervention for child neglect: The empirical knowledge base.* Paper presented at the National Centre on Child Abuse and Neglect Research Symposium on Child Neglect, Washington, DC.

Weakland, J., Fisch, R., Watzlawick, R., & Bodin, A. (1974). Brief therapy: Focused problem resolution. *Family Process, 13,* 141–168.

Whittaker, J. K. (1974). *Social treatment: An approach to interpersonal helping.* Hawthorne, NY: Aldine Publishing.

Whittaker, J. K., Kinney, J., Tracey, E. M. & Booth, C. (Eds.). (1990). *Reaching high-risk families: Intensive family preservation in human services.* Hawthorne, NY: Aldine de Gruyter.

Wickman, E. (1993). *Group treatment in social work.* Toronto: Thompson.

Wilcoxon, S. A. (1991). Clarifying expectation in therapy relationships: Suggestions for written guidelines. *Journal of Independent Social Work, 5*(2), 65–71.

Wilensky, H. L., & Lebeaux, C. N. (1958). *Industrial society and social welfare.* New York: Russell Sage Foundation.

Wood, K. (1978). Casework effectiveness: A new look at the research. *Social Work, 23*(6), 437–458.

part III

TOOLS FOR DOING THE DECIDED

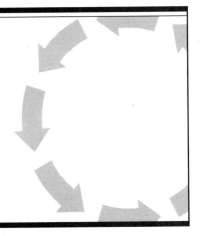

chapter 12

Interventive Methods to Mobilize Client Power

CHAPTER PREVIEW

In the last chapter, we introduced the idea of interventive roles. In this chapter we focus on some specific interventive methods for assisting clients to mobilize their power. These interventive activities can be associated with various roles.

Empowerment is a prominent theme in the social work practice literature (Breton, 1994a; Cox & Parsons, 1994; Dubois & Miley, 1996; Gutierrez, 1994; Hartman, 1993; Kondrat, 1995; Lee, 1994; Mondros & Wilson, 1994; Parsons, 1991; Simon, 1994; Staples, 1990). Key elements of the practice model we have been developing—partnership, working toward client wants, emphasizing client strengths—are consistent with this tradition, but we are uncomfortable with the implication that power is something the social worker gives to the client—that the social worker empowers. We prefer to think in terms of a collaborative process of mobilizing client power. The notion of mobilizing client power was

a part of the engagement, assessment, and service planning phases; likewise, our intervention approaches are intended to assist clients in mobilizing the power needed to solve their problems.

Pinderhughes (1983) defines power as the ability to exert a beneficial influence on forces that affect one's life; powerlessness is the inability to exert such influence. Parsons (1991) speaks of empowerment (in our terminology, mobilizing power) as an active process whose outcome is that clients are strong enough to participate in, take control of, and influence institutions and events that affect their lives. DuBois and Miley (1996) note that "empowerment implies exercising psychological control over personal affairs as well as exerting influence over the course of events in the socio-political arena" (p. 26). For parents with emotionally disturbed children, according to a study, empowerment has three aspects: greater ability to solve their problems and manage their children at home; greater ability to deal with service providers, especially regarding their right to make decisions about services for their children, and their right to knowledge about better services; and greater ability to influence the service system and community to get better services (Koren, DeChillo, & Friesen, 1992). Thus, mobilizing client power means helping clients to take responsibility and control over their own lives and to influence the situation in which they find themselves so as to secure the resources they need. In this chapter, we will be identifying some intervention methods that help clients to mobilize power:

- assisting clients to identify and use the resources of their communities
- assisting clients to become aware of their own behavior
- strengthening clients' communication skills
- providing information to clients
- assisting clients in making decisions
- assisting clients to find meaning in life

In Reading 12-1, Barbara Bryant Solomon identifies strategies you can use to empower families. In Reading 12-2, Anthony N. Maluccio examines ways of enhancing clients' problem-solving skills and promoting competence through action.

SECURING RESOURCES FOR CLIENTS

Social context shapes people's lives. Individuals' ability to solve their problems depends on their ability to secure the resources they need and their power to change the negative impact of environmental conditions. There must be a match between people's coping abilities and their environments. Despite the tendency in some social work to look for the cause of problems within the client and to focus on client pathology, productive interventive efforts may be directed to changing the environment, increasing the client's capacity to deal with environmental blocks, and reducing the negative response to the client by significant others.

Actively Supplying Resources

In Chapter 11, we discussed your ability to bring clients together with resources, as a social broker. You may wish to go further and actually secure concrete resources for clients. If you do so, their energies may be saved for problem-solving work and their life will

become more comfortable; they may feel more able to cope, with a corresponding increase in self-esteem. If clients are able to actively seek out and utilize resources on their own, so much the better, but to require them to do this, at the risk of greatly heightened anxiety or possible failure, is poor practice.

By taking such an active role, will you create client dependency? Not necessarily. Your efforts will be strengthening if the client is fully engaged in decision making and in the allocation of problem-solving tasks. Human beings are socially interdependent; total independence is pathological. People who function well in life do so because they have multiple sources of dependency satisfaction and because they have learned to use each source appropriately. As a social worker, you need to learn how to assess the sources available for meeting clients' dependency needs and to offer resources when they are needed. If you can relieve the client of a dreaded task, you are expressing your concern for that person in a very concrete way.

The social worker in Exhibit 12–1 may want to be very active in securing a back-up care provider for the client. The client's 75-year-old mother may also need assistance in making a decision about moving out but, most likely, she will make the decision as soon as she is comfortable that adequate care is available for her son.

Direct Intervention

You may also choose to intervene directly in the client's transactions with other systems—for example, by discussing a child's problems with the school. To help the client toward better role performance, you will be scrupulous about reporting what you are doing; you will use modeling and identification, set appropriate limits for client behavior, and expect clients to be as active on their own behalf as they can. You will use all the details of the transactions as material for teaching appropriate role behavior.

You may need to help clients see their situation differently (Gutierrez, 1995; Moreau, 1990). Take a look at Exhibit 12–2. What did you see at first? Opportunity is nowhere? Or opportunity is now here? Many clients fail to see the resources available in their environments. As well as identifying and making resources available to clients, you can help them to identify opportunities where initially they see none.

EXHIBIT 12-1	What Next for a Quadriplegic and His 75-Year-Old Care Provider?

Mr. Sandstone, a 37-year-old Native American, is quadriplegic. Two years ago, he was struck by a vehicle while crossing the street. After an 18-month hospital rehabilitation program, Mr. Sandstone was discharged into the community last October. The rehabilitation counselor and social worker found him a wheelchair-accessible apartment and some furniture and took him shopping for clothes. Mr. Sandstone needs assistance with most aspects of daily living, including bathing, transfers, positioning, and bowel and bladder voiding. A home care assistant visits three times a day, seven days a week. His back-up caregiver is his mother, who is 75 years old and has been diagnosed with heart problems. The mother feels obliged to stay and care for her son, who is the youngest of her children. The mother has said, on several occasions, that she is getting too old to provide the care her son needs, that Mr. Sandstone tends to drink a lot, and that she feels she should no longer live with her son because she never drank alcohol in her life. But the mother is presently still the back-up caregiver and has never made an attempt to leave. Mr. Sandstone is dependent on his mother for everything. He doesn't even want to cook for himself or make sandwiches—tasks he was familiar with while in the rehabilitation program.

Organizing

You will also help clients to secure the resources they need by organizing (Breton, 1994b). In Appendix A-3, for example, the worker helps clients organize to improve the quality of their housing. The action plan for the Birky family in (Exhibit 2–15) might include organizing their neighborhood to secure a safe environment for their children. In organizing, you will use interventive methods such as providing information, facilitating decision making, strengthening communication, and rehearsing. In Exhibit 12–3, a social worker, along with a lawyer, assists a group of clients to take political action in order to secure resources to which they believe they are entitled. Social work practice includes assisting clients to function in a democracy, and this involves assisting them to organize to pursue their own interests.

Here's another example. A social worker became aware of a proposed change in the state rules governing a long-term boarding care facility for adults with chroni-cal mental illness. Under the new rules, the facility would be redefined as transitional; residents would be required to move after a fixed time. News of the pending rule change made the residents upset and anxious. However, they were uncomfortable with the idea of testifying at an upcoming hearing on the subject. The social worker suggested that they have their statements videotaped for presentation at the hearing. They agreed, the social worker made the arrangements, and the videotapes made a very powerful impact at the hearing.

INCREASING CLIENT SELF-AWARENESS

When clients do not understand that their behavior—including their thinking and feelings—may be contributing to the problem or that their strengths could solve the problem, the worker needs to enhance clients' self-awareness (Furstenberg & Rounds, 1995; Hepworth, 1993). Several techniques are available.

EXHIBIT 12-2	Opportunities

What does this say?

OPPORTUNITYISNOWHERE.

EXHIBIT 12-3	Social Action with Hmong Veterans

A social action effort has been initiated with Hmong veterans who fought as allies of the United States in Southeast Asia.

The Hmong lived peacefully as farmers in the highland region of Northern Laos before the Vietnam war. In 1960, with a growing fear of the spread of communism in Southeast Asia, the CIA began to recruit the Hmong to help contain the spread of communism in Laos and to provide surveillance of North Vietnamese troop movements. By 1975, an estimate 30,000 Hmong soldiers had been trained, equipped, paid, fed, and directed by the U.S. (Robbins, 1987).

The war disrupted the Hmong economy, leadership patterns, and family structure. Approximately 10% of the population died as a direct result of the war or through related disease and starvation. When the United States withdrew its troops in 1975, those Hmong remaining in Laos were faced with the threat of extermination by the communists; thousands fled to Thailand for safety (Tou-Fou, 1983).

Between 1975 and 1985, over 50,000 Hmong resettled in the United States (Reder, 1985). Life was very difficult for them; their devastating losses could never be forgotten and the barriers to acculturation were immense. Moreover, the United States never officially recognized the role that the Hmong played as its ally in Southeast Asia. Allegedly, the CIA made promises of care and support, should the Hmong ever lose their homeland, but nothing was done (Castle, 1979).

According to Rothman and Tropman (1987), social action represents the efforts of disadvantaged groups to gain the redistribution of resources, power, and/or decision-making capabilities. For the Hmong, the goal of social action was not to gain benefits associated with services rendered to the U.S. Rather, there was hope that, through recognition, they would be able to derive some meaning from their contributions and sacrifices.

The advocacy effort began with a mobilization to present a resolution on the subject at Minnesota precinct caucuses. The resolution was based on information provided by Hmong veterans and a lawyer who was surveying Hmong veterans in the Minneapolis-St. Paul metropolitan area.

Although the resolution was only passed in a few precincts, it did serve some important functions: It provided a sampling of community sentiment on the subject, highlighted the specific features of the proposal that were most likely to evoke resistance, and helped to identify individuals who were interested in the issue and willing to participate in further efforts. Most importantly, the precinct venture revealed the need for increased planning and coordination; because of the eleventh-hour preparations, numerous opportunities to strengthen the caucus turnout were missed.

The first order of business following the caucuses was to organize a task group to facilitate planning for future actions. The task group was relatively small (5–8 people), so that coordinating meetings and activities would not be overly complex. A high priority was placed on gaining Hmong veteran representation, since Hmong interests would be most affected by the social action. Furthermore, the group wanted representation from Vietnam veterans, since they tend to be the most sympathetic to the Hmong's situation. All members of the group identified the problem for work as the lack of support offered by the U.S. government to Hmong veterans for their services in Southeast Asia.

The agreed-upon long-term goal of the social action was to obtain U.S. veterans' benefits for Hmong veterans who fought in alliance with the U.S. between 1960 and 1975. Attention was then directed toward assessing the feasibility of the goal. Critical areas for data collection and investigation were identified, and responsibility for gathering the needed information was delegated. The group decided to identify other similar efforts, potential obstacles and areas of resistance, resources and allies, and to identify unintentional consequences that might arise from the action.

Source: Kathleen Behrens, MSW student, School of Social Work, University of Minnesota.

Providing Feedback

We discussed feedback as a way to clarify communications in Chapters 8 and 10. It can also be used to help clients become more aware of themselves and how they interact with others. Exhibit 12–4 offers guidelines for the use of feedback to assist personal growth. Let's consider some specific forms of feedback: paraphrasing and summarizing; checking perceptions and focusing; clarifying and reflecting; and interpreting.

Paraphrasing and summarizing. In this case, you restate what you saw or heard both as a test of your understanding and so that clients can hear their own productions. To do this, you must listen carefully for the basic message. Then what you communicate to clients must remain very close to what they were expressing; you may simplify to make clear and synthesize what the content, feelings, thinking, or behavior mean to you. Always be tentative in your synthesis. You are submitting

EXHIBIT 12-4	**Using Feedback to Promote Personal Growth**

1. Focus feedback on the behavior, not the person. Focusing on *behavior* is less threatening because it implies that change is possible.
   Example: Say: ``Jordan talked considerably during the meeting.''
   Not: ``Jordan is a loudmouth.''

2. Focus feedback on observations rather than interferences or interpretations.
   Example: Say: ``I noticed you left the meeting early.''
   Not: ``You didn't seem to think the meeting was very important.''

3. Focus feedback on a description of the process rather than a judgment.
   Example: Say: ``I noticed you kept changing the subject and looking at your watch.''
   Not: ``You seemed uncomfortable during our meeting.''

4. Focus feedback on behavior related to a specific situation, the here and now. Feedback is usually most helpful when it is given soon after the observation is made, thus keeping it concrete and relatively free of distortions.

   Example: Say: ``You didn't answer me just now when I asked . . .''
   Not: ``You never answer me when . . .''

5. Focus feedback on the sharing of ideas and information rather than on advice giving. Let the other person decide the most appropriate course of action on the basis of the ideas and information you have given.
   Example: Say: ``Mrs. S. from the school just called and said she's tried to reach you several times and you haven't returned her calls.''
   Not: ``You should return your calls every day.''

6. Focus feedback on the amount of information you think the listener can use, not the amount that you would like to give. If overloaded, the person is less likely to use the feedback effectively.

7. Consider the appropriate time and place when offering feedback. Excellent feedback presented at an inappropriate time can do more harm than good.

---

it for clients' approval, amendment, or rejection. While sharing how you heard the message, watch clients carefully for clues that either confirm or deny the accuracy and helpfulness of the rephrasing. Summarizing can be used to check your understanding and to encourage clients to explore the material more completely.

Checking perceptions and focusing. Perception checking is a way of helping clients realize what they have just said or done. You paraphrase what you believe was said and ask for confirmation or further clarification. Focusing can be used to emphasize a feeling or idea from a vast array of verbalization and also to reduce confusions, diffusion, and vagueness. Thus, you assist clients in focusing on assumptions, ways of thinking, notions, or feelings that may be hidden in the discussion. You will use your own feelings of confusion about the clients' direction as a guide to decide when focusing is appropriate. Questions can be used to lead clients to clarify information, feelings, and experiences and can serve to encourage clients to explore feelings and thinking or to elaborate on those already discussed.

Clarifying and reflecting. Clarifying and reflecting are helpful in improving awareness of behavior. They provide means of connecting feelings, experiences, and thinking that the client left unconnected. In reflecting,

you try to understand the world as the client does. You select and pull together the best mix of context, feelings, and action from your observations of the client, as well as the client's statements, to advance understanding of the client's behavior. Clarifying summarizes core material and brings vague material into sharper focus. You may identify themes that seem to run through the client's behavior. In clarifying, you may make a statement regarding the meaning you attach to your observations and offer it for consideration, along with an admission of your confusion. Alternatively, you may admit confusion about meaning and try to restate what the client has said. You may also ask for clarification, repetition, or illustration from the client if it appears that trying to clarify the situation for you might help the client to understand it.

Interpreting. In interpreting, you explain the meaning of events to clients so that they are able to see their behavior in a new way. You may interpret events from clients' own frame of reference or from the frame of reference of another person. For example, clients may be presented with the target system's frame of reference. You may also reframe the material. If the client sees the glass of water as half empty, the worker points out that it is half full. By reframing the task of whitewashing his Aunt Polly's fence as a privilege, rather than as drudgery, Tom

Sawyer promoted himself from worker to supervisor and profited considerably as his friends bid for the privilege of becoming his workers.

In interpreting, you introduce your idea of what the message or behavior means. This requires considerable skill. We suggest the following guidelines:

1. Keep the language simple and close to the client's message.
2. Offer notions in a tentative way, as a possible contribution.
3. Always solicit the client's evaluation of what the contribution is.
4. If the client denies that the contribution is pertinent, do not insist that it is correct, but do not abandon it. Say, for example, "it may not be a helpful idea, but I would like to do some more thinking about it."

These feedback techniques—paraphrasing and summarizing, checking perception and focusing, clarifying and reflecting, and interpreting—need to be focused on the behavior you observe, rather than on the inferences you make from the behavior. You are providing behavioral descriptions of what took place to help clients become more aware of their own behavior (Fatout, 1995; Millstein, 1993). Behavioral descriptions should be nonjudgmental; they communicate an observation, not an evaluation. Behavioral descriptions are difficult because we tend to process our observations and make statements about our interpretation in terms of motivations, attitudes. We are often unaware that we are inferring. Exhibit 12–5 offers some examples of behavioral descriptions, as well as some corresponding inferences or evaluative statements.

Use of Limits

Though we often think of service in terms of liberation from maladaptive restrictions, setting limits within a

---

EXHIBIT 12–5   Behavioral Descriptions

The skill of behavior description depends on accurate observation which, in turn, depends on being aware of when you are describing and of when you are inferring. A statement must pass two tests to be a behavior description.

1. A behavior description does not report information. It reports specific, observable actions rather than generalizations about the person's motives, feelings, attitudes or personality traits. It states what was observed. It does not infer about why. Here are examples:

Behavior Descriptions	Inferences
Fran walked out of the meeting 30 minutes before it was finished.	Fran was annoyed. Fran has an appointment elsewhere.
Bob's eyes filled with tears.	Bob had a cold. Bob felt sorry for himself.
Becky did not say anything when Bill asked her a question.	Becky did not hear Bill. Becky resented Bill's question. Becky was embarrassed.

2. A behavior description is nonevaluative. It does not say or imply that what happened was good or bad, right or wrong. Evaluative statements (such as name calling, accusations, judgments) usually express what the speaker is feeling and convey little about what behavior was observed. Here are examples:

Behavior Descriptions	Evaluative Statements
Jim talked more than others on this topic. Several times he cut others off before they finished.	Jim is rude. Jim wants to hog the center of attention.
Bob, you've taken the opposite of most statements Sally has made today.	Bob, you're just trying to show Sally up. Bob, you're being stubborn.
Fran walked out of the meeting 30 minutes before it was finished.	Fran doesn't care about others. Fran is irresponsible.
Sam, you cut in before I finished.	Sam you deliberately didn't let me finish.

nurturing relationship may also facilitate client self-awareness. Specifically, the appropriate use of limits may help clients understand and gain control of their impulses. Limits may also build a sense of worth, by demonstrating that we care enough to risk hostility and that we believe clients are strong enough to accept the limits. You will not have to carry the entire burden of limit setting in work with groups and families. Group members will often set limits, either on the behavior of particular members, or for the entire group. The preoccupation of some groups with rules indicates the importance of limits for the growth of the system. In work with individuals, too, rules or limits can be discussed and used to assist clients.

Reassurance

Reassurance involves the recognition and approval of the client's capacities, achievements, feelings, and needs. It is usually seen as a passive technique, in which the worker approves an expression of the client. In social work, however, reassurance can also mean an active search for client strengths—for the areas in which clients are able to cope successfully. Reassurance is primarily used to sustain or restore client capacity but, when used in conjunction with other techniques, it can promote growth. In the one-to-one situation, successful use of reassurance depends on having a positive relationship with the client and on the client's acceptance of your authority. In a group, reassurance may arise from group members' discussion of their common problems and their growing awareness that their feelings and needs are shared by others.

Oral expressions of reassurance should be used cautiously, especially in early contacts with a client. If the client interprets the reassurance as insincere and reflecting a lack of understanding, it will create a barrier to further communication. Reassurance needs to come from your understanding and acceptance of the client and not from your need to say something. Reassurance communicated through being attentive and asking relevant questions will probably be more appropriate than reassurance expressed through your own oral comments. The best way to reassure is to take an active part in identifying strengths with the client; active recognition of the coping strengths will convey your concern and partnership.

Confrontation

Confrontation involves unmasking distortions in clients' feelings, experiences, or behavior; you identify patterns that are inconsistent and may be beyond clients' immediate knowledge. Acceptance of confrontation is difficult for clients, because it implies a challenge to do something about things that have not even been acknowledged. Confrontation must reflect caring and involvement and not a wish to punish or discipline. No other technique offers such a tempting opportunity for you to act out of unacknowledged feelings. When you say that clients need to face honestly what they are doing, the underlying truth may be that you are angry or frustrated with them or that you need to appear powerful and all-knowing.

You must ask how this action would help the client to move toward desired change or to cope with the situation's demands. Done poorly, with a vulnerable system, confrontation can result in the client's quick accommodation to your views or angry withdrawal from contact. Neither is effective in solving problems. Finally, confrontation should be based on a careful evaluation of the relationship and of what the information provided will mean to the client within the partnership already established.

STRENGTHENING CLIENT COMMUNICATION SKILLS

It is important to improve how a client communicates. Communication is involved in many important skills, such as parenting. Most of the interventive methods for increasing clients' awareness of self and behavior can also be used in strengthening or changing patterns of communication. Once aware of their pattern of communication behavior, clients can think about emphasizing some aspects and deemphasizing others or seeking other changes. To help clients strengthen communication skills, you will need to be aware of the misconceptions about communication summarized in Exhibit 12–6.

Teaching Coping Skills

This method goes beyond simply giving information; you will be teaching clients skills in manipulating their environment so as to achieve desired outcomes (Evans,

EXHIBIT 12-6	Ten Misconceptions About Communication

1. Words have meanings. Wrong: Meanings are created in the human mind; different people will associate different meanings with the same word.
2. Communication is verbal. Wrong: Communication is both verbal and nonverbal.
3. Telling is communication. Wrong: Telling is only half of communication; the other half is receiving.
4. Communications will solve all our problems. Wrong: Communication may create more problems than it solves. Careful attention needs to be given to what and how much is communicated.
5. Communication is a good thing. Wrong: Communication is neither good nor bad; it is a tool to facilitate what we want to relay, and this may be good or bad.
6. The more communication, the better. Wrong: The quality is more important; quantity should not override quality.
7. Breakdown can occur in communication. Wrong: Cars break down; communication does not. The more likely problem is that the listener did not hear what he or she wanted to hear or did not understand.
8. Communication is a natural ability. Wrong: Communication skills—both sending and receiving messages—are learned.
9. Interpersonal communication is intimate. Wrong: Intimate communication involves conveying very personal beliefs or feelings; interpersonal communication means talking to another person.
10. Communication competence equals communication effectiveness. Wrong: Knowing how to communicate does not guarantee that the result will be the one desired.

Adapted from: D. Barnes. Survival tips when the diagnosis is poor communication. *Family-Centered Care Networks, 11*(1), 4–5, (1994). (Published by National Center for Family-Centered Care, Bethseda, MD.)

1992; Murphy & Schneider, 1994). You may need to teach clients how to claim their rights and entitlements. Teaching coping skills requires a painstaking consideration of the small details of daily living; it involves helping clients to collect and assess facts and to consider alternative ways of securing what they want. This is time-consuming and demands patience. Some workers find it difficult to use this method without talking down to the client or moving too rapidly. Yet this method is of enormous value for clients who feel hopeless and powerless because of deprivation and lack of nurture in their environment.

Rehearsal

In groupwork, you may ask an individual to practice carrying out a task in the protected social environment of the group. Rehearsal may also be used in interviews with individuals. In either situation, the client is encouraged to role-play the transaction and to think of any obstacles that may appear, the sources of the obstacles, and ways of overcoming them. Rehearsal may be used as a sustaining technique—to help clients accomplish tasks that they have previously been able to handle but now cannot—or as a growth technique, to help clients assimilate new methods of coping.

Modeling

In modeling, you present yourself as an example for the client's consideration; you demonstrate how you might act if confronted with a particular problem. You attempt to leave the client free to adopt or reject this particular pattern. In individual work, however, overcoming your inherent authority may be difficult, unless the client recognizes the modeling of behavior, is ready to use it, and is secure with your concern. The client must have the strength to identify with your strength.

This method is often useful in groupwork, where group members may model behavior; in this context, other members usually feel free to support or reject any model offered.

PROVIDING INFORMATION FOR CLIENTS

Information, Opinions, and Advice

Information and guidance are appropriate parts of the service you provide. On the basis of your professional knowledge and authority, you express an opinion about a course of action to the client, group member, or group. As a rule, this procedure is only used when clients are unable to find their own solution or when they need permissive authority to pursue a course of action. In a group, the members offer each other information and opinions and will become helpers. Because a gain in one area of functioning can, through a redistribution of energies, trigger improvement of functioning in other areas, providing information may be a growth-producing technique if it helps a client deal successfully with an overwhelming situation.

You will give information, suggestions, or opinions:

- to establish a common understanding about the situation
- to share with the client your view of the situation—how you add it up
- to suggest actions the client may want to try
- to communicate new knowledge about the situation

You may suggest alternatives to the client's previous coping efforts and discuss how these alternatives can be used. You may provide information about important aspects of the problem or its possible solution. You may provide information about community resources, how to use them, what to expect from them; information about the client's entitlement to services; and information about how you can act to aid the client's use of resources.

Giving advice is not the same as providing information. Information can be provided in a neutral manner, leaving the client free to use the information or not. However, clients may feel obligated to accept advice, especially from someone in authority. If they disagree, they will find some indirect way of failing to follow through. Avoid giving advice before you understand clients' wants. If a client is asking for advice, try to understand the reason for the request. Be cautious about offering advice unless it is specifically requested by a client. Even then, you will want to label your advice as only your opinion and to be clear that the client is free to accept or reject it. In those circumstances, your advice may save the client energy and demonstrate your concern.

Self-Disclosure

Self-disclosure involves sharing part of your own personal history and life experiences with a client. It goes well beyond sharing information and opinions about a specific situation that the client faces. Social workers debate whether self-disclosure is appropriate and, if so,

under what conditions. In considering these questions, it is helpful to differentiate between self-disclosure initiated by the worker and self-disclosure in response to client's questions.

Worker-initiated self-disclosure. Some social workers see self-disclosure as an essential part of practice (Freud, 1992; Lundy, 1993; MacDonald, 1988; Russell, 1989; Thomas, 1997; Valentich, 1986). They argue that self-disclosure allows the practitioner to share relevant personal experiences and to express emotional responses to the client's experiences and is necessary for building openness and trust (Lundy, 1993). Further, self-disclosure can assist in identifying common social conditions shared by both client and worker (Worell & Remer, 1992). Worker self-disclosure and expression of emotions may be essential to the search for mutual understanding between worker and client (Bricker-Jenkins, 1991) and reduces the role distance and power difference between worker and client (Worell & Remer, 1992).

However, worker-initiated self-disclosure may also confuse clients and lead them to adopt goals that they judge to be important to you, though not to them (Wells, 1994). We recommend that you do not use worker-initiated self-disclosure except after careful planning and discussion with your supervisor. These guidelines may be helpful:

1. Be very comfortable that the self-disclosure is not motivated by your need to share.
2. Do not use self-disclosure as a means to establish your own credibility.
3. Be sure that the self-disclosure relates to the client's struggle and the agreed-upon objective and is meaningful to the client in the current situation.
4. If the client shows disinterest or appears uncomfortable, discontinue self-disclosure.

Responding to client questions. Some clients may ask personal questions of you. In some circumstances such questions may represent honest efforts to secure information, based on a sincere interest in who you are. In others, clients may be testing you and trying to validate their own point of view. For example, it is not uncommon for troubled youths to ask, "Did you ever violate the law?" or "Did you ever use marijuana?" In marriage counseling you may be asked, "Have you ever been married?"

You are not obligated to answer these questions, especially if you feel uncomfortable doing so. In the latter case, we recommend that you simply say, for instance, "I am uncomfortable discussing personal information about me," and then refocus on the client by asking "Can you tell me what's behind your interest?"

If you are comfortable responding to a client's personal question, we recommend a very short answer, followed by similar refocusing on the client. Suppose that an adolescent client asks, "Did you ever smoke marijuana?" We recommend an honest answer,—for instance, "Yes, I did and, as I look back on it, I wish that I hadn't" or simply "Yes, I did" or "No, I haven't." (If you are still smoking marijuana, we do not recommend volunteering this information.) After your short response, refocus by asking, "Can you tell me what's behind your interest in that?" In summary, we suggest the following guidelines when responding to personal questions from clients:

1. You don't need to respond if you are uncomfortable; a simple statement that you are uncomfortable discussing personal matters will be sufficient.
2. If you do respond, keep your answer short and factual; don't explain or defend your behavior.
3. Anything you say should be truthful. This does not mean that you must volunteer the entire truth; leaving things unsaid is not necessarily dishonest.
4. Try to shift the focus to what lies behind the client's question and interest.

Honesty with Clients

Honesty, while necessary as we share vital information with clients, requires care and thought. It would be brutal to say to a distraught client, "You look terrible today." As Exhibit 12–7 illustrates, the cruelty of an honest statement need not be deliberate.

You need to share information in a way that is not hurtful to clients. We suggest the following guidelines:

1. Whatever you do say should be truthful; do not tell lies.
2. You do not need to share everything; the timing may be critical.
3. Many things are best left unsaid; this is especially true of comments, no matter how honest, that might be construed as negative or critical.
4. Try to be sensitive to how the information will be received, and frame your comments in as positive or neutral a manner as possible.
5. Do not use honesty as an excuse to attack or disparage another person.

ASSISTING CLIENTS TO MAKE DECISIONS

Clients have difficulty in making decisions for a number of reasons: lack of experience; difficulty in weighing the options and evidence; or discomfort at taking a risk. In making a decision, we always run the risk of making

EXHIBIT 12-7 Too Much Honesty

Baby Blues cartoon by Jerry Scott and Rick Kirkman © 1997 King Features Syndicate, Inc. Reprinted with special permission of King Features Syndicate.

the wrong choice. Some clients will ask you, directly or indirectly, to make their decisions. You need to scrupulously avoid doing so. Make sure, for example, that a request for advice or information is not a veiled request to make a decision for the client. If making a decision is defined as the problem for work, client and worker can negotiate an appropriate service plan; Exhibit 12–8 provides an example. Having made a decision, the client negotiates with the worker another plan to implement the decision.

Decision Making as Problem Solving

Decision making is a logical problem-solving process. You can involve the client in a discussion of the advantages and disadvantages of one option compared to the advantages and disadvantages of another; it may be helpful to make lists. Try to determine which of the advantages are most important to the client and which of the disadvantages might be neutralized or reduced. In

some cases, the plan may be to gather additional information. Force field analysis (Exhibit 12–9) may help clients to organize their thinking and arrive at a decision.

You will need to encourage clients—or even give them permission—to take risks. Let clients know that risk taking is an essential part of life. If we do not make decisions for ourselves, we become immobilized and someone else is likely to exercise unreasonable control over our lives. An unhelpful decision can usually be reversed as new information comes to light.

Assisting clients to make decisions may seem a cumbersome process, but remember that the skills are transferable: As clients learn how to make decisions in one area, their ability and willingness to engage in decision making in other areas of their life will increase.

Logical Discussion

Logical discussion helps to build the client's capacity for rational behavior. It is most useful when the

---

EXHIBIT 12-8   **A Service Plan to Assist in Decision Making**

BACKGROUND: Richard is the 10-year-old son of Jon and Bonita Jasper. Jon is a merchant seaman and is at sea for extended periods of time, leaving Bonita as the primary provider of child care. Richard has been staying out late at night, is refusing to do household chores, and recently was gone from home overnight. Bonita, in her efforts to control Richard, has used harsh discipline, including beating him with a belt that left welts. The school made a referral to child protection; the child protection agency is holding the case open because Bonita has asked for services from the family service unit of the Maritime Union. This initial plan was developed by Bonita and Sally Harlow, the worker, during a home visit.

DATE: March 5

PROBLEM: Bonita is having difficulty managing Richard without anger, is resorting to harsh punishment, and is considering requesting an out-of-home placement.

OBJECTIVE: Bonita will be able to decide whether to request placement for Richard or to develop a service plan to retain Richard at home.

SERVICE PLAN:

Task	Who Will Do?	To Be Completed by:
1. Meet twice in Bonita's home to discuss the choices available and the pros and cons of each choice.	Bonita and Sally; Sally will visit Bonita at her home for these meetings	1st meeting on March 12; 2nd meeting on March 19.
2. Bonita will make a decision among: (a) requesting placement, (b) developing a service plan for retaining Richard in the home, or (c) discontinuing service.	Bonita	March 23
3. Telephone conference to discuss the decision and schedule another meeting if Bonita decides for (a) or (b).	Worker will call Bonita	March 24

EXHIBIT 12-9	Force Field Analysis

Force field analysis is a structural method for making a decision about a course of action:
1. Identify the situation as it is now.
2. Specify a clear objective (the situation as you would like it to be).
3. Identify the forces operating in the situation that tend to push toward the objective (positive forces), those that tend to push against attaining the objective (negative forces), and those that are neutral or uncommitted (neutral forces). Use a brainstorming technique: Name the forces as fast as possible, with no evaluation. Don't worry about repeating what has already been said. Discussion, clarification, and evaluation come later.
4. Rank the forces in terms of:
   a. Their importance in terms of bringing about change.
   b. The feasibility of bringing about some change.
   c. The clarity or tangibility of the force.
5. Devise action alternatives for altering some of the negative forces, especially those you ranked highest. Consider whether some of the neutral forces could be made positive and how to strengthen the positive forces.

FORCE FIELD ANALYSIS

Forces for (+)	Uncommitted or neutral forces (0)	Forces against (−)

individual or group has strengths in problem solving, the skills and knowledge to permit appraisals of reality, and the ability to see alternatives and consequences. Logical discussion appeals to the client for rational behavior and can serve both to sustain the client and to support growth. However, if the client has no life experience with the problem-solving process, logical discussion may be beyond him and may result in frustration. This technique is less problematic in groupwork, because the members can support each other in openly exploring the group frustration.

Challenging Irrational Beliefs

Some clients will hold beliefs and ideas about themselves, about other persons, or about opportunities within their environment that unnecessarily limit the decisions they can make. These beliefs are irrational: They have limited factual basis or derive from distorted thinking. You can challenge irrational beliefs by means of logical discussion, confrontation, and other approaches. If the beliefs can be challenged, clients may be prepared to consider other ways to behave. Exhibit 12–10 offers examples of irrational beliefs and some possible challenges to them.

ASSISTING CLIENTS TO FIND MEANING IN LIFE

You are likely to encounter clients who feel hopeless and see no meaning in life. Or, in working with young people, you may find that many of them are struggling to find some meaning in the world around them; they are experiencing an existential vacuum. Viktor Franki (1997) has suggested that seeking meaning in life is the

EXHIBIT 12-10 Some Irrational Beliefs

IRRATIONAL BELIEFS THAT LEAD TO UNASSERTIVE RESPONSES

- I must be loved and approved by every significant person in my life; if I'm not, it's awful.

- It would be awful if I hurt the other person.

- It is easier to avoid life difficulties than to face them.

- I need someone stronger than myself on whom to rely.

- Emotional misery comes from external pressure, and I have little ability to control or change my feelings.

IRRATIONAL BELIEFS THAT LEAD TO HOSTILE OR AGGRESSIVE RESPONSES

- When other people behave badly or unfairly, they should be severely condemned, they are rotten individuals.

- It is catastrophic when things are not the way that I like them to be—when I got treated unfairly or rejected.
- The world should be fair and just.

IRRATIONAL IDEAS THAT LEAD TO DEPRESSION OR SELF-DOWNING FOR ASSERTIVE FAILURES

- Things and situations should turn out better than they do and it's terrible if I don't find good solutions to life's grim realities.

- I must be thoroughly competent, adequate and achieving at all times.

EXAMPLES OF WAYS TO CHALLENGE IRRATIONAL BELIEFS

Why would it be terrible if the other person rejected me? How does that make me a worthless, hopeless human being? What do I really have to lose by telling my partner that I don't like the way he behaves toward me? If worst comes to worst and he leaves me, how would that make me a failure, a reject? And what's the evidence that, if this relationship ends, I'll never find another person who will treat me better?

How can I really hurt another person, or become a bad person, simply by making my own well-being and comfort as important as that person's?

Who says life should be easy? It isn't. Change is risky; and the status quo is only easier in the short run—not in the long run.

It might be nice to have someone to rely on; but what law is there that says I can't—even at this late stage—learn new coping skills and take care of myself, if necessary?

No one makes me feel anything; I control my own thinking and feelings.

Why should the other person roast in hell for behaving badly? This behavior doesn't mean she is a totally despicable human being. How can I express my displeasure without calling this person names?

People are going to act the way *they* want—not the way *I* want. I don't like their behavior, but I can stand it.

Why *should* the world be fair? It would be *nice* if it were, but it isn't. How can I try to change what I can change, and lump (or leave) the rest?

What law of the universe says that because I don't like something it shouldn't exist? How does getting myself upset over things really help me to effectively go about trying to change them? Like it or not, the world isn't fair; and I'd just better accept that, trying to change what I can and learning not to upset myself over what I can't change.

Why is it awful if I behave nonassertively (or aggressively)? How does that make me, as a human being, hopeless, worthless, or demeaned? Won't I stand a lot better chance of changing my poor habits and behavior by focusing on where I went wrong—and trying to figure out what to do differently next time—than by beating myself over the head and making myself depressed?

Adapted from: Albert Ellis *A new guide to rational living.* Englewood Cliffs, NJ: Prentice-Hall (1975).

most fundamental of human endeavors and has developed logotherapy, based on religious and secular existentialism, to assist people in finding meaning in life (Guttmann, 1996).

The function of spirituality in assisting people to find meaning in life has been acknowledged in the transpersonal approach to social work practice (Cowley & Derezotes, 1994; Derezotes & Evans, 1995; Lantz & Greenlee, 1990; Randour, 1993; Sermaberkian, 1994), which interprets spirituality as wholeness or integrity, irrespective of religious belief or affiliation (Cowley, 1993). This approach is appropriate for clients whose problems or goals are spiritual in nature, and provides the basis for a holistic assessment of even seemingly mundane problems. Transpersonal social work addresses the decay of moral values in a violent society and the helplessness engendered by nuclear threat, AIDS, homelessness, and dispiration (Cowley, 1993; Cowley & Derezotes, 1994; Smith, 1995; Stretch, 1967).

Transpersonal practice attempts to integrate spiritual experiences into the larger understanding of human development; the ultimate aim of human development is spiritual fulfillment (Smith, 1995). The concept of the person-in-environment is expanded to include the nonhuman world and ultimate reality (Canda, 1988). The validity of mystical experiences is acknowledged; insights achieved during altered states of consciousness or peak experiences are not dismissed as pathology. Some advocates of transpersonal practice challenge the assumptions that linear thinking is the standard for optimal cognitive development, that autonomy is the standard for psychosocial maturity, and that ordinary waking consciousness is the standard for normal mental operation (Canda, 1991).

The suffering associated with a lack of meaning or purpose in life may be a powerful force propelling the individual toward accomplishing objectives (Brown, 1980). The transpersonal model reminds us not to focus so intently on rigid, concrete goals that we miss more subtle—yet significant—internal changes that have taken place (Horowitz, 1991). You help clients find meaning in life by imparting hope, dispelling apprehension, and nurturing the belief that the future beckons with the promise of change (Horowitz, 1991). Your actions communicate hope and affirmation, although you are not their only source.

To assist clients find meaning in life, you may consider the following options:

1. Discuss with clients what they perceive to be the purpose of life and whether they feel that these purposes are being accomplished.

2. Discuss with clients their concept of spirituality and, when appropriate, refer them to a spiritual advisor.

3. Discuss with clients the nature of religious practices and whether they are finding these meaningful. You will support and encourage the practice of religion to the extent that the client wishes to do so. In some cases, you may assist clients to establish contact with religious organizations in their community.

4. Where appropriate, assist clients to find ways that they can serve other persons in their community. Many people find meaning in life through service to others. We will return to this topic in Chapters 14 and 15.

CHAPTER SUMMARY

In carrying out the interventive roles in Chapter 11, you can help clients to mobilize power—to take control of their own lives and decision making and to secure the resources they need—by drawing on a range of interventive methods:

1. Helping clients secure resources. You may provide resources to clients, do things for them, assist them to find resources in their environment, and help them to organize to pursue their interests. Assisting people to participate in a democracy is an essential part of social work practice.

2. Helping clients to become aware of themselves, their behavior, and how they impact others. You may provide feedback to clients through paraphrasing, summarizing, and checking out perception and meaning. You may clarify and reflect what you hear and see and offer interpretations of their communication behavior. You may set limits, gently confront clients, and offer appropriate reassurance.

3. Assisting clients with skill development, especially in communication. Through communication, clients are able to take control over their own lives and influence their situation. You may use role-playing, rehearsal, and modeling and identification or teach coping skills.

4. Providing information to clients. Information is empowering, although it must be shared in a way

that leaves the client free to accept or reject it. This is particularly important in the case of advice, which the client may feel obliged to accept. Offering brief, truthful responses to clients' questions about your own life and experience is appropriate, so long as you are comfortable doing so. However, we urge caution in initiating self-disclosure, which may be driven less by client wants than by worker needs.

5. Assisting clients to make decisions. This will involve both logical discussion, with evaluation of the pros and cons of alternative courses of action, and challenging clients' irrational beliefs that interfere with decision making and action. Your responsibility is to assist clients in making their own decisions; resist the temptation to make clients' decisions for them.

6. Assisting clients to find meaning in life. A sense that life is meaningless is immobilizing. You may discuss with clients what they see as the purpose of life, how they seek meaning in their lives, and whether they are drawn to any religious practices. You may assist them to make use of religious and spiritual advisors. For some people, service to others provides meaning. Explore this possibility with clients and, when they so choose, help them to put it into practice.

A LOOK FORWARD

In Reading 12-1, Barbara Bryant Solomon suggests four methods that you may use to empower families: enabling, linking, catalyzing, and priming. In Reading 12-2, Anthony N. Maluccio discusses action as a tool for promoting competence in clients. He suggests the practice principles of mobilizing motivation for change; redefining assessment as competence clarification; assisting clients in choosing alternative courses of action; recognition of different client and practitioner roles; restructuring the environment; and the use of client feedback.

In the next two chapters, we will examine how you can employ some of these interventive methods to assist clients in utilizing formal and informal social support systems. In Chapter 15, we look at how to develop helping communities, and in Chapter 16 we consider teamwork. Chapter 17 focuses on evaluating practice. In Chapter 18, we examine how to end service. If you are using this text concurrent with your field instruction, we recommend that you turn now to Chapter 18. You will need to start preparing clients for the ending of service well before you reach this point in your classroom course.

READING 12-1   *How Do We Really Empower Families? Strategies for Social Work Practitioners* *

Barbara Bryant Solomon

Despite a history of concern for families and programs aimed at strengthening family life, social workers are more frequently perceived as associated with the creation of problems for families than with the solutions to those problems. For example, George Gilder

(1981) has suggested that the most serious threat to independent, social functioning of individuals and families is the army of welfare workers who seek to provide them with welfare programs rather than economic opportunity.

Professional social workers are quick to point out that welfare workers are not, for the most part, trained social workers and the welfare system in the U.S. is a creation of politicians, not professional social workers. Families have complained, however, that

* Reprinted by permission of the Family Resource Coalition from *Family Resource Coalition Report*, 4(3), pp. 2–3.

in many instances, professionally trained social workers have attempted to utilize a psychodynamic medical model to help families deal more effectively with their problems. This model focuses on family relationships as the source of family dysfunction and gives relatively little attention to the direct and indirect influences of social institutions. Therefore, many families—particularly those with considerable strengths despite difficulties they may be encountering—are likely to reject that kind of "help" which blames the victims.

Fortunately, there are some more recent developments of practice theory within the social work profession which should provide a more acceptable basis for professional assistance to families. Empowerment in general, and family empowerment in particular, represents one such development.

One of the basic tenets of an empowerment approach to assisting families is that different families may need different solutions to the same problems. Bureaucracies tend to develop stereotyped ways of addressing problems. Thus, if a family has an unemployed father, eligibility for assistance is most often based on employment status, and the rights to service of all families with unemployed fathers are the same.

Yet, the actual circumstances of the family might cry out for differential responses. For example, one unemployed father may have a history of successful employment and recent depletion of resources. His family might need basic financial assistance, but the father's greatest need is for a decent job that utilizes his skills and makes it possible for him to support his family without public assistance.

On the other hand, another unemployed father with limited skills and an erratic job history may need to be assisted in improving his skills through a training program while his family will need intensive financial support to sustain them during the training period. Both families may be offered a minimum of financial assistance and a modicum of employment or educational counseling in a manner which is likely to prevent the former father from applying at all, and to reinforce the latter father's feelings of powerlessness and dependency. In this sense, differential assessment and intervention is sacrificed to the notion of "equity" which too often means equally inadequate responses.

How is it possible to develop an approach to helping families which does not foster dependency, recognizes and/or promotes the development of family strengths, and utilizes a mix of family and professional resources to develop the family's capacities for independent, social functioning? This empowerment approach is based on four principles detailed in my book, *Black Empowerment* (Solomon, 1976).

EMPOWERMENT APPROACH PROMOTES DEVELOPMENT OF FAMILY STRENGTHS

A social worker who is utilizing an empowerment model of practice will be able to help families who are experiencing problems recognize that (1) they may not be entirely or even primarily responsible for their problems but they will have to take responsibility for their solution; (2) helping professionals have expertise which can be put at the family's disposal to use in the problem-solving process; (3) resolution of problems will require the collaboration of the family and the "helpers" as peers; (4) their relationship to many external social institutions may influence the etiology and maintenance of their problems, e.g., their relationships with the police department, public housing authority, hospital or neighborhood health clinic, schools, probation department, etc.; and (5) the "system" is not monolithic but made up of many subsystems and effective ways of relating to these external systems can be learned in the same way that relationships with individuals can be learned.

In a three-year research and demonstration project conducted in Los Angeles's inner city, specific empowerment strategies were employed to help families become more effective in their encounters with such institutions as schools, police, welfare departments, health agencies, the courts, and other community agencies. The families had come for counseling at inner-city church sites; however, counseling was not focused solely on family relationships or relationships with the counselor, but rather on the social network in which the families interacted. A description of the strategies utilized by the counselors may be instructive.

ENABLING

This strategy assumes that a family may have considerable resources that are not always recognized as useful in obtaining from a system what the family needs. Enabling refers to actions on the part of the social worker to provide information or contacts which will enable the family to utilize its own resources more effectively.

A family attempting to obtain special support services for a child who was failing in school was frustrated until the counselor made the parents aware of the legal remedies available to them in this situation. Given this new knowledge, the parents were able to confront the school authorities and obtain the services.

A single parent who could read only at a fifth grade level often experienced crisis situations due to the difficulty she encountered in reading utility bills, rental agreements, etc. The parent was helped to see that her teenage daughter could be a useful resource in interpreting written materials until the time that she could master basic reading and writing skills herself. The teenager viewed this request for consultation as an acknowledgement of her own growing maturity.

LINKING

This strategy assumes that families can augment their own strengths by linking with others who can provide new perceptions and/or opportunities. Families may link with others to provide a collective power which can be more successful in confronting a system than that available to any individual family.

Linking, then, refers to actions taken by the social worker to connect families to other families, groups, or networks. In the case of the single, illiterate parent above, she was also helped to join a support group of single parents, many of whom were enrolled in adult education classes. It was their influence which helped her to decide to increase her reading skills.

CATALYZING

This strategy assumes that families have resources, but additional resources may be needed before their own can be fully utilized. For example, if a parent has job skills, he or she will need an actual job before those skills can be used. Catalyzing refers to those actions taken by the social worker to obtain resources which are prerequisite to the family fully utilizing their existing resources.

One family had a relative who lived in another city but was willing to move in with the family and provide child care which the family could not otherwise afford. However, the family's apartment was too small to accommodate another adult and they had been unsuccessful in finding appropriate yet affordable housing. By finding a room for the relative in the same neighborhood, the social worker was able to provide a resource that made it possible for the family to use their own extended family more effectively to meet their needs.

PRIMING

This strategy assumes that many of the systems with which families have negative encounters can respond more positively, but only under conditions which would not be perceived as a "cost" to the system, e.g., any suggestion that the system was not adhering to its own policies and procedures or that the system was "caving in" to some external pressure.

A family was experiencing a great deal of conflict. Their junior high school-age son had become angry and even assaultive with his siblings and parents when he was feeling particularly stressed. The social worker pointed out to the parents that although he had not exhibited the behavior at school, he might do so at any time and the school would very likely suspend him. The mother was able, therefore, to discuss her son's reactions to the stress situation at home with the school counselor and homeroom teacher, indicating that in the case of any unacceptable behavior she could be called to school to handle it. Thus, the social worker assisted the parent in priming the system so that it would respond differently and more positively than it would have otherwise.

CONCLUSION

An empowerment approach to families who are encountering problems in living is based on assumptions of family strengths. At the same time, it does not equate a need for assistance as a sign of weakness or dependency. Perhaps most importantly, the assistance provided is more often directed toward increasing the family's capacity to use its own resources more effectively, particularly in encounters with external social institutions.

READING 12-2 *Action as a Vehicle for Promoting Competence**

Anthony N. Maluccio

Human beings are involved, to one degree or another, in a perpetual struggle toward control of their lives. In this struggle, some of them directly or indirectly ask for help and come to the attention of social workers in diverse settings. Building on an ecological perspective and a problem-solving framework, we address, in this reading, how social workers can respond to this struggle by using action as a vehicle for promoting client competence.

COMPETENCE AND ACTION

Competence

Human or social competence is generally defined as the repertoire of skills that enable the person to function effectively. However, a distinction should be made between discrete skills or competencies and the broader ecological or transactional concept of competence, which, as suggested by Exhibit 12–11, may be defined as the outcome of the interplay among (Maluccio, 1981):

---

* An original reading prepared for this volume. This reading draws from earlier papers by the author, including Maluccio (1974, 1981, 1983), Maluccio & Libassi (1984), and Libassi & Maluccio (1986). The author appreciates Fobin Warsh's contribution of several case examples.

- a person's capacities, skills, potentialities, and other characteristics
- a person's motivation—that is, her interests, hopes, beliefs, and aspirations
- the qualities of the person's impinging environment—such as social networks, environmental demands, and opportunities.

From this perspective flows a set of attitudes, principles, skills, and strategies designed to promote effective functioning in human beings by:

- promoting their empowerment
- focusing on their unique coping and adaptive patterns
- mobilizing their actual or potential strengths
- using their life experiences in a planful way
- emphasizing the role of natural helping networks
- using environmental resources as major instruments of help

Action

Action is an integral component of this competence-oriented perspective; it consists of coping, striving, and goal-directed activities by which individuals endeavor to meet life challenges, attain appropriate control over their lives, achieve their goals, and grow. In this perspective, clients are regarded as active, striving human beings who

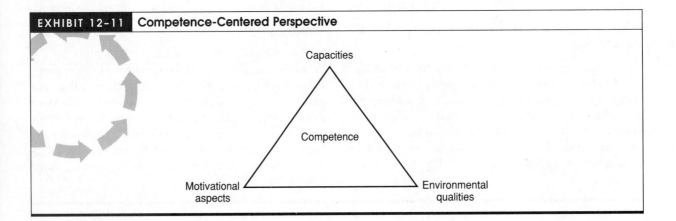

EXHIBIT 12-11 Competence-Centered Perspective

Capacities

Competence

Motivational aspects

Environmental qualities

are capable of organizing their lives and realizing their potentialities, as long as they have appropriate family, community, societal, and environmental resources and supports.

Action includes both natural activities—everyday experiences such as work, play, or social interaction—and artificial activities, including role-playing, play therapy, and participation in activity groups. Artificial activities are used as vehicles for learning, as media of communication, or as opportunities to practice desired behaviors. The client's participation in such activities can serve as preparation for engagement in life itself. Furthermore, the action should be specifically related to people's goals and consonant with their natural growth processes, lifestyles, and significant life events.

Artificial and natural activities may prove complementary. For example, a school social worker found that, following participation in a discussion group on parenting, a mother in an urban school was able to successfully confer with school personnel on behalf of her underachieving child. When she shared her experience with other mothers in the group, she felt a real sense of satisfaction. The example is Exhibit 12–12 suggests that natural activities may be more meaningful and more effective than artificial ones, since they are more closely related to the individual's life processes of growth and adaptation.

An extensive knowledge base supports the use of action as a vehicle for promoting competence (Maluccio, 1983). Especially pertinent are integrative themes from ecology, general systems theory, ego psychology, crisis theory, and learning theory:

1. The concept of human beings as open systems involved in dynamic transactions with their environment. Each person is constantly influenced by—and in turn exerts influence upon—other systems such as family, school, community and work.

2. The related idea of the goodness of fit, or complementarity. In the complex transaction between human beings and their environment, the goodness of fit between people's needs and qualities, on the one hand, and the environment's characteristics and demands, on the other, influences human competence and adaptation.

3. Knowledge about competence development. Knowledge from systems theory, ego psychology, and other disciplines is valuable in understanding how human beings achieve competence and effective functioning through action and through life experiences. Relevant concepts include coping, adaptation, autonomy, and resilience, along with the premise that human beings have an innate motivation to achieve competence.

4. The role of learning. The crucial role of learning in human behavior is central to a competence-centered and action-oriented perspective, and essential to the problem-solving process. Despite their different philosophical assumptions, such perspectives as behaviorism, learning theory, ego psychology, and socialization theory agree that learning through life experiences is a major influence on competence development and human behavior.

PRACTICE PRINCIPLES AND STRATEGIES

These perspectives suggest a range of principles and strategies for the effective use of action in problem solving within diverse agency settings. In problem solving, client and worker employ action—natural or otherwise—to help meet client needs, support client strengths and adaptive strivings, and promote client competence.

Mobilizing Motivation for Change

Early in the helping process, the practitioner needs to consider the readiness of the client to undertake certain activities. As well as the capacity to perform a

EXHIBIT 12-12	**Assistance by Means of Natural Activities**
A family service agency worker had tried to involve Mr. A, an isolated elderly man, in social activities at a neighborhood center. These efforts were unsuccessful, as Mr. A seemed disinterested in contact with his peers or in leaving his home. Eventually, he was faced with the need to relocate owing to demolition of his building.	As the social worker accompanied him on various apartment-hunting trips in different parts of the city, Mr. A began to reminisce about his life experiences, showed much interest in the ways the city had changed, and expressed his desire to move into a setting with opportunities for companionship.

given action, readiness implies some tension needing release and some motivation toward an objective. The tension and motivation can be expressed in different forms, such as anxiety, dissatisfaction, guilt, or even a hopeless dream or a fanciful ambition. The quantity and quality of the client's tension influence the timing of the activity, which should be geared to the person's readiness and spontaneity. In some situations, however, an impulse-ridden person may need help to delay action.

The traditional view of motivation as a client trait is less valuable than "a transactional model dealing with motivation as a process that takes into account the interactions among client, worker, and the environment" (Moore-Kirkland, 1981, p. 33). Such a model builds on the original formulation of the dynamic interaction among motivation, capacity, and opportunity by Ripple, Alexander, and Polemis (1964), especially their emphasis on the pivotal role of motivation in social work intervention. Following such an orientation, the worker redefines resistive behavior as motivation and considers questions such as the following in formulating the assessment and service goals (Moore-Kirkland, 1981).

1. What is the level of anxiety regarding the problem(s), the services, or the relationship with the worker, and what are the specific sources of anxiety or lack of anxiety?
2. How does the client perceive the consequences of achieving the goals of the change effort?
3. What are the effective motivators in the client's life at this time?
4. What practical factors might impede change?

Exhibit 12–13 illustrates ways of mobilizing motivation so as to facilitate effective action and promote competence in a situation involving child abuse, family breakdown, and mother-child separation and eventual reunion.

EXHIBIT 12-13 **Mobilizing Motivation**

Marie W, now divorced, had been married to Tom W for ten years. They have a 9-year-old son, Kevin. Mr. W was physically abusive to both his wife and child. When Kevin was five, his day care provider reported to the state child welfare agency her concerns that Kevin might have been sexually abused. The evaluation, though inconclusive, suggested that the child might have been victimized by a woman. At the same time, Mrs. W, distraught over the breakup of her marriage and ensuing financial difficulties, asked her sister and brother-in-law to provide temporary care for Kevin in their home. The agency then required that Mrs. W participate in a sexual abuse evaluation prior to Kevin's return to her care. Following a long series of delays in initiating the evaluation, which the agency viewed as evidence of Mrs. W's noncompliance, the court awarded Kevin's aunt and uncle temporary guardianship and required that visits with the parents be supervised.

Mrs. W participated in supervised visits at an agency-based visitation center for six months. Each of the visits between Kevin and his mother went very well. However, when a new job took her to a distant part of the state, Mrs. W did not contact her son for seven months. Mrs. W then relocated nearer to Kevin and petitioned the court for his return. The judge appointed a social worker to improve the relationship between Kevin and his mother. Several months into the therapy, Mrs. W disclosed her alcohol abuse. She explained that the trauma of losing her husband and son was overwhelming; she could not tolerate the pain of just visiting with her son, and for that reason she could not participate in parent-teacher conferences, watch Kevin's softball games, or involve herself in other parenting tasks. She indicated that alcohol helped ease the pain, but that more than anything she wanted her son back.

The social worker recognized Mrs. W's disclosure as evidence of the client's trust in her, willingness to confront her problems, and motivation to become a better parent. She used the disclosure to point to Mrs. W's courage and newly found hope that the future might be brighter than she had once thought. With the social worker's support and encouragement, Mrs. W began to attend Alcoholics Anonymous meetings. After a period of proven sobriety, Mrs. W began weekly unsupervised visits with Kevin that were gradually lengthened to a full day and then overnight. She began to feel motivated and confident enough to become more integrated in her son's life.

Mrs. W's sister objected to the social worker's recommendations to increase Mrs. W's time with Kevin. Her sister's attitude initially prompted despair but, helped by the social worker's encouragement, Mrs. W developed a new set of strategies to control her anger and maintain her focus on the goal of reunifying with her son. After two years of continued growth and change by Mrs. W, Kevin returned to his mother's home.

Redefining Assessment as Competence Clarification

In social work practice, interventive plans are based on careful understanding of the client—that is, the special needs, qualities, problems, goals, and behaviors of the person, family, or group. A major purpose of the assessment phase is to understand the client's readiness and competence for change. To do so effectively, the worker needs to complement clinically based assessment procedures with other methods, such as participant observation. As much as feasible and appropriate, the worker should become involved in the client's life situation and seek to understand, through direct experience, what is going on with the client in relevant contexts, such as the family, neighborhood, or school.

Workers should understand, as clearly as possible, each client's competence and the multiple factors affecting it, in order to make professional use of life experiences and strengths as resources for change. Accordingly, the following guidelines will be helpful in assessment (Maluccio, 1981):

1. Clarify the competence of the client. What are the unique capacities, skills, attitudes, motivations, strengths, and potentialities of the client? What are the particular areas of coping strengths? What are indicators of resilience in the person? Which areas of competence need to be reinforced or supported? Which life experiences may be mobilized to stimulate or support the process of change?

2. Clarify the environmental characteristics that influence the coping and adaptive patterns of the client. What are the critical environmental challenges confronting the client? What actual or potential supports are available in the environment? What are the risks and vulnerabilities in the client system? What blocks, obstacles, and deficits interfere with each person's life processes and adaptive strivings?

3. Clarify the goodness of fit between the client system and its environment. Does the environment contain the elements necessary to support, nourish, and challenge the person? What needs to be changed to make the transaction more mutually rewarding, to achieve a better adaptive fit, and to help the person to build on his life experiences? What new experiences or activities should be planned?

The focus on competence clarification also requires that human difficulties be viewed as problems in living or as manifestations of the poor fit between people and their environments. These problems include developmental crises, such as adolescence; life transitions, such as marriage or divorce; and discrepancies between a person's needs and environmental resources, such as a lack of day care services near to a single mother's home.

Problems, needs, or conflicts are not seen as specific weaknesses or properties of the person. They are redefined in transactional terms, so as to suggest ways of intervening in the person-environment transaction. In particular, problems are translated into adaptive tasks or meaningful life experiences, which provide the client with opportunities for action and for competence development. Change efforts can then be directed toward supporting the client's resilience and coping strategies, learning necessary skills, and, in many situations, rising above adversity (Wolin & Wolin, 1993). For example, a parent referred for child neglect is viewed as needing to learn skills in child care and is provided with a homemaker and a parent aide, who offer concrete help and also serve as role models. A couple experiencing marital discord is encouraged to clarify factors that lead to their persistent arguments. A young unmarried mother is seen as having a problem in role transition rather than an underlying personality conflict and is provided with activities that help her to gain competence as a new parent. The use of these principles as a part of the assessment process is illustrated in Exhibit 12–14. Problem definition can lead to the conscious use of life experiences as instruments of change and as opportunities for competence development. Above all, the worker regards clients as human beings who are striving toward growth, can be resources on their own behalf, and have the potential to learn through more positive life experiences.

Choosing Alternative Courses of Action

Another practice strategy is to provide opportunities for clients to consider alternative courses of action—to evaluate various possibilities, test their readiness, and choose the most appropriate alternative. Furthermore, the deliberative process can stimulate clients' cognitive growth and mastery, mobilize their decision-making function, and reinforce the sense of autonomy that comes from involvement in purposive activities consonant with

---

EXHIBIT 12-14 **Assessment as Competence Clarification**

A worker in a halfway house located on the grounds of a large psychiatric hospital began to work with a resocialization group of five middle-aged women who had been diagnosed with schizophrenia. Every one of them had been in the hospital at least four years. They had recently been transferred to the halfway house to test their readiness to return to the community.

In examining the functioning of group members from a competence perspective, the worker was impressed by the variety of existing skills and strengths. For instance, three of the women had been successfully holding part-time jobs in the hospital; one was an excellent cook; another one wrote poetry that delighted the other patients. All of them had been regularly attending group activities. The worker thus identified each client's skills and potentialities for competent functioning. At the same time, she recognized various environmental blocks.

As a result of having been labeled as sick, the women were not receiving positive feedback from their family or from staff members.

The worker set out to improve the goodness of fit between these persons and their environment by changing other people's perceptions of them and their qualities, by offering encouragement and support, and by providing further opportunities for development of their skills and talents. She planned a structured life skills workshop for group members and then helped them to practice their new skills through a variety of specific and repeated activities, such as shopping in local supermarkets, going to the movies in town, and taking the bus to a nearby city. These activities were developed on the basis of the worker's assessment of each person's needs and qualities and were purposively related to specific goals formulated with each client.

---

their needs as well as societal requirements. The worker plays an important role through the provision of information concerning the potential effects of the action, feedback to heighten clients' awareness of their reality, and support in taking a risk. Client-worker interaction becomes more meaningful and productive as both parties go through the process of reaching agreement on specific goals, tasks, and procedures.

It is useful to keep in mind the systems theory principle of equifinality—the notion that the same result can be achieved in different ways. If diverse opportunities for action are identified, the individual is able to look at the world in novel ways and to select the activity most suited to her personal style of coping and drive for competence. People cope differently with similar life crises. Exhibit 12–15 illustrates how a worker who

---

EXHIBIT 12-15 **Helping a Family Cope with a Father's Sudden Death**

Mrs. F was a middle-aged woman who seemed incapable of functioning following her husband's recent death. She became extremely dependent on her adolescent children, who were frightened and frustrated by her behavior. The children avoided her, thus contributing to her loneliness and depression. The family physician referred them to a family service agency.

After helping Mrs. F to work through some of her grief reaction, the social worker involved her and the children in the formulation of multiple tasks designed to promote her independent functioning and to change the family's interactional patterns. For example, instead of constantly avoiding their mother, the children agreed to go with her to visit relatives at least once weekly. Mrs F. agreed to let them go out on their own during the week, rather than feeling that all of them should always stay home to keep her company. The worker instructed the children to sit down individually with their mother and share with her their hopes for the future—something that they had

routinely done with their father. The worker encouraged Mrs. F to make decisions in such areas as planning for necessary housing repairs and also helped her to pursue a variety of activities, such as shopping for some badly needed clothes for herself and beginning to look for a job.

As they performed these varied tasks, Mrs. F and her children developed a new equilibrium in their family system, which had been severely threatened by the loss of the husband and father. New role behaviors and communication patterns emerged, enabling them to offer each other some gratification as a changed family unit. In addition, as she gradually performed her individual tasks with the worker's and children's support, Mrs. F increased her sense of autonomy, gained some desperately needed feelings of competence, and improved her skills in dealing with the environment. All family members thus benefited from engagement in a variety of individual and joint activities and experiences.

understands the person's unique ways of coping and adapting is able to perceive appropriate opportunities for action.

Choosing the most appropriate course of action also involves negotiating short-term goals and formulating specific action plans with clearly defined tasks for members of the client system. Exhibit 12–16 illustrates this in work with a 15-year-old with a learning disability.

Implementing Differential Client and Practitioner Roles

As another feature of a competence-oriented perspective, social work practitioners need to view their clients more explicitly as resources—as human beings with assets and potentialities that can be mobilized on their own behalf—and to help clients to see themselves as resources. Such a perspective suggests that clients should play active roles in such areas as assessment, goal formulation, and the selection of interventive strategies. By exercising their own decision-making powers in these areas, clients increase their autonomy and competence.

As clients take action on their behalf, the role of the social worker is defined in complementary terms. In particular, as suggested by Studt (1968), workers are viewed primarily as catalysts—as enabling agents who help the client to identify and use appropriate experiences or to create new experiences and resources. The worker uses a variety of approaches to help provide the conditions necessary for clients to achieve their pur-

poses. In addition to the role of therapist, a worker may need to serve as guide, strategist, teacher, broker, or advocate.

These changes also affect the relationship between client and practitioner: "The relationship is redefined as one in which two people are working on a shared project. Each brings a special expertise to the task" (Hartman, 1979, p. 264). Moreover, the relationship should be characterized by encouragement of client autonomy, reduction of the authority and power invested in the worker, and the elimination of any hidden agenda (Hartman, 1979).

As much as possible, workers should reduce social distance and promote a relationship in which openness, authenticity, and human caring are nurtured (Germain & Gitterman, 1996). Studies find that clients seem to value the worker's human qualities more than their technical skills. One such study indicated that, from the perspective of clients, the "composite picture of the good or ideal worker is that of someone who is warm, accepting, understanding, involved, natural, genuine, competent, objective, and able to share of himself with the client" (Maluccio, 1979, p. 125). The focus on a redefined client-worker relationship can lead to benefits that at times go beyond the client's immediate need. Exhibit 12–17 provides examples.

As our examples show, mobilizing the potentialities and motivation of clients requires practitioners to select actions that provide opportunities for clients to build on

---

EXHIBIT 12-16 Negotiating Short-Term Goals and Action Plans

Ryan, a shy 15-year-old, had been diagnosed with attention deficit disorder and a learning disability that resulted in poor language comprehension and production. He was doing very poorly in school, which compounded his already low self-esteem. To make matters worse, his older brother, Charley, was an outstanding college freshman, excelling both academically and on the football field. With the school year coming to a close, Ryan told his social worker that he was preparing to quit his part-time job so that he could take the summer off and "just sleep."

The social worker noted that the only time Ryan seemed to talk with any passion and sense of hopefulness was when he described his guitar playing. He played frequently with a group of his friends with whom he had formed a band and wished that

someday he might earn his living as a musician. She explored with Ryan the possibility of his using the summer to work toward this goal. Together they created a list of action steps that he would need to take, such as establishing a regular practice schedule for the band; creating a two-hour show; identifying venues; purchasing a new amplifier; and developing a publicity campaign.

By the end of the summer, Ryan and his friends had accomplished all of their goals and were scheduled to play at a host of school dances through the end of the year. Even Ryan's parents, who had begun to see Ryan as a failure and "just plain lazy," had to admire the energy and drive that their son displayed once he was helped to focus on an aspect of his life that was a strength and that really mattered to him.

EXHIBIT 12-17 Redefining the Worker-Client Relationship

A social worker in a day care center became acquainted with a young mother, Mrs. J when she dropped off and picked up her child each day. Mrs. J began to linger for short conversations with the worker. Eventually, she asked the worker to visit her at home so that they could talk further about some of her concerns.

Mrs. J expressed much dissatisfaction with her life; she felt lonely, unfulfilled, and unhappy over the lack of contact with other adults. People in her neighborhood tended to keep to themselves. Although she was yearning for opportunities to develop her interests and form close relationships with others, her environment provided little challenge or inspiration.

As the worker became aware of Mrs. J's needs and qualities, she encouraged Mrs. J. to try to create an informal support system in the neighborhood, thus making the environment more nurturing. Mrs. J brought considerable knowledge and skills to this task. She had a good understanding of the needs and characteristics of the community and also had skills in arts and crafts. The worker, on the other hand, had information about—and access to—formal agencies and was able to involve appropriate ones in the project.

Mrs. J and the worker began to hold informal arts and crafts events at the day care center for parents and children in the neighborhood. This not only provided an opportunity for families to have fun together but also began to produce the kind of informal support that Mrs. J had wanted.

While playing the role of enabler and community organizer, the worker respected and supported Mrs. J and helped her to create opportunities that were responsive to her needs and talents. In turn, Mrs. J, as an effective leader, attained satisfaction through her participation in meaningful activities and enhanced her sense of competence. At the same time, with the worker's encouragement, she created an environment that was more supportive and challenging for herself, as well as for other mothers in the area.

---

their strengths (Saleebey, 1977). This involves identifying issues of primary concern around which motivation can be awakened and taking into consideration the person's strengths and potentialities and ethnic and racial characteristics, as well as environmental resources and deficits (Iglehart & Becerra, 1995). Above all, it means emphasizing interventions that empower human beings to take action in their own behalf (Parsons & Cox, 1994; Pinderhughes, 1989).

Restructuring the Environment

Competence also flourishes through a nutritive environment that is suited to people's needs and qualities and supports their life processes. Consequently, the worker needs to understand the environment with all of its complexities and to find ways of enriching or restructuring it in a systematic fashion. In many situations, the client environment needs to be modified so as to facilitate coping efforts and adaptive strivings; social networks are especially important in this regard. Indeed, a key characteristic of competent persons is that they are able to identify and use natural helping networks. Some people, however, need help to make effective use of resources within their own actual or potential networks.

Emphasis on the environment of the client system is not new in social work. Typically, however, we have focused on modifying the environment as a means of influencing the helping process. We need to regard environmental resources and supports as instruments of help, rather than simply as influences on help; we need to appreciate the environment's potential to release or inhibit human potentialities for growth, adaptation, and competence. Doing so can lead to more accurate environmental assessment and more effective environmental intervention (Kemp, Whittaker, & Tracy, 1997).

Much can be accomplished by identifying and using environmental instruments—that is, people, resources, social networks or supports, and facilities that exist in the environment or can be added to it. These instruments are integral to intervention (Germain & Gitterman, 1996). In the area of child welfare, for instance, homemakers or parent aides are found to be effective instruments of help in working with parents who abuse or neglect their children. In short, as Exhibit 12–18 suggests, emphasis on changing the environment is as important as—if not more important than—attention to changing people themselves.

EXHIBIT 12-18	Using Environmental Instruments

Mrs. T, a woman in her mid-70s, went to a primary health care facility with health problems, and also complained to the physician that she was lonely and often very blue. The doctor diagnosed her as depressed and referred her to a social worker, who, in turn, made a home visit. Mrs. T's apartment was rather barren and neighbors were cut off from each other, leaving Mrs. T with no one to talk to or confide in. Time hung heavy on her hands. The environment provided neither social supports nor opportunities for activity and involvement.

Building on the competence-centered orientation, the worker found that Mrs. T was an energetic woman who enjoyed people, was motivated toward an active life, was well organized, and had good cognitive skills. She and the worker discussed her interests and potential volunteer jobs that would facilitate socialization, productive activity, and, in essence, a meaningful new role. Eventually, a job was selected in a local library as part of the Retired Seniors Volunteer Program, and opportunities for successful action to promote competence emerged.

The first days on the job were difficult for Mrs. T; she was apprehensive and sensitive to what she perceived as criticisms on the part of the library staff, and she considered resigning. Rather than perceiving these difficulties as a failure on the part of Mrs. T's part, the worker located the problem in the transaction between Mrs. T and the librarian, a busy younger person who was not sufficiently aware of the needs and skills of her new volunteer. The worker's subsequent talk with the librarian was successful in changing the person-environment transaction so that it became mutually satisfying. In other words the worker, as enabler, supported Mrs. T's coping and intervened in restructuring the environment with and for her, until a good match was created.

At termination, after only a few highly focused sessions, Mrs. T had increased her autonomy, enjoyed her new role as a volunteer, and found friends in her apartment and in her work environment. Mrs. T. had learned and practiced new coping skills. In addition, her environment had changed and now provided support and nourishment. The competence-centered approach resulted in increased self-confidence and self-esteem—in sum, positive mental health.

Using Client Feedback

It is important to obtain, on a regular basis, clients' views concerning our helping efforts. Although this may change with the emphasis on consumer satisfaction and outcome evaluation in a managed care environment, workers in general do not systematically elicit client feedback, as worker comments in research interviews illustrate (Maluccio, 1979, p. 175):

- "I often wish I knew what clients think of me—and what we're doing together . . . Maybe I should ask them."
- "How did the client view the objectives of our work together? I don't really know . . . You keep asking me this question and it makes me think about my approach."
- "I think that she [the client] in general felt positive toward me. But I couldn't say specifically how she saw me . . . As you ask about this, I realize that these are things we rarely discuss with our clients."

Client feedback can serve various purposes. It can be a means for the agency to monitor services, carry out program evaluation, and improve service delivery; and it can also be an effective device for workers to monitor practice and improve their skills:

> By being tuned into the clients' perspectives, workers might be better able to determine for themselves which methods or techniques are effective, what they need to modify in their approach in order to make it more relevant to client needs and qualities, and what questions they need to ask about their underlying assumptions regarding human behavior and interpersonal helping. (Maluccio, 1979, 202)

Obtaining feedback in each situation can help ensure that the practitioner is attuned as much as possible to the client's feelings, needs, views, and qualities. Moreover, eliciting the client's view can have positive consequences for the client—by, for instance, providing the individual with opportunities for decision making, reducing the social distance between client and worker, enhancing the sense of mutuality between them, and increasing the client's sense of power and control. In sum, it can promote competence by enhancing the client's self-esteem and autonomy.

More emphasis on client feedback can serve to engage clients even more actively in the helping process. At the same time, it can help workers to examine and revise their approach.

CONCLUSION

Systematic attention to the use of action in social work practice can help to enhance the problem-solving process and ultimately promote client competence. We have delineated a range of practice principles and strategies that can help practitioners achieve such purposes:

- mobilizing motivation for change by building on each person's anxiety and struggles
- viewing human difficulties as manifestations of the poor fit or lack of mutuality between people and their environments
- redefining assessment as the process of clarifying the competence of the client system, the characteristics of

the environment, and the goodness of fit between clients and their environment

- helping clients to choose alternative courses of action
- implementing differential client and practitioner roles, by regarding clients as resources and workers as enabling agents
- restructuring or enriching the client's environment in a purposive and systematic fashion
- obtaining client feedback so as to engage clients more actively in the helping process, enhance their self-esteem, monitor and improve services, and improve practitioner skills

Through deliberate emphasis on action and competence, social workers can promote their own personal and professional growth and redirect the trajectory of coping and adaptation in clients from frustration and despair toward satisfaction, self-fulfillment, and effective functioning.

LEARNING EXERCISES

1. Prepare one- or two-sentence definitions for each of these terms, or briefly explain its meaning to a colleague:
action
advice
artificial activities
behavioral description
catalyzing
checking perceptions
confrontation
direct intervention
existential vacuum
focusing
force field analysis
goodness of fit
irrational beliefs
interpreting
modeling
natural activities
paraphrasing
priming
reassurance
rehearsal
reflecting
self-disclosure
social competence
spirituality

2. In Appendix A-1, how does the worker confront Debbie Smith with the inadequacy of her care for her children? How does this affect the work of Debbie Smith and the worker?

3. In Exhibit 12–1, how would you go about sharing with Mr. Sandstone your views about his need for a back-up care provider and any arrangements you are making for this? Remember that Mr. Sandstone is a Native American client. How will this influence the way in which you share information with him?

4. Assume you are the social worker for Jim in Exhibit 12–19. Which of the methods discussed in this chapter would you use to assist Jim to examine and change how he copes with stress? Explain in detail how you would use the methods you select. How will these help Jim mobilize power?

EXHIBIT 12-19	What's Next for Jim?

Jim, a 45-year-old inmate at Meadow River prison, is married and has three adolescent children. When Jim first approached the worker, he stated his problem as fear and anxiety. Jim was afraid to speak to others and to leave his room. In addition, he suffered from panic attacks. Because of this it was difficult for him to talk about his past; after a few weeks, however, he was more comfortable and he began to open up. He stated that he was wild when he was younger and often got into trouble with the law. At one point he was incarcerated at a correctional institution for the criminally insane. He remembers physical, psychological, and sexual abuse during that incarceration; he believes that much of what happened at the institution has caused his current fears.

Six years ago, Jim was arrested again. He stated that on the way to the police station he became fearful that he may be sent back to the institution for criminally insane; he managed to escape by tying up the police officers and beating them up. He was later arrested and is currently serving time for this offense. While in prison, Jim has joined AA and has become involved with the church.

During the first few meetings, Jim said that his children were doing well in school and excelling in sports. Soon after, he began discussing their problems bit by bit.

Before the holidays in December, Jim broke down and said that two of his children were in foster care and that all of them were continually running away and getting into trouble with the law. He also mentioned that his wife was an alcoholic. By this point, Jim had managed to overcome a lot of his fears and was insistent about the help that he wanted for his family. He began to be quite demanding that someone contact his wife to help her find additional support. Phone calls were made to his wife; however, they were never returned.

In December, Jim had been granted four-hour temporary absences from the institution to attend family counseling in the community. Additionally, he was given a temporary absence to spend Christmas day with his family. During this visit, his family began fighting and he went to his room, pulled out a gun, and said that he was going to shoot himself if everyone didn't sit down and shut up. He felt that this was the only way to calm everyone down. He stayed there the remainder of the day but his wife later called the institution. Jim was quickly transferred from the minimum security camp to maximum security, where he faces more charges and is expected to stay until his release. This transfer was difficult for Jim, because the maximum security unit controls most daily activities. Jim's feeling of anxiety has returned.

REFERENCES

Breton, M. (1994a). On the meaning of empowerment and empowerment-oriented social work practice. *Social Work with Groups, 17*(3), 23–37.

Breton, M. (1994b). Relating competence-promotion and empowerment. *Journal of Progressive Human Services, 5*(1), 27–44.

Bricker-Jenkins, M. (1991). The propositions and assumptions of feminist social work practice. In M. Bricker-Jenkins, H. Hooyman, & N. Gottlieb (Eds.), *Feminist Social Work Practice in Clinical Settings,* (pp. 271–303). Thousand Oaks, CA: Sage Publications.

Brown, J. A. (1980). Child abuse: An existential process. *Clinical Social Work Journal, 8*(2), 108–115.

Canda, E. R. (1988). Spirituality, religious diversity, and social work practice. *Social Casework, 69*(4), 238–247.

Canda, E. R. (1991). East/west philosophical synthesis in transpersonal theory. *Journal of Sociology and Social Welfare, 18*(4), 137–152.

Castle, T. N. (1979). *Alliance in a secret war: The United States and the Hmong of Northeastern Laos.* Unpublished doctoral dissertation, San Diego State University, San Diego, CA.

Cowley, A. (1993). Transpersonal social work: A theory for the 1990s. *Social Work, 38*(5), 527–534.

Cowley, A., & Derezotes, D. (1994). Transpersonal psychology and social work education. *Journal of Social Work Education, 30*(1), 32–40.

Cox, E. O., & Parsons, R. J. (1994). *Empowerment-oriented social work practice with the elderly.* Pacific Grove, CA: Brooks/Cole.

Derezotes, D. S., & Evans, K. E. (1995). Spirituality and religiosity in practice: In depth interviews of social work practitioners. *Social Thought, 18*(1), 39–56.

DuBois, B., & Miley, K. (1996). *Social work: An empowering profession.* Boston: Allyn & Bacon.

Evans, E. H. (1992). Liberation theology, empowerment theory and social work practice with the oppressed. *International Social Work, 35*(2), 135–147.

Fatout, M. F. (1995). Using limits and structures for empowerment of children in groups. *Social Work with Groups, 17*(4), 55–69.

Frankl, V. E. (1997). *Man's search for ultimate meaning*. New York: Insight Books.

Freud, S. (1992). Dropping out: A feminist approach. In C. W. LeCroy (Ed.), *Case studies in social work practice*. Pacific Grove, CA: Brooks/Cole.

Furstenberg, A. L., & Rounds, K. A. (1995). Self-efficacy as a target for social work intervention. *Families in Society, 76*(10), 587–595.

Germain, C. B., & Gitterman, A. (1996). *The life model of social work practice: Advances in theory and practice* (2nd ed.). New York: Columbia University Press.

Gilder, G. (1981). *Wealth and poverty*. New York: Basic Books.

Gutierrez, L. M. (1994). Beyond coping: An empowerment perspective on stressful life events. *Journal of Sociology and Social Welfare, 21*(3), 201–219.

Gutierrez, L. M. (1995). Understanding the empowerment process: Does consciousness make a difference? *Social Work Research, 19*(4), 229–237.

Guttmann, D. (1996). *Logotherapy for the helping professional: Meaningful social work,* New York: Springer.

Hartman, A. (1979). The extended family as a resource for change: Ecological approach to family-centered practice. In C. B. Germain (Ed.), *Social work practice: People and environments* (pp. 239–266). New York: Columbia University Press.

Hartman, A. (1993). The professional is political. *Social Work, 38*(4), 365–366.

Hepworth, D. H. (1993). Managing manipulative behaviour in the helping relationship. *Social Work, 38*(6), 674–682.

Horowitz, R. (1991). Reflections on the casework relationship. Beyond empiricism. *Health and Social Work, 16*(3), 170–175.

Iglehart, A. P., & Becerra, R. M. (1995). *Social services and the ethnic community*. Boston: Allyn & Bacon.

Kemp, S., Whittaker, J. K., & Tracy, E. M. (1997). *Person-environment practice: The social ecology of interpersonal helping*. New York: Aldine de Gruyter.

Kondrat, M. E. (1995). Concept, act, and interest in professional practice: Implications of an empowerment perspective. *Social Service Review, 69*(3), 405–422.

Koren, P. E., DeChillo, N., & Friesen, B. J. (1992). Measurement empowerment in families whose children have emotional disabilities: A brief questionnaire. *Rehabilitation Psychology, 37*(4), 305–321.

Lantz, J., & Greenlee, R. (1990). Existential social work with Vietnam veterans. *Journal of Independent Social Work, 5*(1), 39–52.

Lee, J. (1994). *The empowerment approach to social work practice*. New York: Columbia University Press.

Libassl, M. F., & Maluccio, A. N. (1986). Competence-centered social work: Prevention in action. *Journal of Primary Prevention, 6,* 168–180.

Lundy, M. (1993). Explicitness: The unspoken mandate of feminist social work. *Affilia, 8*(2), 184–199.

MacDonald, S. (1988). Social work interviewing and feminism. *Australian Journal of Social Work, 41*(2), 13–16.

Maluccio, A. N. (1974). Action as a tool in casework practice. *Social Casework, 55,* 30–35.

Maluccio, A. N. (1979). *Learning from clients: Interpersonal helping as viewed by clients and social workers*. New York: Free Press.

Maluccio, A. N. (Ed.). (1981). *Promoting competence in clients: A new/old approach to social work practice*. New York: Free Press.

Maluccio, A. N. (1983). Planned use of life experiences. In A. Rosenblatt & D. Waldfogel (Eds.). *Handbook of clinical social work* (pp. 134–154). San Francisco: Jossey-Bass.

Maluccio, A. N., & Libassi, M. F. (1984). Competence clarification in social work practice. *Social Thought, 10*(2), 51–58.

Millstein, K. H. (1993). Limit setting, coping, and adaptation: A theoretical context for clinicians and caregivers. *Child and Adolescent Social Work Journal, 10*(4), 289–300.

Mondros, J. B., & Wilson, S. M. (1994). *Organizing for power and empowerment*. New York: Columbia University Press.

Moore-Kirkland, J. (1981). Mobilizing motivation: From theories to practice. In A. N. Maluccio (Ed.), Promoting competence in clients: A new/old approach to social work practice (pp. 27–54). New York: Free Press.

Moreau, M. J. (1990). Empowerment through advocacy and consciousness-raising: Implications of structural approach to social work. *Journal of Sociology and Social Welfare, 17*(2), 53–67.

Murphy, K., & Schneider, B. (1994). Coaching socially rejected early adolescents regarding behaviors used by peers to infer liking: A dyad-specific intervention. *Journal of Early Adolescence, 14*(1), 83–95.

Parsons, R. J. (1991). Empowerment: Purpose and practice principles in social work. *Social Work with Groups, 14*(2), 7–21.

Parsons, R. J., & Cox, E. O. (1994). *Empowerment-oriented social work practice with the elderly*. Pacific Grove, CA: Brooks/Cole.

Pinderhughes, E. B. (1983). Empowerment for our clients and for ourselves. *Social Casework: The Journal of Contemporary Social Work, 14*(6), 331–338.

Pinderhughes, E. (1989). *Understanding race, ethnicity, and power.* New York: Free Press.

Randour, M. L. (Ed.). (1993). *Exploring sacred landscapes: Religious and spiritual dimensions in psychotherapy*. New York. Columbia University Press.

Reder, S. (1985). *The Hmong resettlement study, Vol. I, Final report* (Contract No. HHS 600-82-0251). Washington, DC: U.S. Department of Health and Human Services.

Ripple, L., Alexander, E., & Polemis, B. (1964). *Motivation, capacity, and opportunity*. Chicago: University of Chicago, School of Social Service Administration.

Robbins, C. (1987). *The ravens: The men who flew in America's secret war in Laos*. New York: Crown.

Rothman, J., & Tropman, J. E. (1987). Models of community organization and macro practice perspectives: Their mixing and phasing. In F. Cox, J. Erlich, J. Rothman, & J. E. Tropman (Eds.), *Strategies of community organization: Macro practice* (4th ed., pp. 3–26). Itasca, IL: F. E. Peacock.

Russell, M. (1989). Feminist social work skills. *Canadian Social Work Review, 6*(1), 69–79.

Saleebey, D. (Ed.). (1977). *The strengths perspective in social work practice* (2nd ed.). New York: Longman.

Sermaberkian, P. (1994). Our clients, ourselves: The spiritual perspective and social work practice. *Social Work, 39*(2), 178–182.

Simon, B. L. (1994). *The empowerment tradition in American social work: A history.* New York: Columbia University Press.

Smith, E. (1995). Addressing the psychospiritual distress of death as reality: A transpersonal approach. *Social Work, 40*(3), 402–413.

Solomon, B. B. (1976). *Black empowerment: Social work in oppressed communities.* New York: Columbia University Press.

Staples, L. H. (1990). Powerful ideas about empowerment. *Administration in Social Work, 14*(2), 29–42.

Studt, E. (1968). Social work theory and implications for the practice methods. *Social Work Education Reporter, 16*(2), 22–24, 42–46.

Stretch, J. J. (1967). Existentialism: A proposed philosophical orientation for social work. *Social Work, 12,* 97–102.

Tou-Fou, V. (1983). The Hmong of Laos. In Asian American Community Mental Health Training Center (Ed.), *Bridging cultures: Southeast Asian refugees in America* (pp. 73–82). Los Angeles: Special Service for Groups.

Wells, T. L. (1994). Therapist self disclosure: Its effects on clients and the treatment relationship. *Smith College Studies in Social Work, 65*(1), 23–41.

Wolin, S. J., & Wolin, S. (1993). *The resilient self: How survivors of troubled families rise above adversity.* New York: Villard.

Worell, J., & Remer, P. (1992). Feminist perspectives in therapy: An empowerment model for women. New York: Wiley.

chapter 13

Case Management and Formal Social Support

CHAPTER PREVIEW

In the last chapter, we discussed interventive methods you will use to help people mobilize power and effect changes in themselves and their environments. In this and the next chapter, we will look at how you can assist people by providing additional social support (Streeter & Franklin, 1992). In this chapter we will:

- define the concepts of social support and social support networks
- distinguish between formal systems of social support and informal social support networks
- discuss how we can serve as case managers to coordinate formal systems of social support
- discuss the process of effectively making referrals

In the next chapter, we will discuss how to strengthen and enlarge informal networks of social support, including mutual aid and self-help groups.

In Reading 13-1, Miriam M. Johnson and W. David Harrison look at the concept of social care planning. In Reading 13-2, Reima Maglajlic examines the concept of care management adopted in the United Kingdom in coordinating services for persons with disabilities. Social care is a British term (Huxley, 1993); you can think of social care planning as a form of case management.

SOCIAL SUPPORT

Social support has been defined "as the existence or availability of people on whom we can rely, people who let us know that they care about, value, and love

us" (Sarason, Levine, Bashan, & Sarason, 1983, p. 127). It involves the provision of the care and assistance necessary for a person to carry out a social role. Four specific types of social support may be distinguished (Cameron & Cohen & Willis, 1985; Gorlick & Pomfret, 1993; Sarason, Sarason, & Pierce, 1990; Rothery, 1985; Rothery, 1993):

- affiliational support—a feeling of being tightly bound with another person, of being esteemed and valued, and of belonging
- information support—the provision of knowledge and skill (including information about resources) to help us understand and cope with problem events
- emotional support—a feeling that it is safe to express feelings and to discuss emotionally charged events within a particular relationship
- instrumental support—the provision of financial aid or other essential goods and services

Our social support system or social support network is the group of individuals and organizations with whom we interact to receive or exchange social support. (In reality, of course, we do not interact with organizations but rather with individuals within those organizations.)

We can draw social support from both formal and informal sources (Cameron, 1990; Erickson, 1984; Whittaker & Garbarino, 1983). Formal support comes from organizations and agencies, and those who provide the service are usually paid to do so. We will refer to these formally organized agencies and organizations as a social support system. A social support network, by contrast, consists of those individuals—family members, friends, neighbors, workmates, members of community groups, and so forth—who provide informal social support in the course of everyday living. Informal social support involves an exchange; the individuals within a network both give and receive support. We will return to the reciprocity of informal social support in Chapter 14.

CASE MANAGEMENT AND FORMAL SOCIAL SUPPORT

Case Management

One function of social work is to coordinate formal social support (Lauber, 1992; Moore, 1990). This involves assisting clients to identify their social support wants and needs, to determine where these services may be available in the community, and to secure the formal social support services they require. Coordinating the provision of community services, rather than attempting to provide all services directly, is sometimes referred to as case management (Davies, 1992; Douville, 1993; Frankel & Gelman, 1998; Rapp, 1998; Rose, 1992). The functions and principles of case management are summarized in Exhibit 13–1.

Case management is the "process of planning, organizing, coordinating, and monitoring the services and resources needed to respond to an individual's health care and social service needs" (American Hospital Association, 1987, p. 2). Moxley (1989) defines case management as a service delivery system that:

> organizes, coordinates, and sustains a network of formal and informal supports and activities designed to optimize the functioning and well-being of people with multiple needs. Through these activities the case manager seeks to accomplish the following goals:
>
> * to promote when possible the skills of the client in accessing and utilizing these supports and services;
> * to develop the capacity of social networks and relevant human service providers in promoting the functioning and the well-being of the client, and
> * to promote service effectiveness while attempting to have services and supports delivered in the most effective manner possible. (p. 17)

Social work case managers are working with diverse client groups, including children and families (Halfton, Berkowitz, & Klee, 1993; Long, 1995; Thompson & Peebles-Wilkins, 1992; Werrbach, 1996), older individuals (Hennessy, 1993; Soares & Rose, 1994; Sullivan & Fisher, 1994), persons with mental illness (Belcher, 1993; Bertsch, 1992; Degen, Cole, Tamayo, & Dzerovych, 1990; Hornstra, Bruce-Wolfe, Sagduyu, & Riffle, 1993; Rubin, 1992), people who are homeless (Mercier & Racine, 1995), persons with AIDS (Indyk, Belville, Lachapolle, Gordon, & DeWart, 1993; Roberts, Severinsen, Kuehn, Straker, & Fritz, 1992), and persons who abuse drugs or alcohol (Sullivan, Hartman, Dillon, & Wolk, 1994; Freng, Carr, & Cox, 1995;

EXHIBIT 13-1	**Functions and Principles of Case Management for Families and Children**

Case management has five basic functions:
1. *Assessment*—the process of determining needs or problems.
2. *Planning*—the identification of specific goals and the selection of activities and services needed to achieve them.
3. *Linking*—the referral, transfer, or other connection of clients to appropriate services.
4. *Monitoring*—ongoing assurance that services are being delivered and remain appropriate, and the evaluation of client progress.
5. *Advocacy*—intervention on behalf of the client to secure services and entitlements.

Five important case management principles selected by parents are:
1. Parents should have a major role in determining the extent and degree of their participation as case manager.
2. Case managers should have frequent contact with child, family, and other key actors.
3. A single case manager should be responsible for helping families gain access to needed resources.
4. Parents and child should be involved in decision making.
5. Case manager roles and functions should support and strengthen family functioning.

Adapted from: T. J. Early, & J. Poertner. Case management for families and children. *Focal Point*, 7(1), 1–4 (1993). (Published by Research and Training Center on Family Support and Children's Mental Health, Portland State University, Portland, Oregon.)

Sullivan, Wolk, & Hartmann, 1992). The case manager is a single worker who helps clients to navigate the complex network of specialized services that has evolved as a result of

- the historical tendency of policymakers to categorize social needs and problems
- the administrative pressure to specialize in order to make efficient use of labor and resources
- the specialization, underlying the professionalization of services

Case management is needed to coordinate multiple services so that they are efficiently and effectively directed at defined problem areas, individuals, and families. It focuses on the coordination and integration of services at the client level, as opposed to the coordination and integration of policy and program at the planning and administrative level. Other developments that share this perspective have included multiservice centers to provide one-stop social services and multi-agency teams to coordinate services (Healy, 1991). Some critics argue that, because of this focus on individual clients, case management fails to address important issues such as the scarcity of affordable housing, employment, and quality services and the prevalence of welfare policies that discourage family unity (Belcher, 1993; Moore, 1992; Netting, 1992).

Gatekeeping

Lacking the power to manage the system—the services and staff of separate autonomous agencies—the case manager may manage the client by regulating and controlling access to services (Austin, 1993; Dinerman, 1992; Korr & Cloninger, 1991; Moore, 1992)—that is, by acting as a gatekeeper. This application of case management is often used as a cost-containment mechanism (Brennan & Kaplan, 1993), especially in managed care. As the term implies, managed care is a set of practices for managing the provision of care services, in order to contain cost. Devised as a means for employers and insurance companies to contain the escalating costs of providing health services, managed care has become common in mental health and is making inroads in both the child welfare and juvenile justice delivery systems.

As it grows more prevalent, the type of case management used in managed care is provoking concern among many social workers (Shapiro, 1996). However, the impact of managed care is not entirely negative. It may reduce overuse of intrusive and expensive services such as institutional care; and it supports a focus on client's strengths and strengthening informal social support networks. The federal and some state governments are considering regulation to address certain abuses in medical managed care, including arbitrary limits on access to certain kinds of health care, gag agreements that prohibit service providers from sharing information regarding all available services or treatments, and rigid limits on the duration of services.

Your first ethical duty is to your client. Thus, you will be work in partnership with your client to determine her social support wants and to look for means of securing these in the community. In this process, conflict with the options provided by managed care companies is less likely than you might anticipate. In the past, conflict has generally arisen when social workers sought intrusive and expensive services for a client on the basis of their own view of what was needed. However, when a service that you and the client have agreed upon is denied, you will assist the client to use appeal or other remediation processes. You will also document these limitations, as a mechanism for securing changes in managed care policies. Documenting such limitations in pursuit of policy changes has always been a part of our social work obligation (Richmond, 1917).

EFFECTIVE REFERRALS

To coordinate formal social support, you will spend much of your time making and supporting referrals to other services. This social broker role (Chapter 10) involves:

- securing information about available resources
- preparing the client
- preparing the referral agency
- follow-up

Information about Resources

As a social worker, you will operate at the interface between the individual and the formal resource system. To make effective referrals, you must know what resources and services are available—where they are alocated, who provides them (and under what auspices), what kinds of help they offer, and to whom they are available. It is essential to develop and continually update an inventory of important resources. You must also be familiar with various access routes to the resources. What are the entry requirements and appeal procedures of the resource? What are its formal and informal policies?

Ideally, you should have a fairly good idea of what happens from the client's initial contact with a needed resource to the client's effective use of it. To that end, you will need to become personally acquainted with key individuals in the resource system so that you know exactly what you are talking about when you suggest resources to clients. Middleman and Goldberg (1974) have recommended that practitioners cultivate their resources in the long-term interests of their clients. If you maintain contacts with responsive agencies and work to improve the sensitivity of unresponsive agencies at times when no particular crisis demands response, you will be able to quickly and effectively tap a resource using well-established channels of communication when a client is faced with a critical need.

Preparing the Client

Preparation of the client includes discussion of what the referral will involve and what the referral agency expects; you are enabling the client to make effective use of the referral agency. Preparation helps build client competence and strengths and reduces client barriers to the use of services (Moore, 1990; Painter, 1966; Soares & Rose, 1994). Enabling skills are used to help clients deal with their reactions to new agencies or workers.

You will identify the range of resources and services available and appropriate to the client's needs. In partnership with the client, you will weigh the pros and cons of each option. What can the resource offer the client? What is the client entitled to? What might be expected of the client? What might the client expect of individuals within the agency? What steps will be necessary to make use of the resource?

Familiarity with the procedures and the staff at other agencies will help you prepare clients for their likely reception. For example, Mr. Washington was known to be a particularly good youth employment counselor.

He was adept at establishing rapport with young people and had helped many to find their first job in the community. However, youth referred to Mr. Washington first encountered a receptionist who tended to be curt, perfunctory, and hostile. Many of the young people left the office angry or simply failed to show up for their appointment. The staff at the referring agency, puzzled by this lack of follow-through, asked the young people about their experiences and found out about the receptionist's attitude. Using that information, they started preparing the young people, by discussing the reception they could expect at the office. Role playing was used to teach some of the less articulate youth how to ignore rudeness and to quietly, but firmly, request an appointment with Mr. Washington. The staff also considered the possibility of advocacy—approaching the management of Mr. Washington's agency to discuss the reception of clients. However, they decided against this approach, for two reasons: First, they did not want to jeopardize the emerging working relationship between the two agencies; and, second, they thought that, given adequate preparation, dealing with the receptionist would be a good learning experience for the young people. All of us encounter rudeness and insensitivity; the ability to respond without becoming angry and walking away is a useful skill.

Preparing the Referral Agency

Preparation of the referral agency involves sharing information about the client—with the client's full knowledge and usually with the client's consent. If, as sometimes happens, an agency is reluctant to accept a referral and to provide a mandated service, you may need to use mediation or advocacy. It is important to support the client throughout referral.

Generally, preparation of the referral agency will require a telephone conversation. Occasionally, a meeting with a staff person in the agency may be needed; we discourage this, because such meetings are time-consuming and expensive, may not provide the opportunity for client participation, and are usually unnecessary. We encourage you to make the telephone call in the presence of the client; if this is not possible, be sure the client is fully aware of what information you have shared with the referral agency.

You will also communicate with the referral agency by letter and by preparing referral summaries. Exhibit 13–2 presents two versions of a letter sent by a social worker; the first is officious and does not contribute much toward a cooperative working relationship. You would be better advised to adopt the straightforward style of the second version.

Writing is an advocacy tool that can help clients secure the services they want (Waller, Carroll, & Roemer, 1996). In writing referral reports and summaries, avoid jargon, present factual information without overgeneralization, label opinions as such, and include client strengths. According to Cohen (1986), the traditional chronological record is no longer consistent with prac-

---

EXHIBIT 13-2   **A Letter on Behalf of a Client**

Here are two versions of a letter written by a social worker to an attorney. Both the social worker and attorney serve the same client.

VERSION 1

Dear Ms. Trojan:

RE: Nesti, James

As per discussion on April 30, 1993, please be advised that the writer has interviewed said youth on Tuesday, May 4, between 10:00 A.M. and 12:30 P.M. at the Youth Center. Another interview was undertaken on the same date from 2:00 P.M. to 3:00 P.M. at 100 Horseshoe Avenue with the parents. All parties have agreed to holding a family group conference and the first available date is Sunday, May 16, 1993 from 2:30 P.M. to 5:30 P.M.

A concern is that the aforementioned conference cannot be held at the parties' first choice, which is their residence, because once bail is denied there is no provision for writer to escort the youth from the Youth Center to the location proposed for the family group conference. Therefore, arrangements for the family group conference will have to be made for same date and time at the Youth Center. There are no foreseen difficulties with such arrangements.

The people who have agreed to participate in the family group conference are parents, siblings, sister-in-law, other extended family members, previous teacher and a counselor, Native Community Elders, and possibly victims (in either case, victim impact reports will be available).

The agenda for the family group conference is as follows:

a) open circle session with pipe ceremony
b) the youth disclosing circumstances the offense; and
c) family group conference members determining recommendations for disposition.

Trusting this is in order, and please confirm whether as Counsel you are able to attend.

Sincerely,

Social Worker

VERSION 2

Dear Ms. Trojan:

RE: Nesti, James

I interviewed James on Tuesday, May 4 at the Youth Center, and later that day also visited his parents at their home. James and his parents have agreed to a family group conference and one is scheduled for Sunday, May 16, from 2:30 P.M. to 5:30 P.M.

We are concerned that the conference cannot be held at the Nesti home because there is no provision for me to escort James from the Youth Center to his home.

We expect participants in the family group conference to include James, both parents, siblings, a sister-in-law, other extended family members, a previous teacher, a counselor, Native community elders, and possibly victims (in either case, victim impact reports will be available).

The agenda for the family group conference is:

a) open circle session with pipe ceremony
b) James disclosing circumstances the offense; and
c) family group conference members determining recommendations for disposition.

Please confirm whether you are able to attend.

Sincerely,

Social Worker

tice, and content should be organized topically. Use the present tense, include a systematic presentation of observations, be honest about any uncertainty in your sources of information, and be clear about the purpose of the referral report. It is important to be specific about the reasons for requesting this referral. What objectives would you like to have accomplished, and what will be your continuing involvement with the client? We recommend that you share a copy of the referral summary with your client.

Follow-up

After the client makes initial contact with the referral organization, you will follow up with both parties. Follow-up should be a part of the initial planning for the referral, with a follow-up date scheduled as part of the service plan. If follow-up reveals client resistances to continuing the service or the organization's resistance to continuing with the client, you may need to adopt enabling, teaching, mediation, and/or advocacy roles.

Follow-up provides an opportunity to review whether the client is receiving the expected services and is moving toward the objectives. In the event of difficulties, you will need to do some problem solving. Positive feedback regarding the client's experience will encourage your continued use of the referral agency.

If you are still seeing the client as part of the service plan, follow-up can occur as part of one of your regular sessions. If you are not providing ongoing services for the client, you may do follow-up by telephone. The client should not be referred and dropped; follow-up is an essential part of the service you provide.

CHAPTER SUMMARY

Social support—the provision of care and assistance necessary for a person to carry out a social role—has four components: affiliational support, information support, emotional support and instrumental support. In this chapter, we considered formal social support, which is provided by organizations and agencies and usually by paid staff. Case management involves the coordination of formal social support services to assist clients in reaching their goals.

In case management, you adopt the social broker role and refer clients to other services. To do this effectively, you must be familiar with the resources available in the community; prepare your client for referral; include the client in all key decisions; prepare the referral agency, by providing appropriate information; and follow up to ensure that the client is receiving the necessary services.

In your practice, this focus on social brokerage, supplemented by other roles as necessary, will prove very valuable; it is central to the social care discussed in Reading 13-1. This approach calls for skills in humanizing service delivery and in assisting agencies to meet their responsibilities to clients.

A LOOK FORWARD

In Reading 13-1, Miriam Johnson and David Harrison discuss social care, which involves helping to provide socialization, developmental, and counseling services. As an illustration, they describe work with the Milton-Clay extended family. Make a list of all the actions undertaken by the social worker in that case. Note the various interventive roles adopted by the social worker. In this case, worker and client move from problem to problem as their interactions continue; the problem-solving process evolves. As each problem surfaces, the worker discusses it with the client, who participates in the evaluation of alternatives and in decision making about the appropriate intervention.

In Reading 13-2, Reima Maglajlic describes the development of care management for persons with disabilities in the United Kingdom as the result of an ideological shift toward the right; this shift is associated with the dominance of management with business training, decision making by elite managers, and growing sense of alienation among practicing social workers. Theoretically, care management is based on a holistic assessment of client needs, including informal care networks, and involves developing and managing a range of services to provide options for clients. In practice, however, the flexibility and holistic approach of care management are constrained and subverted by rigid institutional structures. To improve care management practice, Maglajlic suggests, social workers need to document unmet need and to increase user involvement.

In Chapter 14, we look at informal social support provided by neighbors, friends, families, and others. In Chapter 15, we will examine how you and your client can work together to develop helping communities.

READING 13-1 *The Social Work Process of Social Care Planning**

Miriam M. Johnson and W. David Harrison

At various points in the human life cycle, we all must be cared for by others, and we must in turn care for others (Aldous, 1994). Mutual caring is one of the essential foundations of human community (Bulmer, 1987; Dokecki, 1992). Social workers are professionally involved in helping people to take care of one another. Using problem-solving processes, they help individuals to meet their social care wants and needs from the community resources available. Often, practitioners strive to make the social care processes of the community more functional (Hadley, Cooper, Dale, & Stacy, 1987).

SOCIAL CARE PLANNING

In this reading, we look at the basic ideas of social care planning and counseling as an application of the problem-solving model. You will encounter an enormous diversity of problems and circumstances in social care planning and counseling. You may need, for instance, to develop a cooperate plan of care for an adolescent in a group home; to coordinate services for an individual moving from a mental hospital to a board and care home; to negotiate the legal system in order to secure permanent homes for the children of an abusive mother; to provide support for long-term caregivers of adults with developmental disabilities; or to persuade a day care provider to take a child with a minor disability.

Services such as foster family and group care or the community care of people with mental disabilities involve what Morris (1977) called caring for as well as caring about people. Social care is central to the personal social services (Harrison & Hoshino, 1984; Kahn & Kamerman, 1982). It involves helping to provide the socialization, developmental, and counseling services and resources that people need in today's complex societies. Demographic trends in Western societies suggest that the need for social care will grow very rapidly (Briar & Kaplan, 1990); already, in many parts of the world, social care and social work are virtually synonymous.

Social care work usually involves integrated planning and counseling. When done well, social care planning is truly social; it involves cooperation between individuals and their communities (for example, Harrison, 1989, 1991; Harrison, Smale, & Hearn, 1992; Johnson, 1992; Martinez-Brawley, 1990; Smale, Tuson, Cooper, Wardle, & Crosbie, 1988; Specht, 1990). This kind of social work is sometimes called case management. However, while case managers often integrate services constructively and provide a supportive relationship (Johnson, 1985), this term is problematic, because it implies that clients are inanimate cases to be managed by someone else, rather than active, self-determining human beings. Where case managers lack professional values and skills, clients may be treated disrespectfully (Netting, 1992). In the United Kingdom, the equivalent term is social care planning (Barclay, 1982), which, in practice, encompasses not only planning but also the emotional, informational, and decision-making aspects of counseling. Regardless of the terminology, it is crucial to recognize the importance of partnership in social care planning. Keith-Lucas' (1973) concept of coplanning is particularly valuable, because cooperative planning is ethically right for social work and is far more productive than planning done to or for people.

The most important human relationships involve caring for others. As infants, we are almost totally dependent on others for our care. As adults, we take care of those we love—our children, our aging parents, our partner, or our friends—when they are sick or in need. When our patterns of care change or break down or when especially difficult needs for care emerge, we often call on specialists, institutions, neighbors, and relatives for assistance, or we seek special training. Social care planning involves helping people to make use of these resources and to come to grips with the difficulties their lives present, so as to improve the quality of care. It encompasses very practical, concrete arrangements, as well as basic issues of human emotion and meaning.

Not limited to work with individuals and families, social care planning also includes collective projects such as adult day care, meals on wheels, and mobility programs. As societal patterns and attitudes change, new

---

*An original reading prepared for this volume.

needs for social care arise. In particular, new opportunities for women in the workplace demand new arrangements for fulfilling their traditional family care roles. Social workers can help individuals, families, communities, and even larger systems adapt to, and shape, these social forces.

Social workers also deal with more severe care problems, such as the difficulty of providing sound socialization and humane care to individuals with serious physical or mental disabilities. In these situations, social care work will often involve a therapeutic dimension.

PROBLEM-SOLVING CONCEPTS IN SOCIAL CARE

Good social care work uses the problem-solving model of practice. The model offers direction as workers focus on providing quality care and helping people cope.

Cognitive psychologists have found that successful problem solving usually involves two processes. First, people must achieve some understanding of the problem. This implies a personally meaningful idea of the current situation and also of a preferred way for things to be—that is, an objective. The current situation may be that things are getting worse, and the objective may be simply to halt the trend. It is often difficult for individuals to see their predicament clearly and to envision something different without skilled and patient help.

Second, humans solving problems invoke some kind of plan—deliberate or haphazard—to reduce the discrepancy between the way things are and the preferred situation (Anderson, 1980; Hayes, 1978; Newell & Simon, 1972; Rubinstein, 1975). Often what appears to be irrational or self-defeating behavior reflects individuals' attempts to deal with problems without some plan or to reduce anxiety without addressing problems directly. A plan is an organized way of working toward solutions; it involves a set of actions and responsibilities, usually with some sequential order. In social care planning, workers and clients must develop this plan together. The problems that they face will be complex and open to a variety of definitions and possible plans of action. Emotions may cloud planning, just as they complicate problem definition. "As problems become less well-defined, greater importance is attached to activities such as interpreting the problem, generating solution possibilities that are minimally suggested by the information given, and evaluating solution attempts" (Bourne, Dominowski, Loftus, & Healy, 1986, p. 237).

Creativity and expertise are important in problem solving. Social workers exercise their creativity by helping people develop plans that fit the situation and lead to desirable results. Hayes (1978) suggests that creativity is promoted by a large knowledge base, an atmosphere that encourages new and more effective ways to deal with problems, and a deliberate search for analogies between the current situation and others.

THE MILTON-CLAY FAMILY

Work with the Milton-Clay family illustrates many aspects of the problem-solving model of social work. James Milton had expected his late 50s to be the golden years. He anticipated that his daughter, Sharon, would be married, and his grandchildren would be a source of pleasure and pride. With his earning power at its peak, his wife Mildred could stay at home and pursue hobbies or take long vacations with him. Unfortunately, a back injury had forced him to quit his construction job. Although he was receiving disability pay, Mildred needed to keep her full-time secretary position in order to cover the monthly bills and to maintain the family's health insurance. His mother-in-law, whom everyone called Nana, lived in their spare bedroom; it meant a loss of privacy, but he'd appreciated her company since his injury. Now the doctor said she needed hip replacement surgery. Mildred would have to be out of work to help out during the long weeks of recovery at home. At the same time, their 31-year-old daughter was again asking for help with her two teenage children. She still seemed more of an adolescent than an adult much of the time, and the Miltons found it hard not to step in when their grandchildren were unsupervised and the home was a wreck. Living within a few blocks of her small apartment was both a convenience and a nuisance.

The Miltons had no close friends. Occasional attendance at church was their only real community contact. It was difficult for them to socialize with people, because their daughter and grandchildren inevitably came up in conversation.

Concerned about his grandchildren, Mr. Milton went to Northwood Family Services, a voluntary agency that he knew had a group foster home program. He spoke to the Family Care Unit worker, Tameeka Arthur, in very precise words and diction, his chin held high. Ms. Arthur could not help but feel for him in his turmoil. Mr. Milton had tried to be supportive to his daughter, but he was afraid that he had actually made matters worse. He explained to Ms. Arthur that his daughter had been a single parent for ten years, since she and her husband divorced. Sharon had a 14-year-old son, Henry, and a 12-year-old daughter, Tina. The Miltons had mixed feelings about Sharon's marriage. She got pregnant during her senior year in high school. Hank Clay seemed like a nice enough fellow, but he had to drop out of his classes at the community college to support her and the baby. After the divorce, Hank moved to another state, remarried, and started a second family. Now his contacts with his first two children were limited to birthday and holiday phone calls. His small child-support checks were often late or didn't come at all, and Sharon had to apply for public assistance when she was between jobs.

After Henry's birth, Sharon spent about six weeks in the state psychiatric hospital with postpartum depression. The Miltons started taking on parental duties for their grandchildren, and there had been little relief in the last 14 years. They were glad to do their part, Mr. Milton stressed, but things had gotten out of hand. Mildred had used up her paid sick leave taking her mother to the doctor, and they couldn't keep running back and forth whenever Sharon's neighbors called to complain that the children had been left without supervision.

Ms. Arthur acknowledged that it seemed now a great strain on the Miltons to feel responsible for three generations at the same time, and indicated that she might be able eventually to help the family make a plan. She asked Mr. Milton what finally had made him decide to ask for help.

Mr. Milton said that he was afraid Sharon was again experiencing a serious bout of depression, although she had been doing well for several months. She had finally put her mind to practical matters and had gotten a job. She had been working 8 to 10 hours a day as a clerk at an auto parts shop, with great enthusiasm. Every night, she was at one night spot or another, almost going without sleep, the children said. Mr. Milton abruptly changed the subject, as if he felt uncomfortable. He said that Mrs. Milton was very stressed with trying to balance her work and care for her mother. He didn't see how she could take on any more, even with his help. In the most measured tones, Mr. Milton said that he and his wife wondered whether their daughter had become a drug addict.

Ms. Arthur said that it was, of course, a possibility, but that it was important not to jump to conclusions. Mr. Milton said that he had never seen any evidence of drug use but he was concerned about the variations in Sharon's mood. He had talked to the children about drugs in the neighborhood and had the impression that they were truly appalled at the idea of drug abuse. He had not been able to confront the issue directly with Sharon.

"Is this not the sort of situation your homes are designed for?" asked Mr. Milton. Ms. Arthur said that sometimes a plan involving group care could be helpful but in these situations, unlike in medicine, it was hard to find the remedy solely on the basis of the symptoms and a diagnosis. She said that usually it was very important to discuss these matters with everyone involved so as to explore the various ways of looking at the situation. She noted that fairly common psychiatric problems other than drug abuse might lead to Sharon's symptoms and that these might be amenable to treatment. Mr. Milton did not think that his daughter had had a mental health consultation recently. He said that he was willing to listen to Ms. Arthur's advice.

Ms. Arthur wondered whether it might be useful for Ms. Clay and maybe her ex-husband to talk with the Miltons and with her about the situation. Mr. Milton thought it would be hard for his wife to take any more time off work. He felt that Hank Clay wouldn't want to be involved and that Sharon, although willing to meet, would probably not want to drive so far without some idea that it would be helpful. In her depressed state, she would see the situation as hopeless. Ms. Arthur wondered what Henry and Tina thought of the situation. She asked whether anyone knew that Mr. Milton was making contact with the agency. He said that Mildred knew. Henry and Tina did not, but they talked very openly about their mother's condition. It might be good to talk with them as soon as possible, Mr. Milton said, because they often felt like they had to tell their mother what to do, anyway. They usually got angry when action was taken without their knowledge and responded by disappearing for a day or two. Even the Department of Social Services had been looking for them once, after the neighbors called to say that something was wrong.

Ms. Arthur said that there was a legal responsibility to inform the Department of Social Services if there was reason to believe that children might have been neglected. She suggested that it might be worthwhile for Mr. Milton to talk to Mr. Bowen from that department, to let him know that she and her agency might be getting involved and to make sure that he knew about the children's situation. Mr. Milton was a bit surprised at this, but he agreed to make the call, saying that he was afraid that everyone was going to know about the situation before they were through.

When Mr. Milton called DSS, he learned that a social worker had been assigned to the family, but that the case had been inactive since Henry and Tina had last come home. Mr. Bowen suggested that Ms. Arthur try to meet with Ms. Clay and get back in touch with him afterward.

Ms. Arthur suggested that Mr. Milton discuss today's conference with his wife and daughter. She asked whether there were any other people in the community who helped Ms. Clay or could look after the children. Mr. Milton said that he had often discussed this with his daughter, but that Sharon seemed completely isolated. Ms. Arthur said that she would be available to meet with them all or with Ms. Clay alone, but that it was not possible to jump in and intervene in Ms. Clay's affairs; that would probably lead to more confusion and friction. If Ms. Clay preferred not to come to the agency at this point, Ms. Arthur could go to her home or to the Miltons'. Ms. Arthur said that she could contact Ms. Clay if necessary. However, Since Mr. Milton had made the first move, it might be best to let him work things out, assuming he still thought that it would be helpful to work with the agency after more thought and discussion.

They talked at some length about how it felt to be a potential client and how Northwood Family Services worked with its clients. The agency tried to work with the whole family; sometimes group home care was part of a plan, but often they were able to work out child care problems without anyone having to move. If placement was part of the plan, they worked very hard on both long-term solutions and the immediate needs and interests of the youngsters. They worked carefully with the Department of Social Services which now had a Permanency Planning Program to make sure that no youngsters got lost in the system without the prospect of a permanent, stable home. Ms. Arthur reassured Mr. Milton that she was not putting down his idea that his grandchildren might benefit from a group home but said that in the light of experience and research, it was most useful to get everyone together working on the same problems,

if possible. He said he would consider what he had learned and agreed to call back no matter what they decided.

Three days later, Mildred Milton telephoned Ms. Arthur. Mrs. Milton said she was glad that Jim had taken it upon himself to do something because, much as she cared for her daughter and her grandchildren, she was too exhausted to even think about the problems anymore. All of her energy was used up worrying about how she was going to care for her mother after surgery. She was glad that someone could help the family think through its options.

Ms. Arthur said she appreciated Mrs. Milton taking her coffee break to call and offered to schedule an evening appointment for the family if needed. She asked if Mrs. Milton had talked to anyone at the Northwood Council on Aging about her mother's needs or if she had requested temporary homemaker chore services. When Mrs. Milton said she had no idea such services existed, Ms. Arthur gave her the name of a colleague at the Council office.

Mrs. Milton thanked Ms. Arthur for her support and told her that she and Jim had talked with their daughter. Since Ms. Arthur had taken some of the fear out of mentioning drug abuse, they had found it possible even to discuss that subject. "Sharon said that she had had nothing to do with drugs." Mrs. Milton asked whether Ms. Arthur could come to the Miltons' home for a conference, not worrying Henry and Tina about a move unless it seemed a real possibility. Ms. Arthur agreed, saying that she would need to involve them as soon as possible if she began to work with their mother.

The meeting occurred at the Milton home as planned. Mrs. Arthur came in the evening, so that neither Mrs. Milton nor Sharon Clay had to miss any time from work. Mrs. Milton's mother joined them at the kitchen table. Almost immediately Ms. Arthur noted that Ms. Clay was seriously depressed; she sat with her eyes fixed on the pattern in the linoleum floor. She talked very little and with an air of complete hopelessness. She confirmed that she had severe ups and downs and had even been tempted to drive off the side of the road at times. She had not consulted any mental health professionals since her hospitalization years before. She said that she had often wondered if the children would be better off somewhere else, but she really had not thought beyond the possibility of her ex and his wife taking them for a while. In her last contact with Hank, two months ago, he said there was no way they could take the kids, but he promised to try to be more prompt with the child-support payments.

Ms. Arthur thought that Sharon might be suffering from a serious cyclic mood disorder. At the same time, the Miltons' need to deal with Nana's upcoming surgery was straining the resources of the family. Ms. Arthur had long ago learned that it was important to share her observations in a deliberate, honest way so that they could really be used by the family; she had not yet even met Henry and Tina. Ms. Arthur suggested that she could probably help develop a plan to support the family now that they were under such stress. She discussed all of the ways that the family had adapted over the years to cope with whatever happened. She said that she hoped that she and the agency might be seen as a new source of support. She wondered whether the adults felt that it would be helpful for Henry and Tina to talk with her and, after some initial uncertainty, they agreed. Ms. Clay said that she would tell her children what was being discussed, and she agreed to telephone Ms. Arthur the next morning. Given the level of concern Ms. Arthur felt over Ms. Clay's depression, she was glad to gain this commitment.

The next day Mr. Milton telephoned Ms. Arthur to thank her for her time. He said that Mildred had called the Council on Aging and was pleased with the alternatives they suggested; she was feeling much less overwhelmed. Mr. Milton said that they would do whatever they could to help Sharon and the children, but they knew that their time might become much more limited soon. Ms. Arthur thought that that would probably be a good way to proceed, letting Ms. Clay take as much responsibility for herself as she could. Mr. Milton did wonder whether Ms. Arthur thought Sharon should see a psychiatrist, and Ms. Arthur said that she was going to suggest a consultation, since she was not really an expert on mental disorders and psychotherapy.

Sharon Clay called as she agreed; and Ms. Arthur made an appointment to meet her at home about an hour before Tina and Henry were to return from school.

The contrast between the Milton home and Sharon Clay's apartment was dramatic. Images of rock stars were on most of the walls, and Henry's collection of baseball caps was prominently displayed on the shelves in the living room. Tina's CDs and tapes were piled high on the floor near the stereo. The house appeared clean, but definitely cluttered. Ms. Clay mumbled an apology for the mess. Pointing to a large pile of papers on the kitchen table, Ms. Clay said that she would have to do something about all these bills and receipts, but she had spent the day just getting them together. She said that she didn't have the energy even to decide what to wear, much less to determine which of her creditors could be paid this month. She went on to say that she had been looking for her will when she found the bills, and she wasn't sure whether to ask her father to sort them out. She hated to do that, but she probably would have to eventually anyway. After asking direct, tactful questions about Ms. Clay's previous reference to driving off the road and her comment about the will, Ms. Arthur learned that the first thing Ms. Clay wanted to do was to go to the hospital for some rest. She said she was worn out, and did not see how she could continue. Ms. Arthur was concerned that Ms. Clay was working on a suicide plan. She shared some of her concern by reflecting how grim the situation seemed to look to Ms. Clay and offered, rather insistently, to take Ms. Clay to the Mental Health Center that afternoon. Ms. Clay seemed relieved that someone was hearing how desperate she felt. Ms. Arthur suggested that Ms. Clay phone the Mental Health Center to see if someone could be prepared for their coming, but Ms. Clay asked Ms. Arthur to call for her. An emergency appointment was scheduled for 5:30 P.M. that day.

Ms. Clay said that she had mentioned going to live with the Miltons to Tina and Henry, but they all knew that that plan would not work for long. Henry had been the first to mention a group home, not very seriously. He knew someone who lived in a group home where the boys went on regular camping trips, and that was of real interest to him. Ms. Clay wondered if the children could be cared for in a group home, at least for the time she was in the hospital. She had told her children that Ms. Arthur was coming, but they seemed not to pay much attention.

Ms. Clay went on to say that she did not really think she could handle the job of parent anymore, that the children were beyond her, and that she was not able to supervise them. They had stopped listening to her and acted as if she were not there much of the time. Now their test grades were dropping, and they were starting to get into trouble at school—nothing serious, just constant hassles. The teacher wanted her to come in for a meeting. The guidance counselor had sent home a note asking permission to test Tina for a learning disability; Ms. Clay thought she still had the permission form somewhere. She had hesitated to sign it for fear that the school would "put Tina in one of those special classes."

The school bus stopped out front and Henry burst in. Far from being disinterested, he was extremely curious about Ms. Arthur's visit. He asked a number of questions about where she came from and what she knew about him. He wondered if she knew that his sister had threatened to run away before they put her away somewhere. Before he could finish, Tina arrived. Ms. Arthur introduced herself. Tina mumbled her name but, when Ms. Arthur asked if she had any questions about what they were discussing, all she would say was, "I don't know."

For the benefit of the children, as well as to make sure that Ms. Clay understood, Ms. Arthur decided to summarize the discussion to that point. She said that several people, including their grandparents and great-grandmother, were concerned about how the family was managing. Ms. Clay had been trying very hard, but she was feeling overwhelmed, and something had to be done.

Tina pointed to her mother and said, "She's what's wrong. She's weird!" Ms. Clay started to cry; she said Tina was right.

"Is my momma crazy?" Tina asked. Ms. Arthur explained that Ms. Clay wasn't crazy; she was just very tired and very unhappy. The situation wasn't anybody's fault—not Ms. Clay's, not the kids', not the grandparents', and not Nana's. But they would all have to work together to figure out what to do next, because Ms. Clay might need to go into the hospital for some tests, to get a rest, and to see if some medicine would help her.

Ms. Clay told the children that they would have to go to the Miltons for the night. The children actually seemed quite happy about this idea. Henry asked if they could rent a video on the way; Ms. Arthur told them that would be up to their grandparents and suggested that they gather a few changes of clothing.

Ms. Clay called her parents, who agreed to pick up the children and even take them out for supper at the local burger place. That done, Henry asked about what life in a group home might be like. Ms. Arthur reminded him that no solution had been selected from the several

alternatives available; they hadn't even decided how long the children would need a place to stay. She hoped that their school attendance wouldn't be interrupted. Ms. Arthur asked about the possibility of talking with others who might care for them in their own neighborhood, but the children could think of no one who had extra space. Ms. Arthur suggested that a foster family home might be an alternative and is usually a first choice—after relatives—for younger children, but that a final placement choice depended on current vacancies. Usually group home facilities were better able to respond to emergencies and to sibling groups. Many teenagers were happier in a group with others their own age, rather than trying to adjust to another family's home. Ms. Arthur was at least happy that they were not actively opposing the idea of placement, as many parents and children did. They would have to work toward some idea of what problems they were up against, and whether a plan for living in a group home would be helpful. Ms. Arthur assured the children that, if they did need to live somewhere other than with their grandparents, they would be encouraged to visit the place first and to meet the adults and some of the children who lived there.

Ms. Arthur agreed to contact the children the following morning at the Miltons. Her overwhelming impression was that they were eager to have someone to help them bring order to their unhappy and sometimes frightening situation. The ambivalence of the children toward their mother was clear. They wished she would act more like other mothers. Sometimes she embarrassed them, and other times they felt they should be taking care of her. Henry, in particular, was worried about how she would manage if he weren't there to be the man of the house.

After Mr. Milton picked up the children, Ms. Arthur and Ms. Clay went to the Mental Health Center. The social worker and psychiatrist there thought that Ms. Clay was seriously depressed and suicidal, probably suffering from a bipolar affective disorder that would respond well to medication. As Ms. Arthur had anticipated, they recommended immediate hospitalization to stabilize Ms. Clay's condition for now and to begin medical treatment. The next morning, Ms. Arthur called to update Mr. Bowen and said that she would be in touch if the children were in need of more attention or if a plan of care were arrived at.

Over the next week, Ms. Arthur had almost daily contact with the hospital staff, Henry and Tina, the Miltons, and Sharon Clay. Nana found the children to be a distraction from worries about her health. Jim and Mildred Milton were happy that Sharon was getting started on a medicine that held promise for her and that Ms. Arthur seemed to be a steadying influence. Nevertheless, the Miltons worried that Sharon would not be able to care for her children right away and that they could not continue to do it after Nana had her surgery.

After a second week, it appeared that Ms. Clay would soon be ready to leave the hospital. A conference was held in which she discussed her situation with the hospital staff, Ms. Arthur, and, at Ms. Clay's request, Mr. Milton. Mr. Milton said that a date had been set for his mother-in-law's surgery and his wife had made arrangements to take off work for three weeks to be with her at the hospital and when she returned home. Ms. Clay asked if the group home placement could be worked out while she got a fresh start. She wanted to stabilize her medicine, attend a day treatment program, take care of the paperwork she had left behind, and maybe apply for a new job.

It was agreed that Ms. Arthur would work with Ms. Clay, Tina, and Henry to pursue this alternative. They decided to arrange for the Clays to meet the counselors and see the facilities that had space available. Ms. Arthur would also need permission to talk over the school situation with the principal and teachers and to have them share the planning with the school in the group home's district. Ms. Clay agreed to go along, but she wanted Ms. Arthur to do the talking. Henry and Tina seemed reassured to learn that, even though the boys and girls were in different homes, they were almost next door to one another.

On the way to the group home, Ms. Arthur told the Clays to think about questions they wanted to ask. She suggested that all three Clays be prepared to discuss why they thought the placement might be useful. She had already talked about how many staff and other children lived there, and had given Henry and Tina a copy of the house rules. She reminded all of them that most families feel anxious and awkward during these visits and that the group home staff understood that.

The visit went smoothly. The children were asked what they were interested in, how they might adapt to some rules and routines, and what specific goals they might want to achieve. Neither Henry nor Tina had thought about things in quite this way before, and it seemed like something of a challenge, especially when they considered some of the privileges and recreational opportunities that went with living in the home. Henry was taken on a tour of the boys' home with his mother, and Tina saw the girls' home with Ms. Arthur. Each child had an opportunity to ask questions of the other teens, who reported that they got tired of some of the rules but that generally things were OK and sometimes even fun. The counselors told Tina she could bring her tapes and told Henry he could put up a poster in his room. Ms. Clay and the children were surprised and reassured to learn that ordinarily there were no restrictions on family visits and telephone calls; in fact, a specific section on family contact was included in the written care plan.

Later, Ms. Arthur commented that Ms. Clay and Henry and Tina seemed to have decided group care would help them take charge of their lives. They agreed, and Ms. Arthur said that it would be important to come to an agreement about their situation and put together a formal plan—a sort of contract to help everyone know what was happening and what they were trying to do. Ms. Arthur said that the staff and the families had found written plans to be particularly helpful. After a good deal of discussion and deciding which points to focus on and which to leave out, a formal plan was drawn up (Exhibit 13–3). Most of it was in the Clays' own words, the product of their own discussions and various perspectives. It was hard to imagine just how much work had gone into such a simple document, but Henry and Tina learned that most of the other residents had been through the same process.

This plan was not a complete solution to the Clays' problems, but it did become an important part of their work on many fronts with Ms. Arthur and others.

A great deal of work had to be done with Henry over the separation from his mother, because he feared she would not be safe without him nearby. One night, he even ran away from the group home with some of the other residents, but he showed up at his mother's front door several hours later. Ms. Clay had already been notified that he was missing, and she was able to reach Ms. Arthur through the agency's after-hours emergency

---

EXHIBIT 13-3 | **A Family Care Plan**

This is a family plan of care developed by Northwood Family Services and Sharon, Henry, and Tina Clay, with the support of the Social Services Department Permanency Planning Program.

The problem leading to this plan is that Ms. Clay is for now unable to provide the care she wants for her children. In the past she has depended on her parents for financial and task support. They have other demands on their time and resources and the Clays would like to be more independent. Ms. Clay has sought psychiatric care for her mental illness and continues to be responsible in following up on medications. Henry and Tina agree that they were reacting to their mother's condition in a way that was unsatisfactory to them and to her. They would like to do better in school.

The objectives developed by the Clay family are as follows:

1. Pleasant, productive living arrangements for Henry and Tina for the next six months (when the plan may be extended) at the Northwood group homes.
2. A return to the Clays living independently as a family.
3. Ms. Clay stabilizing her condition and obtaining steady employment.
4. Less friction and conflict between Henry, Tina, and Ms. Clay than in the recent past.
5. Better academic attendance and grades for both Henry and Tina Clay.

Responsibilities include the following:

1. *Northwood Family Services* agrees to provide ongoing group care services, planning, and counseling. The agency agrees to develop individualized plans with Henry and Tina to find interests they want to pursue and needs they may have and to find ways to achieve their goals while living in the homes. Northwood agrees to work with community resources (for example, schools, employers, neighbors) as much as possible to support reunion of the Clay family.
2. *Sharon Clay* agrees to continue her medical treatment, to enroll in an education or job training program, and to work with Ms. Arthur on planning for the return of Henry and Tina to her care. Ms. Clay agrees to contact her children by telephone at least twice per week, and to visit at least once a week, working out the details with the Northwood staff. Ms. Clay agrees to turn over her child support checks to pay toward the cost of care for her children. Ms. Clay agrees to work with the Department of Social Services as required by law in order to allow for their financial support of the children's care and in documenting her plans and progress.
3. *Henry Clay* agrees to work with his counselors on his objectives and needs while living in the home, to continue to work with Ms. Arthur and Ms. Clay on the goal of returning home, and to attend school. Henry has identified his hot temper and outbursts aimed at his mother as the main things he would like to learn to change.
4. *Tina Clay* agrees to work with her counselors on her objectives and needs while living in the home, to continue to work with Ms. Arthur and Ms. Clay on the objective of returning home, to attend school, and to take new tests to help the school staff figure out the best ways to teach her arithmetic and reading.
5. *The Department of Social Services* agrees to provide an outside review of this planning process at the end of six months and to provide financial and medical support for the children while they are living in the group homes.

A review of this plan can be asked for by anyone involved at any time. At the end of six months a conference will be held to review the plan jointly and to evaluate it and to plan ahead. Everyone involved will have a copy, and the plan will guide everyone's efforts to achieve their goals.

Signed:
Tameeka Arthur   Sharon Clay
Richard Bowen   Tina Clay
Bob Bloom (Group Care Counselor)   Hank Clay
Robin Maple (Group Care Counselor)

Date:

---

number. Ms. Arthur thanked Ms. Clay for calling to let them know Henry was safe. They agreed that Ms. Arthur would pick him up the next day. On the way back to the group home, Ms. Arthur and Henry talked about how getting pressured into misbehaving with peers can be a special problem in group care. Ms. Arthur also said she knew that Henry was worried about his mother. Eventually, with a great deal of support and reassurance, he overcame both the realistic aspects of this fear and also the fantasies involved.

Tina was tested for learning disabilities by the agency's counseling psychologist. He met with her teachers to recommend some special classroom techniques and adaptive study assignments; the recommendations were put in her school file, so that they could be implemented when she returned to her home school.

Ms. Clay benefited greatly from her lithium medication. She saw a psychiatrist at the Mental Health Center once a month to monitor her medication, and participated in a biweekly therapy group. She met every two weeks with Ms. Arthur, usually around specific plans for Henry and Tina and practical things she could do to take control of her life and to become more independent. She became acquainted with relatives of children in the agency's care during parent support group meetings. She remained skeptical of close attachments to new people, but she did seem to feel the other parents understood her situation better than some professionals with whom she had worked. Together with some other mothers, she worked out plans to make treats for the children for special occasions. When Mr. Bowen helped her sign up at DSS for a special program designed to help single mothers get off welfare, Sharon was pleased to learn that one of the other Northwood parents was also involved.

After nine months in care, Henry and Tina returned to live with their mother on a full-time basis. Each maintained contact with some of the adults and teenagers at Northwood. Henry went back for a short-term aftercare counseling group and Tina continued to see the Big Sister who had been assigned to her. One of the clearest changes was that now the entire family seemed able to make use of some of the community supports that were available.

Six months after Tina and Henry returned to her home, Ms. Clay and Ms. Arthur had their last interview. They reviewed the entire agency file, especially the progress detailed in the plans. The last contact of any sort they had was about three months later, when Ms. Clay called to tell Ms. Arthur that she had received her G.E.D. and that both kids had made the Honor Roll. She also reported that Nana was fully recovered and feeling better than ever and that her parents were taking a well-deserved vacation.

READING 13-2 *Social Work, Social Care, Care Management, and User Involvement**

Reima Ana Maglajlic

This reading considers social workers' relationships with politicians, policymakers, other professionals, superiors, and service users, within the arena of social and community care. Parton (1994) argues that these relationships reflect a "hole at the centre of the enterprise" (p. 30).

Social care is an established form of practice in the United Kingdom. In the U.K., as in most of Western Europe, social care refers to a range of activities and care resources provided by the local public social service agencies, informal support (families, friends, and neighbors), and independent (not-for-profit and for-profit)

agencies (Munday, 1993). Social care is only a tiny part of government activity but draws individuals and families to the governmental agenda (Parton, 1994). It could be viewed as a method of indirect social regulation, important for the liberal ideal of maintaining autonomous free individuals who are at the same time governed.

SOCIAL WORK AND THE NEW RIGHT

Social work in the U.K. has had to contend with the disintegration of political consensus about the welfare state (Harris, 1996). Expenditures on social welfare have been declining since the mid-1960s, under the impact of worldwide economic and social trends. The rationale combines fiscal responsibility—the need to halt the steady increase in the social security budget and in

---

* An original reading prepared for this edition.

residential care costs (Holman, 1993; Lewis, Bernstock; Bovell, & Wookey, 1997)—with the New Right dogma of a permanent underclass that is beyond help (Holman, 1993). During the 1970s, social work malpractices were widely publicized, and the profession came to personify the problems of welfarism (Parton, 1994).

For their part, professional, community, and other interest groups (including feminists, radical social workers, and user groups) also wanted changes, but for very different reasons. Concerned about the needs of service users within the welfare state, they were a growing voice for independence from patronizing professional domination. These groups advocated a shift from a medical to a social model of care, as explained by Bewley and Glendinning (1994).

> A medical model of disability focuses on specific, individual impairments, and does not recognize links among the experiences of disabled people in each of the systems of health and social service provision. A social model of disability defines people's experience of disability in terms of institutionalised discrimination against disabled people. The distinction is experienced by disabled people with physical, sensory or mental "impairments." The medical model says that people are disabled by their medical impairments, a social model says that people are disabled by the discriminatory social and political response to their impairment. (p. 5)

The social model does not deny the problems of disability, but locates it "squarely within the society" (Hampshire Coalition of Disabled People, 1995, p. 2).

Community care reforms in the 1980s and the 1990s began to transform the welfare state into welfare pluralism (HMSO, 1989; Department of Health, 1991a, b). For the New Right, the new paradigm included subordination to market forces, a strong managerial class, and the idea of the welfare recipient as a consumer of services, within a new contract culture (Holman, 1993; Harris, 1996). The interest groups saw community-based care and user empowerment. The most visible changes are copious legislation, reduced bureaucracy, budgetary constraints, and an emphasis on private enterprise management (Holman, 1993).

There is a difference of opinion regarding how much resistance social workers mounted to these New Right inroads into the profession. Clapton (cited in Holman, 1993) found no criticisms of the proposals in a two-year search of the social work press, and the same silence is reported from practice (La Valle & Lyons, 1996a).

Brandon and Atherton (1997), however, report long experience of protesting injustices and malpractices within the work setting, as well as the personal and professional consequences of that. According to Cooper (1994), we forgot to ask the most important question. Who needs change?

Today, 15 years after the emergence of community care, the serious consequences of these changes are more apparent: "New welfare can be delivered . . . without anyone having to form a relationship or even see a poor . . . sorry, financially challenged . . . person at all" (Middleton, 1996, p. 4). Within agencies, decision making is increasingly the domain of elite managers removed from the grassroots work (Holman, 1993; Harris, 1996).

MANAGERIALISM IN THE MIXED ECONOMY OF CARE

The managers of the mid-1990s present a professional equivalent of the Mafia—"the macho controllers," as Holman (1993, p. 28) calls them. The historical tensions between social workers and managers, dating back to the Seebohm reforms of 1968 (La Valle & Lyons, 1996b), have become more acute. The older managers are former social workers, although some of those in the Social Service Department are from business backgrounds (Holman, 1993; Thompson, 1995; Lewis et al., 1997). However, even managers with social work background lack recent experience, because they carry no caseloads (Holman, 1993; Thompson, 1995). Managers, in the practitioners' view, have lost social work skills. "They do not feel that principles and ethics of services are their direct concern—that is a problem of the Quality Assurance division" (Anonymous for legal reasons, 1997). There is a lack of shared professional themes between managers and practitioners (La Valle & Lyons, 1996b). Rather than client problems, managers are focused on the wishes of the chief executive and other superiors.

At best, managers and practitioners are uneasy bedfellows (Bamford, cited in La Valle & Lyons, 1996b). Social workers feel like cogs in the managerial chain (Holman, 1993). The major problem is that managers do not consult practitioners regarding the many changes that affect practice (Balloch, 1996), which impairs practitioners' role as change agents (La Valle & Lyons, 1996a).

The emergence of underground newsletters underlines the extent of this communication problem and the feeling of powerlessness among social workers. *News from Sammy's Dad* emerged in one local authority because the climate in social services was perceived as discouraging professional comment on matters that concerned practice; the title is a bitter joke derived from the Russian term *samizdat,* used by dissidents in the former Soviet Union for their underground publications (Sammy's Dad, 1997). Balloch (1996) found that 58% of approximately 1200 social workers interviewed were dissatisfied with department management; almost as many did not perceive managers as a source of support.

These tensions lead to high staff turnover, reduce the numbers of social work staff who see their future as including a managerial post (La Valle & Lyons, 1996b), and open the door for more business professionals. More importantly, who is most affected by this troubled relationship within the mixed economy of care? A letter to Sammy's Dad (1997) gives the answer: "I cannot remember being asked in any recent supervision session what impact a recommendation of mine might have on a client" (Anonymous for legal reasons, 1977, p. 5).

SOCIAL WORKERS AS CARE MANAGERS

The Concept of Care Management

Social workers at the grassroots level assess need and plan care; these functions are performed under the title of care manager. Care management has no widely accepted definition, embraces a variety of meanings, and thus contains both open and hidden agendas (Brandon & Brandon, 1988). One view is that care management is an appropriate tool that offers users a choice of services, and hence a measure of control over their lives (Richardson, 1995), while "containing minimal assumptions about the kind of services people should want" (Hudson, 1993). Care management is the point at which welfare objectives and resource constraints meet—where social and economic criteria must be integrated to balance needs and resources, scarcity and choice (Challis, 1994).

Care management refers to any method of linking, managing, or coordinating services to meet individuals' needs. It evolved in North America during the 1970s and 1980s, as a result of concerns about service fragmentation and cost containment in long-term care (Challis, 1995). Services were to be more flexible and related to needs.

Care management has been defined as an "administrative service that directs client movement through a series of phased involvements with the long term care system" (Capitman, Haskins, & Bernstein, 1986, p. 399). These phased involvements are the seven core tasks of care management:

- publishing information
- determining the level of assessment
- assessing needs
- planning care
- implementing the care plan
- monitoring
- reviewing

Some contrast care management with social casework and service management, because its emphasis is on tailoring services to the individual needs of particular clients, rather than fitting clients into existing service provision (Beardshaw & Towell, 1991). Care managers are generally expected to make a holistic assessment of client needs, encompassing physical and social environments and informal care networks, and then to construct and manage a range of service or living options for clients. These goals are yet to be achieved.

O'Connor (cited in Moore, 1990) made an often-neglected distinction between care management practice and care management systems. Care management practice is direct practice that contributes to the implementation of a care plan. Care management systems are the administrative structures, integration networks, and formal and informal community resources within which care management practice takes place. Dimensions of care management systems include personnel, status, functions, roles, and focus on target and technology. This distinction is helpful in thinking about changes in care management. Such changes must address not only user experiences but the dynamics—or stasis—of the overall system.

In my own research (Maglajlic, 1996), informants (nine care managers, three other professionals, a residential care worker, nine day care workers, and three parents) were asked for their definitions of care management. Some struggled: "I haven't really thought about it." "I guess it's about different types of services on offer." Some stressed the primacy of the practitioner: "You take in all their needs and you monitor it." "It's about how they should be cared for." Others placed the service user at the center of the process: "It's a system where you find what is important to someone and translate it into practical support." "It's about getting the best deal that I can for an individual in terms of meeting his needs-led assessment." No one mentioned a partnership with service users.

All informants were pessimistic about how much these processes are needs-led as opposed to service-led. Most pointed to financial restraints and bureaucracy as major barriers: "In the economics-led climate, people tend to go for what is around." "It's not user led; it's led by finances, bureaucracy, everything but the user."

The Practice of Care Management

In practice, care management is characterized by a preoccupation with agency procedures (Lewis et al., 1997); rigid institutional structures inhibit flexible responses (La Valle & Lyons, 1996a). In the new system, social workers perceive themselves as deskilled and pinned down under large caseloads that allow little client contact. "Community care assessments (form based) are a deskfull; an exercise in administration co-ordination and deforestation" (Anonymous for legal reasons, 1997, p. 8).

Care management practice lacks the expected holistic approach. Professionals in different settings (residential, day services, specialist services) are seldom involved in a coordinated manner (Challis, 1994). Existing communication channels are not used, but there is no incentive to create new ones around the care management process. In a rapidly changing environment, the different professions fear a loss of status or relevance; attacks on professionalism of all kinds in the 1980s and 1990s contributed to this fear. As a result, debates on boundaries among different professions overshadow the ostensible purpose, which is to get the best deal for the service users (Carrier & Kendall, 1995). Interprofessionalism, which requires a willingness to surrender work roles, share knowledge, and integrate procedures on behalf of the service users, may be less useful than a multidisciplinary approach, in which practitioners' retain their specific knowledge but are willing to collaborate across professional boundaries.

The community care reforms introduced a split between the purchaser (usually a public agency) and the provider. The rationale for this was that providers are driven primarily by their own interests, and not those of clients. The split was supposed to remedy this and increase the quality of services on offer. At the same time, market forces were introduced by public encouragement of private and voluntary providers; in 1993/1994, the first year of the community care reforms, local governments were to spend 85% of their allocated budget on the private and voluntary sector (Holman, 1993). Evidence is now accumulating that the purchaser-provider split has encouraged an overadministrative and mechanistic (Lewis et al., 1997) approach.

Within the purchaser-provider split, commitment to a process led by user needs was to be achieved through budget devolution to the lowest possible level; devolution to the care manager level was proven to be most effective (The Sainsbury Centre for Mental Health, 1996). In reality, however, devolution usually stopped at the management level. Care managers thus work toward requirements set by management and administration, and not by service users (Social Services Inspectorate, 1995a). Such a system is disempowering to practitioners and users.

A crisis is slowly developing. Social workers are burdened by lack of resources, vision, and support and by an increase in demand and statutory control requirements (Thompson, 1995). Practitioners who once saw themselves as enthusiastic identifiers of need are now turning into strict rationers (Lewis et al., 1997). One mechanism to resolve conflicts between responsiveness to users' needs and cost containment is advocacy (Challis, 1994). In advocacy, individuals and groups with disabilities press their cases with influential others about situations that affect them directly or try to prevent proposed changes that will leave them worse off (Brandon, Brandon, & Brandon, 1995). Advocacy attracted many social workers into the profession; yet involvement in advocacy on behalf of service users might injure social workers' chances of promotion (Brandon & Atherton, 1997).

The service is no longer universal. Most social service departments now impose eligibility criteria for services. Assessment is offered solely to clients with more complex needs. The judgment regarding whose needs is complex—a new version of the distinction between the deserving and undeserving poor—is not made by social workers but by managers higher up in the hierarchy. While care management is most effective for the clients with the most complex needs (Lightfoot, cited in Cnaan, 1994), there is no justification for the accompanying lack of preventive work (The Sainsbury Centre for Mental Health, 1996). This neglect of prevention further de-skills social workers, since it is inconsistent with their values and training.

Workers have little time to maintain relationships with service users. "No-one mentions the complexity of relationship building, the invasion of personal space by the carer. Surely these two issues alone make all purchased care complex? We should be encouraging agencies to employ people able to grasp these issues and not just anyone prepared to accept the lowest rate of pay" (Annoyed social worker, 1997, p. 8).

Although most social workers are employed in the public sector, they are a minority of the total staff in social service departments; administrative staff predominates (Cooper, 1991; Lewis et al., 1997). While agency guidelines leave some latitude for creative interpretation by workers (Elizabeth, 1997; Lewis et al., 1997), half of the social workers in one study reported lack of clarity over what is expected (Balloch, 1996); thus, they were highly dependent on the personality and preferences of managers (Holman, 1993). Services operate in an ideological vacuum, resorting to whatever works (Thompson, 1995). Whatever it is, "it isn't what we were trained to do" (practitioner cited in Lewis et al., 1997, p. 22). The consequence is disillusionment and cynicism among front-line staff.

In a care management context, social work practice must contend with these circumstances (Harris, 1996):

1. The social market exacerbates the inequalities between different service users.
2. Users are generally uncomfortable with the definition of themselves as consumers.
3. Markets are efficient when individuals have the information and knowledge to be the best judge of their own needs.
4. Little attention is paid to users' opinions.
5. Divisions of class, race, gender, age, disability, and sexual orientation that produce disadvantages within and among social groups are ignored.

The idea of the mixed economy of care lacks the fundamental condition of access to resources (La Valle & Lyons, 1996a). For example, the Community Care (Direct Payments) Act (1997) for which many user groups and professionals campaigned, is still in line with the legacy of the New Right. Many service users—for instance, older individuals—will have no access to the direct payments that the law mandates. Local governments decide who is willing and able to manage their payments, just as they decide, with other community care providers, what need is to be addressed. Rather than service users, the local governments exercise choice and power under the Act.

Service users are also deprived of choice and power under the direct-payment system because of the lack of appropriate information systems. The problems begin when individuals enter the care management system. People who are referred and denied assessment are not provided with any information about care management (The Sainsbury Centre for Mental Health, 1996), while people preparing for assessment are commonly unaware of the elements and possible consequences of the process (Audit Commission, 1995) or are swamped by tides of inappropriate information—written, jargonized, and/or only in English.

IMPROVING CARE MANAGEMENT

Documenting Unmet Need

The challenge to social work posed by care management can be partly remedied by making unmet need a political issue (Lewis et al., 1997). This will entail collecting information about the extent and the nature of needs of service users. Doing so may provide a common ground for partnership between social workers and users, but will require the use of advocacy skills (Brandon & Atherton, 1997).

Notable shortcomings of care provision are a chronic shortage of valued services in the community (Beeforth, Conlon, & Graley, 1994) and the difficulty of ensuring continuity of service for the neediest of users, even with good monitoring (The Sainsbury Centre for Mental Health, 1996). These issues should be set in a wider context; the question is not how to prioritize resources but how we can change a delivery structure in which priorities are not openly negotiated. The criteria governing resource management should be made explicit, with decisions open to challenge and change (Ellis, 1993).

User Involvement

User involvement became a statutory requirement under the National Health Service and Community Care

Act (1990). However, it was legally recognized four years before, in the unimplemented sections of the Disabled Persons Act (1986), which gave individual users and carers the rights to consultation, representation, and information. The Act sought to ensure that service providers were accountable to people with disabilities by conferring these procedural rights at both an individual and collective level of decision making.

Social workers have developed a whole new jargon—quality assurance, consultation, satisfaction surveys, charters, empowerment, partnership, self-advocacy—to make sure that power remains in a firm professional grasp, rather than having more than 50% of users actively involved in all the decision-making bodies (Croft & Beresford, 1993). Few agencies involve users (Arblaster, Conway, Foreman, & Hawtin, 1996). Organizations often suffer from the DATA syndrome: "We're doing all that already" (Fisher & Marsh, cited in Parsloe, 1997).

Users should be involved:

- across all aspects of system organization—within care planning, consultation, strategic planning, and provision of services (Arblaster et al., 1996)
- in trying to influence existing services and developing their own user organizations (Croft & Beresford, 1993)
- in tackling oppression and discrimination and changing organizational culture (The User-Centred Services Group, 1993)
- in addressing common needs of all members of the user group and specific, individual requirements (Poole, 1993)

To promote user involvement, changes will be required in the social care system (Statham, 1996):

1. Efficiency should be evaluated on the basis of the use of time, relationships among service users, professionals, and management, or number of episodes rather than criteria that relate to the nature of the task.
2. Organizational and management systems must promote user involvement, not the culture of blame.
3. The environment in which service users and staff operate is crucial to what can be achieved and should focus on the social nature of needs and social networks.

4. Support networks are needed for workers, who are disempowered and not involved.
5. The influence of the infrastructure of social care (hierarchies and the interdisciplinary approach) must be acknowledged.
6. The goal of independent living must be adopted.
7. Social workers need to learn how to utilize policy conflicts and contradiction in order to secure constructive change for users.

The time has come to move beyond an obligatory, tokenistic consultation that doesn't involve setting the agendas but only comments on decisions already made (Orme, 1996). "Users feel like optional extras, brought in to fine-tune details, but not valued enough to have a central role, so that services they need are flawed" (The User-Centred Services Group, 1993, p. 20). Even in such limited form, user consultation was implemented in only four out of 19 authorities studied by the Social Services Inspectorate (1995b). No attempts were made to specify the machinery for user consultation in legislation, despite its normative recognition (Means & Randall, 1994).

We should remove the hindrances of inappropriate language, incomprehensible and complex systems, and inappropriate meeting style and develop a shared language with service users (Department of Health, 1994). This will require detailed and resourced strategies (Bowl, 1996) to train, inform, and support users (with attention to cultural and disability issues). We need to allow time and flexibility for their involvement, at venues agreeable to all, to pay them for their involvement, to outline the kind of change that is possible, and to secure it as part of the decision-making structures (Arblaster et al., 1996; Croft & Beresford, 1993). Involvement shouldn't focus solely on users' experiences within the system, but should also consider other aspects of their lives and their expectations for the future. This will maintain a framework in which people's lives are more important than service outcomes.

Effective involvement also means providing information: "Victims may not be aware they are victims and do not always know all their real interests" (Means & Randall, 1994, p. 72). Users may be content with receiving services which currently exist, though disillusioned about the nature of services (Brandon & Atherton, 1997). They should not be content with second best

(Gibbs & Priestley, 1996). Information should be available through a one-stop-shop approach (People First, 1990), because contacts with many different people intensify the powerlessness of service users. In addition, information systems are presently constrained by decisions made in crisis (Means & Randall, 1994).

Currently, progress toward user involvement is uneven (Statham, 1996). On the one hand, user groups and radical professional groups are developing new ways of working together. On the other hand, users still do not get a picture of what assessments are about and what options exist, are not actively involved in the process, and do not receive a copy of the assessment (Carpenter & Sberiani, 1996). Also, little attention is given to the users who do not meet eligibility criteria and thus do not receive an assessment (Means & Randall, 1994).

All the stakeholders have fears about user involvement. Users fear that their services will be withdrawn if they complain. Professionals and managers fear that they will be swamped by demands that they cannot meet. There is a history of deep mistrust and unequal power between users and professionals. Professionals are driven by their values and personal commitment, which can be both a force for change and an obstacle (Morris, 1994). Users seek allies within the system (The User-Centred Services Group, 1993), but those efforts are complicated by their need to rely on professionals for advice (Dowson, 1991).

Management may attempt to subvert user involvement by arguing that the service users who do get involved are not representative. As service users have commented, "When we agree with them, we are representative, when we don't, we aren't" (Croft & Beresford, 1993, p. 28). The growing practice of paying users for their involvement and the stronger voice of user organizations may lead to the emergence of professional users. In this context, it is important to support the involvement of users with severe and complex needs—that is, people who have never been heard (Brandon et al., 1995)—and to pressure organizations to provide the training and resources necessary for user involvement (Arblaster et al., 1996). Effective user involvement will depend on strong political commitment at the government level (Arblaster et al., 1996).

Effective involvement requires an acceptance of people, not just as service users, but as equal citizens with equal rights (Croft & Beresford, 1993). Social rights are conceived in terms of needs, not resources (Orme, 1996). They should be legally based, not procedural; most fundamental is the right to income and nondisabling environments (Means & Randall, 1994).

Such an approach is essential for the protection of users against arbitrary professional power (Means & Randall, 1994). We might contrast user involvement with empowerment, which highlights the importance of power (Croft & Beresford, 1993). Empowerment implies citizen control, delegated power, and partnership, all of which are still significantly lacking from the practice of user involvement. We have to keep in mind that the rights that exist are limited. They concern issues that the rest of us take for granted—deciding where to live and what to do during the day, having access to education and employment opportunities. What we call self-advocacy should be part of everyday lives and require no special label; it means, for instance, having the opportunity to say what you want and think and knowing your voice will be heard (Dowson, 1991).

Some social workers (Arblaster et al., 1996; Brandon & Atherton, 1997; Holman, 1993) are advocating a primary relationship with community groups, which thrive on user involvement. Their leaders are elected by local residents and often have first-hand experience of what it means to be a service user. They are also knowledgeable about local needs. Such an approach would alter or remove social works' link to the local government, which is corrosive to professional independence and vitality (Brandon & Atherton, 1997).

Social workers themselves are not consulted within the system, although their input would help to change services (Social Services Inspectorate, 1995b). Mutual partnership between social workers and service users would benefit both groups; in that context, social workers would need to demonstrate their skills in supporting those they are dedicated to serve. An alliance of social workers and service users can provide a sense of vision by communicating outwards and upwards into policy-making (Cooper, 1994; Thompson, 1995). Currently, peer support and development work is not financed by the state because it is not seen as care; the terminology of care should be replaced with one of support (Gibbs & Priestley, 1996).

Concern about Poverty

Concern with poverty has declined among social workers and yet it should be a major issue because most people who approach social service departments have serious financial problems (Holman, 1983). "The existing government is keen to give the status of consumer to parents whose children are at school, patients in hospitals—but extremely reluctant to give it to those who are poor and disabled" (Brandon & Atherton, 1997, p. 18). We may not have skills to abolish poverty, but we should maintain our role as campaigners to keep it on the national agenda, since it adversely affects most of our user groups, particularly young people and the retired (Brandon & Atherton, 1997). Most social work practice ignores the economic and social deficits of poverty, unemployment, bad housing, urban decay, racism, class discrimination, and inadequate public services (Cooper, 1994).

LOOKING TO THE FUTURE

The deficiencies of social work may be traced to its intensely individualistic values (Holman, 1993), which:

- never explain just why all clients are to be valued and have the right to be regarded as citizens
- tend to stress individual practice rather than collective action
- fail to acknowledge that social work may in practice disempower people
- are not a part of the social framework
- are limited to what happens at work and do not extend to the way social workers live their lives

In order to combat managerialism services, training, and research need to be more closely coordinated (Thompson, 1995).

The profession is beset with internal tensions. Academics are perceived as stuck in their ivy tower, and practitioners have yet to be retrieved from stacks of paper and stress-related sick leaves. We have poor skills in taking care of ourselves, which is a paradox in light of the profession we practice. As Walsh (1996) notes, "The cobbler's children are the poorest shod."

A recent study of job satisfaction (Balloch, 1996) shows that 21% of social workers employed by social service departments want to leave the profession; a further 48% want to become independent consultants. British social work has little tradition of private practice (Cooper, 1994). In the United States, by contrast, 15% of all NASW members work privately as primary employment and a further 43% are involved in private practice as secondary, part-time employment (Suppes & Cressy Wells, 1996). An emphasis on private practice would involve rethinking the nature of both social work provision and education in the U.K. In the United States, consumers are making increasing demands for the licensing and certification of social workers. Any move to private social work practice can also be viewed as a move away from the social control of the state over social workers and their practice and, consequently, over service users. My biggest fears are about the generation of social workers born and raised into the profession in the era of marketization. Both privately and professionally, we remember no other practice. Unless we embrace social rights and partnership with service users, we stand an even greater chance of losing the best of our profession (advocacy and community work) and assimilating the worst (market-based, cost-unit thinking and form filling).

LEARNING EXERCISES

1. Provide one- or two-sentence definitions for the following terms; or briefly explain the meaning of each term to a colleague:

affiliational support
care management
care management practice
care management systems
emotional support
formal social support
information support
instrumental support
managed care
social care
social care planning
social support
social support system

2. Reima Maglajlic suggests that care management may be distinguished from traditional social work by its emphasis on tailoring services to the needs of particular clients rather than fitting clients into existing forms of service provision. Do you agree with this distinction? Explain. How might an emphasis on agency function, as we discussed in Chapter 5, contribute to the view of social work as fitting people into existing provision of services?

3. The Milton-Clay case in Reading 13-1 presents many elements of the problem-solving model. Consider the personal and professional qualities that are necessary to put the model into place, as well as the specific characteristics of the model itself.

   3.1. Which characteristics of the problem-solving model do you identify?

   3.2. What might Ms. Arthur have done better in making use of the model?

   3.3. Do you think it was appropriate for Ms. Arthur to take a more active role in seeking emergency help when Ms. Clay sounded suicidal?

   3.4. How do you think each of the Miltons and Clays would have described the family situation before and after they worked with Ms. Arthur? Write a pair of before and after sentences for each person.

   3.5. Mrs. Thomas was the worker at the Northwood Council on Aging who helped Mildred Milton make arrangements for in-home care for her mother. Do you think her interventive roles would have been similar to, or different from, Ms. Arthur's? Explain.

   3.6. Do you think that the Miltons should have been involved in the written plan? Why or why not?

   3.7. A great deal of work was done with each of the Clays after the move to the group home. This is not documented in the material presented. What do you think Ms. Arthur's roles and activities might have been? How might the subsequent plans have looked?

   3.8. Assume that the situation at the beginning of this case example was the same, except that Mr. Milton had talked to his family physician instead of a social worker. How do you think the social care planning and counseling process might have evolved? What do you think would have happened had he approached a mental health center?

   3.9. Do you think that Ms. Arthur should have pursued neighborhood, church, or other local resources more vigorously?

4. Which parts of social care planning do you think would be the most rewarding for you, and which the most challenging?

REFERENCES

Aldous, J. (1994). Someone to watch over me: Family responsibilities and their realization across family lives. In E. Kahana, E. E. Biegel, & M. L. Wykle (Eds.), *Family caregiving across the lifespan* (pp. 42–68). Thousand Oaks, CA: Sage.

American Hospital Association. (1987). *Case management: An aid to quality and continuity of care* (AHA Council Report: Council on Patient Services). Chicago, IL: Author.

Anderson, J. R. (1980). *Cognitive psychology and its implications.* San Francisco: W. H. Freeman.

Annoyed social worker. (1997). The personal and social costs of the market philosophy, *News from Sammy's Dad,* No. 3, 7–8. (Underground Newsletter, Lancashire, England.)

Anonymous for legal reasons. (1997). Why my authority suspended me on suspicion. *News from Sammy's Dad,* No. 3, 8–10 (Underground Newsletter, Lancashire, England.)

Arblaster, L., Conway, J., Foreman, A., & Hawtin, M. (1996). *Asking the impossible? Inter-agency working to address the housing, health and social care needs of people in ordinary housing.* Bristol: Policy Press.

Audit Commission (1995). *Joint review of social service authorities* (Consultation document). London: HMSO.

Austin, C. D. (1993). Case management: A systems perspective. *Families in Society,* 74(8), 471–459.

Balloch, S. (1996). Working in the social services: Job satisfaction, violence and stress. In *Participating in change: Social work profession in social development* (Proceedings of the Joint World Congress of IFSW and IASSW; Hong Kong, pp. 329–32).

Barclay, P. M. (1982). *Social workers: Their roles and tasks.* London: National Institute for Social Work, Bedford Square Press.

Beardshaw, V., & Towell, D. (1991). *Assessment and care management: Implications for the implementation of caring for people* (Briefing Paper No. 10). London: Department of Health.

Beeforth, M., Conlon, E., & Graley, R. (1994). *Have we got views for you: User evaluation of care management.* London: The Sainsbury Centre for Mental Health.

Belcher, J. R. (1993). The trade-offs of developing a case management model for chronically mentally ill people. *Health and Social Work,* 18(1), 20–31.

Bertsch, E. F. (1992). A voucher system that enables persons with severe mental illness to purchase community services. *Hospital and Community Psychiatry, 43*(11), 1109–1113.

Bewley, C., & Glendinning, C. (1994). *Involving disabled people in community care planning.* London: Community Care & Joseph Rowntree Foundation.

Bourne, L. E., Dominowski, R. L., Loftus, E. F., & Healy, A. F. (1986). *Cognitive processes* (2nd ed.). Englewood Cliffs, NJ: Prentice-Hall.

Bowl, R. (1996). Involving service users in mental health services: Social services departments and the NHS and community care act. *Journal of Mental Health, 5*(3), 287–303.

Brandon, D., & Atherton, K. (1997). *A brief history of social work in Britain.* Cambridge: School of Community, Health & Social Studies, Anglia Polytechnic University.

Brandon, D., & Brandon, A. (1988). *Putting people first: A handbook on the practical application of ordinary living principles.* London: Good Impressions.

Brandon, D., Brandon, A., & Brandon, T. (1995). *Advocacy: Power to people with disabilities.* Birmingham: Venture Press.

Brennan, J. P., & Kaplan, C. (1993). Setting new standards for social work case management. *Hospital and Community Psychiatry, 44*(3), 219–222.

Briar, K. H., & Kaplan, C. (1990). *The family caregiving crisis.* Silver Springs, MD: National Association of Social Workers.

Bulmer, M. (1987). *The social basis of community care.* London: Allen & Unwin.

Cameron, G. (1990). The potential of informal support strategies in child welfare. In M. Rothery & G. Cameron (Eds.), *Child maltreatment: Expanding our concept of helping* (pp. 145–168). Hillsdale, NJ: Lawrence Erlbaum.

Cameron, G., & Rothery, M. (1985). *An exploratory study of the nature and effectiveness of family support measures in child welfare.* Toronto: Ontario Ministry of Community and Social Services.

Capitman, J.A., Haskins, B., & Bernstein, J. (1986). Case management approaches in community-oriented long-term care demonstrations. *Gerontologist, 26,* 398–404.

Carpenter, J., & Sberiani, S. (1996). Involving service users and carers in the care programme approach (CPA). *Journal of Mental Health, 5*(5), 483–488.

Carrier, J., & Kendall, I. (1995). Professionalism and interprofessionalism in health and community care: Some theoretical issues. In P. Owens, J. Carrier, & J. Horder (Eds.), *Interprofessional issues in community and primary health care* (pp. 9–36). Basingstoke, England: Macmillan.

Challis, D. (1994). *Implementing caring for people: Care management—Factors influencing its development in the implementation of community care.* London: HMSO.

Challis, D. (1995). Case management: A review of UK developments and issues. In M. Titterton (Ed.), *Caring for people in the community:The new welfare.* (pp. 91–112). London: Jessica Kingsley.

Cnaan, R. A. (1994). The new American social work gospel: Case management of the chronically mentally ill. *The British Journal of Social Work, 24*(5), 553–557.

Cohen, B. Z. (1986). Written communication on social work: The report. *Child Welfare, 65*(4), 399–407.

Cohen, S., & Willis, T. (1985). Stress, social support, and the buffering hypothesis. *Psychological Bulletin, 98,* 310–357.

Cooper, J. (1991). The future of social work: A pragmatic view. In M. Loney, B. Babcock, J. Clarke, A. Cochrane, P. Graham, & M. Wilson (Eds.), *The state or the market: Politics and welfare in contemporary Britain* (2nd ed., pp. 58–69). London: Sage/The Open University.

Croft, S., & Beresford, P. (1993). *Getting involved: A practical manual.* London: Open Services Project/The Joseph Rowntree Foundation.

Davies, B. (1992). *Care management, equity and efficiency: The international experience.* Canterbury, England: University of Kent, Personal Social Services Research Unit.

Degen, K., Cole, H., Tamayo, L., & Dzerovych, G. (1990). Intensive case management for the seriously mentally ill. *Administration and Policy in Mental Health, 17*(4), 265–269.

Department of Health (1994). Implementing caring for people: "It's our lives." Community care for people with learning disabilities. London: HMSO.

Department of Health and Social Services Inspectorate and Scottish Office Social Work Group (1991a). *Care management and assessment: Practitioners' guide.* London: HMSO.

Department of Health and Social Services Inspectorate and Scottish Office Social Work Group (1991b). *Care management and assessment: Managers' guide.* London: HMSO.

Dinerman, M. (1992). Managing the maze: Case management and service delivery. *Administration in Social Work, 16*(1), 1–9.

Dokecki, P. R. (1992). On knowing the community of caring persons: A methodological basis for the reflective-generative practice of community psychology. *Journal of Community Psychology, 20,* 26–35.

Douville, M. L. (1993). Case management: Predicting activity patterns. *Journal of Gerontological Social Work, 20*(3/4), 43–55.

Dowson, S. (1991). *Keeping it safe.* London: Values into Action.

Early, T. J., & Poertner, J. (1993). Case management for families and children. *Focal Point, 7*(1), 1–4. (Published by Research and Training Center on Family Support and Children's Mental Health, Portland State University, Portland, Oregon.)

Elizabeth (1997). Management by whim. *News from Sammy's Dad,* No. 3, 6. (Underground Newsletter, Lancashire, England.)

Ellis, K. (1993). *Squaring the circle: User and carer participation in needs assessment.* London: Joseph Rowntree Foundation.

Erickson, G. D. (1984). A framework and themes for social networks intervention. *Family Process, 23*(2), 187–204.

Frankel, A. J., & Gelman, S. R. (1998). *Case management: An introduction to concepts and skills.* Chicago: Lyceum.

Freng, S. A., Carr, D. I., & Cox, C. B. (1995). Intensive case management for chronic public inebriates: A pilot study. *Alcoholism Treatment Quarterly, 13*(1), 8–90.

Gibbs, D., & Priestley, M. (1996). The social model and user involvement. In *Conference report: Disability rights symposium of the European regions* (pp. 139–150). Southampton, England: Hampshire Coalition of Disabled People.

Gorlick, C., & Pomfret, D. (1993). Hope and circumstance: Single mothers exiting social assistance. In J. Hudson & B. Galaway (Eds.), *Single Parent Families: Perspectives on Research and Policy* (pp. 253–270). Toronto: Thompson Educational Publishing.

Hadley, R., Cooper, M., Dale, A., & Stacy, G. (1987). *A community social worker's handbook*. London: Tavistock.

Halfton, N., Berkowitz, G., & Klee, L. (1993). Development of an integrated case management program for vulnerable children. *Child Welfare, 72*(4), 379–396.

Hampshire Coalition of Disabled People (1995). *The language of disability*. Southampton, England: Author.

Harris, J. (1996). Enforced participation in change: British social work in a changing policy context. In *Participating in change: Social work profession in social development* (Proceedings of the Joint World Congress of IFSW and IASSW, Hong Kong; pp. 274–276).

Harrison, W. D. (1989). Social work and the search for postindustrial community. *Social Work, 34*(1), 73–75.

Harrison, W. D. (1991). *Seeking common ground: A theory of social work in social care*. Brookfield, VT: Gower.

Harrison, W. D., & Hoshino, G. (1984). Britain's Barclay report: Lessons for the United States. *Social Work, 29*(3), 213–218.

Harrison, W. D., Smale, G. G., & Hearn, B. (1992, March). *Toward a practice theory for community social work: Britain's practice and development exchange*. Paper presented at the Council on Social Work Education Annual Program Meeting, Kansas City, MO.

Hayes, J. R. (1978). *Cognitive psychology: Thinking and creating*. Homewood, IL: Dorsey Press.

Healy, J. (1991). Linking local services: Coordination in community centers. *Australian Social Work, 44*(4), 5–13.

Hennessy, C. H. (1993). Modelling case management decision making in a consolidated long-term care program. *The Gerontologist, 33*(3), 333–341.

HMSO (1989). *Caring for people: Community care in the next decade and beyond*. London: Author.

Holman, B. (1993). *A new deal for social welfare*. Oxford: Lion.

Hornstra, R. K., Bruce-Wolfe, V., Sagduyu, K., & Riffle, D. W. (1993). *Hospital and Community Psychiatry, 44* (9), 844–847.

Hudson, B. (1993). *Busy person's guide to care management*. Sheffield: Joint Unit for Social Services Research, Sheffield University.

Huxley, P. (1993). Case management and care management in community care. *British Journal of Social Work, 23*(4), 365–381.

Indyk, D., Belville, R., Lachapolle, S., Gordon, G., & Dewart, T. (1993). A community-based approach to HIV case management: Systematizing the unmanageable. *Social Work, 38*(4), 380–387.

Johnson, M. (1992). Describing the population we serve: Viewing children in a family context. *R & D: Research and Evaluation in Group Care, 21*(1), 18–21.

Johnson, P. J. (1985). Social workers as case managers: A combined methods approach. In A. E. Fink, J. H. Pfouts, & A. Dobelstein (Eds.), *The field of social work* (8th ed.). Hollywood, CA: Sage.

Kahn, A. H., & Kamerman, S. B. (1982). *Helping America's families*. Philadelphia: Temple University Press.

Keith-Lucas, A. (1973). Philosophies of public social service. *Public Welfare, 31*(1), 21–24.

Korr, W. S., & Cloninger, L. (1991). Assessing models of case management: An empirical approach. *Journal of Social Service Research, 14*(1/2), 129–146.

Lauber, M. B. (1992). A taxonomy of case management tasks in community health facilities. *Social Work Research and Abstracts, 28*(3), 3–10.

La Valle, I., & Lyons, K. (1996a). The social worker speaks: Perceptions of recent changes in British social work. *Practice, 8*(2), 5–14.

La Valle, I., & Lyons, K. (1996b). The social worker speaks: Management of change in the personal social services. *Practice, 8*(3), 63–71.

Lewis, J., Bernstock, P., Bovell, V., & Wookey, F. (1997). Implementing care management: Issues in relation to the new community care. *British Journal of Social Work, 27*, 5–24.

Long, D. D. (1995). Attention deficit disorder and case management: Infusing macro social work practice. *Journal of Sociology and Social Welfare, 22*(2), 45–55.

Maglajlic, R. A. (1996). *Four case studies of care planning for adults with learning difficulties who have no speech*. Unpublished master's thesis, School of Community, Health and Social Studies, Anglia Polytechnic University, Cambridge, England.

Martinez-Brawley, E. E. (1990). *Perspectives on the small community: Humanistic views for practitioners*. Silver Spring, MD: National Association of Social Workers.

Means, R., & Randall, S. (1994). *Community care: Policy and practice*. Basingstoke, England: Macmillan.

Mercier, C., & Racine, G. (1995). Case management with homeless women: A descriptive study. *Community Mental Health Journal, 31*(1), 25–27.

Middleman, R. R., & Goldberg, G. (1974). *Social service delivery: A structural approach to social work practice*. New York: Columbia University Press.

Middleton, L. (1996). Editorial. *Practice, 8*(2), 1–4.

Moore, S. T. (1990). Social work practice model of case management: The case management grid. *Social Work, 35*(5), 444–448.

Moore, S. (1992). Case management and the integration of services: How service delivery systems shape case management. *Social Work, 37*(5), 418–423.

Morris, J. (1994). *The shape of things to come? User-led social services* (Social Service Policy Forum Paper No. 3). London: National Institute of Social Workers.

Morris, R. (1977). Caring for versus caring about people. *Social Work, 22*(5), 353–359.

Moxley, D. P. (1989). *The practice of case management*. Newbury Park, CA: Sage.

Munday, B. (1993). Introduction: Definitions and comparisons in European social care. In B. Munday & P. Ely (Eds.), *Social care in Europe* (pp. 1–20). London: Prentice-Hall/Harvester Wheatsheaf.

Netting, F. E. (1992). Case management: Service or symptom? *Social Work, 37*(2), 160–164.

Newell, A., & Simon, H. A. (1972). *Human problem-solving*. Englewood Cliffs, NJ: Prentice-Hall.

Orme, J. (1996). Participation or patronage: Changes in social work practice brought about by community care policies in Britain. In *Participating in change: Social work profession in social development* (Proceedings of Joint World Congress of IFSW and IASSW, Hong Kong; pp. 250–52).

Painter, E. (1966). Ego building procedures that foster social functioning. *Social Casework, 47*(3), 139–145.

Parsloe, P. (1997). Everyday choices may be as important as the grand notion. *Care Plan, 3*(3), 9–12.

Parton, N. (1994). Problematics of government, (post) modernity and social work. *British Journal of Social Work, 24*, 9–32.

People First (1990). *Oi! It's my assessment: Why not listen to me!* London: Author.

Poole, B. (1993). Involving Carers. In the User-Centered Services Group, Building bridges between people who use and people who provide services (pp. 39–40). London: National Institute of Social Workers.

Rapp, C. A. (1998). *The strengths model: Case management with people suffering from severe and persistent mental illness.* New York: Oxford University Press.

Richardson, A. (1995). Care management. In N. Malin (Ed.), *Services for people with learning disabilities* (pp. 240–249). London: Routledge.

Richmond, M. (1917). *Social diagnosis.* New York: Russell Sage Foundation.

Roberts, C. S., Severinsen, C., Kuehn, C., Straker, D., & Fritz, C. J. (1992). Obstacles to effective case management with AIDS patients: The clinician's perspective. *Social Work in Health Care, 17*(2), 27–40.

Rose, S. M. (1992). *Case management and social work practice.* White Plains, NY: Longman.

Rothery, M. (1993). The ecological perspective and work with vulnerable families. In M. Rodway & B. Trute (Eds.), *Ecological family practice: One family, many resources* (pp. 21–50). Queenston, ON: Edwin Mellen.

Rubin, A. (1992). Is case management effective for people with serious mental illness? A research review. *Health and Social Work, 17*(2), 138–150.

Rubinstein, M. A. (1975). *Patterns of problem-solving.* Englewood Cliffs, NJ: Prentice Hall.

Sammy's Dad (1997). Editorial comment: The sterility of oppression. *News from Sammy's Dad,* No. 3, 2–3. (Newsletter, Lancashire, England.)

Sarason, I., Levine, H., Basham, R. & Sarason, B. (1983). Assessing social support: The social support questionnaire. *Journal of Personality and Social Psychology, 44,* 127–139.

Sarason, B. R., Sarason, I. G., & Pierce, G. R. (Eds.) (1990). *Social Support: An interactional view.* New York: John Wiley & Sons.

Shapiro, J. (1996). The downside of managed mental health care. *Clinical Social Work Journal, 23*(4), 441–451.

Smale, G., Tuson, G., Cooper, M., Wardle, M., & Crosbie, D. (1988). *Community social work: A paradigm for change.* London: National Institute of Social Workers.

Soares, H. H., & Rose, M. K. (1994). Clinical aspects of case management with the elderly. *Journal of Gerontological Social Work, 22*(3/4), 143–156.

Social Services Inspectorate (1995a). *Social services department information strategies and systems (with reference to community care): Inspection overview.* London: HMSO.

Social Services Inspectorate (1995b). *Third overview: Report of care management inspection of the work of inspection units in 19 local authorities.* London: HMSO.

Specht, H. (1990). Social work and the popular psychotherapies. *Social Service Review, 64*(3), 345–358.

Statham, D. (1996). *The future of social and personal care: The role of social services organisations in the public, private and voluntary sectors.* London: National Institute of Social Workers.

Streeter, C. L., & Franklin, C. (1992). Defining and measuring social support: Guidelines for social work practitioners. *Research in Social Work Practice, 2*(1), 81–98.

Sullivan, W. P., & Fisher, B. J. (1994). Intervening for success: Strengths-based management and successful aging. *Journal of Gerontological Social Work, 22*(1/2), 61–74.

Sullivan, W. P., Hartman, D. J., Dillon, D., & Wolk, J. L. (1994). Implementing case management in alcohol and drug treatment. *Families in Society, 75*(2), 67–73.

Sullivan, W. P., Wolk, J. L., & Hartman, D. J. (1992). Case management in alcohol and drug treatment: Improving client outcomes. *Families in Society, 73*(4), 195–204.

Suppes, M. A., & Cressy Wells, C. (1996). The future and social work. In M. A. Suppes & C. Cressy Wells (Eds.), *The social work experience: An introduction to the profession and its relationship to social welfare policy* (2nd ed., pp. 461–96). New York: McGraw-Hill.

The Sainsbury Centre for Mental Health (1996). *Care management: Is it working? An executive summary.* London: Author.

The User-Centred Services Group (1993). *Building bridges between people who use and people who provide services.* London: National Institute of Social Workers.

Thompson, M. S., & Peebles-Wilkins, W. (1992). The impact of formal, informal, and societal support networks on the psychological well-being of black adolescent mothers. *Social Work, 37*(4), 322–328.

Thompson, P. (1995). New directions for social services and education. *Practice, 7*(4), 53–61.

Waller, M. A., Carroll, M. M., & Roemer, M. (1996). Teaching writing in social work education: Critical training for agents of change. *Journal of Teaching in Social Work, 13*(1/2), 43–56.

Walsh, E. (1996). Participating in change: The social work profession in social development—W(h)ither social work? In *Participating in change: Social work profession in social development* (Proceedings of the Joint World Congress of IFSW and IASSW, Hong Kong; pp. 31–33).

Werrbach, G. B. (1996). Family strengths-based intensive child care management. *Families in Society, 77*(4), 216–226.

Whittaker, J., & Garbarino, J. (1983). *Social support networks: Informal helping in the human services.* New York: Aldine.

chapter 14

Mobilizing Informal
Social Support

CHAPTER PREVIEW

In Chapter 13, we made the distinction between formal and informal social support. In this chapter, we consider informal social support. We will examine:

- the definition of informal social support
- ways to strengthen networks of informal social support
- the reciprocal nature of informal social support
- ways to expand clients' current social support network
- ways to make use of self-help or mutual aid groups

In Reading 14-1, Elizabeth M. Tracy and James K. Whittaker discuss the importance of social support and provide an assessment tool for determining the social support available to clients. In Reading 14-2, Elijah Mickel provides a historical review of self-help organizations in the African American community.

INFORMAL SOCIAL SUPPORT

Definition

Informal social support refers to the care and assistance provided by families, relatives, friends (Adams & Blieszner, 1993), and neighbors, who form an informal social support network; Specht (1986) defines a social support network as the specific set of interrelated persons with whom an individual engages in social interaction. Informal social support is also offered through leisure activity and church groups, which provide opportunities for socialization (Joyce, Stanley, & Hughes, 1990; Morrison, 1991; Nakhaima, 1994), and through self-help or mutual aid groups (Borkman, 1991; Gitterman & Shulman, 1994; Kurtz, 1990; Strauss et al., 1984). Informal social support embraces a broad range of activities, including assistance with self-care, resource management, home maintenance, assistance with daily activities such as transportation and meal preparation, and emotional support. Individuals' need for informal social support changes throughout life. Social support networks also fluctuate, as a result of factors such as members' death or relocation (Gold, 1987).

According to Olsen (1986), informal networks consist of "self-help groups, friends, neighbors and communities who provide, without payment, a wide range of aid including support, advice, advocacy, transport, friendship, compassion, to those who seek it" (p. 15). Wilson (1986) sees informal social support as "help that is provided within the context of one's personal social network of family, friends and neighbors" (p. 176). The informal social support network consists of "a set of interconnected relationships among a group of people that provides enduring patterns of nurturance (in any or all forms) and provides contingent reinforcement for efforts to cope with life on a day to day basis" (Whittaker, 1986, p. 41). Garbarino (1986) sees informal social support as involving "interconnected relationships, durable patterns of interaction, and interpersonal threads that compromise a social fabric [and] a process of support; a range of interpersonal exchanges that provide an individual with information, emotional reassurance, physical or maternal assistance and a sense of the self as an object of concern" (p. 35). Informal social support is often provided by natural helpers in the individual's environment (Memmott, 1993; Nakhaima, 1994; Patterson, Germain, Brennan, & Memmott, 1988; Patterson, Memmott, Brennan, & Germain, 1992; Wilcox & Taber, 1991)—that is, unpaid people to whom the individual may turn in difficult times because of their concern, interest, and understanding (Patterson & Brennan, 1983). Informal social support is usually provided in face-to-fact contact but can also be provided through telephone networks (Goodman, 1990; King, 1991; Meier, Galinsky, & Rounds, 1995; Rounds, Galinsky & Despard, 1995; Wiener, Spencer, Davidson, & Fair, 1993) and computer networks (Finn & Lavitt, 1994; Weinberg, Schmale, Uken, & Wessel, 1995, 1996).

Benefits of Informal Social Support

There is a positive correlation between supportive social networks and physical and psychological well-being. Informal social support increases immunity to physical and psychological health problems (Specht, 1986); having a larger social support system may even help ward off colds (Cohen, Doyle, Skoner, Robin, & Gwaltney, 1997). Interactions with significant others in a social network can satisfy social and emotional needs, provide socialization and recreation, and protect against loneliness and isolation. People with greater access to supportive human relationships respond better to stressful life events such as divorce (Hughes, Good, & Candell, 1993; Kunz & Kunz, 1995) or job loss (Jones, 1991) and to chronic hardships (Cassel, 1974; Koeske & Koeske, 1990; Ladewig, McGee, & Newell, 1990). Informal social support serves as a buffer against stress for some individuals during major life events or life transitions (Specht, 1986). For example, Saulnier (1996) found that spouses of military personnel on deployment seek social support from friends and neighbors rather than formal programs. A supportive network may facilitate recovery from an acute illness or may promote adaptation to chronic illness.

Informal social support enhances personal well-being, life satisfaction, and quality of life and has been related to individual feelings of self-esteem and connectedness or belonging (Specht, 1986), as well as a sense of purpose (Schilling, 1987).

Informal social support allows older people to remain living in the community as independently as possible (Novak, 1997), slows down the deterioration of their health (Choi & Wodarski, 1996), and may reduce the number of admissions to long-term care facilities (Connidis & McMullin, 1994). Older individuals' informal support networks generally consist of spouses, children, and friends but may also include church groups, self-help groups, or activity groups. Exhibit 14–1 illustrates the importance of social support for a

---

EXHIBIT 14-1   **Informal Support by Friends**

Dear Ann Landers: I am a 55-year-old woman with amyotrophic lateral sclerosis, also known as Lou Gehrig's disease. ALS is a devastating illness that leaves its victims totally paralyzed.

This difficult time has been made bearable by the love and support of my mother and an amazing group of friends. I can never repay the love and kindness these people have shown me, but I would like to honor them by sharing the things they have done on my behalf. Maybe it will inspire your readers to do the same for others who are homebound.

Mary stepped in when my first two caregivers quit on short notice. She came to my apartment every night at 2 A.M. to turn me over. She also assisted with my personal correspondence and business. Lil assisted in my care and kept me company on many occasions. Mary Lee brought gifts to brighten my sickroom and read me books when I could no longer turn the pages.

Bonnie brought special treats, shared her video collection and brought arrangements of lilacs, irises and violets from her garden. Maria cooked my favorite meals and helped me continue entertaining guests in my apartment.

Kristin helped with correspondence and bookkeeping. Bruce picked up and returned my videotapes. Ray handled repairs and modifications to my apartment.

These are just a few of the people who have made difference in my life. If your readers knew the impact these friends have had in maintaining some quality of life for me, then surely they would find it in their hearts to do the same for someone to whom it would mean so much.—Melody in Chicago

From "Ann Landers," August 7, 1997. Copyright © 1997 Universal Press Syndicate. Reprinted with permission.

55-year-old woman with Lou Gehrig's disease; without this help, she would probably be placed in a nursing home.

The isolation of neglectful parents from formal and informal support networks may contribute to child abuse; expanding and strengthening these networks of social support, conversely, may prevent abuse (Beeman, 1995; Fuchs, 1993; Festinger, 1996; Gaudin, Polansky, Kilpatrick, & Shilton, 1993; Moncher, 1995; Thompson, 1995). Exhibit 14–2 suggests that strengthening parents' informal social support system will contribute to a successful return of children from foster care.

Social support may help reduce homelessness (Marin & Vacha, 1994) and delinquency (Shields & Clark, 1995). A Maryland study of 150 adult drug offenders released from custody found that 73% returned to their former neighborhoods but that this did not associate with return to drug use. Dissatisfaction with family life and employment had the strongest correlation with return to drug use; there was no correlation with participation in AA or NA. Employment status was important because it had a positive correlation with whether offenders were getting along with their families (Slaght, 1998). A study of 864 delinquents and their families found that delinquency was affected by the family's natural environment—including influences such as disadvantaged neighborhoods, life distress, social isolation, and lack of partner support; interventions need to be directed to the context in which the family

lives as well as to family processes (Stern & Smith, 1995).

EXPANDING AND STRENGTHENING INFORMAL SUPPORT NETWORKS

Expanding the client's informal support network means increasing the number of persons with whom the client interacts. Strengthening the informal support network has two aspects: increasing the number of interactions with network members and changing the nature of these interactions so that they are more helpful to the client. Exhibit 14–3 illustrates the exploration of informal social support with a 37-year-old single parent diagnosed with schizophrenia. Systematic consideration of Michelle's informal social support network resulted in uncovering strengths in relationships with her brother and a niece and the development of a plan to strengthen these connections. The opportunity to begin communication with a neighbor by responding to the neighbor's greeting may lead to other opportunities for Michelle to strengthen her informal social support network. The social worker might use some of the methods of mobilizing power we discussed in Chapter 11 to help Michelle become more comfortable engaging in informal conversation with the neighbor. For example, role playing these encounters will help Michelle become comfortable with her own skills at social interaction which, in turn, will lead to a strengthening and expanding of her social support network. Finally, there are also opportunities

---

EXHIBIT 14-2 Social Support for Neglectful Parents

A 1981 study of neglectful parents (Polansky, Chalmers, Buttenwieser, & Williams, 1981) pointed to their isolation from informal and formal support networks as a core problem that should be addressed by child welfare providers. Subsequent reports have provided support for this conclusion (Gaudin, Polansky, Kilpatrick, & Shilton, 1993; Polansky, Ammons, & Gaudin, 1985; Zuravin & Greif, 1989). The findings on re-entry in this study strongly underscore the same theme. Yet when the workers in this study were asked to identify caregivers' service needs, counseling or therapy was given the highest priority, consistent with findings from an earlier report (Jones, Neuman, & Shyne, 1976), while parent support groups occupied a much lower

priority. With people as disconnected as the caregivers of re-entrants appear to be, ways must be explored to help them begin to make connections. Various useful approaches to reducing isolation and to enhance parenting skills have been described elsewhere (Boutilier & Rehm, 1993; Carlo, 1993; Fein & Staff, 1993; Gaudin, Wodarski, Arkinson, & Avery, 1990; Lewis, 1991; Polansky et al., 1981; Walton, Fraser, Lewis, Pecora, & Walton, 1993). Yet there is an ongoing challenge to develop ways of reaching out that are sensitive to diverse ethnic and cultural values affecting parental practices as well as family life as a whole (Maluccio, Fein, & Davis, 1982; (National Research Council, 1993).

Source: T. Festinger, Going home and returning to foster care. *Children and Youth Services Review, 18*(4/5), 398 (1996).

EXHIBIT 14-3 Social Support for a Woman with Schizophrenia

Michelle is a 37-year-old woman with schizophrenia. She and her 4-year-old son, Jacob, reside with her 75-year-old father, who supports them financially. Michelle's father has been the primary caregiver of Jacob since birth; because of the severity of her illness, Michelle is unable to adequately care for her son. Michelle does assist in parenting Jacob and usually takes Jacob to the local day care center several days a week. Since being diagnosed with schizophrenia 15 years ago, Michelle has lost contact with all of her friends and has not been able to form new friendships. She is now almost totally socially isolated, especially since the death of her mother last year; Michelle's relationship with her father is strained.

Because there were many areas in Michelle's life that she wanted to work on, our first step was deciding where to start. Michelle thought the main problem was boredom; she had too much free time and no one to visit. I explored these two problem areas with Michelle. She said that she would like to find a job or enroll in a job training program, although she was concerned about how others would perceive her and if she could make friends within these environments. I also asked Michelle how important it was for her to have friends and she stated that this was very important. I asked Michelle whether finding work or forming friendships was more important at this time. Michelle felt that having friends was more important. The problem for work was then defined. Michelle does not have companions to spend time with socially.

The next step was to set objectives. The objectives developed by Michelle include:

- finding a friend to have coffee with
- engaging in some social activities
- building self-esteem, through interacting with people other than professional service providers
- utilizing appropriate communication skills, in order to feel more comfortable in social situations

Several other possible objectives were mentioned, but Michelle didn't want to take on too much at once. She felt that the objectives were attainable and would improve her life.

We then began to develop an intervention plan. We discussed the concept of informal social supports and ways in which they could be utilized. Michelle initially didn't perceive any informal social supports available to her. In exploring, however, we discovered that she had a close relationship with her brother and with a niece who came over to help baby-sit her son when her father was out of town. Michelle stated that her brother came over once a week for dinner and she looked forward to his visits. When I asked what she enjoyed about her brother's company, she said that he made her laugh, he often gave her advice, he would always give her a ride if she needed to go somewhere, and he acted on her behalf if she was having difficulties with her father. Michelle spoke highly of her niece. She and Jacob enjoyed her niece's visits; they often played games or went out to the movies or to dinner. We also discussed other people who might be part of her informal social network. She said that one of her neighbors frequently said hello to her and seemed friendly, although they never engaged in conversation. She also mentioned a mother at Jacob's day care, who recently invited Jacob and Michelle to her son's birthday party, although Michelle wasn't sure if she felt comfortable going.

We then considered ways in which these supports could be utilized. Michelle thought that she could call her brother more if she was having a bad day or if she just wanted to talk. Since Michelle only saw her niece when her father went out of town, we discussed Michelle calling her more often and perhaps getting together on a more regular basis to enjoy social activities. We discussed methods by which she could practice her communication skills and become more comfortable in social situations. She felt that she could do this by initiating phone calls to her brother and niece and by saying hello to her neighbor and the mother at the day-care. I also presented the possibility of Michelle attending a local support group of mothers with young children, who meet weekly. Michelle agreed. We also discussed Michelle volunteering at her son's day care one half day a week; this would give her a chance to meet other mothers and allow her to improve her communication skills. Michelle thought that it would be rewarding to work with children. We also discussed how Michelle's strengths—such as her friendly disposition, her caring attitude toward others, and her desire to make positive changes in her life—would be beneficial in attaining her goals.

Source: BSW student, Faculty of Social Work, University of Manitoba, Winnipeg, Manitoba.

for Michelle's involvement with her son's day care center which would further expand opportunities for her to both receive and give informal social support. We remind you, however, of partialization. You do not want to encourage a client to take on tasks that are overwhelming; thus, some of these tasks in relation to expanding one's social support system were phased in with Michelle.

People give and take social support; thus, it is reciprocal (Tracy, 1990). Part of your work with clients will be to consider how they are being supportive and helpful to others. If Michelle in Exhibit 14–3 volunteers at her son's day care center, she will be helping others and, at the same time, receiving social support. The young paraplegic in Exhibit 14–4, who had been handling his depression with excessive drinking, became active in organizing an AA group; through this process, he both helps himself and provides an important service to others. As you identify client strengths, you will start discovering many ways that clients can help others and contribute to the well-being of their communities.

According to Byrne and Sebastian (1994), listening and empathy are the two most important qualities in providing informal social support, followed by helping, assisting, and guiding. The support provider must convey respect, objectivity, and a nonjudgmental attitude. Social support is characterized by problem solving—that is, assistance with decision making—and

---

EXHIBIT 14-4   **Assisting a Paraplegic to Organize an AA Group**

Jerry, age 35, is physically disabled as a result of a skiing accident three years ago. He is paralyzed from the waist down, with the full use of the left arm but only 40% use of his right arm; he suffered no cognitive impairment. Currently, Jerry lives in an apartment building in which 80% of the residents have a physical disability, while the remaining 20% are able-bodied. Because Jerry had no private disability insurance, he has had to rely on home care service provided by public social assistance. This has resulted in a tight schedule, with very limited flexibility.

Jerry has had trouble coping and has become psychologically and emotionally depressed. Over the past three years, he has developed an alcohol problem and has retreated from both friends and family; he refuses to discuss his problems with anyone. Jerry is a heavy smoker and occasionally smokes marijuana. He is unemployed and does no volunteer work.

Jerry was referred by the manager of his apartment building for drunken and unruly behavior in the halls. Jerry claims that he is tired of being told what to do. His life mostly centers around the home care he receives, which includes bathing, cooking, getting him up from bed, turning him in the middle of the night, shopping for food, and cleaning. Jerry has admitted that he might have a problem with alcohol and has shown a desire to change, but is uncertain how. He says that he feels oppressed and tends to do drugs and alcohol with others in the building. This appears to be Jerry's way of avoiding total isolation.

Jerry and I negotiated the short-term objective that he would quit drinking, stop his abusive behavior, and re-integrate with family and friends. The longer-term goal would be for Jerry to re-enter the mainstream of society. This would involve training for a job, in order to eventually achieve financial independence and control over his life.

The focus of the plan is to link Jerry with his environment and to enable him to cope. We agreed to begin by linking Jerry with his family, friends, and groups within his immediate environment. Essentially, Jerry's role will be to accept face-to-face contact with family and friends and to assume responsibility for his past and present behavior.

Jerry agreed to attend Alcoholics Anonymous, to access information on the problems associated with alcohol and drug abuse, to learn what resources are available for him, and to participate with others in the community. At the initial meetings, Jerry felt encouraged by the progress of other chemically dependent persons. He visited the library and spoke with some residents of a treatment program.

Jerry then expressed an interest in meeting other disabled persons in his building who are chemically dependent. Such networking could help him develop his self-esteem and coping mechanisms to a point where he no longer perceives his disability as a hindrance to life within the community.

I provided Jerry with information regarding the possibility of setting up meetings with other tenants who feel they may have a problem with alcohol or drugs. Thus encouraged, Jerry decided to organize local twelve step meetings. To set up the meetings, Jerry would need access to a meeting room in the building once a week. We agreed that, given management's low opinion of Jerry, I would advocate on his behalf regarding the meeting room.

Jerry decided that, if other tenants were to be aware of these meetings, he would need to post notices on every floor. Jerry's phone number was to be listed, so that he would be directly responsible for organizing the meeting and arranging for other tenants to attend. Jerry was intending that his meetings be for disabled tenants. At my suggestion, he agreed to open the meetings to all tenants, disabled or not. We also agreed to seek out nondisabled tenants to help post the notices. This would not only help Jerry logistically but encourage him to interact socially with nondisabled individuals.

Source: BSW student, Faculty of Social Work, University of Manitoba, Winnipeg, Manitoba.

the ability to be present with an individual (Byrne & Sebastian, 1994). Exhibit 14–5 provides a list of informal helping behavior developed from research interviews with 40 single mothers receiving public assistance (Gottlieb, 1978). You will be helping clients to develop the skills necessary for such behavior, using the methods discussed in Chapter 12.

CREATING AND CHANGING INFORMAL SUPPORT NETWORKS

Simply increasing the size of clients' informal support network is not sufficient. You will need to assist clients in improving their relationships within the support network. You may help clients to create new networks. Furthermore, some social support networks may have negative consequences (Galinsky & Schopler, 1994; Gurowka & Lightman, 1995). For example, you might want to encourage a client to leave a youth gang that endorses illegal behavior. You may consider foster care to remove a child from a troubled family network. Remember, though, that any support system—whether a youth gang or a troubled family—may have both beneficial and harmful aspects. You and your client will need to carefully assess the interactions within the network before making any decisions.

EXHIBIT 14–5 Informal Helping Behavior

CATEGORY	DEFINITION	EXAMPLE
A. Emotionally Sustaining Behaviors		
A1 Talking (unfocused)	Airing or ventilation of general concerns about reference to problem specifics.	"She'll talk things over with me."
A2 Provides reassurance	Expresses confidence in other as a person, in some aspect of other's past or present behavior, or with regard to the future course of events.	"He seems to have faith in me."
A3 Provides encouragement	Stimulates or motivates other to engage in some future behavior.	"She pushed me a lot of times when I was saying, 'Oh, to heck with it.'"
A4 Listens	Listening only, without reference to dialogue.	"He listens to me when I talk to him about things."
A5 Reflects understanding	Signals understanding of the facts of other's problem or feelings.	"She would know what I was saying."
A6 Reflects respect	Expresses respect or esteem for other.	"Some people look down on you; well, she doesn't."
A7 Reflects concern	Expresses concern about the importance or severity of the problem's impact on other or for the problem itself.	"Just by telling me how worried or afraid she is" (for me).
A8 Reflects trust	Reflects assurance of the confidentiality of shared information.	"She's someone I trust and I knew that it was confidential."
A9 Reflects intimacy	Provides or reflects interpersonal intimacy.	"He's just close to me."
A10 Provides companionship	Offers simple companionship or access to new companionships.	"I've always got her and I really don't feel alone."
A11 Provides accompaniment in stressful situation	Accompanies other in a stressful situation.	"She took the time to be there with me so I didn't have to face it alone."
A12 Provides extended period of care	Maintains a supportive relationship to other over an extended period of time.	"She was with me the whole way."

(continued)

EXHIBIT 14-5	Informal Helping Behavior *(continued)*	

CATEGORY	DEFINITION	EXAMPLE
B. Problem-Solving Behaviors		
B1 Talking (focused)	Airing or ventilation of specific problem details.	"I'm able to tell him what's bugging me and we discuss it."
B2 Provides clarification	Discussion of problem details, which aims to promote new understanding or new perspective.	"She makes me more aware of what I was actually saying other than just having the words come out."
B3 Provides suggestions	Provides suggestions or advice about the means of problem solving.	"He offered suggestions of what I could do."
B4 Provides directive	Commands, orders, or directs other about the means of problem solving.	"All Rose told me was to be more assertive."
B5 Provides information about sources of stress	Definition same as category name.	"She keeps me in touch with what my child's doing."
B6 Provides referral	Refers other to alternative helping resources.	"Financially, he put me on to a car mechanic who gave me a tune-up for less than I would pay in a garage."
B7 Monitors directive	Attempts to ensure that other complies with problem-solving directive.	"Making sure that I follow through with their orders."
B8 Buffers from source of stress	Engages in behavior that prevents contact between other and stressor.	"He doesn't offer it (alcohol) to me anymore."
B9 Models or provides testimony of own experience	Models behaviors or provides oral testimony related to the helper's own experience in a similar situation.	"Just even watching her and how confident she seems has taught me something."
B10 Provides material aid or direct service	Lends or gives tangibles (food, clothing, money) or provides service (babysitting, transportation) to other.	"He brought his truck and moved me so I wouldn't have to rent a truck."
B11 Distracts from problem focus	Temporarily diverts other's attention through initiating activity (verbal or action-oriented) unrelated to the problem.	"Or he'll say, 'Let's go for a drive,' some little thing to get my mind off it."
C. Indirect Personal Influence		
C1 Reflects unconditional access	Conveys an unconditional availability to other (without reference to problem-solving actions).	"She's there when I need her."
C2 Reflects readiness to act	Conveys to other readiness to engage in future problem-solving behavior	"He'll do all he can do."
D. Environmental Action		
D1 Intervenes in the environment to reduce source of stress	Intervenes in the environment to remove or diminish the source of stress.	"She helped by talking to the owners and convincing them to wait for the money a while."

Table from *Social and Psychological Research in Community Settings* by Gottlieb and Todd, Muñoz, Snowden and Kelly (eds.), pp. 189–190. Copyright © 1982 Jossey-Bass, Inc. Reprinted with permission.

Mrs. P in Exhibit 14–6 needs to develop a new social support system after a life transition. Since religious connections had been so important to her in her previous community, the worker might help her to connect with a local church group (Nakhaima, 1994).

Individuals with chronic mental illness are sometimes provided with informal social support on the basis of the clubhouse model (Beard, Propst, & Malamud, 1982; Dougherty, 1994; Jackson, Purnell, Anderson, & Schaefer, 1996; Mastboom, 1992; Propst, 1992), which

EXHIBIT 14-6	Diminished Social Network After a Life Transition

Mrs. P, aged 78, was brought into hospital after falling and breaking her hip. Prior to hospitalization, she was living alone in elderly housing. Her husband died almost two years ago. Mr. and Mrs. P raised two children, Karen and Chris, on a farm in rural Manitoba. Karen, 50 years old, is married and lives in Winnipeg; Chris, 47, has been living in Calgary, Alberta, for the past 22 years. Mrs. P came to Canada from Ukraine with her family when she was just a baby. She has two brothers, John and Mike, and a sister Mary, who recently passed away. John (84) has Alzheimer's and lives in a nursing home; Mike (73) lives alone in Winnipeg. Mrs. P was raised and married in rural Manitoba where she and her husband lived together for 58 years. Mrs. P never worked outside of the home; however, she greatly enjoyed helping on the farm and cooking for her family. Their farmhouse was in a close-knit Ukrainian community, which strongly supported the Catholic church. Mrs. P gave up the farm and moved to Winnipeg shortly after husband died. She was diagnosed with cancer three months ago, but up until now has remained independent. Mrs. P will be discharged from hospital next week with a wheeled walker.

In conversations during her hospital stay, Mrs. P reports having a hard time adjusting to the changes in her life. She misses her friends, neighbors, and church from her old community. Also, she doesn't see Karen and her family any more than she did while living on the farm. Mrs. P feels she cannot talk to her daughter about her illness, because Karen cannot accept it so soon after losing her father. Mrs. P also feels Karen is too busy with her own family to deal with any other problems. This is upsetting to Mrs. P who, since losing her husband, realizes more than ever how important family is.

emerged in the 1950s; today more than 180 clubhouses operate in the United States (Lamb, 1994). Clubhouses are communities that provide supportive relationships and opportunities to members and are characterized by (Jackson et al., 1996):

- respect and equality among members and staff
- attention to all aspects of each member's life
- emphasis on the importance of work and accepting responsibility
- focus on members' strengths and competencies

Each community is designed to promote recovery from social isolation (Beard, Propst, & Malamud, 1982) and is centered in a clubhouse building that provides for a full range of members' needs, including food, clothing, shelter, social interaction, meaningful work, and medical care. Supportive relationships develop among members and staff as they participate in the work necessary to operate the clubhouse (Propst, 1992).

MUTUAL AID GROUPS

People come together in mutual aid groups to share a common concern and to help one another cope with, or resolve, problems related to that concern (Toseland & Hacker, 1985). The common concern may be, for instance, recovery from alcoholism, mental health problems, parenting issues, or coping with the stress of a specific illness. Most mutual aid groups provide support to members. Some begin with mutual support and then move outward to social action (Cox, 1991). Some mutual aid groups include social workers in an advisory or facilitating role. Mutual aid groups can provide a network of supportive human relationships for your clients and may be included in service planning (Berkman, 1991; Gitterman & Schulman, 1994; Kurtz, 1990; Powell, 1990). They provide a resource to help clients mobilize power.

Silverman (1986) notes that social workers can work effectively with mutual aid groups through making referrals, serving on advisory boards, providing consultation on request, and initiating efforts to establish new groups. Gartner and Reissman (1984) found extensive social work involvement with mutual aid groups, and Coplon and Strull (1983) found that social workers played several roles in such groups, including educator, resource provider, referral source, link to the greater community, consultant, and group facilitator.

You will need an understanding of the internal workings and ethos of mutual aid and its social and political context in order to help clients tap this valuable resource. Rappaport (1985) suggests that we may need to speak a language of empowerment if we are to collaborate with the mutual aid movement, because medical terminology creates barriers between the sick and the well, between us and them, and between professionals and clients.

In a study, Toseland and Hacker (1985) found that most social workers had a positive view of mutual aid groups and valued the attributes of peer support, mutual sharing of practical ideas for coping, long-term support, and lack of stigma. However, 60% of the social workers surveyed thought that mutual aid groups were biased against professional help and that the groups discouraged members from seeking additional help. Most of the social service agencies for which the respondents worked did not have policies that encouraged the use of mutual aid groups in practice, and 80% of the respondents thought that mutual aid groups were underused by professional social workers. Toseland and Hacker concluded that social workers need to be educated regarding the availability and potential use of mutual aid groups. The attitudes of some professionals may interfere with their collaboration with self-help groups (Salzer, McFadden, & Rappaport, 1994), although professional work can be carried on collaboratively with mutual aid groups (Thompson & Thompson, 1993). Lines of communication between social workers and mutual aid groups need to be developed and strengthened.

We suggest that you become familiar with the range of mutual aid groups available in your community. These are often announced in newspapers, and information about the availability of mutual aid groups is usually available through an information and referral source in your community. The ability of mutual aid groups to meet by telephone (Goodman, 1990; King, 1991; Meier et al., 1995; Rounds et al., 1995; Wiener et al., 1993), and over the Internet (Finn, 1995; Finn & Lavitt, 1994; Weinberg et al., 1995, 1996) makes this type of informal social support widely available even in very sparsely populated areas. As you work with clients, you may explore whether they have been participating in any type of mutual aid or self-help group and, if not, whether this is a resource they might consider. Some of your clients, like Jim in Exhibit 14–4, may be interested in providing leadership to organize a mutual aid group.

INTEGRATING FORMAL AND INFORMAL SUPPORT

While social workers have always worked with the informal social support network, this aspect of practice does not always receive the attention it deserves. In a recent BSW practice seminar, for example, students were asked, first, to review the literature and develop a definition of social support and then to develop a service plan involving social support for one of the clients served in their field placements. Several students made the distinction between formal and informal social support in their definitions, but every plan developed by the 18 students in this practice seminar focused on the formal social support system.

To emphasize the importance of the informal support network, we have considered formal and informal support in separate chapters. In working with clients, however, you will be strengthening both formal and informal social support (Choi & Wodarski, 1996; Koslyk, Fuchs, Tabisz, & Jacyk, 1993; Olsen, 1986; Spence, 1991; Thompson & Peebles-Wilkins, 1992; Whittaker, 1986). Over time, the emphasis in work with any client will tend to shift from formal social support systems to the informal social support network.

CHAPTER SUMMARY

Informal social support—care and assistance by unpaid people in the client's network of family, relatives, friends, neighbors and so forth—is an important resource and serves as a buffer against hardships and stressful life events. Interactions in the client's informal social support network are not always positive; thus, it may be appropriate for the client to reduce some contacts and relationships or to introduce new relationships into his social support network. Possible objectives of intervention include:

- increasing the size of the informal social support network
- strengthening or intensifying the interactions within the network
- changing the interactions within the network
- developing a new network

Social support is reciprocal. Your clients will need to learn how to provide help and support to others. Mutual aid groups provide very accessible forms of social support for many people; they can be found in even the smallest of communities.

While we have treated formal and informal social support in separate chapters, so as to emphasize the importance of informal social support, you are likely to work on both formal and informal social support with most clients. As work with any client proceeds, the balance is likely to shift from formal support to informal support.

A LOOK FORWARD

In Reading 14-1, Elizabeth Tracy and James Whittaker discuss the social network map, which enables us to assess clients' existing informal resources, potential informal resources not presently being used, and possible barriers to accessing social network resources. The social network map has many similarities to the ecomap introduced by Jane Gilgun in Reading 2-4.

In Reading 14-2, Elijah Mickel provides a historical review of self-help organizations in the African American community. As we noted in Chapter 9, many people of color, especially African Americans and Latinos, prefer to seek help from informal networks. Consider carefully how you might strengthen and encourage these practices and, conversely, avoid weakening informal networks.

In Chapter 15, we consider ways that you and your client can work together to develop helping communities. Community development is often regarded as distinct from social work with individuals and families; we think this is unfortunate and prefer to consider ways that you might integrate community development ideas into your work with individuals and families.

READING 14-1 *The Social Network Map: Assessing Social Support in Clinical Practice**

Elizabeth M. Tracy and James K. Whittaker

Clinical practitioners increasingly recognize the importance of their clients' sources of informal social support and make these resources a focal point in case planning and design of service delivery systems (Gottlieb, 1983; Whittaker & Garbarino, 1983). In many ways, the current interest in social support reflects the rediscovery of a concept closely linked to the origins of social work practice (Richmond, 1918). Almost by definition, social work has long recognized the importance of social networks in clients' lives, but in the past decade or so, interest in the significance of informal helpers and their role in the provision of

formal services has been renewed (Collins & Pancoast, 1976; Owne, 1986).

Unfortunately, even though a person-in-environment focus has long been a part of social work tradition, practice technologies for assessment, intervention, and evaluation of supportive environmental helping approaches have, until relatively recently, been less well-developed than have those for person-centered approaches (Grinnel & Kyte, 1975). More often, the "person" has received greater emphasis than the "situation" (Gitterman & Germain, 1981). The development of explicit practice principles and techniques for assessing and intervening with clients' informal social and environmental resources is critically needed (Tracy & Whittaker, 1987). Clients are rarely isolated; rather, they are surrounded by social networks that may either support, weaken, substitute for, or supplement the helping efforts of professionals. Being embedded in a social network and the availability of social resources responsive to stressful events have

*From "The Social Network Map: Assessing Social Support in Clinical Practice" by Elizabeth M. Tracy and James K. Whittaker in *Families in Society: The Journal of Contemporary Human Services*, October, pp. 461–469. Copyright © 1990 by Families in Society. Reprinted with permission.

been shown to have direct and stress-buffering effects on the well-being of clients (Cohen & Wills, 1985). Thus, given the importance of social support, valid and reliable measures of social support resources are needed that can be used in routine assessments and that are clinically useful.

The assessment tool described in this article—the social network map—was developed as part of a larger research and development effort called the Family Support Project (Whittaker, Tracy, & Marckworth, 1989). The goal of this project was to develop practical strategies for assessing and enhancing social support resources for families at risk of disruption as a result of out-of-home placement. The project was undertaken in conjunction with Homebuilders, an intensive family-preservation program designed to prevent unnecessary out-of-home placement (Kinney, Haapala, Booth, & Leavitt, 1990).

This article describes the development and pilot use of the social network map with 45 families served by Homebuilders, along with qualitative findings regarding its clinical utility.[1] A process for social support assessment that focuses both on the structure and function of the personal social network is proposed. The assessment information generated from this approach allows both clinicians and clients to evaluate several aspects of informal support: (1) existing informal resources, (2) potential informal resources not currently utilized by the client, (3) barriers to involving social network resources, and (4) factors to be considered and weighed in the decision to incorporate informal resources in the formal service plan. A final section deals with pertinent questions for assessing social support as well as with strengths and limits of the previously described instrument.

CONCEPTUALIZING AND ASSESSING SOCIAL NETWORKS AND SOCIAL SUPPORT

Social support has been conceptualized in various ways, and it is important at the outset to establish a common definitional and conceptual language. *Social support* here refers to the many different ways in which

---

[1] The Family Support Project Final Report, which contains case illustrations of the social network map and a summary evaluation of the project, can be obtained from the authors.

people render assistance to one another: emotional encouragement, advice, information, guidance, tangible aid, or concrete assistance (Barrera & Ainley, 1983; Gottlieb, 1983; House & Kahn, 1985; Wood, 1984). Social support can be provided spontaneously through the natural helping networks of family and friends or can be mobilized through professional intervention. Social support that is provided through an informal helping network is typically characterized by a mutuality, reciprocity, and informality not often evident in professional helping relationships.

The term *social network* refers to the structure and quantity of a set of interconnected relationships (Mitchell & Trickett, 1980). Barnes's (1954) analyses of relationships in a Norwegian fishing village and Bott's (1957) study of marital patterns among London families are generally thought to be the beginning of what is now referred to as *social network analysis*. A *social support network* refers to a set of relationships that provide nurturance and reinforcement for coping with life on a daily basis (Whittaker & Garbarino, 1983), though not all networks are socially supportive, nor do they always reinforce positive social behaviors.

It is important, then, to distinguish the structural links of the social network from the resources or "supports" exchanged within that network. More social network resources do not necessarily imply more social support, nor is it the case that all exchanges are supportive. For this reason, some authors have viewed social support within social exchange theory (Wellman, 1981; Specht, 1986). In addition, the *perception* that others would be available to render help may be a key factor in mediating stress (Cohen & McKay, 1984; Wethington & Kessler, 1986). Because of these complexities, social support is increasingly viewed as a multidimensional construct, consisting of social network resources, types of supportive exchanges, perceptions of support availability, and skills in accessing and maintaining supportive relationships (Heller & Swindle, 1983).

In recent years, researchers have developed a number of measures for assessing social support (Tardy, 1985). *Structural measures* describe the existence or quality of social relationships, for example, marital status, contacts with friends, church affiliation. *Functional measures* assess various types of supportive exchanges. The supportive functions of social networks are also assessed in various ways. The frequency of specific supportive events can be determined; in addition, the perceived availability or adequacy of support can be evaluated. The difficulty with many social support measurement tools is their length, complexity, and tenuous relationship to direct-practice needs. Many instruments were designed for purposes other than treatment planning, for example, to identify the components of support or the mediating role of social support in stress and coping. Not only were they developed for different purposes, but they were often difficult and time consuming to administer. The dilemma for practitioners is how to assess social support in a clinically meaningful manner.

The eco-map is an extremely useful method for portraying client–environment relationships (Hartman, 1978; Hartman & Laird, 1983). Although the eco-map was designed to help public child welfare workers examine family needs, this tool is now used in a wide variety of practice settings. Although it can be used to illustrate an individual's connections, it is most often used to portray the total family system's relationship with the outside world. The advantages of the eco-map are its visual simulation of connections between a family and the environment, its ability to demonstrate the flow of energy into and from the family, and its depiction of nurturant as well as conflicted relationships. One disadvantage of the eco-map is its imprecise terms, which make it difficult to determine the exact nature of the relationships portrayed. For example, strong versus tenuous relationships can be defined in many different ways. In fact, the eco-map provides a much more complete portrayal of structure than it does of function.

In a manner analogous to the eco-map, social network mapping techniques begin by identifying and visually displaying network composition and membership. However, social network mapping attends to both structure and function in a more detailed fashion than does the eco-map. In general, social networks are constructed for a single individual—an egocentric network—and list each person known to that individual. Social network data collected in this manner have been used to determine a number of variables, including size, composition, and density. Social network mapping techniques are fully compatible

with eco-map procedures but provide more detailed, anchored responses regarding the quality and functioning of social connections.

THE SOCIAL NETWORK MAP

The social network map described here uses a circle mapping technique reported as useful by a number of social network researchers, including Biegel, Shore, and Gordon (1984) in their work with frail elderly, Kahn and Antonucci (1981) in their national study of support networks of older adults, Fraser and Hawkins (1984) and Hawkins and Fraser (1985) in their work with drug abusers, and Lovell and Hawkins (1988) in their study of abusive mothers. The map displays network membership visually but reveals little information in itself about the functioning of network relationships. Therefore, an accompanying grid was included to record responses about the supportive and nonsupportive functions of network relationships, for example, who provided what types of supports, what relationships were reciprocal, what relationships were conflicted, and so forth (R. Catalano, personal communication, June 1987). The advantage of the network grid lies in the added specificity of network functions and the fact that information directly relevant to the target population can be collected. For example, Fraser and Hawkins (1984) used this approach to gather information on a number of drug-related behaviors among network members.

ADMINISTRATION OF THE SOCIAL NETWORK MAP

The social network map collects information on the total size and composition of the network, the extent to which network members provide various types of support, and the nature of relationships within the network as perceived by the person completing the map. Administering the map involves listing network members in each of seven domains: (1) household (people with whom you live); (2) family/relatives; (3) friends; (4) people from work or school; (5) people from clubs, organizations, or religious groups; (6) neighbors; and (7) agencies or other formal service providers. Names or initials of network members are visually displayed on the circle "map" (Exhibit 14–7). After the composition of the network has been identified, a series of questions are asked regarding the nature of network

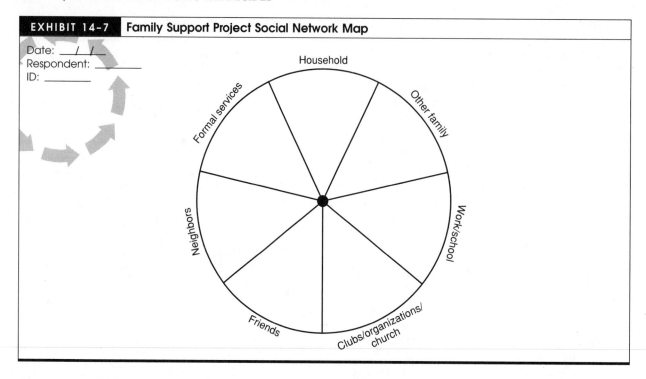

EXHIBIT 14–7 | **Family Support Project Social Network Map**

Date: __/__/__
Respondent: _____
ID: _____

Household

Formal services

Other family

Neighbors

Work/school

Friends

Clubs/organizations/church

relationships (Exhibit 14–8). These questions cover the types of supports available (emotional, informational, and concrete), the extent to which network members are critical of the individual, the direction of help, the closeness of relationships, frequency of contact, and length of relationships. Responses to these questions are recorded on a network grid (Exhibit 14–9).

Specifically, the social network map provides information on the following aspects of social network functioning. For each aspect, both absolute numbers as well as proportions can be calculated; the use of proportions allows for comparisons across social networks of different sizes.

1. *Network size:* total number of people identified in the network
2. *Domain size:* total number/proportions of people in each of the seven domains
3. *Perceived availability of emotional, concrete, and informational support:* proportion of network rated as "almost always" available to provide these types of support
4. *Criticalness:* proportion of network perceived to be "almost always" critical of the individual

5. *Closeness:* proportion of network perceived to be "very close"
6. *Reciprocity:* proportion of network relationships in which "help goes both ways"
7. *Directionality:* proportion of network relationships in which help goes primarily from client to network and proportion of network relationships in which help goes primarily from network to client
8. *Stability:* length of relationships (how long known)
9. *Frequency:* frequency of contact (how often seen)

Social network data collected from 45 families revealed some interesting and clinically useful relationships among these variables. For example, although network size was a poor indicator of perceived social support, network composition appeared to be a relevant factor. Both number and proportion of friends within the network were associated with higher levels of support in this sample. In addition, reciprocity was positively related to concrete support. The proportion of critical network members was negatively related to emotional support. Overall, findings indicated that the families perceived a number of supportive resources within their networks. At the same time,

EXHIBIT 14-8	Instructions/Script for Social Network Map

Step One: Developing a Social Network Map

Let's take a look at who is in your social network by putting together a network map. (Show network map.) We can use first names or initials because I'm not that interested in knowing the particular people and I wouldn't necessarily be contacting any of the people we talk about.

Think back to this past month, say since (date). What people have been important to you? They may have been people you saw, talked with, or wrote letters to. This includes people who made you feel good, people who made you feel bad, and others who just played a part in your life. They may be people who had an influence on the way you made decisions during this time.

There is no right or wrong number of people to identify on your map. Right now, just list as many people as you come up with. Do you want me to write, or do you want to do the writing?

First, think of people in your *household*—whom does that include?

Now, going around the map, what *other family members* would you include in your network?

How about people from *work or school*?

People from *clubs, organizations, or religious groups*—whom should we include here?

What *other friends* haven't been listed in the other categories?

Neighbors—local shopkeepers may be included here.

Finally, list professional people or people from formal agencies whom you have contact with.

Look over your network. Are these the people you would consider part of your social network this past month? (Add or delete names as needed.)

Step Two: Completing the Social Network Grid

(If more than 15 people are in the network, ask the client to select the "top 15" and then ask the questions about only those network members. For each of the questions use the appropriate sorting guide card. Once the client has divided up the cards, put the appropriate code number for each person listed on the network grid.)

Now, I'd like to learn more about the people in your network. I'm going to write their names on this network grid, put a code number for the area of life, and then ask a few questions about the ways in which they help you. Let's also write their names on these slips of paper too; this will make answering the questions a lot easier. These are the questions I'll be asking (show list of social network questions), and we'll check off the names on this grid as we go through each question.

The first three questions have to do with the *types of support* people give you.

Who would be available to help you out in *concrete* ways—for example, would give you a ride if you needed one or would pitch in to help you with a big chore or would look after your belongings for a while, if you were away? Divide your cards into three piles—those people you can hardly ever rely on for concrete help, those you can rely on sometimes, and those you'd almost always rely on for this type of help.

Now, who would be available to give you *emotional support*—for example, to comfort you if you were upset, to be right there with you in a stressful situation, to listen to you talk about your feelings? Again, divide your cards into three piles—those people you can hardly ever rely on for emotional support, those you can rely on sometimes, and those you almost always can rely on for this type of help.

Finally, whom do you rely on for *advice*—for example, who would give you information on how to do something, help you make a big decision, or teach you how to do something? Divide your cards into the three piles—hardly ever, sometimes, and almost always—for this type of support.

Look through your cards and this time select those people, if any, in your network who you feel are *critical* of you (either critical of you or your lifestyle or of you as a parent). When I say "critical," I mean critical of you in a way that makes you feel bad or inadequate. Divide the cards into three piles—those people who are hardly ever critical of you, sometimes critical of you, and almost always critical of you. Again we'll put the code numbers next to their names.

Now look over your cards and think about the *direction of help.* Divide your cards into three piles—those people with whom help goes both ways (you help them just as much as they help you), those whom you help more, and those who help you more. OK, let's get their code numbers on the grid.

Now think about how *close* you are to the people in your network. Divide the cards into three piles—those people you are not very close to, those you are sort of close to, and those you are very close to—and then we'll put a code number for them.

Finally, just a few questions about *how often* you see people and *how long* you've known the people in your network. Divide the cards into four piles—people you see just a few times a year, people you see monthly, people you see weekly, and people you see daily (if you see someone twice or more than twice a week, count that as "daily"). OK, we'll put their numbers on the grid.

This is the last question. Divide the cards into three piles—those people you have known less than a year, from one to five years, and more than five years.

Now we have a pretty complete picture of who is in your social network.

EXHIBIT 14–9 **Family Support Project Social Network Grid**

ID _____

Respondent _____

Name	#	Area of life 1. Household 2. Other family 3. Work/school 4. Organizations 5. Other friends 6. Neighbors 7. Professionals 8. Other	Concrete support 1. Hardly ever 2. Sometimes 3. Almost always	Emotional support 1. Hardly ever 2. Sometimes 3. Almost always	Information/ advice 1. Hardly ever 2. Sometimes 3. Almost always	Critical 1. Hardly ever 2. Sometimes 3. Almost always	Direction of help 1. Goes both ways 2. You to them 3. They to you	Closeness 1. Not very close 2. Sort of close 3. Very close	How often seen 0. Does not see 1. Few times/yr. 2. Monthly 3. Weekly 4. Daily	How long known 1. Less than 1 yr. 2. 1–5 yrs. 3. More than 5 yrs.
	01									
	02									
	03									
	04									
	05									
	06									
	07									
	08									
	09									
	10									
	11									
	12									
	13									
	14									
	15									
	1–6	7	8	9	10	11	12	13	14	15

however, network composition and the functioning of the network could create additional stress and strain (Tracy, 1990).

In order to ease administration and make the network map more engaging to complete, respondents can be supplied sorting cards and slips of paper onto which the names of their network members have been recorded (M. Lovell, personal communication, June 1987). When asked, for example, how close they feel to members of their network, respondents can easily sort the slips of paper into three piles—people with whom they feel very close, somewhat close, and not very close. This method is more visual and tactile than typical paper and pencil tools. Respondents view the process as "fun," more like a game than a test.

Despite the amount of detail the social network map provides, completion of the measures may take surprisingly little time. For the practitioners interviewed, the length of time to complete the social network map with individual family members ranged from 15 minutes to an hour, with an average completion time of approximately 20 minutes. Completion time appears to depend on the size of the network and the extent to which the respondent wants to talk about network members. It should be pointed out that the family members, generally mothers, were in crisis at the point of referral to the agency, and this factor may have influenced administration time to some extent. Most practitioners found administration of the map to be an interactive exercise. Several mentioned the potential of this form of assessment as an ice-breaker or relationship-building activity.

CLINICAL USEFULNESS

As part of the project, practitioners administered the social network map with clients at two points in time, within the first two weeks of intervention and again at termination. A structured qualitative interview was conducted with each of the 23 participating practitioners regarding the use of the map, including administration of the instrument, interpretation of the information gathered, use of this information in service delivery, and barriers to use of social support assessment information. All practitioners indicated that they intended to continue using the map even after the project's completion. Use of the social network map

was cited as helpful in identifying and assessing stressors, strains, and resources within the client's social environment.

The map also enabled therapists to gather information about social and environmental resources in a more systematic manner. Rather than describing social support in global terms (e.g., "relatives live in the area"), practitioners were better able to describe specific aspects of the client's social environment (e.g., types of support, presence or absence of close relationships, the direction of help). Through the use of the social network map, information was often obtained about other potentially useful resources as well as the client's perception of these resources.

In addition to its value as an assessment tool, therapists also cited the social network map as a clinically useful activity. The instrument helped people review their resources and identify potential resources. Often this process revealed unexpected information, indicating more supportive resources than the client or worker had initially realized were present. For example, one client who had initially "bad-mouthed" neighbors realized after completing the social network map how often those same neighbors provided support in various ways.

Another example of the clinical utility of social support assessment is the case of a young single mother who often left her child alone and unattended. When asked about child-care resources, the mother reported none was available. In the process of completing the social network map, two people were identified who could help with babysitting. With therapist coaching, the mother asked these individuals for help and a child-care schedule was established. In this situation, the information gathered about social support was directly relevant to averting the need for placement of the child outside the home.

Similarly, the social network map often provided a vehicle for discussing other issues with the client. These discussions were helpful in understanding current stressors experienced by families. For example, one woman commented that "support from the men in my life is exactly the same as from my children; it's mostly my helping them and they're mostly critical of me." In another example, each member of an entire family placed a deceased relative's name on the social network map, providing an opportunity for the worker to discuss issues of grief and loss. Several workers reported that the map worked well with women in abusive relationships, helping these women to identify what they were actually getting from the relationship. For example, one female client recognized that social support was reciprocal with the majority of her relationships, yet she continued to rely primarily on a particularly abusive one-way relationship with her boyfriend.

Some project practitioners viewed completing the social network map as an empowering activity. Clients began to understand their networks better as well as the steps they could take to get more of their needs met by the network. The visual display of the information gathered made insights readily available to clients. They could be actively engaged in assessing their network and generating options for change. For example, one client realized in working on her map that because she had recently moved, she felt isolated from usual sources of support. A specific intervention was developed to initiate contacts with neighbors.

GUIDELINES FOR ASSESSING SOCIAL SUPPORT

Based on the experience of the practitioners who participated in this project, a number of assessment guidelines and practice principles can be tentatively proposed. It is essential to evaluate social network data in relation to the presenting problems and needs of the client. Practitioners need detailed ways of conceptualizing their client's social resources in order to develop individualized social support goals and accompanying interventions.

The following questions, based primarily on information generated from the social network grid, were helpful in translating social network and social support data into appropriate service goals:

1. Who is in the network, how are they related to the client, and who could be potential members?

2. What are the strengths and capabilities of the social network? In particular, which members of the network provide emotional support, concrete assistance, and information or advice?

3. What are the gaps in social support needs? Is there a lack of fit between the types of support the network is willing or capable of providing and the types of support the client needs or desires?

4. What relationships in the network are based on mutual exchange? Does reciprocity seem to be an issue for the client? Is the client always giving to others and thereby experiencing stress? Or does the client appear to be a drain on the network, with the result that network members are stressed and overburdened?

5. What network members are identified as responsive to requests for help, effective in their helping, accessible, and dependable? Do sufficient numbers of network members meet these conditions?

6. What network members are critical of the client in a negative or demanding way? Is the client surrounded by a network that is perceived as negative, nonsupportive, and/or stress-producing?

7. What obstacles or barriers to utilizing social network resources exist? Does the client lack supportive resources or lack skills in utilizing available resources? For example, the client may lack skills in accessing social network resources or otherwise be reluctant to accept or ask for help. On the other hand, network members may be unable to provide more assistance due to lack of skills or knowledge.

8. How are social support needs prioritized in relation to other presenting problems and needs?

IMPLICATIONS FOR FUTURE CLINICAL APPLICATIONS

With the assessment guidelines presented above, Homebuilder therapists were able to design and develop a variety of social support interventions as part of their clinical work with families. For example, some families were extremely isolated and needed new, additional sources of support. Other families were involved in large social networks, but those networks were not necessarily supportive of the family's efforts to work toward change. For these families, interventions to modify the quality of network relationships were viewed as more appropriate to implement. Through the Family Support Project, a series of case consultations were held in order to assist in clinical decision making. In addition, a social support training module was developed that is now available for use by other family preservation programs. The training module covers both social support assessment and intervention techniques.

Information gathered via the social network map, however, is limited in that the data generated are self-reported and therefore may be affected by recall problems, recent history, and social desirability. For these reasons, social network data are difficult to subject to usual tests of reliability. Little is known about the stability of social network—whether changes in networks represent true changes or unreliable instruments (Tracy, Catalano, Whittaker, & Fine, 1990).

Objective verification of the validity of social network data is a related measurement issue. It is very difficult to determine "true" network size because so much depends on the method of data collection. For example, the time or the manner in which questions are asked could influence the numbers and types of people included in an individual's social network. From a clinical point of view, it is helpful to know the extent to which the network described by the client does, in fact, exist. Perceiving a large supportive network may cushion the experience of stress. Unrealistic expectations of others, however, can also lead to disappointment and feelings of rejection.

Another limitation in the information gathered from the social network map involves the unit of attention, that is, the individual rather than total family focus. The map provides information about an individual's personal social network but does not yield information about the collective impact of personal social networks within a family or group. The family's relation to the social environment would seem to require more than simply summing individual network maps. For example, the overlap—or lack of overlap—in network maps among different family members might be helpful to understand.

Finally, self-reported information about social networks may be influenced by the problem or need precipitating referral for services. It is difficult to know whether social network characteristics are a contributing factor to the presenting problem or a result of the presenting problem, which suggests the need for monitoring changes in social networks over time.

Obviously, more work is needed on the measurement properties of social network assessment information. For example, do the dimensions of support—concrete, emotional, and informational—correlate with other social support measures? In determining the reliability of network data, shorter test–retest intervals are needed in addition to methods of verifying self-reported network membership. It would be helpful to obtain measures of support received in relation to support perceived. The relationship between levels and types of social support and service outcomes needs further examination. Measures of *change* in social support from intake to termination may be correlated with treatment outcomes (Fraser, Pecora, & Haapala, 1988).

CONCLUSIONS

The experiences of family practitioners utilizing the social network map in a very brief intervention highlight the importance of assessing both structural and functional features of clients' social networks. This type of social support assessment information enables practitioners to gain a better sense of the types of support available to clients, the gaps that exist in support availability, and the resources available or potentially available to fill these gaps. It is important to avoid making assumptions about social networks and social support resources; even seemingly isolated clients are often able to identify supportive resources. The need for individualized assessments and corresponding individualized social support interventions is apparent; it is unlikely that one form of intervention will be suitable for all clients.

If social workers are to assess and intervene with client's informal sources of support, then expanded practice models that combine the best of person-centered and environment-centered strategies will be needed (Whittaker, 1986). Social support as a construct can enable practitioners to understand better their client's social environment, the impact of that environment on the client, and how best to create more supportive and nurturant environments. The social network map is one tool that workers can use in gathering specific, clearly defined, and individualized social support assessment information relevant to the planning of social support interventions.

Although the social network map is currently being developed as an assessment tool and practice technique, we believe that it contributes to a new model of practice that links formal and informal helping resources. Consistent with current ecological perspectives, such a practice model helps clients become more competent in dealing with the environment while helping to make the environment more supportive and nurturant of the client (Whittaker, Schinke, & Gilchrist, 1986). A replication of the Family Support Project, including further study of the measurement properties of this tool and its relationship to intervention planning, are currently underway in a large Midwestern youth- and family-serving agency. The practitioners in the project reported in this article, operating within severe time constraints with families in crisis, nonetheless found the instrument clinically useful.

READING 14-2 *Self-Help in African American Communities: A Historical Review**

Elijah Mickel

The traditional approaches to studying poverty and social policy (Federico, 1984; Friedlander, 1968; Harrington, 1962; Huberman, 1963; Jansson, 1990; Merton & Nisbet, 1961; Myrdal, 1962; Prigmore & Atherton, 1986; Rainwater & Yancy, 1967), as well as related issues such as structural adjustment (Meldrum, 1991; Stein & Nafziger, 1991), have not fully appreciated African Americans' contribution to the development of American social welfare (Pollard, 1978; Ross, 1978). The primary form of social welfare in the African American community has been self-help.

The practice of racism has structured the parameters of social welfare in the United States. Discriminatory practices in large part determined who was served and who served. These practices ignored the many strengths of the oppressed and embellished the contributions of the oppressor.

The Africans dragged in chains to these shores came with a range of skills and abilities—as artisans, artists, priests, farmers, and leaders. Colonial slavery was a continuation of the European serf system, with the modification that individuals could be sold apart from the land (Huberman, 1963; Rodney, 1982). Among African Americans, resistance has largely been linked to the religious community, since the early revolts led by Mackandal, Boukman, Gabriel Prosser, Denmark Vessey, Nat Turner, Gullah Jack, and others. Resistance to slavery was the first expression of self-help among Africans in America. The examples in Exhibit 14–10 indicate that resistance began with the first contact with the slavers.

---
*An original reading prepared for this edition.

THE BLACK CHURCH IN AMERICA

The Black Church in America can be traced from the mystery system in ancient Egypt. According to Herodotus (1909), "Almost all the names of the gods came into Greece from Egypt" (p. 252). The secret societies grew out of this system and developed in parallel in other parts of the African continent. When Africans were transported to the American continents, they brought with them memories of these church forms.

During slavery, the principal occasions of worship were ancestral ceremonies, the most important of which in North America was the ring shout (Stuckey, 1987). The Africans brought memories of home, family, and history, as well as a desire to be free. This desire was rooted in their culture and expressed through their religion:

> The slaves, tempered and toughened by the annealing heat of adversity, turned American Christianity inside out, like a glove, infusing it with African-oriented melodies and rhythms and adding new patterns, such as the ring shout, ecstatic seizure and communal call-and-response patterns. The grand outcome was a new creation, which differed strikingly from the white original. The emblem of this creation was the invisible black church of slavery, which centered in the portable "hush-harbors." (Bennett, 1961; p. 99)

One of the first Black Churches in the Americas was at Silver Bluff, South Carolina; Jesse Peters took control of this church in 1783 (Quaries, 1987; Simms, 1888). The first Black Baptist church was founded in Savannah, Georgia in 1788 (Simms, 1888). According to the Georgia historic marker commemorating the church:

> On January 20, 1788, the Reverend Abraham Marshall (white) and the Reverend Jessie Peters (Colored)

EXHIBIT 14-10	Significant Instances of Resistance

YEAR	EVENT
1640	Maryland. John Punch and two white servants found guilty of trying to run away from their master. The whites were given four additional years. John Punch was sentenced to a lifetime of servitude.
1663	Gloster County. African Americans and whites discovered in a conspiracy to overpower their masters and make a break for freedom.
1676	Bacon's Rebellion. Scores of African Americans joined white indentured servants, unemployed workers, and other whites.
1681	Maria and two male companions tried for attempting to burn down the home of their master. One man hanged, one banished. Maria burned at the stake.
1708	Newton, Long Island. A band of slaves killed seven whites. Three of the male slaves were hanged. (One was a Native American.) The women were burned at the stake.
1712	New York City. Twenty-three slaves armed themselves and gathered to set fire to a slaveholder's house. Nine whites killed, six injured. Twenty-one slaves were executed.
1732	Slave plot in Louisiana. One African American woman hanged, four males broken on the wheel. Their heads were stuck on poles at each end of New Orleans.
1739	Stone, South Carolina. Slave revolt led by Jemmy. Twenty-five whites were killed before the insurrection was put down.
1741	Kate and African American boatswain convicted of trying to burn down the entire community of Charlestown, Massachusetts.
1766	Slave woman in Maryland executed for setting fire to her master's home, tobacco house, and outhouse, burning them all to the ground.
1791–1804	Haiti. The second republic in the Western Hemisphere. First successful slave revolt against European domination in history.
1800	Gabriel Prosser and Nancy Prosser. Probably the largest slave revolt in the United States took place near New Orleans in 1811. Four to five hundred slaves gathered after a rising at the plantation of a Major Andry. Armed with cane knives, axes, and clubs, they wounded Andry, killed his son, and began marching from plantation to plantation, their numbers growing. They were attacked by U.S. army and militia forces; 66 were killed on the spot, and 16 were tried and shot by a firing squad.
1822	Charleston, South Carolina. Denmark Vessey led a revolt involving thousands of African Americans, 37 of whom were hanged.
1829	Cincinnati, Ohio. Race riot that resulted in more than 1000 African Americans leaving for Canada.
1831	Southampton County, Virginia. Nat Turner's Rebellion. Some 60 whites were killed.
1811–1839	Florida became a haven for escaped slaves and Native Americans. A point of resistance until 1839.
1839	Joseph Cinquez with fellow slaves killed the captain and took the slave ship Amistad. (Thirty-five Amistad survivors returned to Africa in 1841.)
1841	Slave revolt on the Creole. The ship was sailed to the Bahamas, where the slaves received asylum and freedom.
1848	Seventy-five enslaved individuals armed themselves and attempted to leave Fayette County, Kentucky. All were killed or recaptured.
1850s	During the 1850s about a thousand slaves a year escaped into the North.
1859	John Brown's Rebellion, Harpers Ferry, Virginia. Ended with the capture of John Brown.

Sources: L. Bennett, *Before the Mayflower.* Chicago: Johnson (1961). P. Giddings, *Where and when I enter: Impact of Black women on race and sex in America.* New York: Murrow (1984). H. Zinn, *A people's history of the United States.* New York: Harper & Row (1980).

ordained Andrew Bryan and certified the congregation at a Brampton Barn as the Ethiopian Church of Jesus Christ. The Reverend Bryan moved from place to place with his congregation and was even imprisoned and whipped for preaching ... He persevered and finally bought his and his family's freedom and purchased this lot for his church.

The First African Baptist church in Philadelphia, the African Baptist Church of Boston, and the Abyssinian Baptist Church in New York City were all established in 1809. By 1840, there were more than 300 separate northern black churches (Berry & Blassingame, 1982).

Today, there are thousands of Black churches, with millions of members. These churches are the most powerful, independent social change organizations in the Black community; any intervention in that community must include those institutions if it is to be effective.

SELF-HELP BEYOND THE CHURCH

Self-help organizations also formed independently of churches. In Newport, Rhode Island, for example, a mutual aid society formed in 1780 to record births, marriages, and deaths, to provide for decent burials, to assist members in times of distress, and to apprentice youths to skilled artisans. Under its auspices, the first Black church in Newport was formed in 1824 (Meier & Rudwick, 1966).

From the 1720s on, laws forbidding the formation of fraternal and mutual aid societies were enacted by several states, including Maryland, Virginia, and North Carolina (Berry & Blassingame, 1982). Undaunted, African Americans continued to develop self-help organizations. The African Institute (1835) was the forerunner of Cheney University in Pennsylvania; it began as a program for talented, orphaned African American males.

Self-help organizations embody a basic value system of cooperation, self-determination, and unity. "Regardless of the region, tribe, or community, the helping tradition was deeply rooted in the African way of life. It was to be found almost everywhere that African people existed" (Martin & Martin, 1985, p. 16). African culture mandated an interdependence between free Africans and those who were slaves; it gave Africans a sense of self.

The self-help movement provided a formal structure within which the social service needs of the African American community could be met. Self-help organizations enabled African Americans to develop collective responsibility, economic interdependence, creative purpose, and a belief in themselves.

The early colonizers, too, accepted an obligation to help the needy, but that obligation did not extend to people of color (Trattner, 1979), who had no alternative but to rely on self-help. Mutual support was directed to the alleviation of problems such as hunger, illness, separation, physical disability, physical and spiritual discomfort, and bereavement (Rhone, 1973). Commitment to mutual support is illustrated in the objectives of the Phoenix Society (Exhibit 14–11).

African Grand Lodge 459, founded in 1792 was the first Black freemasons' society in the United States (Crawford, 1914). "The lodge provided its members not just with social recreation, but, more important, with protection against the possibility of enslavement for delinquent debts. It participated in the abolitionist

---

EXHIBIT 14-11   Objectives of the Phoenix Society (1833)

To visit every family in the ward, and make a register of every colored person in it—their name, sex, age, occupation, if they read, write and cyper—to induce them, old and young, and of both sexes, to become members of this society, and make quarterly payments according to their ability—to get the children out to infant, Sabbath, and week schools, and induce the adults also to attend school and church on the Sabbath—to ascertain those persons who are able to subscribe for a newspaper that advocates the cause of immediate abolition of slavery and the elevation of the colored population to equal rights with the whites—to encourage the females to form Dorcas Societies; to help to clothe poor children of color, if they will attend school—the clothes to be loaned, and to be taken away from them if they neglect their schools, and to impress on the parents the importance of having the children punctual and regular in their attendance at school—to establish circulating libraries, formed in each ward, for the use of people of color, on very moderate pay—to establish mental feasts, and also lyceums for speaking and for lectures on the sciences—and to form moral societies—to seek out young men of talents and good moral character, that they may be assisted to obtain a liberal education—to report to the Board all mechanics who are skillful and capable of conducting their trades to procure places at trades, and with respectable farmers, for lads of good moral character—giving a preference to those who have learned to read, write and cypher—and in every other way to endeavor to promote the happiness of the people of color, by encouraging them to improve their minds and to abstain from every vicious and demoralizing practice.

movement and sponsored regular programs to aid the poor" (Carson, 1993, p. 12). Other secret orders—the International Order of Good Samaritans, the Ancient Sons of Israel, the Grand United Order of True Reformers, and the Independent Order of St. Luke— offered insurance against sickness and death, aided widows and orphans of deceased members, and gave opportunities for social interaction (Franklin, 1980).

The Grand United Order of Odd Fellows was founded in 1787, and the Independent Order of Good Samaritans in 1847. "The Odd Fellows burgeoned after the Civil War. It is reported to have had 89 lodges and 4,000 members in 1868 . . . and more than 4,000 lodges and almost 300,000 members by 1904" (Carson, 1993, p. 17).

Some mutual aid organizations assumed an oppressive role within the African American community. In Charleston, South Carolina, for example, the Brown Fellowship Society, founded in 1790, excluded dark-skinned African Americans and prohibited discussions of controversial issues such as slavery (Meier & Rudwick, 1966).

Black benevolent associations met the basic needs of the poor and offered free or subsidized education. They also provided financial and human resources for African Americans to promote their own improvement and confront social injustices (Carson, 1993). In line with the patriarchal attitudes of the time, many of these associations excluded women, who responded by forming their own clubs. One of the first women's organizations was Boston's African American Female Intelligence Society, established in 1832. The society sponsored forums and lectures for the general public and provided its members with health insurance and other services. Other early Bostonian women's organizations were the Daughters of Zion, founded in 1845, and the Female Benevolent Firm, founded in 1850 (Carson, 1993). African American women organized for many purposes:

> The Daughters of Tabor, founded in 1855, was an antislavery society. The Women's Loyal Union was founded in 1892 to help combat lynching. The White Rose Industrial Association, established in New York in 1898, helped young black women migrating from the South find jobs and provided them with a place to live so they would not be lured into prostitution. (Carson, 1993, p. 18)

A TALE OF TWO CITIES

Philadelphia

After 1780, when the Act for the Gradual Abolition of Slavery decreed that no child born in Pennsylvania should be a slave, the city of Philadelphia was regarded as a haven for free African Americans. The city's African American population increased by 176% between 1790 and 1800 (DuBois, 1899). An 1847 study found that African Americans in Philadelphia were employed as mechanics, laborers, seafarers, coachmen, carters, shop-keepers, traders, waiters, cooks, hairdressers, musicians, preachers, physicians, and schoolteachers; the majority of African American women were employed in laundry work or domestic service, while a smaller number were employed in needlework or in other trades (Frazier, 1966).

These Philadelphians donated a portion of their income to mutual aid societies; the Free African Society was founded as early as 1787. "In 1853, there were 108 incorporated Mutual Beneficial Societies in Philadelphia having 8,762 members with an annual income of $29,600 . . . A total of 1385 families was assisted to the amount of $10,292.38" (Jackson, 1973, p. 37). Many of the societies were connected with churches, and others were organized by occupation—for example, the Coachman's Benevolent Society and the Humane Mechanics Society. "The Philadelphia Library Company of Colored Persons maintained a well-furnished room with several hundred volumes and scheduled public debates on moral as well as literary topics" (Meier & Rudwick, 1966, p. 106).

As a result of the self-help organizations, the general conditions of the Black population improved. Although oppressed and excluded, this population used its resources to advance the conditions of the general population in the city.

The condition of the Negroes of the city in the last decade of the eighteenth and the first two decades of the nineteenth century, although without doubt bad, slowly improved; an insurance society, in 1796, took the beneficial features of the old Free African Society. Some small essays were made in business, mostly in small street stands, near the wharves; and many were in the trades of all kinds. Between 1800 and 1810 the city Negro population continued to increase, so that at the latter date there were 100,688 whites and 10,522 blacks in the city, the Negroes thus forming the largest percent of the population of the city that they have ever attained. The free Negroes also began to increase from the effect of the abolition law. The school established in 1770 continued, and was endowed by bequests from whites and Negroes. It had 414 pupils by 1813. In this same year there were six Negro churches and 11 benevolent societies (DuBois, 1899, p. 23).

The number of societies in Philadelphia reflected the sense of community. It showed the commitment of the African American community to freedom. Self-help was perceived as the vehicle that would move the community toward freedom. This was exhibited by their involvement in the number of organizations as well as their faith in the interrelationship of one to the other.

New York

The move toward freedom, equality, and justice is exemplified through Africans in America coming together and using every measure at their disposal to overcome oppression. This included the court system. African Americans were from the beginning convinced that the legal system could be used in their own best interest.

> In 1644, some eighteen years after their arrival, the "Dutch Negroes," as they were called, filed a petition for freedom, the first black legal protest in America. The petition was granted by the Council of New Netherlands, which freed the blacks because they had "served the Company seventeen or eighteen years" and had been long since promised their freedom on the same footing as other free people in New Netherlands. (Bennett, 1961, p. 41)

In New York, as elsewhere in the North, free African Americans formed and funded vigilance committees to protect themselves from those who wished to enslave them. These committees also raised money for the support of the sick and infirm and for widows and orphans of deceased members (Hirsch, 1931).

Testimony to the effectiveness of self-help may be seen in the gradual amelioration in the economic conditions of African Americans in New York:

> A decided improvement in this respect was noted by 1851. So evident was this progress that the colonizationists who had repeatedly referred to the poverty of the Negroes and the prejudice against them in the laboring world as a reason why they should migrate to

Africa, thereafter ceased to say very much about their poverty. (Lindsay, 1921, p. 196)

Frederick Law Olmsted wrote that in New York, during the severe winter of 1854, he did not see a single African American "among the thousands of applicants for soup, bread, and fuel, as charity . . . The poor blacks always manage to keep themselves more decent and comfortable than poor whites" (cited in Hirsch, 1931, p. 435).

African Americans demonstrated their continuing efforts to overcome the oppression inherent to the society. Although at times it was reported that free Africans were only servants, they obtained and maintained skilled jobs. According to Frazier (1966, p. 149), "In spite of the prejudice in New York City against Negro labor, Negroes were engaged in skilled as well as unskilled occupations. Although in the census for 1850 they were listed chiefly as servants and laborers, some had found a place in the skilled occupations as carpenters, musicians, and tailors."

Mutual aid may also be given much of the credit for a decrease in African American mortality rates in New York and Philadelphia. It appears that a joint population of 37,000 free colored have diminished their ratio of mortality from 1 in 17 in Philadelphia, and 1 in 21 in New York in 1820; to 1 in 40, in both places in 1843, being a distinct improvement in condition of at least 100 percent in 23 years!" (Aptheker, 1951, p. 241).

IMPLICATIONS FOR PRACTICE

The major themes within the history of African American self-help are freedom, justice, mutuality, and social change. These values are fundamental to social work. Practitioners can draw upon an understanding of secret orders and societies, mutual aid organizations, and self-help groups in developing community practice. The history of self-help demonstrates the efficacy of participation by the oppressed in their own liberation struggle and reminds us of the need to mobilize client strengths. Community organizations must be involved in decisions that affect their lives.

The financial basis of self-help organizations is of particular interest. The church-based organization was a successful model. Church organizations existed on the financial contribution of members, as well as their volunteer labor. The leader was charged with building the budget and the goal was usually defined before the collection was taken. This model still exists within many communities.

In times of crisis, practitioners must evaluate many models for self help. Practitioners should not be afraid to look at successful self-help models regardless of the political implications. Simply because we do not agree with the theoretical underpinnings, dare we ignore the possible contribution? Social workers must take a serious look at the women's clubs, secret societies, fraternal and benevolent groups, many of which began with only the desire to change social conditions and the concomitant practices emanating from the community's attitude

and oppressive structure. There are answers which can be gleaned from the past. African Americans have provided a successful methodology. Practitioners must do a thorough analysis of the contribution of the past and relate it to the present using it to prepare for the future. Utilizing a nonpathological approach, practitioners can assess the self-help movement and use its strengths.

The historic vision underpinning African American self-help provides a foundation for current social work practice. This vision allowed the self-help groups to effectively challenge poverty and to resist mental, physical, and spiritual oppression.

LEARNING EXERCISES

1. Write a one- or two-sentence definition for the following terms or briefly explain each term to a colleague:

    expanding social support networks
    informal social support
    informal social support network
    mutual aid group
    reciprocal nature of social support
    strengthening social support networks

2. If a clubhouse program exists in your community, try to visit and learn the philosophy of the program. Otherwise, write for information about program development to the Center for Clubhouse Develop-

ment, c/o Fountain House, 425 West 47th Street, New York, NY 10036, or call 212-582-0340.

3. Read the letter to Ann Landers in Exhibit 14–12 and write a brief response (no more than 150 words) suggesting ways to strengthen the informal social support network for No Name, No City's mother. Compare your response to Ann Landers' reply, given in Appendix C. Which do you think would be more likely to strengthen the mother's informal support network?

4. The movie *Mask* is based on the true story of Rocky Dennis. After watching the video (the 1994 movie starring Cher and directed by Peter Bogdanovich, not

---

EXHIBIT 14-12 Her Mom is in Deep Denial

Dear Ann Landers: Here's the situation. My mother, an attractive woman in her mid-50s, has been living with a man for 10 years. "Sam" told her he was divorced but puts off discussing getting married. In recent years, Mom has quit working because Sam supports her.

The truth is that Sam is still married to his first wife. I found out accidentally seven years ago when I saw Sam driving around town with her when he was supposed to be out of state on business. I told Mom I had seen him, and she became very upset with me and said, "You don't know what you're talking about." After that, I decided I wouldn't interfere.

Sam frequently "works" on holidays. I know it hurts her that he is away, but it kills me that she

defends him, constantly making excuses for his absences on her birthday, Christmas and so on. She insists that he is very important to his company and that no one else can do his job. I know he is actually spending the holiday weekend with his wife, kids and grandchildren right here in town because I have seen him.

I get very angry and frustrated with Mom for not seeing the obvious. At the same time, I know how much her pride would be damaged if she actually had to acknowledge the situation. Is there any way I can help Mom get out of this no-win relationship without making her angry with me?—No Name, No City

From "Ann Landers," August 11, 1997. Copyright © 1997 Universal Press Syndicate. Reprinted with permission.

the later movie with a similar name), contrast the professional help that Rocky received to the help he received from the motorcycle gang. In what specific ways did the motorcycle gang provide support? Over-

all, do you consider this social support helpful or harmful? As a social worker, would you try to strengthen or weaken Rocky's ties to the motorcycle gang? Explain.

REFERENCES

Adams, R. G., & Blieszner, R. (1993). Resources for friendship intervention. *Journal of Sociology and Social Welfare, 28*(4), 159–175.

Aptheker, H. (1951). *A documentary history of the Negro people in the United States.* New York: Carol Publishing.

Barnes, J. A. (1954). Class and communities in a Norwegian island parish. *Human Relations, 7*(1), 39–58.

Barrera, M., & Ainley, S. L. (1983). The structure of social support: A conceptual and empirical analysis. *Journal of Community Psychology, 11,* 133–144.

Beard, J., Propst, R., & Malamud, T. (1982). The Fountain House model of psychiatric rehabilitation. *Psychosocial Rehabilitation Journal, 5*(1), 47–53.

Beeman, S. (1995). Reconceptualizing social support: The results of a study on the social networks of neglecting mothers. In E. Wattenberg (Ed.), *Children in the shadows: The fate of children in neglecting families* (pp. 61–84). Minneapolis: Center for Urban and Regional Affairs, University of Minnesota.

Bennett, L. (1961). *Before the Mayflower.* Chicago: Johnson.

Berry, M. F., & Blassingame, J. W. (1982). *Long memory.* New York: The Oxford Press.

Biegel, D. E., Shore, B. K., & Gordon, E. (1984). *Building support networks for the elderly: Theory and application.* Beverly Hills, CA: Sage.

Borkman, T. J. (Ed.). (1991) Self help groups. *American Journal of Community Psychology* (special issue), *19*(5).

Bott, E. (1957). *Family and social network.* London: Tavistock.

Boutiller, L., & Rehm, D. (1993). Family reunification practice in a community-based mental health center. In B. A. Pine, R. Warsh, & A. N. Maluccio (Eds.), *Together again: Family reunification in foster care* (pp. 51–64). Washington, DC: Child Welfare League of America.

Byrne, C., & Sebastian, L. (1994). The defining characteristics of support. *Journal of Psychosocial Nursing, 32*(6), 33–38.

Carlo, P. (1993). Parent education vs. parent involvement: Which type of efforts work best to reunify families? *Journal of Social Service Research, 17*(1 & 2), 135–150.

Carson, E. D. (1993). *Early roots of Black philanthropy.* Washington, DC: Joint Center for Political and Economic Studies.

Cassel, J. (1974). Psychosocial processes and stress: Theoretical formulations. *International Journal of Health Services, 4*(3), 471–482.

Choi, N. G., & Wodarski, J. S. (1996). The relationship between social support and health status of elderly people: Does social support slow down physical and functional deterioration? *Social Work Research, 20*(1), 52–63.

Cohen, S., Doyle, W. J., Skoner, D. P., Robin, B. S., & Gwaltney, J. M. (1997). Social ties and susceptibility to the common cold. *Journal of the American Medical Association, 227*(24), 1940–1944.

Cohen, S., & McKay, G. (1984). Social support, stress and the buffering hypothesis: A theoretical analysis. In A. Baum, J. E. Singer, & S. E. Taylor (Eds.), *Handbook of psychology and health* (vol. 4, pp. 78–89). Hillsdale, NJ: Lawrence Erlbaum.

Cohen, S., & Wills, T. A. (1985). Stress, social support and the buffering hypothesis. *Psychological Bulletin, 98*(2), 310–357.

Collins, A. H., & Pancoast, D. L. (1976). *Natural helping networks: A strategy for prevention.* Washington, DC: National Association of Social Workers.

Connidis, I. A., & McMullin, J. A. (1994). Social support in older age: Assessing the impact of marital and parent status. *Canadian Journal of Aging, 13*(4), 510–527.

Coplon, J., & Strull, J. (1983). Roles of the professional in mutual aid groups. *Social Casework: The Journal of Contemporary Social Work, 64*(5), 259–266.

Cox, E. O. (1991). The critical role of social action in empowerment oriented groups. *Social Work with Groups, 14*(3/4), 77–90.

Crawford, G. W. (1914). *Prince Hall and his followers.* New York: The Crisis.

Dougherty, S. J. (1994). The generalist role in club house organizations *Psychosocial Rehabilitation Journal, 18*(1), 95–108.

DuBois, W. E. B. (1899). *The Philadelphia Negro.* New York: Benjamin Blom.

Federico, R. C. (1984). *The social welfare institution.* Lexington, MA: D. C. Heath.

Fein, E., & Staff, I. (1993). Goal-setting with biological families. In B. A. Pine, R. Warsh, & A. N. Maluccio (Eds.), *Together again: Family reunification in foster care* (pp. 67–92). Washington, DC: Child Welfare League of America.

Festinger, T. B. (1996). Going home and returning to foster care. *Children and Youth Services Review, 18*(4/5), 398.

Finn, J. (1995). Computer-based self-help groups: A new resource to supplement support groups. *Social Work with Groups, 18*(1), 109–117.

Finn, J., & Lavitt, M. (1994). Computer-based self-help groups for sexual abuse survivors. *Social Work with Groups, 17*(1/2), 21–46.

Franklin, J. H. (1980). *From slavery to freedom: A history of Negro Americans.* New York: Alfred A. Knopf.

Fraser, M. W., & Hawkins, J. D. (1984). The social networks of opioid abusers. *International Journal of the Addictions, 19*(8), 903–917.

Fraser, M. W., Pecora, P. J., & Haapala, D. A. (1988). *Families in crisis: Final report on the family-based intensive treatment project*. Salt Lake City, UT: Social Research Institute, University of Utah.

Frazier, E. F. (1966). *The Negro family in the United States*. Chicago: University of Chicago Press.

Friedlander, W. A. (1968). *Introduction to social welfare*. Englewood Cliffs, NJ: Prentice-Hall.

Fuchs, D. (1993). Building on the strengths of family and neighborhood social network ties for the prevention of child maltreatment: An ecological approach. In M. R. Rodway & B. Trute (Eds.), *The ecological perspective in family-centered therapy* (pp. 69–98). Queenston, ON: Edwin Mellen.

Galinsky, M. J., & Schopler, H. H. (1994). Negative experiences in support groups. *Social Work in Health Care, 20*(1), 77–95.

Garbarino, J. (1986). Where does social support fit into optimizing human development and preventing dysfunction? *British Journal of Social Work, 16*(supplement), 23–37.

Gartner, A. & Reissman, F. (Eds.) (1984). *The self-help revolution*. New York: Human Sciences Press.

Gaudin, J. M., Polansky, N. A., Kilpatrick, A. C., & Shilton, P. (1993). Loneliness, depression, stress and social supports in neglectful families. *American Journal of Orthopsychiatry, 63*(4), 597–605.

Gaudin, J. M., Jr., Wodarski, J. S., Arkinson, M. K., & Avery, L. S. (1990). Remedying child neglect: Effectiveness of social network interventions. *Journal of Applied Social Sciences, 15*, 97–123.

Gitterman, A., & Germain, C. B. (1981). Education for practice: Teaching about the environment. *Journal of Education for Social Work, 17*(3), 44–51.

Gitterman, A., & Shulman, L. (1994). *Mutual aid groups: Vulnerable populations and the life cycle*. New York: Columbia University Press.

Gold, D. (1987). Sibling in older age: Something special. *Canadian Journal on Aging, 6*(3), 199–227.

Goodman, C. (1990). Evaluation of a model self-help telephone program: Impact on natural networks. *Social Work, 35*(6), 556–562.

Gottlieb, B. H. (1983). *Social support strategies*. Beverly Hills, CA: Sage.

Gottlieb, B. H. (1978). The development and application of a classification scheme of informal helping behaviors. *Canadian Journal of Behavioral Science, 10*(2), 105–115.

Grinnel, R. M., & Kyte, N. S. (1975). Environmental modification: A study. *Social Work, 20*(4), 313–318.

Gurowka, K. J., & Lightman, E. S. (1995). Supportive and unsupportive interactions as perceived by cancer patients. *Social Work in Health Care, 21*(4), 71–83.

Harrington, M. (1962). *The other America: Poverty in the United States*. Baltimore: Penguin.

Hartman, A. (1978). Diagrammatic assessment of family relations. *Social Casework, 59*(8), 465–476.

Hartman, A., & Laird, J. (1983). *Family-centered social work practice*. New York: Free Press.

Hawkins, J. D., & Fraser, M. W. (1985). The social networks of street drug users: A comparison of descriptive propositions from control and differential association theories. *Social Work Research and Abstracts, 21*(1), 3–12.

Heller, K., & Swindle, R. W. (1983). Social networks, perceived social support and coping with stress. In R. D. Felner, L. A. Jason, J. Morisugu, & S. S. Farber (Eds.), *Preventive psychology: Theory, research and practice* (pp. 87–103). New York: Pergamon.

Herodotus (1909). *The history of Herodotus*. (Translated from the ancient Greek by G. Rawlinson). New York: Tandy-Thomas.

Hirsch, L. H. (1931). The Negro and New York, 1783–1865. *Journal of Negro History, 16*, 415–473.

House, J. S., & Kahn, R. L. (1985). Measures and concepts of social support. In S. Cohen & S. L. Syme (Eds.), *Social support and health* (pp. 83–108). Orlando, FL: Academic.

Huberman, L. (1963). *Man's worldly goods*. New York: Monthly Review Press.

Hughes, R., Good, E. S., & Candell, K. (1993). A longitudinal study of the effects of social support on the psychological adjustment of divorced mothers. *Journal of Divorce and Remarriage, 19*(1/2), 37–56.

Jackson, W. S. (1973). *Social service delivery system in the Black community during the ante-bellum period (1619–1860)*. Atlanta: Atlanta University School of Social Work.

Jackson, R. L., Purnell, D., Anderson, S. B., & Sheafor, B. W. (1996). The clubhouse model of community support for adults with mental illness: An emerging opportunity for social work education. *Journal of Social Work Education, 32*(2), 173–180.

Jansson, B. (1990). *Theory and practice of social welfare policy*. Belmont, CA: Wadsworth.

Jones, L. P. (1991). Unemployment: The effect on social networks, depression, and reemployment organizations. *Journal of Social Service Research, 15*(1/2), 1–22.

Jones, M. A., Neuman, R., & Shyne, A. W. (1976). *A second chance for families: Evaluation of a program to reduce foster care*. New York: Child Welfare League of America.

Joyce, B., Stanley, D., & Hughes, L. (1990). Staying well: Factors contributing to successful community adaptation. *Journal of Psychosocial Nursing and Mental Health Services, 28*(6), 18–24.

Kahn, R. L., & Antonucci, T. C. (1981). *Convoys of social support: A life course approach*. In S. B. Kiesler, J. N. Morgan, & V. C. Oppenheimer (Eds.), *Aging: Social change* (pp. 383–405). New York: Academic.

King, H. (1991). A telephone reassurance service: A natural support system for the elderly. *Journal of Gerontological Social Work, 16*(1/2), 159–177.

Kinney, J., Haapala, D., Booth, C., & Leavitt, S. (1990). The Homebuilders model. In J. K. Whittaker, J. Kinney, E. M. Tracy, & C. Booth (Eds.), *Reaching high-risk families: Intensive family preservation in the human services* (pp. 31–64). New York: Aldine de Gruyter.

Koeske, G. F., & Koeske, R. D. (1990). The buffering effect of social support on parental stress. *American Journal of Orthopsychiatry, 60*(3), 440–451.

Koslyk, D., Fuchs, D., Tabisz, E., & Jacyk, W. R. (1993). Combining professional and self help group intervention: Collaboration in co-leadership. *Social Work with Groups, 16*(3), 111–123.

Kunz, J., & Kunz, P. R. (1995). Social support during the process of divorce: It does make a difference. *Journal of Divorce and Remarriage, 24*(3/4), 111–119.

Kurtz, L. F. (1990). The self-help movement: Review of the post decade of research. *Social Work with Groups, 13*(3), 101–115.

Ladewig, B. H., McGee, G. W., & Newell, W. (1990). Life strains and depressive affect among women: Moderating effects of social support. *Journal of Family Issues, 11*(1), 36–47.

Lamb, H. R. (1994). A century and a half of psychiatric rehabilitation in the United States. *Hospital and Community Psychiatry, 45*(10), 1015–1020.

Lewis, K. G. (1991). A three step plan for African-American families involved with foster care: Sibling therapy, mothers' group therapy, family therapy. *Journal of Independent Social Work, 5*(3/4), 135–147.

Lindsay, A. G. (1921). The economic condition of the Negroes of New York prior to 1861. *Journal of Negro History, 6*(2), 190–199.

Lovell, M. L., & Hawkins, J. D. (1988). An evaluation of a group intervention to increase the personal social networks of abusive mothers. *Children and Youth Services Review, 10,* 175–188.

Maluccio, A. N., Fein, E., & Davis, I. P. (1982). Family reunification: Research findings, issues, and directions. *Child Welfare, 53,* 489–504.

Marin, M. V., & Vacha, E. F. (1994). Self-help strategies and resources among people at risk of homelessness: Empirical findings and social services policy. *Social Work, 39*(6), 649–657.

Mastboom, J. (1992). Forty clubhouses: Model and practices. *Psychosocial Rehabilitation Journal, 16*(2), 9–23.

Meier, A., Galinsky, M. J., & Rounds, K. A. (1995). Telephone support groups for caretakers of persons with AIDS. *Social Work with Groups, 18*(1), 99–108.

Meier, A. & Rudwick, E. M. (1966). *From plantation to ghetto: An interpretive history of American Negroes.* New York: Hill & Wang.

Meldrum, A. (1991, November-December). ESAP'S fables. *Africa Report,* 56–60.

Memmott, J. L. (1993). Models of helping and coping: A field experiment with natural and professional helpers. *Social Work Research and Abstracts, 29*(3), 11–21.

Merton, R. K., & Nisbet, R. (1961). *Contemporary social problems.* New York: Harcourt Brace Jovanovich.

Mitchell, R. E., & Trickett, E. J. (1980). Social networks as mediators of social support. *Community Mental Health Journal, 16*(1), 27–43.

Moncher, F. J. (1995). Social isolation and child abuse risk. *Families in Society, 76*(7), 421–433.

Morrison, J. D. (1991). The Black church as a support system for black elderly. *Journal of Gerontological Social Work, 17*(1/2), 105–120.

Myrdal, G. (1962). *An American dilemma: The Negro problem and modern democracy.* New York: Pantheon.

Nakhaima, J. M. (1994). Network family counselling: The overlooked resource. *Arete, 19*(1), 46–56.

National Research Council (1993). *Understanding child abuse and neglect.* Washington, DC: National Academy Press.

Novak, M. W. (1997). *Aging and Society: A Canadian Perspective* (3rd ed.). Toronto: ITP Nelson.

Olsen, R. F. (1986). Integrating formal and informal social care: The utilization of social support networks. *British Journal of Social Work, 16*(supplement), 15–22.

Owne, D. (1986). Formal and informal patterns of social care. *British Journal of Social Work, 16*(suppl.), 5–14.

Patterson, S. L., & Brennan, E. M. (1983). Matching helping roles with the characteristics of older natural helpers. *Journal of Gerontological Social Work, 5,* 55–66.

Patterson, S. L., Germain, C. B., Brennan, E. M., & Memmott, J. (1988). Effectiveness of rural natural helpers. *Social Casework, 69*(5), 272–279.

Patterson, S. L. Memmott, J. L. Brennan, E. M., & Germain, C. B. (1992). Patterns of natural helping in rural areas: Implications for social work research. *Social Work, 28*(3), 22–28.

Polansky, N. A., Ammons, P. W., Gaudin, J. M. (1985). Loneliness and isolation in child neglect. *Social Casework, 66*(1), 38–47.

Polansky, N. A., Chalmers, M. A., Buttenwieser, E., & Williams, D. P. (1981). *Damaged parents: An anatomy of child neglect.* Chicago: University of Chicago Press.

Pollard, W. L. (1978). *A study of Black self help.* San Francisco: R & E Research Associates.

Powell, T. J. (1990). *Working with self help.* Washington, DC: NASW.

Prigmore, C. S., & Atherton, C. R. (1986). *Social welfare policy.* Lexington, MA: D. C. Heath.

Propst, R. (1992) Standards for Clubhouse programs: Why and how they were developed, *Psychosocial Rehabilitation Journal, 16*(2), 25–30.

Quarles, B. (1987). The Negro in the making of America. New York: Collier Books.

Rainwater, L., & Yancey, W. L. (1967). *The Moynihan report and the politics of controversy.* Cambridge, MA: M.I.T. Press.

Rappaport, J. (1985). The power of empowerment language. *Social Policy, 16*(2), 15–21.

Rhone, J. (1973). Social services delivery system among slaves 1619–1790. In W. S. Jackson, J. V. Rhone, & C. L. Sanders (Ed.), *Social service delivery system in the Black community during the ante-bellum period (1619–1860).* (pp. 3–10) Atlanta: Atlanta University School of Social Work.

Richmond, M. (1918). *Friendly visiting among the poor.* New York: Macmillan.

Rodney, W. (1982). *How Europe underdeveloped Africa.* Washington, DC: Howard University Press.

Ross, E. L. (1978). *Black heritage in social welfare, 1860–1930.* Metuchen, NJ: Scarecrow Press.

Rounds, K. A., Galinsky, M. J., & Despard, M. R. (1995). Evaluation of telephone support groups for persons with HIV disease. *Research in Social Work Practice, 5*(4), 442–459.

Salzer, M. S., McFadden, L., & Rappaport, J. (1994). Professional views of self-help groups. *Administration and Policy in Mental Health, 22*(2), 85–95.

Saulnier, M. R. (1996). Accessing support in times of need. *The Social Worker, 64*(3), 97–106.

Schilling, R. F. (1987). Limitations of social support. *Social Service Review, 61*(1), 19–31.

Shields, G., & Clark, R. D. (1995). Family correlates of delinquency: Cohesion and adaptability. *Journal of Sociology and Social Welfare,* 22(2), 93–106.

Silverman, P. R. (1986). The perils of borrowing: Role of the professional in mutual help groups. *The Journal for Specialists in Group Work,* 11(2), 68–73.

Sims, J. M. (1888). *The first colored Baptist church.* Philadelphia: J. P. Lippincott.

Slaght, E. F. (1998). Focusing on the family in the treatment of substance abusing criminal offenders. *Journal of Drug Education,* 29(1),

Specht, H. (1986). Social support, social networks, social exchange, and social work practice. *Social Service Review,* 60(2), 218–240.

Spence, S. A. (1991). Social support for the black elderly: Is there a link between informal and formal assistance? *Journal of Sociology and Social Welfare,* 18(3), 149–158.

Stein, H., & Nafziger, E. W. (1991). Structural adjustment, human needs, and the World Bank agenda. *Journal of Modern African Studies,* 29(1), 173–189.

Stern, S. B., & Smith, C. A. (1995). Family processes and delinquency in an ecological context. *Social Service Review,* 64(4), 703–731.

Strauss, A., Corbin, J., Fagerhaugh, S., Glaser, B., Maines, D., Suczek, B., & Wiener, B. (1984). *Chronic illness and the quality of life.* Toronto: C. V. Mosby.

Stuckey, S. (1987). *Slave culture.* New York: Oxford University Press.

Tardy, C. H. (1985). Social support measurement. *American Journal of Community Psychology,* 13, 187–202.

Thompson, D. L., & Thompson, J. A. (1993). Working the 12 steps of Alcoholics Anonymous with a client: A counselling opportunity. *Alcoholism Treatment Quarterly,* 10(1/2), 49–61.

Thompson, M. S., & Peebles-Wilkins, W. (1992). The impact of formal, informal, and societal support networks on the psychological well-being of black adolescent mothers. *Social Work,* 37(4), 322–328.

Thompson, R. A. (1995). *Preventing child maltreatment through social support: A critical analysis.* Thousand Oaks, CA: Sage.

Toseland, R. W., & Hacker, L. (1985). Social workers' use of self-help groups as a resource for clients. *Social Work,* 30(3), 232–237.

Tracy, E. M. (1990). Identifying social support resources of at-risk families. *Social Work,* 35(3), 252–258.

Tracy, E. M., Catalano, R. F., Whittaker, J. K., & Fine, D. (1990). Reliability of social network data. *Social Work Research and Abstracts,* 26(2), 33–35.

Tracy, E. M., & Whittaker, J. K. (1987). The evidence base for social support interventions in child and family practice: Emerging issues for research and practice. *Children and Youth Services Review,* 9, 249–270.

Trattner, W. I. (1979). *From poor law to welfare state.* New York: Free Press.

Walton, E., Fraser, M. W., Lewis, R. E., Pecora, P. J., & Walton, W. K. (1993). In-home family-focused reunification: An experimental study. *Child Welfare,* 72(5), 473–487.

Weaver, H. N. (1992). African-Americans and social work: An overview of the ante-bellum through progressive eras. *Journal of Multicultural Social Work,* 2(4), 91–102.

Weinberg, N., Schmale, J. D., Uken, J., & Wessel, K. (1995). Computer-mediated support groups. *Social Work with Groups,* 17(4), 43–54.

Weinberg, N., Schmale, J., Uken, J., & Wessel, K. (1996). Online help: Cancer patients participate in a computer mediated support group. *Health and Social Work,* 21(1), 24–29.

Wellman, B. (1981). Applying network analysis to the study of support. In B. H. Gootlieb (Ed.), *Social networks and social support* (pp. 171–200). Beverly Hills, CA: Sage.

Wethington, E., & Kessler, K. C. (1986). Perceived support, received support, and adjustment to stressful life events. *Journal of Health and Social Behavior,* 27, 78–89.

Whittaker, J. K. (1986). Integrating formal and informal social care: A conceptual framework. *British Journal of Social Work,* 16(supplement), 39–62.

Whittaker, J. K., & Garbarino, J. (1983). *Social support networks: Informal helping in the human services.* New York: Aldine.

Whittaker, J. K., & Schinke, S. P., & Gilchrist, L. D. (1986). The ecological paradigm in child, youth, and family services: Implications for policy and practice. *Social Service Review,* 60(4), 483–503.

Whittaker, J. K., Tracy, E. M., & Marckworth, M. (1989). *The family support project: Identifying informal social support resources for high risk families.* Seattle, WA: University of Washington, School of Social Work.

Wiener, L. S., Spencer, E. D., Davidson, R., & Fair, C. (1993). National telephone support groups: A new avenue toward psychosocial support for HIV-Infected children and their families. *Social Work with Groups,* 16(3), 55–71.

Wilcox, J. A., & Taber, M. A. (1991). Informal helpers of elderly home care clients. *Health and Social Work,* 16(4), 258–265.

Wilson, P. A. (1986). Informal care and social support: An agenda for the future. *British Journal of Social Work,* 16, 173–179.

Wood, Y. R. (1984). Social support and social networks: Nature and measurement. In P. McReynolds & G. J. Chelvne (Eds.). *Advances in psychological assessment* (vol. 6, pp. 312–353). San Francisco: Jossey-Bass.

Zuravin, S., & Greif, G. S. (1989). Normative and child-maltreating AFDC mothers. *Social Casework,* 70(2), 76–84.

chapter 15

Building Helping Communities

CHAPTER PREVIEW

Social work celebrated its centennial in 1998; the first formal training program for social workers was established by the New York Charity Organization Society in the summer of 1898. Our 100-year history has been marked by conflict between those who advocate for community development, community organizing, and social action and those who emphasize services to persons experiencing stress and crisis (Franklin, 1990). The literature on community organizing and community development (Banks & Mangan, 1997; Buffum & MacNair, 1994; Fisher, 1994; Galaway & Hudson, 1994; Homan, 1994; Meenaghan & Gibbons, 1998; Midgley, 1995; Mandros & Wilson, 1994; Tropman, 1997; Weil, 1997; Wharf & Clague, 1997; Woliver, 1993) has presented these approaches to community change as distinct from direct work with individuals and families.

Finding ways to integrate these two traditions into the practice of all social workers is an important challenge facing the profession (Adams & Nelson, 1995; Barber, 1995; Elliott, 1993). In this chapter, we will consider contributions that practitioners and their individual and family clients can make to the development of helping communities. Participation in social support networks and in communities is reciprocal; clients both receive benefits from communities and contribute to them.

Practitioners and their clients may contribute to their communities by:

- contributing to social capital
- seeking advice and consultation from natural helpers
- initiating communications
- contributing to peaceful solutions for conflicts
- organizing to meet community needs

In Reading 15-1, John McKnight argues that we have lost too much control of our activities to institutions with either therapeutic or advocacy visions; we need to return to a community vision, in which citizens freely associate to care for each other.

CONTRIBUTING TO SOCIAL CAPITAL

Social scientists have developed the concept of social capital to help explain why collective actions fail in some communities and succeed in others.

> By analogy with notions of physical capital and human capital—tools and training that enhance individual productivity—social capital refers to features of social organization, such as networks, norms, and trust, that facilitate coordination and cooperation for mutual benefit. Social capital enhances the benefits of investment in physical and human capital. (Putnam, 1993)

Robert D. Putnam (1993) studied 20 powerful regional governments established in Italy in 1970. Some were dismal failures; they were inefficient, lethargic and corrupt. Others, however, were very successful in creating innovative programs and administering policy. Putnam attributed the difference to the presence of social capital in the successful communities (Exhibit 15–1). Social capital consists of networks of social relationships—what we have called informal social support networks. Communities with dense social networks have high social capital; those with sparse social networks have low social capital. The density of the social networks increases as people in a community participate in more social networks, the higher the proportion of the members of the community participating in the social networks, and the extent to which the social networks

EXHIBIT 15-1	Social Capital

Robert D. Putnam studied 20 new regional governments that were established in Italy in 1970. Some of the new governments proved to be dismal failures—inefficient, lethargic, and corrupt. Others have been remarkably successful, however, creating innovative day care programs and job-training centers, promoting investment and economic development, pioneering environmental standards and family clinics—managing the public's business efficiently and satisfying their constituents.

These communities did not become civic simply because they were rich. The historical record strongly suggests precisely the opposite: They have become rich because they were civic. The social capital embodied in norms and networks of civic engagement seems to be a precondition for economic development, as well as for effective government. Development economists take note: Civics matters.

By analogy with notions of physical capital and human capital—tools and training that enhance individual productivity—``social capital'' refers to features of social organization, such as networks, norms, and trust, that facilitate coordination and cooperation for mutual benefit. Social capital enhances the benefits of investment in physical and human capital.

How does social capital undergird good government and economic progress? First, networks of civic engagement foster sturdy norms of generalized reciprocity: I'll do this for you now, in the expectation that down the road you or someone else will return the favor. ``Social capital is akin to what Tom Wolfe called the 'favor bank' in his novel, *The Bonfire of the Vanities*'' notes economist Robert Frank. A society that relies on generalized reciprocity is more efficient than a distrustful society, for the same reason that money is more efficient than barter. Trust lubricates social life.

Networks of civic engagement also facilitate coordination and communication and amplify information about the trustworthiness of other individuals. Students of prisoners' dilemmas and related games report that cooperation is most easily sustained through repeat play. When economic and political dealing is embedded in dense networks of social interaction, incentives for opportunism and malfeasance are reduced. This is why the diamond trade, with its extreme possibilities for fraud, is concentrated within close-knit ethnic enclaves. Dense social ties facilitate gossip and other valuable ways of cultivating reputation—an essential foundation for trust in a complex society.

Finally, networks of civic engagement embody past success at collaboration, which can serve as a cultural template for future collaboration. The civic traditions of north-central Italy provide a historical repertoire of forms of cooperation that, having proved their worth in the past, are available to citizens for addressing new problems of collective action.

Reprinted with permission from *The American Prospect*, 13, Spring. Copyright © 1993 The American Prospect, P.O. Box 383080, Cambridge, MA 02138. All rights reserved.

overlap so that there is an interconnectedness within the community.

Access to social capital enhances family well-being (Boisjoly, Duncan, & Hofferth, 1995). The loss of social capital and the withering of community life may contribute to emotional disorders (Maher, 1992) and crime (Bellair, 1997). Cullen (1994) argues that variations in social control, individual involvement in crime, and crime rates correlate with social support—that is, the availability of social networks that provide coping resources for citizens. As social support in a community increases, the crime rate falls (Cullen, 1994). Communities that enmesh their citizens in mutual ties of trust, empathy, and obligation insulate them from the social precipitators of crime (Braithwaite, 1989; Cullen, 1994; Messner & Rosenfeld, 1994). Further, crime rates may be lower in communities that encourage citizens to participate in altruistic activities (Chamlin & Cochran, 1997).

If social capital increases as persons participate in informal associations and social networks, then clients can contribute to the social capital of their communities by participating in sporting clubs, recreational organizations, neighborhood groups, religious organizations, PTAs, and so forth. Where clients participate is less important than that they become involved. Remember, however, that social capital depends on active participation: playing on a team, rather than observing a sporting event; joining a community chorus, rather than attending a concert; and working on a broadcast at a local public access cable station, rather than going to a movie.

You may discuss with clients how they are contributing to the social capital of their communities. If their connections are tenuous or sparse, strategize ways of increasing their participation in informal associations and social networks.

CONSULTING INFORMAL HELPERS

Clients may be invited—or encouraged—to seek consultation and advice from family, friends, and community members (Memmott, 1993). Some may be reluctant to seek advice or to discuss matters of concern. But people do not need to live alone, isolated, and relying totally on professionals. A 1997 survey of mid-life Americans, for example, found that 64% did not foresee difficulty talking to their aging parents about the parents' ability to live independently, although 68% had never done so (Barrett, 1997). Of the 29% who had spoken with their aging parents, 70% reported that it was easy to do.

All of us must make important decisions in our lives, and some of these are difficult. We can benefit from the advice of natural helpers (Patterson, Memmott, Brennan, & Germain, 1992) in our informal support networks. Some of these helpers will have had more life experiences than us, some will have a particular expertise, and others will have alternative viewpoints. Generally people appreciate being asked for advice and consultation. The process itself will strengthen support networks.

Professionals sometimes actively or passively discourage clients from seeking advice from friends, neighbors, and family. For example, in Exhibit 12–9, where a mother needed to decide whether to request the placement of her 12-year-old son or to seek assistance in managing his behavior within the home, the service plan only included consultation with the social worker. Exhibit 15–2 provides an alternative service plan for the same client, which includes consultation with her minister, a sister, and two friends.

As professionals, we must remember that people in our clients' informal support systems are an important resource for consultation about decisions. Informal helpers are available to clients at all hours and will be a part of client's communities long after we have left. Helping clients use these resources will involve three sets of activities:

- identifying which individuals within the client's informal networks may be a helpful source of advice and including consultation with these people in the service plan;
- reviewing the advice received and assisting the client in determining how useful it is;
- taking the advice into consideration and arriving at a decision.

You will help clients to understand that they are not bound by the advice received; taking into consideration the information obtained, they will make their own decisions.

BUILDING TRUST THROUGH COMMUNICATION

North American societies are characterized by a pervasive fear and lack of trust. A 1995 national survey found that, in the United States, only 35% of respondents believed that most people could be trusted; the figure had been 76% in 1964 (Morin & Balz, 1996). Fear and distrust inhibit us from engaging with others (Exhibits 15–3 and 15–4).

Building trust is essential if we are to develop helping communities. This process can best occur from the grassroots level, as individuals take responsibility for their own lives and environments and learn to communicate with others. We see three ways for you and your client to reduce fear and distrust.

First, carefully consider whether you are overemphasizing fear—especially fear of strangers—in your work together. We all need to balance the risks of living with our responsibilities to build helping communities. That we need to lock our homes should not convince us that all youths are dangerous. That a woman abused by her spouse needs a safety plan does not mean that all men are dangerous. Fear is more likely to be overcome with collective action; thus, we may wish to encourage clients to meet regularly with others to take strolls in their neighborhoods and to spend time on the streets and in public places.

Second, there are many ways to engage people, even strangers, rather than avoiding them. Can we say good morning to a group of teenagers loitering in a shopping center, rather than walking around them? Can we stop for a few minutes to chat with a panhandler? A friendly greeting to people we meet on the street or in stores can help us develop comfort and skill in reaching out to others.

Third, encourage your clients not to jump to conclusions when people appear surly or unfriendly. As Exhibit 15–5 illustrates, a kind word and a pleasant greeting may be the best response. Try to understand rather than judge.

EXHIBIT 15-2   **Revised Service Plan to Assist Bonita to Make a Decision**

BACKGROUND: Richard is the 12-year-old son of Jon and Bonita Jasper. Jon is a merchant seaman and is at sea for extended periods of time, leaving Bonita as the primary provider of child care. Richard has been staying out late at night, is refusing to do household chores, and recently was gone from home overnight. Bonita, in her efforts to control Richard, has used harsh discipline, including beating him with a belt that left welts. The school made a referral to child protection; the child protection agency is holding the case open because Bonita has asked for services from the family service unit of the Maritime Union. This initial plan was developed by Bonita and Sally Harlow, the worker, during a home visit.

DATE: March 5

PROBLEM: Bonita is having difficulty managing Richard without anger, is resorting to harsh punishment, and is considering requesting an out-of-home placement.

OBJECTIVE: Bonita will be able to decide whether to request placement for Richard or to develop a service plan to retain Richard at home.

SERVICE PLAN:

Task	Who Will Do?	To Be Completed by:
1. Meet twice in Bonita's home to discuss the choices available and the pros and cons of each choice.	Bonita and Sally; Sally will visit Bonita at her home for these meetings	1st meeting on March 12; 2nd meeting on March 19
2. Consult with the following people to seek their advice regarding decision: • Rev. Clarke, minister of Bonita's church • Bonita's sister, Anna • Bonita's two friends, Corie and Denise	Bonita	March 19
3. Bonita will make a decision among: (a) requesting placement, (b) developing a service plan for retaining Richard in the home, or (c) discontinuing service.	Bonita	March 23
4. Telephone conference to discuss the decision and schedule another meeting if Bonita decides for (a) or (b).	Worker will call Bonita	March 24

EXHIBIT 15-3   **Fear of Helping Children**

Ralph Smith, a nationally known child advocate from Philadelphia, was just a daddy one afternoon, picking up his son at child care.

He walked toward the back, near the bathrooms when a girl walked out, tights around her ankles, an unhappy look on her face. No one else was there. He bent down to help her pull the tights up. Then he froze. What if someone saw this tableau and misinterpreted it?

"I pulled the tights up so fast," he says now, embarrassed at his fear.

How do we help other people's children?

Adults' inability to nurture or correct someone else's kids is "one of the most tragic social changes to impact on children," said David Popence, co-chairman of the Council on Families in America and a sociology professor at Rutgers University.

Source: M. Dubin, Adults fear helping kids of others. *Omaha World-Herald*, p. 42 (1996, July 23).

EXHIBIT 15-4   Semi Silences SOS Pleas

An elderly Gretna couple frantically trying to wave down help by the roadside were ignored by several motorists—some of whom even swerved to avoid them—before they were finally run over and killed.

But RCMP (Royal Canadian Mounted Police) say no one stopped for Jacob Neufeld, 78, and his wife Mary, 77, until it was too late.

RCMP Cpl. Richard Graham said the Neufelds were struck down after they moved onto the road in an effort to get a semi-trailer to stop at about 8 p.m. on an isolated strip of the highway about 13 kilometres south of Morris.

Graham said the couple were on their way home to Gretna after having dinner at their daughter's home in Grunthal. He said it appears they turned off Highway 75 and onto a side road by mistake, then got stuck in a ditch when they tried to turn around.

Graham said the couple walked about half a kilometre back to the main highway and—likely cold and exhausted—began trying to flag down passing vehicles, waving their arms and walking onto the highway.

"People are afraid to stop for anyone these days," he said.

From "Semi Silences SOS Pleas" by P. Wiecek in the *Winnipeg Free Press*, February 4, 1995, p. 1. Reprinted with permission.

PEACEMAKING

Bishop Tutu and the South African Truth and Reconciliation Commission provide a powerful example of peacemaking under very difficult circumstances. Families have been able to forgive those who admit to torturing and killing family members during Apartheid. Perpetrators have avoided prosecution by facing up to the families, sharing the truth, and helping to locate remains. This has provided the families with an oppor-tunity for closure and healing. Some critics complain that justice has not been done, because the perpetrators have not been punished, but Bishop Tutu argues that reconciliation is occurring and the nation is being spared bloody conflict and many additional deaths. Are we able to modify demands for vengeance and punishment in order to build peaceful, helping communities?

In order to contribute to peaceful communities, we must admit fault when we are at fault and offer forgive-

---

EXHIBIT 15-5   A Lesson Learned

Dear Ann Landers: I want to share a recent discovery that has made me a better person. Maybe some of your readers will see themselves.

I used to assume that a wealthy woman I knew slightly was an arrogant snob because she rarely spoke and never smiled. I also had the notion that the woman in the supermarket with the whining children was a lousy mother.

Then one day, as I stood in line at the grocery store, I noticed that the clerk never smiled at the customers and ignored polite conversation. I was tempted to tell her what I thought of her sour attitude when the elderly woman in front of me took a different approach.

She said, "Honey, you look like you're having a bad day." The clerk looked up with the saddest eyes I've ever seen and said, "My husband lost his job yesterday, and I just found out I'm pregnant!"

The woman patted her hand and said, "Dear, things will work out."

When it was my turn, the clerk had tears in her eyes, but she smiled, and I felt ashamed of myself for being so intolerant.

That incident made me realize that people usually aren't rude because they are mean and want to make my life miserable. They are unpleasant because they have problems on their mind and a heavy heart. My entire outlook on life changed that day.

I now assume the frowning woman might be worried about the results of a biopsy, the rude young driver could be on his way to the emergency room to meet an injured relative, and the distracted mother with the screaming child in the supermarket may need my smile and a kind word—perhaps the only ones she will get all day.

This change in attitude has made those around me happier, but the greatest benefit is mine. I am less angry and more serene, and I like myself better.—**Older and Wiser**

From "Ann Landers," April 5, 1997. Copyright © 1997. Universal Press Syndicate. Reprinted with permission.

ness when we have been harmed. No one is expected to be perfect; we all make mistakes. You can help clients contribute to peace when you assist them in accepting responsibility for their mistakes, extending apologies to persons they have harmed, and developing plans by which they can make redress. Accepting responsibility for the harm we have caused to others is one of the twelve steps on which Alcoholics Anonymous and other self-help programs are based.

If clients have been harmed by others, their ability to accept apologies, consider redress, and offer forgiveness will contribute to their personal growth (Di Blasio, 1993; Di Blasio & Proctor, 1993) and to helping communities (Norell & Walz, 1994). Both apologies and forgiveness need to be freely offered and not coerced. In talking with clients who have been harmed by others, you may explore their views about forgiveness.[1]

ORGANIZING HELPING COMMUNITIES

You and your client contribute to helping communities by developing and participating in:

- mentoring and support organizations
- community economic development organizations
- consumer and social action organizations

---

[1]Information about forgiveness is available from the International Forgiveness Institute, P.O. Box 6153, Madison, WI 53716.

Mentoring and Support Organizations

Altruism, as a part of human motivation (Schwartz, 1993; Wakefield, 1993), underlies mutual assistance programs, such as those that provide mentors for youth, especially in multicultural urban settings, to assist with school performance and positive self-identification (Freedman, 1993; Keenan, Dyer, Morita, & Shaskey-Setright, 1990; Mech, Pryde, & Rycraft, 1995; Zippay, 1995). Families may serve as mentors to other families where child abuse is present, to assist with stress management and the development of parenting skills (Kiam, Green, & Pomeroy, 1997). In some communities, seniors who provide volunteer services for older seniors can earn credits for assistance with transportation, food preparation, and other needs (Fort & Associates, 1990). Many of your clients will experience personal growth and satisfaction by serving as volunteers in their communities (Vorrath & Bendtro, 1985; Rosemond, 1994).

Churches and other religious organizations are increasingly involved in support services for low-income families and others; a helping community intended to provide supervision and support for offenders is described in Exhibit 15-6. Constructed constellations of helpers are very promising for the development of helping communities (Delgado & Rose, 1994).

In this context, you and your client may:

- help community groups organize mentoring and support programs, especially as you become enmeshed in a network of associations within the community

| **EXHIBIT 15-6** | **One Church–One Offender** |

One Church–One Offender provides an alternative to incarceration for nonviolent offenders through placement with volunteer committees sponsored by local churches. Our mission is:

To offer nonviolent offenders a better alternative to overcrowded, expensive jails through a partnership with judicial, social and religious agencies cooperating to provide a program of community based advocacy, health care, education and spiritual nurture.

To encourage positive behavior and to provide an environment conducive to the growth of self-esteem, confidence, independence and hopefulness in the offender.

To intervene in the client's life to influence productive ways of living useful to the client and the community.

Trained committees of caring people work with a nonviolent offender to help that person become a productive citizen. The program rests on the willingness of community volunteers to become involved in addressing the current rate of crime and on the determination of the courts to resolve problems of overcrowding in jails and prisons that do nothing to reform behavior. It also relies on the desire of the individual offender to change and work for a better life for him and his family. One Church–One Offender is making a difference in the lives of offenders and making our neighborhoods a better place to live.

Source: One Church–One Offender, Inc., 227 E. Washington Blvd., Suite 205, Fort Wayne, IN 46802. Phone: 219-422-8688.

- identify, assess, and make use of existing mentoring and support services
- explore client strengths and how these may contribute to a helping community, so that the client may become a provider of mentoring and support services

Community Economic Development

Community economic development is an effort to integrate social development, community development, and economic development (Galaway & Hudson, 1994; Midgley, 1996). It generally involves small-scale, local activities designed to improve economic conditions, increase participation within a community, and strengthen the community's helping ability. North American community development can learn much from the African experience, with its focus on creating economic and social infrastructure and the enhancement of productive activities and social well-being (Kabadaki, 1995). Midgley (1993) notes that, while the eradication of poverty will require a massive national effort, "community programs that seek to enhance incomes and improve social conditions at the local level have an obvious . . . role to play" (p. 277). In your work with individual clients, two aspects of community economic development may be particularly helpful: microbusinesses and cooperatives.

Microbusinesses. Some of your clients, including young people entering adulthood, may be interested in establishing small businesses and developing markets for their services (Else & Raheim, 1992; Raheim, 1996). Individuals can often offer services—such as day care, word processing, home maintenance and repair, home cleaning, and yard maintenance—at more competitive rates than can large organizations, because of lower overheads and administrative costs. Self-employment may enhance economic empowerment and self-sufficiency for women (Raheim & Bolden, 1995). However, many clients lack (1) skills in areas such as developing a business plan, marketing, and financial management and (2) the capital necessary to establish a small business; even a modest home-operated business will require some capital.

Microlending programs address both of these limitations. They are well-established in Asia and Africa as a mechanism for making very small loans to enable low-income persons—often women—to establish small businesses and move their family out of poverty (From sandals to suits, 1997). As a condition of the loan, microlending programs often require participation in a group for training in business practices. The group members provide support and encouragement to each other. In some of the programs, the group guarantees the loans to individuals; thus, all the group members have a stake in helping each business succeed. Pilot microlending programs are being developed in North America to provide assistance to low-income persons. If microlending programs are available in your community, you may choose to help clients access this resource, as a step toward self-support. If no programs are available, you may wish to consider establishing one. Exhibit 15–7 identifies sources of information about microlending.

Cooperatives. Participation in cooperatives may also be appropriate for some of your clients (Fairbairn, Bold, Fulton, Ketilson, & Ish, 1991; Fulton, 1989; Quarter, 1992). There are both producer and consumer cooperatives. In producer cooperative, a group of people who produce a product or a service band together to jointly market and sell the goods or services. Farmers in North America for example, have formed producer cooperatives to market their products. In consumer cooperatives, a group of consumers bands together to collectively buy and distribute goods or services. Examples include babysitting clubs, food purchasing clubs, cooperative grocery stores, service stations, credit unions, and even cooperative funeral services. Generally, cooperatives can offer services at lower costs than other businesses. In addition, cooperatives provide opportunities for members' active participation in the business; some require donated work, which helps lower the cost of the product. Your clients are likely to be more interested in consumer cooperatives than in producer cooperatives, unless several have successfully established related businesses and can market their services together. Some may even wish to help initiate a cooperative in their neighborhood or community, to meet a specific need. Information about organizing cooperatives is readily available on the Internet; some other sources of information are identified in Exhibit 15–8.

EXHIBIT 15-7   Microlending and Microenterprise Resources

Corporation for Enterprise Development
777 North Capital Street, NE Suite 410
Washington, DC 20002
202/408-9788

Association for Enterprise Opportunity
70 East Lake Street
Suite 620
Chicago, IL 60601
312/357-0177

Economic Opportunities Program (Self Employment Learning Project)
The Aspen Institute
1333 New Hampshire Ave., NW
Suite 1070
Washington, D.C. 20036
202/736-5807

National Congress of Neighborhood Women
604 Seventh Street, SW
Washington, D.C. 20024
202/484-2943

Women's Initiative for Self Employment
450 Mission Street, Suite 420
San Francisco, CA 94105
415/442-7983

Appalachian Center for Economic Networks (ACENET)
94 North Columbus Road
Athens, OH 45701
614/592-3854

Community Economic Development Project Missouri Association for Social Welfare
621 Lee Street
St. Louis, MO 63119
314/963-9227

EXHIBIT 15-8   Cooperatives Resources

Coady International Institute
St. Francis Xavier University
P.O. Box 5000
Antigonish, Nova Scotia B2G 2WE
Canada
Phone: 902-867-3961
Fax: 902-867-3907
email: mtoogood@stfx.ca
www address: www.stfx.ca/institutes/coady

Center for Cooperatives
University of Wisconsin
230 Taylor Hall
427 Lorch Street
Madison, WI 53706
Phone: 608-262-3981
Fax: 608-262-3251
email: reynolds@aae.wisc.edu
www address: http://www.wisc.edu/uwcc/

Wales Cooperative Center
Llandaff Court
Fairwater Road
Cardiff
South Glamorgan CF5 2XP
Wales
Phone: 01222-554955
Fax: 01222-578568
www address: www.cf.ac.uk/ccin/main/socecon/co-op

International Cooperative Alliance
15, route des Movillons
1218 Grand-Saconnet
Geneva, Switzerland
phone: 41-022-929-8888
fax: 41-022-798-4122
email: ica@coop.org
www address: www.coop.org/

Canadian Cooperative Association
400-275 Bank Street
Ottawa, Ontario K2P 2L6
phone: 613-238-6711
fax: 613-567-0658
www address: www.coopcca.com

Social Action Groups

Engaging in collective action to promote change is fundamental to a democratic society. Part of your service to clients may be to help them identify and join social action groups whose goals they share. Groups of social service consumers have successfully secured changes to create more helping communities for their members (Breton, 1995; Checkoway, 1995; Cohen & Wagner, 1992; Cox, 1991; Tower, 1994; Weiss, 1993). Ask your clients if they hold membership in a consumer organization and, if not, whether that is of interest to them. You may also consider ways that clients may actively involve themselves in consumer organizations in order to promote the kinds of helping communities they desire.

Sometimes no social action organization promoting the changes that clients desire may exist at the local level. For example, the Birky family (Exhibit 2–15) may not find a local organization prepared to take on the problem of the uncovered ditch; Mrs. Iverson (Exhibit 5–3) may not find an organization prepared to lobby for a foster home placement for her daughter. Social action organizations often focus on changes in larger systems—at the national, state, or city level. These are important changes, but many of the problems that clients encounter are at the local level—for instance, the need for traffic lights, more frequent garbage pickup, adequate street lighting, or increased availability of teachers for parent consultation. You may need to assist your clients in taking leadership in such change efforts and to become an advisor, consultant, and participant in those efforts.

CHAPTER SUMMARY

Participation in a helping partnership is one of the key themes of this book. In this chapter, we have expanded the notion to include clients' participation in their communities. It is through participation that we build helping communities.

You and your clients may participate in your community by:

- becoming active in voluntary associations and organizations, and thereby contributing to the social capital of the community

- seeking advice from friends, neighbors, and respected community members
- striving to reduce fear through communication with others—especially strangers—in the community
- becoming a peacemaker—both by accepting responsibility for your errors and apologizing and by offering forgiveness when others do the same
- organizing helping communities—by using and offering services as a mentor or volunteer, participating in community economic development, and participating in social change groups

We hope that you will encourage and support your clients' community participation. It is equally important, however, to make sure that you are not doing or saying anything to hinder clients' community participation (Swenson, 1994). Give careful thought to these questions:

1. Am I doing anything to discourage or interfere with the client's participation in voluntary associations and community organizations?

2. Am I in any way discouraging this client from discussing personal matters and key decisions with trusted family members, friends, or others?

3. Am I doing or saying anything that may exaggerate or increase the client's fear?

4. Am I encouraging this client to consider ways of making peace within his or her community, by acknowledging and apologizing for errors and forgiving those who have done wrong?

5. Am I encouraging the client to use and provide volunteer service, to join cooperatives, and to participate in social action organizations?

A LOOK FORWARD

In Reading 15-1, John McKnight argues that social policymakers focus too much on institutions and individuals and undervalue communities and voluntary associations. He suggests that we need a vision of the community as the context for enabling people to participate, contribute their gifts, and meet their wants.

In Chapter 16, we examine teamwork in social work practice. The remaining chapters are devoted to the steps you will take to evaluate your practice, end service with a client, and avoid burnout.

READING 15-1 *Regenerating Community**

John McKnight

Each of us has a map of the social world in our mind, and the way we act, our plans and opinions are the result of that map.

The people who make social policy also have social maps in their minds. They make plans and design programs based upon their map. Indeed, if you carefully examine their programs, you can detect the nature of their mental map.

Using this method, we have found that the most common social policy map has two locations: institutions and individual people. By institutions we mean large structures such as corporations, universities, and government mental health systems. These structures organize a large group of people so that a few of them will be able to control the rest of them. In this structure, there is ultimately room for one leader. It is a structure initially created to produce goods such as steel and automobiles.

In the last few decades, the structure has also been used to design human service systems. While these newly designed hierarchical, managed service systems do not produce goods such as steel, they do produce needs assessments, service plans, protocols, and procedures. They are also thought, by some policymakers, to produce health, education, security, or justice.

If it is correct that these systems can produce these service commodities, then it is possible to imagine that there are consumers of their products. For example, we have all heard that there are now people called "health consumers." They are the *individuals* who are the other part of the social map created by most social policymakers. They make a complete economic world by acting as the users (consumers) of the products of managed institutional producers of such commodities as mental health, health, education, and justice. Thus, we can see that it was necessary to create health consumers once we had systems that could produce health. Otherwise, there would be no purpose for these large hierarchical, managed systems.

Once we understand this social map of institutions and individuals we can see why we have mental health providers and mental health consumers. We can also see how our developing service economy works.

Because the gross national product is the sum of the goods and *services* produced each year, many policy experts have come to believe that the well-being of our society significantly depends upon the amount of the commodities called services that are produced by institutions and used by consumers. For example, a person with a perilous and extended illness (a health consumer) contributes significantly to our economic growth by using large amounts of the commodities produced by the health system. Indeed, a very ill person disabled for a considerable amount of time could cause production of much more medical dollar value through their illness than the value of their own production were they healthy.

This amazing development is possible, in part, because of the unusual two-place map used by many social policymakers in designing social service programs. Unfortunately, this map and the program designs that flow from it have recently encountered three major problems.

The first problem is that in spite of ever-growing inputs into institutionalized service systems, many individuals continue to reject their roles as consumers. This is the problem of intractability that has resulted in an increasing focus upon the "compliance" issue. Especially in our big cities, many intractable young individuals continue to refuse to learn in spite of heightened resources and managerial inputs to school systems. This is commonly known as the educational problem.

Similarly, there are many other intractable individuals who refuse to behave in spite of our correctional institutions. This is the crime problem.

There is also the nutrition problem created by intractable people who refuse to eat the right food. And the chemical dependency problem created by intractable people who insist on smoking and drinking incorrectly. There is also the ever-growing number of intractable people who refuse to flourish in institutions created for labeled people, in spite of all the professional and managerial improvements designed by the systems.

* From "Regenerating Community" by John L. McKnight in *Social Policy*, pp. 54–58. Copyright © 1987 Social Policy Corporation. Reprinted with permission.

Indeed, there are so many intractable people refusing to consume institutional services that we are now designing new systems that surround these individuals with professionally administered services. Thus, one can now see individuals whose lives are bounded by institutions "targeting" their services at an intractable individual through teachers, doctors, trainers, social workers, family planners, psychologists, vocational counselors, security officers, and so forth. This is usually called a "comprehensive, multidisciplinary, coordinated, interagency service system." It is the equivalent of institutionalization without walls or the design of an environment to create a totally dependent service system consumer.

The second problem with programs based upon the typical social policy map is that the sum of their costs can be greater than the wealth of the nation. In a recent white paper entitled "A Time to Serve," a group of Swedish government planners described the escalating costs of their much-acclaimed social service system. They point out that at present rates of growth, the system could consume the entire nation's wealth within a few decades. Therefore, they propose that the government begin to "tax" people's time by requiring the Swedish people to contribute unpaid work to the maintenance and growth of their social service system.

While it is clearly the case that the United States is not in immediate danger of the Swedish economic dilemma, we are contributing substantial amounts to social service systems. A recent study by the Community Services Society of New York found that approximately $7,000 per capita of public and private money is specifically allocated to the low-income population of that city. Thus, a family of four would be eligible on a per capita basis for $28,000 that would place them in the moderate-income category. However, only 37 percent of this money actually reaches low-income people in income. Nearly two-thirds is consumed by those who service the poor.

The third problem with the typical social policy map is that programs based upon its suppositions are increasingly ineffective and even counter-productive. For example, we now understand that our "correctional systems" consistently train people in crime. Studies demonstrate that a substantial number of people, while in hospitals, become sick or injured with maladies worse than those for which they were admitted. In many of our

big city schools we see children whose relative achievement levels fall further behind each year. Thus, we have come to recognize the possibility that we can create crime-making corrections systems, sickness-making health systems, and stupid-making schools based upon a social model that conceives of society as a place bounded by institutions and individuals.

It is obvious, upon the briefest reflection, that the typical social policy map is inaccurate because it excludes a major social domain—the community. By community, we mean the social place used by family, friends, neighbors, neighborhood associations, clubs, civic groups, local enterprises, churches, ethnic associations, temples, local unions, local government, and local media. In addition to being called the community, this social environment is also described as the informal sector, the unmanaged environment, and the associational sector.

THE STRUGGLE BETWEEN COMMUNITY AND INSTITUTION

These associations of community represent unique social tools that are unlike the social tool represented by a managed institution. For example, the structure of institutions is a design established to create *control* of people. On the other hand, the structure of associations is the result of people acting through *consent*. It is critical that we distinguish between these two motive forces because there are many goals that can only be fulfilled through consent, and these are often goals that will be impossible to achieve through a production system designed to control.

There are many other unique characteristics of the community of associations:

• The associations in community are interdependent. To weaken one is to weaken all. If the local newspaper closes, the garden club and the township meeting will each diminish as they lose a voice. If the American Legion disbands, several community fund-raising events and the maintenance of the ballpark will stop. If the Baptist Church closes, several self-help groups that meet in the basement will be without a home and folks in the old people's home will lose their weekly visitors. The interdependence of associations and the dependence of community upon their work is the vital center of an effective society.

• The community environment is constructed around the recognition of fallibility rather than the ideal. Most institutions, on the other hand, are designed with a vision imagining a structure where things can be done right, a kind of orderly perfection achieved, and the ablest dominate.

In contrast, community structures tend to proliferate until they create a place for everyone, no matter how fallible. They provide vehicles that give voice to diversity and assume that consensual contribution is the primary value.

In the proliferation of community associations, there is room for many leaders and the development of leadership capacity among many. This democratic opportunity structure assumes that the best idea is the sum of the knowings of the collected fallible people who are citizens. Indeed, it is the marvel of the democratic ideal that people of every fallibility are citizens. Effective associational life incorporates all of those fallibilities and reveals the unique intelligence of community.

• Associations have the capacity to respond quickly. They do not need to involve all of the institutional interests incorporated in a planning committee, budget office, administrative staff, and so forth.

A primary characteristic of people who need help is that their problem is created by the unexpected tragedy, the surprise development, the sudden change. While they will be able to stabilize over the long run, what they often need is immediate help. The rapid response capacity of associations, and their interconnectedness, allows for the possibility of immediate and comprehensive assistance without first initiating a person into a system from which they may never leave.

• The proliferation and development of community associations allow for the flowering of creative solutions. Institutions tend to require creative ideas to follow channels. However, the nonhierarchical nature of the field of associations allows us to see all of the budding ideas and greatly increases our opportunities for social innovation.

• Because community associations are small, face-to-face groups, the relationship among members is very individualized. They also have the tradition of dealing with non-members as individuals. Institutions, on the other hand, have great difficulty developing programs or activities that recognize the unique characteristics of each individual. Therefore, associations represent unusual tools for creating "hand-tailored" responses to those who may be in special need or have unique fallibilities.

• Our institutions are constantly reforming and reorganizing themselves in an effort to create or allow relationships that can be characterized as "care." Nonetheless, their ministrations consistently commodify themselves and become a service. For many people with uncommon fallibilities, their need is for care rather than service. While a managed system organized as a structure of control can deliver a service, it cannot deliver care. Care is a special relationship characterized by consent rather than control. Therefore, its auspices are individual and associational. For those who need care, we must recognize the community as the appropriate social tool.

• Finally, associations and the community they create are the forum within which citizenship can be expressed. Institutions by their managed structure are definitionally unable to act as forums for citizenship. Therefore, the vital center of democracy is the community of associations. Any person without access to that forum is effectively denied citizenship. For those people with unique fallibilities who have been institutionalized, it isn't enough that they be deinstitutionalized. In order to be a citizen, they must also have the opportunity for recommunilization.

In summary, the community of associations provides a social tool where consent is the primary motivation, interdependence creates holistic environments, people of all capacities and fallibilities are incorporated, quick responses are possible, creativity is multiplied rather than channeled, individualized responses are characteristic, care is able to replace service, and citizenship is possible. When all of these unique capacities of community are recognized, it is obvious why the social policy map that excludes community life has resulted in increasing failures. To exclude from our problem-solving capacities the social tool of community is to have taken the heart out of America.

Why is it, then, that social policy maps so often ignore community? One reason is that there are many institutional leaders who simply do not believe in the capacities of communities. They often see communities as collections of parochial, inexpert, uninformed, and biased people. Indeed, there are many leaders of service systems who believe that they are in direct competition with communities for the power to correctly define problems, provide scientific solutions and professional services.

In this competitive understanding, the institutional leaders are correct. Whenever hierarchical systems become more powerful than the community, we see the flow of authority, resources, skills, dollars, legitimacy, and capacities away from communities to service systems. In fact, institutionalized systems grow at the expense of communities. As institutions gain power, communities lose their potency and the consent of community is replaced by the control of systems; the care of community is replaced by the service of systems; the citizens of community are replaced by the clients and consumer of institutional products.

VISIONS OF SOCIETY

Today, our society is the site of the struggle between community and institution for the capacities and loyalties of our people. This struggle is never carried out in the abstract. Instead, it occurs each day in the relations of people, the budget decisions of systems, and the public portraits of the media. As one observes this struggle, there appear to be three visions of society that dominate the discourse.

The first is the *therapeutic vision*. This prospect sees the well-being of individual as growing from an environment composed of professionals and their services. It envisions a world where there is a professional to meet every need, and the fee to secure each professional service is a right. This vision is epigrammatically expressed by those who see the ultimate liberty as "the right to treatment."

The second prospect is the *advocacy vision*. This approach foresees a world in which labeled people will be in an environment protected by advocates and advocacy groups. It conceives an individual whose world is guarded by legal advocates, support people, self-help groups, job developers, and housing locaters. Unlike the therapeutic vision, the advocacy approach conceives a

defensive wall of helpers to protect an individual against an alien community. It seeks to ensure a person's right to be a functioning individual.

The third approach is the *community vision*. It sees the goal as "recommunilization" of exiled and labeled individuals. It understands the community as the basic context for enabling people to contribute their gifts. It sees community associations as contexts to create and locate jobs, provide opportunities for recreation and multiple friendships, and to become the political defender of the right of labeled people to be free from exile.

Those who seek to institute the community vision believe that beyond therapy and advocacy is the constellation of community associations. They see a society where those who were once labeled, exiled, treated, counseled, advised, and protected are, instead, incorporated in community where their contributions, capacities, gifts, and fallibilities will allow a network of relationships involving work, recreation, friendship, support, and the political power of being a citizen.

Because so many labeled people have been exiled to a world expressing the professional and advocacy vision of an appropriate life, the community vision has frequently been forgotten. How will people know when they are in community? Our studies suggest that this universe is distinctive and distinguished from the environment of systems and institutions. The community experience incorporates a number of strands.

Capacity

We all remember the childhood question regarding how to describe a glass with water to its mid-point. Is it half full or half empty? Community associations are built upon the recognition of the fullness of each member because it is the sum of their capacities that represents the power of the group. The social policy map makers, on the other hand, build a world based upon the emptiness of each of us—a model based upon deficiency. Communities depend upon capacities. Systems commodify deficiencies.

Collective Effort

It is obvious that the essence of community is people working together. One of the characteristics of this community work is shared responsibility that requires many talents. Thus, a person who has been labeled deficient can find a "hammock" of support in the collective capacities of a community that can shape itself to the unique character of each person. This collective process contrasts with the individualistic approach of the therapeutic professional and the rigidity of institutions that demand that people shape themselves to the needs of the system.

Informality

Associational life in the community is a critical element of the informal economy. Here transactions of value take place without money, advertising, or hype. Authentic relationships are possible and care emerges in place of its packaged imitation: service.

The informality of community is also expressed through relationships that are not managed. Communities viewed by those who only understand managed experiences and relationship appear to be disordered, messy, and inefficient. What these people fail to understand is that there is a hidden order to community groups that is determined by the need to incorporate capacity and fallibility.

While institutions and professionals war against human fallibility by trying to replace it, cure it, or disregard it, communities are proliferations of associations that multiply until they incorporate both the capacities and the fallibilities of citizens. It is for this reason that labeled people are not out of place in community because they all have capacities and only their fallibilities are unusual. However, because there are so many community associations, there are always some sets of associational relationships that can incorporate their fallibilities and use their unique gifts.

Stories

In universities, people know through studies. In businesses and bureaucracies, people know by reports. In communities, people know by stories. These community stories allow people to reach back into their common history and their individual experience for knowledge about truth and direction for the future.

Professionals and institutions often threaten the stories of community by urging community people to count up things rather than communicate. Successful community associations resist efforts to impose the foreign language of studies and reports because it is a tongue that ignores their own capacities and insights. Whenever communities come to believe that their common knowledge is illegitimate, they lose their power and professionals and systems rapidly invade their social place.

Celebration

Community groups constantly incorporate celebrations, parties, and social events in their activities. The line between work and play is blurred and the human nature of everyday life becomes part of the way of work. You will know that you are in community if you often hear laughter and singing. You will know you are in an institution, corporation, or bureaucracy if you hear the silence of long halls and reasoned meetings. Associations in community celebrate because they work by consent and have the luxury of allowing joyfulness to join them in their endeavors.

Tragedy

The surest indication of the experience of community is the explicit common knowledge of tragedy, death, and suffering. The managed, ordered, technical vision embodied in professional and institutional systems leaves no space for tragedy; they are basically methods for production. Indeed, they are designed to deny the central dilemmas of life. Therefore, our managed systems gladly give communities the real dilemmas of the human condition. There is no competition here. To be in community is to be an active part of associations and self-help groups. To be in community is to be a part of ritual, lamentation, and celebration of our fallibility.

Knowing community is not an abstract understanding. Rather, it is what we each know about all of us.

As we think about ourselves, our community and institutions, many of us recognize that we have been degraded because our roles as citizens and our communities have been traded in for the right to clienthood and consumer status. Many of us have come to recognize that as we exiled our fallible neighbors to the control of managers, therapists, and technicians, we lost much of our power to be the vital center of society. We forgot about the capacity of every single one of us to do good work and, instead, made some of us into the objects of good works—servants of those who serve.

As we think about our community life, we recognize that something has happened to many of us as institutions have grown in power. We have become too impotent to be called real citizens and too disconnected to be effective members of community.

There is a mistaken notion that our society has a problem in terms of effective human services. Our essential problem is weak communities. While we have reached the limits of institutional problem solving, we are only at

the beginning of exploring the possibility of a new vision for community. It is a vision of regeneration. It is a vision of reassociating the exiled. It is a vision of freeing ourselves from service and advocacy. It is a vision of centering our lives in community.

We all know that community must be the center of our life because it is only in community that we can be citizens. It is only in community that we can find care. It is only in community that we can hear people singing. And if you listen carefully, you can hear the words: "I care for you, because you are mine, and I am yours."

LEARNING EXERCISES

1. Write one- or two-sentence definitions for the following terms, or briefly explain each term to a colleague:

   consumer cooperatives
   dense social networks
   microlending
   natural helper
   social capital

2. Exhibit 15–9 suggests that absentee human services systems contribute to the problems of poor urban neighborhoods. Do you agree? Explain. Do you think social workers should be expected—or

   required—to live in their clients' neighborhoods? Why or why not?

3. In *Sacred Clowns,* a novel by Tony Hillerman, Jim Chee, a Navajo police officer, solves a case of manslaughter resulting from drunk driving. After reading the book, explain whether you agree with the way Chee resolved the case. Do you think the resolution helped make the community a better place to live? Why or why not?

4. Can you identify ways that social work practice might contribute to fear in communities? How might we reduce this possibility?

EXHIBIT 15-9 **Absentee Human Service Systems**

The current remote and bureaucratized systems must be changed in order to end the economic mistargeting of our existing human-service spending. In any poor urban neighborhood, tens of millions of dollars are spent each year on human needs—health services, foster care, recreation, environmental clean-up, drug education and treatment, nutrition and housing improvements. Almost every dollar of this investment currently goes to teachers, police officers, day care providers, nurses, outreach workers, probation officers, foster families, social workers, health care professionals, planners, managers, landlords, administrators, and service contractors who live some place else. The second time these dollars are spent, they are spent somewhere else. We are used to decrying the problems of absentee landlords and absentee merchants, but we have largely ignored the absentee human-service system we have so consistently sustained. Community-planned and community-managed human-service systems would not only work better for clients, they would also contribute jobs, enterprise, and development to the neighborhoods that need them most.

Source: Community empowerment: Making human services a community enterprise. *AEC Focus,* 4(1), 3 (1994). (Published by the Annie E. Casey Foundation, One Lafayette Place, Greenwich, CT 06830.)

REFERENCES

Adams, P., & Nelson, K. (1995). *Reinventing human services: Community and family practice*. Hawthorne, NY: Aldine de Gruyter.

Banks, C. K., & Mangan, M. (1997). *The company of neighbours: Community development action research*. Toronto: University of Toronto Press.

Barber, J. G. (1995). Politically progressive casework. *Families in Society, 76*(1), 30–37.

Barrett, L. (1997). *Independent living: Adult children's perceptions of their parents' needs*. Washington, D.C.: American Association of Retired Persons.

Bellair, P. E. (1997). Social interaction and community crime: Examining the importance of neighbor networks. *Criminology, 35*(4), 677.

Boisjoly, J., Duncan, G. J., & Hofferth, S. (1995). Access to social capital. *Journal of Family Issues, 16*(5), 609–631.

Braithwaite, J. (1989). *Crime, shame and reintegration*. Cambridge, England: Cambridge University Press.

Breton, M. (1995). The potential for social action in groups. *Social Work with Groups, 18*(2/3), 5–13.

Buffum, W. E., & MacNair, R. H. (Eds.). (1994). Commitment to social action: Introduction. *Journal of Community Practice* (special issue), *1*(2).

Chamlin, M. B., & Cochran, J. K. (1997). Social altruism and crime. *Criminology, 35*(2), 203–227.

Checkoway, B. (1995). Six strategies of community change. *Community Development Journal, 30*(1), 2–20.

Cohen, M. B., & Wagner, D. C. (1992). Acting on their own behalf: Affiliation and political mobilization among homeless people. *Journal of Sociology and Social Welfare, 19*(4), 21–40.

Cox, E. O. (1991). The critical role of social action in empowerment oriented groups. *Social Work with Groups, 14*(3/4), 77–90.

Cullen, F. T. (1994). Social support as an organizing concept for criminology. *Justice Quarterly, 11*, 527–559.

Delgado, J. R., & Rose, M. K. (1994). Caregiver constellations: Caring for persons with AIDS. *Journal of Gay and Lesbian Social Services, 1*(1), 1–14.

Di Blasio, F. A. (1993). The role of social workers' religious beliefs in helping family members forgive. *Families in Society, 74*(3), 163–170.

Di Blasio, F. A., & Proctor, J. H. (1993). Therapists and the clinical use of forgiveness. *American Journal of Family Therapy, 21*(2), 175–184.

Elliott, O. (1993). Social work and social development: Towards an integrative model for social work practice. *International Social Work, 36*(1), 21–36.

Else, J. F., & Raheim, S. (1992). AFDC clients as entrepreneurs. *Public Welfare, 50*(4), 36–41.

Fairbairn, B., Bold, J., Fulton, M., Ketilson, L. H., & Ish, D. (1991). *Cooperatives and community development: Economics in social perspective*. Saskatoon, SK: University of Saskatchewan.

Fisher, R. (1994). *Let the people decide: Neighbourhood organizing in America*. New York: Twayne.

Fort, R., & Associates. (1990). *Spices of life: A well being handbook for older Americans*. Washington, DC: Center for Responsive Law.

Franklin, D. L. (1990). The cycles of social work practice: Social action vs. individual interest. *Journal of Progressive Human Services, 1*(2), 59–80.

Freedman, M. (1993). *The kindness of strangers: Adult mentors, urban youth, and the new voluntarism*. San Francisco: Jossey-Bass.

From sandals to suits: Microlending and the microcredit summit. (1997, February 1). *The Economist, 342*, 75.

Fulton, M. (Ed.) (1989). *Capital formation in cooperatives: Social and economic considerations*. Saskatoon, SK: University of Saskatchewan.

Galaway, B., & Hudson, J. (Eds.). (1994). *Community economic development: Perspectives on policy and research*. Toronto: Thompson Educational Publishing.

Homan, M. S. (1994). *Promoting community change: Making it happen in the real world*. Pacific Grove, CA: Brooks/Cole.

Kabadaki, K. (1995). Rural African women and development. *Social Development Issues, 16*(2), 23–35.

Keenan, L. D., Dyer, E., Morita, L., & Shaskey-Setright, C. (1990). Toward an understanding of mentoring in rural communities. *Human Services in the Rural Environment, 14*(2), 11–18.

Kiam, R., Green, C., & Pomeroy, E. (1997). *Families empowering families through community partnerships*. Orlando, FL: School of Social Work, University of Central Florida.

Maher, T. F. (1992). The withering of community life and the growth of emotional disorders. *Journal of Sociology and Social Welfare, 19*(2), 125–146.

Mandros, J., & Wilson, S. (1994). *Organizing for power and empowerment*. New York: Columbia University Press.

Mech, E. V., Pryde, J. A., & Rycraft, J. R. (1995). Mentors for adolescents in foster care. *Child and Adolescent Social Work Journal, 12*(4), 317–328.

Meenaghan, T. M., & Gibbons, W. E. (1998). *Generalist practice and skills in larger systems*. Chicago: Lyceum.

Memmott, J. L. (1993). Models of helping and coping: A field experiment with natural and professional helpers. *Social Work Research and Abstracts, 29*(3), 11–21.

Messner, S. F., & Rosenfeld, R. (1994). *Crime and the American dream*. Belmont, CA: Wadsworth.

Midgley, J. (1993). Promoting a development focus in the community organization curriculum: Relevance of the African experience. *Journal of Work Education, 29*(3), 269–278.

Midgley, J. (1995). *Social development: The development perspective in social welfare*. London, England: Sage.

Midgley, J. (Ed.). (1996). Social work and economic development. *International Social Work, 39*(1), 5–12.

Morin, R., & Balz, D. (1996, January 28). Americans losing trust in each other and institutions. *The Washington Post*, pp. A1, A6.

Norell, D., & Walz, T. (1994). Reflections from the field toward a theory and practice of reconciliation in ethnic conflict resolution. *Social Development Issues, 16*(2), 99–111.

Patterson, S. L., Memmott, J. L., Brennan, E. M., & Germain, C. B. (1992). Patterns of natural helping in rural areas: Implications for social work research. *Social Work Research and Abstracts, 28*(3), 11–21.

Putnam, R. D. (1993). The prosperous community: Social capital and public life. *The American Prospect, 13*(spring), 35–42.

Quarter, J. (1992). *Canada's social economy: Cooperatives, non-profits, and other community enterprises.* Toronto: James Lorimer.

Raheim, S. (1996). Micro-enterprise as an approach for promoting economic development in social work: Lessons from the Self-employment Investment Demonstration. *International Social Work, 39*(1), 69–82.

Raheim, S., & Bolden, J. (1995). Economic empowerment of low-income women through self-employment programs. *Affilia, 10*(2), 138–154.

Rosemond, J. K. (1996, March). Volunteering for kids: Help your children learn that service—not self-interest—holds our world together. *The Rotarian,* pp. 16–17.

Schondel, C., Boehm, K., Rose, J., & Marlow, A. (1995). Adolescent volunteers: An untapped resource in the delivery of adolescent preventive health care. *Youth and Society, 27*(2), 123–135.

Schwartz, B. (1993). Why altruism is impossible . . . and ubiquitous. *Social Service Review, 30*(1), 314–343.

Swenson, C. R. (1994). Clinical practice and the decline of community. *Journal of Teaching in Social Work, 10*(1/2), 195–212.

Tower, K. D. (1994). Consumer centered social work practice: Restoring client self-determination. *Social Work, 39*(2), 191–196.

Tropman, J. E. (1997). *Successful community leadership: A working guide.* Washington, DC: NASW.

Vorrath, H. H., & Bendtro, L. K. (1985). *Positive peer culture* (2nd ed.). Chicago: Adline de Gruyter.

Wakefield, J. C. (1993). Is altruism part of human nature? Toward a theoretical foundation for the helping professions. *Social Service Review, 67*(3), 406–458.

Weiss, J. O. (1993). Genetic disorders: Support groups and advocacy. *Families in Society, 79*(4), 213–220.

Weil, M. (1997). *Community practice.* Binghampton, NY: Haworth Press.

Wharf, B., & Clague, M. (Eds.). (1997). *Community organizing: Canadian experiences.* Toronto: Oxford University Press.

Woliver, L. R. (1993). *From outrage to action: The politics of grass-roots dissent.* Urbana, IL: University of Illinois Press.

Zippay, A. (1995). Expanding employment skills and social networks among teen mothers: A case study of a mentor program. *Child and Adolescent Social Work Journal, 12*(1), 51–69.

Teamwork for Social Work Practice

CHAPTER PREVIEW

The capacity to operate as a productive member of a team is an important social work practice skill. You will need this skill when, in the role of broker (Chapters 11 and 13), you link clients with various services that they require but you cannot supply. Moreover, a service you are able to offer—such as the care of children away from their homes—may require you to become part of a team in order to ensure effective service delivery.

In this chapter, we will consider:

- teamwork as a problem-solving process
- intraprofessional, interdisciplinary, and natural helper teams
- obstacles to effective teamwork
- difficulties due to competition among team members
- difficulties due to different professional or agency cultures
- the relationship between teamwork and advocacy
- skills for working on a team with natural helpers
- some disadvantages of teams, including the negative client impacts of dysfunctional teams, the relatively high costs of teams, and the possibility that teams will serve professional rather than client interest

In Reading 16-1, John Compher identifies some of the harmful consequences for individuals and families when social workers from different agencies do not work effectively as a team.

THE PROBLEM-SOLVING APPROACH TO TEAMWORK

Teamwork as a Resource

Teamwork involves the cooperative effort of an organized group to achieve a common goal. The purpose of coming together in a team is to use the different capacities brought by team members in order to expand the knowledge and range of skills available to the client in problem solving. If they maintain this problem-solving focus, team members are able to communicate around the defined task. They must work out their own problems of communication and relationship so as to offer the client the most effective help possible.

If you conclude that you cannot offer all the service a client needs or wants, what do you do? First, you should obtain your supervisor's suggestions as to where you and the client might turn for help. Another important step is to talk with the client. You may describe outside services as a necessity in light of the problem, the objectives, and the limits on your service—for instance, by telling parents who need to place a child about foster home services and what they involve—or as a topic for discussion and decision making with the client; for example, you may say that your assessment of the situation might benefit if the client can talk with a psychiatrist on the agency staff.

We suggest that you ask clients whether they want to participate in team meetings and planning or whether they prefer you to take on this role. Practitioners working as a team sometimes develop a pattern of meeting without the client to pool their knowledge of the problem and to decide how to proceed; further, professionals talk differently when clients are not present (Sands, 1994). Sometimes clients are told about this meeting, and sometimes they are not. We think clients should be actively involved in considering how different professionals can be of help and told about all relevant professional consultations (Saltz & Schaefer, 1996). We much prefer to offer clients the opportunity to participate in the deliberations with the other professionals so that they may speak for themselves (Williams, 1988).

Involving Clients in Teams

Before approaching another agency, talk with the client about what it can offer, how it may be used, and what information will need to be shared. Gang members may have a number of concerns if an outreach worker suggests to a street gang that an organized agency could offer a meeting place and opportunities for recreation. What will the worker tell the agency about the gang members? Will the agency admit them if it knows their behavioral history? Will the agency try to control them? The parents of an angry, acting-out daughter may have similar questions if a worker suggests foster home placement as a temporary measure to help both child and parents think things out. Will the foster parents need to be told that the girl steals? What will the foster parents expect of them? Under what conditions will they be able to see their daughter? To take her home? How can foster parents help when they, her own parents, can not? You and the client will need to discuss how the new service will be contacted and involved in the client's affairs; expectations and requirements of the new service will be discussed and understood. You will consider what information about the client is to be shared. It is usually helpful to ask clients what they think the agency should be told about them.

The rule of thumb is that you provide team members with the information they need in order to work toward solution of the problem in the way the client and you have decided. Sharing information with others is not a simple issue. We must always consider how the other person will use the information. For instance, placing children in foster homes involves difficult decisions: What should foster parents be told about the children and about the natural parents? We need to present clients in a positive light, but how much information can be kept secret when foster parents and children live intimately as a family? We must develop an answer in each particular case. It is essential, however, to keep the client aware of what is being shared and why. Whenever possible, involve the client directly in the sharing. In planning foster care placement, for example, the birth parents and foster parents may meet to exchange information.

A case conference is very useful for joint planning and monitoring when more than one worker is involved with the same client system. Clients should be told about these conferences and their outcomes or invited to participate. You and your clients should consider these questions:

1. Will attending the conference help clients in their analysis of the problem?

2. Will it help give clients a sense of being in control of their own destiny?

3. Will clients feel overwhelmed by the professionals and by the problems identified in the situation?

4. Will the decisions at the conference demand specific behavior of the clients or relate primarily to agency policies and the parameters of service?

5. Is it possible for the clients to provide meaningful input to the conference?

The Team Leader

If more than one agency or professional is involved with the same client, you will need at least one face-to-face planning session, in order to work together successfully. This meeting is essential; lack of time is not an adequate excuse. Letters and telephone calls are not a satisfactory alternative.

In each case conference, someone is appointed leader, with responsibility:

- for seeing that all agencies and persons involved are included in the conference
- for defining the purpose and focus of the conference
- for seeing that everyone present is heard
- for clarifying the plan of action—who is to do what and when
- for helping to resolve any conflicts

The conference should result in group acceptance of the part each agency is to play; the conclusions of the conference are recorded. Everyone receives a copy of the plan and has a chance to correct it. Once the corrected plan has been adopted, each agency has a responsibility to follow through on it. The leader monitors implementation of the plan by each agency and thus becomes the captain of the service team. Who is to serve in this role and how that person is to be selected should be decided before the team begins the action phase of the work with the client. The team leader is granted power and authority and must be willing to use them responsibly. Difficult working relationships among the members of the team must be approached as problems to be solved and worked through to some acceptable conclusion; otherwise, they will distort the team's relationship to the client (Fargason, Barnes, Schneider, & Galloway, 1994; Sands, Stafford, & McClelland, 1990; Sessa, 1996).

Types of Teams

You will be working on various types of teams (Exhibit 16–1). We often think of interdisciplinary teams, such as when members of different profes-sions in a hospital meet to coordinate services for a client (Poulin, Walter, & Walker, 1994), or of teams consisting of members of the same profession, as when social workers representing different agencies meet to coordinate services to a family. Exhibit 16–1 identifies two additional types of teams: (1) the Type E team, in which you work with natural helpers or paraprofessionals within your own agency—for example, working with foster parents, with agency volunteers, or with mental health consumers as peer service providers (Solomon & Draine, 1996); and (2) the Type F team in which you collaborate with natural helpers outside your agency, including self-help or mutual aid groups (Chapter 14). The emergence of thousands of mutual aid groups in this country creates an exceptional opportunity for collaboration. In this chapter, we will consider:

- how to function as a member of interdisciplinary (Type A and B) and multidisciplinary (Type C and D) teams
- how to work with natural helpers both within and outside your agency (Type E and F teams)
- problems of competition and differing professional and agency cultures

EXHIBIT 16–1 Typology of Teams

	Within your organization (intraagency)	With another organization (interagency)
Social work team	Type A *Example:* Foster care worker and adoption worker from the same agency work together to develop and implement permanent plan for child in foster care	Type B *Example:* Child protection worker, school social worker, and probation officer meet regularly to coordinate services for a family in which youth behavior problems relate to a pattern of intrafamily abuse
Interdisciplinary team	Type C *Example:* Hospital social worker, nurse, doctor, and physical therapist meet to coordinate discharge plan for a client/patient	Type D *Example:* Public health nurse, adult protection worker, and senior citizen center worker meet to develop a protection and activity plan for a vulnerable older person living alone
Natural helper team	Type E *Example:* Social worker and foster parent develop service plan for youth in care	Type F *Example:* Social worker and Parent Anonymous mutual aid group work to provide mutual aid and support to parents who, under stress, may abuse their children.

- methods of effective planning and sharing as a team member

INTRAPROFESSIONAL AND INTERDISCIPLINARY TEAMS

For much of its history, social work has been concerned about the fragmentation of helping services. There have been periodic efforts to establish methods of collaboration between the various community agencies. In the early 1900s, with Dr. Cabot's employment of social workers in the hospital setting, collaboration across professional lines became a pressing problem. Since then, relatively little progress has been made in understanding how professionals work together. However, without effective teamwork, clients and families in the social service system are caught in a nightmarish fragmentation of care, as John Compher points out (Reading 16-1). They face the burden of resolving professional conflicts, reconciling incongruities, and acting on contradictory advice.

Obstacles to Effective Teamwork

A man crossing the street was hit by a truck. When passers-by rushed over to help, they saw the man crawling away as fast as he could, on hands and one knee, dragging one leg helplessly. They said, "Where are you going? Don't you realize you've just been hit by a truck. You need help." The man replied, "Please leave me alone. I don't want to get involved." Like the man, social workers are often reluctant to get involved in teamwork and interdisciplinary collaboration. However, collaboration in service provision is essential to your effectiveness and can be a satisfying experience (Poulin et al., 1994). Why is it, then, that we have such trouble in working across professional lines? Let's look at some of the obstacles.

The myth of good intentions. Social workers sometimes assume that a spirit of cooperation is enough to ensure effective teamwork. If we are friendly, outgoing, and thoughtful of others, surely good interdisciplinary collaboration must follow? This rests on two erroneous notions: (1) that getting along with others is easy for anyone and is not a professional skill; and (2) that teamwork rests totally on personality variables and thus no specific knowledge or skills are required. Personality

is certainly relevant, but we are lost if we reduce the collaborative process to its psychological dimensions. Teamwork skills must be learned and refined.

There is, however, one important psychological factor: the tendency to evaluate difference in terms of right and wrong. Rather than accepting that two opinions may be different but of equal validity, we tend to assume that one must be preferable to the other. However, members of a helping team must be open to difference of opinion, comfortable with conflict, and willing to enter into negotiations to resolve the differences or to accept the legitimacy of different views.

Helplessness in the face of authority. In almost all host settings—that is, environments, such as schools and hospitals, in which social work is not the dominant profession—social workers complain of feeling helpless in the face of the authority of another profession (Dane & Simon, 1991); Exhibit 16–2 provides an example. The central message in such complaints is: "There is nothing we can do to influence the course of things when we have such limited power." We must come to grips with our conception of power and authority if we are to work collaboratively.

Remember that there are two types of authority—the authority of position and the authority of competence. The authority of competence is granted us by our colleagues, with whom we interact each day. Thus, when we see a colleague as having more authority than we do, we have given that person a part of this authority. If we are to be effective, all professionals need power and authority—the power and authority to help. Thus, while granting to other professionals the authority necessary to carry out their responsibilities, we must retain the authority that we need to carry out our job. One reason social workers see ourselves as powerless may be, paradoxically, that we want to be omnipotent. If we cannot solve a problem that has plagued people for a generation, we feel that we are failures. Our expectations need to be more realistic.

Professional boundaries. Professionals on a helping team will have certain areas of overlapping competence, certain tasks that either could do. These areas can be effectively handled by negotiation around individual situations. Otherwise, conflict over who does what may cause bitter feelings and deter collaboration. Professionals tend to see their turf as all-encompassing, and to consign other professions to peripheral roles. Social

---

EXHIBIT 16-2 | **Resistant Team Members**

The social worker is part of the facility's multidisciplinary team at a long-term care facility.

The client is a 75-year-old woman. Her diagnosis includes: schizophrenia (delusions and paranoia), dementia, and Parkinson's disease. The physical assessment reveals: ambulates and transfers independently, hearing and vision is good. The mental functioning and psychological assessment reveals: alert, oriented to person and place, poor cognition and perception, paranoid with new people, occasional outbursts/screaming, occasionally will exhibit aggressive hitting-out behavior when feeling threatened, and sings when anxious. Her social skills are limited to one-on-one interaction (loves to talk about clothing); she becomes agitated and anxious in groups. Her verbal skills are limited. Of her six siblings; only one visits occasionally.

The client began to experience problems as a teenager. Her mother died when she was 21, and she lived in group homes until admission. She has worked in a sewing room and in a cafe.

She was admitted on September 22 for a probationary six-month trial (because of behavior problems). The first care conference was held in December. The social worker made the following recommendations: use gentle calm approach; let client make the first move; keep voice level low; respect client's right to privacy and allow client to make decision to have her door closed; and praise client regarding appearance and behavior. Shortly after the care conference, the social worker made these observations:

1. Her recommendations had not been included on care plan. The social worker spoke to Head Nurse, who said it was not necessary to include these recommendations as all staff are aware of the approach to use with clients.

2. Staff continue to leave client's door open and enter without knocking.

---

workers are especially inclined to behave in this way, because of the poorly defined boundaries of the profession. At the other extreme, some professionals insist that any member of the staff can deal effectively with any problems. We need to work on defining areas of overlap, as well as areas of special competence. Role negotiation is an important collaborative skill; it allows us to identify what the profession is and is not sanctioned to do, to develop appropriate ways of broadening our sanction, and to bargain for turf.

Professional differences. Knowledge of human growth and development, of the genesis of human problems, and of ecosystems is copious and sometimes contradictory. Each profession selects the knowledge that is most related to its function and that best supports its methods of practice. As a result, professions may hold different beliefs, assumptions, and expectations about human nature and human conduct. Correspondingly, each profession develops different styles of communication and methods of problem solving. Professions may also have different notions of what is an effective outcome. Thus, conflicts between professionals may arise out of these very different beliefs and expectations about how people act and how they should be treated (Sands et al., 1990). Parker (1987), for example, analyzes

the confusion that can result in an interdisciplinary team serving children in a psychiatric setting when some staff adopt a causal approach to the problems, while others operate from a systems theory framework and a relational understanding of conflict.

Professions do not need to see things from the same perspective. In difference, there is strength. If I have an accident, I do not want a physician at the scene to focus on helping me understand my pain; the physician should address the physical damage. But if my injuries are extensive and disabling, I expect the physician to explore the possibility of social work help. Physicians seek cure; social workers seek greater social competence and expanded ways of coping with social life. These goals are not incongruent, but they often generate conflict over which is of more value. In teamwork, we need to recognize the inevitability of conflicts and differences; we must learn to negotiate them, in the best interests of clients and their families (Fargason et al., 1994; Sands et al., 1990).

Competition

When helping persons, groups, or organizations work together on a common problem shared by a common client, their relationship will include both cooperative and competitive elements. There are infinite possibilities for competitive behavior: "I understand the needs of those children better than the foster mother or the teacher"; "My work is more central than yours to the client's welfare"; "My supervisor knows more than your supervisor"; "My agency is where the action really is."

The prevalence of competition in areas where it is inappropriate—and even destructive to the rational interests of the competing individuals—has been highlighted by experiments in game theory, which seeks to understand the problems of human interaction and decision making from the perspective of strategic games. To determine the conditions under which players will cooperate, it is interesting to study the nonzero-sum game. In contrast to win-lose games, where there is a winner and a loser, these games are structured so that it is absurd to play uncooperatively; a player who declines to cooperate has no chance of winning and considerable chance of losing. Nevertheless, uncooperative play frequently predominates. What's more, players tend to become even more competitive as the games go on and the negative effects of competition become more apparent.

What explains this behavior? Players can be classified into three categories: (1) maximizers, who are interested only in their own payoffs; (2) rivalists, who are interested only in defeating their partners and are not concerned with the result of the game itself; and (3) cooperators, who are interested in helping both themselves and their partners. Comparison of nonzero-sum games under conditions in which communication between players is impossible and is encouraged shows that improved communication only increases cooperation in the case of the cooperators; it fails to change the behavior of the maximizers or the rivalists (David, 1970).

In social work practice, the client is hurt by competitive relationships between practitioners. We can work toward changing a maximizer (interested only in personal gain) or a rivalist (interested only in putting others down) into a cooperator (interested in helping the client) by the kind of climates we establish. For example, we can actively recognize the importance of each team member. Too often, child care staff, who carry the daily stress of living with disturbed and deviant children, find that their efforts go unrewarded by the professional staff, who assume only they really know what the child needs. Do we support people who propose a change in a particular way of working or do we see their suggestions as something to shoot down? Do we actively encourage and explore new ideas or do we immediately come up with reasons why they won't work? Rivalists often develop skill in the use of professional language and use this ability to argue that any new proposal reflects a simple-minded misunderstanding of the underlying dynamics. This is a cheap shot; ultimately, the client bears the cost.

Competition is devastating to teamwork. Members' ego involvement with their own professional orientation may block their ability to consider the opinions or perspectives of others (Mouzakitis & Goldstein, 1985). It is essential for team members to develop relationships that foster trust and mutual respect (Mouzakitis & Goldstein, 1985). A team must also be clearly focused on its purpose—to harness the expertise of individual members in the interests of problem solving. As leader, you may need to remind the team of this common goal.

Different practitioners bring to the team different value systems, principles, frames of reference, moral language, and definitions of what makes good practice (Abramson, 1984). Strong disagreements may surface about such things as client involvement in treatment planning; conflict may arise when team members disagree about for whom to advocate (child or parent, victim or offender). In these conditions, outcomes may be borne out of compromise rather than consensus, even though all members of a group are held responsible. A study of interdisciplinary teams that experienced conflict found that members saw themselves primarily as representatives of their own discipline, rather than as members of a team (Sands et al., 1990); if they are to be effective, team members need to develop a common value base, language, and conceptual framework.

Abramson (1984) provides guidelines on enhancing collective responsibility in interdisciplinary collaboration. Team members need to establish:

- shared meanings of ethical concepts such as confidentiality and autonomy; a priority order of values and ethical principles
- a regular procedure for analyzing complex ethical dilemmas when they arise

The ethics committees of your professional organization and agency are resources for this purpose. Members who still cannot agree with the rest of the group can record their dissent and be excused from that particular case (Abramson, 1984). Team members must be informed that silent disagreement will not excuse them from their responsibility for group decisions.

A commitment to team functioning sometimes leads members to avoid disagreement at all costs. This poses the risk of groupthink, in which individuals feel less accountable for what happens and consequently becoming less thorough. One way to avoid this is to assign rotating team members to the role of devil's advocate. If decisions are routinely challenged, the chances of overlooking potential problems will be reduced.

Differences in Professional and Agency Culture

Effective collaboration requires that helping persons demonstrate respect, trust, and acceptance in their interactions. We are all taught the importance of accepting and respecting clients, but we seldom examine what this means when applied to colleagues.

An important part of all professional education and staff development is the attempt to socialize workers to their agency and their profession (Chapter 6). As you internalize the values and culture of the profession, you are constrained to work in certain ways and to take certain positions; this is the only meaningful protection clients have in using a professional's services. However, internalization can cause problems in interagency collaboration, unless we become aware of our values and culture and learn to recognize and respect the values and culture of the other agency.

The way in which you define the problems for work will be shaped by your agency, its value system, and its accepted ways of operating. You will need both to be a part of your agency and to be analytical about it; in teamwork, you cannot afford to be trapped within a particular way of approaching problems. In order to work effectively with other community services, you will need to understand the structure, values, and operating practices of those agencies. Unless understood, different conceptions of how people in need act and can be helped can result in bitter conflict.

On a team, we obtain an intimate view of our colleagues. The questionable competence of a team member's performance can be a very touchy issue, especially

if that person has more power and authority (Abramson, 1984). Many social workers stress the need for skill building in this area. All participants need to understand the basics of effective teamwork; it does little good for one profession to strive for an atmosphere of mutual respect if other professions assume roles of self-appointed authority. The smoothness with which a team functions will reflect the degree to which the power base of the institution supports the team process (Nason, 1983). This support can be demonstrated by trainings in group problem solving and team building.

Teamwork and Advocacy

Exhibit 16–3 illustrates some of the challenges of teamwork. The social worker on an interdisciplinary (Type C) team feels caught between the views of the team and the view of the client about an appropriate discharge plan; dilemmas of this type are common on interdisciplinary teams (Abramson, Donnelly, King, & Mailick, 1993). What do you think this worker should do? What is her obligation to the client? How might she respond to her team? Mailick and Ashley (1981) discuss conflict between advocacy and teamwork and offer three guidelines for integrating these aspects of social work practice:

1. Be comfortable with the area of competency that you bring to the team. Recognize that all team members bring valuable competencies and that no team member is omnipotent. Advocate on behalf of clients within your area of competence.

2. Time advocacy carefully. Set priorities to guide decisions as to which issues will be deferred and which you will fight for. This will require political acumen.

3. Learn how to advocate. As in other settings, an important skill is the ability to present a well-reasoned position without anger or attacking other positions.

NATURAL HELPER TEAMS

You will also be working with natural helper (paraprofessional) teams. Two situations may be distinguished: (1) collaboration within your own agency with, for instance, volunteers, child care workers, and foster parents, all of whom bring expertise and make unique contributions to the service plan; and (2) collaboration

---

EXHIBIT 16–3 Disagreements Regarding Discharge Planning

Tom, a 22-year-old African American, entered the Regional Treatment Center about six months ago, through a district court commitment for mental illness. At the time of hospitalization, Tom was in a decompensated state, with significant disorganization of thought. Early treatment was complicated by difficulties in adjusting medications, with severe side effects. Tom is consistent in denying the mental illness and will either state no memory of dysfunctional behavior or offer a different interpretation of events. Tom's family support is strong. The family includes the patient's mother, an infant grandchild in her care, and an adult daughter who lives outside of this home. The treatment team perceives the family as mistrustful; their interactions with team members have been abrupt and conflict-filled. Discharge planning was underway at the time the case was assigned to me.

Tom's condition is considered stabilized. He is participating in selected group programs, his mood is generally consonant with the situation, his thinking is organized and lucid, and he is responsible in providing for his basic needs. Tom has been unable to

specify goals beyond his desire to leave the treatment center. He is compliant with the medication, but verbalizes no insight into its necessity or benefits. He will talk about undesirable side effects, which he agrees have been worse in the past. Tom has had no significant experience with independent living. The team is recommending discharge to a group home, because of Tom's history of poor medication compliance and need for monitoring for side effects. Tom is in agreement with discharge but disagrees with the team's plan.

I am responsible for implementation of the discharge plan and have had four interviews with Tom on the subject of discharge. Tom expressed many negative ideas about group homes. He agreed to visit a group home to expand his information and clarify perceptions about group homes; the visit seemed to reduce Tom's apprehensions but his determination to return to his mother's home did not change. The significant disagreement regarding discharge planning is producing conflict and alienation between the treatment team and Tom and his family.

Source: Paulette Anderson, MSW student, University of Minnesota School of Social Work, Minneapolis.

---

with natural helpers within the community, including members of clients' informal social support networks and mutual aid or self-help groups (Chapter 14).

All of the ideas we discussed about interdisciplinary and intraprofessional teams apply to work with a natural helper team. Working with these teams is difficult for some social workers, however, because it involves sharing power and authority with other team members (Hazel, 1989; Hazel & Fenyo, 1993; Blüml et al., 1989). A team is a task-centered group; your job as the facilitator will be to assist the team to come to a decision and to carry it out. Review the material in Exhibit 11–6 on helping a group reach a decision.

Guidelines for working cooperatively with natural helper teams are provided in Exhibit 16–4. Let's apply these principles to a situation involving a social worker and a foster parent team. After six months in a foster home, where she was placed because of sexual assaults by her stepfather, 16-year-old Rose is making a good adjustment. Recently, however, she has been showing signs of depression and withdrawal. A psychologist has recommended family therapy with her and the foster parents. The foster parents want therapy for Rose but believe family therapy with them is unnecessary. How would you handle this situation with your team members—the foster parents? Would you expect them

---

EXHIBIT 16–4 Facilitating a Natural Helper Team

Here are some principles to guide your work with natural helper teams:
1. Recognize differing expertise.
2. Share all information.
3. Involve all team members in all phases of planning.
4. Allow team members to express differing opinions.
5. Discuss differences of opinion, and negotiate action plans.
6. Expect responsible behavior from all team members.
7. Discuss performance problems openly.

to undergo therapy with Rose and attempt to enforce this as a condition of their service? If not, how would you deal with the psychologist?

In our opinion, the psychologist's request that the foster parents undergo therapy with Rose was inappropriate; we should not expect members of a service team to enter into therapy with their clients. Members of a team can be expected to consider how suggestions from other professionals can be incorporated into their work with clients; this is consultation, not therapy. Further, if there are performance problems on the part of a team member, discuss them openly as part of a team meeting and develop a plan for their resolution.

Here's another example. Jack, age 16, has been in foster family care for about two months and is making a reasonably good adjustment. Jack's mother, whom he sees irregularly, promised to visit him over the weekend. On Thursday, she telephoned to say she would not be able to visit. On Friday, Jack skipped school. The social worker believes that Jack skipped school because of his disappointment about his mother's not visiting and that no disciplinary action is necessary. The foster parents, however, have told Jack that he must spend all day Saturday in the house studying. As the social worker, how would you address this difference? To what extent does the notion of differing expertise play a role in your decision? Do you respect the decision of your team member or overrule it?

In our opinion, the social worker should probably respect the team members' decision; being grounded for a day and required to study does not seem an unreasonable response to skipping school for a day. Alternative ways to handle disappointment might become the focus of some immediate work with Jack. In a team meeting, you might also discuss your different opinion and try to negotiate an agreement with the foster parents about how this type of problem will be dealt with in the future.

In work with natural helper teams, it is very important to respect the team members' expertise. As Exhibit 16–5 argues, the work done by foster and adoptive parents is likely to be more helpful to children than the work done by professionals. The same may be said for child care staff, volunteers, and clients' neighbors and family members. Your role as a professional will be largely to support and assist the natural helper and to assist the client in making use of the natural

helper, rather than to provide interventive services yourself.

DISADVANTAGES OF TEAMWORK

You need to consider certain disadvantages and risks before you decide to use a team. A poorly functioning team in which differences among the professionals remain unresolved may be destructive rather than helpful for the client (Huslage & Stein, 1985; Parker, 1987). If there are legitimate differences of view to be resolved, a meeting for that purpose may be necessary. Another disadvantage is that clients are often excluded from team meetings. This is inconsistent with social work practice; the social worker should ensure that the client is present at the team meeting, or at least has the opportunity to be present. As a minimum, the client must be fully informed of the team meeting and a mechanism for the input of client views into team decision making must be established.

Cost is another consideration. Team meetings requiring several professionals represent a considerable expenditure of resources (Poulin et al., 1994). For example, a case conference that involves five professionals meeting for two hours (not to mention travel time) consumes the equivalent of more than a workday; this time might have otherwise been available to provide direct services to clients. During a field placement in a child protection agency in a rural county, a student observed that child protection teams—consisting of a social worker from social services, a police officer, a public health nurse, and a school official—spent more time talking among themselves than interacting with the family about the allegations of child abuse or neglect. You will need to evaluate carefully whether the benefits of a team meeting justify the costs. If the function is coordination of services, for example, you should consider whether careful case management would be more efficient (Kane, 1982). Despite frequent claims that geriatric interdisciplinary teams provide superior care, there have been few studies of their effectiveness (Schmitt, Farrell, & Heinemann, 1988).

Finally, team meetings can be used to meet the needs of professionals, rather than clients (Sands et al., 1990), as Exhibit 16–6 wryly illustrates. Going to meetings and talking with colleagues is sometimes easier—and even more enjoyable—than the hard work of assisting clients

| EXHIBIT 16-5 | Helping Foster and Adoptive Children |

There is often an unnecessary, irrelevant and counterproductive boundary between therapist, caseworkers and the family. Many traditional interventions focus in one of two directions: one, individual psychotherapy of the child with token consultation to the parents; and two, family therapy that has a "submerged" goal of smoking out problems in the parents or in their marriage. In the former case, the oft-times well-intended therapist unwittingly undermines the placement through efforts at forming an exclusive "special relationship" with the child. Involvement with the parents is reduced to informing them about the highlights of therapeutic progress. In the latter case (in family therapy), treatment is directed away from the problem child and onto the parents (foster/adoptive) as the core of the problem. With disturbed children such approaches are myopic and amount to a "prescription of failure." We have often heard, much to our chagrin, that psychotherapy was successful right up to the time that the placement failed—a failure in fact which is laid on the already hunched shoulders of the beleaguered parents.

Overanalyzing of the parents and solo treatment of the child are hazardous in the special situation of disturbed foster and adoptive children. Faced with the task of parenting and treating the formerly maltreated child, it is critical that all forces come together. The inherent differences and distrust that often underlie the relationships between and among the family, agencies and processionals must be put aside.

We have found that a therapeutic team comprised of mental health professional, family, caseworker and school personnel—all striving with unified goals—has great synergistic power. That is, their helping impact is greater than the sum of individual parts. In a collaborative approach, they are less apt to be "split" apart from each other by the child's attempts to ally with some and to reject others. The acknowledgement and support of members of the team can inflate deflated parents, offer support and advice, and, in a sense, inoculate them against "imported pathology."

THE FAMILY AS PRIMARY AGENT OF CHANGE

There is not a school teacher, nor a therapist, nor a friendly neighbor, nor any other well-intended individual that can make the difference in the disturbed child's life the way his family can. (In many instances this is the foster and adoptive family. However, sometimes this may also involve the biological family, in situations where they are still an active part of the child's life.) While many individuals can have a positive place in the child's world, the changes each can make are at times secondary. It is the moment-by-moment, interaction-by-interaction, day-to-day struggles that primarily lead to the building of bonds, the mitigation of past injuries and abuses and the re-socialization of the child. Given the importance of the family—foster or adoptive—it is mandatory that they be supported, nurtured, respected and recognized for their primary role in treatment of the child.

From *Troubled transplants* by R. T. Delaney and F. R. Kunstal. Copyright © 1993 Wooden Barns Publishing Company. Reprinted with permission.

with problems. An even more insidious practice is to use team meetings as a means of protecting professional turf. You may, of course, need meetings to work out professional differences; the purpose of these meetings, however, must be explicit and they should not be disguised as a client service.

We suggest asking these questions before encouraging a team meeting:

1. Is the purpose for the meeting clear?
2. Can all the participants contribute to the purpose?
3. Can the purpose be accomplished equally in some less labor-intensive—and thus more efficient—way?

CHAPTER SUMMARY

In this chapter, we have discussed teamwork as a means of offering the client help in problem solving. You may be working with teams drawn from within your agency, interagency teams, interdisciplinary teams, and teams with natural helpers and mutual aid groups. If possible, clients should be involved as direct participants in teams and team decision making. As a minimum, clients must be fully informed of the reasons for team meetings, so that they have an opportunity to raise matters for discussion, and fully informed of the results of meetings.

EXHIBIT 16-6 Meetings to Avoid Work

Dilbert cartoon by Scott Adams © 1994 United Features Syndicate, Inc. Reprinted by permission.

Obstacles to effective teamwork include the misguided belief that a spirit of cooperation is all that is required, a feeling of helplessness when the team includes a person of considerable power or authority, disputes about professional boundaries, and clashes between the values and assumptions of different professions. Competition among team members must be minimized if the team is to serve clients effectively. Differing professional and agency cultures will impact on the effectiveness of the team. Finally, the expectation of loyalty to team decisions may limit your ability to serve as an effective client advocate.

Much of your work will involve coordinating natural helper teams. Natural helpers include foster parents, volunteers, clients' neighbors and friends, and mutual aid groups. Do not think of these helpers as a source of competition or threat. They may be the primary service providers, while you provide support and assistance to them.

Finally, you need to be aware of certain disadvantages of teamwork, including the harmful effects of dysfunctional teams, the high cost of teams, and the possibility that teams may exist to serve the needs of professionals rather than clients. We suggest that you always ask whether the purpose for which the team was created can be accomplished equally well or more efficiently by good case management.

A LOOK FORWARD

In Reading 16-1, John Compher identifies four dysfunctional patterns of interaction among agencies and social workers that may interfere with family work: (1) the blind system, in which agencies do not know what the other agencies are doing; (2) the conflicted system, characterized by battles among agencies that set up divergent goals for the client; (3) the rejecting system, in which agencies are focused on their own operational needs, rather than clients' needs; and (4) the underdeveloped system, which can be strengthened by providing clients with careful, coordinated referrals.

In Chapter 17, we examine ways of evaluating practice. How can you and your client evaluate the interventions you are using? We will also consider program-level evaluations and, because records are an important evaluation tool, we will take another look at record keeping. In chapter 18, we discuss the process of ending service with clients and, in Chapter 19, we offer some parting comments on burnout.

READING 16-1 *The Dance beyond the Family System**

John Victor Compher

The bold admonition to recast the roles of the family therapist and the social worker in a way that makes it "difficult [for one] to separate the specialist in 'emotional' problems from the specialist in 'community' problems" is not a new challenge (Auerswald, 1968; Hoffman & Long, 1969). Systems thinking has revolutionized clinical therapy, creating a flourishing literature and numerous family-therapy schools. However, the broader vision of the family in community and the systematic entanglements of these multisystems have produced only a sparse (yet growing) body of knowledge. The family's dependence on helping-agent networks is especially evident in the child welfare realm. Family-centered services have developed as a concept and as a means to strengthen the family's internal functioning as well as the family's ability to relate

*Copyright 1987, National Association of Social Workers, Inc. from *Social Work*, vol. 32, No. 2, March–April 1987, pp. 105–108. Reprinted with permission.

effectively to powerful public agents (Bryce & Maybanks, 1979; Hartmann & Laird, 1983).

However, social agencies (which often refer families for clinical treatment), children and family services, courts, schools, mental hospitals, and day programs often unwittingly create negatively charged triangulated relationships requiring direct and conjoint communication and case treatment planning (Carl & Jarkovie, 1983; Compher, 1984). For example, internal conflict among the helping agents of delinquency control is believed to be a contributing factor to the maintenance or exacerbation of delinquent patterns (Emerson, 1969; Miller, Baum, & McNeil, 1968; Miller, 1958). Similarly, the child's dual environments of family and school create contextual and relational dissonances that at times necessitate intervention into the adult relationships of both settings in order to promote the child's development (Aponte, 1976; Compher, 1982; Tucker & Dyson, 1976).

A full-systems therapeutic approach, therefore, widens the lens of assessment and intervention beyond the family system to the interactive patterns of the family's immediate community and service systems. The dance of the various parties is clearly observable and demonstrates that the service-community network relationships clearly have an impact on treatment outcomes. Because the dysfunctional extrafamilial processes may serve to maintain, exacerbate, or create symptomatic behaviors, it seems neither helpful nor accurate to characterize these interchanges as outgrowths of family pathology but rather to understand them as interdependent contributions.

Assessment characteristics of the interactional process of the family in community suggest at least four rather common dysfunctional modes. The blind, or dispersed, system operates in a vacuum of disengagement, abdicating responsibility and control. The conflicted interinstitutional system usually sets up a pattern of triangulation in which the family suffers setbacks. The rejecting system is characterized by ideological bias, struggles for reimbursement, or overwhelmed states of operation that create discontinuity and provoke a family's feelings of being cast about. Finally, the underdeveloped system affords the practitioner an opportunity to create optimal, reliable referrals that are coordinated through active conference work.

"BLIND" SERVICE NETWORK

The seemingly "blind" service network is composed of dispersed service entities that deal with the client in a manner that demonstrates little or no knowledge of others' involvements. The client controls the information flow and finds that he or she can reduce factors that might produce change by misinforming or not informing the network of various behaviors. Some important service or monitoring parties will have very little contact with the client because they feel overwhelmed by large caseloads. The more active service participants will feel impotent and wonder why their well-intended work is not favorably influencing the client. An illusion that there is no substantial problem may also operate. The client's defense mechanisms will exploit the service network's detachment, until at some point of desperation, symptomatic behavior will escalate. In sum, the professionals have allowed their own distraction or seduction.

The O family demonstrates classic roles of child and spouse abuse; the suspicious alcoholic husband, after gaining control over his parenting conduct, became increasingly prone toward violence with his wife. Mrs. O's lack of differentiation and threatened position seemed to cripple her from taking sufficient protective action for herself. Perhaps she also feared the engagement of protective services, which could remove the child. Because the father's original attack on the child had been life threatening, criminal charges led to his prosecution and to three years of reporting probation. The abused child was moved for six months to the grandparents' home in another city.

During the first year of probation, Mr. O told his probation officer and the child protective school worker that he was faithfully attending a counseling program and that he was no longer drinking. He was proud that he had two part-time jobs and that his wife was employed. His wife, however, was frightened and intimidated by him and believed that the therapy was making him worse. Indeed, on those days for which Mr. O alleged attendance, he returned home more agitated and more threatening than ever, which led Mrs. O to place a secret call to the child protective worker indicating that she was contemplating a move into a women's shelter because of her husband's direct threats.

The alarm of the child protective worker and her supervisor over the wife's fear of danger prompted an urgent case meeting with the probation officer, the therapist, the child protective worker, the supervisor, and subsequently with Mr. O. It became quite clear to all the professionals at their first meeting that indeed their own lack of communication with each other had contributed to the illusion that the client was improving. The therapist had accepted the client's cordiality and persistent denial of drinking and other problems and had agreed to hold monthly rather than weekly meetings. Until the spousal crisis occurred, the child protective worker had believed that there was little reason to be in contact with the therapist. The probation officer, with a caseload of nearly 250 clients, had not taken time to monitor the client closely or to verify his claims of keeping his appointments for treatment. In short, each of the parties had operated in a vacuum with little knowledge of the others' existence and without an understanding of each other's professional role in relation to the client family. Indeed, involvement with the family had in general been sporadic and minimal.

As a result of the case meeting, clinical therapeutic goals and service objectives were developed by the interagency representatives to include (1) strengthening the wife's status and concept of self (2) enabling the wife to be in frequent communication with the support system, (3) regular reporting by the therapist to the probation officer, (4) further psychological testing and use of a new, intensive group for battering husbands, and (5) ongoing case conferences at about six-week intervals to assess progress and further interventions, including consideration of a detoxification program and marital counseling.

Although there had been some initial concern that Mr. O might react to the professional system's tighter controls through spousal violence or threats to his wife, it became clear that instead his symptomatic behavior was for the first time decreasing. Indeed, a correlation was evident in this case between the presence of acting out behavior on the part of the family and the professional community's ability to coordinate its own communication and intervention in an effective way.

CONFLICTED SERVICE NETWORK

The conflicted service network is characterized by overt, often intransigent, ideological battles and battles among service agencies in relation to the client. The client will experience varying degrees of triangulation by the parties who direct or support the client toward divergent goals. The splitting of service participants among themselves or by the client effectively eliminates the achievement of change and maintains the status quo. Differing values concerning maintaining family life versus placement or institutionalization frequently arouse such systemic conflict. In court-related matters, such as child-protection cases, an adversarial position may be unavoidable. When opposing parties are in a fiscal contract with each other, higher executive intervention may help resolve problems. If problem-solving efforts fail, a new and more compatible configuration of service participants will be necessary, along with a period of time to overcome setbacks and psychological damage to the family.

In the W family case, a single-parent mother demonstrated behaviors toward her son that fluctuated from angry physical assaults to extreme disengagement and depression. Mrs. W demanded that the boy, age 13, change his problem-filled behaviors—in this instance, stealing at home, acting out at school, and running away. Her practice of overwhelming him with orders and ultimatums and punishment through withdrawal and emotional distancing contributed to the maintenance of his chaotic and volatile behaviors. For the sake of her own coping, she demanded, within the family system and service system, the absolute right to engage or disengage at will. This behavior expressed itself particularly around placement issues.

Over a period of several years, the mother, with her son intermittently in placement, participated in a number of therapeutic attempts with a range of separate therapists who were invited to operate quite independently with the family, apart from the service and legal network. The mother sought constantly to bring her son back home from placement at the times he demonstrated the most progress away from home. She asserted that because he had improved and seemed well, she could manage him. A recommendation from her therapist coupled with a plea from her attorney completed the triangulation in regard to the placement facility and the child protective agency, setting in motion a judicial system that awarded the mother custody of her child with little consideration for whether or not the mother's relationship with him had actually changed.

A systems treatment modality was then instituted to bring together service planning in the context of family treatment. The child would remain in placement while the family attended biweekly sessions. At least monthly, key service personnel or legal representatives would be brought into sessions to monitor progress and to work cooperatively, if possible, toward the timing of another reunification attempt. The approach was embraced by the family's legal representatives and the current placement social worker; the family therapist and systems case manager from the child protective agency did the choreography.

A major setback to this new and positive momentum occurred, however, when the original social worker from the placement agency left the agency and was replaced by a new and quite inexperienced worker who promoted an agenda of his own. The new worker observed the newly emerging strengths of the family. To meet his administrator's strong demands for another bed in the short-term placement center, the worker operated outside the framework of the treatment team, allying himself with the mother's and the son's desire for a highly premature placement discharge and a temporary return home. Opposing the recommendations of the therapist and child protective case manager, Mrs. W seized the opportunity for an extended visit, which set in motion again the negative dynamics, resulting in one more failed attempt by the mother to discipline her son. Higher level administrative intervention was not available, and the team sustained a prolonged and serious setback in relationship to this mother and son and the original treatment goals.

When such a split occurs in the interagency team effort, the family's original maladaptive dynamics will prevail. The family, having been challenged either through its voluntary or involuntary involvement to try new, constructive behaviors, finds that it is now able to exploit or to be exploited by the irrational dynamics of the service system that had been defined as "helper." The family's inherent difficulties are thus reinforced, making future treatment efforts all the more difficult.

REJECTION BY SERVICE SYSTEMS

When a system is first and foremost responsive to its own operational needs and unresponsive to a client's specific concerns, the client not surprisingly feels rejected. The service system may be overwhelmed with too high a volume of work or it may be anxious about the possibility of not being paid, either by the client or by the client's insurance plan. In the large public sector, considerable case turnover—for example, movement of a case from intake to a series of other specialized services or from worker to worker—disallows sufficient opportunity for meaningful relationships to develop between the counselor and client. Gaps in service may also exist during transfers of staff. These factors contribute to the maintenance of behaviors and hold the client in the system for extended periods. If the client family demonstrates considerable emotional distress, the discontinuous transactions will usually cause an escalation of problems to emergency situations as the client seeks to reengage rejecting parties or elements of the service. Poorly planned discharges from mental health institutions provide tragic examples, on a massive scale, of rejected, deteriorating

patients. Similar phenomena are occurring all too frequently with children's services, health care, aging, and other services.

In the M family's case, a single-parent mother who was a former drug abuser suffering from acquired immune deficiency syndrome (AIDS) was denied readmittance to a large metropolitan hospital because of an enormous outstanding bill that was not yet covered by medical assistance. The hospital argued that her condition was chronic, not acute, and that, although she was slowly dying, so were many other patients, including cancer patients who could not be maintained at the hospital. Further, the hospital recommended nursing home care because Ms. M was too frail to care for her own needs. No private nursing home in the city was found that would admit her, however. High-level executive intervention was needed to gain her admission into the single public nursing home facility. The employees' union then balked, refusing to provide care to her out of fear of contagion. Because she contracted pneumonia during this time, she was finally readmitted to the original hospital as an acutely ill patient.

After her pneumonia subsided, she was abruptly discharged without adequate community discharge planning and was delivered by ambulance to the yet unoccupied and unfurnished house of a supportive friend. Two days later, the newly assigned community nurse was appalled to find her in a hot, fly-infested vacant room lying near her own unemptied bedpan. Because of the acting-out behaviors exhibited by her young children in this traumatic context and allegations of child abuse from a caretaker aunt, child protective service and counseling for the family were provided.

The family's grief extended not only to the mother's misery and imminent death, but to the rejecting treatment of this modern health care system. Counseling was effective in large part because it acknowledged the service system's dysfunction as a key element of the traumatic and tragic circumstances. The practitioner intervened to help organize case conferences with hospital personnel, the community nursing system, a community-based AIDS task force, and a homemaker service. Stabilization of the turbulent system enabled the family to better focus on Ms. M's and their own needs and to appropriately grieve her death when it occurred several months later.

In summary, the rejecting nature and disarray of the original service system greatly contributed to an increase of stress and dysfunction in the M family. The original health problem was exacerbated as another family member became abusive and two of the children then tried to run away. This escalation likewise provided another signal for help by the extended family after their earlier, more rational protestations had fallen on deaf ears. An empathic professional response developed finally out of the reorganized service community. This development led to a rather rapid, yet lasting, amelioration of the problems of the extended family members. The health needs of the mother and the caretaking needs of the children were jointly resolved by the multiple professional parties, who had now begun to communicate with each other on behalf of the entire family. The formal joint meetings of the various services that were organized by the social worker provided a setting for public accountability and advocacy, which reduced the rejecting tendency of the original services.

UNDERDEVELOPED SYSTEM

It is not uncommon to discover in socially isolated families or in families new to the service system significant cultural deprivation, including an absence of key service providers. A careful therapeutic intake process that is systems-oriented will, therefore, determine the client's current range and degree of involvement within the service community. This service community may include schools, health centers, doctors, legal personnel, and religious institutions.

Because the inexperienced client may also feel insecure around professionals and be easily overwhelmed, he or she needs a good deal of support in establishing an effective network and in following through after professional contacts have begun. There is nothing more unhelpful to such a client than to refer him or her to unresponsive or inappropriate sources. It is therefore essential that the systems practitioner know the referral resources. Making a personal call, accompanying the client, or inviting the other professionals into sessions provides a clear, visible means of establishing interagency team relationships. Careful preparation, including role play and agenda settings, prepares the client for successful relationships within the network. Crisis

points may be the best times to establish the coordinated services of a network.

Ms. R, a mother in her early 20s, entered the service network involuntarily through a child protective report and investigation. Her relative isolation had been a contributing factor to her frustration and to the physical abuse of her 6-year-old son, Timmy. She was also burdened by the demands of an active 4-year-old daughter. Although she felt at first quite defensive toward the protective service agency, claiming that she was being harrassed, she responded with interest and a sense of relief when advocacy was offered around Timmy's acknowledged school problems. She had had several unsuccessful encounters with a punitive principal and was understandably distressed that Timmy was so frequently suspended from school. The school, she believed, was not dealing with Timmy or his problems, and it thus had alienated her as well. Although she was illiterate and was quite simple in her speech and manner, Ms. R was nevertheless ready to redress Timmy's school problems (with the assistance of an advocate).

The development of new and functioning relationships within the school system also provided opportunities for building trust and rapport between the client and the worker. Based on this relationship with the client, a second referral was initiated, this time to a clinical therapist and educational treatment program. In this instance, the systems worker selected a personally known source and attended the initial session to introduce the client to the new therapist and to clarify treatment goals. The clinical intake process revealed that Timmy had been conceived by a rape, which had contributed to his mother's negative, vindictive attitude toward him.

While the therapist-client relationship developed, the social worker, operating as a team member with the therapist, linked the client's family to additional services as needs were identified. These services included a day care program for the 4-year-old girl and, later, a family shelter for the mother and her children when she moved out of her own home to avoid abuse from her mate. The therapist also extended the network by arranging for an educational specialist to work with each child and for a case conference with Timmy's teacher. Joint efforts of the therapist and social worker promoted the client's emotional development and a system of tangible supports in the community. In summary, the client's isolation and abusive behaviors were mitigated through the client's engagement with an evolving supportive treatment and an evolving service community.

EXPLORING JOINT PRACTICE

From an ecological-systems perspective, the behavioral patterns of the family may be linked directly with those of the service-system providers. This linkage may be profound, particularly in cases in which the family's acting out violates social norms in a way that requires powerful interventions from society—for example, in the adult criminal justice, child welfare, juvenile justice, and mental health systems—or in cases in which a family member may be exceedingly vulnerable, as in the healthcare context. The client, as if dealing with a series of powerful parental figures after the initial intervention, must reckon with the accountable presence, for better or worse, of various service personnel. Further dysfunctional family behavior may be correlated with the patterns, often irrational, of the complex service system itself.

How well the service community network recognizes the joint involvement and influence in relationship to the family will have a great impact on treatment and service effectiveness. The blind, triangulated, and rejecting service configurations are particularly apt to invite from certain families an escalation and reinforcement of presenting difficulties, but awareness by service staff of the potential to be part of a supportive community can provide an essential context for positive change.

Finally, although there has been some cross-fertilization among the related service fields and some broadening of clinical social work roles, in particular, in recent years, the frontier that combines individual, family, and social-systems assessment and operations into a sophisticated joint practice continues to remain open for active exploration. Families with serious problems, also intertwined in the dysfunctional social web, can only benefit from such expansionary approaches.

LEARNING EXERCISES

1. Please write a one- or two-sentence definition of these key concepts, or briefly explain each one to a friend:

   blind service network
   conflicted service network
   interdisciplinary team
   intraprofessional team
   mutual aid group
   rejecting service network
   teamwork
   undeveloped service network

2. Exhibit 16–2 illustrates a problem in team performance. If you were this social worker, how would you go about resolving the problem? Present your plan using the format for service agreements introduced in Chapter 11: statement of the problem for work, objective, and action plan.

3. Reread section 1.07 of the NASW code of ethics or Section 5 of the CASW code of ethics. (We recommended that you acquire these codes in Chapter 6.) How might this apply to the use of teams?

4. A social worker made this statement to a 13-year-old youth being placed in foster family care: "Part of my job is to make sure the foster parents do what they are supposed to." What do you think may have been the reason for the statement? How might a statement such as this affect team functioning?

5. Here is a problem encountered in a natural helper team: "This foster parent reprocesses things two or three times, her phone calls are lengthy, and she rambles on. She tends to call during the evening even though there is not a specific crisis. During these discussions, I often feel emotionally exhausted." How would you handle this?

6. How would you define the problems for work in Exhibit 16–7 Are any of John Compher's dysfunctional networks relevant here? If you were working in this center, what action would you recommend to solve the problems?

EXHIBIT 16-7	Manipulative Trainees

In a Caribbean nation, young people, ages 16–25, have the opportunity to apply to a one-year occupational training program. Entrance is voluntary but, once accepted, the young people are expected to adhere to program rules. No trainee is allowed to leave the campus during school days between 8 A.M. and 5 P.M. unless there is a medical or domestic emergency at home. Any trainee wishing to go home for a weekend must apply, by 4 P.M. Wednesday, for a weekend pass. The application is to be made through the director of the residence hall to the social service department. While off campus, every trainee is expected to be in possession of a leave card, signed by the social worker. Only the social worker is authorized to grant leave.

However, many of the trainees are finding ways to manipulate the system. They go to the health services and pretend to be ill; the nurse then writes a permission to the social workers, who automatically issue a pass. Some trainees attempt to develop a relationship with the nurse, so that she will sign these pass requests regularly. Some trainees have been sending telegrams to themselves reporting a death or sickness in the family, which they then use as a basis for requesting emergency leave. Some have been attempting to develop a relationship with the gate guard, so he will permit them to come and go without passes.

Instead of applying for weekend passes on Wednesday, trainees are coming into the office in large numbers on Friday and pressuring the social workers to grant weekend leaves. Some bring letters from teachers, often fraudulent, granting permission to leave campus. If the social worker denies leave, trainees may go to the nurse or the gate guard or simply climb over the fence. Some trainees forge their social worker's name on the leave card.

REFERENCES

Abramson, M. (1984). Collective responsibility in interdisciplinary collaboration: An ethical perspective for social workers. *Social Work in Health Care, 10*(1), 35–43.

Abramson, J. S., Donnelly, J., King, M. A., & Mailick, M. D. (1993). Disagreements in discharge planning: A normative phenomenon. *Health and Social Work, 18*(1), 57–64.

Aponte, H. J. (1976). The family-school interview: An ecostructural approach. *Family Process, 15*(3), 303–311.

Auerswald, E. H. (1968). Interdisciplinary versus ecological approach. *Family Process, 7*(2), 202–215.

Blüml, H., Gudat, U., Langreuter, J., Martin, B., Schettner, H., & Schumann, M. (1989). Changing concepts of social work in foster family care. *Community Alternatives: International Journal of Family Care, 1*(1), 11–22.

Bryce, M., & Maybanks, S. (1979). *Home-based services for children and families.* Springfield, IL: Charles C. Thomas.

Carl, D., & Jarkovic, G. J. (1983). Agency triangles: Problems in agency-family relationships. *Family Process, 22*(4), 441–451.

Compher, J. V. (1982). Parent, school, child systems: Triadic assessment and intervention. *Social Casework: The Journal of Contemporary Social Work, 63*(7), 415–423.

Compher, J. V. (1984). The case conference revisited: A systems view. *Child Welfare, 63*(5), 411–418.

Dane, B. O., & Simon, B. L. (1991). Resident guests: Social workers in host settings. *Social Work, 36*(3), 208–213.

David, M. (1970). *Game theory.* New York: Basic Books.

Emerson, R. (1969). *Judging delinquents: Context and process in juvenile court.* Chicago: Aldine.

Fargason, C. A., Barnes, D., Schneider, D., & Galloway, B. W. (1994). Enhancing multi-agency collaboration in the management of child sexual abuse. *Child Abuse and Neglect, 18*(10), 859–869.

Hartman, A., & Laird, J. (1983). *Family centered social work practice.* New York: Free Press.

Hazel, N. (1989). Adolescent fostering as a community resource. *Community Alternatives: International Journal of Family Care, 1*(1), 1–10.

Hazel, N., & Fenyo, A. (1993). *Free to be myself: The development of teenage fostering.* St. Paul, MN: Human Service Associates.

Hoffman, L., & Long, L. (1969). A systems dilemma. *Family Process, 8*(3), 211–234.

Huslage, S., & Stein, F. (1985). A systems approach for the child study team. *Social Work in Education, 7*(2), 114–123.

Kane, R. A. (1982). Teams: Thoughts from the bleachers. *Health and Social Work, 7*(1), 2–4.

Mailick, M., & Ashley, A. (1981). Politics of interprofessional collaboration: Challenge to advocacy. *Social Casework: The Journal of Contemporary Social Work, 62*(3), 131–137.

Miller, W. B. (1958). Inter-institutional conflict as a major impediment to delinquency prevention. *Human Organization, 17*(3), 20–23.

Miller, W. B., Baum, R. C., & McNeil, R. (1968). Delinquency prevention and organizational relations. In S. Wheeler (Ed.), *Controlling delinquents* (pp. 61–100). New York: Wiley.

Mouzakitis, C., & Goldstein, S. (1985). A multidisciplinary approach to treating child neglect. *Social Casework: The Journal of Contemporary Social Work, 66*(4), 218–224.

Nason, F. (1983). Diagnosing the hospital team. *Social Work in Health Care, 9*(2), 25–45.

Parker, T. (1987). Dilemmas resulting from the application of extemporaneous ethics in interdisciplinary team decision making. *Family Therapy, 14*(3), 201–211.

Poulin, J. E., Walter, C. A., & Walker, J. L. (1994). Interdisciplinary team membership: A survey of gerontological social workers. *Journal of Gerontological Social Work, 22*(1/2), 93–107.

Saltz, C. C., & Schaefer, T. (1996). Interdisciplinary teams in health care: Integration of family caregivers. *Social Work in Health Care, 22*(3), 59–70.

Sands, R. G. (1994). A comparison of interprofessional and team-parent talk of an interdisciplinary team. *Social Work in Education, 16*(4), 207–219.

Sands, R. G., Stafford, J., & McClelland, M. (1990). I beg to differ: Conflict in the interdisciplinary team. *Social Work in Health Care, 14*(3), 55–72.

Schmitt, M. H., Farrell, M. P., & Heinemann, G. D. (1988). Conceptual and methodological problems in studying the effects of interdisciplinary geriatric terms. *The Gerontologist, 28*(6), 753–764.

Sessa, V. I. (1996). Using perspective talking to manage conflict and affect in teams. *Journal of Applied Behavioral Science, 32*(1), 101–115.

Solomon, P., & Draine, J. (1996). Service delivery differences between consumer and non-consumer case managers in mental health. *Research on Social Work Practice, 6*(2), 193–207.

Tucker, B. Z., & Dyson, E. (1976). The family and the school: Utilizing human resources to promote learning. *Family Process, 15*(1) 125–141.

Williams, B. C. (1988). Parents and patients: Members of an interdisciplinary team on an adolescent inpatient unit. *Clinical Social Work Journal, 16*(1), 78–91.

chapter 17

Evaluating Practice

CHAPTER PREVIEW

Evaluation is the final phase of the problem-solving process. Through evaluation, you and your client make decisions as to whether you are carrying out the service plan as intended and the objectives are being accomplished. On the basis of the evaluation, you and your client may change the problem for work, change your objectives, change the service plan, or carry out the service plan in a different way.

Social workers, along with other human service professionals, must verify the efficiency and effectiveness of services and intervention plans. Are they accomplishing their intended objectives? And at what cost of money, time, and other resources (Moore, 1995)? Evaluation may involve:

- assessing, with your clients, the efficiency and effectiveness of the intervention plan you are following
- determining whether you and your clients are carrying out your service plans as intended
- working with colleagues to assess the programs and services offered by your agency
- using knowledge generated by program evaluation to assist you and your clients in selecting effective approaches
- being vigilant for unintended consequences and taking reasonable steps to guard against harmful effects of intervention
- keeping records for use in evaluating service plans

We present a framework for thinking about program or practice evaluation.

In Reading 17-1, Robert W. Weinbach introduces single case designs as a tool for practice evaluation. In Reading 17-2, John McKnight addresses unintended negative consequences of intervention.

PROGRAM EVALUATION AND PRACTICE EVALUATION

Some social workers and schools of social work make a sharp distinction between program evaluation and practice evaluation. Program evaluation refers to efforts to measure the effectiveness or efficiency of programs, such as family counseling, case management, and foster family care. Practice evaluations are carried out by individual social workers and their clients to measure the efficiency and effectiveness of an intervention plan in relation to a specific client problem and set of objectives. Hudson and Grinnell (1989) have identified five categories of program evaluation:

1. *Needs assessment*—determining the feasibility of establishing a program.

2. *Evaluability assessment*—determining whether a program can be evaluated. The resources required by a program, the expected program activities, and the intended program results are defined, as well as the logic that links resources to activities and activities to intended results.

3. *Process analysis* (sometimes called formative evaluation)—the study of program processes; in which program interventions are monitored and measured.

4. *Outcome analysis* (sometimes called summative evaluation)—the measurement of program results, to determine program effectiveness. When combined with measurement of program costs, outcome analysis yields cost-effectiveness or cost-benefit statements. Cost-benefit studies consider a broader range of benefits than do cost-effectiveness studies.

5. *Program monitoring*—the ongoing, continuous collection and analysis of program data (about resources, activities, and results) and the reporting of program

information. Whereas process and outcome analysis may be one-time studies, monitoring is continuous; it usually involves a computer-based information system.

Evaluation is the application of scientific methods to measure both change processes and their outcomes. Evaluation procedures are the same for programs and for specific intervention plans; accordingly, a sharp distinction between program evaluation and social work practice evaluation is not warranted. Evaluation is directed toward measuring the results (dependent variables) of programs or interventions, and the nature of the interventions themselves (the independent variables), with a research design that allows the outcome to be attributed to the change processes. *Summative* evaluation is the study of program or intervention outcomes or effectiveness; *formative* evaluation is the study of program processes. Both types of evaluation occur on two levels. At the program level, social workers are asked to measure the impact and the nature of programs such as child protection, family counseling, and community development; this may be referred to as program evaluation research. At the level of individual worker-client relationships, evaluation research focuses on the nature of a particular intervention, its presumed results, and the evidence that it led to the results.

An Evaluation Model

Social workers sometimes have difficulty with the program evaluation literature because of the nomenclature. However, despite differences in terminology, the same conceptual framework can be adopted for either program or practice evaluation. Hudson and Grinnell (1989) offer a useful model (Exhibit 17–1). The structure of an evaluation—whether a program or a practice evaluation—will involve four sets of variables: inputs, activities, outputs, and outcomes.

Inputs are the resources necessary to implement the program or the intervention. At the program level, resources may include money, particular types of staff (such as licensed social workers), and, of course, clients or customers for the service. At the worker-client level, resources will include your time, skill, and access to the information and resources required by the service plan.

At the program level, activities are what agencies do to try to produce changes—in other words, the services provided, such as intake interviewing, counseling, and referral. At the worker-client level, activities are what you and your client do to implement the service plan—in other words, interventions. In this model, activities correspond to the independent variables described in research courses.

Outputs are the immediate results of the program or service plan—the objectives, in the terminology used in this book. For example, the output of a service plan designed to assist an unemployed person might be securing a job. But securing a job may also have longer-term benefits, such as increasing self-esteem, self-support, and financial independence. We refer to these longer-term benefits as outcomes. The difference between outputs and outcomes is not always clear; one distinguishing characteristic is that outputs are generally stepping stones to some further benefit, whereas outcomes provide the socially justifying reason for the intervention or program; outcomes stand on their own and do not require any further justification. For example, at the program level, an intervention designed

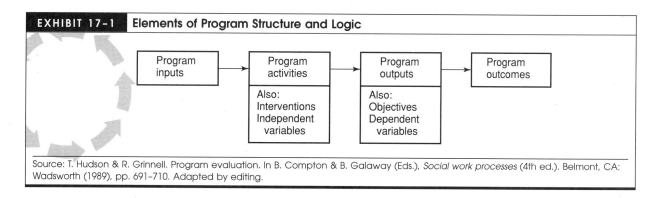

EXHIBIT 17-1 Elements of Program Structure and Logic

Program inputs → Program activities → Program outputs → Program outcomes

Program activities — Also: Interventions Independent variables

Program outputs — Also: Objectives Dependent variables

Source: T. Hudson & R. Grinnell. Program evaluation. In B. Compton & B. Galaway (Eds.), *Social work processes* (4th ed.). Belmont, CA: Wadsworth (1989), pp. 691–710. Adapted by editing.

to increase the availability of day care in a particular community might have an output of increasing the number of days of day care provided. But this may not be a sufficient justification for the program, in the absence of longer-term benefits such as providing opportunities for self-support for mothers, improved employment opportunities for parents, or improved child care for preschool children.

For example, the desired output (or objective) of the intervention plan in Exhibit 12–9 is a decision on the part of the client to proceed in one direction or another, whereas an outcome might well be an improvement in parent-child relations or stable living arrangements for the adolescent. Thus, outputs are the dependent variables or the intended result of the intervention. Note that a variable might be both independent and dependent, depending on where it lies in the causal chain of events. In our earlier example, getting a job was a dependent variable for the interventive efforts, but an independent variable in relation to increasing self-support. In Exhibit 12–9 a decision by Bonita is a dependent variable of the worker-client meetings (the interventions, or independent variables) but is an independent variable of what may follow in the planning for Bonita and Richard. In Chapter 11, we said that the objectives of intervention should be specific, concrete, and proximate. Thus, the objectives of worker-client intervention will correspond to the concept of outputs in Exhibit 17–1, although clearly these outputs will also be connected to what clients desire to permit a less stressful and more comfortable life.

The Linking Logic

Binding together the four key concepts—inputs, activities, outputs, and outcomes—is a linking logic. Why do we believe that, if the resources are provided, the activities will occur? Or that, if the activities occur, the outputs will result? Or that, if the outputs occur, the outcomes will result? For example, day care is often promoted as an intervention necessary to reduce the number of persons on public assistance, and federal financial support is often cited as a resource (input) necessary to develop day care. The linking logic, however, will need to explain why increased federal appropriations for day care will expand the number of day care facilities available for low-income families. Second, we will

need to establish how increasing day care facilities for low-income families will result in a reduction in the public assistance caseload. And, of course, we should make the further connection to some socially justifying outcome. What is the reason for believing that reducing the public assistance caseload will bring about any improvement in social conditions or the quality of life of low-income persons?

As another example, intensive family intervention programs are often promoted as means of curtailing out-of-home placement of children and youth, and professionally trained social workers are thought to be necessary to carry out such programs. In this example, the professionally trained social worker is an input, the intensive family intervention program is an activity or independent variable, and the reduction of out-of-home placement is the output or dependent variable. The linking logic would need to explain why professionally trained social workers are necessary for intensive family intervention, and why intensive family intervention will reduce out-of-home care. Again, we should also draw a connection between the output (reduction of out-of-home care) and some socially justifying outcome, such as meeting the developmental needs of children and youth. The linking logic constitutes the intervention or program theory; it explains the connections. Often, we do not think much about the linking logic but, if we take seriously our responsibilities as scholar-researcher-practitioners, we will learn to explain the linking logic more explicitly. And we will become familiar with the knowledge base that supports it.

Many of us tend to think in terms of summative program evaluation—an attempt to assess the extent to which a program is reaching its objectives and goals. While summative evaluations are useful in making judgments about the worth of a program, they have little usefulness unless the interventions used are well conceptualized and understood. Knowing that objectives are being accomplished is of little use unless we also know how they are being accomplished. Likewise, knowing that objectives are not being accomplished is not useful unless we are clear about what interventions failed to accomplish the desired objectives. For example, if we find a reduction in child abuse after a parent skills training program, we could say that a laudable goal has been accomplished. The finding is of little practical value, however, unless we clearly understand the nature of the training program that apparently led to the reduction in abuse; we cannot replicate the program unless we know what it was. Now assume that you are working with a senior citizens group toward an objective of securing more adequate police protection in their neighborhood. Even if the objective is accomplished—say, more foot patrols are assigned to the neighborhood at hours when senior citizens would like to be on the streets—the finding is of limited value and will not contribute to the knowledge base of the profession unless you can document how this goal was accomplished.

THE SOCIAL WORKER AS PRACTITIONER-RESEARCHER
Evaluation as a Client Service

As part of the client services you provide, you will be called on to be a researcher—to apply sound scientific methodology to an understanding of interventions and the measurement of results (Rosen, 1996). You and your clients will ask: What are our activities (independent variables)? What are our goals (dependent variables)? And how can we relate activities to the goals? In Chapter 2, we noted that we test our assumptive knowledge, contribute to knowledge development for the profession, and use program evaluation concepts in our practice as we carry out our obligations to be competent researchers with our clients. Meeting these obligations is difficult (Elks & Kirkhart, 1993; Gerdes, Edmonds, Hoslam, & McCartney, 1996; Owens & Nease, 1993).

Our independent variables (the program or intervention methods used) are often poorly conceptualized. Thus, efforts to measure outputs and outcomes may be premature unless we also simultaneously engage in formative evaluations directed toward conceptualizing and measuring the nature of the intervention. Studies of program and interventive processes are essential to the development of the knowledge base of the profession and are a prerequisite to summative evaluations. Before talking about program or intervention effectiveness (that is, summative evaluations), we need to answer a series of questions about the program or intervention itself:

1. What are we attempting to accomplish? What objectives have you and your client set for the program or intervention? Clarity about objectives is essential for any evaluation.

2. What is the population for which these objectives are to be accomplished? It may be an individual, a group of clients, a neighborhood, or an even larger aggregation.

3. What components of the program or intervention plan are necessary to accomplish the objectives for the defined population or client? You should be able to specify all relevant program components or interventions.

4. How do the components of the program or intervention fit together? Do some need to precede others? Are some concurrent? Flow charts might be drawn to illustrate the relationships among the various intervention activities and the objectives.

5. What are the reasons and supporting evidence for believing that the intervention activities will accomplish the objectives? In other words, what is the linking logic? You must have some hypotheses that link the objectives to the intervention plan. Part of evaluation is to test these hypotheses—to test assumptive knowledge and expand the knowledge base of the profession.

As an illustration, let's go back to the senior citizens working to increase public safety in the neighborhood. These seniors like to be out during the late afternoon and early evening; however, they feel insecure in their immediate neighborhood because of concern about muggings and purse snatchings. Suppose that their objective is to have a pair of police officers assigned to patrol the neighborhood on foot from 3 to 11 P.M.

The next step is to develop an intervention plan that will lead to the objective. The seniors decide that, first, they need to secure the police chief's support for the notion of a foot patrol in their neighborhood and, second, they need to influence the city council to secure some additional resources for the neighborhood. Thus, in implementing this plan, they will need to bring two kinds of pressure to bear—factual and political. They will need to assemble facts concerning the number of crimes against seniors in the neighborhood and the extent to which seniors' activities are limited by fear of street crime. Even with that knowledge, they will need to mobilize a show of political support if they are to get the city council's attention. After considerable brainstorming and planning, you and the seniors may develop an intervention plan similar to Exhibit 17–2. This simplified flow chart indicates the various components (activities or independent variables) of the intervention plan and their relationship. A formative evaluation can be directed

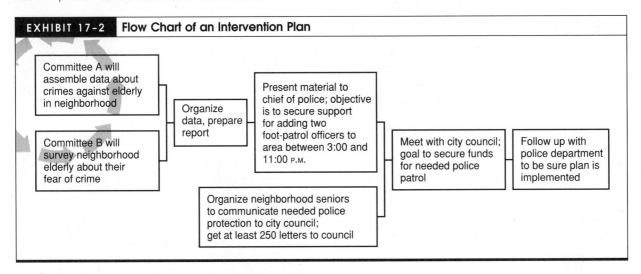

EXHIBIT 17-2 | **Flow Chart of an Intervention Plan**

Committee A will assemble data about crimes against elderly in neighborhood

Committee B will survey neighborhood elderly about their fear of crime

Organize data, prepare report

Present material to chief of police; objective is to secure support for adding two foot-patrol officers to area between 3:00 and 11:00 P.M.

Organize neighborhood seniors to communicate needed police protection to city council; get at least 250 letters to council

Meet with city council; goal to secure funds for needed police patrol

Follow up with police department to be sure plan is implemented

at monitoring the extent to which each of these activities occurs. If the persons responsible for gathering the evidence fail to do so, and the group then fails to have an impact on the police chief, you and the seniors will have a clearer understanding of what went wrong in accomplishing the objective. Alternatively, the plan may be fully implemented but still the objectives are not accomplished. This is a summative evaluation. On that basis, you and the seniors may make a judgment that the plan itself was not appropriate. You would then consider alternative plans and strategies—perhaps working to unseat some city council members or forming coalitions with other organizations so as to bring additional political pressure to bear.

This example also illustrates the distinction between outputs and outcomes. The output of the intervention was the assignment of a team of foot patrol officers to the neighborhood; the desired outcome was a reduction in crime against senior citizens. Whether the output—the two patrol officers—will actually lead to the outcome is a separate research question that will be of interest to you and the clients.

Confronting

Formative evaluations address a key question: Is the program activity or service plan being implemented as designed? Let's focus for a moment on service plans, although the same procedures hold true for programs. We can address the question at both the conceptual and operational levels. The conceptual level is the service plan: What did we agree to do? The plan is often in written form. The operational level consists of the intervention activities: What do we actually do? Formative evaluation examines whether we did what we said we were going to do.

Many of your evaluation activities with clients will involve determining whether the agreed-upon service plan was carried out. Sometimes it is not; clients or workers may not follow through. For example, a formative evaluation of the intervention plan in Exhibit 17–3 might reveal that Committee A did not collect the necessary evidence or did not do so in a timely fashion. The intervention in Exhibit 12–9 may not have been implemented because the worker was unable to schedule the second visit with Bonita. If the evaluation reveals that the plan has not been implemented as scheduled, decisions must be made about how to proceed.

Consider this example. Sixteen-year-old Ron broke into a small owner-operated business and did about $480 of damage. As part of the service plan, Ron and the social worker, Mr. Garcia, have agreed to meet with the victim to negotiate a way of making amends (Exhibit 17–3). Mr. Garcia follows through on his part of the plan by contacting the victim, learns that the victim is willing to meet with Ron, schedules a meeting, and communicates this to Ron by telephone. Ron, however, fails to meet with Mr. Garcia to prepare for negotiation with the victim and fails to appear for the meeting with

---

EXHIBIT 17-3 **A Service Plan for Tom**

DATE: January 20.
PROBLEM: Ron has committed a burglary and has been told by the judge that he will be expected to make restitution to the victim.

OBJECTIVE: To develop and present to the court a restitution plan that is acceptable to both the victim and Ron.

SERVICE PLAN:

What Is to Be Done?	By Whom?	When?
1. Meet with Mr. Higby (victim) to determine if he is willing to meet with Ron to work out a restitution plan. Try to secure his agreement to meet.	1. Mr. Garcia (social worker)	1. February 1
2. Telephone Ron to let him know results of meeting with Mr. Higby and to schedule meetings 3 and 4.	2. Mr. Garcia	2. February 2
3. Meet at office to prepare for meeting with Mr. Higby.	3. Ron and Mr. Garcia	3. February 7
4. Meet with Mr. Higby to develop restitution plan; Mr. Garcia to serve as mediator.	4. Ron and Mr. Garcia	4. February 15
5. Present restitution plan to judge at disposition hearing.	5. Ron, with assistance from Mr. Garcia as needed	5. February 20

---

the victim. The plan has not been implemented as agreed. What do we do?

Formative evaluations will lead you to confront clients who do not follow through on agreements. Confrontation is a specialized form of feedback (Chapter 8) that addresses discrepancies between statements and actions. In Reading 8-2, Cournoyer and Byers discussed confrontation in groups; in Chapter 12, we examined confronting as a way to help clients mobilize power. You will often use confrontation to assist clients in following through on agreements.

We offer some guidelines for confronting in Exhibit 17–4. Essentially, you gently but firmly draw attention to the discrepancy between words and actions. You do not make any type of judgment about the client, and

you do not express anger. Once the discrepancy has been noted and discussed, you involve the client in the resolution of the problem, exactly as in all previous planning. You have a responsibility to follow up on situations in which the intervention plan is not being followed and to confront the client.

In Ron's case, Mr. Garcia made arrangements to visit Ron the next evening, and this conversation ensued.

Garcia: Ron, I thought we ought to talk a bit about what happened that you didn't show up for the meeting with me and with Mr. Higby.
Ron: OK.
Garcia: Can you tell me what happened?
Ron: I don't know, I just didn't make it. [Silence.]

EXHIBIT 17-4 **Guidelines for Confronting**

1. The purpose of confronting is to point out a discrepancy between a verbal commitment and behavior and to involve the client in solving this problem.
2. Confronting is *not* an expression of worker anger or frustration.
3. Confronting relates to specific behavior.
4. Limit confronting to the behavioral discrepancy; do *not* make any judgment about the person.
5. Do not offer answers or explanations for the discrepancy.
6. Explore—and, whenever possible, use—the client's solution to the discrepancy as the basis for reinstituting or revising the plan.

Garcia: Ron, are you a little uncomfortable with the idea of talking with Mr. Higby?

Ron: Not really, I can handle it.

Garcia: How would you like to proceed from here?

Ron: I'll meet with the guy.

Garcia: Ron, there are at least two ways that we can proceed with this. We can go ahead and try to arrange for a meeting so you can see if you can negotiate an arrangement with Mr. Higby or we can ask the judge to decide what would be fair in terms of restitution in this situation.

Ron: I'd rather meet with him.

This led to some further exploration about how such a meeting might go and how Ron handles himself in an unpleasant situation. Mr. Garcia worked to prepare Ron for the meeting, which was held the following week. Ron was able to participate in conversations with the victim; together, they developed a plan for Ron to provide 45 hours of labor to the business as payment for his share of the damages.

This case illustrates some important elements of confronting. The worker did not allow the situation to be ignored; the focus was on the specific behavior; the discrepancy itself became the focus of the problem, with exploration of how Ron handled such situations; and the plan was implemented. In some situations, confronting may result in a revision in the plan. For example, Ron might well have let the judge decide the restitution and so avoided meeting the victim. Had he chosen this option, the focus of work would have been to prepare Ron for the hearing and to explore the kind of proposal he would like to make to the court.

Evaluation as a Continuous Process

You have a responsibility to be a researcher. You might begin by conceptualizing and measuring your intervention activities. Before you can do this, you need a clear picture of what they are and why they would lead to the chosen objectives. You can then begin thinking about summative evaluation—that is, measuring the extent of objective attainment. Research and evaluation form a continuous process and provide a flow of data for ongoing reassessment of objectives, intervention plans, and even the problem definition.

Evaluation provides feedback loops in the problem-solving process, so that you and your clients can continuously reassess the problem for work, the objectives, and the intervention plans (Exhibit 17–5). Your evaluation may indicate a need to redefine the problem (or define a new problem), to reassess objectives (or develop new objectives), or to modify the intervention plan. The evaluation feedback loops reduce the linearity of the problem-solving model and render it dynamic, systemic,

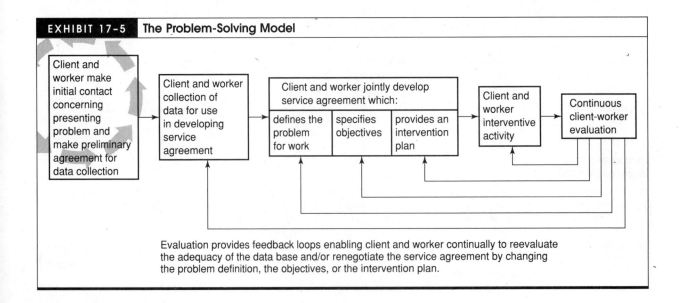

EXHIBIT 17–5 The Problem-Solving Model

Client and worker make initial contact concerning presenting problem and make preliminary agreement for data collection → Client and worker collection of data for use in developing service agreement → Client and worker jointly develop service agreement which: defines the problem for work | specifies objectives | provides an intervention plan → Client and worker interventive activity → Continuous client-worker evaluation

Evaluation provides feedback loops enabling client and worker continually to reevaluate the adequacy of the data base and/or renegotiate the service agreement by changing the problem definition, the objectives, or the intervention plan.

and constantly changing. However, any changes arising out of evaluation must be negotiated with the client, and any intervention activities undertaken must be based on a clearly specified service agreement. Experience with interventive activities may indicate a need for a change in the agreement, but changes cannot be made unilaterally.

Clear specification of objectives is a prerequisite to evaluation. Without clear objectives, evaluation of progress toward their accomplishment is impossible. Likewise, clear specification of the service plan is necessary to assess whether client-worker activities are appropriate for reaching the objectives.

Goal Attainment Scaling

Specification of measurable, concrete objectives is often difficult. Goal attainment scaling was developed (Kiresuk & Lund, 1977; Kiresuk, Smith, & Cardillo, 1994) as a tool to evaluate patient progress in mental health programs; the procedures can be used in any situation that involves goal setting—for instance, in measuring client progress toward service objectives (Fleuridas, Leigh, Rosenthal, & Leigh, 1990; Karr, 1990), student progress toward learning goals, and agency progress toward organizational objectives. Goal attainment scaling is particularly useful for social work, because it permits individualized objectives. There is no effort to impose predetermined or standardized objectives; rather, you and your client work toward objectives

individually tailored to a particular situation. The procedures, however, only measure the extent of goal or objective attainment. They do not measure the importance of the objectives themselves, nor do they determine the intervention methods. How objectives are achieved is not a part of goal attainment scaling.

The grid used in goal attainment scaling (Exhibit 17–6) provides for the development of scales—with five levels of predicted attainment after a specified period of time; the levels range from the most unfavorable to the most favorable result thought likely, with the expected result at the midpoint on each scale. At least one scale should be developed for each objective and a heading provided for each scale; as many scales as are necessary may be developed. Once the scale headings have been provided, a follow-up date is set. Where do you and your client expect to be at that date? The entire objective may not have been attained; indicate on the scale the level of accomplishment that you expect. Then specify the most unfavorable result and the most favorable result at follow-up, and finally select the intermediate levels of less than expected success and more than expected success. Specification of the five levels must be objective enough to permit reliable scoring. Quantification is desirable, whenever possible, but is not absolutely essential in establishing the scale levels.

Be sure that each scale is both exhaustive (that is, the scale levels account for all outcome possibilities) and

| EXHIBIT 17-6 | Goal Attainment Follow-Up Grid |

Program using goal attainment scaling _____	Date of scale construction _____ Follow-up date _____			
Levels of predicted attainments	Scale headings and scale weights			
	scale 1 ($w_1 =$)	scale 2 ($w_2 =$)	scale 3 ($w_3 =$)	scale 4 ($w_4 =$)
Most unfavorable results thought likely				
Less than expected success				
Expected level of success				
More than expected success				
Most favorable results thought likely				

mutually exclusive (that is, none of the five levels overlap). Once developed, the scales can be set aside until the designated follow-up date. Scoring consists of checking what has been accomplished on each scale at the designated follow-up date. Kiresuk and Garwick (1974) present a formula for calculating an overall goal attainment scale score and discuss procedures for weighting scales if some are thought more important than others. Exhibit 17–7 illustrates a set of goal attainment scales that might have been developed with Mrs. B in Exhibit 11–11.

Single System Designs

The practitioner research that we have been discussing involves a research sample of one rather than a group of subjects; this is often known as the single system design (Berlin, 1983; Grinnell, 1997; Tripodi, 1984).

EXHIBIT 17-7   Goal Attainment Follow-up Grid: Case Example

Program using GAS   Intercity Head Start

Client   Mrs. B

Date of scale construction   August 1

Follow-up date   September 1

Levels of predicted attainments	Scale headings and scale weights			
	Scale 1: Relation to Jimmy ($w_1 = $)	Scale 2: Relation to Loneliness ($w_2 = $)	Scale 3: Return to Clinic ($w_3 = $)	Scale 4 ($w_4 = $)
Most unfavorable results thought likely	Mrs. B reports angrily yelling at Jimmy daily or more often during last week in August.	No action or discussion of Mrs. B's loneliness.	No discussion or action about returning to clinic.	
Less than expected success	Mrs. B reports angrily yelling at Jimmy more than three times but less than daily during last week in August.	Mrs. B discusses her loneliness but cannot make plans to deal with it.	Mrs. B is discussing her reaction to the clinic but has not formulated plans to return.	
Expected level of success	Mrs. B reports angrily yelling at Jimmy no more than three times during last week in August.	Mrs. B is discussing her loneliness and making plans to join a group.	Mrs. B has discussed her reaction to the clinic and plans to secure a return appointment.	
More than expected success	Mrs. B has discontinued angrily yelling at Jimmy but has not discovered another way to discipline him.	Mrs. B has initiated contacts with a group.	Mrs. B has telephoned the clinic for a return appointment.	
Most favorable results thought likely	Above, and Mrs. B is using another form of discipline before becoming angry with Jimmy.	Mrs. B has attended one group meeting.	Mrs. B has been to the clinic for a return appointment.	

Sharon Berlin (1983) has described the use of this design with a client with symptoms of depression. Robert Weinbach discusses its use at length in Reading 17-1.

ASSISTING WITH PROGRAM EVALUATION

As a practitioner, you will be involved in program evaluation within your agency in several ways. You will be requested to provide data for the program evaluation effort, usually by completing data forms. Beyond this, however, you might also be involved in formulating the questions to be addressed by a program evaluation, and you might use the program evaluation results in determining, along with clients, the most appropriate intervention in a given set of circumstances.

As different people in an agency plan program evaluation, different views of agency objectives and outcomes may emerge, along with different views of the purpose of the evaluation (Exhibit 17–8). This is likely to occur in agencies that have not operationalized a mission statement by developing more immediate objectives. Without shared objectives, the agency will waste resources by moving in divergent directions.

In Chapter 6, we identified your ethical duty to keep track of current developments and research affecting your practice. Thus, in addition to continuous evaluation of your own practice and involvement in agency-level program evaluation, you will also share information from literature evaluations of various interventions with clients for consideration in decision making.

RECORDING

Keeping records is an important client service; it provides the data necessary to evaluate your practice, data to document that services have been provided (Corcorin & Gingerich, 1994; Gelman, 1992), data for program evaluation, and data for purposes of accountability.

In Reading 4-1, Susan Tebb described a recording model in which the client is involved in writing the case record. This creative approach furthers the important notion of partnership. Regardless of who writes the case record, however, you are responsible for seeing that it is done in a timely fashion, and that the record is complete and accurate. Exhibit 17–9 presents an overview of social

---

EXHIBIT 17-8	Differing Views About Objectives and Evaluation

Helping Families, Inc., is a small (eight professional staff plus a director) family service agency that provides family counseling, marital counseling, individual counseling, and family life education services. The agency receives funds from the United Way, fees, and a contract for service. Recently the United Way and the local welfare department, which purchases services from Helping Families, Inc., have mandated that all agencies develop a plan for evaluation of their services. The evaluation plan must include procedures to determine if the agency is accomplishing its goals.

Helping Families, Inc., has never formulated very clear outcome goals, other than broad mission statements having to do with helping individuals and families cope with the strains of living. The agency has created a committee to address the evaluation mandate. A program evaluation researcher has been retained as a consultant and is assisting the committee to formulate objectives that are reasonably measurable. The committee members have strong views about evaluation.

Sally Dogooder, a social worker, is committed to helping clients. She doesn't think there is a need for evaluation and is concerned that the effort may consume some of the already limited time available to serve clients.

Gene Helpinghand, also a social worker, is moderately favorable to evaluation. He agrees that the agency needs to develop a better understanding of what it is doing, both to provide information to the community and to improve the delivery of services. Gene is concerned about the basis for evaluation, however, and believes strongly that assisting clients to feel better is the primary mission of the agency.

I. M. Hardpressed, the harried executive of Helping Families, is frequently called on to defend the agency to the community and to justify expenditures. She wants to know if services are being delivered in the most efficient manner possible and is particularly interested in being able to document services and costs.

Francis Powerstructure, president of the board of Helping Families, Inc., and a leading member of the business community, is interested in documenting that the agency is delivering a useful product and wants to know if the agency is providing the community with a worthwhile service.

EXHIBIT 17-9	Social Work Recording

WHY RECORD?

In all contacts with clients, their families, and community resources, it is necessary to record what took place so that (1) the worker remembers what happened; (2) other people may know; (3) service program and objectives may be reviewed; and (4) teaching and learning may occur. Thus, records are for use.

WHAT GOES INTO A RECORD?

A case record—the account of what the social worker did in a particular situation—should fit the needs of the case. The purpose of the recording should determine its length and scope, and what is written should meet the interests of its intended readers. Good recording is based on factual reporting, good thinking, and sound evaluative judgment. The social worker is not a journalist but might apply the fundamental journalistic questions: What? Who? Where? When? How? Why? The last of these is the most difficult; heed the researcher's dictum not to go beyond data—that is, to support any speculations with at least some relevant facts.

THE FORMS OF RECORDING

There are three major forms of recording: (1) narrative; (2) summary; and (3) assessment and evaluative.

Narrative

Narrative recording—sometimes known as process recording—is used when it is necessary to report as many facts as you can remember—for example, in a critical situation or transaction that others, including a supervisor or a psychiatrist, need all the information possible to evaluate it. A narrative recording of an interview may also be used in order to make sense of the interaction and to better understand the associated dynamics. Narrative recordings can be useful tools for learning, especially early in the worker's career. However, they will waste the worker's time, the secretary's time, and the supervisor's time if done routinely, mechanically, and without a specific purpose. Thus, narrative recording in social work practice should be used sparingly. Workers may sometimes find it helpful to record an interview in narrative form, so as to become more aware of the interaction. For most ongoing treatment, though, summary recording is preferred.

Summary

There are several types of summary recordings:

1. Intake summaries succinctly state what brought the client to the agency, including the nature of the presenting problem and what is asked of the agency. Agencies usually provide an outline to guide the worker in this phase. A complete biography or family chronology is not necessary in the first interview. However, a foundation for future work with the client should be laid, with a focus on the problem and what can be done about it.

2. Discharge summaries put the discharge plan in writing, so that there can be no misunderstanding about the situation and about what interventions are planned for the future. The discharge summary should be geared to the future prospects of the case and should spell out at least some of the factors that led to the discharge plan.

3. Transfer or closing summaries state why a case was closed or transferred, review briefly what was accomplished, and say what remains to be done by the client, with or without further help. The nature of the closing contract—how it was fulfilled and what the client's understanding is—should be specified. In all discharge, transfer, or closing summaries, it is necessary to summarize what went on during the social work contact, why the case was closed, and what the closing or transfer arrangements were.

4. A block summary encapsulates all the contacts over a period of time. How often such block summaries should be done—especially in periods when there is little contact or little change in a situation—depends on the nature of the case. Allowing months to go by without recording client contacts may create the erroneous impression that a case situation has been completely dormant. To minimize time-consuming narrative recordings, block recordings can be interspersed with narratives of particularly important transactions.

Assessment and Evaluative Statements

In a sense, all recordings contain elements of judgment, perception, and applications of knowledge; accordingly, all recordings, except transcriptions from tapes, are impressionistic in one way or another. To introduce adjectives and adverbs is to make evaluative comments. This is all to the good, but you must provide evidence for your thinking. It is often helpful to include a brief paragraph of impressionistic assessment at the end of a particular recording. Clinical diagnosis is not necessary, but there is no reason why the worker cannot state an informed opinion. Basically, recordings, whatever their form, should at some point convey the worker's impression of how the client looks, feels, thinks, and acts. Inclusion of the worker's own reaction to the client is also appropriate.

Source: John Goldmeier, Professor, School of Social Work and Community Planning, University of Maryland.

work recording. Many social workers find recording onerous and tend to slight this part of their professional responsibility. We hope that you will take recording as seriously as other parts of your practice. Here are some guidelines:

1. Keep your records up to date. It is much easier to keep records current than to try to catch up after you have fallen behind.

2. Record all contacts—as a minimum, the dates, who the contact was with, and the place of the contact.

3. Keep your records factual and based on your observations of what was seen and heard.

4. Avoid vague words or phrases, such as *uncooperative, euphoric, bizarre, resistant,* and *stubborn.*

5. Keep your records as short as possible but do not leave out any crucial information.

6. Record any agreements made by you or your client that require follow-up.

7. Be sure your recording relates to the purpose at hand.

We are not suggesting a specific recording format; your agency will have a required format. You may also record by keying the information directly into a recording format on your computer screen (Modai & Rabinowitz, 1993).

Recording will also be an important tool for your professional development. Process recording (Graybeal & Ruff, 1995) is an effort to capture the interchange between you and your client. On the basis of such records, an instructor or consultant can help you identify your practice strengths and weaknesses and learn how to improve your practice skills. At one time, process recording involved the worker's written recollections of interactions with the client. Direct observation and electronic (video or audio) recording are now also widespread. Process recording will certainly be a part of your student experience and may continue as the basis for a learning interchange with your agency supervisor or with a consultant. Service to clients will improve as we develop our skills. We have an ethical duty to learn throughout our careers; this may require us to regularly prepare process recordings.

UNINTENDED CONSEQUENCES

Evaluation usually focuses on whether we accomplish our objectives. Did we do the good that we intended? Seldom do we seek evidence of the unintended—perhaps harmful—consequences of our work. All of our summative evaluations, of both practice and program, should seriously examine the possibility of such consequences. It may be more important to know whether we are causing harm than whether we are doing good.

Sieber (1981) argues that any social intervention may have unintended effects—either side effects or regressive effects. *Side effects* result from the intervention but have no direct bearing on the problem itself. For example, in medicine, some chemotherapies for cancer may cause hair loss, dizziness, nausea, or other reactions that do not relate directly to the cancer itself. Side effects may be classified as positive, neutral, or negative. Some side effects may benefit the client, although they do not directly address the problem for work. For example, as we have seen, a possible service plan for the Birky family, introduced in Exhibit 2–15, might include helping the Birkys to organize their neighbors politically, with the goal of covering the ditch in which their son died. Possible positive side effects from such a plan might be an expansion of the Birkys' informal support system or a change in their views about African Americans.

Regressive effects have a direct bearing on the problem the intervention was designed to resolve but make the condition worse. Thus, they occur when the results of an intervention are the opposite of what was intended. Exhibit 17–10 contains an interesting example of unintended regressive effects, from a well-designed study involving random selection of a group of juvenile offenders to three types of intervention—restitution, probation supervision, and mental health counseling; a fourth group both made restitution and received mental health counseling. Before and after data on delinquent behavior were collected for each group of offenders and then standardized to provide a measure of the rate of delinquent incidents per 100 youths over a period of one year. The results indicate that the delinquent behavior of the youths who received mental health counseling alone increased after treatment—a regressive effect; the delinquent behavior of youths in the other groups decreased or remained unchanged. A single study does not, of course, provide justification for discontinuing mental health treatment to delinquent youth, but such studies do require us to consider the possibility of regressive effects.

Note that, in the research reported in Exhibit 17–10, the independent variable, mental health treatment, was never operationalized; this is a common problem in program evaluation. However, if useful results are to be obtained, the treatment must be described very clearly. Mental health treatment could include many very different types of intervention. Some of these might be harmful, and others helpful.

Social workers often deal with people who are vulnerable and under stress; we discuss intimate details of clients' lives; and we intrude into their social systems. Any intrusive service has the potential for harm (Burr & Christensen, 1992; Durst, 1992; Howitt, 1993; McNulty & Wardle, 1994). We need to be aware of this possibility and take reasonable steps to prevent any negative side effects or regressive effects. One important step is to move toward partnership with the client. By involving the client in decision making and functioning within the framework of what the client wants, we reduce the risk of imposing intrusive procedures that may have harmful effects. A second step is to make a commitment to think carefully about the possibility of doing harm in each client situation.

CHAPTER SUMMARY

Your evaluation efforts will proceed at two levels. With your client, you will continuously evaluate the extent to which the goals of the service contract are being accomplished. This evaluation provides feedback loops in the problem-solving process and an ongoing opportunity to renegotiate the problem for work, the objective, and the service plan. You will also be called on to assist with agency program evaluation. Such efforts provide information regarding the interventive approaches that seem most effective in particular circumstances. At both levels, evaluation requires an explicit statement of goals and interventive means or program activities. Interventions must be described precisely and in detail; evaluation is not possible otherwise. Goal attainment scaling provides one means of measuring client progress. Recording yields the data necessary for evaluation, serves as the basis for practitioner and agency accountability, and is a tool for professional development. Finally, it is important to systematically consider the possibility of unintended negative consequences from interventions; partnership with clients helps to prevent negative consequences.

A LOOK FORWARD

In Reading 17-1, Robert Weinbach introduces single system research, which, he argues, is compatible with good social work practice. As an illustration, he applies this design to the evaluation of a group program for pediatric diabetes clients who need to reduce their sugar intake.

EXHIBIT 17-10 | **Example of Regressive Effects**

This study involved random assignment of youth adjudicated delinquent to four treatment strategies—restitution either to community or victim; mental health counseling for a diagnostic session followed by therapy; probation supervision and mental health counseling; and probation supervision alone. The outcome goal for all the treatment strategies was to reduce the incidence of delinquent behavior. Here are the results. What evidence do you see of regressive effects?

	Restitution only	Restitution and mental health counseling	Mental health counseling	Probation only
Rate of delinquent incidents per 100 youth for year before intervention.	101	55	64	75
Rate of delinquent incidents per 100 youth for one year beginning with intervention.	74	47	84	75

Source: A. Schneider, Restitution and recidivism rates of juvenile offenders: Results from four experimental studies, *Criminology, 24,* 533–552 (1986). Copyright 1986 by American Society of Criminology. Reprinted by permission. Findings presented in this exhibit are from the Clayton County, Georgia, Juvenile Restitution Program.

In Reading 17-2, John McKnight examines why public policies that intend to produce positive benefits may actually have serious unintended negative consequences. As McKnight demonstrates, we cannot assume that good intentions will produce good results.

In Chapter 18, we discuss endings in social work. How can we reduce the harmful impacts of endings and convert them to a positive experience for clients? In Chapter 19, we take a final look at what it means to be a social worker and how to avoid burnout.

READING 17-1 *Does My Intervention Make a Difference? Single System Research*

Robert W. Weinbach

Relatively few social workers have the opportunity to design and implement program evaluations; a larger percentage participate in them. But *all* social workers should be involved in evaluating whether their methods of intervention are achieving their objectives. The most common method for doing so is single system research (also known as single subject research, $N = 1$ research, single case designs, or ideographic research).

ACCOUNTABILITY AND PRACTICE

The impetus for social work practitioners to evaluate the effectiveness and efficiency of their practice cannot be traced to any one event. Over the past 30 years, many interrelated phenomena have contributed to this impetus, including:

- conservative politicians who spotlight the supposed failures of human service programs (especially public assistance) and demand proof that tax dollars are being used productively
- a reduction in resources for human services, with an accompanying withdrawal of government and charitable funding from programs and services that cannot demonstrate that they work
- attempts by human service professionals, faced with financial constraints, to identify those services that, if cut, would represent the least loss to client groups
- the argument by vocal consumer advocates that clients have a right to be involved in planning for services and a right to expect that programs and services will accomplish their objectives

- mushrooming litigation in which consumers of services seek compensation not only for professional malpractice, but also for promised results that have not been achieved
- meta-analysis of research reports on the effectiveness of intervention methods
- professional organizations' emphasis, for over a decade, on the utilization of research by practitioners (Grasso & Epstein, 1992)
- the advent of managed care in the 1990s, with its emphasis on cost containment
- recent action by the Council on Social Work Education (1992a, b), which accredits social work education programs, ensuring that future social workers will have some understanding of methods for evaluating the effectiveness of their practice

RESEARCH FOR AND BY THE PRACTITIONER

Methods for evaluating the effectiveness of programs and services employ many of the established procedures of scientific inquiry. But they also differ markedly from more traditional research in a number of ways, most dramatically in their objectives. For example, most traditional group research studies attempt to study a sample or portion of the research population. Their goal is to identify relationships between variables within the sample. Statistical methods are used to determine whether the relationships within the sample are likely to be true of the population. In this way, general knowledge is developed for use by others. In program evaluation and single system research, by contrast, we are less concerned with developing general knowledge than with determining whether a given program is working within a given organization (program evaluation) or whether a given

---

* An original reading revised for this edition.

treatment appears to be effective with a given case (single system research). The external validity, or generalizability (Rubin & Babbie, 1997), of findings from a program evaluation—that is, the likelihood that those findings would be true of similar or identical programs—is assumed to be low. No two programs are exactly alike; what we learn about one may not be true of another. The results of a single system study are also assumed to have little or no external validity (Marlow, 1998), because, as we know, no two clients or client systems are alike.

With single system research, the social worker wants to know, "Does my intervention method appear to be effective in my work with *this* client or client system?" Single system research is conducted by responsible practitioners to provide feedback for their own use.

There is little reason why a client or client group should object to being a part of single system research. It involves doing what clients expect a good social worker to do anyway—to conscientiously and objectively monitor their progress toward some objective. For this reason, single system research generally does not require prior approval from an institutional review board or other similar groups that protect the rights of research participants within more traditional group research studies.

When conducting single system research with families, individuals, or groups, there is rarely any need for deception. Clients often participate in identifying and setting treatment objectives. Thus, there is no reason why they cannot be aware that research is occurring; they often participate in collecting and recording data.

In many ways, single system research is more like good practice than like research. Its similarities to traditional group research designs are quite superficial (Yegidis & Weinbach, 1996). Single system research studies a single case, but that is about the only similarity to the exploratory, qualitative research design that researchers usually call a case study. It makes repeated, ongoing measurements of the same variable (such as a behavior or attitude that the social worker is seeking to influence); that is a characteristic of all forms of longitudinal research, but longitudinal studies usually have a slightly different purpose—to learn when and under what conditions certain changes occur. As we have noted, single system research does not seek to make generalizations, as most longitudinal research does.

Single system research has been compared to experimental research. Some authors even refer to certain single system designs as experimental (Bloom, Fischer & Orme, 1995). Single system research uses a kind of quasi-control group (observations of those times when the intervention is not being offered). It also introduces or manipulates what can be regarded as the independent or predictor variable (the intervention). But it does not meet all of the requirements of a classical experimental research design. Most importantly, the sample (the client system studied) is not selected randomly; it is selected for study because it seems especially appropriate for single system research.

While it is probably employed most with individual clients, single system research is equally suitable for work with couples, families, groups, organizations, or communities (Thyer, 1993). It can be used as long as the social worker can: (1) conceptualize and specify the intervention method being used; and (2) operationalize and accurately measure the behavior, attitude, or other problem that the intervention is designed to influence. Of course, these conditions are not always present.

Sometimes, single system research is not appropriate for another reason. It requires the presence of a clear pattern in the target problem (the dependent or criterion variable, in research terminology). That pattern can be rising, falling, steady, or even fluctuating in some consistent way over time. But it cannot appear to be simply random in its incidence.

The target problem in single system research is most often a behavior, but it may be some other attribute like an attitude or a perception that can be measured repeatedly and accurately. It may be the principal problem experienced by a client or client system, or it may be just one symptom or manifestation of the problem. The target problem may be something undesirable or dysfunctional that the intervention is designed to decrease or extinguish. But it can also be something desirable (for example, assertiveness) that the intervention is designed to increase.

The target problem is measured at regular time intervals, and these measurements are systematically recorded. Any one of several aspects of a problem might be used; the measurements thus generated would reflect different levels of measurement precision (Tripodi, 1994). For example, we could record the frequency (ratio level), duration (interval level), or magnitude (ordinal level) of temper tantrums by a client's 3-year-old child or the length of the interval between them (ratio level). Or we could simply note whether a tantrum occurred during the previous week (nominal level). Which of these measurements would a social worker choose? It depends on the objective of intervention, which should have been agreed upon in partnership with the client. Relevant questions might include:

1. What type of change is sought and what realistic objectives have been set?
2. What is the best way to demonstrate whether or not progress is being made toward achieving the objective of intervention?
3. What would success or lack of success for the intervention look like?

There is an almost infinite number of target problems that a social worker might select as the dependent variable in single system research, for example:

- the number of hours that a mother helps a child with homework
- the number of self-esteem enhancing comments to a child by a parent
- the intervals between family activities
- the number of times that spouses disagree without blaming
- the duration of meals with all family members present
- the number of discussions about child-rearing issues between parents
- the percentage of members who verbally participate in a treatment group
- the number of participants in a group who have sought employment
- the number of workdays lost because of calling in sick
- the number of times that legislators request a social worker's opinion on pending social legislation
- the percentage of registered voters within a community
- the incidence of hate crimes within a community

Note that most of these target problems are expressed in positive terms. While this is not always feasible, it is desirable, because it is consistent with social work values and processes: We seek to increase what is positive, rather than focusing on the negative aspects of problems. Note also that most of these examples involve a behavior that is easily measured. With single system research, simple is almost always better.

Often, single system research involves an innovative intervention that we think may prove effective, or an intervention that is generally believed to be effective with one problem or client but has yet to be tried with another one. Single system research is exploratory; the social worker thinks, "I wonder if I can demonstrate that this is associated with a difference?" It is often the precursor to replication with other similar clients who have the same target problem or, ultimately, to various forms of group research designed to have more external validity.

SINGLE SYSTEM RESEARCH AS GOOD SOCIAL WORK PRACTICE

Do good social workers evaluate their practice using single system research, or is single system research really just a form of good social work practice? That's an academic question. The truth is that single system research methods are very consistent with good practice. Much of what is done in conducting single system research is what a good practitioner would do anyway—except that, perhaps, single system research helps us to do it in a more systematic way. For example, it has been suggested elsewhere in this book that, in social work practice, the independent variable (the intervention) is often poorly conceptualized. One of the most important steps in planning for single system research is to develop a clear conceptualization and specification of the intervention. It is not enough to merely conduct research that asks, "Did my intervention make a difference?" We want to know exactly *what* made a difference; that is the only way that we can learn from our efforts.

Similarly, measuring the dependent (or criterion) variable forces the social worker to clearly define and specify the treatment goal and to develop or find objective ways of measuring it. This is also very consistent with sound social work practice. For example, if alcohol abuse is the general problem, what is the treatment objective—total abstinence, not drinking on the job, drinking that does not involve abuse of family members, or some other type of alcohol-related behavior? In the participatory planning process, what did the social worker and the client adopt as a realistic objective? Would the substitution of another substance be indicative of treatment success or failure? Should the dependent variable be the amount of alcohol consumed over a time period, the frequency of bouts of drinking, their duration, their magnitude, or the length of time between them? The specification and measurement of the dependent variable will inevitably depend on what objective was agreed upon, as will any good treatment planning. Note the other similarities between the steps in planning single research in Exhibit 17–11 and the usual questions asked in good social work assessment and treatment planning.

Step 6 in Exhibit 17–11 alludes to ethical concerns. On the surface, it might seem that single system research can produce numerous ethical dilemmas for the social worker. However, most of these concerns stem from a misunderstanding. Whenever single system research is conducted, strict adherence to professional ethical standards is emphasized. Clients are not denied access to needed treatment. Rather, the intervention method that the social worker is evaluating is offered as an adjunct to the usual treatment or intervention—not usually as a replacement for it. For example, while a patient in an inpatient psychiatric facility participates in occupational therapy, group treatment, physical therapy, and medication therapy, a social worker might employ intervals during which some other intervention is alternately offered and not offered. Then, the data could be examined to see if the presence or absence of the intervention is associated with some behavior—for example, a reduction in acting-out. In this way, the withdrawal of the intervention (a requirement of the research design) is not an ethical problem.

In accordance with social work values, single system research must always be subordinate to clients' welfare. It can be terminated prior to its completion for ethical reasons. If, for example, a social worker concludes that an intervention is associated with an undesirable fluctuation in the target problem, it should not be reintroduced, even if the research design calls for its reintroduction. Conversely, another social worker may decide that, in the client's best interest, an intervention that appears to be highly effective should be continued indefinitely, even though the research design calls for its withdrawal.

The various single system research designs are all, in a sense, variations on a theme. In all such designs, the target problem is subjected, alternately, to periods when the specific intervention is offered (B phases) and periods when it is not (baseline or A phases); a chart is kept of its fluctuations. The simplest design, known as AB, consists of an observation period in which the dependent variable is measured and recorded but the intervention (independent variable) is not offered (A) and then a period in which the dependent variable is measured and recorded with the inclusion of the intervention (B). This design is generally used when the social worker believes that the effects of the intervention are likely to be permanent. For example, an intervention to increase assertiveness might be tested using an AB design because it is believed that assertiveness, once learned, is self-reinforcing.

| **EXHIBIT 17-11** | **Planning for Single System Research** |

1. Briefly describe the client's problem or at least its manifestation.
2. Specify the target behavior, attitude, or other factor (the dependent variable) and how you propose to measure it. Remember, it may be just a symptom of an underlying problem if that symptom is to be the focus of some intervention.
3. Identify what pattern of the dependent variable exists (stable, rising, falling, and so on).
4. In 50 words or (preferably) less, specify the treatment or intervention to be used (the independent variable), and how it will relate to other, ongoing services to the client.
5. Conduct a literature review. Identify research studies or professional literature suggesting that your treatment may produce the desired results.
6. Select the single system design most suitable for examining the relationship between the independent and dependent variables. Specify why it is

the best, given such factors as time and ethical constraints.
7. Determine which pattern of the dependent variable would indicate that your intervention may be related to a desired effect with your client—that is, the goal of treatment that you and the client have agreed upon.
8. Determine what pattern(s) would suggest the possibility that your intervention may have promoted unhealthy dependency or some other unintended consequence.
9. Conduct the research, carefully graphing the fluctuations in the dependent variable.
10. Carefully analyze the research results relative to steps 7 and 8. If the pattern in step 7 is observed, speculate on what other clients might find the intervention helpful.
11. Replicate the research with similar clients or with other clients who might benefit from the intervention.

Other designs add one or more A or B phases. For example, an ABA design adds a second A phase after intervention to see if the dependent variable changes when treatment is withdrawn. An ABAB (reversal) design adds both second baseline (A) and second intervention (B) phases to see what happens to the dependent variable when the intervention is withdrawn and then re-introduced. Another specialized design is ABCABC, which monitors the effects of twice introducing two different successive interventions on a single dependent variable, while multiple baseline designs measure outcomes across clients, across settings, and across clients' multiple target problems (Thyer, 1993). More complicated designs attempt to ensure that any difference in the dependent variable is indeed a function of an intervention; that is, they try to increase the internal validity (Rubin & Babbie, 1997). Such designs probably produce more definitive answers about a social worker's practice effectiveness, but they involve a loss of simplicity. They may require that a social worker receive advanced research training and devote more time to single system research than can be justified.

Ideally, research begins in an A phase of observation, with no intervention, so that a baseline can be established; longer A phases are desirable because they "contain enough points to establish the unlikelihood that extraneous events affecting the target problem will coincide only with the onset of intervention" (Rubin & Babbie, p. 322). However, requiring an initial A phase may pose ethical concerns. What if the dependent variable is a behavior that represents a serious problem or is even life-threatening, such as unsafe sex practices? Sometimes a valid retrospective baseline can be based on a recollection of what has occurred in the recent past. If this is impossible, can we ethically withhold a potentially effective intervention during the baseline phase? Of course not! We could select a research design that begins with an intervention phase (such as BAB), even though it may not be the design of choice from a purely research perspective.

Note that the research can start after treatment has been in progress for months or even years. Alternatively, if a design calls for the research to end in an A phase (for example, an ABA design), an intervention that seems to correlate with desirable changes in the target problem can always be reinstituted after the final A phase.

INTERPRETING FINDINGS

Once a design is selected and implemented, the social worker records and plots the frequency, duration, and other aspects of the target problem at regular intervals and observes the patterns that develop. Computer software packages for personal computers store and graphically display data and provide appropriate statistical analysis (Bloom, Fischer & Orme, 1995); hand-generated graphs can also be used. The time dimension (hours, days, weeks, months, number of interviews, and so on) is displayed along the horizontal axis, while the measurements of the dependent variable are displayed along the vertical axis. The social worker can use the chart for ongoing feedback and is constantly seeking to interpret it. The research graph or chart might provide the focus for a discussion of treatment progress with the client. For example, the social worker might suggest that, according to the graph, a recovering stroke patient seems to be spending more time in performing activities of daily living. Client and worker might also examine together the degree of consistency of any pattern observed. When the research has been completed, the social worker and client can look at the entire pattern of the dependent variable. Practice knowledge, values, and skills will suggest many questions, for example:

1. What else was going on in the client's life during the research?
2. What components of the treatment package besides the independent variable may have contributed to changes in the dependent variable?
3. How may the passage of time or normal physical processes have influenced the dependent variable?
4. How much dependency on the social worker is reflected in the fluctuations in the dependent variable, and is this desirable?
5. How efficient (costly) is the intervention, given the results documented?
6. How likely is the pattern to continue after permanent discontinuation of the intervention?
7. Overall, how consistent are the results with treatment goals and objectives?

AN EXAMPLE: INTERVENTION IN A SUPPORT GROUP

The social work research literature includes many examples of single system research with individual clients. The following case illustrates its use in a group context.

Rhoda, a social worker in a large general hospital, was leading a support group for 10 children with Type I (insulin dependent) diabetes who were having trouble controlling their blood sugar. In reading about juvenile diabetes and talking to colleagues, she learned that many children continue to eat sugar-flavored foods, despite the hazards to their health, because they think they won't like the taste of foods prepared with sugar substitutes. She wanted to see if regular exposure to a pleasant-tasting snack made with sugar substitutes and other low-calorie ingredients might contribute to better control of blood glucose level among her group members. She defined her intervention as "bringing in a home-cooked sugar-free snack and spending five minutes of each group session with all group members tasting it and discussing it." Her dependent variable was a measurement already in use and available—the results of the children's blood test taken three days after each group session. At the testing, clinic staff recorded whether each child was within the optimum blood glucose range.

Rhoda selected an ABAB design for her research. Since the target problem was not immediately life-threatening for the children, she felt that, ethically, she could begin her research in a nonintervention (A) phase. She also believed that ABAB, with its four phases, would allow a pattern of relationship between the dependent and independent variables to develop, if the intervention made a difference. She recognized the major limitations of the research. She knew that the glucose reading taken in the hospital may not have been typical for any or all of the children. She also could not control the other two major influences on blood glucose level (besides diet): insulin intake and exercise. But, she knew that single system research seeks association between variables and does not attempt to uncover relationships of cause and effect. Rhoda implemented her research and kept a chart of the results (Exhibit 17–12). Was her intervention effective? As with most single system research efforts, there were few conclusive findings. But she made three important observations that influenced her future practice as a group leader:

1. Overall, the children showed a desirable change in the dependent variable over the course of the research.

2. There were no dramatic changes when the intervention was introduced or withdrawn.

EXHIBIT 17–12 | **ABAB Design for the Tuesday Afternoon Group**

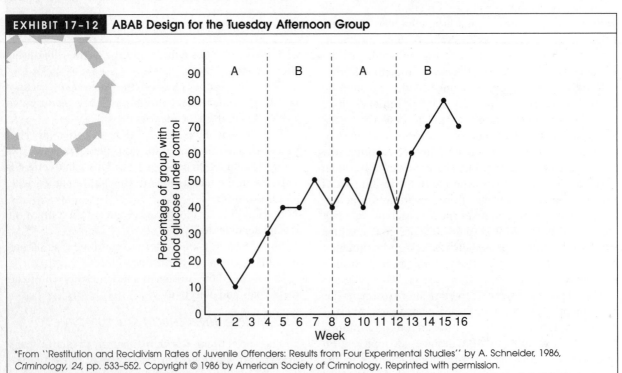

*From ``Restitution and Recidivism Rates of Juvenile Offenders: Results from Four Experimental Studies'' by A. Schneider, 1986, *Criminology, 24*, pp. 533–552. Copyright © 1986 by American Society of Criminology. Reprinted with permission.

3. Verbal participation by group members, while not a target for change, increased dramatically over the course of the research. By week 16, all children were active participants.

These findings suggested many question, for instance:

1. Given that the percentage of children with their blood glucose level in control consistently and dramatically improved over the 16 weeks, should the intervention be regarded as successful?

2. If so, does the research suggest that the periodic reinforcement method used is the best way to employ the intervention?

3. Does the lack of a decline in the dependent variable when the treatment was withdrawn indicate that the treatment was not closely associated with changes in the dependent variable or that it had a healthy carryover effect?

4. Would a decline at these points have been consistent with treatment goals of independent blood sugar management?

5. Would the changes in the dependent variable have occurred even without the intervention, because of experience, learning, maturation, time, or some other factor?

6. Did the increased verbal interaction within the group contribute to change in the dependent variable or was it, perhaps, the other way around?

7. Did the intervention contribute more to increased verbal participation in the group than to changes in the dependent variable? If so, what are the treatment implications?

Rhoda could not isolate any cause-effect relationships between her intervention and the dependent variables using the ABAB design. However, the intervention had been associated with two desirable changes—the group's improved blood glucose level and the increase in their verbal participation—both of which, in her experience, did not usually occur until later in a group's existence. Did it matter exactly how and why these desirable changes occurred? Probably not, at least not at this early stage of her inquiry. She decided to replicate her research with a diabetic support group that was about to begin.

STRENGTHS AND WEAKNESSES

Single system research will never replace group research as a means of generalized knowledge building for the social work profession. Findings derived from single system research have limited external validity; only through replication with similar clients can more generalized knowledge regarding practice effectiveness be generated. Single system research is also vulnerable to charges that it lacks internal validity (Marlow, 1993), in that we can only speculate on the degree to which changes in the dependent variable might have resulted from something other than the intervention. Further, single system research is difficult to use with some problems, especially those that are not easily measured. It is most suitable when the client has one major problem, rather than in situations where the client system has a multitude of equally severe and interrelated problems. However, if the problems are mutually reinforcing, single system research can be used to see if an interaction is associated with changes in one of them that may help to break up the cycle.

Single system research requires administrative support and encouragement. The results should be used only for candid feedback to the individual social worker; they should never be used for administrative evaluation by a supervisor.

The limitations of single system research are common to social work practice, which must often depend on the self-report of clients or their significant others for data on the dependent variable. The social worker must assume that the information received is truthful, which is questionable when working with problems characterized by denial or distortion. It is also difficult to know about— much less to control—other factors that may be influencing the target behavior. Moreover, when clients substitute one problem for another—for example, cocaine dependency for alcohol dependency—how can the success of an intervention be judged? Defining the dependent variable broadly—for example, as substance abuse—will help in this case.

The advantages of single system research clearly outweigh its limitations and demands. It is inexpensive, both in dollars and in time required. The basics are easily taught and understood in a one-day workshop. Single system research raises few ethical issues because it is consistent with good professional practice. In contrast to many group research studies, utilization of findings is virtually guaranteed. Findings, while always tentative, can provide good early feedback on the effectiveness of a new intervention, which can be discarded if it appears to make no difference or reevaluated through replication.

Single system research is well-suited to task-centered, problem-solving methods of practice. It is consistent with a wide variety of methods and social work processes that stress the importance of sound, accountable social work practice. It is also well suited to the participatory methods of social work practice described elsewhere in this book.

READING 17-2 *Do No Harm: Policy Options That Meet Human Needs**

John McKnight

The medical profession has long understood that its interventions have the potential to hurt as well as to help. The Hippocratic oath, repeated by physicians to this day, concludes with the primary mandate: "This above all, do no harm." The harmful capacity of medicine is recognized in what current medical language calls iatrogenic disease—doctor-created maladies.

Much of the positive reputation of the medical profession flows from the ethic that assumes a good doctor, before undertaking any intervention, always asks: "Will this initiative help more than hurt?" Responsible professionals are bound by Hippocrates to consider the balance before acting. Indeed, in the most ethical practice, the burden of proof for efficacy is upon the physician.

The traditional ethical code that prominently displays the Hippocratic principle in the foreground of the medical profession stands in stark contrast to the theory, research, and practice of most other "human service" professions. In the fields of social work, developmental disabilities, physical disability, or care of the elderly, no tradition of routinely analyzing possible negative side-effects exists. Instead, evaluation usually focuses on whether an intervention "made a difference." The intervention is presumed to help if it has any effect at all, and if it has no measurable effect, it is assumed not to have hurt.

Some observers suggest the lack of accounting for negative effects in the human services is a consequence of those interventions not being "powerful" ones when compared to the chemicals and scalpels of medicine.

Instead, there is an unstated assumption that these non-medical professions are searching for something that "works" within fields characterized by effective, neutral or abandoned initiatives, none of which could have basically injured their clients. It is this naive assumption that has degraded the nonmedical human service professions and contributed to popular impressions that many of the clients of these professions are not worth a public investment. Indeed, we now hear the constant claim that the clients of human service professionals—the poor, disadvantaged, disabled, young and old—have not been helped by "pouring money on the problem." The client is usually blamed for not blooming under this "rain of dollars." What has actually happened, however, is that money has been "poured" into the programs of human service professionals (Executive Office of the President, 1986) and we have no knowledge of whether the effects of their ministrations have been iatrogenic. Instead, the labeled and vulnerable in our society are blamed.

If we are to recover the potential of public policy as an asset for those who are labeled, exploited and excluded, it is critical that we begin to understand the iatrogenic aspects of the major agent of public policy—the human service professions. When we can conceptualize the structurally negative effects of their interventions, we can begin a reasoned decision-making process regarding the two basic questions that should determine social policy:

- "Which of the competing human service solutions have more efficacy than negative side effects?"
- "Is there a less iatrogenic solution that does not involve human service methods?"

* From "Do No Harm: Policy Options That Meet Human Needs" in *Social Policy,* Summer, pp.5–15. Copyright © 1989 Social Policy Corporation. Reprinted with permission.

This latter question is a critical element of the policy-making process. We often forget that a human service is only one response to a human condition. There are always many other possibilities that do not involve paid experts and therapeutic concepts.

Mark Twain reminds us that "If your only tool is a hammer, all problems look like nails." While the human service tool has undoubted efficacy in particular situations, like the hammer, it can also do great harm when used inappropriately. All the problems of those who are vulnerable, exploited, excluded, or labeled are not nails. They do not always "need" human services. More often, they may "need" justice, income, and community.

This paper is an attempt to formulate a conceptual framework to assess the iatrogenic effects of the tool called human services (Illich, 1976). What structurally negative effects does it incorporate? When is it inappropriately used? And what methods might test the iatrogenic potential?

There are at least four structurally negative characteristics of the human service tool.

The first is the consequence of seeing individuals primarily in terms of their "needs." Each of us can be conceived as a half-glass of water.

We are partly empty. We have deficiencies.

We are also partly full. We have capacities.

Human service professionals focus on deficiencies, call them "needs," and have expert skills in giving each perceived deficiency a label. The negative effects of this diagnostic process have been thoroughly explored in the literature regarding labelling theory (Wolfensberger, 1975). As a result, we are generally aware that to be diagnosed and labelled as "mentally ill" or "disadvantaged" carries a heavy negative social consequence.

What is less well understood is the fact that the labelling professions force us, structurally, to focus on the empty half when the appropriate focus may be the full half. For example, many people labeled "developmentally disabled" or "physically disabled" are never going to be "fixed" by the service professions. Nonetheless, they are frequently subjected to years of "training" to write their name or tie their shoes. These same people may have many capacities that are unused and unshared while their lives are surrounded by special services that will demonstrably fail to fix the deficiency. Denying opportunities to express capacities is often the structurally iatrogenic effect of the use of ineffective therapeutic tools.

For those whose "emptiness" cannot be filled by human services, the most obvious "need" is the opportunity to express and share their gifts, skills, capacities, and abilities with friends, neighbors, and fellow citizens in the community. As deficiency-oriented service systems obscure this fact, they inevitably harm their client and the community by preempting the relationship between them (O'Connell, 1988).

The second structurally negative effect of the use of the human service tool is its effect on public budgets. It is clear to every elected official that the public purse is limited. Contemporary legislative process is mainly about the division of that purse. To give more to one activity (defense) usually means giving less to another (agriculture or education). Therefore, a realistic approach to public policy and expenditure always requires an understanding of trade-offs—who or what gets less as something else gets more.

This process occurs between major expenditure categories such as education, highways, defense, medicine, and agriculture. Trade-offs also take place within each of these categories. Should we have more land-based bombers or more missiles? There is a choice to be made.

The same process occurs within the human service budget. Here, however, it is less well understood because the basic competition for the limited funds available for the "disadvantaged" is between the human service system and cash income for labeled people. Service system lobbyists and advocates see the competition for limited public resources as a jockeying between various service providers and systems. They rarely recognize or acknowledge, however, that the net effect of their lobbying is to limit cash income for those they call "needy" and increase the budget and incomes of service programs and providers.

As a federal study showed, between 1960 and 1985 federal and state cash assistance programs grew 105 percent in real terms, while non-cash programs for services and commodities grew 1,760 percent. By 1985, cash income programs amounted to $32.3 billion, while commodity and service programs received $99.7 billion (Executive Office of the President, 1986). While commodity programs and vouchers such as food stamps and housing vouchers represent a minority of these dollars, they are often preferable to human service allocations because they provide a greater range of choice and are appropriated for more basic life requirements.

The service system's preemption of public wealth designated for the "disadvantaged" is also demonstrated by studies of poverty allocations in New York City and Chicago (Grossman & Smolka, 1984; Kallenback & Lyons, 1989). Both studies demonstrate that over 60 percent of all public funds allocated in those cities for low-income people are allocated for services rather than for income.

The effect of trading cash for human services is devastating for people whose lives cannot be "fixed" by service intervention. Nonetheless, we have no effective measures that allow legislators or policy-makers to assess whether public investments for services would be more enabling as cash income. As a consequence, most legislative debate surrounding labelled people is about which services to fund, and for how much.

The third structurally negative effect of the human service tool is its impact upon community and associational life. The community, a social space where citizens turn to solve problems, may be displaced by the intervention of human service professionals as an alternative method of problem solving. Human service professionals with special expertise, technique, and technology push out the problem-solving knowledge and action of friend, neighbor, citizen, and association. As the power of profession and service system ascends, the legitimacy, authority, and capacity of citizens and community descend (Illich, 1977). The *citizen* retreats. The *client* advances. The power of community action weakens. The authority of the service system strengthens. And as human service tools prevail, the tools of citizenship, association, and community rust. Their uses are even forgotten. Many local people come to believe that the service tool is the only tool, and that their task as good citizens is to support taxes and charities for more services.

The consequence of this professional persuasion is devastating for those labeled people whose primary "need" is to be incorporated in community life and empowered through citizenship. These people include those frequently labeled as developmentally disabled, physically disabled, elderly, ex-convicts. They desperately "need" incorporation into community life but the community of citizens and associations has often been persuaded by human service advocates that vulnerable people:

- need to be surrounded by professional services in order to survive
- are therefore appropriately removed from community life in order to receive these special service programs in special places
- cannot be incorporated into community life because citizens don't know how to deal with these special people

The result of this professional pedagogy is a disabled citizenry and impotent community associations, unable to remember or understand how labeled people were or can be included in community life.

Instead of recognizing the crucial need most labeled people have for the empowerment of joining community life as a citizen, expressing capacities and making choices, many good-willed citizens volunteer to assist service systems free of charge. In this simple act, citizen volunteers trade off their unique potential to bring a labelled person into their life and the associational life of community in exchange for the use of their time as an unpaid agent for a service system. The community group that might ask a disabled or vulnerable person to join as a member decides, instead, to raise money for wheelchairs and rehabilitation centers. The associations of community life are led to support segregated, professionally controlled athletic events rather than incorporating a labelled person into a church bowling league.

In working to meet this need for incorporation, it is necessary to recognize that the human service tool typically limits, weakens or replaces community, associational and citizen tools. This is in the nature of any approach built on the premise that vulnerable people will be better because an expert knows better.

The fourth structurally negative consequence of using human service programs is that they can create, in the aggregate, environments that contradict the potential positive effect of any one program. When enough programs surround a client, they may combine to create a new environment in which none of the programs will be efficacious.

This particular iatrogenic effect is difficult to comprehend because it grows from the use of programs, any one of which might seem reasonable standing alone. Indeed, most individual service programs appear reasonable and "needed" when presented to legislators. What is invisible is the effect of the program when it is joined by many other service programs as they surround a labeled person. With enough services surrounding a life, a new environment emerges that has its own peculiar system of incentives, rewards, and penalties.

The process is analogous to an aggregation of trees. In an urban neighborhood there are usually trees in yards and parkways. We would not say, however, that people in that neighborhood live in a forest, even though the trees in a forest may be of the same kind. We would not call an area a forest until it has enough trees to create a new environment that does not exist in the neighborhood. In the forest, the shade and fallen leaves kill off grasses. In their place appear new wild flowers and bushes. The grassland animals are replaced by those that live in trees. Prairie birds are replaced by forest birds. The forest flora and fauna create a different world; most people even act differently in a forest, even though it is a place comprised of trees familiar from their neighborhood.

By way of analogy, each individual service program is like a tree. But when enough service programs surround people, they come to live in a forest of services. The environment is different from the neighborhood or community. And people who have to live in the service forest will act differently than those people whose lives are principally defined by neighborhood relationships.

We all recognize the forests of services that are called institutions. They are places where people live wholly surrounded by service professionals, programs, and plans. The uniqueness of this environment is emphasized by large buildings, walls, fences, and so on. Nonetheless, forests of services can be created without walls or large buildings. Places called group homes, halfway houses, and convalescent homes are usually service forests. Also, some labeled individuals who live with their families can be so fully served by professionals that their life is lived in a forest although their residence is in a neighborhood.

There are also low-income neighborhoods where so many people live lives surrounded by services that the neighborhood itself becomes a forest. People who live in this neighborhood forest are now called the "underclass." This is an obvious misnomer. Instead, we should say that the neighborhood is a place where citizens act as anyone else would if their lives were similarly surrounded and controlled by paid service professionals. A more accurate

label than "underclass" would be "dependent on human service systems." A more accurate differentiation of status would be to say the residents are "clients" rather than "citizens."

When the services grow dense enough around the lives of people, a circular process develops. A different environment is created for these individuals. The result of a non-community environment is that those who experience it necessarily act in unusual and deviant ways. These new ways, called inappropriate behavior, are then cited by service professionals as proof of the need for separation in a forest of services and the need for more services.

The disabling effect of this circular process is devastating to the client and to our communities. The public is understandably mystified. Each individual program appears to be reasonably needed and appropriate. However, in the aggregate, each program has become ineffective and often harmful. The situation is analogous to a person who dies of taking 20 different pills, any one of which might have been helpful.

Physicians have long recognized this interactive iatrogenic effect. Service systems have not. Instead, human service systems nearly always prescribe more programs, more services, more "targeting," and larger forests. The result is predictably counterproductive. Costs increase. Programs proliferate. Forests grow. Clients multiply. People adapt their behavior to the forest and are called maladaptive. The cycle spirals downward and the failures are blamed on the victims.

In summary, these iatrogenic effects tell us that policymakers and practitioners should be constantly aware that the use of human service tools places a person at risk of: a reduced sense of self worth; poverty; segregation from community life; and disempowerment as a citizen (Exhibit 17–13). The risks demand the most serious reevaluation of policies that empower human service professionals and systems to intervene in the lives of labelled and vulnerable people.

A practical framework for this policy reevaluation would begin by placing the burden of proof upon those who propose a human service intervention as a means of helping a person with a particular condition. This "burden" is analogous to that understood by the Food and Drug Administration as it evaluates the use of various medical interventions. The intervenor has the responsibility to identify the negative side effects and to prove the benefits are greater.

EXHIBIT 17-13	Four Structurally Negative Effects on Human Services	
1. Human services emphasize deficiencies.	→	1. Undermines the sense of capacity and self worth of a client.
2. Human services create a demand on public budgets.	→	2. Reduces the cash income and market choices of the client.
3. Human services focus on problem solving by experts and systems.	→	3. Decreases participation in community life by the client.
4. A dense environment of services surrounds individuals and communities on all sides.	→	4. Intensifies dependency, stimulates deviance, and neutralizes the positive potential of individual programs of service intervention.

This is an excellent model for evaluating proposed human service interventions. The service advocate should be required to identify the negative effects, present evidence of the benefits, and demonstrate that the benefits outweigh the negative effects. The effect of such a rigorous evaluation would create a positive new force in the lives of labeled people. The service agency, department, or professional would be asked by legislators, public executives, boards of directors, foundations, or groups of labelled people to specify the negative effects of their proposals. This wholesome new discipline placed upon the service advocates would often create a revolutionary reexamination of their assumptions and practices.

In addition to the burden of proof regarding negative effects and benefits of a particular service intervention, the service advocate should also be required to present evidence that the intervention will not be used cumulatively, creating a service forest. Just as the ethical medical professional recognizes and protects against the negative effects of the interaction among many drugs, the human service professional should be required to identify the negative effect of aggregating programs around a person's life and define the safeguards that will be used to protect against the dependency and deviance that so frequently result from a "forest" of services.

Once both requirements are met by service advocates and the particular and interactive negative effects are clarified, policymakers should quickly recognize that the use of a particular human service tool is not necessarily good or even neutral. They should see that a service is a potentially injurious tool and begin to ask whether other kinds of non-service resources, activities, or opportunities might be appropriate for the person said to be in need of a service. They could begin to ask, "Is there a different kind of approach that doesn't involve a human service

that might be more effective and have less negative effect?"

Here again, the medical analogy is helpful. While the Food and Drug Administration may approve a medicine as being more beneficial than harmful, an ethical physician does not assume that it should therefore be prescribed. Instead, the physician asks whether there are other, more effective ways of dealing with the condition that do not involve use of the drug and its negative effects.

The current protocol for high blood pressure provides a good example. All the approved medicines have some significant negative effects. Therefore, ethical physicians first seek non-medical alternatives before risking use of the medicine. This often involves advising clients to undertake an exercise program, reduce their weight, and decrease their salt intake. Similarly, a review of policy options to address conditions of vulnerable and labeled people should systematically examine non-human service responses that might provide the same or better results with fewer or no negative side effects.

This policy-options review requires that policymakers have a set of alternatives to test against proposed human service interventions. Fortunately, there are at least three alternatives that have historically proven effective in addressing the conditions of many who are vulnerable, labelable, or said to be in need.

The first option is to identify the capacities, skills, or potential contributions of the persons said to be in need. What policies, resources, or activities could result in the exercise, expression, visibility, and magnification of those assets? For example, many people labeled "developmentally disabled" have been found to thrive and flourish when they escape a "forest" of professional services and are provided community opportunities to express their unique gifts (O'Connell, 1988). Similarly, low-income people, neighborhoods, and public housing developments experience regeneration when they focus on their capacities rather than an exclusive emphasis upon problems, deficiencies, and needs (McKnight, 1987). However, in the case of both groups of people, the files of the local human service agencies and authorities are filled with descriptions of their needs, deficiencies, diagnoses, and problems. Therefore, those agencies are not useful as a resource for capacity-oriented development. Policymakers will need to find other activities and supports if the assets and capacities of people and communities are to be viewed as the basic problem-solving tools.

The second option is to provide cash income in lieu of access to prepaid or vouchered human services. This option provides an opening to many new opportunities and even creates better services. The advantages of income over services include:

- providing empowering choices in a free market
- providing choices between services, thus creating a competitive market that should improve services
- creating a market in low-income areas where mainline enterprises will have an incentive to reach out to low-income people

There is, of course, the stereotypic concern that "disadvantaged" people might not use their income wisely. However, there is no evidence that, as a group, these people are less wise in the use of their money than doctors, psychologists, social workers, or other professionals who are now the primary beneficiaries of dollars appropriated for low-income and other labeled people.

The third option is to seek participation in community life and citizenship activities instead of human service interventions. This option flows from the fact that many vulnerable people are primarily disabled by their segregation from community life in institutions, "special" programs, or service ghettos (Rothman, 1971). Paradoxically, their lives often improve significantly when they leave service systems and become effectively incorporated in community life (Woodson, 1981). Therefore, the challenge is to create policies that stimulate the hospitality of citizen associations and community groups so that they will incorporate and share the capacities and gifts of those who have been excluded because of their labels.

My purpose in this analysis has been to establish two basic premises:

1. Human service interventions have negative effects as well as benefits.
2. Human service interventions are only one of many ways to address the condition of people who are labeled.

Many of our failed reforms and programs during the last two decades are the result of our failure to recognize these two realities. When policymakers begin to evaluate human service proposals from the perspective of these two premises, we will create much more effective means of problem solving. Making these premises operational is reasonably simple. They can be expressed in five basic questions that can be asked by any person responsible for policies affecting those citizens who are especially vulnerable, disadvantaged, or exploited:

1. What are the negative effects of the human service proposed to help the class of people?
2. What are the situations where the proposed service may be applied with many other services and what interactive negative effects will result?
3. Will a focus on the capacities of the class of people be more effective than a service program's focus on deficiencies and needs?
4. Will providing the dollars proposed for funding the human service provide greater benefits if given to the clients as cash income?
5. Will incorporation into community life be more beneficial than special, separating service treatments?

The last three questions incorporate the central values of a free and democratic society. They recognize that the greatest "service" our society provides is the opportunity to express our unique capacities, to have a decent income and join with our fellow citizens in creating productive communities. No human service professional or program will ever equal the healing and empowering effect of those three democratic opportunities. Therefore, policies that support citizen capacity, income, and community should have preference over other forms of intervention that are necessarily second-rate and second-best responses. Effective democratic policy is guided by three powerful principles: citizenship, income, and community.

LEARNING EXERCISES

1. Prepare one- or two-sentence definitions for the following concepts or briefly explain each concept to a colleague:

   AB design
   ABA design
   ABAB design
   baseline
   effectiveness
   efficiency
   formative evaluation
   goal attainment scaling
   iatrogenic
   inputs
   outcomes
   outputs
   practice evaluation
   program evaluation
   regressive effects
   side effects
   single subject designs
   summative evaluation

2. If you are in a field placement, discover if your agency has a written policy regarding program evaluation. If so, how does it compare with the policy in Exhibit 17–8?

3. Goal attainment scaling procedures can be used in any situation where objectives are set; thus, goal attainment scaling can be learned without actually working with clients. Set personal learning objectives for yourself for next term: How many books will you read? How many articles? What are your objectives for grades? What percentage of written assignments will you complete on time? Develop a set of goal attainment scales to measure the extent to which you accomplish your objectives.

4. What guidance do the NASW and CASW codes of ethics offer for your participation in program evaluation activities?

5. Team up with four other classmates and role-play a meeting of the committee in Exhibit 17–9. Ask one or two other students to observe your committee meeting and offer feedback on the reasons you could or could not come to agreement. What was the role of the program evaluation consultant?

REFERENCES

Berlin, S. (1983). Single-case evaluation: Another version. *Social Work Research and Abstracts, 19*(1), 3–11.

Bloom, M., Fischer, J., & Orme, J. (1995). *Evaluating practice: Guidelines for the accountable professional* (2nd ed.). Boston: Allyn & Bacon.

Burr, W. R., & Christensen, C. (1992). Undesirable side effects of enhancing self-esteem. *Family Relations, 41*(4), 460–464.

Corcoran, K., & Gingerich, W. J. (1994). Practice evaluation in the context of managed care: Case recording methods for quality assurance reviews. *Research on Social Work Practice, 4*(3), 326–337.

Council on Social Work Education. (1992a). *Curriculum policy statement for master's degree programs in social work education.* Alexandria, VA: Author.

Council on Social Work Education. (1992b). *Curriculum policy statement for BSW programs in social work education.* Alexandria, VA: Author.

Durst, D. (1992). The road to poverty is paved with good intentions: Social interventions and indigenous peoples. *International Social Work, 35*(2), 191–202.

Elks, M. A., & Kirkhart, K. E. (1993). Evaluating effectiveness from the practitioner perspective. *Social Work, 38*(5), 554–563.

Executive Office of the President (1986). *Up from dependency* (suppl. 1, vol. 1). Washington, DC: U.S. Government Printing Office.

Fleuridas, C., Leigh, G. K., Rosenthal, D. M., & Leigh, T. E. (1990). Family goal recording: An adaptation of goal attainment scaling for enhancing family therapy and assessment. *Journal of Marital and Family Therapy, 16*(4), 389–406.

Gelman, S. R. (1992). Risk management through client access to case records. *Social Work, 37*(1), 73–79.

Gerdes, K. E., Edmonds, R. M., Hoslam, D. R., & McCartney, T. L. (1996). A statewide survey of licensed clinical social workers' use of practice evaluation procedures. *Research on Social Work Practice, 6*(1), 27–39.

Grasso, A., & Epstein, I. (1992). *Research utilization in the social services.* New York: Haworth Press.

Graybeal, C. T., & Rulf, E. (1995). Process recording: It's more than you think. *Journal of Social Work Education, 31*(2), 169–181.

Grinnell, R. M. (1997). *Social work research and evaluation* (5th ed.). Itasca, IL: F. E. Peacock.

Grossman, D., & Smolka, G. (1984). *New York City's poverty budget.* New York: Community Service Society of New York.

Howitt, D. (1993). *Child abuse errors: When good intentions go wrong.* New Brunswick, NJ: Rutgers University Press.

Hudson, J., & Grinnell, R. (1989). Program evaluation. In B. Compton & B. Galaway (Eds.), *Social work processes* (4th ed., pp. 691–710). Belmont, CA: Wadsworth.

Illich, I. (1976). *Medical nemesis.* New York: Pantheon.

Illich, I. (1977). *Disabling professions.* London: Marion Boyers.

Kallenbach, D., & Lyons, A. (1989). *Government spending for the poor in Cook County, Illinois: Can we do better?* Evanston, IL: Center for Urban Affairs and Policy Research, Northwestern University.

Karr, J. (1990). Goal attainment scaling in the treatment of children with behavior disorders. *School Social Work Journal, 15*(1), 14–20.

Kiresuk, T. J., & Garwick, G. (1974). Basic goal attainment scaling procedures. *Program Evaluation Report* (Chapter 1). Minneapolis, MN: Program Evaluation Project, Hennipen County Health Center.

Kiresuk, T. J., & Lund, S. H. (1977). Goal attainment scaling. In C. C. Attkisson, W. A. Hargreaves, M. J. Horowitz, & S. E. Sorenson (Eds.), *Evaluation of human service programs.* New York: Academic.

Kiresuk, T., & Sherman, R. E. (1968). Goal attainment scaling: A general method for evaluating comprehensive community health programs. *Community Mental Health Journal, 4,* 443–453.

Kiresuk, T. J., Smith, A., & Cardillo, J. E. (1994). *Goal attainment scaling: Applications, theory, and measurement.* Hillsdale, NJ: L. Erlbaum Associates.

Marlow, C. (1998). *Research methods for generalist social work* (2nd ed.). Pacific Grove, CA: Brooks/Cole.

McKnight, J. (1987). *The future of low-income neighborhoods and the people who reside there.* Evanston, IL: Center for Urban Affairs and Policy Research, Northwestern University.

McNulty, C., & Wardle, J. (1994). Adult disclosure of sexual abuse: A primary cause of psychological distress? *Child Abuse and Neglect, 18*(7), 549–555.

Modai, I., & Rabinowitz, J. (1993). Why and how to establish a computerized system for psychiatric case records. *Hospital and Community Psychiatry, 44*(11), 1091–1097.

Moore, S. T. (1995). Efficiency in social work practice and administration. *Social Work, 40*(5), 602–608.

O'Connell, M. (1988). *The gift of hospitality.* Evanston, IL: Center for Urban Affairs and Policy Research, Northwestern University.

Owens, D. K., & Nease, R. F. (1993). Development of outcome-based practice guidelines: A method for structuring problems and synthesizing evidence. *Journal on Quality Improvement, 19*(7), 249–264.

Rosen, A. (1996). The scientific practitioner revisited: Some obstacles and prerequisites for fuller implementation in practice. *Social Work Research, 20*(2), 105–111.

Rothman, D. J. (1971). *The discovery of the asylum.* Boston: Little, Brown.

Rubin, A., & Babbie, E. (1997). *Research methods for social work* (3rd ed.). Pacific Grove, CA: Brooks/Cole.

Sieber, S. (1981). *Fatal remedies.* New York: Plenum.

Thyer, B. A. (1993). Single system research designs. In R. M. Grinnell (Ed.), *Social work research and evaluation* (4th ed.). Itasca, IL: F. E. Peacock.

Tripodi, T. (1994). *A primer on single-subject design for clinical social workers.* Washington, DC: NASW.

Wolfensberger, W. (1975). *The origin and nature of our institutional models.* Syracuse, NY: Human Policy Press.

Woodson, R. (1981). *A summons to life.* Cambridge, MA: Ballinger.

Yegidis, B., & Weinbach, R. (1996). *Research methods for social work.* White Plains, NY: Longman.

chapter 18

Endings in Social Work

CHAPTER PREVIEW

For many social workers, ending a working relationship with a client is one of the most difficult phases of the problem-solving process. In this chapter, we will consider:

- circumstances under which endings occur
- preparation of clients for endings
- responding to clients' reactions
- assisting clients to use endings as a learning and growth-producing experience
- being aware of our own feelings and reactions to endings

In Reading 18-1, Howard Hess and Peg McCartt Hess provide a context for understanding the ending phase, along with some practical suggestions.

TYPES OF ENDINGS

Endings occur under different sets of circumstances. They may occur when the service agreement has been satisfactorily completed and the client does not require continuing services or when you and the client agree that nothing more can be done, even though the objectives may not have been fully achieved. Sometimes, the relationship ends because you are leaving the agency or taking on different duties; the client will then be transferred to another worker within your agency. Finally, a client who requires a service that your agency does not provide will be referred elsewhere; in such cases, in contrast to the referrals discussed in Chapter 13, there is no expectation that service will continue from your agency.

Whether the ending occurs because of discontinuation of services, internal transfer of the client, or referral to an external agency, the process is essentially the same. You must prepare clients for ending by assisting them with their reactions. To do this, and to achieve a positive and growth-producing ending for clients, you must also be aware of your own feelings and reactions.

CLIENT REACTIONS

Clients may react to termination of the helping relationship in various ways:

- by behaving as though it were not going to happen, in an attempt at denial
- by returning to earlier behavior patterns or reintroducing problems or tasks
- by explosive behavior and assertions that the worker is wrong to say the client can go it alone
- by a precipitate break in the relationship, as if to preempt the worker's intention of leaving

Clients may feel deserted. They may feel that you are breaking the service agreement and resent what they perceive as your irresponsibility and lack of concern. The reaction will depend on the particular client, the problem, and the particular relationship between worker and client. For clients addressing emotional difficulties, your departure may evoke all the accumulated pain of prior separations. For a task-centered group working toward community change, the sense of betrayal and desertion may be overshadowed by concerns about the competence of the new worker who will be helping them. The reactions of a group of adolescent girls to termination are described in Exhibit 18–1.

Consider this example. A worker informed his client, Sal, that he was leaving the agency in six weeks. He

EXHIBIT 18-1	Does the Group End?

The Let's-Talk-About-It group was composed of five adolescent girls, all on probation; the girls were selected for the group because they appeared to be shy, somewhat withdrawn, and lacking in social skills. The group leader was an outgoing, knowledgeable, yet sensitive volunteer with the probation agency. Each girl had discussed the group with her probation officer, and with the volunteer group worker, prior to the first group meeting. The group volunteer worker had also had a joint meeting with all the girls and their parents to arrive at a contract for the group.

The purpose of the group was to improve the girls' social skills, including their ability to communicate. The group agreed to meet for five sessions. At the first meeting, after a period of initial nervousness and giggling, the girls showed excellent ability to become part of a group, to enter into discussions, and to plan. One girl, the 17-year-old, quickly established herself as a spokesperson for the group and at one point in the first meeting expressed her feelings, as well as the temperature of the group, by saying, ``We all feel a little tongue-tied and have to have time to think that over.'' At a later meeting this same girl remarked, on hearing the tape of the previous week's meeting played back, that she had no idea she had talked so much. Nevertheless, she continued to be more active verbally throughout the sessions.

They chose to have a hair stylist talk to them in the second meeting, and a modeling instructor in the fourth meeting, leaving the third and fifth meetings for discussion. There was not much apparent interest in the social event, but it later seemed clear to us that this related to the girls' social deprivation rather than their disinterest. The girls' use of individual meetings with probation officers to make the group experience more meaningful; several asked their probation officers to give them ideas about social activities so they could help plan the event. This also serves to point out the necessity of checking out meaning with a client; in this instance, the girls' silence could have been interpreted as meaning

something other than their lack of experience and knowledge.

The content of the five weekly meetings will be summarized. In contrast to their inability to discuss plans for a social event spontaneously, with only a suggestion from the worker, they launched into active discussion of such topics as whether to drop out of school, what to do when one is invited to a boy's house and wants to go but is too shy, and whether adults can ever really help a kid who is in trouble. A question such as, ``Has anything happened since last week that anyone would like to talk about?'' was enough to get the discussion started. The use the girls made of the discussion was evident in comments such as, ``Maybe now we won't be so scared,'' as well as in their improved ability to communicate in the group meetings and in individual interviews.

The termination of the group provided both professional staff and volunteers with some insight and learning. None of the girls appeared for the fifth and final meeting. All but one did, however, contact the worker by phone or in person. One girl arrived 20 minutes after the scheduled meeting time and explained that she had missed her bus. Another girl phoned to explain that she was ill and that her sister, also a member of the group, would miss the meeting because she had to stay after school. A fourth girl arrived 45 minutes later with her boyfriend, and explained that she was delayed and therefore could not attend the meeting. The fifth girl, reached later by phone, explained her absence by saying she had to stay after school and explained her failure to call in by saying she had been unable to use the phone at school.

The next day, one of the sisters phoned the worker at home to say that she and her sister wondered if they really had to end the group meetings. She was told that this could be discussed at the rescheduled final session. With the evidence of the girls' reluctance to give up the group experience, the staff considered negotiating several more sessions with them.

promised to introduce Sal to his new probation officer and help them to get started together. Sal, an adolescent with a long history of theft and assault, had never had a trusting relationship with anyone until he met the worker. Over the year that they had worked together, he had made tremendous changes in his behavior; there had been no new offenses. Thus, the worker was surprised to hear that Sal had stolen a car and resisted arrest

when apprehended. When the two met, Sal greeted the worker by saying, "Now you can't leave. I'm in a new mess and you can't leave until you go to court with me and get me straightened out again." What happens to his ability to form trusting relationships when the worker explains that he must go regardless of the client's need? What can the worker do to ease the pain and to support Sal's ability to trust?

Clients' reactions to termination will probably involve their usual coping and behavioral patterns in response to stress, including

- denial
- attempts to control the worker and the situation by creating new problems
- direct expression of feelings of abandonment and anger toward the worker
- indirect expression of anger by avoidance—for instance, by missing appointments, as in Exhibit 18–1

PREPARING CLIENTS FOR ENDINGS

The need for termination should be discussed well in advance of the termination date (Northern, 1969; Philip, 1994). Endings are less hurtful and destructive when there is time for client and worker to deal with their reactions and, in transfers, for new workers to get involved in an orderly manner. Clients may regard it as desertion when you leave the agency. They may feel that you would stay with them if they were important to you

or, worse yet, if they were good clients. Clients need to participate with you in planning the transfer to another worker or termination of their contact with the agency. You should invite clients to discuss their feelings about termination. At times, particularly in group situations, clients can be encouraged to role-play the transfer—from concern about your departure through beginning with a new worker. They can discuss or role-play their thoughts about the new worker. In Exhibit 18–2, Helen Northern identifies some of the clues that a group members may be ready for termination.

Clients need opportunities to meet the new worker. The first time, the new worker may just stop in for a minute to be introduced. You may discuss with clients their feelings and thoughts about the new worker after this introduction. The second time, the new worker may attend as an observer if the client is a group, or sit in on an interview, if the client is an individual or a family; the new worker is there to get acquainted. At the third encounter, you and the new worker operate as a team, and the new worker gradually assumes the primary professional role. The two of you can talk together, to

---

EXHIBIT 18–2 Ending a Group

The purposeful nature of social work implies that from time to time it is necessary to assess the desirability of continuing service to the members. The judgment may be that there has been progress toward the achievement of goals and there is potential for further improvement, in which case the service should be continued. Another decision may be that little, if any, progress has been made; if this is combined with little potential for changing the situation, the service should be discontinued. Still another evaluation may be that progress toward the achievement of goals has been sufficient, and the service should be terminated. Social workers have undoubtedly anticipated termination from the beginning of their work with the group and have clarified with the members its possible duration, so that the goals and means toward their achievement have been related to the plans for both individuals and the group. Nevertheless, there comes a time when the worker and the members must face the fact of separation from each other and often, also, the end of the group itself (p. 222).

As the group moves toward readiness for termination, there are clues to guide practitioners in their activities with the group. The goals that members have for themselves and each other have been partially achieved, at least, although movement in the group may have been faster for some than for others. Members come to talk about some of the changes that have taken place in them and in the group. Attendance becomes irregular unless the worker makes special efforts to motivate members to continue until the final meeting . . . The structure tends to become more flexible . . . Cohesiveness weakens as the members find satisfactions and new relationships outside the group.

The time span between the initial information about termination and the final meeting of the group will vary with many factors, including the group's purpose, the length of time the group has been together, the problems and progress of the members, their anticipated reactions to termination, and the press of the environment on them (p. 228).

Source: H. Northern, *Social work with groups.* New York: Columbia University Press (1969), p. 225.

assess where you are and how the new worker understands and evaluates the contract, with the client as observer. In this way, the client obtains a clear idea of what the new worker is told and what his or her commitment is.

Social workers usually terminate services when the service has been successful (Fortune, Pearlingi, & Rochelle, 1991); in that case, both clients and the workers are likely to report a sense of pride and accomplishment (Fortune, Perlingi, & Rochelle, 1992). We suggest a brief ceremony when the service agreement has been completed; you can decide what is appropriate on the basis of the client's wishes, your agency, and the nature of the work. Groups may end service with a planned social event. With a family, simple refreshments can be served at your agency or you may wish to go out with the family for refreshments or even for lunch. With an individual client, you may wish to go out for lunch or coffee; if you don't feel comfortable with that, you may consider giving the client a letter of commendation for the work done. Keep in mind that the purpose is simply to celebrate the conclusion of very important work. Do not attempt to convert a professional relationship into a social relationship.

When clients are leaving the agency because nothing more can be done or because they are unhappy with the services provided; an ending ceremony would probably not be appropriate. We recommend open discussion of the situation and, if progress has been made, a letter of commendation for the work done. Leave the door open for these clients to return when they require assistance in the future; use the word *when,* not *if.* Clients who leave the agency when their work is finished should also be made aware that they can initiate future contact. Many individuals and families will need social services on an intermittent basis.

As evaluation of the client's progress continues, you may begin to think that the objectives are in sight, and you may introduce the matter of ending. Or clients may indicate that they are ready to move on to a new experience and leave you behind. If clients begin to miss appointments or indicate with pride that they took some unilateral action toward the objective, they may be telling you that they can go it alone and that ending service is appropriate.

To sum up, these guidelines will be helpful in preparing clients for endings.

1. Discuss endings as far in advance as possible. If the ending date is known when the service agreement is negotiated, discuss the ending then.

2. When ending occurs by transfer, introduce the client to the new worker as far in advance of the ending as possible. Invite the new worker to at least one joint meeting with you and the client.

3. Help clients to cope with their reactions to the end of the helping relationship.

ENDINGS AS A LEARNING EXPERIENCE

The tasks of termination are:

- working out the conflict—for both worker and client—between acknowledging improvement and goal achievement and relinquishing help
- working out the client's fear of losing the helping relationship and the support of a concerned person
- examining the experience and recognizing the progress made
- considering how this experience can be transferred to other life problems
- examining what is involved in stabilizing the gains made
- encouraging the client to seek help in the future, if needed

Planning for endings often provides an opportunity for a growth-producing experience (Siebold, 1992). Clients will respond to the perceived loss with stereotyped behavior patterns that they have previously adopted in response to stress. This offers an opportunity to analyze those reactions and to consider alternative ways that the client might behave.

For example, consider Sal, who stole another car in a misguided effort to avoid losing his worker. Had Sal's previous delinquencies been attempts to retaliate against others or to control a situation he did not like? Did the behavior accomplish those ends? Could Sal learn ways to handle disappointment and anger that would not have unpleasant consequences for him or others? Analyzing such questions could result in a growth experience for Sal.

Likewise, consider the avoidance behavior used by the teenagers in Exhibit 18–1. Is this their usual way of handling disappointment? How else might it be handled? The worker might help them to practice talking about and sharing their sense of loss. Alternatively, recognizing that these girls had a very positive experience with the group, the worker might meet with the clients and their probation officers and help them identify groups in their communities that could offer similar experiences.

WORKER REACTIONS TO ENDINGS

Termination may also be difficult for you. You may feel that you are betraying the client and violating the service agreement. You may feel that no other worker can take your place; by subtly imparting this judgment, you will increase the client's feelings of uncertainty. If you are leaving the agency, painful feelings of separation may arise. You may be so anxious about the demands of the new job that you do not give the problems of transfer your full attention. All of these feelings may churn within you. The situation is different if the transfer occurs because the client has a problem with you. In that case, you should examine your own feelings carefully, to be sure that you do not set obstacles in the client's way.

Termination stirs up emotions both about your professional activities and about your clients. You will feel pleased that progress has been made but also a sense of loss and grief. You may find that termination stirs up guilt about not having been able to do better and fear of the client's efforts to go ahead independently. Some workers consider continuing a limited relationship with former clients. We discourage this; worker-initiated contacts are seldom helpful. Even such limited activities as sending birthday or holiday cards primarily reflect your own need and difficulty with separation.

Professional relationships should not be converted to personal or social relationships, but common sense and courtesy suggest that, for example, you should feel free to greet and speak briefly with a former client who is waiting to see another worker in your agency. If you see a former client on the street or in a social setting, you are free to say hello and exchange a few words, especially if the client acknowledges you. You may occasionally receive an invitation to a former client's college gradua-

tion or wedding. You are under no obligation to accept these invitations, but doing so poses no particular problem, as long as the invitation is initiated by the former client and you do not use this occasion establish a longer-term social relationship.

Transfer may also pose problems for the client's new worker, who may wonder whether they can offer as effective help as their predecessor did and may meet clients with defensiveness and a determination to prove themselves. As a result, they may move forward too rapidly with new ideas; feeling angry and hurt about the transfer and still feeling loyalty to you, clients may need to mark time and do some testing before they are willing to move on. Some clients will lose their trust of workers and will feel reluctant to establish a relationship with another person who may also leave. The new worker must recognize clients' right to have their feelings and take the time they need to deal with them.

CHAPTER SUMMARY

Endings occur when service is completed, when you leave the agency or take on different responsibilities, or when you refer a client to another agency that can provide the service needed. Ending a relationship is difficult. You should expect reactions of loss from clients, who may develop new problems, express anger, or avoid you by missing appointments.

You have a responsibility to prepare clients for endings. Be explicit if you are providing a time-limited service and the ending date is known when you begin. If you are transferring the case, let the client know as soon as you are aware of the pending change. If service is being completed, discuss this several sessions in advance of the expected ending, and plan to use one of your final sessions for evaluation. Prepare clients for transfer or referral by introducing them to the new worker. Try to involve the new worker in at least one session, which can be spent in reviewing progress and identifying further work to be done; this could be the evaluation session.

Discuss clients' reactions to the ending and, if appropriate, help them to cope. Endings may be a learning and growth experience for clients. They are likely to handle their reactions to termination by resorting to their usual mechanisms for coping with stress. You may be able to help clients identify and consider other ways of handling their feelings or to reinforce other work that you have been doing. A closing ceremony is important, especially when the objectives of the service plan have been accomplished.

Endings may also be difficult for you; you need to be aware of—and responsible for—your own feelings. In particular, you may experience a sense of loss. After termination, we discourage contact with clients, especially if initiated by you. Sending birthday cards or holiday cards, for example, may not be helpful to the client. You may occasionally receive invitations to special events, such as a former client's wedding. You are under no obligation to accept such invitations, but it is appropriate to do so, as long as you do not attempt to initiate a continuing social relationship.

Finally, you must ensure that clients feel free to return to the agency if they require future assistance. Social work services, like health services, may be an ongoing resource in clients' lives.

A LOOK FORWARD

In Reading 18-1, Howard Hess and Peg McCartt Hess provide a context for understanding termination. They note that endings, while they often prompt denial and distancing on the part of both clients and social workers, offer an opportunity to build a bridge between the service provided and the client's subsequent problem-solving activities.

In the final chapter, we share some further thoughts on the process of becoming a social worker. We focus specifically on how to avoid burnout, which is a professional hazard in our intensely demanding field.

READING 18-1 *Termination in Context**

Howard Hess and Peg McCartt Hess

A distinctive characteristic of the worker-client interaction—whether a single interview for the purpose of assessment and referral or a therapeutic relationship, extending over a series of interviews—is that it must end. Termination raises issues of separation and self-sufficiency and will also require both client and social worker to evaluate their work together. Because of these issues of separation and evaluation, ending can be difficult for both client and practitioner (Fox, Nelson, & Bolman, 1969; Shulman, 1992; Siebold, 1991; Siporin, 1975; Webb, 1985). In many instances, ambivalence about the ending causes both to vacillate in their judgments about an appropriate conclusion to their work. Their ability to resolve this ambivalence determines the quality of the termination experience.

In mastering termination, clients must accomplish two general tasks: First, they must confront and begin to accept the impending separation from their helpers; and, second, they must come to terms with the outcome of the helping process. Client awareness of both loss and outcome is stimulated by the encroaching time limit. At

no other phase in the process is time such a powerful influence.

Because clients and practitioners often form close attachments, termination typically involves working through the grief associated with a break in these ties; as well as a clear evaluation or review of accomplishments. If the goals of working together have been accomplished, clients can be helped to acknowledge the appropriateness of ending. Conversely, if the goals have not been accomplished, the client can be helped to determine whether the goals were realistic and how problem solving can continue after the end point with the practitioner. When the helping process is disrupted, the termination work should clarify the nature of the necessary referral or transfer. As the work is reviewed, clients often experience a blend of pride in accomplished change, hope for the future, and sorrow about the loss of a valued resource.

The interrelationship between loss and evaluation during termination is clear in the following extract from a final interview:

Student: We haven't talked very much about the fact that this is my last visit to you. I just wanted to hear how you're feeling about that.

_____
*An original paper revised for this volume.

Client: I'd rather you'd stay on . . . and still come . . . In a way I hated for you even to come today because I said I won't see her from now on . . . I said, well maybe I'll just leave the house and that way she might have to come back . . . I said no, I'll just wait.

Student: Endings are hard, C, and it's hard for me, too, because you've been a very important person to me these last months.

Client: You've helped me a lot. When nobody else could. Just sitting down and talking. Other people say you're wrong, you're wrong. You're crazy. You think you are crazy. What's wrong with you? That's all I ever hear from B. I can't talk to B about nothing.

Student: It feels good to be able to talk and to say what's on your mind and not be judged. I'm glad that it has been helpful to you to have someone to talk to. I think you've done some things for yourself, too, C. That's kind of what I'd like to pay attention to just now.

Client: What?

Student: I'd like to talk about what you've been doing for yourself that has been helping.

Client: Yeah, but you know I just started almost not wanting to go back to the doctor's and the only thing that made me really want to go back was that I started bleeding yesterday.

Student: Uh-huh.

Client: 'Cause I really started feeling again like I just didn't care no more.

Student: I wonder . . .

Client: Easy let down . . . It's easy for me to feel let down like that. Very easy.

Student: I wondered . . . I was thinking about what you had said last time. That you didn't want to be dependent on anybody and so forth. If that might have something to do with the fact that you had grown dependent on me over these past few months and that I was going to let you down just like everybody else has.

Client: I was thinking about how I'll feel about that other social worker. I don't know if I'll be able to talk to her like I've been able to talk to you. I might feel angry toward her. I've been thinking about that and feeling if maybe I'd feel angry because she's trying to take S's place. And it won't be the same.

THE CONTEXT OF TERMINATION

Although the termination phase is unique, it cannot be accurately understood except in the context of an entire course of treatment. Decisions made early about focus and goals directly determine the potential for review during termination. A theme that continues throughout the entire treatment process is the attachment between client and helper that develops during early and middle phases. Consequently, the practitioner's awareness of differential relationship patterns is crucial in planning and managing termination. In addition, termination always occurs within a specified social context, including the organization that sponsors and shapes the helping process.

Problem Definition

Clarity about the focus of the helping process is necessary to successful termination. The determination of how long the treatment will continue and how activities will be structured follows from the specification of client problems and agreement about objectives. The objectives are then reworked throughout the helping process and reflected in the specific termination plan. In this respect, the quality of review at termination depends directly on the clarity of the treatment objectives. Lack of precision in the early and middle phase of the work creates difficulty in measuring the extent to which the objectives have been achieved (Chapter 17). Correspondingly, the point of termination is more difficult to establish, and relationship may become the focus of the work, rather than the vehicle.

If client problems are developmental, the termination might be designed to allow periodic checking in with the practitioner as the developmental progression continues (Golan, 1981). If the client problems are related to specific material or physical difficulties, on the other hand, a fixed end point might be appropriate. When the expectations of the outcome of the helping process are shared and based upon a skillful assessment, the format of termination will have already been suggested.

Client's expectations concerning what will be derived from the helping process are maintained by hopes for specific change, as well as the subjective meaning or value of the helping relationship. As the work progresses, the practitioner must monitor and maintain the appropriate balance between objective achievement and relationship gratification. Termination decisions should reflect that balance.

The Helping Relationship

The attachment between client and social worker is one source of the feelings experienced in termination.

The impending separation runs counter to many clients' hope that this attachment would continue indefinitely. Accordingly, termination may engender ambivalence in both client and practitioner; in a sense, this ambivalence mirrors the ambivalence about the beginning of the work together. Our knowledge about the separation or individuation process verifies the presence of strong and often contradictory feelings about leaving valued others (Kauff, 1977). Mastery of termination requires both client and practitioner to experience and share a variety of reactions to the ending.

One way that social workers can prepare for termination is to teach clients about the predictable reactions to loss and to assist them in identifying those reactions when either directly or indirectly expressed. Various authors have written about the predictable stages of the grief process: denial, anger, sadness, acceptance, and disengagement (Germain & Gitterman, 1996; Kubler-Ross, 1969; Lindemann, 1956; Webb, 1985). For example, clients who have previously experienced multiple or traumatic losses may react with sadness and feelings of abandonment. On the other hand, clients who have succeeded in achieving desired gains in treatment may be particularly proud and self-confident during termination (Fortune, 1987). Do not assume that all clients uniformly transverse these stages in lock-step fashion or that all clients react to termination with the same intensity. However, both clients and practitioners tend to deal with termination initially with denial and/or distancing. This may take many forms, varying from general detachment to premature discontinuation of sessions. Initially, these reactions may provide the client with space for adaptation; appropriate focus by the practitioner often aids in surmounting the denial and allows open exchange about the discomfort and confusion associated with loss. If they experience uncertainty about their own capacity to deal with the ending, however, practitioners may encourage clients to remain in a state of denial as a form of self-protection. As noted earlier, separation and ending inevitably evoke self-examination regarding competence and accomplishment; social workers and clients alike are forced to confront their own limitations.

It is the responsibility of the practitioner to guide the ending process, through appropriately timed interventions and self-disclosure. Honest expression of the practitioner's own reactions during the termination phase facilitates the client's expression of responses stimulated by termination. Through this mutual exchange or sharing of reactions, the reality of the ending is verified.

A major task of termination is to construct a bridge between the services provided and the clients' subsequent problem-solving efforts. In part, this may be accomplished through a synthesis of termination evaluation and future planning. Clients should be empowered, through termination, to embark on a self-directed course of action based upon a realistic assessment of their problem-solving strengths. Successful termination supports client self-esteem, reinforces the client's hope that progress will continue, and also frees the client to reinvest energy in appropriate life tasks and ongoing relationships that support problem solving.

DIFFERENTIAL PATTERNS OF ATTACHMENT

So far, feelings related to loss in termination have been discussed in the context of the open-ended helping relationship between an individual client and practitioner. However, individual counseling is only one type of social work process. Many clients present problems related to inadequate resources or information and have limited need for counseling. In addition, many clients are best helped within their families or in small groups.

Variations in client problems and goals and in the modality used are associated with important qualitative differences in the nature of termination. In different types of work, the nature of the client-practitioner attachment varies, as does the focus and length of time required for the termination phase. Variations in termination as a function of the primary intervention activities and system size are summarized in Exhibit 18–3. Let's consider these variations in more detail, for each of the primary activities.

Counseling

Individual counseling often allows for the development of a high degree of mutual attachment, which tends to increase as the process continues. Termination of individual counseling is quite likely to prompt elements of the grieving process for client and practitioner. Termination of a predominantly counseling relationship may be time-consuming. For example, in treatment of a year's duration, the last eight weeks would be utilized for ending, as would two of the last 8–12 interviews in short-term treatment (Reid & Epstein, 1972; Shulman, 1992; Webb, 1985). Inattention to termination or prolonged denial may provoke regression and circumvent

EXHIBIT 18-3	Variations in Termination

Primary activities	System size		
	Individual	Group	Family
Counseling	Attachment may be intense	Attachment may be intense but shared among group worker, group as a whole, and other members.	Attachment may be intense, but is shared with other family members.
	Loss in termination may include considerable avoidance and/or grief, which must be openly managed and processed in mutual interaction.	Grief may be considerable; when formed groups terminate, focus must be on ending and multiple separations. In natural groups, loss is moderated by ongoing ties between members. Termination should include support of groups' ongoing motivation to support members.	Loss moderated by family's continuation. Termination focus is on improved attachments and communication within family system.
Education	Attachment may be of moderate intensity.	Attachment usually more moderate in intensity.	Attachment often more moderate in intensity.
	Ending often preset in original plan and focuses on success in learning and generalization beyond treatment setting.	Differences persist between formed and natural groups, but have less impact upon the nature of termination. Emphasis in both groups is on evaluation of learning. Some formed groups may continue after treatment ends.	As family is usually ongoing, termination includes focus on members' mutual support and application of learning that has occurred.
Resource mobilization (referral, brokerage, mediation, advocacy)	Attachment may be intense, but transitional and/or intermittent.	Attachment may be intense but is present among multiple group members.	Attachment may be intense and may have strengthened family relationships.
	Loss moderated by attachment to new resource and/or need satisfaction. Focus is on evaluation of mobilization, with door open for return. Loss not usually a theme in termination discussion.	Termination should enhance group's capacity to locate and utilize resources independently. During this phase, some formed groups will develop into natural groups and maintain their ties.	Termination should enhance the family's capacity to locate and utilize resources independently. Specific skills regarding resource use may be consolidated during termination.

solidification of gains. The practitioner's role is to monitor and persistently call attention to the dynamics of the ending phase.

Counseling with families and small groups can also entail an intense relationship between clients and practitioner. The major distinction between family or group and individual treatment is that any single client's attachment is to multiple others. In fact, one of the practitioner's major goals in work with families and small groups is to facilitate individuals' communication with others, as well as to solidify members' attachments with one another; the attachment between the individual client and practitioner is diffused throughout the client system. Although a family's termination with the practitioner may be difficult for individual family members, the experience of loss is often modified by the reality that the family is likely to remain intact and members can turn to one another for support. The practitioner's role during termination is to underscore the family's interpersonal resources. Loss of the practitioner is moderated by the attachments shared by family members and by review of the system's shared treatment accomplishments.

In the group, several phenomena may be present (Shulman, 1992). If the group is ongoing or naturally formed—for instance, a neighborhood group, classroom, or cottage unit—individual group members may turn to one another for assistance during and following termination. In a group that disbands at termination (a formed group, in the terminology of Exhibit 18–3), termination can be quite emotionally charged, because members lose the group as a whole, other group members, and the group worker. The group practitioner must facilitate the members' ability to detach from the group. In this instance, the practitioner places major emphasis on the group members' efforts to deal with the loss of one another and acts as a catalyst, encouraging member interactions.

Educational Interventions

Educational interventions tend to maintain a focus upon cognitive processes; the major goal is learning, rather than emotional change or stabilization. Although intimate relationships certainly can develop when the helping goals and supporting interventions are educational, the attachment between client and practitioner may be less intense than in counseling situations. The point of termination is often preset by the nature and amount of material to be learned. There is typically less client concern that termination will endanger the maintenance of what has been learned and more emphasis on utilization of the new skills beyond treatment. The practitioner's educational interventions encourage generalization of learning through rehearsal, practice, and positive reinforcement in the client's natural environment. A clear focus on evidence of the client's learning and self-sufficiency is the most effective method of solidifying gains during the ending period. Educational interventions with families (family life education) or groups (parent education groups) are not likely to result in intense attachments between clients and practitioners or, correspondingly, in feelings of loss at termination.

Resource Mobilization

Interventions focused on resource mobilization may include referral, mediation, brokerage, and/or advocacy. In these instances, the relationship is often intense, and attachment develops rapidly between client and practitioner, either because of the urgency of the identified problem or because client and worker participate closely in a mobilization effort directed toward an outside source. However, in spite of the intensity of the effort, the worker is acting as a way station to an additional helping resource somewhere else. Consequently, termination is focused heavily on the success of resource mobilization and less on the attendant interaction between client and practitioner. Resource mobilization with families and groups is also highly task-focused. Termination is expected when the resource is activated but might include a provision for additional contact should resource problems reappear. Although attachments may be strong throughout a specific period, the relationship expectations are clearly limited. Therefore, termination may be less emotionally charged and may require an emphasis on evaluation of outcomes rather than issues of loss or grief.

Certain general statements can be made about differences in the helping relationship associated with the primary activities and the system size:

1. More exclusive relationships between client and practitioner will usually result in more intense attachment. Greater intensity of attachments typically necessitates greater attention to the grieving process.

Generally, family and group systems provide multiple resources for resolution of grief; feelings of loss are diffused and shared with other clients.

2. Termination is likely to be more emotionally charged as the attachment between client and practitioner increases. The ending phase of such relationships will require sensitive support and encouragement toward self-sufficiency. As already noted, certain interventions more typically result in greater client reliance on the practitioner.

3. Reactions to the loss of the practitioner will be more limited if clients can continue in relationships that were a part of the helping process. Clients in families and ongoing groups are more likely to substitute one another for the lost practitioner and thereby more readily resolve the grieving process.

4. Themes of loss and evaluation can be expected in the termination of each helping relationship, and therefore clients' ideas and feelings with regard to each theme should be recognized and explored.

ORGANIZATIONAL INFLUENCES UPON TERMINATION

Termination will also be shaped by the organizational context within which social work intervention occurs. The organizational mission sets limits on the nature of the client problems that can be addressed and the typical or preferred treatment modalities utilized. Intra- and interorganizational factors may also affect the timing and character of termination.

The impact of the organizational mission is most evident in settings where social workers provide a secondary service, such as hospitals, schools, emergency shelters, and the workplace. In such settings, clients are typically eligible for the practitioner's assistance only for the duration of their involvement with the primary service. Thus, the relationship with a social worker is usually terminated when patients are discharged from the hospital, children reach the end of the school year, clients leave an emergency shelter, or employees quit or are fired. While such setting-specific endings are planned and anticipated openly by the client and practitioner together, the ending itself may be experienced as an unnatural or premature closure. A social worker in a children's hospital comments, "Each morning when I come in to work, the first thing I do is check the census to see who's missing." Such abrupt endings may be accompanied by a brief follow-up period for attention to termi-

nation issues or by referral of the client for continuing services. However, provision of time to accomplish the tasks of termination is crucial both for clients, whether or not they seek services elsewhere, and for practitioners.

Settings in which social services are the primary organizational mission also structure beginnings and endings of client-practitioner relationships through available program options and preferred treatment modalities. For example, a public agency mandated to serve all persons requesting services in a geographic area, such as a community mental health center, may develop guidelines limiting the duration of client services or designating the modalities to be utilized, such as crisis intervention, solution-focused treatment, or group treatment. In negotiating the service agreement, you should inform clients of such agency guidelines, to ensure the realistic definition of treatment goals.

Other organizational factors also affect the helping process. For example, requirements for practitioners' productivity or for third-party reimbursement for agency services may place subtle or explicit pressures upon practitioners. There may be an expectation that social workers will continue with clients beyond contracted services in order to inflate the direct service time or will terminate prematurely because the client's reimbursement benefits have been exhausted. Practitioners may also be expected to extend services up to a client's benefit limit regardless of need (Strom-Gottfried 1997) or to terminate prematurely in order to shrink the agency's waiting list. Managed care companies may also preempt decisions about the timing of termination: "For clients who have been approved for some managed care payments, the social worker's report of positive treatment outcomes frequently inclines the case reviewer to stop payment for further services because the client's needs are then determined to be not great enough" (Davidson & Davidson, 1996, p. 209). The possibility that a client's personal information is maintained in the managed care company's file after termination is also troubling (Davidson & Davidson, 1996). Pressures regarding the timing and management of termination increasingly present ethical dilemmas for the individual social worker, as well as for the organization. These dilemmas require skillful balancing of client need and organizational demands (Reamer, 1995) and inevitably impact on the practitioner's feelings about the employing agency and about beginnings and endings with clients.

If clients have been referred involuntarily by the courts or other systems, such as the workplace or a school, potential difficulties in termination arise when the problem definition and/or length of treatment are determined externally and as a condition for a child's return home from foster care, an employee's return to work, or a continuation of probation.

Organizational commitments to professional training also shape the termination process. An exploratory study of students' termination of individual clinical work at the end of an academic year found that students in the sample appeared to learn about termination primarily from their agency supervisors (Gould, 1978). Students' first-year field agency supervisors, as well as several of the second-year supervisors, had encouraged students not to discuss the predictable training-related ending of treatment with their clients until the latter part of treatment (Gould, 1978). This policy could potentially have a destructive impact on the helping process, particularly in the termination phase. "By contrast, where agencies are open and direct about their training function and present their students as supervised learners, clients expect the student's departure at the end of the academic year, and termination and transfer are likely to be viewed as legitimate (though some people do 'forget' they were told at the start)" (Germain & Gitterman, 1996, pp. 312–313).

Because the organizational context influences the nature of the help offered and received, it is crucial that inter- and intraorganizational factors be fully and openly weighed early in the process, as the client and practitioner explore goals, options, and tasks together, and in the ending phase, as feelings and ideas regarding loss and evaluation emerge.

SELF-AWARENESS IN TERMINATION

In the ending phase, the worker must be open to a range of intense feelings and reactions from the client, including sadness, anger, and negative evaluation of their work together. Clients may also express relief, increased self-esteem, and diminished need for the worker's assistance. These predictable themes suggest important areas for the social worker's introspection and action.

Continuing self-examination and self-awareness is fundamental to professional competence. Social workers necessarily explore their own attitudes, values, experiences, and feelings in order to ensure that their interactions with clients are guided by the clients' needs and concerns, rather than their own. In termination, these include the worker's lifelong experiences with and feelings about separations generally; feelings and concerns about the worker's competence as a helping person; and feelings about a specific client system and the ending of work together.

The predictable stirring of memories and feelings associated with separation is the major theme in descriptions of termination: "The ending process in a helping relationship can trigger feelings of the deepest kind in both worker and client. This is the reason why there is potential for powerful work during this phase as well as ineffective work if the feelings are not dealt with" (Shulman, 1992, p. 174). The social worker's ability to deal with these feelings in the helping interaction builds on awareness of the personal meaning of separation. Therefore, the practitioner's own experiences with separation and assumptions about clients' feelings emerge as areas for reflection. Thus, practitioners' experiences with death, divorce, geographic moves, or other losses or transitions may affect their ability to individualize the meaning of the ending to specific clients. Painful or recent separation experiences may prompt a practitioner to deny the importance of the ending to the client, in order to avoid remembering or reexperiencing painful feelings.

When the termination is based upon the practitioner's own timetable and needs, rather than those of the client, self-awareness is particularly important. For example, practitioners leaving an agency or students completing a semester of agency-based practicum training may experience conflict because they are acting out of self-interest rather than concern for the client (Gould, 1978; Moss & Moss, 1967; Siebold, 1991). As a second-year social work student commented, "I haven't yet had any real terminations with clients—all my cases have ended when the placement is over. I feel so guilty to quit working with my clients because my time is over, not because we're through. I have offered to volunteer here at the agency when the placement is over." At the end of professional training, student practitioners are also typically in the process of separating from the university, from the student role, from practicum agency and field instructor, and from classmates. Therefore, client terminations become part of a broader separation experience.

It is important for the student practitioner to explore and understand the multifaceted nature of this transition period (Husband & Scheunemann, 1972).

Inevitably, the evaluative component of ending raises the questions: "Have I done well by this client? Could I have done more?" It is not possible to evaluate and review client goal accomplishment without scrutiny of the practitioner's sensitive and skilled use of self in the process. Practitioners must be aware of their reactions to the evaluation of their own performance. While the major reason for professional inattention to termination as a phase of treatment "seems to be the general sensitivity to loss and separation" (Fox, Nelson, & Bolman, 1969, p. 62), another contributing factor may be the profession's general sensitivity to accountability and evaluation. However, as Germain and Gitterman (1996) emphasize, "Endings are especially valuable in building professional knowledge and refining skills. Joint assessment of outcomes with clients, identifying what was helpful and what was not helpful, and why, can be gradually generalized to practice principles" (p. 335). Objective evaluation and conceptualization of one's own practice is preceded by self-examination and acknowledgement of one's level of training and experience, as well as the professional expectation of continued growth. Each termination provides further information regarding the practitioner's strengths and professional learning needs.

Feelings of inadequacy or guilt about difficulties in helping a particular client, however, should be shared and examined with one's supervisor, consultant, or colleagues to determine the reality of this assessment and to prevent transmission of the message that the client should either reassure the practitioner of his or her worth or confirm the lack of worth.

The specific meaning for the practitioner of a particular client and of that client's termination also merits self-examination. For example, has this client been particularly gratifying? Or ungratifying? Is this client terminating with little accomplished? Has the client's success or lack of success taken on a special meaning for the practitioner personally or within the organization? Does the practitioner wish to have a continuing relationship with the client? Is there relief at the idea of terminating with this client? Have organizational pressures become an issue in the treatment and termination? As Levinson (1977) notes, "During treatment the therapist has an opportunity to participate in a creative process in which a new or modified self emerges . . . Saying good-bye to the patient by the therapist can be akin to saying good-bye to a part of himself" (p. 483). The meanings of termination are uniquely personal to the practitioner. Anticipating these meanings is an important aspect of preparation for the disciplined and conscious use of self in termination with the client.

SUMMARY

The intent of the helping process, whether brief or long-term, is to make a positive difference in the life of the client. This difference can be understood, evaluated, and maintained by means of skillful termination. The major task of the practitioner during this phase is to help the client move from denial or avoidance of the inevitable ending to exploration of ideas and feelings related to the outcome of the helping process and to termination of the helping relationship. The ability to accomplish this task will depend upon the practitioner's self-awareness and skills, as well as the practitioner's understanding of the context within which termination occurs: the client's problems and goals, the particular helping relationship, and the sponsoring organization. Thus, each termination can be uniquely anticipated and sensitively completed.

LEARNING EXERCISES

1. In Appendix A-2, how much time elapsed between the worker's suggestion that Mrs. Stover's case be closed and the actual closing of the case? What do you think was accomplished by engaging the client in an evaluation of what had been accomplished? What did the worker do to preserve the gains that Mrs. Stover had made?

2. How was the ending in the Debbie Smith case (Appendix A-1) handled differently from that for Mrs. Stover? Which ending do you think is more helpful for the client? Explain.

3. If you were the social worker supervising the volunteer in Exhibit 18–1, what would be your response to the ending problems? Should the group continue? Give the reasons for your recommendation.

4. Sara, age 35, recently moved to the area to be near her aging mother. Over a period of three months, you have supported her decision to place her mother in a nursing home and worked with her to minimize her feelings of grief, loss, and guilt. As you are preparing to terminate the relationship, Sara asks if you can be friends, especially since she has no friends or family in the area. How do you respond? Give your reasons.

REFERENCES

Davidson, J. & Davidson, T. (1996). Confidentiality and managed care: Ethical and legal concerns. *Health and Social Work, 21*(3), 208–215.

Fortune, A. (1987). Grief only? Client and social worker reactions to termination. *Clinical Social Work Journal, 15*(2), 159–171.

Fortune, A., Pearlingi, B., & Rochelle, C. (1991). Criteria for terminating treatment. *Families in Society: The Journal of Contemporary Human Services, 72*(6), 366–370.

Fortune, A., Pearlingi, B., & Rochelle, C. (1992). Reactions to termination of individual treatment. *Social Work, 37*(2), 171–178.

Fox, E., Nelson, M., & Bolman, W. (1969). The termination process: A neglected dimension in social work. *Social Work, 14*(4), 53–63.

Germain, C., & Gitterman, A. (1996). *The life model of social work practice* (2nd ed.). New York: Columbia University Press.

Golan, N. (1981). *Passing through transitions.* New York: Free Press.

Gould, R. (1978). Students' experience with the termination phase of treatment. *Smith College Studies in Social Work, 48*(3), 235–269.

Husband, D., & Scheunemann, H. (1972). The use of group process in teaching termination. *Child Welfare, 51*(5), 505–513.

Kauff, P. (1977). The termination process: Its relationship to the separation individuation phase of development. *International Journal of Group Psychiatry, 27*(1), 3–18.

Kubler-Ross, E. (1969). *On death and dying.* New York: Macmillan.

Levinson, H. (1977). Termination of psychotherapy: Some salient issues. *Social Casework, 58*(8) 480–498.

Lindemann, E. (1956). Symptomatology and management of acute grief. In H. Parad (Ed.), *Crisis intervention: Selected readings* (pp. 7–21), New York: Family Service Association.

Moss, S., & Moss, M. (1967). When a caseworker leaves an agency: The impact on worker and client. *Social Casework, 48*(7) 433–437.

Northern, H. (1969). *Social work with groups.* New York: Columbia University Press.

Philip, C. E. (1994). Letting go: Problems with termination when a therapist is seriously ill or dying. *Smith College Studies in Social Work, 64*(2), 169–179.

Reamer, F. (1995). *Social work values and ethics.* New York: Columbia University Press.

Reid, W. J. & Epstein, L. (1972). *Task-centered casework.* New York: Columbia University Press.

Shulman, L. (1992). *The skills of helping individuals, families, and groups* (3rd ed.). Itasca, IL: F. E. Peacock.

Siebold, C. (1991). Termination: When the therapist leaves. *Clinical Social Work Journal, 19*(2), 191–204.

Siebold, C. (1992). Forced termination: Reconsidering theory and technique. *Smith College Studies in Social Work, 63*(1), 325–341.

Siporin, M. (1975). *Introduction to social work practice* New York: Macmillan.

Strom-Gottfried, K. (1997). The implications of managed care for social work education. *Journal of Social Work Education, 33*(1), 7–18.

Webb, N. B. (1985). A crisis intervention perspective on the termination process. *Clinical Social Work Journal, 13*(4), 329–340.

chapter 19

Avoiding Burnout

CHAPTER PREVIEW

You are reaching the end of this book, but you are still at the beginning of your journey to becoming a social worker. The material we have presented is complex and will demand further thought, study, and experimentation. One exciting thing about social work is that it is a never-ending learning experience.

Given the complexity and interdependence of human beings, we hope that you find problem solving both challenging and satisfying. We hope you care deeply about your clients' troubles, have the strength to stand with them as they struggle to solve their problems, and respect their wisdom and courage as they do so. You will also need to understand the shaping power of the environment in human endeavors. All of us have much to learn about human growth, development, and change. Are you willing to engage in constant inquiry, so as to add to our professional understanding?

As a social worker, you will experience stresses and tensions; they come with the territory. Accordingly, you will need to find a way to recognize and address them. As Jones (1993) points out, role conflicts can either lead to burnout or be energizing, depending on your response. One way of lessening stress is to find or establish a support group.

In Reading 19-1, Jan Hagen defines burnout and reviews the research on its sources. She offers suggestions for avoiding burnout.

SELF-AWARENESS

As social workers, we need to cultivate self-awareness. We must work at knowing and accepting ourselves—at knowing what we can do and accepting what we can't.

We need to recognize our particular vulnerabilities and explore ways of dealing with them. Feeling empathy for our client is essential, but we cannot make objective assessments of the problem if we identify too closely with the client (Koeske & Kelly, 1995). We may over-identify with a client whose problem resembles one with which we have struggled.

Social workers often demand too much of themselves. Suppose that you cannot establish a helping relationship with a particular client. You will feel disappointment and a sense of failure, but don't be too hard on yourself. You need to accept that the client has a part in establishing the relationship. Some clients will not only decline to engage with you but will behave in intentionally provoking ways. In that case, you will probably feel anger and frustration. If you are unaware of these feelings, they will cloud your judgment. If you are aware of them, however, you can treat them as a problem to be understood and resolved. Our responses to clients do not come out of nowhere; they develop from our relationships with important people in our life and from our interactions with other clients. We should not be afraid to examine them, nor should we blame ourselves if they seem inappropriate. The task is to analyze the interaction, assess the problem, and attempt to resolve it. If we find our client's behavior irritating, other people will probably respond in similar ways. It may be important to help make the client recognize the impact of this behavior on his or her relationships with others.

In developing self-awareness, we need to examine our expectations for ourselves, our clients, and the outcome of our work. We need to accept that clients' problems are usually the products of complex social interaction over some period of years, during which many hurtful things have happened. We cannot undo what has been done, and blaming those involved is unhelpful. We need to help the client accept what happened as a reality and figure out where to go from here. We cannot remake lives, but we can help people deal in more satisfying ways with the life they now have.

The pace of human change is slow. We often expect far too much of ourselves; no one can make changes overnight. Look at the amount of time that the worker invested in Mrs. Stover (Appendix A-2) and at the pace of the gains. Although Mrs. Stover was not actively appreciative of the time the worker invested, she was very aware of change, and the school noted significant change in the children. The work had tremendous impact in helping Mrs. Stover and her children solve their problems.

You will seek satisfaction from your work with clients. But ask yourself whether you expect the clients themselves to be a source of satisfaction or whether you seek satisfaction from competent problem solving. Do you want your clients to like you? In reality, the clients who most need help are likely to find taking responsibility for themselves difficult and to reject your offers of help. Their anger and rejection are a response to the social context in which they find themselves. You will need to work at separating personal from professional needs and at recognizing your ambivalent feelings toward clients who reject you. Such ambivalent feelings do not mean you are a failure; they simply present you with a problem to solve. Recognize them as such and share them with a support group.

If you expect too much of yourself, you will regard negative feelings or problems you can't seem to solve as weaknesses or evidence of incompetence. Feeling guilty or ashamed, you may then be reluctant to ask for appropriate professional help or support from your colleagues. Likewise, you may have difficulty in setting limits on client demands in order to make time for your own and your family's legitimate needs. However, you will need time for yourself if you are to have resources to give to others.

Finally, you must be clear about your feelings regarding agency constraints on your work. You should be able to inform clients of agency policies without apology. While it is perfectly appropriate for you to work toward changes in those policies, it is not helpful to join the client in impotent anger. However, if a certain policy clearly undermines the welfare of a number of clients, you may wish to help them form an advocacy group to have the policy modified.

THE NEED TO CONTROL

The need to control is a widespread problem in human service professions. The client wants help, and the worker, through access to agency and community resources, has the power to help. If you feel you know how a problem should be solved, you may try and use your power to control the client's behavior.

Social work is a collaborative partnership. Do not try to control the client's behavior and do not take responsibility for the client's actions. Instead, discuss alternative courses of action and likely consequences from each one. Control is inimical to partnership. Further, attempts to control another person are likely to leave you emotionally exhausted or cynical about human beings and unable to provide help to anyone.

Control can take subtle forms. Taking on responsibilities for clients, for example, may be an indirect form of control; it deprives them of the opportunity to be responsible for themselves. Unnecessarily intensive services, especially if unwanted by the client, may also be a form of control. Knowledge can be used to control clients rather than as a resource to reach their goals. Any attempt to regulate and control another person will lead to frustration and defeat. These problems are illustrated in Exhibit 19-1, which describes the disappointment of a social worker who left the profession after two job experiences.

REALISTIC OBJECTIVES

A written statement of the client's problem, objective, assessment, and plan will help keep you from expecting too much. When you come back from seeing Mrs. X, who seems to be functioning no better than she was three interviews ago, you may feel frustrated and defeated. But if you look at your plan and it reminds you that you can expect only slow change in Mrs. X's situation, you may feel a sense of satisfaction with the gains that have been made. Focus on realistic objectives.

If you have an overwhelming caseload, you may feel defeated and discouraged because you know you can't help all these people. To overtax yourself in the attempt is going to help no one. Accept the situation without

EXHIBIT 19-1 Interview with a Former Social Worker

I asked if she had expectations about the duties of the social worker. She said that she felt that she could remake people's lives—that she could help people adjust to their problems in order to have a healthy personality. When she started work, she found she couldn't remake people's lives, because she had a lot of paper work and reports dealing with her clients. She said she could not change people's patterns of behavior as easily as she expected. These behavior patterns are so incorporated into the person's life that it is difficult to change them. She didn't have enough time to do all that she wanted to help the client.

Her second job was at a private agency, where she took care of adoptions and unwed mothers. In this job, she had more time with her clients. But she realized that she just didn't have answers for all the problems of her clients. When a client was really open with her, she felt that she didn't know quite how to handle the situation. She said she couldn't run to a supervisor in the middle of an interview, asking what to do.

self-blame (you didn't create it) and make realistic plans to do what you can. Sit down with your supervisor and decide how many cases you can serve to your fullest, how many will absolutely explode without regular visits, and how many can get along with fewer. Select from your caseload two groups of clients to prioritize: those who just have to be seen; and a few clients whom you would like to work with for the sake of your own learning and satisfaction. These you should plan to see regularly. To the other clients, provide only the minimum service that they need or the agency mandates. You should make a plan for those clients, however, and record what you intend to do and why. You do need to work toward lower caseloads but, in the meantime, you will do what you can. Because you must have opportunities to learn if you are to find satisfaction in your work, you need to seek out those opportunities.

In our experience, workers tend to focus too much on clients' weaknesses and pathology. It would help to search more for client strengths. Also, ask clients how things are going. Regularly sit down with them and evaluate gains made and battles lost; clients are usually more aware of positive changes than you are. Ask clients about their pleasures in life. Information about clients helps you to understand them and to set realistic objectives with them.

SUPPORT

A sense of personal well-being (Koeske & Kirk, 1995) and a social support system (Himle, Jayaratne, & Thyress, 1991; Koeske & Koeske, 1989, 1993) will help you weather the stresses of your work. You may find it helpful to have regular group meetings with your colleagues. Such meetings are informal, with loose agendas; they provide an opportunity for workers to talk about their feelings, their defeats, their successes, and the new things they have tried. In this way, you come to understand that you are not alone; you build a structure of group support.

You will also find it helpful to read histories of social work and biographies of social workers. You need to take a long view of the profession—to understand the struggles waged and the gains made by those who have gone before us. You may often feel frustrated at the sexism and racism in the profession; you will marvel, for example, at women's courage as you read about the hostility of senators early in the 20th century to female social workers' proposal for an act to support maternal and child health. Social workers have made great strides in improving the lives of vulnerable people. We should be proud of our profession; but we need to understand that these gains did not come overnight.

To avoid burnout, you will also need relationships and interests outside of work. Do not build your whole life around your profession. Remember that you must be more than your profession if you are to serve it well. Many social workers are so enmeshed with their work that their whole sense of meaning in life derives from interaction with their workmates. Interaction with agency colleagues is important, but we encourage you to develop an informal support group outside of your work setting. You may choose to become involved in hobbies, arts, civic activities, recreational groups, or neighborhood groups. Build a support system with persons outside your agency and engage in activities to divert your attention from the immediate stresses of work.

CHAPTER SUMMARY

Research suggests that social workers may experience less burnout than do comparable occupational groups (Söderfeldt, Söderfeldt, & Lars-Erik, 1995). Nevertheless, it is an occupational hazard with which you must contend. We suggest these guidelines for making your working life more satisfying and enjoyable:

1. Work at becoming aware of your own feelings, views, and biases and the ways that these may affect your perception of others.

2. Choose limited objectives that are achievable.

3. Avoid attempting to control others, which is time-consuming, emotionally draining, and usually self-defeating.

4. Take responsibility for your own behavior, but remember that you are not responsible for decisions made by clients or any other person or for the consequences that may follow from them.

5. Develop support systems within your agency, your profession, and your community. It is especially important to pursue interests outside of social work, so that your sense of self-worth does not depend entirely on your professional identity and your job.

A LOOK FORWARD

In Reading 19-1, Jan L. Hagen discusses burnout and how social workers can deal with exhaustion and defeat. We hope that this final contribution will help you to pay attention to your own welfare and ways to help yourself.

So we come to the end of our book. We both started social work practice in our mid-20s and, between us, we now have over 75 years of experience; we have never regretted our decisions to become social workers. We wish for you a satisfying and exciting career.

READING 19-1 *Burnout: An Occupational Hazard for Social Workers**

Jan L. Hagen

In general, social workers are regarded as being at high risk for burnout. As Meyerson (1994) notes, "Social workers face ambiguity in their technologies (e.g., talking to clients), their goals (e.g., to provide empathy and caring), their evaluation criteria (e.g., sensitivity) and occupational boundaries (e.g., who is and is not a social worker)" (p. 629). Social workers often enter the profession with an idealized sense of mission to help others and yet they must work within sometimes severe bureaucratic constraints. Accordingly, burnout may be particularly high during the initial years of practice, as social workers confront the realities of their jobs, their clients, and their own competence (Cherniss, 1980; Edelwich & Brodsky, 1980). Practitioners may describe their dissatisfaction in various ways:

- "I am only 31 years old and feel that my job has stifled my ability and drive. I hope to get a job which will bring my old self out; where I can think for myself, plan, use my brain again. It is hard to recover from burnout but I plan to."
- "Workers here are unappreciated. Administrators do not care about their people and it filters down from there. Only failures are noted, so morale is very low. The goal of 100% excellence is impossible to reach. Therefore, some stop trying while others get ulcers trying to stay afloat."

Burnout is costly to practitioners, organizations, and clients. For the individual practitioner, burnout may mean physical and emotional exhaustion; depression and general malaise; feelings of helplessness and hopelessness; physical problems such as headaches, ulcers, hypertension, fatigue, and backaches; and the development of personal problems such as marital conflict and

---

*An original reading prepared for this edition.

drug and alcohol abuse (Maslach, 1976, 1982; Pines, Aronson, & Kafry, 1981). For the organization, burnout results in inefficient workers, low morale, absenteeism, and high turnover. For clients, burnout among service providers means impersonal, dehumanized, and uncaring services.

Burnout, however, is not yet a clearly defined concept, nor has a clearly articulated theoretical model been developed. This reading reviews definitions of burnout, specifies variables contributing to it, and examines strategies for prevention and intervention by both individuals and agencies. Practitioners will be better prepared to prevent and alleviate burnout by knowing the personal, organizational, and societal variables that contribute to it.

DEFINING BURNOUT

Freudenberger (1974), a psychoanalyst, first used the term *burnout* to describe emotional and physical exhaustion brought about by conditions at work and identified types of personalities prone to burnout: the dedicated worker who takes on too much work with an excess of intensity; the overcommitted worker whose outside life is unsatisfactory; and the authoritarian worker who needs extensive control in his or her job (Karger, 1981). Freudenberger's conceptualization of burnout highlights the role of individual psychological characteristics and excludes the interactions between people and their environments.

Maslach and Pines propose a broader social/psychological view of burnout that examines the relationship between individuals and their work environments (Maslach, 1978, 1982; Pines et al., 1981; Pines & Maslach, 1978). Based on her numerous investigations, Maslach (1978) has concluded that

> burn-out is best understood (and modified) in terms of the social and situation sources of job related stresses. Although personality variables are certainly relevant in the overall analysis, the prevalence of the phenomenon and the range of seemingly disparate staff people who are affected by it suggest that the search for causes is better directed away from identifying the bad people and toward uncovering the characteristics of the bad situations where many good people function. (p. 114)

For Maslach (1982), burnout is

> a syndrome of emotional exhaustion, depersonalization, and reduced personal accomplishment that can occur

among individuals who do "people work" of some kind. It is a response to the chronic emotional strain of dealing extensively with other human beings, particularly when they are troubled or having problems. (p. 3)

The variables to consider in this formulation of burnout include: (1) the personal characteristics of the practitioner; (2) the job setting, in terms of supervisory and peer support as well as agency rules and regulations; and (3) the actual work with individual clients.

On a societal level, Karger (1981) argues that professional burnout is very similar to industrial alienation as defined by Marx. In Marxian theory, burnout and dissatisfaction are logical outgrowths of a capitalist system in which workers become alienated from work; they are "reactions to the fragmentation of work, to competition within the workplace, and to the loss of worker autonomy" (Farber, 1983, p. 8). By including larger societal issues—how work is structured and valued in society—a Marxist analysis is helpful in conceptualizing burnout among human service providers. However, as Farber (1983) has noted, the helping professions are unique in numerous ways, and a class analysis of their role within society is inadequate.

As we see, these approaches disagree about the nature of burnout and its causes; they do agree, however, that the symptoms of burnout include attitudinal, physical, and emotional components.

It is most useful to think of burnout as a work-related strain, the "outcomes of experienced stress-emotions and behaviors that deviate from the individual's normal response" (Jayaratne, Tripodi, & Chess, 1983). It is distinct from, although not unrelated to, job dissatisfaction, which is another work-related strain. As a strain, burnout produces at least three outcomes: (1) emotional exhaustion—a lack of emotional energy to use and invest in others; (2) depersonalization—a tendency to respond to others in callous, detached, emotionally hardened, uncaring, and dehumanizing ways; and (3) a reduced sense of personal accomplishment and a sense of inadequacy in relating to clients (Maslach, 1982).

STRESSORS THAT CONTRIBUTE TO BURNOUT

Stressors that contribute to burnout may be identified in the individual, the helping relationship, the work environment, and society. There is still little agreement as to which of these are most important.

The Individual

The initial work on burnout focused on individual psychology and personality structures. These certainly play a role in burnout, though not the only role. While excessive emotional demands in a work situation place anyone at risk for burnout, personality characteristics make some individuals more vulnerable. Low self-esteem and lack of confidence increase vulnerability to burnout, as does a lack of understanding about self-limitations, strengths, and weaknesses. As Maslach (1982) notes, "All too often providers feel completely responsible for whether a client succeeds or fails, lives or dies—and are emotionally overwhelmed by this heavy burden" (p. 65). When asked why they entered social work, practitioners often note the desire to help others, to make a contribution to the betterment of others, or to create a just world. The loftiness of these ideals contributes to burnout (Chemiss, 1980a, b; Edelwich & Brodsky, 1980). Practitioners will quickly become disillusioned with both themselves and their clients if these ideals generate unrealistic goals and expectations—for example that clients' problems require only simple solutions, that problems will be solved quickly, that practitioners can work effectively with anyone, that practitioners' work will drastically alter clients' lives, and that clients will show the utmost appreciation for the practitioners' efforts (Edelwich & Brodsky, 1980).

Other reasons for entering social work include personal needs such as recognition, approval, affection, power and control, and intimacy. In and of themselves, these needs neither help nor hinder work with clients. The risk of burnout increases, however, if practitioners expect clients to fulfill these personal needs.

In general, men and women experience burnout similarly, although some gender differences have been noted. Women are more likely to experience emotional exhaustion and to experience it more intensely, whereas men are more prone to depersonalization, characterized by callousness toward clients (Maslach, 1982; Jayaratne et al., 1983). Vulnerability to burnout appears to be related to age: Younger workers are more likely to experience burnout than older workers, who not only have more time on the job but also tend to have a more balanced perspective (Maslach, 1982; Poulin & Walter, 1993).

Investigating the role of education, Maslach (1982) found that those who had some college but did not graduate were at lower risk for burnout than those with postgraduate education; those with four years of college were at highest risk for burnout. This, too, may be related to age and practitioners' unrealistic expectations.

Relationships with family members and friends also influence burnout. As part of the practitioner's social support system, family and friends can have a buffering effect on the stresses of work (Koeske & Koeske, 1989). Research indicates that, as these personal relationships become more positive, the likelihood of burnout falls (Pines et al., 1981). A longitudinal study of intensive case managers suggests that it is the level of current, rather than previous, social supports that affects worker outcomes (Koeske & Kirk 1995). However, if relationships with family members and friends are stressful, they may contribute to burnout by creating additional demands and obligations that conflict with work roles (Cherniss, 1980b).

The Helping Relationship

The helping relationship is a major contributor to burnout. In fact, burnout has been defined as the "result of constant or repeated emotional pressure associated with an intense involvement with people over long periods of time" (Pines et al., 1981, p. 15). The helping relationship exists for the primary benefit of the client, and the emotional giving in the relationship is exclusively from the practitioner to the client. Constant emotional giving and sharing the intense feelings of others may result in emotional depletion. Some client problems are more emotionally draining than others: Incest, child abuse, wife battering, and rape, for example, place tremendous emotional demands on the practitioner. Moreover, what is emotionally stressful and depleting will be different for different individuals, depending on previous life experiences. Nevertheless, unless practitioners have an adequate knowledge base, a commitment to individualization, and sufficient awareness of personal responses, they may develop callous and hostile attitudes toward clients as a result of prolonged exposure to emotionally charged situations. Additionally, burnout is likely if practitioners overidentify with clients and get caught up in their emotions (Koeske & Kelly, 1995).

When clients come for services, they are not functioning at their optimal level. Often, by the time they reach a social worker, they have exhausted their own resources—including informal social supports—in trying to solve their problems. They may feel hopeless and at their wit's end. Many times, work focuses exclusively on clients' problems and deficiencies; their strengths, abilities, and resources are ignored. This not only limits practitioners' effectiveness but also fosters cynical attitudes to clients and depersonalization.

Social work practitioners tend to focus on unsuccessful interventions with clients. Certainly, evaluation of failed interventions can be helpful, as a means of building knowledge and skills, but successes need to be evaluated as well. In general, client feedback reduces the likelihood of burnout (Pines & Kafry, 1978). Practitioners need to build ongoing and systematic evaluation into their practice.

The Work Environment

Within the past few years, research has begun to address the larger social, organizational, and societal factors that contribute to burnout. Arches (1991) identified two factors: the worker's perceived lack of autonomy and the influence of funding sources on agencies. In this section, we'll look at the impact of workload, role ambiguity, and role conflict; relationships with co-workers and supervisors; and agency goals and procedures.

An early study (Pines & Kafry, 1978) identified caseload size as related to burnout, particularly the development of negative attitudes toward clients, Maslach (1982) also links excessive caseload to emotional withdrawal and impersonal service. More recent studies suggest that the critical factor is not the actual size of the workload but the worker's perception that the workload is too large. Additionally, the role of workload dissatisfaction in burnout seems to be different in different settings—for example, child welfare services or family services (Jayaratne & Chess, 1984).

Important stressors in the work environment are role ambiguity, defined as lack of clarity regarding a worker's rights, responsibilities, methods, goals, status, or accountability, and role in which the practitioner experiences conflict, inconsistent, incompatible, or inappropriate demands (Farber, 1983). Role ambiguity and role conflict reduce the clarity of goals and expectations

in work with clients and impair relationships with co-workers and supervisors, on account of confusion regarding work responsibilities.

Using job satisfaction as an indirect indicator of burnout, Harrison (1980) found that high levels of role ambiguity and role conflict related to low levels of job satisfaction among child protective workers. However, in studies of social workers generally, Jayaratne and Chess (1983) found that role conflict and role ambiguity "do not play a significant role in either the assessment of job satisfaction or in the reporting of burnout" (p. 137). Again, however, the importance of role ambiguity and role conflict in burnout may vary by job position and setting (Jayaratne & Chess, 1984). For example, a qualitative study of public child welfare administrators suggests that role conflict may be energizing for individual administrators and that the process of resolving conflicts contributes to team work, coalition building, and networking among diverse groups (Jones, 1993).

Relationships with co-workers and supervisor also have a bearing on burnout. These relationships may be an additional source of stress if they are competitive or conflicted. However, co-workers and supervisors are an important source of social support; they play vital roles in helping practitioners learn new skills, evaluate the effectiveness of their work, develop competence in their positions, and understand the purpose and function of the agency. A study of social service workers found that workers who had positive relationships with co-workers, had someone to discuss work problems with, and received feedback from both co-workers and supervisors were less likely to experience burnout (Pines & Kafry, 1978). Poulin and Walter (1993) note that an increase in supervisor support helped to decrease burnout among social workers. Informational and instrumental support from supervisors and co-workers have also been found to buffer the impact of various work stresses on burnout (Himle et al., 1991).

Agency goals and procedures may foster burnout. If the agency's goals are unclear or ambiguous, role ambiguity or role conflict result. Ambiguous goals contribute to difficulties in measuring the effectiveness of interventions and hinder the provision of helpful feedback from co-workers and supervisors. Agency procedures—such as the mandatory collection of certain data on all clients, regardless of its relevance to the clients' problems—also interfere with the client-worker relationship and with worker effectiveness.

Research suggests that many sources of job-related stress—such as financial rewards, mastery, predictability, and workload—may be reduced if an agency setting is culturally sophisticated—that is, promotes policies and practices facilitating appropriate services for culturally diverse clients (Gant, 1996). However, culturally sophisticated workplaces did little to reduce worker burnout, and Gant (1996) suggests that "psychological stresses may simply be an enduring consequence of working in the human services" (p. 168).

Adequacy of organizational resources has been related to burnout (Poulin & Walter, 1993). If funding is inadequate agency staff have insufficient resources and support to meet demands for service. While staff may be reduced, the workload of the agency seldom is, and practitioners must contend with increased and often inappropriately large caseloads.

Societal Factors

Three societal factors are particularly relevant to social work: social welfare policy, changing expectations of work, and sexism.

The development of social welfare policy in the United States is primarily a political process. Although this is one of the strengths of a democratic society, the policy directions and program goals that result are often vaguely stated, which may lead to conflicting, ambiguous, and excessive role demands on social workers. If legislation is intended as a symbolic statement and its objectives exceed its funding, service providers must negotiate high consumer expectations with inadequate resources. Further, ambiguous legislation results in a lack of job specificity, lack of program structure, and excessive paperwork in pursuit of accountability (Dressel, 1982).

Cherniss (1980b) has identified unfulfilled expectations as a major source of burnout among human service providers, especially with "the growing belief during the last 40 years that ... a job had to be a vehicle for self-actualization as well as economic security" (p. 150). Seeking self-actualization through work—and only through work—fosters burnout by creating unrealistic expectations for the work setting.

Discrimination based on gender has been well documented in society and in social work. Sexism contrib-

utes to burnout among women through its influence on salary levels, promotions, organizational influence and power, job assignments, and role expectations (Edelwich & Brodsky, 1980). Sexism in the workplace may foster a sense of helplessness and powerlessness, decrease the availability of feedback on performance, and interfere with social support from co-workers and supervisors (Finn, 1990).

PREVENTING AND ALLEVIATING BURNOUT

Techniques recommended for stress management and stress reduction include relaxation techniques, physical exercise, proper nutrition and rest, and the reduction of coffee, cigarette, drug, and alcohol consumption. Important as they are for health promotion and well-being, these methods address the symptoms of burnout, rather than the causes. Strategies for addressing burnout must focus on stressors at the individual level, including the client-worker relationship, and the organizational and societal level.

Individual Strategies

While the importance of organizational factors cannot be denied, individual practitioners bear some responsibility for burnout. New practitioners, driven by idealized notions of professional performance, may experience a crisis of competence (Cherniss, 1980a). Building on White's theory (1959, 1963) that a sense of competence may be developed by acting in the environment and meeting its challenges, Harrison (1980) suggests that "workers are able to develop positive affective responses to their jobs only if there is some certainty that what they do is valuable and makes a difference in the lives of clients" (p. 42). One aspect of competence is "the worker's skill, including techniques, judgment, and the ability to use him or herself effectively" (Harrison, 1983, p. 32). Thus, by developing skill, the individual contributes toward a positive work experience.

Practitioners have an ongoing responsibility to expand their knowledge base, by keeping up with the professional literature, participating in continuing education programs and in-service trainings, and learning from clients, peers, and supervisors. A strong knowledge base is vital for understanding the client's current situation and goals and designing appropriate practice interventions. It is particularly important to develop an awareness of, and sensitivity to, cultural factors in the client's situation.

Practitioners must learn to set realistic goals. By establishing realistic goals for the work environment, the practitioner will be able to measure progress, to have a sense of accomplishment, and to feel mastery. While noble ideals of fighting injustice or providing well-being to all motivate many social workers, progress toward those goals is difficult to measure without more specific and realistic indicators along the way. The same principles apply to direct work with clients. In partnership, client and practitioner must formulate realistic goals, accompanied by specific subgoals to mark progress. By attending to the client's wishes, the practitioner is less likely to set inappropriate goals, and the chance of a successful outcome is increased. Worker-practitioner partnership also tends to reduce beginning practitioners' sense of total responsibility for clients' well-being.

Focusing on clients' strengths, abilities, and resources reduces the risk of burnout. With an understanding of these assets, the practitioner develops a more complete and realistic perspective of clients and of appropriate interventions. A practitioner who focuses solely on problems and deficiencies will be less able to design effective interventions and more likely to adopt a negative attitude to clients.

Self-awareness also reduces the likelihood of burnout. First, if we understand our personal limitations, we will not accept inappropriate responsibility, we will set achievable goals, and our work expectations will be realistic. Second, if we are aware of our personal needs, we might realize that they are being inappropriately met in work with clients; in that case, we can develop other resources to address these needs. Third, if we are self-aware, we can recognize and deal with our subjective reactions to clients that hinder effective work. Because the use of self is critical in work with clients, awareness of our emotional responses is vital for the well-being of both client and practitioner.

To develop competence and to avoid burnout, practitioners must actively seek feedback about their work with clients. This includes direct feedback from clients, through systematic and continual evaluation of progress toward goals. Developments in clinical research have provided resources for gathering information about effectiveness. Additionally, feedback may be gathered

indirectly by evaluation of the clients' progress in treatment. Colleagues and supervisors are also essential sources of feedback.

Building a social support system at work is critical in reducing the likelihood of burnout. Co-workers and supervisors fulfill a number of social support functions, including listening without judgment, technical support, technical challenge, emotional support, emotional challenge, and sharing social reality (Pines, 1983). Energy invested in developing relationships with colleagues is repaid many times over through access to their expertise and support.

Research indicates that a fulfilling and enriching personal life contributes to more positive attitudes toward work. As Maslach (1982) notes:

> When your whole world is your work and little else, then your whole world is more likely to fall apart when problems arise on the job. Your sense of competence, your self-esteem, and your personal identity are all based on what you do in life, and they will be far more shaky and insecure if that base is a narrow one. (p. 104)

Setting boundaries on your work is often the first step toward a satisfying personal life (Maslach, 1982). Taking leisure time is not enough, however; it must be used for personally rewarding activities, such as fostering personal relationships and exploring personal interests.

Organizational and Societal Strategies

Agencies must assume responsibility for creating work environments that decrease vulnerability to burnout. A strategy frequently suggested is the development of training programs. Programs in stress or time management are less important than programs designed to increase practitioners' skills and knowledge—in particular, interpersonal skills and information about the clients served, realistic goals for that population, and practice models appropriate for intervention, as well as information about evaluation techniques. This type of training enhances practitioners' sense of competency.

To reduce burnout, agencies should review their policies. First, agency policies and procedures must be responsive to client needs. If the requirements regarding data collection and documentation or the mandated procedures for intervention, interfere with the helping relationship, they will contribute to burnout. Second, agency policies and procedures, both formal and informal, must provide clarity of job function and tasks, to minimize role ambiguity and conflict for both supervisors and practitioners. Third, agency policy that fosters the development of supportive relationships with co-workers and supervisors will reduce burnout. Fourth, agency policies and procedures, both formal and informal, should be nonsexist. All workers, regardless of gender, expect to be treated equally and equitably in the work environment.

Specific strategies have been proposed to deal with the emotional energy that work with clients demands (Daley, 1979; Pines & Kafry, 1978; Zastrow, 1984). One alternative is to rotate assignments. This allows practitioners to experience variety—and perhaps challenge—in their work but, unless employed with caution, it may undermine the development of competency. A more useful alternative is to balance work assignments so that particularly demanding cases are distributed among the staff. Work assignments should also be flexible, so as to meet individual practitioner needs in terms of caseload composition; providing a variety of case assignments reduces the risk of burnout. Another alternative is time-outs, which allow practitioners to assume less stressful work assignments for a time. As a general rule, agencies should make efforts to reduce caseload size if they want to minimize burnout, with its costly consequences of

absenteeism, worker inefficiency, and turnover. Other options include job sharing, job splitting, quality circles for participatory management, and flexible benefit plans (McNeeley, 1988).

Finally, it is appropriate for both agency representatives and individual practitioners to become involved in the political process—for instance, by designing social welfare legislation responsive to clients' needs, with realistic program goals and adequate funding. In political action, it is usually more effective to join an organized group. The National Association of Social Workers actively lobbies on both state and federal levels in support of legislation consistent with the principles and goals of the profession.

CONCLUSION

Social workers are at risk for burnout by virtue of who they are, the work they do, and the environments in which they work. Once burnout has developed, it is extremely difficult to reverse, and the costs of burnout are a burden for the client, the practitioner, and the agency. Prevention is a more successful strategy. Agencies have a responsibility to create a work environment that does not foster burnout. However, the individual practitioner is able to reduce the risk of burnout by becoming aware of the various stressors and implementing strategies for their minimization.

LEARNING EXERCISES

1. Develop your own burnout prevention plan. First, make a list of the stressors identified in Reading 19-1. Second, classify each stressor in terms of the amount of control that you, as a new professional, might reasonably be able to exercise over it. We suggest two categories: those that you can reasonably expect to control; and those over which you will have limited control. Try to state (in one sentence) what you will do to exercise control over each of the stressors in your first list and thus reduce your risk of burnout.

REFERENCES

Arches, J. (1991). Social structure, burnout, and job satisfaction. *Social Work, 36*(3), 202–206.

Cherniss, C. (1980a). *Professional burnout in human service organizations.* New York: Praeger.

Cherniss, C. (1980b). *Staff burnout.* Beverly Hills: Sage.

Daley, M. R. (1979). Burnout: Smoldering problem in the protective services. *Social Work, 24*(5), 375–379.

Dressel, P. L. (1982). Policy sources of work dissatisfaction: The case of human services in aging. *Social Service Review, 56*(3), 406–423.

Edelwich, J., & Brodsky, A. (1980). *Burn-out.* New York: Human Services Press.

Farber, B. A. (1983). Introduction: A critical perspective on burnout. In B. A. Farber (Ed.), *Stress and burnout in the human service professions* (pp. 1–20). New York: Pergamon.

Finn, J. L. (1990). Burnout in the human services: A feminist perspective. *Affilia, 5*(4), 55–71.

Freudenberger, H. J. (1974). Staff burn-out. *Journal of Social Issues, 30*(1), 159–165.

Gant, L. M. (1996). Are culturally sophisticated agencies better workplaces for social work staff and administrators? *Social Work, 41*(2), 163–171.

Harrison, W. D. (1980). Role strain and burnout in child protection service workers. *Social Service Review, 54*(1), 31–44.

Harrison, W. D. (1983). A social competence model of burnout. In B. A. Farber (Ed.), *Stress and burnout in the human service professions* (pp. 29–39). New York: Pergamon.

Himle, D. P., Jayaratne, S., & Thyness, P. (1991). Buffering effects of four social support types on burnout among social workers. *Social Work Research and Abstracts, 27*(1), 22–27.

Jayaratne, S, & Chess, W. A. (1983). Job satisfaction and burnout in social work. In B. A. Farber (Ed.), *Stress and burnout in the human service professions* (pp. 129–141). New York: Pergamon.

Jayaratne, S., & Chess, W. A. (1984). Job satisfaction, burnout, and turnover: A national study. *Social Work, 29*(5), 448–453.

Jayaratne, S., Tripodi, T., & Chess, W. A. (1983). Perceptions of emotional support, stress, and strain by male and female social workers. *Social Work Research and Abstracts, 19*(2), 19–27.

Jones, M. L. (1993). Role conflict: Causes of burnout or energizer? *Social Work, 38*(2), 137–141.

Karger, H. J. (1981). Burnout as alienation. *Social Service Review, 55*(2), 270–283.

Koeske, G. F., & Kelly, T. (1995). The impact of overinvolvement on burnout and job satisfaction. *American Journal of Orthopsychiatry, 65*(2), 282–292.

Koeske, G. F., & Kirk, S. A. (1995). The effect of characteristics of human service workers on subsequent morale and turnover. *Administration in Social Work, 19*(1), 15–31.

Koeske, G. F., & Koeske, R. D. (1989). Workload and burnout: Can social support and perceived accomplishment help? *Social Work, 34*(3), 243–248.

Koeske, G. F., & Koeske, R. D. (1993). A preliminary test of a stress-strain-outcome model of reconceptualizing the burnout phenomenon. *Journal of Social Service Research, 17*(3/4), 107–135.

Maslach, C. (1976). Burned-out. *Human Behavior, 5*(9), 16–22.

Maslach, C. (1978). The client role in staff burn-out. *Journal of Social Issues, 34*(4), 111–124.

Maslach, C. (1982). *Burnout: The cost of caring.* Englewood Cliffs, NJ: Prentice-Hall.

McNeely, R. L. (1988). Five morale enhancing innovations for human services. *Social Casework, 69*(4), 204–213.

Meyerson, D. E. (1994). Interpretation of stress in institutions: The cultural production of ambiguity and burnout. *Administrative Science Quarterly, 39*(4), 628–653.

Pines, A. (1983) On burnout and the buffering effects of social supports. In B. A. Farber (Ed.), *Stress and burnout in the human service professions* (pp. 158–160). New York: Pergamon.

Pines, A., Aronson, E., & Kafry, D. (1981). *Burnout: From tedium to personal growth.* New York: Free Press.

Pines, A., & Kafry, D. (1978). Occupational tedium in the social services. *Social Work, 23*(6), 499–507.

Pines, A., & Maslach, C. (1978). Characteristics of staff burnout in mental health settings. *Hospital and Community Psychiatry, 29*(4), 233–237.

Poulin, J. E., & Walter, C. A. (1993). Social workers' burnout: A longitudinal study. *Social Work Research and Abstracts, 29*(4), 5–11.

Söderfeldt, M., Söderfeldt, B., & Lars-Erik, W. (1995). Burnout in social work. *Social Work, 50*(5), 638–646.

White, R. W. (1959). Motivation reconsidered: The concept of competence. *Psychological Review, 66*(5), 297–344.

White, R. W. (1963). *Ego and reality in psychoanalytic theory.* New York: International Universities Press.

Zastrow, C. (1984). Understanding and preventing burn-out. *British Journal of Social Work, 14*(2), 141–155.

Appendix A: Case Materials

The Debbie Smith Case*

Debbie Smith was a disgusting hunk of humanity. That was clear. At least it was clear to all of the previous caseworkers, who didn't hesitate to moralize at length about her in the case record.

A 22-year-old woman who had dropped out of school in the tenth grade, Ms. Smith had gotten pregnant twice by men old enough to be her father. She was receiving AFDC for her two children, Angelia, 5, and Tommy, 3. She was described as a poor housekeeper, a negligent mother, and a person without any motivation. She had been active with protective services for some time because of concern about neglect of her children.

On the first visit, I went to her apartment and knocked several times without receiving an answer. As I was leaving, a neighbor came out and said in a disgusted voice: "She's in there. You just have to pound and pound." She directed me back to the apartment, a partially converted garage, and loudly knocked and shouted. After a while, an obese woman in a dirty robe came to the door. She looked much older than 22 years old, and her skin was crusted over with eczema sores. She acted sleepy but warmly invited me in. The other woman left after making a snide remark.

The front room of the apartment served as a living room and a bedroom to Ms. S; it was small, dreary, and dirty. The shades were drawn and the temperature was in the high 80s with a heater going full blast, although it was a beautiful, bright afternoon outside. In the first interview, I introduced myself and attempted to establish rapport. I didn't mention the condition of the house nor

---

*This is a case carried and recorded by a student at Indiana University School of Social Work.

the fact that she could not adequately supervise the children when she was asleep. Fortunately, the second point was not of immediate importance since the neighbor I'd met was Ms. S's aunt and was keeping an eye on them. Debbie Smith went to get the children, at her own initiative, to introduce them to me. She talked with pride of their accomplishments. Angelia seemed to be an alert, bright child but somewhat shy. Tommy seemed quite affectionate and outgoing but mentally slow.

My initial impression was not of disgust, but more of pity. I felt Miss S was bright and articulate and had a great deal of affection for her children. I was impressed by the fact that she wanted me to meet them and by the obvious interest she had in them. She seemed to have so little meaning in her life other than the children.

THE PRELIMINARY ASSESSMENT

I made five more weekly visits. In these visits, I tried to understand Ms. Smith's view of her problems, to collect data, and to establish a relationship of trust.

My assessment was based on the three members of the S family. Biogenetically, there were several problems. Ms. S had medical problems, most noticeably obesity and eczema. I suspected that she had metabolism problems, which possibly contributed to obesity, to her desire for high temperatures, and to her lethargy. There were indications that the children were not receiving balanced, nutritious meals, partly as a result of their mother's inattention.

Cognitively, Ms. S showed her greatest strength. She was not only bright and articulate but was easily motivated in this area. Angelia appeared to share her talents, but Tommy appeared slow for his age.

Psychosocially, this was a poorly adjusted family. Ms. S had spent a short time as a child with her mother, who had grown up in a middle-class family. All the other family members had gone to college and had been successful, but Ms. S's mother had shocked the family by becoming pregnant repeatedly, by men whom the family classed as undesirable. An aunt who had no children of her own had offered to take Ms. S and raise her. Already under financial strain, the mother agreed. As a result, Ms. S was raised in a city quite distant from her mother; her aunt and uncle provided material support but gave her little emotional support. The aunt was cold and punitive, and her attitude toward sex was extremely prudish.

My contacts with the aunt confirmed what Ms. S told me of her. The aunt informed me at length that Debbie was worthless and would end up in the gutter. Ms. S was subjected to these lectures daily. Ms. S disliked her aunt but felt that she was dependent upon her and that she had a moral obligation to be thankful for what the aunt has done for her. She blamed her mother for having rejected her and for having given her to an aunt who was so devoid of human emotion.

Ms. S wanted to provide more warmth and love for her children than she had experienced but she was hampered by an inadequate model of family functioning. In addition, her own problems interfered with her ability to nurture the children. She gave them sincere, showy affection at times but was inconsistent in her behavior. Because of the long hours of sleeping each day, she mainly avoided them. Sometimes she would express her frustration by shouting at them; then she would feel guilty and hug and kiss them. She did not show preference toward either of them, in spite of Angelia's obviously superior intelligence. She recognized that they had different areas of strength and encouraged them in these areas.

The environment in which Ms. S lived was overwhelmingly hostile. Her aunt was constantly nagging her about what she should do (get out of bed and clean the house), what she was (a no-good tramp), and what she should not do (get into trouble again). This advice had been reinforced by a long series of social workers. She had no positive social experience and indeed had become a total recluse. She spent large portions of her time in bed, seemingly as an escape. Her children had few experiences; their great-aunt occasionally took them someplace.

The situation is a good example of a mismatch of coping patterns and impinging environment, which results in feedback that creates further mismatching. This vicious circle involves an increasing number of people (basically offspring) and contributes to an ever greater dysfunction. Ms. S's strengths were her hopes and aspirations for her children and her desire to do more for them. The fact that she was bright and articulate and enjoyed discussing her situation was also positive.

I hoped to break the circle of mismatchings, but I had to decide the most effective point of intervention. Alleviation of medical problems seemed a logical starting point. My efforts in providing access to medical resources would be a concrete example of nurturing and supporting. If medical problems could be overcome, then the family members might be able to function at maximum physical strength and to cope more effectively with their other problems. It would also provide an opportunity to assess Ms. S's motivation and willingness to follow through on a plan mutually developed.

I decided to explore with Ms. S the necessity of seeking treatment and to suggest possible treatment resources. With her permission, I would make a referral to the visiting public health nurse, who could explain health problems and give advice on how to minimize them. She would also be able to help Ms. S plan balanced diets. For Tommy, it might be advisable to make use of a special fund available for a work-up to explore the possibility of developmental disability. In the event of disability, appropriate plans could be made before he began school.

The community had two nursery schools, which could offer the children a wider range of experiences. I hoped to interest Ms. S in the cooperative school because this would involve her in an activity and would help her to develop techniques of child care.

THE WORKING ASSESSMENT

At the next interview, I had hoped to explore these suggestions with Ms. S, but I was so appalled by the condition of the house that I changed my plans. The living room bedroom had debris piled four or five inches thick over the entire floor. In order to sit down, I had to remove a pile of records and clothing from a chair and then clear off a section of the floor on which to set the chair. Ms. S was lying between sheets so incredibly filthy that it was hard to believe they had ever been gray, much less white; they must not have been washed in weeks. The condition of the apartment represented a health and safety hazard to the children and Ms. S. A confrontation was necessary. I decided to focus on the children's welfare, a matter with which she was concerned. I pointed out, firmly and directly, that it was unfair to subject the children to these kinds of conditions and that rats and cockroaches were inevitable if things did not improve. She listened attentively and then admitted that she had not considered the possible effect on the children nor the likely health and safety hazards. It seemed to make an impression on her that I was rational and unemotional and did not couch the discussion in terms of how evil she was. I tried to show her that I respected her even though I did not like her behavior in this instance. She promised to clean up the house if I would return in a week to see it. Far more importantly, however, the incident presented an opportunity for her to unleash her feelings about herself.

She informed me that her apartment was like herself—dirty. Having her aunt nag at her constantly only served to reinforce this opinion. When I explored why she felt she was dirty, she was surprised that it was not obvious to me. This appeared to be her first feedback that others might not agree with her self-perception. (Generally, they probably did.) She explained that having had three illegitimate pregnancies, having dropped out of school, and having to depend on welfare support were indications that she was dirty. In fact, everything she did was an indication that she was a worthless, dirty person.

This was the first that I had heard of a third child. Her aunt had arranged for her first child to be given to a friend. Debbie had no choice in the matter, just as she had no choice when her aunt declared that she was to keep the second child as punishment for having gotten into trouble again. This left her with unresolved feelings about her first child; she had a desire to see the child and feared that the child would feel rejected by her. Unavoidably, she also had feelings that Angelia was a source of punishment, even though she loved her very much.

The incident and the new knowledge I had of Ms. S changed my assessment and my strategy of intervention. I decided that I could expect little movement until her self-image was improved and that this would have to take priority over the other goals. I knew she would have to feel that a change in self-esteem was necessary and possible and that this would have to be incorporated into her value system. Since the topic had arisen and she seemed receptive to discussing her feelings, I felt that we should begin immediately. We discussed on a very intellectual plane how one develops a self-image and the philosophical idea of the basic worth of each person.

She was then able to apply the abstract ideas to her own life experiences and to examine how she came to have a negative self-image. She recalled how miserable she had been as a teenager. Her aunt lectured her continually on the evils of sex. These ideas were in contradiction to those of her peers. Sex was an area in which she could most threaten her aunt, and in retrospect she sees her actions as a way of punishing her aunt. In addition, she felt that she was searching for a relationship that provided warmth and love, which she had never received from her mother or her aunt and uncle. She did not find this type of relationship, however. All three children were the result of casual affairs with older men whom she saw as socially undesirable. She felt unworthy of any other man, however. The parallel between her actions and those of her mother hardly seems accidental. In a sense it was a self-fulfilling prophecy. Many times her aunt had accused her of being like her mother, and it was small wonder that she chose this way in which to rebel.

As a result of the second pregnancy she was moved into her present apartment, which was fashioned out of one half of a garage. The other half housed the latest-model Cadillac. Ms. S felt that moving from the house was both punishment and rejection. She offered to show the worker the apartment, and it became apparent that Angelia did not live with her. Ms. S said that Angelia had a room in the house (and by implication, room in the aunt's heart) but ate with Tommy and her. The aunt had special affection for Angelia and had strongly hinted that Angelia should stay with her if Ms. S were ever to break the ties and move from her present situation. Ms. S though that this might be the best situation for her daughter, since she had so little to offer Angelia.

At this point, I felt that we had begun to define and prioritize problems and had a more adequate assessment of Ms. S's situation. She had expressed awareness of problems and the desire for change. With the relationship that had already been established, it appeared that a plan of action could be mutually worked out and first steps at redirection taken.

Our plan was to begin by helping Ms. S to become independent from her aunt. Separation from the hostile environment was valuable in itself but, in addition, it would prove to Ms. S that she was capable of managing on her own and could be self-sufficient. It would also mean leaving the dreary surroundings, hopefully for more pleasant ones. Separation presented a financial problem, however, because the public welfare grant provided a small housing allowance that was inadequate to pay the rent anywhere else. Finally, separation would force her to address her feelings about Angelia. If she gave her daughter up, she would be behaving in the same way as her own mother. She needed to realize that she had a real contribution to make to her daughter.

The original goal of getting medical treatment could be incorporated into the self-image building attempts. Improving her body image could help boost her self-esteem.

On the next few visits, rapid movement was evident. We began to explore alternative ways to the goals we had set. Ms. S made strides toward cleaning her house, and I praised her. But I looked forward to a day when she would do it for herself, not for me. We discussed her situation and I shared what I saw as her strengths. She was flattered by my feeling that she was bright and enthusiastically agreed to be tested by City College. Our interview served to strengthen her self-esteem.

Ms. S began to make actual change efforts in the next three months. Her testing at City College showed that she had a high IQ, and her aptitude scores for college subjects were so good that the school was willing to accept her as a freshman without a high school diploma. She went for counseling and decided to take a review course and get her General Educational Development diploma before going to college; she felt that it would give her more security. She was showing a great deal of maturity in her decisions. She got psychology and philosophy books from library to enlighten herself (and to impress me). She was able to understand Freud's concepts of id, ego, and superego with little difficulty. Health problems had been explored. Extracting teeth improved her general state of health; the gum disease had been depressing her immune system.

Tommy was found to have an average IQ but was behind his age group developmentally because of very severe hearing loss. He was referred to a charity for children with disabilities, which sponsored corrective surgery.

The public health nurse came weekly to help plan a balanced diet for the children and a weight reduction diet for Ms. S. I coordinated my efforts with the nurse, and she reinforced my efforts to build Debbie's self-esteem.

During this upward climb, there were periods of regression. I had to get Ms. S out of bed on many occasions. More often, however, the house was cleaner, the shades were up, and the heat was reasonable. I could see improvement in her skin, and she seemed happier.

The children were visited, and they finally enrolled in the nursery school. When I visited, they would run up to tell me what they had been doing, and I got the same kind of excited reaction from Ms. S.

Each success Ms. S achieved helped convince her that she could build a satisfying life.

THE CONTINUING REASSESSMENT

A point came at which we were ready to begin the generalization and stabilization of change. Two major considerations marked this period. One was that Ms. S's aunt decided to tear down the garage and build several apartment units instead. This meant that Ms. S would be forced by circumstances to make the desired separation. The second was the need to counteract Ms. S's attempts at structuring our relationship into a friendship rather than a professional relationship. The present relationship had been used purposefully to motivate Ms. S to follow through on proposed projects. However, I had had to resist her attempts to let visits become book review sessions or social calls. In a sense, she was resisting attempts to go further and to use the knowledge she had gained to help herself; it was a tactic to resist change. I decided to clarify the nature of the relationship and to set a new goal—that of widening social contacts so that others in the community could provide the friendship she so much desired.

Thus, successful separation from her aunt and successful establishment of social contacts became goals during this period. She used agency policy to give her support in moving Angelia with her: She explained to her aunt that the public welfare agency could not give her money for a child who was not living with her. Ms. S had come to believe that she had more to offer Angelia but was still finding it difficult to confront her aunt directly.

The new apartment was larger and more cheerful, and the neighbors were friendly. She thrived in the new environment and this helped her to broaden her social contacts. She began going to church fellowship meetings and did volunteer work for a civil rights group while the children were in nursery school. She was so efficient that she soon became an officer in the group. She made a good child care arrangement with a neighbor for her evenings at the GED review course. At Christmas, she got a job as a gift wrapper at a large department store.

Ms. Smith developed enough friends so that she was happy to use our relationship in a professional way. She discussed her feelings toward people visiting in the home. She became anxious and did not want people in her apartment for too long. She had used her apartment as a protective womb for such a long time that she was threatened by friends coming there. We worked through many such fears, or at least relieved her anxiety about holding such beliefs.

Her apartment was consistently clean, partly because she knew guests might drop in at any time. Her eczema was rapidly disappearing, and she bragged of having lost 50 pounds. Her change of attitude was reflected in the behavior of the children and in her care of them. She was more consistent in her discipline, and they were more responsive.

She took the children on a bus trip to visit her mother. It was a very good experience. Her mother was glad to see her and the children, and Ms. S was able to satisfy herself that her mother loved her. She felt she had made peace with her mother after all these years.

Soon afterward, she began dating a man who was a college graduate, an accountant. After several months, she became engaged to him and was extremely happy. Problems arose, however. His parents were unhappy that he had chosen a high school dropout who had illegitimate children. Their pressure was sufficient to break up the relationship. As soon as I learned of the broken engagement, I made a home visit. I was sure that this would result in regression, and I wanted to head it off. I could visualize a dirty apartment, drawn shades, and extreme temperature. When I arrived, the apartment was spotless, and she was smiling. I told her what I had expected and she laughed. "The relationship was a good one for me. I know now that someone who is handsome, intelligent, and well-educated can love me. But I wouldn't touch Robert with a ten-foot pole; he's a momma's boy. Any man who can't make decisions for himself isn't worth having. I'm going to college next year and will have the opportunity to meet all kinds of men. I'm not going to settle for a weak man; I want one that will think of me first." It appeared we were ready to terminate our relationship. Debbie Smith no longer needed me. She had the inner strength to make her own decisions and to motivate herself.

READING A-2 *The Stover Family**

This family was referred to Family Service Agency from the child protection unit of the County Department of Public Welfare. At the time of referral, the family included Earl (husband and father), age 43; June (wife and mother), age 39; and three children. The two oldest children (George, age 12, and Larie, age 5) are June Stover's children by a previous marriage; Eileen, age 4, is of this marriage.

Mr. and Mrs. Stover had been active with 22 social agencies during the past 15 years. Mrs. Stover has had three marriages, the first after she became pregnant in high school. She never lived with her first husband. Her

*A case study prepared for this text.

second husband was a ward of the state with serious developmental disability. Three of her four children with him were placed for adoption. She became involved with Mr. Stover while still married to her second husband; her first child by Mr. Stover arrived four months after their marriage. Mrs. Stover has shown other signs of instability and attempted suicide eight years ago.

Mr. Stover has been known to the Veterans Administration since his army discharge 10 years ago as a psychoneurotic. He is reportedly alcoholic. During contacts with Family Service three years ago, Mrs. Stover reported a number of episodes of physical abuse of herself and the children by Mr. Stover.

Since the present marriage there have been six complaints of neglect of the children. These have originated from Mrs. Stover's relatives, her former husband and his relatives, the school nurse, and the minister. The Child Protection Unit has found insufficient evidence to proceed on these charges. Workers have found it difficult to work with Mrs. Stover; when contacted by a worker, she is superficially cooperative but then avoids workers whenever possible. If an appointment is made in advance, she is never home. Family Service was reluctant to reopen the case, as indications were that this woman couldn't use help. However, on plea from the Public Welfare Department, we decided to make another attempt to provide service.

Eileen Stover, the 4-year-old, has a condition believed to be muscular dystrophy. Previous workers have found Mrs. Stover unrealistic in her attitude toward Eileen's condition.

MARCH 20 TO APRIL 15

Since Family Services accepted the case, I have tried to contact the Stover family without any success. The Public Welfare worker says it is impossible to find Mrs. Stover at home if she knows who is coming and that she is not to be trusted at all; she agrees to everything and does nothing: On April 13, I sent a note saying I would call on April 15; this time Mrs. Stover was home.

The Stovers have two rooms on the second floor of a large house, the ground floor of which is in the process of being remodeled. Mrs. Stover indicated that she couldn't talk to me since her husband was sleeping. She is of medium height, quite dirty in appearance, with old slacks, a man's shirt hanging out, and bare feet. Mrs. Stover is in her seventh month of pregnancy. I referred to the previous contacts of Family Services and other agencies and explained we had decided to come to see her as we knew about a number of problems she had been having. I indicated that I was aware of her previous marital difficulties and the fact that she had temporarily left her husband last March; we knew that this resulted in difficulties for the family as a whole. Mrs. Stover's reaction was to say that the situation has cleared up and she feels that the marital relationship is ok. She did, however, appear responsive to interest in her problems and accepted an office interview for April 23.

APRIL 23

Mrs. Stover did not keep the appointment. On repeated calls in person, I did not find her home. I made two appointments by telephone, neither of which she kept.

JUNE 24

I finally located the Stover family when welfare called to say they had moved to Jonesville. On this date I found them both home. Their present housing is a four-room shack raised about five feet from the ground on stilts beside the river. The home was flooded out two years ago. There is no foundation; the beams and supporting joists in the house were seriously weakened by the flood. The sides and interior partitions are still caked with dirt from the flood.

There is no sign of paint on the interior or exterior of the house, which is barely habitable. The front door has a drop of about four feet to the ground, with only a crude ladder. The home has two bedrooms, a living room, and kitchen; these are adequate in size. Toilet facilities are outdoor. The shack was previously owned by an elderly bachelor, who died. The house was in estate when the Stovers moved in, and they are paying a low rent, which may be applied toward a purchase price if the Stovers decide to stay.

Mr. and Mrs. Stover were both present. Mr. Stover is a small-built man, neatly dressed, unshaven, and quiet. Mrs. Stover had made him aware that I had seen her earlier. He said that they were getting on well now, outside of the fact that he is unemployed. He stated that the previous difficulties between himself and Mrs. Stover had been due largely to his alcoholic problem. Quarrels occurred usually when he was drinking; he would get angry and has a strong temper. He said that there have been no such happenings for the last 10 months. I asked him to what he attributed the change. He feels that difficulties arose because of his nervousness and unemployment. When he is nervous, he starts drinking, and they go round and round again. He said that he had been employed pretty steadily during the last summer and fall, mostly on temporary jobs. The reason he can't get employment now as a carpenter is that the employer must insure him and in order to do this he must pass a physical examination. Thus, he finds himself confined largely to odd jobs and casual labor. Another thing that bothers him about employment is that he gets nervous working too close to too many people and that he dislikes working for other people. Small things bother him; he is easily irritated. He would prefer to work for himself. His ambition would be to get a small farm of his own where he could grow vegetables for market. The problem is lack of capital, and he doubts if he will get a chance to do this. The Stovers appear to present a united front to the world. However, Mrs. Stover neither nodded nor spoke in support of much of what her husband said. She did make a point of saying in his presence that she felt his drinking had improved.

JULY 17

Again, I failed to find the Stovers at home on visits I made by appointment. On July 15, it appeared as though they had moved again. The Public Welfare Department had no new address. But, on this date, to my surprise Mrs. Stover came into the office. She was neatly dressed in a clean dress and had her hair done up. She seemed uneasy about the story she had to tell and was trying to be placating. Mrs. Stover said she had decided to leave her husband, because he has been drinking heavily, mostly wine, and has been beating her and the kids. She is afraid of what will happen. He was on the wagon up to June but started drinking again. Mrs. Stover felt this had something to do with the troubles with housing. Also, Mr. Stover has picked up with a neighbor who drinks, and they have been going out together. Mr. Stover, she said, "gets nervous and edgy." He orders the kids and Mrs. Stover around. Nothing she does pleases him. He calls her all sorts of names when he gets drunk. Mr. Stover pushed Eileen down in the yard because she got in his way.

Mrs. Stover hasn't notified Public Welfare of the change in circumstances. She is out of money and the baby is due shortly. I gave her a check for immediate needs and advised her to go immediately to the Welfare Board and get things straightened out with them. She was obviously attempting to charm me into helping her with this, as she says the Welfare Board won't do anything for her. I agreed to talk to AFDC about her application there.

JULY 18 TO SEPTEMBER 1

Together, Mrs. Stover and I made application for AFDC and arranged for care of the children during her confinement. I visited with her twice in the hospital. After the baby's birth, Mrs. Stover moved in with her sister, without notifying Public Welfare. I pointed out to her that this was why she had trouble with AFDC. She complained they couldn't trust her, but this behavior certainly seemed to prove their point. Mrs. Stover said she was planning on moving again. She promised to notify AFDC and workers of her new address; this time she did.

SEPTEMBER 15. AFDC VISIT TO MRS. STOVER

Mrs. Stover, Eileen, and Peter, the baby, were at home; the two children played happily in the apartment. Eileen has come to know me. The apartment consists of three good-sized rooms in a row in an old apartment building. Mrs. Stover has the apartment neat and clean. She was dressed in slacks and noticeably cleaner and paying more attention to her appearance. Mrs. Stover mentioned she has bought winter clothes for the children, but not all she needs yet. She showed me her AFDC budget, which includes funds to be signed over by Mr. Stover from his disability pension. Mr. Stover held up signing the documents, but instead gave Mrs. Stover some money himself in September, and is offering to do this every month. Mrs. Stover refused this offer and reported the whole matter to the VA office. By law, she feels, he will be required to sign the document, since part of his disability pension is for his wife and children. She feels Mr. Stover is still trying to spoil her plans or to get back and live with her. I raised the question of Mrs. Stover's plans regarding the marriage. Mrs. Stover seems quite sure at this point that she wants a permanent separation. She would want a rule that Mr. Stover would visit the children, but only when sober, and could only visit his two children—that is, Peter and Eileen. Mrs. Stover again admitted ambivalent feelings about Mr. Stover. She has always felt she needed him and couldn't get along without him. She was ready to put up with his drinking to some extent; she was always afraid of being alone in the world. Moreover, she regards him as an intelligent man, who is not at all hard to get along with when not drinking. However, she now feels his drinking has got to the point where he can't control it, and he won't admit it. She is risking her own safety and realizes now that staying with Mr. Stover may cost her the family. The children could be harmed, or it might be necessary for an agency to place them.

At the present time, Mrs. Stover doesn't know where Mr. Stover is.

SEPTEMBER 22

I suggested that Mrs. Stover make her need for a stove known to her AFDC worker. She doesn't wish to. I pointed out that she could be cheating herself, since it is my understanding that AFDC can assist with a need of this kind. I indicated that her reluctance to approach them seemed to indicate that all was not yet well in her relationship to AFDC and asked what the trouble was. Mrs. Stover again said she doesn't trust them. Checks have been held up when she didn't fully appreciate the reason. She has been given to understand that she is a babysitter for her own children. AFDC, she feels, are paying her in that capacity and have given her to understand that they may fire her at any time. I brought up incidents indicating that there had been reasons for concern about the children in the past. I commented that dangers to the children seemed to lie more in Mrs. Stover's disturbed marriages. In my view, I told her, she has feeling for the children, she wants to keep them, and she is capable of caring for them. On the other hand, we have to consider the emotional effect on the children, as well as possible physical dangers because of the violence in her marriages. Mrs. Stover again said she knows that my primary concern is with the children. She indicated that she doesn't resent this from me, because she knows I support her effort to get out of the tangled marital situation. She does resent this from AFDC workers; on the other hand, she recognizes that she has given AFDC workers reason for concern because of her avoidance of them. I pointed out that Mrs. Stover can improve her relationship with AFDC by informing them of changes and needs. Mrs. Stover noted that lately she has been phoning her AFDC worker about every change and circumstance. We decided that Mrs. Stover would explore the possibility of getting the stove from her landlord and, failing this, will think further about approaching AFDC. She is reluctant to ask for extra things from AFDC for fear that she will be thought too demanding. She has considerable doubt about the idea that a request of this kind might help convince AFDC that she wants to meet her family's needs.

Mrs. Stover said that she thinks perhaps they regard her as lacking in intelligence. I challenged this by pointing out that AFDC records show her to be of very superior intelligence (reported IQ is 142). Mrs. Stover indicated that she knows her IQ is 142, though she doesn't recall who told her this. I explained this placed her within the upper 1% of the population in intelligence, whereupon Mrs. Stover demanded, "Where has it got me?" She went on to say, "My life is a complete mess," pointing out her three unhappy marriages at 39. She mentioned that she didn't do as well in school as she should have, always had her nose in a book, has always had a liking for books, but cannot use this information in her own life. Her dream is to be a librarian. At times, she thinks that after five years or so, when Peter is older and in school, she would like some kind of training for work; her first choice would be library work. Her future plans are in terms of working and supporting her children, and she stressed that she wants *no more men*.

Mrs. Stover asked how she could have made such a mess of her life. I pointed out that feelings are often as important as brains in determining what we do and suggested that she work on the problem of how her experiences and her feelings have landed her where she is. She can still use books to acquire knowledge and training, but this is not enough by itself. Mrs. Stover seemed very taken by this.

OCTOBER 13

Mrs. Stover volunteered that she is not feeling well and has been cranky lately. This she attributes to her current concern about her husband. At times she feels lonely. Most of the time, however, she is contented to stay apart from him. Still she gets restless and starts to move things around in the apartment. I commented that the children are cleaner and better clothed, that I had noticed her giving instructions to the children, and that they seemed to obey her willingly. Mrs. Stover feels (particularly with regard to housework) this is a gain she has made since the change in her marital situation. Her housing is much improved; she has less on her mind, is less confused, and knows what she is after; and she finds more satisfaction in doing housework. There is a certain satisfaction for her in being able to make some decisions without having to turn to her mother.

OCTOBER 20

Discussed with Mrs. Stover that Public Welfare had requested a conference, so that we might work together better. I told her what material I would be sharing with them. I invited her comments but she was upset and angry, as she was sure they wanted to discontinue AFDC.

OCTOBER 26. CONFERENCE WITH PUBLIC WELFARE

Public Welfare is concerned about Mrs. Stover's record of unstable marriages and the fact that they have often been unable to keep in touch with her or to keep up with her changes of address. The agency is prepared to keep AFDC in cash but fears a repetition of her unsatisfactory marital experience: Can she really keep Mr. Stover at arm's length? There is also worry that she might attempt suicide again. However, a review of developments in the case by Family Service indicates that Mrs. Stover is presently trying to free herself of anxiety regarding the situation. Because Mrs. Stover shows good feeling for the children and capacity to meet their needs, a decision was made to continue AFDC in cash while Mrs. Stover works out her problems in relation to men and her marriages. Mrs. Stover's distrust of AFDC was examined in some detail; the AFDC worker will try to create an opportunity to discuss this at some length with Mrs. Stover and thus reassure her of the agency's interest and frankness with her.

NOVEMBER 3. VISIT TO MRS. STOVER BY APPOINTMENT

Eileen and Peter were taking their regular afternoon sleep and the other children were in school. Mrs. Stover now seems to have the household well organized, and the children are regular in sleeping habits. There is a marked improvement in the appearance of the apartment; all floors are swept, the dust is off the furniture, and the kitchen is in good order. Mrs. Stover was dressed in blue denims for housework, but was neat and clean; she is apparently paying more attention to her personal appearance. The interview began with a discussion of the meeting with Public Welfare. Mrs. Stover acknowledged that she had had considerable apprehension about the meeting—in particular, concern that there might be plans to cancel her allowance again. Since the last interview, her AFDC worker had visited and spent an hour with her. Mrs. Stover felt this interview helped a great deal; she is now more satisfied that AFDC is on her side. She was greatly relieved, she indicated, by the assurance that her allowance would not be arbitrarily cut

off unless the AFDC worker was unaware of her whereabouts. Mrs. Stover brought up a further problem in connection with running the household. As she gets more interested in cooking, she is realizing how little she knows. She attempted to cook a goose for the family but spoiled it through lack of proper cleaning. She claims the food that she knows how to prepare is plain and unattractive. The children do some complaining about the food; George recently pointed out that other children he knows get more variety. I arranged to bring Mrs. Stover a recipe file containing a large variety of recipes and some instructions on food preparation and menus. Mrs. Stover is also interested in tackling her budget problems in a more organized fashion; using budget envelopes from the agency, she will be able to keep track of her expenses for two months, so as to gain a more accurate idea of where her money is going.

NOVEMBER 10. VISIT TO MRS. STOVER BY APPOINTMENT

She indicated that, since starting divorce action, she has been feeling edgy; and she had trouble sleeping last night. Mrs. Stover feels she has a need to get married. After divorce, it is open season, and there is some danger that she would make another mistake, although she reiterates that she is through with men. Mrs. Stover feels that the first step is to get used to living without a man in the household. She feels that possibly she picks husbands whom she feels sorry for. Her father was a man who needed reforming. At this point I relayed information from her family's record regarding her father, to the effect that he was a smooth dapper man who was openly unfaithful to his wife and had an alcoholic problem. Mrs. Stover said this described him to a T. She realizes that her mother was trying to reform her father and perhaps she behaves the same way. Mrs. Stover expressed considerable hostility toward her father, pointing out that it was all take on his part and no give. Her mother played right into this attitude, since she did everything for him without much protest and never drew the line. Mrs. Stover has had the attitude, too, that a man is someone who bosses you around. She feels that she expects this from men and obeys them. She catered to her husband, did everything possible to pacify, didn't complain about his drinking, didn't draw the line beyond which he couldn't go. Instead, she let the abuse go on without really facing him, until she finally ran out on the situation. She related this again to her mother, pointing out that her mother was just as much at fault as her father. As an adolescent, she became aware that her mother was encouraging the father in his behavior by being too forgiving. Mrs. Stover is sure that this has also been her pattern with men.

Realizing all these things about herself makes her feel guilty, edgy, and anxious. At least she is now less doubtful about what she wants to do. I pointed out that her anxiety is a natural part of finding out about herself. Mrs. Stover admitted that she still has ambivalent feelings about her husband—a feeling of loneliness and the realization that she could have him back just by asking. At times she is tempted to do this. However, she has held the line firmly and, as she accomplishes more, the temptation diminishes. At the moment, she realizes the need for larger housing, since there is no privacy for George. She handles periods of anxiety by getting busy in the apartment—cleaning, preparing meals, or sewing. Time doesn't hang heavily on her hands, especially with her young children. She feels that she is now giving them more attention than ever, and maybe giving Peter too much attention. During the period at his grandmother's, he got used to having somebody playing with him and frequently interrupts her housework. Mrs. Stover's own tendency with the children, as she admits, has been to do too much for them. Larie hasn't yet fully learned how to dress herself, because Mrs. Stover has taken too much responsibility for this.

I asked Mrs. Stover what she has been looking for in a husband. Mrs. Stover feels she wanted someone to look after her, someone who would in a sense be a good father for her. She laughed at how little her actual choice of husbands reflected that wish.

NOVEMBER 25. HOME VISIT TO MRS. STOVER BY APPOINTMENT

Because Mrs. Stover was in the middle of moving and was up on a ladder installing curtains, I did not prolong the interview. However, Mrs. Stover wanted to tell me about a new angle instead. This is the first time that she has lived alone with her children following disruptions of her marriages. Before that, she always went home to mother and, from her mother's home, she picked up with another man. When Mrs. Stover came to the present building, her mother told her that she would be lonely living by herself, that she would never make a

go of it, that she ought to stay in the mother's home. Mrs. Stover realized that this was typical of her mother's attitude. There is some tendency here for her mother to keep her tied to her, and Mrs. Stover recognized that she was a willing participant in this. She has never felt capable of managing her own life or making decisions on her own and has had to turn to her mother all through her life, for even small decisions. She made moving to her present apartment a sort of test case; she took the decision herself and made a point of not telling anybody about it until she had rented the apartment. After doing this, she felt as if she had really accomplished something. She then described how she was the good little girl at home all her life. Her mother seemed to expect her to take a lot of responsibility for her younger brother and later her sister. She changed, dressed, and bathed them when they were toddlers, though at the time she was only 9 or 10 herself. Part of this was because her mother was frequently sick. When Mrs. Stover was in grade 10, her mother was ill in the hospital for a considerable time, during which she left Mrs. Stover, then 15, with total responsibility for the household. This situation was intolerable for her, and it was at this time that she got involved with her first husband. He was an older man who offered her companionship. He seemed to take it for granted that she would sleep with him, and she did. At the time, she acted largely on impulse, meeting her needs—or the man's needs—without much thought. Her first marriage only lasted a few days. Her husband seemed at first to offer her affection and wouldn't endlessly criticize her, as the father did.

DECEMBER 8. VISIT WITH MRS. STOVER BY APPOINTMENT

I suggested during a telephone conversation that we review where we had gotten to date; Mrs. Stover agreed.

On my arrival, she showed me her new apartment, which has a large living room, kitchen, and two bedrooms; it will permit George to have his own room, where he can be later joined by Peter. Mrs. Stover made the decision without advance consultation with her mother or with myself. She felt this was something of a gain in itself, since she used to have so much trouble making decisions.

Mrs. Stover also mentioned that the children are getting more attention than they used to. In fact, she feels they may be getting too much attention, particularly Peter.

Mrs. Stover said that she feels more secure with herself. This is the first time she has ever had her own place. When her marriages failed in the past, she always went back to mother.

I asked Mrs. Stover how she felt she had been able to change this. Mrs. Stover mentioned first the fact that she has nice neighbors. They are friendly and cooperate with her; she gets a real feeling of support from them. For example, the family across the hall, who have a car, drive her to the supermarket, since there is no supermarket in the immediate area.

Mrs. Stover also mentioned that she had some activity with the school. She laughingly commented, "I'm all tangled up with the school around planning parties." The school had asked some parents to act as party room mothers, to help look after the children. Mrs. Stover and a neighbor, Mrs. Kirby, had done so and have been asked by the school to recruit 11 more mothers. Mrs. Stover has been on the phone a lot about this. While it is a chore and a nuisance, she enjoys it, and she has a lot of respect for the school principal. It makes her feel good to know the school trusts her with such a job.

In response to my further questions as to why she is functioning differently, Mrs. Stover mentioned her increased self-confidence. She related this to her contact with Family Service and AFDC, since the two agencies have demonstrated a lot of confidence with her. She said, "You must have this confidence in me or you wouldn't have spent as much time helping me as you did." She also used to lie awake at night worrying about whether her AFDC check would come. Now, she doesn't. She described also, in relation to Family Service, a feeling of having someone available to her if things go wrong or get difficult.

Mrs. Stover also brought up some negatives. She said that thinking about herself makes her feel like "she is peeking inside other people." At times it makes her edgy and nervous. She sees other people making the same mistakes and having the same problems she did. This sometimes makes her uncomfortable.

Mrs. Stover went on to discuss her concern about Eileen, who will be old enough to start school next fall. Mrs. Stover doubts if this will be possible, however, because Eileen clings to her mother. Mrs. Stover said that Eileen simply can't keep up with the other children, nor can she follow their games.

In response to my question, Mrs. Stover clarified that her concern is not with Eileen's present behavior so much as that it may be difficult to get her started in any kind of educational program next fall. She hopes to use the time between now and next fall to foster a little independence in Eileen. I supported this idea, pointing out several ways in which Mrs. Stover could achieve this: through encouraging Eileen in outdoor play and deliberately conditioning her to stay with the neighbor—for short periods at first and longer periods later. I also suggested giving Eileen encouragement for anything she can accomplish, since she is aware of her inability to keep up with the other children.

I suggested that Eileen could have an aptitude test at the school's Guidance Office and mentioned the possibility of Eileen's enrolling in the nursery school for children with special needs. Mrs. Stover was skeptical about this plan. She wasn't sure she wanted to ask the school about this. I pointed out that this was the way she felt about AFDC too, and that things worked out better when she bared her problems with them.

JANUARY 16

Mrs. Stover called to inquire whether I thought she should move. She has been offered an apartment in the same building a floor above her existing apartment; it is cleaner, has more closet space, and would have more privacy for George and more living space in general. Mrs. Stover wound up by wondering if I ought to look at and approve the new apartment. I indicated willingness to do this but said that I trusted her own decision on the matter.

JANUARY 19

Mrs. Stover announced that she had decided against moving. As soon as she talked it over with the children, they became very anxious and edgy, except for Peter. This made her realize the extent to which the children had been upset by previous moves. She said, "I figured I'd be losing more than I gained by moving now." Mrs. Stover had also been concerned about the fire hazard on the third floor, because she had recently heard that the old building is a big firetrap and would burn rapidly. This is a particular problem for Mrs. Stover since not only Peter but Eileen would need special help in any emergency.

JANUARY 25. HOME VISIT BY APPOINTMENT

Mrs. Stover was washing clothes; she explained that she has been borrowing the neighbor's washing machine whenever she can.

I explained to Mrs. Stover her eligibility for supplementary assistance from AFDC for a washing machine and outlined the procedure. She was initially lukewarm to this idea. When I asked why, she repeated her view that it wasn't smart to ask AFDC worker for too much. I took issue with this, pointing out that AFDC is aimed at enabling her to bring up children, and its purpose can be frustrated unless she takes responsibility for letting the AFDC worker know of her needs. Mrs. Stover accepted this and mentioned that she is expecting a visit from the AFDC worker.

Mrs. Stover said that she enjoys calling the parents for the school party. It makes her feel that she is helping the school out.

I mentioned PTA as an aid to any feelings of isolation that Mrs. Stover might have. Mrs. Stover said she liked the idea of PTA or something that will "broaden my life out a little bit," but at the same time her family keeps her busy; time, if anything, goes too fast.

FEBRUARY 8

According to Mrs. Stover, the AFDC worker didn't like the apartment because of the lack of play space for the children. Mrs. Stover had raised problem of the washing machine and bedding with the AFDC worker, who said to make arrangements to get the bedding on time payments if necessary. Mrs. Stover has gone ahead and done this. She is awaiting a chance to get three estimates on the washing machine.

In a surprise move, Mr. Stover had sent toys for the children; his mother had delivered them. Mrs. Stover had accepted them without question, because she thought the mother-in-law possibly didn't know that she was averse to taking anything from him. Mrs. Stover was very angry that Mr. Stover had used this deception. I wondered if Mrs. Stover could explain her attitude in this matter-of-fact manner as soon as possible to the mother-in-law, to prevent any repetitions of this ploy. Mrs. Stover accepted this idea. She is on good terms with the mother-in-law and feels she could explain the situation to her quite readily.

MARCH 15

Mrs. Stover says that Mr. Stover has again phoned the lady upstairs. I made a suggestion to Mrs. Stover for handling these calls as follows: Ask the person calling to leave his name and number. If he calls again, encourage the neighbor to tell him that she is not taking any more calls for Mrs. Stover. Mrs. Stover seemed pleased at this plan.

MARCH 22

Mrs. Stover said that Eileen is starting to go outside on her own without being urged to do so. Since our recent clarification, Mrs. Stover has felt more relaxed about this and is also letting Eileen go out on the back porch. She formerly had done this, but kept running out every few minutes. I brought out again that I thought there was an intermediate stage between school and home—that is, a stage in which Eileen would have a place to go to develop a range of activity and to play with other children.

Mrs. Stover said that she feels more confident about Eileen now and that much of the problem was probably her own attitude. She brought up the possibility of the East School summer program for prekindergarten children, which she had heard about last year. The idea of this program, as Mrs. Stover understands it, is to give the children some experience of being away from their parents and getting used to the school building. This was discussed at the last PTA meeting that Mrs. Stover had attended.

George is continuing to get good school reports but does not like some aspects of school work. He doesn't like writing stuff down. She handles this by encouraging George to recognize that school can't be all pleasurable activities, nor will he necessarily like all of his teachers. The thing for him to do is to try to put up with these unpleasant aspects, because there are so many things about school he likes. I supported Mrs. Stover in this, pointing out the desirability of consistently encouraging George in responsible attitudes.

APRIL 12

Mrs. Stover discussed the Easter party at school. At the party, the teacher had noticed that Eileen was attached to her mother. Eileen nonetheless went cheerfully to play with the other children and allowed

Mrs. Stover to go in and see the teacher by herself. The teacher had said also that she feels Eileen should be able to start with the others in kindergarten. The teacher had apparently liked Eileen and felt she would be very glad to have her in the class. She had indicated to Mrs. Stover that, at the end of the kindergarten year, a decision could be made regarding a special class for Eileen.

Mrs. Stover also wanted to tell me something her AFDC worker had said: that "the welfare had found Mrs. Stover could be relied on." Mrs. Stover was very pleased about this. The welfare also bought her a washing machine, Mrs. Stover having finally gotten the three estimates.

APRIL 15

Psychological report received regarding Eileen. Eileen scored at the borderline defective intelligence level in this examination, with an IQ of 74.

APRIL 18. VISIT TO MRS. STOVER BY APPOINTMENT

We discussed the report from the psychologist, which I had brought with me. It became evident that Mrs. Stover was having difficulty accepting that Eileen is developmentally disabled.

In relation to planning a school program based on the report, Mrs. Stover felt that she would like to take the teacher up on her statement that Eileen could do well in the kindergarten group the first year, with an evaluation of her progress and the probability of a special class or school after that. Mrs. Stover prefers this to a nursery for children with developmental disabilities.

MAY 3. HOME VISIT BY APPOINTMENT

Mrs. Stover began the interview by some further remarks regarding Eileen. She felt the last two discussions had helped clarify her own thinking. She is more relaxed with Eileen, and Eileen is continuing to play outside a good deal with other children.

I asked Mrs. Stover how she feels about the divorce. She said that she still feels that it may as well sit. She has not had much recent trouble with Mr. Stover and is hoping that he had decided not to bother her. She will take divorce action only if Mr. Stover becomes a problem. In the meantime, she is keeping her mind open on the whole subject.

Mrs. Stover went on to say that she would like some further help with the problem of raising her kids. At the moment, she is concerned about George, who is having problems in school. He comes home at noon crying. She and one of George's teachers don't get along, either. Mrs. Stover feels that this teacher is extremely punitive toward George; she is rapping George over the knuckles with a ruler. On Monday, George had been ill, and Mrs. Stover phoned the school explaining this. It had been arranged that Mrs. Stover would phone back when George was ready to return. She did this Tuesday morning as George returned to school. Later in the morning, Mrs. Stover received a call from the teacher claiming that George was playing hooky, though it was subsequently verified that George was in school. George didn't even have a class with the teacher that morning. George had recently made a mistake on his arithmetic calculations, and the teacher made him stay after school and do them over 200 times each. Shortly after this, she had sent home a paper that she had refused to mark because the writing was too faint. Mrs. Stover showed the paper to me, and the writing was quite legible and clear. As a result of this, George had had to do these calculations a total of 600 times. George says that when he gets out of school he feels like killing somebody. As a result of the punitive treatment by the teacher, George is now taking the attitude "to heck with school." Mrs. Stover says that George really knows he has no choice in the matter of attending school, nor is he at all likely to truant.

I offered to visit the school and to review the problem with the principal and the school social worker, with Mrs. Stover present or not as she desired. In advance of this, we could discuss how to present the problem to the school—not strictly as a complaint against the teacher, but on the basis of concern about George and his discouragement about the school situation. Mrs. Stover said she liked this approach, but she wanted to try it out on her own.

This led to a discussion of how she should handle this with George. Mrs. Stover has been very careful not to side completely with George and paint the teacher as the villain. When he comes home crying, she puts her arm around him and comforts him. On the other hand, she has tried to help him see that he is likely to meet other teachers like this one, that this is part of going to school. George has wanted a transfer to another school but she thinks it is too late in the year. I supported Mrs. Stover in her stand with George and her plan to go to the school to discuss it.

MAY 10

Mrs. Stover was quite angry at Public Welfare, because her budget has been reduced by $15 a month. She talked in terms of going off AFDC and going to work. I asked her to examine this carefully in terms of what it would mean to try to manage the children and work at the same time. I concurred in the idea of her working as a long-term goal but suggested very careful consideration of this as something she could do soon. After this, Mrs. Stover calmed down and said she realized this was not a constructive thing to do. I brought up the possibility of using a home economist as a consultant to help Mrs. Stover get the most out of her present budget. Mrs. Stover said, "I'm all for that," but added that she felt she is managing pretty economically at present. She doesn't see where she is going to manage with a $15 decrease.

I later saw the home economist briefly and a joint visit with home economist was planned for May 24.

MAY 25

On a brief home visit, I took clothing supplied by the home economist, including a dress for Mrs. Stover, three small comforters for the younger children, and a jacket for Eileen.

JUNE 6. VISIT TO MRS. STOVER BY APPOINTMENT

We initially discussed Mrs. Stover's arrangements with the home economist regarding the budget. Mrs. Stover said, "She showed me how I could cover all my expenses and a little extra." She remained somewhat skeptical, but she planned to give it a try and to confer further with the home economist on any difficulties that come up.

She has recently heard indirectly that Mr. Stover is planning to get married. I inquired what Mrs. Stover's reaction was, and she said she feels greatly relieved. It had made her feel free of him and had also made her realize how protective toward him she still feels; this, more than anything else, had been a barrier to her taking divorce action. The latest news takes the decision out of her hands; it gets her off the hook. She had always felt that it was her duty to stay with Mr. Stover no matter what he did, since he needed to be looked after.

I asked where Mrs. Stover feels she is at with this problem. She described her former pattern of running from one situation into a worse one; she wouldn't allow anybody to help her or to get close enough to help her. She feels now she understands more why she got into this series of messes and is less apt to jump before she looks. She cites her impulse to throw over AFDC as an example of how she used to operate, but now she stops and thinks before she makes a decision of this kind.

Mrs. Stover said that she now feels she has something of her own and she is not afraid any more of losing it. She feels comfortable also in her attitude of not having anything to do with men. She said, "My way of looking at a man now is in terms of what can he give me as a husband that is better than what I've got now. So far I haven't met anybody who I thought could measure up to this." She is not going to feel any responsibility to save a man.

She added that she and men just don't mix. Basically she has no use for men, and this would prevent her ever having a productive relationship with a man. On the other hand, she does worry about the effects of her extreme dislike of men on the children; she doesn't want the girls to be prejudiced against men, and she has an adolescent boy.

I suggested that, in future interviews, we could discuss the specific methods she may use in teaching the children about such matters and in cultivating attitudes toward men.

JUNE 14

Returning to the question of Mrs. Stover's instruction of the children, I went over some material abstracted from a recent book dealing with adolescents' attitudes toward the opposite sex. Mrs. Stover said that she felt the book would be useful to her. The children do not volunteer much in this area, nor do they ask many questions. She tries to deal with these on a factual basis as they come up.

Mrs. Stover indicated that she feels it is her own attitudes that are important. Nonetheless, she can perhaps avoid giving the children a biased attitude toward men. I suggested presenting Mr. Stover and his problems in as favorable a light as possible to the children and attempting to avoid running him down. Mrs. Stover thought this would be possible. The children speak little of Mr. Stover but seem settled in the attitude that he doesn't want to be with the family. George shows some resentment, occasionally commenting that they are better off now that Mr. Stover is not around. Mrs. Stover accepted my suggestion that, when George makes such remarks, she could point out that Mr. Stover has his problems but also has his good points, and had wanted to be a father to the family but hadn't been equal to the task.

JUNE 28. VISIT TO MRS. STOVER BY APPOINTMENT

Mrs. Stover was flying around in a complete dither and made the remark, "I ain't going to talk to you long." Her AFDC worker had informed her that the apartment is not a fit place for the children to live. The worker had told Mrs. Stover to go to the housing project and apply for an apartment. Mrs. Stover had done this and had been told that she should be prepared to move in three days. Mrs. Stover talked at first as though she hadn't been given any choice in the matter. When I inquired about this, however, she agreed that it is her decision as to whether she goes to the housing project. She feels that circumstances are forcing her to move so quickly. By this, she means that she has to take an apartment while it can be got.

Later Mrs. Stover phoned again, wanting to know if I had any information as to why the county might have held up her check, since she did not receive it. Later, Mrs. Stover found out that the check had been sent to her new address by the county but, since Mrs. Stover's name was not on the mailbox, the check had been returned. It will now be sent back to her again and it will likely be two or three days before she receives it. Mrs. Stover is angry at AFDC again, as she says the worker had advised her not to get too excited, that to make such a big fuss over a check being late was neurotic.

JULY 6. HOME VISIT TO MRS. STOVER'S NEW APARTMENT IN THE HOUSING PROJECT

The family has a two-bedroom unit, Mrs. Stover and the girls have one room and the boys have the other.

The most recent incident has aroused considerable fresh hostility in Mrs. Stover toward the AFDC. Mrs. Stover said, "I can't do anything with the Welfare." A further difficulty was that, when the family got to the apartment, the electricity was not connected. Two days later, the company had come out and connected it.

We tried to analyze Mrs. Stover's part in the difficulties with AFDC. I pointed out that she showed good capacity to plan in her dealings with our agency. Why

was there this difference? Mrs. Stover felt that it might be because she has greater feeling about the AFDC and, in her doings with AFDC, she is tense and more apt to fly off the handle, partly from past conflict and partly from the fact that the AFDC in a more authoritative position with her than is Family Service, since they have control over the purse strings. Mrs. Stover agrees that, being in this frame of mind, she is especially likely to have misunderstandings or antagonism with the AFDC. On the other hand, she feels that the agency contributes to this by the hurried manner in which everything is handled, and the fact that AFDC workers visit her place unexpectedly and surprise her with things such as the order to move to the new apartment, which seemed to come out of the blue. On top of this, Mrs. Stover feels pushed around by AFDC. She sees no solution at present; she never hit it off with welfare and finds it difficult to imagine she ever will. Her current attitude is to do what they tell her, try to avoid breaking any regulations, and keep out of trouble. Mrs. Stover said she guessed the main thing in her dealings with AFDC would be to try to keep from getting excited and losing her head.

In the remainder of the interview, we discussed future plans and goals. Mrs. Stover was aware of my coming vacation and the possibility of termination. Mrs. Stover gave some evaluation at this point of what she thought the relationship with Family Service means to her. She sees it largely as a control on her impulsive behavior. Before acting, she phones me and I help her think things through, so that she doesn't act on the spur of the moment. Despite her recent difficulties with AFDC, she feels there has been real improvement; they at least have greater trust in her, and she some greater trust in them. Then, too, she has had less difficulty with her husband for a long time and has made some progress in getting Eileen ready for school. In the light of all this, she feels that, objectively considered, her situation is better and she can probably handle it more easily than in the past. The vacation could be a kind of planned period to see how she manages. A tentative appointment was set for a follow-up visit in August.

AUGUST 30

Mrs. Stover obviously has mixed feelings about the termination plan. On the one hand, she reiterates that she has fewer problems and is better able to manage them. On the other, her tie to the agency implies some security for her, inasmuch as she knows that, if things do take a downturn, she can always turn to the agency. I explained that she could do this in any case, but she wants to defer termination. I agreed, at least for the present.

SEPTEMBER 18

The school social worker telephone regarding Eileen. Mrs. Stover started Eileen in kindergarten at the beginning of this month. The school's health record shows that Eileen has muscular dystrophy, and the teacher had spoken to the social worker about this, wanting further clarification. The teacher had also observed that Eileen showed no ability to relate to other children in her group. Eileen is, after all, only 4 and won't be 5 until October, but Mrs. Stover had, during visits to the school last May and June, talked the problem over with the school staff, and they had agreed to start Eileen.

The school social worker felt that continuing Eileen in kindergarten might be good in view of the mother's overprotection of Eileen and the mother's continuing work on her own behavior. If Eileen's limitations are accepted in the group and not much is expected of her in the way of either skills or sociability, it is quite likely that she will be able to make an adjustment to the kindergarten situation. Failing this, Eileen's admission to a school for children with developmental difficulties should be considered. Matters were left that the school social worker will call us in about six weeks, and that period will be used to see how Eileen gets along.

Later in the day, I dropped in on Mrs. Stover to discuss the school's report. Mrs. Stover said that she recognized Eileen is behind the group in sociability, and we briefly reviewed the report obtained in April regarding her intellectual state.

At the same time, Mrs. Stover was pleased Eileen had been able to separate herself from her mother and sister without apparent difficulty. Mrs. Stover wants to visit the school soon, to see the teacher and get more information for herself.

A further appointment will be scheduled in a month, after Mrs. Stover visits the school. Despite the previous plan to terminate, both Mrs. Stover and the school want the agency to stay, at least until Eileen's problem has been worked out.

SUMMARY. OCTOBER 18 THROUGH DECEMBER 1

Mrs. Stover had visited the school in October and got a very favorable report on Eileen. The teacher told Mrs. Stover that Eileen cannot comprehend things with the rest of the children, but her behavior is not abnormal, nor does it in any way hamper the class or harm the other children. Eileen plays very little with the other children, but the teacher pointed out that lots of children play by themselves in the classroom. On November 16, a further brief report from the school social worker confirmed the information from Mrs. Stover.

SUMMARY. DECEMBER 1 THROUGH JANUARY 8

The two interviews with Mrs. Stover during this period were concerned largely with working through her feelings about the agency closing its case.

However, another incident reactivated Mrs. Stover's hostilities toward AFDC. This led to a lengthy discussion about Mrs. Stover's family, which has been on welfare as far back as she can remember and has built up certain more or less fixed attitudes toward the welfare agency. These include a feeling of being pushed around, worthlessness, and not being treated as an individual. She heartily agreed with my point that partly this stemmed from being chronically on the receiving end and never having a feeling of being able to give to others. In addition, Mrs. Stover's belief that the welfare agency is an almost all-powerful agency, which is apt to do anything without any explanation, seems unshakable at this point.

FEBRUARY 15. LAST VISIT

In this termination interview, Mrs. Stover summed up her feelings as follows: "We've changed in the fact that we are more settled, more of a family instead of five people. Each is different, that is to be expected, but we are more united, kind of. That's the biggest change, more secure in ourselves as a family. Larie and George and I each worried about ourselves instead of all of us. Now it isn't so much a personal worry as how is this family going to get along. We think of the good of the family rather than for each one. It's not so much what you've said and done as what you've listened to. I could talk things over and sort them out, kind of. I could bring up things that I wouldn't ordinarily be able to tell people. If I told these things to others, they would get all mixed up in my problem, but you don't."

"I think too, I've found out there is always a reason for the way welfare acts. And, if I try, I can usually find out what it is. And the school is so much help to me with Eileen. They trust me."

ENTRY FOR RECORD: APRIL 23

I received a call from Mrs. Stover, whom I referred to Miss Bithy, the social worker at the school for children with developmental disabilities, regarding Eileen.

ENTRY FOR RECORD: JUNE 17

The school social worker called to report on the family. The school has been asking, "What kind of casework did Mrs. Stover receive?" There has been remarkable change in the children. Physical care has greatly improved. Larie is described as "top girl in her class." Eileen has made a great deal of progress in relating to other children. The school is wondering what has happened to account for the change. The social worker and I agreed that it is a cumulation of things over two years rather than anything recent and dramatic. She will talk further to the teachers. I later telephoned Mrs. Stover and relayed the school's message. She was very pleased and said that she herself notices a big change in Eileen. Application is pending for Eileen's admission to the school for children with developmental disabilities.

ENTRY FOR RECORD: SEPTEMBER 11

Mrs. Stover called to say Eileen is enrolled at the special school and is enjoying the experience. Eileen is very tired when she gets home. However, she leaves the home readily in the morning, much to Mrs. Stover's surprise.

READING A-3 *The House on Sixth Street**

Francis P. Purcell and Harry Specht

The extent to which social work can affect the course of social problems has not received the full consideration it deserves.[1] For some time the social work profession has taken account of social problems only as they have become manifest in behavioral pathology. Yet it is becoming increasingly apparent that, even allowing for this limitation, it is often necessary for the same agency or worker to intervene by various methods at various points.

In this paper, the case history of a tenement house in New York City is used to illustrate some of the factors that should be considered in selecting intervention methods. Like all first attempts, the approach described can be found wanting in conceptual clarity and systematization. Yet the vital quality of the effort and its implications for social work practice seem clear.

THE PROBLEM

"The House on Sixth Street" became a case when Mrs. Smith came to an MFY [Mobilization for Youth] Neighborhood Service Center to complain that there had been no gas, electricity, heat, or hot water in her apartment house for more than four weeks. She asked the agency for help. Mrs. Smith was 23 years old, black, and the mother of four children, three of whom had been born out of wedlock. At the time she was unmarried and receiving Aid to Families with Dependent Children. She came to the center in desperation because she was unable to run her household without utilities. Her financial resources were exhausted—but not her courage. The Neighborhood Service Center worker decided that, in this case the building—the tenants, the landlord, and circumstances affecting their relationships—was of central concern.

*Copyright 1965, National Association of Social Workers, Inc. from *Social Work*, 10(4), October 1965, pp. 66–76. Reprinted with permission.
[1] Social work practitioners sometimes use the term *social problem* to mean "environmental problem." The sense in which it is used here corresponds to the definition developed by the social sciences: That is, a social problem is a disturbance, deviation, or breakdown in social behavior that (1) involves a considerable number of people and (2) is of serious concern to many in the society. It is social in origin and effect, and is a social responsibility. It represents a discrepancy between social standards and social reality. Also, such socially perceived variations must be viewed as corrigible (see Merton & Nisbet, 1961, pp. 6, 701).

A social worker then visited the Sixth Street building with Mrs. Smith and a community worker. Community workers are members of the community organization staff in a program that attempts to encourage residents to take independent social action. Like many members in other MFY programs, community workers are residents of the particular neighborhood. Most of them have little formal education; their special contribution being their ability to relate to and communicate with other residents. Because some of the tenants were Puerto Rican, a Spanish-speaking community worker was chosen to accompany the social worker. His easy manner and knowledge of the neighborhood enabled him and the worker to become involved quickly with the tenants.

Their first visits confirmed Mrs. Smith's charge that the house had been without utilities for more than four weeks. Several months before, the city Rent and Rehabilitation Administration had reduced the rent for each apartment to one dollar a month because the landlord was not providing services. However, this agency was slow to take further action. Eleven families were still living in the building, which had 28 apartments. The landlord owed the electric company several thousand dollars. Therefore, the meters had been removed from the house. Because most of the tenants were welfare clients, the Department of Welfare had "reimbursed" the landlord directly for much of the unpaid electric bill and refused to pay any more money to the electric company. The Department of Welfare was slow in meeting the emergency needs of the tenants. Most of the children (48 from the 11 families in the building) had not been to school for a month because they were ill or lacked proper clothing.

The mothers were tired and demoralized. Dirt and disorganization were increasing daily. The tenants were afraid to sleep at night because the building was infested with rats. There was danger of fire because the tenants had to use candles for light. The 17 abandoned apartments had been invaded by homeless men and drug addicts. Petty thievery is common in such situations. However, the mothers did not want to seek protection from the police for fear that they would chase away all men who were not part of the families in the building (some of the unmarried mothers had men living with them—one of the few means of protection from physical danger available to these women—even though mothers

on public assistance are threatened with loss of income if they are not legally married). The anxiety created by these conditions was intense and disabling.

The workers noted that the mothers were not only anxious but "fighting mad"; not only did they seek immediate relief from their physical dangers and discomforts but they were eager to express their fury at the landlord and the public agencies, which they felt had let them down.

The effect of such hardships on children is obvious. Of even greater significance is the sense of powerlessness generated when families go into these struggles barehanded. It is this sense of helplessness in the face of adversity that induces pathological anxiety, intergenerational alienation and social retreatism. Actual physical impoverishment alone is not nearly so debilitating as poverty attended by a sense of unrelieved impotence that becomes generalized and internalized. The poor then regard much social learning as irrelevant, since they do not believe it can effect any environmental change (Purcell, 1964).

INTERVENTION AND THE SOCIAL SYSTEMS

Selecting a point of intervention in dealing with this problem would have been simpler if the target of change were Mrs. Smith alone, or Mrs. Smith and her co-tenants, the clients in whose behalf intervention was planned. Too often, the client system presenting the problem becomes the major target for intervention, and the intervention method is limited to the one most suitable for that client system. However, Mrs. Smith and the other tenants had a multitude of problems emanating from many sources, any one of which would have warranted the attention of a social agency. The circumstantial fact that an individual contacts an agency that offers services to individuals and families should not be a major factor in determining the method of intervention. Identification of the client merely helps the agency to define goals; other variables are involved in the selection of method. As Burns and Glasser (1963) have suggested:

> It may be helpful to consider the primary target of change as distinct from the persons who may be the primary clients. . . . The primary target of change then becomes the human or physical environment toward which professional efforts via direct intervention are aimed in order to facilitate change. (p. 423)

The three major factors that determined MFY's approach to the problem were (1) knowledge of the various social systems within which the social problem was located (i.e., social systems assessment), (2) knowledge of the various methods (including non–social work methods) appropriate for intervention in these different social systems, and (3) the resources available to the agency.

The difficulties of the families in the building were intricately connected with other elements of the social system related to the housing problem. For example, seven different public agencies were involved in maintenance of building services. Later, other agencies were involved in relocating the tenants. There is no one agency in New York City that handles all housing problems. Therefore, tenants have little hope of getting help on their own. In order to redress a grievance relating to water supply (which was only one of the building's many problems) it is necessary to know precisely which city department to contact. The following is only a partial listing:

1. No water—Health Department
2. Not enough water—Department of Water Supply
3. No hot water—Buildings Department
4. Water leaks—Buildings Department
5. Large water leaks—Department of Water Supply
6. Water overflowing from apartment above—Police Department
7. Water sewage in the cellar—Sanitation Department

The task of determining which agencies are responsible for code enforcement in various areas is not simple, and in addition one must know that the benefits and services available for tenants and for the community vary with the course of action chosen. For example, if the building were taken over by the Rent and Rehabilitation Administration under the receivership law, it would be several weeks before services would be re-established, and the tenants would have to remain in the building during its rehabilitation. There would be, however, some compensations: tenants could remain in the neighborhood—indeed, in the same building—and their children would not have to change schools. If, on the other hand, the house were condemned by the Buildings Department, the tenants would have to move, but they would be moved quickly and would receive top relocation priorities and maximum relocation benefits.

But once the tenants had been relocated—at city expense—the building could be renovated by the landlord as middle-income housing. In the Sixth Street house, it was suspected that this was the motivation behind the landlord's actions. If the building were condemned and renovated, there would be 28 fewer low-income housing units in the neighborhood.

It is obvious, even limiting analysis to the social systems of one tenement, that the problem is enormous. Although the tenants were the clients in this case, Mrs. Smith, the tenant group, and other community groups were all served at one point or another. It is even conceivable that the landlord might have been selected as the most appropriate recipient of service. Rehabilitation of many slum tenements is at present nearly impossible. Many landlords regard such property purely as an investment. With profit the prime motive, needs of low-income tenants are often overlooked. Under present conditions it is financially impossible for many landlords to correct all the violations in their buildings even if they wanted to. If the social worker chose to intervene at this level of the problem, he might apply to the Municipal Loan Fund, make arrangements with unions for the use of non-union labor in limited rehabilitation projects, or provide expert consultants on reconstruction. These tasks would require social workers to have knowledge similar to that of city planners. If the problems of landlords were not selected as a major point of intervention, they would still have to be considered at some time since they are an integral part of the social context within which this problem exists.

A correct definition of interacting social systems or of the social worker's choice of methods and points of intervention is not the prime concern here. What is to be emphasized is what this case so clearly demonstrates: that, although the needs of the client system enable the agency to define its goals, the points and methods of intervention cannot be selected properly without an awareness and substantial knowledge of the social systems within which the problem is rooted.

DEALING WITH THE PROBLEM

The social worker remained with the building throughout a four-month period. In order to deal effectively with the problem, he had to make use of all the social work methods as well as the special talents of a community worker, lawyer, city planner, and various civil rights organizations. The social worker and the community worker functioned as generalists; with both individuals and families calling on caseworkers as needed for specialized services or at especially trying times, such as during the first week and when the families were relocated. Because of the division of labor in the agency, much of the social work with individuals was done with the help of a caseworker. Group work, administration, and community organization were handled by the social worker, who had been trained in community organization. In many instances he also dealt with the mothers as individuals, as they encountered one stressful situation after another. Agency caseworkers also provided immediate and concrete assistance to individual families, such as small financial grants, medical care, homemaking services, baby-sitting services, and transportation. This reduced the intensity of pressures on these families. Caseworkers were especially helpful in dealing with some of the knotty and highly technical problems connected with public agencies.

With a caseworker and a lawyer experienced in handling tenement cases, the social worker began to help the families organize their demands for the services and utilities to which they were legally entitled but which the public agencies had consistently failed to provide for them.

The ability of the mothers to take concerted group action was evident from the beginning, and Mrs. Smith proved to be a natural and competent leader. With support, encouragement, and assistance from the staff, the mothers became articulate and effective in negotiating with the various agencies involved. In turn, the interest and concern of the agencies increased markedly when the mothers began to visit them, make frequent telephone calls, and send letters and telegrams to them and to politicians demanding action.

With the lawyer and a city planner (an agency consultant), the mothers and staff members explored various possible solutions to the housing problem. For example, the Department of Welfare had offered to move the families to shelters or hotels. Neither alternative was acceptable to the mothers. Shelters were ruled out because they would not consider splitting up their families, and they rejected hotels because they had discovered from previous experience that many of the "hotels" selected were flop-houses or were inhabited by prostitutes.

The following is taken from the social worker's record during the first week:

> Met with the remaining tenants, several black men from the block, and [the city planner]. . . . Three of the mothers said that they would sooner sleep out on the street than go the Welfare shelter. If nothing else, they felt that this would be a way of protesting their plight . . . One of the mothers said that they couldn't very well do this with most of the children having colds. Mrs. Brown thought that they might do better to ask Reverend Jones if they could move into the cellar of his church temporarily. . . . The other mothers got quite excited about this idea because they thought that the church basement would make excellent living quarters.

After a discussion as to whether the mothers would benefit from embarrassing the public agencies by dramatically exposing their inadequacies, the mothers decided to move into the nearby church. They asked the worker to attempt to have their building condemned. At another meeting, attended by tenants from neighboring buildings and representatives of other local groups, it was concluded that what had happened to the Sixth Street building was a result of discrimination against the tenants as Puerto Ricans and blacks. The group—which had now become an organization—sent the following telegram to city, state, and federal officials:

> We are voters and Puerto Rican and black mothers asking for equal rights, for decent housing and enough room. Building has broken windows, no gas or electricity for four weeks, no heat or hot water, holes in floors, loose wiring. Twelve of 48 children in building sick. Welfare doctors refuse to walk up dark stairs. Are we human or what? Should innocent children suffer for landlords' brutality and city and state neglect? We are tired of being told to wait with children ill and unable to attend school. Black and Puerto Rican tenants are forced out while buildings next door are renovated at high rents. We are not being treated as human beings.

For the most part, the lawyer and city planner stayed in the background, acting only as consultants. But as the tenants and worker became more involved with the courts, and as other organizations entered the fight, the lawyer and city planner played a more active and direct role.

RESULTANT SIDE-EFFECTS

During this process, tenants in other buildings on the block became more alert to similar problems in their buildings. With the help of the community development staff and the housing consultant, local groups and organizations such as tenants' councils and the local chapter of the Congress of Racial Equality were enlisted to support and work with the mothers.

Some of the city agencies behaved as though MFY had engineered the entire scheme to embarrass them—steadfastly disregarding the fact that the building had been unlivable for many months. Needless to say, the public agencies are overloaded and have inadequate resources. As has been documented, many such bureaucracies develop an amazing insensitivity to the needs of their clients (Bendix, 1952). In this case, the MFY social worker believed that the tenants—and other people in their plight—should make their needs known to the agencies and to the public at large. He knew that when these expressions of need are backed by power—either in numbers or in political knowledge—they are far more likely to have some effect.

By the time the families had been relocated, several things had been accomplished. Some of the public agencies had been sufficiently moved by the actions of the families and the local organizations to provide better services for them. When the families refused to relocate in a shelter and moved into a neighborhood church instead, one of the television networks picked up their story. Officials in the housing agencies came to investigate and several local politicians lent the tenants their support. Most important, several weeks after the tenants moved into the church, a bill was passed by the city council designed to prevent some of the abuses that the landlord had practiced with impunity. The councilman who sponsored the new law referred to the house on Sixth Street to support his argument.

Nevertheless, the problems that remain far outweigh the accomplishments. A disappointing epilogue to the story is that in court, two months later, the tenants' case against the landlord was dismissed by the judge on a legal technicality. The judged ruled that because the electric company had removed the meters from the building it was impossible for the landlord to provide services.

Some of the tenants were relocated out of the neighborhood and some in housing almost as poor as that they had left. The organization that began to develop in the neighborhood has continued to grow, but it is a painstaking job. The fact that the poor have the strength to continue to struggle for better living conditions is something to wonder at and admire.

IMPLICATIONS FOR PRACTICE

Social work helping methods as currently classified are so inextricably interwoven in practice that it no longer seems valid to think of a generic practice as consisting of the application of casework, group work, or community organization skills as the nature of the problem demands. Nor does it seem feasible to adapt group methods for traditional casework problems or to use group work skills in community organization or community organization method in casework. Such suggestions—when they appear in the literature—either reflect confusion or, what is worse, suggest that no clear-cut method exists apart from the auspices that support it.

In this case it is a manifestation of a social problem—housing—that was the major point around which social services were organized. The social worker's major intellectual task was to select the points at which the agency could intervene in the problem and the appropriate methods to use. It seems abundantly clear that in order to select appropriate points of intervention the social worker needs not only to understand individual patterns of response, but the nature of the social conditions that are the context in which behavior occurs. As this case makes evident, the social system that might be called the "poverty system" is enduring and persistent. Its parts intermesh with precision and disturbing complementarity. Intentionally or not, a function is thereby maintained that produces severe social and economic deprivation. Certain groups profit enormously from the maintenance of this system, but larger groups suffer. Social welfare—and, in particular, its central profession, social work—must examine the part it plays in either maintaining or undermining this socially pernicious poverty system. It is important that the social work profession no longer regard social conditions as immutable and a social reality to be accommodated as service is provided to deprived persons with an ever increasing refinement of technique. Means should be developed whereby agencies can affect social problems more directly, especially through institutional (organizational) change.

The idea advanced by MFY is that the social worker should fulfill his professional function and agency responsibility by seeking a solution to social problems through institutional change rather than by focusing on individual problems in social functioning. This is not to say that individual expressions of a given social problem should be left unattended. On the contrary, this approach is predicated on the belief that individual problems in social functioning are to varying degrees both cause and effect. It rejects the notion that individuals are afflicted with social pathologies, holding, rather, that the same social environment that generates conformity makes payment by the deviance that emerges. As Nisbet points out ". . . socially prized arrangements and

values in society can produce socially condemned results" (Merton & Nisbet, 1961, p. 7). This should direct social work's attention to institutional arrangements and their consequences. This approach does not lose sight of the individual or group, since the social system is composed of various statuses, roles, and classes. It takes cognizance of the systemic relationship of the various parts of the social system, including the client. It recognizes that efforts to deal with one social problem frequently generate others with debilitating results.

REFERENCES

Bendix, R. (1952). Bureaucracy and the problem of power. In R. K. Merton, A. Gray, B. Hockey, & H. C. Sebrin (Eds.), *Reader in bureaucracy* (pp. 114–134). New York: Free Press.

Burns, M. E., & Glasser, P. H. (1963). Similarities and differences in casework and groupwork practice. *Social Service Review,* 37(4), 416–428.

Merton, R. K., & Nisbet, R. A. (Eds.) (1961). *Contemporary social problems.* New York: Harcourt Brace Jovanovich.

Purcell, F. P. (1964). The helping professions and problems of the brief contact. In F. Reissman, J. Cohen, & A. Pearl (Eds.), *Mental health of the poor* (pp. 431–434). New York: Free Press.

Appendix B:
Professional Associations

READING B-1 *Chapters of the National Association of Social Workers (U.S.)*

The names of chapter executive directors and current addresses are available on the NASW world wide website: http://www.naswdc.org.

ALABAMA CHAPTER
Governors Park II
2921 Marti Lane, #G
Montgomery, AL 36116
334-288-2633
334-288-1398 (fax)

ALASKA CHAPTER
1727 Wickersham Drive
Anchorage, AK 99507
907-563-4502
907-563-4504 (fax)
e-mail:
NASWAK@ALASKA.NET

ARIZONA CHAPTER
610 W. Broadway, #116
Tempe, AZ 85282
602-968-4595
602-894-9726 (fax)
e-mail: NASW
AZ@PRIMENET.COM

ARKANSAS CHAPTER
1123 S. University #101
Little Rock, AR 72204
501-663-0658
800-797-6279
501-663-6406 (fax)
e-mail:
NASWAR@CEI.NET

CALIFORNIA CHAPTER
1016 23rd Street
Sacramento, CA 95816
916-442-4565
800-538-2565
916-442-2075 (fax)
e-mail:
NASWCA@AOL.COM

COLORADO CHAPTER
6000 E. Evans
Bldg. #1, Suite #121
Denver, CO 80222
303-753-8890/91
e-mail:
CNASW@AOL.COM

CONNECTICUT CHAPTER
2139 Silas Deane Hwy.
Suite 205
Rocky Hill, CT 06067
860-257-8066
860-257-8074 (fax)

DELAWARE CHAPTER
3301 Green Street
Claymont, DE 19703
302-792-0646
302-792-0678 (fax)
e-mail: NASWDE@
DIAMOND.NET.UDEL.EDU

FLORIDA CHAPTER
345 South Magnolia Dr.
Suite #14-B
Tallahassee, FL 32301
904-224-2400
800-352-6279
904-561-6279 (fax)

GEORGIA CHAPTER
3070 Presidential Drive
Atlanta, GA 30340
404-234-0567
404-234-0565 (fax)

HAWAII CHAPTER
200 N. Vineyard Blvd
Honolulu, HI 96817
808-521-1787
808-521-3299 (fax)
e-mail:
NASWHI@ALOHA.NET

IDAHO CHAPTER
200 North 4th Street
Boise, ID 83702
208-343-2752
208-385-0166 (fax)
e-mail:
NASWID@RMCI.NET

ILLINOIS CHAPTER
180 N. Michigan Avenue
Suite #400
Chicago, IL 60601
312-236-8308
312-236-6627 (fax)
e-mail:
OFFICE@2.NASWIL.ORG

INDIANA CHAPTER
1100 West 42nd St.
Suite #316
Indianapolis, IN 46208
317-923-9878
317-925-9364 (fax)

INTERNATIONAL CHAPTER
CMR 419 Box 1913
APO, AE 09102
011-49-622-131-5915
e-mail:
ANNESIEGEL@AOL.COM

IOWA CHAPTER
4211 Grand Avenue
Level 3
Des Moines, IA 50312
515-277-1117
515-277-2277 (fax)
e-mail:
NASWIOWA@AOL.COM

KANSAS CHAPTER
Jayhawk Towers
700 SW Jackson St.
Suite 901
Topeka, KS 66603-3740
913-354-4804
800-776-4806
913-354-1456 (fax)
e-mail: NASWKS@MAIL.
CJNETWORKS.COM

KENTUCKY CHAPTER
310 St. Clair
Frankfort, KY 40601
502-223-0245
502-223-0525 (fax)

LOUISIANA CHAPTER
700 N. 10th St. #200
Baton Rouge, LA 70802
504-346-1234
504-346-5035 (fax)
e-mail:
NASWLA@AOL.COM

MAINE CHAPTER
99 Western Ave. #2
10 Lobbe Office Park
P.O. Box 5065
Augusta, ME 04332
207-622-7592
207-623-4860 (fax)
e-mail:
NASW99ME@AOL.COM

MARYLAND CHAPTER
5710 Executive Drive, #105
Baltimore, MD 21228
410-788-1066
410-747-0635 (fax)
e-mail:
MOYAA@JUNO.COM

MASSACHUSETTS CHAPTER
14 Beacon St. #409
Boston, MA 02108
617-227-9635
617-227-9877 (fax)
e-mail: CHAPTER@
NASWMA.ORG

METRO DC CHAPTER
2025 Eye St. NW, #106
Washington, DC 20006
202-457-0492
202-296-5106 (fax)

MICHIGAN CHAPTER
230 N. Washington Sq.
Suite #212
Lansing, MI 48933
517-487-1548
517-487-0675 (fax)

MINNESOTA CHAPTER
480 Concordia Avenue
St. Paul, MN 55103
612-293-1935
612-293-0952 (fax)

MISSISSIPPI CHAPTER
P.O. Box 4228
Jackson, MS 39216
601-981-8359
800-543-7098
601-981-6922 (fax)

MISSOURI CHAPTER
Parkade Ctr/Suite 138
601 Business Loop
70 West
Columbia, MO 65203
573-874-6140
800-333-6279
573-874-8738 (fax)
e-mail: NASWMO@
SOCKETIS.NET

MONTANA CHAPTER
900 N. Montana Ave #5-B
Helena, MT 59601
406-449-6208
406-449-2533 (fax)
e-mail:
CH1717@AOL.COM

NEBRASKA CHAPTER
P.O. Box 83732
Lincoln, NE 68501
402-477-7344
800-737-6279
402-476-6547 (fax)
e-mail:
ASSOC@NAVIX.NET

NEVADA CHAPTER
1651 E. Flamingo Road
Las Vegas, NV 89119
702-791-5872
702-791-5873 (fax)
e-mail:
NASWNV@AOL.COM

NEW HAMPSHIRE CHAPTER
c/o NH Assoc. for the Blind
25 Walker Street
Concord, NH 03301
603-226-7135
603-226-7135 (fax)
e-mail: MAILERV@
PSC.PLYMOUTH.EDU

NEW JERSEY CHAPTER
110 West State Street
Trenton, NJ 08608
609-394-1666
609-394-0200 (fax)
e-mail:
NASWNJ@AOL.COM

NEW MEXICO CHAPTER
1503 University Blvd, NE
Albuquerque, NM 87102
505-247-2336
505-246-8761 (fax)

NEW YORK CITY CHAPTER
15 Park Row
20th Floor
New York, NY 10038
212-577-5000
212-577-6279 (fax)

NEW YORK STATE CHAPTER
225 Lark Street
Albany, NY 12210
518-463-4741
800-724-6279 (in state)
518-463-6446 (fax)
e-mail:
NASWNYS@AOL.COM

N. CAROLINA CHAPTER
P.O. Box 27582
Raleigh, N.C. 27611-7581
919-828-9650
800-280-6207
919-828-1341 (fax)
e-mail:
NASWNC@AOL.COM

N. DAKOTA CHAPTER
P.O. Box 1775
Bismarck, ND 58502-1775
701-223-4161
701-224-9824 (fax)
e-mail: TPXC69A@
PRODIGY.COM

OHIO CHAPTER
42 E. Gay St., #700
Columbus, OH 43215
614-461-4484
614-461-9793 (fax)

OKLAHOMA CHAPTER
116 E. Sheridan, #210
Oklahoma City, OK 73104
405-239-7017
405-236-3638 (fax)
e-mail:
NASWOK@IONET.NET

OREGON CHAPTER
7688 SW Capitol Hwy
Portland, OR 97219
503-452-8420
503-452-8506 (fax)
e-mail:
NASW@EARTHLINK.NET

PENNSYLVANIA CHAPTER
1337 N. Front Street
Harrisburg, PA 17102
717-232-4125
717-232-4140 (fax)
e-mail: ALOMAN@
NASWPA.ORG

PUERTO RICO CHAPTER
P.O. Box 192051
San Juan, PR 00919-2051
787-758-3588
787-281-8433 (fax)

RHODE ISLAND CHAPTER
260 W. Exchange Street
Providence, RI 02903
401-274-4940
401-274-4941 (fax)
e-mail:
RINASW@AOL.COM

S. CAROLINA CHAPTER
P.O. Box 5008
Columbia, SC 29250
803-256-8406
803-254-4116 (fax)
e-mail:
SCNASW@JUNO.COM

S. DAKOTA CHAPTER
830 State Street
Spearfish, SD 57783
605-642-0711
605-642-0822 (fax)
e-mail: SDNASW@
BLACKHILLS.COM

TENNESSEE CHAPTER
1720 West End Avenue
Suite #607
Nashville, TN 37203
615-321-5095
615-327-2676 (fax)

TEXAS CHAPTER
810 West 11th Street
Austin, TX 78701
512-474-1454
800-888-6279
512-474-1317 (fax)
e-mail: NASWTEX@
REALTIME.NET

UTAH CHAPTER
University of Utah
Graduate School of Social Work
Salt Lake City, UT 84112
801-583-8855
801-583-6218 (fax)
e-mail:
UTNASW@AROS.NET

VERMONT CHAPTER
P.O. Box 1348
Montpellier, VT 05601
802-223-1713
802-457-4489 (fax)

VIRGIN ISLANDS CHAPTER
Havensight Secretarial Services
2 Buccaneer Mall
St. Thomas, VI 00802
809-776-3424
809-777-8108 (fax)

VIRGINIA CHAPTER
The Virginia Building
1 North 5th St. #410
Richmond, VA 23219
804-643-1833
804-643-1845 (fax)

WASHINGTON CHAPTER
2601 Elliott Avenue
Suite 4175
Seattle, WA 98121
206-448-1660
800-864-2078
206-448-1674 (fax)

W. VIRGINIA CHAPTER
1608 Virginia St. East
Charleston, WV 25311
304-343-6141
304-345-6279
304-343-3295 (fax)
e-mail: NASWWV@AOL.COM

WISCONSIN CHAPTER
14 Mifflin Street
Suite #104
Madison, WI 53703
608-257-6334
608-257-8233 (fax)
e-mail: NASWI@AOL.COM

WYOMING CHAPTER
P.O. Box 701
Cheyenne, WY 82003
307-634-2118
307-634-7512 (fax)
e-mail:
KCEMMONS@JUNO.COM

READING B-2 *Social Work Associations in Canada*

Alberta Association of Registered Social Workers
#52, 9912-106 St
Edmonton, AB T5K 1C5
403-421-1167
403-421-1168 (fax)
800-661-3089 (Alberta residents only)

British Columbia Association of Social Workers
Suite 402, 1755 West Broadway
Vancouver, BC V6J 4S5
604-730-9111
604-730-9112 (fax)
800-605-4747 (BC residents only)

Manitoba Association of Social Workers
103-2015 Portage Avenue
Winnipeg, MB R3J OK3
204-888-9477
204-889-0021 (fax)
e-mail: maswmagic.mb.ca

New Brunswick Association of Social Workers
P.O. Box 1533, Postal Station A
Fredericton, NB E3B 5G2
506-459-5595
506-457-1421 (fax)

Newfoundland and Labrador Association of Social Workers
P.O. Box 5244, East End Post Office
St. John's, NF A1C 5W1
709-753-0200
709-753-0120 (fax)
e-mail: nlasw@voyager.newcomm.net

Nova Scotia Association of Social Workers
1891 Brunswick St., Ste 106
Halifax, NS B3J 2G8
902-429-7799
902-429-7650 (fax)
e-mail: nsasw@fox.nstn.ca

Ontario Association of Social Workers
410 Jarvis St.
Toronto, ON M4Y 2G6
416-923-4848
416-923-5279 (fax)
e-mail: oasw@web.net

Ordre professionnel des travailleurs sociaux du Québec
5757, avenue Decelles, bureau 335
Montréal (PQ) H3S 2C3
514-731-3925
514-731-6785 (TC/fax)

Prince Edward Island Association of Social Workers
81 Prince St.
Charlottetown, PE C1A 4R3
902-368-5362
902-368-7180 (fax)

Saskatchewan Association of Social Workers
2110 Lorne St.
Regina, SK S4P 2M5
306-545-1922
306-545-1895 (fax)

READING B-3 *American Social Work Licensing Boards**

Alabama
State Board of Social Work Examiners
Folsom Administrative Building
64 North Union Street, Suite 129
Montgomery, AL 36130
205-242-5860

Alaska
Bd. of Clinical Social Work Examiners
Division of Occupational Licensing
Dept. of Commerce & Econ. Develop.
P.O. Box 110806
Juneau, AK 99811-0806
907-465-2551

Arizona
Bd. of Behavioral Health Examiners
1400 West Washington, #350
Phoenix, AZ 85007
602-542-1882

*Information from American Association of Social Work Boards (800-225-6880).
Source: American Association of State Social Work Boards (AASSWB) Phone: 1-800-225-6880

California
Bd. of Behavioral Science Examiners
400 R Street, Suite 3150
Sacramento, CA 95814-6240
916-445-4933

Colorado
Board of Social Work Examiners
1560 Broadway, Suite 1340
Denver, CO 80202
303-894-7766

Connecticut (no board)
Department of Health Services
150 Washington Street
Hartford, CT 06106
860-566-1039

Delaware
Board of Social Work Examiners
Cannon Building, Suite 203
P.O. Box 1401
Dover, DE 19903
302-739-4522 x220

District of Columbia
Board of Social Work
614 H Street, NW, Room 923
Washington, DC 20001
202-727-7823
202-727-7454

Florida
Board of Clinical Social Work, Marriage & Family
    Therapy, and Mental Health Counselling
1940 N. Monroe Street
Tallahassee, FL 32399-0753
904-487-2520

Georgia
Composite Bd. of PC, Social Workers and Marriage &
    Family Therapists
166 Pryor Street, SW
Atlanta, GA 30303
404-656-3989

Hawaii (no board)
Social Work Program
1010 Richards Street
Honolulu, HI 96813
808-586-3000

Idaho
State Board of Social Work Examiners
Bureau of Occupational Licensing
Owyhee Plaza/1009 Main St., Ste. 220
Boise, ID 83702
208-334-3233

Illinois
SW Examining & Disciplinary Board
Dept. of Professional Regulation
320 West Washington Street, 3rd Floor
Springfield, IL 62786
217-785-0800

Indiana
SW Certification and Marriage & Family Therapists
    Credentialing Board
Health Professions Bureau
Indiana Government Center
402 West Washington St., Room 041
Indianapolis, IN 46204
317-233-4443

Iowa
Board of Social Work Examiners
IA Department of Public Health
Bureau of Professional Licensure
Lucas State Office Building
321 E. 12th Street
Des Moines, IA 50319-0075
515-281-4422

Kansas
Behavioral Sciences Regulatory Board
712 S. Kansas Avenue
Topeka, KS 66603-3817
913-296-3250

Kentucky
Board of Examiners of Social Work
Berry Hill Annex
Louisville Road, Box 456
Frankfort, KY 40602
502-564-3296

Louisiana
State Board of BCSW Examiners
18258 John Broussard
P.O. Box 345
Prairieville, LA 70769
504-673-3010

Maine
State Board of Social Work Licensure
35 State House Station
Augusta, ME 04333
204-624-8603

Maryland
State Board of Social Work Examiners
Dept. of Health & Mental Hygiene
4201 Patterson Avenue
Baltimore, MD 21215-2299
410-764-4788

Massachusetts
Bd. of Registration of Social Workers
100 Cambridge Street
Boston, MA 02202
617-727-3073

Michigan
Board of Examiners of Social Work
P.O. Box 30246
Lansing, MI 48909
517-373-1653

Minnesota
Board of Social Work Examiners
2700 University Ave., West, Suite 22
St. Paul, MN 55114-1095
612-643-2580

Mississippi
Social Work Advisory Council
Dept of Health/Professional Licensure
P.O. Box 1700
Jackson, MS 39215-1700
601-987-4153

Missouri
Adv. Committee for Lic. Clinical SWs
3605 Missouri Boulevard
P.O. Box 1335
Jefferson City, MO 65102-0085
573-751-0885

Montana
Board of Social Work Examiners
111 North Jackson, Arcade Building
Helene, MT 59620-0407
406-444-4285

Nebraska
Bureau of Examining Boards
301 Centennial Mall South
P.O. Box 95007
Lincoln, NE 68509-5007
702-688-2555

New Hampshire
Board of Examiners of Psychology and Mental Health
   Practice
105 Pleasant Street, Box 457
Concord, NH 03301
603-271-6762

New Jersey
State Board of Social Work Examiners
P.O. Box 45033
Newark, NJ 07101
201-504-6495

New Mexico
Board of Social Work Examiners
1599 St. Francis Drive
P.O. Box 25101
Santa Fe, NM 87504
505-827-7554

New York
State Board of Social Work
NY State Education Department
Cultural Education Center, Rm #3041
Albany, NY 12230
518-474-4974

North Carolina
NC Social Work Board
130 South Church Street
P.O. Box 1043
Asheboro, NC 27204
910-625-1679

North Dakota
Board of Social Work Examiners
P.O. Box 6145
Bismarck, ND 58506-6145
701-222-0255

Ohio
Social Work Board
77 South High Street, 16th Floor
Columbus, OH 43266-0340
614-466-0912

Oklahoma
Board of Licensed Social Workers
4145 NW 61st Terrace
Oklahoma City, OK 73112
405-946-7230

Oregon
State Board of Licensed Clinical SWs
3218 Pringle Road, SE, Suite 140
Salem, OR 97302-6310
503-378-5735

Pennsylvania
State Board of Social Work Examiners
P.O. Box 2649
Harrisburg, PA 17105-2649
717-783-1389

Puerto Rico (no Board)
c/o NASW, Puerto Rico Chapter
271 Ramon Ramos
Urb. Roosevelt
Hata Rey, PR 00918
809-758-3588

Rhode Island
Division of Professional Regulation
RI Department of Health
3 Capitol Hill, Room 104
Providence, RI 02908-5097
401-277-2827

South Carolina
Board of Social Work Examiners
3600 Forest Drive, Suite 101
P.O. Box 11329
Columbia, SC 29211-1329
803-734-4242

South Dakota
Board of Social Work Examiners
P.O. Box 654
Spearfish, SD 57783-0654
605-642-1600

Tennessee
Board of SW Certification & Licensure
Tennessee Department of Health
283 Plus Park Boulevard
Nashville, TN 37247-1010
615-367-6207

Texas
State Board of Social Work Examiners
1100 West 49th Street
Austin, TX 78756-3183
512-719-3521

Utah
Social Work Licensing Board
Occupational & Professional Licensing
160 East 300 South
P.O. Box 45805
Salt Lake City, UT 84145-0805
801-530-6551

Vermont
Office of the Secretary of State
Licensing & Registration Division
109 State Street
Montpelier, VT 05609-1106
802-828-2390

Virginia
Board of Social Work
6606 West Broad Street, 4th Floor
Richmond, VA 23230-1717
804-662-9914

Virgin Islands
Board of Social Work Licensure
No. 1 Subbase, 2nd Floor, Room 205
St. Thomas, VI 00802
809-774-3130

Washington
Mental Health Q. Assurance Council
Dept. of Health Counsellors Section
P.O. Box 47869
Olympia, WA 98504-7869
360-664-4375

West Virginia
Board of Social Work Examiners
P.O. Box 5459
Charleston, WV 23561
304-558-8816

Wisconsin
Board of Social Workers, MFTs, and Professional
    Counsellors
Department of Regulation & Licensing
1400 E. Washington Avenue
Madison, WI 53708-8935
608-267-7223

Wyoming
Prof. Counselors, MFTs, SWs, & Chemical Dependency
    Licensing Board
2301 Central Avenue
Barrett Building, Room 349
Cheyenne, WY 82002
307-777-7788

Appendix C: Solutions

Here is the solution to Exhibit 8–13 (Chapter 8):

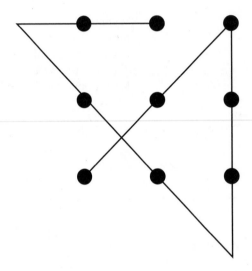

Here is the response from Ann Landers to No Name, No City in Exhibit 14–12 (Chapter 14):

Dear N.N., N.C.: It should be apparent to you that your mom is in deep denial about this relationship. I'm sure the rational side of her brain knows what's going on, but she doesn't want to acknowledge it. Abandon your efforts to save her. She doesn't wish to be "saved."

Index

A

Abramson, M., 442
Abstract values, 104–105
Abstract writing, 156
Abuse
  child
    engaging respondents in situations of, 207
    reporting of, 161
    unannounced home visits and, 204
  family reunification and, 320–321, 322
  of power, 153–154
  spousal/domestic, 67–80, 332
    first interview in, 71–75
    initial assessment in, 67–71
    planning interventions in, 76
    summary discussion in, 76–78
  in strengths perspective, 16
Acceptance, 178
  in client-worker partnership, 103
  of differences, 184–185
Accessibility, in engagement process, 205
Accountability, 469
  dignity through, 108–109
  professional, 134
Achieved roles, 40
Action plans, 305–308
  alternative, data collection and, 259–260
  definition of, 302
  in family reunification programs, 324
  and focusing on results, 307–308
  for groups, 306–307
  limitations on worker activity and, 308
  negotiating, 359
  objectives and, 263–264
  time limits in, 306

Action system, 33
Actions, to promote client competence, 354–362
Activities
  in evaluation, 457
  to promote client competence, 355
Adoptive children, 446
Advice, in intervention, 344–345
Advocacy, 157–160, 312
  in care management, 383
  misdirected, culture groups and, 234
  in strengths perspective, 22
  teamwork and, 443
Affective level of response, 268
African cultures
  African Americans
    communication styles with, 234
    help-seeking behaviors of, 233
    self-help history of, 410–415
    use of agency services by, 234
    worker race and, 238
  confidentiality and, 166–167
  cultural variation among, 236
Agency
  administrators, 307
  authority from, 129–130, 132–133
  board committees, 143
  and burnout, 504–505, 506–507
  as client, 126
  conflicts with, 131, 159
  function of, 130, 132
  intraorganizational change and, 140–147
  as limitation on worker activity, 308
  vs. professional expectations, 133–134
  and teamwork, 443
Agency method focus, 6

IN-BOOK SURVEY

At Brooks/Cole, we are excited about creating new types of learning materials that are interactive, three-dimensional, and fun to use. To guide us in our publishing/development process, we hope that you'll take just a few moments to fill out the survey below. Your answers can help us make decisions that will allow us to produce a wide variety of videos, CD-ROMs, and Internet-based learning systems to complement standard textbooks. If you're interested in working with us as a student Beta-tester, be sure to fill in your name, telephone number, and address. We look forward to hearing from you!

In addition to books, which of the following learning tools do you currently use in your counseling/human services/social work courses?

_____ **Video** _____ in class _____ school library _____ own VCR

_____ **CD-ROM** _____ in class _____ in lab _____ own computer

_____ **Macintosh disks** _____ in class _____ in lab _____ own computer

_____ **Windows disks** _____ in class _____ in lab _____ own computer

_____ **Internet** _____ in class _____ in lab _____ own computer

How often do you access the Internet? _____

My own home computer is:

_____ Macintosh _____ DOS _____ Windows _____ Windows 95

The computer I use in class for counseling/human services/social work courses is:

_____ Macintosh _____ DOS _____ Windows _____ Windows 95

If you are NOT currently using multimedia materials in your counseling/human services/social work courses, but can see ways that video, CD-ROM, Internet, or other technologies could enhance your learning, please comment below:

_____

_____

_____

Other comments (optional): _____

_____

Name _____ Telephone _____

Address _____

School _____

Professor/Course _____

You can fax this form to us at (408) 375-6414; e:mail to: info@brookscole.com; or detach, fold, secure, and mail.

FOLD HERE

- -

NO POSTAGE
NECESSARY
IF MAILED
IN THE
UNITED STATES

BUSINESS REPLY MAIL

FIRST CLASS   PERMIT NO. 358   PACIFIC GROVE, CA

POSTAGE WILL BE PAID BY ADDRESSEE

ATT: MARKETING

**Brooks/Cole Publishing Company
511 Forest Lodge Road
Pacific Grove, California 93950-5098**

- -

FOLD HERE

TO THE OWNER OF THIS BOOK:

We hope that you have found *Social Work Processes,* Sixth Edition, useful. So that this book can be improved in a future edition, would you take the time to complete this sheet and return it? Thank you.

School and address: _____

Department: _____

Instructor's name: _____

1. What I like most about this book is: _____

_____

_____

2. What I like least about this book is: _____

_____

_____

3. My general reaction to this book is: _____

_____

4. The name of the course in which I used this book is: _____

_____

5. Were all of the chapters of the book assigned for you to read? _____

   If not, which ones weren't? _____

6. In the space below, or on a separate sheet of paper, please write specific suggestions for improving this book and anything else you'd care to share about your experience in using the book.

_____

_____

_____

_____

_____

Optional:

Your name: _____ Date: _____

May Brooks/Cole quote you, either in promotion for *Social Work Processes,* Sixth Edition,
or in future publishing ventures?

Yes: _____ No: _____

Sincerely,

Beulah R. Compton
Burt Galaway

FOLD HERE

NO POSTAGE
NECESSARY
IF MAILED
IN THE
UNITED STATES

BUSINESS REPLY MAIL

FIRST CLASS   PERMIT NO. 358   PACIFIC GROVE, CA

POSTAGE WILL BE PAID BY ADDRESSEE

ATT: *Beulah R. Compton & Burt Galaway*

**Brooks/Cole Publishing Company
511 Forest Lodge Road
Pacific Grove, California 93950-5098**

FOLD HERE